Business Ethics

◆ ◆ ◆

BUSINESS ETHICS
A Philosophical Reader

♦ ♦ ♦

THOMAS I. WHITE
Rider College

PRENTICE HALL
Upper Saddle River, New Jersey 07458

Library of Congress Cataloging-in-Publication Data

White, Thomas I.

Business ethics: a philosophical reader / Thomas I. White.

p. cm.

Includes bibliographical references and index.

ISBN 0-02-427221-3

1. Business ethics. I. Title.

550'1'51474—dc20   CIP

Editor: Maggie Barbieri

Production Supervisor: Ann-Marie WongSam

Production Managers: Muriel Underwood and Paul Smolenski

Cover Designer: Russ Maselli

This book was set in Janson by Digitype, Inc.

Printed in the United States of America

10

ISBN   0-02-427221-3

Prentice-Hall International (UK) Limited,London

Prentice-Hall of Australia Pty. Limited, Sydney

Prentice-Hall Canada Inc., Toronto

Prentice-Hall Hispanoamericana, S.A., Mexico

Prentice-Hall of India Private Limited, New Delhi

Prentice-Hall of Japan, Inc., Tokyo

Pearson Education Asia Pte. Ltd., Singapore

Editora Prentice-Hall do Brasil, Ltda., Rio de Janeiro

To Marilyn
Angel of light

Preface

◆ ◆ ◆

Business ethics remains, relatively speaking, a new branch of philosophy. Cosmology, metaphysics, epistemology, political philosophy, and logic begin with the Milesians, Plato, and Aristotle. Ethics originates with Socrates. And while this last ancient thinker confronts his fellow Athenians in the marketplace, he confronts issues related to living in general, not the ethical problems of doing business. It is the canyons of Wall Street, not the dusty paths of the Athenian agora, that have given rise to contemporary business ethics in the past twenty-five years.

Despite its relatively new status, business ethics has been maturing, and this anthology aims to reflect that development. This collection does contain many standard, if less philosophical, pieces in the field, such as Milton Friedman's discussion of the social responsibility of business. However, I have tried mainly to select essays of a high level of philosophical sophistication, that is, articles that demonstrate that business ethics is an area of inquiry with its own philosophical integrity. Most of this anthology consists of what might be called the "second generation" research in business ethics.

This book thus aims to serve the needs of philosophers who prefer to approach business ethics almost exclusively through philosophical readings, rather than a combination of ethical, legal, and managerial essays. Nonetheless, each chapter ends with case studies which illustrate the theoretical issues under investigation. I welcome any suggestions for improving this current collection.

Like all books, this one springs from the efforts of many people, and I would like to express my thanks to them at this time. Helen McInnis, now of Oxford University Press, initiated this project. Maggie Barbieri, my editor, oversaw the book to completion with encouragement and patience. Ann-Marie WongSam steered it through the rapids of production. And Douglas Anderson, Penn State University; Robert Corrington, Drew University; Paul Edwards; William Langenfus, Iowa State University; Robert Stewart, California State University – Chico; and Anthony Weston, State University of New York – Stony Brook, served as readers of various proposals and earlier drafts. I would also like to express my gratitude to my faculty and administrative colleagues at Rider College. I have been a philosopher in the business school since 1989, and this experience has been both challenging and enriching. I hope that this book is worthy of the support that all of these people have so generously given me.

Thomas I. White
Princeton, New Jersey

vii

Contents

◆ ◆ ◆

PREFACE   vii

CHAPTER 1   *Ethics and Business*   1

ETHICS 1
Philosophical Ethics 1
Virtue and the Human Personality: Socrates, Plato,
   and Aristotle 2

EVALUATING THE ETHICAL
CHARACTER OF ACTIONS 4
Teleological Ethics 4
Deontological Ethics 8
Evaluating the Moral Character of Actions 11

ETHICAL ISSUES IN BUSINESS 11
Capitalism 12
   The Ethics of Capitalism *12*
Corporations 13
   Corporations and Ethics *16*
How Corporations Are Run 18
   The Ethics of Corporate Organization *21*
Customers 22
   Ethics and Customer Relations *23*
Business and Government 24
   Business, Ethics, and the Law *25*
Business and the Environment 25
   Business, Ethics, and the Environment *26*
Business and Ethics: A Final Word 26

ADDITIONAL READINGS 27

CHAPTER 2   *The Morality of Business and Capitalism*   29

JAMES H. MICHELMAN, "Some Ethical Consequences
of Economic Competition"   30

RICHARD McCARTY, "Business and Benevolence"   41

MICHAEL NOVAK, "What Is Democratic Capitalism?"   53
"Virtuous Self-Interest"   56

JEFFREY REIMAN, "Exploitation, Force,
and the Moral Assessment of Capitalism"   60

DISCUSSION QUESTIONS   72

CASE 2.1 ◆ Tobacco and Addiction   73

CASE 2.2 ◆ The Catholic Challenge   76

ADDITIONAL READINGS   78

CHAPTER 3   *Distributive Justice*   79

JOEL FEINBERG, "Distributive Justice"   80

JOHN RAWLS, "A Theory of Justice"   89

ROBERT NOZICK, "Distributive Justice"   100

J. J. C. SMART, "Distributive Justice and Utilitarianism"   110

MILTON FISK, "Economic Justice"   115

DISCUSSION QUESTIONS   125

CASE 3.1 ◆ The Distribution of Wealth   125

CASE 3.2 ◆ Executive Salaries   128

ADDITIONAL READINGS   130

CHAPTER 4   *Work and Human Well-Being*   131

A. R. GINI AND T. SULLIVAN, "Work:
The Process and the Person"   132

E. F. SCHUMACHER, "Buddhist Economics: Work"   141

KARL MARX, "Estranged Labour"   144
"Division of Labour"   149

KAI NIELSEN, "Alienation and Work"   151

DISCUSSION QUESTIONS   155

CASE 4.1 ◆ The End of the Assembly Line   156

CASE 4.2 ◆ Gender and Management Styles   157

ADDITIONAL READINGS   160

CHAPTER 5   *Corporate Social Responsibility*   161

MILTON FRIEDMAN, "The Social Responsibility
of Business Is to Increase Its Profits"   162

THOMAS DONALDSON, "Constructing
a Social Contract for Business"   167

FRED D. MILLER, JR., AND JOHN AHRENS,
"The Social Responsibility of Corporations"   187

KENNETH E. GOODPASTER, "Business Ethics and
Stakeholder Analysis"   205

DISCUSSION QUESTIONS   221

CASE 5.1 ◆ Ben & Jerry's   221

CASE 5.2 ◆ Stakeholders, Pensions, and Health Benefits   224

ADDITIONAL READINGS   226

CHAPTER 6   *Corporations, Responsibility and Personhood*   227

PETER A. FRENCH, "The Corporation
as a Moral Person"   228

JOHN LADD, "Corporate Mythology
and Individual Responsibility"   236

CHRISTOPHER MEYERS, "The Corporation,
Its Members, and Moral Accountability"   251

JOHN D. BISHOP, "The Moral Responsibility
of Corporate Executives for Disasters"   261

DISCUSSION QUESTIONS   269

CASE 6.1 ◆ Corporate Persons and Free Speech   269

CASE 6.2 ◆ Harmful Products, Bankruptcy, and
          Responsibility   271

ADDITIONAL READINGS   274

CHAPTER 7   *Corporate Punishment*   275

PETER A. FRENCH, "The Hester Prynne Sanction"   276

J. ANGELO CORLETT, "French on
Corporate Punishment: Some Problems"   287

SHANNON SHIPP, "Modified Vendettas
as a Method of Punishing Corporations"   294

ROBERT J. RAFALKO, "Corporate
Punishment: A Proposal"   307

DISCUSSION QUESTIONS   322

CASE 7.1 ◆ Beech-Nut's Imitation Apple Juice   322

CASE 7.2 ◆ Sentencing a Corporation to Prison   324

ADDITIONAL READINGS   325

CHAPTER 8   *Business and Honesty*   327

ALBERT Z. CARR, "Is Business Bluffing Ethical?"   328

NORMAN E. BOWIE, "The Ethics of Bluffing and Poker"   338

THOMAS L. CARSON, RICHARD E. WOKUTCH,
AND KENT F. MURRMANN, "Bluffing in Labor
Negotiations: Legal and Ethical Issues"   347

JENNIFER JACKSON, "Honesty in Marketing"   358

DISCUSSION QUESTIONS   368

CASE 8.1 ◆ The Borland Scam   369

CASE 8.2 ◆ Truth and Business School   370

CASE 8.3 ◆ The Latest Books of "Late" Authors   371

ADDITIONAL READINGS   372

CHAPTER 9   *Insider Trading*   373

BILL SHAW, "Should Insider Trading
Be Outside the Law?"   374

WILLIAM B. IRVINE, "Insider Trading:
An Ethical Appraisal"   379

PATRICIA H. WERHANE, "The Ethics
of Insider Trading"   399

JENNIFER MOORE, "What Is Really
Unethical About Insider Trading?" 404

DISCUSSION QUESTIONS 419

CASE 9.1 ◆ The Small Investor 420

CASE 9.2 ◆ Printers and Reporters 421

ADDITIONAL READINGS 423

CHAPTER 10 *Employee Rights* 425

DAVID W. EWING, "A Proposed Bill of Rights" 426

PATRICIA H. WERHANE, "Employee and Employer
Rights in an Institutional Context" 430

ANITA M. SUPERSON, "The Employer–Employee
Relationship and the Right to Know" 435

ROBERT A. DAHL, "Democracy in the Workplace:
Is It a Right or a Privilege?" 446

TIBOR R. MACHAN, "Human Rights, Workers' Rights,
and the 'Right' to Occupational Safety" 455

DISCUSSION QUESTIONS 460

CASE 10.1 ◆ The Rights of Current Employees Versus
the Rights of Their Unconceived Children 460

CASE 10.2 ◆ Firings, Libel, and Due Process 462

ADDITIONAL READINGS 464

CHAPTER 11 *Employee Privacy* 465

GEORGE G. BRENKERT, "Privacy,
Polygraphs, and Work" 466

JOSEPH R. DES JARDINS, "Privacy in Employment" 479

RICHARD L. LIPPKE, "Work, Privacy, and Autonomy" 487

JOSEPH R. DES JARDINS and RONALD DUSKA,
"Drug Testing in Employment" 496

DISCUSSION QUESTIONS 510

CASE 11.1 ◆ Love and Business 510

CASE 11.2 ◆ High-Tech Invasions of Privacy   512

ADDITIONAL READINGS   513

CHAPTER 12   *Whistleblowing*   515

RICHARD T. DE GEORGE, "Whistle Blowing"   516

GENE G. JAMES, "Whistle Blowing:
Its Moral Justification"   531

DAVID THEO GOLDBERG, "Tuning in
to Whistle Blowing"   545

RONALD DUSKA, "Whistleblowing
and Employee Loyalty"   551

NATALIE DANDEKAR, "Can Whistleblowing Be
FULLY Legitimated? A Theoretical Discussion"   556

DISCUSSION QUESTIONS   568

CASE 12.1 ◆ The Pattern of Retaliation   569

CASE 12.2 ◆ More Questions and Alternative
            Scenarios for the Challenger Disaster   570

ADDITIONAL READINGS   571

CHAPTER 13   *Advertising*   573

ROBERT L. ARRINGTON, "Advertising
and Behavior Control"   574

RICHARD L. LIPPKE, "Advertising and
the Social Conditions of Autonomy"   585

JOHN WAIDE, "The Making of
Self and World in Advertising"   600

LYNN SHARP PAINE, "Children as Consumers: An Ethical
Evaluation of Children's Television Advertising"   607

DISCUSSION QUESTIONS   629

CASE 13.1 ◆ Airfares   629

CASE 13.2 ◆ Sexual Persuasion   631

ADDITIONAL READINGS   634

CHAPTER 14   *Affirmative Action and Discrimination*   635

THOMAS NAGEL, "A Defense of Affirmative Action"   636

LEO GROARKE, "Affirmative Action
as a Form of Restitution"   640

EVELYN B. PLUHAR, "Preferential Hiring
and Unjust Sacrifice"   648

LAURA M. PURDY, "In Defense of Hiring
Apparently Less Qualified Women"   657

SIDNEY HOOK, "Rationalizations for
Reverse Discrimination"   663

DISCUSSION QUESTIONS   667

CASE 14.1 ◆ Did It Work?   668

CASE 14.2 ◆ Life-Style Discrimination?   669

ADDITIONAL READINGS   671

CHAPTER 15   *Sexual Harassment and
Comparable Worth*   673

SUSAN M. DODDS, LUCY FROST, ROBERT
PARGETTER, AND ELIZABETH W. PRIOR,
"Sexual Harassment"   674

LARRY MAY AND JOHN C. HUGHES,
"Is Sexual Harassment Coercive?"   686

JUNE O'NEILL, "An Argument
Against Comparable Worth"   693

LAURIE SHRAGE, "Some Implications
of Comparable Worth"   705

JUDITH OLANS BROWN, PHYLLIS TROPPER
BAUMANN, AND ELAINE MILLAR MELNICK, "Equal
Pay for Jobs of Comparable Worth: An Analysis of the
Rhetoric"   720

DISCUSSION QUESTIONS   726

CASE 15.1 ◆ Ontario's Ground-Breaking
                 Comparable Worth Program   727

CASE 15.2 ◆ New Forms of Harassment   728

ADDITIONAL READINGS   731

CHAPTER 16   *Mergers and Acquisitions*   733

MICHAEL C. JENSEN, "Takeovers:
Folklore and Science"   734

PATRICIA H. WERHANE, "Two Ethical
Issues in Mergers and Acquisitions"   752

LISA H. NEWTON, "Charting Shark-Infested Waters:
Ethical Dimensions of the Hostile Takeover"   758

LISA H. NEWTON, "The Hostile Takeover:
An Opposition View"   767

DISCUSSION QUESTIONS   778

CASE 16.1 ◆ ESOPs   779

CASE 16.2 ◆ Should Investors Have to
                       Give Some Money Back?   780

ADDITIONAL READINGS   782

CHAPTER 17   *Doing Business in a Global Economy*   783

RICHARD T. DE GEORGE, "Ethical Dilemmas for
Multinational Enterprise: A Philosophical Overview"   784

NORMAN E. BOWIE, "Business Ethics
and Cultural Relativism"   790

THOMAS DONALDSON, "Multinational Decision-Making:
Reconciling International Norms"   799

THOMAS DONALDSON, "The Ethics
of Risk in the Global Economy"   810

DISCUSSION QUESTIONS   824

CASE 17.1 ◆ The Ethics of Prison Labor   825

CASE 17.2 ◆ The Mequiladoras   826

ADDITIONAL READINGS   828

CHAPTER 18   *Business and the Environment*   829

W. MICHAEL HOFFMAN, "Business
and Environmental Ethics"   830

DAVID P. HANSON, "The Ethics of Development
and the Dilemmas of Global Environmentalism"   841

PETER SINGER, "The Place of Nonhumans
in Environmental Issues"   849

ERIC KATZ, "Defending the Use of Animals by Business:
Animal Liberation and Environmental Ethics"   855

DISCUSSION QUESTIONS   863

CASE 18.1 ◆ Nuclear Power   863

CASE 18.2 ◆ The Ethics of Dolphin/Human Interaction   865

ADDITIONAL READINGS   867

Business Ethics

◆ ◆ ◆

CHAPTER 1

◆ ◆ ◆

Ethics and Business

Thirty years ago, "business ethics" was a term used only by comedians looking for a cheap laugh. Together with "jumbo shrimp" and "military intelligence," "business ethics" was supposed to be a classic oxymoron. Today, matters of business ethics are too sobering to be funny. Financial scandals landed many Wall Street luminaries, including two of its most powerful men —Ivan Boesky and Michael Milken—in prison. The savings and loan debacle will cost American taxpayers hundreds of billions of dollars. "Love Canal" became a symbol of corporate wrongdoing of the first order. And defense contractors scandalized the nation with huge cost overruns and astronomical prices for mundane objects. By the 1990s, Boesky's remark that it is possible to feel good about being greedy had revealed itself as the moral equivalent of fool's gold.

Fortunately, corporate America responded to these crises in a positive way. Many companies established departments to deal with ethical issues and instituted programs in ethics for employees. Business schools began requiring courses in ethics for their students. The former chairman of the Securities and Exchange Commission, John Shad, even donated $20 million of his personal fortune to establish an ethics program at the Harvard Business School. Johnson & Johnson's courageous handling of the Tylenol poisonings showed that a major corporation was willing to do the right thing even when that meant sustaining substantial financial losses.

Numerous philosophers also took this moral crisis seriously, and business ethics has now become a thriving area of philosophical inquiry. Once seen as a disreputable second cousin to "real" philosophy, business ethics is now one of the most lively and interesting areas of contemporary ethics.

However, before we can consider the defining characteristics of business ethics, we need to begin with an examination of philosophical ethics in general.

ETHICS

Philosophical Ethics

Ethics is the branch of philosophy that explores the nature of moral virtue and evaluates human actions. Philosophical ethics differs from legal, religious,

1

cultural, and personal approaches to ethics by seeking to conduct the study of morality through a rational, secular outlook that is grounded in notions of human happiness or well-being. A major advantage of a philosophical approach to ethics is that it avoids the authoritarian bases of law and religion as well as the subjectivity, arbitrariness, and irrationality that may characterize cultural or totally personal moral views.[1]

Virtue and the Human Personality: Socrates, Plato, and Aristotle

Ethics began in ancient Greece when philosophers focused primarily on the nature of moral virtue. Socrates (469–399 B.C.) took a practical approach, regularly accosting his fellow Athenians and challenging them to think about virtue and the "health of the soul." Comparatively little is known about Socrates' teaching about ethics, except that he believed that vice resulted from ignorance and that a Socratic-assisted examination of one's deepest beliefs could free an individual from the snares of confused and contradictory thinking and pave the way to virtue. Accordingly, Socrates' main ideas about ethics related to convincing people to be virtuous.

Socrates' major ethical claims were that happiness is impossible without moral virtue and that unethical actions harm the person who performs them more than the people they victimize. Although it is not totally clear what Socrates meant by these notions, he seems to have believed that an unethical person is weak, even psychologically unhealthy. He apparently thought that what we today would call cognitive and noncognitive capacities are harmed as the unethical person gives into his or her desires and ultimately becomes enslaved by them. Someone in the grip of corruption can no longer be satisfied and endlessly seeks new pleasures. In addition, the individual's intellect and moral sense are impaired. Socrates thus saw someone steeped in vice as lacking the freedom, self-control, and intellectual clarity that are needed to live happily.[2] The immoral person literally becomes a slave to his or her desires.

Socrates' focus on the relationship between ethics and the human personality was continued by his student Plato (428–348 B.C.), who described moral virtue in terms of a proper balance and harmony among different aspects of the "soul"—reason would rule over the physical desires with the assistance of the emotions.[3] Like Socrates, Plato saw moral virtue as necessary for the health of the soul, but he thought that genuine virtue was difficult to attain and ultimately depended on learning highly sophisticated, metaphysical truths that required years of study. For Plato, then, moral virtue was rooted in the intellect.

Plato's pupil Aristotle (384–322 B.C.) saw moral virtue differently than his teacher did, however, linking it less to the intellect and more to what we today

---

[1]Although some thinkers differentiate between "ethics," "morals," "ethical," and "moral," this discussion will use these terms synonymously.

[2]For a fuller explanation of this reading of Socrates, see "Socrates: Vice Harms the Doer" in my *Discovering Philosophy* (Englewood Cliffs, NJ: Prentice Hall, 1991), 210–224.

[3]Plato does not use "soul" in the Christian sense of a nonmaterial, spiritual entity that inhabits a physical body. As seen by his claim that the soul's three parts are reason, the emotions, and the physical appetites, he has in mind the combination of forces that characterize and animate the human being.

refer to as character or personality. Indeed, Aristotle defined virtue in the *Nicomachean Ethics* "not . . . according to the nature of the actions, but according to the disposition of the doer."[4] Aristotle also argued that moral virtue was developed in the same way as physical skills — through practice and habit.

Aristotle's concept of moral virtue, then, involved our hearts as well as our heads. In essence, Aristotle offered a personality type as his moral standard: the virtuous person. "Acts are called just and temperate," he wrote, "when they are such as the just or temperate man would perform. The temperate and just man is not he who does these acts, but he who does them in the way in which just and temperate men do them" (1105b). This means, according to Aristotle, choosing to do the right thing for its own sake and "from a firm and unshakable disposition" (1105a – b). Doing the right thing resentfully or to enhance one's reputation or after a torturous struggle with conflicting desires does not count as virtue.

The way to develop the character type Aristotle had in mind, however, is relatively simple — we practice. "Moral virtue," he wrote, "is produced by habit" (1103a). It is the same basic process as learning a technical skill:

> [W]e acquire the know-how by actually doing. For example, people become builders by actually building, and the same applies to lyre players. In the same way, we become just by doing just acts; and similarly with "temperate" and "brave." . . . By acting in affairs that involve a contract with others, some of us become just, some unjust. By acting in dangerous situations and being trained to show fear or confidence, we become brave or cowardly. The same can be said of desire and temper: some become moderate and controlled, others immoderate and bad tempered, from actually behaving in such or such a way in cases where desire or temper is involved. In short, like practices produce like dispositions. (1103a – b)

Socrates, Plato, and Aristotle discussed ethics in a way that probably feels foreign to contemporary sensibilities. People at the end of the twentieth century generally do not talk about virtue as "psychic harmony," or about vice as "harming the doer," or about doing things as "the just or temperate man would." Nonetheless, these Greek philosophers took up central ethical questions that are too frequently ignored: Why be ethical? And, what does being ethical really mean?

Socrates and Plato answered the first question by asserting a close relationship between moral virtue and the healthy human personality. They argued that no matter what vice looks like on the surface or what it achieves — wealth, power, fame, romance — it is actually a sign of weakness, not strength. Aristotle answered the second question by stressing the inner dimension of human action. Virtue depends on character, not deeds, and our character is shaped by every action that we perform.

The ideas of these three thinkers thereby underscore the relationship between ethics and the very core of our being. Socrates, Plato, and Aristotle

---

[4]*The Philosophy of Aristotle*, Renford Bambaugh, ed. (New York: New American Library, 1963), 1105a.

showed that what we do helps or hurts ourselves as much as, if not more than, the people with whom we deal. These philosophers therefore forcefully demonstrated that our welfare is ultimately in our own hands; they argued for the seriousness of taking care of the moral character of our actions; and they gave an interesting twist to what it really means to "look out for number 1." In contrast to the pervasive belief in our culture that satisfying an ever-expanding list of physical and material wants will lead to happiness, Socrates and Plato suggested precisely the opposite. Their ethical outlook, then, is a sobering caution about the difficulty of remaining in control of our lives. By making our character, will, and intentions central elements of moral virtue, Aristotle pointed out how critical it is to study our motivations and master the inner forces that could lead to moral compromises.

EVALUATING THE ETHICAL CHARACTER OF ACTIONS

If ancient ethics concentrated on the nature of moral virtue and its rationale, modern ethics has focused on determining the ethical character of actions and has developed two competing traditions. One argues that actions have no intrinsic ethical character but acquire their moral status from the consequences that flow from them. The other tradition claims that actions are inherently right (e.g., telling the truth) or wrong (e.g., cheating or stealing). The former is called a *teleological* approach to ethics, the latter, *deontological*.

Teleological Ethics

A teleological outlook is particularly appealing because it takes a pragmatic, commonsense, even unphilosophical approach to ethics. Generally speaking, teleological thinkers claim that the moral character of actions depends on the simple, practical matter of the extent to which actions actually help or hurt people. Actions that produce more benefits than harm are right; those that do not are wrong. This outlook is best represented by utilitarianism, a school of thought originated by the British thinker Jeremy Bentham (1748–1832) and refined by John Stuart Mill (1806–1873).

Strongly influenced by the empiricism of David Hume, Bentham aimed at developing a "moral science" that was more rational, objective, and quantitative than other ways of separating right from wrong. Bentham particularly argued against the ascetic religious traditions of eighteenth-century England that held up suffering and sacrifice as models of virtue.

Bentham began with what he took as the self-evident observations that (1) pleasure and pain govern our lives, and (2) the former makes life happier, while the latter makes it worse. These two concepts anchor Bentham's ethical outlook. "Nature has placed mankind," he wrote in his *Introduction to the Principles of Morals and Legislation*, "under the governance of two sovereign masters, *pain* and *pleasure*. It is for them alone to point out what we ought to do, as well as to determine what we shall do. On the one hand the standard of right and wrong, on the other the chain of causes and effects, are fastened to their throne."[5]

[5]Jeremy Bentham, *Introduction to the Principles of Morals and Legislation*, Ch. I, i, in *Ethical Theories*, A.I. Melden, ed. (Englewood Cliffs, NJ: Prentice Hall, 1967), 367.

From this insight about pleasure and pain, Bentham developed as his ethical touchstone the notion of *utility:*

> that property in any object, whereby it tends to produce benefit, advantage, pleasure, good or happiness, (all this in the present case comes to the same thing) or (what comes again to the same thing) to prevent the happening of mischief, pain, evil, or unhappiness to the party whose interest is considered: if that party be the community in general, then the happiness of the community: if a particular individual, then the happiness of that individual. (Ch. I, ii)

Utilitarianism therefore contends that something is morally good to the extent that it produces a greater balance of pleasure over pain for the largest number of people involved, or, as it is popularly described, "the greatest good of the greatest number." Pleasure is Bentham's ultimate standard of morality because "the greatest happiness of all those whose interest is in question . . . [is] the right and proper, and only right and proper and universally desirable, end of human action. (Ch. I, i, n)"

Aiming to make ethics practical, Bentham proposed a system for measuring the amount of pleasure and pain that an action produces. Called the *hedonistic calculus*, Bentham's system identifies seven aspects of an action's consequence that can be used to compare the results of different deeds: the intrinsic strength of the pleasurable or painful feelings produced (intensity), how long they last (duration), how likely it is that these sensations will be produced by a given action (certainty or uncertainty), how soon they will be felt (propinquity or remoteness), whether these feelings will lead to future pleasures (fecundity) or pains (purity), and the number of people affected (extent).

The great advantage of the hedonistic calculus is that it provides a method for talking about ethics that is open, public, objective, and fair. The benefits and harms produced by actions can be identified and measured. Furthermore, although everyone's happiness counts, no one individual's happiness counts for more than another's. Utilitarianism is in many ways very democratic.

For example, Bentham's system readily shows why it is wrong to steal money from people at knife point. The theft will surely make the robber happy. But this pleasure is short-lived, lasting only until the money from each robbery runs out; the thief must also live with the worry of being caught. Moreover, the robber's happiness is outweighed by the victims' unhappiness. The negative feelings of the thief's targets will be intense and, very possibly, long term. Furthermore, more people experience pain from the thefts than feel any pleasure. Bentham would therefore see such theft as clearly wrong, producing a greater balance of unhappiness over happiness among all those involved in the situation.

Notice that this discussion makes no appeal to rights, a difficult moral theory, personal attitudes, or religious teachings. One need not be a lawyer, philosopher, person of good conscience, or religious believer in order to uncover the moral status of actions. All that is required for determining whether or not an action is morally defensible is careful, thorough, and fair examination of whom the action helps or hurts and in what ways.

Bentham's version of utilitarianism contains major flaws, however. This is evident as soon as we change some of the details of the previous scenario, because the scales of the hedonistic calculus would tip the other way. Imagine that the thief is a Robin Hood-like character who steals only exotic cars of rich people and uses his gains to feed many desperately hungry people. He neither threatens nor physically injures anyone, and his victims are reimbursed by insurance companies. These firms spread the cost out over all policyholders, who surely experience this more as "inconvenience" than "pain." It is hard to see how Bentham's system would label the robberies as wrong. As long as the thief is appropriately altruistic with his bounty, his actions seem to produce more pleasure than pain.

John Stuart Mill, Bentham's godson and intellectual heir, was sensitive to the fact that utilitarianism appeared to defend actions that most people felt intuitively were wrong, such as lying and stealing. Accordingly, Mill revised utilitarianism, adding the idea that pleasures and pains could be classified according to quality as well as by amount. He also stressed the far-reaching effects of wrongdoing more explicitly than Bentham did.

Mill's version of utilitarianism rejects one of Bentham's fundamental premises — that all pleasures are equal. Bentham is disturbingly plain about this. He wrote,

> Let a man's motive be ill-will, call it even malice, envy, cruelty; it is still a kind of pleasure that is his motive: the pleasure he takes at the thought of the pain which he sees, or expects to see, his adversary undergo. Now even this wretched pleasure, taken by itself, is good: it may be faint; it may be short: it must at any rate be impure: yet while it lasts, and before any bad consequences arrive, it is good as any other that is not more intense. (Ch. X, X, n)

Mill contends in his essay *Utilitarianism*, however, that

> It is quite compatible with the principle of utility to recognize the fact that some kinds of pleasure are more desirable and more valuable than others. It would be absurd that, while, in estimating all other things, quality is considered as well as quantity, the estimation of pleasures should be supposed to depend on quantity alone.[6]

Accordingly, Mill opened the door for distinguishing what we might call "high quality" versus "low quality" pleasures and pains. Pleasures that Mill regarded as intrinsically superior include those associated with intelligence, education, sensitivity to others, a sense of morality, and physical health. Inferior pleasures include those arising from sensual indulgence, indolence, selfishness, stupidity, and ignorance.

A small amount of high quality pleasure could, then, outweigh a larger amount of low quality pleasure. Similarly, a small amount of high quality pleasure that is accompanied by substantial amounts of unhappiness would count as more pleasure than a greater amount of purer, but lower quality pleasure. When confronted with the issue of who determines the qualities of pleasures and pains, Mill replied that it would be those with the greatest experience of both: "It is better to be a human being dissatisfied than a pig satisfied; better to be Socrates dissatisfied than a fool satisfied. And if the fool, or the pig, are of a

---

[6]John Stuart Mill, *Utilitarianism*, Oskar Piest, ed. (Indianapolis, IN: Bobbs-Merrill, 1957), p. 12.

different opinion, it is because they only know their own side of the question. The other party to the comparison knows both sides. (12–13)"

Mill also took pains to examine the far-reaching consequences of actions. Concerned that utilitarianism might seem to defend lying, for example, Mill argued that the wide-ranging, social harm that it does far outweighs the good experienced by its beneficiaries. "Thus it would often be expedient," wrote Mill,

> for the purpose of getting over some momentary embarrassment, or attaining some object immediately useful to ourselves or others, to tell a lie. But inasmuch as the cultivation in ourselves of a sensitive feeling on the subject of veracity is one of the most useful, and the enfeeblement of that feeling one of the most hurtful, things to which our conduct can be instrumental; and inasmuch as any, even unintentional, deviation from truth does that much toward weakening the trustworthiness of human assertion, which is not only the principal support of all present social well-being, but the insufficiency of which does more than any one thing that can be named to keep back civilization, virtue, everything on which human happiness on the largest scale depends — we feel that the violation, for a present advantage, of a rule of such transcendent expediency is not expedient, and that he who, for the sake of convenience to himself or to some other individual, does what depends on him to deprive mankind of the good, and inflict upon them the evil, involved in the greater or less reliance which they can place in each other's word, acts the part of one of their worst enemies. (29)[7]

Mill's revisions of utilitarianism would probably take care of the most obvious weaknesses of Bentham's ideas. Mill would probably object to our Robin Hood scenario, then, by positing eventual harm to the thief and to society. The thief could become desensitized to the point that he might be less discriminating about the financial status of his victims, more tolerant of a less altruistic brand of thievery, more willing to resort to threats and violence, and so certain of the superiority of his personal moral compass that he becomes dangerously self-righteous. Word of his exploits could lead to his being imitated by others in a way that impedes the broad social benefits that flow from respecting rights of ownership.

Yet even Mill's brand of utilitarianism cannot avoid certain difficulties. First, some questions arise about the mechanism of distinguishing types of pleasures. Mill's reliance on personal experience initially seems sensible. You would hardly ask someone who knew nothing about sound equipment to help you pick out a new audio system. You trust that the people you do ask know that the pleasure you will get from the stereo will outweigh the immediate pain of the high price you are paying. Why shouldn't it be the same with ethics? How

---

[7]Another way of talking about Mill's insight here is that in the face of Bentham's *act-utilitarianism*, Mill suggests *rule-utilitarianism*. That is, whereas act-utilitarianism dictates that moral calculation should consider only the particular actions in question and their specific consequences, rule-utilitarianism sees the issue more as one of the moral character of rules, norms, or policies. Thus, although Mill conceded that a particular act of lying might be beneficial, he suggested that the consequences of adopting a moral rule to the effect that "lying is acceptable when it is to your private advantage" would be socially disastrous.

could someone who had lived a life of cruel and selfish treatment of others be expected to understand the pleasures that come from being a good and decent person? How could someone who had always been scrupulously honest know the full range of negative consequences that come from lying? Yet recognizing only certain, experienced people as qualified to make moral judgments could jeopardize the fair, open, impartial, and objective method of assessing consequences that a teleological outlook seeks. Many groups throughout human history have used claims of special moral insight to advance selfish and unscrupulous ends, defending the superiority of a certain class, race, religion, or gender. Subjective decisions are not necessarily arbitrary, but the danger remains that they could be.

The central weakness of Mill's approach to ethics, however, is that as long as an action or policy produces enough high quality pleasure, any action is theoretically defensible. Imagine, for example, that benevolent slavery of only 1 percent of the world's population for the next century could somehow lead to permanent peace, the end of poverty and hunger, and the discovery of cures for all major diseases. Our slaves would be the subjects of a crash program of social, political, and medical experiments sponsored by the United Nations and involving the brightest people from all countries. The aim is to solve the planet's worst problems once and for all. Imagine, further, that once these solutions are found, they are offered free to all countries. It is hard to imagine that the pain and suffering of the slaves would be greater than the centuries of benefits that would be enjoyed by billions of humans to come.

Nonetheless, this flaw should not overshadow the genuine advantages of a teleological approach to ethics. For the most part, it makes great common sense to link the ethical character of actions or policies to their practical outcome. Bentham's attempt to scrupulously catalog the consequences of actions points out the numerous ways that pleasures and pains can differ. It also imposes an objectivity and impartiality on ethical analysis that protects against prejudice, stupidity, or self-interest masquerading as moral wisdom. Mill's revisions of Bentham's ideas enjoy these same virtues, and Mill's discussion of types or kinds of pleasure and pain provides us with yet another important way to identify the consequences of actions.

The difficulty of employing a teleological approach should not be underestimated, however. As Mill's ideas imply, a full account of an action's results means not only careful analysis of the immediate consequences to all involved and astute discernment of the quality and comparative value of the sensations experienced, but also an uncovering of the subtle, indirect, far-reaching, and long-term results as well. An accurate teleological analysis requires great patience, impressive powers of observation, and a keen understanding of how people actually respond to various experiences.

Deontological Ethics

The second major tradition in philosophical ethics is the deontological approach. This outlook is based on an idea that teleological thinkers flatly deny — that actions have intrinsic moral value. Some actions are considered inherently good (truth telling, keeping promises, respecting the rights of others); others are inherently bad (dishonesty, coercion, theft, manipulation). No matter how much good comes from lying, argues a deontological thinker, the action will never be right.

Philosophy's most representative deontological thinker is Immanuel Kant (1724 – 1804). Kant believed that he had discovered the fundamental moral law that would determine the ethical character of an action without regard to its consequences. Kant called his moral law the *categorical imperative* — a command that holds no matter what the circumstances. He believed further that the validity of this ethical principle stemmed from reason itself and from our nature as free and rational moral agents with inherent value.

Even more so than with Aristotle, Kant assessed the moral character of actions by focusing on the internal, particularly the rational aspect of human conduct. Kant saw the validity of his ethics as being so steeped in reason that commentators have noted that his *Foundations of the Metaphysics of Morals* could have been called *Ethics Based on Reason*. Kant noted that the basis of moral obligation "must not be sought in the nature of man or in the circumstances in which he is placed, but sought a priori solely in the concepts of pure reason."[8]

For an action to be good, Kant believed that it must not simply conform to a moral law but must be done for the sake of a moral law. Indeed, Kant claimed that the only thing inherently good is a good will, that is, one that follows reason's guidance and acts from a sense of duty. A good will chooses what it does simply and purely because it is the right thing to do, not because it is inclined to do some deed or because the deed has positive consequences. Moreover, Kant claimed that reason dictates that the principle according to which one is acting, what Kant terms an action's *maxim*, should be able to be a universal law. As Kant expressed it in his first formulation of the categorical imperative: "Act only according to that maxim by which you can at the same time will that it should become a universal law of nature. (39)"

Kant's initial formulation of the categorical imperative reflected the belief that because ethics is essentially a rational enterprise, ethical principles should have the same character as such rational activities as logic and mathematics. For example, they should be internally consistent and universally valid. Kant argued that if one can will the maxim of one's action as a universal law, the principle on which one's deed is based meets these requirements and thereby conforms to a sense of duty. Maxims that fail this test are, by contrast, self-defeating and contradictory. Kant illustrated this with the example of a false promise. He wrote:

> [A] man finds himself forced by need to borrow money. He well knows that he will not be able to repay it, but he also sees that nothing will be loaned him if he does not firmly promise to repay it at a certain time. He desires to make such a promise, but he has enough conscience to ask himself whether it is not improper and opposed to duty to relieve his distress in such a way. Now, assuming he does decide to do so, the maxim of his action would be as follows: When I believe myself to be in need of money, I will borrow money and promise to repay it, although I know I shall never do so. Now this principle of self-love or of his own benefit may very well be compatible with his whole future welfare, but the

---

[8]Immanuel Kant, *Foundations of the Metaphysics of Morals*, Lewis White Beck, trans. (Indianapolis, IN: Bobbs-Merrill, 1959), p. 5.

question is whether it is right. He changes the pretension of self-love into a universal law and then puts the question: How would it be if my maxim became a universal law? He immediately sees that it could never hold as a universal law of nature and be consistent with itself; rather it must necessarily contradict itself. For the universality of a law which says that anyone who believes himself to be in need could promise what he pleased with the intention of not fulfilling it would make the promise itself and the end to be accomplished by it impossible; no one would believe what was promised to him but would only laugh at any such assertion as vain pretense. (40)

The false promise, then, is morally wrong because the maxim on which it is based is internally inconsistent. Universalizing it destroys the very concept of the promise that it aims to use. Such a principle of volition is illogical. The behavior of anyone who follows such a principle is morally flawed because it is literally irrational.

Kant's initial account of the moral law focused on our rational nature, but later in the *Foundations* he defined the categorical imperative in terms of human dignity and freedom. He wrote: "Act in such a way that you treat humanity, whether in your own person or in the person of any other, always at the same time as an end and never simply as a means." Kant believed that we each have a dignity that must be respected in our dealings with each other. Treating people as ends requires seeing them as autonomous beings who are entitled to control their own fate and not to be deceived or manipulated. Actions that are consistent with the dignity and autonomy of moral agents are intrinsically good. Treating people simply as a means, however, is to regard them as something that we use for our own purposes without their full and free consent. Such actions are inherently wrong.

Kant returns to the issue of the false promise to illustrate this idea:

[A] man in need finds himself forced to borrow money. He knows well that he won't be able to repay it, but he sees also that he will not get any loan unless he firmly promises to repay it within a fixed time. He wants to make such a promise, but he still has conscience enough to ask himself whether it is not permissible and is contrary to duty to get out of difficulty in this way. . . . [He] will immediately see that he intends to make use of another man merely as a means to an end which the latter does not likewise hold. For the man whom I want to use for my own purposes by such a promise cannot possibly concur with my way of action toward him and hence cannot himself hold the end of this action. (40, 48)

The person who was deceived by the false promise was tricked into doing something that he or she would not have consented to had all the facts been known. Even if the debt is ultimately paid, it does not change the fact that one person imposed his or her will on another and treated that person simply as a means to an end. Moral agents, for Kant, are free and autonomous. Being used against their will simply as a means to someone else's end violates this freedom.

Kant's discussions of the categorical imperative reveal the heart of a deontological outlook, but the details of his philosophy are complex. A less technical way of describing a deontological approach, however, might be to say that the ultimate ethical standard is whether an action fits with, is consistent with, or is appropriate to the fact that it is done to or performed by a being of a special sort — one who is rational and free. Indeed, this is the basic premise of claims that humans have *rights*. To say that we have basic human rights is to claim that we are entitled to treatment of a certain sort simply because of the very fabric of our being. That is why these rights are sometimes spoken of as *inalienable*. They reflect characteristic and defining features of our nature. Legal rights are created and bestowed by governments, but fundamental moral rights inhere in our nature and are simply recognized, not granted, by countries. A deontological approach to ethics, then, sees rights to fairness, equality, justice, honesty, and the respect of our dignity as rooted in the fundamental characteristics that define our nature.

Like the teleological approach to ethics, the deontological outlook has much to commend it. Analyzing an ethical dilemma takes on a much narrower focus than when approached teleologically. The only question is: Which actions are inherently good? Instead of engaging in complex projections of the primary and secondary consequences of some act, we focus simply on the deed itself. Does it respect the basic human rights of everyone involved? Does it avoid deception, coercion, and manipulation? Does it treat people equally and fairly?

The primary difficulty with this approach, however, is its inflexibility. If lying is intrinsically wrong, there is no way to justify it even when it produces more good than harm. If we lie or steal in order to help someone, for example, a deontological approach still condemns it. And this total lack of compromise makes a deontological standard a difficult one to live by.

Evaluating the Moral Character of Actions

With the teleological and deontological approaches to ethics, then, we see the basic elements that can be used in determining the ethical character of actions. One school of thought points to the results, the other to the actions themselves. So between them they reveal a wide array of internal and external factors of human actions that have moral consequences. Although these two outlooks conflict in theory, they complement one another in practice. In the pragmatic challenge of identifying and resolving ethical dilemmas, neither should be ignored; each acts as a check on the limitations of the other.

ETHICAL ISSUES IN BUSINESS

Business is one of the most pervasive elements of American society. We run into it daily — as employees, employers, customers, or the audience for commercials. Testifying to the centrality of business, Calvin Coolidge once observed that "the business of America is business." But what is business? And what are the areas in business that are most likely to produce ethical difficulties? What are the major ethical dilemmas that will arise? Where is debate over the relative weight of harms and benefits most likely to happen? Which business actions violate fundamental moral principles?

Business is actually a simple notion — making and selling goods or services for a profit. The shape of business in contemporary capitalism, however, is complex. Tiny "mom and pop" operations exist, but larger corporations are more often the norm. A vast majority of the work force is employed by small companies, but the few huge corporations that employ thousands of workers and annually take in billions of dollars wield enormous power. As seen in Flint, Michigan, the economies of entire cities and towns can depend on a single corporation's decisions — in this case, those of General Motors. Some companies are owned by one or a few individuals, but the ownership of other firms is spread among the people who own shares of the companies' stock. In larger corporations, managers run the firm with oversight by a board of directors. Employees in some companies have a major say in what happens, while other firms are characterized by hostile, adversarial relationships between employer and employees. And government has increasingly made its presence felt in the business world through legislation and regulations that often have economic ends, but just as often social and political ones. A wide array of characters — workers, managers, directors, stockholders, bondholders, banks, consumers, suppliers, competitors, corporate raiders, legislators, and regulators — vie for influence over corporate decisions.

So let's sort through the complexity and get a clear picture of just what business is and where the ethical issues arise.

Capitalism

In order to understand business, it is essential to start with the type of the economic system in which profit-making ventures ordinarily operate — capitalism. *Capitalism* is an economic system based on private property and the competition of the free market. Businesses respond to consumer desires by offering what they hope will be satisfying products. The price of these goods and services is theoretically set by free, voluntary, individual agreements to buy and sell. Capitalism generally rejects central economic planning, preferring to let the market determine which products are available and how much they will cost. The fact that businesses vie with each other for customers is supposed to ensure responsiveness to consumer wants and to encourage efficiency and creativity. As a result, customers should get what they want; they should receive good value for their money; and inefficient or greedy firms should either reform or go out of business. Capitalism is also characterized by the pursuit of self-interest and an uneven distribution of wealth. A critical defense of capitalism contends that the "common good" is actually promoted by everyone's acting selfishly. As Adam Smith explained it in his *Wealth of Nations:*

> [An individual] intends only his own gain, [but] he is . . . led by an invisible hand to promote an end which was no part of his intention. . . .
> By pursuing his own interest he frequently promotes that of the society more effectually than when he really intends to promote it.[9]

The Ethics of Capitalism

The distinctive features of capitalism present us with a variety of ethical questions.

[9]Adam Smith, excerpt from *The Wealth of Nations* in *The Varieties of Economics*, vol. 1, Robert Lekachman, ed., (New York: Meridian Books, 1962), 197.

- Capitalism is based on the right to own private property. Is such a right morally defensible? Should it be subject to any restrictions?
- The goods and services for sale in a capitalistic economy are supposed to stem from what consumers want. Are there any ethical problems with the fact that capitalism offers products that can be harmful or addictive, such as guns, gambling, tobacco, and alcohol? Should the freedom of the market be respected or should the government restrict what can be bought and sold? Are there ethically defensible reasons for making prostitution illegal? If guns can be sold, why shouldn't sex be as well?
- The process of buying and selling frequently involves negotiations. Accordingly, the most skillful negotiators get the best deals. A common tactic in negotiation is to bluff or to misrepresent one's actual position. Is bluffing dishonest? Is it lying? Or can it be defended as an ethical strategy?
- Capitalism also works by competition. Does this breed hostile and anti-social attitudes? Does it lead us to see each other more as enemies to beat rather than as neighbors and friends to work with?
- Capitalism encourages the accumulation of wealth and is characterized by a dramatically uneven distribution of wealth. Does this inequality lead to the "greatest good of the greatest number"? Should it have to? Can wealth be justified when it coexists with poverty in the same economy? Should wealth be limited or should the wealthy at least be forced to invest their money in a way that will have greater social benefits? Could this be done without violating individual freedom, rights to ownership, or personal control of one's property?
- Proponents of capitalism argue that it promotes freedom through every aspect of its activities. Every transaction between buyers and sellers is voluntary. All investment decisions are voluntary. No one forces a worker to work for a particular company. Dissatisfied employees can leave at any time to work for other firms or even establish businesses of their own. No one forces a business to produce a particular product. Similarly, no one prevents it from making and selling what it wants. Does the extent to which capitalism respects human freedom make it a deontological thinker's dream? Does capitalism actually deliver as much freedom as it seems to promise?
- Because capitalism is market driven, businesses probably increase their chances of success by appealing to the tastes of the lowest common denominator of a society. Does this encourage the proliferation of what Mill would regard as lesser pleasures? What are the long-term consequences of this? Does mass capitalism encourage lower quality pleasures in place of higher quality ones? Even if it does, is there anything wrong with that?
- Capitalism is based on maximizing one's own interest. Is this morally acceptable, or does capitalism encourage people to cross the line to selfishness, greed, and callous indifference toward others?

Corporations

Businesses are generally organized as *corporations*. Born in medieval Europe, a corporation originally was any group of people who joined together for a common purpose. Universities, for example, started as corporations of scholars. Common parlance now generally reserves the term *corporation* for profit-making, business organizations.

A corporation, however, is more than just a shorthand way of referring to the group of individuals who own a business enterprise. Corporations have a distinct legal status, and the law grants them specific benefits. Corporations are considered to be persons, for example, and they have many of the same rights as biological persons. Corporations also enjoy limited liability. That is, claims against a corporation and its owners can be made only against corporate resources. If a corporation goes bankrupt but still owes money, its owners' private holdings are protected.

The owners of corporations hold stock in the company — shares of ownership. (Stock is often also referred to as *equity*.) Corporations sell stock in order to raise money to fund the business. Stockholders (or shareholders) are promised only that they will share in any profits. If the company goes "belly up," they are last in line to be paid off. The shareholders' higher risk associated with the absence of any guarantees, however, is supposed to be balanced by higher profits in the form of *dividends* — the amount of money per share that stockholders receive as their portion of the profits. Major stockholders include private individuals, pension funds and other institutional investors, insurance companies, employees, banks, other corporations, and the corporation itself.

Stock is a share of ownership, but it is also a commodity. Some investors buy stock intending to hold onto it for years. But many people see stock mainly as a commodity with a fluctuating value, and they try to capitalize on this by speculating on which way the stock will move. Stock is sold at an initial price, but its value rises or falls depending on how the company is viewed by stock markets. (In the United States, most stock is bought and sold on the New York Stock Exchange and the American Stock Exchange.) As a result, shareholders can make money from their stock not only by receiving dividends, but also by selling the stock at a higher price than they paid for it. It is possible to make money whether a stock's price rises or falls. The latter is called "selling a stock short" and involves borrowing shares of someone else's stock, usually without their knowing it, selling it at the current price, waiting for the price to drop, buying back the requisite number of shares at a lower price, returning the shares and pocketing the difference. There is also a market in *warrants*, a certificate that simply gives the holder the right to buy a certain amount of stock at a specified time at a designated price. *Stock options* involve a similar right but are usually limited to a company's employees.

Issuing stock is a favorite way for corporations to raise money because it carries no commitment to repay the investment. Companies, however, will also raise money by issuing *bonds* at a fixed rate of interest that they promise to pay on a given schedule, frequently over decades. Bonds are thus a more secure investment than stock, but in exchange for the security, bondholders generally receive lower returns than stockholders.

One drawback of a corporation's issuing stock, however, is that anyone can buy it on the open market, including an individual or company interested in taking over the corporation. Such maneuvers are called *hostile takeovers. Corporate raiders* look for companies whose stock price is undervalued, that is, lower than they believe it is worth based on the value of the company. They offer to buy stock from shareholders at a premium price, assuming that once they control the company, they will manage it — or sell some or all of it — so as to make a profit on their investment. In response to a corporate raider, companies will often seek out a friendly buyer (a "white knight"). Sometimes a group of senior executives will buy the company; this is known as a leveraged buy-out (LBO). (The term comes from the fact that a company that is heavily in debt is said to be heavily "leveraged.") Some companies try to ward off takeovers by making themselves too unattractive to buyers in the first place. They use various financial disincentives ("poison pills") that are designed to make a takeover too expensive to succeed. One common tactic is for senior executives to receive huge settlements (known as "golden parachutes,") if they are removed from their positions as a result of the takeover.

Whether takeovers are friendly or hostile, they can produce dramatic changes in a company. Takeovers are usually financed by borrowed money (for example, high-yield, high-risk, "junk" bonds), and the target company may be broken up and profitable divisions sold off to decrease the debt. Operations are streamlined and jobs may be lost. Similar pressure is felt in leveraged buy-outs because the purchase is also financed by debt. The company thereby takes on substantial interest payments in the hope that future profits will cover them.

Because stock ownership is spread out among hundreds or thousands of people, ultimate authority in such companies is vested in a *board of directors*, a group of individuals responsible for seeing that the company is run properly. Traditionally, this has been understood to mean that business is conducted so that the interests of the owners, that is, the stockholders, will be maximized.

Board members have a legally enforceable fiduciary responsibility to advance the interest of shareholders, but the number and variety of stockholders can lead to disagreement about what this entails. Some shareholders argue that promoting their interests means keeping the market price of the stock as high as possible and even selling the company if a sufficiently profitable offer comes along. Other investors prefer stability and security and are more concerned with the size of their dividends. Employee stockholders will readily compromise both market value and dividends for corporate policies that guarantee job security. Shareholders will occasionally sue their own board of directors, charging them with failure to protect their interests.

Some people contend, however, that corporations should not be run exclusively for the interests of the stockholders. Rather, companies are said to have a *corporate social responsibility* that requires them to promote the interests of the communities and the nation in which they are located. According to this idea, being a good corporate citizen means more than simply obeying the law. Combating environmental pollution, reducing hard-core unemployment, protecting the local economy, contributing to charity, and supporting schools and other local causes are just a few of the social responsibilities companies are said to have.

Another way that the idea of expanded corporate responsibilities is expressed is to say that the corporation is responsible for protecting not only the stockholders' interests, but also the interests of anyone affected by corporate actions, that is, anyone who holds a stake in the outcome. *Stakeholders*, then, include employees, suppliers, customers, and members of the surrounding community. These groups claim an equal footing with stockholders when corporate decisions are made.

Many corporations focus all of their efforts in one industry. Apple Computers, for example, makes virtually all of its profits from computer products. Other companies branch out. Sears, for instance, originated as a retailer with its department stores and catalog business but moved into financial services. Other companies go even further afield. General Electric is involved in consumer electronics, aerospace, nuclear power, and communications. Similarly, USX (formerly U.S. Steel) has businesses in the steel, real estate, and petroleum industries. Such diversified corporations are called *conglomerates*. Some conglomerates exist simply to own, buy, and sell companies. That is, they have no primary allegiance to a particular industry. These companies, such as Texron, are known as holding companies.

Throughout the last thirty years, business has become increasingly international, and a major consequence of this is that many corporations are now genuinely global entities. They may be based in one country, but they have operations in many others. Such corporations are called multinational corporations (MNCs) and can buy the raw materials and labor that they need at the lowest price available on the globe and then sell their goods in countries where the prices are highest. They may also produce products that may be banned in the country they are made in but are legal to sell in other countries. The operation of a multinational is subject to local laws, but the entire corporation is actually free to determine its own international strategy. Multinational corporations are one of a handful of genuinely transnational institutions.

Another tendency in recent decades is for American corporations to concern themselves less with the production of goods than with the delivery of services. Because more basic manufacturing is now being done at lower costs in other countries, the majority of American workers are employed in service industries. These include everything from management consulting, financial services, and health care to travel and entertainment.

Corporations and Ethics

Corporations are interesting from an ethical standpoint. We speak of them as identifiable, autonomous entities, but they really are not. They are based on the principle of *delegated agency*, whereby managers and employees are supposed to act in the best interests of the genuine owners — the absent stockholders. But this idea has been attacked as too narrow. What, then, are the primary ethical issues raised by the nature of a corporation?

- What does it mean for the law to call the corporation a person? What rights does this imply? Free speech? Life?
- What responsibilities does a corporation have? Does it have social responsibilities? If so, what are they? Where would such responsibilities originate?
- Do the higher risks that stockholders accept and the rights of ownership that they acquire by buying stock establish them as the group whose interests must be advanced above all others? Does a company have obligations to its stakeholders? Does the fact that a company's actions will help or hurt identifiable groups of people thereby obligate the company to take their interests into account in making business decisions? In whose interest should the company be run?
- What are the ethical implications of limited liability? Are the rights of lenders sufficiently protected by the limited liability of a corporation's owners? Corporations can also receive temporary protection from creditors by declaring bankruptcy and restructuring how they will pay their debts. Is this an allowable strategy when, as in the case of the Manville Corporation described in

Chapter 6, those liabilities largely resulted from health claims and legal awards for people who had been injured by the company's product?

• How responsible can directors and executives be for their actions when they act only as agents for the shareholders? Does this fiduciary/agent relationship limit their moral responsibility? What should an executive do if he or she realizes that the company can profit by doing business with a firm notorious for unethical, but legal, conduct toward its employees? Is the executive morally obligated to pursue the profit because of a duty to advance the interests of the stockholders?

• What ethical guidelines should be followed in the attempt to profit from trading in a company's stock? Insider trading is against the law, but is it unethical? Is there a victim to this crime? What is inside information? Is it unethical to trade on a "hot tip"? Who is barred from using inside information? What about a printer who comes across such information while doing a job for another company? What if someone profited from using inside information to buy and sell stock options rather than stock itself? Does this make any difference?

• Do owners of large blocks of stock have different responsibilities than small owners? What should the manager of a pension fund that owns millions of shares of a particular company do when that firm is the target of a hostile takeover? Selling the fund's stock to the raider will produce a windfall for the fund, but a successful takeover may lead to the company's being broken up and many people losing their jobs. Whose interests take precedence?

• What are the ethical issues connected with takeovers? Some argue that the increasing amount of debt carried by corporations is bad not only for the companies but also for the economy. Debt, it is argued, jeopardizes the health of otherwise successful companies, ties up money that could do more good elsewhere, and causes some people to lose their jobs. The average success rate in mergers and acquisitions is only 50 percent, so do the benefits outweigh the risks? Corporate raiders used to engage in a practice called *greenmail*: Raiders would begin buying a target company's stock, threaten a takeover, but then agree to sell the stock to the company for a premium. This practice is now illegal, but was it unethical? Are golden parachutes ethically defensible?

• Do multinational corporations have any special moral obligations? Is there anything unethical about moving part of an MNC's operation from a country with expensive labor to one with cheap labor? Country A makes it illegal to sell a certain product; is there anything wrong with a company in country A making these products to sell in country B, where the product is legal? If the moral and/or legal norms of two countries in which the MNC operates are different, what should it do? For example, one country might be trying to eradicate discrimination or environmental pollution, while another country has no interest in either issue. Would simply obeying the law in each country be morally sufficient? Or should the corporation always enforce the higher standards throughout its entire global operation? If required antidiscrimination or antipollution programs increase a company's costs, is it morally acceptable for the company to move its operations to countries without such laws?

• Were MNCs that profited from doing business in South Africa doing anything morally questionable? What if they profited from selling arms to the South African military?

• Do companies doing business with third world countries have special responsibilities to protect the interests of the people they deal with there? Nestlé, for example, was criticized for promoting infant formula in countries where mothers' milk was often a healthier alternative. Was this a legitimate complaint?

• Do American-based corporations have any obligation to resist the temptation to move manufacturing operations offshore? Such moves have led to the loss of thousands of high-paying, blue-collar jobs. The jobs that rose in their place have for the most part been in the service industry at lower salaries. Can domestic companies be internationally competitive if they have a strong national loyalty?

How Corporations Are Run

As previously described, corporations are usually owned by so many different stockholders that ultimate authority and the responsibility for oversight are placed in the hands of a board of directors. Directors are generally men and women with business experience outside the company. They may include large stockholders, but they hardly ever include employees. Directors are elected by the shareholders after being nominated by the board. The executive committee of the board of directors, including the chairperson of the board, usually consists of executives from the corporation itself. From a practical standpoint, this is the most powerful group in the corporation for determining a company's general direction and its major policies.

Directors do not involve themselves in the corporation's ordinary business decisions. These day-to-day judgments are made by numerous senior and junior managers. Top executives include the chief executive officer (CEO), chief operating officer (COO), and chief financial officer (CFO). These officials are followed by executive vice-presidents, senior vice-presidents, vice-presidents, and a variety of assistant vice-presidents and managers. Each area of the company has its own head or director. Different divisions of large companies also have their own presidents.

Corporations are organized in a hierarchical, quasi-military fashion and are characterized by relationships of authority. Everyone has a boss. Even the CEO is responsible to the board, and the board is responsible to the shareholders. In the workplace, managers wield considerable authority over those they supervise.

The corporate hierarchy is also characterized by wide differences in salary. Managers generally make more than workers. Senior managers earn much more. The CEO of an average U.S. corporation is annually paid approximately seventy to eighty times more than the average American worker.

The main areas or functions of corporations are divided into *line* and *staff*. The former are those parts of the company directly connected with generating profits, for example, manufacturing, operations, marketing, and sales. The latter are support services: accounting, finance, legal, and human resources (formerly called personnel). Line positions usually have more prestige. CEOs virtually always come from line rather than staff functions. Lee Iacocca's background, for example, is in marketing. Success in moving up the corporate hierarchy comes more from having the ability to manage increasingly large numbers of people and less from being an exceptional accountant, engineer, chemist, or salesperson.

A particularly important staff function is accounting. A corporation's chief accountant is the controller (also comptroller). The controller's office is responsible for overseeing the financial status of the corporation, investigating signs of financial impropriety, and preparing reports on the company's financial condition. Accounting is not an exact science, however, and part of an accountant's job is to decide which methods and procedures will be used in preparing financial statements. These statements, however, are annually reviewed for accuracy by auditors from an outside accounting firm.

The primary task of managers is to determine how the business of the corporation will be conducted and to oversee the people under them. The major principle that has governed business in this regard since the beginning of the industrial revolution is the *division of labor*, which is best represented by the assembly line, where the complicated process of manufacturing a product is broken down into small, easily mastered, repetitive steps. A variation of this principle is also employed in offices and in the service industry. Managers and supervisors control who performs which tasks and how and when they are done. Managers aim to design work to optimize efficiency, even if it makes it less interesting. The work environment is characterized by an endless search to find ways that workers can produce more at lower costs. It is fair to say that workers and their managers frequently stand in an adversarial relationship to one another.

This adversarial relationship is most frequently expressed in the idea that labor and management are always and fundamentally in conflict over how to run the business. Management, it is said, wants to get the most out of labor for the least amount of money, while labor wants the most amount of money for the least amount of work. Sometimes this tension produces a situation in which employees join a union and establish the terms of a contract through collective bargaining with management. Roughly 20 percent of the American work force is unionized. Even in nonunion workplaces, however, the interests of the company and those of its employees are frequently considered to be at odds with one another.

When employers and unions cannot agree on the terms of a contract, workers will frequently resort to a variety of job actions to try to exert pressure on the company. They may call in sick, work more slowly, or even refuse to work and go on strike. Unions will also form picket lines for the purpose of persuading other people (customers, suppliers, other employees) to stay away from the company. Companies will usually negotiate with workers on strike, but they will sometimes replace them with new workers.

All employees receive a salary that is established either through collective bargaining or by prevailing wage rates. Most employees also receive various benefits, for example, health care insurance, disability insurance, and contributions to a pension fund. Pension funds are generally invested in stocks and bonds, and in many corporations, the funds have performed so well that the plans are overfunded — that is, they contain more money than is needed for their current obligations. Some companies have drawn this money out of the pension fund for immediate corporate needs. Some pension funds were the source of substantial profits made by corporate raiders. Some paid insurance companies to set up annual payments (annuities) for pensioners and then kept the rest of the pension funds for themselves. In other companies, difficult financial times have led to decreases in the pensions and health care benefits of retirees.

Tensions regularly arise in many companies over the question of how much authority a corporation has over its employees and what it can require as conditions of employment. Many employers now require drug tests, and some screen prospective employees for other health problems. Many companies give their employees psychological tests. Some corporations refuse to hire smokers because they will raise insurance premiums and health care costs. Others have rules about dating fellow workers or a competitor's employees. Some corporations practice "employment at will," a doctrine that gives a company maximum flexibility by claiming the right to terminate a worker for no just cause whatsoever. A common practice in the past, but now largely illegal, was requiring employees to take a lie detector test in connection with a company investigation of wrongdoing.

Adversarial relationships between corporations and their workers are not universal, however. Progressive corporations are characterized by an awareness by all parties involved that their welfare is interconnected. In such businesses, cooperation and mutual respect have replaced adversarial relationships. Trust has revealed the waste and inefficiency of distrust. Employees are regarded as the company's primary resource. Management and labor have benefited from seeing one another as partners in a common endeavor. In some firms there are even committees to which a fired employee can appeal the decision — committees that actually do overrule managers and rescind terminations. Following European and Japanese models, many American companies have also been changing the way work is designed. More companies are stressing quality and excellence rather than quantity. Self-planning teams of workers are replacing mindless, assembly line labor. Managers are giving up authority and letting decisions be made at the lowest levels of the organization.

All corporations are not alike in how they are run, however. Each is characterized by identifiable values and conventions that produce a distinct *corporate culture*. Corporate cultures vary as much as individuals do. Some firms are replete with policies, while in others, decisions are made as situations call for them. Some companies are highly ethical, while in others, moral and legal compromise is a way of life. Some corporations regard employees as their primary asset; others see workers as expendable and stupid pawns to be ordered about. In some corporations, success is measured by quarterly profits, stock price, and return to shareholders. Such companies may also rely on other companies to develop new ideas and products that they then use. Other corporations, however, focus more on the long range and invest in their own research and development. The atmosphere in some corporations is tense and hostile; the culture is so political as to be Byzantine. In essence, more effort goes into personal success and survival than into the real job at hand. Other firms, by contrast, are characterized by a friendlier atmosphere, shared authority, a sense of common purpose, and a spirit of cooperation.

A major factor that will force increased flexibility in corporate cultures across the board, however, is the demographic change taking place in the work force. Business in America used to be exclusively a white male's province, but by the year 2000, a vast majority of the new workers in the work force will be women or nonwhites. Corporate cultures, however, have been shaped largely by white men, and this has hampered the progress that women and minorities have been able to make in business. In essence, the first phase of the racial and sexual integration of business amounted to allowing women, blacks, and Hispanics into business as long as they conformed to the rules and norms established by the dominant white male culture. A principal challenge in the coming decades, however, is whether corporations can move to a more advanced stage of integration, altering their cultures so that they are genuinely receptive to differences among people.

The Ethics of Corporate Organization

The structure of corporate governance, the design of work, employer–employee relationships, and corporate cultures raise numerous ethical issues.

- The average member of a board of directors is a white, male, politically conservative, senior manager. Even though shareholders elect board members, boards nominate their own replacements; not surprisingly, they usually nominate people like themselves. Is there anything ethically questionable about this structure of corporate governance? Should it be more representative and more democratic? Specifically, should American corporations follow the German model and include employee representation on boards? In light of the public impact of corporate decisions, should there be community representatives on boards? Whether they are stockholders or not, do employees and the public have a right to be involved in decisions that will affect their lives? Should corporations be more democratic?
- Is the vast difference in salaries in corporations ethically defensible? Do top executives make too much money? In a market system, does it even make sense to ask whether anyone makes "too much" money? Executives generally make less than entertainers and sports figures. Does this imply that they are underpaid?
- Despite the popular picture of an accountant as a dull "bean counter," accountants probably face more ethical dilemmas in business than anyone else. They are under constant pressure to show the company's financial condition in the best light. They may be the first to see evidence of financial dishonesty. What is an accountant's moral responsibility, however? At what point does using accounting conventions become misrepresenting the truth? If a junior accountant reports dishonesty to the controller and the controller ignores the evidence, does the accountant have a responsibility to go to the CEO or to the board of directors? If an outside audit uncovers financial wrongdoing, should it be reported to legal officials, stockholders, or just senior management?
- Accountants are not alone in facing dilemmas about whether to "blow the whistle" on corporate wrongdoing. But all potential whistleblowers face the same issues. At what point is whistleblowing allowable? At what point is it required? Does it make any difference whether the dilemma stems from stealing money from the corporation or from something that may lead to someone's being hurt? Is whistleblowing disloyal to one's fellow workers or to one's company? Whistleblowers are often punished or ostracized for what they do. Is there anything morally wrong with this action? Does the likelihood of retribution relieve whistleblowers of any moral obligation?

• Is there any ethical requirement for work to be designed in a particular way? Is there anything wrong with designing work so that it is dull and boring, even if extremely efficient? Are systems that give employees some control over the design of their work morally superior or just different?

• From an ethical standpoint, is there anything intrinsically questionable about the frequently adversarial character of relationships in business, particularly between management and labor? Is cooperation intrinsically superior?

• Is there anything ethically wrong with strikes? Picket lines? Replacing workers on strike? Being one of those new workers?

• Is there anything unethical about using the money from an overfunded pension plan for other purposes? Whose money is it — the retirees' or the corporation's? Is it a benefit or deferred income? Is it morally acceptable for corporate raiders to buy annuities for retirees and appropriate what's left for themselves? What kind of obligation does a corporation have to its retirees? Is it morally obligated to increase pensions as the cost of living increases? Is a company morally obligated to avoid decreasing its former workers' medical benefits?

• What rights are employees entitled to? In the United States, corporations do not necessarily have to respect the same rights for its employees that the government must for all its citizens. Is this ethically defensible? Should employees, for example, have rights to due process? What kind of rights to free speech should an employee have? Should an employee be able to be fired for criticizing the company?

• How much privacy are employees morally entitled to? Do drug tests violate their privacy? Are companies entitled to regulate aspects of an employee's private life that can affect the corporation?

• How defensible is the practice of employment at will?

• How does one evaluate corporate cultures from an ethical perspective?

• What actions are corporations morally obligated to undertake in order to prevent racial or sexual discrimination?

Customers

The whole point of what goes on inside corporations, of course, is to produce goods or services that people outside the company will buy. A corporation's customers include private individuals; other businesses; and local, state, and federal governments. Customers may be domestic or foreign.

Primary responsibility for promoting products to customers falls to those in the company's marketing department. They try to identify the most likely audience for their company's goods or services as well as the most effective way to reach that audience. Marketing departments also keep track of the competition.

Advertising is obviously one of the most important ways to communicate with potential consumers. A sales force is another major way to make contact with buyers. Coupons and rebates are used to induce customers to buy certain products, as are special sales.

Customers look for safe, effective products at a fair price. Although the price of products is usually set by some combination of the cost of production, consumer demand, and the supply available, companies are sometimes caught engaging in collusion to keep prices high. Companies and industries vary according to pricing strategy. For example, the profit margins for the food in a grocery store are relatively low while those of designer clothing, pharmaceuticals, and eyeglasses are relatively high. The profits on items with lower margins and for discount stores in general, therefore, come from a higher volume of sales.

Companies frequently try to reassure consumers about the quality of a product by offering guarantees or warranties. Companies will also sometimes recall products that have been found defective or dangerous.

Ethics and Customer Relations

Despite the simplicity with which a business's relationship to its customers can be described, this area of business raises many ethical issues.

- Corporations' attempts to keep track of the competition's plans raise various ethical questions. Where is the line between legitimate research and industrial espionage? Is there anything wrong with trying to learn another company's secrets?
- When is advertising misleading and deceptive? When does an ad cross the line from putting the best face on a product and become a case of misrepresenting its nature? Is there anything ethically questionable about the extensive use of sex in contemporary advertising? How should products be advertised to children so as not to take advantage of their youth and inexperience? Is there anything wrong with celebrities from the worlds of entertainment or sports endorsing products?
- Are any sales practices unethical? What about trying to talk a buyer up to a more expensive product, so-called "bait and switch" tactics? If a salesperson knows that a new and improved version of a product will be available shortly, does he or she have an obligation to tell the customer? What if it means that the customer will delay buying and that the store will be stuck with more inventory of a soon-to-be obsolete product?
- A very small number of people who are induced to buy because of a rebate offer actually send for the rebate. The figure might be as low as 2 percent. How do coupons and rebates look from an ethical point of view? Should a company simply put the product on sale for everyone?
- From an ethical standpoint, are there conditions that have to be met for a sales promotion to be a genuine sale? The catalog of one retailer, for example, advertises its products as "up to 50 percent off" — for example, "Regular Price $45 — YOUR COST ONLY $29.95." The order form, however, states: "Regular Prices are a general guide for reference purposes only. This indicates our determination of comparable prices for similar merchandise at retail outlets across the country. It is not our present or former selling price." Are the claims of savings in this catalog morally dubious, or is the disclaimer — placed so that it should catch the attention of any serious buyer — a sign of a scrupulously honest retailer? Would it be more honest to say "price elsewhere" rather than "regular price"?
- If the market will bear it, is there anything wrong with making, say, a 60 percent profit on an item? Does it ever make sense to say that a consumer was overcharged? Aren't all transactions between buyer and seller completely voluntary? Aren't there always competitors to keep prices in line? Is there anything wrong with high profit margins?

- Is there anything wrong with corporations conspiring to fix prices? What if it results in the continued financial health of these firms and ultimately protects the jobs of hundreds of workers?
- Some corporations have been found to have secret warranties. A product might have a problem that the company chooses not to announce publicly, but if a customer complains after the warranty has expired, the company will fix or replace the product. Is there anything morally questionable about this practice?
- There have been cases in which products with a defective design caused serious injury to consumers. In return for a settlement, however, the company required the injured consumer to agree not to say anything publicly about the case. Apparently, the company feared that such publicity would hurt sales and lead to other complaints and settlements. Is there anything wrong with this practice?

Business and Government

In theory, the role of government in free market capitalism is limited. Government's job is simply to enforce the laws and prevent monopoly. In reality, however, government has a pervasive presence in contemporary business.

Laws and regulations affecting business emanate from the local, state, and federal levels. They touch virtually every aspect of business. The Securities and Exchange Commission regulates the investment industry. The Department of Justice can stop a merger that it believes violates antitrust laws. Judges can prevent the importing of products from countries that fail to follow certain restrictions. Courts can overturn firings and order reinstatement, back pay, and punitive damages. There are laws relating to salary (minimum wage and other compensation issues), allowable working age, labor relations, environmental pollution, workplace safety, consumer protection, product liability, and deceptive advertising. The most common way of punishing corporations that break the law is through fines. However, there have been cases of executives being jailed for actions they took in the name of the company.

Government regulation of business sometimes stems from a desire to ensure that competition is open and fair. But laws frequently aim to advance a policy considered to be in the national interest, for example, the prohibition of child labor. One of the most far-reaching attempts to advance social ends is federal legislation aimed at eliminating discrimination in the workplace. American businesses responded to various civil rights acts and employment discrimination laws with affirmative action programs designed to increase the representation of women and racial minorities in business. Such programs were compulsory for companies doing business with the federal government, but voluntary for all others. Nonetheless, affirmative action has received the strong support of the nation's business leaders.

Even after a quarter century of implementation, however, affirmative action remains controversial. One set of critics charges that it has gone too far and permits so-called "reverse discrimination" and hiring quotas based solely on race or sex. Other critics claim that current programs are too weak and point to ongoing income disparities between whites and blacks and to the small numbers of female and minority senior executives.

The desire of women to advance in business has also brought attention to special difficulties they face. The problem of sexual harassment in the workplace received extensive national attention during the confirmation hearings of Supreme Court Justice Clarence Thomas. Many women also claim that they continue to earn less than men. They argue not that men and women still earn different amounts for doing the same job, but that women are paid less than men for jobs of *comparable worth*. Supporters of comparable worth claim that positions that are traditionally filled by women have been undervalued and undercompensated in comparison to jobs that require similar amounts of responsibility, training, and experience but are normally filled by men — for example, the job of the nurse versus the job of the electrician. The concept of comparable worth has been accepted for municipal workers by various states, cities, and towns in the United States and applies to all employees — public and private — in the Canadian province of Ontario. It has also made headway in corporations under the label of "job evaluation" programs. Nonetheless, the idea remains highly controversial.

Business, Ethics, and the Law

Although the legal character of an action is not the same as its ethical character, examining the aspects of business that governments seek to regulate reveals numerous moral issues.

- What should happen when a corporation breaks the law? Is it possible to penalize such an entity? Who should be responsible for corporate wrongdoing? Executives? Board members? Stockholders? Is it fair to punish executives for corporate actions when they act simply as agents for the stockholders? Fines are the most common way to punish corporations, but the cost of punishment can simply be passed along to consumers.
- How should discrimination in American society be combated? Are affirmative action programs ethically defensible? Are they too weak or too strong? What constitutes reverse discrimination? Do affirmative action programs aid those people who have been most damaged by discrimination?
- What is the difference between innocent flirting or friendly joking, on the one hand, and sexual harassment, on the other? Precisely what makes sexual harassment ethically questionable?
- Is the concept of comparable worth ethically defensible? Opponents of the idea argue that women freely choose the jobs they have. Others contend that parents, guidance counselors, and hiring officers "steer" women to lower paying careers. Is legislation the proper way to correct ongoing discrimination in this area?

Business and the Environment

For the last century, industrial capitalism has generally regarded the planet's natural resources as something businesses can use as they see fit. Little thought was given to environmental pollution, overuse of resources, preservation of resources for future generations, or the interests of animals. Indeed, such concerns are frequently seen as costly impediments to economic development. Between environmental legislation and a heightened awareness by consumers about the dangers of continued pollution, however, many corporations are seeking to conduct their businesses in an environmentally responsible fashion.

Business, Ethics, and the Environment

Environmental ethics is one of the newest and most challenging areas of business ethics. In many cases, resolving these problems calls for dramatic shifts in conventional ways of thinking.

• Do future generations have rights? If so, must we change the way we do business? Should we limit the amount of natural resources we use annually? Are the rights of future generations violated by our use of nuclear power, that is, by our generating wastes that are dangerous for thousands of years?

• Is there a way of harmonizing economic development and environmental pollution? Do more developed countries have a greater responsibility not to pollute than less developed countries? Do the developed nations have a moral responsibility to cut back their way of life?

• Does business's attempt to get consumers to increase their level of consumption have adverse environmental consequences? Does it encourage waste and misuse of limited resources?

• Do animals have rights? Should animals be used in testing products? Should the interests of animals be taken into account when a business wants to develop an area for profit? Are farm animals entitled to live under particular conditions before they are slaughtered? Is it ethical at all to raise animals for food?

• What obligations do businesses have in order to be environmentally responsible? Must they shift production to recycled or recyclable substances? Should they decrease the amount of material used in packaging?

• What does it mean to say that a product is "green," that is, environmentally friendly? Do companies have a moral obligation to produce only "green" products?

Business and Ethics: A Final Word

The essence of business — the fairly simple idea of buying and selling things for profit in a competitive, free market — leads to an enormous array of ethical issues. The previous discussion points to most of the basic ones, but many more would surface as one explored the fine points of business.

In the readings and cases that follow, you will encounter many of the ethical dilemmas mentioned here. Yet despite the great variety of issues, they can all be viewed in terms of the basic questions set by teleological and deontological approaches to ethics. How do business practices measure up against a standard of human happiness or well-being? Who will be helped or hurt and in precisely what way? What course of action will produce the greatest overall benefits, both in terms of quantity and quality? Are the actions or policies in question appropriate to the fact that they are done by and to beings of a special sort? Are people being used as merely a means to an end? Are their rights being violated?

ADDITIONAL READINGS

Ethics

Frankena, William K., *Ethics* (Englewood Cliffs, NJ: Prentice Hall, 1973).
Melden, A. I., *Ethical Theories* (Englewood Cliffs, NJ: Prentice Hall, 1967).
Rachels, James, *The Elements of Moral Philosophy* (New York: Random House, 1986).
Solomon, Robert C., *Ethics: A Brief Introduction* (New York: McGraw-Hill, 1984).
White, Thomas I., *Right and Wrong: A Brief Guide to Understanding Ethics* (Englewood Cliffs, NJ: Prentice Hall, 1988).

Ethics and Business

Beauchamp, Tom L., and Norman E. Bowie, eds., *Ethical Theory and Business*, 3rd ed. (Englewood Cliffs, NJ: Prentice Hall, 1988).
De George, Richard T., *Business Ethics*, 3rd ed. (New York: Macmillan, 1990).
Des Jardins, Joseph R., and John J. McCall, eds., *Contemporary Issues in Business Ethics*, 2nd ed. (Belmont, CA: Wadsworth, 1990).
Donaldson, Thomas, *Corporations and Morality* (Englewood Cliffs, NJ: Prentice Hall, 1982).
———, and Patricia Werhane, eds., *Ethical Issues in Business: A Philosophical Approach*, 3rd ed. (Englewood Cliffs, NJ: Prentice Hall, 1988).
Hoffman, W. Michael, and Jennifer Mills Moore, eds., *Business Ethics: Readings and Cases in Corporate Morality*, 2nd ed. (New York: McGraw-Hill, 1990).
Iannone, A. Pablo, ed., *Contemporary Moral Controversies in Business* (New York: Oxford, 1989).
Regan, Tom, ed., *Just Business* (New York: Random House, 1983).
Shaw, William H., and Vincent Barry, *Moral Issues in Business*, 5th ed. (Belmont, CA: Wadsworth, 1992).
Snoeyenbos, Milton, Robert Almeder, and James Humber, eds., *Business Ethics: Corporate Values and Society* (Buffalo, NY: Prometheus Books, 1983).
Velasquez, Manuel G., *Business Ethics: Concepts and Cases*, 3rd ed. (Englewood Cliffs, NJ: Prentice Hall, 1992).

CHAPTER 2

◆ ◆ ◆

The Morality of Business and Capitalism

Although business ethics deals with specific ethical dilemmas such as insider trading, discrimination, employee rights, and deceptive advertising, there are also fundamental ethical questions that relate to the economic system in which business takes place. Accordingly, this chapter asks about the morality of business and capitalism

We begin with observations about the conflict between our ordinary moral sensibilities and common business conduct — observations made by someone who has been in business for nearly thirty years, James Michelman. Michelman explores the troubling insight that the demands of economic competition seem to dictate morally questionable actions and attitudes. The issue of the overall ethical character of business is also pursued by Richard McCarty, who, after rejecting the traditional defenses of business selfishness, offers a strategy for combining business and benevolence. Concentrating on the motives underlying business decisions, McCarty argues that there is "a virtuous way to be selfish [that is,] a virtuous way to practice business." Similarly supportive of the economic system in which business in America is done is Michael Novak. Novak recognizes the traditional charges leveled at capitalism, but he defends the system as being based on "virtuous self-interest," not mere greed and envy. Next, we encounter Jeffrey Reiman's contention that even if capitalism is exploitative, it may nonetheless have a moral defense.

James H. Michelman
SOME ETHICAL CONSEQUENCES OF ECONOMIC COMPETITION

I would like to discuss some fundamental questions regarding business ethics that stem (for me) from personal observations I've made over twenty-five years of responsible activity in the world of free enterprise.

I

First, I note that a conflict exists between attitudes and actions demonstrated by myself and my associates when related to business, and attitudes and actions shown in more private affairs. I am aware of acts of charity, kindness, and public service performed by my co-workers in their private lives. In their dealings with me, they are truthful and faithful; we share common goals. Yet, in our dealings with customers and suppliers neither our truthfulness nor our fidelity can be assumed. If we are truthful and faithful it is because of (economically) rational or sentimental reasons, not because we are determined by moral law. We excuse ourselves by assuming a similar lack of truthfulness and fidelity in our trading partners. And they too, we believe, assume the same of us. Sometimes we are dealt with openly — all cards on the table. In that case, we assume laziness or sentimentality. These attitudes, actions, and reactions derive from the many years we have spent surviving in competitive markets. They are pragmatic; they are learned from experience.

We are seldom kind. When large sums are at stake, kindness is irrelevant. Nor do we look for kindness. Thus sympathy and compassion are excluded from those attitudes and expectations determining our course. The obligation of mutual aid is irrelevant, too. Suppliers are those you buy cheaply from; customers those to whom you sell as dearly as possible. We view competitors as the enemy and suppose that we are the enemy to them. Our relations with them are formal; our attitudes, dislike and fear. An act dictated by thoughts of beneficence toward any of them by any of us would be considered by the rest of us to be a foolish act at best, and, at worst, an act of betrayal. With respect to competing for orders or resources, our gain is our competitors' loss; and we rejoice at our gain. Thus we are undismayed at their loss to which we have contributed. Again, we suppose like feelings on their part. We take none of these attitudes, dispositions, and actions to be exceptional, but rather expect that they are more or less universal in the business world. They seem to be rational attitudes and actions; and their rightness also seems to be confirmed by the (business) benefits they confer, and the (business) losses which follow when their controlling precepts are ignored. Now I have not observed these statements to be always true, of course. But they hold as to primary tendencies.

Certainly, the reader should not rely only upon my personal observations. My business or industry may be peculiar. It is possible that my views are

From *Journal of Business Ethics* 2 (1983), 79–87. Copyright © 1983 by D. Reidel Publishing Co., Dordrecht, Holland and Boston, U.S.A. Reprinted by permission of Kluwer Academic Publishers.

distorted. If the reader is, or has been, engaged in commerce, he can reflect on his own observations to see how they jibe with mine. In addition there are two more investigations he can make. He can examine the daily press to see if the stories printed about business tend to confirm or contradict my reports. And the reader can construct hypothetical situations and note what he would expect the responses of the actors to be.

The press seems to afford confirmation. As an exercise in preparing this paper I noted in *The New York Times* and *The Wall Street Journal* during the period March 9, 1982–April 2, 1982, many articles either stating directly or strongly implying attitudes and actions on the part of persons engaged in business or the professions, or who were 'investors', that we probably would take to be violations of accepted moral rules.[1] Two examples illustrate the point clearly.

1. *The Wall Street Journal*, March 11, 1982, headlined 'Comparative Ads Are Getting More Popular, Harder Hitting'. Comparative advertising, of course, directly compares the advertiser's product to that of his competitor(s). The competing products are often disparaged; sometimes it is suggested that they are dangerous. The *Journal* quoted the director of broadcast standards and practices at one of the major networks. "Competitors are taking each other by the throat". The imagery is apt. Although almost all advertising carries with it the implication that if successful it will contribute to the unsuccess of the advertiser's competitors, this implication may be ignored by the audience and denied by those who conceive and execute it. But this masking must grow much less effective when the ads become 'hard hitting'. Ultimately, it is not other advertisers and other firms, but rather other *people* that are being attacked and presumably will suffer from the success of the 'hard hitting' campaign. The executives, copywriters, and art people of the agency whose campaign is less successful will suffer; they may lose their jobs. The persons responsible for merchandising the product under attack will be damaged in some proportion to the rise in fortunes of the attackers.

2. *The Wall Street Journal*, April 2, 1982, headlined 'The Workout Crew. Bankers Who Step In If Loans Go Bad Reveal Lenders' Other Face. There Isn't Any Smile on It; Teams Tell Ailing Clients To Make Changes Or Else. "We See a Management Void"'. This long lead article begins by stating that ". . . workout specialists, the bankers who take over when a business loan goes bad" are known as "undertakers, morticians, black hats, or goons". They are dreaded. They force firings. Sometimes they are known by euphemisms because "Sometimes ailing companies extricate themselves from workout at one bank by borrowing from another institution. If the new banker, unaware of the customer's less-than-perfect status, calls the old one for information and hears 'workout', he will run the other way." "A [client] company's change in status from master to slave often comes abruptly . . . 'It's always interesting to watch them walk down that corridor, look at that sign (Institutional Recovery Management) [a euphemism] and watch their faces change as it dawns on them they might be in trouble', chuckles [a senior banking officer]." "Bankers say they have only one concern . . . : getting their money back. 'We have the right to get paid and they have an obligation to pay us. . . . The bank didn't cause the company to make bad investments or whatever it was that caused them to lose money'". The sense of this article is fear and humiliation on the

part of the executives of the company in difficulty, contempt and rationality by the bankers.

Neither of these articles (nor the others) conveys any feeling that the actions and attitudes of the participators are unacceptable or even unexpected. Their activities are interesting and so newsworthy. But they are not subject to moral judgment. Yet the comparative advertisers are engaging in an obviously male-ficent enterprise (even if unacknowledged by themselves). The workout crews — as described in the article — are brutal. These attributes — maleficence and brutality — are not, of course, those that we would wish our friends and neighbors to hold and express in their dealings with us. Nor may they be warranted by reasoning from a certain justifying premise of free enterprise — one that holds least-cost efficiency to be a proper end of economic activity. For in the case of the advertisers, maleficent effort has been expended merely to induce purchasers to substitute one consumer product for a similar one.[2] With respect to the workout crews, brutality is irrelevant. Yet, until we have reason to think that maleficent persons are attracted to the advertising industry and brutal ones to banks, we must concede that maleficence and brutality are characteristics of the job rather than the person.

To further investigate if there is a tendency for business morality to diverge from private, the reader might consider several scenarios and suppose what his own responses would be.

For example, he might suppose himself a purchasing agent, right now in the midst of buying a large quantity of raw material. Would he inform one of his regular suppliers that all the others raised their prices just this week? Or would he do his best to conceal the news? What if the supplier's salesman put the question to him directly? Would he claim ignorance? And if he answered the question truthfully, would he have occasion to feel that he had not fulfilled his obligation to his firm? If he then switched sides of the desk and became the salesman asking the question of the buyer, what assumptions should he make regarding the buyer's response?

Suppose the reader gives himself a promotion. He becomes president of the firm. What would he want — and expect — of his purchasing agent? Truthfulness, or shrewd dealing, assuming that these were in conflict?

Or the reader might suppose himself removed from the world of commercial negotiation. Rather he is an investor who, betting on a weak economy with high unemployment and falling interest rates, has bought fixed income securities. But the economy strengthens, workers are re-hired, and rates rise. How would he respond? Would he be pleased that the misery of hard times has begun to abate? Or would he grieve at the principal losses of his bonds? Suppose that it was not his own money that he had invested, but that of a charitable foundation of which he was trustee. Would this difference alter his response?

All these examples — my own observations, press reports, and reflections by the reader — at least begin to suggest that viewed from a certain standpoint, business competition simply may be amoral. This possibility raises another question — one that asks if there are *necessary* contradictions between generally accepted moral obligations and the laws and rules that flow from the logic of economic competition?

II

Business competition — free enterprise — is a rational undertaking. Profit maximization is the overriding consideration in the competitive universe, and profit maximization is achieved through rationality. These remarks, commonplace in microeconomic theory, may be justified as follows.

Unless a firm can bid successfully for factors of production it cannot survive. And only if it earns at least an average rate of return on its invested capital, will it be able to stay in the auction. The market validates this premise every day. A firm earning less than its competitors loses its ability to pay its more talented employees that wage which they could get elsewhere, and they will leave. Its credit rating sinks; its cost of funds rises. It may have difficulty borrowing regardless of cost. Thus its access to raw materials becomes restricted, and it is unable to pay for new plant and equipment. As a result its unit cost of production increases. These short examples are not exhaustive. But they illustrate real forces which logically must, and ultimately do, drive that firm to bankruptcy or voluntary liquidation.

One could postulate a universe of firms all initially earning about the same rate of return on invested capital but *not* maximizing income. But this universe would be unstable for unless there were legal constraints on return of capital the very engine of free enterprise — the profit motive — would immediately drive at least some firms to maximize profits. Once these became some small significant fraction, that fraction could, and would, outbid the rest for productive resources. Hence, relative stability occurs only when *all* are running their hardest; that is when *all* are seeking to maximize income. The laggards have already fallen by the wayside; future laggards will suffer the same fate.

To maximize profit the firm is obliged to make the most efficient use of its productive factors among which — often the most important — are persons; to choose products for sale which optimize its revenue; to purchase resources — again including persons — at the lowest possible cost, in short, to operate rationally. Else, it is failing to maximize return on invested capital and, sooner or later, must lose out to its competitors and cease to be a firm.

These simple considerations lead to profound ethical consequences.

First, consider our normal sense of what kind of persons we feel we ought to be. What are the attitudes and actions that we would like to think are part of our own moral makeup and that we would wish others to exhibit in their relationships with us? A non-exhaustive list surely includes courage and intelligence, kindness, compassion, honesty, loyalty, respect for others, adherence to the social duties of mutual aid and non-maleficence, and self-respect. Call this set of characteristics our *desired moral character* or the *human virtues.*

What characteristics would we look for in the managers of a company in which we held an important stake? Whatever this catalog turns out to be, call it the *desired business character.* It also certainly includes intelligence and a certain type of courage. But here we value intelligence and courage only insofar as they aid our managers to maximize the profits of our firm.

Next, if we analyze the role of persons as employees of firms engaged in free enterprise we discover an immediate moral paradox. Note that treating an employee as other than a productive factor stems from a philanthropic judgment rather than a business one. It may be rational for a firm to treat (some of) its employees considerately and reward them well, but only up to that point where finally there is no marginal benefit from doing so. Considerations of kindness and sympathy, for example, are irrelevant. A manager's obligation is to his firm, not its employees; and as we have already seen, he has no real choice in the matter if his firm is to survive. But it is clear that in following this reasoning we are struck at once with a contradiction which can be expressed by asking the question, What is the manager's duty to himself? If the discharge of his corporate responsibilities requires him to run counter to his desired moral character and so to violate his own basic self, must he do so? The necessity of profit maximization provides the answer. If the firm is to survive, the manager's obligation must be to it, not to himself. It follows, then, that free enterprise can require the violation of the individual's most basic duties to himself.

As a firm thrives, so do its responsible employees. But *regardless of their own well-being* their duty is to act so as to further the firm's interests which are to maximize its income, to make more and more money, amass more and more wealth. It is likely that these goals will be severely limited since all the firm's competitors, having the very same goals, prevent any single firm from outdistancing the others. But if the firm's policies — and so those of its responsible employees — are not fixed on the main chance, it is bound to fail. Once the firm enters the competition, it must abide by the rules of that competition. And all these rules are comprehended by the single Rule: Let the maxim of your action be that which advances the profitability of your firm. It seems a fair argument that once a rational being enters into — becomes an employee — of a firm (putting aside of course his motive for doing so) insofar as he acts *as an employee*, the maxim of his action must ignore his own moral interest and regard only his duty to make his firm as profitable as possible.

Nor is this all. Rationality demands that vendors rationalize their customers (sell at the highest possible price) and users rationalize their suppliers (buy at the lowest possible cost). Rationality demands that competitors seek the same orders, the same resources, the same employees — seek that is, their advantage at the expense of others. Given the set of demands engendered by, and inseparable from, the universe of economic competition, it therefore becomes a clear contradiction for an employee of one firm to act upon the laws generated by competition and will also that his suppliers, his customers, his competitors, act upon, and benefit from, those laws as well. For he then would be willing that they do what they can to negate his will. He would be willing war on himself.[3]

In sum, we find that the responsible firm employee must regard co-workers, vendors, and customers only as means to his firm's advantage; and that he himself is mere means to this end. We may conclude that insofar as he is fulfilling the obligation of his job — doing that for which he draws compensation — a corporate executive (for example) is foreclosed from acting toward his associates (superior, peers, subordinates) out of humane considerations, foreclosed from considering the interests of his suppliers and customers, foreclosed from beneficent acts toward his competitors, or indeed toward anyone with whom he has a commercial relationship. He is also thereby foreclosed from acting in accordance with his own moral character. He may, of course, perform *seeming* acts of beneficence or fidelity toward any of these persons or toward himself, but in that case the acts would be the end of rational calculation. If not seeming, they must be neutral acts or done *in spite of* his duty to his firm.

III

In addition to the general moral consequences of economic competition, we can identify specific consequences. Some of the more apparent are cataloged below.

1. When any business prize — a sale, a purchase, an order to deliver, a contract to perform — is sought by two or more firms, the duties both of mutual aid and of non-maleficence become contradictory. The contradiction of the duty of mutual aid follows at once from the fact of the competition. The impossibility of non-maleficence follows almost as immediately. For under competition there is a winner (or winners), and there is a loser (or losers). Let us think, for example, of two salesmen competing for a contract. The successful salesman, if his compensation is by commission, has benefited directly. It is possible that his life's prospects have been enhanced. If he is a good salesman, that is, a frequent winner, they will have been. But by winning he has hurt his competitor. The loser may suffer real psychic pain, and through loss of prospective income and damaged expectations, real physical injury as well. But all this is of no matter to the winner. For merely by entering the competition he has willed that his competitors be injured.

2. The obligation to tell the truth is contradicted by the requirements of commercial negotiation. We see this by noting that if there is to be negotiation, rather than a fixed or coerced price[4] there must be *room* for negotiation — call it a negotiating range. The range is defined by the highest price the buyer will pay and the lowest the seller will accept. Within those limits a deal can be struck. Now one or the other must make a statement, else the negotiation could not begin. The statement, however, must be misleading. If the buyer reveals the highest price he is willing to pay (the top of the range) the deal will be made at that figure. Nor can the seller reveal the lowest price he will take. The *duty* of either is to make his opposite believe that the top (bottom) of the possible range is lower (higher) than it really is. And to mislead someone is, of course, to tell him an untruth or, at the least, let him infer what is not the truth. Truth in commercial negotiation is a casualty of the responsibility of the participants to the business entity for whom they work.

3. The duty of respect for others is irrelevant in determining product choices. At any time, a firm has a limited product transformation function. It cannot make everything. From those things that it can produce it will select the ones that will maximize its profit. Considerations of social benefit or damage have no place. But ideas of social benefit or damage derive ultimately from the idea of respect for others. Hence respect for others has no place in the free market.

Consider the tobacco industry. Surely this is a paradigm example. There exists substantial respected testimony that blames smoking for significant numbers of deaths from cancer, heart, and other diseases. Recent articles in *The New York Times* report that senior U.S. officials, among them the Surgeon General, testified before a House subcommittee that, " . . . Government findings . . . blame smoking for 340,000 deaths a year and . . . call it the chief preventable cause of illness and premature death in the nation". But the Tobacco Institute fought a proposal for more specific labeling about the dangers from smoking on cigarette packages and in advertising. The "chairman of the institute's executive committee said, that the proposal for five labels . . . was a 'thinly veiled effort further to harass and ultimately eliminate an important American Industry'". The *Times* also reported that a Rockefeller Foundation study found "The beneficiaries [of the tobacco support program] may be farmers, but they are also doctors and lawyers, churches and banks, mill workers and truck drivers, and in many cases, widows".[5]

It simply is impossible to conceive of persons engaging in the production or merchandising of products for smoking and at the same time observing the precepts encompassed by the obligation to respect your fellow. A defense based upon a spurious premise of freedom of choice is, of course, negated by the vigorous advertising and merchandising campaigns conducted by the industry.

IV

To this point we have focused mainly, though not entirely, on actions. When we turn to attitudes the matter becomes more complex. I have already introduced the problem in suggesting that a corporate executive carrying out his responsibilities might have to distort his nature. But this possibility itself has more than one aspect. Suppose that he must ignore what is (or has been) his (more or less) settled disposition to act in accordance with the human virtues — to act kindly, generously, truthfully, etc. Does he then override his nature consciously, or finally become unaware? For under the circumstances of competition we might expect that he would develop habitual attitudes of rationality expressed by hardness, shrewdness, and single-mindedness. These attitudes, or some of them, might begin to determine his actions under private circumstances. Or, on one occasion they may overwhelm, and on another be overwhelmed by, the set of softer dispositions.

Because firms are teams and responsible employees generally team members, attitudes congruent with the business characteristics are reinforced. Consider a purchasing agent. He cannot prudently assume that his supplier is dealing with him truthfully. And he has an obligation to his fellow team members not to let them down, to do his job — which is to purchase materials as cheaply as possible — as best he can. These are powerful motives for him to deal shrewdly with no special considerations for truth. Nor are the motives, given their ground, unreasonable.

But we need not stick to particular cases. Ultimately, all firms are engaged in a single overarching competition for capital and return on capital. In any block of time there is only a certain amount of money to be invested or lent, a certain number of good employees to be hired, a certain amount of income to be distributed. As a result of this unremitting, relentless competition, both specific and general, responsible firm members do develop, in greater or lesser amounts, a team morality. It is 'us agin them'. Consequently, the defeat of the opposition becomes a goal in itself. Consequently also, the business characteristics become justified and in terms of the competition they come to be constituents of a certain higher morality. Though by besting a competitor, whether in a single small event such as getting an order, or in actually driving him out of business, the winner causes the loser real harm, that moral fact never enters the consciousness of the actors as such. The loser does not feel himself ill-used, and as a business competitor he has no moral grounds for resentment. Feelings of beneficence, even of compassion, are effectually blocked; they have no place in this world.

V

If the analyses set down above are correct in the main, what conclusions can we draw from them? The most apparent, and in a way the least helpful, is that free enterprise, like other social schemes in this imperfect world, is a flawed undertaking. Perhaps examining its flaws in some detail will be more helpful.

First, only in the immediate sense is free enterprise free. For, as I have tried to show, it imposes rigid constraints — all stemming from the a priori of profit maximization — on those who operate in its universe. Within a given industry, one firm, by way of policy, may commence to commit what other citizens could look upon as a series of enormities. But if that firm, because of its policy, say, of dumping untreated wastes into rivers and acid particulates into the atmosphere, reduces its cost of production, the others must follow. The remedy, of course, is legislation and enforcement. But, absent that remedy, the executives of the competing firm are choiceless: they too must pollute. Now, even if it is likely that the business characteristics are a part of their settled attitudes, it does not follow that a propensity to poison the environment is ingrained in their psychologies. In fact there is no reason to assume that such an idea is not repugnant to them as moral individuals. To the reader it certainly is repugnant. So the polluters, seeking to maximize the profits of their firms, are forced to attack themselves as moral beings. Justification from considerations of reciprocity becomes in this case very difficult. It appears, in fact, that justification from considerations of corporate survival is the sole possibility. Hence, I suggest that in this example, and in analogous cases, the participants inflict real damage upon their own self-respect. They themselves are damaging perhaps the most important constituent of their own lives.

The demand that participants attack their own self-respect is not limited to some set of corporate executives. We can see this by observing that ultimately all production, except for government use and private investment, is for private consumption; and so firms increase sales and presumably profit by taking measures to increase and differentiate consumption (differentiation being that means of getting off a horizontal demand curve where it is impossible to earn an economic profit and onto a downward sloping curve where, at appropriate volumes, profits are made). Thus all individuals in the free enterprise system are subject to constant substantial pressures to buy. All, but for a few who for one reason or another exhibit a peculiar indifference — or moral strength — of character, will respond to a degree. But this response is equivalent to a need for extra income and wealth and these — in the free market scheme — are gained through competition. No one, whether he is an assembly line worker, a chief operating officer, a licensed professional or an 'investor', sees himself as a producer of social wealth. Rather we view ourselves, and we must view ourselves, as *competitors* for those true economic (scarce) goods, income and jobs to get income. As such we are subject to the laws of competition, and as such our actions are defined at least as much by the devilish among us as by the angelic. The employee always competes with his employer for money, and typically competes with his co-workers as well. If one is an entrepreneur, he competes with the world. Virtue, being displaced by rationality, has no place in this competition; and the individual is obliged to make a choice between virtue and money. We might sketch an indifference function showing virtue vs income. [See Figure 1.]

This curve seems reasonable enough. At high levels of virtue, but low income, it assumes the individual will sacrifice a great deal of it (and presumably, his self-respect) in order to gain income. If he already has a large income, he probably will not inflict further damage on his self-respect in order to gain more. In fact, he might cede income in order to gain virtue. But if his (perceived) income is low, and by sacrificing (perceived) virtue he can increase it, he probably will do so. At least to a point. For in order to live other than meanly he must have a decent income. In order to have a decent income he is obliged to compete for it. And if the devilish are willing to sacrifice virtue for income, then so must everyone.

Now those who are obliged to sacrifice their humanity, either in the discharge of corporate duties, or in the pursuit of a decent share of material wealth, cannot call themselves free.

Next, I assume — this journal assumes — that most men would wish to lead lives in which they can express in their work the human virtues. Similarly, they would wish to forego behavior which demonstrates hardness, shrewdness, and single-mindedness. And almost everyone would choose to live in that bright world postulated by John Rawls where it is publicly known that the acceptance of the duty of mutual aid brings "a sense of confidence and trust in other men's good intentions and the knowledge that they are there if we need them".[6] The logic of competition shoves all this aside — an intolerable knowledge which men must deny in order to believe themselves truly human.

Thus the compartmentalization of our souls; the acceptance, but non-acknowledgement of hypocrisy, and so the impossibility of ever achieving a happy society — which can exist nowhere but in the souls of its members. The reader might here object that no one really is forced into the competition, that one *can* live and not compete, or compete minimally. But this objection would be mistaken. If no one competed, society would no longer be competitive — it would be a different society. And if only the ethically indifferent among us competed, ethical indifference would wholly define our economic universe. But most of us, vigorous competitors or not, are not ethically indifferent. Very few of us make always wholly rational competitive judgements, otherwise we

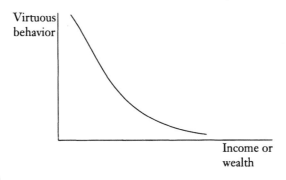

FIGURE 1

would be monsters, not men. It is *that* dichotomy which finally represents the great flawed detail of free enterprise.

Why stress it so? My answer is that otherwise we must fall into a trap which indeed has snared many. The trap is nothing else but the enchantment of the logical beauty of the free market and the seeming freedom it affords. As we have seen, viewed from the standpoint of individual morality, its freedom is largely illusory. Although, as markets approach the conditions of perfect competition, they approach Paretian efficiency, that fact by itself should not stand as sufficient warrant to build an economy on the foundations of free enterprise. The ethical implications, which I have tried to outline here, ought also to be taken into account.

Now all this does not mean that a society necessarily is to reject free-enterprise in favor of some other economic scheme. For one thing, the system simply works. And regardless of whether society attempts to solve its economic problems by economic competition or in some other fashion, moral dilemmas will inevitably present themselves. For example, if we would avoid the patent evils of a free enterprise system, then we must subject ourselves to the patent evils — loss of liberty — of a command system. Nevertheless, I do not think that the immoralities inherent in economic competition can be overemphasized. For to admit the imperfectability of men and their institutions is not to concede that they cannot be made better. But first we will have to have a clearer understanding of the nature of our current imperfections. If society is to move forward, it better have some collective awareness of what it is about.

Notes

* I am grateful to John McMurtry for suggesting this paper and for his valued criticisms. I am also indebted to Barbara Kelly for her wise criticism and her constant encouragement.

1. *Wall Street Journal* Staff Reporter, Washington. 'Doctor Group Tried To Bar Fees, Services From Ads, FTC Says', *The Wall Street Journal*, 9 March, 1982, p. 12, col. 3.

Linda Greenhouse, Special to *The New York Times*, Washington, March 23. 'Justices Uphold Right of Doctors To Solicit Trade — Affirm Order by F.T.C. Allowing Advertising', *The New York Times*, 24 March, 1982, p. A16, cols. 1–5.

Robert Reinhold, Special to *The New York Times*, Denver. 'Competition Held Key to Lower Medical Cost', *The New York Times*, 1 April, 1982, p. A1, cols. 2–4, p. D23, cols. 1–4.

Editorial. 'Deregulating the Doctors', *The Wall Street Journal*, 2 April, 1982, p. 22, cols. 1–2.

Special to *The New York Times*, Raleigh, N.C., March 8. 'Farmers Back Tobacco Plan They Would Finance', *The New York Times*, 11 March, 1982, p. B8, cols. 2–5.

Washington, March 11 (UPI). 'U.S. Health Officials Endorse Stronger Cigarette Warnings', *The New York Times*, 12 March, 1982, p. A15, cols 2–3.

Washington, March 12 (AP). 'Tobacco Institute Denounces Cigarette Labeling Proposal', *The New York Times*, 13 March, 1982, p. 9, col. 1.

Bill Abrams, 'Comparative Ads Are Getting More Popular, Harder Hitting', *The Wall Street Journal*, 11 March 1982, p. 29, col. 1.

Wall Street Journal Staff Reporter, Washington. 'New Chief of FTC Urges Congress to Limit Commission's Authority to Challenge Ads', *The Wall Street Journal*, 19 March, 1982, p. 12, cols. 2–3.

Wall Street Journal News Roundup. 'PepsiCo's Reaction To 7-UP Ads Is Said To Draw FTC Study', *The Wall Street Journal*, 19 March, 1982, p. 12, col. 3.

Wall Street Journal News Roundup. 'Gasoline Price War Delights Motorists; Analysts Watch for Increase in Driving', *The Wall Street Journal*, 9 March, 1982, p. 14, cols. 2–3.

Brenton R. Schlender, Staff Reporter of *The Wall Street Journal*, Dallas. 'American Airlines

Gets a "Bad Guy" Image in Dallas From Its Harsh Attacks on Braniff', *The Wall Street Journal*, 12 March, 1982, p. 25, cols. 3–5, p. 39, col. 1.

Philip Shabecoff, Special to *The New York Times*, Washington, March 11. 'Witnesses Clash Over Rule On Burying of Toxic Waste', *The New York Times*, 12 March, 1982, p. A12, cols. 1–2.

Philip Shabecoff, Special to *The New York Times*, Washington, March 17. 'U.S. Reversing Stand on Burial of Toxic Liquid — Drops Move to Ease Rule for Drums in Landfills', *The New York Times*, 18 March, 1982, p. A1, col. 2, p. A22, col. 1.

Janet Guyon, Staff Reporter of *The Wall Street Journal*, White Plains, N.Y. 'New Recipe: General Foods Says It Has Finally Solved Its Profit Problems, but Doubts Linger On', *The Wall Street Journal*, 2 April, 1982, p. 42, cols. 1–6.

Claudia Waterloo, Staff Reporter of *The Wall Street Journal*, Storm Lake, Iowa. 'Season of Stress: Farm Life is Changed As Perilous Economics Undermine Confidence — Tension Cuts Neighborliness, Leaves Some Wondering Where to Turn for Help — The Tragedy of a Hog Raiser', *The Wall Street Journal*, 9 April, 1982, p. 1, col. l, p. 11, cols. 1–5.

Robert Pear, Special to *The New York Times*, Washington, March 20. 'Schweiker Declares Nursing Home Rules Will Not Be Relaxed', *The New York Times*, 21 March, 1982, p. 1, col. 1, p. 18, cols. 1–4.

James M. Perry, Staff Reporter of *The Wall Street Journal*, Washington. 'The Power Brokers: Affable Lobbyist Aids United Technologies In Jet-Engine Battle — By Serving as Contact Man, Clark Mac Gregor Fights GE Bid for a Major Order — Saying a Word to Mrs. Meese', *The Wall Street Journal*, 1 April, 1982, p. 1, col. 1, p. 18, cols. 1–2.

Julie Salamon, 'The Workout Crew: Bankers Who Step In If Loans Go Bad Reveal Lenders' Other Face — There Isn't Any Smile on It; Teams Tell Ailing Clients To Make Changes or Else—"We See a Management Void"', *The Wall Street Journal*, 2 April, 1982, p. 1, col. 6, p. 16, col. 1–3.

2. The article lists toilet-bowl cleaners, mouthwashes, soft drinks, pizza, and shampoos among others.

3. It is true that this is a general conclusion which can be drawn from the premises of competition as such, but what we are discussing here is a special kind of competition. It is pervasive, it in large measure defines our lives, and it is impossible to withdraw from it entirely. As we have seen, it forces the competitors to run as fast as they can, without rest. It is well worth focusing on the consequences of *economic* competition, even if some of these may be deduced from the fact of competition itself.

4. A price set by coercion or bribery would itself be the result of an immoral act.

5. Washington, March 11 (UPI). 'U.S. Health Officials Endorse Stronger Cigarette Warnings'.

Washington, March 12 (AP). 'Tobacco Institute Denounces Cigarette Labeling Proposal'.

Special to *The New York Times*, Raleigh, N.C., March 8. 'Farmers Back Tobacco Plan They Would Finance'.

6. J. Rawls, *A Theory of Justice* (Harvard University Press, Cambridge, MA, 1971), pp. 338–339.

Richard McCarty
BUSINESS AND BENEVOLENCE

Business activity, it seems, is the very model of cold, calculating, selfish conduct. Though some business persons sheepishly acknowledge this, many others openly celebrate ruthless selfishness, extolling the profit motive, even greed, as business virtues.[1] Yet if selfishness is a business virtue, while selfless benevolence is a moral virtue, then it seems that good persons cannot be good at business, and that the successful business person is a moral failure. While this hasty conclusion ignores the ample room for benevolent activities in one's non-business, personal life, it nevertheless suggests that something about business is incompatible with morality. *Business ethics* is a contradiction in terms, according to a familiar jest; and perhaps a subtle truth underlying that quip is just that the selfish profit motive successful business requires is intrinsically at odds with part of the requirements of morality.

In order to take business ethics seriously, then, it is necessary to harmonize the apparent opposition between business selfishness and moral benevolence. Blending business and benevolence is the project of the present study, a project in which we shall find it fruitful to examine various traditional moral defenses of business and the profit motive. Though often used in conjunction, two separate strategies for addressing this problem are prominent: one challenges the moral indictment of self-interest or selfishness, attempting to exonerate the profit motive; another tries to justify business selfishness through its beneficial consequences. Finding both traditional strategies ultimately unsatisfactory, I show in the end how business and benevolence can be combined in profitable business activities which can also be morally virtuous.

I. SELF-INTEREST, SELFISHNESS AND GREED

The first traditional justification of the profit motive involves a defense of business selfishness; by demonstrating that self-interest need not be immoral, or vicious, it appears to follow that profit-seeking is morally blameless. Some variations on this theme see self-interest as amoral; ethical egoists see selfishness in business, and everywhere else, as morally praiseworthy.

Defenders of selfishness typically object to common tendencies to imbue the term with an immoral or vicious quality, condemning selfishness in advance through linguistic convention. It is better, they argue, to begin with a morally neutral definition, so that vicious selfishness may be distinguished from amoral, permissible or virtuous selfishness.[2] To accommodate this suggestion, we shall begin with *self-interest* as an abstract kind of self-regard, and we shall stipulate the following morally neutral definition: *seeking satisfaction of one's desires or attainment of one's goals.* Now since it is plausible that people can have moral desires or seek moral goals, on this definition one can be both self-interested and morally good or virtuous. Indeed, since to be virtuous is to desire morally

From *Business and Professional Ethics Journal* 7, no. 2 (1987), 63–83. Reprinted by permission of the author.

good states of affairs or to make the goals of morality one's own, self-interest so defined becomes a necessary condition for moral virtue, and also probably for life itself.[3] In this neutral sense, *self-interest* can correctly characterize the profit motive as well as the moral saint's voluntary self-sacrifice.

Our morally neutral definition of *self-interest*, however, lacks any reference to the desires and goals of others. But both selfishness and selflessness seem to be essentially "other-related" characteristics. One could be neither selfish nor selfless on a deserted island, since there would be no one over whom to prefer oneself or for whom to sacrifice oneself. In solitude, one can be, at best, self-interested. *Selfishness*, then, seems more correctly defined in relation to others, as: *giving overriding importance to satisfying one's own desires or attaining one's own goals when doing so conflicts with proper desires and goals of others*. On this definition, then, the profit motive is selfish to the extent that it conflicts with the natural desires of others to pay less, to take fewer risks, or to expend less effort. Altruistic behavior, accordingly, is not selfish in this sense, though it may be self-interested in the very broad sense defined above. Selfishness and altruism, on this scheme, are *ways* of being self-interested.

Now although selfishness here is opposed to selflessness, it is not obvious that there is anything necessarily immoral about it; though in some forms it may indeed be vicious. In casual games, for example, players pursue their own goals in opposition to the desires or goals of opponents. If games and similar competitions are morally permissible, then selfishness may be permissible, and need not be immoral. The selfish profit motive, accordingly, may be exonerated provided we can see business activity as friendly competition or as morally permissible selfishness.[4] Business activities and competitive games may take an immoral or vicious turn, however, and we can reserve the term, *greed* for such vicious selfishness. Just as selfishness is a way of being self-interested, greed is a way of being selfish.

So long as business activity avoids vicious selfishness, then, it is morally blameless. But can business persons avoid vicious selfishness? As business is often conceived and practiced, I think, they cannot. Selfishness will be vicious when it (*a*) leads one to do wrong by violating others' legal or moral rights; or when it (*b*) precludes acting on one's moral obligations toward others, or prevents one from being virtuous.[5] Now, however, respectful of others' moral and legal rights persons may be in their selfish business activities, it is difficult to see how such activities permit fulfilling even minimal moral obligations of beneficence toward others. *Business is not charity.*

At this point in the argument it may seem reasonable to object along the following lines: Since business does not have obligations of beneficence, it cannot neglect such obligations; business selfishness is vicious, then, only to the extent that it tends toward transgressions of others' rights. This objection begins by denying business' moral obligations of beneficence. If the point of this denial is simply that *businesses* lack such obligations, then although it may be true, it is irrelevant. (We shall return to this question briefly at the end.) The issue, it will be recalled, is whether the profit motive of business *persons*, who, as persons, *do* have such obligations, is vicious selfishness; whether business selfishness precludes one's fulfilling his or her moral obligations or beneficence. Since business, as often conceived and practiced, excludes even minimal beneficence as a matter of principle, the profit motive appears to be vicious selfishness, or greed.[6] This traditional defense of selfishness, then, cannot resolve the opposition between business and ethics unless we can find a way for business activity to provide opportunities for at least some beneficence.

II. BENEFICENCE AND BENEVOLENCE

The second type of traditional moral defense of business often employs an "end-state" moral justification of the profit motive. The idea is that the interests of morality are served best by business selfishness, even by some kinds of greed. Here we might recall Adam Smith's well-known praise of the selfish profit motive. In the view frequently attributed to him, everyone's selfish activity enables an "invisible hand" to secure public benefits. On this view, the way to be beneficent, to contribute to the good of others and the wider public good, is to be selfish.[7] Yet this leaves us with a rather limited notion of beneficence. If our moral obligations toward others can be completely satisfied by such meager contributions to the social good as most individual business people blindly contribute through seeking profits, then business selfishness can be morally justified. Yet it is clear that in our relations with others as employees, customers, business associates, needy fellow citizens and even fellow human beings, morality requires personal commitments beyond the minimal ties that bind mere atomistic economic participants in the wider social good.

H. B. Acton, in friendly criticism of Smith on this point, attempts to show that beneficence pervades the market economy.

> It is not that each individual seeks his own interest and that some "invisible hand," to use Adam Smith's famous expression, sees to it that this results in benefits for all. . . . It is rather that the very structure or system of free exchange in a society with division of labor and limited resources is one in which what each party produces is for some others to have in return for what the producer would like to have from them. Benefitting oneself by providing what others need is the *raison d'etre* of the whole affair. It is not that the good of others is a contingent by-product of selfishness, but that each party can only benefit himself by benefitting others.[8]

In Smith's view, the way to be beneficent is to be selfish; Acton, however, suggests that in the market economy, the only way to realize selfish aims, to benefit oneself, is to benefit others directly through business activities. Instead of an "end-state" justification, we may call this a "concomitant" justification; for Acton sees the moral merit of business activity not in an "end-state" of social benefit, but in the individual actions themselves, or in their immediate beneficial consequences. In competitive markets, he writes,

> individuals, whether firms or persons, provide for others in working for themselves. We might equally well say that in working for others they work for themselves. Hence, someone who was averse to helping other people would, once he understood the logic of the system, be rather disconcerted if he had to play a part in it. For business success depends on supplying people with what they want, and hence involves helping them.[9]

Now this "market of favors," as I shall call it, is an interesting but problematic twist on the traditional consequentialist justification of the profit motive. The first problem to note lies embedded in the last sentence quoted above. Acton notes rightly that one secures profits by supplying people with what they want, but this does not necessarily involve helping them, as he claims. In fact, supplying people with what they want in certain types of profitable business activities may be quite harmful to them. Drug dealers, for example, profit by keeping their customers satisfied, though they do them great harm. It is true that the drug buyer shares guilt with the drug dealer, that the buyer shouldn't purchase and use harmful drugs; nevertheless, the concomitant of profit-motivated drug dealing, and similar activities, is quite the opposite of beneficence. Thus, while Acton suggests the profit motive requires beneficence, we see that it actually requires only satisfying others' desires.

Most people, however, generally desire what is good for them; or so it is reasonable to assume. Hence, Acton's view may be satisfactory so long as we restrict it to business activities supplying essential human goods. People desire safe, efficient, environmentally acceptable means of transportation. Automobile companies seek profit by supplying automobiles with the desired capabilities to meet this demand, and so provide what is for many people an essential human good. People also desire steady employment in safe working conditions at a fair wage; and profit-seeking automobile companies must employ thousands of workers, thereby benefitting employees.

Even here, however, automakers' providing products and jobs may not easily count as beneficence. We have seen in recent years how American auto manufacturers have resisted progress in developing safer, more fuel-efficient and pollution-free cars. The dramatic increase in government regulation of the auto industry's reluctant progress toward these goals is evidence that the automakers' profit motive is not well tuned to benefitting the car-buying public. As industry designers know well, profit does not require benefitting the consumer on an absolute scale of benefits; rather, sizable profits may be secured merely by providing *relative advantages*, or selling points slightly greater than those offered by competitors. Similarly, auto workers are attracted to their jobs not through the companies' absolute beneficence, but because they find their jobs most advantageous, given their skills and the location of their homes, in comparison with other available jobs.

These considerations of relative advantage seem to tarnish the supposed beneficence of profit-seeking producers and employers. Yet insofar as relative advantages are indeed advantages and constitute goods which may be more difficult or impossible to secure in a nonprofit economy, the tarnished beneficence of producer/employers may yet secure a moral exoneration of the profit motive. Further analysis, however, seriously threatens the beneficence Acton finds pervading business activities; for his characterization of that beneficence betrays a confused, one-sided view of business activities when he writes, as quoted above, that "Benefitting oneself by providing what others need is the *raison d'etre* of the whole affair . . . each party can only benefit himself by benefitting others."

Here Acton suggests that producer/employers *benefit themselves* by benefitting others; yet this is not quite an accurate description of the market of favors. Players in the market economy benefit others and *the others* benefit them. More accurately, producer/employers offer or advertise benefits to consumers and employees, but they refuse to confer those benefits until consumers and employees first benefit them. Acton, on the contrary, casts business profit as a kind of "self-beneficence" following on one's beneficence to others. In so doing he obscures the obvious strings attached to business beneficence. He hides the fact that profit usually comes from the hard-won economic resources of consumers and the hard work of employees; that business transactions are not one-sided beneficence, but, ideally, simply fair trade.

A more accurate picture of business activity shows us not that the profit motive requires genuine beneficence, as Acton seems to suggest, but that it requires merely a tarnished, "strings-attached" provision of relative advantages. We may now reasonably question whether this "strings-attached beneficence" necessary for business profit can provide a moral justification for the profit motive, resolving the apparent incompatibility between business and ethics.

If it makes no moral difference how beneficence comes about, then the fact that some benefits come with strings attached should be irrelevant. Yet it is quite clear that the circumstances and motives which give rise to an act of beneficence are morally relevant. A secret revolutionary attempting a political assassination but accidentally killing instead another assassin carrying out a similar plot, may actually save the person he intended to kill. He might well be praised as a hero; that is, so long as his motives remain secret. By all appearances, he has done a good deed; yet we cannot truly say it was an act of beneficence, for whether acts are truly beneficent depends partly on their motives. In Acton's "strings-attached beneficence," therefore, it is clear that the motives of such "business benefactors" disqualify their normal business transactions from counting as genuine beneficence. Genuine, morally praiseworthy beneficence requires benevolent motives. A true benefactor, one with morally praiseworthy benevolent motives, does good to others with no strings attached.

Now Acton notes that a business person may benefit others without such strings attached by making gifts, "or what comes to the same thing in a market, by selling below what he knows to be the market price. But persistently to do this would be to opt out of the system, the very functioning of which requires service to be by exchange rather than by gift."[10] Benevolence, we must conclude, is alien to the business system, as Acton sees it. On his view, business remains essentially incompatible with even the minimal altruistic demands of morality. Unless we can find some way to blend the profit motive and benevolence, business remains partly at odds with ethics.

Andrew Carnegie, whose name is readily associated with both business success and generous philanthropy, provides, in theory and practice, a model for coordinating the profit motive with genuine benevolence. Carnegie's view is similar to Smith's, in that he appears to offer an "end-state" justification which sees the profit motive as furthering the public good; yet rather than leave such beneficence up to an impersonal invisible hand, he places it in the highly conspicuous hands of wealthy business tycoons. In their capable hands, according to Carnegie, only the best charitable causes will be advanced; and benevolently, since philanthropists do not profit from their administration of wealth. Carnegie writes:

> This, then, is held to be the duty of the man of wealth: To set an example of modest, unostentatious living, shunning display or extravagance; to provide moderately for the legitimate wants of those dependent upon him; and, after doing so, to consider all surplus revenues which come to

him simply as trust funds, which he is called upon to administer, and strictly bound as a matter of duty to administer in the manner which, in his judgment, is best calculated to produce the most beneficial results for the community — the man of wealth thus becoming the mere trustee and agent for his poorer brethren, bringing to their service his superior wisdom, experience, and ability to administer, doing for them better than they would or could do for themselves.[11]

In Carnegie's view, though, only very few business persons are qualified for this benevolent administration of surplus wealth. These are the best business minds who, while sufficiently selfish, are distinguished chiefly by their uncommon business talent and are rewarded accordingly with great fortunes. The common run of merely competent business persons, according to Carnegie, are unfit for philanthropy both because they lack fortunes, and accordingly also because they lack the ability to administer benevolent projects to the best advantage of humanity.[12] Consequently, on this view, business and benevolence are only rarely compatible, in persons of wealth; yet we have reason to suspect that even this rare coordination is all it appears to be.

Carnegie himself, as is evident in the above quotation, sees wealthy philanthropists as "trustees" of their surplus. This seems to imply that the great fortunes they possess and administer rightfully belong to the less fortunate, from whom, after all, they won their fortunes.[13] Carnegie pictures philanthropists as individualistic, competitive and highly talented business persons throughout most of their lives, accumulating wealth which still belongs, in some sense, to others. Near the end of their productive years in business, when their accumulation of others' wealth amounts to a fortune beyond their capacities for enjoyment, they return the wealth they have won, with some kind of interest. This picture, however, begins to resemble Acton's picture of business beneficence. Insofar as philanthropists are merely trustees, investing others' wealth throughout their lives and returning it with interest in later years, the benefits they impart to humanity are simply their end of a life-long bargain. Yet if we expand our focus on the lives and practices of these philanthropists, we may be able to see how they can, in the larger picture, enter the life-long bargain with praiseworthy benevolent motives.

Instead of choosing other traditionally benevolent professions such as the clergy, medicine or social work, young, talented people benevolently wishing to benefit humanity in some way may enter business hoping to accumulate vast fortunes to be philanthropically administered. Eventual success in such a benevolent life-plan requires a long career generating wealth under the profit motive, after which such selfishness can be supplanted by the original benevolence. We need not limit these wider benevolent opportunities to only a few naturally selected business champions, as Carnegie did, but we may see such opportunities open to business people of all talents; the less talented merely administering less wealth, though no less benevolently. At last, then, it seems that business and true benevolence can be generally coordinated. Coordinated though they may be, however, they remain, as yet, incompatible.

On this model, in which original benevolence gives way to selfishness but ultimately returns, the coordination of benevolence and the profit motive is cyclical; yet the cycle preserves their opposition. Business remains, after all, a thoroughly selfish enterprise; and successful business people can atone for their selfishness, perhaps only in part, through philanthropy in their retirement years. If this cyclical coordination of business and benevolence were the best we could hope for, then we ought to celebrate it. The cycle is morally dangerous, however, and we therefore have an incentive to continue our investigation in search of a satisfactory synthesis of business and benevolence. The moral danger lurking in the cyclical coordination is this: The most ruthless and unfair business practices can seem to be justified as the means to future benevolence. On the cyclical model, because there is a time for selfishness and another time for benevolence, it can easily appear to business people that there is a time for business and another time for ethics.

III. BENEVOLENT BUSINESS

If we are to make business and ethics fully compatible, we must find ways for business people occasionally to carry out their business activities benevolently, in fulfillment of their obligations toward others. We cannot rely on a cyclical coordination of the profit motive and benevolence which preserves their opposition, we must dissolve that opposition by introducing benevolence into business activity, by finding ways for it to co-exist in the same consciousness as the selfish profit motive. Though this appears impossible, continued reflection on selfishness and benevolence may show how they can be compatible. Selfishness, as defined above, is *giving overriding importance to satisfying one's desires and attaining one's goals when doing so conflicts with proper desires and goals of others.* It is morally objectionable, or vicious, we said, when it precludes fulfilling moral obligations toward others. Benevolence, as we have noted, is properly motivated beneficence. A benevolent act is a gesture of good will (*bene, vol*); and gestures of good will are also freely given to others, with no strings attached.[14] How, then, can one be both selfish and benevolent?

Selfishness and benevolence, we have seen, are "other-directed" character traits or motives. Now if selfishness is giving preference to self above *all* others, and benevolence is acting with good will toward *all* others, then the two can never be compatible; it is also doubtful that anyone ever could be selfish or benevolent, on such a universal understanding of those terms. On the more limited and commonly accepted view of selfishness and benevolence, however, it is possible to deal selfishly with one person or group while dealing benevolently with another. This distinction between others with whom one deals selfishly and others with whom one is benevolent provides for the possibility of a synthesis of the profit motive and benevolence. To actualize that possibility, we need to show how one can, in the course of profit-seeking business dealings with the person or group, direct those dealings with good will in a manner beneficial to other persons or groups. In this way, gestures of good will can be carried out with selfish, profit-seeking motives.

There is no more contradiction in a gesture of good will for a selfish purpose than there is in a good-faith promise for a deceitful purpose, especially not if the promisor and the deceived are different people. If a man can borrow a new car with a good-faith promise, he may do so for the purpose of misrepresenting himself as the owner of the car to impress business associates. Similarly, one may selfishly seek profit from one person by acting benevolently toward another.

Corporate charitable contributions serving public-relations purposes are perhaps the most common and simplest form of profitable benevolence. Such donations to worthy causes are almost universally recognized as good for business. Insofar as they are truly gifts, with no strings attached, they are gestures of good will; yet as Acton failed to see, or did not fully appreciate, one can profit in the market economy as a consequence of benevolent gifts.

In the wake of recent cutbacks in public funding of worthy causes, some corporations initially reluctant to take up the slack have discovered that the pull-out of government funds has created a marketing vacuum. The highly profitable 1984 Summer Olympics was one of the first examples of how marketing "tie-ins" to popular causes could yield generous profits. American Express, somewhat earlier, launched a successful *cause-related marketing* campaign making a small donation to the restoration of the *Statue of Liberty* for each credit-card charge. Similarly, MasterCard's 1987 "Choose To Make A Difference" campaign guaranteed at least $2 million in donations to several non-profit service organizations. Benevolent, cause-related marketing appears as profitable as traditional advertising gimmicks and sweepstakes prizes, perhaps more so.[15]

Business donations to worthy causes which enhance corporate images and profits can be selfish benevolence, satisfying both the profit motive and moral obligations toward others. Unlike other forms of beneficence we have considered, such donations or good works can directly address particular individuals' or groups' immediate needs; they can be offered with no strings attached; and they are part of the business system, not alien to it.

The possibilities and potentials of business benevolence have scarcely been explored. Creative business minds are far from exhausting the many possible ways to benefit their own business enterprises and others in need at the same time. In this country's earliest example of corporate philanthropy, railroad executives financed YMCA hostels in small towns, providing inexpensive lodging for railroad employees. More recent examples include: B. Dalton Booksellers' millions of dollars in donations to fight illiteracy; McDonald's "Ronald McDonald Houses" providing support for hospitalized children and families; Southern Bell's project raising $25,000 in donations for a Florida boy needing a liver transplant by donating 50 cents for every Custom Calling feature sold in July 1985.[16]

Among the many possible ways business can contribute to worthy causes, however, it is important to note a continuum between actions or programs which border on the merely beneficent, and those which are truly benevolent. Texaco, for example, has supported radio broadcasts of the *Metropolitan Opera* since 1940. The company behind Neiman-Marcus, Carter Hawley Hale Stores, Inc., recently shifted donations from various charities it supported to visual and performing arts programs, hoping to reach upscale consumers more effectively.[17] While no visible strings may be attached to donations like these, a kind of subtle dragnet is thrown out with the benefits. The primary purpose of such donations is to offer benefits to potential or loyal customers. These seem sharply distinguished from benevolent contributions to identifiable groups or needy individuals from whom no return business or favors are expected. Between these two poles are questionably benevolent programs where donors oversee the management of their gifts, with some strings attached, ensuring that their own interests are served.[18] The most praiseworthy model of business benevolence we have identified is that of gestures of good will toward some, which bring profits from others. There may be many modifications of this model which serve business interests and the interests of others, though the less they give toward good-will gestures with no strings attached, the farther they move from genuine benevolence.

Not everyone, however, sees such good works in a morally favorable light.[19] Milton Friedman, for instance, in criticizing "business social responsibility," uses phrases such as "hypocritical window-dressing," and "tactics approaching fraud" to describe donations by a corporation attempting to "generate goodwill as a by-product of expenditures that are entirely justified in its own self-interest."[20] Now Friedman here is writing about a slightly different though closely related issue, and there is therefore a danger of taking him out of context. His general point, however, is that it is deceitful to cast selfishly motivated corporate donations as fulfilling business' social responsibilities or moral obligations. Since this is exactly what we have done above, however, it seems reasonable to see Friedman's remarks as critical of the view presented here.

We may note in passing, however, that in the context of his overall view, the point Friedman expresses here is highly paradoxical. Readers familiar with Friedman's arguments on the social responsibility of business will recall that he *does* think business has a social obligation to increase profits. Thus, he must admit that selfishly motivated gestures of good will do indeed contribute toward fulfilling business' social responsibility, and therefore they cannot be seen as hypocritical or fraudulent.

On the other hand, to be more faithful to Friedman's stated intentions, we must understand his criticism as insisting that there is a fundamental opposition between fulfilling moral obligations, "social responsibilities," and increasing profits: that actions motivated by profit cannot, no matter how beneficial the outcome, count as morally praiseworthy or virtuous.[21] Assuming we agree with this point straightforwardly, we must concede that someone touting his selfishly motivated actions on others' behalf as morally worthy is indeed hypocritical. Friedman's point, therefore, seems quite reasonable and is a potentially devastating criticism of our whole project here. If selfishly motivated actions cannot properly count as virtuous, then no matter how benevolently business people administer profitable donations, so long as their benevolence is tainted with the profit motive, moral virtue eludes them; and business remains, therefore, not fully ethical.

We can respond to this criticism, however, in a manner similar to the way we salvaged the genuine benevolence of Carnegie's philanthropists: by expanding our focus on the motives people display in entering business careers or in practicing business. Earlier we imagined how benevolent motives might lead people into careers in business, though at that point we saw no way to make business activity itself benevolent; opportunities for benevolence came only after a long career of selfishness. Having seen how business enterprises may be benevolent, though, we may now consider business persons' morally informed choices of the way they will practice business. Will they engage in purely selfish business, seeking *continually* to maximize personal and corporate profits both immediately and in the long run, or will their careers consciously include *occasional* projects of benevolent business, even if on the whole somewhat less profitable than purely selfish business?

Now the person who chooses to do business always seeking maximum profits may indeed encounter circumstances where philanthropic business activities similar to those discussed above are the most profitable use of available resources. Such a person makes good-will gestures *only when they secure maximum profits*; but this pervasively selfish attitude toward business is indeed incompatible with moral virtue. On the other hand, someone may choose to include occasional benevolent projects in her business career, or as part of the goals of her business, even if such projects are not the most profitable use of resources; and if she chooses to practice business in this manner because morality requires such beneficence, then she is a genuinely virtuous business person.[22]

To display the complicated structure of motivation which makes room for virtuous activity in business, we may distinguish two general levels of motivation in business: the *performance* level and the *practice* level. On the *performance* level, we may examine the motivations for particular business actions or performances. When we consider business activity as described in Acton's market of favors at this level, for example, we see business people performing such favors with a selfish motive, expecting a somewhat greater favor in return. The motives behind benevolent business actions we have illustrated above, however, cannot be displayed this simply, but require a bifurcation of motives on the *performance* level. Thus, the complex motives behind a benevolent action in business will include, on one sublevel, simply motives of good will, expecting no favors in return. On a higher sublevel, however, there is an ulterior, selfish motive: seeking profit from some as a consequence of one's good will toward others.

On the still higher level of *practice*, more general motives are operative, along with a corresponding range of ways to practice business.[23] On one extreme, a greedy person may choose to practice business in whatever manner secures maximum profit. For such a person, laws and others' moral rights and needs are important only so far as they affect his own profit maximization. If illegal or immoral business performances promise greater profits, this person does not hesitate to seek those profits. Another person may practice business less viciously, drawing the line at breaking laws and transgressing others' moral rights, though still seeking maximum profit within only those restrictions. It is always conceivable, however, that circumstances may arise where such persons can maximize profits through beneficent business performances. Here, even the thoroughly vicious business person above, following his unrestricted motive of profit maximization, will do business beneficently. Yet because of his vicious motive on the practice level, even though his acts are good-will gestures, he is not morally praiseworthy, as Friedman would agree.

Another person, however, may practice business in a virtuous manner. This person recognizes the importance of profit in business, even of profit maximization in selected business performances. She does not, however, go to the vicious extreme of always consciously selecting only those business performances or activities which constitute the most profitable use of available resources; nor is she content with the less viciously selfish practice of profit maximization within only those limitations set by laws and others' moral rights. Sensitive to her obligations toward others, she chooses at least some business activities which allow her benevolently to contribute to others' welfare, even if these are not the most profitable alternatives. So motivated, she may seek profit in these business enterprises while acting on morally praiseworthy motives. Such a virtuous motive on the *practice* level is consistent with the profit motive on a sublevel of the *performance* level, which is in turn consistent with benevolent motives, or good will gestures on the lowest sublevel.

IV. SUMMARY AND CONCLUSION

With this complicated structure of motivation we see how business people, motivated by profit, can perform actions of good will toward others, without selfish strings attached, and how they can do so ultimately from morally praiseworthy motives. Selfishness, as we saw above, is not simply a matter of seeking fulfillment of one's desires, but a matter of the way one does so: in relation to the desires and goals of others. Greed, we also saw, is a vicious way to be selfish: either violating rights, or, as a matter of principle, looking only after one's own best interests, never willing to sacrifice profits for the good of others. A greedy person may indeed perform beneficent business actions, freely giving to some when doing so realizes maximum profits from others; but he will do so only under those conditions. Because business can be practiced benevolently, however, there is a virtuous way to be selfish, or a virtuous way to practice business, by performing beneficent business from moral motives.

Although we have occasionally mentioned the general issue of the moral obligations or social responsibilities of businesses or corporations, our focus has been on the obligations and motives of business *persons* as moral agents. Yet these moral features of persons can have important implications for the business activities and institutions in which they participate. The central question of this discussion has been: Must virtuous people abandon benevolent motives in their business activities, with the consequence that their profit motive becomes vicious selfishness, or is there room in business for virtuous moral agents to act benevolently? If the former, then the vicious selfishness business activity requires infects business institutions and business in general. If the latter, however, then business can be fully ethical.

Having shown here how virtuous business people can practice business benevolently, we have demonstrated conditions under which business activities and institutions can be described as fully ethical, or as constituting or conducting virtuous, benevolent business. Virtuous persons practice business within the limitations set by laws and others' moral rights, but also with a conscious commitment to perform at least some benevolent business activities, even at the cost of failing to maximize profits overall. Corporations of virtuous business persons, then, should exhibit such virtuous commitments in their stated purposes and projects. Corporations lacking such commitments cannot be described as fully ethical, and virtuous persons will have a reason to favor the corporations' adoption of such commitments, or to avoid participation in such corporations altogether. We need not maintain that businesses or corporations have obligations of beneficence, but only that persons ought occasionally to be benevolent in their business activities, and ought to structure business institutions in which they participate accordingly.

Notes

*I gratefully acknowledge Norman Bowie's helpful criticisms of an earlier draft of this paper.

1. Consider, for example, Ivan Boesky's remark in a commencement address: "I think greed is healthy. You can be greedy and still feel good about yourself"; quoted in Adam Smith, "Wall

Street's Outrageous Fortunes," *Esquire* vol. 107 (April 1987): 73–74. See also William Safire, "Ode to Greed," *The New York Times* (Jan. 5, 1986): E21.

2. Compare Ayn Rand, *The Virtue of Selfishness: A New Concept of Egoism* (New York: Signet, 1964), pp. vii–xi.

3. Compare Michael Novak, *The Spirit of Democratic Capitalism* (New York: Simon & Schuster, 1982), pp. 92–95. Novak displays a fundamental confusion when he attempts to defend capitalism against the charge of vicious selfishness by demonstrating that self-interest, as I use the term here, is a precondition of virtue.

4. Compare Ted Levitt, "The Mixed Matrix of Greed," *Harvard Business Review* vol. 65 (Nov–Dec 1987): 6–7.

5. Compare Anthony Flew, "The Profit Motive," *Ethics* vol. 86 (July 1976): 312–322, esp. 314. To argue here that we have moral obligations of beneficence toward others would be beyond the scope of this paper. That we do have "duties of charity" or "Good-Samaritan obligations" is often demonstrated by sensational examples of people's refusal, without justification, to give aid to others in need. The example of Kitty Genovese is often cited in this respect. See John Simon, Charles W. Powers and Jon P. Gunnemann, *The Ethical Investor: Universities and Corporate Responsibility* (New Haven: Yale, 1972), pp. 15–26. See also Immanuel Kant, *The Doctrine of Virtue*, trans. Mary Gregor (New York: Harper & Row, 1964), pp. 115–146.

6. Compare Kant: About duties of virtue he writes, "To fulfill them is *merit* (*meritum* = +a); but to transgress them is not so much *guilt* (*demeritum* = −a) as rather mere *lack of* moral *worth* (= 0), unless the agent makes it his principle not to submit to these duties" (*Ibid.*, p. 49). The last clause, condemning principled selfishness, is especially relevant here. It may also be recalled how Kant demonstrates in a famous passage that a maxim or policy of refusing to benefit others when one can cannot be consistently willed as universal law, and therefore that adopting such a policy is morally blameworthy. (See Immanuel Kant, *Foundations of the Metaphysic of Morals*, trans. L. W. Beck (Indianapolis: Bobbs-Merrill, 1959), p. 41/Ak 424.) Insofar as business activity requires such a policy, therefore, it is blameworthy. Although whether one *can* benefit others in business remains at this point a relevant but open question, the rest of this discussion offers an affirmative answer.

7. Arguably, Smith held a view more closely resembling that of Andrew Carnegie, to be discussed below. See Irving Kristol, "A Capitalist Conception of Justice," in *Ethics, Free Enterprise and Public Policy*, ed. De George and Pilcher (Oxford, 1978), pp. 60–63.

8. H. B. Acton, *The Morals of Markets: An Ethical Exploration* (London: Longman Group, 1971), pp. 15–16.

9. *Ibid.*, 17.

10. *Ibid.*, 16.

11. Andrew Carnegie, *The Gospel of Wealth, And Other Timely Essays*, ed. Edward C. Kirkland (Cambridge, MA: Belknap Press, 1962), p. 25.

12. *Ibid.*, 26–29.

13. See *Ibid.*, 28.

14. I put aside, for the moment, the specifically moral, or Kantian, sense of "good will," though in addition to the absence of strings attached, genuine benevolence also requires this moral motive, as will become evident below.

15. See Beth Resler Walters, "Credit Card Philanthropy," *Pace* vol. XV (April 1988): 86–91; and Jeffrey Kutler, "MasterCard Bets on Charity As a Way to Get to Customers, *American Banker*, vol. 152 (August 11, 1987): 6; John Boal, "The Corporate Bottom Line: It's Better To Give Than To Receive," *Esquire*, vol. 101 (March 1984): 255–256; Albert Walker, "The Good That They Do: The Case For Corporate In-Kind Contributions," *Public Relations Quarterly*, vol. 32 (Spring 1987): 15; Monci Jo Williams, "How To Cash In On Do-Good Pitches," *Fortune*, vol. 113 (June 9, 1986): 71.

16. These and related examples are discussed in Timothy S. Mescon and Donn J. Tilson, "Corporate Philanthropy: A Strategic Approach to the Bottom Line," *California Management Review*, vol. XXIX (Winter 1987): 49–61; See also John W. Dienhart, "Charitable Investments: A Strategy for Improving the Business Environment," *Journal of Business Ethics* vol. 7 (January–February 1988): 63–71.

17. See Mescon and Tilson, 54–56.

18. A vigorous debate has arisen around "strings-attached" donations to colleges and universities. See Robert H. Malott, "Corporate Support of Education: Some Strings Attached," and Louis W. Cabot, "Corporate Support of Education: No Strings Attached," *Harvard Business Review* (July–August 1978): 133–144. See also Richard I. Morris and Daniel A. Biederman, "How to Give Money Away Intelligently," *Harvard Business Review*, (November–December 1985): 151–159; Jeffrey Kovach, "Charitable Investments: Is This Growing Practice True Philanthropy?" *Industry Week*, vol. 223 (October 1, 1984): 29; and Dienhart, *op cit.*

19. For specific criticisms of "cause-related marketing" see Maurice G. Gurin, "Cause-Related Marketing in Question," *Advertising Age* vol. 58 (July 27, 1987). Dienhart responds to similar criticisms, see pp. 70–71.

20. Milton Friedman, "The Social Responsibility of Business Is to Increase Its Profits," *The New York Times Magazine* (September 13, 1970): 124.

21. This Kantian assumption is shared by Louis W. Fry, G. D. Keim and R. E. Miners, "Corporate Contributions: Altruistic or For-Profit?" *Academy of Management Journal*, vol. 25, no. 1 (1982): 94–106.

22. She might, as a matter of contingent fact, secure maximum profit from her benevolent business enterprises; because in her circumstances, there may be no more profitable way to invest the donated resources. But since her motivation for including these projects in her business activities is a moral motive and not ultimately a selfish one, she is morally praiseworthy.

23. John Rawls discusses the moral significance of *practices* in "Two Concepts of Rules," *The Philosophical Review*, vol. LXIV (1955); see also B. J. Diggs, "Rules and Utilitarianism," *American Philsophical Quarterly*, vol. 1 (1964). Because I am concerned here specifically with levels of motivation, my use of *practice* diverges slightly from Rawls's, though there is some overlap. In discussing business as a practice, and ways of practicing business, I employ a usage of the term similar to that of a physician's "medical practice" or a lawyer's "legal practice." On the practice level, motives guide us in determining both general practices to adopt (business, medicine, etc.) and how to practice them.

Michael Novak

WHAT IS DEMOCRATIC CAPITALISM?

Throughout the world, capitalism evokes hatred. The word is associated with selfishness, exploitation, inequality, imperialism, war. Even at home, within the United States, a shrewd observer cannot fail to note a relatively low morale among business executives, workers, and publicists. Democratic capitalism seems to have lost its spirit. To invoke loyalty to it because it brings prosperity seems to some merely materialistic. The Achilles' heel of democratic capitalism is that for two centuries now it has appealed so little to the human spirit.

This failure is not commanded by stars conjoining in the sky. It is a failure not of iron necessity but of intellect. If the system in which we live is better than any theory about it, as Reinhold Niebuhr has suggested, the guardians of its spirit — poets and philosophers and priests — have not penetrated to its secret springs. They have neither deciphered nor taught its spiritual wisdom. They have not loved their own culture.

From Michael Novak, "What Is Democratic Capitalism?" in *The Spirit of Democratic Capitalism* (New York: Simon & Schuster, 1982), 31–35. Reprinted by permission of Sterling Lord Literistic, Inc. Copyright © 1982 by Michael Novak.

Clearly, this deficiency shows something wrong at the heart of democratic capitalism. In recent years, Daniel Bell in *The Cultural Contradictions of Capitalism* has tried to name the flaw. A generation ago, Joseph Schumpeter with uncanny accuracy foretold its course.

The ironic flaw which such writers discern in democratic capitalism is this: that its *successes* in the political order and in the economic order *undermine* it in the cultural order. The more it succeeds, the more it fails. Here are a few of the most commonly heard indictments.

1. *The corruptions of affluence.* Moral discipline yields successes. But success corrupts moral discipline. Thus the system's ironical momentum heads toward hedonism, decadence, and that form of "self-fulfillment" which is like gazing into the pool of Narcissus. Instead of seeking discipline, citizens seek "liberation." Instead of saving, individuals spend and borrow. Instead of committing themselves to hard work, citizens live for "weekends." The health of a democratic republic depends upon a disciplined citizenry, but the political order of democratic capitalism is undermined by laxity. The economic system depends upon a sense of duty, disciplined innovation, and savings, but it also emits siren calls of pleasure. Productivity falls; debts grow; inflation roars; the system stagnates. In this sense, the new phenomenon encountered by economists — "stagflation" — is at bottom a disease of the spirit, which silently spreads decay even when unobserved by economic indicators. Citizens desire something for nothing — and they get it. Inflation and recession follow.

2. *Advertising and moral weakness.* The leaders of the economic system permit advertising to appeal to the worst in citizens. They encourage credit-card debt, convenience purchasing, the loosening of restraint. Their workers, their customers, and they themselves — following such solicitations — reap the whirlwind.

3. *Structural irresponsibility.* The leaders of the political order take advantage of a structural weakness in all democratic societies. Unable to depend on strong political parties, political leaders face the people alone and vulnerable, clothing themselves in symbolism and wishes. Their promises of benefits have become a special form of bribery endemic to democracy. Since each politician is on his own, none has an institutional reason to worry about who will eventually pay the costs. The careers of political leaders are shorter than the consequences of their actions. The state acquires ever heavier financial responsibilities, and yet the public incessantly clamors for *"More!"* The political leader spends, spends — an undignified activity Mr. Dooley would have lucidly diagnosed as bribes, bribes — since votes are seldom to be won by *lowering* benefits. All sectors of society desire more, so politicians promise more. They spend money not their own, money the system does not have. The structural flaw in all welfare democracies is the desire of every population to live beyond its means. Weak human nature triumphs over common sense, in public as in private life.

4. *An ambitious adversarial class.* The number of persons grows who see in expanded government empires to conquer, personal security and wealth to accumulate, and personal power to acquire. Moreover, these growing numbers are increasingly led by an intelligent, able, persistent, and ambitious elite strong enough to rival the business elite in brains and purpose and power. In order to grow wealthy and powerful in a welfare democracy, two roads now lie open where only a short time ago one lay open. This single road used to lie through

the private sector. Now a high road has been opened through the public sector. Like Mt. Everest, the limited state once towered in solitary silence, waiting to be taken. The occupying troops have multiplied. The state has become an anthill of activity. Those in control of it are gaining control over the private sector as well. For the private sector is under law while those who make, multiply, and enforce laws have powers of coercion. Lust for power — *superbia* — is deeper, more pervasive, and more widespread than lust for wealth — *cupiditas*.

5. *The declining status of aristocracy*. The leaders of the moral-cultural sector have long suffered under the market system of democratic capitalism from a profound loss of status (which through domination in the media they have recently been regaining). In traditional societies, an archbishop holds status he cannot possibly command under a fully differentiated system separating church from state. In traditional societies, scholars and artists received patronage and status they cannot readily command in the commercial marketplace. Truly rare works of genius can be appreciated by a very few; the market discerns them poorly. In the old days, artists and scholars hoped to bring their patrons (and themselves) immortality. They belonged to an aristocracy of spirit within an aristocratic culture. Aristocratic elites cherished artistic elites so that the two might forevermore be linked: excellence of intellect and aristocratic taste. In Great Britain, the artist may be "knighted," so inscribed into the aristocratic order.

By contrast, the dominant class within democratic capitalism has been the commercial class. The standards of the market are only rarely the standards of artistic and intellectual excellence. The mass market may indeed recognize great talents like those of Dickens, but for the most part it seems to favor those talents which flatter the conventional wisdom. In the marketplace, the claims of high excellence are much attenuated.

A socialist state affords its artists and intellectuals higher status. Authoritarian schemes of life enforce respect, affording honor and privilege to compliant intellect. Bourgeois cultures offer liberty but confer little of the status which systems of the traditional or of the socialist sort have it in their power to confer.

6. *Envy*. In democratic capitalism, the resentments of the intellectuals are bound to fester. Monetary rewards for high intellectual and artistic talents, while in the vagaries of the market sometimes lavish, are more frequently less than rewards for top performers in corporate management, athletics, and entertainment. That fan dancers command moneys many a scholar can scarcely dream of cries to heaven for justice. That a top talent in the field of corporate management commands a salary commensurate with that of a movie star rankles in the breasts of top academic and artistic talents. A less gifted brother of a brilliant social scientist goes to work for a corporation and draws a higher salary. Is that fair? Is this meritocracy? The Lord Jehovah, knowing its potency in the human breast, forbade covetousness twice in ten commandments.

7. *Taste*. The culture of democratic capitalism is loathed — with perhaps the deepest loathing — for its "bourgeois" and "philistine" tastes. Yet some corporate managers seem to have tastes at least as high as some professors of sociology. Thus the loathing is most exactly directed at the market mechanism, toward which, as Yugoslav socialist Bogdan Denitch puts it, "socialist theorists with rare exceptions" cherish a "dogmatic, almost puritanical attitude," being offended by the passion of Eastern European youths for jeans. The market

encourages a "consumer sovereignty that socialist intellectuals all too often think is bad for ordinary mortals." Denitch adds:

> There are two sides to this aversion. One is a predilection of socialist intellectuals toward neat, organized plans run by experts not too unlike themselves; the other is a notion that if customers of the lower orders are turned loose, they will not choose things that are good for them.[1]

Free to choose, a democratic people luxuriously manifests vulgarity. Plastic roses offend the sensitive. Rudeness and vulgarity in "shopping strips" assault the intellectuals. The tastes of ordinary citizens in Hamtramck, Newark, and South Boston scrape against refined tastes like a fingernail across a blackboard.

Trouble arises because both markets and democratic procedures introduce leveling pressures. Majorities of consumers, like political majorities, often choose what some think is not good for them. Socialists who are intellectuals frequently desire the democratization of the economic system, offended both by the existence of economic elites and by the aesthetics and moral mediocrity of free market consumers. Socialism is a neat solution to both grievances. It raises up a new elite to a position empowering it to impose a better way. Thus its attack upon the aesthetics of democratic capitalism is an important step toward "the reintegration of the political and the economic."[2] Such a "reintegration" embodies a moral-cultural vision which is to be obligatory for all.

In sum, democratic capitalism appears to the orderly eye a morass of cultural contradictions. Not many poets, philosophers, artists, or theologians have smiled kindly upon it. It seethes with adversarial spirit.

To these complaints must be added scores of others. It is charged that the skies, water, and lands are polluted. Discarded chemicals "poison" populations. The new civilization is called "cancerous." The wealthy, it is claimed, get wealthier, while the criminal-justice system oppresses the poor. The great corporations are viewed as internally undemocratic and hardly compatible with democracy at all. The "imperialism of money" keeps the Third World in "dependency." The material success of developed nations "causes" the poverty of the less-developed nations. It is hardly any wonder that, for those who believe these things, capitalism is an evil system. . . .

VIRTUOUS SELF-INTEREST

R. H. Tawney described the age of capitalism as the age of acquisitiveness. Marx described it as the reduction of every human relation to the cash nexus. Pamphleteers for generations have denounced its licensing of greed. Yet

---

[1]Bogdan Denitch, untitled essay, in Robert L. Heilbroner et al., "What Is Socialism?" *Dissent* 25 (Summer 1978): 353.
[2]Michael Harrington, in Heilbroner et al., "What Is Socialism?" p. 357.

simple reflection upon one's own life and the life of others, including the lives of those critics who denounce the system from within, suggests that there are enormous reservoirs of high motivation and moral purpose among citizens in democratic capitalist societies. The history of democratic capitalism is alive with potent movements of reform and idealistic purpose. As the world goes, its people do not in fact seem to be more greedy, grasping, selfish, acquisitive, or anarchic than citizens in traditional or in socialist societies. If democratic capitalism is to be blamed for sins it permits to flourish, the virtues it nourishes also deserve some credit.

In practice, the bone of contention seems most often to be the central concept of self-interest. A system committed to the principle that individuals are best placed to judge their real interests for themselves may be accused of institutionalizing selfishness and greed — but only on the premise that individuals are so depraved that they never make any other choice.

The founders of democratic capitalism did not believe that such depravity is universal. Furthermore, they held that the laws of free economic markets are such that the real interests of individuals are best served in the long run by a systematic refusal to take short-term advantage. Apart from internal restraints, the system itself places restraints upon greed and narrowly construed self-interest. Greed and selfishness, when they occur, are made to have their costs. A firm aware of its long-term fiduciary responsibilities to its shareholders must protect its investments for future generations. It must change with the times. It must maintain a reputation for reliability, integrity, and fairness. In one large family trucking firm, for example, the last generation of owners kept too much in profits and invested too little in new technologies and new procedures, with the result that their heirs received a battered company unable to compete or to solve its cash-flow problems. Thus a firm committed to greed unleashes social forces that will sooner or later destroy it. Spasms of greed will disturb its own inner disciplines, corrupt its executives, anger its patrons, injure the morale of its workers, antagonize its suppliers and purchasers, embolden its competitors, and attract public retribution. In a free society, such spasms must be expected; they must also be opposed.

The real interests of individuals, furthermore, are seldom merely self-regarding. To most persons, their families mean more than their own interests; they frequently subordinate the latter to the former. Their communities are also important to them. In the human breast, commitments to benevolence, fellow-feeling, and sympathy are strong. Moreover, humans have the capacity to see themselves as others see them, and to hold themselves to standards which transcend their own selfish inclinations. Thus the "self" in self-interest is complex, at once familial and communitarian as well as individual, other-regarding as well as self-regarding, cooperative as well as independent, and self-judging as well as self-loving. Understood too narrowly, self-interest destroys firms as surely as it destroys personal lives. Understood broadly enough, as a set of realistic limits, it is a key to all the virtues, as prudence is.

Like prudence in Aristotelian thought, self-interest in democratic capitalist thought has an inferior reputation among moralists. Thus it is necessary to stress again that a *society* may not work well if all its members act always from benevolent intentions. On the other hand, democratic capitalism as a system deliberately enables many persons to do well by doing good (or even purporting to do good). It offers incentives of power, fame, and money to reformers and moralists.[1]

The economic system of democratic capitalism depends to an extraordinary extent upon the social capacities of the human person. Its system of inheritance respects the familial character of motivation. Its corporate pattern reflects the necessity of shared risks and shared rewards. Its divisions both of labor and of specialization reflect the demands of teamwork and association. Its separated churches and autonomous universities reflect the importance of independent moral communities. The ideology of individualism, too much stressed by some proponents and some opponents alike, disguises the essential communitarian character of its system.

Regrettably, the theory of democratic capitalism was left too long to economists. While economists are entitled to specialize, theologians also have such rights. A theology of democratic capitalism requires a larger view, of which economists freely concede the legitimacy. Thus, Milton and Rose Friedman in their best-selling *Free to Choose* consciously stress

> . . . the broad meaning that must be attached to the concept of "self-interest." Narrow preoccupation with the economic market has led to a narrow interpretation of self-interest as myopic selfishness, as exclusive concern with immediate material rewards. Economics has been berated for allegedly drawing far-reaching conclusions from a wholly unrealistic "economic man" who is little more than a calculating machine, responding only to monetary stimuli. That is a great mistake. Self-interest is not myopic selfishness. It is whatever it is that interests the participants, whatever they value, whatever goals they pursue. The scientist seeking to advance the frontiers of his discipline, the missionary seeking to convert infidels to the true faith, the philanthropist seeking to bring comfort to the needy — all are pursuing their interests, as they see them, as they judge them by their own values.[2]

Under self-interest, then, fall religious and moral interests, artistic and scientific interests, and interests in justice and peace. The interests of the self define the self. In a free society, persons are free to choose their own interests. It is part of the function of a free economy to provide the abundance which breaks the chains of the mere struggle for subsistence, and to permit individual persons to "find themselves," indeed to define themselves through the interests they choose to make central to their lives.

In brief, the term "self-interest" encodes a view of human liberty that far exceeds self-regard, selfishness, acquisitiveness, and greed. Adam Smith attempted to suggest this by speaking of *rational* self-interest, by which he meant a specification of human consciousness not only intelligent and judgmental, beyond the sphere of mere desire or self-regard, but also guided by the ideal of objectivity. In *The Theory of Moral Sentiments* (1759), he argued that what is truly rational must be seen to be so not merely from the point of view of the

---

[1]See Kathleen Nott, *The Good Want Power: An Essay in the Psychological Possibilities of Liberalism* (New York: Basic Books, 1977).

[2]Milton and Rose Friedman, *Free to Choose* (New York: Harcourt Brace Jovanovich, 1980), p. 27.

self-interested party but from that of a disinterested rational observer as well. He called the achievement of such realistic judgment "the perfection of human nature." The whole system, as he imagined it, is aimed toward the acquisition of such realism: "We endeavour to examine our own conduct as we imagine any other fair and impartial spectator would examine it." Again: "To feel much for others, and little for ourselves . . . to restrain our selfish, and to indulge our benevolent, affections, constitutes the perfection of human nature."[3]

Democratic capitalism, then, rests on a complex theory of sin. While recognizing ineradicable sinful tendencies in every human, it does not count humans depraved. While recognizing that no system of political economy can escape the ravages of human sinfulness, it has attempted to set in place a system which renders sinful tendencies as productive of good as possible. While basing itself on something less than perfect virtue, reasoned self-interest, it has attempted to draw from self-interest its most creative potential. It is a system designed for sinners, in the hope of achieving as much moral good as individuals and communities can generate under conditions of ample liberty.

Can human society imitate Providence?

[3]Adam Smith, *The Theory of Moral Sentiments* (Indianapolis: Liberty Classics, 1969), pp. 204, 71.

Jeffrey Reiman

EXPLOITATION, FORCE, AND THE MORAL ASSESSMENT OF CAPITALISM

INTRODUCTION: THE FORCE-INCLUSIVE DEFINITION OF EXPLOITATION

Marxists and non-Marxists alike would profit from a common understanding of the meaning of the Marxian concept of exploitation and the angle of vision it provides. Towards this end, I want to discuss and defend the following definition of *exploitation*: "A society is exploitative when its social structure is organized so that unpaid labor is systematically forced out of one class and put at the disposal of another." Note that *both* unpaid labor *and* force are included here in the definition of exploitation.[1] It is not underpaid labor, but unpaid labor; and not only unpaid labor, but forced unpaid labor. On this definition, exploitation (in any economic system, capitalist or other) is a kind of coercive "prying loose" from workers of unpaid labor. I call this the "force-inclusive definition," in order to distinguish it from what I call the "distributive definition," which defines exploitation as some form of maldistribution to which force is an external support.

Defending a definition of exploitation that includes both force and unpaid labor requires showing that it is worthwhile to view social processes characterized by both of these as unitary phenomena. There is nothing unusual about this. We do an analogous thing when we separate out "robbery" — which includes both theft and force — from other forms of theft. One reason that it is worthwhile to view processes that force unpaid labor out of workers as unitary phenomena is that such processes are arguably forms of slavery, and thus worthy of special moral scrutiny.

Marxists hold that workers in capitalism work more hours for their bosses than the number of hours of work it takes to produce the real equivalent of the wages their bosses give them in return, and thus that they work in part without

From *Philosophy and Public Affairs*, 16, no. 1 (Winter 1987), 3–19, 40–41. Copyright © 1987 by Princeton University Press. Reprinted by permission of Princeton University Press.

I am grateful to G. A. Cohen for his generous and helpful comments on an earlier draft of this essay. I thank also the Editors of *Philosophy & Public Affairs* for many thought-provoking suggestions.

[1] I claim no particular originality for this definition. Nancy Holmstrom, for example, takes the "features common to exploitation" to be "that it involves forced, surplus, and unpaid labor, the product of which is not under the producers' control" (Nancy Holmstrom, "Exploitation," *Canadian Journal of Philosophy* 7, no. 2 [June 1977]: 359). She presents arguments to support the claim that the force-inclusive definition is the best interpretation of what Marx seems to have meant by exploitation. Though I agree with many of Holmstrom's points, my defense of this definition and of the conditions of its application to capitalism takes a substantially different form than hers does. This is due to the fact that Marxist writers have recently posed questions about exploitation and force that raise doubts about whether the concept of exploitation ought to be kept irrespective of "what Marx meant." I want to defend the force-inclusive definition in a way that shows that these doubts can be dealt with. I hope also to convince non-Marxists that the concept of exploitation is a valuable and usable tool of social analysis.

60

pay. And, with capitalists owning all the means of production, workers must do this in order to get a chance at making a living, and thus a chance at living at all. Therefore, workers are said to be forced to work without pay, and capitalism is said to be a form of slavery. If this sounds odd, it is because the term "slavery" normally refers to a specific historical form of forced extraction of unpaid labor (the "classical slavery" of the ancient world or antebellum America) in which individuals "owned" others — and this is not to be found in the other modes of production which Marxism calls exploitative, namely, feudalism and capitalism. Holding that these systems are forms of slavery requires thinking of the defining feature of slavery as *forced unpaid labor* which can be realized in various forms, one of which is the classical form where individuals are directly owned by other individuals. In what follows, I shall mean by "slavery" this essential core of "forced unpaid labor," and reserve the term "classical slavery" for the particular form it took in the ancient world or antebellum America. On the force-inclusive definition of exploitation, any exploitative society is a form of slavery. . . .

One point of this exercise is to set up the issues in a way that enables us to see what follows for the moral assessment of capitalism if Marxian theory is essentially correct. By this moral assessment, I mean primarily the determination of the justice of capitalism. And by that, I do not mean the determination of what Marx thought about capitalism's justice, but what we should think, in light of *our* conception of justice, if the Marxian analysis of capitalism is essentially correct.[2] I shall not try to complete the moral assessment of capitalism that would determine whether it is just or not. Rather, I try to spell out the nature of exploitation as a necessary preparation for that assessment, and attempt to show how that assessment is affected by the determination that capitalism is exploitative.

---

[2]There is a substantial literature on the question of whether capitalism is unjust according to Marxism. See articles in M. Cohen, T. Nagel, T. Scanlon, eds. *Marx, Justice, and History* (Princeton, NJ: Princeton University Press, 1980); K. Nielsen and S. Patten, eds., *Marx and Morality* (*Canadian Journal of Philosophy*, Supplemental Volume VII, 1981), and J. Pennock and J. Chapman, eds., *Marxism: Nomos XXVI* (New York: New York University Press, 1983); as well as G. A. Cohen, "Freedom, Justice, and Capitalism," *New Left Review* 126 (March/April 1981): 3–16; and more recently, Norman Geras's review of the whole discussion, "The Controversy About Marx and Justice," *New Left Review* 150 (March/April 1985): 47–85. Geras concludes, quite wisely I think, that "Marx did think that capitalism was unjust but he did not think he thought so" (p. 70). As the convoluted nature of this answer should suggest, this literature is dogged by unclarity about what question it should be asking. Allen Wood, for example, presents convincing textual evidence showing at least that Marx calls capitalism just, and then Wood goes on to conclude that Marx's problem with capitalism was not a problem about its injustice at all, but about the fact that it is a form of servitude (Allen Wood, "The Marxian Critique of Justice," in Cohen, Nagel, and Scanlon, eds., *Marx, Justice, and History*, pp. 1–41). In my view, it is of little more than historical interest whether Marx called capitalism just. And saying that Marx's problem with capitalism was its servitude not its injustice, assumes that justice is distributive justice and that servitude is not an issue of justice, neither of which assumptions seems true or helpful. As recent arguments about the injustice of slavery have evidenced, contemporary conceptions of justice cover issues of servitude. In my view, the relevant question is whether capitalism is unjust *according to our conception of justice* if the *Marxian analysis of capitalism is essentially correct*. This is the question we must answer to determine our stance toward capitalism. See my "The Possibility of a Marxian Theory of Justice," in Nielsen and Patten, eds., *Marx and Morality*, pp. 307–322.

I. EXPLOITATION, LABOR, STRUCTURAL FORCE, AND MORALITY

In this section, I present an extended gloss on the force-inclusive definition of exploitation. I argue that it depends on a *general* version of the labor theory of value, and on a *structural* conception of force, and that establishing that capitalism is exploitative according to this definition leaves open the question of its justness.

Consider first the notion of "unpaid labor" in the proposed definition. When Marxists say that workers (in any mode of production) labor without pay, they take this to follow automatically from the claim that the workers give more labor than they receive back in the form of compensation. In capitalism, Marx held that workers work without pay because they give their bosses more labor-time than the amount of labor-time they get back in the form of their wage. A worker works, say, a forty-hour week and receives back a wage which will purchase some amount of goods that it takes (whoever produces them) less than forty hours of labor to produce. The worker gives a surplus of labor over the amount he receives in return, and this surplus labor is held to be unpaid.

But from the fact that I give my boss more labor than I get back from him, it does not automatically follow that the surplus I give is unpaid. It only follows automatically if labor is the proper measure of what my boss and I have exchanged. If, by contrast, the proper measure is, say, marginal utility, then it is possible that my wage (meaning the goods it will purchase) represents marginal utility for me equivalent to what my work represents for my boss, even if I must work longer to produce his utility than wage-good workers worked to produce mine. Since the application of the definition of exploitation to capitalism rests on the assumption that surplus labor is unpaid because it is surplus, it requires the doctrine that labor is the proper measure of what bosses and workers trade. That means that it requires something like "the labor theory of value." And, since the Marxian charge of exploitation in any mode of production always rests on the notion that surplus labor is ipso facto unpaid labor, I take it that the definition of exploitation generally depends on something like the labor theory of value.

I say "something like" the labor theory of value because I do not mean the whole of the theory by that name which Marx develops in *Capital*. In its specific application to capitalism, this theory holds that the market values of commodities tend to reflect (through various refractions) the relative amounts of time upon which they have been labored. This in turn is taken as implying that the prices of commodities could ultimately be transformed into the amounts of labor-time normally expended in their production. And this is widely thought to be impossible, thus rendering the labor theory of value generally vulnerable and many Marxists willing to jettison it. I shall not try to defend the theory as a theory of price-formation. But I do think that a more general version of the theory, which makes no claim to account for prices, is defensible and must be defended if the Marxian notion of exploitation is to be applied to capitalism, and to any other social system.

To see this more general version, consider that the labor theory of value might be thought of as a two-storied theory. On the ground floor is the notion that labor-time is the sole measure of the real value that produced things have as a result of being produced. On the floor above is the notion that capitalism works (via the market, competition, and so forth) to bring the prices of produced things into some systematic relationship with the amount of time labored on them.[3] Notice that "value" means something different in this upper-floor theory, which we can call the "special labor theory of value," than it means in the ground-floor theory, which we can call the "general labor theory of value." In the former, value means something like "what a product will bring on the market," while in the latter, it means something like "what ultimately matters about a product." Though the two senses are distinct, there is an understandable relationship between them: The special labor theory of value claims that capitalism has built-in mechanisms that bring the prices of things into systematic relationship with what ultimately matters about them in any system of production.

Marx obviously held the special labor theory of value with respect to capitalism, and I think he implicitly held the general labor theory of value for all modes of production.[4] If he didn't, I contend he should have, since it is the minimum necessary to make the concept of surplus labor imply unpaid labor in any mode of production, not just one in which the capitalist price-formation mechanisms are operating. The general theory supports the charge of exploitation in capitalism even when doubts about the special theory are raised; and it can be plausibly defended, even if there are fatal flaws in the special theory.[5] Crudely and by no means completely stated, the defense is this.

An economic system is some organization of the productive labor of society and of the distribution of the products of that labor among the members of society. Such a system works by means of a system of ownership, understood in the broadest sense as any system of recognized claims on parts of the social product (including the resources that went into it). By means of a system of

---

[3]By "some systematic relationship" I include the fact that Marx held the value of a commodity to be determined by "socially necessary labor-time" (the average amount necessary to produce such a commodity at the time it comes on the market) rather than by the actual amount labored on it, and that Marx showed in great detail the structural reasons why prices deviate from socially necessary labor-time. Karl Marx, *Capital* (New York: International Publishers, 1967), vol. I, p. 39 and vol. III, pp. 142ff. Hereafter, references to *Capital* will be cited in the text as "*C*" followed by the volume number and the page number.

[4]Marx writes that "however varied the useful kinds of labour . . . may be, it is a physiological fact, that they are functions of the human organism, and that each such function, whatever may be its nature or form, is essentially the *expenditure* of human brain, nerves, muscles, &c. . . . In all states of society, the labour-time that it costs to produce the means of subsistence, must *necessarily be an object of interest to mankind.* . . . And lastly, from the moment that men in any way work for one another, their labour assumes a *social* form" (*C*, I, p. 71; emphasis mine). This does not of course amount to a statement of the general theory, but the emphasized terms do represent most of its basic elements.

[5]This is an important dividend of separating out the general from the special labor theory of value. Cohen has argued for separating the concept of exploitation from the labor theory of value because the socially necessary labor constituting value is not the same as the actual labor that went into products, and thus appropriation of surplus value is not appropriation of actual labor. And Roemer has taken as one reason for suspicion about the Marxian concept of exploitation, the fact that the labor theory, with which it is linked, seems subject to insuperable theoretical objections. Without commenting on the validity of these points, note that in both cases the difficulties are with the special and not the general labor theory of value. Separating out the general theory allows the concept of exploitation to stay tied to the labor theory of value even if Cohen and Roemer are right about the liabilities of the special theory. See Cohen, *LT*, passim; and Roemer, *PR*, p. 283.

ownership, an economic system works so that different people end up possessing products that others have worked on.

Suppose, now, that we are surveying the various economic systems that have existed in history so that we might assess them morally. We shall surely want a neutral way of characterizing what it is that people give one another in the various systems (where "give" is understood very broadly to refer to any way in which some person undergoes a loss that ends up a gain to another). By neutral, I mean a way of characterizing that does not presuppose the validity of any of the systems of ownership that are under inspection. Accordingly, we cannot say that what people give others is equivalent to "what they give of what they own." The reason is that if ownership is not valid, then in giving what I (invalidly) "own," I may really not be giving anything but only passing on what is actually given by someone else. Indeed, it is precisely such matters that we would want to be able to identify for purposes of our moral assessment. More generally, since an economic system includes its system of ownership, measuring what people give one another in an economic system in terms of what they own in that system effectively builds a bias in favor of that system into our measurement (it allows that system to supply the measure of what is to count as giving). Thus we need a way of characterizing what people give each other in an economic system that is independent of ownership. Then, while remaining neutral on its validity, we will be able to say of any ownership system how it works to get some people to give things to others.

When nothing that presupposes the validity of the system of ownership can be used, all that remains that workers give in production is their time and energy, in a word, their labor, or as Marx had it, their "labor-time" (which he understood to include a standard measure of energy exerted).[6] And this labor-time is really *given* in the sense that it is "used up" — as finite human beings workers have only finite time and energy, and thus less left over when they have given some up. The same cannot be said, for example, of their talents. First of all, their talents are the result of their natural gifts plus the time and energy they devoted to developing those gifts. This time and energy counts of course, and it must be factored into labor-time, so that the talented labor devoted to producing something now must include some measure of the earlier labor that went into producing that level of talent. But the "natural gifts" themselves are, as the word suggests, given to the worker and thus merely passed on by him. What's more, talents are not used up in exercising them. If anything, they are augmented by use rather than depleted. Outside of ownership, labor, and talent, all that is left in any part of the social product are the natural materials that went into it. And these (less the labor that went into extracting them or working them up into usable form) are not given by anyone to anyone else unless they are owned.

Try the following thought experiment. Suppose that A and B are equal in their talents, and that C enslaves them both, forcing A to work two eight-hour days and B to work one eight-hour day at the same level of intensity (relative to their capacities). I expect that readers will agree that what happens to A here is worse than what happens to B and that it is roughly twice as bad (or, equivalently, that what C does to A is worse, roughly by a factor of two, than what he

---

[6]"The labour-time socially necessary is that required to produce an article under the normal conditions of production, and with the average degree of skill and *intensity* prevalent at the time" (*C*, I, p. 39; emphasis mine).

does to B). Suppose that A and B are each forced to work one eight-hour day, though A is forced to work at twice the level of intensity that B is (again relative to their capacities). Here too, I expect that readers will agree that what happens to (or what C does to) A is worse than what happens to (or what C does to) B and that it is roughly twice as bad. Suppose now that X is twice as talented as Y, though both have devoted the same amount of time and energy to reaching their respective levels of talent, and that Z enslaves them both, forcing them each to work at their respective levels of talent for one eight-hour day at the same level of intensity. Is X's enslavement twice as bad as Y's? Is it worse at all? I think the reader will agree that their enslavements (thought of either as their fates or as what Z does) are equally bad. Doesn't it follow from this that (*ceteris paribus*) taking more time and energy from one person than from another amounts to taking more from the first, while taking more talented labor from one than from another does not? I think this reflects the recognition that what people give in laboring is their time and energy and not their talents.

It might be objected that counting labor as given by workers presupposes that workers *own* it. But I think that it only presupposes that labor is physically their *own*, in the way that their pains and their deaths are their own. And this I take to be a natural fact. People give themselves in laboring; they literally use themselves up. *Labor done, however willingly or even joyously, is life itself spent.* I suspect that it is this natural fact that accounts for the lingering appeal of the labor theory of value, and for the reluctance of many Marxists to part with the theory in the face of apparently unanswerable objections to it. In any event no stronger notion of ownership is implied here than is implied in the standard Marxist usage of the term "alienation."

It might also be objected that the general labor theory of value is itself a moral theory, in that it seems to give a kind of moral priority to labor-time for purposes of moral assessment of economic systems. I grant this point, but I do not regard it as an objection. We arrive at the general labor theory looking for a way of characterizing what people give in productive arrangements that is neutral, not cosmically neutral, but neutral regarding the validity of systems of ownership. As long as the general theory can be formulated neutrally in this respect, it will do what we want even if it is not morally neutral in some ultimate sense. That we reach it by looking for means to assess economic systems morally already suggests that what we will find is something that matters morally, and that it will have some moral implications about how we determine the validity of ownership systems. But it will do its job as long as it does no more than this while leaving open the final determination of their validity.[7] In fact, rather than an objection, this is a confirmation. As Marx and Marxists use the

---

[7] Rather than determine the validity of ownership systems, what the general theory does is strip away the halo of legitimacy that normally surrounds titles of ownership, and allow us to see any economic system in terms of what ultimately matters, that is, as a distribution of the labor-time that goes into the products produced. And this means that any economic distribution is a system of relations in which people can be said to be *laboring for* others in varying proportions — irrespective of whether they are *forced to*, or whether they are laboring for others *without compensation*. I contend that this gives us the appropriate neutral standpoint from which to evaluate property systems morally. I have developed the implications of this approach to evaluating distributions in "The Labor Theory of the Difference Principle." *Philosophy & Public Affairs* 12, no. 2 (Spring 1983): 133–159.

term exploitation, it is a descriptive notion which carries a strong negative moral presumption with it. The general labor theory accounts for this peculiar quasi-moral nature of the concept of exploitation.

Consider now the term "force" in the proposed definition. The force in capitalism is as elusive as the unpaid nature of surplus labor in capitalism. This is because, unlike the masters of classical slaves, capitalists are normally prohibited from using physical violence against their workers either on the job or at the negotiating table. Consequently, that workers are forced to work in order not to starve (or more recently, in order not to be reduced to surviving minimally on the dole) appears as no more than the natural fact that food doesn't fall from the sky and thus people must work in order to eat. The invisibility of exploitative force in capitalism results from the fact that, in capitalism, overt force is supplanted by force built into the very structure of the system of ownership and the classes defined by that system. Because there is the human institution of private ownership of means of production by a small class of people, the members of the class of nonowners are forced to work *for those people* — though not necessarily forced *by* those people — in order to get a crack at a living at all. Accordingly, I take it that the force in our definition must apply not only to overt violence, but to force that is "structural," both in its effects and in its origins.

Take the effects first: Unlike the usual strongarm stuff that singles out particular individuals as its targets, this force works on people by virtue of their location in the social structure (that is, for example, *qua* members of some class), and it affects individuals more or less "statistically." By this I mean that *such force affects individuals by imposing an array of fates on some group while leaving it open how particular individuals in that group get sorted, or sort themselves, into those fates*. The term "structural" is appropriate for such force because it works the way that a physical structure such as a bottleneck (in the road) imposes fates on groups, forcing a majority of cars to slow down while leaving it to chance and other factors who makes up that majority and who gets into the minority that slips easily through.

This force is structural in its origin also: Though the force works to transfer labor from one class to another, it is not the benefiting class that forces the losing one — rather the structure of the ownership or class system itself forces the transfer. (Among the roles constituting a structure, some will be assigned the dirty work of administering violence; but I take this to be a tool of structural force, not the thing itself.)

To get a handle on the notion of structural force, picture a large crowd of spectators who must pass through a human bottleneck as they leave a stadium. I mean "human bottleneck" quite literally. Imagine that people are standing shoulder to shoulder in the shape of a bottleneck and that the crowd must pass through this human funnel to get out of the stadium. The people making up the human bottleneck are there with varying degrees of intentionalness, some are there just minding their own business and some are there because they want the crowd to have to pass through just this sort of shape. But all are inclined to stay where they are because they want to, or believe they should or must, or because they are conditioned to, or some combination of these. If people in the crowd try to break through the human bottleneck, they will at least be resisted, and where they succeed in making an opening, people from other points on the bottleneck will move to seal it up and prevent their passing through. And other bottleneckers will at least support this and even offer to lend a hand. The crowd leaving the stadium, then, will find in this bottleneck varying degrees of resistance to their attempts to break through it, but enough so that they will have to adapt their flow to the shape.

It seems to me that we can say here that the crowd is forced into a certain pattern by the structure of the human bottleneck. Note that this force works its effects "statistically." Some people — say, those who move quickly to the head of the crowd — will hardly be slowed or constrained at all, they may follow the same path they would have had there been no one else there. And the force originates structurally. To be sure, the bottleneck structure is manned by real individuals, but they play their roles more or less unthinkingly, and none of those who play their roles thinkingly could succeed in keeping the crowd in the shape were it not for the rest of the people making up the bottleneck. The result of their all generally playing their roles is to force the crowd to take on the shape of the bottleneck, while leaving undetermined which individual will end up in each particular spot inside that shape.

The institution of private property is like the human bottleneck. A large number of people play roles — as judges, lawyers, police officers, laborers, consumers, real estate agents, voters, and so on — in that institution, thinkingly and unthinkingly, more or less actively. And it is the overall shape of those roles that forces a certain pattern of options on the people subject to it, while leaving it open exactly which options are forced on which particular individuals.[8]

I shall not launch a full-scale justification of using the term "force" in this way. Note, however, that the features of standard cases of force are here in recognizable if somewhat altered form. First, in the standard cases we take force to limit people's options by making all their alternatives but one either unacceptable or prohibitively costly (as in "your money or your life"). With structural force, people's options are limited by their social position to a *range* of things they can do, with options outside this range unacceptable or prohibitively costly. So, by virtue of occupying a social position defined, say, by lack of access to means of production, a person will be limited to a range of ways in which he can achieve a living, because alternatives outside this range (such as starvation or begging or crime) are unacceptable or prohibitively costly. Second, in the standard cases of force, it is exercised intentionally by human beings. Structural force is a kind of leverage over people to which they are vulnerable by virtue of their location in the social structure. But the social structure — say, a caste or property system — is nothing but a pattern of human behavior.[9] So, while structural force need not be exercised intentionally, there is no doubt that

---

[8]There is no logical problem with people playing roles in the structures that limit their freedom. A military command structure, for example, forces obedience on every soldier by the general likelihood that other soldiers will obey orders to punish disobedients, and these others are forced (and thus likely) to obey because of yet others, and so on. Each individual soldier is among the "other soldiers" for everyone else. It follows that every soldier plays a role in the structure that limits every soldier's freedom. Insofar as workers pay taxes, respect "No Trespassing" signs, and the like, they play roles in the structure of private ownership that in turn constrains their freedom.

[9]"The social system is not an unchangeable order beyond human control but a pattern of human action" (John Rawls, *A Theory of Justice* [Cambridge, MA: Harvard University Press, 1971], p. 102).

it is exerted by human beings.[10] And if it is not intentional, it is in principle something that, by making people aware of the effects of their actions, could be made intentional; and in fact, if enough people became aware, they could alter this force or rightly be held to intend it.

More controversial is the following. In the standard cases, the target of force has no real choice over his fate, either because all his alternatives save one are unacceptable, or because he has no alternatives at all (perhaps he has been bound or drugged). In structural force, by contrast, there is some *play*. Structural force works to constrain a group of individuals to some array of situations, leaving it to them or to other factors to determine how they are distributed among those situations. Therefore, between the forcing structure and its effects there can be room for the operation of free and rational choice on the part of individuals affected. That is, while people are constrained to the set of situations in the array (because alternatives outside the array are unacceptable or prohibitively costly), they may be able to exercise real choice among those in the array, selecting the one that they find most desirable. Nonetheless, I contend that, as long as the group is constrained such that its members must end up distributed among all the situations in the array determined by the structure, all the individuals are "forced into" the particular situations in which they end up — even if they exercised some choice on the way. In short, structural force can operate through free choice. And the reason for this is that force need not only take advantage of your fear (say, of dying) — it can also work, indeed often more effectively, by taking advantage of your rationality.

Suppose an outlaw is laying in wait for a stagecoach, in which he knows there will be six passengers each wearing a gold watch worth twenty dollars and each carrying about that amount in cash. Our outlaw wants to emerge with three watches and sixty dollars but is indifferent about who gives which. He resolves then to give the passengers a chance to choose which they will give, although if their choices don't arrive at his desired outcome he will rescind the privilege and just take three watches and sixty dollars. Stopping the coach, gun in hand, he orders the passengers to give him either their watch or their cash. The passengers are utility maximizers who regard their watches and their twenty dollars as comparably desirable, though each has a decided if small preference for one or the other. As luck would have it, their preferences match the outlaw's desired outcome, and three give up their watches and three their cash.

Now, take one passenger at random who, say, has given up his watch. Is it not the case that he was forced to give up the watch? It certainly seems odd to say that he wasn't forced to give up his watch because he had an acceptable alternative. To say that seems to focus excessively on what happens in the last moment just before the passenger handed over his watch and to pay too little attention to the fact that the situation had been set up so that there was a good chance that by allowing him (and the others) to choose (rationally, in light of their preferences), the outlaw would succeed in subordinating their wills to his ends.

Suppose that at the moment our outlaw stops the coach and makes his threat another stranger passes by and offers to protect the three passengers who would

[10]Cohen writes "where relations of production force people to do things, people force people to do things" (*SP*, p. 6). Cohen, by the way, allows that people can also be forced without being forced by people, but adopts, for the present argument, the narrower view that they can only be forced by people. I do the same.

have given up their watches. Our protector, however, wants sixty dollars for his trouble. Suppose now that the passengers decide to give up their watches (on the same grounds that they decided this in the first example), and thus turn down the offer of protection. If you held that the passenger in the first example was not forced to give up his watch, mustn't you hold that now? If so, you would have to say that the passenger freely chose to be robbed, or that he was not robbed but gave away his watch freely — which is preposterous. I take it then that a person can be said to be forced to do something even if he has rationally chosen that thing from among other acceptable alternatives, provided that the whole array of alternatives can be said to be forced upon him.

This will be no news to con artists and spy-story authors. They well know that a free choice can be the last link in the chain that ties a person to a forced fate. It is possible to get someone to do your bidding by setting up a situation in which doing your bidding is your victim's most rational choice, even if there are other choices which are acceptable though less rational for him. It is easy to overlook this, since when a person does what is most rational for him because it is most rational, and not just because it is the only thing acceptable, he seems to be acting freely. And, to an extent he is. But rather than showing that he is thus not forced, what that shows is that force can work through his free choice. An intelligent forcer can take advantage of the fact that, left free, people will normally do what is most rational for them. And this is an advantage because when people do another's bidding this way, they are less likely to see (or feel) that they are being forced. Accordingly, force can be more effective because less visible if it can work through people's predictable free choices. For this very reason we must free ourselves from the notion that force occurs only when a person is presented with alternatives all of which are unacceptable but one. Otherwise, we shall miss the way in which social structures force fates on people while appearing to leave their fates up to them.

When Marx wrote that the wage-worker "is compelled to sell himself of his own free will" (*C*, I, p. 766), he was not being arch or paradoxical. He was telling us both how force works in capitalism *and* why it is unseen. Indeed, I contend that what Marxists call capitalist ideology boils down to little more than the invisibility of structural force. And libertarian capitalism is the theory that results when the lover of freedom falls prey to that invisibility.[11]

How much real choice people have over which of the situations they end up in will be a matter of how much play there is in the structural force. I shall say that where people can choose among the situations in the array to which they are constrained, the relative acceptability of the alternative situations one can choose among determines whether one is "tightly" or "loosely" forced into the situation one ends up in. Suppose then, that a structure imposes on people an array of two situations, A and B, while leaving it to them to choose which they will end up in. If B is considerably less acceptable than A, I would say that those who end up in A have been (relatively) tightly forced (by the structure) into A. If A and B are roughly comparable in acceptability, I would say that those who end up in A have been (relatively) loosely forced there (by the structure) — though still truly forced. And in general, the greater the number of acceptable nonre-

[11]See my "The Fallacy of Libertarian Capitalism," *Ethics* 92 (October 1981): 85–95.

dundant alternatives in an array, the more loosely individuals are forced into the ones in which they end up.

Bear in mind that the array of situations determined by a social structure is not an arbitrary matter. Unless a structure deploys enough of its people in each of the situations necessary to its functioning, that structure will soon break down. Accordingly, we should not be surprised to find that structures normally have play in them up to the point that leaving outcomes to choice will yield the needed distribution of individuals — just as much play as there was in our outlaw's force.

. . . If it still sounds strange to speak this way, consider the possibility that our language has been shaped in ways that serve structural force by making us unlikely to label it. What if this is just how we have to be able to talk about societies in order to morally assess them correctly? What if the fact that there is a role for choice blinds us to the force that is at work determining the shape of the larger terrain within which we choose? What if the very salience of the standard forms of direct or violent force blinds us to the less visible indirect ways in which force can work? I contend that all a social structure has to do to count as forcing fates on its members is force them into an array of fates among which they will be distributed or distribute themselves in some manner within the limits of tolerance necessary to the functioning of that structure. This is all that is necessary, because, for the purpose of moral assessment of social structures, what is crucial is how they constrain people's lives, and that is so even if there is enough play in that constraint to allow a role for choice. To insist on more, in determining what should count as force, is to be overly dominated in one's imagination by the image of one person physically forcing or threatening another.[12]

Marx counsels that the illusion about the nature of capitalism "vanishes immediately, if, instead of taking a single capitalist and a single labourer, we take the class of capitalists and the class of labourers as a whole" (*C*, I, p. 568). Applied to force, this would require us to open ourselves to the possibility of a kind of force that operates from the shape of the social structure itself and on classes as a whole. I contend that something like this is necessary to free ourselves from illusions about how force operates in capitalism. And more generally, it is necessary if we are to give concrete sense to claims such as Rawls's that "unjust social arrangements are themselves a kind of extortion, even violence."[13]

Note that, as the force in exploitation is structural, so is the exploitation itself. Unpaid labor is extracted from the class of laborers as a whole and put at the disposal of the other class as a whole, rather than individual laborers each dumping their quantum of unpaid labor into the hands of individuals in the receiving class. Thus, even if some highly paid workers in fact receive more labor-time in their wage than they give on the job, it can still be said that the working class is exploited as long as the total time it labors is more than the

---

[12]I have explored the way this domination of our imaginations limits our conception of crime to the kinds of things that poor people do, in *The Rich Get Richer and the Poor Get Prison: Ideology, Class, and Criminal Justice*, 2d ed. (New York: John Wiley, 1984), pp. 45–76. See, also, my "The Marxian Critique of Criminal Justice," *Criminal Justice* 6, no. 1 (Winter/Spring 1987).

[13]Rawls, *A Theory of Justice*, p. 343.

labor-time it gets back in wages. Here too, the structure affects individuals in a statistical way.

The final feature of the definition on which I shall comment (briefly) is its relation to morality. I contend that the claim that capitalism is exploitative is compatible with its being just, or at least being the most just system actually possible. In defense of this, I shall make three points. The first, and most obvious, is that the fact that a system is exploitative and thus slavery creates a presumption against its justice, but no more. In principle that presumption could be overridden. Even those who think that slavery is invariably evil generally allow that there are conceivable conditions under which it could be just.[14] And this is given added support by the fact that, since capitalist slavery is not classical slavery, it is possible that some of the features that make the latter particularly awful are absent or can be moderated in the former. Second, social systems must be assessed as systems, not piecemeal. That it is exploitative is only one feature of capitalism. Capitalism is also a system (as Marx well saw) that dramatically increases the productivity of labor, and thus that has the capacity to raise the standard of material well-being while reducing the amount of labor needed to produce it. Marx understood this as capitalism's historical mission (*C*, III, pp. 441 and 819–820). Moreover, advanced capitalist societies have been characterized by an undeniably large range of personal and political freedom, which materialists at least must suspect is somehow linked to the structure of the capitalist mode of production. I shall have more to say about this at the end of this article. For the present, it suffices to say that if capitalism is judged as a whole system, and if its productivity and freedom are in some way inextricably linked to its mode of extracting unpaid labor, the overall judgment of capitalism's justice cannot be determined exclusively by the fact of its exploitativeness.

Third, social systems must be assessed in terms of what is really possible in history, not just what is in principle desirable. Marx actually said very little about the socialism and communism he hoped or expected would replace capitalism. In his writings, these appear as little more than theoretical constructs arrived at by negating the troublesome features of capitalism. If capitalism is exploitative because of private ownership of the means of production, then we can project in theory the remedy for this in the form of collective ownership, first via the state in socialism, and then directly in communism. But judgments about capitalism cannot fairly be made by comparing its reality with some ideal system. It must be compared with what is actually possible. And here it is an open question whether systems of collective ownership can actually be made to function in a way which overall is superior to the way in which capitalism does function. Thus, even if capitalism is exploitative, it might, as a matter of historical fact, be the most just system actually possible. My point here is not to assert this, but to make clear that it is not foreclosed by finding capitalism exploitative. . . .

Even if we grant that capitalism is exploitative according to the force-inclusive definition, and that workers are forced to continue to sell their labor power . . . , it remains significant *that they have a choice and that they pass it up.* I want to emphasize the separate significance of these two facts. The first signifies that

---

[14]See, for example, ibid., p. 248.

capitalist slavery is freer than classical slavery, and the second signifies that capitalist slavery is less awful than classical slavery. The capitalist variety is imposed by looser force than the classical variety. It cannot be denied that a society that allows its workers to choose its slavery from among acceptable alternatives constrains their freedom less than one that does not. And to that extent, [this] freedom . . . counts in the positive column in any moral assessment of capitalism. Moreover, that workers pass up acceptable alternatives to selling their labor power suggests that, whatever the disabilities of selling labor power may be, they are not intolerable. It would be hard to imagine many classical slaves passing up a similar way of escaping from their situation. Thus [this] freedom . . . must also count to reduce the sum in the negative column in any moral assessment of capitalism.

As I see it, the implication of [this] argument, then, is that capitalist slavery is a substantially milder thing than classical slavery, and no Marxist can rightly call capitalism slavery with the intention of conveying that it is as bad as the classical variety. Capitalism might be, or might be made into, a relatively mild form of slavery. But this possibility must be viewed alongside another. No one who is aware of the power conferred by ownership of means of production can ignore the potential danger involved in handing ownership of the means of production over to the state. Capitalist slavery might be mild in part because in it ownership of means of production is private and thus power is decentralized. This could be the material condition of the looseness in capitalist structural force. The space between a plurality of centers of power may be just the space in which freedom occurs, and conflicts between the centers may work to keep that space open. State ownership, by contrast, might not be slavery at all, in that, by means of the state, the people themselves would own the means of production, and people cannot be slaves to themselves. But as a material fact, state ownership might still represent a condition in which people were more vulnerable to, or less able to resist or escape from, force than they are in capitalism. It follows that, even if socialism ends capitalist slavery, it remains possible, on materialist grounds, that some achievable form of capitalism will be morally superior to any achievable form of socialism. And this remains possible even if capitalism is exploitative according to the force-inclusive definition.

DISCUSSION QUESTIONS

1. Michelman asks whether it is necessary for there to be "contradictions between generally accepted moral obligations and the laws and rules that flow from the logic of economic competition." In other words, must you act unethically in order to succeed in business? Is business in a free, competitive, capitalistic, market economy morally corrupt?

2. McCarty observes that it might be argued that "the selfish profit motive successful business requires is intrinsically at odds with part of the requirements of morality." Do you agree or disagree with this idea?

3. McCarty offers some examples of "benevolent business." Are these

merely exceptions to the rule, as it were, or is it possible for every transaction to flow from moral motives?

4. Novak notes that "the leaders of the moral-cultural sector have long suffered under the market system of democratic capitalism from a profound loss of status." Nothing exemplifies this more than the use of rock stars and sports figures to endorse products. Some would argue that this practice weakens society because it enshrines the wrong group of people as cultural icons. Critics suggest that physicians, successful executives, teachers, and clergy, for example, would be better role models for young people. What is your reaction to this?

5. Novak says that "democratic capitalism . . . has attempted to set in place a system which renders sinful tendencies as productive of good as possible." Do you agree with this characterization? Are these tendencies indeed "sinful"? Does the system succeed? What is your evaluation of the moral character of such a system? Would it be better for an economic system to try to eradicate rather than harness the energies responsible for vice?

6. Reiman observes that "capitalism might be, or might be made into, a relatively mild form of slavery." He says this in defense of capitalism. What is your reaction to Reiman's moral assessment of capitalism?

CASE 2.1

Tobacco and Addiction

When we speak of the tragedy of drug addiction, we usually mean the deaths resulting from heroin, cocaine, or alcohol abuse. Cocaine kills approximately 8,000 people each year, and alcohol is responsible for more than ten times that number of deaths. Yet these figures pale beside the nearly 400,000 deaths produced annually by diseases related to smoking, that is, to nicotine addiction. The morality of alcohol use was attacked during Prohibition, and alcohol abuse is no longer considered chic in American society. The "war on drugs" has called into question the ethical defensibility of illegal drugs. Yet, despite the harm that is produced by tobacco, smoking is generally not challenged as an ethical issue by the general public. Are there truly no serious ethical problems here or is this an oversight?

Smoking has traditionally been described as a practice that individuals freely choose. Smokers, it is argued, have full knowledge of the risks associated with tobacco. Indeed, smokers can hardly avoid knowing these risks because of the Surgeon General's warnings printed in every cigarette ad and on the side of every pack of cigarettes: "Smoking causes lung cancer, heart disease, emphysema, and may complicate pregnancy"; "Smoking by pregnant women may result in fetal injury, premature birth, and low birth weight"; "Quitting smoking now greatly reduces serious risks to your health"; and "Cigarette smoke contains carbon monoxide."

Defenders of smoking claim that such explicit warnings remove any ethical concerns associated with tobacco. Smokers freely and rationally choose the pleasure of smoking over the dangers that they are well aware of. Smokers are neither deceived nor coerced by cigarette manufacturers. Nonsmokers may not approve of the habit or understand the choice, but smokers argue that they have the right to make such a choice and inflict whatever harm they choose on their own bodies.

Cigarette manufacturers claim that they are doing nothing unethical in supplying the demand for cigarettes and promoting their products. The major ethical issue faced by the $60-billion-per-year industry seems to revolve around how cigarette manufacturers should advertise so as not to encourage smoking among people too young to make a fully informed decision. Cigarette manufacturers claim that their ads are meant only to generate brand loyalty among adults who already smoke.

Critics of smoking, however, object to this account and point to a central fact that is not mentioned in any of the Surgeon General's warnings — tobacco is addictive. Opponents claim that smoking meets all of the criteria for classification as a drug addiction: Nicotine easily enters the bloodstream and alters the smoker's mood; despite the fact that smoking does physiological damage, most smokers compulsively continue the practice; most smokers have unsuccessfully tried to stop smoking; there are withdrawal symptoms when a smoker tries to quit; and these symptoms are so painful that most smokers who try to stop relapse in order to avoid them. Indeed, the addiction appears to be so powerful that half of the smokers who have heart and lung surgery continue to smoke. From an ethical standpoint, then, if nicotine is addictive, the free choice argument might be called into question.

Critics of smoking also claim that cigarette ads misrepresent the nature of the product and that advertising is indeed aimed at young people. They object to "life-style" ads that portray smokers as young, glamorous, sexy, and healthy and to the fact that cigarette companies advertise in magazines with a heavy teenage readership, such as *Rolling Stone, National Lampoon,* and *Movies U.S.A.* They object to the way that cigarette companies promote themselves by sponsoring sporting events. Opponents claim that the image of cigarettes that is cultivated is so far from what is actually the case as to be considered unethical, that is, false and deceptive.

Opponents also stress the ethical significance of the young age at which most smokers take up cigarettes. A 1987 survey of high school sophomores revealed that more than 60 percent of fifteen- and sixteen-year-olds were already smoking and that more than 10 percent of them had started when they were eight or nine. About 50 percent of smokers begin by age thirteen, and 90 percent by age twenty-one. Critics claim that young teenagers do not fully appreciate the risks of smoking. Another survey showed that 35 percent of high school seniors did not think that smoking a pack of cigarettes a day produced any serious harm. If teenagers are not actually considering the risks of smoking in their decisions about whether or not to smoke, can they be said to be making free and informed decisions? Are the tobacco companies taking advantage of their youth and inexperience?

Finally, taking a purely utilitarian point of view, opponents argue that the harm that smoking does to society outweighs the benefits. Smokers may get pleasure and companies may get profits, but critics argue that the rest of the society pays the costs. One government study estimates that each pack of cigarettes sold generates more than $2.00 in costs related to health care, lost productivity, and the like. When one realizes that there are approximately 70 million smokers in the United States, the enormous impact of these costs on the economy becomes apparent. But because these expenses are not paid for by the smokers themselves but by higher insurance premiums and consumer prices passed on to everyone else, a question can be raised about whether this is an ethically acceptable practice.

Discussion Questions

1. What, if any, are the tobacco companies' responsibilities? Should all cigarette ads be banned?

2. Does the fact that nicotine is addictive blunt the free choice argument? Does the fact that tobacco's addictive quality is not publicized mean that smokers are not fully informed about the nature of the product? Is life-style cigarette advertising false and misleading?

3. Can young teenagers make decisions that are fully free and informed? And even if their decisions can be questioned, whose responsibility is it to address this? The tobacco companies? Parents? Society?

4. Is there anything unethical about marketing a product that can produce such harm, even if the choice to use it is totally voluntary? Are tobacco companies involved in anything unethical?

5. Does the fact that a product that is alleged to do such harm is so widely available say positive or negative things about the morality of business and capitalism?

Sources

Green, Mark, "Warning: RJR May Endanger Kids' Health," *New York Times*, March 13, 1990, A29.

Miller, Angela B., and Richard Miller, "Problems of Nicotine Addiction," *San Francisco Chronicle*, December 6, 1989, 9.

Molotsky, Irvin, "Surgeon General Rebukes Tobacco Industry Over Combative Ads," *New York Times*, January 12, 1990, D1.

Ramirez, Anthony, "Tobacco Campaign Set to Warn Off Teen-Agers," *New York Times*, December 11, 1990, D1, D11.

Wald, Matthew L., "Using Liability Law to Put Tobacco on Trial," *New York Times*, February 14, 1988, F11.

◆ ◆ ◆

The Catholic Challenge

The question of the moral legitimacy of capitalism has been taken up not only by secular writers such as those in this chapter, but also by religious thinkers. In particular, the Catholic church has issued two noteworthy challenges to the economy over the last decade. In 1986 American Catholic bishops published *Economic Justice for All*, a pastoral letter that examines the U.S. economy from an ethical perspective. The bishops found it lacking on a variety of fronts, especially the growing levels of poverty and unemployment in such a wealthy economy. The bishops observed that from 1968 to 1978, nearly a quarter of the U.S. population lived in poverty part of the time and received welfare benefits in at least one year. Objecting to the tradition of using strictly financial measures to evaluate the economy, the bishops wrote, "The fundamental moral criterion for all economic decisions, policies, and institutions is this: They must be at the service of *all people, especially the poor*."

In 1991 the Catholic church again spoke to issues regarding the morality of capitalism through an encyclical entitled "Centesimus Annus" ("The Hundredth Year") issued by Pope John Paul II. The Pope generally praises capitalism. However, he also calls into question the ethical character of two features of the economy that most businesspeople probably take as givens — *profit* and the *market*. The Pope defends "the legitimate role of profit as an indication that a business is functioning well," but he states that it is not the only standard for measuring a business. "It is possible," he writes,

> for the financial accounts to be in order, and yet for the people — who make up the firm's most valuable asset — to be humiliated and their dignity offended. . . . In fact, the purpose of a business firm is not simply to make a profit, but is to be found in its very existence as a community of persons who in various ways are endeavoring to satisfy their basic needs, and who form a particular group at the service of the whole of society. Profit is a regulator of the life of a business, but it is not the only one; other human and moral factors must also be considered which, in the long run, are at least equally important for the life of a business.

Similarly, the free market is praised as "the most efficient instrument for utilizing resources and effectively responding to needs." Yet, the Pope immediately adds,

> this is true only for those needs which are "solvent," insofar as they are endowed with purchasing power, and for those resources which are "marketable," insofar as they are capable of obtaining a satisfactory price. But there are many human needs which find no place on the market. It is a strict duty of justice and truth not to allow fundamental human needs to remain unsatisfied, and not to allow those burdened by such needs to perish. . . . There are collective and qualitative needs which cannot be satisfied by market mechanisms. There are important human needs which escape its logic. There are goods which by their very nature cannot and must not be bought or sold.

76

Neither Pope John Paul II nor the American bishops denounce capitalism in general or the American economy in particular from a moral point of view. Yet their remarks are trenchant criticisms of fundamental features of contemporary free market economies.

Discussion Questions

1. What is your reaction to the challenge posed by the Pope and the American bishops?
2. Do unemployment and poverty signal a flaw in the economy or do they result from weaknesses in individual people?
3. Is it even possible to do business rationally without relying exclusively on strictly financial measures and traditional market values?
4. Do you agree that there are needs that cannot be met by market mechanisms? Is so, what are they?
5. Do you agree with the Pope's claim that there are goods that should not be bought or sold? What kind of goods is he referring to?
6. Does the market ever allow for buying and selling in a way that strikes you as clearly unethical?

Sources

Briggs, Kenneth A., "Catholic Bishops Ask Vast Changes in Economy of U.S.," *New York Times*, November 12, 1984, A1, B11.

"The Church and Capitalism," *Business Week*, November 12, 1984, 104–112.

"Excerpts from Draft of Bishops' Letter on the U.S. Economy," *New York Times*, November 12, 1984, B10.

Excerpts from Final Draft of Bishops' Letter on the Economy," *New York Times*, November 14, 1986, A14.

"Excerpts from the Pope's Encyclical: On Giving Capitalism a Human Face," *New York Times*, May 3, 1991, A10.

National Conference of Catholic Bishops, *Economic Justice for All: Pastoral Letter on Catholic Social Teaching and the U.S. Economy* (Washington, DC: United States Catholic Conference, 1986).

Sciolino, Elaine, "Applying Roman Catholic Tradition to U.S. Economy," *New York Times*, November 13, 1984, A23.

Steinfels, Peter, "Papal Encyclical Urges Capitalism to Shed Injustices," *New York Times*, May 3, 1991, A1, A10.

Suro, Roberto, "John Paul's Economics of Compassion," *New York Times*, September 7, 1986, F1, F8.

◆ ◆ ◆

ADDITIONAL READINGS

Camenisch, Paul F., "Profit: Some Moral Reflections," *Journal of Business Ethics*, 6 (1987), 225 – 231.

Flew, Anthony, "The Profit Motive," *Ethics*, 86 (July 1976), 312 – 322.

Friedman, Milton, *Capitalism and Freedom* (Chicago: University of Chicago Press, 1962).

Harrington, Michael, "Corporate Collectivism: A System of Social Injustice," in *Ethics, Free Enterprise & Public Policy*, edited by Richard T. De George and Joseph A. Pichler (New York: Oxford University Press, 1978), 43 – 56.

Haworth, Alan, "Capitalism, Freedom and Rhetoric: A Reply to Tibor R. Machan," *Journal of Applied Philosophy*, 6, no. 1 (1989), 97 – 107.

Machan, Tibor R., "The Virtue of Freedom in Capitalism," *Journal of Applied Philosophy*, 3, no. 1 (1986), 49 – 58.

Pichler, Joseph A., "Capitalism in America: Moral Issues and Public Policy," in *Ethics, Free Enterprise & Public Policy*, edited by Richard T. De George and Joseph A. Pichler (New York: Oxford University Press, 1978), 19 – 39.

CHAPTER 3

◆ ◆ ◆

Distributive Justice

The issue of *distributive justice* — the fairness of the distribution of economic benefits throughout a society — is a major element in assessing the ethical character of any economy. However, it is especially important in evaluating a capitalist economy in which wealth is normally distributed unequally. Is such inequality morally defensible?

This chapter begins with a discussion of some different ideas about how distributive justice might be achieved. Joel Feinberg describes and evaluates five different principles that have been suggested: equality, need, merit, contribution, and effort. Then we consider the two most influential positions on distributive justice advanced by contemporary philosophers, as well as two responses to their arguments. John Rawls argues from the standpoint of social contract theory and suggests two principles of justice that people might reasonably agree to in an imaginary "original contract." Robert Nozick, however, rejects Rawls's approach in favor of a libertarian reading of justice based on rights of ownership and transfer. J. J. C. Smart and Milton Fisk respond to Rawls and Nozick, albeit differently. Smart is a utilitarian thinker who does not accept Rawls's ideas about liberty and equality, on the one hand, and Nozick's emphasis on rights, on the other. Fisk is a Marxist who, in the course of rejecting the main defenses of the economic inequality in the United States, objects to Nozick's ideas of entitlement and challenges the practicality and validity of Rawls's principles.

Joel Feinberg

DISTRIBUTIVE JUSTICE

The term "distributive justice" traditionally applied to burdens and benefits directly distributed by political authorities, such as appointed offices, welfare doles, taxes, and military conscription, but it has now come to apply also to goods and evils of a nonpolitical kind that can be distributed by private citizens to other private citizens. In fact, in most recent literature, the term is reserved for *economic* distributions, particularly the justice of differences in economic income between classes, and of various schemes of taxation which discriminate in different ways between classes. Further, the phrase can refer not only to acts of distributing but also to de factor states of affairs, such as *the fact that* at present "the five percent at the top get 20 percent [of our national wealth] while the 20 percent at the bottom get about five percent.[1] There is, of course, an ambiguity in the meaning of "distribution." The word may refer to the *process* of distributing, or the *product* of some process of distributing, and either or both of these can be appraised as just or unjust. In addition, a "distribution" can be understood to be a "product" which is *not* the result of any deliberate distributing process, but simply a state of affairs whose production has been too complicated to summarize or to ascribe to any definite group of persons as their deliberate doing. The present "distribution" of American wealth is just such a state of affairs.

Are the 5 percent of Americans "at the top" really different from the 20 percent "at the bottom" in any respect that would justicize the difference between their incomes? It is doubtful that there is any characteristic — relevant or irrelevant — common and peculiar to all members of either group. *Some* injustices, therefore, must surely exist. Perhaps there are some traits, however, that are more of less characteristic of the members of the privileged group, that make the current arrangements at least approximately just. What could (or should) those traits be? The answer will state a standard of relevance and a principle of material justice for questions of economic distributions, at least in relatively affluent societies like that of the United States.

At this point there appears to be no appeal possible except to *basic attitudes*, but even at this level we should avoid premature pessimism about the possibility of rational agreement. Some answers to our question have been generally discredited, and if we can see why those answers are inadequate, we might discover some important clues to the properties any adequate answer must possess. Even philosophical adversaries with strongly opposed initial attitudes may hope to come to eventual agreement if they share *some* relevant beliefs and standards and a common commitment to consistency. Let us consider why we all agree (that is, the author's assumption) in rejecting the view that differences in race, sex, IQ, or social "rank" are the grounds of just differences in wealth or income. Part of the answer seems obvious. People cannot by their own voluntary choices determine what skin color, sex, or IQ they shall have, or which

From Joel Feinberg, "Economic Income" in *Social Philosophy* (Englewood Cliffs, NJ: Prentice Hall, 1973), 107–117. Joel Feinberg, *Social Philosophy*, © 1973, pp. 107–117. Reprinted by permission of Prentice Hall, Englewood Cliffs, New Jersey.

[1] "T.R.B. from Washington" in *The New Republic*, Vol. CLX, No. 12 (March 22, 1969), p. 4.

hereditary caste they shall enter. To make such properties the basis of discrimination between individuals in the distribution of social benefits would be "to treat people differently in ways that profoundly affect their lives because of differences for which they have no responsibility."[2] Differences in a given respect are *relevant* for the aims of distributive justice, then, only if they are differences for which their possessors can be held responsible; properties can be the grounds of just discrimination between persons only if those persons had a *fair opportunity* to acquire or avoid them. Having rejected a number of material principles that clearly fail to satisfy the "fair opportunity" requirement, we are still left with as many as five candidates for our acceptance. (It is in theory open to us to accept two or more of these five as valid principles, there being no a priori necessity that the list be reduced to one.) These are: (1) the principle of perfect equality; (2) the principle[s] of need; (3) the principles of merit and achievement; (4) the principle of contribution (or due return); (5) the principle of effort (or labor). I shall discuss each of these briefly.

(i) EQUALITY

The principle of perfect equality obviously has a place in any adequate social ethic. Every human being is equally a human being, and . . . that minimal qualification entitles all human beings equally to certain absolute human rights: positive rights to noneconomic "goods" that by their very natures cannot be in short supply, negative rights not to be treated in cruel or inhuman ways, and negative rights not to be exploited or degraded even in "humane" ways. It is quite another thing, however, to make the minimal qualification of humanity the ground for an absolutely equal distribution of a country's *material wealth* among its citizens. A strict equalitarian could argue that he is merely applying Aristotle's formula of proportionate equality (presumably accepted by all parties to the dispute) with a criterion of relevance borrowed from the human rights theorists. Thus, distributive justice is accomplished between A and B when the following ratio is satisfied:

$$\frac{A\text{'s share of P}}{B\text{'s share of } P} = \frac{A\text{'s possession of } Q}{B\text{'s possession of } Q}$$

Where P stands for economic goods, Q must stand simply for "humanity" or "a human nature," and since every human being possesses *that* Q equally, it follows that all should also share a society's economic wealth (the P in question) equally.

The trouble with this argument is that its major premise is no less disputable than its conclusion. The standard of relevance it borrows from other contexts where it seems very little short of self-evident, seems controversial, at best, when applied to purely economic contexts. It seems evident to most of us that merely being human entitles *everyone* — bad men as well as good, lazy as well as industrious, inept as well as skilled — to a fair trial if charged with a crime, to equal protection of the law, to equal consideration of his interests by makers of national policy, to be spared torture or other cruel and inhuman treatment, and to be permanently ineligible for the status of chattel slave. Adding a right to an

[2] W. K. Frankena, "Some Beliefs About Justice," *The Lindley Lecture*, Department of Philosophy Pamphlet (Lawrence: University of Kansas, 1966), p. 10.

equal share of the economic pie, however, is to add a benefit of a wholly different order, one whose presence on the list of goods for which mere humanity is the sole qualifying condition is not likely to win wide assent without further argument.

It is far more plausible to posit a human right to the satisfaction of (better: to an opportunity to satisfy) one's *basic* economic needs, that is, to enough food and medicine to remain healthy, to minimal clothing, housing, and so on. As Hume pointed out,[3] even these rights cannot exist under conditions of extreme scarcity. Where there is not enough to go around, it cannot be true that everyone has a right to an equal share.[4] But wherever there is moderate abundance or better — wherever a society produces more than enough to satisfy the *basic needs of everyone* — there it seems more plausible to say that mere possession of basic human needs qualifies a person for the opportunity to satisfy them. It would be a rare and calloused sense of justice that would not be offended by an affluent society, with a large annual agricultural surplus and a great abundance of manufactured goods, which permitted some of its citizens to die of starvation, exposure, or easily curable disease. It would certainly be *unfair* for a nation to produce more than it needs and not permit some of its citizens enough to satisfy their basic biological requirements. Strict equalitarianism, then, is a perfectly plausible material principle of distributive justice when confined to affluent societies and basic biological needs, but it loses plausibility when applied to division of the "surplus" left over after basic needs are met. To be sure, the greater the degree of affluence, the higher the level at which we might draw the line between "basic needs" and merely "wanted" benefits, and insofar as social institutions create "artificial needs," it is only fair that society provide all with the opportunity to satisfy them.[5] But once the line has been drawn between what is needed to live a minimally decent life by the realistic standards of a given time and place and what is only added "gravy," it is far from evident that justice still insists upon absolutely equal shares of the total. And it is evident that justice does *not* require strict equality wherever there is reason to think that unequal distribution causally determines greater production and is therefore in the interests of everyone, even those who receive the relatively smaller shares.

Still, there is no way to *refute* the strict equalitarian who requires exactly equal shares for everyone whenever that can be arranged without discouraging total productivity to the point where everyone loses. No one would insist upon equal distributions that would diminish the size of the total pie and thus leave smaller slices for *everyone*; that would be opposed to reason. John Rawls makes this condition part of his "rational principle" of justice: "Inequalities are arbitrary unless it is reasonable to expect that they will work out to everyone's advantage. . . ."[6] We are left then with a version of strict equalitarianism that is by no means evidently true and yet is impossible to refute. That is the theory that purports to apply not only to basic needs but to the total wealth of a society, and allows departures from strict equality when, *but only when*, they will work

[3] David Hume, *Enquiry Concerning the Principles of Morals* Part III (LaSalle, Ill.: The Open Court Publishing Company, 1947). Originally published in 1777.

[4] Except in the "manifesto sense" of "right" discussed on p. 67.

[5] This point is well made by Katzner, "An Analysis of the Concept of Justice," pp. 173–203.

[6] John Rawls, "Justice as Fairness," *The Philosophical Review*, LXVII (1958), 165.

out to everyone's advantage. Although I am not persuaded by this theory, I think that any adequate material principle will have to attach great importance to keeping differences in wealth within reasonable limits, even after all basic needs have been met. One way of doing this would be to raise the standards for a "basic need" as total wealth goes up, so that differences between the richest and poorest citizens (even when there is no real "poverty") are kept within moderate limits.

(ii) NEED

The principle of need is subject to various interpretations, but in most of its forms it is not an independent principle at all, but only a way of mediating the application of the principle of equality. It can, therefore, be grouped with the principle of perfect equality as a member of the equalitarian family and contrasted with the principles of merit, achievement, contribution, and effort, which are all members of the nonequalitarian family. Consider some differences in "needs" as they bear on distributions. Doe is a bachelor with no dependents; Roe has a wife and six children. Roe must satisfy the needs of eight persons out of his paycheck, whereas Doe need satisfy the needs of only one. To give Roe and Doe equal pay would be to treat Doe's interests substantially *more* generously than those of anyone in the Roe family. Similarly, if a small private group is distributing food to its members (say a shipwrecked crew waiting rescue on a desert island), it would not be fair to give precisely the same quantity to a one hundred pounder as to a two hundred pounder, for that might be giving one person all he needs and the other only a fraction of what he needs — a difference in treatment not supported by any relevant difference between them. In short, to distribute goods in proportion to basic needs is not really to depart from a standard of equality, but rather to bring those with some greater initial burden or deficit up to the same level as their fellows.

The concept of a "need" is extremely elastic. In a general sense, to say that S needs X is to say simply that if he doesn't have X he will be harmed. A "basic need" would then be for an X in whose absence a person would be harmed in some crucial and fundamental way, such as suffering injury, malnutrition, illness, madness, or premature death. Thus we all have a basic need for foodstuffs of a certain quantity and variety, fuel to heat our dwellings, a roof over our heads, clothing to keep us warm, and so on. In a different but related sense of need, to say that S needs X is to say that without X he cannot achieve some specific purpose or perform some specific function. If they are to do their work, carpenters need tools, merchants need capital and customers, authors need paper and publishers. Some helpful goods are not strictly needed in this sense: an author with pencil and paper does not really need a typewriter to write a book, but he may need it to write a book speedily, efficiently, and conveniently. We sometimes come to rely upon "merely helpful but unneeded goods" to such a degree that we develop a strong habitual dependence on them, in which case (as it is often said) we have a "psychological" as opposed to a material need for them. If we don't possess that for which we have a strong psychological need, we may be unable to be happy, in which case a merely psychological need for a functional instrument may become a genuine need in the first sense distinguished above, namely, something whose absence is harmful to us. (Cutting across the distinction between material and psychological needs is that between "natural" and "artificial" needs, the former being those that can be expected to develop in any normal person, the latter being those that are manufactured or contrived, and somehow implanted in, or imposed upon, a person.) The more abundant a society's material goods, the higher the level at which we are required (by the force of psychological needs) to fix the distinction between "necessities" and "luxuries"; what *everyone* in a given society regards as "necessary" tends to become an actual, basic need.

(iii) MERIT AND ACHIEVEMENT

The remaining three candidates for material principles of distributive justice belong to the nonequalitarian family. These three principles would each distribute goods in accordance, not with need, but with *desert*; since persons obviously differ in their deserts, economic goods would be distributed unequally. The three principles differ from one another in their conceptions of the relevant *bases of desert* for economic distributions. The first is the principle of *merit*. Unlike the other principles in the nonequalitarian family, this one focuses not on what a person has *done* to deserve his allotment, but rather on what kind of person he is—what characteristics he has.

Two different types of characteristic might be considered meritorious in the appropriate sense: skills and virtues. Native skills and inherited aptitudes will not be appropriate desert bases, since they are forms of merit ruled out by the fair opportunity requirement. No one deserves credit or blame for his genetic inheritance, since no one has the opportunity to select his own genes. Acquired skills may seem more plausible candidates at first, but upon scrutiny they are little better. First, all acquired skills depend to a large degree on native skills. Nobody is born knowing how to read, so reading is an acquired skill, but actual differences in reading skill are to a large degree accounted for by genetic differences that are beyond anyone's control. Some of the differences are no doubt caused by differences in motivation afforded different children, but again the early conditions contributing to a child's motivation are also largely beyond his control. We may still have some differences in acquired skills that are to be accounted for solely or primarily by differences in the degree of practice, drill, and perseverance expended by persons with roughly equal opportunities. In respect to these, we can propitiate the requirement of fair opportunity, but only by nullifying the significance of acquired skill as such, for now skill is a relevant basis of desert only to the extent that it is a product of one's own effort. Hence, *effort* becomes the true basis of desert (as claimed by our fifth principle, discussed below), and not simply skill as such.

Those who would propose rewarding personal *virtues* with a larger than average share of the economic pie, and punishing defects of character with a smaller than average share, advocate assigning to the economic system a task normally done (if it is done at all) by noneconomic institutions. What they propose, in effect, is that we use retributive criteria of distributive justice. Our criminal law, for a variety of good reasons, does not purport to punish people for what they are, but only for what they do. A man can be as arrogant, rude, selfish, cruel, insensitive, irresponsible, cowardly, lazy, or disloyal as he wishes; unless he *does* something prohibited by the criminal law, he will not be made to suffer legal punishment. At least one of the legal system's reasons for refusing to penalize character flaws as such would also explain why such defects should not be listed as relevant differences in a material principle of distributive justice. The apparatus for detecting such flaws (a "moral police"?) would be enormously cumbersome and impractical, and its methods so uncertain and fallible that none of us could feel safe in entrusting the determination of our material allotments to it. We could, of course, give roughly equal shares to all except those few who have *outstanding* virtues — gentleness, kindness, courage, diligence, reliability, warmth, charm, considerateness, generosity. Perhaps these are traits that deserve to be rewarded, but it is doubtful that larger economic allotments are the appropriate vehicles of rewarding. As Benn and Peters remind us, "there are some sorts of 'worth' for which rewards in terms of income seem inappropriate. Great courage in battle is recognized by medals, not by increased pay."[7] Indeed, there is something repugnant, as Socrates and the Stoics insisted, in paying a man to be virtuous. Moreover, the rewards would offer a pecuniary motive for certain forms of excellence that require motives of a different kind, and would thus tend to be self-defeating.

The most plausible nonequalitarian theories are those that locate relevance not in meritorious traits and excellences of any kind, but rather in prior doings: not in what one is, but in what one has done. Actions, too, are sometimes called "meritorious," so there is no impropriety in denominating the remaining families of principles in our survey as "meritarian." One type of action-oriented meritarian might cite *achievement* as a relevant desert basis for pecuniary rewards, so that departures from equality in income are to be justicized only by distinguished achievements in science, art, philosophy, music, athletics, and other basic areas of human activity. The attractions and disadvantages of this theory are similar to those of theories which I rejected above that base rewards on skills and virtues. Not all persons have a fair opportunity to achieve great things, and economic rewards seem inappropriate as vehicles for expressing recognition and admiration of noneconomic achievements.

(iv) CONTRIBUTION OR "DUE RETURN"

When the achievements under consideration are themselves contributions to our general economic well-being, the meritarian principle of distributive justice is much more plausible. Often it is conjoined with an economic theory that purports to determine exactly what percentage of our total economic product a given worker or class has produced. Justice, according to this principle, requires that each worker get back exactly that proportion of the national wealth that he has himself created. This sounds very much like a principle of "commutative justice" directing us to *give back* to every worker what is really his own property, that is, the product of his own labor.

The French socialist writer and precursor of Karl Marx, Pierre Joseph Proudhon (1809–1865), is perhaps the classic example of this kind of theorist. In his book, *What is Property?* (1840), Proudhon rejects the standard socialist

---

[7]S. I. Bean and R. S. Peters, *Social Principles and the Democratic State* (London: George Allen and Unwin Ltd., 1959), p. 139.

slogan. "From each according to his ability, to each according to his needs."[8] in favor of a principle of distributive justice based on contribution, as interpreted by an economic theory that employed a pre-Marxist "theory of surplus value." The famous socialist slogan was not intended, in any case, to express a principle of distributive justice. It was understood to be a rejection of all considerations of "mere" justice for an ethic of human brotherhood. The early socialists thought it unfair, in a way, to give the great contributors to our wealth a disproportionately small share of the product. But in the new socialist society, love of neighbor, community spirit, and absence of avarice would overwhelm such bourgeois notions and put them in their proper (subordinate) place.

Proudhon, on the other hand, based his whole social philosophy not on brotherhood (an ideal he found suitable only for small groups such as families) but on the kind of distributive justice to which even some capitalists gave lip service:

> The key concept was "mutuality" or "reciprocity." "Mutuality, reciprocity exists," he wrote, "when all the workers in an industry, instead of working for an entrepreneur who pays them and keeps their products, work for one another and thus collaborate in the making of a common product whose profits they share among themselves."[9]

Proudhon's celebrated dictum that "property is theft" did not imply that all *possession* of goods is illicit, but rather that the system of rules that permitted the owner of a factory to hire workers and draw profits ("surplus value") from *their* labor robs the workers of what is rightly theirs. "This profit, consisting of a portion of the proceeds of labor that rightfully belonged to the laborer himself, was 'theft.'"[10] The injustice of capitalism, according to Proudhon, consists in the fact that those who create the wealth (through their labor) get only a small part of what they create, whereas those who "exploit" their labor, like voracious parasites, gather in a greatly disproportionate share. The "return of contribution" principle of distributive justice, then, cannot work in a capitalist system, but requires a *fédération mutualiste* of autonomous producer-cooperatives in which those who create wealth by their work share it in proportion to their real contributions.

Other theorists, employing different notions of what produces or "creates" economic wealth, have used the "return of contribution" principle to support quite opposite conclusions. The contribution principle has even been used to justicize quite unequalitarian capitalistic status quos, for it is said that capital as well as labor creates wealth, as do ingenious ideas, inventions, and adventurous risk-taking. The capitalist who provided the money, the inventor who designed a product to be manufactured, the innovator who thought of a new mode of production and marketing, the advertiser who persuaded millions of customers to buy the finished product, the investor who risked his savings on the success of the enterprise — these are the ones, it is said, who did the most to produce the

---

[8]Traced to Louis Blanc. For a clear brief exposition of Proudhon's view which contrasts it with that of other early socialists and also that of Karl Marx, see Robert Tucker's "Marx and Distributive Justice," in *Nomos VI: Justice*, ed. C. J. Friedrich and J. W. Chapman (New York: Aldine-Atherton Press, 1963), pp. 306–325.

[9]Tucker, "Marx and Distributive Justice," p. 310.

[10]Tucker, "Marx and Distributive Justice," p. 311.

wealth created by a business, not the workers who contributed only their labor, and of course, these are the ones who tend, on the whole, to receive the largest personal incomes.

Without begging any narrow and technical questions of economics, I should express my general skepticism concerning such facile generalizations about the comparative degrees to which various individuals have contributed to our social wealth. Not only are there impossibly difficult problems of measurement involved, there are also conceptual problems that appear beyond all nonarbitrary solution. I refer to the elements of luck and chance, the social factors not attributable to any assignable individuals, and the contributions of population trends, uncreated natural resources, and the efforts of people now dead, which are often central to the explanation of any given increment of social wealth.

The difficulties of separating out causal factors in the production of social wealth might influence the partisan of the "return of contribution" principle in either or both of two ways. He might become very cautious in his application of the principle, requiring that deviations from average shares be restricted to very clear and demonstrable instances of unusually great or small contributions. But the moral that L. T. Hobhouse[11] drew from these difficulties is that *any* individual contribution will be very small relative to the immeasurably great contribution made by political, social, fortuitous, natural, and "inherited" factors. In particular, strict application of the "return of contribution" principle would tend to support a larger claim for the *community* to its own "due return," through taxation and other devices.

In a way, the principle of contribution is not a principle of mere *desert* at all, no matter how applied. As mentioned above, it resembles a principle of commutative justice requiring repayment of debts, return of borrowed items, or compensation for wrongly inflicted damages. If I lend you my car on the understanding that you will take good care of it and soon return it, or if you steal it, or damage it, it will be too *weak* to say that I "deserve" to have my own car, intact, back from you. After all, the car is *mine* or my due, and questions of ownership are not settled by examination of deserts; neither are considerations of ownership and obligation commonly outbalanced by considerations of desert. It is not merely "unfitting" or "inappropriate" that I should not have my own or my due; it is downright *theft* to withhold it from me. So the return of contribution is not merely a matter of merit deserving reward. It is a matter of a maker demanding that which he has created and is thus properly his. The ratio — A's share of X is to B's share of X as A's contribution to X is to B's contribution to X — appears, therefore, to be a very strong and plausible principle of distributive justice, whose main deficiencies, when applied to economic distributions, are of a practical (though severe) kind. If Hobhouse is right in claiming that there are social factors in even the most pronounced individual contributions to social wealth, then the principle of due return serves as a moral basis in support of taxation and other public claims to private goods. In any case, if A's contribution, though apparently much greater than B's, is nevertheless only the tiniest percentage of the total contribution to X (whatever that may mean and however it is to be determined), it may seem like the meanest quibbling to distinguish very seriously between A and B at all.

[11] L. T. Hobhouse, *The Elements of Social Justice* (London: George Allen and Unwin Ltd., 1922). See especially pp. 161–163.

(v) EFFORT

The principle of due return, as a material principle of distributive justice, does have some vulnerability to the fair opportunity requirement. Given unavoidable variations in genetic endowments and material circumstances, different persons cannot have precisely the same opportunities to make contributions to the public weal. Our final candidate for the status of a material principle of distributive justice, the *principle of effort*, does much better in this respect, for it would distribute economic products not in proportion to successful achievement but according to the degree of effort exerted. According to the principle of effort, justice decrees that hard-working executives and hard-working laborers receive precisely the same remuneration (although there may be reasons having nothing to do with justice for paying more to the executives), and that freeloaders be penalized by allotments of proportionately lesser shares of the joint products of everyone's labor. The most persuasive argument for this principle is that it is the closest approximation to the intuitively valid principle of due return that can pass the fair opportunity requirement. It is doubtful, however, that even the principle of effort fully satisfies the requirement of fair opportunity, since those who inherit or acquire certain kinds of handicap may have little opportunity to *acquire the motivation* even to do their best. In any event, the principle of effort does seem to have intuitive cogency giving it at least some weight as a factor determining the justice of distributions.

In very tentative conclusion, it seems that the principle of equality (in the version that rests on needs rather than that which requires "perfect equality") and the principles of contribution and effort (where nonarbitrarily applicable, and only *after* everyone's basic needs have been satisfied) have the most weight as determinants of economic justice, whereas all forms of the principle of merit are implausible in that role. The reason for the priority of basic needs is that, where there is economic abundance, the claim to life itself and to minimally decent conditions are, like other human rights, claims that all men make with perfect equality. As economic production increases, these claims are given ever greater consideration in the form of rising standards for distinguishing basic needs from other wanted goods. But no matter where that line is drawn, when we go beyond it into the realm of economic surplus or "luxuries," nonequalitarian considerations (especially contribution and effort) come increasingly into play.

John Rawls
A THEORY OF JUSTICE

1. THE ROLE OF JUSTICE

Justice is the first virtue of social institutions, as truth is of systems of thought. A theory however elegant and economical must be rejected or revised if it is untrue; likewise laws and institutions no matter how efficient and well-arranged must be reformed or abolished if they are unjust. Each person possesses an inviolability founded on justice that even the welfare of society as a whole cannot override. For this reason justice denies that the loss of freedom for some is made right by a greater good shared by others. It does not allow that the sacrifices imposed on a few are outweighed by the larger sum of advantages enjoyed by many. Therefore in a just society the liberties of equal citizenship are taken as settled; the rights secured by justice are not subject to political bargaining or to the calculus of social interests. The only thing that permits us to acquiesce in an erroneous theory is the lack of a better one; analogously, an injustice is tolerable only when it is necessary to avoid an even greater injustice. Being first virtues of human activities, truth and justice are uncompromising.

These propositions seem to express our intuitive conviction of the primacy of justice. No doubt they are expressed too strongly. In any event I wish to inquire whether these contentions or others similar to them are sound, and if so how they can be accounted for. To this end it is necessary to work out a theory of justice in the light of which these assertions can be interpreted and assessed. I shall begin by considering the role of the principles of justice. Let us assume, to fix ideas, that a society is a more or less self-sufficient association of persons who in their relations to one another recognize certain rules of conduct as binding and who for the most part act in accordance with them. Suppose further that these rules specify a system of cooperation designed to advance the good of those taking part in it. Then, although a society is a cooperative venture for mutual advantage, it is typically marked by a conflict as well as by an identity of interests. There is an identity of interests since social cooperation makes possible a better life for all than any would have if each were to live solely by his own efforts. There is a conflict of interests since persons are not indifferent as to how the greater benefits produced by their collaboration are distributed, for in order to pursue their ends they each prefer a larger to a lesser share. A set of principles is required for choosing among the various social arrangements which determine this division of advantage and for underwriting an agreement on the proper distributive shares. These principles are the principles of social justice: they provide a way of assigning rights and duties in the basic institutions of society and they define the appropriate distribution of the benefits and burdens of social cooperation. . . .

From John Rawls, *A Theory of Justice* (Cambridge, MA: Harvard University Press, 1971), 3–4, 7, 11–13, 14–15, 17–20, 60–63, 63–65, 100–104. For permission to photocopy this selection please contact Harvard University Press. Reprinted by permission of the publishers from *A Theory of Justice* by John Rawls, Cambridge, Mass.: The Belknap Press of Harvard University Press, Copyright © 1971 by the President and Fellows of Harvard College.

2. THE SUBJECT OF JUSTICE

Many different kinds of things are said to be just and unjust: not only laws, institutions, and social systems, but also particular actions of many kinds, including decisions, judgments, and imputations. We also call the attitudes and dispositions of persons, and persons themselves, just and unjust. Our topic, however, is that of social justice. For us the primary subject of justice is the basic structure of society, or more exactly, the way in which the major social institutions distribute fundamental rights and duties and determine the division of advantages from social cooperation. By major institutions I understand the political constitution and the principal economic and social arrangements. Thus the legal protection of freedom of thought and liberty of conscience, competitive markets, private property in the means of production, and the monogamous family are examples of major social institutions. Taken together as one scheme, the major institutions define men's rights and duties and influence their life-prospects, what they can expect to be and how well they can hope to do. The basic structure is the primary subject of justice because its effects are so profound and present from the start. The intuitive notion here is that this structure contains various social positions and that men born into different positions have different expectations of life determined, in part, by the political system as well as by economic and social circumstances. In this way the institutions of society favor certain starting places over others. These are especially deep inequalities. Not only are they pervasive, but they affect men's initial chances in life; yet they cannot possibly be justified by an appeal to the notions of merit or desert. It is these inequalities, presumably inevitable in the basic structure of any society, to which the principles of social justice must in the first instance apply. These principles, then, regulate the choice of a political constitution and the main elements of the economic and social system. The justice of a social scheme depends essentially on how fundamental rights and duties are assigned and on the economic opportunities and social conditions in the various sectors of society. . . .

3. THE MAIN IDEA OF THE THEORY OF JUSTICE

My aim is to present a conception of justice which generalizes and carries to a higher level of abstraction the familiar theory of the social contract as found, say, in Locke, Rousseau, and Kant.[1] In order to do this we are not to think of the original contract as one to enter a particular society or to set up a particular form of government. Rather, the guiding idea is that the principles of justice for the basic structure of society are the object of the original agreement. They are the principles that free and rational persons concerned to further their own inter-

---

[1] As the text suggests, I shall regard Locke's *Second Treatise of Government*, Rousseau's *The Social Contract*, and Kant's ethical works beginning with *The Foundations of the Metaphysics of Morals* as definitive of the contract tradition. For all of its greatness, Hobbes's *Leviathan* raises special problems. A general historical survey is provided by J. W. Gough, *The Social Contract*, 2nd ed. (Oxford, The Clarendon Press, 1957), and Otto Gierke, *Natural Law and the Theory of Society*, trans. with an introduction by Ernest Barker (Cambridge, The University Press, 1934). A presentation of the contract view as primarily an ethical theory is to be found in G. R. Grice, *The Grounds of Moral Judgment* (Cambridge, The University Press, 1967).

ests would accept in an initial position of equality as defining the fundamental terms of their association. These principles are to regulate all further agreements; they specify the kinds of social cooperation that can be entered into and the forms of government that can be established. This way of regarding the principles of justice I shall call justice as fairness.

Thus we are to imagine that those who engage in social cooperation choose together, in one joint act, the principles which are to assign basic rights and duties and to determine the division of social benefits. Men are to decide in advance how they are to regulate their claims against one another and what is to be the foundation charter of their society. Just as each person must decide by rational reflection what constitutes his good, that is, the system of ends which it is rational for him to pursue, so a group of persons must decide once and for all what is to count among them as just and unjust. The choice which rational men would make in this hypothetical situation of equal liberty, assuming for the present that this choice problem has a solution, determines the principles of justice.

In justice as fairness the original position of equality corresponds to the state of nature in the traditional theory of the social contract. This original position is not, of course, thought of as an actual historical state of affairs, much less as a primitive condition of culture. It is understood as a purely hypothetical situation characterized so as to lead to a certain conception of justice.[2] Among the essential features of this situation is that no one knows his place in society, his class position or social status, nor does any one know his fortune in the distribution of natural assets and abilities, his intelligence, strength, and the like. I shall even assume that the parties do not know their conceptions of the good or their special psychological propensities. The principles of justice are chosen behind a veil of ignorance. This ensures that no one is advantaged or disadvantaged in the choice of principles by the outcome of natural chance or the contingency of social circumstances. Since all are similarly situated and no one is able to design principles to favor his particular condition, the principles of justice are the result of a fair agreement or bargain. For given the circumstances of the original position, the symmetry of everyone's relations to each other, this initial situation is fair between individuals as moral persons, that is, as rational beings with their own ends and capable, I shall assume, of a sense of justice. The original position is, one might say, the appropriate initial status quo, and thus the fundamental agreements reached in it are fair. This explains the propriety of the name "justice as fairness": it conveys the idea that the principles of justice are agreed to in an initial situation that is fair. The name does not mean that the concepts of justice and fairness are the same, any more than the phrase "poetry as metaphor" means that the concepts of poetry and metaphor are the same.

Justice as fairness begins, as I have said, with one of the most general of all choices which persons might make together, namely, with the choice of the first

[2]Kant is clear that the original agreement is hypothetical. See *The Metaphysics of Morals*, pt. I (*Rechtslehre*), especially §§47, 52; and pt. II of the essay "Concerning the Common Saying: This May Be True in Theory but It Does Not Apply in Practice," in *Kant's Political Writings*, ed. Hans Reiss and trans. by H. B. Nisbet (Cambridge, The University Press, 1970), pp. 73–87. See Georges Vlachos, *La Pensée politique de Kant* (Paris, Presses Universitaires de France, 1962), pp. 326–335; and J. G. Murphy, *Kant: The Philosophy of Right* (London, Macmillan, 1970), pp. 109–112, 133–136, for a further discussion.

principles of a conception of justice which is to regulate all subsequent criticism and reform of institutions. Then, having chosen a conception of justice, we can suppose that they are to choose a constitution and a legislature to enact laws, and so on, all in accordance with the principles of justice initially agreed upon. Our social situation is just if it is such that by this sequence of hypothetical agreements we would have contracted into the general system of rules which defines it. . . .

. . . It may be observed, however, that once the principles of justice are thought of as arising from an original agreement in a situation of equality, it is an open question whether the principle of utility would be acknowledged. Offhand it hardly seems likely that persons who view themselves as equals, entitled to press their claims upon one another, would agree to a principle which may require lesser life prospects for some simply for the sake of a greater sum of advantages enjoyed by others. Since each desires to protect his interests, his capacity to advance his conception of the good, no one has a reason to acquiesce in an enduring loss for himself in order to bring about a greater net balance of satisfaction. In the absence of strong and lasting benevolent impulses, a rational man would not accept a basic structure merely because it maximized the algebraic sum of advantages irrespective of its permanent effects on his own basic rights and interests. Thus it seems that the principle of utility is incompatible with the conception of social cooperation among equals for mutual advantage. It appears to be inconsistent with the idea of reciprocity implicit in the notion of a well-ordered society. Or, at any rate, so I shall argue.

I shall maintain instead that the persons in the initial situation would choose two rather different principles: the first requires equality in the assignment of basic rights and duties, while the second holds that social and economic inequalities, for example inequalities of wealth and authority, are just only if they result in compensating benefits for everyone, and in particular for the least advantaged members of society. These principles rule out justifying institutions on the grounds that the hardships of some are offset by a greater good in the aggregate. It may be expedient but it is not just that some should have less in order that others may prosper. But there is no injustice in the greater benefits earned by a few provided that the situation of persons not so fortunate is thereby improved. The intuitive idea is that since everyone's well-being depends upon a scheme of cooperation without which no one could have a satisfactory life, the division of advantages should be such as to draw forth the willing cooperation of everyone taking part in it, including those less well situated. Yet this can be expected only if reasonable terms are proposed. The two principles mentioned seem to be a fair agreement on the basis of which those better endowed, or more fortunate in their social position, neither of which we can be said to deserve, could expect the willing cooperation of others when some workable scheme is a necessary condition of the welfare of all.[3] Once we decide to look for a conception of justice that nullifies the accidents of natural endowment and the contingencies of social circumstance as counters in quest for political and economic advantage, we are led to these principles. They express the result of leaving aside those aspects of the social world that seem arbitrary from a moral point of view. . . .

---

[3]For the formulation of this intuitive idea I am indebted to Allan Gibbard.

4. THE ORIGINAL POSITION AND JUSTIFICATION

I have said that the original position is the appropriate initial status quo which insures that the fundamental agreements reached in it are fair. This fact yields the name "justice as fairness." It is clear, then, that I want to say that one conception of justice is more reasonable than another, or justifiable with respect to it, if rational persons in the initial situation would choose its principles over those of the other for the role of justice. Conceptions of justice are to be ranked by their acceptability to persons so circumstanced. Understood in this way the question of justification is settled by working out a problem of deliberation: we have to ascertain which principles it would be rational to adopt given the contractual situation. This connects the theory of justice with the theory of rational choice.

If this view of the problem of justification is to succeed, we must, of course, describe in some detail the nature of this choice problem. A problem of rational decision has a definite answer only if we know the beliefs and interests of the parties, their relations with respect to one another, the alternatives between which they are to choose, the procedure whereby they make up their minds, and so on. As the circumstances are presented in different ways, correspondingly different principles are accepted. The concept of the original position, as I shall refer to it, is that of the most philosophically favored interpretation of this initial choice situation for the purposes of a theory of justice.

But how are we to decide what is the most favored interpretation? I assume, for one thing, that there is a broad measure of agreement that principles of justice should be chosen under certain conditions. To justify a particular description of the initial situation one shows that it incorporates these commonly shared presumptions. One argues from widely accepted but weak premises to more specific conclusions. Each of the presumptions should by itself be natural and plausible; some of them may seem innocuous or even trivial. The aim of the contract approach is to establish that taken together they impose significant bounds on acceptable principles of justice. The ideal outcome would be that these conditions determine a unique set of principles; but I shall be satisfied if they suffice to rank the main traditional conceptions of social justice.

One should not be misled, then, by the somewhat unusual conditions which characterize the original position. The idea here is simply to make vivid to ourselves the restrictions that it seems reasonable to impose on arguments for principles of justice, and therefore on these principles themselves. Thus it seems reasonable and generally acceptable that no one should be advantaged or disadvantaged by natural fortune or social circumstances in the choice of principles. It also seems widely agreed that it should be impossible to tailor principles to the circumstances of one's own case. We should insure further that particular inclinations and aspirations, and persons' conceptions of their good do not affect the principles adopted. The aim is to rule out those principles that it would be rational to propose for acceptance, however little the chance of success, only if one knew certain things that are irrelevant from the standpoint of justice. For example, if a man knew that he was wealthy, he might find it rational to advance the principle that various taxes for welfare measures be counted unjust; if he knew that he was poor, he would most likely propose the contrary principle. To represent the desired restrictions one imagines a situation in which everyone is deprived of this sort of information. One excludes the knowledge of those contingencies which sets men at odds and allows them to be guided by their prejudices. In this manner the veil of ignorance is arrived at in a natural way. This concept should cause no difficulty if we keep in mind the constraints on arguments that it is meant to express. At any time we can enter the original position, so to speak, simply by following a certain procedure, namely, by arguing for principles of justice in accordance with these restrictions.

It seems reasonable to suppose that the parties in the original position are equal. That is, all have the same rights in the procedure for choosing principles; each can make proposals, submit reasons for their acceptance, and so on. Obviously the purpose of these conditions is to represent equality between human beings as moral persons, as creatures having a conception of their good and capable of a sense of justice. The basis of equality is taken to be similarity in these two respects. Systems of ends are not ranked in value; and each man is presumed to have the requisite ability to understand and to act upon whatever principles are adopted. Together with the veil of ignorance, these conditions define the principles of justice as those which rational persons concerned to advance their interests would consent to as equals when none are known to be advantaged or disadvantaged by social and natural contingencies.

There is, however, another side to justifying a particular description of the original position. This is to see if the principles which would be chosen match our considered convictions of justice or extend them in an acceptable way. We can note whether applying these principles would lead us to make the same judgments about the basic structure of society which we now make intuitively and in which we have the greatest confidence; or whether, in cases where our present judgments are in doubt and given with hesitation, these principles offer a resolution which we can affirm on reflection. There are questions which we feel sure must be answered in a certain way. For example, we are confident that religious intolerance and racial discrimination are unjust. We think that we have examined these things with care and have reached what we believe is an impartial judgment not likely to be distorted by an excessive attention to our own interests. These convictions are provisional fixed points which we presume any conception of justice must fit. But we have much less assurance as to what is the correct distribution of wealth and authority. Here we may be looking for a way to remove our doubts. We can check an interpretation of the initial situation, then, by the capacity of its principles to accommodate our firmest convictions and to provide guidance where guidance is needed. . . .

11. TWO PRINCIPLES OF JUSTICE

I shall now state in a provisional form the two principles of justice that I believe would be chosen in the original position. In this section I wish to make only the most general comments, and therefore the first formulation of these principles is tentative. As we go on I shall run through several formulations and approximate step by step the final statement to be given much later. I believe that doing this allows the exposition to proceed in a natural way.

The first statement of the two principles reads as follows:

First: each person is to have an equal right to the most extensive basic liberty compatible with a similar liberty for others.

Second: social and economic inequalities are to be arranged so that they are both (a) reasonably expected to be to everyone's advantage, and (b) attached to positions and offices open to all.

There are two ambiguous phrases in the second principle, namely "everyone's advantage" and "open to all." . . .

By way of general comment, these principles primarily apply, as I have said, to the basic structure of society. They are to govern the assignment of rights and duties and to regulate the distribution of social and economic advantages. As their formulation suggests, these principles presuppose that the social structure can be divided into two more or less distinct parts, the first principle applying to the one, the second to the other. They distinguish between those aspects of the social system that define and secure the equal liberties of citizenship and those that specify and establish social and economic inequalities. The basic liberties of citizens are, roughly speaking, political liberty (the right to vote and to be eligible for public office) together with freedom of speech and assembly; liberty of conscience and freedom of thought; freedom of the person along with the right to hold (personal) property; and freedom from arbitrary arrest and seizure as defined by the concept of the rule of law. These liberties are all required to be equal by the first principle, since citizens of a just society are to have the same basic rights.

The second principle applies, in the first approximation, to the distribution of income and wealth and to the design of organizations that make use of differences in authority and responsibility, or chains of command. While the distribution of wealth and income need not be equal, it must be to everyone's advantage, and at the same time, positions of authority and offices of command must be accessible to all. One applies the second principle by holding positions open, and then, subject to this constraint, arranges social and economic inequalities so that everyone benefits.

These principles are to be arranged in a serial order with the first principle prior to the second. This ordering means that a departure from the institutions of equal liberty required by the first principle cannot be justified by, or compensated for, by greater social and economic advantages. The distribution of wealth and income, and the hierarchies of authority, must be consistent with both the liberties of equal citizenship and equality of opportunity.

It is clear that these principles are rather specific in their content, and their acceptance rests on certain assumptions that I must eventually try to explain and justify. A theory of justice depends upon a theory of society in ways that will become evident as we proceed. For the present, it should be observed that the two principles (and this holds for all formulations) are a special case of a more general conception of justice that can be expressed as follows.

All social values — liberty and opportunity, income and wealth, and the bases of self-respect — are to be distributed equally unless an unequal distribution of any, or all, of these values is to everyone's advantage.

Injustice, then, is simply inequalities that are not to the benefit of all. Of course, this conception is extremely vague and requires interpretation.

As a first step, suppose that the basic structure of society distributes certain primary goods, that is, things that every rational man is presumed to want. These goods normally have a use whatever a persons' rational plan of life. For simplicity, assume that the chief primary goods at the disposition of society are rights and liberties, powers and opportunities, income and wealth. . . . These are the social primary goods. Other primary goods such as health and vigor, intelligence and imagination, are natural goods; although their possession is influenced by the basic structure, they are not so directly under its control. Imagine, then, a hypothetical initial arrangement in which all the social primary goods are equally distributed: everyone has similar rights and duties, and income and wealth are evenly shared. This state of affairs provides a benchmark for judging improvements. If certain inequalities of wealth and organizational powers would make everyone better off than in this hypothetical starting situation, then they accord with the general conception.

Now it is possible, at least theoretically, that by giving up some of their fundamental liberties men are sufficiently compensated by the resulting social and economic gains. The general conception of justice imposes no restrictions on what sort of inequalities are permissible; it only requires that everyone's position be improved. We need not suppose anything so drastic as consenting to a condition of slavery. Imagine instead that men forego certain political rights when the economic returns are significant and their capacity to influence the course of policy by the exercise of these rights would be marginal in any case. It is this kind of exchange which the two principles as stated rule out; being arranged in serial order they do not permit exchanges between basic liberties and economic and social gains. The serial ordering of principles expresses an underlying preference among primary social goods. When this preference is rational so likewise is the choice of these principles in this order. . . .

The fact that the two principles apply to institutions has certain consequences. Several points illustrate this. First of all, the rights and liberties referred to by these principles are those which are defined by the public rules of the basic structure. Whether men are free is determined by the rights and duties established by the major institutions of society. Liberty is a certain pattern of social forms. The first principle simply requires that certain sorts of rules, those defining basic liberties, apply to everyone equally and that they allow the most extensive liberty compatible with a like liberty for all. The only reason for circumscribing the rights defining liberty and making men's freedom less extensive than it might otherwise be is that these equal rights as institutionally defined would interfere with one another.

Another thing to bear in mind is that when principles mention persons, or require that everyone gain from an inequality, the reference is to representative persons holding the various social positions, or offices, or whatever, established by the basic structure. Thus in applying the second principle I assume that it is possible to assign an expectation of well-being to representative individuals holding these positions. This expectation indicates their life prospects as viewed from their social station. In general, the expectations of representative persons depend upon the distribution of rights and duties throughout the basic structure. When this changes, expectations change. I assume, then, that expectations are connected: by raising the prospects of the representative man in one position we presumably increase or decrease the prospects of representative men in other positions. Since it applies to institutional forms, the second principle (or rather the first part of it) refers to the expectations of representative individuals. As I shall discuss below, neither principle applies to distributions of particular goods to particular individuals who may be identified by their proper names. The situation where someone is considering how to allocate certain commodities to needy persons who are known to him is not within the scope of the principles. They are meant to regulate basic institutional arrangements. We must not assume that there is much similarity from the standpoint of justice between an administrative allotment of goods to specific persons and the appropriate design of society. Our common sense intuitions for the former may be a poor guide to the latter.

Now the second principle insists that each person benefit from permissible inequalities in the basic structure. This means that it must be reasonable for each relevant representative man defined by this structure, when he views it as a going concern, to prefer his prospects with the inequality to his prospects without it. One is not allowed to justify differences in income or organizational powers on the ground that the disadvantages of those in one position are outweighed by the greater advantages of those in another. Much less can infringements of liberty be counterbalanced in this way. Applied to the basic structure, the principle of utility would have us maximize the sum of expectations of representative men (weighted by the number of persons they represent, on the classical view); and this would permit us to compensate for the losses of some by the gains of others. Instead, the two principles require that everyone benefit from economic and social inequalities. . . .

17. THE TENDENCY TO EQUALITY

I wish to conclude this discussion of the two principles by explaining the sense in which they express an egalitarian conception of justice. Also I should like to forestall the objection to the principle of fair opportunity that it leads to a callous meritocratic society. In order to prepare the way for doing this, I note several aspects of the conception of justice that I have set out.

First we may observe that the difference principle gives some weight to the considerations singled out by the principle of redress. This is the principle that undeserved inequalities call for redress; and since inequalities of birth and natural endowment are undeserved, these inequalities are to be somehow compensated for.[4] Thus the principle holds that in order to treat all persons equally, to provide genuine equality of opportunity, society must give more attention to those with fewer native assets and to those born into the less favorable social positions. The idea is to redress the bias of contingencies in the direction of equality. In pursuit of this principle greater resources might be spent on the education of the less rather than the more intelligent, at least over a certain time of life, say the earlier years of school.

Now the principle of redress has not to my knowledge been proposed as the sole criterion of justice, as the single aim of the social order. It is plausible as most such principles are only as a prima facie principle, one that is to be weighed in the balance with others. For example, we are to weigh it against the principle to improve the average standard of life, or to advance the common good.[5] But

---

[4]See Herbert Spiegelberg, "A Defense of Human Equality," *Philosophical Review*, vol. 53 (1944), pp. 101, 113–123; and D. D. Raphael, "Justice and Liberty," *Proceedings of the Aristotelian Society*, vol. 51 (1950–1951), pp. 187f.

[5]See, for example, Spiegelberg, pp. 120f.

whatever other principles we hold, the claims of redress are to be taken into account. It is thought to represent one of the elements in our conception of justice. Now the difference principle is not of course the principle of redress. It does not require society to try to even out handicaps as if all were expected to compete on a fair basis in the same race. But the difference principle would allocate resources in education, say, so as to improve the long-term expectation of the least favored. If this end is attained by giving more attention to the better endowed, it is permissible; otherwise not. And in making this decision, the value of education should not be assessed solely in terms of economic efficiency and social welfare. Equally if not more important is the role of education in enabling a person to enjoy the culture of his society and to take part in its affairs, and in this way to provide for each individual a secure sense of his own worth.

Thus although the difference principle is not the same as that of redress, it does achieve some of the intent of the latter principle. It transforms the aims of the basic structure so that the total scheme of institutions no longer emphasizes social efficiency and technocratic values. We see then that the difference principle represents, in effect, an agreement to regard the distribution of natural talents as a common asset and to share in the benefits of this distribution whatever it turns out to be. Those who have been favored by nature, whoever they are, may gain from their good fortune only on terms that improve the situation of those who have lost out. The naturally advantaged are not to gain merely because they are more gifted, but only to cover the costs of training and education and for using their endowments in ways that help the less fortunate as well. No one deserves his greater natural capacity nor merits a more favorable starting place in society. But it does not follow that one should eliminate these distinctions. There is another way to deal with them. The basic structure can be arranged so that these contingencies work for the good of the least fortunate. Thus we are led to the difference principle if we wish to set up the social system so that no one gains or loses from his arbitrary place in the distribution of natural assets or his initial position in society without giving or receiving compensating advantages in return.

In view of these remarks we may reject the contention that the ordering of institutions is always defective because the distribution of natural talents and the contingencies of social circumstance are unjust, and this injustice must inevitably carry over to human arrangements. Occasionally this reflection is offered as an excuse for ignoring injustice, as if the refusal to acquiesce in injustice is on a par with being unable to accept death. The natural distribution is neither just nor unjust; nor is it unjust that persons are born into society at some particular position. These are simply natural facts. What is just and unjust is the way that institutions deal with these facts. Aristocratic and caste societies are unjust because they make these contingencies the ascriptive basis for belonging to more or less enclosed and privileged social classes. The basic structure of these societies incorporates the arbitrariness found in nature. But there is no necessity for men to resign themselves to these contingencies. The social system is not an unchangeable order beyond human control but a pattern of human action. In justice as fairness men agree to share one another's fate. In designing institutions they undertake to avail themselves of the accidents of nature and social circumstance only when doing so is for the common benefit. The two principles are a fair way of meeting the arbitrariness of fortune; and while no doubt imperfect in other ways, the institutions which satisfy these principles are just.

A further point is that the difference principle expresses a conception of reciprocity. It is a principle of mutual benefit. We have seen that, at least when chain connection holds, each representative man can accept the basic structure as designed to advance his interests. The social order can be justified to everyone, and in particular to those who are least favored; and in this sense it is egalitarian. But it seems necessary to consider in an intuitive way how the condition of mutual benefit is satisfied. Consider any two representative men A and B, and let B by the one who is less favored. Actually, since we are most interested in the comparison with the least favored man, let us assume that B is this individual. Now B can accept A's being better off since A's advantages have been gained in ways that improve B's prospects. If A were not allowed his better position, B would be even worse off than he is. The difficulty is to show that A has no grounds for complaint. Perhaps he is required to have less than he might since his having more would result in some loss to B. Now what can be said to the more favored man? To begin with, it is clear that the well-being of each depends on a scheme of social cooperation without which no one could have a satisfactory life. Secondly, we can ask for the willing cooperation of everyone only if the terms of the scheme are reasonable. The difference principle, then, seems to be a fair basis on which those better endowed, or more fortunate in their social circumstances, could expect others to collaborate with them when some workable arrangement is a necessary condition of the good of all.

There is a natural inclination to object that those better situated deserve their greater advantages whether or not they are to the benefit of others. At this point it is necessary to be clear about the notion of desert. It is perfectly true that given a just system of cooperation as a scheme of public rules and the expectations set up by it, those who, with the prospect of improving their condition, have done what the system announces that it will reward are entitled to their advantages. In this sense the more fortunate have a claim to their better situation; their claims are legitimate expectations established by social institutions, and the community is obligated to meet them. But this sense of desert presupposes the existence of the cooperative scheme; it is irrelevant to the question whether in the first place the scheme is to be designed in accordance with the difference principle or some other criterion.

Perhaps some will think that the person with greater natural endowments deserves those assets and the superior character that made their development possible. Because he is more worthy in this sense, he deserves the greater advantages that he could achieve with them. This view, however, is surely incorrect. It seems to be one of the fixed points of our considered judgments that no one deserves his place in the distribution of native endowments, any more than one deserves one's initial starting place in society. The assertion that a man deserves the superior character that enables him to make the effort to cultivate his abilities is equally problematic; for his character depends in large part upon fortunate family and social circumstances for which he can claim no credit. The notion of desert seems not to apply to these cases. Thus the more advantaged representative man cannot say that he deserves and therefore has a right to a scheme of cooperation in which he is permitted to acquire benefits in ways that do not contribute to the welfare of others. There is no basis for his making this claim. From the standpoint of common sense, then, the difference principle appears to be acceptable both to the more advantaged and to the less advantaged individual. Of course, none of this is strictly speaking an argument for the principle, since in a contract theory arguments are made from the point of view of the original position. But these intuitive considerations help to clarify the nature of the principle and the sense in which it is egalitarian.

Robert Nozick
DISTRIBUTIVE JUSTICE

The minimal state is the most extensive state that can be justified. Any state more extensive violates people's rights. Yet many persons have put forth reasons purporting to justify a more extensive state. It is impossible within the compass of this book to examine all the reasons that have been put forth. Therefore, I shall focus upon those generally acknowledged to be most weighty and influential, to see precisely wherein they fail. In this chapter we consider the claim that a more extensive state is justified, because necessary (or the best instrument) to achieve distributive justice. . . .

The term "distributive justice" is not a neutral one. Hearing the term "distribution," most people presume that some thing or mechanism uses some principle or criterion to give out a supply of things. Into this process of distributing shares some error may have crept. So it is an open question, at least, whether *re*distribution should take place; whether we should do again what has already been done once, though poorly. However, we are not in the position of children who have been given portions of pie by someone who now makes last minute adjustments to rectify careless cutting. There is no *central* distribution, no person or group entitled to control all the resources, jointly deciding how they are to be doled out. What each person gets, he gets from others who give to him in exchange for something, or as a gift. In a free society, diverse persons control different resources, and new holdings arise out of the voluntary exchanges and actions of persons. There is no more a distributing or distribution of shares than there is a distributing of mates in a society in which persons choose whom they shall marry. The total result is the product of many individual decisions which the different individuals involved are entitled to make. . . .

THE ENTITLEMENT THEORY

The subject of justice in holdings consists of three major topics. The first is the *original acquisition of holdings*, the appropriation of unheld things. This includes the issues of how unheld things may come to be held, the process, or processes, by which unheld things may come to be held, the things that may come to be held by these processes, the extent of what comes to be held by a particular process, and so on. We shall refer to the complicated truth about this topic, which we shall not formulate here, as the principle of this topic, which we shall not formulate here, as the principle of justice in acquisition. The second topic concerns the *transfer of holdings* from one person to another. By what processes may a person transfer holdings to another? How may a person acquire a holding from another who holds it? Under this topic come general descriptions of voluntary exchange, and gift and (on the other hand) fraud, as well as reference to particular conventional details fixed upon in a given society. The complicated truth about this subject (with placeholders for conventional details) we shall call the principle of justice in transfer. (And we shall suppose it also includes principles governing how a person may divest himself of a holding, passing it into an unheld state.)

If the world were wholly just, the following inductive definition would exhaustively cover the subject of justice in holdings.

1. A person who acquires a holding in accordance with the principle of justice in acquisition is entitled to that holding.
2. A person who acquires a holding in accordance with the principle of justice in transfer, from someone else entitled to the holding, is entitled to the holding.
3. No one is entitled to a holding except by (repeated) applications of 1 and 2.

The complete principle of distributive justice would say simply that a distribution is just if everyone is entitled to the holdings they possess under the distribution.

A distribution is just if it arises from another just distribution by legitimate means. The legitimate means of moving from one distribution to another are specified by the principle of justice in transfer. The legitimate first "moves" are specified by the principle of justice in acquisition.[1] Whatever arises from a just situation by just steps is itself just. The means of change specified by the principle of justice in transfer preserve justice. As correct rules of inference are truth-preserving, and any conclusion deduced via repeated application of such rules from only true premises is itself true, so the means of transition from one situation to another specified by the principle of justice in transfer are justice-preserving, and any situation actually arising from repeated transitions in accordance with the principle from a just situation is itself just. The parallel between justice-preserving transformations and truth-preserving transformations illuminates where it fails as well as where it holds. That a conclusion could have been deduced by truth-preserving means from premises that are true suffices to show its truth. That from a just situation a situation *could* have arisen via justice-preserving means does *not* suffice to show its justice. The fact that a thief's victims voluntarily *could* have presented him with gifts does not entitle the thief to his ill-gotten gains. Justice in holdings is historical; it depends upon what actually has happened. We shall return to this point later.

---

[1]Applications of the principle of justice in acquisition may also occur as part of the move from one distribution to another. You may find an unheld thing now and appropriate it. Acquisitions also are to be understood as included when, to simplify, I speak only of transitions by transfers.

Not all actual situations are generated in accordance with the two principles of justice in holdings: the principle of justice in acquisition and the principle of justice in transfer. Some people steal from others, or defraud them, or enslave them, seizing their product and preventing them from living as they choose, or forcibly exclude others from competing in exchanges. None of these are permissible modes of transition from one situation to another. And some persons acquire holdings by means not sanctioned by the principle of justice in acquisition. The existence of past injustice (previous violations of the first two principles of justice in holdings) raises the third major topic under justice in holdings: the rectification of injustice in holdings. If past injustice has shaped present holdings in various ways, some identifiable and some not, what now, if anything, ought to be done to rectify these injustices? What obligations do the performers of injustice have toward those whose position is worse than it would have been had the injustice not been done? Or, than it would have been had compensation been paid promptly? How, if at all, do things change if the beneficiaries and those made worse off are not the direct parties in the act of injustice, but, for example, their descendants? Is an injustice done to someone whose holding was itself based upon an unrectified injustice? How far back must one go in wiping clean the historical slate of injustices? What may victims of injustice permissibly do in order to rectify the injustices being done to them, including the many injustices done by persons acting through their government? I do not know of a thorough or theoretically sophisticated treatment of such issues.[2] Idealizing greatly, let us suppose theoretical investigation will produce a principle of rectification. This principle uses historical information about previous situations and injustices done in them (as defined by the first two principles of justice and rights against interference), and information about the actual course of events that flowed from these injustices, until the present, and it yields a description (or descriptions) of holdings in the society. The principle of rectification presumably will make use of its best estimate of subjunctive information about what would have occurred (or a probability distribution over what might have occurred, using the expected value) if the injustice had not taken place. If the actual description of holdings turns out not to be one of the descriptions yielded by the principle, then one of the descriptions yielded must be realized.[3]

The general outlines of the theory of justice in holdings are that the holdings of a person are just if he is entitled to them by the principles of justice in acquisition and transfer, or by the principle of rectification of injustice (as specified by the first two principles). If each person's holdings are just, then the total set (distribution) of holdings is just. To turn these general outlines into a specific theory we would have to specify the details of each of the three principles of justice in holdings: the principle of acquisition of holdings, the

[2]See, however, the useful book by Boris Bittker, *The Case for Black Reparations* (New York: Random House, 1973).

[3]If the principle of rectification of violations of the first two principles yields more than one description of holdings, then some choice must be made as to which of these is to be realized. Perhaps the sort of considerations about distributive justice and equality that I argue against play a legitimate role in *this* subsidiary choice. Similarly, there may be room for such considerations in deciding which otherwise arbitrary features a statute will embody, when such features are unavoidable because other considerations do not specify a precise line; yet a line must be drawn.

principle of transfer of holdings, and the principle of rectification of violations of the first two principles. I shall not attempt that task here. (Locke's principle of justice in acquisition is discussed below.)

HISTORICAL PRINCIPLES AND END-RESULT PRINCIPLES

The general outlines of the entitlement theory illuminate the nature and defects of other conceptions of distributive justice. The entitlement theory of justice in distribution is *historical*; whether a distribution is just depends upon how it came about. In contrast, *current time-slice principles* of justice hold that the justice of a distribution is determined by how things are distributed (who has what) as judged by some *structural* principle(s) of just distribution. A utilitarian who judges between any two distributions by seeing which has the greater sum of utility and, if the sums tie, applies some fixed equality criterion to choose the more equal distribution, would hold a current time-slice principle of justice. As would someone who had a fixed schedule of trade-offs between the sum of happiness and equality. According to a current time-slice principle, all that needs to be looked at, in judging the justice of a distribution, is who ends up with what; in comparing any two distributions one need look only at the matrix presenting the distributions. No further information need be fed into a principle of justice. It is a consequence of such principles of justice that any two structurally identical distributions are equally just. (Two distributions are structurally identical if they present the same profile, but perhaps have different persons occupying the particular slots. My having ten and your having five, and my having five and your having ten are structurally identical distributions.) Welfare economics is the theory of current time-slice principles of justice. The subject is conceived as operating on matrices representing only current information about distribution. This, as well as some of the usual conditions (for example, the choice of distribution is invariant under relabeling of columns), guarantees that welfare economics will be a current time-slice theory, with all of its inadequacies.

Most persons do not accept current time-slice principles as constituting the whole story about distributive shares. They think it relevant in assessing the justice of a situation to consider not only the distribution it embodies, but also how that distribution came about. If some persons are in prison for murder or war crimes, we do not say that to assess the justice of the distribution in the society we must look only at what this person has, and that person has, and that person has, . . . at the current time. We think it relevant to ask whether someone did something so that he *deserved* to be punished, deserved to have a lower share. . . .

PATTERNING

The entitlement principles of justice in holdings that we have sketched are historical principles of justice. To better understand their precise character, we shall distinguish them from another subclass of the historical principles. Consider, as an example, the principle of distribution according to moral merit. This principle requires that total distributive shares vary directly with moral merit; no person should have a greater share than anyone whose moral merit is greater. (If moral merit could be not merely ordered but measured on an interval or ratio scale, stronger principles could be formulated.) Or consider the principle that results by substituting "usefulness to society" for "moral merit" in the previous principle. Or instead of "distribute according to moral merit," or "distribute according to usefulness to society," we might consider "distribute according to the weighted sum of moral merit, usefulness to society, and need," with the weights of the different dimensions equal. Let us call a principle of distribution *patterned* if it specifies that a distribution is to vary along with some natural dimension, weighted sum of natural dimensions, or lexicographic ordering of natural dimensions. And let us say a distribution is patterned if it accords with some patterned principle. (I speak of natural dimensions, admittedly without a general criterion for them, because for any set of holdings some artificial dimensions can be gimmicked up to vary along with the distribution of the set.) The principle of distribution in accordance with moral merit is a patterned historical principle, which specifies a patterned distribution. "Distribute according to I.Q." is a patterned principle that looks to information not contained in distributional matrices. It is not historical, however, in that it does not look to any past actions creating differential entitlements to evaluate a distribution; it requires only distributional matrices whose columns are labeled by I.Q. scores. The distribution in a society, however, may be composed of such simple patterned distributions, without itself being simply patterned. Different sectors may operate different patterns, or some combination of patterns may operate in different proportions across a society. A distribution composed in this manner, from a small number of patterned distributions, we also shall term "patterned." And we extend the use of "pattern" to include the overall designs put forth by combinations of end-state principles.

Almost every suggested principle of distributive justice is patterned: to each according to his moral merit, or needs, or marginal product, or how hard he tries, or the weighted sum of the foregoing, and so on. The principle of entitlement we have sketched is *not* patterned.[4] There is no one natural dimension or weighted sum or combination of a small number of natural dimensions that yields the distributions generated in accordance with the principle of entitlement. The set of holdings that results when some persons receive their marginal products, others win at gambling, others receive a share of their mate's income, others receive gifts from foundations, others receive interest on loans, others receive gifts from admirers, others receive returns on investment, others

---

[4]One might try to squeeze a patterned conception of distributive justice into the framework of the entitlement conception, by formulating a gimmicky obligatory "principle of transfer" that would lead to the pattern. For example, the principle that if one has more than the mean income one must transfer everything one holds above the means to persons below the mean so as to bring them up to (but not over) the mean. We can formulate a criterion for a "principle of transfer" to rule out such obligatory transfers, or we can say that no correct principle of transfer, no principle of transfer in a free society will be like this. The former is probably the better course, though the latter also is true.

Alternatively, one might think to make the entitlement conception instantiate a pattern, by using matrix entries that express the relative strength of a person's entitlements as measured by some real-valued function. But even if the limitation to natural dimensions failed to exclude this function, the resulting edifice would *not* capture our system of entitlements to *particular* things.

make for themselves much of what they have, others find things, and so on, will not be patterned. . . .

To think that the task of a theory of distributive justice is to fill in the blank in "to each according to his _____" is to be predisposed to search for a pattern; and the separate treatment of "from each according to his _____" treats production and distribution as two separate and independent issues. On an entitlement view these are *not* two separate questions. Whoever makes something, having bought or contracted for all other held resources used in the process (transferring some of his holdings for these cooperating factors), is entitled to it. The situation is *not* one of something's getting made, and there being an open question of who is to get it. Things come into the world already attached to people having entitlements over them. From the point of view of the historical entitlement conception of justice in holdings, those who start afresh to complete "to each according to his _____" treat objects as if they appeared from nowhere, out of nothing. A complete theory of justice might cover this limit case as well; perhaps here is a use for the usual conceptions of distributive justice.[5]

So entrenched are maxims of the usual form that perhaps we should present the entitlement conception as a competitor. Ignoring acquisition and rectification, we might say:

> From each according to what he chooses to do, to each according to what he makes for himself (perhaps with the contracted aid of others) and what others choose to do for him and choose to give him of what they've been given previously (under this maxim) and haven't yet expended or transferred.

This, the discerning reader will have noticed, has its defects as a slogan. So as a summary and great simplification (and not as a maxim with any independent meaning) we have:

> *From each as they choose, to each as they are chosen.*

HOW LIBERTY UPSETS PATTERNS

It is not clear how those holding alternative conceptions of distributive justice can reject the entitlement conception of justice in holdings. For suppose a distribution favored by one of these nonentitlement conceptions is realized. Let us suppose it is your favorite one and let us call this distribution D_1; perhaps everyone has an equal share, perhaps shares vary in accordance with some dimension you treasure. Now suppose that Wilt Chamberlain is greatly in demand by basketball teams, being a great gate attraction. (Also suppose contracts run only for a year, with players being free agents.) He signs the following sort of contract with a team: In each home game, twenty-five cents from the

---

[5]Varying situations continuously from that limit situation to our own would force us to make explicit the underlying rationale of entitlements and to consider whether entitlement considerations lexicographically precede the considerations of the usual theories of distributive justice, so that the *slightest* strand of entitlement outweighs the considerations of the usual theories of distributive justice.

price of each ticket of admission goes to him. (We ignore the question of whether he is "gouging" the owners, letting them look out for themselves.) The season starts, and people cheerfully attend his team's games; they buy their tickets, each time dropping a separate twenty-five cents of their admission price into a special box with Chamberlain's name on it. They are excited about seeing him play; it is worth the total admission price to them. Let us suppose that in one season one million persons attend his home games, and Wilt Chamberlain winds up with \$250,000, a much larger sum than the average income and larger even than anyone else has. Is he entitled to this income? Is this new distribution D_2, unjust? If so, why? There is *no* question about whether each of the people was entitled to the control over the resources they held in D_1; because that was the distribution (your favorite) that (for the purposes of argument) we assumed was acceptable. Each of these person *chose* to give twenty-five cents of their money to Chamberlain. They could have spent it on going to the movies, or on candy bars, or on copies of *Dissent* magazine, or of *Monthly Review*. But they all, at least one million of them, converged on giving it to Wilt Chamberlain in exchange for watching him play basketball. If D_1 was a just distribution, and people voluntarily moved from it to D_2, transferring parts of their shares they were given under D_1 (what was it for if not to do something with?), isn't D_2 also just? If the people were entitled to dispose of the resources to which they were entitled (under D_1), didn't this include their being entitled to give it to, or exchange it with, Wilt Chamberlain? Can anyone else complain on grounds of justice? Each other person already has his legitimate share under D_1. Under D_1, there is nothing that anyone has that anyone else has a claim of justice against. After someone transfers something to Wilt Chamberlain, third parties *still* have their legitimate shares; *their* shares are not changed. By what process could such a transfer among two persons give rise to a legitimate claim of distributive justice on a portion of what was transferred, by a third party who had no claim of justice on any holding of the others *before* the transfer?[6] To cut off objections irrelevant here, we might imagine the exchanges occurring in a socialist society, after hours. After playing whatever basketball he does in his daily work, or doing whatever other daily work he does, Wilt Chamberlain decides to put in *overtime* to earn additional money. (First his work quota is set; he works time over that.) Or imagine it is a skilled juggler people like to see, who puts on shows after hours. . . .

[6]Might not a transfer have instrumental effects on a third party, changing his feasible options? (But what if the two parties to the transfer independently had used their holdings in this fashion?) I discuss this question below, but note here that this question concedes the point for distributions of ultimate intrinsic noninstrumental goods (pure utility experiences, so to speak) that are transferrable. It also might be objected that the transfer might make a third party more envious because it worsens his position relative to someone else. I find it incomprehensible how this can be thought to involve a claim of justice.

Here and elsewhere in this chapter, a theory which incorporates elements of pure procedural justice might find what I say acceptable, *if* kept in its proper place; that is, if background institutions exist to ensure the satisfaction of certain conditions on distributive shares. But if these institutions are not themselves the sum of invisible-hand result of people's voluntary (nonaggressive) actions, the constraints they impose require justification. At no point does *our* argument assume any background institutions more extensive than those of the minimal night-watchman state, a state limited to protecting persons against murder, assault, theft, fraud, and so forth.

The general point illustrated by the Wilt Chamberlain example and the example of the entrepreneur in a socialist society is that no end-state principle or distributional patterned principle of justice can be continuously realized without continuous interference with people's lives. Any favored pattern would be transformed into one unfavored by the principle, by people choosing to act in various ways; for example, by people exchanging goods and services with other people, or giving things to other people, things the transferrers are entitled to under the favored distributional pattern. To maintain a pattern one must either continually interfere to stop people from transferring resources as they wish to, or continually (or periodically) interfere to take from some persons resources that others for some reason chose to transfer to them. . . .

Proponents of patterned principles of distributive justice focus upon criteria for determining who is to receive holdings; they consider the reasons for which someone should have something, and also the total picture of holdings. Whether or not it is better to give than to receive, proponents of patterned principles ignore giving altogether. In considering the distribution of goods, income, and so forth, their theories are theories of recipient justice; they completely ignore any right a person might have to give something to someone. Even in exchanges where each party is simultaneously giver and recipient, patterned principles of justice focus only upon the recipient role and its supposed rights. Thus discussions tend to focus on whether people (should) have a right to inherit, rather than on whether people (should) have a right to bequeath or on whether persons who have a right to hold also have a right to choose that others hold in their place. I lack a good explanation of why the usual theories of distributive justice are so recipient oriented; ignoring givers and transferrers and their rights is of a piece with ignoring producers and their entitlements. But why is it *all* ignored?

Patterned principles of distributive justice necessitate *re*distributive activities. The likelihood is small that any actual freely-arrived-at set of holdings fits a given pattern; and the likelihood is nil that it will continue to fit the pattern as people exchange and give. From the point of view of an entitlement theory, redistribution is a serious matter indeed, involving, as it does, the violation of people's rights. (An exception is those takings that fall under the principle of the rectification of injustices.) From other points of view, also, it is serious.

Taxation of earnings from labor is on a par with forced labor.[7] Some persons find this claim obviously true: taking the earnings of n hours labor is like taking n hours from the person; it is like forcing the person to work n hours for another's purpose. Others find the claim absurd. But even these, *if* they object to forced labor, would oppose forcing unemployed hippies to work for the benefit of the needy.[8] And they would also object to forcing each person to work five

[7]I am unsure as to whether the arguments I present below show that such taxation merely *is* forced labor; so that "is on a part with" means "is one kind of." Or alternatively, whether the arguments emphasize the great similarities between such taxation and forced labor, to show it is plausible and illuminating to view such taxation in the light of forced labor. This latter approach would remind one of how John Wisdom conceives of the claims of metaphysicians.

[8]Nothing hangs on the fact that here and elsewhere I speak loosely of *needs*, since I go on, each time, to reject the criterion of justice which includes it. If, however, something did depend upon the notion, one would want to examine it more carefully. For a skeptical view, see Kenneth Minogue, *The Liberal Mind*, (New York: Random House, 1963), pp. 103–112.

extra hours each week for the benefit of the needy. But a system that takes five hours' wages in taxes does not seem to them like one that forces someone to work five hours, since it offers the person forced a wider range of choice in activities than does taxation in kind with the particular labor specified. (But we can imagine a gradation of systems of forced labor, from one that specifies a particular activity, to one that gives a choice among two activities, to . . . ; and so on up.) Furthermore, people envisage a system with something like a proportional tax on everything above the amount necessary for basic needs. Some think this does not force someone to work extra hours, since there is no fixed number of extra hours he is forced to work, and since he can avoid the tax entirely by earning only enough to cover his basic needs. This is a very uncharacteristic view of forcing for those who *also* think people are forced to do something *whenever* the alternatives they face are considerably worse. However, *neither* view is correct. The fact that others intentionally intervene, in violation of a side constraint against aggression, to threaten force to limit the alternatives, in this case to paying taxes or (presumably the worse alternative) bare subsistence, makes the taxation system one of forced labor and distinguishes it from other cases of limited choices which are not forcings.[9]

The man who chooses to work longer to gain an income more than sufficient for his basic needs prefers some extra goods or services to the leisure and activities he could perform during the possible nonworking hours; whereas the man who chooses not to work the extra time prefers the leisure activities to the extra goods or services he could acquire by working more. Given this, if it would be illegitimate for a tax system to seize some of a man's leisure (forced labor) for the purpose of serving the needy, how can it be legitimate for a tax system to seize some of a man's goods for that purpose? Why should we treat the man whose happiness requires certain material goods or services differently from the man whose preferences and desires make such goods unnecessary for his happiness? Why should the man who prefers seeing a movie (and who has to earn money for a ticket) be open to the required call to aid the needy, while the person who prefers looking at a sunset (and hence need earn no extra money) is not? Indeed, isn't it surprising that redistributionists choose to ignore the man whose pleasures are so easily attainable without extra labor, while adding yet another burden to the poor unfortunate who must work for his pleasures? If anything, one would have expected the reverse. Why is the person with the nonmaterial or nonconsumption desire allowed to proceed unimpeded to his most favored feasible alternative, whereas the man whose pleasures or desires involve material things and who must work for extra money (thereby serving whomever considers his activities valuable enough to pay him) is constrained in what he can realize? Perhaps there is no difference in principle. And perhaps some think the answer concerns merely administrative convenience. (These questions and issues will not disturb those who think that forced labor to serve the needy or to realize some favored end-state pattern is acceptable.) In a fuller discussion we would have (and want) to extend our argument to include interest, entrepreneurial profits, and so on. Those who doubt that this extension can be carried through, and who draw the line here at taxation of income from labor,

[9]Further details which this statement should include are contained in my essay "Coercion," in *Philosophy, Science, and Method*, ed. S. Morgenbesser, P. Suppes, and M. White (New York: St. Martin, 1969).

will have to state rather complicated patterned *historical* principles of distributive justice, since end-state principles would not distinguish *sources* of income in any way. It is enough for now to get away from end-state principles and to make clear how various patterned principles are dependent upon particular views about the sources or the illegitimacy or the lesser legitimacy of profits, interest, and so on; which particular views may well be mistaken.

What sort of right over others does a legally institutionalized end-state pattern give one? The central core of the notion of a property right in X, relative to which other parts of the notion are to be explained, is the right to determine what shall be done with X; the right to choose which of the constrained set of options concerning X shall be realized or attempted.[10] The constraints are set by other principles or laws operating in the society; in our theory, by the Lockean rights people possess (under the minimal state). My property rights in my knife allow me to leave it where I will, but not in your chest. I may choose which of the acceptable options involving the knife is to be realized. This notion of property helps us to understand why earlier theorists spoke of people as having property in themselves and their labor. They viewed each person as having a right to decide what would become of himself and what he would do, and as having a right to reap the benefits of what he did.

This right of selecting the alternative to be realized from the constrained set of alternatives may be held by an *individual* or by a *group* with some procedure for reaching a joint decision; or the right may be passed back and forth, so that one year I decide what's to become of X, and the next year you do (with the alternative of destruction, perhaps, being excluded). Or, during the same time period, some types of decisions about X may be made by me, and others by you. And so on. We lack an adequate, fruitful, analytical apparatus for classifying the *types* of constraints on the set of options among which choices are to be made, and the *types* of ways decision powers can be held, divided, and amalgamated. A *theory* of property would, among other things, contain such a classification of constraints and decision modes, and from a small number of principles would follow a host of interesting statements about the *consequences* and effects of certain combinations of constraints and modes of decision.

When end-result principles of distributive justice are built into the legal structure of a society, they (as do most patterned principles) give each citizen an enforceable claim to some portion of the total social product; that is, to some portion of the sum total of the individually and jointly made products. This total product is produced by individuals laboring, using means of production others have saved to bring into existence, by people organizing production or creating means to produce new things or things in a new way. It is on this batch of individual activities that patterned distributional principles give each individual an enforceable claim. Each person has a claim to the activities and the products of other persons, independently of whether the other persons enter into particular relationships that give rise to these claims, and independently of whether they voluntarily take these claims upon themselves, in charity or in exchange for something.

Whether it is done through taxation on wages or on wages over a certain amount, or through seizure of profits, or through there being a big *social pot* so that it's not clear what's coming from where and what's going where, patterned

---

[10]On the themes in this and the next paragraph, see the writings of Armen Alchian.

principles of distributive justice involve appropriating the actions of other persons. Seizing the results of someone's labor is equivalent to seizing hours from him and directing him to carry on various activities. If people force you to do certain work, or unrewarded work, for a certain period of time, they decide what you are to do and what purposes your work is to serve apart from your decisions. This process whereby they take this decision from you makes them a *part-owner* of you; it gives them a property right in you. Just as having such partial control and power of decision, by right, over an animal or inanimate object would be to have a property right in it.

J. J. C. Smart

DISTRIBUTIVE JUSTICE AND UTILITARIANISM

INTRODUCTION

In this paper I shall not be concerned with the defense of utilitarianism against other types of ethical theory. Indeed I hold that questions of ultimate ethical principle are not susceptible of proof, though something can be done to render them more acceptable by presenting them in a clear light and by clearing up certain confusions which (for some people) may get in the way of their acceptance. Ultimately the utilitarian appeals to the sentiment of generalized benevolence, and speaks to others who feel this sentiment too and for whom it is an over-riding feeling. (This does not mean that he will always act from this over-riding feeling. There can be backsliding and action may result from more particular feelings, just as an egoist may go against his own interests, and may regret this.) I shall be concerned here merely to investigate certain consequences of utilitarianism, as they relate to questions of distributive justice. The type of utilitarianism with which I am concerned is act utilitarianism, which is in its normative aspects much the same as the type of utilitarianism which was put forward by Henry Sidgwick, though I differ from Sidgwick over questions of moral epistemology and of the semantics of ethical language.

THE PLACE OF JUSTICE IN UTILITARIAN THEORY

The concept of justice as a *fundamental* ethical concept is really quite foreign to utilitarianism. A utilitarian would compromise his utilitarianism if he allowed principles of justice which might conflict with the maximization of happiness (or more generally of goodness, should he be an 'ideal' utilitarian). He is concerned with the maximization of happiness and not with the distribution of

From J. J. C. Smart, "Distributive Justice and Utilitarianism," in *Justice and Economic Distribution*, 2nd ed., edited by John Arthur and William H. Shaw (Englewood Cliffs, NJ: Prentice Hall, 1991, 106–110, 115–116. Reprinted by permission of the author.

it. Nevertheless he may well deduce from his ethical principle that certain ways of distributing the means to happiness (e.g. money, food, housing) are more conducive to the general good than are others. He will be interested in justice in so far as it is a political or legal or quasi-legal concept. He will consider whether the legal institutions and customary sanctions which operate in particular societies are more or less conducive to the utilitarian end than are other possible institutions and customs. Even if the society consisted entirely of utilitarians (and of course no actual societies have thus consisted) it might still be important to have legal and customary sanctions relating to distribution of goods, because utilitarians might be tempted to backslide and favour non-optimific distributions, perhaps because of bias in their own favour. They might be helped to act in a more nearly utilitarian way because of the presence of these sanctions.

As a utilitarian, therefore, I do not allow the concept of justice as a fundamental moral concept, but I am nevertheless interested in justice in a subordinate way, as a *means* to the utilitarian end. Thus even though I hold that it does not matter in what way happiness is distributed among different persons, provided that the total amount of happiness is maximized. I do of course hold that it can be of vital importance that the *means* to happiness should be distributed in some ways and not in others. Suppose that I have the choice of two alternative actions as follows: I can either give $500 to each of two needy men, Smith and Campbell, or else give $1000 to Smith and nothing to Campbell. It is of course likely to produce the greatest happiness if I divide the money equally. For this reason utilitarianism can often emerge as a theory with egalitarian consequences. If it does so this is because of the empirical situation, and not because of any moral commitment to egalitarianism as such. Consider, for example, another empirical situation in which the $500 was replaced by a half-dose of a life saving drug, in which case the utilitarian would advocate giving two half doses to Smith or Campbell and none to the other. Indeed if Smith and Campbell each possessed a half dose it would be right to take one of the half doses and give it to the other. (I am assuming that a whole dose would preserve life and that a half dose would not. I am also assuming a simplified situation: in some possible situations, especially in a society of non-utilitarians, the wide social ramifications of taking a half dose from Smith and giving it to Campbell might conceivably outweigh the good results of saving Campbell's life.) However, it is probable that in most situations the equal distribution of the means to happiness will be the right utilitarian action, even though the utilitarian has no ultimate moral commitment to egalitarianism. If a utilitarian is given the choice of two actions, one of which will give 2 units of happiness to Smith and 2 to Campbell and the other of which will give 1 unit of happiness to Smith and 9 to Campbell, he will choose the latter course.[1] It may also be that I have the choice between two alternative actions, one of which gives − 1 unit of happiness to Smith and + 2 to Smith and + 2 to Campbell. As a utilitarian I will choose the former course, and here I will be in conflict with John Rawls' theory, whose maximin principle would rule out making Smith worse off.

UTILITARIANISM AND RAWLS' THEORY

Rawls deduces his ethical principles from the contract which would be made by a group of rational egoists in an 'original position' in which they thought behind a 'veil of ignorance,' so that they would not know who they were or even what generation they belonged to. Reasoning behind this veil of ignorance, they would apply the maximin principle. John Harsanyi earlier used the notion of a contract in such a position of ignorance, but used not the maximin principle but the principle of maximizing expected utility.[2] Harsanyi's method leads to a form of rule utilitarianism. I see no great merit in this roundabout approach to ethics *via* a contrary to fact supposition, which involves the tricky notion of a social contract and which thus appears already to presuppose a moral position. The approach seems also too Hobbesian: it is anthropologically incorrect to suppose that we are all originally little egoists. I prefer to base ethics on a principle of generalized benevolence, to which some of those with whom I discuss ethics may immediately respond. Possibly it might show something interesting about our common moral notions if it could be proved that they follow from what would be contracted by rational egoists in an 'original position,' but as a utilitarian I am more concerned to advocate a normative theory which might replace our common moral notions than I am to explain these notions. Though some form of utilitarianism might be deducible (as by Harsanyi) from a contract or original position theory, I do not think that it either ought to be or need be defended in this sort of way.

Be that as it may, it is clear that utilitarian views about distribution of happiness do differ from Rawls' view. I have made a distinction between justice as a moral concept and justice as a legal or quasi-legal concept. The utilitarian has no room for the former, but he can have strong views about the latter, though *what* these views are will depend on empirical considerations. Thus whether he will prefer a political theory which advocates a completely socialist state, or whether he will prefer one which advocates a minimal state (as Robert Nozick's book does[3]), or whether again he will advocate something between the two, is something which depends on the facts of economics, sociology, and so on. As someone not expert in these fields I have no desire to dogmatize on these empirical matters. (My own private non-expert opinion is that probably neither extreme leads to maximization of happiness, though I have a liking for rather more socialism than exists in Australia or U.S.A. at present.) As a utilitarian my approach to political theory has to be tentative and empirical. Not believing in moral rights as such I can not deduce theories about the best political arrangements by making deductions (as Nozick does) from propositions which purport to be about such basic rights.

Rawls deduces two principles of justice.[4] The first of these is that 'each person is to have an equal right to the most extensive basic liberty compatible with a similar liberty for others,' and the second one is that 'social and economic inequalities are to be arranged so that they are both (a) reasonably expected to be to everyone's advantage, and (b) attached to positions and offices open to all.' Though a utilitarian could (on empirical grounds) be very much in sympathy with both of these principles, he could not accept them as universal rules. Suppose that a society which had no danger of nuclear war could be achieved only by reducing the liberty of one percent of the world's population. Might it not be right to bring about such a state of affairs if it were in one's power? Indeed might it not be right greatly to reduce the liberty of 100% of the world's population if such a desirable outcome could be achieved? Perhaps the present generation would be pretty miserable and would hanker for their lost liberties. However we must also think about the countless future generations which might exist and be happy provided that mankind can avoid exterminating itself, and we must also think of all the pain, misery and genetic damage which would be brought about by nuclear war even if this did not lead to the total extermination of mankind.

Suppose that this loss of freedom prevented a war so devastating that the whole process of evolution on this planet would come to an end. At the cost of the loss of freedom, instead of the war and the end of evolution there might occur an evolutionary process which was not only long lived but also beneficial: in millions of years there might be creatures descended from *homo sapiens* which had vastly increased talents and capacity for happiness. At least such considerations show that Rawls' first principle is far from obvious to the utilitarian, though in certain mundane contexts he might accede to it as a useful approximation. Indeed I do not believe that restriction of liberty, in our present society, could have beneficial results in helping to prevent nuclear war, though a case could be made for certain restrictions on the liberty of all present members of society so as to enable the government to prevent nuclear blackmail by gangs of terrorists.

Perhaps in the past considerable restrictions on the personal liberties of a large proportion of citizens may have been justifiable on utilitarian grounds. In view of the glories of Athens and its contributions to civilization it is possible that the Athenian slave society was justifiable. In one part of his paper, "Nature and Soundness of the Contract and Coherence Arguments,"[5] David Lyons has judiciously discussed the question of whether in certain circumstances a utilitarian would condone slavery. He says that it would be unlikely that a utilitarian could condone slavery as it has existed in modern times. However he considers the possibility that less objectionable forms of slavery or near slavery have existed. The less objectionable these may have been, the more likely it is that utilitarianism would have condoned them. Lyons remarks that our judgments about the relative advantages of different societies must be very tentative because we do not know enough about human history to say what were the social alternatives at any juncture.[6]

Similar reflections naturally occur in connection with Rawls' second principle. Oligarchic societies, such as that of eighteenth century Britain, may well have been in fact better governed than they would have been if posts of responsibility had been available to all. Certainly to resolve this question we should have to go deeply into empirical investigations of the historical facts. (To prevent misunderstanding, I do think that in our present society utilitarianism would imply adherence to Rawls' second principle as a general rule.)

A utilitarian is concerned with maximizing total happiness (or goodness, if he is an ideal utilitarian). Rawls largely concerns himself with certain 'primary goods', as he calls them. These include 'rights and liberties, power and opportunities, income and wealth.'[7] A utilitarian would regard these as mere means to the ultimate good. Nevertheless if he is proposing new laws or changes to social institutions the utilitarian will have to concern himself in practice with the distribution of these 'primary goods' (as Bentham did).[8] But if as an approximation we neglect this distinction, which may be justifiable to the extent that there is a correlation between happiness and the level of these 'primary goods,' we may say that according to Rawls an action is right only if it is to the benefit of the least advantaged person. A utilitarian will hold that a redistribution of the means to happiness is right if it maximizes the general happiness, even though some persons, even the least advantaged ones, are made worse off. A position which is intermediate between the utilitarian position and Rawls' position would be one which held that one ought to maximize some sort of trade off between total happiness and distribution of happiness. Such a position would imply that sometimes we should redistribute in such a way as to make some persons, even the least advantaged ones, worse off, but this would happen less often than it would according to the classical utilitarian theory.

. . . .

UTILITARIANISM AND NOZICK'S THEORY

General adherence to Robert Nozick's theory (in his *Anarchy, State, and Utopia*) would be compatible with the existence of very great inequality indeed. This is because the whole theory is based quite explicitly on the notion of *rights*: in the very first sentence of the preface of his book we read 'Individuals have rights. . . . ' The utilitarian would demur here. A utilitarian legislator might tax the rich in order to give aid to the poor, but a Nozickian legislator would not do so. A utilitarian legislator might impose a heavy tax on inherited wealth, whereas Nozick would allow the relatively fortunate to become even more fortunate, provided that they did not infringe the *rights* of the less fortunate. The utilitarian legislator would hope to increase the total happiness by equalizing things a bit. How far he should go in this direction would depend on empirical considerations. He would not want to equalize things too much if this led to too much weakening of the incentive to work, for example. Of course according to Nozick's system there would be no reason why members of society should not set up a utilitarian utopia, and voluntarily equalize their wealth, and also give wealth to poorer communities outside. However it is questionable whether such isolated utopias could survive in a modern environment, but if they did survive, the conformity of the behaviour of their members to utilitarian theory, rather than the conformity to Nozick's theory, would be what would commend their societies to me.

SUMMARY

In this article I have explained that the notion of justice is not a fundamental notion in utilitarianism, but that utilitarians will characteristically have certain views about such things as the distribution of wealth, savings for the benefit of future generations and for the third world countries and other practical matters. Utilitarianism differs from John Rawls' theory in that it is ready to contemplate some sacrifice to certain individuals (or classes of individuals) for the sake of the greater good of all, and in particular may allow certain limitations of personal freedom which would be ruled out by Rawls' theory. *In practice*, however, the general tendency of utilitarianism may well be towards an egalitarian form of society.

Notes

1. There are of course difficult problems about the assignment of cardinal utilities to states of mind, but for the purposes of this paper I am assuming that we can intelligibly talk, as utilitarians do, about units of happiness.

2. John C. Harsanyi, 'Cardinal Utility in Welfare Economics and the Theory of Risk-Taking', *Journal of Political Economy*, 61 (1953), 434–435, and 'Cardinal Welfare, Individualistic Ethics, and Interpersonal Comparisons of Utility', ibid., 63 (1955), 309–321. Harsanyi has discussed Rawls' use of the maximin principle and has defended the principle of maximizing expected utility instead, in a paper 'Can the Maximin Principle Serve as a Basis for Morality? A Critique of John Rawls's Theory', *The American Political Science Review*, 69 (1975), 594–606. These articles have been reprinted in John C. Harsanyi, *Essays on Ethics, Social Behavior, and Scientific Explanation* (Dordrecht, Holland: D. Reidel, 1976).

3. Robert Nozick, *Anarchy, State, and Utopia* (Oxford: Blackwell, 1975).

4. Rawls, *A Theory of Justice* (Cambridge, Mass.: Harvard University Press, 1971), p. 60.

5. In Norman Daniels (ed.), *Reading Rawls* (Oxford: Blackwell, 1975), pp. 141–167. See pp. 148–149.

6. Lyons, op. cit. p. 149, near top.

7. Rawls, op. cit., p. 62.

8. On this point see Brian Barry, *The Liberal Theory of Justice* (London: Oxford University Press, 1973), p. 55.

Milton Fisk

ECONOMIC JUSTICE

Defenders of the capitalist form of society do not defend a right to economic equality. Economic inequality is, they argue, to everyone's advantage. Yet some of these defenders of capitalism are also supporters of liberal democracy. They must then recognize limits to economic inequality beyond which even capitalism should not go. Vast concentrations of economic wealth are sources of political power that strangle the basic liberties of a democratic society. But many defenders of capitalist society maintain that in the US at least these limits to economic inequality have not been reached.

The purpose of this chapter is to show that the arguments justifying the existing high degree of economic inequality fall apart. To show this it will not be necessary to defend, or to reject, the right to complete economic equality. Nonetheless, this chapter points to an egalitarian direction. For it shows also that the degree of economic inequality inevitable within even a reformed capitalist society cannot be justified from the perspective of working-class morality.

1. ECONOMIC INEQUALITY

According to many writers on US society, the stage of widespread affluence has been reached within the US. There is, on the one hand, a reduced level of economic inequality, and there is, on the other hand, an elimination of the lower classes as a majority in favour of a large and prosperous middle class. The misery and inequality that characterized nineteenth and early twentieth-century capi-

From Milton Fisk, "Economic Justice," in *Ethics and Society: A Marxist Interpretation of Value* (New York: New York University Press, 1980), 224–237. Reprinted by permission of the publisher.

talism have been redeemed with the arrival of the 'affluent society'. This picture, however, conceals the urgent problem of economic inequality within the US. As Gabriel Kolko notes in his pathbreaking dissenting work on income distribution, 'The predominantly middle-class society is only an image in the minds of isolated academicians.'[1]

First let us look at the distribution of before-tax personal, as opposed to corporate, income during the period 1910–1970 to get some idea as to whether there has been a significant trend toward equality. To do this we can consider families as broken up into five groups of equal size, ranging from those with the highest to those with the lowest income. (People living in families make up roughly 90 per cent of the US population.) *In the sixty-year period considered, families in the highest fifth received between 40 and 45 per cent of all family income.* That is, they received at least two times more than they would have if every family received the same income. Despite variations from year to year, there is no overall trend in this period toward a significantly smaller share of the national income for the richest fifth. The middle fifth has received between 15 and 18 per cent of all family income. This means that it received over the entire sixty-year period less than it would have if income were egalitarian. For this group the trend, within these narrow limits, has been for a slight rise in its share of income, but after World War II that rise stopped completely. Finally, what about the families in the poorest quintile? That group has received between 4 and 6 per cent of the national personal income, which runs up to five times less than it would receive under equality. The overall trend has been for families in this bottom group to get proportionally the same during the sixty-year period. As regards income in the US, then, there is significant and continuing inequality.[2] The top fifth as a whole takes six to ten times more of the national family income than does the bottom fifth. (Data for non-family persons shows even greater inequality.)

Our data has so far been taken on before-tax income. Will not taxation make the picture one of greater equality? It does change the picture as regards equality but only in an insignificant way. Many taxes are regressive: they are a larger fraction of lower than of higher incomes. Social security taxes, property taxes, and sales taxes are all regressive. It cannot be expected that these would provide a shift toward equality. But even the federal income tax, which is progressive, has failed to do more than decrease by two per cent the share of national income of the top fifth. The increase in the share of the bottom fifth resulting from federal income taxes has remained a fraction of a per cent. Moreover, the percentage of all taxes coming from the non-owning classes has been rising steadily since World War II. Taxes have, then, failed to equalize income significantly.[3]

We are dealing with a society in which private ownership of the means of production is a fundamental feature. Some personal income comes from ownership, to be sure, but one cannot say exactly how wealth is distributed simply on the basis of knowing how income is distributed. For one thing, a significant but variable share of returns from ownership is invested in new means of production and does not appear as dividend income. Nonetheless, in a capitalist society we can predict that wealth, like income, is unevenly distributed. It is highly concentrated in the hands of a very few owners: they own the plants, the trucks, the warehouses, the mines, the office buildings, the large estates, and the objects of art. The poor are often net holders of 'negative wealth' because of their debts.

Between 1810 and 1969, the concentration of wealth has remained remarkably constant; the top one per cent as regards wealth has held between 20 and 30 per cent of all the wealth in the US. In 1962 the poorest 20 per cent held less than one-half of one per cent of the nation's wealth.[4]

Nonetheless, some currency has been given to the view that corporate ownership has become widespread and that workers are now significant owners. Stock ownership is, indeed, more widespread, but this has not seriously affected the high degree of concentration of stock ownership in the hands of the wealthiest.

By 1962, the wealthiest one per cent of the population still held 72 per cent of the nation's corporate stock. In that year, the wealthiest one per cent also held 48 per cent of the nation's bonds, 24 per cent of the loans, and 16 per cent of the real estate.[5] Clearly then wealth is even less equitably distributed than income in the US, and the inequality has been one of long duration. Pensions for workers account for nearly ten per cent of corporate stock. This may provide workers with security after retirement, but it does not give them the power of wealth holders. The reason is that they have no control over these pension funds, which merely add power to the financial institutions that manage them.

Is it not possible to have affluence alongside inequality? The thesis that the US has become 'middle class' may still stand if it can be shown that the lower income quintiles are experiencing affluence. Two things are to be noted in this regard. First, the official unemployment rates between World War II and 1975 have averaged 4.8 per cent of the workforce. Many people do not show up in the statistics since they have dropped out of the workforce due to the discouraging job picture. When all hidden sectors of unemployment are taken into account, the actual unemployment figures may have averaged 8 to 10 per cent of the workforce. Unemployment compensation, even for those eligible for it, would not be an adequate means of keeping these workers and their families affluent if they were unemployed for long periods. In 1970, 23 per cent of all factory production workers were unemployed for at least three months. Clearly, then, unemployment alone keeps a sizeable part of the lowest quintile from affluence.

Second, the cost of the means of satisfying survival needs has skyrocketed due to a variety of socio-economic factors. For example, a car is often a necessity for getting to work due to widespread inadequacy of public transportation. A telephone is a necessity when work for those laid off depends on being called-in only a few hours in advance. As a result of these and numerous other changes, the amount of income needed to meet the bare necessities has skyrocketed. The increased purchasing power of workers' incomes does not mean affluence. It signifies the greater difficulty of satisfying survival needs in an advanced capitalist society.

An income that allows a family these more expensive necessities but that provides no savings either for long-term investment or for children's education would be the minimum needed to keep a family beyond the poverty line. The US Bureau of Labor Statistics has defined a 'modest but adequate budget' as one that allows a family to meet the expenses of food, clothing, cheap housing, used car, minimum school outlays, one TV set in ten years, nine movies per year, and no savings. This modest budget lies, then, just above the poverty line. In 1967 an urban family of four could afford this budget with an income of $9,076. Yet 54 per cent of all US families lived on less than this income and thus fell below what is in effect the poverty line. In 1973, $12,626 was needed for this budget, which was $600 more than the median family income. In 1977 the modest-but-adequate line was $17,106, considerably above the median income of $12,436 for families with one wage earner. The supposedly affluent factory worker who is not laid off or put on part-time during the year made, on the average, $8,600 in 1973, which was $4,000 less than the BLS modest budget.[6]

A large prosperous middle class has by no means replaced the struggling lower classes as the majority class. With more than half of the people living below the modest but adequate budget of the BLS, the underbelly of the US capitalist society is a deprived majority, just as it was fifty years ago. 'In advanced capitalist societies, the costs of staying out of poverty (i.e. of satisfying invariant subsistence needs) grows as the economy grows. Consequently, there is no long-term tendency in advanced capitalist societies for the incidence of poverty to decrease significantly as the economy grows.'[7] The economic inequality of US society is not just relative inequality, for it is an inequality that means deprivation for a sizeable chunk of the society.

2. OWNERSHIP AND PRODUCTIVITY

There are several strategies used by spokespersons of the ruling class to defend the situation of inequality described above. The first defence rests on the rights of ownership. The second rests on the need for inequality in order to increase productivity. In the next section, a third strategy will be discussed: it rests on the notion of a fair wage.

According to the *first defence* of inequality, those who have put their hard-earned money into a business enterprise have the right to appropriate the fruits of that enterprise and divide them according to their own decisions. Thus the product that workers have made is controlled by owners and not by the workers. Owners are within their rights to divide the product in such a way that inequality is great and poverty widespread. An entire web of ideology has been woven on this basic frame of the rights of ownership. Part of that web is the system of law, backed by police force, entitling the owner to the fruits of the worker. From the perspective of members of the working class, there are several holes in this defence. These holes show that what is built on the frame of ownership rights is indeed only ideology.

On the one hand, if ownership rights lead to continued inequality and poverty, then from a working-class perspective there simply are no such rights. The attitude that ownership of the means of production is sacred merely protects the owners at the expense of those who suffer the resulting inequality. A right is more than such an attitude; it must be justified and indeed justified from a class standpoint. Economic inequality can be justified by ownership rights only if there are such rights. There may well be such rights from the perspective of the ruling class. Yet the continued inequality and poverty resulting from ownership are evidence favouring the view that relative to the working class owners have no legitimate right to the fruits of enterprise.

On the other hand, the basis given for the justification of the owner's right to the fruits of enterprise is not adequate. That basis was the hard work of the investor. Investment, however, is an on-going process in a viable firm. The initial investment is followed by many subsequent investments. Let us grant that the owner has worked hard — whether in the form of the honest toil of the self-employed person or in the form of the forcible plunder of the syndicated criminal — to accumulate the initial investment. But when the plant is rebuilt or expanded, the new investment will be possible only because of the hard work of the workers. Once new investment has been made, there is no longer the same basis for saying that the original owner has the right to control the entire product of the new investment. The logic of 'hard work' applies here too. If the owner worked hard to accumulate the initial investment, it is equally true that the workers worked hard to make the new investment possible. Thus, in a viable firm, the workers should, on the logic of hard work, have a right to appropriate an ever increasing share of the product. The capitalist's own logic backfires!

A modified version of the hard-work defence of inequality has been devised by economists. According to it *both* the contribution of the capitalist *and* that of the worker to the production of a commodity have to be recognized. By measuring what each contributes, one can say what share of the product each should get. The shares will in fact be such that inequality and poverty result. But, according to the modified defence, this arrangement is perfectly just since deserts are strictly according to contributions.

The theory behind this modified defence has recently been shown to be untenable.[8] Very simply, the theory is circular. How does one measure the contribution of the capitalist to determine the capitalist's share of the product? One can do this, according to the theory, by finding out how much added units of capital increase the value of the entire product. But this requires that different kinds of capital goods have a price so that units of capital can be compared. The prices of capital goods do not just drop from the blue. They are determined, it turns out, by the ratio of wages to profits. Here is where the circularity comes in. For wages and profits are precisely the shares going to workers and owners. The defence of unequal shares on the basis of unequal contributions is worthless since it must resort to explaining unequal contributions in terms of unequal shares.

According to the *second defence* of inequality, significant inequality with poverty at the bottom is a necessary condition for making the society as affluent as it is. In a widely published newspaper article entitled 'Morality and the Pursuit of Wealth' appearing in July 1974, the President of the US Chamber of Commerce, Arch Booth, said the realization of equality by the transfer of wealth from the haves to the have-nots would lessen the 'work incentive of the most productive members of society' and endanger 'the ability of the economic system to accumulate capital for new productive facilities'. Booth's solution is to let the rich keep on investing in productive facilities thereby increasing the share the poor get through better wages and higher employment.

There is one glaring fallacy in this argument. It is the logical fallacy of an 'incomplete disjunction'. The disjunction Booth offers us is that *either* we have a forced redistribution of income within capitalism *or* we let the income of the non-owners rise naturally by increasing investment. But the disjunction needs to be expanded to include at least one more alternative: beyond capitalism, it is possible to expand productive facilities through the investment of collective rather than of private capital. In one form of collective ownership, workers would manage the investment of collective capital in order to advance their interests. In this case, the inequality in both wealth and income needed for growth under private capitalism becomes unnecessary. Without significant inequality, private capitalism would lack the centres of economic power needed to put large amounts of labour to work in order to produce a surplus for growth. The model here for a system of collective ownership of the means of production is not that of nationalized industry run by a bunch of officials who are not controlled by workers. This would be the bureaucratic model found in places like the USSR which are no longer private capitalist societies. Rather, the model is that of a workers' democracy in which democracy extends down to the workplace and in which workplaces are coordinated by a council of representatives from each. This socialist alternative is sufficient to make Booth's disjunction incomplete.

But why do we need such a third alternative? The reason is that Booth's two do not solve the problem of poverty. He is demonstrably wrong in holding that continuing to invest will eliminate poverty. As was pointed out in Section 1, growth under capitalism makes staying out of poverty increasingly more difficult. But he is absolutely correct in holding that taking from the rich to equalize economic status will reduce the ability of those still left with wealth to expand productive facilities significantly. Thus sticking with the two alternatives advanced by Booth gives a depressing conclusion: the only way to increase production in order to overcome society-wide scarcity leads to chronic inequality and poverty. This conclusion would be inescapable were it not for a third alternative like the socialist alternative uncovered when asking whether Booth's disjunction was complete.

A workers' democracy can afford greater equality and an elimination of poverty while at the same time increasing productive facilities. It can do this because investments in productive facilities are made from wealth that is not just produced by but also managed by the workers rather than by a ruling minority. If investment is made with private capital, there will be economic stagnation where there is not great inequality. Moreover, where investment is made with private capital and hence for private capital, investment slows down, whatever the human need for it, when profits fall. There is, then, not only chronic inequality and poverty but also a periodic recurrence of shortages of the supply of goods to meet survival needs.

In a workers' democracy all of this is changed. (a) Since capital is collectively controlled by workers, the surplus produced is controlled by those producing it. There is, then, no need for an unequal economic power, as there is when people have to be put to work to produce a surplus they will not control. (b) Eliminating poverty will not result in a setback to constructive growth. In the first place, the vast production of waste items — war materials, luxuries for the rich, advertising — needed to stabilize the system of private profits will be rechannelled into production for the satisfaction of survival needs. This will go a long way toward eliminating poverty. In the second place, poverty is a drain on the productive potential of those caught in it. This potential will be released for producing even more social wealth. (c) The full productive capacity of industry can be employed without the capitalist's fear of driving the rate of profit down. So long as the products of industry provide a basis for making people and plants more productive, there is, in a workers' democracy, no reason to run industry at much less than full capacity. By contrast, capitalist industry slows down when people cannot buy more, not when people do not need more. In short, in a workers' democracy, relative equality, the absence of poverty, and the expansion of means to satisfy needs are compatible goals.

3. A FAIR WAGE

A *third strategy* for defending the inequality and the poverty that is to be found today in the US introduces the concept of compensation for work. The defence is that labour is sold on the free market and, on the whole, the free market determines a *just* price for things. Thus, since inequality and poverty are, in part, a result of the free market for labour, there is no *right* to economic equality or even to a 'modest budget'. A free market must not involve the use of power by those who exchange their goods and services within it to coerce those with whom they exchange.

This argument seems to leave open the possibility that wages should mount and thus that the worker should come closer to the owner in economic status. But in fact this possibility is not open. As pointed out in Section 1, the range of inequality and the degree of poverty in the US have remained remarkably constant. The majority of the people are at or below the level of existence provided by the modest budget. Because of the greater power and organization of the owning class, the wages and salaries of workers remain at a level that allows them merely to perform their jobs well and to raise a new generation of workers. (Differences between the wages of, say, industrial and clerical workers need to be viewed against the background of a general pull toward this subsistence level.) To perform well and to reproduce themselves they have been forced to purchase the ever more elaborate and hence more expensive means of satisfying survival needs and the needs specific to their jobs. Short-term variations in the supply of and demand for labour are only part of this long-term pattern of compensating workers at a subsistence level. At this level, there is nothing much left over for savings and investments that might narrow the gap between them and the owning class. The BLS's moderate but adequate budget is the changing upper limit of the subsistence wage. So long as the owning class is a ruling class, workers' compensation will be held under this limit.

It is not, then, the free market that determines this long-term level of wages. This level is determined by the power of the owning class. The market only provides variations on it. From the perspective of the owning class, a wage that provides a subsistence appropriate to a worker of a given kind is a fair wage. It is a fair wage precisely because, on the one hand, higher wages would erode profits, and, on the other hand, lower wages would destroy the possibility of having the healthy, well trained, and contented workforce needed for production. The appeal to the free market is only a veil for these interests of the owning class. Ruling-class interest and the power at its disposal, not the free job market, allows the owners to call a wage fair that insures inequality.

What, then, is a fair wage from the perspective of the working class? Suppose we are calves who face the prospect of going to slaughter as one-year olds. The farmers who send us to slaughter find that this is the age at which to realize a maximum profit on us. So one year is the 'fair' time, from the perspective of the farmers, for calves to enjoy themselves before slaughter. An inquisitive calf poses the question, 'What is the true "fair" time for cattle to live before slaughter? Is it two years, or even three?' A selfish calf who has no regard for the farmer and the future of cattle farming generally shouts, 'Stop quibbling; we should demand a moratorium on beef eating. An end to the slaughter of cattle!' Similarly, Marx said that the slogan, 'A fair day's wage for a fair day's work!' should be replaced by the slogan, 'An end to the wage system!'[9] Instead of the wage system, work should be done in such a way that the workers' compensation is not just a function of the greater power of a non-working ruling class.

The wage system is a system that in advanced industrial countries has been central to the domination of lower classes by a ruling class. Through that system people are set to work in order to preserve or increase the control of wealth by and, thus, the power of a minority class. They are thus given from what they produce only what is needed to reproduce their labour. When part of the product of workers is used in this way to perpetuate and strengthen the domination of a non-working class, workers are properly said to be 'exploited'. Acceptance of the wage system and plans to reform it from within do not face up to the key role wages play in domination. When workers themselves decide how they are to be compensated out of what they produce, the wage system has ceased to exist and along with it exploitation.

The struggle of workers for higher income under capitalism is no less important because of all this. But it must be placed in a proper perspective. The struggle is important because without it workers would gain less in prosperity and lose more in recession than would be necessary and the ranks of the unemployed would swell beyond their chronically high bounds. But two things must be remembered. The *first* is that this struggle is not aiming at a wage that is 'fair' in an absolute way. The idea that there is such a thing as an absolute fair wage implies that within the wage system there is some point at which a proper division can be made of the fruits of enterprise between owners and workers. That there is no such point is clear since we are not dealing with classes whose aims can eventually be harmonized but with classes whose inner historical needs are in conflict on the very point of wages themselves.

The *second* thing is that the struggle for higher income begins the organization of people for the collective action that is needed to abolish the wage system itself. This long-term perspective has for some time been forgotten by trade unions everywhere. Their leaders advocate accommodation with the existing system of domination of working people. These leaders talk about a fair wage but they mean only the wages and benefits they think they can wheedle out of the owners. Their conception of fairness and of rights is no longer a class conception. A class conception makes overthrowing the wage system a right of working people.

4. A JUST DISTRIBUTION

Let us leave defences of present economic inequality and take up a proposal for limiting inequality. If capitalist arguments justifying present inequality fail, then where is the line to be drawn for an acceptable degree of inequality? Our problem is how to distribute a product that has come about through the combined efforts of people in different roles. Since isolated producers are the exception, we cannot start with the assumption that there is a product to which an individual producer is 'entitled' because he or she is 'responsible' for that product.[10] In deciding on a principle of just distribution there are two factors to be considered.

On the one hand, there is the average amount of goods per individual in the population, and, on the other hand, there is the degree of inequality with which goods are actually parcelled out to individuals. Increasing the average amount of goods per individual might increase the inequality of distribution, whereas decreasing the inequality in distribution might decrease the average per individual. In capitalism we saw that inequality of wealth is a condition of economic growth. Also, inequality of income within the working class weakens solidarity, making possible a greater surplus and hence greater growth. If strict equality means poverty all around, we might recoil from strict equality and look for a balance between a large average amount and considerable equality. But so far we have no clue as to where to strike this balance.

John Rawls has recently proposed an interesting way of balancing a high average amount of goods with a low degree of inequality.[11] The idea is that we are to avoid demanding such a low degree of inequality that the worst off are penalized by getting less than they would with a higher degree of inequality. We are to avoid only those high degrees of inequality that are arrived at by preventing the worst off from getting the most they could get.

Rawls formulated this in his Principle of Difference which tells us to 'maximize the expectations of the least favoured position'. If what goes to the most favoured could have gone to the least favoured without reducing the expectations of future goods coming to the least favoured, then it should indeed go to the least favoured. Maximizing the goods that go to the least favoured group has, then, the effect of preventing the kind of drop in the average amount of goods that would cause general deprivation. At the same time, it has the effect of preventing excessive inequality, since distribution to the well off is limited by maximizing the expectations of the least well off. We have the best of both worlds — a higher level of affluence than with excessive egalitarianism and a lower level of inequality than with less benefits for the worst off. A beacon seems to have been lighted for the groping reformers!

Without denying the brilliance of this suggestion, it is well to insert two cautionary remarks concerning any distribution scheme that leads to reform of present inequality. The *first* remark takes us back to historical materialism. . . . It is that Rawls talks about distribution without relating it to production. He assumes wrongly that the validity of his principle is absolute, rather than relative to circumstances within production. Marx criticized the Social Democracy for its failure to consider that,

> The distribution of the means of consumption at any time is only a consequence of the conditions of production themselves. . . . Vulgar socialism (and from it in turn a section of democracy) has taken over from the bourgeois economists the consideration and treatment of distribution as independent of the mode of production and hence the presentation of socialism as turning principally on distribution.[12]

But Rawls has a blueprint for distribution considered in abstraction from any mode of production.

In what kind of organization of human and material potential to overcome scarcity will such a distribution scheme be practical? One thing is certain: in capitalist society there is not the least chance that the Rawlsian scheme could be put into practice. The reason is simply that the organization of production in a capitalist society centres around increasing productive facilities through the making of profits. The class of owners would not advance the interests characteristic of their class by agreeing to maximize the expectations of the least favoured. Given its power, this class would block the realization of the scheme.

Suppose, though, that some mode of production would allow for distribution in accordance with the Principle of Difference. Should not one simply choose to bring about such a mode of production? Certainly — if the Principle of Difference is valid. But its validity is relative to production in the following way. Validity in general is relative to classes, and classes are essential roles in a given mode of production. One should, then, choose to realize the principle only if it is valid relative to one's class. Nonetheless, that class might have to change the existing mode of production in order to realize the new distribution. Even though the capitalist mode of production excludes the application of the Principle of Difference, it may be a valid principle for one of the lower classes within capitalism.

A distributional plan is not just because it is elegant or intuitive but because it answers to needs arising in production. Not only the actual but also the just distribution is dependent on production.

The *second* remark on Rawls' Principle of Difference concerns its relation to the lower classes. Can it function as an ideal for the lower classes? After all, the whole trade-union struggle for higher wages and better working conditions seems to point to the fact that the working class is dedicated to maximizing its expectations, even if this cannot be accomplished within the capitalist system. But there is a fatal difficulty. There is one thing better for the least advantaged than working to maximize the expectations of the group of the least advantaged. That is their working to change the group from being least advantaged. The least advantaged — however this group is delimited — has, as a group, a right to move out of the position of being least advantaged. 'The last shall be first and the first last.'[13]

Moving out of the position of being least advantaged has two possible implications. *Either* some other group is placed in the category of least advantaged. To maintain its advantage the newly advantaged group cannot allow groups under it to maximize their expectations. The situation then reproduces that of the old order. *Or* all groups become equally advantaged relative to their needs, ending the system of differential advantages. The possibility for maximizing the advantages of the least advantaged comes only when there are no longer any advantaged groups to be protected by not maximizing the advantages of the least advantaged.

Thus the Principle of Difference cannot be realized so long as there are differences in advantages and is irrelevant once differences in advantages have been abolished. But it would be utopian to put strict equality on the immediate agenda. The equal satisfaction of needs is an ideal that we can choose to realize only down the road within a fully developed democratic organization of production that has little resemblance either to private capitalist or to bureaucratic organizations of production.

Notes

1. Gabriel Kolko, *Wealth and Power in America*, Praeger, New York, 1962, p. 108.

2. These data are based on tables in Kolko, *Wealth and Power in America*, p. 14, and in Frank Ackerman and Andrew Zimbalist, 'Capitalism and inequality in the United States', in *The Capitalist System*, 2nd ed., p. 298.

3. Kolko, *Wealth and Power in America*, Ch. II, and Ackerman and Zimbalist 'Capitalism and inequality in the United States', in *The Capitalist System*, 2nd ed., p. 303. In Sweden, by contrast, taxes change the ratio of the bottom third to that of the top third from 38 to 48 per cent.

4. Lititia Upton and Nancy Lyons, *Basic Facts: Distribution of Personal Income and Wealth in the United States*, Cambridge Institute, 1878 Massachusetts Ave., Cambridge, Mass., 1972, p. 6, and Ackerman and Zimbalist, 'Capitalism and inequality in the United States', in *The Capitalist System*, 2nd ed., p. 301.

5. Upton and Lyons, *Basic Facts*, p. 31.

6. Arnold Cantor, 'The widening gap of incomes', *The AFL-CIO American Federationist*, March 1975.

7. Bernard Gendron, 'Capitalism and poverty', *Radical Philosophers' Newsjournal*, 4, January 1975, p. 13. This essay appears as Ch. XII of Gendron's *Technology and the Human Condition*, St. Martin's Press, New York, 1977.

8. A major piece in this exciting but technical attack on capitalist economics is P. Garegnani's 'Heterogeneous capital, the production function, and the theory of distribution', in *A Critique of Economic Theory* eds. E. K. Hunt and G. Schwartz, Penguin, Harmondsworth, 1972, pp. 245–291.

9. Karl Marx, *Wages, Price, and Profit* (1865), Foreign Language Press, Peking, 1970, Ch. XIV.

10. On entitlement, see Robert Nozick, *Anarchy, State, and Utopia*, Basic Books, New York, 1974, Ch. VII.

11. Rawls, *A Theory of Justice*, pp. 78–80.

12. Karl Marx, *Critique of the Gotha Programme* (1875), ed. C. P. Dutt, International Publishers, New York, 1970, pp. 10–11.

13. Matthew 20: 16.

◆ ◆ ◆

DISCUSSION QUESTIONS

1. Which of Feinberg's five principles should govern how a society's wealth is distributed?

2. Imagine yourself in Rawls's "original position," choosing from behind a "veil of ignorance." Would you agree to the two principles that he develops?

3. Some thinkers have objected to Rawls's attempt to generate such an important ethical principle as justice by using such a contrary-to-fact presupposition as the original position. Do you approve of Rawls's strategy?

4. Does Nozick's example using Wilt Chamberlain prove what the author claims it does?

5. Fisk offers several arguments against the economic inequality in the United States. How persuasive are they?

CASE 3.1

The Distribution of Wealth

A critical issue in evaluating the ethical character of an economic system is the relative distribution of burdens and benefits among the members of a society. Capitalism regularly produces a wide gap between the richest and the poorest members of the economy — something its foes are quick to criticize.

Throughout most of the twentieth century, the distribution of family income has been relatively constant with the top 20 percent holding 40 – 45 percent and the bottom 20 percent holding 4 – 6 percent. The specific breakdown in 1989 was

highest quintile	46.7%
second quintile	24.0%
third quintile	15.9%
fourth quintile	9.6%
bottom quintile	3.9%

In the same year, the distribution of income levels was as follows:

Income Level	*Percentage of Households*
$75,000 and over	7.4
$50,000 –$74,999	13.4
$35,000 –$49,999	17.3
$25,000 –$34,999	16.0
$15,000 –$24,999	18.6
$10,000 –$14,999	10.3
$5,000 –$9,999	10.8
Under $5,000	6.2

Median family income was $28,906.

Differences in wealth, however, are not necessarily unethical in themselves. Conservative economists claim that such differences actually foster the general good as benefits "trickle down" from rich to poor in the form of increased investment and spending that spur production and create jobs. And, as you know from your reading in this chapter, John Rawls argues that "while the distribution of wealth and income need not be equal, it must be to everyone's advantage." Does our uneven distribution of wealth satisfy enough conditions to be ethically justifiable?

You be the judge of that. Over the last fifteen years, the richest 5 percent of the population (those families with incomes over $102,000) saw their incomes grow nearly 60 percent, after adjusting for inflation. The top 1 percent experienced an increase of more than 100 percent. By contrast, the income of the bottom 60 percent of the population decreased approximately 15 percent after inflation through the same period. And to make matters worse, the poverty rate increased to more than 13 percent of the population —32 million people. (In this context, *poverty* is defined as a family of four receiving less than $13,359 a year, that is, less than 40 percent of the country's median income.) Apparently, few benefits trickled down to either the poor or even the middle class.

It also seems that groups discriminated against in the past continue to be disproportionately represented at the low end of the economic spectrum. White households have approximately twice the income of black households and ten times the wealth (savings, real estate, automobiles, stocks, bonds, and other assets). Twenty percent of all children in the United States live in poverty, but 50 percent of all black children under the age of six live in poverty. Even higher education, a traditional path out of poverty, did not always help blacks. Despite having a college degree, one out of three black male graduates and one

out of two black female graduates earned poverty wages in 1987. It is difficult to
see, then, how the good fortune of those at the top of the economy was to
everyone's advantage.

Perhaps the best way to evaluate the current distribution of wealth is to
consider whether the dollars are spread around in a way that allows everyone,
or at least the average person, to live a reasonably comfortable life. One way to
do this is to determine how far the income of an average family goes. What
kind of life does the median family income — something less than $30,000 —
allow? Take that figure as your starting point and see how well it covers the
following expenses. Keep in mind, however, that when you work with the
median family income, you are looking at a figure that is higher than that
earned by 50 percent of the population.

Gross Income	*$30,000*
Taxes	_____
Housing	
Rent	_____
Furnishings	
Utilities	_____
Food	_____
Clothing	_____
Transportation	
Car payments	_____
Insurance	_____
Maintenance and gas	_____
Health expenses	
Medical and dental	_____
Insurance	_____
Miscellaneous	
Education	_____
Life insurance	_____
Entertainment	_____
Vacation	_____
Gifts	_____
Personal	_____
Debt (loans, credit cards)	_____
Savings	_____

Discussion Questions

1. What do your calculations and all of the statistics suggest to you?
2. Is the current distribution of wealth ethically justifiable? If so, how do
you account for poverty and how should it be handled? If not, what can be done
about it that would be morally defensible?

Sources

"America's Income Gap: The Closer You Look, The Worse It Gets," *Business Week*, April 17, 1989, 78–79.

Pear, Robert, "Rich Got Richer in 80's; Others Held Even," *New York Times*, January 11, 1991, A1, A20.

"The Rich Are Richer—And America May Be the Poorer," *Business Week*, November 18, 1991, 85, 88.

U.S. Bureau of the Census, *Current Population Reports*, series P-60, Nos. 166 and 168.

"The Widening Income Gap," *Business Week*, January 15, 1990, 16.

CASE 3.2

Executive Salaries

As we just saw, a broad view of the economy reveals considerable differences in wealth. Not surprisingly, similar differences appear within individual companies with executives at the top making much more money than the workers at the bottom. How do these differences fare from an ethical point of view?

In 1990, the average chief executive officer (CEO) of an American corporation received anywhere from $500,000 to $2 million in compensation (salary, bonus, stock options, etc.). The median figure was $1.7 million—approximately 50 percent more than Japanese CEOs and nearly twice as much as Canadian, British, and German executives. As high as this seems, however, it pales in comparison to the amounts received by the most highly paid CEOs: $18.3 million by UAL's Stephen Wolf, $16.7 million by Apple Computer's John Sculley, and $14.8 million by Paul Fireman of Reebok. Yet even this is not as steep as it gets. In 1987 Charles Lazarus of Toys R Us received $60 million. Two years later Michael Eisner of Walt Disney received $40 million. In 1990 the special conditions of two mergers produced bonanzas for Time Warner's Steven Ross ($78.1 million) and LIN Broadcasting's Donald Pels ($186.2 million).

It is difficult to know how to assess such salaries from an ethical perspective. With family income averaging $30,000, there is little question that CEO salaries far outstrip those of most people in corporations. Yet if these CEOs are responsible for generating new jobs and high profits for the entire organization, such huge compensation packages would seem to be deserved. Is there a close connection between pay and performance? Here we get a mixed picture. The companies of some highly paid CEOs do poorly, while the companies of more modestly paid executives do quite well—the two biggest names the athletic shoe business, Nike and Reebok, are an example. During 1988–1990, Nike's Philip Knight received $1 million while his company and shareholders did extremely well. Reebok's Fireman, by contrast, received $40.9 million as the company lost its number one spot to Nike and repaid investors less well than did its rival. Similarly, Lee Iacocca received a 25 percent raise in 1990 at the same time that Chrysler's earnings fell 79 percent. In general, the picture is not reassuring. Corporate profits rose 78 percent over the last decade, but CEO compensation increased 212 percent.

In addition to asking whether such high salaries are deserved, we can ask whether they are fair to all concerned. That is, how does the income of the CEO compare with that of other people in the organization? The average CEO earns 70 to 80 times that of the average worker, and the $18 million received by UAL's Wolf is 1,200 times that of the salary of a new flight attendant. The president of the United States, by comparison, earns 25 times more than someone earning the federal minimum wage. German CEOs make 23 times and Japanese CEOs 17 times what the average worker earns.

Some American companies, however, do have policies that limit the difference between the top and bottom of the pay scales. Office furniture manufacturer Herman Miller has a limit of 20 times the average salary of a factory worker at the firm. Ben & Jerry's Ice Cream goes even lower, not allowing top salaries to rise more than seven times that of the lowest salaries. At what point does the difference become too much?

Another question of fairness is raised by the fact that the difference in earnings between the lowest and highest paid employees has steadily increased. In 1960, CEOs generally made 40 times more than the average worker. But during the 1980s, CEO compensation rose by 212 percent, while the salary of factory workers increased by a significantly lower 53 percent. Critics of the high salaries also point to the fact that CEOs frequently receive raises at the same time that workers are being laid off. In 1991, for example, defense contractor General Dynamics reduced its 86,000 person work force by 12,000 because of lower defense spending. Yet the top 25 executives of the company shared $18 million in bonuses tied to an increase in the stock price. ◆

Discussion Questions

1. What is your reaction to all of this? How do you evaluate CEO compensation from an ethical perspective?

2. Do CEOs deserve salaries that are higher than everyone else's in the company? How much higher?

3. How do you determine how much more valuable one person is than another in the company? In a free market economy, does it even make sense to suggest that anyone is making too much money? Isn't it simply a function of market forces — in this case, the labor market?

4. Isn't executive talent in short supply? Doesn't it take special skills to be a chief executive officer? Shouldn't those skills be rewarded?

Sources

"CEO Pay Envelopes Are Lighter North of the Border," *Business Week*, June 24, 1991, 26.

Cox, Craig, and Sally Power, "Executive Pay: How Much Is Too Much?," *Business Ethics*, 5 no. 5 (September – October 1991), 18 – 24.

"The Flap over Executive Pay," *Business Week*, May 6, 1991, 90 – 96.

"How CEO Paychecks Got So Unreal," *Business Week*, November 18, 1991, 20, 24.

"Layoffs on the Line, Bonuses in the Executive Suite," *Business Week*, October 21, 1991, 34.

Uchitelle, Louis, "No Recession for Executive Pay," *New York Times*, March 18, 1991, D1, D10.

"Where U.S. CEOs Have Foreign Rivals Beat: Paychecks," *Business Week*, February 5, 1990, 18.

◆ ◆ ◆

ADDITIONAL READINGS

Arthur, John, and William H. Shaw, eds., *Justice and Economic Distribution* (Englewood Cliffs, NJ: Prentice Hall, 1978).

Bowie, Norman, *Towards a New Theory of Distributive Justice* (Amherst: University of Massachusetts Press, 1971).

Daniels, Norman, ed., *Reading Rawls: Critical Studies of a Theory of Justice* (New York: Basic Books, 1976).

Held, Virginia, *Property, Profits and Economic Justice* (Belmont, CA: Wadsworth Publishing, 1980).

Kipnis, Kenneth, and Diana T. Meyers, *Economic Justice* (Totowa, NJ: Rowman & Littlefield, 1985.)

Paul, Jeffrey, ed., *Reading Nozick: Essays on Anarchy, State and Utopia* (Totowa, NJ: Rowman & Littlefield, 1981).

Stewart, Robert M., ed., *Readings in Social and Political Philosophy* (New York: Oxford University Press, 1986).

CHAPTER 4

◆ ◆ ◆

Work and Human Well-Being

As much as questions related to distributive justice and the nature of business pose ethical challenges to the very essence of capitalism, no less a challenge surfaces when we consider the concept of *work*. The popular attitude about work is probably that it is best avoided: "The best work is no work." But what we do with our productive energies is actually a critical element of human happiness and, therefore, significant from an ethical perspective. Some thinkers argue that capitalism extracts too high a price from our work life by forcing work to be designed in an intrinsically unsatisfying way. Are jobs that are so alienating that they make human happiness impossible the price we pay for the material prosperity we enjoy with capitalism? Do we have a right to meaningful work? Do we have a right to work of any sort?

A. R. Gini and T. Sullivan begin our consideration of work by claiming that satisfaction with life is closely related to satisfaction with work. E. F. Schumacher also sees work as both positive and necessary for human development. Schumacher's "Buddhist Economics" implies a powerful criticism of the way work is thought of in contemporary capitalism. The classic critic of work in the capitalist system, however, is Karl Marx. The famous Communist philosopher argues that capitalism's success depends on intrinsically unsatisfying labor, and his remarks about "alienated labor" and the "division of labor" strike at the heart of capitalism. Kai Nielsen echoes Marx with his brief account of alienation in the contemporary economy.

A. R. Gini and T. Sullivan
WORK: THE PROCESS AND THE PERSON

For the most of us, working is an entirely nondiscretionary activity, an inescapable and irreducible fact of existence. Work is, well, work – an activity required to sustain life. In its very worst light, work is seen as something evil, a punishment, the grindingly inevitable burden of toil laid, along with mortality, upon the human situation.[1] At best, work looms so large and problematic in most of our lives that we either take it for granted and forget about it or we actively suppress its significance on our lives. Work is simply *there*, as illness, death, taxes and mortage payments are there, something to be endured.[2] *Chicago Tribune* columnist Mike Royko accurately captures the spirit of the "common man's" feelings about work when his alter-ego in the column, Slats, says:

> . . . why do you think the lottery is so popular? Do you think anybody would play if the super payoff was a job on the night shift in a meat packing plant? People play it so if they win they can be rich and idle . . . like I told you years ago — if work is so good, how come they have to pay us to do it?[3]

The common laments against work, however, are not simply based on the fact that most of us are part of the captive work force and hence accept work as inevitable. In well over 100 studies in the last twenty-five years, workers have regularly depicted their jobs as physically exhausting, boring, psychologically diminishing or personally humiliating and unimportant.[4] Over 109 million people constitute the American work force. This vast army of workers labors in 25000 different full-time occupations, each of which defines its practitioners by income, education, social status, living standard and life style.[5] During the 1970s a great deal of attention was given to "workers' dissatisfaction", (i.e. "white-collar woes" and "blue-collar blues.") Indications are that the problems enumerated in the 1970s will not simply go away in the 1980s and 90s. Indeed, recent surveys indicate increasing job dissatisfaction as well as a direct increase in the commonality of complaints across the spectrum of occupations. The cry of uninteresting, unchallenging, non-stimulating, non-creative work is no longer the exclusive lament of the assembly line, lower status, blue-collar worker. Managers and laborers, office workers and mechanics can now be heard to chorus their disapproval of their occupations. While it is still the case that managers, overall, are more satisfied with their work than are clerical, hourly and piece-work employees, the distinctions and specific issues that once clearly separated management from all other types of employees are becoming blurred.[6]

The results of a 1979 survey published by the University of Michigan indicated that worker dissatisfaction was at its highest point in over a decade. Sixty percent of the workers surveyed wanted new jobs. Thirty-nine percent

From *Journal of Business Ethics* 6 (1987), 649–655. Copyright © 1987 by D. Reidel Publishing Co., Dordrecht, Holland and Boston, U.S.A. Reprinted by permission of Kluwer Academic Publishers.

132

thought they were underpaid. Thirty-six percent said they had unused skills. Thirty-six percent felt over-qualified for their jobs, and fifty-five percent wanted more time off. Unlike their parents' generation, contemporary workers do not see their jobs as a simple contract: A day's work for a day's pay. Labor-relations analyst John R. Browning has said, "Today's workers want much more. They want nothing less than eight hours of meaningful, skillfully guided, personally satisfying work for eight hours pay and that's not easy for most companies to provide."[7] In 1974, Daniel Yankelovich offered a limited but staggering statistic when he claimed that only one out of every five men (women were not included in the survey) feels that his work fills his psychological as well as economic needs.[8]

The question before us is "Why are so many people so unhappy in their work?" Simply put, the reason people don't like their jobs is that they have bad jobs, or to use E. F. Schumacher's term they have "bad work."

According to Schumacher, bad work is:

> Mechanical, artificial, divorced from nature, utilizing only the smallest part of man's potential capabilities; it sentences the great majority of workers to spending their working lives in a way which contains no worthy challenge, no stimulus to self perfection, no chance of development, no element of Beauty, Truth, or Goodness . . . [9]

For Schumacher one of the darkest aspects of contemporary work life is the existence of an appalling number of men and women condemned to work which has no connection with their inner lives, no spiritual meaning for them whatever. Bad work for Schumacher offers no opportunity for the individual to become more than he or she already is, offers no potential for growth, no sense of beauty and delight, no feelings of completeness and no sense of well-being.

Work for too many is perceived as down-time, something that has to be done, but seldom adding to who we are. Too many workers accurately talk of jobs as having nothing to do with their inner sense of self. Studs Terkel in his now classic *Working* tells us that work for many is a purely alien occupation. One of the people he interviewed remarked, "Unless a guy's a nut, he never thinks about or talks about it. Maybe about baseball or about getting drunk the other night or he got laid or he didn't get laid. I'd say one out of a hundred actually gets excited about work."[10]

To put Schumacher's argument into a more classical perspective, bad work alienates workers both from themselves and from their work. An alienated worker engages in activities that are not intrinsically rewarding, that might be demanding in some respects but permit little or no originality, no latitude and discretion and no sense of fulfillment and completion. Sociologist Robert Kahn suggests that for most workers the only choice is between no work (usually accompanied by severe economic penalties as well as a conspicuous lack of meaningful alternatives) or a job burdened with negative qualities (routine, compulsory scheduling, dependency etc.) In these circumstances, says Kahn, the individuals have no difficulty with their choice. They choose work as the only real alternative and then pronounce themselves moderately satisfied if not stimulated, enraptured or excited with what they do.[11] Some workers adjust to their tasks by viewing work in purely instrumental terms or as a means to other ends. George Strauss has pointed out that a significant number of workers deliberately take on high paying but boring jobs in order to support their real interests.[12] This is the kind of compromise that many people make. In essence what they say is: "I don't like what I do, but it allows me to do what I like."

These claims of disappointment and distress, however, seem to fly in the face of a study published in the mid-1950s and frequently replicated since then. In 1955 sociologists Nancy Morse and Robert S. Weiss of the University of Michigan's Survey Research Center published the results of a study of more than 400 men. They asked the question, "If by chance you inherited enough money to live comfortably without working, do you think you would work anyway?" The vast majority (80%) of all respondents replied positively even though the percentages were slightly higher for professional and lower white-collar workers (86%) than for the blue-collar workers (76%).[13]

At regular intervals over the next twenty-eight years this survey was expanded (both in numbers surveyed and by the inclusion of women) and repeated by various research organizations. The results of these follow-up surveys essentially reaffirmed the original survey results: the percentage of those choosing to work ranged from 67.4% (1969, University of Michigan), 71.5% (1977, University of Michigan), 73% (1974, Yankelovich, *The New Morality*) to 75% (1978, Renwich and Lawler).[14]

The most recent and perhaps the most comprehensive findings on this topic come from a group of researchers at the University of Kentucky in 1983. Of the 7281 adults polled nationwide, 74% of the men and 64% of the women surveyed said they would continue to work. While married men were more inclined than married women to say they would keep working, single men and women were equally likely to report that they would stick with it. Younger, better educated respondents with more prestigious jobs were more inclined to say that they would stay employed, compared with older individuals and less educated respondents. But the majority of all groups still reported that they would stay at work.[15]

The question before us now is "If so many people are so unhappy in their work, why, other than necessity, do people express a desire to work?" A practical response to this question is that one wants to work to occupy time, to have something, anything, to do to avoid the greater burden and stress of deadtime versus downtime. There is certainly, the pressure, when answering surveys, to give a socially acceptable answer. The ethic of generations tells us that we *ought* to want to work, that to admit to be willing to retire before one's time is to be somehow weak. Beyond that, however, is a deeper need to be fully occupied, to do good work or, failing that, any work. People want to work because they are intuitively aware that work, be it "bad" or "good," helps to shape them. It gives them a sense of direction and it allows for personal creativity and fulfillment.

The personal meaning of work is as important as its economic and social meaning. Where we live, how well we live, whom we see socially, what and where we consume and purchase, how we educate our children — all of these factors are dominated by the work we do to make a living.[16] While many people don't like their specific jobs, they want to work because they are aware at some level that work plays a crucial and perhaps unparalleled psychological role in the formation of human character. Work is not just a course of livelihood, it is also one of the most significant contributing factors to an inner life. And yet, as Schumacher points out, the question "what the work does to the worker," is seldom asked.[17] It is precisely this question on which I would like to focus attention. I want to examine what work does to and for us no matter what the nature of the product we produce by our labors.

People need to work. People must work to finish, define and refine their nature; work makes us human because we make something of ourselves through work. Even more than personal survival, mankind creates its own history through his work.[18] Sociologist Peter Berger has said "to be human and to work appear as inextricably intertwined notions."[19] In his earliest philosophical writings in the 1840s, Karl Marx defined the person as a worker. For Marx, persons acquire self-definition through labor. Work is the means by which we become unique individuals; we create ourselves in our work.[20] In Marx we can find full-scale analysis of the meaning of work in human development as well as what he saw as the distortion of this development in capitalistic society.

In the western world, Marx's critique of the work place, and its effect on the individual, gets lost in his overall analysis of capitalism and his attacks on bourgeois society. While many scholars feel that his writings are extremely critical of lay 19th century capitalism as a social political system, his real focus and purpose was an examination of the effects of work on the person and how the person affects work. A significant portion of his doctrine of historical materialism is devoted to his belief that the "material conditions of life" and specifically "the mode of production of the material means of existence" determine much else in human life, consciousness and society. For Marx, the essence of the human being rests upon their work:

> As individuals express their life (sic), so they are. What [individuals] . . . are . . . coincides with their production, both with what they produce and with how they produce. The nature of individuals thus depends on the material conditions determining their production.[21]

As Schumacher has pointed out in Marx's regard, it is a great error to overlook or to underestimate the effects of the "modes of production" upon people's lives. How people work and what they produce necessarily affects what they think and how they perceive their own sense of freedom and independence.[22] In other words, both the process and the product of our work help us to know who and what we are.

A somewhat unexpected but nonetheless important affirmation of Marx's overall thesis on work is Pope John Paul II's 1981 encyclical *Laborem exercens, On Human Work:*

> Man is made to be in the visible universe an image and likeness of God Himself, and he is placed in it in order to subdue the earth. From the beginning he is called to work. . . . Only man is capable of work, and only man works, at the same time by work occupying his existence on earth. Thus work bears a particular mark of man and of humanity, the mark of a person operating within a community of persons.[23]

That by labor or work man "occupies his existence on earth" means that mankind literally creates its own reality by virtue of work. In work mankind creates and defines the world, and in the process simultaneously becomes more human. According to the encyclical, the human world is not a simple given or a fixed thing. It is rather a "fact" continuously being produced by human labor. Work, the encyclical claims, is a good thing. It is good in the sense that is it useful or something to enjoy. It is good because it expresses and expands human dignity. Individuals not only transform nature, adopting it to their own needs through work, but they also achieve fulfillment as human beings and, in a sense, become "more a human being."[24] For Pope John Paul II it is through work that people constitute themselves as subjects of their own lives and, collectively, of their common history. He further emphasizes that what happens to the "subject of work" at work is more important than what "the work produces." The dignity and honor which work communicates to people is derived not from the "object achieved" but from the individual's "actual engagement" in the process, that is, from the labor of one's hands and mind. In the labor the transformation experienced by the subject is of greater value and importance than the object produced. "The preeminence of the subjective meaning of work over the objective one" is a principle that plays an important part in the reasoning of the entire encyclical. However true it may be that mankind is "destined for work" and "called to work" what must always be kept in clear perspective is that "work is for man and not man for work."[25]

Freud has written that at the very least work gives one "a secure place in the human community."[26] It is also the case that work helps establish the regularity of life, its basic rhythms and cycles of day, week, month and year. Without work, time patterns become confused, days are without pattern.[27] Further, work organizes, routinizes and structures our lives. It allows a safe outlet for our competitive strivings and often helps to keep us sane. More than this, as the German philosopher Martin Heidegger stated, "You are your projects."[28] In the vocabulary of metaphysics, Heidegger is implying that through "projects" (work) and the projection and continuation of these "projects" into the future, individuals posit their "being" in the world. Heidegger is suggesting that "You are what you do." Identity is largely a function of concerted action or productive achievement. We are known by others and we know and define ourselves primarily by the projects we devise, by the products we create and by the occupations which represent these productive pursuits. A person who cannot point to achievements does not and cannot feel like a full person. Subjective experience is simply too diffuse for self-identity. To say "I feel it" is not as definitive as to say "I did it." Nothing else in our lives can give us the sense of objective identity that work can.[29]

When psychiatrists and psychologists talk of "ego boundaries" they mean that a well-balanced people have clear perspectives on the limits and outlines of their own identities. They do not suffer from "boundary diffusion" and possess a clear sense of integrity and continuity. For most of us, the primary source of life's labels and "ego boundaries" is our work. In work we come both to know ourselves and orient ourselves to the external world. Work allows us to establish a "coherent web of expectations" of the rhythm, direction and definition of our lives.[30] Self-definition implies the ability to feel contained within precise outlines. The more descriptive we can be about ourselves the greater our sense of self-definition. Nothing is so uniquely personal, so active a representation of individuals as their skills and works.[31] To use Gregory Baum's handsome phrase, "labor is the axis of human self-making." Work is a necessary attribute of the human personality. Work molds the person and work is the mark of a person. To work is an act of personal freedom, self-assertion, self-fulfillment and self-realization.

If there is a congruence between personality and work, then a partial explanation of why people need good work can be found in ways people respond psychologically to the stimuli of work. It is well established that work stress can lead to physical illness, especially heart disease, and ulcers — as well as to alcoholism, drug addiction, and a host of psychosomatic ailments. However, the impact of routine or subjectively boring work is less clear and somewhat difficult to measure. A high percentage of people who do objectively routine work report having happy and uncomplicated home lives, but there are enough who do not that statistical studies point to a direct correlation between routine, low skilled work and off-the-job dissatisfaction. These studies imply that at the level of mental health, interesting work is a requirement of adult life. The underlying thesis here is one borrowed from the philosopher Adina Schwartz. According to Schwartz, when persons work for considerable lengths of time at jobs that involve repetitive mechanical activity, they tend to be made less capable of, and less interested in, rationally and independently framing, pursuing and adjusting their own plans during the rest of their non-work time. They thereby lead less autonomous, less interesting and less fulfilling lives.[32]

This thesis is echoed in recent longitudinal studies. In one such study Melvin L. Kohn and Carmi Schooler argue that there is a reciprocal relationship between the substantial complexity of work and intellectual flexibility. Their data indicate that "current job demands affect current thinking processes. . . . If two men of equivalent intellectual flexibility were to start their careers in jobs differing in substantive complexity, the man in the more complex job would be likely to outstrip the other in further intellectual growth."[33] A direct implication of Kohn and Schooler's research is that routine and boring jobs do not simply prevent persons from acting autonomously while at work, but that they also hinder us from developing the intellectual abilities that we must have in order to rationally pursue plans during non-work time. Routine jobs cause persons to be less inclined, in all aspects of their lives, to engage in the purposeful striving that is characteristic of autonomous individuals. Kohn and Schooler conclude that jobs tend to determine personalities more than personalities determine jobs.

Arthur Kornhauser's classic *Mental Health of the Industrial Worker: A Detroit Study*, speaks to this point:

> . . . factory employment, especially in routine production tasks, does give evidence of extinguishing workers' ambition, initiative, and purposeful directions towards life goals. . . . The unsatisfactory mental health of working people consists in no small measure of their dwarfed desires and deadened initiative, reduction of their goals and restriction of their efforts to a point where life is relatively empty and only half meaningful.[34]

Kornhauser's study of the Detroit automobile worker concludes that mental health at work, like job satisfaction, varies according to status. "Mental health is poorer among factory workers as we move from skilled, responsible, varied types of work to jobs lower in those respects."[35] Kornhauser also concluded that mental health was low among those workers who felt that they had no chance to use their abilities.[36] It was suggested that low-grade work caused lowered self-esteem, discouragement, futility, and feelings of failure and inferiority in contrast to a sense of personal growth and self-fulfillment resulting from more varied, responsible, challenging undertakings that afford opportunity to develop and use one's ideas and skills.[37]

The point here is that given what you do, you cannot avoid being who you are. I take it to be the case that each person, having chosen a job, shapes its content. And to a greater or lesser extent the content of the job shapes the person. Not only are we affected by what we do; we tend to become what we do. A person's activities determine self-identity, and in western culture paid employment is, rightly or wrongly, the main activity by which we define and assess ourselves and others.[38]

I think it is true that only a statistical minority of the work force is able to find meaning in work beyond the basic reward of the pay check.[39] Nevertheless, satisfaction with life seems to be related to satisfaction on the job.[40] The quality of our lives is dependent on the quality of the work we do — those who are unhappy with their jobs are also likely to be unhappy with life in general. Moreover, to be denied work is to be denied far more than the things that work can buy; it is to be denied the ability to define and respect one's self; and it is to be denied a basic and primary organizing principle in life. As Theodore Roszak quite correctly points out — "the doing is as important as what gets done, the making as valuable as the made."[41]

Good work is the ideal, but clearly good work is hard to find. Perhaps the only realistic compromise available to most of us is to find and embellish whatever good is possible in our work. As individuals we must find work that is good for us, as a society we must create work that is good for individuals. No matter how optimistic the technological forecasts for the future, there is no real possibility that work itself will become obsolete and unnecessary. The challenge will be to make it available and fulfilling.[42] Employment must have meaning beyond the trading of labor for money. If the pursuit of happiness is a good, not to say an inalienable right, then happiness must be sought in the way we spend our days. It quite clearly cannot be attained in the face of eight daily hours of misery and the converse appears more likely to be true; i.e. to be happy in our work is to be happy. The conclusion remains Marx's dictum, "As individuals express their life (sic), so they are."

Notes

1. 'What Is the Point of Working?' *Time Magazine*, May 11, 1981, pp. 93, 94.
2. Lee Braude, *Work and Workers: A Sociological Analysis* (New York: Praeger Publications, 1975), p. 3.
3. Mike Royko, 'Silver Spoons Fits, Why Not Wear It?", *Chicago Tribune*, November 11, 1985, Sect. I, p. 3.
4. *Work in America: Report of a Special Task Force to the Secretary of Health Education and Welfare* (Cambridge Mass.: MIT press, 1980), p. 13.
5. Melvin Kranzberg, Joseph Gies, *By the Sweat of Their Brow — Work in the Western World* (New York: G. P. Putnam's, 1975), p. 4.
6. One of the most important surveys to directly deny this contention is: M. R. Cooper, B. S. Morgan, P. M. Foley, and L. B. Kaplan, 'Changing Employee Values: Deepening Discontent?', *Harvard Business Review*, Jan/Feb. 1979, pp. 117–125.

7. 'New Breed of Workers', *U.S. News and World Report*, September 3, 1979, pp. 35, 36.

8. Daniel Yankelovich, 'The Meaning of Work', in *The Worker and the Job: Coping with Change*, ed. Jerome M. Rosow (Englewood Cliffs: Prentice Hall, Inc., 1974), pp. 44, 45.

9. E. F. Schumacher, *Good Work* (New York: Harper Colophan Books, 1980), p. 27.

10. Studs Terkel, *Working* (New York: Pantheon Books, 1974), p. xxxiv.

11. Robert L. Kahn, 'The Meaning of Work: Interpretations and Proposals for Measurement', in *The Human Meaning of Social Change*, ed. Angus Campbell, Philip Converse (New York: Basic Books, 1972).

12. George Strauss, 'Workers: Attitudes and Adjustment', in *The Worker and the Job: Coping with Change*, ed. Jerome M. Rosow (Englewood Cliffs: Prentice Hall, Inc., 1974), p. 83.

13. Nancy Morse and Robert Weiss, 'The Function and Meaning of Work', *American Sociological Review* 20, No. 2 (April 1966), pp. 191–198.

14. Michael Maccoby and Katherine A. Tersi, 'What Happened to the Work Ethic?" *The Work Ethic in Business*, ed. W. Michael Hoffman and Thomas J. Wyly (Cambridge, Mass.: Oelgeschlager, Gunn & Hain Publishers, 1981), p. 33.

15. Wm. B. Lacy, J. L. Bokemeier, and J. M. Shepard, 'Job Attribute Preferences and Work Commitment of Men and Women in the United States', *Personnel Psychology*, 1983, 3, pp. 315–329.

16. Daniel Yankelovich, 'The Meaning of Work', in *The Worker and the Job: Coping with Change*, p. 19.

17. E. F. Schumacher, *Good Work*, pp. 2, 3.

18. Gregory Baum, *The Priority of Labor* (New York: Paulist Press, 1982), p. 9.

19. Bernard Lefkowitz, *Breaktime* (Hathorn Books, Inc., 1979), p. 14.

20. Gregory Baum, *The Priority of Labor*, p. 12.

21. Karl Marx, 'The German Ideology', ed. trans by Loyd Easten, Kurt Guddat, in *Writings of the Young Marx on Philosophy and Society* (New York: Doubleday, 1967), p. 409.

22. E. F. Schumacher, *Good Work*, pp. 41, 42.

23. *Laboren exercens*, Encyclical Letter of Pope John Paul II, in Gregory Baum, *The Priority of Labor*, p. 95.

24. *Ibid.*, p. 112.

25. *Ibid.*, pp. 104–106.

26. Nathan Hale, 'Freud's Reflections of Work and Love', in *Themes of Work and Love and Adulthood*, ed. Neil J. Smelser and Erik A. Erikson (Cambridge Mass: Harvard University Press, 1980), p. 30.

27. *Work in America: HEW Task Force Report*, p. 8.

28. Martin Heidegger, *Being and Time*, trans. by John Macquarrie, Edward Robinson (New York: Harper and Row, 1962), pp. 102–186. Martin Heidegger, *The Basic Problems of Phenomenology* trans. by Albert Hofstadter (Bloomington, In: University of Indiana Press, 1982), pp. 168–171.

29. Erik A. Erikson, 'Themes of Adulthood in the Freud–Jung Correspondence', in *Themes of Work and Love in Adulthood*, pp. 43–74.

30. Bernard Lefkowitz, *Breaktime*, pp. 16, 17.

31. Erik A. Erikson, 'Themes of Adulthood in Freud–Jung Correspondence', pp. 55–58.

32. Adina Schwartz, 'Meaningful Work', *Ethics* 92 (July 1982), pp. 634–646.

33. Melvin L. Kohn and Carmi Schooler, 'The Reciprocal Effects of the Substantive Complexity of Work and Intellectual Flexibility: A Longitudinal Study', *American Journal of Sociology* 84 (1978): 24–52, pp. 43–48.

34. Arthur Kornhauser, *Mental Health of the Industrial Worker: A Detroit Study* (New York: John Wiley & Sons, 1964), pp. 252–270.

35. *Ibid.*, p. 262.

36. For a detailed analysis of the theory that human satisfaction is a function of the perceived fit between what a person has (abilities, resources) and what a person needs and/or wants, see:

R. D. Caplan, 'Social Support, Person–Environment Fit', in *Mental Health and the Economy*, ed. by L. A. Ferman and J. P. Gordus (Kalamazoo, Michigan, Upjohn Institute, 1979), pp. 89–137.

'Person–Environment Fit: Past, Present, and Future', in *Stress Research*, ed. by C. L. Cooper (New York: John Wiley and Sons, 1983), pp. 35–77.

R. V. Harrison, 'Person–Environment Fit and Job Stress', in *Stress at Work*, ed. by C. L. Cooper and R. Payne (New York: John Wiley, 1978), pp. 175–205.

'The Person–Environment Fit Model and the Study of Job Stress', in *Human Stress and Cognition in Organizations: An Integrated Perspective*, ed. by T. D. Beehr and R. S. Bhagat (New York: John Wiley, 1982).

For an overview of the topic of *Multiple Discrepancies Theory* also see:

Alex C. Michalos, 'Multiple Discrepancies Theory', *Social Indicators Research* 16 (1985), pp. 347–413.

37. In recent years, at least five major studies have indicated that job satisfaction increases with a worker's sense of involvement and personal sense of development through work.

T. J. Bergmann, 'Managers and Their Organizations: An Interactive Approach to Multimentional Job Satisfaction', *Journal of Occupational Psychology* 54 (1981), pp. 275–288.

G. J. Groothuis, L. A. Ten Horn, and J. Scheele, 'Attitudes and Work Simplification in a Retail Organization', *Mens en Onderneming* 33 (1979), pp. 501–518.

H. S. Leonard, H. Margolis, and D. J. Keating, 'Silent Factors Influencing Resident Advisor Turnover: An Exploratory Study', *Child Care Quarterly* 10 (1981), pp. 329–333.

D. E. Skodol and J. S. Maxman, 'Role Satisfaction Among Psychiatric Residents', *Comprehensive Psychiatry* 22 (1981), pp. 174–178.

S. Venkataraman and R. N. Anantharaman, 'Need Satisfaction and Need Importance Among Managerial Personnel', *Journal of Psychological Researches* 25 (1981), pp. 15–20.

For a complete review of the literature on job satisfaction and quality of work life issues see:

Alex C. Michalos, 'Job Satisfaction, Marital Satisfaction and the Quality of Life: A Review and a Preview', in *Research and the Quality of Life*, ed. by Frank M. Andres (Ann Arbor Michigan: University of Michigan Press, 1986), pp. 57–83.

38. Robert I. Kahn, *Work and Health* (New York: John Wiley, 1981), p. 11.

39. Studs Terkel, *Working*, p. xi.

40. A number of independent studies corroborate the thesis that satisfaction with life as a whole is positively correlated to job satisfaction.

Alex C. Michalos, 'Satisfaction and Happiness', *Social Indicators Research* 8 (1980), pp. 385–422.

C. S. Morgan, 'Female and Male Attitudes Toward Life: Implications for Theories of Mental Health', *Sex Roles* 6 (1980), pp. 367–380.

R. Rose, 'Who Can't Get No Satisfaction?', *New Society* 53 (1980), pp. 265–266.

D. J. Vredenburgh and J. E. Sheridan, 'Individual and Occupational Determinates of Life Satisfaction and Alienation', *Human Relations* 32 (1979), pp. 1023–1038.

T. H. White, 'The Relative Importance of Work as a Factor in Life Satisfaction', *Relations Industrielles* 36 (1981), pp. 179–191.

41. Theodore Roszak, *Person/Planet* (New York: Doubleday, 1979), p. 227.

42. Robert Kahn, *Work and Health*, p. 16.

E. F. Schumacher

BUDDHIST ECONOMICS: WORK

'Right Livelihood' is one of the requirements of the Buddha's Noble Eight-fold Path. It is clear, therefore, that there must be such a thing as Buddhist economics.

Buddhist countries have often stated that they wish to remain faithful to their heritage. So Burma: "The New Burma sees no conflict between religious values and economic progress. Spiritual health and material wellbeing are not enemies: they are natural allies."[1] Or: "We can blend successfully the religious and spiritual values of our heritage with the benefits of modern technology."[2] Or: "We Burmans have a sacred duty to conform both our dreams and our acts to our faith. This we shall ever do."[3]

All the same, such countries invariably assume that they can model their economic development plans in accordance with modern economics, and they call upon modern economists from so-called advanced countries to advise them, to formulate the policies to be pursued, and to construct the grand design for development, the Five-Year Plan or whatever it may be called. No one seems to think that a Buddhist way of life would call for Buddhist economics, just as the modern materialist way of life has brought forth modern economics.

Economists themselves, like most specialists, normally suffer from a kind of metaphysical blindness, assuming that theirs is a science of absolute and invariable truths, without any presuppositions. Some go as far as to claim that economic laws are as free from 'metaphysics' or 'values' as the law of gravitation. We need not, however, get involved in arguments of methodology. Instead, let us take some fundamentals and see what they look like when viewed by a modern economist and a Buddhist economist.

There is universal agreement that a fundamental source of wealth is human labour. Now, the modern economist has been brought up to consider 'labour' or work as little more than a necessary evil. From the point of view of the employer, it is in any case simply an item of cost, to be reduced to a minimum if it cannot be eliminated altogether, say, by automation. From the point of view of the workman, it is a 'disutility'; to work is to make a sacrifice of one's leisure and comfort, and wages are a kind of compensation for the sacrifice. Hence the ideal from the point of view of the employer is to have output without employees, and the ideal from the point of view of the employee is to have income without employment.

The consequences of these attitudes both in theory and in practice are, of course, extremely far-reaching. If the ideal with regard to work is to get rid of it, every method that 'reduces the work load' is a good thing. The most potent method, short of automation, is the so-called 'division of labour' and the classical example is the pin factory eulogised in Adam Smith's *Wealth of Nations.*[4] Here it is not a matter of ordinary specialisation, which mankind has practised from time immemorial, but of dividing up every complete process of production into minute parts, so that the final product can be produced at great speed without anyone having had to contribute more than a totally insignificant and, in most cases, unskilled movement of his limbs.

The Buddhist point of view takes the function of work to be at least three-fold: to give a man a chance to utilise and develop his faculties; to enable him to overcome his ego-centredness by joining with other people in a common task; and to bring forth the goods and services needed for a becoming existence. Again, the consequences that flow from this view are endless. To organise work in such a manner that it becomes meaningless, boring, stultifying, or nerve-racking for the worker would be little short of criminal; it would indicate a greater concern with goods than with people, an evil lack of compassion and a soul-destroying degree of attachment to the most primitive side of this worldly existence. Equally, to strive for leisure as an alternative to work would be considered a complete misunderstanding of one of the basic truths of human existence, namely that work and leisure are complementary parts of the same living process and cannot be separated without destroying the joy of work and the bliss of leisure.

From the Buddhist point of view, there are therefore two types of mechanisation which must be clearly distinguished: one that enhances a man's skill and power and one that turns the work of man over to a mechanical slave, leaving man in a position of having to serve the slave. How to tell the one from the other? "The craftsman himself," says Ananda Coomaraswamy, a man equally competent to talk about the modern west as the ancient east, "can always, if allowed to, draw the delicate distinction between the machine and the tool. The carpet loom is a tool, a contrivance for holding warp threads at a stretch for the pile to be woven round them by the craftsmen's fingers; but the power loom is a machine, and its significance as a destroyer of culture lies in the fact that it does the essentially human part of the work."[5] It is clear, therefore, the Buddhist economics must be very different from the economics of modern materialism, since the Buddhist sees the essence of civilisation not in a multiplication of wants but in the purification of human character. Character, at the same time, is formed primarily by a man's work. And work, properly conducted in conditions of human dignity and freedom, blesses those who do it and equally their products. The Indian philosopher and economist J. C. Kumarappa sums the matter up as follows:

"If the nature of the work is properly appreciated and applied, it will stand in the same relation to the higher faculties as food is to the physical body. It nourishes and enlivens the higher man and urges him to produce the best he is capable of. It directs his free will along the proper course and disciplines the animal in him into progressive channels. It furnishes an excellent background for man to display his scale of values and develop his personality."[6]

If a man has no chance of obtaining work he is in a desperate position, not simply because he lacks an income but because he lacks this nourishing and enlivening factor of disciplined work which nothing can replace. A modern economist may engage in highly sophisticated calculations on whether full employment 'pays' or whether it might be more 'economic' to run an economy at less than full employment so as to ensure a greater mobility of labour, a better stability of wages, and so forth. His fundamental criterion of success is simply the total quantity of goods produced during a given period of time. "If the marginal urgency of goods is low," says Professor Galbraith in *The Affluent*

Society, "then so is the urgency of employing the last man or the last million men in the labour force."[7] And again: "If . . . we can afford some unemployment in the interest of stability — a proposition, incidentally, of impeccably conservative antecedents — then we can afford to give those who are unemployed the goods that enable them to sustain their accustomed standard of living."

From a Buddhist point of view, this is standing the truth on its head by considering goods as more important than people and consumption as more important than creative activity. It means shifting the emphasis from the worker to the product of work, that is, from the human to the subhuman, a surrender to the forces of evil. The very start of Buddhist economic planning would be a planning for full employment, and the primary purpose of this would in fact be employment for everyone who needs an 'outside' job: it would not be the maximisation of employment nor the maximisation of production. Women, on the whole, do not need an 'outside' job, and the large-scale employment of women in offices or factories would be considered a sign of serious economic failure. In particular, to let mothers of young children work in factories while the children run wild would be as uneconomic in the eyes of a Buddhist economist as the employment of a skilled worker as a soldier in the eyes of a modern economist.

Notes

*"Buddhist Economics" first published in *Asia: A Handbook*, edited by Guy Wint, published by Anthony Blond Ltd., London, 1966.

1. *The New Burma* (Economic and Social Board, Government of the Union of Burma, 1954)
2. *Ibid*
3. *Ibid*
4. *Wealth of Nations* by Adam Smith
5. *Art and Swadeshi* by Ananda K. Coomaraswamy (Ganesh & Co., Madras)
6. *Economy of Permanence* by J. C. Kumarappa (SarvaSeva Sangh Publication, Rajghat, Kashi, 4th edn., 1958)
7. *The Affluent Society* by John Kenneth Galbraith (Penguin Books Ltd., 1962)

Karl Marx

ESTRANGED LABOUR[1]

We have proceeded from the premises of political economy. We have accepted its language and its laws. We presupposed private property, the separation of labour, capital and land, and of wages, profit of capital and rent of land — likewise division of labour, competition, the concept of exchange-value, etc. On the basis of political economy itself, in its own words, we have shown that the worker sinks to the level of a commodity and becomes indeed the most wretched of commodities; that the wretchedness of the worker is in inverse proportion to the power and magnitude of his production; that the necessary result of competition is the accumulation of capital in a few hands, and thus the restoration of monopoly in a more terrible form; that finally the distinction between capitalist and land-rentier, like that between the tiller of the soil and the factory-worker, disappears and that the whole of society must fall apart into the two classes — the property-*owners* and the propertyless *workers*.

Political economy proceeds from the fact of private property, but it does not explain it to us. It expresses in general, abstract formulae the *material* process through which private property actually passes, and these formulae it then takes for *laws*. It does not *comprehend* these laws — i.e., it does not demonstrate how they arise from the very nature of private property. Political economy does not disclose the source of the division between labour and capital, and between capital and land. When, for example, it defines the relationship of wages to profit, it takes the interest of the capitalists to be the ultimate cause; i.e., it takes for granted what it is supposed to evolve. Similarly, competition comes in everywhere. It is explained from external circumstances. As to how far these external and apparently fortuitous circumstances are but the expression of a necessary course of development, political economy teaches us nothing. We have seen how, to it, exchange itself appears to be a fortuitous fact. The only wheels which political economy sets in motion are *avarice* and the *war amongst the avaricious — competition*.

Precisely because political economy does not grasp the connections within the movement, it was possible to counterpose, for instance, the doctrine of competition to the doctrine of monopoly, the doctrine of craft-liberty to the doctrine of the corporation, the doctrine of the division of landed property to the doctrine of the big estate — for competition, craft-liberty and the division of landed property were explained and comprehended only as fortuitous, premeditated and violent consequences of monopoly, the corporation, and feudal property, not as their necessary, inevitable and natural consequences.

Now, therefore, we have to grasp the essential connection between private property, avarice, and the separation of labour, capital and landed property;

From Karl Marx, "Estranged Labour," in *Economic and Philosophic Manuscripts of 1844*, in *The Marx-Engels Reader*, edited by Robert C. Tucker, 2nd ed. (New York: Norton, 1978), 56–63. Reprinted by permission of the publisher.

[1] *Die Entfremdete Arbeit*. [In some other translations this phrase appears as "alienated labour." R. C. Tucker.]

between exchange and competition, value and the devaluation of men, monopoly and competition, etc.; the connection between this whole estrangement and the *money*-system.

Do not let us go back to a fictitious primordial condition as the political economist does, when he tries to explain. Such a primordial condition explains nothing. He merely pushes the question away into a grey nebulous distance. He assumes in the form of fact, of an event, what he is supposed to deduce — namely, the necessary relationship between two things — between, for example, division of labour and exchange. Theology in the same way explains the origin of evil by the fall of man: that is, it assumes as a fact, in historical form, what has to be explained.

We proceed from an *actual* economic fact.

The worker becomes all the poorer the more wealth he produces, the more his production increases in power and range. The worker becomes an ever cheaper commodity the more commodities he creates. With the *increasing value* of the world of things proceeds in direct proportion the *devaluation* of the world of men. Labour produces not only commodities; it produces itself and the worker as a *commodity* — and does so in the proportion in which it produces commodities generally.

This fact expresses merely that the object which labour produces — labour's product — confronts it as *something alien*, as a *power independent* of the producer. The product of labour is labour which has been congealed in an object, which has become material: it is the *objectification* of labour. Labour's realization is its objectification. In the conditions dealt with by political economy this realization of labour appears as *loss of reality* for the workers; objectification as *loss of the object* and *object-bondage*; appropriation as *estrangement*, as *alienation*.[2]

So much does labour's realization appear as loss of reality that the worker loses reality to the point of starving to death. So much does objectification appear as loss of the object that the worker is robbed of the objects most necessary not only for his life but for his work. Indeed, labour itself becomes an object which he can get hold of only with the greatest effort and with the most irregular interruptions. So much does the appropriation of the object appear as estrangement that the more objects the worker produces the fewer can he possess and the more he falls under the dominion of his product, capital.

All these consequences are contained in the definition that the worker is related to the *product of his labour* as to an *alien* object. For on this premise it is clear that the more the worker spends himself, the more powerful the alien objective world becomes which he creates over-against himself, the poorer he himself — his inner world — becomes, the less belongs to him as his own. It is the same in religion. The more man puts into God, the less he retains in himself. The worker puts his life into the object; but now his life no longer belongs to him but to the object. Hence, the greater this activity, the greater is the worker's lack of objects. Whatever the product of his labour is, he is not. Therefore the greater this product, the less is he himself. The *alienation* of the worker in his product means not only that his labour becomes an object, an *external* existence, but that it exists *outside him*, independently, as something alien to him, and that

---

[2]"Alienation" — *Entausscrung*. An alternative and perhaps better translation of *Entausscrung* would be "externalization." The term translated "estrangement" in the above passage is *Entfremdung*. [R. C. Tucker]

it becomes a power of its own confronting him; it means that the life which he has conferred on the object confronts him as something hostile and alien.

Let us now look more closely at the *objectification*, at the production of the worker; and therein at the *estrangement*, the *loss* of the object, his product.

The worker can create nothing without *nature*, without the *sensuous external world*. It is the material on which his labor is manifested, in which it is active, from which and by means of which it produces.

But just as nature provides labor with the *means of life* in the sense that labour cannot *live* without objects on which to operate, on the other hand, it also provides the *means of life* in the more restricted sense — i.e., the means for the physical subsistence of the *worker* himself.

Thus the more the worker by his labour *appropriates* the external world, sensuous nature, the more he deprives himself of *means of life* in the double respect: first, that the sensuous external world more and more ceases to be an object belonging to his labour — to be his labour's *means of life*; and secondly, that it more and more ceases to be *means of life* in the immediate sense, means for the physical subsistence of the worker.

Thus in this double respect the worker becomes a slave of his object, first, in that he receives an *object of labour*, i.e., in that he receives *work*; and secondly, in that he receives *means of subsistence*. Therefore, it enables him to exist, first, as a *worker*; and, second, as a *physical subject*. The extremity of this bondage is that it is only as a *worker* that he continues to maintain himself as a *physical subject*, and that it is only as a *physical subject* that he is a *worker*.

(The laws of political economy express the estrangement of the worker in his object thus: the more the worker produces, the less he has to consume; the more values he creates, the more valueless, the more unworthy he becomes; the better formed his product, the more deformed becomes the worker; the more civilized his object, the more barbarous becomes the worker; the mightier labour becomes, the more powerless becomes the worker; the more ingenious labour becomes, the duller becomes the worker and the more he becomes nature's bondsman.)

Political economy conceals the estrangement inherent in the nature of labour by not considering the direct relationship between the worker (labour) *and production.* It is true that labour produces for the rich wonderful things — but for the worker it produces privation. It produces palaces — but for the worker, hovels. It produces beauty — but for the worker, deformity. It replaces labour by machines — but some of the workers it throws back to a barbarous type of labour, and the other workers it turns into machines. It produces intelligence — but for the worker idiocy, cretinism.

The direct relationship of labour to its produce is the relationship of the worker to the objects of his production. The relationship of the man of means to the objects of production and to production itself is only a *consequence* of this first relationship — and confirms it. We shall consider this other aspect later.

When we ask, then, what is the essential relationship of labour we are asking about the relationship of the *worker* to production.

Till now we have been considering the estrangement, the alienation of the worker only in one of its aspects, i.e., the worker's *relationship to the products of his labour.* But the estrangement is manifested not only in the result but in the *act of production* — within the *producing activity* itself. How would the worker come to face the product of his activity as a stranger, were it not that in the very act of production he was estranging himself from himself? The product is after all but the summary of the activity of production. If then the product of labour is alienation, production itself must be active alienation, the alienation of activity, the activity of alienation. In the estrangement of the object of labour is merely summarized the estrangement, the alienation, in the activity of labour itself.

What, then, constitutes the alienation of labour?

First, the fact that labour is *external* to the worker, i.e., it does not belong to his essential being; that in his work, therefore, he does not affirm himself but denies himself, does not feel content but unhappy, does not develop freely his physical and mental energy but mortifies his body and ruins his mind. The worker therefore only feels himself outside his work, and in his work feels outside himself. He is at home when he is not working, and when he is working he is not at home. His labour is therefore not voluntary, but coerced: it is *forced labour*. It is therefore not the satisfaction of a need; it is merely a *means* to satisfy needs external to it. Its alien character emerges clearly in the fact that as soon as no physical or other compulsion exists, labour is shunned like the plague. External labour, labour in which man alienates himself, is a labour of self-sacrifice, of mortification. Lastly, the external character of labour for the worker appears in the fact that it is not his own, but someone else's, that it does not belong to him, that in it he belongs, not to himself, but to another. Just as in religion the spontaneous activity of the human imagination, of the human brain and the human heart, operates independently of the individual — that is, operates on him as an alien, divine or diabolical activity — in the same way the worker's activity is not his spontaneous activity. It belongs to another; it is the loss of his self.

As a result, therefore, man (the worker) no longer feels himself to be freely active in any but his animal functions — eating, drinking, procreating, or at most in his dwelling and in dressing-up, etc.; and in his human functions he no longer feels himself to be anything but an animal. What is animal becomes human and what is human becomes animal.

Certainly eating, drinking, procreating, etc., are also genuinely human functions. But in the abstraction which separates them from the sphere of all other human activity and turns them into sole and ultimate ends, they are animal.

We have considered the act of estranging practical human activity, labour, in two of its aspects. (1) The relation of the worker to the *product of labour* as an alien object exercising power over him. This relation is at the same time the relation to the sensuous external world, to the objects of nature as an alien world antagonistically opposed to him. (2) The relation of labour to the *act of production* within the *labour* process. This relation is the relation of the worker to his own activity as an alien activity not belonging to him; it is activity as suffering, strength as weakness, begetting as emasculating, the worker's *own* physical and mental energy, his personal life or what is life other than activity — as an activity which is turned against him, neither depends on nor belongs to him. Here we have *self-estrangement*, as we had previously the estrangement of the *thing*.

We have yet a third aspect of *estranged labour* to deduce from the two already considered.

Man is a species being, not only because in practice and in theory he adopts the species as his object (his own as well as those of other things), but — and this is only another way of expressing it — but also because he treats himself as the actual, living species; because he treats himself as a *universal* and therefore a free being.

The life of the species, both in man and in animals, consists physically in the fact that man (like the animal) lives on inorganic nature; and the more universal man is compared with an animal, the more universal is the sphere of inorganic nature on which he lives. Just as plants, animals, stones, the air, light, etc., constitute a part of human consciousness in the realm of theory, partly as objects of natural science, partly as objects of art—his spiritual inorganic nature, spiritual nourishment which he must first prepare to make it palatable and digestible—so too in the realm of practice they constitute a part of human life and human activity. Physically man lives only on these products of nature, whether they appear in the form of food, heating, clothes, a dwelling, or whatever it may be. The universality of man is in practice manifested precisely in the universality which makes all nature his *inorganic* body—both inasmuch as nature is (1) his direct means of life, and (2) the material, the object, and the instrument of his life-activity. Nature is man's *inorganic body*—nature, that is, in so far as it is not itself the human body. Man *lives* on nature—means that nature is his *body*, with which he must remain in continuous intercourse if he is not to die. That man's physical and spiritual life is linked to nature means simply that nature is linked to itself, for man is a part of nature.

In estranging from man (1) nature, and (2) himself, his own active functions, his life-activity, estranged labour estranges the *species* from man. It turns for him the *life of the species* into a means of individual life. First it estranges the life of the species and individual life, and secondly it makes individual life in its abstract form the purpose of the life of the species, likewise in its abstract and estranged form.

For in the first place labour, *life-activity, productive life* itself, appears to man merely as a *means* of satisfying a need—the need to maintain the physical existence. Yet the productive life is the life of the species. It is life-engendering life. The whole character of a species—its species character—is contained in the character of its life-activity, and free, conscious activity is man's species character. Life itself appears only as *a means to life*.

The animal is immediately identical with its life-activity. It does not distinguish itself from it. It is *its life-activity*. Man makes his life-activity itself the object of his will and of his consciousness. He has conscious life-activity. It is not a determination with which he directly merges. Conscious life-activity directly distinguishes man from animal life-activity. It is just because of this that he is a species being. Or it is only because he is a species being that he is a Conscious Being, i.e., that his own life is an object for him. Only because of that is his activity free activity. Estranged labour reverses this relationship, so that it is just because man is a conscious being tha the makes his life-activity, his *essential* being, a mere means to his *existence*.

In creating an *objective world* by his practical activity, in *working-up* inorganic nature, man proves himself a conscious species being, i.e., as a being that treats the species as its own essential being, or that treats itself as a species being. Admittedly animals also produce. They build themselves nests, dwellings, like the bees, beavers, ants, etc. But an animal only produces what it immediately needs for itself or its young. It produces one-sidedly, whilst man produces universally. It produces only under the dominion of immediate physical need, whilst man produces even when he is free from physical need and only truly produces in freedom therefrom. An animal produces only itself, whilst man reproduces the whole of nature. An animal's product belongs immediately to its physical body, whilst man freely confront his product. An animal forms things in accordance with the standard and the need of the species to which it belongs, whilst man knows how to produce in accordance with the standard of every species, and knows how to apply everywhere the inherent standard to the object. Man therefore also forms things in accordance with the laws of beauty.

It is just in the working-up of the objective world, therefore, that man first really proves himself to be a *species being*. This production is his active species life. Through and because of this production, nature appears as *his* work and his reality. The object of labour is, therefore, the *objectification of man's species life*: for he duplicates himself not only, as in consciousness, intellectually, but also actively, in reality, and therefore he contemplates himself in a world that he has created. In tearing away from man the object of his production, therefore, estranged labour tears from him his *species life*, his real species objectivity, and transforms his advantage over animals into the disadvantage that his inorganic body, nature, is taken from him.

Similarly, in degrading spontaneous activity, free activity, to a means, estranged labour makes man's species life a means to his physical existence.

The consciousness which man has of his species is thus transformed by estrangement in such a way that the species life becomes for him a means.

Estranged labour turns thus:

(3) *Man's species being*, both nature and his spiritual species property, into a *being alien* to him, into a *means* to his *individual existence*. It estranges man's own body from him, as it does external nature and his spiritual essence, his *human* being.

(4) An immediate consequence of the fact that man is estranged from the product of his labour, from his life-activity, from his species being is the *estrangement of man* from *man*. If a man is confronted by himself, he is confronted by the *other* man. What applies to a man's relation to his work, to the product of his labour and to himself, also holds of a man's relation to the other man, and to the other man's labour and object of labour.

In fact, the proposition that man's species nature is estranged from him means that one man is estranged from the other, as each of them is from man's essential nature.[3]

DIVISION OF LABOUR

One capitalist can drive another from the field and capture his capital only by selling more cheaply. In order to be able to sell more cheaply without ruining himself, he must produce more cheaply, that is, raise the productive power of labour as much as possible. But the productive power of labour is

[3]"Species nature" (and, earlier, "species being") — *Gattungswesen*; "man's essential nature" — *menschlichen Wesen*.

From Karl Marx, *Wage Labour and Capital* and *The Manifesto of the Communist Party* in *The Marx-Engels Reader*, edited by Robert C. Tucker, 2nd ed. (New York: Norton 1978, 211–212, 214–215, 479. Reprinted by permission of the publisher.

raised, above all, by a *greater division of labour*, by a more universal introduction and continual improvement of *machinery*. The greater the labour army among whom labour is divided, the more gigantic the scale on which machinery is introduced, the more does the cost of production proportionately decrease, the more fruitful is labour. Hence, a general rivalry arises among the capitalists to increase the division of labour and machinery and to exploit them on the greatest possible scale. . . .

We see how in this way the mode of production and the means of production are continually transformed, revolutionised, *how the division of labour is necessarily followed by greater division of labour, the application of machinery by still greater application of machinery, work on a large scale by work on a still larger scale.* . . .

Further, as the *division of labour* increases, labour *is simplified.* The special skill of the worker becomes worthless. He becomes transformed into a simple, monotonous productive force that does not have to use intense bodily or intellectual faculties. His labour becomes a labour that anyone can perform. Hence, competitors crowd upon him on all sides, and besides we remind the reader that the more simple and easily learned the labour is, the lower the cost of production needed to master it, the lower do wages sink, for, like the price of every other commodity, they are determined by the cost of production.

Therefore, as labour becomes more unsatisfying, more repulsive, competition increases and wages decrease. The worker tries to keep up the amount of his wages by working more, whether by working longer hours or by producing more in one hour. Driven by want, therefore, he still further increases the evil effects of the division of labour. The result is that *the more he works the less wages he receives*, and for the simple reason that he competes to that extent with his fellow workers, hence makes them into so many competitors who offer themselves on just the same bad terms as he does himself, and that, therefore, in the last resort he *competes with himself, with himself as a member of the working class.*

Machinery brings about the same results on a much greater scale, by replacing skilled workers by unskilled, men by women, adults by children. It brings about the same results, where it is newly introduced, by throwing the hand workers on to the streets in masses, and, where it is developed, improved and replaced by more productive machinery, by discharging workers in smaller batches. We have portrayed above, in a hasty sketch, the industrial war of the capitalists among themselves; *this war has the peculiarity that its battles are won less by recruiting than by discharging the army of labour. The generals, the capitalists, compete with one another as to who can discharge most soldiers of industry.* . . .

Owing to the extensive use of machinery and to division of labour, the work of the proletarians has lost all individual character, and consequently, all charm for the workman. He becomes an appendage of the machine, and it is only the most simple, most monotonous, and most easily acquired knack, that is required of him. Hence, the cost of production of a workman is restricted, almost entirely, to the means of subsistence that he requires for his maintenance, and for the propagation of his race. But the price of a commodity, and therefore also of labour,[1] is equal to its cost of production. In proportion, therefore, as the repulsiveness of the work increases, the wage decreases. Nay more, in proportion as the use of machinery and division of labour increases, in the same proportion the burden of toil also increases, whether by prolongation of the working hours, by increase of the work exacted in a given time or by increased speed of the machinery, etc.

Kai Nielsen

ALIENATION AND WORK

Many people are skeptical about moral judgments. They believe no one can really show that something is good or bad, right or wrong. However, a careful look at the workplace will tell us why that skeptical view is problematic.

There is something very paradoxical about ethical skepticism in the face of what we know about our lives. We have experienced destructive wars that achieved no morally acceptable end. The life work of many is useless, frustrating, and not under their own control; still, as bad as their jobs are, given the alternatives, they are fortunate to have them, and hence cling to them — that is the depth of their alienated condition. We see pollution and the destruction of our environment and racism and sexism as pervasive features of our lives, and in the face of all this, we feel powerless.

Are there not certain conditions — those just mentioned — that are plainly wrong and those — their opposites — that are plainly right? It seems to me that we have good reasons for saying that there are some things — things that are a part of the very fiber of our social lives — that are plainly evil.

What are these ills that are so pervasive and so alienating in our society? I believe, if we think concretely and nonevasively about work and the conditions surrounding it, we'll see that there are deep evils in our world that are by no means inevitable or necessary. What I am saying here needs to be concretized and exemplified. Following is an extreme case, but a true one:

When black school children in South Boston were bused into white schools, they were violently assaulted. They saw, as their buses passed through white neighborhoods, black mannequins hung in effigy, white power signs, and, on one school wall, a sign announcing in four-foot-high letters, "Hitler was Right." Inside the school, even with police protection, they were violently

---

[1]Subsequently Marx pointed out that the worker sells not his labour but his labour power.

From Kai Nielsen, "Alienation and Work," in *Moral Rights in the Workplace*, edited by Gertrude Ezorsky (Albany: State University of New York Press, 1987), 28–34. Reprinted from *Moral Rights in the Workplace* edited by Gertrude Ezorsky by permission of the State University of New York Press. Copyright © 1987 State University of New York Press.

attacked by antibusing gangs. It was painfully clear that police sympathies lay with the whites. Even a few teachers were viciously prejudiced. Ask yourself what happens to a young child under such an assault. What must be the effect of such unprovoked hatred on the personality and self-respect of a child? Such actions can have no justification. We know that something is happening here that is morally intolerable.

Like racism, sexism is often grossly obvious and widespread. The hiring and treatment of secretaries is sometimes a dramatic case in point. To be told: "We usually don't hire married girls. We want young, pretty, available girls around the office" is to be evaluated on qualities irrelevant to the position for which you are interviewing. If obtaining a job and advancing within a company means tolerating sexual harassment, then you are being treated merely as an object. Again we have human conditions that are morally intolerable, though often tolerated in our society.

Then there is the plight of the elderly, who because unproductive are expendable. In the extreme, although not statistically insignificant, cases, you will find elderly people living in dilapidated residential hotels with two-burner hot places and less than minimal food, heat, and hot water. They are isolated, lonely, and fear eviction. Again, we have a widely tolerated but still morally intolerable situation.

People complain about welfare "bums," but there are people in North America and Europe who try but are not able to find work. (In 1983, 35 million people were out of work in the capitalist societies of the West.) Many of the habitually unemployed are caught in an endless cycle of poverty and ignorance. Most come from uneducated and poverty-stricken backgrounds. Deprived of a decent education, they're thrown into the work force at a very young age, with little experience and no training. Because of their lack of education, their job prospects are very limited, and without a job that pays well, that education may never be achieved. Such people are caught in an endless cycle of poverty that saps the will, undermines dignity, and destroys their lives and the lives of their children. In this way a relatively permanent class of unemployables is created. Again we have a situation of the morally intolerable being routinely tolerated.

Finally, let us look at consumerism and work. Eleanor Langer, in her expose of life inside the New York Telephone Company, points out one very strong, largely socially imposed, motivation for those women working within the company in alienating and emotionally exhausting circumstances.[1] Through social manipulation, they become trapped by their love of objects. Their work affords them no satisfaction or any basis for developing self-respect. A telltale showing of this was in their endless purchasing of new and different wigs. So, with incessant company encouragement, they try to find their identities in consumerism. Theirs is an endless quest for objects. We have — to make a general statement — a pervasive consciousness industry, combined with frustrating conditions at work and in our families, pushing us into largely senseless patterns of consumption. We, in this example, have people being manipulated in a way that is morally unacceptable.[2]

Let us turn to our reflection on work. Work is something in our societies that is for many of us deeply unsatisfying, debilitating, dehumanizing, or, as the catch phrase has it, alienating — though still usually preferable to welfare. As Albert Camus put it, "Without work all life goes rotten." But it is equally plain, as he knew, that when work is soulless — as in an assembly line, a typing pool — "life stifles and dies." To make our lives satisfying, we must have meaningful work. Again we have something that is plainly evil.[3]

Why are these things I have mentioned so deeply embedded and pervasive in our social and working lives, and why are they evil? They are evil because they cause people to suffer needlessly; they undermine our self-respect and autonomy. People are simply used, treated as a means, manipulated, and deceived; their hopes for themselves and their children are destroyed. Their health (both physical and mental) is damaged, and they are exploited by their employers. They have nothing even remotely like equal chances in life.

As study after study shows, there is considerable dissatisfaction of workers with the work in our societies.[4] It is not that people do not want to work at all; it is the particular work they do under conditions of supervision and control, that is so dissatisfying. Yet even when work affords them little satisfaction, most people would prefer to work, as a lesser evil, rather than retirement. They want to continue working not because they enjoy it but, as one worker put it, "only to fill time."[5] A task force report as to the secretary of Health, Education and Welfare, *Work in America*, summarized a central conclusion of over a hundred studies done over a period of twenty years: "Workers want most . . . to become masters of their immediate environment and to feel that their work and they themselves are important. . . ."[6] These feelings are crucial elements in self-respect. Yet modern working conditions militate against their fulfillment. Work is very often authoritarian. The very idea of democracy in the workplace is often thought an outrage. Yet the fact is that work typically takes place under close supervision and dictation in an authoritarian atmosphere not unlike the military.[7]

People learn to do routine and fragmented tasks, often having little conception of the overall process. However, when management introduces labor-saving machines — machines that under socioeconomic circumstances could be liberating to workers — the workers must resist their adoption in order to keep their wretched jobs. As Adam Smith recognized before Karl Marx, work under such conditions is a thoroughly dehumanizing experience that "so stunts our understanding and our sensibilities that we generally, if we are formed under such employment, become as stupid and ignorant as it is possible for a human creature to become."[8] Our very human capacities are stunted, and we suffer self-estrangement and alienation.

Our alienation is deepened because we feel powerless to change our situation, to alter the fact that we must sell ourselves in order to work at all. (Recall that while in the middle of the nineteenth century, less than half of all employed people were wage and salary workers. By 1970 only 9 percent were not salaried employees — a drop from 18 percent in 1950. The idea that most of us, if we chose to take the risk, could work for ourselves is pure illusion.[9]

Work is often perceived as meaningless because it contributes very little to our well-being. It certainly does not give us a sense of pride to make products designed to become obsolete. Often workers know they are making junk, sometimes needlessly polluting junk, yet they must continue to make it anyway. They also very frequently make things that are a waste of our natural resources and energy and may even be harmful, for example, electric toothbrushes, snowmobiles (except for very limited purposes), food additives, and valium (in many instances).

Suppose a salesperson sells insurance to someone who doesn't need it or persuades someone to buy a product they don't need to replace a product that is good for them. Or suppose you are a secretary who types documents that teach companies how to avoid taxation or pollution controls. Suppose you are an accountant paid to "doctor" a firm's books. How can such pursuits be considered meaningful work and how could it not undermine your self-respect?

In our societies, workers have very little input into decisions about what is to be produced and how it is to be produced; therefore, a genuine work community never develops, where workers "come together to determine through their social interaction the important decisions governing production.[10] Under such circumstances work become drudgery, an instrument for gaining money and material security.

To work under such conditions is alienating and self-estranging. This state is often masked in various forms of self-deception: dissatisfaction with ourselves and with the world. And with this dissatisfaction come feelings of powerlessness, senselessness, and isolation. But alienation has an objective sense as well. Alienation occurs, as Herbert Gintis puts it, "when the structure of society denies you access to life-giving and personally rewarding activities and relationships."[11] When elements in your personal and social life become meaningless, fragmented, out of reach, you begin to feel, as existentialists have stressed, the absurdity and the pointlessness of your life. When this is your situation, you are alienated, though such alienation can take more disguised, less self-conscious forms.

The debilitating effects of many workers' jobs carry over into their personal lives. Alcoholism and drug addiction are very high among many workers. Also, work in which one has little control or responsibility engenders a general passivity. "The worker who is denied participation and control over the work situation is unlikely to be able to participate effectively in community or national decision making, even if there are formal opportunities to do so.[12] Without democracy in the workplace, we are unlikely to achieve meaningful democracy in community affairs.[13] What we too often see are alienated, passive human beings who feel utterly powerless before forces they can neither control nor understand.

Their nonpassivity, like the return of the repressed, comes out in authoritarian behavior at home, a preoccupation with sex — for males a preoccupation with how many women they can seduce — and as is seen on television, a preoccupation with sex and violence. The politically impotent, the supervised and drilled male, can at least be boss in his own bed and home if not at work. In the extreme cases, this often leads to spouse and child abuse. Alienation at work creates deep alienation throughout one's life, destroying the possibility for healthy emotional development.[14] "To be alienated is to be separated in concrete and specific ways from 'things' important to well-being," principally social roles that involve respectful collaboration with others.[15] Whether there are these social roles that are essential for giving sense to one's life depends on the social structures in which one lives. "Alienation arises when the social criteria determining the structure and development of important social roles are *essentially* independent of individual needs.[16] Work relationships are social relationships, and in our society their authoritarian structures dull our sensibilities, intellectual capacities, initiative, creativity, and autonomy.

I have discussed conditions of life in the workplace that, contrary to moral skepticism, are obvious moral evils. Indeed, if any theory were to imply that these conditions were not evil, I would believe the theory to be plainly mistaken.

Notes

1. Eleanor Langer, "Inside the New York Telephone Company," *The Capitalist System*, 2d ed., ed. Richard C. Edwards et al (Englewood Cliffs, N.J.: Prentice Hall), 4–11.

2. Hans Magnus Enzensberger, *The Consciousness Industry* (New York: Seabury Press, 1974).

3. See Harry Braverman, *Labor and Monopoly Capital* (New York: Monthly Review Press, 1974); Samuel Bowles and Herbert Gintis, *Schooling in Capitalist America* (New York: Basic Books, 1976).

4. *Work in America: Report of a Special Task Force to the Secretary of Health, Education, and Welfare* (Cambridge, Mass.: MIT Press, 1973).

5. Ibid.

6. Ibid.

7. Langer, *The Capitalist System*, 4–11; Harry Braverman, *Labor and Monopoly Capital.*

8. Adam Smith, *The Wealth of Nations* (New York: Modern Library, 1937), 734.

9. Gintis, *Schooling in Capitalist America*, 293–317.

10. Ibid., 275.

11. Ibid., 276.

12. Langer, *The Capitalist System*, 267.

13. Ibid., 267.

14. Ibid., Gintis, *Schooling in Capitalist America*, 277.

15. Ibid.

16. Ibid.

DISCUSSION QUESTIONS

1. Gini and Sullivan call work "the axis of human self-making." Do you agree?

2. Conventional American society would define a "good job" primarily as one with high pay. Schumacher would say that a good job would be one that lets people use and develop their talents, become part of a group, and produce necessary goods and services. Which viewpoint is correct?

3. When Marx describes the evils of alienated labor and the division of labor, he obviously has factory work in mind. Yet he would say that these criticisms apply just as readily to any kind of work going on under capitalism — work in the service industry, sales, office work, and so on. Describe what white-collar alienation would look like.

4. Nielsen points out that for many of us, work is "deeply unsatisfying, debilitating, dehumanizing," and he claims that this is "plainly evil." In capitalism, however, no one is compelled by the state to work at a particular job. Don't our jobs result from individual choices? Does this fact weaken the force of Marx's and Nielsen's critiques?

CASE 4.1

◆ ◆ ◆

The End of the Assembly Line

As the readings in this chapter have made clear, the benefits of the industrial revolution carried with them a steep cost — alienation. Machines, the assembly line, and a style of management based on authority and obedience made it possible to boost output and reduce the price of goods. But making work less demanding also made it less challenging and less interesting. Expecting workers to follow mindlessly the orders of management bred passivity and resentment. The resulting alienation led to boredom, absenteeism, apathy, inefficiency, and shoddy performance on the job. This phenomenon is not limited to the factory floor. Authoritarian, inflexible methods of organizing work among white-collar workers as well as the spread of computers and other new technologies may similarly increase alienation.

Critics of today's work environments, however, consider them to be unethical as well as uncomfortable and uninteresting. Work is so central to a basic sense of human well-being, they argue, that it is immoral for companies to subject their employees to a work life that is so unsatisfying and alienating. From an ethical standpoint, the substance and structure of work should respect the dignity of the worker. Work should enhance self-esteem and develop talents. The workplace should empower workers, not force them to act like children. Anything less, to borrow Kant's terminology, treats an individual "as a means only" rather than "an end in itself."

Change in the methods of production is taking place, however. Corporations are moving away from the assembly line and managers' monopoly on decision making. Instead, work is beginning to be arranged around teams that require workers not only to perform numerous tasks to complete a job but to make decisions about how that job will be accomplished. This is happening in at least one very surprising place — General Motors — a corporation hardly known for being organizationally nimble and experimental. In 1985, GM established the Saturn Corporation. Its aim was not simply to build new cars, but to build cars in new ways. Among its innovations were a heavy emphasis on quality, employee training, management–labor cooperation, consensus and teamwork. An agreement with the United Auto Workers guarantees job security and that work will be done in teams with considerable autonomy. Also the assembly line is designed to be more comfortable for workers.

Even more revolutionary, however, are the changes Volvo has adopted. Sweden has been a pioneer in designing work around teams, and Volvo has used teams for a number of years. But Volvo went a step further when it built a plant in Uddevalla, Sweden, that has no assembly line at all. The plant is organized totally around teams of seven to ten workers who are responsible for assembling entire cars with little supervision. The teams manage themselves and perform such traditional management functions as hiring, quality control, and scheduling. Volvo's Uddevalla teams boast low absenteeism and high morale, and they reportedly produce better quality cars more quickly than do the automaker's other plants. ◆

Discussion Questions

1. The core ethical issue in how work is designed is whether the traditional assembly line/management-authority model goes so much against the grain of the human spirit as to be unethical. If so, a team-based model that encourages employee autonomy and respects the dignity of workers has much to be said for it. But does the traditional way that work is structured genuinely hurt workers?

2. Is workplace alienation harmful? If so, does that mean that the vast majority of workers who labor in traditional settings are the victims of morally indefensible practices? Is it, then, unethical for companies not to reconfigure themselves along the lines of Saturn's and Volvo's practices? Also, would it matter if a team-based, participatory way of organizing work were actually less efficient than the traditional way? Would a company have a moral obligation to forego maximum profits in order to provide workers with more satisfying jobs?

Sources

"Here Comes GM's Saturn," *Business Week*, April 9, 1990, 56–62.
Lohr, Steve, "Making Cars the Volvo Way," *New York Times*, June 23, 1989, D1, D5.
"Volvo's Radical New Plant: 'The Death of the Assembly Line'?," *Business Week*, August 28, 1989, 92–93.

CASE 4.2

♦ ♦ ♦

Gender and Management Styles

As traditional as the assembly line is as a way of structuring work, so is a management style based on authority. The typical large corporation is organized as a quasi-military, bureaucratic hierarchy in which orders flow from management to labor. Managers set the goals of the organization and determine how work will be done. The implicit assumption is that management is brighter and more knowledgeable than labor — thus, more capable of deciding what will make the business efficient and profitable. The proper role of labor, in this management style, is to acquiesce to the superior insights of managers and, quite simply, to obey.

Some thinkers would argue that structuring an organization around such an authoritarian outlook fails to meet the demands of human dignity and is therefore morally problematic. A standard reply to this objection, however, is that hierarchical organizations and authoritarian management styles merely reflect the nature of business. Maximum efficiency in an advanced economy requires that someone have the authority to give orders about how things should be done. The inefficiencies of democracy may be tolerable, even virtuous, in the political realm. But, so goes the argument, they are self-defeating in business and would cost profits and jobs. In essence, the defender of the traditional business arrangement offers a utilitarian argument. Whatever un-happiness workers experience will be more than offset by a secure, well-paying job for themselves and by the material benefits for others in the society.

Recent studies suggest, however, that the typical way of running a business may be less a product of the nature of business than of the gender of those who have been in charge. At least two experts in management have proposed that women have dramatically different management styles than men do. Because this alternate style is characterized less by authority than by communication, consensus building, cooperation, empowerment, and mutual respect, one could argue that it is a preferable style from an ethical viewpoint. Do female managers have more humane ideas about how business should be done? Is there a link between gender and business ethics?

Management consultant Marilyn Loden argues that each gender is trained to value traits that are so different that they produce genuinely different world-views. For example, Loden claims that the male worldview values competition, the need for control, aggressive behavior, and the ability to think analytically and strategically. The result of these values in business, then, is a masculine model of leadership that employs a competitive operating style in a hierarchical organizational structure, with the basic objective of winning, and a rational problem-solving style. Loden identifies the key characteristics of this model as: high control, strategic, unemotional and analytical.

By contrast, Loden argues that women tend to rely on emotional as well as rational data and place greater value than do men on the aesthetic, social, and religious dimensions of life. Consequently, a feminine model of leadership prefers a cooperative operating style in an organization structured around a team, with the basic objective being quality output, and a problem-solving style that is both intuitive and rational. The key characteristics of this model, claims Loden, are less controlling, empathic, collaborative, and high-performance standards. "In short," observes Loden,

> feminine leaders are apt to be more concerned with maintaining close personal relationships with others. They are more likely to consider feelings as well as the basic facts in decision-making—to strive for solutions in which everyone is a winner and to avoid situations where someone must lose. They are also more inclined to subordinate short-term, personal advancement to improve the long-term health of the orga-nization that they and their associates mutually depend on. (62)

Similar findings about gender differences come from researcher Judy B. Rosener, who contrasts how men and women describe their ideas about leader-ship. She writes in her controversial *Harvard Business Review* article, "Ways Women Lead,"

> The men are more likely than the women to describe themselves in ways that characterize what some management experts call "transactional" leadership. That is, they view job performance as a series of transactions with subordinates—exchanging rewards for services rendered or pun-

ishment for inadequate performance. The men are also more likely to use power that comes from their organizational position and formal authority.

The women respondents, on the other hand, described themselves in ways that characterize "transformational" leadership — getting subordinates to transform their own self-interest into the interest of the group through concern for a broader goal. Moreover, they ascribe their power to personal characteristics like charisma, interpersonal skills, hard work, or personal contacts rather than to organizational stature. . . . [T]hese women actively work to make their interactions with subordinates positive for everyone involved. More specifically, the women encourage participation, share power and information, enhance other people's self-worth, and get others excited about their work. All these things reflect their belief that allowing employees to contribute and to feel powerful and important is a win – win situation — good for the employees and the organization. (120)

As previously noted, the ethical significance of these differences in management styles is that some might argue that the allegedly feminine style appears to meet higher ethical standards. It treats people with respect, gives them control over their lives, and shares information and power. Moreover, claim these management experts, this style is quite effective in business. That is, it can turn a profit just as well as the masculine style. ◆

Discussion Questions

1. Does it seem plausible to you that the differences described by Loden and Rosener are associated with gender? Do you observe similar differences among your friends and associates?

2. Is it accurate to say that the feminine style meets higher ethical standards than the masculine one? Or are these differences just that — differences, with neither style better or worse than the other?

3. How important is management style in assessing how satisfying an employee's work life is?

4. How important is management style in determining how ethically a business operates?

Sources

Loden, Marilyn, *Feminine Leadership, or How to Succeed in Business Without Being One of the Boys* (New York: Random House, 1985).

Judy B. Rosener, "Ways Women Lead," *Harvard Business Review*, November–December 1990, 119–125.

ADDITIONAL READINGS

Braybrooke, David, "Work: A Cultural Ideal Ever More in Jeopardy," *Midwest Studies of Philosophy*, 7 (1982), 321–341.

De George, Richard T., "Workers' Rights: Employment, Wages, and Unions," in *Business Ethics*, 3rd ed. (New York: Macmillan, 1990), 308–331.

Ezorsky, Gertrude, ed., *Moral Rights in the Workplace* (Albany: State University of New York Press, 1987).

CHAPTER 5

♦ ♦ ♦

Corporate Social Responsibility

In the same way that the structure of a capitalist economy raises fundamental ethical questions, so does the structure of the main institution that conducts business in that economy — the corporation. One basic issue hotly debated throughout the last two decades has been the responsibilities of corporations and the managers who run them. Is a manager responsible for achieving only financial goals or are there other responsibilities as well? What does it mean to claim that a corporation has "social responsibilities"? What do managers owe stockholders? Do managers have any duties to other groups affected by the corporation, such as employees, customers, or vendors?

Perhaps the most famous essay on this issue is Milton Friedman's "The Social Responsibility of Business Is to Increase Its Profits." Friedman takes a hard, narrow line and argues vigorously against the claim that corporations have broad responsibilities. The contemporary philosopher Thomas Donaldson, however, works with the notion of the social contract, describes the terms of a "social contract for business," and argues against Friedman's position. Fred Miller and John Ahrens consider some of the major arguments for and against treating the corporation as a public, rather than a private, institution. And Kenneth Goodpaster offers a way for managers to take account of the interest of all stakeholders.

Milton Friedman

THE SOCIAL RESPONSIBILITY OF BUSINESS IS TO INCREASE ITS PROFITS

When I hear businessmen speak eloquently about the "social responsibilities of business in a free-enterprise system," I am reminded of the wonderful line about the Frenchman who discovered at the age of 70 that he had been speaking prose all his life. The businessmen believe that they are defending free enterprise when they declaim that business is not concerned "merely" with profit but also with promoting desirable "social" ends; that business has a "social conscience" and takes seriously its responsibilities for providing employment, eliminating discrimination, avoiding pollution and whatever else may be the catchwords of the contemporary crop of reformers. In fact they are — or would be if they or anyone else took them seriously — preaching pure and unadulterated socialism. Businessmen who talk this way are unwitting puppets of the intellectual forces that have been undermining the basis of a free society these past decades.

The discussions of the "social responsibilities of business" are notable for their analytical looseness and lack of rigor. What does it mean to say that "business" has responsibilities? Only people can have responsibilities. A corporation is an artificial person and in this sense may have artificial responsibilities, but "business" as a whole cannot be said to have responsibilities, even in this vague sense. The first step toward clarity in examining the doctrine of the social responsibility of business is to ask precisely what it implies for whom.

Presumably, the individuals who are to be responsible are businessmen, which means individual proprietors or corporate executives. Most of the discussion of social responsibility is directed at corporations, so in what follows I shall mostly neglect the individual proprietor and speak of corporate executives.

In a free-enterprise, private-property system, a corporate executive is an employe of the owners of the business. He has direct responsibility to his employers. That responsibility is to conduct the business in accordance with their desires, which generally will be to make as much money as possible while conforming to the basic rules of the society, both those embodied in law and those embodied in ethical custom. Of course, in some cases his employers may have a different objective. A group of persons might establish a corporation for an eleemosynary purpose — for example, a hospital or a school. The manager of such a corporation will not have money profit as his objective but the rendering of certain services.

In either case, the key point is that, in his capacity as a corporate executive, the manager is the agent of the individuals who own the corporation or establish the eleemosynary institution, and his primary responsibility is to them.

Needless to say, this does not mean that it is easy to judge how well he is

From *New York Times Magazine*, September 13, 1970, 32–33, 122–126. Copyright © 1970 by The New York Times Company. Reprinted by permission.

performing his task. But at least the criterion of performance is straightforward, and the persons among whom a voluntary contractual arrangement exists are clearly defined.

Of course, the corporate executive is also a person in his own right. As a person, he may have many other responsibilities that he recognizes or assumes voluntarily — to his family, his conscience, his feelings of charity, his church, his clubs, his city, his country. He may feel impelled by these responsibilities to devote part of his income to causes he regards as worthy, to refuse to work for particular corporations, even to leave his job, for example, to join his country's armed forces. If we wish, we may refer to some of these responsibilities as "social responsibilities." But in these respects he is acting as a principal, not an agent; he is spending his own money or time or energy, not the money of his employers or the time or energy he has contracted to devote to their purposes. If these are "social responsibilities," they are the social responsibilities of individuals, not of business.

What does it mean to say that the corporate executive has a "social responsibility" in his capacity as businessman? If this statement is not pure rhetoric, it must mean that he is to act in some way that is not in the interest of his employers. For example, that he is to refrain from increasing the price of the product in order to contribute to the social objective of preventing inflation, even though a price increase would be in the best interests of the corporation. Or that he is to make expenditures on reducing pollution beyond the amount that is in the best interests of the corporation or that is required by law in order to contribute to the social objective of improving the environment. Or that, at the expense of corporate profits, he is to hire "hard-core" unemployed instead of better-qualified available workmen to contribute to the social objective of reducing poverty.

In each of these cases, the corporate executive would be spending someone else's money for a general social interest. Insofar as his actions in accord with his "social responsibility" reduce returns to stockholders, he is spending their money. Insofar as his actions raise the price to customers, he is spending the customers' money. Insofar as his actions lower the wages of some employes, he is spending their money.

The stockholders or the customers or the employes could separately spend their own money on the particular action if they wished to do so. The executive is exercising a distinct "social responsibility," rather than serving as an agent of the stockholders or the customers or the employes, only if he spends the money in a different way than they would have spent it.

But if he does this, he is in effect imposing taxes, on the one hand, and deciding how the tax proceeds shall be spent, on the other.

This process raises political questions on two levels: principle and consequences. On the level of political principle, the imposition of taxes and the expenditure of tax proceeds are governmental functions. We have established elaborate constitutional, parliamentary and judicial provisions to control these functions, to assure that taxes are imposed so far as possible in accordance with the preferences and desires of the public — after all, "taxation without representation" was one of the battle cries of the American Revolution. We have a system of checks and balances to separate the legislative function of imposing taxes and enacting expenditures from the executive function of collecting taxes and administering expenditure programs and from the judicial function of mediating disputes and interpreting the law.

Here the businessman — self-selected or appointed directly or indirectly by stockholders — is to be simultaneously legislator, executive and jurist. He is to decide whom to tax by how much and for what purpose, and he is to spend the proceeds — all this guided only by general exhortations from on high to restrain inflation, improve the environment, fight poverty and so on and on.

The whole justification for permitting the corporate executive to be selected by the stockholders is that the executive is an agent serving the interests of his principal. This justification disappears when the corporate executive imposes taxes and spends the proceeds for "social" purposes. He becomes in effect a public employe, a civil servant, even though he remains in name an employe of a private enterprise. On grounds of political principle, it is intolerable that such civil servants — insofar as their actions in the name of social responsibility are real and not just window-dressing — should be selected as they are now. If they are to be civil servants, then they must be selected through a political process. If they are to impose taxes and make expenditures to foster "social" objectives, then political machinery must be set up to guide the assessment of taxes and to determine through a political process the objectives to be served.

This is the basic reason why the doctrine of "social responsibility" involves the acceptance of the socialist view that political mechanisms, not market mechanisms, are the appropriate way to determine the allocation of scarce resources to alternative uses.

On the grounds of consequences, can the corporate executive in fact discharge his alleged "social responsibilities"? On the one hand, suppose he could get away with spending the stockholders' or customers' or employes' money. How is he to know how to spend it? He is told that he must contribute to fighting inflation. How is he to know what action of his will contribute to that end? He is presumably an expert in running his company — in producing a product or selling it or financing it. But nothing about his selection makes him an expert on inflation. Will his holding down the price of his product reduce inflationary pressure? Or, by leaving more spending power in the hands of his customers, simply divert it elsewhere? Or, by forcing him to produce less because of the lower price, will it simply contribute to shortages? Even if he could answer these questions, how much cost is he justified in imposing on his stockholders, customers and employes for this social purpose? What is his appropriate share and what is the appropriate share of others?

And, whether he wants to or not, can he get away with spending his stockholders', customers' or employes' money? Will not the stockholders fire him? (Either the present ones or those who take over when his actions in the name of social responsibility have reduced the corporation's profits and the price of its stock.) His customers and his employes can desert him for other producers and employers less scrupulous in exercising their social responsibilities.

This fact of "social responsibility" doctrine is brought into sharp relief when the doctrine is used to justify wage restraint by trade unions. The conflict of interest is naked and clear when union officials are asked to subordinate the interest of their members to some more general social purpose. If the union officials try to enforce wage restraint, the consequence is likely to be wildcat strikes, rank-and-file revolts and the emergence of strong competitors for their jobs. We thus have the ironic phenomenon that union leaders — at least in the U.S. — have objected to Government interference with the market far more consistently and courageously than have business leaders.

The difficulty of exercising "social responsibility" illustrates, of course, the great virtue of private competitive enterprise — it forces people to be responsible for their own actions and makes it difficult for them to "exploit" other people for either selfish or unselfish purposes. They can do good — but only at their own expense.

Many a reader who has followed the argument this far may be tempted to remonstrate that it is all well and good to speak of government's having the responsibility to impose taxes and determine expenditures for such "social" purposes as controlling pollution or training the hard-core unemployed, but that the problems are too urgent to wait on the slow course of political processes, that the exercise of social responsibility by businessmen is a quicker and surer way to solve pressing current problems.

Aside from the question of fact — I share Adam Smith's skepticism about the benefits that can be expected from "those who affected to trade for the public good" — this argument must be rejected on grounds of principle. What it amounts to is an assertion that those who favor the taxes and expenditures in question have failed to persuade a majority of their fellow citizens to be of like mind and that they are seeking to attain by undemocratic procedures what they cannot attain by democratic procedures. In a free society, it is hard for "good" people to do "good," but that is a small price to pay for making it hard for "evil" people to do "evil," especially since one man's good is another's evil.

I have, for simplicity, concentrated on the special case of the corporate executive, except only for the brief digression on trade unions. But precisely the same argument applies to the newer phenomenon of calling upon stockholders to require corporations to exercise social responsibility (the recent G.M. crusade, for example). In most of these cases, what is in effect involved is some stockholders trying to get other stockholders (or customers or employes) to contribute against their will to "social" causes favored by the activists. Insofar as they succeed, they are again imposing taxes and spending the proceeds.

The situation of the individual proprietor is somewhat different. If he acts to reduce the returns of his enterprise in order to exercise his "social responsibility," he is spending his own money, not someone else's. If he wishes to spend his money on such purposes, that is his right, and I cannot see that there is any objection to his doing so. In the process, he, too, may impose costs on employes and customers. However, because he is far less likely than a large corporation or union to have monopolistic power, any such side effects will tend to be minor.

Of course, in practice the doctrine of social responsibility is frequently a cloak for actions that are justified on other grounds rather than a reason for those actions.

To illustrate, it may well be in the long-run interest of a corporation that is a major employer in a small community to devote resources to providing amenities to that community or to improving its government. That may make it easier to attract desirable employes, it may reduce the wage bill or lessen losses from pilferage and sabotage or have other worthwhile effects. Or it may be that, given the laws about the deductibility of corporate charitable contributions, the stockholders can contribute more to charities they favor by having the corporation make the gift than by doing it themselves, since they can in that way contribute an amount that would otherwise have been paid as corporate taxes.

In each of these — and many similar — cases, there is a strong temptation to rationalize these actions as an exercise of "social responsibility." In the present climate of opinion, with its widespread aversion to "capitalism," "profits," the "soulless corporation" and so on, this is one way for a corporation to generate goodwill as a by-product of expenditures that are entirely justified in its own self-interest.

It would be inconsistent of me to call on corporate executives to refrain from this hypocritical window-dressing because it harms the foundations of a free society. That would be to call on them to exercise a "social responsibility"! If our institutions, and the attitudes of the public make it in their self-interest to cloak their actions in this way, I cannot summon much indignation to denounce them. At the same time, I can express admiration for those individual proprietors or owners of closely held corporations or stockholders of more broadly held corporations who disdain such tactics as approaching fraud.

Whether blameworthy or not, the use of the cloak of social responsibility, and the nonsense spoken in its name by influential and prestigious businessmen, does clearly harm the foundations of a free society. I have been impressed time and again by the schizophrenic character of many businessmen. They are capable of being extremely far-sighted and clear-headed in matters that are internal to their businesses. They are incredibly short-sighted and muddle-headed in matters that are outside their businesses but affect the possible survival of business in general. This short-sightedness is strikingly exemplified in the calls from many businessmen for wage and price guidelines or controls or incomes policies. There is nothing that could do more in a brief period to destroy a market system and replace it by a centrally controlled system than effective governmental control of prices and wages.

The short-sightedness is also exemplified in speeches by businessmen on social responsibility. This may gain them kudos in the short run. But it helps to strengthen the already too prevalent view that the pursuit of profits is wicked and immoral and must be curbed and controlled by external forces. Once this view is adopted, the external forces that curb the market will not be the social consciences, however highly developed, of the pontificating executives; it will be the iron fist of Government bureaucrats. Here, as with price and wage controls, businessmen seem to me to reveal a suicidal impulse.

The political principle that underlies the market mechanism is unanimity. In an ideal free market resting on private property, no individual can coerce any other, all cooperation is voluntary, all parties to such cooperation benefit or they need not participate. There are no "social" values, no "social" responsibilities in any sense other than the shared values and responsibilities of individuals. Society is a collection of individuals and of the various groups they voluntarily form.

The political principle that underlies the political mechanism is conformity. The individual must serve a more general social interest — whether that be determined by a church or a dictator or a majority. The individual may have a vote and a say in what is to be done, but if he is overruled, he must conform. It is appropriate for some to require others to contribute to a general social purpose whether they wish to or not.

Unfortunately, unanimity is not always feasible. There are some respects in which conformity appears unavoidable, so I do not see how one can avoid the use of the political mechanism altogether.

But the doctrine of "social responsibility" taken seriously would extend the scope of the political mechanism to every human activity. It does not differ in philosophy from the most explicitly collectivist doctrine. It differs only by professing to believe that collectivist ends can be attained without collectivist means. That is why, in my book "Capitalism and Freedom," I have called it a "fundamentally subversive doctrine" in a free society, and have said that in such a society, "there is one and only one social responsibility of business — to use its resources and engage in activities designed to increase its profits so long as it stays within the rules of the game, which is to say, engages in open and free competition without deception or fraud."

Thomas Donaldson

CONSTRUCTING A SOCIAL CONTRACT FOR BUSINESS

In a speech to the Harvard Business School in 1969, Henry Ford II stated:

The terms of the contract between industry and society are changing . . . Now we are being asked to serve a wider range of human values and to accept an obligation to members of the public with whom we have no commercial transactions.

The "contract" to which Henry Ford referred concerns a corporation's *indirect* obligations. It represents not a set of formally specified obligations, but a set of binding, abstract ones. A social contract for business, if one exists, is not a typewritten contract in the real world, but a metaphysical abstraction not unlike the "social contract" between citizens and government that philosophers have traditionally discussed. Such a contract would have concrete significance, for it would help to interpret the nature of a corporation's indirect obligations, which are notoriously slippery.

The aim of this chapter is to discover a corporation's indirect obligations by attempting to clarify the meaning of business's so-called "social contract." The task is challenging. Although people speak frequently of such a contract, few have attempted to specify its meaning. Although businesspeople, legislators, and academics offer examples of supposed infractions of the "contract," few can explain what justifies the contract itself. Consider the assertion that Chisso

From Thomas Donaldson, "Constructing a Social Contract for Business," in *Corporations and Morality* (Englewood Cliffs, NJ: Prentice Hall, 1982), 18–35. Thomas Donaldson, *Corporations and Morality,* © 1982, pp. 18–35. Reprinted by permission of Prentice Hall, Englewood Cliffs, New Jersey.

Corporation violated its "contract" with society when it knowingly dumped toxic mercury into the ocean, or that the Nestlé Corporation violated its "contract" when it promoted sales of infant formula in Third World countries. What serves as the ultimate basis for such claims? No contract can be pulled from a drawer and pointed to; no signatures can be checked for authenticity. Just what, then, *is* the social contract?

A good starting point is the so-called "social contract" that philosophers have spoken of between society and the state. This political contract has usually been viewed as a theoretical means for justifying the existence of the state. Philosophers have asked, "Why should people let a government exist at all?" in other words, "Why should people prefer to have a government control much of their actions — to impose taxes, raise armies, and punish criminals — instead of having no government at all?" They never doubted for a moment the need for a state, but they believed raising such questions would clarify not only the justification for the state's existence, but also the reciprocal obligations between the state and its citizens. If a government began to abuse its citizenry, to trample on its rights or to diminish social welfare, then according to such philosophers it had broken the tenets of the social contract and could be overthrown. Such a theory in the hands of the seventeenth-century English philosopher John Locke, provided much of the theoretical support for the American Revolution and design of the Declaration of Independence and the U.S. Constitution.

The political social contract provides a clue for understanding the contract for business. If the political contract serves as a justification for the existence of the state, then the business contract by parity of reasoning should serve as the justification for the existence of the corporation.

Thus, crucial questions are: Why should corporations exist at all? What is the fundamental justification of their activities? How can we measure their performance and say when they have achieved their fundamental purpose? Consider a case involving General Motors and the production of automobiles. The automobiles that General Motors produced during the 1950s and 1960s all had noncollapsible steering wheels (called by Ralph Nader "ram-rodding" steering wheels), and evidence indicated that they contributed to hundreds of thousands of highway deaths. But General Motors and other auto manufacturers kept them on the cars anyway, claiming the added expense of collapsible steering wheels would reduce car sales and profits. Their claim may well have been true. However, by refusing to install safer steering wheels, had they failed to achieve a fundamental corporate mission? Had they violated a tenet of an implied social contract between them and society? Or had they just attended to business — although in a way which had unfortunate consequences for society? To answer these questions, we must first know what justifies General Motors' existence.

It is reasonable to look for a fundamental purpose, or set of purposes, that justifies corporate existence. Doing so makes conceptual sense, despite the fact one would never look for what justifies, say, human existence. As we learned in the last chapter, corporations, unlike humans, are artifacts, which is to say *we* create them. We *choose* to create corporations and we might choose either not to create them or to create different entities. Corporations thus are like political states in their need for justification.

But, one might ask, aren't corporations justified already? Do they not already contribute to society by supplying it with goods and services? And do they not possess an inherent *right* to exist? These questions suggest that one might explain corporate existence without struggling to articulate the tenets of a "social contract."

One might attempt to justify corporate existence by appealing simply to corporate productivity: to the automobiles, irons, tools, clothing, and medical equipment corporations create. Because society demands such items, it seemingly also requires the corporations that produce them. Adam Smith, the eighteenth-century Scottish philosopher, emphasizes productivity when he justifies a set of economic practices through their contribution to the wealth of nations. But although productivity is surely a crucial piece in the puzzle of corporate justification, it fails to provide a full solution. To say that an organization produces wealth for society is not sufficient to justify it from a moral perspective, since morality encompasses the entire range of human welfare. To say something produces wealth is to say something morally good about it — assuming that wealth is counted as a human good — but it fails to tell us what else the thing does, or how its process of creation affects society. Consider the example of a nuclear power reactor. To say that a nuclear reactor generates electricity is to say something good about it, but it fails to consider the reactor in the context of the possibility of melt-downs, the storage of nuclear waste, the costs of alternative production, and so forth. And this is true even if we suppose that ultimately nuclear reactors are fully justified. The logic of the problem of corporate justification is similar. To achieve a complete moral picture of a corporation's existence, we must consider not just its capacity to produce wealth, but rather the full range of its effects upon society: its tendencies to pollute or to harm workers, or, alternatively, its tendencies to help employees by providing jobs and other benefits for society.

Suppose, on the other hand, that one tried to justify corporate existence simply through the inherent "right" of corporations to exist. We remember that one of the two rival interpretations of the corporation sees it as a product of free human association: people freely come together for the purpose of conducting business, and they constitute the corporation. And we remember that in the United States since the mid-nineteenth century corporate status has been regarded as a right, not a privilege. Why, then, is there even a need to justify corporate existence?

Again, this line of reasoning falls short of providing a complete justification. Granted the act of incorporation does not happen in a vacuum; at a minimum there must be a petitioning group of persons. But even granting that individuals, by virtue of their freedom, are allowed to create these superpersonal entities, and even granting that the entities themselves should possess unlimited longevity and limited liability, these facts by themselves say nothing about *why* people ought to do such a thing. An analogy reveals the distinction: people may, by virtue of their freedom, be allowed to become drunk nightly; but it is abundantly clear that their *right* to do so fails to justify their nightly drunkenness. Similarly, even if there were a right to incorporate, it would fail to justify corporate existence in the sense of showing why corporations *ought* to exist. Doing so requires more than merely showing that people have a right to incorporate.

THE HISTORY OF THE SOCIAL CONTRACT

Because neither method of justification appears satisfactory, let us return to the idea of a social contract. Other methods, such as traditional utilitarianism, are available and promising, and should not be ruled out. But the focus of this chapter's efforts will be upon the method of social contract. The aim will be to determine what a social contract for business might look like. Since none has been constructed, the best strategy will be to look again at its counterpart, the *political* social contract. Perhaps if we discover the inner workings of the contract between citizens and the state, a blueprint will emerge for constructing the contract between society and corporations.

In the hands of political philosophers the term "social contract" has referred not to an item, but to a method for justifying and explaining the state. The most renowned classical philosophers adopting it were the English philosophers, Thomas Hobbes (1588–1679) and John Locke (1632–1704), and the French philosopher Jean-Jacques Rousseau (1712–1778). Each first imagined society *without* a civil state (without, that is, any government), and then society with it. The strategy was to highlight the benefits that society should expect to receive from the state. Yet, despite similarity of method, each reached different conclusions. Hobbes argued that people must obey the king, or sovereign, because the social contract itself is a contract between sovereign and people. Without such a contract, i.e., in the state without government which Hobbes called a "state of nature," only a condition of "war" could exist, with each person being pitted against his or her fellow human, and no power or authority to make peace among them.

John Locke, writing after Hobbes, repudiated such pessimism. The state of nature preceding the contract, Locke contended, was not one of war, but rather a tolerable, though mildly unruly situation in which people possessed natural rights, such as the right to property and freedom. Indeed they lacked only an efficient means to arbitrate their disputes and protect their rights. To remedy these drawbacks, society must construct the social contract. However, the agreement is not, as Hobbes thought, between the people and a sovereign. Instead, people first establish "civil society," and afterwards civil society negotiates an agreement (a fiduciary trust) to establish a legislative power, or government, that will protect society's rights.[1] If the government fails to protect society's rights, then the trust is broken and revolution is justified. Locke is more wary of government abuses than Hobbes. For Locke, the relationship between people and legislative power is not one of contract; rather it is the same kind that exists between employer and employee, that is, a "trust" between principal and agent. "This conception," J. W. Gough remarks, "fitted Locke's intention admirably, for unlike the contract of government, in which rights and duties were reciprocal, it left the duties on the side of the government, and the rights on the side of the people."[2]

Rousseau's version of the social contract differs from the earlier two. According to him, the contract is created when rights are surrendered *in toto* by individuals to the whole community. As he puts it paradoxically, "Each, giving himself to all, gives himself to nobody." With this, the state is born. The state's

---

[1] J. W. Gough, *The Social Contract* (Oxford: Clarendon Press, 1936), p. 143.
[2] Gough, *The Social Contract*, p. 143.

desire for its own welfare, dubbed by Rousseau the "general will," thus becomes the yardstick by which all government actions are to be measured. This complex version of the contract has struck many as odd, but it has a special aim: to place the moral underpinnings of the state squarely with the desires and well-being of its people. Ernest Barker sums it up:

> [Rousseau] was hardly concerned with practical necessities; he was hot in pursuit of the logical symmetry of an ideal scheme of popular sovereignty.[3]

This chapter cannot do full justice to the arguments of the social contract philosophers; instead, a few general observations about their methods must suffice. *First*, the tradition of social contract theory is a tradition of social change and reform. This holds not only for the arguments of Hobbes, Locke, and Rousseau, but for ones less well known. The Huguenots, a persecuted Protestant group in France, used a social contract argument in the sixteenth century to defend religious tolerance; and the English Whigs, a political group, used it in the seventeenth century to bolster the cause of civil liberty. Consider Robert Ferguson's remark in his *Brief Justification of the Prince of Orange's Descent into England*: "No government is lawful," Ferguson writes, "but what is founded upon compact and agreement between those chosen to govern and those who condescend to be governed."[4] Social contract arguments have unsettled the clergy, shaken monarchies, and brought on revolution. There may never have been a pen and ink contract, but remarkably enough, thousands of people have acted *as if* there were.

The contract has been used as a moral ideal, as a law higher even than the state, against which the state must be evaluated. It is not unlike the "higher law" invoked by the Greeks and Romans. We are reminded of Sophocles' play, *Antigone*, in which a grief-stricken woman learns that her brother's body has been condemned to rot outside the city's walls, stripped even of the honor of a burial. She defies the orders of the king and risks her own life to bury her brother. When asked why she disobeys, she tells the king that his laws have less authority than the ones she obeys: the eternal, unwritten laws of the gods.

Second, two basic forms of the contract can be distinguished. The first postulates people as being in a "state of nature," and agreeing to create an organized society. By "state of nature" is meant a situation prior to the emergence of government, prior, that is, to legislatures, courts of law, police, and public officials. The government is seen as a creation of the people; it emerges from the people and owes its very existence to them. The second approach does not imagine people *creating* government, but rather defining the terms of an implied contract between them and an existing government. This implied contract imposes obligations upon both parties: upon the government and the people. In the seventeenth century, for example, the people of England who wished to overthrow James II claimed that he had violated an implied contract: although this contract was not understood to explain the structure and formation of James' government, it was viewed as setting down certain conditions which he and the people were bound to follow.[5]

<hr/>

[3]Ernest Barker, *Social Contract* (London: Oxford University Press, 1947), p. xxxvi.
[4]Gough, *The Social Contract*, p. 130.
[5]Gough, *The Social Contract*, p. 213.

Third, amid the various versions of the social contract theory a common strand exists: an emphasis on the *consent* of the parties. Most versions invite one to imagine the situation in which rational people, outside ordinary society, must consent to a proposal about the structure of social institutions. The characteristics of the situation — for example, what information people are presumed to have, what interests they bring to the decision, or what issues they are to decide — vary from theory to theory. Yet each version relies upon the consent of the parties: force cannot be a factor, nor can techniques of persuasion.

Critics have repeatedly attacked the social contract for its failure to represent historical fact. No one, the critics charge, could seriously believe that people once gathered in the woods to establish a contract for the world's first governments. Marx and other theorists (such as Paley, Maine, and Blackstone) have made this very point. What is more, modern anthropology appears to confirm their suspicions.

But perhaps such criticism misses the mark, since, as was noticed already, social contract theories have typically been used to analyze *existing* institutions rather than to create new ones. Locke wanted to discover the moral foundation for English government, not dig up the historical causes of the Sumerian or Egyptian kingdoms. Even if no pen and ink contracts ever existed, many would argue that an abstract contract exists, not unlike the invisible laws of the gods, which obliges governments to serve the social welfare. Even if no pen and ink contract ever existed, they would argue that the point of the social contract is to clarify the *logical* presuppositions, not the historical antecedents, of political power.

APPLYING THE CONTRACT TO BUSINESS

The social contract has typically (though not always) been applied to governments. Is there any reason to suppose it is applicable to economic institutions? To productive organizations such as General Motors? One reason for doing so is that companies like General Motors are social giants. They affect the lives of millions of people, influence foreign policy, and employ more people than live in many countries of the world. Equally important is the fact that General Motors exists only through the cooperation and commitment of society. It draws its employees from society, sells its goods to society, and is given its status by society. All of this may suggest the existence of an implied agreement between it and society. If General Motors holds society responsible for providing the condition of its existence, then for what does society hold General Motors responsible? What are the terms of the social contract?

Before we attempt to spell out the terms of the social contract, a prior issue must be settled; namely, *who* are the parties to the contract? So far we have spoken of a contract between society and business, but the concepts of both "business" and "society" are vague. "Business" might include, for example, independent businesspeople such as professional entertainers or craftsmen, as well as large corporations; or it might include *all* corporations, including nonproductive ones. For clarity, let us stipulate, then, that "business" refers to productive organizations: ones where people cooperate to produce at least one specific product or service. Productive organizations would include corporations (of the productive sort), manufacturing partnerships, and service organizations. Later this definition will need to be restricted further, but it will suffice for now.

By attempting to find the moral underpinnings of all productive organizations, we will indirectly be searching for the moral underpinnings of corporations. This happens because virtually all corporations, as we saw earlier, are productive organizations. Once the moral underpinnings of productive organizations are known, it will be possible to answer from a moral perspective questions such as why does General Motors exist and what is General Motors' fundamental purpose? Or, speaking more precisely, it will be possible to answer such questions about General Motors when General Motors is considered *as a member of the class of productive organizations*.

The term "society" is similarly vague. It might refer to the aggregate of individuals who make up society, or to something over and above the sum of those individuals. On the second interpretation, "society" might be construed as having interests (like Rousseau's "general will") which are not the direct products of its members' interests. For clarity, let us stipulate that the contract is between productive organizations and *individual members of society*, not between productive organizations and some supra-individual, social entity.

CONSTRUCTING A CONTRACT

The simplest way of understanding the social contract is in the form: "We (the members of society) agree to do X, and you (the productive organizations) agree to do Y." Applying this form to General Motors (or any productive organization) means that the task of a social contract argument is to specify X, where X refers to the obligations of society to productive organizations, and to specify Y, where Y refers to the obligations of productive organizations to society.

It is relatively easy in this context to specify X, because what productive organizations need from society is:

1. Recognition as a single agent, especially in the eyes of the law.
2. The authority: (a) to own or use land and natural resources, and (b) to hire employees.

It may appear presumptuous to assume that productive organizations must be warranted by society. Can one not argue that any organization has a *right* to exist and operate? That they have this right *apart* from the wishes of society? When asking such questions, one must distinguish . . . between claims about rights of mere organizations and claims about rights of organizations with special powers, such as productive organizations. A case can be made for the unbridled right of the Elks Club, whose members unite in fraternal activities, to exist and operate (assuming it does not discriminate against minorities or women); but the same cannot be said for Du Pont Corporation, which not only must draw on existing stores of mineral resources, but must find dumping sites to store toxic chemical by-products. Even granted that people have an inalienable right to form and operate organizations, and even granted that this right exists apart from the discretion of society, the productive organization requires special status under the law and the opportunity to use society's resources: two issues in which every member of society may be said to have a vested interest.

Conditions 1 and 2 are obviously linked to each other. In order for a productive organization to use land and hire employees (conditions of 2), it must have the authority to perform those acts as if it were an individual agent (the condition of 1). The philosophical impact of 1 should not be exaggerated. To say that productive organizations must have the authority to act as individual agents is not necessarily to affirm that they are abstract, invisible persons. Rather it is a means of stating the everyday fact that productive organizations must, for a variety of purposes, be treated as individual entities. For example, a corporation must be able to hire new employees, to sign contracts, and to negotiate purchases without getting the O.K. from *all* its employees and stockholders. The corporation *itself*, not its stockholders or managers, must be considered to be the controller of its equipment and land; for its stockholders or managers may leave, sell their shares, or die. If they do, the organization still controls its resources; it still employs its work force, and it still is obligated to honor its previous contracts and commitments.

Defining the *Y* side of the contract is as difficult as defining the *X* side is easy. It is obvious that productive organizations must be allowed to exist and act. But it is not obvious precisely why societies should allow them to exist, that is, what specific benefits society should hope to gain from the bargain. What specific functions should society expect from productive organizations? What obligations should it impose? Only one assumption can be made readily: that the members of society should demand at a minimum that the benefits from authorizing the existence of productive organizations outweigh the detriments of doing so. This is nothing other than the expectation of all voluntary agreements: that no party should be asked to conclude a contract which places him or her in a position worse than before.

The task of specifying society's terms for the social contract is a challenging one. To do so, let us return to a traditional device in social contract theory, the device of imagining society *without* the institution that is being analyzed. In short, let us consider society without productive organizations, in a "state of nature." Instead of the traditional state of nature where people live without government, we shall consider a state where people live without *productive organizations*. To avoid confusing this state with the traditional ones, let us call it the "state of individual production." Thus, the strategy involves:

1. Characterizing conditions in a state of individual production (without productive organizations).
2. Indicating how certain problems are remedied by the introduction of productive organizations.
3. Using the reasons generated in the second step as a basis for specifying a social contract between society and its productive organizations.

Such a strategy has obvious advantages. If step 2 indicates the specific benefits which society should expect from productive organizations, it should help specify the terms of the social contract.

The details must be spelled out. How are we to imagine the state of individual production? What people occupy it? Are they selfish? Charitable? How do they labor?

At a minimum the people in the state of individual production should be imagined as having "economic interests," i.e., as being people for whom it is desirable to have some things or services produced by human labor. Under such a definition almost any human would qualify, except perhaps ascetics or persons who prefer death to life. Thus, the people envisioned by the present strategy are ordinary, economically interested persons who have not yet organized themselves, or been organized, into productive organizations.

Should they be imagined as purely egoistic, wanting only to satisfy their own selfish interests, or as purely benevolent, wanting only to satisfy the interests of others? In the real world both characterizations are extreme — ordinary people are neither devils nor saints — and thus is suggested the strategy of assuming the same about people in the state of individual production. Let us adopt this strategy; if the contract has application to ordinary people, it will help to keep ordinary people in mind.[6]

To imagine a state of individual production, i.e., without productive organizations, is to imagine a society in which individuals produce and work alone. It is to imagine society without factories, banks, hospitals, restaurants, or railroads, since all these organizations, as well as many others, count as productive organizations, that is, they are organizations in which people cooperate to produce at least one specific product or service. (For our purposes, noneconomic factors such as family structure, religious attitudes, and educational interests shall be disregarded.) Now in such a state we may imagine any level of technology we wish. The only crucial fact is that people produce *individually*.

THE TERMS OF THE CONTRACT

Two principal classes of people stand to benefit or be harmed by the introduction of productive organizations: (1) people who consume the organizations' products, i.e., consumers; and (2) people who work in such organizations, i.e., employees. The two classes are broadly defined and not mutually exclusive. "Consumer" refers to anyone who is economically interested; hence virtually anyone qualifies as a consumer. "Employee" refers to anyone who contributes labor to the productive process of a productive organization, including managers, laborers, part-time support personnel, and (in corporations) members of the board of directors.

Benefits for Consumers

From the standpoint of our hypothetical consumers, productive organizations promise to *enhance the satisfaction of economic interests*. That is to say, people

---

[6]Some social contract theorists, e.g., Thomas Hobbes and John Rawls, have adopted a different approach, preferring to emphasize people's self-interested tendencies in the state of nature. This view has some definite advantages, since one can say "Even self-interested people will agree to such and such a principle," and, in turn, one's argument gains a persuasive edge. Rawls does not literally assume that people are egoists, but he does assume that they wish to maximize their possession of primary goods. But in the present instance, no compelling reasons exist for representing people worse than they are, and one good reason does exist for representing them as they are: the presence of even ordinary (i.e., non-self-interested) motives can help clarify the conditions of the social contract.

could hope for the introduction of productive organizations to better satisfy their interests for shelter, food, entertainment, transportation, health care, and clothing. The prima facie benefits for consumers include:

1. *Improving efficiency* through:
   a. Maximizing advantages of specialization.
   b. Improving decision-making resources.
   c. Increasing the capacity to use or acquire expensive technology and resources.
2. *Stablizing levels of output and channels of distribution.*
3. *Increasing liability resources.*

Each benefit, of course, needs explanation.

The first benefit, improving efficiency, is the special excellence of productive organizations. Productive organizations tend to generate products that are equal or better in quality and price, with lower expenditures of human labor, than is possible in the state of individual production. Let us examine a few of the reasons for this remarkable capacity.

1A. Maximizing the Advantages of Specialization

Adam Smith's well-known thought-experiment in the *Wealth of Nations* provides ready evidence for the truth that two can often be more efficient than one. He showed that in the production of pins, one person working alone could account for a mere handful of pins, whereas in a system of first-order specialization — where one cuts the wire, another points the wire, and so on — the proportionate share of pins per worker increases dramatically. The same is true today. To produce clocks, erasers, and antibiotics efficiently, an enormous degree of cooperative specialization is required: the mere existence of products like the space shuttle owes itself to such specialization. Economists agree that many products are further subject to *economies of scale*; that is, their efficient production is dependent not only upon cooperative specialization, but on a certain level of it. Because of this factor, a company like American Motors may be too small to compete successfully with General Motors in the production of automobiles.

The greater efficiency which derives from productive organizations is partially dependent upon the level of technology. At minimal levels it may be less efficient to have such systems. One person working alone with stone implements may be able to clean and prepare vegetables as efficiently as three working in concert. At higher levels of technology this would not be true. The reverse is also possible: advanced technology may allow one person to be efficient in a situation where, minus the technology, he or she would not be. Equipped with a mechanical combine, one individual may be efficient at harvesting wheat, whereas without it six or more would be required. But no matter what the level of technology, some tasks benefit from cooperative specialization. Even in a futuristic, thoroughly technological society, a group of scientists who cooperate to perfect an additional piece of technology should, all other things being equal, be more efficient than an aggregate of individual scientists working without contact among themselves.

1B. Improving Decision-making Resources

Productive organizations share with individual persons the tendency to err in decision-making. Despite this, such organizations have decision-making advantages. First, they can utilize the ongoing talents of people with different backgrounds. Thus, a decision by Westinghouse, Inc., to manufacture a new appliance may call on the knowledge of chemists, accountants, engineers, and marketing specialists. One person could never possess such knowledge.

Second, they can increase information storage. In the same way a person can collect and remember information on a small scale, organizations do so on a large scale. Productive organizations can have superhuman memories: some corporations have libraries larger than those in universities, where all their information bears either directly or indirectly upon productive success.

1C. Increasing the Capacity to Use and Acquire Expensive Technology and Resources

This advantage is nearly self-evident. All other things being equal, two or more people will have greater financial resources than one; hence productive organizations can make capital expenditures on a larger scale than single individuals. Often the use of large, expensive equipment is important not only for increasing production, but for generating higher quality production, since expensive equipment is frequently necessary to improve productive efficiency. An individual who intends to produce bread cannot compete in today's world without mechanical ovens, assembly lines, and mechanical bread-slicers. Yet few individuals can afford such items, much less attempt to operate them single-handedly. By combining their energies and resources in a productive organization, people can increase the cost effectiveness of production.

2. Stabilizing Levels of Output and Channels of Distribution

The imaginary inhabitants of our state of individual production stand to benefit by the merging of individual craftsmen into organizations which are relatively stable, and whose level of output and pattern of distribution are relatively constant. Individual craftsmen are subject to illness, psychological problems, and the need for rest. For example, to rely on an individual mail carrier for the delivery of one's mail is riskier than depending on a large postal organization. Individuals must sleep, eat, and rest, but a large postal organization never sleeps, never eats — it even grows larger at Christmas. In general, then, productive organizations promise to stabilize the market for the benefit of the consumer.

3. Increasing Liability Resources

Under this heading are grouped the benefits that consumers reap because organizations, in contrast to individuals, have "deep pockets." In short, they are better able to compensate injured consumers. In the late 1970's Ford Motor Company was forced by the courts to compensate victims of the Ford Pinto's exploding gas tank. Because of design defects, the Pinto's tank was prone to ignite when hit from behind. The money paid by Ford to victims (and relatives of victims) was astounding; it ran into the millions of dollars. Although few productive organizations are as large as Ford, it remains true that organizations are better able to back their products with financial resources than individuals.

Contrast the capacity of any automobile company in this regard with the capacity of the individual person who builds an auto in his or her backyard.

Benefits for Employees

These, then, are the prima facie benefits from introducing productive organizations for consumers. But productive organizations should also be viewed from the standpoint of their effects on people as workers, that is, from the standpoint of their effects upon individual laborers and craftsmen in the state of individual production who opt to work for productive organizations.

It is not difficult to discover certain prima facie benefits, such as the following:

1. Increasing income potential (and the capacity for social contributions).
2. Diffusing personal liability.
3. Adjusting personal income allocation.

1. Increasing Income Potential and Capacity for Social Contributions

This benefit follows immediately from the earlier fact that cooperative specialization increases productive efficiency. The person, like Smith's hypothetical pin maker, who joins others in the production of pins is able to make many times more pins than he would alone. This increase also represents an increase in his chance to receive a higher income.

It also increases, if he is so inclined, his overall capacity to contribute to society. For if he feels some personal obligation to contribute productively to society, or if he merely wishes to be benevolent, his increased productivity increases his power of doing so. Two options are available: he can either accept lower than normal personal remuneration, thus increasing his net contribution; or he can accept normal remuneration and give some of it away. An example of the former would be those who work in voluntary organizations, e.g., the Women's Service League or the Peace Corps. An example of the latter is the person who works for a major company, but who donates some of his salary to charity. In any case, the person who increases his productivity by joining a productive organization thereby increases, all other things being equal, *both* his income potential and his capacity for contribution. Of course ambitious owners or unjust economic arrangements may deprive workers of the additional income which they (the workers) have generated. But this is a by-product of the particular owners or of particular economic systems, and not a feature of productive organizations per se.

2. Diffusing Personal Liability

A second prima facie benefit from the standpoint of workers lies in the capacity of an organization to diffuse liability, or in short, to insure the individual against the risk of massive compensation demands. A worker in the state of individual production who sells faulty, dangerous products is morally liable for the damages her product causes. If she negligently drops poison in the medicine she manufactures, then she is ethically bound to compensate the victim. But the extent of this liability can exceed her capacity to pay. Therefore she stands to gain by working with others in a productive organization, for it then becomes the productive organization, not she, who assumes ultimate liability.

3. Adjusting Personal Income Allocation

The increased resources of the productive organization allow the worker to participate in an income-allocation scheme which is detached from the vicissitudes of his capacity to produce, and which is more closely tied to his actual needs. The vicissitudes of the worker's capacity include occasional illness, disabling accidents, and a tendency to lose speed and strength as he ages. Yet his needs persist and sometimes even increase in the face of these vicissitudes. The employee can work harder when he is healthy; but he needs as much money, and sometimes more, when he is ill. The worker may not be able to produce more when he is 50 than when he was 20, but if he marries and has a family his need for income may be greater at 50. When the worker joins a productive organization, the organization can allocate personal income according to a scheme more equitable for him and everyone else. Income may, for example, be raised in accordance with length of service, even in a proportion greater than the individual's productivity, and it can continue to be distributed to workers even when they are ill and disabled.

These prima facie benefits to the worker may be added to the prima facie consumer benefits discussed earlier. Together they constitute a set of reasons which rational people living in a state of individual production might use to justify the introduction of productive organizations. Indeed, if some such set of prima facie benefits did *not* exist, then people would be foolish to introduce such organizations; there would be nothing to gain.

It now becomes possible in light of this analysis to begin the task of specifying the general character of a hypothetical social contract. From the standpoint of society, the goal of a productive organization may be said to be *to enhance the welfare of society through a satisfaction of consumer and worker interests*. In turn, each of the prima facie benefits that we have discussed can be construed as specific terms of the social contract. Productive organizations should attempt to satisfy consumer interests through enhancing efficiency, stabilizing output, and augmenting liability, and they should attempt to satisfy employee interests through increasing income potential, diffusing personal liability, and adjusting income allocation. These terms of the contract thus constitute fundamental positive goals of productive organizations.

It is not in society's interest to settle for less instead of more. As mentioned earlier, it can choose either not to create productive organizations, or to create ones with different standards. A rational group of people in the state of individual production will *a fortiori* choose to create organizations that observe the highest standards — to maximize welfare — and will build such standards into the bargain.

Drawbacks for Consumers and Employees

An obvious question arises. If people in the state of individual production must agree upon the terms of the social contract, and if these terms directly relate to the task of enhancing society's welfare, then why stop with maximizing prima facie benefits? Why not also minimize prima facie drawbacks? John Locke employed a similar strategy in structuring his political social contract: he not only specified the positive goals of government, but, recognizing government's tendency to abuse privilege, also saw fit to specify certain pitfalls that government must avoid. Are there prima facie drawbacks to introducing productive organizations as well? Are there drawbacks from the standpoint of consumers? Of workers?

Our imaginary consumer stands to benefit because productive organizations, along with the technology they encourage, improve productivity and put more shoes, clothing, electricity, and automobiles on the market. But there is an unwanted consequence of which twentieth-century consumers are painfully aware: increased production tends to deplete natural resources while increasing pollution. More shoes, clothing, electricity, and automobiles require more leather, cotton, coal, and iron. The world has a finite supply. Moreover, the amazing machines so well adapted to productive organizations — the gas engines, the coal furnaces, and the nuclear reactors all generate by-products which render the environment less fit for human life.

The problem of the increased pollution and depletion of natural resources is more obvious than a second problem, which is the diffusion of individual moral responsibility which sometimes occurs in productive organizations. In the state of individual production, the consumers buy their goods from the individual craftsman who stands behind his product, or at least if he does not, the consumers know where to go. When the cobbler sells a pair of shoes to John Doe and the shoes fall apart, he must confront Doe face to face. Contrast this situation with that of productive organizations, in which workers never see the consumer. To the employee, the consumer is faceless, and the employee's level of psychic accountability tends to lower along with a rise in consumer anonymity. The employee is responsible for his behavior, but to his superior, not to the customer; and his superior sometimes is more apathetic than he. In extreme instances the employee may participate in a form of rebellion unknown to the independent craftsman: "industrial sabotage," where workers retaliate against management by intentionally damaging products.

While speaking of potential drawbacks of productive organizations, one must also acknowledge that the political power of productive organizations is sometimes used to enhance individual interests. Such power sometimes is used to secure favors from government which damage both consumer interests and the interests of the general public. Organizations can receive favors which bolster monopoly power and aggravate inefficiency, as when the railroads in the United States in the late nineteenth century used government grants and privileges to develop a stranglehold on public transportation. Organizations can also use power to divert government expenditures from consumer items to items that actually harm the consumers' interests. In Germany prior to World Wars I and II, for example, large munitions manufacturers used their political influence to increase taxation, and thus decrease consumers' buying power, for massive purchases of cannons, tanks, fighter planes, and warships. Undeniably, from the overall standpoint of the German public, these purchases were disastrous.

From the perspective of consumers these problems represent potential drawbacks often associated with the introduction of productive organizations. But drawbacks also exist for employees.

Workers in the state of individual production possess a few obvious advantages. For one, they are close to the product and able to take pride in their own creations and the fact that their hands were responsible for the lamp, the soap, or the shirt being sold. But workers in productive organizations are typically removed from the product. They are, in the words of Marx, "alienated" in a way that may block their very capacity for self-expression. During World War II the U.S. aircraft manufacturers discovered that alienation was hampering production. Production was shown to increase when the draftsmen, riveters, and sheetmetal workers were taken to *see* the finished product they had worked on — the airplane itself.

In addition to possible alienation and loss of pride, the worker may also suffer from losing control over the design of the product and of his or her work structure. Whereas the individual craftsman can structure her hours and conditions to suit herself, the organizational worker must suit the needs of the overall organization. A man or woman working on an assembly line is powerless to improve the design of the product, and equally powerless to change the design of the work process. The look of the product, the speed of the conveyor belt, and even the number of steps to perform the task all have been determined by others, who are frequently strangers to the worker. Seldom even does the worker have control over safety arrangements or levels of in-plant pollutants.

The increased capacity of productive organizations (over individuals) to use large, expensive technology and massive resources reveals on the other side a decreased capacity of the workers to control their lives. They must adapt to the machines. If a machine operates most efficiently at a certain pace, then the worker must, like the spool boys of the nineteenth-century cotton industry, hurry to meet that pace. In such cases it is as if the machine were controlling the person instead of the person controlling the machine. Similarly, the increased efficiency which results from specialization reveals, on its reverse, the monotony of the simple task repeated thousands of times. The man who knocked the struts into place on the wheels of Henry Ford's Model T was far more efficient than the old craftsman who built a carriage from the bottom up. But the Ford worker knocked struts in place on wheels every minute of every working day.

These prima facie *drawbacks* may be seen as reasons for *not* introducing productive organizations. Unless the prima facie benefits discussed earlier outweigh these prima facie drawbacks, no contract will be concluded because rational people will not choose a lesser over a greater good. And if the benefits outweigh the drawbacks, it follows that in order maximally to enhance welfare, productive organizations should both pursue positive goals and minimize negative ones. Thus, using our discussion as a basis for this list of negative goals, we have:

From the standpoint of *consumers*, productive organizations should minimize:

1. Pollution and the depletion of natural resources.
2. The destruction of personal accountability.
3. The misuse of political power.

From the standpoint of *workers*, productive organizations should minimize:

1. Worker alienation.
2. Lack of worker control over work conditions.
3. Monotony and dehumanization of the worker.

Thus the social contract will specify that these negative consequences be minimized.

Trade-Offs

The social contract sketched out requires, then, that productive organizations maximize goods and minimize evils relative to consumer and worker welfare. But how will an organization know how to make the inevitable trade-offs between maximizing and minimizing, and between consumer interests and worker interests? For example, a corporate decision may impair worker interests while at the same time enhancing consumer interests. Consider the age-old trade-off between higher salaries and lower consumer prices. If coffee workers are paid higher salaries, then coffee drinkers pay higher prices. Conversely, if doctors are paid lower salaries, then patients pay lower prices. These trade-offs are common not only in the area of salaries, but in many others as well. Where does one draw the line?

How would the rational inhabitants of our state of individual production answer this question? Because the contract specifies that the function of productive organizations is to enhance the welfare of society, our inhabitants might choose a utilitarian standard for making trade-offs, that is, a standard that would specify that organizational policies or action should aim for *the greatest good for the greatest number*. On the other hand, they might prefer a nonutilitarian, or deontological standard, which would specify that *organizational action should accord with general policies or rules which could be universalized for all productive organizations* (i.e., which society would want all productive organizations to adopt).

Whatever the standard — and it must be acknowledged that determining the standard is difficult — two things seem certain. First, society does acknowledge that trade-offs often must be made. Society could not reasonably expect productive organizations to maximize worker interests come what may, say by adopting the policy of paying workers the absolute maximum possible at a given time, for to do so would grossly neglect consumers. If General Motors expended every bit of its resources on employees, the result for society would be catastrophic. Similarly, the consumer must not receive all the attention. Such a policy would result in poor working conditions, low salaries, and frustrated workers (no matter how satisfied employees might be in their life as consumers).

Because trade-offs must be made, it remains logically possible that people in the state of individual production would choose to introduce productive organizations and to establish the social contract, even when they expected either worker interests or consumer interests to be less satisfied than in the state of nature — so long as *overall* welfare were enhanced. In other words, the inhabitants might believe that, on balance, people as workers stand to lose from the introduction of productive organizations, and that potential alienation, loss of control, and other drawbacks make the overall condition of the worker worse than before. But if the benefits to people as consumers fully *overshadowed* these drawbacks, we should still expect the contract to be enacted.

Justice

There is a caveat which has application to the overall contract. People would make a trade-off of the kind just discussed only on the condition that it did not violate certain minimum standards of justice, however these are specified. For example, they would refuse to enact the contract if they knew that the existence of productive organizations would systematically reduce a given class of people to an inhuman existence, subsistence poverty, or enslavement.

This point, in turn, provides a clue to one of the specific tenets of the contract. Although the contract might allow productive organizations to undertake actions requiring welfare trade-offs, it would prohibit organizational acts of injustice. It might allow a corporation to lay off, or reduce the salaries of, thousands of workers in order to block skyrocketing production costs; here, worker welfare would be diminished while consumer welfare would be enhanced. But it is another matter when the company commits gross injustices in the process — for example, if it lies to workers, telling them that no layoffs are planned merely to keep them on the job until the last minute. Similarly, it is another matter when the organization follows discriminatory hiring policies, refusing to hire blacks or women, in the name of "consumer advantage." These are clear injustices of the kind that society would want to prohibit as a condition of the social contract. We may infer, then, that a tenet of the social contract will be that productive organizations are to remain within the bounds of the general canons of justice.

Determining what justice requires is a notoriously difficult task. The writings of Plato, Aristotle, and more recently, John Rawls, have shed considerable light on this subject, but unfortunately we must forego a general discussion of justice here. At a minimum, however, the application of the concept of justice to productive organizations appears to imply *that productive organizations avoid deception or fraud, that they show respect for their workers as human beings, and that they avoid any practice that systematically worsens the situation of a given group in society.* Despite the loud controversy over what justice means, most theorists would agree that justice means at least this much for productive organizations.

An Overview of the Contract

Our sketch of a hypothetical social contract is now complete. By utilizing the concept of rational people existing in a state of individual production, we have indicated the terms of a contract which they would require for the introduction of productive organizations. The questions asked in the beginning were: Why should corporations exist at all? What is the fundamental justification for their activities? How can we measure their performance, to say when they have performed poorly or well? A social contract helps to answer these questions. Corporations considered as productive organizations exist to enhance the welfare of society through the satisfaction of consumer and worker interests, in a way which relies on exploiting corporations' special advantages and minimizing disadvantages. This is the *moral foundation* of the corporation when considered as a productive organization. The social contract also serves as a tool to measure the performance of productive organizations. That is, when such organizations fulfill the terms of the contract, they have done well. When they do not, then society is morally justified in condemning them.

Productive organizations (whether corporations or not) that produce quality goods at low prices, that reject government favoritism, and that enhance the well-being of workers receive high marks by the standards of the social contract. Those that allow inefficiency, charge high prices, sell low-quality products, and fail to enhance the well-being of workers receive low marks. The latter organizations have violated the terms of the social contract. They must reform themselves, or lose their moral right to exist.

It is well to notice that such a social contract does not specify additional obligations or rights which *corporations* have in contrast to *productive organizations* in general. The social contract justifies corporations as *productive organizations*, not as *corporations*. Presumably, then, further reasons remain to be discovered for society's establishing a certain type of productive organization, such as the corporation — with limited liability, stockholder ownership, and its other characteristics. The important task of discovering those reasons, however, must wait for another occasion. Our development of the social contract has fallen short of a full moral comprehension of corporations, but it has secured a solid footing in an equally important area: comprehending the moral underpinnings of productive organizations.

THE SOCIAL RESPONSIBILITY OF BUSINESS

Assuming that such a contract exists, it clashes with the argument of the controversial economist Milton Friedman, in his article entitled "The Social Responsibility of Business Is to Increase Its Profits."[7] There Friedman condemns "social responsibility" by appealing to the "fiduciary" duties of managers. He argues that when stockholders bring a company into existence through buying stock, they do so on the condition that corporate managers will follow their wishes — usually, to make a profit. A moral obligation is thus generated for managers, namely, to serve as fiduciaries for profit-seeking investors; and it follows that using the stockholders' money otherwise, say, to conform to the social contract, is tantamount to stealing.[8]

This argument owes its credibility to the sanctity we give to voluntary agreements. We champion voluntary agreements and believe people have a right to make them, good or bad. When a person has freely obligated himself — as a manager presumably does to the stockholder who contributes capital we balk at meddling with the agreement, at inserting additional conditions.

It is obvious, however, that the social contract could not jeopardize *all* voluntary agreements and contracts, but only those whose consequences would

---

[7] "The Social Responsibility of Business Is to Increase Its Profits," *The New York Times Magazine*, September 13, 1970.

[8] As will be shown later, however, the U.S. courts have disagreed with this principle, allowing corporations to give up to 5 percent of profit to charity.

commit managers to act contrary to the terms of the social contract. Not even commitments by managers to pursue profits are excluded, but only commitments to pursue profits in a way that conflicts with the contract. Nor does it follow that commitments that violate the contract should be made *illegal*. The contract possesses a *moral* force in the sense of providing the moral foundations for productive organizations, yet its legal implications have not yet been clarified.

The significant question, then, is whether the moral force of the contract is in conflict with the right of managers to make voluntary agreements with stockholders. The answer is that it is not. To begin with, almost no theory of natural rights understands rights as exceptionless principles: rights can conflict. One's right to own the fruits of one's labor does not permit one to *own* one's children, even if one is a woman who bore the children, because children have a right to liberty which *outweighs* the earlier right.[9] Similarly, if managers have rights to conclude agreements with stockholders, then workers and consumers also have rights which may take priority. For example, if managers voluntarily agree to pursue profits even at the expense of workers' lives, then the workers' right to life clearly takes precedence.

But although one right can sometimes outweigh another, can the social contract ever outweigh a right? Can something other than a right outweigh a right? Frequently nonrights considerations do outweigh certain rights. For example, people are said to have the right to control their property, yet an exception is made when governments condemn property for public purposes, say, to build a road. The act is justified by an overriding public interest. Thus, the fact that the social contract is not itself a right does not preclude its overriding rights under certain circumstances. To take an obvious example: the social contract's requirement that productive organizations serve consumer interests would *outweigh* the rights of a stockholder and manager to agree to market an inherently dangerous product.

Thus Friedman's claim that the social responsibility of business is merely to increase its profits is either in error or incomplete. It is in error if it is meant to imply that the force of a hypothetical fiduciary agreement between manager and stockholder prevents managers from using the social contract as the yardstick for responsible managerial activity. This is because even the right to make voluntary agreements has been shown to have exceptions; and, as also demonstrated, there may be overriding moral considerations (such as the social contract). Friedman's argument is incomplete, on one other hand, if it is meant to imply that the existence of a voluntary agreement generates a prima facie obligation for the manager to pursue profit. That implication is correct as far as it goes, but it neglects to mention that there may be other responsibilities which are incumbent on the manager stemming from different sources — in this case, from a moral obligation generated through a social contract.

In fairness both to Friedman and others who take similar positions, it must be admitted that considerations other than the right to undertake voluntary agreements can be invoked to defend the propriety of profit maximizing. For example, Friedman argues elsewhere that a system in which productive organizations

---

[9]Lawrence C. Becker, "The Labor Theory of Property Acquisition," *Journal of Philosophy*, 73 (1976), 657.

attempt to maximize profit yields *maximum consumer satisfaction.*[10] It might even be claimed that the social contract is *best* satisfied when business managers pursue exclusive profit maximization. If this were true, the social responsibility of business would remain with satisfying the social contract, but the way to satisfy it would be through profit maximization. It would be a bit like telling a golfer *not* to aim at his target but to aim left of it to counteract his slice. The possibility that the social contract is served by profit maximization will be investigated in detail in the next chapter.

IMPLICATIONS OF THE SOCIAL CONTRACT

It might be imagined that the social contract implies that consumers and workers should participate in the management of productive organizations since the interests of these groups are the basis of the contract itself. Many corporate reformers recommend co-determination of the corporation by all affected parties. Some endorse experiments with worker-controlled factories similar to those in Yugoslavia, and others recommend placing public and employee representatives on boards of directors in accordance with the West German model (West Germany has incorporated co-determination into the governing mechanism of many of her corporations). It might be argued that such proposals are directly supported by the social contract.

Caution, however, is in order. As noted above, even arguments for profit maximization can be launched in the name of the social contract. An attempt also could be made to prove that the contract is best fulfilled when organizations are controlled by professional managers. Whether the empirical evidence justifies such a view is the crucial issue. From the perspective of the social contract, the questions of organizational structure must be decided in terms of how well various structures satisfy the contract. What the preceding analysis has shown is that any organizational structure *must take into account* the interests of consumers and rank-and-file workers. Functional myopia must be avoided: the productive organization exists to satisfy more than one privileged group in society.

To conclude, it must be said that the most important application of the social contract sketched out in this chapter is evaluation of the performance of productive organizations from a moral perspective. We have seen that the productive organization cannot be viewed as an isolated moral entity unconstrained by the demands of society, for its very reason for existing lies with its capacity to satisfy certain social interests. Productive organizations, whether U.S. corporations or not, are subject to moral evaluations which transcend the boundaries of the political systems that contain them. The underlying function of all such organizations from the standpoint of society is to enhance social welfare through satisfying consumer and worker interests, while at the same time remaining within the bounds of justice. When they fail to live up to these expectations, they are deserving of moral criticism. When an organization, in the United States or elsewhere, manufactures a product that is inherently dangerous, or when it pushes its employees beyond reasonable limits, it de-

---

[10]Milton Friedman, *Capitalism and Freedom* (Chicago: University of Chicago Press, 1962).

serves moral condemnation: the organization has failed to live up to a hypothetical contract — a contract between itself and society.

When Henry Ford II referred to the social contract, he left the term "social contract" undefined. This chapter has attempted to sharpen the focus of what such a contract might mean, and thereby clarify the content of a corporation's indirect obligations. Clearly, other methods of specifying the contract are possible, and the version presented in this chapter should not be regarded as the last word. Whatever form it takes, however, the social contract expresses an underlying conviction that corporations exist to serve more than themselves. This conviction emerges in the speeches of businesspeople as well as in the writings of philosophers. It is the conviction expressed by the inventor of the Model T, the grandfather of Henry Ford II, when he said: "For a long time people believed that the only purpose of industry is to make a profit. They were wrong. Its purpose is to serve the general welfare."[11]

Fred D. Miller, Jr., and John Ahrens
THE SOCIAL RESPONSIBILITY OF CORPORATIONS

In recent decades, large corporations have come to play an increasingly important role in the economy of the United States. Corporations like AT&T, IBM, and General Motors, because they are able to pool the resources of millions of investors, exert enormous influence on their respective industries and affect the life and well-being of every American. It is thus no surprise that such corporations are the targets of a great deal of criticism. Many social and economic theorists argue that the modern corporation, because of its size and special legal status, cannot be treated simply as one of the kinds of organizations that individuals form for their private benefit. Instead, they contend, the modern corporation is a *public* institution, a creature of the state, so that it can and must be held to a higher *social responsibility* — that is, to more stringent standards of legal and moral responsibility — than the traditional business firm.

This chapter considers some of the major arguments for and against treating the corporation as a public rather than a private institution. Section I examines alternative theories of the structure and legal status of corporations. Section II reviews opposing theories of corporate social responsibility and their application to some of the more pressing public-policy issues of the day. Section III addresses the specific problem of the size and consequent political power of the modern corporation. Section IV explores the ethical responsibilities that a corporation may have beyond making profits for its stockholders. Finally,

[11]Quoted in David Ewing, *Freedom Inside the Organization* (New York: McGraw-Hill, 1977), p. 65.

From Fred D. Miller, Jr., and John Ahrens, "The Social Responsibility of Corporations," in *Commerce and Morality*, edited by Tibor R. Machan (Totowa, NJ: Rowman & Littlefield, 1988), 140–160. Reprinted by permission of publisher.

Section V considers whether the ideal of "economic democracy" could be most fully realized by transforming corporations into political entities or by preserving their traditional character.

I. THE MODERN CORPORATION: PRIVATE PROPERTY OR PUBLIC INSTITUTION?

What is a corporation? At first glance, the answer to this question seems obvious: a corporation is simply one of the more complicated organizations individuals have developed to facilitate the pursuit of profit.[1] However, this obvious answer is not universally accepted. Some critics of the modern corporation argue that it cannot be justified within the ideological framework of free-market capitalism. Some also argue that the modern corporation is really a public rather than a private organization and should be treated accordingly. These critics justify their claims by reference to legal and structural characteristics that seem to be unique to the modern corporation. These characteristics include the following: corporations are formed by means of "corporate charters" requiring legal sanction. In nearly all corporations with publicly owned stock, the owners (stockholders) are, for the most part, not the managers. The owners of a corporation are protected by the doctrine of "limited liability" from any loss in excess of their investments. (A stockholder of a chemical company, for example, cannot be held personally liable if the company causes harm by dumping hazardous wastes.) Corporations possess a great deal of economic power, in virtue of which they influence the lives of everyone in modern society. These features have prompted many critics of the corporation to argue that corporations are *"quasi-public"organizations* resembling political states or that they are *creatures of the law* established by acts of government and endowed with special legal privileges. Opposed to these theories is the doctrine that the corporation is essentially private, arising from individual contracts. These theories will be examined in turn.

The Corporation as a Quasi-Public Organization

One of the most conspicuous structural characteristics of modern corporations, especially the larger ones, is that most of the owners — the stockholders — have little or no input into the corporate decision-making process. Whether voluntarily or otherwise, most of the owners of modern corporations have turned over the responsibility for managing their property to professionals. And this characteristic of corporations disturbs even defenders of capitalism such as Irving Kristol. This separation of ownership and management, Kristol argues, indicates that "the large corporation has ceased being a species of private property, and is now a 'quasi-public' institution."[2] The problem now, in Kristol's view, is to preserve the corporation by redesigning it in ways that reflect the change in its nature.

Kristol's argument for interpreting the separation of ownership and management as a transition from private property to public institution is twofold: (1) the modern corporation deviates from the model of private property as it was understood by such early defenders of capitalism as Adam Smith.[3] In Smith's model, the free market involved myriads of businesspeople in competition to sell goods to myriads of consumers. Property was owned by individuals who decided directly and for themselves how it was to be used in their firms. The modern corporation, because it gives a small elite of professional managers the power "to make economic decisions affecting the lives of tens of thousands of citizens,"[4] is inconsistent with the liberal-democratic ideals on which this country's political and economic system is founded. Hence, the modern corporation is *not* private property and may not claim the protections and immunities normally granted to private property.

Both of these arguments have been criticized. The first argument rests upon a controversial interpretation of the nature of capitalism and, as one critic argues:

> There is no justification for equating capitalism with a particular configuration of small firms run by their owners, and Adam Smith's preferences are not binding upon persons who prefer to create some other arrangement. The essence of capitalism is the inviolability of individual rights, including the right to use or invest wealth as one chooses and the right to associate with others for any purpose and under any mutually acceptable terms of association.[5]

In short, Kristol's appeal to authority is irrelevant; capitalism has evolved since the time of Adam Smith.

Kristol's second argument, based on the separation of ownership and management, may be criticized on the grounds that such a separation is objectionable only if it is involuntary on the part of stockholders. But it is obvious that stockholders make a voluntary and deliberate decision to entrust some of their resources to *professional* managers. And if stockholders find this arrangement unacceptable and the authority of management too onerous, they have only to sell their stock in order to regain control of their resources.[6] Therefore, the separation of ownership and management that characterizes the modern corporation is consistent with the ideals of liberal democracy. The authority of managers does not undermine individual autonomy and self-determination because it derives from a voluntary or consensual arrangement between owners and managers. And the freedom of stockholders to sell their stock if they are dissatisfied serves to discourage the arbitrary exercise of managerial authority.

Indeed, it might be argued that the modern corporation is, in fact, an economic analog to the only political arrangement designed to preserve liberal-democratic ideals, i.e., representative government. In the United States, at least, it is representative government that is supposed to preserve individual autonomy by giving each citizen an equal voice in government and to prevent arbitrary exercise of political authority by allowing citizens to review and replace their representatives. The stockholder in a modern corporation has at least this much control over managers, if not more. Potential stockholders can choose to invest in any of a vast array of different corporations with different management philosophies, or they can invest in none at all. And they can prevent or escape the arbitrary exercise of authority simply by selling their stock. Where do citizens have this much control over their political fate?

The Corporation as a Creature of the State

Some have argued that the special legal status of the corporation renders it a public rather than a private institution. Ralph Nader, an outspoken critic of the modern corporation, argues that corporations are and always have been creatures of the state. They are, he claims, dependent on the state for their very existence, because they are created by the government for the benefit of the public rather than for the private benefit of stockholders and managers. Hence, corporations may legitimately be held to higher standards of social responsibility than traditional business firms.

Why are corporations creatures of the state, even though they are owned by private citizens? Nader's answer seems to be that a corporation requires the government's permission — a government charter — in order to do business[7] and that there are features peculiar to the modern corporation that can only be granted by law.[8] Nader discusses a number of these special features, but the most important by far is *limited liability*. Corporate stockholders, unlike the owners of more traditional firms, are not liable to the extent of their total personal assets for the debts and torts (wrongful acts) of the corporation; rather, their liability is limited by law to their investment in the corporation. This is a substantial hedge against economic risk and a powerful incentive to invest in corporate stock. And it is a privilege that can only be granted by the state.

Nader's account of the corporation as a creature of the state has also been criticized on two main points. First, it is pointed out that what Nader calls a "corporate charter" is just the articles of incorporation, which do not constitute any sort of governmental authorization and do not bind the corporation to the service of public rather than private interests. The articles of incorporation contain the name, purpose, and intended duration of the business, the amount of start-up capital, the names of the incorporators, and other information of a similar nature. The state's role is to record this information, just as it records information concerning births, marriages, land sales, and so forth. In all these cases, filing the appropriate documents with the government gives legal validity to private contracts. But, as Robert Hessen argues, this does not make the corporation, any more than birth or marriage, a creature of the state:

> On the contrary, procedural requirements apply to virtually all contracts. For example, to be legally valid, a marriage contract must follow specific procedural requirements: it must be performed by someone authorized by the state, it must be witnessed, and a signed certificate must be filed with the state. If these requirements make the state a party to a contract, then every marriage is a *ménage à trois:* bride, groom, and government. Quite literally, government plays a smaller role in the creation of a corporation than of a marriage. Yet who, for that reason, would describe marriage as a creature of the state or claim that a marriage certificate contains a promise to serve the public interest.[9]

According to Hessen, the state does not create corporations; it merely recognizes and records their creation.

It has also been objected against Nader's theory that features like limited liability for debts and torts do not have to be explained as special privileges granted by the state. Limited liability for debts needs no special explanation because it is not a privilege that is *guaranteed* to corporations. That is, a potential creditor is within his (legal) rights to refuse to extend credit to a corporation unless some or all of the stockholders assume personal liability for the debt. And limited liability for torts or wrongful acts does not need to be construed as any special and valuable privilege granted only to corporate stockholders. The strongest argument for treating limited liability as such is based on the doctrine of vicarious liability. According to this doctrine, individuals are (legally) responsible for damages or wrongful acts performed by their employees or agents. For example, if Jones, an employee of Smith, makes an illegal kickback to a public official to obtain special advantages for Smith's business firm, it follows by this doctrine that *Smith* is vicariously responsible for the illegal kickback. If the doctrine of vicarious liability were extended to corporate stockholders, then each stockholder would be held personally liable for the wrongful acts committed by the corporation or its agent (e.g., the illegal disposal of hazardous wastes). And, the argument goes, vicarious liability should extend to all owners, including all corporate stockholders. But limited liability provisions in the law shield stockholders from penalties for debts or torts of the corporation beyond the value of their stock. Hence, corporations enjoy a special privilege that is not granted to ordinary persons under the law.

This argument has been criticized on the ground that the first premise — that the doctrine of vicarious liability should extend to *all* stockholders — is false.

> Vicarious liability should apply only to shareholders who play an active role in managing the enterprise or in selecting and supervising its employees and agents. The tort liability of inactive shareholders ought to be the same as that of limited partners, that is, limited to the amount invested. The same rationale applies to both because inactive shareholders and limited partners contribute capital but do not participate actively in management and control.[10]

On this account, therefore, limited liability is not a privileged status granted to corporate stockholders; it is simply a recognition of their limited responsibility.

The Corporation as Created by Contract

Not all contemporary theorists regard corporations as radically different from other forms of business organizations. Robert Hessen, for example, argues that corporations, just like other businesses, are created by contract and that the apparently unique features of corporations can be explained in terms of their contractual origins. Hessen's arguments for this view, which he calls the *inherence theory*, are really just extensions of the criticisms of the theories of the corporation discussed previously.

Once it is recognized that the so-called "corporate charter" is, in fact, merely the articles of incorporation, it is not difficult to see that the corporation is born of a contract. This is a contract between individuals who wish to pool some of their resources and, perhaps, delegate some of the responsibility for managing these resources. The same contract, quite obviously, accounts for the separation of ownership and management in the modern corporation. Hessen's justification of these arrangements is simple: so long as we recognize that they are the result of voluntary agreements, they need not be seen as either mysterious or illegitimate. Limited liability for debts is also the result of a contract; it is a contract between stockholders and creditors, and one that potential creditors are not obliged to make.[11]

The principle difficulty for Hessen's inherence theory is limited liability for torts, for it seems unlikely that the victims of corporate wrongful acts would voluntarily agree to an arrangement that protects the personal assets of stockholders from damage claims. However, Hessen argues, this arrangement is not always or even usually much of an advantage to stockholders or disadvantage to tort victims, especially when a large corporation is involved. Most large corporations have assets far in excess of the assets of any of their stockholders, and they carry substantial liability insurance. Hence, it is not clear that stockholders in large corporations need this protection for their personal assets or that tort victims would benefit to any great extent if stockholders were personally liable. Further, Hessen rejects the doctrine of vicarious liability discussed above and, hence, believes that the limited liability arrangement simply gives legal recognition to the fact that most corporate stockholders play no role whatsoever in the management of the corporation and thus are not personally responsible for corporate torts. Those who do take an active role in management can and should be held liable; but to make inactive stockholders personally liable for corporate torts would be to commit an injustice.[12]

Some critics of this theory object that it misses the point of the corporate social responsibility debate. Modern corporations are huge concentrations of economic power that exert enormous influence on the condition of modern society and the welfare of every human being. And, continue the critics, the real concern of those who claim that the corporation is a public institution is to bring these economic giants under greater public control. Although there are attempts to find a justification for this view in the legal tradition, the argument that has carried the most conviction has been the *social responsibility argument:* the public's interests must be protected, and the vast economic power of corporations must be harnessed for everyone's benefit. Corporations must, in other words, be held to higher standards of social responsibility than mere individuals. For even if the theory is correct that corporations are private property originating in contracts, corporations have *public effects* that are so great that they cannot be ignored.

II. THEORIES OF CORPORATE SOCIAL RESPONSIBILITY

What are the social responsibilities of corporations? Even amongst those who agree that corporations are public institutions, there is considerable disagreement about the correct answer to this question. Some merely want corporate management to be more sensitive to the social impact of their decisions, others want to see more effective policing of abuses of corporate power, and still others want to see corporations undertake extensive programs for the melioration of social ills. Proposals for accomplishing these goals range from more effective regulation and enforcement of criminal statutes to direct public or governmental management of large (or all) corporations. At the other end of the spectrum are those who argue that the social responsibilities of corporations are essentially those described in Adam Smith's theory of the "invisible hand" and that social ills must be addressed by some means other than the "nationalization" of corporations. In order to clarify the most important ethical issues in the social responsibility debate, this section will examine two diametrically opposed views of what the social responsibilities of corporations are and how we can ensure that corporate management undertakes these responsibilities.

Cases Calling for Corporate Social Responsibility

First, however, it is necessary to provide a context in terms of which different theories of corporate social responsibility can be understood. Numerous social ills are attributed in whole or in part to corporate activity, but three sorts of cases will serve to indicate the importance of the corporate social responsibility debate.

Plant Closings: As corporations have grown larger and larger, many communities have become thoroughly dependent on one or a few companies for their tax base and for jobs. When a company decides to scale down operations at a plant or close or relocate it, the economic consequences for the community can be catastrophic.

Product Safety: The modern marketplace offers a bewildering array of products designed to improve the quality of leisure, increase mobility, extend communication, relieve the day-to-day aches and pains of the body and spirit, enhance natural beauty, and so forth. Many of these products are the result of extremely complicated advances in science and technology, which the consumer is but little prepared to understand. And, as recent phenomena like thalidomide babies and the toxic effects associated with many cosmetics and feminine hygiene products indicate, the human costs that result from an error in judgment can be extremely high.

Deterioration of the Environment: Recent decades have witnessed rapid growth in the level of industrial activity and, consequently, rapid proliferation of new industrial processes and substances. Not all of these activities and processes and substances are benign; some produce significant and harmful changes in our natural environment.

Corporations, because they play such an important role in our economy, have undeniably contributed to the emergence of these and other problems, whether intentionally or otherwise.[13] And this is the impetus behind the corporate social responsibility debate and the variety of proposals designed to enlist the aid of corporations in attempts to solve these problems.

Corporate Democracy as a Vehicle for Social Responsibility

One approach to these problems is the corporate democracy theory. This approach is illustrated by the Corporate Democracy Act of 1980. This bill (which failed to gain passage) was introduced in Congress as H.R. 7010 and was actively supported by consumer activists like Ralph Nader and his associates. The bill, which would apply to all nonfinancial corporations with assets or annual sales of more than $250 million or more than 5,000 employees, includes the following significant provisions:

- A majority of the board members of corporations subject to the Act must be independent; i.e., they cannot have been officers or managers of the corporation for a period of five years prior to their election to the board and they cannot have been officers, directors, employees, or more than 1% equity owners of any organization providing significant service to the corporation for a period of three years prior to their election to the board.

- Among the committees of the board there must be a public policy committee, which will be responsible for policies concerning community relations, consumer protection, and environmental protection. A majority of the members of this committee must be independent directors.
- Corporations must give notice two years in advance of any plant closing or relocation that will significantly reduce employment in the area and must compensate local governments for the resultant decrease in tax revenues.

The intent of the Corporate Democracy Act was to reduce the control the managers and stockholders would have over corporate decisions and to bring corporations under substantial and direct public control. If this act had passed, corporations would have become essentially public institutions.[14]

An important objection that has been leveled against the corporate democracy approach is that it would substantially reduce the efficiency with which corporations can do business. Expertise in deciding policy for a business requires experience, but the Corporate Democracy Act effectively ensures that the majority of the directors of large corporations will lack the necessary experience. Further, the provision concerning plant closings and relocations would reduce management's ability to preserve the economic health of corporations by choosing the most advantageous sites for corporate activities. And this is certainly contrary to the interests of both stockholders and society as a whole. Efficiency is not the only virtue of economic institutions, but it is certainly one of their virtues and one which proposals like the Corporate Democracy Act seem certain to undermine.

Another objection turns on the ethical difficulties raised by this attempt and others like it to restrict the rights of property owners. The right to own property is a central principle of capitalism that is protected in the United States Constitution. And there is a long tradition of social and legal theory that views private property as an important shield against the arbitrary, capricious, and oppressive exercise of political power: if control of the resources people need to survive and prosper is decentralized, rather than concentrated in the hands of political authorities, it is more difficult for these political authorities to deprive people of their civil liberties.[15] Of course, one might argue that the gravity and urgency of the social problems discussed above outweigh the risks of placing substantial economic power in the hands of political authorities. But it seems reasonable that this drastic alteration in the economic system of the United States should only be undertaken as a last resort and after other ideas have failed. The existence of competing theories of corporate social responsibility suggests that we have not yet reached this impasse.

Profit Making Within the Rules as Social Responsibility

A theory of corporate social responsibility, which lies at the opposite end of the spectrum from the corporate democracy theory, is proposed by Milton Friedman. Like Hessen, Friedman believes that corporations are a species of private property and, consequently, that they have exactly the same social responsibility as other businesses in a capitalist economy:

> In such an economy, there is one and only one social responsibility of business — to use its resources and engage in activities designed to increase its profits so long as it stays within the rules of the game, which is to say, engages in open and free competition, without deception or fraud. . . . It is the responsibility of the rest of us to establish a framework of law such that an individual in pursuing his own interest is, to quote Adam Smith again, "led by an invisible hand to promote an end which was no part of his intention."[16]

In short, the social responsibility of business is just what it has always been supposed to have been — to increase its profits within the framework of the law. And if we want to enlist the aid of business in solving social problems, the only legitimate way of doing so is to effectively police the fraudulent and deceptive practices that contribute to these problems and to frame our laws in such a way that businesses are able to profit by providing for social needs. This theory, defended by Friedman, is referred to as the *fundamentalist theory of social responsibility*.

In view of the seriousness of many of the problems facing contemporary society, this view may seem nothing more than a callous and shortsighted defense of private interests. But this appearance of callousness and short-sightedness fades on closer examination. For Friedman is not suggesting that we should ignore the economic power of corporations, or that we must resign ourselves to being unable to enlist this power in attempts to address social problems. He is, rather, suggesting that bringing corporations under more direct public control is neither a legitimate nor a particularly effective means of ensuring that their vast economic power is used for socially beneficial ends. We should instead adopt means that preserve the economic freedom that has served as a hedge against political oppression and that has contributed so much to the high standard of living enjoyed by so many Americans.[17]

Applying Friedman's theory to the social problems discussed above will help to clarify this point. What, for example, is the capitalist solution to the problem of unsafe products? The answer is really quite simple. The marketplace already provides unbiased information on the safety and quality of a broad range of goods and services in news reports and in publications like *Consumer Reports*. The fact that a consumer is not himself qualified to judge the claims of sellers does not mean that he must either accept these claims at face value or turn to the government for protection. If consumers feel a need for unbiased information, and surely they will if deceptive advertising or the marketing of unsafe or ineffective products is at all widespread, the market itself will satisfy this need. And if consumers are forewarned, unsafe or ineffective goods and services are no threat since consumers can avoid them. Hence, the market itself provides consumer protection. And Friedman would probably add that it provides it at a lower price than government can.

Plant closings and relocations pose a somewhat different problem. If the only responsibility of business is to increase its profits, then the responsible manager will close or relocate plants whenever he can improve the profitability of his operations by so doing. Thus, it would seem that only government intervention in the economic decision-making process can prevent the disruption of communities this causes. And this is probably true, but it is worth noting that government intervention is often the cause of this problem rather than the solution; and even when it is not the cause, it is not always a *desirable* solution. When a company decides to close or relocate a plant because the goods it produces are no longer saleable, or because the source of raw materials has shifted, or some similar reason, it is hard to condemn the decision. While the change may produce temporary disruptions in a particular community, it makes for more efficient use of resources and thus benefits society as a whole; it is, in other words, the socially responsible thing to do. Quite often, however, the decision to relocate operations is a result of the fact that some local governments offer lower tax rates or free services, or have pursued policies that reduce labor costs (e.g., antiunion policies). If government did not have the power to offer these incentives, i.e., to exploit some members of the community for the benefit of others, many plant closings and relocations simply would not occur. In cases such as these, the solution is not less economic freedom but more.

And the same is true of the environmental problems that threaten to destroy us all. Air pollution, water pollution, and the depletion of other resources that are not readily replaceable, have reached crisis proportions because these resources are, for the most part, public rather than private property. They are owned by government rather than by individuals; and since government is supposed to represent the interests of all people, it must give the interests of those who would pollute and pillage equal consideration with the interests of those who would nurture and preserve. Unfortunately, the activities of the former quite often render the demands of the latter pointless. If these resources were owned by individuals, the owners would have a strong economic incentive to preserve their property so it would be adaptable to a variety of uses and retain its value over time. Again, the solution is not less economic freedom, but more.[18]

Friedman's fundamentalist theory has, not surprisingly, been sharply attacked by most critics of the corporation. Two sorts of criticisms are especially worth noting here. First, Friedman's theory of corporate social responsibility presupposes a very sanguine view of the way in which a capitalist economy would function in the absence of government controls, and some critics object that his view is too optimistic. For even if it is true that unfettered capitalism would constitute the best treatment for social ills, one might question whether or not unfettered capitalism is attainable. Economic power can be used to acquire political power, especially in a democracy like the United States, in which public opinion is determined primarily by the media and by respect for the views of "experts." According to the critics, corporations will use their vast resources to ensure that legislation and public policy favor their interests over the interests of society and that they are never subjected to the rigors of competitive capitalism. It is evident from this objection that an understanding of corporate social responsibility requires a consideration of the political power of corporations, which is discussed in Section III.

Secondly, Friedman's theory has been criticized on the ground that it does not take into account many important ethical dimensions of the decisions that corporate managers make. In defining social responsibility, he seems to hold that managers should consider only two factors as morally relevant: honoring their commitment to the stockholders to maximize the profits of the corporation and following "the rules of the game." According to his interpretation, the rules of the game require that one "engage in open and full competition, without deception or fraud." Friedman's critics ask why these "rules" are so important and why other values should not also be given equal weight, e.g., supporting the local community even when this requires losses. Friedman's interpretation of "the rules of the game" is bound to seem arbitrary unless it is supported with an explicit, defensible ethical theory. Moreover, critics also characterize his fundamentalist theory as suffering from a type of ethical "tunnel vision." They argue that there are other moral goals besides the pursuit of profits, that these other goals are more often than not in conflict with profit-maximizing, and that when this happens, profits should take the back seat. In view of such objections, it will be necessary in Section IV to examine the *moral* dimensions of social responsibility.

III. THE POLITICAL DIMENSION OF SOCIAL RESPONSIBILITY

The economic power of corporations can be translated into political power in a variety of ways, and many of the more effective ways are completely legal and aboveboard. Former Senator Fred Harris has called for extensive revision of the laws governing campaign financing and corporate income tax deductions. He cites examples of business practices that influence politicians such as contributions to campaigns and political action committees (PACs), intensive lobbying, political advertising, and giving jobs to former government officials. Corporations are able to influence judicial decisions, legislation, and regulatory policy because they have the wherewithal to sway public opinion and to ensure that their interests are effectively represented before Congress and the government's regulatory agencies. And one need not resort to charges of collusion or bribery to explain the disproportionate influence of corporations. Our political system provides numerous legal avenues to power and influence for those with sufficient wealth.[19]

Harris and other critics who make similar claims are no doubt correct, but one must be cautious in condemning the disproportionate political power of corporations and even more cautious in prescribing a remedy that includes federal chartering of corporations and more vigorous antitrust enforcement to break up large corporations. If government officials have been lax thus far in designing and enforcing regulations to protect the public's interests, is the situation likely to be improved by giving them the additional power to decide which corporations shall exist and how large they shall be?

Even if there were legislative means to prevent corporations from exercising olitical power, some would argue that we should not use it. For the apparently dispropo. ionate political power of corporations seems less intimidating if we remember that large corporations are owned by thousands or even millions of stockholders. When the lobbyists of a large corporation represent corporate interests before government officials, it is the interests of all these stockholders that are really at stake. Moreover, it would be impossible to restrict corporate support for political advertising, PACs, and lobbies without violating the civil liberties of the owners and managers of corporations.

If the political power of corporations still seems threatening, we should consider whether or not there are alternatives to further politicizing the corporation by annexing it to the state. One alternative is suggested by Milton Friedman's theory of corporate social responsibility: we should strip government of the functions that allow officials to exercise their power on behalf of corporations rather than "the public." For many of the political activities of corporations are directed at gaining special advantages through existing or proposed legislation: for example, protection from foreign competition through tariffs or "domestic content" legislation, special subsidies, price supports, low-interest or no-interest loans (as in the Chrysler bailout), government enforced monopolies (as in the case of utilities and local cablevision companies), special tax breaks (such as depletion allowances), and government contracts. As government has come to control the economy to an increasing extent, corporations have felt compelled to resort to political tactics rather than traditional economic competition. For example, corporations frequently use antitrust suits to defeat or destroy their competitors. It seems inevitable that as long as this arsenal of political weapons exists, corporations will use them, especially while the same weapons are available to other corporations, to organized labor, and to various groups dedicated to bringing corporations under total governmental control. According to Friedman, the solution to this is disarmament: curbing the governmental powers that the contending interest groups are seeking to use to their own advantage. There is, as we said earlier, no guarantee that this can be accomplished. But neither is there any guarantee that further politicizing the corporation will produce any beneficial effect. And, as Friedman points out, it is not only corporations who have "social responsibilities"; it is also the responsibility of each individual to ensure that there is a framework of laws and political institutions that brings private and "public" interests into harmony.[20] Perhaps, in the present context, the way to carry out that responsibility is not through any positive exercise of political power, but rather through the refusal to give any further economic power to political officials.

IV. THE ETHICAL DIMENSION OF SOCIAL RESPONSIBILITY

Closer examination of Milton Friedman's fundamentalist view of corporate social responsibility also indicates that ethical principles need to be taken into account. His view is that, in a capitalist economy, "there is one and only one social responsibility of business — to use its resources and engage in activities designed to increase its profits so long as it stays within the rules of the game, which is to say, engages in open and free competition, without deception or fraud." The managers of a corporation should use available assets to make investments that are expected to maximize the shareholder's profits rather than to engage in charitable contributions or follow "enlightened" but nonprofitable business practices. On the other hand, the managers should not attempt to make a profit by engaging in deception, fraud, or coercion against competitors. Although this view may have a certain pragmatic appeal to businesspeople, Friedman unfortunately does not support it with any explicit ethical arguments. Consequently, it is not clear why one should accept *his* view of social responsibility, rather than an opposite view: for example, "The social responsibility of a corporation is to make a profit — no ifs, ands, or buts about 'the rules of the game'" (the pure profit-making view), or "The social responsibility of a corporation is to serve the community by providing employment opportunities for all, improving the environment, promoting justice worldwide . . . even if it costs the shareholders money" (the community service view).

Respect for Rights

An ethical theory can provide a basis for defending one view of corporate social responsibility against others. One such ethical theory, which has been extremely important in the United States, is the theory of individual human rights. On this theory, individuals are free to pursue their own goals (provided that they do not prevent others from pursuing their goals), and other people have the duty not to interfere in this pursuit. Since the most flagrant form of interference involves the use of force or coercion, the theory of individual rights requires that individuals abstain from the use of force except in the defense of rights against violations by others. Threats of force against others also prevent them from pursuing their goals, so threats are also violations of rights. Individual rights include the right to produce and own property — so thefts or invasions of property are also infringements of rights. When individuals enter into voluntary contracts with each other, each person has a duty to keep the agreement. To take property from another by means of a false promise is to steal that person's property. Thus, fraud is a violation of the rights of others. Individual rights have a basically *negative* character. If Jones has the right to "life, liberty and the pursuit of happiness," this means that Smith has the duty not to interfere with Jones's exercise of this right. It does not mean that Smith has the duty to provide Jones with positive benefits. Smith can justifiably be forced to provide Jones with a positive benefit only if Smith has voluntarily assumed an obligation towards Jones, e.g., by signing a contract. If Smith has not voluntarily assumed an obligation but is forced to serve Jones's purposes anyway, then Smith is nothing but a slave whose rights are being violated.

This theory of individual rights provides support for Friedman's view as opposed to the pure profit-making view or the community service view.[21] For on this theory the individuals in a corporation have the duty to respect the rights of other individuals. Hence, they may not use force against workers or fraud against consumers in order to make greater profits, for this would be to violate the rights of the workers or consumers. Nor may they use force or coercion to drive out their competitors in order to increase profits, for this would again involve violating the competitors' rights. Thus, the theory of individual rights cannot support the pure profit-making view of social responsibility. Nor can it support the community service view. For managers have taken the stockholders' money with the understanding that it will be invested to make a profit and thereby benefit the stockholders. If the managers were to use the money for another purpose, they would be failing in their contractual obligations to the stockholders and thus be violating their rights. This is obvious if managers divert corporate funds for selfish purposes. But even if managers have unselfish motives, for example, to help the community, they will be in the same moral position as a person who forced Smith to serve Jones without his consent and thereby treated Smith as a slave. In general, then, if corporate social responsibility is understood as the theory that a corporation should respect individual human rights, it leads to a view like Friedman's rather than to the pure profit-making view or the community service view.[22]

Morals versus Profits?

The discussion of the ethical dimension of corporate social responsibility has, so far, been in terms of the respective duties and rights of managers, shareholders, consumers, workers, and competitors. Another ethical issue concerns whether or not profit-maximization is the only goal that should concern corporations and their owners. Should they be concerned about other values? Often this is presented as an "either-or" issue. Either the basic concern is with economic values such as productivity or efficiency, in which case corporations should concentrate on making profits and steer clear of social involvements, or else "social and human values" are the primary concern and business should assume greater social commitments even at the expense of profits.

But the argument that there is a dichotomy between morals and profits rests on a crucial assumption: that it is obvious to business managers which course of action out of many alternatives will lead to the greatest profits or smallest losses. For on this assumption, the obligation to maximize profits will severely limit the courses of action open to responsible managers. Managers will have very little flexibility in carrying out their primary directive to maximize profits. They will, in effect, function like profit-maximizing robots. But it is far from obvious that this assumption is true: in the real world it is not so simple for managers to determine which course of action is profit maximizing.[23]

For the question of what will enhance a corporation's profitability is ambiguous, and, consequently, so is Friedman's theory that the manager's social responsibility requires maximizing the profits of the corporation. One ambiguity concerns whether decisions are made with a view to *long-run* or to *short-run* profitability.

Friedman's theory does not specify which of these two strategies of "maximizing profits" should be followed, and it could be argued that it should not do so. For just as individual people have strikingly different views about the relative importance for them of benefits they will enjoy, or costs they must bear one year, three years, or ten years in the future, so also the managers of different corporations have different attitudes toward the future. It could be argued that in a free market, investors should be free to seek out the corporations with an attitude on profitability with which the investors feel secure. For consumers and investors have the right to decide for themselves just how long- or short-run their thinking will be under varying circumstances. Moreover, different investors and managers may well elect different strategies for return on equity because of different circumstances, abilities, and knowledge.

What many people would call "socially responsible" behavior on the part of business may turn out to be long-run profit seeking as well. For example, William C. Norris, founder of the Control Data Corporation, holds that "social problems provide profit-making opportunities." Norris developed a strategy of investing corporate resources in "inner city" areas to produce learning centers. These centers, containing Control Data products, are meant to develop entrepreneurial skills in disadvantaged populations, thereby creating future customers for Control Data. Such a strategy might require ten years or more to pay off. But it nevertheless illustrates the wide range of options open to "profit seekers" in the free market.

A further ambiguity in the idea of profitability is whether the factors contributing to profits are to be exclusively quantitative. Qualitative factors such as image, public relations, good will, and popular opinion can have an impact on profitability that may be indirect and hard to quantify, but are nonetheless important. Hence, one should not assume that certain types of corporate behavior are invariably inimical to profitability. Friedman, for example, mentions charitable contributions to universities as profit-reducing. This is to overlook the possibility that such philanthropy may enhance qualitative factors of the community, which are in turn favorable to corporate profitability. The Ford Motor Company was mistakenly criticized for ignoring profitability in 1914 when it reduced the workday to eight hours and raised wages to $5 a day.

The dichotomy between profits and morality may also be criticized on the grounds that it makes an overly simplistic assumption about how two values can be related: it assumes that either one of the values is a mere means to achieving the other (e.g., going to the dentist for the sake of keeping one's teeth healthy), or that the two values are in conflict with each other. But as Aristotle observed in his *Nicomachean Ethics*, a person can value a thing for its own sake and at the same time value it as a means to a further end. For example, you may decide to have a good vacation. You also value friendships for their own sake. Given these values, you plan your vacation to include frequent visits with friends. In such a case, you are both valuing your visits with friends for their own sakes and valuing them as a means to having a good vacation. It would be quite unfair for someone to criticize you for "just using" your friends as a means. You could sincerely protest that you do value their friendship for its own sake. The same kind of reasoning can and does occur when managers make corporate decisions.

Consider a case in which the manager of a corporation is trying to deal with the problem of alcoholism among his employees. The manager might be committed both to maximizing the profits of the stockholders and to treating the employees fairly and humanely. In the course of considering whether the company should finance a rehabilitation program for employees with an alcohol problem, he finds that it would be no more expensive to introduce such a program than to fire the employees and retrain new ones. He may also have reason to think that such a program would enhance the prospect for better employees in the future. The manager may introduce the rehabilitation program on the grounds that it is morally correct in terms of both profitability and the welfare of his workers. The manager in such a case clearly is not concerned only about profits. But what if the manager discovers that the company cannot afford such a program given its marginal market position? He might then conclude that he has no choice but to fire or lay off employees with a drinking problem. But even in this case the manager can be concerned not only with profits but also with the well-being of his employees.

Three Principles of Social Responsibility

Douglas Den Uyl, a professor of business ethics, has formulated three principles that define the ethical dimensions of social responsibility:

1. *The principle of respect for individual rights.* This is the principle that managers should respect the rights of their shareholders and of other persons with whom they deal: consumers, workers, competitors. By the same token, government and the critics of corporations should respect the rights of managers and owners of the corporations.

2. *The principle of responsible recommendation.* This principle recognizes the central place of profitability in the development and, indeed, the survival of the corporation. Shareholders invest their money in a corporation with a view to making a profit, and managers have an obligation to them. It is not responsible

to recommend policies to corporations that would prevent managers from meeting this obligation.

3. *The principle of moral consideration.* This principle states that because managers generally have a degree of flexibility in pursuing the overall goals of the corporation, they should be open to the moral dimension in making decisions. They should take into account the interests of others and how their decisions are affecting others.

To see how Den Uyl's principles would be applied, suppose that the managers of a corporation decide that because of a drop in demand, it is necessary to close a plant on which a small community is heavily dependent for employment. This could qualify as a "socially responsible" action on the three principles, provided that the corporation fulfilled all of its contractual obligations to workers and members of the community as well as investors (principle 1), it determined that closing the plant was necessary to maintain the corporation's profitability (principle 2), and the managers took into account the interests of the local community and sought out alternatives (consistent with principles 1 and 2), which would minimize the adverse impact of the plant closing (principle 3).

Organizations critical of American corporations, such as the Interfaith Council on Corporate Responsibility, frequently submit proxy resolutions at shareholder meetings that are intended to make the corporation more "responsible." A typical example is a proxy resolution submitted to Caterpillar Tractor Company dealing with plant closings and layoffs:

> Be it therefore resolved that the shareholders request the Board of Directors to adopt a written policy for permanent or indefinite plant closings and mass layoffs, affecting 100 employees or more, which would include: (1) Committing Caterpillar to provide financial, technical and other assistance in retraining workers who are being laid off permanently or indefinitely so that they may qualify for current and future job openings; (2) Providing workers with information about current and expected job openings in their region as well as vocational counseling; (3) Providing advance public notice of at least six months of a plant closing and at least four months of a mass layoff; (4) Giving dislocated workers first priority for jobs in other plants; (5) Placing new installations in or near plants which are closing or losing operations.[24]

Such a resolution would not be supported by any of Den Uyl's three principles of social responsibility. It most clearly violates principle 2, responsible recommendation. For although the group that made this proposal is concerned about the future employment of the workers laid off, it shows little or no concern for the financial viability or improvement of the corporation. For example, the fifth proposal, requiring Caterpillar to put new installations near plants that are closing or losing operations, is to demand that Caterpillar make itself vulnerable to economic forces that have already destroyed other companies. The framers of this resolution evidently intend to solve a "social problem" by transferring wealth from Caterpillar's shareholders to unemployed workers. Further, in closing a plant, the company would not violate the rights of the workers, since the employees do not have a right to those jobs beyond what the company contractually agreed to provide. So principle 1, respect for individual rights, does not support the resolution's proposals. Nor does it receive support from principle 3, which only implies that a responsible management would handle the plant closing humanely and take whatever steps it can to ease the transition. For this proxy resolution goes much further than this. In fact, it considers only the benefits that would be brought to particular localities. It does not consider other geographical areas that might benefit from new plants. Nor does it give indication of any concern for those who will bear the cost of implementing such a proposal. Hence, such resolutions themselves violate principle 3, since they fail to take fully into account how the interests of others would be affected if the resolutions were adopted.

V. CONCLUSION: CORPORATIONS AND ECONOMIC DEMOCRACY

The corporate social responsibility debate is largely the result of a rising tide of sentiment in favor of what has been called "economic democracy." The ideal of economic democracy is the analog of the ideal of political democracy. The latter is achieved by erecting political institutions that give each person an equal voice in government and thereby protect us from the arbitrary and oppressive exercise of political power. The former, we may presume, is to be achieved by giving each person an equal voice in important decisions concerning the disposition of society's resources, thereby protecting us from the arbitrary and harmful exercise of economic power. And most proposals for accomplishing this include politicizing economic decisions and bringing corporations (and perhaps other businesses as well) under the direct control of the political process.

But perhaps the evolution of the modern corporation as a *private* economic institution is an even more significant step in the direction of economic democracy. It is possible for private corporations to operate in such a way that they do not usurp political power and for them to pursue the goal of profitability in an ethically responsible manner. It is true, of course, that not every citizen, nor even every stockholder, has an equal voice in the economic decisions that affect his welfare; this will probably never be achieved, and some of the theories we have discussed suggest that it should not be. But the modern corporation, operating in an environment of economic freedom, gives each of us the opportunity to use our resources in a responsible way to influence economic decisions and to protect ourselves from their consequences. And this, after all, is the point of economic democracy.

Notes

1. Of course, not all corporations and perhaps not even most are created for the purpose of making profits in the narrow economic sense. There are numerous so-called "nonprofit" corporations that are devoted to charitable, artistic, and other purposes. However, we will restrict our remarks to the former, since it has been the subject of virtually all the criticism directed at the modern corporation.

2. Irving Kristol, "On Corporate Capitalism in America," *The Public Interest*, no. 41 (Fall, 1975), p. 138.

3. Ibid., p. 125.

4. Ibid., p. 128.

5. Robert Hessen, "A New Concept of Corporations," *The Hastings Law Journal*, vol. 30 (May, 1979), pp. 1342–1343.

6. Ibid., pp. 1344–1349.

7. Ralph Nader, "The Case for Federal Chartering," in *Corporate Power in America*, Ralph Nader and Mark Green, eds. (New York: Grossman Publishers, 1973), pp. 81–84.

8. Ralph Nader, Mark Green, and Joel Seligman, *Taming the Giant Corporation* (New York: W. W. Norton, 1976), pp. 33–61.

9. Hessen, op. cit., p. 1337.

10. Ibid., pp. 1333–1334.

11. Hessen provides a detailed account of these and other features of the modern corporation in his *In Defense of the Corporation* (Stanford, Cal.: Hoover Institution Press, 1979), esp. chapters 1–4.

12. Ibid., pp. 18–22.

13. A more detailed and substantially more vituperative discussion of corporate contributions to contemporary social ills is provided by Ralph Nader, op. cit., pp. 15–32.

14. For a complete text of the Corporate Democracy Act, as well as texts of some of the testimony given to Congress in support of something like this type of legislation, see *Protection of Shareholders Rights Act of 1980*, U.S. Government Printing Office, Nov. 19, 1980 [y 4.B 22/3:P 94/8].

15. For an extended discussion of the relationship between economic liberty and political liberty, see F. A. Hayek, *The Road to Serfdom* (Chicago: University of Chicago Press, 1944).

16. Milton Friedman, *Capitalism and Freedom* (Chicago: University of Chicago Press, 1962), p. 133.

17. Ibid., pp. 133–136.

18. For a more detailed discussion of the relationships between economic freedom and environmental issues, see John Ahrens, *Preparing for the Future* (Bowling Green, Ohio: The Social Philosophy and Policy Center, 1983), esp. chapter IV.

19. Fred R. Harris, "The Politics of Corporate Power," in Nader, op. cit., pp. 25–41.

20. See note 16.

21. For a more systematic and detailed presentation of the theory of individual rights, see Ayn Rand, *Capitalism: The Unknown Ideal* (New York: New American Library, 1967), and Robert Nozick, *Anarchy, State, and Utopia* (New York: Basic Books, 1974).

22. It should be noted that the theory of individual rights is part of the classic ideal of *libertarianism*. As has been noted earlier, this ideal has been an important intellectual tradition in the United States, but there are other classic ideals (including, most obviously, Marxism, socialism, and facism) that would reject both individual rights and Friedman's view.

23. This section owes a good deal to the analysis in Douglas Den Uyl, *The New Crusaders* (Bowling Green, Ohio: The Social Philosophy and Policy Center, 1984).

24. Den Uyl, op. cit., p. 48.

Kenneth E. Goodpaster
BUSINESS ETHICS AND STAKEHOLDER ANALYSIS

> So we must think through what management should be accountable for;
> and how and through whom its accountability can be discharged. The
> stockholders' interest, both short- and long-term, is one of the areas. But
> it is only one.
>
> Peter Drucker, 1988
Harvard Business Review

What is ethically responsible management? How can a corporation, given its economic mission, be managed with appropriate attention to ethical concerns? These are central questions in the field of business ethics. One approach to answering such questions that has become popular during the last two decades is loosely referred to as "stakeholder analysis." Ethically responsible management, it is often suggested, is management that includes careful attention not only to stockholders *but to stakeholders generally* in the decision-making process.

This suggestion about the ethical importance of stakeholder analysis contains an important kernel of truth, but it can also be misleading. Comparing the ethical relationship between managers and stockholders with their relationship to other stakeholders is, I will argue, almost as problematic as ignoring stakeholders (ethically) altogether — presenting us with something of a "stakeholder paradox."

DEFINITION

The term "stakeholder" appears to have been invented in the early '60s as a deliberate play on the word "stockholder" to signify that there are other parties having a "stake" in the decision-making of the modern, publicly-held corporation in addition to those holding equity positions. Professor R. Edward Freeman, in his book *Strategic Management: A Stakeholder Approach* (Pitman, 1984), defines the term as follows:

> A stakeholder in an organization is (by definition) any group or individual who can affect or is affected by the achievement of the organization's objectives. (46)

Examples of stakeholder groups (beyond stockholders) are employees, suppliers, customers, creditors, competitors, governments, and communities. *Exhibit 1* illustrates one way of picturing the conventional stakeholder groups along with the two principal channels through which they often affect the corporation, law and markets.

From *Business Ethics Quarterly*, 1, no. 1 (January 1991), 53–73. Reprinted by permission.

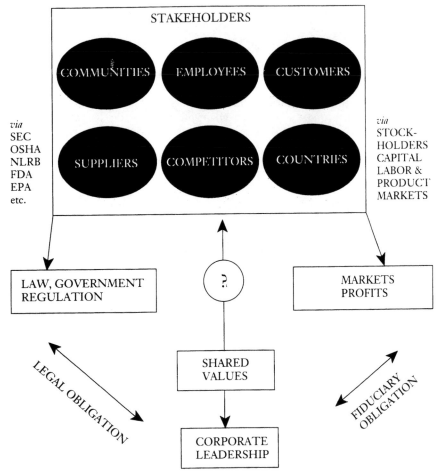

EXHIBIT 1   *Business Decision-Making and Ethical Values*

Another metaphor with which the term "stakeholder" is associated is that of a "player" in a game like poker. One with a "stake" in the game is one who plays and puts some economic value at risk.[1]

Much of what makes responsible decision-making difficult is understanding how there can be an ethical relationship between management and stakeholders that avoids being too weak (making stakeholders mere means to stockholders' ends) or too strong (making stakeholders quasi-stockholders in their own right). To give these issues life, a case example will help. So let us consider the case of General Motors and Poletown.

THE POLETOWN CASE[2]

In 1980, GM was facing a net loss in income, the first since 1921, due to intense foreign competition. Management realized that major capital expenditures would be required for the company to regain its competitive position and profitability. A $40 billion five year capital spending program was announced that included new, state-of-the-art assembly techniques aimed at smaller, fuel-efficient automobiles demanded by the market. Two aging assembly plants in Detroit were among the ones to be replaced. Their closure would eliminate 500 jobs. Detroit in 1980 was a city with a black majority, an unemployment rate of 18% overall and 30% for blacks, a rising public debt and a chronic budget deficit, despite high tax rates.

The site requirements for a new assembly plant included 500 acres, access to long-haul railroad and freeways, and proximity to suppliers for "just-in-time" inventory management. It needed to be ready to produce 1983 model year cars beginning in September 1982. The only site in Detroit meeting GM's requirements was heavily settled, covering a section of the Detroit neighborhood of Poletown. Of the 3,500 residents, half were black. The whites were mostly of Polish descent, retired or nearing retirement. An alternative "green field" site was available in another midwestern state.

Using the power of eminent domain, the Poletown area could be acquired and cleared for a new plant within the company's timetable, and the city government was eager to cooperate. Because of job retention in Detroit, the leadership of the United Auto Workers was also in favor of the idea. The Poletown Neighborhood Council strongly opposed the plan, but was willing to work with the city and GM.

The new plant would employ 6,150 workers and would cost GM $500 million wherever it was built. Obtaining and preparing the Poletown site would cost an additional $200 million, whereas alternative sites in the midwest were available for $65-80 million.

The interested parties were many — stockholders, customers, employees, suppliers, the Detroit community, the midwestern alternative, the Poletown neighborhood. The decision was difficult. GM management needed to consider its competitive situation, the extra costs of remaining in Detroit, the consequences to the city of leaving for another part of the midwest, and the implications for the residents of choosing the Poletown site if the decision was made to stay. The decision about whom to talk to and *how* was as puzzling as the decision about *what* to do and *why*.

I. STAKEHOLDER ANALYSIS AND STAKEHOLDER SYNTHESIS

Ethical values enter management decision-making, it is often suggested, through the gate of stakeholder analysis. But the suggestion that introducing "stakeholder analysis" into business decisions is the same as introducing ethics into those decisions is questionable. To make this plain, let me first distinguish between two importantly different ideas: stakeholder analysis and stakeholder synthesis. I will then examine alternative kinds of stakeholder synthesis with attention to ethical content.

The decision-making process of an individual or a company can be seen in terms of a sequence of six steps to be followed after an issue or problem presents itself for resolution.[3] For ease of reference and recall, I will name the sequence PASCAL, after the six letters in the name of the French philosopher-mathematician Blaise Pascal (1623 – 1662), who once remarked in reference to ethical decision-making that "the heart has reasons the reason knows not of."

1. PERCEPTION or fact-gathering about the options available and their short- and long-term implications;
2. ANALYSIS of these implications with specific attention to affected parties and to the decision-maker's goals, objectives, values, responsibilities, etc.;
3. SYNTHESIS of this structured information according to whatever fundamental priorities obtain in the mindset of the decision-maker;
4. CHOICE among the available options based on the synthesis;
5. ACTION or implementation of the chosen option through a series of specific requests to specific individuals or groups, resource allocation, incentives, controls, and feedback;
6. LEARNING from the outcome of the decision, resulting in either reinforcement or modification (for future decisions) of the way in which the above steps have been taken.

We might simplify this analysis, of course, to something like "input," "decision," and "output," but distinguishing interim steps can often be helpful. The main point is that the path from the presentation of a problem to its resolution must somehow involve gathering, processing, and acting on relevant information.

Now, by *stakeholder analysis* I simply mean a process that does not go beyond the first two steps mentioned above. That is, the affected parties caught up in each available option are identified and the positive and negative impacts on each stakeholder are determined. But questions having to do with processing this information into a decision and implementing it are *left unanswered*. These steps are not part of the *analysis* but of the *synthesis, choice,* and *action.*

Stakeholder analysis may give the initial appearance of a decision-making process, but in fact it is only a *segment* of a decision-making process. It represents the preparatory or opening phase that awaits the crucial application of the moral (or nonmoral) values of the decision-maker. So, to be informed that an individual or an institution regularly makes stakeholder analysis part of decision-making or takes a "stake-holder approach" to management is to learn little or nothing about the ethical character of that individual or institution. It is to learn only that stakeholders are regularly identified — *not why and for what purpose.* To be told that stakeholders are or must be "taken into account" is, so far, to be told very little. Stakeholder analysis is, as a practical matter, morally *neutral.* It is therefore a mistake to see it as a substitute for normative ethical thinking.[4]

What I shall call "stakeholder synthesis" goes further into the sequence of decision-making steps mentioned above to include actual decision-making and implementation (S,C,A). The critical point is that stakeholder synthesis offers *a pattern or channel by which to move from stakeholder identification to a practical response or resolution.* Here we begin to join stakeholder analysis to questions of substance. But we must now ask: What kind of substance? And how does it relate to *ethics?* The stakeholder idea, remember, is typically offered as a way of integrating *ethical* values into management decision-making. When and how does substance become *ethical* substance?

Strategic Stakeholder Synthesis

We can imagine decision-makers doing "stakeholder analysis" for different underlying reasons, not always having to do with ethics. A management team, for example, might be careful to take positive and (especially) negative stakeholder effects into account for no other reason than that offended stakeholders might resist or retaliate (e.g., through political action or opposition to necessary regulatory clearances). It might not be *ethical* concern for the stakeholders that motivates and guides such analysis, so much as concern about potential impediments to the achievement of strategic objectives. Thus positive and negative effects on relatively powerless stakeholders may be ignored or discounted in the synthesis, choice, and action phases of the decision process.[5]

In the Poletown case, General Motors might have done a stakeholder analysis using the following reasoning: our stockholders are the central stakeholders here, but other key stakeholders include our suppliers, old and new plant employees, the City of Detroit, and the residents of Poletown. These other stakeholders are not our direct concern as a corporation with an economic mission, but since they can influence our short- or long-term strategic interests, they must be taken into account. Public relation's costs and benefits, for example, or concerns about union contracts or litigation might well have influenced the choice between staying in Detroit and going elsewhere.

I refer to this kind of stakeholder synthesis as "strategic" since stakeholders outside the stockholder group are viewed instrumentally, as factors potentially affecting the overarching goal of optimizing stockholder interests. They are taken into account in the decision-making process, but as external environmental forces, as potential sources of either good will or retaliation. "We" are the economic principals and management; "they" are significant players whose attitudes and future actions might affect our short-term or long-term success. We must respect them in the way one "respects" the weather—as a set of forces to be reckoned with.[6]

It should be emphasized that managers who adopt the strategic stakeholder approach are not necessarily *personally* indifferent to the plight of stakeholders who are "strategically unimportant." The point is that in *their role as managers*, with a fiduciary relationship that binds them as agents to principals, their basic outlook subordinates other stakeholder concerns to those of stockholders. Market and legal forces are relied upon to secure the interests of those whom strategic considerations might discount. This reliance can and does take different forms, depending on the emphasis given to market forces on the one hand and legal forces on the other. A more conservative, market-oriented view acknowledges the role of legal compliance as an environmental factor affecting strategic choice, but thinks stakeholder interests are best served by minimal interference from the public sector. Adam Smith's "invisible hand" is thought to be the most important guarantor of the common good in a competitive economy. A more liberal view sees the hand of government, through legislation and regulation, as essential for representing stakeholders that might otherwise not achieve "standing" in the strategic decision process.

What both conservatives and liberals have in common is the conviction that the fundamental orientation of management must be toward the interests of stockholders. Other stakeholders (customers, employees, suppliers, neighbors) enter the decision-making equation either directly as instrumental economic factors or indirectly as potential legal claimants. (See again *Exhibit 1*.) Both see law and regulation as providing a voice for stakeholders that goes beyond market dynamics. They differ about how much government regulation is socially and economically desirable.

During the Poletown controversy, GM managers as individuals may have cared deeply about the potential lost jobs in Detroit, or about the potential dislocation of Poletown residents. But in their role as agents for the owners (stockholders) they could only allow such considerations to "count" if they served GM's strategic interests (or perhaps as legal constraints on the decision).

Professor Freeman (1984, cited above) appears to adopt some form of strategic stakeholder synthesis. After presenting his definition of stakeholders, he remarks about its application to any group or individual "who can *affect* or is *affected by*" a company's achievement of its purposes. The "affect" part of the definition is not hard to understand; but Freeman clarifies the "affected by" part:

> The point of strategic management is in some sense to chart a direction for the firm. Groups which can affect that direction and its implementation must be considered in the strategic management process. However, it is less obvious why "those groups who are affected by the corporation" are stakeholders as well . . . I make the definition symmetric because of the changes which the firm has undergone in the past few years. Groups which 20 years ago had no effect on the actions of the firm, can affect it today, largely because of the actions of the firm which ignored the effects on these groups. Thus, by calling those affected groups "stakeholders," the ensuing strategic management model will be sensitive to future change . . . (46)

Freeman might have said "who can actually or potentially affect" the company, for the mind-set appears to be one in which attention to stakeholders is justified in terms of actual or potential impact on the company's achievement of its strategic purposes. Stakeholders (other than stockholders) are actual or potential means/obstacles to corporate objectives. A few pages later, Freeman writes:

> From the standpoint of strategic management, or the achievement of organizational purpose, we need an inclusive definition. We must not leave out any group or individual who can affect or is affected by organizational purpose, *because that group may prevent our accomplishments.* (52) [Emphasis added.]

The essence of a strategic view of stakeholders is not that stakeholders are ignored, but that all but a special group (stockholders) are considered on the basis of their actual or potential influence on management's central mission. The basic normative principle is fiduciary responsibility (organizational prudence), supplemented by legal compliance.

Is the Substance Ethical?

The question we must ask in thinking about a strategic approach to stakeholder synthesis is this: Is it really an adequate rendering of the *ethical* component in managerial judgment? Unlike mere stakeholder *analysis*, this kind of synthesis does go beyond simply *identifying* stakeholders. It integrates the stakeholder information by using a single interest group (stockholders) as its basic normative touchstone. If this were formulated as an explicit rule or principle, it would have two parts and would read something like this: (1) Maximize the benefits and minimize the costs to the stockholder group, short- and long-term, and (2) Pay close attention to the interests of other stakeholder groups that might potentially influence the achievement of (1). But while expanding the list of stakeholders may be a way of "enlightening" self-interest for the organization, is it really a way of introducing ethical values into business decision-making?

There are really two possible replies here. The first is that as an account of how ethics enters the managerial mind-set, the strategic stakeholder approach fails not because it is *im*moral; but because it is *non*moral. By most accounts of the nature of ethics, a strategic stakeholder synthesis would not qualify as an ethical synthesis, even though it does represent a substantive view. The point is simply that while there is nothing necessarily *wrong* with strategic reasoning about the consequences of one's actions for others, the kind of concern exhibited should not be confused with what most people regard as *moral* concern. Moral concern would avoid injury or unfairness to those affected by one's actions because it is wrong, regardless of the retaliatory potential of the aggrieved parties.[7]

The second reply does question the morality (*vs.* immorality) of strategic reasoning as the ultimate principle behind stakeholder analysis. It acknowledges that strategy, when placed in a highly effective legal and regulatory environment and given a time-horizon that is relatively long-term, may well avoid significant forms of anti-social behavior. But it asserts that as an operating principle for managers under time pressure in an imperfect legal and regulatory environment, strategic analysis is insufficient. In the Poletown case, certain stakeholders (e.g., the citizens of Detroit or the residents of Poletown) may have merited more *ethical* consideration than the strategic approach would have allowed. Some critics charged that GM only considered these stakeholders *to the extent that* serving their interests also served GM's interests, and that as a result, their interests were undermined.

Many, most notably Nobel Laureate Milton Friedman, believe that market and legal forces are adequate to translate or transmute ethical concerns into straightforward strategic concerns for management. He believes that in our economic and political system (democratic capitalism), direct concern for stakeholders (what Kant might have called "categorical" concern) is unnecessary, redundant, and inefficient, not to mention dishonest:

> In many cases, there is a strong temptation to rationalize actions as an exercise of "social responsibility." In the present climate of opinion, with its widespread aversion to "capitalism," "profits," the "soulless corporation" and so on, this is one way for a corporation to generate good will as a by-product of expenditures that are entirely justified in its own self-interest. If our institutions, and the attitudes of the public make it in their self-interest to cloak their actions in this way, I cannot summon much indignation to denounce them. At the same time, I can express admiration for those individual proprietors or owners of closely held corporations or stockholders of more broadly held corporations who disdain such tactics as approaching fraud.

Critics respond, however, that absent a pre-established harmony or linkage between organizational success and ethical success, some stakeholders, some of the time, will be affected a lot but will be able to affect in only a minor way the interests of the corporation. They add that in an increasingly global business environment, even the protections of law are fragmented by multiple jurisdictions.

At issue then is (1) defining ethical behavior partly in terms of the (nonstrategic) decision-making values *behind* it, and (2) recognizing that too much optimism about the correlation between strategic success and virtue runs the risk of tailoring the latter to suit the former.

Thus the move toward substance (from analysis to synthesis) in discussions of the stakeholder concept is not necessarily a move toward ethics. And it is natural to think that the reason has to do with the instrumental status accorded to stakeholder groups other than stockholders. If we were to treat all stakeholders by strict analogy with stockholders, would we have arrived at a more ethically satisfactory form of stakeholder synthesis? Let us now look at this alternative, what I shall call a "multi-fiduciary" approach.

Multi-Fiduciary Stakeholder Synthesis

In contrast to a strategic view of stakeholders, one can imagine a management team processing stakeholder information by giving the same care to the interests of, say, employees, customers, and local communities as to the economic interests of stockholders. This kind of substantive commitment to stakeholders might involve trading off the economic advantages of one group against those of another, e.g., in a plant closing decision. I shall refer to this way of integrating stakeholder analysis with decision-making as "multi-fiduciary" since all stakeholders are treated by management as having equally important interests, deserving joint "maximization" (or what Herbert Simon might call "satisficing").

Professor Freeman, quoted earlier, contemplates what I am calling the multi-fiduciary view at the end of his 1984 book under the heading *The Manager As Fiduciary To Stakeholders*:

> Perhaps the most important area of future research is the issue of whether or not a theory of management can be constructed that uses the stakeholder concept to enrich "managerial capitalism," that is, can the notion that managers bear a fiduciary relationship to stockholders or the owners of the firm, be replaced by a concept of management whereby the manager *must* act in the interests of the stakeholders in the organization? (249)

As we have seen, the strategic approach pays attention to stakeholders as to factors that might affect economic interests, so many market forces to which companies must pay attention for competitive reasons. They become actual or potential legal challenges to the company's exercise of economic rationality. The multi-fiduciary approach, on the other hand, views stakeholders apart from their instrumental, economic, or legal clout. It does not see them merely as what philosopher John Ladd once called "limiting operating conditions" on management attention.[8] On this view, the word "stakeholder" carries with it, by the deliberate modification of a single phoneme, a dramatic shift in managerial outlook.

In 1954, famed management theorist Adolf Berle conceded a long-standing debate with Harvard law professor E. Merrick Dodd that looks in retrospect very much like a debate between what we are calling strategic and multi-fiduciary interpretations of stakeholder synthesis. Berle wrote:

> Twenty years ago, [I held] that corporate powers were powers in trust for shareholders while Professor Dodd argued that these powers were held in trust for the entire community. The argument has been settled (at least for the time being) squarely in favor of Professor Dodd's contention. (Quoted in Ruder, see below.)

The intuitive idea behind Dodd's view, and behind more recent formulations of it in terms of "multiple constituencies" and "stakeholders, not just stockholders" is that by expanding the list of those in whose trust corporate management must manage, we thereby introduce ethical responsibility into business decision-making.

In the context of the Poletown case, a multi-fiduciary approach by GM management might have identified the same stakeholders. But it would have considered the interests of employees, the city of Detroit, and the Poletown residents *alongside* stockholder interests, not solely in terms of how they might *influence* stockholder interests. This may or may not have entailed a different outcome. But it probably would have meant a different approach to the decision-making process in relation to the residents of Poletown (talking with them, for example).

We must now ask, as we did of the strategic approach: How satisfactory is multi-fiduciary stakeholder synthesis as a way of giving ethical substance to management decision-making? On the face of it, and in stark contrast to the strategic approach, it may seem that we have at last arrived at a truly moral view. But we should be cautious. For no sooner do we think we have found the proper interpretation of ethics in management than a major objection presents itself. And, yes, it appears to be a *moral* objection!

It can be argued that multi-fiduciary stakeholder analysis is simply incompatible with widely-held moral convictions about the special fiduciary obligations owed by management to stockholders. At the center of the objection is the belief that the obligations of agents to principals are stronger or different in kind from those of agents to third parties.

The Stakeholder Paradox

Managers who would pursue a multi-fiduciary stakeholder orientation for their companies must face resistance from those who believe that a strategic orientation is the only *legitimate* one for business to adopt, given the economic mission and legal constitution of the modern corporation. This may be disorienting since the word "illegitimate" has clear negative ethical connotations, and yet the multi-fiduciary approach is often defended on ethical grounds. I will refer to this anomalous situation as the *Stakeholder Paradox:*

> It seems essential, yet in some ways illegitimate, to orient corporate decisions by ethical values that go beyond strategic stakeholder considerations to multi-fiduciary ones.

I call this a paradox because it says there is an ethical problem whichever approach management takes. Ethics seems both to forbid and to demand a strategic, profit-maximizing mind-set. The argument behind the paradox focuses on management's *fiduciary* duty to the stockholder, essentially the duty to keep a profit-maximizing promise, and a concern that the "impartiality" of the multi-fiduciary approach simply cuts management loose from certain well-defined bonds of stockholder accountability. On this view, impartiality is thought to be a *betrayal of trust*. Professor David S. Ruder, a former chairman of the Securities and Exchange Commission, once summarized the matter this way:

> Traditional fiduciary obligation theory insists that a corporate manager owes an obligation of care and loyalty to shareholders. If a public obligation theory unrelated to profit maximization becomes the law, the corporate manager who is not able to act in his own self interest without violating his fiduciary obligation, may nevertheless act in the public interest without violating that obligation.[9] (226)

Ruder continued:

> Whether induced by government legislation, government pressure, or merely by enlightened attitudes of the corporation regarding its long range potential as a unit in society, corporate activities carried on in satisfaction of public obligations can be consistent with profit maximization objectives. In contrast, justification of public obligations upon bold concepts of public need without corporate benefit will merely serve to reduce further the owner's influence on his corporation and to create additional demands for public participation in corporate management. (228–229)

Ruder's view appears to be that (a) multi-fiduciary stakeholder synthesis *need not* be used by management because the strategic approach is more accommodating than meets the eye; and (b) multi-fiduciary stakeholder synthesis should not be invoked by management because such a "bold" concept could threaten the private (*vs.* public) status of the corporation.

In response to (a), we saw earlier that there were reasonable questions about the tidy convergence of ethics and economic success. Respecting the interests and rights of the Poletown residents might really have meant incurring higher costs for GM (short-term as well as long-term).

Appeals to corporate self-interest, even long-term, might not always support ethical decisions. But even on those occasions where they will, we must wonder about the disposition to favor economic and legal reasoning "for the record." If Ruder means to suggest that business leaders can often *reformulate* or *re-present* their reasons for certain morally grounded decisions in strategic terms having to do with profit maximization and obedience to law, he is perhaps correct. In the spirit of our earlier quote from Milton Friedman, we might not summon much indignation to denounce them. But why the fiction? Why not call a moral reason a moral reason?

This issue is not simply of academic interest. Managers must confront it in practice. In one major public company, the C.E.O. put significant resources behind an affirmative action program and included the following explanation in a memo to middle management:

I am often asked why this is such a high priority at our company. There is, of course, the obvious answer that it is in our best interest to seek out and employ good people in all sectors of or society. And there is the answer that enlightened self-interest tells us that more and more of the younger people, whom we must attract as future employees, choose companies by their social records as much as by their business prospects. *But the one overriding reason for this emphasis is because it is right.* Because this company has always set for itself the objective of assuming social as well as business obligations. Because that's the kind of company we have been. And with your participation, that's the kind of company we'll continue to be.[10]

In this connection, Ruder reminds us of what Professor Berle observed over twenty-five years ago:

> The fact is that boards of directors or corporation executives are often faced with situations in which they quite humanly and simply consider that such and such is the decent thing to do and ought to be done . . . They apply the potential profits or public relations tests later on, a sort of left-handed justification in this curious free-market world where an obviously moral or decent or humane action has to be apologized for on the ground that, conceivably, you may somehow make money by it. (*Ibid.*)

The Problem of Boldness

What appears to lie at the foundation of Ruder's cautious view is a concern about the "boldness" of the multi-fiduciary concept [(b) above].[11] It is not that he thinks the strategic approach is always satisfactory; it is that the multi-fiduciary approach is, in his eyes, much worse. For it questions the special relationship between the manager as agent and the stockholder as principal.

Ruder suggests that what he calls a "public obligation" theory threatens the private status of the corporation. He believes that what we are calling multi-fiduciary stakeholder synthesis *dilutes* the fiduciary obligation to stockholders (by extending it to customers, employees, suppliers, etc.) and he sees this as a threat to the "privacy" of the private sector organization. If public obligations are understood on the model of public sector institutions with their multiple constituencies, Ruder thinks, the stockholders loses status.

There is something profoundly *right* about Ruder's line of argument here, I believe, and something profoundly *wrong*. What is right is his intuition that if we treat other stakeholders on the model of the fiduciary relationship between management and the stockholder, we will, in effect, make them into quasi-stockholders. We can do this, of course, if we choose to as a society. But we should be aware that it is a radical step indeed. For it blurs traditional goals in terms of entrepreneurial risk-taking, pushes decision-making towards paralysis because of the dilemmas posed by divided loyalties and, in the final analysis, represents nothing less than the conversion of the modern private corporation into a public institution and probably calls for a corresponding restructuring of corporate governance (e.g., representatives of each stakeholder group on the board of directors). Unless we believe that the social utility of a private sector

The American Law Institute

PRINCIPLES OF CORPORATE GOVERNANCE:

ANALYSIS AND RECOMMENDATIONS

Tentative Draft No. 2
(April 13, 1984)

Part II

THE OBJECTIVE AND CONDUCT OF THE BUSINESS CORPORATION

ANALYSIS AND RECOMMENDATION

§201.   The Objective and Conduct of the Business Corporation

A business corporation should have as its objective the conduct of business activities with a view to enhancing corporate profit and shareholder gain, except that, whether or not corporate profit and shareholder gain are thereby enhanced, the corporation, in the conduct of its business

(a) is obliged, to the same extent as a natural person, to act within the boundaries set by law,

(b) may take into account ethical considerations that are reasonably regarded as appropriate to the responsible conduct of business, and

(c) may devote a reasonable amount of resources to public welfare, humanitarian, educational, and philanthropic purposes.

EXHIBIT 2

has disappeared, not to mention its value for individual liberty and enterprise, we will be cautious about an interpretation of stakeholder synthesis that transforms the private sector into the public sector.

On the other hand, I believe Ruder is mistaken if he thinks that business ethics requires this kind of either/or: either a private sector with a strategic stakeholder synthesis (business without ethics) or the effective loss of the private sector with a multi-fiduciary stakeholder synthesis (ethics without business).

Recent debates over state laws protecting companies against hostile take-overs may illustrate Ruder's concern as well as the new challenge. According to one journalist, a recent Pennsylvania anti-takeover law

> does no less than redefine the fiduciary duty of corporate directors, enabling them to base decisions not merely on the interests of share-holders, but on the interests of customers, suppliers, employees and the community at large. Pennsylvania is saying that it is the corporation that directors are responsible to. Shareholders say they always thought they themselves were the corporation.

Echoing Ruder, one legal observer quoted by Elias (*ibid.*) commented with reference to this law that it "undermines and erodes free makets and property rights. From this perspective, this is an anticapitalist law. The management can take away property from the real owners."[12]

In our terms, the state of Pennsylvania is charged with adopting a multifidu-ciary stakeholder approach in an effort to rectify deficiencies of the strategic approach which (presumably) corporate raiders hold.

The challenge that we are thus presented with is to develop an account of the moral responsibilities of management that (i) avoids surrendering the moral relationship between management and stakeholders as the strategic view does, while (ii) not transforming stakeholder obligations into fiduciary obligations (thus protecting the uniqueness of the principle-agent relationship between management and stockholder).

II. TOWARD A NEW STAKEHOLDER SYNTHESIS

We all remember the story of the well-intentioned Doctor Frankenstein. He sought to improve the human condition by designing a powerful, intelligent force for good in the community. Alas, when he flipped the switch, his creation turned out to be a monster rather than a marvel! Is the concept of the ethical corporation like a Frankenstein monster?

Taking business ethics seriously need not mean that management bears *additional* fiduciary relationships to third parties (nonstockholder constituen-cies) as multi-fiduciary stakeholder synthesis suggests. It may mean that there are morally significant *nonfiduciary* obligations to third parties surrounding any fiduciary relationship (See *Figure 1*.) Such moral obligations may be owed by private individuals as well as private-sector organizations to those whose free-dom and well-being is affected by their economic behavior. It is these very obligations in fact (the duty not to harm or coerce and duties not to lie, cheat, or

	Fiduciary	Non-fiduciary
Stockholders	●	
Other stakeholders		●

FIGURE 1   *Direct Managerial Obligations*

steal) that are cited in regulatory, legislative, and judicial arguments for constraining profit-driven business activities. These obligations are not "hypothetical" or contingent or indirect, as they would be on the strategic model, wherein they are only subject to the corporation's interests being met. They are "categorical" or direct. They are not rooted in the *fiduciary* relationship, but in other relationships at least as deep.

It must be admitted in fairness to Ruder's argument that the jargon of "stakeholders" in discussions of business ethics can seem to threaten the notion of what corporate law refers to as the "undivided and unselfish loyalty" owed by managers and directors to stockholders. For this way of speaking can suggest a multiplication of management duties *of the same kind* as the duty to stockholders. What we must understand is that the responsibilities of management toward stockholders are of a piece with the obligations that *stockholders themselves* would be expected to honor in their own right. As an old Latin proverb has it, *nemo dat quod non habet*, which literally means "nobody gives what he doesn't have." Freely translating in this context we can say: No one can expect of an *agent* behavior that is ethically less responsible than what he would expect of himself. I cannot (ethically) *hire* done on my behalf what I would not (ethically) *do* myself. We might refer to this as the "Nemo Dat Principle" (NDP) and consider it a formal requirement of consistency in business ethics (and professional ethics generally):

> (NDP) Investors cannot expect of managers (more generally, principals cannot expect of their agents) behavior that would be inconsistent with the reasonable ethical expectations of the community.[13]

The NDP does not, of course, resolve in advance the many ethical challenges that managers must face. It only indicates that these challenges are of a piece with those that face us all. It offers a different kind of test (and so a different kind of stakeholder synthesis) that management (and institutional investors) might apply to policies and decisions.

The foundation of ethics in management — and the way out of the stakeholder paradox — lies in understanding that the conscience of the corporation is a logical and moral extension of the consciences of its principals. It is *not* an expansion of the *list* of principals, but a gloss on the principal-agent relationship itself. Whatever the structure of the principal-agent relationship, neither principal nor agent can ever claim that an agent has "moral immunity" from the basic obligations that would apply to any human being toward other members of the community.

Indeed, consistent with Ruder's belief, the introduction of moral reasoning (distinguished from multi-fiduciary stakeholder reasoning) into the framework of management thinking may *protect* rather than threaten private sector legitimacy. The conscientious corporation can maintain its private economic mission, but in the context of fundamental moral obligations owed by any member of society to others affected by that member's actions. Recognizing such obligations does *not* mean that an institution is a public institution. Private institutions, like private individuals, can be and are bound to respect moral obligations in the pursuit of private purposes.

Conceptually, then, we can make room for a moral posture toward stakeholders that is both *partial* (respecting the fiduciary relationship between managers and stockholders) and *impartial* (respecting the equally important non-fiduciary relationships between management and other stakeholders). As philosopher Thomas Nagel has said, "In the conduct of life, of all places, the rivalry between the view from within and the view from without must be taken seriously."[14]

Whether this conceptual room can be used *effectively* in the face of enormous pressures on contemporary managers and directors is another story, of course. For it is one thing to say that "giving standing to stakeholders" in managerial reasoning is conceptually coherent. It is something else to say that it is practically coherent.

Yet most of us, I submit, believe it. Most of us believe that management at General Motors *owed* it to the people of Detroit and to the people of Poletown to take their (nonfiduciary) interests very seriously, to seek creative solutions to the conflict, to do more than use or manipulate them in accordance with GM's needs only. We understand that managers and directors have a special obligation to provide a financial return to the stockholders, but we also understand that the word "special" in this context needs to be tempered by an appreciation of certain fundamental community norms that go beyond the demands of both laws and markets. There are certain class-action suits that stockholders ought not to win. For there is sometimes a moral defense.

CONCLUSION

The relationship between management and stockholders is ethically different in kind from the relationship between management and other parties (like employees, suppliers, customers, etc.), a fact that seems to go unnoticed by the multi-fiduciary approach. If it were not, the corporation would cease to be a private sector institution — and what is now called business ethics would become a more radical critique of our economic system than is typically thought. On this point, Milton Friedman must be given a fair and serious hearing.

This does not mean, however, that "stakeholders" lack a morally significant relationship to management, as the strategic approach implies. It means only that the relationship in question is different from a fiduciary one. Management may never have promised customers, employees, suppliers, etc. a "return on investment," but management is nevertheless obliged to take seriously its extra-legal obligations not to injure, lie to or cheat these stakeholders *quite apart from* whether it is in the stockholders' interests.

As we think through the *proper* relationship of management to stakeholders, fundamental features of business life must undoubtedly be recognized: that corporations have a principally economic mission and competence; that fiduciary obligations to investors and general obligations to comply with the law cannot be set aside; and that abuses of economic power and disregard of corporate stewardship in the name of business ethics are possible.

But these things must be recognized as well: that corporations are not solely financial institutions; that fiduciary obligations go beyond short-term profit and are in any case subject to moral criteria in their execution; and that mere compliance with the law can be unduly limited and even unjust.

The *Stakeholder Paradox* can be avoided by a more thoughtful understanding of the nature of moral obligation and the limits it imposes on the principal-agent relationship. Once we understand that there is a practical "space" for identifying the ethical values shared by a corporation and its stockholders — a space that goes beyond strategic self-interest but stops short of impartiality — the hard work of filling that space can proceed.

Notes

This paper derives from a conference in Applied Ethics, *Moral Philosophy in the Public Domain*, held at the University of British Columbia, in June 1990. It will also appear in an anthology currently in preparation at the UBC Centre of Applied Ethics.

1. Strictly speaking the historical meaning of "stakeholder" in this context is someone who literally *holds* the stakes during play.

2. See Goodpaster and Piper, *Managerial Decision Making and Ethical Values*, Harvard Business School Publishing Division, 1989.

3. See Goodpaster, PASCAL: A Framework For Conscientious Decision Making (1989).

4. Actually, there are subtle ways in which even the stakeholder identification or inventory process might have *some* ethical content. The very process of *identifying* affected parties involves the use of the imagination in a way that can lead to a natural empathetic or caring response to those parties in the synthesis, choice and action phases of decision-making. This is a contingent connection, however, not a necessary one.

5. Note that including powerless stakeholders in the analysis phase may indicate whether the decision-maker cares about "affecting" them or "being affected by" them. Also, the inclusion of what might be called secondary stakeholders as advocates for primary stakeholders (e.g., local governments on behalf of certain citizen groups) may signal the values that will come into play in any synthesis.

6. It should be mentioned that some authors, most notably Kenneth R. Andrews in *The Concept of Corporate Strategy* (Irwin, Third Edition, 1987) employ a broader and more social definition of "strategic" decision-making than the one implied here.

7. Freeman writes: "Theoretically, 'stakeholder' must be able to capture a broad range of groups and individuals, even though when we put the concept to practical tests we must be willing to ignore certain groups who will have little or no impact on the corporation at this point in time." (52–53)

8. Ladd observed in a now-famous essay entitled "Morality and the Ideal of Rationality in Formal Organizations" (*The Monist*, 54, 1970) that organizational "rationality" was defined solely in terms of economic objectives: "The interests and needs of the individuals concerned, as individuals, must be considered only insofar as they establish limiting operating conditions. Organizational rationality dictates that these interests and needs must not be considered in their own right or on their own merits. If we think of an organization as a machine, it is easy to see why we cannot reasonably expect it to have any moral obligations to people or for them to have any to it." (507)

9. Public Obligations of Private Corporations," *U. of Pennsylvania Law Review*, 114 (1965). Ruder recently (1989) reaffirmed the views in his 1965 article.

10. "Business Products Corporation — Part 1," HBS Case Services 9-337-077.

11. "The Business Judgement Rule" gives broad latitude to officers and directors of corporations, but calls for reasoning on the basis of the long-term economic interest of the company. And corporate case law ordinarily allows exceptions to profit-maximization criteria only when there are actual or potential *legal* barriers, and limits charitable and humanitarian gifts by the logic of long term self-interest. The underlying rationale is accountability to investors. Recent work by the American Law Institute, however, suggests a rethinking of these matters. See *Exhibit 2*.

12. Christopher Elias, "Turning Up the Heat on the Top," *Insight*, July 23, 1990.

13. We might consider the NDP in broader terms that would include the relationship between "client" and "professional" in other contexts, such as law, medicine, education, government, and religion, where normally the community's expectations are embodied in ethical standards.

14. T. Nagel, *The View from Nowhere*, Oxford U. Press (1986), p. 163.

◆ ◆ ◆

DISCUSSION QUESTIONS

1. Friedman claims that the doctrine of corporate social responsibility is essentially "taxation without representation." He observes that an executive "is exercising a distinct 'social responsibility,' rather than serving as an agent of the stockholders or the customers or the employees, only if he spends the money in a different way than they would have spent it. But if he does this, he is in effect imposing taxes, on the one hand, and deciding how the tax proceeds shall be spent, on the other." Is Friedman correct? If so, can you support such a fundamentally "un-American" idea?

2. Does Donaldson successfully refute Friedman?

3. Miller and Ahrens refer to the provisions of a proposed Corporate Democracy Act aimed to bring corporations under greater public control. Do you think that such a law should be enacted? Why or why not?

4. Apply Goodpaster's suggestions for how to take care of the interest of stakeholders to the Poletown case, and decide how it should be resolved.

CASE 5.1

◆ ◆ ◆

Ben & Jerry's

One of America's most unusual companies must surely be Ben & Jerry's Ice Cream, headquartered in Waterbury, Vermont. The company's founders, Ben Cohen and Jerry Greenfield, established the company with modest goals —to make a high-quality, all natural ice cream and to work together. They never aspired to the extraordinary success they now enjoy. Founded in 1978 in a renovated gas station on a $12,000 investment ($4,000 of it borrowed), Ben & Jerry's was hailed in 1981 by *Time* magazine for making "the best ice cream in the world." The company had sales of more than $70 million in 1990, and it continues to grow.

Ben and Jerry themselves are unlikely models of corporate moguls (you can find their picture on the top of their ice cream cartons), but what is particularly unusual about the company is its strong sense of corporate social responsibility. "We believe that business can be profitable and improve the quality of life for people at the same time," explains Ben. This belief is expressed more fully in the firm's "Statement of Mission":

Ben & Jerry's is dedicated to the creation and demonstration of a new corporate concept of linked prosperity. Our mission consists of three interrelated parts:

Product Mission—To make, distribute, and sell the finest quality, all-natural ice cream and related products in a wide variety of innovative flavors made from Vermont dairy products.

Social Mission—To operate the company in a way that actively recognizes the central role that business plays in the structure of society by initiating innovative ways to improve the quality of life of a broad community—local, national, and international.

Economic Mission—To operate the company on a sound financial basis of profitable growth, increasing value for our shareholders, and creating career opportunities and financial rewards for our employees.

Underlying the mission of Ben & Jerry's is the determination to seek new and creative ways of addressing all three parts, while holding a deep respect for the individuals, inside and outside the company, and for the communities of which they are a part.

Central to this notion of "linked prosperity" is the company's decision to donate 7.5 percent of its pretax earnings to nonprofit and charitable causes. More significant, however, is that the company's ordinary business operations are infused with a sense of moral purpose. Ben & Jerry's chocolate-coated "Peace Pop" promotes "1% for Peace," an initiative aimed at directing 1 percent of the defense budget to activities that will promote peace. The dairy ingredients used in the company's products are purchased from a cooperative of Vermont family farms. The peaches in Fresh Georgia Peach ice cream are bought from a family farm in Georgia. Rainforest Crunch ice cream is made from nuts from Brazilian rainforest trees, and sales of the flavor indirectly benefit efforts to preserve the rainforest. Chocolate Fudge Brownie ice cream is made from brownies bought from a New York organization that provides jobs and training for the homeless. The blueberries in Wild Maine Blueberry come from the Passamaquoddy Indians in Maine. As a way of demonstrating commitment to the company's surrounding community, one of the company's stock offerings was limited to people from Vermont. And the company has a policy whereby the highest paid employee cannot earn more than seven times what the lowest paid employee earns. "We do this," the company explains, "because we believe that most American corporations overpay top management, and underpay entry-level employees—and because everyone who works at Ben & Jerry's is a major contributor to our success."

Ben & Jerry's also regularly takes actions that more traditional corporations would judge as being too controversial. It sponsored a billboard opposing a nuclear power plant in New Hampshire. It signed a full-page ad in the *New York Times* before the war in the Persian Gulf opposing military action and encouraging an energy policy based on conservation. It opposed approval of bovine growth hormone, a genetically engineered hormone designed to increase milk production. And it has used its facilities for voter registration drives, offering a free cone to new voters.

What we ultimately see with Ben & Jerry's is a direct, practical challenge to the tired cliché that business and ethics are antithetical. As Ben writes to his shareholders,

> The most amazing thing is that our social values . . . have actually helped us to become a stable, profitable, high growth company. This is

especially interesting because it flies in the face of those business theorists who state that publicly held corporations cannot make a profit and help the community at the same time, and moreover that such companies have no business trying to do so. The issues here are heart, soul, love and spirituality. Corporations which exist solely to maximize profit become disconnected from their soul — the spiritual interconnectedness of humanity. Like individuals, businesses can conduct themselves with the knowledge that the hearts, souls and spirits of all people are interconnected; so that as we help others, we cannot help helping ourselves.

It makes no sense to compartmentalize our lives — to be cutthroat in business, and then volunteer some time or donate some money to charity. For it is business that is the most powerful force in our society. Multinational corporations are the most powerful force in the world — stronger even than nation states. So, if business is the most powerful force in the world, it stands to reason that business sets the tone for our society. Nonprofits and charities cannot possibly accomplish their objectives if business does not use its power to help people. ◆

Discussion Questions

1. What is your reaction to the way Ben & Jerry's conducts business? Do you agree with Ben that the company succeeds because of, not in spite of, its commitment to social values? If it turns out that the company's commitment to certain causes leads to a loss of some business, what should it do? If it chooses to stay the course, would it be falling short on its responsibilities to its stockholders? If it chooses to give up that cause, would it be falling short of its moral responsibilities?

2. Ben's claim about the power of business is extremely important because it implies that corporations could choose to produce a tremendous amount of good in society. Does every corporation have a responsibility to conduct itself the way that Ben & Jerry's does? What is your reaction to the claim that corporations that focus simply on the bottom line are morally culpable because of the good they fail to do? That is, it could be claimed that by failing to advance a social agenda similar to Ben & Jerry's, these companies are morally negligent. At what point could it be argued that if a business has a social and political agenda, it should be subject, in a democratic society, to social and political control?

Sources

Ben & Jerry's Ice Cream, "About Ben & Jerry's."
———, *Ben & Jerry's 1990 Annual Report.*
———, "Ben & Jerry's Time Line."
———, "Benefits à la Ben & Jerry."
———, "Human Development."
———, "Sharing the Wealth."

CASE 5.2

Stakeholders, Pensions, and Health Benefits

Running a business in a way that promotes the interests of all stakeholders is an appealing goal. But putting the idea into practice is difficult. This is especially apparent in recent controversies involving pensions and health benefits.

Throughout the 1980s, the assets of American pension funds more than tripled to a value of $2.6 trillion. This figure included $600 billion more than companies needed to meet their current pension obligations and sounds like good news. The funds were full (overfunded) and pensioners must surely be secure.

Not so, however. Throughout the same decade, numerous corporations viewed these funds as sources of capital, and they drew from them for a variety of purposes. In several cases, pension funds were used to save companies from failure. But in the worst cases, companies closed the pension plans altogether, provided their pensioners with minimal annuities purchased from insurance companies, and used the surplus any way they chose. Unlike a pension, an annuity is not insured by the Federal Pension Benefit Guaranty Corporation. Whether or not the annuities will be paid, then, depends on the future financial health of the insurance company, and there has been at least one failure. Also, an annuity is a fixed sum, whereas companies sometimes add cost-of-living increases to pensions.

A central question is to whom does the money in a pension fund actually belong? Workers claim that it is theirs and see it as deferred wages. A surplus is protection against an uncertain, possibly inflationary future. Management, however, sees any surplus over current obligations as money that can be used to benefit other stakeholders. When Exxon withdrew $1.6 billion from its $5.6 billion pension fund in 1986, for example, it argued that its shareholders would be better served.

The most controversial cases involve the fate of pension funds in acquisitions. For example, in 1982 North Carolina's Cannon Mills was sold by the Cannon family to David H. Murdock. Murdock sold the mill to Fieldcrest Mills in 1985. But first he terminated Cannon's $102.7 million pension plan, paid $67 million to provide workers with annuities from the Executive Life Insurance Company, and kept roughly $30 million of the surplus. In 1991, however, Executive Life was seized by California regulators. The company had invested too heavily in high-risk, high-yield junk bonds and collapsed when the junk bond market soured. Cannon pensions were cut by 30 percent while regulators sought ways to return the pensions to their full total. A similar fate befell retirees from Pacific Lumber, a company purchased in 1985 by Charles E. Hurwitz. Hurwitz terminated Pacific's pension plan and used the surplus to reduce his debt from the purchase. He, too, replaced the company pension plan with annuities bought from Executive Life, a company that at the time was receiving high marks from rating agencies.

Another area in which there has been competition between stakeholders involves health benefits. Particularly if a company covers its employees' health costs itself, there are few rules by which it must operate. Indeed, a 1991 federal appeals court ruled that companies that self-insure can sharply reduce benefits for employees who develop expensive illnesses. A Houston music store, for example, discontinued its health benefits policy with a private insurance company and self-insured in order to reduce its costs. Yet it also lowered an employee's maximum benefit from $1 million to $5,000, despite the fact that one employee was already undergoing expensive treatment for AIDS. Even though the savings benefit some of the stakeholders, employees who experience a catastrophic illness could be decimated financially.

A similar controversy involving competing stakeholder interests and health benefits arose during the liquidation of Eastern Airlines. By the time Eastern Airlines declared bankruptcy in January 1991, the company owed about $2.4 billion to creditors and former employees. Eastern, however, was also paying $3.6 million per month for health benefits for 10,800 retired employees younger than 65 and thus ineligible for Medicare. In light of the fact that the airline's liquidation was projected to raise only $66.5 million to pay claims, Martin R. Shugrue, the trustee overseeing the liquidation, asked the bankruptcy court to suspend medical benefits for the retirees.

Eastern's unions objected, claiming that in determining how the liquidation fund should be distributed, priority should be given to the retirees. They argued that the loss of benefits would leave seriously ill retirees without any health care coverage because insurance companies would not accept them. And healthy retirees, they claimed, could not afford health insurance premiums because of their small, fixed incomes. The unions also argued that the money would make more of a difference to the retirees than to corporate creditors, who expected to receive less than 3 cents on every dollar they were owed. "It is simply beyond dispute," argued the union, "that each dollar spent is of more significance to the individuals being faced with the medical and financial crisis posed by Eastern's dissolution than to business creditors, which have proportionally larger budgets by factors in the millions." The creditors, not surprisingly, found the unions' position unfair. "The discouraging reality of the Eastern bankruptcy," they contended, "is that virtually all the holders of a claim or interest have been harmed. Although it is unfortunate, it is not inequitable that the retirees share this hardship as well."

In terms of the ordinary workings of the economy, it is perfectly legitimate for Shugrue and the creditors to ask for the suspension of the retirees' benefits. In fact, after declaring bankruptcy in 1988, the LTV Corporation suspended health and life insurance benefits for about 78,000 retirees. ◆

Discussion Questions

1. How would you resolve these issues? What should happen when various stakeholders compete for the same resources? Does it matter that the benefits received by various stakeholders — shareholder dividends, retirees' pensions, employees' health benefits — differ?

2. To whom does the money in a pension fund belong?

3. If Murdock and Hurwitz bought Executive Life's annuities in good faith, assuming that employees would be protected, are they entitled to do whatever they want with the surplus in the pension fund?

4. If providing employees with generous pensions and health care benefits is

expensive, does a company have the responsibility to spend the money? What if doing so decreases profits? What if limiting health care coverage or lowering pensions will prevent layoffs?

5. Do Eastern's creditors have a legitimate claim on the airline's assets? How does their claim compare to that of the pensioners?

6. How do you implement stakeholder theory fairly in such difficult circumstances as those described in this case study?

Sources

Applebome, Peter, "Mill Town Pensioners Pay for Wall Street Sins," *New York Times*, July 30, 1991, A1, A16.

"The Fury over Pension Funds," *Business Week*, July 3, 1989, 31.

Greenhouse, Steven, "Just Whose Money Is in an Employee Pension Plan?," *New York Times*, February 1, 1987, E7.

Pear, Robert, "Court Approves Cuts in Benefits in Costly Illnesses," *New York Times*, November 27, 1991, A1, B7.

"The Power of Pension Funds," *Business Week*, November 6, 1989, 154–158.

"Retired Mill Employees Assured on Pensions," *New York Times*, August 7, 1991. A16.

"The Retiring Kind Are Getting Militant about Benefits," *Business Week*, May 28, 1990, 29.

Salpukas, Agis, "Fight over Liquidation of Eastern," *New York Times*, May 20, 1991, D4.

———, "Eastern Claimants May Find Smaller Pie in Liquidation," *New York Times*, May 22, 1991, D, 17.

"In Search of the Vanishing Nest Egg," *Business Week*, July 30, 1990, 46.

Williams, Winston, "Raking in Billions from the Company Pension Plan," *New York Times*, November 3, 1985, F1, F8.

ADDITIONAL READINGS

Hodapp, Paul F., "Can There Be a Social Contract with Business?," *Journal of Business Ethics*, 9 (1990), 127–131.

Kultgen, John, "Donaldson's Social Contract for Business," *Business & Professional Ethics Journal*, 5 (1985), no. 1. 28–50.

Levitt, Theodore, "The Dangers of Corporate Social Responsibility," *Harvard Business Review*, September-October 1958, 41–50.

Mulligan, Thomas, "A Critique of Milton Friedman's Essay 'The Social Responsibility of Business Is to Increase Its Profits,'" *Journal of Business Ethics*, 5 (1986), 265–269.

———, "Justifying Moral Initiative by Business, with Rejoinders to Bill Shaw and Richard Nunan," *Journal of Business Ethics*, 9 (1990), 93–103.

Sharplin, Arthur, and Lonnie D. Phelps, "A Stakeholder Apologetic for Management," *Business & Professional Ethics Journal*, 8 (1988), no. 2. 41–53.

Shaw, Bill, "A Reply to Thomas Mulligan's 'A Critique of Milton Friedman's Essay "The Socal Responsibility of Business Is to Increase Its Profits"'," *Journal of Business Ethics*, 7 (1988), 537–543.

CHAPTER 6

◆ ◆ ◆

Corporations, Responsibility and Personhood

It is one thing to make the general claim that corporations do or do not have some social responsibility. A more precise and problematic issue related to the concept of responsibility, however, is how to determine and interpret its scope. We know what it means to hold an individual responsible for his or her actions, but what does it mean to say that a corporation is morally culpable? Is a corporation somehow different from the collection of individuals comprising it? If so, how? And what are the ethical implications of this distinction? For example, are individuals who act as agents of a corporation personally responsible for what they do?

This chapter focuses on the debate about whether corporations can be held responsible. We begin with a classic piece by Peter French, who argues that the internal decision structures of corporations allow us to speak of "corporate intentions," and these intentions make corporations morally responsible. John Ladd opposes this point of view and claims that ethical concepts cannot be applied directly to corporations as if they were persons. Christopher Meyers holds that both corporations and their individual members should be held accountable for corporate decisions. The question of the individual responsibility of senior executives is explored by John Bishop, who argues that corporate executives have the minimal moral obligation to prevent disasters.

Peter A. French

THE CORPORATION AS A MORAL PERSON

In one of his *New York Times* columns of not too long ago Tom Wicker's ire was aroused by a Gulf Oil Corporation advertisement that "pointed the finger of blame" for the energy crisis at all elements of our society (and supposedly away from the oil company). Wicker attacked Gulf Oil as the major, if not the sole, perpetrator of that crisis and virtually every other social ill, with the possible exception of venereal disease. It does not matter whether Wicker was serious or sarcastic in making his charges (I suspect he was in deadly earnest). I am interested in the sense ascriptions of moral responsibility make when their subjects are corporations. I hope to provide the foundation of a theory that allows treatment of corporations as members of the moral community, of equal standing with the traditionally acknowledged residents: biological human beings, and hence treats Wicker-type responsibility ascriptions as unexceptionable instances of a perfectly proper sort without having to paraphrase them. In short, corporations can be full-fledged moral persons and have whatever privileges, rights and duties as are, in the normal course of affairs, accorded to moral persons.

It is important to distinguish three quite different notions of what constitutes personhood that are entangled in our tradition: the metaphysical, moral and legal concepts. The entanglement is clearly evident in Locke's account of personal identity. He writes that the term "person" is "a *forensic* term, appropriating actions and their merit; and so belongs only to *intelligent agents*, capable of law, and happiness, and misery."[1] He goes on to say that by consciousness and memory persons are capable of extending themselves into the past and thereby become "concerned and *accountable*."[2] Locke is historically correct in citing the law as a primary origin of the term "person." But he is incorrect in maintaining that its legal usage somehow entails its metaphysical sense, agency; and whether or not either sense, but especially the metaphysical, is interdependent on the moral sense, accountability, is surely controversial. Regarding the relationship between metaphysical and moral persons there are two distinct schools of thought. According to one, to be a metaphysical person is to be a moral one; to understand what it is to be accountable one must understand what it is to be an intelligent or a rational agent and vice versa; while according to the other, being an agent is a necessary but not sufficient condition of being a moral person. Locke holds the interdependence view with which I agree, but he roots both moral and metaphysical persons in the juristic person, which is, I think, wrongheaded. The preponderance of current thinking tends to some version of the necessary pre-condition view, but it does have the virtue of treating the legal person as something apart.

It is of note that many contemporary moral philosophers and economists both take a pre-condition view of the relationship between the metaphysical and moral person and also adopt a particular view of the legal personhood of corporations that effactually excludes corporations *per se* from the class of moral persons. Such philosophers and economists champion the least defensi-

From *American Philosophical Quarterly* 3 (1979), 207–215. Reprinted by permission.

ble of a number of possible interpretations of the juristic personhood of corporations, but their doing so allows them to systematically sidestep the question of whether corporations can meet the conditions of metaphysical personhood.[3]

Many philosophers, including, I think, Rawls, have rather uncritically relied upon what they incorrectly perceive to be the most defensible juristic treatment of collectivities such as corporations as a paradigm for the treatment of corporations in their moral theories. The concept of corporate legal personhood under any of its popular interpretations is, I want to argue, virtually useless for moral purposes.

Following many writers on jurisprudence, a juristic person may be defined as any entity that is a subject of a right. There are good etymological grounds for such an inclusive neutral definition. The Latin "*persona*" originally referred to *dramatis personae*, and in Roman law the term was adopted to refer to anything that could act on either side of the legal dispute. [It was not until Boethius' definition of a person "*Persona est naturae rationabilis individua substantia* (a person in the individual subsistence of a rational nature)" that metaphysical traits were ascribed to persons.] In effect, in Roman legal tradition persons are creations, artifacts, of the law itself, i.e., of the legislature that enacts the law, and are not considered to have, or only have incidentally, existence of any kind outside of the legal sphere. The law, on the Roman interpretation, is systematically ignorant of the biological status of its subjects.

The Roman notion applied to corporations is popularly known as the Fiction Theory. . . .

The Fiction Theory's major rival in American jurisprudence and the view that does seem to inform Rawls' account is what I shall call "the Legal Aggregate theory of the Corporation." It holds that the names of corporate bodies are only umbrellas that cover (but do not shield) certain biological persons. The Aggregate Theory treats biological status as having legal priority and corporate existence as a contrivance for purposes of summary reference. (Generally, it may be worth mention, Aggregate Theorists tend to ignore employees and identify corporations with directors, executives and stockholders. The model on which they stake their claim is no doubt that of the primitive partnership.) I have shown elsewhere[4] that to treat a corporation as an aggregate for any purposes is to fail to recognize the key logical differences between corporations and mobs. The Aggregate Theory, then, despite the fact that it has been quite popular in legislatures, courtrooms, and on street corners, simply ignores key logical, socio-economic and historical facts of corporate existence. It might prove of some value in clarifying the dispute between Fiction and Aggregate theorists to mention a rather famous case in the English law. (The case is cited by Hallis.) It is that of *Continental Tyre and Rubber Co., Ltd.* vs. *Daimler Co., Ltd.* Very sketchily, the Continental Tyre company was incorporated in England and carried on its business there. Its business was the selling of tires made in Germany, and all of its directors were German subjects in residence in Germany, and all but one of its shares were held by German subjects. The case arose during the First World War, and it turned on the issue of whether the company was an English subject by virtue of its being incorporated under the English law and independent of its directors and stockholders, and could hence bring suit in an English court against an English subject while a state of war existed. The majority opinion of The Court of Appeals (5-1) was that the corporation was an entity created by statute and hence was "a different person altogether from the subscribers to the memorandum or the share-holders on the register."[5]

Underlying all of these interpretations of corporate legal personhood is a distinction, embedded in the law itself, that renders them unhelpful for our purposes. Being a subject of rights is often contrasted in the law with being an "administrator of rights." Any number of entities and associations can and have been the subjects of legal rights. Legislatures have given rights to unborn human beings, they have reserved rights for human beings long after their death, and in some recent cases they have invested rights in generations of the future.[6] Of course such subjects of rights, though they are legal persons, cannot dispose of their rights, cannot administer them, because to administer a right one must be an agent, i.e., able to act in certain ways. It may be only an historical accident that most legal cases are cases in which "the subject of right X" and "the administrator of right X" are co-referential. It is nowhere required by law, under any of the three above theories or elsewhere, that it be so. Yet, it is possession of the attributes of an administrator of rights and not those of a subject of rights that are among the generally regarded conditions of moral personhood. It is a fundamental mistake to regard the fact of juristic corporate personhood as having settled the question of the moral personhood of a corporation one way or the other.

Two helpful lessons however, are learned from an investigation of the legal personhood of corporations: (1) biological existence is not essentially associated with the concept of a person (only the fallacious Aggregate Theory depends upon reduction to biological referents) and (2) a paradigm for the form of an inclusive neutral definition of a moral person is provided: "a subject of a right." I shall define a moral person as the referent of any proper name or description that can be a non-eliminatable subject of what I shall call (and presently discuss) a responsibility ascription of the second type. The non-eliminatable nature of the subject should be stressed because responsibility and other moral predicates are neutral as regards person and *personum* prediction.[7] Though we might say that the Ox-Bow mob should be held responsible for the death of three men, a mob is an example of what I have elsewhere called an aggregate collectivity with no identity over and above that of the sum of the identities of its component membership, and hence to use "the Ox-Bow mob" as the subject of such ascriptions is to make summary reference to each member of the mob. For that reason mobs do not qualify as metaphysical or moral persons.

There are at least two significantly different types of responsibility ascriptions that should be distinguished in ordinary usage (not counting the laudatory recommendation, "He is a responsible lad.") The first type pins responsibility on someone or something, the who-dun-it or what-dun-it sense. Austin has pointed out that it is usually used when an event or action is thought by the speaker to be untoward. (Perhaps we are most interested in the failures rather than the successes that punctuate our lives.)

The second type of responsibility ascription, parasitic upon the first, involves the notion of accountability. "Having a responsibility" is interwoven with the notion "Having a liability to answer," and having such a liability or obligation seems to imply (as Anscombe has noted[8]) the existence of some sort of authority relationship either between people or between people and a deity or in some weaker versions between people and social norms. The kernel of insight that I find intuitively compelling, is that for someone to legitimately hold someone else responsible for some event there must exist or have existed a responsibility relationship between them such that in regard to the event in question the latter was answerable to the former. In other words, "X is responsible for *y*," as a second-type ascription, is properly uttered by someone Z if X in respect to *y* is or was accountable to Z. Responsibility relationships are created in a multitude of ways, e.g., through promises, contracts, compacts, hirings, assignments, appointments, by agreeing to enter a Rawlsian original position, etc. The right to hold responsible is often delegatable to third parties; though in the case of moral responsibility no delegation occurs because no person is excluded from the relationship: moral responsibility relationships hold reciprocally and without prior agreements among all moral persons. No special arrangement needs to be established between parties for anyone to hold someone morally responsible for his acts or, what amounts to the same thing, every person is a party to a responsibility relationship with all other persons as regards the doing or refraining from doing of certain acts: those that take descriptions that use moral notions.

Because our interest is in the criteria of moral personhood and not the content of morality we need not pursue this idea further. What I have maintained is that moral responsibility, although it is neither contractual nor optional, is not a class apart but an extension of ordinary, garden-variety, responsibility. What is needed in regard to the present subject then is an account of the requirements for entry into any responsibility relationship, and we have already seen that the notion of the juristic person does not provide a sufficient account. For example, the deceased in a probate case cannot be held responsible in the relevant way by anyone, even though the deceased is a juristic person, a subject of rights.

A responsibility ascription of the second type amounts to the assertion of a conjunctive proposition, the first conjunct of which identifies the subject's actions with or as the cause of an event (usually an untoward one) and the second conjunct asserts that the action in question was intended by the subject or that the event was the direct result of an intentional act of the subject. In addition to what it asserts it implies that the subject is accountable to the speaker (in the case at hand) because of the subject's relationship to the speaker (who the speaker is or what the speaker is, a member of the "moral community," a surrogate for that aggregate). The primary focus of responsibility ascriptions of the second type is on the subject's intentions rather than, though not to the exclusion of, occasions. Austin wrote: "In considering responsibility, few things are considered more important than to establish whether a man *intended* to do A, or whether he did A intentionally."[9] To be the subject of a responsibility ascription of the second type, to be a party in responsibility relationships, hence to be a moral person, the subject must be at minimum, what I shall call a Davidsonian agent.[10] If corporations are moral persons, they will be non-eliminatable Davidsonian agents.

For a corporation to be treated as a Davidsonian agent it must be the case that some things that happen, some events, are describable in a way that makes certain sentences true, sentences that say that some of the things a corporation does were intended by the corporation itself. That is not accomplished if attributing intentions to a corporation is only a shorthand way of attributing intentions to the biological persons who comprise e.g. its board of directors. If that were to turn out to be the case then on metaphysical if not logical grounds there would be no way to distinguish between corporations and mobs. I shall argue, however, that a *C*orporation's *I*nternal *D*ecision Structure (its CID Structure) is the requisite redescription device that licenses the predication of corporate intentionality.

Certain events, that is , actions, are describable as simply the bodily movements of human beings and sometimes those same events are redescribable in terms of their upshots, as bringing about something, e.g., (from Austin[11]) feeding penguins *by* throwing them peanuts ("by" is the most common way we connect different descriptions of the same event[12]), and sometimes those events can be redescribed as the effects of some prior cause; then they are described as done for reasons, done in order to bring about something, e.g., feeding the penguins peanuts in order to kill them. Usually what we single out as that prior cause is some desire or felt need combined with the belief that the object of the desire will be achieved by the action undertaken. (This, I think, is what Aristotle meant when he maintained that acting requires desire.) Saying "someone (X) did *y* intentionally" is to describe an event (*y*) as the upshot of X's having had a reason for doing it which was the cause of his doing it.

It is obvious that a corporation's doing something involves or includes human beings doing things and that the human beings who occupy various positions in a corporation usually can be described as having reasons for *their* behavior. In virtue of those descriptions they may be properly held responsible for their behavior, *ceteris paribus*. What needs to be shown is that there is sense in saying that corporations and not just people who work in them, have reasons for doing what they do. Typically, we will be told that it is the directors, or the managers, etc., that really have the corporate reasons and desires, etc., and that although corporate actions may not be reducible without remainder, corporate intentions are always reducible to human intentions.

Every corporation has an internal decision structure. CID Structures have two elements of interest to us here: (1) an organizational or responsibility flow chart that delineates stations and levels within the corporate power structure and (2) corporate decision recognition rule(s) (usually embedded in something called "corporation policy"). The CID Structure is the personnel organization for the exercise of the corporation's power with respect to its ventures, and as such its primary function is to draw experience from various levels of the corporation into a decision-making and ratification process. When operative and properly activated, the CID Structure accomplishes a subordination and synthesis of the intentions and acts of various biological persons into a corporate decision. When viewed in another way, as already suggested, the CID Structure licenses the descriptive transformation of events, seen under another aspect as the acts of biological persons (those who occupy various stations on the organizational chart), to corporate acts by exposing the corporate character of those events. A functioning CID Structure *incorporates* acts of biological persons. For illustrative purposes, suppose we imagine that an event E has at least two aspects, that is, can be described in two non-identical ways. One of those aspects is "Executive X's doing *y*" and one is "Corporation C's doing *z*."

The corporate act and the individual act may have different properties; indeed they have different causal ancestors though they are causally inseparable. (The causal inseparability of these acts I hope to show is a product of the CID Structure, X's doing y is not the cause of C's doing z nor is C's doing z the cause of X's doing y although if X's doing y causes event F then C's doing z causes F and vice versa.)

Suppose, for illustrative purposes, we activate a CID Structure in a corporation, Wicker's favorite, the Gulf Oil Corporation. Imagine that three executives X, Y and Z have the task of deciding whether or not Gulf Oil will join a world uranium cartel. X, Y, and Z have before them an Everest of papers that have been prepared by lower echelon executives. Some of the papers will be purely factual reports, some will be contingency plans, some will be formulations of positions developed by various departments, some will outline financial considerations, some will be legal opinions and so on. Insofar as these will all have been processed through Gulf's CID Structure system, the personal reasons, if any, individual executives may have had when writing their reports and recommendations in a specific way will have been diluted by the subordination of individual inputs to peer group input even before X, Y and Z review the matter. X, Y and Z take a vote. Their taking of a vote is authorized procedure in the Gulf CID Structure, which is to say that under these circumstances the vote of X, Y and Z can be redescribed as the corporation's making a decision; that is, the event "XYZ voting" may be redescribed to expose an aspect otherwise unrevealed, that is quite different from its other aspects, e.g., from X's voting in the affirmative. Redescriptive exposure of a procedurally corporate aspect of an event, however, is not to be confused with a description of an event that makes true a sentence that says that the corporation did something intentionally. But the CID Structure, as already suggested, also provides the grounds in its other type of recognitor for such an attribution of corporate intentionality. Simply, when the corporate act is consistent with an instantiation or an implementation of established corporate policy, then it is proper to describe it as having been done for corporate reasons, as having been caused by a corporate desire coupled with a corporate belief and so, in other words, as corporate-intentional.

An event may, under one of its aspects, be described as conjunctive act "X did a (or as X intentionally did a) & Y did a (or as Y intentionally did a) & Z did a (or as Z intentionally did a)" (where $a =$ voted in the affirmative on the question of Gulf Oil joining the cartel). Given the Gulf CID Structure, formulated in this instance as the conjunction of rules: when the occupants of positions A, B and C on the organizational chart unanimously vote to do something and if doing that something is consistent with an instantiation or an implementation of general corporate policy and *ceteris paribus*, then the corporation has decided to do it for corporate reasons, the event is redescribable as "The Gulf Oil Corporation did j for corporation reasons f" (where j is "decided to join the cartel" and f is any reason (desire + belief) consistent with basic policy of Gulf Oil, e.g. increasing profits) or simply as "Gulf Oil Corporation intentionally did j." This is a rather technical way of saying that in these circumstances the executives' voting is, given its CID Structure, also the corporation deciding to do something, and that regardless of the personal reasons the executives have for voting as they do and even if their reasons are inconsistent with established corporate policy or even if one of them has no reason at all for voting as he does, the corporation still has reasons for joining the cartel; that is, joining is consistent with the inviolate corporate general policies as encrusted in the precedent of previous corporate actions and its statements of purpose as recorded in its certificate of incorporation, annual reports, etc. The corporation's only method of achieving its desires or goals is the activation of the personnel who occupy its various positions. However, if X voted affirmatively purely for reasons of personal monetary gain (suppose he had been bribed to do so) that does not alter the fact that the corporate reason for joining the cartel was to minimize competition and hence pay higher dividends to its shareholders. Corporations have reasons because they have interest in doing those things that are likely to result in realization of their established corporate goals regardless of the transient self-interest of directors, managers, etc. If there is a difference between corporate goals and desires and those of human beings it is probably that the corporate ones are relatively stable and not very wide ranging, but that is only because corporations can do relatively fewer things than human beings, being confined in action predominately to a limited socio-economic sphere. The attribution of corporate intentionality is opaque with respect to other possible descriptions of the event in question. It is, of course, in a corporation's interest that its component membership view the corporate purposes as instrumental in the achievement of their own goals. (Financial reward is the most common way this is achieved.)

It will be objected that a corporation's policies reflect only the current goals of its directors. But that is certainly not logically necessary nor is it in practice true for most large corporations. Usually, of course, the original incorporators will have organized to further their individual interests and/or to meet goals which they shared. But even in infancy the melding of disparate interests and purposes gives rise to a corporate long-range point of view that is distinct from the intents and purposes of the collection of incorporators viewed individually. Also, corporate basic purposes and policies, as already mentioned, tend to be relatively stable when compared to those of individuals and not couched in the kind of language that would be appropriate to individual purposes. Furthermore, as histories of corporations will show, when policies are amended or altered it is usually only peripheral issues that are involved. Radical policy alteration constitutes a new corporation, a point that is captured in the incorporation laws of such states as Delaware. ("Any power which is not enumerated in the charter and the general law or which cannot be inferred from those two sources is *ultra vires* of the corporation.") Obviously underlying the objection is an uneasiness about the fact that corporate intent is dependent upon policy and purpose that is but an artifact of the socio-psychology of a group of biological persons. Corporate intent seems somehow to be a tarnished illegitimate offspring of human intent. But this objection is another form of the anthropocentric bias. By concentrating on possible descriptions of events and by acknowledging only that the possibility of describing something as an agent depends upon whether or not it can be properly described as having done something (the description of some aspect of an event) for a reason, we avoid the temptation to look for extensional criteria that would necessitate reduction to human referents.

The CID Structure licenses redescriptions of events as corporate and attributions of corporate intentionality while it does not obscure the private acts of executives, directors, etc. Although X voted to support the joining of the cartel because he was bribed to do so. X did not join the cartel, Gulf Oil Corporation joined the Cartel. Consequently, we may say that X did something for which he should be held morally responsible, yet whether or not Gulf Oil Corporation should be held morally responsible for joining the cartel is a question that turns on issues that may be unrelated to X's having accepted a bribe.

Of course Gulf Oil Corporation cannot join the cartel unless X or somebody who occupies position A on the organizational chart votes in the affirmative. What that shows, however, is that corporations are collectivities. That should not, however, rule out the possibility of their having metaphysical status, as being Davidsonian agents, and being thereby full-fledged moral persons.

This much seems to me clear: we can describe many events in terms of certain physical movements of human beings and we also can sometimes describe those events as done for reasons by those human beings, but further we can sometimes describe those events as corporate and still further as done for corporate reasons that are qualitatively different from whatever personal reasons, if any, component members may have for doing what they do.

Corporate agency resides in the possibility of CID Structure licensed redescription of events as corporate-intentional. That may still appear to be downright mysterious, although I do not think it is, for human agency as I have suggested, resides in the possibility of description as well.

Although further elaboration is needed, I hope I have said enough to make plausible the view that we have good reasons to acknowledge the noneliminatable agency of corporations. I have maintained that Davidsonian agency is a necessary and sufficient condition of moral personhood. I cannot further argue that position here (I have done so elsewhere). On the basis of the foregoing analysis, however, I think that grounds have been provided for holding corporations *per se* to account for what they do, for treating them as metaphysical persons *qua* moral persons.

Notes

1. John Locke, *An Essay Concerning Human Understanding* (1960), Bk. II, Ch. XXVII.
2. Ibid.
3. For a particularly flagrant example see Michael Jensen and William Meckling, "Theory of the Firm: Managerial Behavior, Agency Costs and Ownership Structure." *Journal of Financial Economics*, vol. 3 (1976), pp. 305–360. On p. 311 they write, "The private corporation or firm is simply one form of legal fiction which serves as a nexus for contracting relationships. . . ."
4. "Types of Collectivities and Blame," *The Personalist*, vol. 56 (1975), pp. 160–169, and in the first chapter of my *Corporate and Collective Responsibility*, Columbia University Press, 1984.
5. "Continental Tyre and Rubber Co. Ltd. vs. Daimler Co., Ltd." (1915) K.B., p. 893.
6. And, of course, in earlier times animals have been given legal rights.
7. See Gerald Massey, "Tom, Dick, and Harry, and All The King's Men." *American Philosophical Quarterly*, vol. 13 (1976), pp. 89–108.
8. G. E. M. Anscombe, "Modern Moral Philosophy," *Philosophy*, vol. 33 (1958), pp. 1–19.
9. J. L. Austin, "Three Ways of Spilling Ink," in *Philosophical Papers* (Oxford, 1970), p. 273.
10. See, for example, Donald Davidson, "Agency," in *Agent, Action, and Reason*, ed. by Binkley, Bronaugh, and Marras (Toronto, 1971).
11. Austin, p. 275.
12. See Joel Feinberg, *Doing and Deserving* (Princeton, 1970), p. 134f.

John Ladd

CORPORATE MYTHOLOGY AND INDIVIDUAL RESPONSIBILITY

The far-reaching powers of corporations in our society and their pervasive influence over our daily lives, make it increasingly imperative for moral philosophers to inquire into questions about corporations and morality. There are many questions that need to be asked. Some of them are new, while others are old questions in a new context. Many of the latter are questions familiar to students of political philosophy and they reflect the same kinds of theoretical and practical perplexities. They are problems such as the problem of authority and obedience, of the allocation of benefits and burdens, of paternalism and autonomy, of liberty and human rights, of justice, the public interest and the common good.

I stress the seriousness, urgency, variety and complexity of ethical questions, problems and issues relating to corporations because many of my critics have interpreted my theories about formal organizations and corporations to imply that they are outside the domain of ethics altogether.[1] That is not my position at all. Rather, my position is simply that ethical concepts cannot be applied directly to corporations as if they were persons; that is not to say at all that they cannot be applied to them indirectly by applying them, say, to individuals and groups of individuals associated with corporations in some way or other. The principal purpose of this essay will be to explain and defend my position on the subject by sorting out some moral questions concerning corporations and indicating ways in which the ethics of corporations might be developed.

Throughout this essay, I shall take the general position that the modern corporation is a social institution comparable to other institutions of a society, such as the state, the family, the church, the schools, the professions, or even more generally, private property or that "peculiar institution, slavery." Following Parsons, I shall take an institution to be a "complex of institutionalized role integrates . . . a complex of patterned elements in role-expectations . . . "[2] Generally speaking, social institutions, like those just mentioned, are complexes of practices, norms and concepts that dominate and regulate specific aspects of social life, social relations and social interactions. Corporations in our society provide institutionalized mechanisms for organizing the production and distribution of goods and services.

A few preliminary remarks about social institutions in general may help to set my remarks about corporations in perspective. First, social institutions are always subject to moral review, criticism and evaluation. Consequently, an institution may be moral, immoral or morally indifferent—in part or as a whole. Second, institutions are constantly changing; old institutions often disappear and are replaced by new ones. Sometimes such changes are for better and sometimes they are for worse. (The "peculiar institution" of slavery illustrates both these points about evaluation and change.) If one is a utilitarian, which I am

From *The International Journal of Applied Philosophy*, 2 (Spring 1984), 1–21. Reprinted by permission.

not, the tendency of a particular institution to promote utility would be the governing factor in evaluating it and determining whether institutional changes represent progress or the reverse. But regardless of whether or not one is a utilitarian, the point remains that all social institutions are and must be subject to ethical scrutiny, critique and evaluation, although I am not prepared to offer simple rules for doing so here. The modern corporation, as a social institution, is like other social institutions in these two respects. As with other social institutions, however, moral problems concerning corporations are not all black and white: they are much more subtle and complicated than that. In particular, if we find certain features of corporations as an institution to be ethically objectionable, change rather than abolition may in the long run be the wisest course.

Social institutions of the sort intended here almost always, perhaps always, have an ideology as an essential component; for it is generally important and perhaps even necessary for people to be able to rationalize and defend their practices; sometimes the mere survival of an institution requires justifying it against the criticisms of reformers, skeptics, and rebels. For such reasons, it has often been claimed that particular institutions, such as the family or the state, were founded by the gods. It is not uncommon, then, to find a body of myths, a mythology, as part of the ideology of a social institution.

Since mythology is an important concept in this essay, I should explain what I mean by the word. By "mythology" I mean a coherent body of social beliefs that, taken literally rather than figuratively, are patently false. For example, they may be about supernatural beings with supernatural powers, like the Greek gods or the Navaho Holy People. Despite their ostensibly literal falsity, they are "believed in" and consequently perform important social functions of one sort or another, in particular they serve to confer authority and legitimacy on particular institutions, practices and establishments. Both social contract and divine rights theories of the state illustrate the use of mythology in political and social philosophy to legitimize political systems, in this case quite different ones.[3] Because of their important social functions and their use to support social institutions, they must be taken very seriously from an ethical point of view; for quite apart from the fact that a particular mythology is literally false, its functions may be benign or pernicious, sometimes even disastrous, depending on whether the social practice it is used to support is moral or not.[4] To demythologize an institution therefore is to attack (or criticize) not only the mythology but the institution itself. For example, the attack on slavery is an institution involved at the same time an attack on the mythology behind it. Similarly, the demythologization of corporate mythology must lead to the repudiation of particular practices founded on it.

At this juncture, a few remarks about my methodology will help to explain the structure of my argument. First, I shall approach the issues from the ethical point of view and thus my analysis and argument is concerned with an ethical evaluation of the underlying premises, presuppositions, implications and consequences of the views that I am examining. I shall treat institutional ideologies, such as the corporate mythology, as examples of what Wittgenstein called "language games," that is, a practice *cum* language with a "logic" of its own. The connections between language, logic and practice are captured by Wittgenstein's phrase a "way of life." As such, a language game provides certain kinds of reasons for conduct, under which may be included decision-making, planning, and policy-making as well as the structuring of attitudes. Practical reasons of this sort are important for ethics, because they determine our social relations and our social interactions, which, according to my philosophy, constitute the domain of morality. Roughly speaking, then, I shall approach a particular corporate ideology as a language game with special kinds of reasons for action that are based on the mythology that corporations are moral persons.

LEGAL CORPORATIONS FOR FORMAL ORGANIZATIONS

I should make it clear at the very beginning that this essay is not concerned with corporations in the purely legal sense but with corporations as a social institution; for a purely legal conception of corporations, and of related concepts such as the legal concept of corporate responsibility, does not give rise to any questions of special interest to a moral philosopher, apart from more general questions of the philosophy of law. As far as corporations in the legal sense are concerned, it is a commonplace among lawyers that a corporation is legal fiction; that is, corporations are simply legally created artificial persons that, for purely legal purposes, are invested with certain sorts of legal rights and obligations that are customarily connected with legal personality. It has been said of legal fictions of this sort that they are like scaffolding; they can be thrown away once the building has been erected.[5] The particular moral issues connected with corporations that concern us as moral philosophers cannot, however, be discarded as easily as scaffolding, for mythologies cannot be simply thrown away like legal fictions. With regard to slavery, for example, the mythology of a divinely decreed separation of the races is of a totally different order from a simple legal fiction.

When we approach corporations as a social institution, however, although there may be important legal similarities between little corporations consisting of a small group of individuals or of a single person (e.g. John Doe, MD, Inc.) and large multi-national corporations, from a larger moral point of view, the differences between these two kinds of corporations in function, structure and scale place them in entirely different sociological and moral categories. For purposes of this essay, then, I shall concentrate on the kind of corporations found in the Fortune 500 list, that is, large-scale corporations with large numbers of employees, large assets and large incomes, corporations that are almost always multi-national conglomerates.

There are two aspects of large-scale corporations that are important for ethics: first, in these corporations management is divorced from ownership (the stockholders) and second, they are bureaucracies, that is, formal organizations with complex structures involving centralized control and hierarchies of managers and workers, etc. I shall comment briefly on each of these items.

First, the divorce of management from ownership in the modern corporation has important ethical consequences for such things as moral responsibility. It means, for example, that we can no longer use the traditional ethical notion of ownership-responsibility to deal with issues of moral responsibility in corporate contexts. Formerly, ownership-responsibility made some sense because employers were at one and the same time owners and managers and could therefore personally be held morally and legally responsible for the operations of their companies and for the impact of their operations on others: employees, clients and the general public. The separation of ownership and management in the modern corporation has radically changed the moral as well as the legal relationships between all these parties. It clearly no longer makes sense to hold that the owners (i.e. the stockholders) have the ultimate responsibility for the conduct of "their" corporation, since personally they have no control over the corporation's operations or policies, except purely nominally. In reality, stockholders are simply investors, lenders of capital, rather than entrepreneurs. For this reason, when corporate management speaks, as it does in stock reports, of its responsibility to the stockholders, it is simply talking rubbish — ethically speaking — at least, in any meaningful sense of "responsibility"; for responsibility implies control, that is, the power of influence outcomes, which is something that the stockholders do not have.

An even more important aspect of corporations of the Fortune 500 type as far as ethics is concerned is their enormous scale. The effect of the scale of these organizations and their activities, is to submerge the individual in the impersonal vastness of their operations, projects and plans. Even managers appear to lose their identity as individuals when they function as decision-makers in a corporate organization. Impersonality and anonymity are the hallmark of relationships and interactions within the modern corporation.

The most significant features of modern corporations morally come from their being formal organizations, that is, bureaucracies. Consequently, the chief moral problems and ethical issues that relate to corporations are more akin to those that relate to public organizations such as the Post Office, the IRS or the FBI, than they are to those arising in small personally owned companies like Dr. Doe, Inc. or like Adam Smith's pin factory, which has only ten workers. What is ethically significant as far as a large corporation is concerned is organizational complexity rather than ownership. For, in fact and from a moral point of view, as far as function, structure and social organization is concerned, a private airline corporation is hardly different from a publicly owned airline and the moral problems relating to one are comparable to those relating to the other.

The essential irrelevance, from a moral point of view, of the ownership of corporations, i.e. whether they be private or public, is even more obvious when we turn to their function in society; for major corporations in a society like ours play a public role as well as the ostensible private goal of making money. Indeed, the goal of making money may not be decisive at all, for, although they are geared to profit-making, many of our large corporations are in fact on the rocks financially and depend on government subsidies to continue in operation. A large corporation may go bankrupt but society will not let it go out of business, as it might a small company. The reason for this is obvious, for large corporations are enormous establishments providing essential public services, they employ large numbers of people, and, in general, they control large sectors of the economy. The important thing from an ethical point of view is that corporations, as large formal organizations, are centers of power and dominate our whole social life. At best large corporations serve society, but at worst they exploit society for their own private purposes with the result that individuals connected with them as employees, clients and consumers, may be reduced to the status of captives and victims. In sum, the pressing ethical questions relating to large corporations concern their use and abuse of power in relation to the public good. These questions, in turn, lead to questions of how to control this power and turn it to good rather than questionable purposes. Indeed, as far as the fate of the individual in modern corporate society is concerned, if John Stuart Mill were alive today, he would most likely be as critical of the tyranny of organizations (e.g. giant corporations) as he was, in his day, of the tyranny of the majority.

The most urgent issue to be addressed in the ethics of corporations is, as I have said, the issue of power and the control of power.[6] Corporations in our society pose a special problem in that regard. For, although they are like governments in that they wield enormous power and their actions and decisions have far-reaching consequences, they are unlike government as far as control over their power is concerned — both in theory and in practice; for government is, or is supposed to be representative and answerable to the public. In contrast to government, corporations might, to borrow Popper's term, be said to be *closed societies*, which means that they are immune from public accountability. A *de facto*, if not a *de jure*, existence as a "closed society" is a characteristic trait of formal organizations in general, including governmental bureaucracies.

But, in contradistinction to democratic political theory, the notion of corporations as "closed societies" is built into the theory of corporations, or at least into the "ideology." Thus, the mythological personification of corporations provides a ready-made rationale for their being closed societies, which, in different words, amounts to the claim that corporations are or ought to be "morally autonomous." As far as this claim is concerned, I shall argue later that autonomy is a vice rather than a virtue in formal organizations; organizational autonomy is not something to be encouraged and protected as it is in individuals, rather it is something that should be viewed with uneasiness, if not apprehension.[7] Secrecy about public affairs, whether it be in government or in corporations, is a threat to the public good. But that is a long story that cannot be explored further in this essay.

CORPORATIONS AND THE COMMON GOOD

It is commonly taken for granted that formal organizations in general, and corporations in particular, tend to be socially useful and beneficial. As soon as we discard our rosy glasses, however, we can see that formal organizations, whether they be private corporations or governmental bureaucracies, in fact frequently fail to serve the common good and sometimes even subvert it. Furthermore, Weber to the contrary notwithstanding, formal organizations have not always been the paradigm of rationality. In this century, as we all know, many of society's formal organizations, private and public, have gone berserk — they have led the people into wars, depressions, dislocations, and are even now pushing us towards the ultimate disaster of a nuclear holocaust. Far from being rational in the ordinary sense, it is in the nature of large-scale formal organizations to steam ahead blindly in pursuit of pre-established goals without any regard to the consequences of their actions for the public interest, namely, the health, welfare and safety of society.[8]

We need not enter here into economic questions such as the question which system provides the most efficient kind of social organization for the production and distribution of goods and services, e.g. whether socialism or capitalism is the most efficient economic system. The problems that I am concerned with in this essay are moral problems of a more general nature and problems that are created by formal organizations of all types, in the USSR as well as in progressive countries like ours; to put it succinctly, they are the sort of problems that are connected with the moral category of the public responsibility of individuals.

For simplicity's sake, it is convenient to divide the moral problems connected with corporations into macro-ethical problems, that is, large-scale moral problems relating to society in general, and micro-ethical problems, that is, problems concerning relationships between individuals and between individuals and corporations. On the macro-ethical level, in addition to issues about power and accountability that have already been mentioned, there are problems relating to waste, inefficiency, negligence, and lack of regard for safety and for the environment. These are problems that people usually have in mind when they use the term "corporate responsibility."

On the micro-level, there is a congeries of moral problems concerning the relationships between individuals, inside and outside the corporation, and concerning what individuals ought or ought not to do to others in their capacity as managers, as employees, or as clients. Since the corporate environment is, in many ways, different from other social environments, the kinds of moral problems connected with corporations will inevitably be somewhat different from moral problems arising in other contexts.

The point that I wish to stress in listing these various problems is the multiplicity and variety of moral problems relating to corporations that need to be investigated by philosophers. The rest of this essay will be concerned, however, with what might be called *meta-ethical problems* about the ethical concepts and categories that ought to be used in dealing with these moral problems. What models should we use in our ethical analysis of corporations?

AN ALLEGED ANALOGY BETWEEN CORPORATIONS AND INDIVIDUALS

One approach to problems concerning morality and corporations that seems to me to be utterly mistaken attempts to assimilate corporate morality to the morality of individual persons. Thus, Goodpaster contends that Plato's analogy between the state and the individual can be "inverted" and individual morality can be "projected" onto the corporation.[9] Those who follow this route generally seem to take for granted some such position as Nozick's that: "Since we may have only weak confidence in our intuitions and judgments about the whole structure of society, we may attempt to aid our judgments by focusing on microsituations that we do have a firm grasp of."[10] There is, in my opinion, a remarkable want of argument for either of the two propositions asserted here, *vis.*, that we have confident intuitions about morality in microsituations and that there is a moral isomorphism between individuals and organizations.[11] In view of the *prima facie* implausibility of the hypothesized isomorphism, surely the burden of proof rests on its advocates to furnish a few arguments to defend it.

I shall not repeat all the arguments that I have given elsewhere against the assimilation of the morality of corporations and of formal organizations in general to the morality of persons. My argument in a nutshell is that moral notions cannot be applied directly to formal organizations because the logical framework of organizational decision-making automatically and necessarily excludes the kind of moral reasoning that we demand of and attribute to individuals when they engage in moral deliberation, moral discussions and moral decision-making. My conclusion is that "since formal organizations (e.g. corporations) cannot have moral obligations, they cannot have moral responsibilities in the sense of having obligations towards those affected by their actions because of the power they possess. Organizations have tremendous power, but no responsibilities."[12] I have tried to forestall misunderstanding of my position regarding ethics and corporations by reiterating that my contentions about moral responsibility relate only to organizations as alleged moral beings. As I have persistently argued, it does not follow from the denial of moral personhood to corporations that morality has nothing to do with corporations and, in particular, that individuals within them, e.g., managers and workers, or individuals that have dealings with them, e.g., clients, inspectors and public officials, have to forget about morality altogether when they relate to corporations.[13]

I shall now examine in more detail some views about the moral status of corporations that are opposed to mine and the arguments that might be and have been presented for them. The views in question generally take the form that corporations have moral obligations, moral rights, and moral responsibilities in *exactly the same sense* as individuals have them. Furthermore, these corporate obligations, rights, and responsibilities are distinct from, over and above, or in addition to those of particular individuals within the corporations or connected with them in one way or other. That is, corporate obligations, rights and responsibilities are not "reducible" to obligations, rights and responsibilities of individuals. I shall call this general position "corporativism."

As I have already pointed out, it is impossible to find any clear-cut and cogent arguments for corporativism. Therefore it will be necessary for me to try to reconstruct them. I shall begin with a general, vague, and intuitive argument that appears rather frequently in one form or another. I shall call it *the moral import argument*. It runs somewhat as follows: corporations play a morally important role in society and bring about many things that have moral import, either positive or negative. Furthermore, we often apply moral predicates to corporations, calling them "good" or "bad", "fair" or "unfair," "responsible" or "irresponsible," etc. However, the argument continues, the actions of a corporation cannot strictly speaking be identified with or reduced to the actions of particular individuals, e.g. particular managers, and so cannot be imputed to particular individuals. Therefore, if morality is to be applied to corporations at all, it must be applied to them in the same way as it is applied to individuals. Basically, then, it is assumed in this argument that we are forced to choose between two positions: either corporations are beyond the pole of morality altogether or else they must be brought under the scope of morality by according them the moral status of persons.[14] Before I can answer the "moral import argument," it first needs to be "tightened up." The next few sections of the essay will be devoted to this task.

CORPORATIVISM

Corporativism may take one of two forms, either that corporations are real full-fledged moral persons or that morality applied to them *as if* they were persons, that is, they are persons by analogy. The first version of corporativism will be called *corporativism in the strong sense*. The second version, which holds that, although corporations are not strictly moral persons, some moral concepts may be predicated of them by analogy with natural moral persons, will be called *corporativism in the weak sense*. It is hardly necessary to add that both positions are inconsistent with my own.

Corporativism in the strong sense is stated most clearly and unequivocally by Peter French. He writes:

> In short, corporations can be full-fledged moral persons and have whatever privileges, rights and duties are, in the normal course of affairs, accorded moral persons.[15]

Weaker forms of corporativism deny the moral persons view, but retain some of its paraphernalia, such as the application of personal moral categories to corporations. Thus, although Donaldson explicitly rejects what he calls the "Moral Person View" of corporations, in his subsequent discussions of morality and corporations, he attributes moral obligations and responsibilities to corporations *as if* they were persons.[16] In other words, he seems inclined to personify corporations, albeit with qualifications. His view is therefore what I call corporativism in the weak sense.[17]

THREE ARGUMENTS FOR CORPORATIVISM

Instead of the rather vague argument that I have called the moral import argument, it is possible to identify three more specific kinds of argument for corporativism (and against my position). Each of these arguments contains a partial truth but also, I shall argue, makes an incorrect inference from that partial truth. The three arguments are based on three separate premises: (1) that corporations are and must be held morally responsible for untoward outcomes, (2) that corporations are moral actors, and (3) that corporations as collectivities cannot be reduced to aggregates of individuals. I shall call them, respectively: (1) The fixation of responsibility argument, (2) The corporate actor argument, and (3) The irreducibility argument. Taken together, the three premises purport to show, in one way or another, that corporations possess a special kind of identity and unity that makes it possible, if not necessary, to apply moral predicates to them directly.

I shall now examine in turn each of these three arguments for corporativism as I have reconstructed them.

THE FIXATION OF RESPONSIBILITY ARGUMENT

This argument focuses on the fixing of responsibility or blame on a person. It rests on the basic premise that in order to attribute responsibility and blame, it is necessary to be able to fix it on a person. It runs as follows:

(a) C is to be "blamed," i.e. held responsible, for an untoward event E if C was the cause of E.[18] When corporation C is the cause of an untoward event E, then blame must be 'pinned on' the corporation as contrasted with particular individuals within it, because no one particular individual can be blamed for what the corporation did, that is, no particular individual was its cause.

Substituting our term "responsibility" for French's term "blameworthiness' and using corporations as examples of what he calls "conglomerate collectivities," the conclusion in French's words is:

> . . . when we say that a conglomerate collectivity (e.g. a corporation) is blameworthy we are saying that other courses of collectivity action were within the province of the collectivity and that had the collectivity acted in those ways the untoward event would not likely have occurred and that no exculpatory excuse is supportable as regards the collectivity.[19]

Underlying arguments of this sort is the questionable premise that responsibility does not (or cannot) exist unless it can be fixed, that is, "pinned" on someone or something *to the exclusion of someone else or something else.*

Now "responsibility" is a weasel word and means many different things.[20] In one common meaning of "responsibility," however, untoward events can happen where it is impossible determinately and exclusively to pinpoint the responsibility on one identifiable person or set of persons, in the kinds of situations we are considering this is due to the fact that social causation is complex, multi-dimensional and overdetermined. (Who can say which person or set of persons was responsible for Viet Nam? How can we 'pin' the blame for this untoward event or set of events?) In any case, the notion of causation that is invoked in attributions of responsibility is complicated and subtle; it is not a simple uni-linear affair. For these and other reasons, large scale social responsibility is shared rather than divided, and is not uniquely determinable.

I have argued elsewhere that the concept of fixing responsibility is primarily a legal or a legalistic concept rather that a moral concept *per se.*[21] To fix responsibility (or blame) is to fix "liability," for purposes of determining who is to pay, who is to be reprimanded or who is to be punished. In the liability sense, if responsibility cannot be fixed (pinned), then the concept has no use. On the other hand, legal liability is often tied to causal responsibility, although it need not be; in vicarious liability someone other than the causal agent is held responsible, often because he has more money! For this reason, if we need to determine who is to pay for an untoward event, e.g. an automobile accident, then it makes sense to fix the liability on a corporation, e.g. GM, or even to "blame" GM for an accident. I submit, however, that it is fallacious to argue from legal concepts, so if we reject the identification of the moral concept of responsibility with the legal concept of responsibility, then the argument in question loses its cogency. After all, our concern in this essay is the moral status of corporations not their legal status.

THE MORAL ACTOR ARGUMENT

The second argument is based on the contention that corporations are moral agents and therefore persons, or at least that they have some characteristic features of persons.[22] I find the term "agent" to be misleading and a source of confusion, because the word has several standard meanings that need to be kept separate; for example, "agent" may mean causal agent, as applied, e.g. to acids, or it may mean a legal agent, e.g. a representative or deputy. I shall therefore use the term *actor* instead. By "actor" I intend an individual who performs or is capable of performing acts in the full-blown sense of voluntary, intentional and deliberate acts as performed by adult human beings.[23] As I reconstruct the argument under discussion here, its proponents allege that corporations are actors in this sense. The argument is set forth most strongly and clearly by French in his article "The Corporation as a Moral Person."[24]

The argument for the proposition that corporations are moral actors (= agents) is that they do such things as make decisions, transfer property, make contracts, make plans, deliberate, and have the kinds of things that are presupposed by activities like deliberation, namely, purposes, goals and interests.[25] Furthermore, the argument goes, when a corporation performs any of the acts just mentioned the acts are distinguishable and, in some sense, separable from the acts of the individuals who are its agents, e.g. managers and directors. In other words, the acts of corporations (their interests, etc.) cannot be reduced without remainder to the acts of individuals, e.g. managers.

It would be absurd, of course, to deny this kind of irreducibility, i.e. an irreducibility of meaning. For there is clearly a sense in which to say that XCo. did A means something different from saying that Mr. Smith, CEO of XCo., did A, although existentially the acts are identical, e.g. concluding a contract. Not only are the specific act-descriptions different, but the rationale for them are also entirely different. The "logic of corporate decision-making" is different from the "logic" of an individual person's decision to act on behalf of the corporation. Their motivation might be quite different. In his capacity of manager, Mr. Smith is not acting for himself, as it were, but for XCo. and the act is ascribed to the XCo. rather than to Mr. Smith.[26]

The question at issue in cases like this is whether two different act-descriptions imply that there are two different acts and two different actors. Or, as seems more likely, there are simply two different act-descriptions of one and the same act imputable to one and the same actor (= Mr. Smith). Moreover, it is necessary to ask whether responsibility attaches to acts by virtue of a particular act-description alone without regard to other act-descriptions; for example, if X is the signing of a contract by XCo., then is someone different responsible for it from Mr. Smith, who was the one who affixed his signature to it?[27] Finally, we must ask whether an act-description that is transferable, i.e. that can be performed under the same act-description by different actors at different times, implies that there is only one actor, represented, say, by a number of agents. Behind these questions are deeper questions relating to what happens when one person acts for or on behalf of another, as his representative or agent. But here we must add that the person represented *does not exist* as a person at all, in the literal sense. The problem will become clearer as we proceed.

DRAMATIS PERSONAE

Two analogies come to mind as ways of explaining the difference between XCo.'s and Mr. Smith's act, i.e. differences between what they are doing, why they are doing it, and who is the person who is actor, while also recognizing the ontological (or existential) identity of the corporate act and the manager's act. The first analogy is with a stage-production, say, of *Hamlet*. When John Gielgud says "To be or not to be" we ascribe the words to Hamlet, not to Mr. Gielgud, although it is actually Mr. Gielgud who utters them. The words and actions of Hamlet fit into a pattern, make sense in terms of his beliefs, values and aspirations. We have to understand them in that light. To explain them by reference to the personal idiosyncrasies of Mr. Gielgud means to miss the point of the play. By the same token, to explain XCo.'s actions by reference to Mr. Smith's personal idiosyncrasies is to miss the point, once again.

Now suppose, however, that during the play Mr. Gielgud were to stab the man playing Polonius and actually to wound him mortally: who is to blame? who is responsible? Hamlet or Mr. Gielgud? Since Hamlet does not in reality exist, he cannot be held responsible. Would not the same hold true of Mr. Smith? Sure enough, XCo.'s acts are XCo.'s acts, but they are also Mr. Smith's acts, just as the wielding of the sword is Hamlet's act and also Mr. Gielgud's act. But what is true in and for the play, is not true in and for real life. For in real life the man is killed by Mr. Gielgud or the contract is signed by Mr. Smith. XCo.'s acts may be compared to what transpires in the play; it has a certain logic and can be understood without reference to real persons. But existentially it has no separate existence. Insofar as responsibility and morality in general concern the real world, it is a category mistake to apply them to the play world of the corporation.

There are, of course, certain disanalogies between XCo. and Hamlet, but it is not clear that they are relevant. First, the script of the part to be played by Hamlet is ready-made, as it were, and Mr. Gielgud is obliged to follow the text. In contrast, the managers of XCo., such as Mr. Smith, write the text as they go along; they make it up. Second, *Hamlet* as we know it is fiction: we are supposed to suspend belief while it is being played. We all know that it is false that Hamlet exists. What the corporation, XCo., does is not fictitious in this sense. The corporate acts take place in this world, not on the stage. Unlike *Hamlet*, reality is somehow attributed to XCo.'s acts and in that sense they must be taken seriously.

CORPORATIONS AND THE GREEK GODS

These points suggest a second analogy, namely, the analogy between corporations and mythological beings. Suppose that we are ancient Greeks and we attribute acts to the gods, such as the Trojan War. Let us assume that the Greeks really believed that the gods did the things attributed to them. These beliefs influence their conduct, even to the extent of sacrificing their lives for the gods. We ourselves know that the Greek gods do not in fact exist, but those who believed in the mythology thought that they existed and that their acts were part of the real world.

It is interesting to note that the mythology to which I refer played an important role in Greek politics; for the oracles, particularly the one at Delphi, were constantly consulted by the political and military leaders of the City-States before they undertook any important projects. Apollo spoke through the priestesses to those who wanted direction. The priestesses were the intermediaries and through their power as representatives of the god, they were able to manipulate people for what may be considered to be political ends. One author goes so far as to attribute the survival of the multiplicity of city-states to the way in which the oracles acted to preserve the unity of Greek society.[28]

There are striking resemblances between the belief that corporations are real persons and the Greek mythology that took Apollo to be a real person. (Both are immortals!) Managers may be compared to the priestesses, who manipulated society for their own interests or for what they superstitiously took to be the god's interest (= what the managers take to be the corporation's interest).

Mythologies, ancient and modern, can be benign, so we should not dismiss them simply because they are literally false. Their falsity may not be as relevant to ethics as their use and their social consequences. By the same token, we should be wary of myths that are not only false but also mischievous, i.e. do more evil than they do good. Like the Greek mythology of the oracles, the mythology of corporations can be used and often is used to manipulate the public and to advance the interests of a particular class. Furthermore, just as the Greek mythology relieved individuals of responsibility for their actions and projected it onto the gods, so also the corporate mythology enables individuals to abdicate their responsibility for collective action and to "project" responsibility, instead, onto the corporation.

THE IRREDUCIBILITY ARGUMENT

We now turn to the third and most instructive argument for corporativism, the argument that rests on the contention that corporations are the sort of collective entities that are irreducible to the individuals who happen for a time to compose them. Thus, French argues that corporations are "conglomerate collectivities" as distinguished from "aggregate collectivities" where "a change in A's membership always entails a change in the identity of A." Unlike an aggregate, a corporation preserves its identity as the identity of its managers, employees and clients changes through time. French calls it a "conglomerate collectivity," one whose "identity does not entirely consist in (is not exhausted by) the identities of its membership."[29] Inasmuch as a corporation has an "independent identity and continuity," not reducible to that of the individuals composing it, moral judgments regarding corporations are not reducible to moral judgments regarding individuals, Q.E.D.

The key issue here is the independent identity and continuity of a group of individuals. For convenience, I shall call such groups *associations*. Corporations are often compared in regard to their continuing identity to nations, universities, churches and clubs, that is, associations that remain the same even when there is a complete turnover of membership. A nation or a club that lasts for centuries is not a different nation or club simply because one generation of members has died and another generation has come into being. There is a kind of identity possessed by associations that, as it were, transcends their membership.

The argument just outlined is fallacious, however, because it is based on the assumption of an exhaustive dichotomy between kinds of associations. There is a much greater variety of associations than is assumed in the argument; what is more important is that distinctions between various kinds of association carry with them crucially different ethical implications. From an ethical point of view, there are enormous differences between nations, clubs and corporations, to mention only a few kinds of associations. A brief survey will help to highlight some of the ethical issues we need to consider.

I shall begin by distinguishing between *abstract associations* and *concrete associations*. Abstract associations are associations that are set up to promote an end of some kind or other. Consequently, an abstract association is identified and defined by reference to its goal and structure, rather than by reference to the individuals within it or to their individual goals. Individuals in abstract associations are not ordinarily used to define the association or to determine its goals. The obvious example of an abstract association is a corporation or a formal organization such as a governmental bureaucracy; we do not identify or define either by reference to individuals, e.g. they do not "belong" to nameable individuals. Abstract associations are, in other words, structures that are set up for certain purposes, which may or may not be the same as the purposes of individuals in the association.

A concrete association, on the other hand, is a collection of individuals that is defined and identified by its membership rather than by its structure. It is the collection of all persons who are members, may have been or will be members of it. Membership, in turn, is generally defined by reference to characteristics that belong to individuals as such, such as a particular historical characteristic or set of characteristics: being from the same locality, the same family, the same school, the same race or religion. Thus, the American nation is the collection of all Americans, present, past and future. The Adams family is the collection of all individuals descended, say, from John Adams or related to them affinally. The church is the body of persons who have been baptized into it.[30]

Now, membership in a concrete association carries with it certain obligations, rights and responsibilities. As I have argued elsewhere members of a concrete association have collective and individual responsibility for the other members of the association. Members of a family, of a community, or of a nation have responsibility for each other. That is the essence of the virtue of loyalty. Families, communities, universities, churches, and nations properly and appropriately are founded on loyalty and may properly and appropriately demand loyalty from their members.[31]

It is important to bear in mind that concrete associations, as such, do not have goals. The individuals in them may have goals and they may share goals, but there are no goals of the association as distinct from those of individuals in it. Families and nations, i.e. communities in the broad sense, achieve their unity through common group membership and the sharing of values and responsibilities, perhaps even a common history rather than dedication to a pre-determined goal.[32]

There is, however, a third kind of association that needs to be mentioned, namely, *cooperative associations*. They are abstract in one sense and are structured by goals, but the goals of these associations are shared by their individual members, because they serve them. Examples would be labor unions, social clubs and football teams. In them, the members come together and work together for a goal or end that they all have in common: they all want the same kind of thing and so create an organization to get what they want. Such cooperative associations are, nevertheless abstract: they are set up for a specific purpose, goal or end, and are identified and defined by them.

If we reflect on the differences between these three kinds of associations, we can see that the moral implications of belonging to one or other of them are quite different. This can be seen if we reflect for a moment on what "glues" people together in each kind of association. In a formal organization or a corporation the glue is provided by contracts and by self-interest. An employee works hard for the company because that is his job, that is what he is paid for, and so on. The goals of the company, i.e. the corporation, are separate and distinct from the goals of its individual constituents — managers, employees, and customers.[33] In a cooperative association, on the other hand, the glue is a common interest, a sharing of goals: for a football team it is winning. A cooperative association holds its members together because it provides the facilities for achieving the goals of its members. Finally, a concrete association like a nation or a family, which I call a *community*, provides a completely different kind of glue binding its members. It is not a common goal, but a common heritage or a common experience that binds the members of a community together. They "belong to each other." The alumni of a university are a community, that is, are bound together, by the fact that they are graduates of the same university. Family members are bound together by the fact that they have common ancestors, common histories, and common experiences; it does not have to be the case that they have common goals. In fact, the members of a community may have quite divergent goals. Indeed, perhaps they *should* have different goals![34]

Now, what has all this to do with the morality of corporations. Simply this: we make an egregious mistake, not only a category mistake but also a serious moral mistake, when we "project" the moral commitments required by and belonging to one type of association to other types. The truth is that corporations are not families, they are not nations, and, of course, they are not clubs. Consequently, the moral commitments required in the corporate context are quite different from those required in associations like families or clubs.

To be more specific, moral concepts like obligation, rights and responsibility apply to concrete associations, because, after all, their constituents, members, are the individuals belong to them, even though the membership may be constantly changing. Since abstract associations, as such, are not collections of individuals, but organizational structures, these moral concepts do *not* apply to them. People, individually or in groups, can have obligations, rights and responsibilities. But, as I have argued at some length, corporations are not people but *organizations* of people. To confuse them is to fall prey to a moral confusion that has serious moral consequences.[35]

I reached the same conclusion by a somewhat different route in my earlier essay on the subject. In the earlier essay, however, I emphasized the mistake as a category mistake. In this essay, I want to stress the absurd and morally disastrous consequences resulting from this confusion of categories. As a moralist, I hope that the lesson will not be lost!

Notes

1. The theory that I refer to was first set forth in "Morality and the Ideal of Rationality in Formal Organizations." MONIST, Vol. 54, No. 4 (October, 1970). Hereafter I shall refer to this article as *MIR*.

2. Talcott Parsons, *The Social System*. New York: Free Press, 1964, p. 39.

3. For an interesting discussion, see Margaret MacDonald, "The Language of Political Theory," in Antony Flew, ed. *Logic and Language*, first series. Oxford: Basil Blackwell, 1952. MacDonald calls them "pictures," "images," or "analogies." Political theories differ "in picturing political relationships with the help of two very different images." (p. 172).

4. See Ernst Cassirer, *The Myth of the State*. New Haven: Yale University Press, 1947. Cassirer stresses the connections between political mythology and violence, the prime example being the myths of Nazism. His attitude towards myths is ambiguous, but in the end he concludes

that the power of myth needs to be "tamed and subdued" and that "human culture . . . could not arise until the darkness of myth was fought and overcome." p. 375.

5. See Lon L. Fuller, *Legal Fictions*. Stanford: Stanford University Press, 1967, p. 70. The scaffolding idea is attributed to J. C. Gray.

6. There is a large literature on this important subject. One of the most valuable discussions, from the point of view advocated here, is Christopher D. Stone, *Where the Law Ends: the Social Control of Corporate Behavior*. New York: Harper Torchbooks, 1975.

7. See *MIR*.

8. For further discussion, see *MIR*.

9. Kenneth E. Goodpaster and John B. Matthews, Jr., "Can a Corporation have a Conscience?" *Harvard Business Review*, Vol. 60, No. 1 (February, 1982).

10. Robert Nozick, *Anarchy, State and Utopia*. New York: Basic Books, 1974, p. 204. Goodpaster quotes this passage in the article mentioned just cited.

11. For a critique of the analogy, see Renford Bambrough, "Plato's Political Analogies," reprinted in Gregory Vlastos, *Plato, A Collection of Essays*, II. Garden City, N.Y.: Doubleday, 1971. If we look at Bambrough's critique, we can see why the analogy does not hold whichever way it is used.

12. Ladd, *MIR*, p. 508.

13. I mention this because a common misperception of my position is that corporate officials "should not let their personal moral notions supersede the ends of the corporation." My view is exactly the opposite, namely, that the ends of the corporation should not supersede the individual's moral notions.

14. The argument from moral import might be extended by analogy to an argument to the effect that because nuclear armaments have moral import, we ought to be able to ascribe moral obligations, rights and responsibilities to nuclear bombs!

15. "The Corporation as a Moral Person," *American Philosophical Quarterly*, Vol. 16, No. 3 (July, 1979), p. 207.

16. See Thomas Donaldson, *Corporations and Morality*. Englewood Cliffs, N.J.: Prentice-Hall, 1982; see also, Goodpaster's review of Donaldson's *Corporations and Morality*, in *Business and Professional Ethics Journal*, Vol. 1., No. 3 (Spring, 1982), pp. 101–105.

17. See also, David T. Ozar, "The Moral Responsibility of Corporations," in Thomas Donaldson and Patricia H. Werhane, eds., *Ethical Issues in Business*. Englewood Cliffs, N.J.: Prentice-Hall, 1979, pp. 294–300.

18. The argument I present here is an adaptation from one found in Peter French, "Types of Collectivities and Blame," *The Personalist*, Vol. LVI (1975). French writes: "'X is to blame for y' pins something on X: X was the cause of the event y." and "Statements ascribing blame to a conglomerate collectivity are not reducible to a conjunction of statements ascribing blame to the collectivity's membership without remainder." (164). He uses corporations such as the Honeywell Corporation as examples of "conglomerate collectivities." They are irreducible because blame in these cases is indivisible.

19. *Op. cit.*, p. 166.

20. I have discussed responsibility in a number of writings. See, for example, "Philosophical Remarks on Professional Responsibility in Organizations." *Applied Philosophy*, Vol. I, No. 2 (Fall, 1982).

21. *Ibid.*

22. Donaldson, *op. cit.*, wants to make a distinction between moral persons and moral agents. My arguments are directed against both conceptions.

23. Whether or not babies, idiots and animals are actors in this sense is immaterial to the present inquiry.

24. For reference, see note 15.

25. French claims that for that reason corporations are "Davidsonian" agents. I do not completely understand his argument, for as I read Davidson on "Agency," agency depends in the final analysis on "primitive actions" which are bodily movements. (Donald Davidson, *Actions and Events*. Oxford: Claredon Press, 1980, p. 49.) Do corporations have bodies?

26. There are standard ways used by philosophers to capture the distinction that is involved here. Essentially, it relates to Frege's distinction between sense (meaning) and reference (identity).

27. I have discussed the question of how to identify acts for moral purposes in "Positive and Negative Euthanasia," in J. Ladd, ed., *Ethical Issues Relating to Life and Death*. New York: Oxford University Press, 1979, pp. 175–180.

28. See Mario Attilio Levi, *Political Power in the Ancient World*. London: Weidenfeld and Nicolson, 1965, especially Chapter 2. Also Martin P. Nilsson, *Cults, Myths, Oracles, and Politics in Ancient Greece*. Lund: Gleerup, 1951.

29. *Ibid.*

30. The distinction between abstract and concrete association resembles in important respects Tönnies's distinction between *Gesellshschaft* and *Gemeinschaft*. See Ferdinance Tönnies, *Community and Society*. Tr. Charles P. Loomis. New York: Harper and Row, 1957.

31. See my article on "Loyalty," in *The Encyclopedia of Philosophy*, ed. Paul Edwards. New York: Macmillan, 1967, Vol. 5, pp. 97–98.

32. So-called "community studies" in sociology also start from the premise that they are defined territorially and in terms of multiplicity of social interactions, rather than in terms of goals. "A community is that collectivity the members of which share a common territorial area as their base of operations for daily activities." Talcott Parsons, *The Social System*. New York: Free Press, 1951, p. 91.

33. It should be borne in mind that we are talking here about theory, not actual practice; for in actual practice, managers often manipulate corporations for their own self-interest without regard to what is in the interest of the corporation. For examples, see Paul Solman and Thomas Friedman, *Life and Death of the Corporate Battlefield*. New York: Simon and Schuster, 1982.

34. I am prepared to argue that diversity of goals and interests is at least a *desideratum*, if not a necessary condition of a flourishing community, such as a village, a university or a family.

35. A detailed discussion of some of these objectionable consequences would be the first order of business in another essay on the ethics of corporations. An example is the extension to corporations of concepts like privacy and autonomy, which are valid and necessary when applied to individuals but exactly the opposite when applied to corporations.

Christopher Meyers

THE CORPORATION, ITS MEMBERS, AND MORAL ACCOUNTABILITY

Should corporations, as corporations, be held morally accountable for their actions? Or, more fundamentally, are corporations the kinds of entities to which responsibility ascriptions can appropriately be assigned? Moral tradition has long argued that only *moral agents*, entities with particular metaphysical qualities, can legitimately be held accountable for their actions. Do corporations have the requisite qualities of moral agency? Or are they mere legal fictions, artificially created to provide legal protection for the persons who make them up?

Take, for example, the Hooker Chemical Company; is it the kind of entity that can legitimately be held responsible for its poisoning of the Love Canal area in New York? There is much to suggest that it is: It has a corporate personality;

it made decisions; these decisions led to harmful actions; and it made additional decisions and took further actions in response to those harms. On this account, the Hooker Chemical Company is indeed a unique, individual agent, one who can and should be held accountable for its actions.

But then if the company is itself an agent, what of the persons who make it up? If we hold the corporation, as a whole, accountable, this would seem to preclude blaming any of the individual decision-makers. Thus the manager or division chief who made the actual decision not to properly dispose of the Love Canal chemicals would not be held accountable. An either/or dilemma seems to emerge: Either we hold the company responsible for immoral behavior and exempt its members from accountability, or we condemn the individual members and conceive of the corporation as nothing more than a legal fiction.

I argue in this paper that this is in fact a false dilemma, that it is possible to view the corporation as a moral agent responsible for its actions while at the same time holding individual decision-makers personally accountable for their decisions and actions. To make this case, I will first briefly establish what sorts of characteristics an entity must have for responsibility ascriptions to be legitimately applied, that is, what one must have or do to be a moral agent. I will then show why certain types of corporations[1] qualify as moral agents and how, despite this metaphysical/moral status, it is nonetheless possible also to hold individuals within those corporations personally accountable.

MORAL AGENCY

Let me start with a basic definition of moral agency: A moral agent is any entity who possesses the minimal conditions necessary to judge it as a holder of rights and obligations and to which responsibility ascriptions are appropriate. To acknowledge an entity as a moral agent is to acknowledge it as having a substantial status in the moral community. It is to recognize that the entity has a legitimate claim on others to respect it as a moral entity; i.e., it is to recognize that the agent may hold others as duty-bound in their relations toward it and it is to hold the agent as having certain duties toward others.

While a moral agent must be one capable of engaging in moral relations with others, it is not necessary that the agent be regarded, in Kantian fashion, as an end-in-itself. While the latter condition may be a requirement for being a moral *person*,[2] it is not necessary for being a moral *agent*, a distinction that is fundamental to my argument. Unlike others writing in this area,[3] I do not wish to claim that corporations have the same status as persons; for example, corporations do not have a right to life, as any number of corporations discovered during the takeover-frenzied days of the 1980s.

Recent work in animal rights theory has shown, however, that being a member of the moral community is not an all-or-nothing proposition; rather, it falls upon a continuum, as determined by the entity's inherent capabilities. Thus, since many animals are capable of experiencing pleasures and pains, a strong case can be made that they have a right not to be tortured, even if these same animals do not have a right to life.[4] And, as I will argue, since many corporations are capable of engaging in intentional and reflective behavior, they too are holders of certain rights and obligations and can be legitimately held accountable for their actions.

Indeed, it is this latter condition, of accountability, that places corporations high upon the moral status continuum. For this condition requires not only that the entity is deserving of certain basic protections, but that because of its decision-making capabilities, others appropriately hold it responsible for its decisions and actions. In French's terms, for an entity to be justly held accountable, it must be capable of being "an administrator of rights. To administer a right one must be an agent; i.e., able to act in certain ways" (French, 1979, p. 210). The heart of this point, I take it, is that while any number of entities are afforded *legal* rights and protections,[5] in order for an entity to be transculturally recognized as a moral agent accountable for its actions, it must have a particular metaphysical status, that of *intentional agency*.

Four Conditions

The concept of agency clearly depends upon the entity being capable of causing events to occur. But causality alone is insufficient, for otherwise we would hold rocks that cause destructive landslides and tornadoes that cause devastation to life and property morally accountable. Thus causality is a necessary but not a sufficient condition of agency.[6]

In addition to being able to attribute the cause of a decision or event to an agent, responsibility ascriptions require a complex level of intentionality. French struggles with this problem, concluding that responsibility ascriptions are legitimately assigned to "Davidsonian agents" (French, 1979, p. 211), i.e., those for whom a true description of an event is that they "did it intentionally" (Davidson, 1971, p. 7). Davidson's task here is to correlate specific actions to specific sources so that we may determine whether person P brought about event X, in particular in cases of mistaken identity.

This represents an important first step toward capturing the type of intentionality necessary for accountability in that it provides a means for determining which events may be appropriately attributed to which causes. But it seems accountability demands a fuller analysis of intentionality since on this account the rock to which the cause of the landslide may be truthfully attributed would be deemed the intentional and thus accountable agent.

What is missing from Davidson's and French's accounts, I think, is a description of the intentional agent's subjective state. Dennett's discussion of *second-order* intentions, of "reciprocity," fills the gap here. According to Dennett, an entity to which responsibility ascriptions are appropriate is "one to which we ascribe not only simple beliefs, desires and other Intentions, but beliefs, desires and other Intentions *about* beliefs, desires and other Intentions" (Dennett, 1976, pp. 178, 181, his emphasis). Responsibility ascriptions are thus appropriately assigned if an entity has intentions, beliefs or desires about some other entity's intentions, beliefs or desires, or, in the case of self-reflection, about its own intentions, beliefs or desires.

There are two reasons why this type of reflective intentionality is fundamental to responsibility ascriptions. First, in order to hold an agent accountable, we must be able truthfully to say that it is capable of taking other moral beings' concerns into account. It is precisely when such concerns are either not considered and should have been, or when such concerns are considered with malevolence, that we declare the agent morally culpable. If an entity is incapable of considering others' concerns, if it does not possess second-order intentionality, it makes no sense to nonetheless hold it accountable for how its actions affect those concerns. In the language of classical moral theory, "Ought implies can"; i.e., to say an entity ought to be concerned with others implies that it is capable of doing so. Without this condition, we would end up holding entities accountable to do things they cannot do.

The second reason why second-order intentionality is fundamental to responsibility ascriptions is that it is the means by which agents *identify* with decisions and actions. That is, after considering how an action would affect others, the morally accountable agent must also be able to reflect back on the choice and contemplate whether to proceed. And it is through this process that the agent is able to determine whether the choice is one she or he truly wants; through this process the choice becomes his or her *own*.

Thus two of the necessary conditions for a high level of moral agency are first, that the entity plays a causal role in the event and, second, that it does so while being capable of engaging in second-order intentionality.[7] A third necessary condition is that the entity must exist in a moral relationship with others. As French notes, a moral agent is in a moral relationship with another, and is thus accountable to him, her, or it, when the first agent's actions would affect another in a way that an accurate description of the event would include "moral notions" (French, 1979, p. 211). These relationships need not, though they may, arise out of contractual or other formal arrangements. Instead, they may arise simply because the parties exist in the moral community in a way such that when one agent acts, others are morally affected.

These three conditions combine to produce the final — that the agent must be an individual, a single entity to whom moral ascriptions can be assigned. This final condition allows the possibility of assigning praise or condemnation. There must be some*one* or some*thing* to admire or to blame. The question now, then, is whether corporations qualify as these types of moral agents. Do they meet all the necessary (and, when combined, sufficient) conditions?

CORPORATIONS AS MORAL AGENTS

There certainly is a popular sentiment that corporations are moral agents, that they should be blamed or praised for their behavior. Recall, for example, public reaction to the Exxon Valdez's massive Alaskan oil spill. Although the tanker's captain was eventually convicted of negligence, most of the public's wrath was directed at *Exxon*, as a distinct, blameworthy entity.

But upon what are these types of sentiments based? Part of it may be a yearning to affix blame when problems arise; part of it may be an unjustified anthropomorphism; part of it may be a simple rationalization to justify social benefit positions like the so-called "deep-pockets" argument.[8] Much of the sentiment, however, seems based upon a recognition that we do, in many ways, respect corporations as moral agents. That is, going back to my definition of moral agency, we respect our moral obligations toward corporations. When we enter into a contract with a corporation, either an employment contract or a business contract, we hold ourselves as being morally obliged to respect the contract and thereby to respect the corporation *qua* partner to the contract. Further, we recognize the corporation as having certain rights; e.g., the right to property ownership, the right to due process under the law, the right to freedom of expression, etc. And, if my criteria for moral agency are valid, this respect for the corporation's status in the moral community should be accompanied by a reciprocal respect; i.e., the corporation should in turn respect the rights of other moral agents or be held accountable for not doing so.

The previous argument, however, is purely a descriptive one. That is, our society does at least partially respect a corporation's status in the moral community and so we expect the respect to be returned. But *should* we respect the corporation as a moral agent? Does it, the corporation itself, satisfy the criteria of moral agency; i.e., does it cause events, does it exist as an individual, does it exist in a moral relationship with other moral agents, and is it capable of second-order intentionality? Or is the corporation simply an aggregate of the persons who make it up, persons to whom any appropriate responsibility ascriptions should be made?

Causality and Individuality

The easiest of the conditions to satisfy is that of causality. It should be obvious that corporate actions produce a wide range of effects, both positive and negative.

It is not so obvious that corporations can be unique and distinct individuals. French and John Ladd convincingly argue, however, that because of their structure, at least some corporations satisfy the individuality criterion. This structure creates a "formal organization," one that exists on its own, separate from the specific individuals working within it. Ladd:

> The general characteristics of all these organizations are that they are "planned units, deliberately structured for the purpose of attaining specific goals," and such that each formal organization is a "continuous organization of official functions bound by rules." One of the distinctive features of formal organizations of the type we are interested in is that they are ordinarily hierarchical in structure; they not only have a "horizontal" division of labor but a "vertical" one as well—a "pyramid of authority." [Further,] individual office-holders are in principle replaceable by other individuals without affecting the continuity or identity of the organization. In this sense, it has sometimes been said that an organization is "immortal" (Ladd, 1970, pp. 488–489).

French further develops Ladd's analysis to show that this metaphysical status exists prior to any legal process of incorporation, a process the law "recognizes . . . for its own [socially benefitting] purposes" (French, 1976, p. 209). Part of this purpose has historically been directed toward assigning accountability to these formal organizations, as revealed in early skirmishes involving the East India Company in 1612,[9] the 1938 Act of Congress which subjected corporations to legal guilt, liability, and punishment, and a 1978 Supreme Court ruling granting corporations rights of free speech.[10]

Moral Relationships

It is also clear that corporations exist in moral relationships with other agents. They frequently engage in activities which have profound moral effects on others. Further, those effects often stem from other than contractual or other formal relationships. The residents of the Love Canal area had no established formal relationship with Hooker Chemical, but they were morally affected in significant and negative ways by the company's actions. Further, those residents have, in turn, significantly affected Hooker Chemical, by attempting to abrogate some of its property rights in compensation for their harms.

Intentionality

Many decisions that emerge from corporations are plainly of the intentional, second-order type. When American Airlines lowers its transcontinental fare, it does so with due consideration of how it will affect the desires or intentions of competitors, consumers, regulators, etc. If American Airlines feels United Airlines will become angered or indignant and threaten a price war, it may decide to back off from its decision. Either way, its intention to bring about certain kinds of actions includes beliefs, desires, and intentions about the same in others.

What is much more difficult to establish is that these intentional decisions can be ascribed to the *corporation*, as opposed to the members within the corporation. Again, both French, with his account of the Corporate Internal Decision (CID) structure, and Ladd, with his appeal to a language-game understanding of the decision-making process, provide perceptive and plausible accounts of why this kind of ascription makes sense. Ladd's account, though, falls short in that it excludes moral considerations. In his view, certain constitutive-type rules or policies define the corporation; decisions which adhere to these rules are not *personal* decisions, but are rather *corporate* decisions. Ladd attempts to prove this point by appeal to a confusing claim that corporate rules and goals must be empirically verifiable. He thus excludes moral considerations as "relevant to the operations of a formal organization" (Ladd, 1970, p. 498). Given that Ladd uses Wittgenstein's notion of the "language game" as the basis for his argument, and given that for Wittgenstein the *social context* is key to the make-up of a particular language game, his exclusion of moral considerations as being a valid component of the corporate language game, of corporate goals and policies, is both odd and implausible.

French's account is similar to Ladd's in that he describes what he calls the "corporate decision recognition rules" (French, 1979, p. 212), which function in the same constitutive way as Ladd's. French, however, does not exclude moral considerations from the legitimate goals or policies of a corporation. He recognizes that much of a corporation's enterprise is morally significant and stresses not only the legitimacy, but also the importance, of holding corporations morally accountable.

Hence, by combining Ladd's and French's accounts, we establish corporations' formal and thus metaphysical and moral status. What we need to do is go beyond their positions to show how *both* the corporation and its principal members can be held morally accountable for corporate actions. For, even in French's view, the implication is that *only* the corporation can be held accountable. The members within it, so long as their decisions adhere to the recognition rules, are not, he argues, morally accountable for corporate actions. They, like the Nuremberg defendants, have the ultimate defense: "I was doing it for the company."

PERSONAL RESPONSIBILITY

The first concern is determining both the nature and the source of the goals or policies of the corporation to which the recognition rules must adhere. French's point that the goals and policies of a corporation need to be the personal ones of the current directors is an important, if too weak, start (French, 1979, p. 214). What he needs to say is that the goals and policies *must* not strictly be the personal ones of the directors, for if they are, then emerging decisions would have the strictly personal nature we have been trying to avoid.

Incorporator Responsibility

But, assuming the goals and policies are not those of the current directors, assuming instead that they can be traced to the *original* incorporators, does that mean they are simply those incorporators' personal goals? French's response is interesting, though again inadequate. He suggests, "even in infancy the melding of disparate interests and purposes gives rise to a corporate long range point of view that is distinct from the interests and purposes of the collection of incorporators viewed individually" (French, 1979, p. 214). Two comments are in order. First, his is an empirical claim about the formation of a corporation that surely does not hold in all cases. Often corporations evolve, generally for tax purposes, from previously established, individually controlled companies. In these cases the policies have already been established by an individual or very small group of individuals and hence are much more personal in nature.

Second, even in those cases where there was a true disparity of interests, the individual incorporators certainly agreed upon whatever compromise of these interests was established. And as parties to that agreement, even if the terms were not ideally what, individually, they would have desired, they are accountable for the actions that emerge from that agreement.

I wish to emphasize that in both circumstances the decisions should still be regarded as *corporate* decisions carrying *personal* responsibility. The kinds of policies established in a corporation's infancy are of a broad nature; they give direction to decision-making, but it is through their specific implementation (i.e., in their being filtered through the CID structure) that they become corporate intentions.[11]

Hence we begin to see a breaking down of the "either the corporation is responsible or the individuals are" dichotomy. The original incorporators or policy makers maintain responsibility for at least the general direction of corporate decisions.

Managerial Responsibility

But what of those cases in which the policy makers are either deceased or no longer affiliated with the company and its actions? Can we assign personal responsibility in addition to corporate responsibility? And to whom would it be assigned? I think we can and to see how, let us return to Ladd's game analogy.

Using this analogy, we can think of a game in which there are some very strict, if general, constitutive rules for the proper playing of the game. As the players engage in the activity, they attempt to implement these rules in specific ways so as to advantage themselves or their team. As both sides attempt to implement the rules so as to gain advantage,[12] in order for the game to be well-played, there must be a final arbitrator or referee who judges whether the specific implementation of a rule adheres to the more general rules or policies that define the game. She or he judges whether a particular action is consistent with the original intention of the gamewright.

Relating this to the CID structure, the original incorporators act as the gamewrights. They establish strict, if most often general, policies or constitutive rules for acceptable corporate behavior. Clearly, these cannot include many, if any, specific rules about specific behaviors,[13] given the enormous range of behaviors and corresponding restrictions that would be applicable. As lower-level employees go about their work, they will try to accomplish their either implicit or explicit job descriptions through specific implementation of the rules, as they deem appropriate according to their interpretation of corporate goals and policies. But such implementations will often involve misunderstandings of true corporate policy, and it is at this point that the arbitrator or referee steps in to make a judgment. In the CID structure, that arbitrator is the supervisor, manager, division chief, whoever has the final authority as to whether a particular decision, project, or design will be acted upon. This person is thus not only responsible for determining feasibility, but for whether the decision adheres to corporate policy, for whether it is the type of decision the corporation would want to do.

But the manager has another task as well, and it is at this point that personal moral accountability again enters. In addition to determining whether the particular decision adheres to corporate policy, the manager/arbitrator has the responsibility to determine whether the corporate policies are themselves morally sound. If she or he does not make this second determination and a corporate decision harms others, that manager/arbitrator, in addition to the corporation, is accountable for the harm. If she or he feels a decision is consistent with corporate policy but is nonetheless immoral, she or he has an obligation at least to express those concerns to a supervisor.[14]

A frequently cited example of corporate decision-making, Kurt Vandivier's "Why Should My Conscience Both Me?" (Vandivier, 1972), helps clarify this process. In his account, he describes B.F. Goodrich's strong desire to establish contracts with companies that manufactured aircraft for the U.S. Air Force. This general goal was implemented, in the case described, in a way that eventually involved considerable amounts of deception and fraud. As the project evolved, lower-level engineers saw this deceit and fraud developing and voiced their concerns to supervisors. This process found its way to the individual who had final control over whether to proceed with the project, in this case the manager of the plant's technical services division. It was this manager's job to determine whether the project was consistent with company policy. He determined that it was and through this consistency, and through the formal nature of the decision-making process, the project became a *corporate* project, one for which the corporation could be held accountable. But it was also a *personal* decision. That manager, seeing the decision was consistent with company policy and seeing that it was potentially illegal or immoral, had a further obligation to attempt to alter either company policy or the project. By not doing so he placed the values inherent in the game structure/corporation above those of the society in which the game/corporation existed. And it is this decision for which society may legitimately hold him personally accountable.

SUMMARY AND CONCLUSION

To briefly summarize, an entity has the status of being a moral agent if it is an individual who causes events, who is capable of second-order intentionality, and who exists in a moral relationship with other moral agents. A corporation acquires this status through a combination of its formal nature (its CID structure) and its effect on and relationship with other moral agents. As such, the corporation can and should be held morally accountable for its actions.

It is also by making appeal to the corporation's formal nature and the analogy to language-games that managers, supervisors, division chiefs, etc., acting in the role of arbitrator/referee of company policy, acquire some measure of personal accountability for corporate actions. An analysis of the delineation of that measure, of the degree to which the corporation as opposed to its members should be held accountable, is beyond the scope of this paper, though such an analysis will necessarily involve consideration of the specifics of the individual case.

If these arguments are sound, they reveal the breakdown of the "either the corporation or its members" dichotomy. In the case of the Hooker Chemical Company, both the company and the manager(s) who made the decision not to dispose of the chemicals properly should be held morally accountable for the subsequent harms.

The next step in the discussion should involve trying to understand what it means to hold a corporation morally accountable. As I suggested earlier, there are important differences between moral agents and moral persons, and we need to better understand the nature of those differences. For example, what are the appropriate kinds of punishment for a corporation?[15] Given the complex nature of retributively punishing such an entity, should we strive only for restitution? If so, should we then treat its decision-making members in the same way? These questions provide amply evidence of the complexity of the notion of corporate responsibility as well as evidence that the work done here represents only a mere beginning.[16]

Notes

1. My focus here is upon larger corporations, those with the kind of complex decision-making structure described later in the paper.

2. See, for example, Dennett, 1976, pp. 177–178.

3. See, for example, Peter French's seminal article, "The Corporation as Moral Person" (French, 1979), a piece from which I will otherwise borrow much in developing my own case.

4. See Singer, 1991, pp. 343–346.

5. That is, a particular society may deem that certain creatures or objects are of such value relative to their culture that they are deserving of civil protection—for example, cadavers, artworks, endangered species, etc. This status, though, needs to be distinguished from holding a natural right, from being the type of entity such that *any* just society would provide it protection.

6. Whether the cause must be a *first cause*, i.e., removed from deterministic considerations, can be for my purposes here a mute question. While this may be another of the conditions that distinguishes a moral person from a moral agent, I will appeal to a type of compatabilist position for assigning responsibility ascriptions to corporations. That is, given an adequately sophisticated level of corporate intentional decision-making, the *original* source of the cause is unimportant. For a related approach to this issue, see Ladd, 1970, pp. 512–516.

7. That the agent need only be capable of second-order intentionality is to account for

culpability in cases of negligence, i.e., for cases where the agent *could* and *should* have reflected upon the choice but did not do so.

8. See Brenkert, 1984, pp. 346–347.

9. See Stone, 1975, p. 14. Chapters Two, Three, and Four of his book give an informative account of the historical legacy of the law's relationship with corporations.

10. See Donaldson, 1982, p. 19.

11. So long, that is, as the original policy setter does not act in a veto position, in which case the decision would be his or her personal decision.

12. It might be suggested that this competitive element causes the analogy to collapse at this point. But there need not be competition for there to be discrepancies in specific implementations of general rules; competition merely brings these discrepancies to the forefront. Further, we should not disregard the often severely competitive interaction between various departments in the same company.

13. They may, however, include the kind of rules that Stone refers to as "informal constraints" (Stone, 1975, p. 5).

14. What his or her obligations are beyond this — e.g., whether she or he has an obligation to "whistle blow" — is beyond the scope of this paper.

15. French attempts to tackle some of these issues in "The Hester Prynne Sanction" (French, 1985), to which Warren Kessler gave a very insightful critique at a recent APA meeting (Kessler, 1989).

16. I am particularly grateful to Professor George Brenkert, from whose seminar this paper originally emerged.

Bibliography

Brenkert, George. "Strict Products Liability and Compensatory Justice," in *Business Ethics: Readings and Cases in Corporate Morality*, W. Michael Hoffman and Jennifer Mills Moore, Editors (New York: McGraw-Hill, 1984).

Davidson, Donald. "Agency," in *Agent, Action, and Reason*, Robert Binkley et al., Editors (Toronto: University of Toronto Press, 1971).

Dennett, Daniel. "Conditions of Personhood," in *The Identities of Persons*, Amelie Rorty, Editor (Berkeley: University of California Press, 1976).

Donaldson, Thomas. *Corporations and Morality* (Englewood Cliffs, NJ: Prentice-Hall, 1982).

French, Peter. "The Corporation as a Moral Person," *American Philosophical Quarterly*, Vol. 16, no. 3, July 1979.

———. "The Hester Prynne Sanction," *Business and Professional Ethics Journal*, Vol. 4, no. 2, Winter 1985.

Kessler, Warren. "Punishing Corporate Criminals," presented at the *Pacific Division Meetings of the American Philosophical Association*, Los Angeles, CA, March 1989.

Ladd, John. "Morality and the Ideal of Rationality in Formal Organizations," *The Monist*, Vol. 54, no. 4, October 1970.

Stone, Christopher. *Where the Law Ends* (New York: Harper and Row, 1975).

Singer, Peter. "All Animals Are Equal," in *Contemporary Moral Problems* 3rd Edition, James E. White, Editor (St. Paul: West Publishing Co., 1991).

Vandivier, Kurt. "Why Should My Conscience Both Me?" in *In the Name of Profit*, Robert Heilbroner et al., Editors (New York: Doubleday and Company, 1972).

John D. Bishop

THE MORAL RESPONSIBILITY OF CORPORATE EXECUTIVES FOR DISASTERS

I. INTRODUCTION

When large corporations are criticized for causing disasters, the senior executives of those corporations usually protest their personal innocence, and deny that they should bear any moral responsibility for the tragedy. They often protest that they were not given information which could have warned them of impending problems even though they made honest efforts to obtain such information. Subsequent investigations have sometimes revealed that others in the corporation (often engineers) knew of safety problems, but that this information failed to reach decision making executives. Examples of this phenomenon include the cargo door problem on the DC-10, and the explosion of the Challenger — both tragedies involving loss of life.

This denial of moral responsibility intuitively conflicts with the high remuneration that CEOs and other executives receive in return for being responsible for corporations. In particular, it conflicts with the bonus remuneration which they receive if the corporation performs well. If they benefit when the corporation flourishes, should they not accept responsibility when things go horribly wrong?

The denial also conflicts with the current trend in our society of holding senior executives more socially responsible (Brooks, 1989). To note a single example, a U.S. District Judge recently insisted that the CEO of Pennwalt Corp. should personally attend his court to enter a guilty plea on a toxic spill charge. Note that the judge was not making a legal point, (corporate lawyers could have just as easily entered the plea), but a point about social responsibility (Globe and Mail, 1989).

This paper will analyse to what extent we can or should hold executives morally responsible for disasters. In particular, it will examine the case in which knowledge indicating impending problems is available to someone in the corporation, but has failed to reach decision making executives.

To help clarify the issues that the rest of the paper will deal with, the next section will eliminate some cases in which executives clearly are not responsible. Section III will elaborate on the reasons executives give for denying responsibility; in particular this paper concentrates on the case in which executives claim that they did not have and could not be expected to have had information vital to preventing the disaster. The reasons why apparently powerful executives cannot get information from their own corporation needs to be examined carefully (Section IV) before moving on in the final two sections to analysing to what extent we are justified in holding executives morally responsible.

From *Journal of Business Ethics*, 10 (1991), 377–383. Copyright © 1991 Kluwer Academic Publishers. Reprinted by permission of Kluwer Academic Publishers.

It perhaps should be made clear at the outset that moral responsibility, or the lack of it, does not have direct implications for legal liability. The legal aspects of this problem are complicated, especially when the tragedy is in one country, and the corporate head office is in another. Legal issues are not dealt with in this paper.

II. LIMITS ON EXECUTIVE RESPONSIBILITY

It is commonplace in discussing morality that people should not be held responsible for events over which they have no influence or control. In this section, several types of events over which executives have no influence are eliminated from discussion. Executives cannot be held responsible for acts of God, nor, in their role as executives, for actions which are not performed on behalf of the corporation. Events not excluded in this section are not necessarily the moral responsibility of executives, but they are the actions which will be the basis of discussion in the rest of this article.

It can be accepted that executives are not responsible for obvious "acts of God". This does not mean that they should not be held accountable for the results of a natural event, for they may well be in a position to determine the outcome even when the event itself is inevitable. For example, suppose an earthquake causes a factory to collapse, killing several workers. Obviously, we cannot hold the executives of the company which owns the factory responsible for the earthquake itself; earthquakes are natural events which are beyond human control. However, we might hold the executives responsible for the factory being built in an earthquake zone, or we might hold them responsible for the use of money saving construction methods which caused the building to collapse. In these cases, we would consider the executives at least partly responsible for the workers' deaths. The fact that a person has no influence or control over an event does not necessarily exempt him or her from responsibility for the consequences of that event. What we hold him or her responsible for are the actions which determined those consequences.

Corporate executives, in their role as executives, should also not be held responsible for events which are not the result of the corporation's activities. The concepts of the "executive's role" and of the "corporation's activities" both need explaining.

Executives, because they are people, have moral responsibilities, as citizens, neighbours, parents, etc. Such responsibilities, while not being denied, will not be discussed in this paper. The purpose of the present discussion is limited to the moral responsibility of executives in their role as executives. However, this should not be taken to mean that the moral principles that apply to persons acting in the role of executives are any different from those which apply in the rest of their lives. Although it is sometimes argued that the morality of professional activities differs from the morality of everyday life (Carr, 1968), that is a position which cannot be applied to executives without the most careful examination (Callahan, 1988-A; Gillespie, 1983; Nagel, 1978). We will not go into this debate here; since this paper does not discuss the actual moral duties of executives as executives, we need not discuss how they differ from their other duties.

The notion of "corporate activities" also needs expanding. It has been argued that corporations are moral entities in their own right, and that corporations can commit actions (French, 1977). This is a position which I reject for the sorts of reasons outlined in Danley (1980). However, in this paper, I will avoid further discussion of this issue because it is not relevant to the current topic. Even if corporations are moral agents and as such are held responsible for corporate activities, this does not exempt the people in the corporation from also being held responsible for their role in those activities. Moral responsibility is not a fixed quantity; its assignment to one moral entity does not necessarily reduce the responsibility of other moral agents. Thus corporate executives can be held morally accountable for the same events for which the corporation is also accountable, though not necessarily to the same degree or for the same reasons. Because of this, we do not have to decide on corporate moral responsibility to discuss the issue of the responsibility of executives for their role in corporate actions.

"Corporate activities" can also refer to the actions of the corporation's employees which are done in their capacity as employees. Presumably, executive are in a position to influence such actions on the part of employees, and it is their responsibility for such actions that the rest of this paper will be concerned with. Executives may, for social reasons, be in a position to influence employee behaviour off the job, but the use of such influence does not concern us here. We will confine our examination to events which result from the actions of employees while on the job. To hold the executives responsible for such events (if we decide to do so) is to hold them responsible for the actions of others, but it is assumed that executives have some influence or control over the actions of employees. The question we need to discuss is to what extent the executive has such influence and control, and whether it extends only to actions the executive directly instigates, or to all actions and omissions of employees as employees.

Even though we will confine the discussion to executive responsibility for actions employees commit in their capacity as employees, for convenience sake such employee actions will sometimes be referred to as the actions of the corporation. This should not be taken to imply that corporations can actually commit actions; the phrase is used as shorthand. Similarly, by employee actions, we mean only those committed as employees.

III. WHY EXECUTIVES MAY NOT BE MORALLY RESPONSIBLE

When things go horribly wrong, executives sometimes deny responsibility on the grounds that they did not know, and could not be expected to know, the information they needed to prevent the disaster. They maintain this even when some of the corporation's employees knew, or ought to have known, the relevant information.

Consider the case of DC-10 Ship 29, which crashed near Paris on March 3, 1974 when its cargo doors flew off. All 346 people aboard were killed. Subsequent investigations revealed that McDonnell-Douglas, the manufacturer of the aircraft, was aware of the cargo door problem, and that Ship 29 had been returned to the corporation for FAA ordered corrections to the door locking mechanism (French, 1984; Eddy *et al.*, 1976). These corrections were never made, though stamped inspection sheets indicated they had been. John Brizendine, President of the Douglas division of McDonnell-Douglas, denied all knowledge of this failure to fix the doors (French, 1982), though it is clear that at least some people in the company must have known. Since there is no reason to question Brizendine's honesty, we will assume that the information that could have prevented the disaster failed to reach him. (We will also assume that he would have acted on the information if he had received it.)

As a second example, consider the explosion of the Challenger space shuttle, again with loss of life. Engineers at Morton Thiokol, which manufactured the solid rocket booster, had repeatedly expressed concerns, in written memos and verbally, about possible failure of O-ring seals on cold weather launches (Grossman, 1988). These concerns failed to reach decision making management at NASA, who maintain that they would have stopped the launch had they been aware of the engineers' opinion (Callahan, 1988-B). Again, vital information that could have prevented disaster failed to reach executives responsible for the final decision.

I do not want to raise the issue of the honesty of the executives when they claim they did not know. It has transpired in some cases that executives knew more than they were willing to admit — such was the case in the Dalkon shield tragedy (Mintz, 1985), or the knowledge of tobacco executives about early cancer studies (White, 1988). However, it is clear that executives often do not know, and are not told even if others in the corporation have the information. The immorality of lying, and of being able to stop a disaster and not doing so, are beyond doubt; the responsibility (if any) of executives when they actually are not told is more problematic, and is the central topic of this paper. It will be assumed that in the cases cited (the DC-10 cargo door problem and the Challenger disaster), executives were in fact in the dark about impending problems.

IV. NEGATIVE INFORMATION BLOCKAGE

Can executives be taken seriously when they claim that they cannot be expected to know about impending tragedy? After all, they have the authority to demand that information be given to them. And it is their job to know what is going on in their corporation. If someone in the company has or can get the information (which is the most interesting case), then why cannot the executives simply send a memo to all employees saying such information is to be sent directly to their attention? This question needs to be examined carefully if we are to determine whether executives are responsible when disaster strikes, or whether we should accept the claim that they did not know and could not have known the information needed to prevent the tragedy.

The problem with getting information to executives is a well-known phenomenon in corporate and other hierarchical organizations which I will call "negative information blockage". In brief, information regarding the riskiness of a corporation's plans is stifled at source or by intervening management, even when senior executives have demanded that such information be sent on to them. This phenomenon needs to be analysed further.

The notion of negative information requires the distinction between a corporation's objectives and its constraints. The objectives (or goals — I will use the two words interchangeably) of a corporation are what its senior executives are perceived as wanting to achieve. These objectives are, of course, the executive's, but it is convenient to refer to them as the corporation's. These goals may or may not be what the executives think they want to achieve, or what they say they want to achieve; corporate mission statements may not be honest or may not be believed. The actual goals of the executives (or the corporation) can only be identified by examining what sorts of behaviour the executives reward, as will be discussed below.

The constraints on a corporation are those facts which affect the pursuit of its goals, and which cannot be changed, at least in the short run. Some constraints are physical, and cannot be violated by anyone in the corporation even if they wanted to. For example, the cabins on jet aircraft need to be pressurized — that need is a fact which no manufacturer can do anything about. Other constraints are moral, legal, or mandated by safety. These constraints can be ignored by a corporation or its employees, and it is these sorts of constraints which interest us.

Objectives and constraints are very different concepts, though sometimes constraints are recognized in statements of a company's objectives. For example, the objective of an aircraft manufacturing corporation might be stated as: "To produce aircraft which can be safely operated." Here safety, which is a constraint, looks like it is part of the objective, but this appearance does not stand up to analysis. The objective is to produce operable aircraft; safety is actually a constraint on that goal because airplanes cannot be operated if they fall out of the sky. Safety is not a separate or secondary goal, but a condition of achieving the actual goal of making operable aircraft.

Within a corporation, goals and constraints are treated very differently. Rewards are given for employee behaviour which appears to help the company achieve its goals. Observing legal, moral, and safety constraints is seldom rewarded; it tends to be assumed that employees will observe such constraints without reward. Instead, employees in companies which enforce constraints are usually punished when violation of the constraint is discovered; they are not usually rewarded just for observing constraints. Complete failure of a corporation to enforce legal, moral or safety constraints raises obvious moral problems; this discussion will be centered on the more interesting case in which constraints are enforced by the corporation (i.e., by the executives), but ignored by some of the employees. Why they are ignored, even under the threat of punishment, has to do with the different ways in which executives encourage employees to pursue goals, and discourage them from violating constraints.

In general, employee behaviour which enhances corporate goals is rewarded, observing constraints is not. Hindering objectives is almost always punished. Constraints are constraints on the pursuit of the company's goals, and hence observing them can threaten an employee's rewards. In fact, observing constraints and asking one's management to do so as well may impede the company's goals to the point where the behaviour itself is punished. Surely this encourages violation of constraints.

There are other pressures on employees to put rewards for pursuing goals before the observance of constraints. Violation of constraints is only punished if one is caught; hence there is an element of gamble involved. The time factor also plays a major role; rewards are usually immediate, while discovery of violated constraints may be months or years away, by which time the employee has had his promotion and is safely elsewhere.

To complicate matters further, corporations are hierarchical. If an employee does resist temptation and observes constraints at the risk of losing rewards, his manager, or his manager's manager, may not. If getting a company to observe a constraint requires escalating concerns to the senior executive level (and this is the case we are concerned with in this article), then a single failure to resist temptation may block the concern from reaching the executives. This is the phenomenon of negative information blockage.

Since negative information blockage is inherent in the nature of goals, constraints, rewards and punishments, then to what extent can executives be held responsible for getting information past the blockage? The next section will consider two possible views on this topic.

V. EXECUTIVE RESPONSIBILITY AND NEGATIVE INFORMATION BLOCKAGE

The first of the two views is that executives are responsible for doing whatever they can to prevent negative information blockage. They have a moral duty to structure the corporation to ensure that risks of disaster are discovered and made known to themselves (and then, of course, to act on the information.) They have a moral responsibility to do as much as they can to prevent tragedy.

What exactly executives can do I will not discuss in detail; a few examples will suffice. They can offer rewards of information brought to them; they can keep an "open door" policy so junior employees can go around the blockages; they can set a personal example of concern for moral, legal, and safety constraints. These ideas are generally discussed in business ethics literature under the topic of whistleblowing, since whistleblowing is often the result of frustration with negative information blockage. (See, for example, Callahan, 1988-C). Without going into further detail on what executives can do, we can summarize the first view of corporate executive responsibility by suggesting they should do whatever is reasonably possible to prevent knowledge of potential disasters from being blocked before it reaches them.

The second view is that executives, especially CEOs, are responsible for preventing tragedy, excepting only those cases, such as acts of God, which were discussed above in Section II. This view is radically different from the first; just how different can be seen if we consider how executives would be judged in the event of a tragedy. On the first view, the impartial spectator making moral judgements would inquire what steps the executives had taken prior to the tragedy to make sure information on the impending disaster had been conveyed to them. And, of course, they would ask whether the executives had acted on anything they knew. On the second view, the impartial spectator would hold the executive morally responsible for the failure to acquire sufficient information to prevent the tragedy, regardless of whether or not steps had been taken to circumvent negative information blockage. This view is essentially holding that since the tragedy happened, the steps taken were obviously not sufficient, and hence the executives are morally culpable.

It should be noted that on the second view, we are holding executives morally responsible even though they did not know the disaster might happen, and even though they may have taken some steps to acquire the knowledge. We are holding them morally responsible for the result, not the effort. The first view holds them responsible only for the effort.

There are many cases in life where people are held responsible for results rather than effort: it is one of the painful lessons we learn as children. For example, on examinations, students, especially in such subjects as medicine and engineering, are quite rightly marked on results, not the amount of effort they put into studying. And executives themselves do not hesitate to hold employees responsible for getting results

Demanding results on the job, not just effort, is acceptable because it is necessary. When an engineer designs a bridge, it is important to society that it does not collapse. It is important to society that doctors are competent, not just that they are doing their best. We are often justified in holding people responsible for doing their job well.

If people fail in their jobs, they may or may not be held legally liable depending on the circumstances, but in any case their careers suffer, and they may lose their jobs. The fact that they are held responsible is reflected in the impact on their professional standing when they succeed or fail. To distinguish this type of responsibility from legal and moral responsibility, I will refer to it as professional responsibility.

The case of professional responsibility that best parallels the situation of executives is that of cabinet ministers in a parliamentary system. When things go wrong in an area of ministerial responsibility, the minister is held accountable and is expected to resign. They are not supposed to argue that they tried, that they have not been negligent, or that they are not legally liable. Thus Lord Carrington resigned when Argentina invaded the Falklands; he did not stay on protesting that it was not his fault (though it probably was not). The questions we must now deal with are: should we apply professional responsibility to executives? And secondly, how does professional responsibility relate to moral responsibility?

VI. PROFESSIONAL RESPONSIBILITY

The concept of professional responsibility applies when the outcome of a professional activity is of great concern to a person or people other than the person doing the activity. It especially applies if the outcome is of concern over and above any contract the professional has with some other person, or if the outcome is of great concern to bystanders. Let me illustrate these points with an example.

When I buy a pair of shoes and find them faulty, I take them back to the shoe store and generally will be satisfied if I am given back my money. The responsibility is limited to reversing the contract. When I go to a doctor for an operation, I am not interested in hearing that he or she will refund me the cost of the operation if it goes wrong, especially if I die. We can say in this case that the doctor has a professional responsibility which goes beyond the "contract." It goes beyond because the consequences of failure go beyond the contract. Similarly, if an engineer designs a bridge that collapses, then refunding the money he or she received for the design hardly helps those who were on the bridge when it collapsed. It helps so little that that course of action is seldom pursued. The engineer, in this case, has a professional responsibility.

Liability laws generally reflect the fact that responsibility can extend far beyond reversing the original contract, but this discussion is not an attempt to define legal liability. The point is that professional responsibility arises when the consequences of failure have effects on other people (customers or bystanders) which exceed the confines of the initial contract.

Clearly, this applies to executives. If they fail to create a corporate culture which overcomes negative information blockage and disaster results, it often involves the death of their customers (or of their customers' customers, as in the case of the DC-10s). It is clear that we are justified in holding executives professionally responsible when tragedy happens. In other words, we hold them professionally responsible for failing to obtain the information needed to prevent the disaster, whether or not they tried to.

But is holding executives professionally responsible different from holding them morally responsible? In the cases we have been examining, there is a close connection between the two.

Executives and everyone else have a moral responsibility to ensure that their activities do not result in the deaths of others if that result can be prevented. Executives, therefore, have a moral responsibility to do their best to obtain the information needed to prevent disasters. They have a professional responsibility, as we have seen, not just to do their best, but to actually succeed in preventing avoidable disasters. The latter grows out of the former in the sense that executives have a professional responsibility to succeed in fulfilling their moral responsibilities. (Of course, they also have professional responsibilities with other origins as well.) Thus, although normally a person only has a moral responsibility for trying to avoid immoral results, in this case (and in others) a person has a professional responsibility to succeed in fulfilling the underlying moral responsibility.

This conclusion has a major implication for judging executives; namely, when tragedy happens, we are justified in holding them responsible based on moral values. If they object that they did not have the information necessary to prevent the disaster and that they had made an honest effort to obtain that information, then we can accept that as individuals they have fulfilled their moral obligations. (We are assuming honesty.) But as professional executives, they have failed to fulfil their professional obligation to carry out moral requirements. We are still justified in holding them responsible based on moral considerations.

References

Brooks, L. J.: 1989, 'Corporate Ethical Performance: Trends, Forecasts, and Outlooks', *Journal of Business Ethics* 8, No. 1, pp. 31–38.

Callahan, J. C.: 1988-A, *Ethical Issues in Professional Life* (Oxford University Press, Oxford), pp. 49–50.

Callahan, J. C.: 1988-B, *Ethical Issues in Professional Life* (Oxford University Press, Oxford), p. 342.

Callahan, J. C.: 1988-C, *Ethical Issues in Professional Life* (Oxford University Press, Oxford), pp. 337–339.

Carr, A. Z.: 1968, 'Is Business Bluffing Ethical?', *Ethical Issues in Professional Life*, C. Callahan, ed. (Oxford University Press, Oxford), pp. 69–72.

Danley, J. R.: 1980, 'Corporate Moral Agency: the case for Anthropological Bigotry', *Ethical Issues in Professional Life*, J. C. Callahan, ed. (Oxford University Press, Oxford), pp. 269–274.

French, Peter A.: 1977, 'Corporate Moral Agency', *Ethical Issues in Professional Life*, J. C. Callahan, ed. (Oxford University Press, Oxford), pp. 265–269.

Gillespie, Norman Chase: 1983, 'The Business of Ethics, *Ethical Issues in Professional Life*, J. C. Callahan, ed. (Oxford University Press, Oxford), pp. 72–76.

Globe and Mail: 1989, 'Polluting firm's chairman hauled into court by U.S. judge', Associated Press, Globe and Mail, August 10 1989, p. B10.

Grosman, Brian A.: 1988, *Corporate Loyalty: A Trust Betrayed* (Penguin Books, Markham Ont.), pp. 177–179.

Mintz, Morton: 1985, *At Any Cost: Corporate Greed, Women, and the Dalkon Shield* (Random House, Inc., New York).

Nagel, Thomas: 1978, 'Ruthlessness in Public Life', *Ethical Issues in Professional Life*, J. C. Callahan, ed. (Oxford University Press, Oxford), pp. 76–83.

White, Larry C.: 1988, *Merchants of Death: The American Tobacco Industry* (Beech Tree/Morrow, New York).

◆ ◆ ◆

DISCUSSION QUESTIONS

1. French claims that corporations, and not just people who work in them, have reasons for doing what they do. Does this imply corporate rather than personal responsibility, as French thinks?

2. How does Ladd's view differ from French's? Which do you support?

3. Meyers, like French, ties the notion of responsibility to decision making. Accordingly, when Meyers argues that employees are personally responsible for corporate actions, he cites "managers, supervisors, division chiefs, etc.," that is, people traditionally thought of as deciding corporate policy. At what point, however, do lower-level employees share moral responsibility? Meyers writes, "The Hooker Chemical Company *should* be held morally accountable for its poisoning of Love Canal, *as well as* should the manager who made the final decision to dump the chemicals." What about the employees who actually dumped the chemicals? What, if any, responsibility, did they have?

4. Bishop argues that senior executives should be held professionally and morally responsible for tragedies, even if they did not have the information needed to prevent the disaster. How fair is this?

5. From a practical standpoint, what does it mean to hold an executive morally responsible for corporate wrongdoing or a preventable disaster? Should the executive resign, be fired, be fined, publicly apologize, perform community services, or be jailed?

CASE 6.1

◆ ◆ ◆

Corporate Persons and Free Speech

Although philosophers continue to debate whether or not corporations are moral persons, the United States Supreme Court decided more than a century ago that corporations are legal persons. A corporation may differ from a "natural" person in being, as the Court described it, an "artificial being, invisible, intangible, and existing only in contemplation of law." But corporations nonetheless enjoy many of the constitutional protections accorded living and breathing persons. Corporations have defended themselves by citing the Fourth Amendment's prohibition against unreasonable searches and seizures, and the Fifth Amendment's ban on double jeopardy. Perhaps most controversial, however, is the extent to which the Court recognizes corporations' First Amendment rights to free speech.

The landmark case in this regard was the Supreme Court's 1978 decision that ruled unconstitutional a Massachusetts law limiting corporate speech. The statute had barred corporations from making contributions or spending organizational money for the purpose of "influencing or affecting the vote on any question submitted to the voters, other than one materially affecting any of the property, business or assets of the corporation." In other words, in the case of a referendum whose outcome would directly affect their interests, corporations could address the electorate as much as they wanted. However, absent any such impact, they had to stay on the political sidelines. The case at issue involved a Massachusetts referendum on a proposal to amend the state constitution to allow the legislature to enact a graduated personal income tax. Two banking associations and three corporations announced their plan to spend corporate funds to oppose the idea. The Massachusetts attorney general prevented them from doing so, on the grounds that the corporations had no direct interest in the matter.

The Supreme Court ruled that these corporations had guarantees of free speech that should have allowed them to speak as they chose. As Justice Lewis Powell wrote, "In the realm of protected speech, the legislature is constitutionally disqualified from dictating the subjects about which persons may speak and the speakers who may address a public issue." The heart of the Supreme Court's ruling rests on the idea that the value of the message for informing the public is more important than its source. The ruling clearly treats corporations as though they are "persons" with all the accompanying rights.

Yet two dissenting opinions in this and a later case contain points that are relevant to the question of the extent to which corporations should be thought of as persons. In this case, Justice Byron White wrote that "what some have considered to be the principal function of the First Amendment, the use of communication as a means of self-expression, self-realization, and self-fulfillment, is not at all furthered by corporate speech." In Justice White's judgment, the corporate statements at issue in the Massachusetts case "in the last analysis are the purely personal views of the management, individually or as a group." Yet if a corporation is a person, shouldn't it have some sort of a "self" that can be expressed, realized, and fulfilled? Shouldn't it have some kind of intellect? Echoing Justice White's reservations, in a different case eight years later, Justice William Rehnquist wrote that to "ascribe to such artificial entities an 'intellect' or 'mind' is to confuse metaphor with reality."

Yet another issue is raised by Justice Rehnquist's reminder that corporations differ from natural persons in being the creations of law. As such, he argues, there is nothing wrong with the law placing them under restrictions not appropriate for natural persons. ◆

Discussion Questions

1. Do any of the points raised by Justices White and Rehnquist successfully undermine the idea that corporations are persons?

2. All of us speak of many sorts of corporations—business, educational, medical—as though they have a single identity. We easily say, for example, "The university is wrong in what it's doing." When we speak like this, are we, as Justice Rehnquist suggests, confusing "metaphor with reality"? Or are we expressing a commonsense insight that corporations are indeed so close to being persons that they can be said to have intentions, rights, and responsibilities?

Sources

First National Bank of Boston et al., Appellants, v. *Francis X. Bellotti, etc.,* U.S. Supreme Court 435 U.S. 765, 1978, 55 L Ed 2d 707.

Nader, Ralph, and Carl J. Mayer, "Corporations Are Not Persons," *New York Times,* April 9, 1988, 131.

CASE 6.2

◆ ◆ ◆

Harmful Products, Bankruptcy, and Responsibility

One of the most perplexing issues in business ethics is who should be held responsible when a corporation markets a product that turns out to be harmful. Should the corporation alone be held responsible or should individual executives also share that burden? And how extensive should this responsibility be? Should the company be obligated to the extent that it puts its future at risk? If a corporation believes that fully accepting this responsibility will destroy the company, is it justified in declaring bankruptcy in order to avoid or at least limit its responsibility?

Bankruptcy is ordinarily used by companies that are in such serious financial shape that they cannot pay their current bills. By filing under Chapter 11 of the bankruptcy laws, companies may continue in business but are protected against their creditors and have enough freedom to determine if they can reorganize their business and their debt so that they can resume normal operations. At least two prominent and apparently healthy corporations, however, have taken the highly unusual step of filing for bankruptcy to protect themselves from future liability stemming from the manufacturing or marketing of harmful products. In 1982, the Manville Corporation (formerly Johns-Manville) filed for Chapter 11 bankruptcy because of the large number of lawsuits stemming from the harm associated with the asbestos it produced years earlier.

Similarly, the pharmaceutical firm of A. H. Robins filed under Chapter 11 because of liability suits alleging harm from its Dalkon Shield intrauterine device. Both companies emerged from bankruptcy with controversial plans to handle the damages from those lawsuits. Also, corporate executives at the companies were protected from being sued individually; in essence, they were absolved of responsibility for any wrongdoing.

The Manville Corporation was a leading producer of asbestos, a substance that has excellent insulating and fire protecting properties. Unfortunately, if asbestos fiber is inhaled, severe harm — even death — can result. The damage does not surface, however, from anywhere from ten to forty years after initial exposure. This is precisely what happened to thousands of workers who began claiming in the 1950s that they were becoming seriously ill because of exposure to Manville's product decades earlier. Claims were made as far back as the 1930s that asbestos posed at least some threat to workers. Yet it was not until the 1960s that the full extent of the danger was established. Critics of the company claim that Manville suppressed information about the danger of asbestos, but the company denies such allegations. Moreover, Manville argues that it was not the sole author of the harm asbestos did. During World War II, asbestos was used extensively in naval vessels. Manville's asbestos operation broke no laws; it had operated according to federal specifications for the product during the war and according to the federal postwar guidelines for handling the product. Manville thus claimed that the federal government should share responsibility for the workers' diseases.

Manville's bankruptcy filing stunned the financial community because the company was, at that time, in excellent shape. The rationale for the filing, however, was that the cost of the asbestos lawsuits could reach $2 to $5 billion, well above the company's $1.1 billion net worth. Without bankruptcy protection and a plan for keeping the cost of settlements manageable, Manville argued, the company would slowly die, especially because Manville was caught in a war between its insurance companies over how to assess responsibility for reimbursing Manville for workers' claims. One group of insurers claimed that they were responsible only if they were insuring Manville when a worker's disease surfaced. The other group countered that responsibility should be traced to whoever covered Manville when the affected workers were exposed. Until the dispute could be resolved, the insurance companies refused to pay Manville for its liabilities. The company was thereby thrown on its own resources and foresaw financial disaster if this continued. Lawsuits would gradually deplete the company's resources to the point that it could no longer stay in business. And if that happened, not only would its entire work force be unemployed, but thousands of claimants would receive no settlement at all. Bankruptcy thus seemed the logical course of action.

The settlement that let Manville emerge from bankruptcy in 1988 created a trust fund that would be responsible for settling all claims. But it also effectively took control of the corporation. The trust was established with $2.5 billion from Manville and its insurers, received ownership of as much as 80 percent of Manville's stock, and was promised up to 20 percent of its yearly profits. The reorganization plan also protected Manville executives and its insurance companies from lawsuits. By the end of 1989, however, the trust fund was running out of money. Twenty-three thousand cases were settled, but legal and administrative costs had consumed about two-thirds of the fund's resources. As a result, many of the 90,000 remaining claimants, some with cancer, were told that they would not be paid for at least another ten years. In 1990, the trust was reorganized by a federal judge.

The A. H. Robins Company had a similar story. From 1971 to 1974, Robins marketed an IUD known as the Dalkon Shield. Robins discontinued the product when women began to sue the company, claiming that they had been harmed by the device. These women claimed that the shield could produce life-threatening pelvic infections, birth defects, and even sterility. Critics of the company claim that the initial research on the product had been insufficient and overly optimistic. Subsequent studies showed that it was neither as effective for preventing pregnancy nor as safe as originally thought. In early 1985, Robins set up a $615 million fund to handle claims, but it quickly became apparent that this would not be enough. Like Manville, Robins was in solid financial shape. But also like Manville, Robins faced a mounting number of lawsuits. And so in August 1985, the company filed for bankruptcy under Chapter 11. Robins argued that it had not done anything illegal or intentionally harmed anyone. Robins's critics, however, claim not only that the company had early warnings that the initial research was faulty but also that company officials destroyed material that had been requested by federal authorities. American Home Products subsequently bought Robins and, following the Manville model, established as $2.5 billion trust fund for claimants. The settlement with the bankruptcy court also protected Robins's officials from additional suits and from being assessed punitive damages. ◆

Discussion Questions

1. By declaring bankruptcy, both Manville and Robins hoped to avoid the possibility of financial devastation because of future liabilities. The trust funds were established to compensate victims but also to allow the companies to end their liability once and for all and to get back to business. In handling the problem in this way, did these corporations fulfill their responsibilities to the people who were injured by their products? Did the individual executives who made decisions about these products fulfill their responsibilities?

2. Should executives be held personally responsible when they act in the interests of their firms? (If you think that the companies or executives fell short, remember that one of the defining features of a corporation is that it is an entity with limited liability and that its managers are simply agents for the firm's owners.)

3. Both companies argue that they marketed products in a legal manner according to the best information they had at the time. Should they be held responsible for what they did not know about their products' dangers? Should the government have a responsibility in cases like this? Were any government agencies negligent in these cases?

4. Critics of Manville and Robins claim that these companies shirked their responsibility to their victims by violating the spirit of bankruptcy protection when they were not really in immediate financial trouble. Do you agree? Does your view of this case change if officials at either company in fact had firm knowledge or at least good reason to suspect their products?

Sources

"Back in Jeopardy at Manville," *Business Week*, June 25, 1990, 28–29.

Coplon, Jeff, "When Did J-M Know?" *Village Voice*, March 1, 1983, 16.

Des Jardins, Joseph R., and John J. McCall, "Manville's Bankruptcy and Asbestos Litigation" and "A. H. Robins and the Dalkon Shield," *Contemporary Issues in Business Ethics*, 2nd ed. (Belmont, CA: Wadsworth Publishing Company, 1990), 248–249.

Gini, A. R., "Manville: The Ethics of Economic Efficiency?" *The Journal of Business Ethics*, 3 (1984), 63–70.

——, and T. Sullivan, "A. H. Robins: The Dalkon Shield," in *Ethical Issues in Business: A Philosophical Approach*, 3rd ed., edited by Thomas Donaldson and Patricia H. Werhane (Englewood Cliffs, NJ: Prentice Hall, 1988), 414–424.

Labaton, Stephen, "Manville's Trust for Asbestos Victims Runs Low," *New York Times*, October 24, 1989, A18.

——, "Revamping of Manville Trust Is Proposed," *New York Times*, November 20, 1990, D1.

ADDITIONAL READINGS

French, Peter, "What Is Hamlet to McDonnell-Douglas or McDonnell-Douglas to Hamlet: DC-10," *Business & Professional Ethics Journal*, 1, no. 2 (1981), 1–12.

Friedman, Marilyn, and Larry May, "Corporate Rights to Free Speech," *Business & Professional Ethics Journal*, 5, nos. 3 & 4 (1985), 5–30.

Garrett, Jan Edward, "Unredistributable Corporate Moral Responsibility," *Journal of Business Ethics*, 8 (1989), 535–545.

Goodpaster, Kenneth E., "The Concept of Corporate Responsibility," *Journal of Business Ethics*, 2 (1983), 1–22.

——, "The Principle of Moral Projection: A Reply to Professor Ranken," *Journal of Business Ethics*, 6 (1987), 329–332.

——, and John B. Matthews, "Can a Corporation Have a Conscience?," *Harvard Business Review*, January-February 1982, 132–141.

Ladd, John, "Morality and the Ideal of Rationality in Formal Organizations," *The Monist*, October 1970, 488–516.

Manning, Rita C., "Corporate Responsibility and Corporate Personhood," *Journal of Business Ethics*, 3 (1984), 77–84.

Ozar, David T., "Do Corporations Have Moral Rights?," *Journal of Business Ethics*, 4 (1985), 277–281.

Pfeiffer, Raymond S., "The Central Distinction in the Theory of Corporate Moral Personhood," *Journal of Business Ethics*, 9 (1990), 473–480.

Ranken, Nani L., "Corporations as Persons: Objections to Goodpaster's 'Principle of Moral Projection,'" *Journal of Business Ethics* 6 (1987), 633–637.

Surber, Jere, "Individual and Corporate Responsibility," *Business & Professional Ethics Journal*, 2, no. 4 (1982), 67–88.

Velasquez, Manual, "Why Corporations Are Not Morally Responsible for Anything They Do," *Business & Professional Ethics Journal*, 2, no. 3 (Spring 1983), 1–18.

Werhane, Patricia H., "Corporate and Individual Moral Responsibility: A Reply to Jan Garrett," *Journal of Business Ethics*, 8 (1989), 821–822.

CHAPTER 7

◆ ◆ ◆

Corporate Punishment

The preceding chapter introduced the debate over whether or not corporations can be held responsible for their actions. Those who claim that corporations are responsible, however, have another major issue to address—what then? It is easy enough to punish an individual, but how does one punish a corporation? And how does one do so justly?

One of the most discussed proposals for corporate punishment is Peter French's "The Hester Prynne Sanction." French suggests that corporations be shamed, that is, that they be subject to adverse publicity that threatens their "prestige, image, and social standing." French's proposal is found wanting on several counts by J. Angelo Corlett and Shannon Shipp. Corlett merely details his objections, but Shipp suggests that in addition to government-initiated economic sanctions, corporations be subject to "modified vendettas," that is, "organized attempts by nongovernment groups to influence corporations through the application of economic and noneconomic sanctions." Yet another proposal—"corporate beheading"—is offered by Robert J. Rafalko.

Peter A. French

THE HESTER PRYNNE SANCTION

Perhaps the most quoted line in the long history of the discussion of corporate criminal liability is attributed to Edward, First Baron Thurlow, Lord Chancellor of England. The line is:

> Did you ever expect a corporation to have a conscience, when it has no soul to be damned, and no body to be kicked?[1]

Baron Thurlow was concerned with how effectively to punish a corporation that had committed a serious crime when the corporation cannot be thrown into jail, when large fines can usually be passed on to consumers, and so on. This is a crucial practical issue because the idea of corporate criminality will be an empty theoretical one if the courts have no effective means of punishing a corporation that has been found guilty of criminal violation, and the courts have been busy lately in hearing corporate criminal cases.[2] ("Corporate crimes," as I use the term, are not to be confused with "white-collar crimes." White-collar crimes are typically perpetrated by managers, accountants, etc., against their own corporations. Corporate crimes are those that involve general corporate policy or decisionmaking, for example, the manufacture of defective, life-threatening products, pollution of the environment, wrongful death in certain airline disasters, antitrust violations, and price fixing.)[3]

Baron Thurlow's dictum is firmly cemented in the foundation of the retributive views that sustain our penal system. The firm hand of retribution, with its biblical "eye for an eye" authority, still commands the high ground of our thinking about the punishment of criminals,[4] and perhaps it should. If a corporation has no body to kick (leaving to God the business of souls and eternal damnation), how can it retribute its felonious behavior? It has no eye to be exchanged for an eye it has blinded by unsafe working conditions. It has no neck to stretch for the wrongful deaths it has caused in product explosions. Or so the story is meant to go.

Retributivism, however, does not have to be understood in strict biblical, in-kind terms. Capital punishment in the case of human murderers, for example, in many jurisdictions has been replaced by life sentences that carry possible parole stipulations, and the old Anglo-Saxon notion of wergeld is frequently utilized in settling wrongful-death suits. The price of a human life may not always come cheap, but it is being set by the courts and paid by corporate offenders or their insurance carriers. In the famous Ford Pinto case in Indiana the company used the insurance industry figure of $200,000 as the value of a human life when it defended its cost-benefit analysis regarding the redesign of the gas tanks on the Pinto. The particulars of how that figure is determined are not important. If I may mention, however, I have had some direct dealings with wergeld that produced a substantially larger sum for the value of human life. In Minnesota a few years ago, I was hired as a consultant to a legal firm to develop the case for a farm family suing a trucking company for the wrongful death of

From *Business and Professional Ethics Journal*, 4, no. 2 (1984), 19–32. Reprinted by permission of the author.

their eleven-year-old son. The firm argued that because the child was the fifth in the family and was not essential to productive operation of the farm, the most it should have to pay was the relatively standard $200,000. To counter that position I presented the view that the family must be adequately compensated for its nonfinancial losses: the unrequitable affection for the child, the loss of familial association, the value of future tender relationships between parents and siblings and the dead child. The wrongful death of the child induced a vacancy in a family that had not only a financial and emotional investment in the child, but an identity relationship to the child. There were no firm legal precedents for my arguments, but it proved successful and the family received a wergeld settlement many times greater than the original offer.

The idea that a corporation can pay a court fine or a set sum to the relatives of its victim in a homicide case and thereby expiate its guilt is, however, regarded by many people as a shocking affront to justice.[5] After all, the price of such a punishment can be written off as just another cost of business, and in the normal course of events it may be passed on to the consumers of the corporation's products or services. The penal effect of the punishment is absorbed by the innocent. But what are the alternatives? Certainly a whole corporation cannot, as Baron Thurlow knew, be tossed in jail, and when the crime is a truly corporate one it will strain the concept of justice to punish individual employees or managers or directors if, as is normally the case, such persons can demonstrate that they did not have the relevant intentions nor the required capacities to constitute the *mens rea* required by the law for successful criminal prosecution.[6] Vicarious liability or guilt by association in these instances is hardly likely to satisfy the demands of justice. Frankly, very few of these cases are really reducible to matters of individual negligence, let alone intentional recklessness.[7] Most of the existing penal options, such as license or charter revocation, are usually ineffective. Furthermore, fines and forced closings tend to hurt those who are the least closely associated with the relevant corporate decisionmaking: stockholders and low-level employees.

Stockholders, however, need not be of much concern to us. They are protected by SEC regulations and if they suffer from corporate punishment, that is a risk they undertook when entering the market. Often stockholders benefit for a period of time from the undetected crime. I see no reason why they ought not bear some of the burden of its retribution. The stockholders, after all, are free to trade their holdings in the market and never were assured of a clear profit. Also, the stockholders might consider pressing a civil suit against the corporation that cost them a significant value in stock because of its criminal behavior. A class-action suit by stockholders who claim damage under such conditions could even have a second-level retributive result. If the corporation were forced to pay stockholders for losses resulting from corporate crime, some deterrent aims of punishment might also be accomplished.

It is likely, as we know, that corporations will try to recover heavy fines in the form of higher prices. The limit to that kind of practice, thankfully, is set by the marketplace. The only exceptions would be in public utilities or in other monopoly or semimonopolistic enterprises where consumers must deal with the criminal corporation or forego the service. Such corporations are generally regulated by government agencies, and pricing increases to offset penalties could be prevented if those agencies act in the best interests of the community at large.

It should be mentioned with respect to the harming of innocent employees that when a human being is convicted of a felony and punished, his or her family and dependents are frequently cast into dire financial straits. The harm done to them, though they may be totally innocent of any complicity in the crime, may, in fact, far outweigh that done to the incarcerated felon. After all, the convicted criminal receives three meals a day and lodging. His or her family may be reduced to penury and find that meals are only a sometime thing, and then hardly nutritious. In many jurisdictions, little or no official interest is paid to these innocent sufferers. Why should we be concerned with the employees who work for offending corporations?[8]

These problems, then, are not major, but the fining of corporations is just not perceived in the corporate world as punishment comparable to incarceration of the human felon. Because of that fact, many believe that, at least as a practical matter, and regardless of whether punishment is morally justified, corporations should not even be subject to the criminal law.[9] Such a view, however, can lead to a number of socially unacceptable outcomes, perhaps the worst of which is that many offenses will go unpunished because the offense is of a peculiarly corporate nature. An important form of social control of the most powerful institutions in our community will then be relinquished to the reasonable demands of our canons of individual criminal justice. Do we then have no viable theoretical and practical options?

I propose to commend an alternative type of punishment, though I must stress that in isolation from other available sanctions, such as fines and probation orders, the punishment I have in mind will not likely have the full reformative or deterrent effects a concerned citizenry would desire. In some cases it will best be used only to augment other sentences, though in many cases it may be sufficient punishment and have all of the generally desired retributive, and even deterrent, effects.

The moral psychology of our criminal legal system is guilt-based,[10] and guilt is an economic notion. Guilt historically has been viewed as a form of debt, either or both to the specific victim harmed or to the society as a whole. Crime unbalances the books. To expiate guilt, the guilty party must repay, compensate, or restore — hence the fine system and the wergeld practices. Punishment is an institutional vehicle of repayment and restoration. When the debt is retired the original *status quo* is restored. This idea has deep roots. The Latin *debitum* in the Lord's Prayer was rendered in Old English as *gylt*, and, of course, there is that popular expression, "paying one's debt to society."

Guilt is a threshold notion and so depends upon a sense of boundaries and limits, usually as set by rules or laws. Guilt is centrally a transgression, a trespass. Either the defendant is guilty as charged or not guilty. Guilt is a minimum maintenance notion. In short, guilt avoidance involves meeting only basic standards of behavior. As should be expected, guilt-based moralities are statute-dominated. To feel guilty is to feel one has done something that is forbidden or restricted. For the more sophisticated, it may also be to realize or believe that one has done something that falls beneath the minimal behavior requirements of the society.

In contrast to cultures having a guilt-based morality, certain cultures, and in part our own, place primary emphasis on the personal worth and image of the members of society. In such moralities the central notion is shame rather than guilt.[11] Shame, in fact, may be a more primitive moral notion than guilt. There are no natural expressions of guilt as there surely are for shame, for example, blushing. We do say, of course, that someone "looks guilty," meaning that he or she is displaying certain kinds of behavior—for example, shifty eyes and nervousness—but nothing so directly relates to guilt as blushing, hanging one's head, or covering one's face to communicate one's sense of shame.

In a shame-based morality, evaluation of behavior is not primarily made against rules or laws that have established minimal constraints. Moral and personal worth is usually measured against role or identity models. To have shame or to be shameful a person must regard his or her behavior as being below or short of what is expected of or associated with the role, station, or type with which he or she identifies himself or herself. The feeling of shame is the feeling of inadequacy or inferiority.

Shame involves a subjective feeling of self-reference. Experiences of shame are experiences of exposure, characterized by a sense of loss of the identity one thought one had. A crucial element in a shame-based morality is a stress on the individual's self-conception as measured against ideal models that are accepted by the person as appropriate to that individual's way of life. Shame, then, has both a private and a public aspect. (In fact, the Greeks and the French have two words for these two sides of shame.)

Shame is a visual concept. Its root meaning is to cover one's face or hide. It relates to the way one looks to oneself and to the way one thinks one looks to others. If you are ashamed, you want to cover yourself. You do not want to be seen.

Interestingly, the language indicates that being without shame, being shameless, is not a respectable thing, though being guiltless is. The most dangerous persons are the brazen incorrigibles who in Zephaniah's words "knoweth no shame."[12] To be unaffectable by shame is to be antisocial and, worse than that, to have no concern for self-image. Shame operates in the field of honor and self-respect rather than being associated with following legal and social rules. Shame is also described as the experience of having shattered a trust or of having been implicated in a shattering of trust. Self-respect, honor, personal worth, and trust provide the conceptual structure of a shame-based moral constraint system. They are also central notions of free-enterprise business.

An adept penal system would be one that could induce shame when there has been a notable incongruity with appropriate models, when trust has been shattered, and that could utilize the visual and media capabilities of the society to heighten and focus the awareness in the offender, as well as the community at large, of serious shameful behavior.

But why is shame so valuable a moral emotion in a criminal context? The answer uncovers the penal virtues of shame over guilt. Shame cannot be purged by mere repayment. Shame is not translatable to debt, and wergeld in no way relieves shame. Paying a fine cannot restore the *status quo* disrupted by shameful actions. It cannot reestablish worth or trust. Regaining worth, reclaiming identity, is not a question of purchase. The shameful person must act in positive, creative, possibly even heroic ways so that he or she may again see himself or herself and be seen as worthy. The greater the shame the more extraordinary and prolonged must be the behavior that reestablishes worth. Confession relates to guilt. Guilty-feeling persons seem almost compelled to communicate. Shameful people have no desire to talk of their shame and confession does not dent the shame. Notice the difference between condemnation and contempt.

The society condemns the guilty, but it holds the shameful in contempt; it derogates the social status of the shameful person, whereas only a price is extracted from the guilty. There is also something very spontaneous about the social reaction to the shameful person, who is abandoned, exiled, or cast out. The response to the guilty is not extemporaneous. Punishment is contrived as an instrument of restoration through which, by suffering, the guilty's relationship to the rest of society is repaired.

Our current penal system only incidentally, accidentally, induces shame in offenders. There is, however, a sanction that specifically derives its force from the concept of shame, that could be purposefully utilized in this country (as it once was), and that could have especially sanguine effects in corporate criminal cases. For obvious reasons, I shall call it the Hester Prynne Sanction. Recall *The Scarlet Letter?*[13]

> "The penalty thereof is death. But in their great mercy and tenderness of heart, they have doomed Mistress Prynne to stand only a space of three hours on the platform of the pillory, and then and thereafter, for the remainder of her natural life, to wear a mark of shame upon her bosom."
> "A wise sentence!" remarked the stranger gravely bowing his head. "Thus she will be a living sermon against sin."[14]

The Hester Prynne sanction, it should be noticed, is not directly a monetary penalty. Adverse publicity could contribute to the achievement of monetary retributive effects by costing the corporation business. That is not, however, the reason for utilizing the sanction. Primarily, the Hester Prynne Sanction threatens prestige, image, and social standing. It really works only when the offender comes to regard himself or herself as having acted disgracefully, as having broken a trust, or as having failed to measure up to personal and social standards. The offender should come to view the sanction as a legitimate damaging blot on his or her reputation; as a mark of a shortcoming; as an indicator of the disgust of others; as a signal that identity must be rebuilt.

The Hester Prynne Sanction is particularly suited to corporate offenders because image, reputation, and social acceptance are at the very heart of modern corporate life.[15] Little sustained success has ever been enjoyed by a company with a bad reputation. Official censure is not an inconsequential matter where corporate achievement depends on communal standing. In fact, the Hester Prynne Sanction could prove far more effective in dealing with corporate offenders than with human criminals. For a corporation to survive, it simply must garner and nurture a good image among the constituents of its marketplace. Furthermore, writing corporate punishments in terms of adverse-publicity orders is more likely to minimize the kinds of unwanted externalities that plague the monetary sanctions now used by the courts against corporate offenders.[16] It is noteworthy that the U.S. National Commission on reform of Federal Criminal Laws in its 1970 draft report supported the use of a tactic that sounds remarkably like the punishment of Hester Prynne:

> When an organization is convicted of an offense, the court may in addition or in lieu of imposing other authorized sanctions, . . . require the organization to give appropriate publicity to the conviction . . . by advertising in designated areas or in designated media. . . .

Sadly, the Commission's *Final Report*[18] lacked this recommendation because of strong corporate lobbying. My argument is directed toward a revival of the basic idea.

Despite the almost universal corporate aversion to a tarnished image, it should be pointed out, "bad press" is hardly penal and can be countered by corporate media campaigns intended "to put a different face on the matter." Quite simply, if the Hester Prynne Sanction is to be retributively penal, the convicted corporation must regard the adverse publicity as not only noxious, but a *justified* communal revelation of the corporation's disgrace, its shameful actions.

A shame-based sanction functions, as previously noted, only in relation to some sort of model identity against which the offender judges himself and expects to be judged by the institutions of social order and justice. Where do we find such models for corporations? *The Scarlet Letter* provides only the structural or formal aspects of the matter. Hester was judged unworthy against a model of human fidelity that was deeply embedded in the puritanical society of early Boston. That model was understood and internalized throughout her community. It was not a *product* of law, though surely many of the old Bostonian laws were derived from the same set of conceptions that engendered the model.

Throughout the centuries we have articulated human ideal models,[19] though we seem less intent on this enterprise in recent decades. These models are a part of our history, legend, education, religion, and literature. There surely are corporate ideal models in our culture as well, though they are of a more recent origin. The content of such models need not here be specified, though we should expect to find such features as profitability, social responsiveness, industriousness, and humaneness in them. In fact, we may now have better pictures of these corporate ideal models than we have for ordinary human beings. In short, we seem to have a number of generally shared basic ideas about what a socially responsible corporation ought to look and act like and, by and large, most corporations embrace these ideals, at least in their documents, codes of employee conduct, and public relations releases. The particulars of our corporate model especially seem to take shape in the forefront of our thinking when we witness things that have gone corporately wrong, as, for example, in the recent disaster in Bhopal, India.

The courts have the authority and the social credibility to force corporations to confront their failures, to live up to the community expectations engendered by their roles and public images. Court-ordered adverse publicity could provide an official revelatory apparatus, the modern substitute for the pillory, where the corporate offender stands contemptible before its community, forced to confront the fact of its inadequacy. Shame is, after all, an identity crisis.

The exciting aspect of the Hester Prynne Sanction, however, is that the suffering of adverse publicity does not restore the offender's social status. It does not relieve the shame. Only positive corrective acts can do that. But look where this gets us: the imposition of the Hester Prynne Sanction on a corporation broadcasts a corporate offender's behavior, thus arousing (I) appropriate social contempt, (2) a recognition of a failure to measure up, and (3) the kind of adjustments to operating procedures, policies, and practices that are required for the corporate offender to regain moral worth in both its own eyes and those of the community. Rehabilitation is thereby served by retribution.

It will surely be noted that the Hester Prynne Sanction, as I have described its potential use in corporate criminal cases, has clear affinities to sanctions that are already commonly used in professional organizations. Most professional societies, in fact, use censure and publicity as their primary penalty against members or associated institutions that violate their codes of professional ethics. The American Society of Civil Engineers, for example, imposes such a penalty and may also require censured members to discuss their offenses in professional public meetings.[20] For years the AAUP has used a censure list devised to shame institutions that have violated academic freedom. The major difference between the Hester Prynne Sanction and these censure techniques is that it is a court-ordered and supervised sanction. It relates to the whole community rather than to a professional body and it is imposed for criminal offenses and not just violations of professional codes.

The Hester Prynne Sanction might have significant retributive and deterrent effects on corporate offenders, but as a primary penal device some legal theorists have thought it prone to fail for a number of practical reasons.

In the first place, as we all know, government is a rather poor propagandist.[21] It is not very persuasive, and very rarely is it pithy. (Have you ever seen a catchy piece of government-written prose that could rival the output of Madison Avenue?) For the adverse-publicity sanction to have the desired effects, for it to have a genuine impact on an offending corporation's established image, the courts will have to employ clever writers and publicists, not the run-of-the-mill bureaucratic scribblers who crank out the government's literature.

Such a concern can be easily addressed. Courts have the power to write their orders in such a way that the cost of the adverse publicity is paid by the criminal corporation from its own advertising budget to a competitive agency (other than ones that carry its accounts), which will then manage a campaign as approved by an officer of the court (perhaps a college professor trained in advertising and marketing). The corporation will have to submit its previous year's advertising budget to be used as a starting line, a percentage of the advertising budget will be set aside for the adverse-publicity campaign, and that percentage will be carried through all annual budgets until the expiration of the order. In this way, even if the corporation increases its advertising budget to attempt to entice sales, it will have to pay a higher adverse-publicity cost. The court-appointed overseer will instruct the agency to expend all funds in the adverse-publicity budget annually and to do so in outlets roughly equivalent to those used by the usual corporate advertising agencies. For example, the agency will not be allowed to place adverse publicity in obscure small-town newspapers if the corporation does not generally advertise in such ways. The private sector would then be actively engaged in the penal process and a whole new and respectable area of advertising will provide jobs and new paths of expression for the creative imagination to wander.

A frequently voiced second concern is that the level of anticorporate "noise" in our society is so great as to devalue the effect of specific adverse-publicity orders.[22] The newspaper editorialists, the campaigning politicians, the special interest groups, the conservationists, the Naderites, the assorted movie and TV actors and actresses with various causes all contribute to a confusing cacophony of charges that are usually indirect, unsubstantiated, and certainly not properly adjudicated. Can this noise be controlled? Probably not, and it is not a good idea to pursue such a line in a free country. Against this noise, however, a well-developed adverse-publicity campaign, identified clearly as court-ordered, is still likely to draw special attention. The public may never be very discriminating, but generally the fact that a court has ordered a certain publicity campaign as punishment for a particular criminal offense should pierce the shield of apathy behind which the public hides from the onslaught of ordinary corporate criticism.

It will be suggested that corporations can dilute the Hester Prynne Sanction through counterpublicity.[23] There is no denying the power of Madison Avenue agencies to create clever and effective image building, even in the face of severe public or government criticism. But the sanction can be written in such a way, as suggested above, to offset any corporate counterattack. Furthermore, the court has the power to order the corporation not to engage in any advertising directed specifically toward rebutting or diluting the sentence. If the corporation were to promote its own case after having lost in court and received an adverse-publicity sentence, it would be in contempt of the court and sterner measures would be justified. Oil companies like Mobil, it might be remembered, mounted effective replies to the media charges leveled against them during the energy crisis. Also, corporations after *Central Hudson Gas & Electric Corp.* v. *Public Service Commission* [447 U.S. 557 (1980)] clearly have First Amendment rights to express opinions on matters of public concern.[24] Corporate rebuttals to adverse-publicity orders, however, would not be protected by *Central Hudson*, and the Mobil commercials were certainly not attempts to minimize the effectiveness of any court orders. The oil companies had been charged only in the field of public opinion and their response was a totally appropriate defense in that venue.

The Hester Prynne Sanction may prove efficacious in fraud, public safety, and felony cases, but some doubt it can be equally effective in regulatory cases. Gulf Oil, for example, was convicted of illegal campaign contributions in connection with the Watergate scandals.[25] The publicity was profuse, but there is little evidence that it hurt Gulf Oil sales. Two responses seem appropriate. The first is to point out that in the regulatory cases adverse publicity occurred in the ordinary media coverage of the events. It was not court-ordered in lieu of or in addition to some other penal sanction, such as a stiff fine. In effect, it was incidental and as the story faded from the front page or the first fifteen minutes of the telecast, its intensity diminished. But, it just may be the case that the Hester Prynne Sanction does not produce significant desired effects in the case of certain crimes. I make no claim that adverse-publicity orders will always suffice to achieve the retributive ends of the legal system. A mix of sanctions will undoubtedly be required. I would argue that adverse-publicity orders are more likely than most other sanctions to produce what might be called "rehabilitative outcomes," reformed corporations. Fines certainly are too easily assimilated to business costs.

The Hester Prynne Sanction, however, may produce some of the same externalities as fines.[26] After all, if it is really effective, some say that it should lead to decreased sales and the corporation's employees at the lowest levels could be made to suffer layoffs and other unwanted effects.[27] This should not overly concern us. Such externalities plague penal sanctions of all kinds. More to the point, however, the true question is whether the Hester Prynne Sanction is justifiable over the simple assessment of a fine when both produce basically equivalent externalities. I think that I have offered some firm reasons for the court to prefer, at least with regard to certain crimes, the Hester Prynne Sanction rather than or in addition to fines. It is worth briefly noting that in a recent study of seventeen major corporations that have suffered adverse publicity over an offense or serious incident (though such publicity was not court-ordered) executives at the middle and higher levels of management reported that loss of corporate prestige was regarded as a very major corporate concern.[28] Indeed, the loss of prestige was regarded as far more serious than the payment of a stiff fine. The payment of the fine and the suffering of court-ordered and supervised adverse publicity are simply not equivalent punishments.

The Hester Prynne Sanction is also, for moral reasons, to be preferred over community-service orders. The celebrated case of *United States* v. *Allied Chemical Company* [(1976) 7 Env. Rep. (BNA) 29; File CR-76-0129-R (U.S. Dist. Ct., Eastern Div. of Va., Richmond Div. 1976)], in which Allied Chemical was fined $13.24 million after a no-contest plea to 940 counts of pollution of the James River and other Virginia waterways, is often cited as an example of creative sentencing leading to the development of an alternative to the traditional sanctions.[29] The Allied Chemical fine was reduced to $5 million when the company agreed to give $8,356,202 to the Virginia Environmental Endowment. Strictly speaking, the court did not order community service, but it did accept the company's establishment of the endowment as mitigatory. In another case, *United States* v. *Olin Mathieson* [Criminal No. 78-30 (U.S. Dist. Ct., Dist. of Conn. June 1, 1978)], the company pleaded no contest to the charge of conspiracy involving the shipment of rifles to South Africa. The judge imposed a $45,000 fine after Olin Mathieson agreed to set up a $500,000 New Haven Community Betterment Fund. (The maximum penalty could have been $510,000.)

Although neither of these cases really involved the imposition of a community-service sanction (the defendants essentially wrote a check), some legal theorists have recently argued that the lessons learned in them indicate the desirability of providing the court with such a sentencing option.[30] There are certain practical problems with this approach that warrant only brief mention. Perhaps the most serious is that the corporation's costs in buying or performing community service are tax-deductible charity contributions and standard court-imposed fines are, of course, nondeductible. However, legislation could correct this deficiency.

It must also be realized that the performance of community service is a positive, image-enhancing action. It can be expected to elevate the public's opinion of the criminal corporation. In fact, the results of corporate community-service projects and charitable contributions are likely to make a rather favorable impression on the members of society, while the reasons the donor corporation embarked on its apparently altruistic ventures are likely to be forgotten or lost in the outpouring of grateful sentiment. There is, however, an obvious corrective for this difficulty: to invoke the Hester Prynne Sanction in conjunction with community-service sentencing. Simply, the court can require that the service project be clearly identified as court-ordered as a penalty for a specific criminal offense. Every association drawn by the corporation to its beneficence would have to include an adverse-publicity reference to its criminal conviction as the reason for the service. Although community service does not seem to stand on a par with the Hester Prynne Sanction and the traditional sentencing options, should it be encouraged? I think there are reasons that its use should be very restricted and that it should never be used in isolation from more penal sanctions.

The socially conciliatory aspect of community service, the fact that such endeavors can restore lost prestige and polish tarnished images, makes such civic contributions a major avenue for corporations to regain status and acceptance lost through conviction and broadcast in accord with the imposition of a Hester Prynne sentence. A shamed company, as earlier noted, cannot simply buy its way back to social grace. It needs to perform especially worthy deeds to achieve restoration. Community service is certainly of the type of actions it needs to perform to achieve such ends. But for there to be worth in the doing of such deeds, they must be voluntary. If they are performed under a form of duress, they are not actions of the person compelled to perform them. Insofar as none of our principles of responsibility capture them for that person, they do not accrue to the moral credit of that person. They would seem to be extended acts of the judge who decided to whom and how much. The convicted corporation is little more than an instrument of the court's conception of social need. A recent Nebraska sentence is a case in point. A corporation convicted of bid rigging in highway construction contracts was ordered to donate $1.4 million to establish a permanent professional chair in business ethics at the state university.[31]

The community-service sanction, when conjoined to the Hester Prynne Sanction (ideally) or to a fine, can, however, have a certain morally desirable outcome, beside the fact that some good was done (the service was performed or the donation to a worthy cause was made) and regardless of the reasons for its performance. Forced charitable deeds might serve to inculcate a habit of social concern in the corporation. At the very least, the sentenced corporation might come to view a continuation of community involvement as a way of currying future judicial favor. Aristotle maintained that a person is good by doing good deeds, by getting into the habit of doing such things.[32] A community-service sentence could start a corporation on the path to virtue. Hence, there may be a rehabilitative value in the sanction despite the involuntary nature of the service performed by the convicted company.

There is, however a notable amount of uncertainty that such an outcome will ensue from this type of sentencing. It does not seem likely enough to be a justifying reason for use of the sanction. In fact, the best reason for a judge to order community service would be to achieve the charitable ends themselves. The rehabilitation of the offending corporation would seem to be an incidental upshot. Judges, however, are not necessarily in the best position to decide on our social or charitable needs. Furthermore, other than monetary or time loss, the penalty relationship of the sentence to the crime may be remote.

All of these factors militate against the use of community-service orders in corporate criminal cases, unless they are augmented by stiff fines and/or the Hester Prynne Sanction. In comparison with the other discussed sanctions, adverse publicity, with its primary shaming function, would seem to be preferable on both practical and moral grounds. In any event, it is clear that there are effective and morally justifiable sentencing options (though community service is the least preferable) that support the inclusion of corporate entities among those persons who are subject to the criminal law. Baron Thurlow's demurral on the notion of corporate criminal liability may be set aside. Corporations are not only intentional agents, moral persons, they are proper subjects of the criminal law and all its fury. They can be stigmatized and they can be "kicked" in ways comparable to those visited on human offenders.

Notes

1. *The Oxford Dictionary of Quotations*, 2d ed. (Oxford: Oxford University Press, 1966), p. 547.

2. See, generally, Marshall B. Clinard and Peter C. Yeager, *Corporate Crime* (New York: Free Press, 1980).

3. See, e.g., Brent Fisse and John Braithwaite, *The Impact of Publicity on Corporate Offenders* (Albany, NY: State University of New York Press, 1983), chaps. 2 – 18, p. 317.

4. See, e.g., J. Murphy, *Retribution, Justice, and Therapy* (Boston: D. Reidel, 1979); R. Singer, *Just Deserts: Sentencing Based on Equality and Desert* (Cambridge, MA: Ballinger, 1979); A. Von Hirsch, *Doing Justice: The Choice of Punishments* (New York: Hill and Wang, 1976). But see John Braithwaite, "Challenging Just Deserts: Punishing White-Collar Criminals," *Journal of Criminal Law and Criminology* 73 (1982): 723 – 763.

5. See, generally, Victoria Lynn Swigert and Ronald A. Farrell, "Corporate Homicide: Definitional Processes in the Creation of Deviance," *Law & Society Review* 15 (1980): 161 – 182; Brent Fisse, "Reconstructing Corporate Criminal Law: Deterrence, Retribution, Fault, and Sanctions," *Southern California Law Review* 56 (1983): 1141 – 1246.

6. See, further, Peter A. French, *Collective and Corporate Responsibility* (New York: Columbia University Press, 1984), chap. II.

7. See, e.g., Fisse and Braithwaite, *The Impact of Publicity on Corporate Offenders*, p. 303.

8. See, generally, John C. Coffee, Jr., " 'No Soul to Damn: No Body to Kick': An Unscandalized Inquiry into the Problem of Corporate Punishment," *Michigan Law Review* 79 (1981): 386 – 459, pp. 401 – 402.

9. See, e.g., Gerhard Mueller, "*Mens Rea* and the Corporation," *University of Pittsburgh Law Review* 19 (1957): 21 – 50.

10. See, generally, Walter Kaufmann, *Without Guilt and Justice* (New York: Delta, 1973).

11. See, further, Peter A. French, "It's a Damn Shame," unpublished manuscript (1984). For a psychodynamic analysis of shame, see Helen M. Lynd, *On Shame and the Search for Identity* (London: Routledge & Kegan Paul, 1958).

12. Zephaniah 3:5.

13. Nathaniel Hawthorne, *The Scarlet Letter* (1850; New York: Pocket Books, 1954).

14. Ibid., p. 63.

15. See, e.g., Wally Olins, *The Corporate Personality: An Inquiry into the Nature of Corporate Identity* (New York: Mayflower Books, 1981); Charles Channon, "Corporations and the Politics of Perception," *Advertising Quarterly* 60, 2 (1981): 12 – 15; Nancy Yashihara, "$1 Billion Spent on Identity: Companies Push Image of Selves, Not Products," *Los Angeles Times*, 10 May 1981, pt. 6, pp. 1, 17.

16. See Fisse and Braithwaite, *The Impact of Publicity on Corporate Offenders*, pp. 308 – 309.

17. U.S. National Commission on Reform of Federal Criminal Laws, *Study Draft* (Washington, DC: U.S. Government Printing Office, 1970), #405.

18. U.S. National Commission on Reform of Federal Criminal Laws, *Final Report* (Washington, DC: U.S. Government Printing Office, 1971), #3007.

19. See, generally, Kaufmann, *Without Guilt and Justice*; Fred L Polak, *The Image of the Future: Enlightening the Past, Orienting the Present, Forecasting the Future* 1 and 2 (New York: Oceana Publications, 1961).

20. See Stephen H. Unger, *Controlling Technology* (New York: Holt, Rinehart, and Winston, 1982).

21. See, further, Coffee, ' "No Soul to Damn,' " pp. 425 – 426; Fisse and Braithwaite, *The Impact of Publicity on Corporate Offenders*, pp. 291 – 292.

22. Coffee, " 'No Soul to Damn,' " p. 426. See, further, Fisse and Braithwaite, *The Impact of Publicity on Corporate Offenders*, pp. 294 – 295.

23. See, further, Coffee, " 'No Soul to Damn,' " p. 426; Fisse and Braithwaite, *The Impact of Publicity on Corporate Offenders*, pp. 295–298.

24. See, generally, Herbert Schmertz, *Corporations and the First Amendment* (New York: Amacom, 1978); William Patton and Randall Bartlett, "Corporate 'Persons' and Freedom of Speech: The Political Impact of Legal Mythology," *Wisconsin Law Review* 1981: 494–512.

25. See John J. McCloy, *The Great Oil Spill* (New York: Chelsea House, 1976).

26. Coffee, " 'No Soul to Damn,' " pp. 427–428.

27. But see Fisse and Braithwaite, *The Impact of Publicity on Corporate Offenders*, pp. 306–309.

28. Ibid., chap. 19.

29. See, further, Brent Fisse, "Community Service as a Sanction against Corporations," *Wisconsin Law Review* 1981: 970–1017.

30. Fisse, "Community Service as a Sanction against Corporations."

31. *New York Times*, July 29, 1983, p. 1.

32. Aristotle, *Nicomachean Ethics*, trans. M. Ostwald (Indianapolis: Bobbs-Merrill, 1962), p. 33.

J. Angelo Corlett

FRENCH ON CORPORATE PUNISHMENT: SOME PROBLEMS

In *Corporate and Collective Responsibility* (New York: Columbia University Press, 1984), Peter A. French argues that corporations as well as corporate-individuals can and should be held morally responsible for untoward events of which they are intentional agents. Moreover, he argues, guilty corporations can and ought to be punished for their wrongdoings. The purpose of this paper is to examine his theory of corporate punishment, and to show why it is problematic. One assumption I shall make is that corporations can be guilty of and responsible for wrongdoing.

The punishment of corporations, which I shall refer to as corporate punishment, is a primary stumblingblock to French's collective and corporate responsibility theory. Retribution, he states, need not always be made in kind. The reason why this is so is because the corporation has no eye to exchange for an eye that it might have destroyed. Straightaway, then, there is a difficulty in effectively and sufficiently punishing a corporation which is responsible and guilty for causing an untoward event (French, p. 188).

Take the recent Union Carbide toxic chemical leakage in Bhopal, India, where Union Carbide is responsible (I shall assume) for approximately two thousand deaths and several more short and long-term illnesses of Indian people. The question here is how to administer punishment to Union Carbide so that both parties are treated justly. Thus a main question regarding the punishment of guilty corporations is how to effectively and sufficiently deal with corporations that are found guilty of untoward events.

From *Journal of Business Ethics*, 7 (1988), 205–210. ©1988 by D. Reidel Publishing Company. Reprinted by permission of Kluwer Academic Publishers.

I am grateful to Burleigh T. Wilkins, Philosophy Department, University of California, Santa Barbara, and B. Celeste Corlett, Psychology Department, University of California, Santa Barbara, for their comments on earlier drafts of this paper.

French explores some proposed methods of corporate punishment and notes why these are problematic. First, he argues that fining a guilty corporation is inadequate because the cost of the fines can be easily absorbed by raising consumer prices. Second, French argues that the revocation of a guilty corporation's charter or license to operate in a given locale is problematic for at least two reasons: (a) The corporation might be able to reconstruct itself under a new charter, management and a new name in that locale or elsewhere in order to resume corporate activities; (b) Innocent employees of the corporation are likely to be adversely affected economically by a charter revocation (French, p. 188). Insofar as the Bhopal incident is concerned, fining Union Carbide or revoking its charter are inadequate penalties for its wrongdoing. For both such punishments are likely to be passed on to the consumer in the form of higher prices for Union Carbide products. What, then, can be done to effectively and sufficiently punish corporations that are found guilty of untoward events?

As a remedy for this puzzle of corporate punishment French suggests what he calls the "Hester Prynne Sanction." The Hester Prynne Sanction consists largely of an institutionalized psychological punishment administered to the corporation that is found guilty of wrongdoing. It takes the form of a court ordered adverse publication of the corporation the cost of which is paid by the guilty corporation. The aim of the sanction is to create a psychological disposition of shame within the corporation for that of which it is guilty. French thinks that such shame, when the guilt of the corporation is made public, is most fatal to any corporation because public shame damages a corporation's prestige. According to higher-level management, a corporation's loss of prestige is the worst thing that can happen to it (French, p. 200).

There are, however, a number of difficulties which plague the utilization of the Hester Prynne Sanction against guilty corporations. First, the loss of prestige of a corporation may contribute to the financial failure of that corporation. In turn, this will adversely affect the economic condition of that corporation's work force, causing undue immiseration to its workers. (Here I assume that the work force does not play a primary role in that which makes the corporation guilty of wrongdoing.)

To this criticism French replies that the adverse economic affects that the Hester Prynne Sanction might have on a guilty corporation's work force "should not overly concern us" (French, p. 200). But this *is* a concern unless and until French can provide a successful argument which shows that it ought to be of no concern. Such an argument would at least have to consist in his showing that there is a genuine and significant causal connection between the untoward event and the work force of the corporation that is found guilty of that untoward event. If this is not shown, and if the Hester Prynne Sanction is imposed on a corporation the work force of which is not causally related to an untoward event in question, then the work force is punished unfairly. French himself uses this criticism against the suggestion of charter revocations and fines for corporations that are found guilty of wrongdoing. But he fails to see that this criticism also applies to his suggestion that the adverse economic affects the Hester Prynne Sanction might have on a corporation's work force ought not to overly concern one.

A second problem with the use of the sanction against guilty corporations is that the corporation might escape such financial loss and the immiseration of its workers by passing on the cost of the sanction to consumers in the form of higher prices. French uses this as an argument against the suggestion of fining corporations that are found guilty of wrongdoing. However, he does not see that the adverse effects of the Hester Prynne Sanction may be evaded by a corporation in the same manner. If a corporation is punished by means of French's sanction, then it may raise the prices of its products to the consumers in order to make up for the loss of profit due to the adverse publicity brought on by the sanction. On French's view, there is nothing which ensures against this possibility.

A third problem with the use of the Hester Prynne Sanction against guilty corporations is that the guilty corporation can simply, if it knows that it is economically advantageous for it to do so, recharter itself under another name, management, etc, in order to avoid the shame occasioned by the sanction. That is, the corporation can simply file bankruptcy and reorganize itself in such a way that one would not recognize the new corporation as being (for the most part) the same as the previous corporation, rather than suffer the embarrassment and costliness of the sanction. There are at least two ways that a corporation might recharter itself. First, it can recharter itself under a new name while continuing to do business in the same industry. Second, it can recharter itself under a new name while taking up business in another industry. An example of the first sort of reorganization would be an oil company simply changing its name in order to avoid the social stigma attached to it by the Hester Prynne Sanction. An example of the second sort would be that oil company's rechartering and entering into a different field of business altogether, say, computer technology. In this latter case, a corporation could escape the adverse affects of the sanction by making itself unrecognizable to both the media (which is said to be the primary tool used by the court to execute the Hester Prynne Sanction) and to the public. On French's view, there seems to be nothing stopping a guilty corporation from evading the affects of the sanction in this manner. Moreover, French argues against the revocation of charters for guilty corporations on the ground that innocent people related to the corporation are negatively affected. But he fails to realize that this argument also applies to the Hester Prynne Sanction. French provides no reason why a corporation found guilty of wrongdoing could not recharter itself in order to avoid the humiliation of the sanction. Again, French's arguments are turned against him.

A fourth weakness of the Hester Prynne Sanction against guilty corporations is that it depends too much on the reliability of the media to effectively carry out the sanction insofar as publicity is concerned. This is especially true if the corporation in question has significant ties with the media. Under such conditions the media might be prone to tone down its coverage of the corporation in question out of either a loyalty to the guilty corporation or out of a fear that the sanction might spell the demise of that corporation upon which the media is itself financially dependent. Thus any damage to the reputation of the guilty corporation by the sanction might also lead to the demise of the media itself because of its significant economic ties to the guilty corporation. On French's view, there seems to be no doubt about the media's motives or ability to carry out the Hester Prynne Sanction effectively.

A fifth puzzle with the use of the Hester Prynne Sanction against guilty corporations is that its scope is limited. It may indeed work in a situation where a corporation is found guilty of systematically abusing its workers, or where a corporation is found guilty of producing and selling, say, automobiles which malfunction slightly. In these cases the sanction might serve well as a deterrent to the continuation of such unacceptable business procedures. However, the sanction is unable to effectively and sufficiently punish corporations that are found guilty of gross forms of negligence. For example, the effect of the Hester Prynne Sanction on Union Carbide for the Bhopal incident would in no way do justice to the immensity of Union Carbide's responsibility to the families of those who were killed and severely injured by the toxic chemical leakage. The public shame of Union Carbide is at best only a necessary punishment. It is not a sufficient punishment for the incident of which Union Carbide is responsible. Neither the short nor long-term effects of the Hester Prynne Sanction on Union Carbide could begin to render a just punishment for the fatal occurrence at Bhopal.

Furthermore, even if it is a statistical fact that, generally speaking, corporate management thinks that the loss of prestige resulting from the Hester Prynne Sanction (or something akin to it) is the most devastating punishment that a corporation guilty of wrongdoing can receive, this is irrelevant. In the case of Union Carbide it is certainly in the corporation's best interest to be publically shamed because justice actually requires that somehow the corporation ought to recompense for the deaths and illnesses of thousands of Indian people. In such a case Union Carbide would obviously accept public shame over a much more severe punishment, say, the death penalty or long-term imprisonment with no chance of parole for certain constituents of the corporation who are the primary responsible agents of the Bhopal incident. So it is simply a mistake to punish corporations according to a standard with which they agree or find acceptable. The very fact that the management of such corporations considers the publicity of guilty corporations and the shame that ensues to be an acceptable punishment might serve to destroy or severely limit the deterrent force of the Hester Prynne Sanction. Punishing guilty corporations according to a standard which their membership accepts is akin to punishing a criminal according to what that criminal finds to be an acceptable punishment! The Hester Prynne Sanction is only useful in cases of minor corporate offences; it is an ineffective and insufficient punishment for instances of more significant corporate wrongdoing.

To this French might reply that the implementation of more stringent penalties on corporations that are found guilty of gross forms of wrongdoing would tend to render such corporations impotent in the marketplace of trade and competition. Moreover, it might stifle business and technological growth altogether if corporations are to be severely punished for the unfortunate results of what are otherwise quite "natural" business practices. To this reply I simply answer that justice cannot be tailored to the methods of business or technological manifest destiny. This is the sort of morality that leads to corporate wrongdoing in the first place. Rather, corporations must themselves act according to the dictates of what justice requires in given circumstances. The circumstances of justice must determine the practices of corporations, not vice versa.

French states that the Hester Prynne Sanction might be more effective as a punishment for corporate wrongdoing if it is coupled with a planned and enforced community service project the cost of which is covered by the guilty corporation (French, pp. 200–201). An example of this might be punishing an oil company guilty of environmental pollution by having it pay for high-level research in ecological and environmental preservation.

But there are puzzles with French's suggestion. One is that the financial status of such research is directly dependent on the financial stability of the funding corporation. But if the corporation is adversely affected by the sanction, then it might fall on economic hard times, threatening the operation of the environmental research. Moreover, since the corporation funds the research, it can in some way influence and hence bias the reports coming out of the research so that such reports do not further complicate the adverse conditions of the corporation or industry. For example, the corporation might strongly suggest or even dictate that the research be done in areas of environmental studies which reflect a positive outlook toward the corporation rather than a negative one. Even if this is not the case, the researchers might come to the realization that their wages can be threatened if they produce and publicize any environmentally negative studies related to the guilty corporation. And if the public considers these studies, the stock of that corporation could drop to a drastic level, not to mention the fact that the public could boycott the purchase of that corporation's manufactured products enough to force it into dire financial conditions, leaving its research institute and its employees without funding. A further problem with French's position on this matter of a guilty corporation's being punished by having to fund research projects is that such a penalty in no way serves as a recompense for gross forms of corporate wrongdoing. For example, forcing Union Carbide to fund, say, chemical engineering research in no way amounts to a fair punishment for its responsibility and guilt regarding the Bhopal incident. Even if such research is not problematic in the ways I describe, and even if such a punishment is coupled with the Hester Prynne Sanction, a punishment much more severe is needed to effectively and sufficiently penalize Union Carbide for the magnitude of the untoward event of which it is responsible. Moreover, linking the Hester Prynne Sanction with community service might yield another undesirable consequence. French is concerned with creating an attitude of corporate shame for corporate wrongdoing. But he fails to realize that linking the sanction to community service (whether it be environmental research, support of the arts, or whatever) may serve as a guilty corporation's opportunity to boast — as is often done — of its community service achievements, thereby deceiving the public regarding the actual reason why the corporation is performing such services.

A seventh problem with the Hester Prynne Sanction is that it is to some degree hypocritical. It is the context of corporate competition that creates a problem of hypocrisy for corporate punishment theories like French's. The same system that encourages corporate competition and corporate success is the same one which seeks to punish corporations for pursuing such ideals. The hypocritical nature of the Hester Prynne Sanction, then, consists in the fact that it seeks to punish corporations for doing what they are encouraged to do (i.e., making a profit and bettering the economic achievements of all other corporations) as corporate enterprises.

Since French takes the name of his sanction from Hawthorne's *The Scarlet Letter*, an illustration from that story will suffice to suggest the hypocritical nature of the Hester Prynne Sanction. The reader will recall that in Hawthorne's story Hester Prynne commits adultery with the town cleric. She is "tried" and sentenced to the humiliation of having to wear a scarlet letter in order to publicize her wrongdoing. Now there are several things to note about this story. First, Hawthorne is widely known as a *critic* of the Puritan culture. The point of his story, secondly, is to suggest the hypocritical nature of that culture. The townspersons are not genuinely concerned about the welfare of this woman who is caught in the web of a most complex human relationship. Their concern is punishment. They are unconcerned with the fact that Hester Prynne is a victim of the social situation in which she finds herself. They are unconcerned with the fact that the society is "set up" in such a manner that only certain "crimes" (or "sins") are socially apparent (i.e., adultery in the case of some women) while other "crimes" are not obvious to the public, but are regularly practiced by the very persons who condemn Hester Prynne. Certainly the story of Hester Prynne is a seething indictment of the intolerance and self-righteousness of the Puritan culture. Just as the Puritan culture fosters a way of life which gives rise to various wrongdoing, so does the social order in which corporations operate. And just as it is hypocritical for the Puritans to adversely publicize the "sinful" deed of Hester Prynne, it is also hypocritical for corporations to be adversely publicized for socially unacceptable practices. How can French suggest punishment for guilty corporations when the "free market" system itself forces corporations (if they desire to be successful) to compete under terms which encourage such abuses? Will the corporations which are without sin cast the first stone?

Now I am in no way hinting that French intends to punish corporations guilty of wrongdoing in an intolerant or self-righteous way. However, French does not explain the court's procedural fairness in punishing corporations that are found guilty of causing untoward events. He does not show how the system will operate in a fair manner when punishing such corporations. There seems to be no reason why one should not expect to find the same arbitrary and politically and economically motivated procedures in punishing guilty corporations which exists presently, i.e., where a corporation is punished for wrongdoing, but other corporations which contributed indirectly to the same untoward event are not punished. Certainly equal punishment under the law applies to the corporate realm. Moreover, French's utilization of the term "Hester Prynne Sanction" perhaps betrays an ignorance regarding the fundamental points of Hawthorne's story. Hester Prynne, according to Hawthorne, is treated *wrongly* for her "offence," suggesting that any mode of punishment akin to that which she receives is equally wrong. Perhaps French ought to rename his suggested method of corporate punishment.

Furthermore, French states that the Hester Prynne Sanction is an effective means of corporate punishment in a shame based society like our own (French, pp. 192 — 193). It is true that the success of the sanction depends on the guilty corporation's ability to feel shame for what it has done wrong. But what if it has little or no capacity for such a feeling under any circumstance? What if, moreover, the corporation is perfectly willing to delude the courts, media and the public into thinking that it is shameful about doing a wrongful deed, but it in fact places more emphasis on profit-making than on moral practices in business? What if a guilty corporation is perfectly willing to undergo the Hester Prynne Sanction so long as it does not interfere with significant profit-making? Does not the sanction then lose its sting? Can the Hester Prynne Sanction be of help in punishing such corporations? French seems to have assumed, rather naively, that all corporations will feel shameful regarding their corporate wrongdoing. Moreover, he assumes that in the light of such shame corporations will be deterred from repeat offences by way of the sanction. I believe this is false at least in some cases. The primary reason that some corporations feel shameful for doing something which is deemed unacceptable is because they are caught. This can, however, hardly be seen as shame if by "shame" one means a genuine remorse for one's actions and a genuine effort to change one's ways. I submit, then, that corporations are not automatically shameful of their wrong actions. A case in point is Union Carbide, which (as far as I am aware) offers no more than $2000 to the surviving families of each dead victim of the Bhopal incident, while it offers nothing to the thousands of surviving victims of that disaster. Obviously, a corporation which is clearly responsible for, and feels genuine remorse for, an untoward event of this magnitude would make a much more generous offer to both the families of those who died and to those who survived the chemical leakage. Thus, the Hester Prynne Sanction assumes that guilty corporations will feel shameful about their wrongful acts, but it is by no means clear that corporations will or do exhibit such a feeling. As long as a guilty corporation can find avenues to increase its profits, there seems to be no reason for that corporation not to continue in its wrongful ways, despite the effects on it as a result of the Hester Prynne Sanction. This undercuts the sanction because if there is no guarantee that guilty corporations will feel such shame, then the possibility of corporate rehabilitation is wanting, making the Hester Prynne Sanction an ineffective means of corporate punishment.

In conclusion, nothing on French's view of the use of the Hester Prynne Sanction against guilty corporations ensures against the following: (1) The unjust immiseration of the guilty corporation's work force; (2) The ability of the guilty corporation to escape the financial penalty of the sanction by raising its prices for the consumer, (3) The ability of the guilty corporation to reorganize itself and thereby escape the public shame of the sanction; (4) The possibility of the media's ineffectiveness in carrying out the sanction; (5) The limited scope of the sanction on those corporations guilty of gross forms of wrongdoing; (6) The guilty corporation's ability to control the findings and operations of its court appointed research facility; (7) The hypocritical nature of the sanction; (8) The possibility that some corporations will not feel shameful about their wrongful deeds. These are eight reasons why the utilization of French's Hester Prynne Sanction is problematic as a punishment for corporate wrong-doing.

Although the Hester Prynne Sanction is useful in some cases of minor corporate wrongdoing, it is not useful as a punishment for corporations guilty of gross wrongdoing, such as the Union Carbide incident in Bhopal. What French needs in order to ensure the success of his claims regarding corporate punishment is a general theory of punishment which is capable of giving an effective and sufficient punishment to corporations guilty of gross wrongdoing. What he needs is a theory of corporate punishment which: (1) does not permit a corporation found guilty of wrongdoing to evade the guilt, shame and negative effects of the punishment; (2) does not permit the punishment to adversely affect (in any way) innocent employees or the general public in any significant manner; (3) does not permit the guilty corporation a way by which to benefit financially from the punishment; and (4) has a genuine rehabilitative intent and effect (instead of a crippling one) on the punished corporation. Moreover, such a theory of corporate punishment must be based on an adequate concept of corporate moral personhood. How such a theory might be explicated is the subject of another paper.

Shannon Shipp

MODIFIED VENDETTAS AS A METHOD OF PUNISHING CORPORATIONS

Did you ever expect a corporation to have a conscience, when it has no soul to be damned, and no body to be kicked?

Baron Thurlow

Punishment is a method of social control that may be used to secure values which are legitimately served within a just social order (Lyons, 1984). Punishment is part of the "bargain" between the individual and the society in which he or she lives to ensure maximum freedom is enjoyed by all members of society. As legal individuals, corporations are part of this implied bargain.

Punishing corporations is much different from punishing individuals. It is difficult to punish a "person" who has no conscience or corpus. Yet those charged with regulating the actions of corporations face that situation whenever a corporation breaks a law or fails to act morally responsible. The difficulties of punishing corporations for actions which lead to criminal liability have led to a great deal of controversy in philosophy and business ethics. One controversial area is what institution (or institutions) has (have) the duty to punish errant corporations. While government and market mechanisms have legislated corporate behavior for centuries, non-government institutions such as consumer groups and unions have received much recent attention as alternatives or replacements for government sanctions.

This paper explores how non-government institutions punish corporations through modified vendettas (MVs). A vendetta is a blood feud in which the relatives of an injured party try to harm the injurer. In this paper, the vendetta concept is modified in that those using this method are not necessarily harmed directly or related to those harmed by the corporation. It is also modified in that those carrying on the vendetta cannot bloody the corporation's nose. It can be shown, however, without stretching the analogy too far, that a MV can impair the corporation's cash flow, which is its economic lifeblood. For instance, a public-interest group may carry on a MV when it supports a boycott of a firm's products because of perceived criminally or morally irresponsible corporate behavior.

This paper is concerned with three practical philosophical questions about using MV to punish corporations.

1. Is the MV necessary for punishing corporations?
2. How effective is the MV?
3. Can the MV be justified from a theoretical perspective?

From *Journal of Business Ethics*, 6 (1987), 603–612. ©1987 by D. Reidel Publishing Company. Reprinted by permission of Kluwer Academic Publishers.

To answer these questions, the paper is composed of three sections. The first section will trace the evolution of corporate structure, and illustrate the concurrent evolution in the manner in which corporations are punished. From this historical analysis, the necessity of the MV or other non-government forms of corporate punishment becomes apparent. The second section, through two case examples, will illustrate MVs used against two corporations. The discussion following the two case studies will use stakeholder analysis as a framework for assessing the effectiveness of the MVs. The third section will evaluate current corporate punishment methods from a philosophical perspective to determine whether the methods meet standards for utility and maintenance of individual and corporate rights.

1. HISTORY OF CORPORATE PUNISHMENT

Methods of corporate punishment have changed as corporations themselves have evolved. Donaldson (1982) states that corporations have evolved through four stages. Within each stage, organizational structural characteristics differed, along with the institutions responsible for punishing criminal corporations and the locus of culpability within the firm.

In the first stage, corporations were organized for reasons other than economic benefit. For example, the Church was an early corporation, as was the guild. These groups were primarily self-regulating, in that they were the only organizations with the skills to assess the degree to which one of their laws had been violated. Culpability for corporate action was typically assumed by all members of the corporation.

Corporations in the second stage were used as repositories for trading rights. Members of the corporation were able to exercise the trading rights. The members did not share capital, however, and each member had total liability for his or her trading expeditions. Punishment was meted out by the government through the revocation of charter for severe offenses involving the corporation as a whole, while individual entrepreneur's offenses were punished by the corporation. Culpability for individual and corporate actions fell to the individual entrepreneurs.

When the liability for an expedition became too high for even wealthy individuals to bear, the third stage of corporate development began. In this stage, capital was pooled, liability was shared, and power was placed in the hands of a ruling governor or board. The modern corporation, with its ability to endure beyond the natural lives of its founders, its ability to sue and be sued, and its ability to provide investors with a vehicle in which their liability is limited to the size of their investment, first appears in this stage. The difference between the third and fourth stage centers on restrictions in chartering new corporations, an issue which does not affect this discussion.

Corporations in the third and fourth stages posed great problems in assessing culpability. With limited liability as an organizational characteristic, investors denied responsibility for the actions of managers, while managers ascribed responsibility for their actions on behalf of the corporation to the owners of the corporation, i.e. the investors. Since it was difficult to determine individuals responsible for corporate actions, and it was not possible to imprison corporations, the preferred method of corporate punishment became fines administered by the judicial system.

The justification for the system of fines to curb corporate excesses has been stated by Friedman (1962). In his view, punishing corporations through fines allows the marketplace to regulate corporate wrongdoing. The cost of those fines will place the wrongdoing firm at a competitive disadvantage *vis-à-vis* its competitors who act according to statute. As a result, firms who break the law will suffer in the marketplace. According to this rationale, firms should always act in accordance with statutes from a purely economic perspective.

If this model is correct, why do some corporations intentionally break the law? One answer is that the model above oversimplifies the corporate environment. Wrongdoing will not always be detected, and even if it is, due to the vagaries of the legal process, will not always be followed by punitive sanctions. It is also possible that the sanctions provided for in the statute are not sufficient to place the offending corporation at a competitive disadvantage. In a sense, the existence of these conditions encourages the corporation to perform a cost-benefit analysis to determine whether it should or should not adhere to the law.

One might suggest at this point that all that is needed to ensure corporate compliance with statutes is for society to enact tougher laws and more stringent enforcement procedures. Stone (1975) argues that neither the marketplace nor more stringent enforcement procedures are sufficient to regulate corporate performance. He offers three reasons as support for his claim. First, there is a time lag problem. Law is primarily a reactive institution. By the time legislation is passed against a harmful corporate practice, grievous damage can already be inflicted. At the same time, until the law is passed, the offending corporation has an unfair competitive advantage compared to firms who do not act in a harmful fashion. Second, the industry is often involved in making or monitoring compliance with the laws designed to regulate its behavior. This situation is not inherently unsatisfactory, as industry cooperation is needed to develop standards and monitor compliance. Unfortunately, to the extent that corporations refuse to release internal information that indicates unsafe practices or need for changes in standards, regulatory agencies, because of lack of information and staffing, are not able to develop new regulations to alter the behavior of firms in the industry. Lastly, implementation of legal action against a corporation is difficult. In a model tort case involving one individual suffering an injury at the hands of another individual, the injured party knows of the injury, knows who has caused the injury, knows or can ascertain the nature and extent of his or her injuries, and can apply common experience in showing cause and effect between the action of the injuring party and the injury itself. In the case of an individual harmed by a large corporation, it is rare that all of the circumstances above can be established. Identifying and punishing an offender is difficult unless all of the conditions above are met.

Other complaints against overreliance on legal sanctions are raised by Donaldson (1982), who maintains that legal sanctions are often overstandardized and likely to encourage adversarial relationships between corporations and those monitoring corporate behavior. Overstandardized solutions fail to account for extenuating circumstances. Adversarial relationships are not preferred because many of the conditions which require regulation are first noted by the industry itself. If those firms identifying conditions in their industry that require additional regulation are subject to legal sanctions, it is not likely that the firms will be forthcoming in identifying such conditions.

While the discussion above illustrates that legal sanctions may not be sufficient to regulate corporate behavior, the intention is not to suggest that laws are unnecessary. The point is made, however, that merely tightening current laws will not be sufficient to cause corporations to adherer to laws. Something more is needed; and this is the point where philosophers disagree. In the following section, some alternates to tightening current laws will be discussed.

To move beyond the problems of the traditional solution of punishing corporations by fines imposed through the legal system, one might ask in what other ways corporations could be punished. At least two other possibilities exist (see Figure 1). Monetary sanctions meted out by the government are the traditional method, but non-monetary sanctions by government and non-government institutions exist as well.

French (1984) identifies the "Hester Prynne" sanction as a non-monetary means for the government to punish corporations. Hester Prynne was the heroine in Nathaniel Hawthorne's novel *The Scarlet Letter*. She committed adultery, was found out, and as a condition of her punishment was forced to wear the letter "A" on her bosom for the rest of her life. This was not a penalty of restricting freedom, such as imprisonment, but one based on shame. When used against a corporation, the Hester Prynne sanction is a blot on corporate prestige. Much as individuals prefer to be well-thought of, it seems that corporations are averse to adverse publicity. Millions of dollars and years of hard work go into building a corporation's reputation. Although it is difficult to place a dollar value on reputation, there are few executives who would prefer or be satisfied with a bad corporate reputation. As a result, French suggests supplementing or substituting legal sanctions with advertising campaigns which publicize the corporation's wrongdoing. These sanctions would be administered through the same legal institutions already applying legal sanctions, and would be conducted by the corporation convicted of wrong-doing. An example of this sanction is the order by the FTC which required Warner-Lambert to run corrective advertising to counteract its previous claims that Listerine could reduce the severity or incidence of colds.

Unfortunately, the Hester Prynne sanction is beset with many of the same problems as legal remedies. Time lags between corporate actions and sanctions by courts, the need for industry participation in detecting problems, and difficulty in assessing culpability for criminal actions are still issues needing resolution.

The MV method of corporate punishment differs from the Hester Prynne sanction in that MV relies on non-government bodies to punish corporations.

	Monetary	Non-monetary
Government	System of fines	Hester Prynne
Non-government Groups	Modified vendetta	Modified vendetta

Sanctioning institution(s)

FIGURE 1 *Sanction*

MVs can include both monetary sanctions, such as boycotts, and non-monetary sanctions, such as anti-corporate publicity campaigns. MVs are improvements over fines and the Hester Prynne sanction for several reasons. First, since government intervention is not required, the time lag problem may be alleviated. Further, MV sanctions are important because they are not merely a supplement or substitute for fines, as is the case with the Hester Prynne sanction. Instead, they are often called into play when the corporation is performing activities which are legal but morally irresponsible, at least from the perspective of the sanctioners. While it is not the aim of this paper to enter the discussion of the moral status of corporations, it is important to note that individuals often ascribe moral characteristics to corporations. In common usage, we ascribe benevolence to corporations that donate generously to charitable causes, and speak disparagingly of corporations who do not act in accordance with commonly accepted moral principles (May, 1983). The MV sanction is an outgrowth of ascribing moral characteristics to corporations. When corporations perform acts which are legal, but morally irresponsible, the MV sanction is often the only recourse of affected groups.

II. CASE STUDIES OF MVS

This section uses two case studies to illustrate the use of MVs. The situations are analyzed from a stakeholder perspective to illustrate the interrelationships of the groups trying to influence the corporation's behavior. The MV sanctions are evaluated in terms of how effectively they accomplished their stated goals. These cases were selected due to the amount of published material on the efforts of outside groups to change the corporations' behavior.

J. P. Stevens

J. P. Stevens, a large textile manufacturer, had a 17-year history of fighting attempts by the Amalgamated Clothing and Textile Workers Union (ACTWU) to organize its workforce (see Buzzard, 1978; Kovacks, 1978; *Forbes*, May 25, 1981, p. 116; *Business Week*, February 22, 1982, p. 60 for a history of the Stevens–ACTWU struggle). The standoff finally ended in 1982, with ACTWU becoming the bargaining agent for 10 of Stevens' 70 manufacturing facilities.

The conflict between the union and Stevens featured disputed union elections and numerous appeals to the National Labor Relations Board and the courts by both sides. According to the union, the primary disputes between the union and Stevens were seniority, job bidding, distribution of work loads, and pay practices.

Throughout the course of the battle between ACTWU and Stevens, a variety of tactics were used by both sides to force the other to change its behavior. Stevens trained its plant managers to be anti-union, and offered benefits to its workers for remaining non-union. ACTWU organized consumer boycotts and adverse publicity campaigns against Stevens. The union's efforts seemed to have little effect on Stevens until it began a systematic campaign to isolate Stevens from its lenders and business peers. James Finley

(Stevens' chairman) was forced off the board of Manufacturers Hanover Trust after the union threatened to pull its pension fund deposits. Two of Stevens' board members, David Mitchell (chairman of Avon) and R. Manning Brown Jr. (chairman of New York Life) were forced to resign after the union threatened to conduct a proxy fight over control of their companies. Metropolitan Life, holder of $97 million of Stevens' $226 million in long-term debt, was threatened with a similar proxy fight if it did not divest its Stevens holdings. Metropolitan Life estimated that the cost of handling proxies to its 23 million policyholders would be $5 - 7 million. Shortly after the union's threat to Metropolitan Life, peace broke out between Stevens and the union.

Nestlé

Nestlé, a multinational food processing firm, was the subject of a 7 year boycott by numerous church and activist groups. These groups charged Nestlé with selling powdered infant formula in Third World countries where lack of readily available clean water virtually ensured contamination of the formula, with a resulting increase in infant mortality.

Nestlé's initial handling of the case was maladroit (*Fortune*, Dec. 27, 1982). It adopted a public stance of righteous indignation while quietly reducing promotion of infant formula in Third World countries. Nestlé also began channeling funds to groups with positions favoring Nestlé, giving rise to suspicions that Nestlé was purchasing favorable public opinion.

In 1977, a consumer boycott, organized by Infant Formula Action Committee (INFACT), and supported by the National Council of Churches and other church organizations, began against Nestlé. This boycott eventually involved most Nestlé products sold in grocery stores, and was in force in 10 countries, including the U.S.

As a result of pressure from these groups, the World Health Organization (WHO), a U.N.-sponsored group, issued nonbinding guidelines in 1981 regarding the sale and distribution of infant formula in Third World countries. These guidelines banned all advertising and also prohibited almost all distribution of formula, including direct approaches to mothers and free samples, except for doctors and other health workers. The guidelines did not have the force of law, however, unless the affected countries adopted similar statutes.

The industry trade association refused to operate according to these guidelines in 1981, claiming that they were anti-business and too restrictive. INFACT and other groups continued their boycott. In 1983, 7 years into the boycott, INFACT set up centers in Boston, Chicago and Minneapolis to increase pressure on Nestlé. These centers coordinated the efforts of churches and women's groups to force Nestlé to change its marketing practices of baby formula. One tactic used was to collect signatures and present petitions to grocery stores carrying Nestlé products. These petitions encouraged retailers to bring pressure on Nestlé to change its actions (personal communication, Minneapolis INFACT office, August, 1985).

As a result of external pressure, Nestlé agreed to adopt the WHO guidelines in 1983. INFACT stopped its boycott in 1984. To monitor its compliance with those guidelines, Nestlé set up an Infact Mortality Audit Commission (IFAC). IFAC is a nine-member commission composed of doctors, scientists and churchmen. It is headed by former Secretary of State Edmund Muskie (*Science*, 10 February, 1984).

Discussion

The campaigns against Stevens and Nestlé exemplified the MV concept. Non-government groups orchestrated monetary and non-monetary sanctions in hopes of changing corporate behaviors which could not be altered by existing legal remedies.

No individual group, however, was strong enough to change the corporation's actions single-handedly, as would be the case with the application of legal sanctions by the government. To show how the groups together accomplished changes in corporate behavior none could have achieved alone, stakeholder analysis is used as an analytical framework.

One guide to understanding how the actions of external groups affect corporate behavior is through applications of stakeholder theory. According to Freeman (1984) a stakeholder is a person or group who affects or is affected by the achievement of the organization's objectives. Through non-legal sanctions, a number of groups sought to affect Nestlé's and J.P. Stevens' actions. In the Stevens case, the union, workers, sympathetic outside unions, consumers, business peers and lending institutions all affect Stevens' ability to continue in business. Nestlé is affected by the groups organizing the boycott, consumers following the boycott and grocers subjected to petitions from boycotting groups. To clarify the power and stake positions of each of these groups, stakeholder maps of each case appear in Figures 2 and 3.

A stakeholder map is a historical analysis of the positions of the stakeholders in a firm. Each stakeholder is shown in terms of its relationship to the target firm. Freeman (1984) uses two dimensions, power and stake, to construct stakeholder maps. Power is defined as the ability to use resources to cause certain events to occur. The power dimension has three major classifications; voting, economic and political. Owners can exert power in terms of voting for the organization to pursue certain policies. Customers and suppliers exert economic power in terms of their ability to switch firms, raise prices or request price concessions. Government and quasi-government bodies can exert political power in terms of their ability to enact legislation which affects corporate actions. The groups in the Nestlé case used economic power (boycotts and pickets) and political power (influence on WHO to develop its non-binding guidelines). In the J. P. Stevens case, groups used economic power (boycotts against Stevens) and combinations of voting power and economic power (pressure on lenders and business peers by purchasing a stake or by threatening to remove assets).

Groups have a stake when the actions of a firm affect them in some way. The stake dimension is a continuum with three classifications; equity, market, and influence. Groups with equity stakes include owners and directors. Market stakes are held by customers, suppliers, unions, owners and debt-holders. Groups with influence stakes include trade associations, government, federal agencies and the SEC. In the Nestlé case, consumers and grocery stores held market stakes, while INFACT, church groups and WHO had influence stakes. In the Stevens case, the business peers had equity stakes, while the unions, consumers and lenders had market stakes.

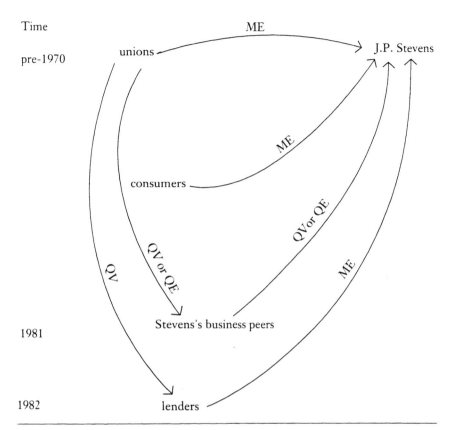

*The letters on the lines between the groups refer, respectively, to the stakes of each group and the types of power used by one group to influence the other.

Stakes	Types of Power
Q = Equity	E = Economic
I = Influence	P = Political
M = Market	V = Voting

FIGURE 2   *J.P. Stevens Stakeholder Map*

Figures 2 and 3 are modifications of Freeman's two-dimensional approach to developing stakeholder maps. Two reasons necessitated these modifications. First, Figures 2 and 3 show the interactions among the stakeholders themselves as well as their relationships to the target firm. In both cases, the interactions between the stakeholders were important in determining the amount of pressure brought against the target firm. In the Nestlé case, grocers were pressured by petitions and boycotters to remove Nestlé products from their shelves. Although little published information exists on this point, it would be difficult to imagine that the grocers did not report these actions to Nestlé and request

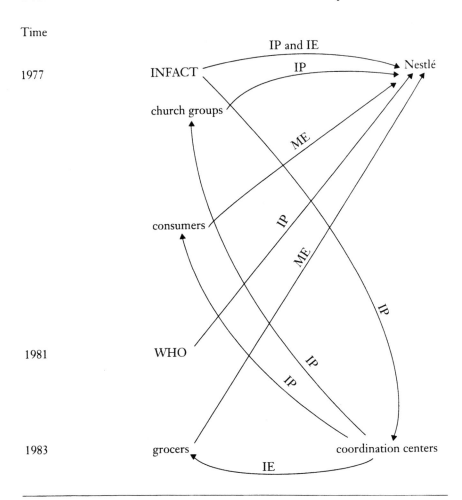

Time

*The letters on the lines between the groups refer, respectively, to the stakes and types of power used by one group to influence the other.

Stakes	Types of Power
Q = Equity	E = Economic
I = Influence	P = Political
M = Market	V = Voting

FIGURE 3   *Nestlé Stakeholder Map*

something be done. In the Stevens case, the company was forced to adopt a more conciliatory attitude towards the union as a result of the union's campaign to isolate Stevens from its lenders and outside directors.

Second, the two-dimensional stakeholder map is a static representation of reality. It is not possible to distinguish temporal precedence in the actions of any of the stakeholders. In both cases, however, not all stakeholders were pressing the target firm for action throughout the conflict. INFACT, for example, waged its boycott for four years before WHO instituted its guidelines, and for five or six years before going directly to grocery stores to request Nestlé products be removed from the shelves. ACTWU had a long history of disputes with Stevens, but corporate peers and lenders were not pressured to use their influence on Stevens until two or three years before the union was formally recognized as the bargaining agent for 10 of Stevens' plants. To show the dynamic aspect, the stakeholders are arranged from top to bottom by their length of participation in the conflict, with those in the dispute longest at the top.

Assessing the effectiveness of the Modified Vendetta is not simple. French (1984) and Donaldson (1982) state the effectiveness of any method of punishment can only be assessed in terms of how well it meets the goals of society. Unfortunately, the goals of the groups comprising society are often conflicting, with each side claiming to speak for society's interests. If one is willing to accept the stated goals of INFACT to improve nutritional conditions for infants in Third World countries, and the stated goals of ACTWU to ensure the rights of workers, both of which seem laudable as a reflection of society's desires, the changes in corporate behavior brought about by the actions of these groups were effective. If one accepts Nestlé's contention that adoption of the guidelines led to a decrease in consumer choice for mothers in Third World countries, and Stevens' contention that the closed shop mandated by the union restricted a worker's right to associate, the changes were not effective.

Thus far we have explained the MV form of corporate punishment and evaluated its effectiveness in two cases. Stakeholder analysis has been used to explain how MV operates to influence corporations to change their behavior. MV has not, however, been philosophically justified as an appropriate method of redressing corporate actions not susceptible to legal remedies. Justification will be attempted by comparing MV to theory of punishment which combines retributive and utilitarian principles.

III. PHILOSOPHICAL JUSTIFICATION OF THE MV

Lyons (1984) argues that preferred results from punishment arise out of two basic justifications. The first is retribution, which is the idea that the offender deserves the same treatment he or she inflicted on someone else, or in the least that the offender be deprived of good treatment by others. The second is utilitarian. It is based on the idea that punishment is useful, or justified in terms of the good it provides the community or that it deprive the offender of the ability or opportunity to do further harm.

Lyons suggests the ideal justification for punishment is one that combines utilitarian and retributive principles. While utilitarian principles justify coercive punishments on a nonretributive basis and the concentration of the right to punish in the hands of the state or some disinterested third party, Kantian retributive principles argue for the acceptance of mitigating circumstances, and against strict liability, vicarious liability, exemplary punishments and the punishment of innocent individuals to achieve good for a greater number.

Therefore, it seems that the justification for punishment combining retributive and utilitarian principles, hereafter referred to as the combination justification, provides the most justice for the greatest number while preserving the rights of individuals. To justify the MV as a method of corporate punishment, it can be compared to the combination justification. That comparison will show areas where modifications should be made, based on the relative agreement or disagreement between the combination justification and MV. While a complete analysis is not possible, three critical comparisons will be made between the combination justification and MV. First, does the combination justification allow the MV to bypass government institutions charged with monitoring and controlling the behavior of organizations? Second, are the rights of individual corporations subjected to a MV preserved? Third, are the Kantian principles against strict liability and vicarious liability violated when MV is used?

The use of extra-legal means clearly places the groups using the combination technique of corporate punishment into a position of "going over government's head." However, do these groups usurp government's role in corporate punishment? I think not, for several reasons. First, as Stone points out, governments often pass laws based on the activism of groups who see gaps in existing law. To the extent that these new laws reflect the preferences of society, the activist groups perform a valuable function in ensuring the responsiveness of government.

Second, the firm always has the option of changing its behavior to that desired by the activist groups, with no intervention from the government or other interested groups. In this case, the activist groups act as an early warning system to the corporation, emphasizing areas where changes in corporate behavior are worth examining before government interference occurs.

Third, if the corporation feels the external groups' claims are incorrect or misleading, it has the option of going to court to obtain a cease and desist order or monetary judgement against the groups. Slander and libel laws are designed to protect corporations, as well as individuals, against false and malicious statements.

Fourth, unlike government decrees, corporations can simply ignore the issues raised by the activist groups. Activists' pronouncements do not have the force of law, and some corporations may elect to disregard them and hope they will go away.

The answer to the question of whether groups employing a MV usurp government's role in punishing corporations is negative. They cannot force corporations to change their behavior. These groups can, however, lead government to make laws where they are needed or to focus society's attention on areas deserving concern.

The second issue is whether corporations' rights are preserved. Clearly in some instances these rights are denied by activists, generally on behalf of a right they perceive takes precedence. For example, for the past several years, Honeywell's annual meeting in Minneapolis has been disrupted by anti-nuclear activists questioning Honeywell's production of nuclear weapons and other war material. While Honeywell has the right to free speech in providing a forum for its stockholders to ask questions about company performance, anti-nuclear activists abrogate that right by disrupting the meeting on the grounds that they are ensuring individuals' right to life.

The precedence of different rights is a question pondered by several philosophers, including Singer (1979). Singer's argument is that while rights should be honored, it is clear that certain rights take precedence over others. For example while individuals have a right to pursue their own projects, if *A* could save *B*'s life with a minimum of inconvenience to *A*'s projects, *A* should save *B*'s life. The generalized statement of this is that if an action is in our power to avert great harm without great sacrifice, we should take that action. The Honeywell activists are using this argument to justify disrupting the Honeywell annual meeting. In their view, production of nuclear weapons is a great harm which through their disruption of the annual meeting might be stopped or reevaluated.

Honeywell management, on the other hand, sees a tenuous connection between production and/or use of nuclear weapons and their annual meeting. They argue that production of nuclear weapons is necessary for the purposes of defense. Disruption of the annual meeting is unlikely to affect their production of weapons or research on defense-related issues, and is a violation of shareholders right to question management's actions.

Regardless of which side is right, the difficulty of Singer's argument is evident. Different groups see opposing goals as occupying the moral high ground. There are a number of instances where neither goal occupies a higher moral position than the other. As a result, it is not clear if the combination justification condones the violation of corporate rights unless it is clear which of the competing goals has the moral high ground. Determining which goals occupy the moral high ground is difficult and subject to debate but must occur before a MV is justified. If the MV is justified, this provides the "excuses" sought by Kant to pardon the behavior of the groups conducting the MV.

The last issue is the extent to which a MV can apply vicarious liability to those working in organizations the groups are seeking to punish. Vicarious liability is the practice of punishing people for acts performed by others. Reports of churches chastising those who work in plants making nuclear weapons are one such instance of imputing vicarious liability. Although Lyons states that vicarious liability is undesirable, others, notably May (1983) and Goldman (1983) disagree. May's argument is that merely by becoming a member of an organization one does not leave one's morality at the office or plant entrance. A similar argument is advanced by Goldman (1983), who states that the members of corporations have weak role differentiation between their private lives and their lives as members of the corporations. In other words, acting in one's corporate capacity is not an excuse for not following the rules of individual morality. The result of both arguments is the same; individuals are morally responsible for the actions they take in the name of the corporation. As a result, it is justified for groups composing a MV to ascribe moral responsibility to individual employees for corporate actions.

From the discussion of these three issues, it seems evident that the Modified Vendetta is at least partially justified by a theory of punishment incorporating retributive and utilitarian principles. The three issues discussed here, while not exhaustive, are key to the acceptance of any form or model of corporate punishment.

CONCLUSION

Punishing corporations is different, and in some ways much more difficult than punishing individuals. Punishing corporations through traditional systems of fines administered through the legal system is not adequate to curb criminal corporate behavior. This paper described MVs, which are proposed to be the next stage in the evolution of methods of punishing corporations. The effectiveness of MVs was assessed through two case examples. In both cases, the MV worked reasonably well, although not necessarily speedily.

Use of the MV was justified by comparing it to a theory of punishment based on a combination of utilitarian and retributive principles. The MV was found to increase society's control over corporations by allowing non-government groups to take actions to change unacceptable (to them) corporate behavior. Corporations' rights to operate were preserved, since both legal and public relations counter-efforts could be mounted by corporations to stop unwarranted or frivolous MVs.

References

Business Week, February 22, 1982. p. 60.

Buzzard, W.: 1978, 'How the Union Got the Upper Hand on J.P. Stevens', *Fortune* (June 19) 86.

Donaldson, Thomas: 1982, *Corporations and Morality*, Englewood Cliffs, New Jersey: Prentice-Hall.

Forbes, May 25, 1981. p. 116.

Fortune, December 27, 1982. p. 109.

Freeman, R. Edward: 1984, *Strategic Management: A Stakeholder Approach*, Boston: Pitman Publishing.

French, Peter: 1984, *Corporate and Social Responsibility*, pp. 186–202.

Friedman, Milton: 1962, *Capitalism and Freedom*, Chicago: University of Chicago Press.

Goldman, Alan: 1983, 'Authority, Autonomy, and Institutional Norms', *Ethical and Policy Issues Perspectives on the Professions* (March/June), Vol. 3, Nos. 1, 2.

Kant, Immanuel: 1797 *Metaphysical Elements of Justice*, trans. John Ladd (1965), New York: Bobbs-Merrill.

Kovacks, K.: 1978, 'How the Union Got the Upper Hand on J.P. Stevens', *Fortune* (June 19), 86.

Lyons, David: 1984, *Ethics and the Rule of Law*, Cambridge: Cambridge University Press.

May, Larry: 1983, 'Vicarious Agency and Corporate Responsibility', *Philosophical Studies* 43, 69–82.

Science, February 10, 1984. p. 35.

Singer, Peter: 1979, 'Rich and Poor', in *Practical Ethics* (New York: Cambridge University Press), pp. 166–179.

Stone, Christopher: 1975, *Where the Law Ends*, New York: Harper and Row.

Robert J. Rafalko
CORPORATE PUNISHMENT: A PROPOSAL

A disturbing anomaly exists in the way U.S. law treats American corporations. Ever since Chief Justice John Marshall described the corporation as
"an artificial being, invisible, intangible, and existing only in the contemplation
of the law"[1] the boundaries for the rights and responsibilities of corporations
have been hotly and, for the most part, inconclusively disputed. Never have we
encountered a more misused metaphor than Marshall's, but few others have
been quoted more often. Perhaps, just because of the metaphor's lack of illumi-
nation, it can mean all things to all people and, subsequently, each of us can
quote it to his own purpose. In any case, that's undoubtedly why answers to
questions about corporate rights and liabilities are so muddled in business, legal
and philosophical discussions. The following essay is an exercise in logic and
creative thinking. I shall argue that no good reasons exist for the supposition
that corporations have rights independent of the rights and interests of the
persons they serve and that the error of treating corporations as though they do
have autonomous rights derives from a sloppy argument from analogy. I shall
further argue that the analogy of corporations to citizens, though pushed too far
by some courts and lawmakers, remains a useful analogy if its logical relations
can be cleaned up and clarified. Finally, I shall conclude this essay by employing
the refurbished analogy in such a way that it yields a proposal for more effective
criminal punishment for corporate wrongdoing.

Part of my intent in writing this paper is satirical. I believe that much of the
analysis on this subject has been due to pressing some faulty analogies too far.
When we allow metaphors and analogies to get out of control, the result can be
humor as well as confusion. We've taken the confused thesis too seriously too
long. I hope the reader will find that my proposal has a humorous as well as an
insightful side to it.

I. SETTING UP THE PROBLEM

The problem is one of moral and legal liability where corporations have trans-
gressed acceptable bounds of conduct. The problem of corporate legal liability
is one of justification, and the familiar hardware of legal justification is precedent and the calculation of competing interests and rights. Precedent is, in the
last analysis, a special sort of appeal to authority, and authority in this instance
rests on no more than prior pronouncements made on like cases. These pronouncements presumably rest on further moral types of justification. Therefore, the problem of legal liability reduces in the last instance to a problem of
moral liability.

The difficulty, however, arises when we ask questions about the nature of
the corporation. Can an abstract, collective entity be the sort of thing that
assumes moral identity? If we answer "Yes," and we are able to make good our

From *Journal of Business Ethics*, 8 (1989), 917–928. © 1989 Kluwer Academic Publishers.
Reprinted by permission of Kluwer Academic Publishers

answer, then most moral and legal theoreticians instinctively view the problem of the justification of corporate moral liability claims as a clash of competing interests — most often, as a clash between the rights of the corporation and the interests of workers, consumers, and the community-at-large. If we answer "No," then, for many, the problem ends right there. The corporation is a creature bound by its charter. Regulations and restrictions may be (or may not be) appropriate, but no further talk about liability or punishment is conceptually appropriate.[2]

My contention is that the adherents of the arguments on both sides of this position are mistaken. First, the stubbornly persistent manner of viewing claims about liability and punishment as a weighting of competing rights and interests will get us nowhere; but, second, the analogy of corporations to moral persons is useful if not exact, and without appeal to such an analogy we are destined to succumb to a blind moral debility whose catastrophic effects to the environment, the community, and the worker no free market jingoism can palliate.

Regarding corporations as analogous to moral persons has one overriding drawback. Corporations are designed to limit liability, whereas no moral person is so exempted. The history of the evolution of the corporation is quite clear on this matter. Many people commonly think of the corporation as existing solely or exclusively for the purpose of making a profit, but this view is clearly mistaken. Corporate charters were originally granted to universities, monasteries, the guilds and boroughs in order to separate jurisdictions and divide responsibilities.[3] As early as the 15th century, English courts had come to recognize the corporate principle of limited liability: "*Si quid universitati debetur, singulis non debetur, nec quod debet universitas, singuli debent.*"[4] Later, companies such as the Hudson Bay Company and the East India Company were incorporated with the intention of encouraging investment by means of the principle of limited liability. The sharing of responsibility among shareholders served three purposes: first, a creditor usually stood to gain more by suing the shareholders as a unit than he would be suing any one individual; secondly, the shareholder became liable only to the extent of his original investment — his other assets could not be touched; and thirdly, these limits on liability served to make investment more attractive, thus establishing the modern close link between profit and shared liability.

Moreover, even modern corporations do not exist solely — and many, not at all — for the purpose of reaping profits. Some corporations, for example, the University of North Carolina, are chartered as non-profit, their corporate status serving to define responsibilities and to place limits on the liability of their members.

The corporation, I submit, is best defined as a liability-limiting mechanism. Given this definition, no wonder the courts have so much difficulty meting out just punishment to corporations when they engage in misconduct! Rarely can the courts legally pierce the corporate veil to prosecute individuals thought responsible for corporate wrong-doing. Even when they can, the courts tend to display a reluctance to do so — we may suspect that that reluctance is the result of confusion regarding the range of liability pertaining to corporations and the well-entrenched personification of the corporation as moral agent.

When the courts attempt to place responsibility on the corporation itself, the appropriate punishment is deemed to be monetary. However, when a corporation engages in repeated instances of gross misconduct, the courts are reluctant to levy truly heavy fines — as in the case of Hooker Chemical Company, despite a history of repeated violations of the law over a period of four decades. Good reason exists for the court's caution. A truly ponderous fine, the sort of fine necessary to act as a deterrent to such a community might be left stranded without its major industry, or consumers might be deprived of a much-needed or much-wanted product.

At the heart of the problem is the inability of legislators, jurists, businessmen, and philosophers to find innovative solutions to these and like problems.

One of the misconceptions that we may judge to be in part responsible for this sort of inflexible thinking is the supposition that if indeed corporations are like moral agents, then corporations have moral rights which must be weighted against the interests of the community. In the next section, I question this assumption and argue that we more properly ought to regard the existence of the corporation as a socially conferred privilege, which does not entail any supposition of a corporation's moral right to exist, or moral rights of any other kind.

II. DO CORPORATIONS HAVE RIGHTS?

Our question concerns the normative justifications for the supposition that corporations have rights analogous to First Amendment guarantees offered to all citizens of the United States. If corporations do have such rights, then we may be tempted to infer that they also possess a right to exist analogous to a human's right to life. Were that so, it would have a significant impact on any considerations we might devise regarding the proper punishment to be accorded incorrigibly law-breaking corporations. However, let us see if that is really so.

If we were to phrase our question as, "Do corporations have *human* rights?" — the answer would be, "No," for obvious reasons: corporations do not eat, drink, breathe, sleep or procreate; they are not human beings. Some philosophers even cogently dispute the contention that human beings have such rights as "Human Rights," but that is not at issue here. What is at issue is whether there is good and compelling reason to offer the guarantees of the Bill of Rights of American corporations.

Some philosophers, such as Thomas Donaldson, believe the issue is already settled: corporations *do* enjoy such guarantees. Donaldson's strategy is an admirable one: he hopes that by making such concessions to the ownership of such rights, then, by the force of analogy, corporations can be brought into tow, morally speaking. Rights entail moral responsibilities, so, by making such a concession, Donaldson constructs a social contract basis for moral censures against irresponsible and incorrigible corporations. However, as is clear from the passage quoted below from his book, *Corporations and Morality*, Donaldson concedes far too much:

> With the passage of the Fourteenth Amendment to the Constitution, U.S. corporations acquired full status as abstract persons, complete with rights to life, liberty, and state citizenship. (Most U.S. corporations are citizens

of the state of Delaware.) Although modern U.S. corporations do not possess certain features of personhood — i.e. they neither eat, require medical attention, nor vote — they are treated as persons in a multitude of ways: they must pay taxes, are liable for damages, can enter into legal agreements, and have the right to freedom of speech. Modern corporations are created by persons, but they are created in the image of their creators.[5]

This is a beguiling passage, but we see at once what's wrong with it: it is not an argument; it is an assertion, coupled with a few factual references. Moreover, Donaldson has some of his facts wrong. If the Fourteenth Amendment "grants" such rights as free speech to the corporation, it does so only in a way that is derivative from the rights of the persons whom the corporation serves.

Corporations are not persons, and cannot thereby be entitled to the rights of persons. However, we grant some of the protections of the Fourteenth Amendment to corporations because we find such actions suitable on occasion — especially the due-process and equal protection provisions, and especially where they pertain to the deprivation of *property*. But where we find such *ad hoc* applications suitable, we can also find other applications unsuitable. For example, we do not find First Amendment guarantees for freedom of assembly suitable whenever corporations engage in collusion over price fixing. And God forbid that we should ever grant U.S. corporations the inalienable right to bear arms!

Sometimes people (mostly corporation lawyers, but sometimes philosophers as well) argue that corporations are deserving of due process and equal protection of all First Amendment rights because so esteemed a personage as Justice Marshall said that they are "invisible persons," but we are already wise to this rhetorical device; it is a run-away metaphor, and a fallacious appeal to authority as well. Sometimes it is useful to think of the corporation as though it were an "invisible person," but an actual person, decidedly, it is not. If we wish to grant such rights to the corporation, we must always in the first instance ask the simple question, "Why? Is such a declaration expedient? In the national interest? In the interests of the individuals served by the corporation?" The answers will vary with the circumstances: sometimes treating corporations as though they have certain rights is expedient in some of these ways; sometimes not.

Donaldson is also incorrect when he supposes that the courts have recognized that American-based corporations have the First Amendment rights of free speech. Nothing I have been able to uncover in Supreme Court decisions corroborate that belief. In the landmark case of *First National Bank of Boston v. Bellotti*, for example, — the case that I surmise Donaldson had in mind when he made his assertion — the Court did not rule that corporations (meaning *all* corporations, or even *all U.S. based* corporations) have the right of freedom of speech. Nor did the Court — interestingly enough — rule that First National Bank of Boston had the right to free speech. The majority opinion, written by Justice Powell, is especially enlightening in this regard. Justice Powell writes:

> The proper question therefore is not whether corporations have First Amendment rights and, if so, whether they are coextensive with those of natural persons. Instead the question must be whether "the statute in question" abridges expression that the First Amendment was meant to protect. We hold that it does. . . . [6]

Justice Powell clearly did not mean to commit the Court to the ascription of Human Rights to abstract entities — a wise precaution to my mind. In a fashion that would please William of Occam, Justice Powell avoided ontological commitment to abstract entities. Justice Powell ruled just that, *in this instance*, abridging free speech to First National Bank of Boston would be less expedient than prohibiting such expression. Yet, we also infer from the decision that in other cases, prudence might dictate the need to abridge corporate free expression — for example, Justice Powell mentions the restrictions on trading on the basis of inside information.

I take Judge Powell's decision to be based on an appeal to the principle of the greatest liberty compatible with a like liberty for all. That may be relevantly applicable in the case of *First National Bank of Boston v. Bellotti*, but improper where price-fixing or inside trading is concerned. Each case must be taken on its respective merits with regard to the principle of greatest liberty.

The lesson to be learned from this case is that we *can* make good sense of the corporation as a legal entity, a *persona ficta* with *iures fictus* (rights of a certain but derivative sort). Yet, any conclusion which supposes that a corporation has an autonomous right to exist apart from the interests it serves is unwarranted. Therefore, the corporation is enough like a moral person to make moral and legal demands of it — that would seem to follow from any grant of *rights* to it, for the correlative of rights is responsibilities; but no basis exists for the supposition that the corporation is somehow entitled to the same degree of protection or of compassion or of mercy that the courts accord to real persons when they break the law. Surely, the faulty conclusion which portrays corporations as beaters of autonomous rights could only follow as a result of a misplaced reliance on the strength of the analogy involved when corporations are compared to persons, and a greater understanding of the worth of argument by analogy is necessary to clarify the degree to which we should credence the personification of the modern corporation. This is a subject which I shall develop in the next section.

III. THE ARGUMENT FROM ANALOGY

Philosophers have been suspicious of the argument from analogy ever since David Hume made his celebrated and concerted attack against William Paley's argument from design for the existence of God.

We now know that arguments from analogy have special strengths and special drawbacks. Monroe Beardsley sums up the difficulties with analogical argument, saying that it is indeed "a distinctive form of argument" but "not a cogent (one)."[7] Because arguments from analogy have the virtue of plausibility, and wide acceptance in popular use, we must know how to deal with them, but in fact analogical arguments do not render the conclusion any probability whatever.

Consider just how the argument from analogy fails on the test of cogency: Compare two entities A and B by searching for whatever properties they share. If entities A and B share properties X, Y, and Z, we are in no way justified in leaping to the conclusion that if A has further property a, then so also will B. The only way we could be sure that B had a is if we knew in advance of the argument the truth of the further premise that B and A are identical. Then, by virtue of Leibnitz' Law of the Identity of Indiscernibles, we would then and only then be justified in inferring that B also has a.

However, critical inquiry is not the only basis for argument. We have the familiar distinction between critical thought and creative thought. Beardsley suggests that analogies can help us put objects in a new light, and they can prompt new and creative hypotheses.[8] Such is the real value of analogical arguments.

We would do well to draw a distinction here between the use of the argument from analogy as "deductively binding," and the argument from analogy as "critically explorative." When an analogical argument is used in a deductively binding way, it is faulty in the sorts of ways that a David Hume and Monroe Beardsley describe. Such an argument speculates on the independent existence of certain relations or entities — but this is speculation only; such relations or entities are not *observed*, nor is any evidence offered beyond the analogical exercise itself which confers any degree of likelihood or certainty on the conclusion of the argument.

We may detect, however, a more legitimate basis for this argument form: we may say that an analogical argument is "critically explorative" just in case it is used in a manner which opens up new avenues of thought, or if it employed in a way that expands our options in finding solutions to problems, or in clarifying relations between otherwise unlike objects. The difference between "critically explorative" and "deductively binding" uses of the argument from analogy is very much the difference between mapmaking and consulting a ready-made map (except that, in the former case, we also may be creating some of the landscape even as we're charting it.)

Recall, once more, Justice Marshall's personification of the corporation as "an artificial being." The problem is twofold: First, Marshall's juridical descendants used the analogy in precisely the form of which Monroe Beardsley disapproves — what we've called here, "the deductively binding" form. The analogy is taken much too literally and we run the danger of looking for (or, worse: assuming the existence of) attributes of personhood in the corporation where none exist. The danger is compounded by the second feature of the Marshall definition of the corporation: the fact that the analogy is cast in a *metaphorical* form. Metaphors, we must emphasize, have especially regrettable propensities in such critical contexts since they may be said to be "analogies in disguise."

What separates the metaphor from the more clearly analogical simile is the implicit suggestion in the metaphor that the analogy to be made entails a correspondingly tight fit between shared properties of distinct entities. A stronger presumption exists, then, that if A has property a, then so also will B. Such figures of speech are fraught with perils from a logical point of view, especially when argumentative appeals are made to the metaphors coined by illustrious personages on the part of individuals in a legal system that is by its nature exceedingly literal-minded. Beardsley wisely cautions us that metaphors have two hidden dangers: first, metaphors are hard to control. They often run away from us, and cause us to seem to be saying more than we intended. Second, we can get locked into favorite metaphors, causing us to see matters only through the point of view which the metaphor prompts. Such metaphors may obscure other possible interrelationships, so that coming to think in new and more productive ways becomes more and more difficult.[9] The greatest contribution that analogies have to make to our thinking — their potential for creativity —

can be defeated by a metaphor that has too familiar a use. I fear that both of these drawbacks are present in the legal, moral and business reliance on the Marshall metaphor, and I attribute our inability to find new and creative solutions to the problem of corporate misconduct tied to the worn-out and over-used metaphor of corporations as "abstract beings."

We may rush to Justice Marshall's defense, and rightly so, for he clearly shows us the dissimilarities between persons and corporations within the very context of these oft-quoted remarks: persons are not invisible, neither are they intangible nor existing only in the contemplation of law. But this metaphor has in the first place, entranced subsequent users into disregarding the dis-analogies. Even so cautious a thinker as Thomas Donaldson sometimes inadvertently slips into the habit of describing corporations as "invisible persons."[10] The problem is that Justice Marshall's metaphor has controlled our thinking too rigidly: it has attained the status of a legal presupposition. As a result, solutions to problems of corporate wrongdoing continue to elude us.

Philosophy may well be defined as the discipline which seeks to uncover, and challenge, basic presuppositions about life, conduct, knowledge and reality — presuppositions which may be widely shared, largely unrecognized, and stand as roadblocks to appropriate or innovative solutions. It is my contention that such unrecognized presuppositions have hold of us here.

The method by which philosophers must often uncover these presuppositions is through the device known as a "thought-experiment." Thought-experiments share both a critical and a creative function. Once a presupposition of import is uncovered, then constructive critical analysis can begin, but in the first instance thought-experiments are creative enterprises. They may pose the question, "What if matters were otherwise?" By so asking, a philosopher can look at a problem from a new vantage point. An example of this device at work in political philosophy is the time-honored mechanism of the "State of Nature" theory, which Thomas Hobbes and John Locke, among others, have used to good effect. The problem each seeks to solve is the nature of government, its purposes and justification. The State of Nature thought-experiment is an aid here in supposing what conditions might have been like before any government whatever existed. Depending on how one sets up the experiment, radically different results ensue (as was the case between the theories of Hobbes and Locke.) Thereupon, critical analysis can proceed. However, I repeat, in the first instance the exercise is always a creative one, and that usually proceeds along an analogical base.

My proposal is to do some creative thinking of our own. If some corporations act irresponsibly and threaten the life and well-being of law-abiding citizens in the community, then surely some device more effective than the levying of fines can be found as a way of deterring such misconduct in the future. To find the answer, treating recalcitrant corporations as on a par to hardened criminals might well be an illuminating analogy. Notice that by so proposing such an analogy, I do not endorse an exact correspondence. That would be to miss the point of the thought-experiment. The analogy proposed has a creative, not a critical, intention.

IV. CIVIL VS. CRIMINAL PROSECUTION

Consider the familiar case history of Hooker Chemical Company. In a period that stretches from 1942 to 1979, Hooker Chemical and Plastics Corporation demonstrated a remarkable disregard for the health and well-being of residents living adjacent to disposal sites and chemical discharges. Most notable of these transgressions was the incident at Love Canal, but a long series of such abuses is on record. In 1972, at Hyde Park, N.Y., the manager of an adjacent plant complained to Hooker of "an extremely dangerous condition affecting our plant and employees. . . ." The manager traced the source to a Hooker disposal site. In 1976, the New York Department of Environmental Conservation was forced to ban consumption of several species of fish from Lake Ontario because of discharges of the chemical Mirex from the Hooker Niagara Falls Plant. In 1976–1977, Hooker was named as a defendant for supplying raw materials for the manufacture of Kepone dust, which had induced illness in employees of Life Science Company, Virginia. In 1977, Hooker paid a fine of $176,000 for discharging HCCPD into a lake in Michigan. Michigan officials also sued Hooker in 1979 for pollution around its plant in Montague. In 1979, the town of Niagara Falls filed suit against Hooker based on a NY State Health Department survey of residents near Hyde Park.[11] Again, in 1979, Hooker was convicted of polluting the air with fluoride at White Springs, Florida.[12]

Despite these cases, Hooker Chemical and Plastics Company has shown no evidence of a "change of heart" in its policies regarding chemical discharges and disposal sites. In fact, as far as we are able to determine, to date no fine or suit has been able to deter Hooker from its modus operandi. The fines have been negligible in both amount and in effect.

Union Carbide's Bhopal incident serves as another case in point, where 2000 people lost their lives. Less than one year later, an accident occurred at the Union Carbide site in West Virginia, and just prior to the Bhopal incident, Union Carbide was fined $3.9 million for delaying reporting of new carcinogenicity information on the chemical, diethyl sulfate, to the Environmental Protection Agency. In these cases, fines have proved (and may continue to be) costly to Union Carbide. Nevertheless, a pattern of abuses has developed in the company's safety procedures.[13]

There are some promising developments in prosecutorial aggressiveness directed against individuals in the corporation who may be made out to be more responsible than others when the decision-making process results in grievous transgressions of the law. For instance, in the cases of the General Dynamics Corporation overcharges to the U.S. Military, attempts have been made to pierce the "corporate veil" and prosecute the individuals who are allegedly responsible for the decision which led the company into wrongdoing. Such charges have been leveled at three senior executives of General Dynamics regarding the overcharges. Even more aggressive is the set of charges leveled against Lester Crown, owner of 23% of General Dynamics' 65 million shares of stock, with respect to an Illinois bribery case which may result in the suspension of his security clearance.[14] Such attempts are not entirely without precedent, but they do represent a challenge to the very boundary lines of corporate liability sharing. Nevertheless, good reasons exist for those boundaries, and, by virtue of those good reasons, nothing may come of those attempts by the courts. Moreover, such legal actions are the exception to the rule and, as Neil Glixon argues, that is a major reason such corporations remain recalcitrant. He writes:

> The idea of personal responsibility is evidently passe. Responsibility is diffused into the corporation, and finally fades away into misdemeanors

whose perpetrators must perform community service, as if they had been guilty of writing graffiti on subway walls.[15]

Glixon goes on to point out that Union Carbide's Chairman, Warren M. Anderson, begged off from any blame, either for himself or for his company, for the accident at Bhopal, India. Glixon comments: "The problem is that in today's corporate structures the causal chain is always extended. One can easily understand how a Warren Anderson may find it difficult to identify himself as a culprit in so extended a chain. . . ."[16] However, Glixon here overlooks Anderson's earlier pronouncements of personal moral responsibility for the accident, when he claimed he would devote the rest of his life to helping the people who suffered during the tragedy. He reversed himself a year later, in an interview for *Business Week*, where he stated that when he made his remarks about moral responsibility, he had "overreacted." What brought on this hardening of the heart? The issue is insightfully discussed in the "Notes and Comment" heading of the New Yorker magazine:

> His company, pursued by lawyers seeking billions of dollars in compensation for the dead and injured (and sizable fees,) is facing a critical court decision about whether the case will be tried in India or in America, where damage awards are expected to be higher. . . .
>
> What Mr. Anderson meant. . . . perhaps, is that at first he reacted as a private man but in the intervening months he has remembered — or been reminded — that he is the head of a corporation. Murray Kempton pointed out in a recent edition of *Newsday* that as Mr. Anderson was talking about the "moral responsibilities" of his company its stock was collapsing; now the company, defiant . . . has seen its shares rise to a price more than a third above their level on the day before Bhopal.[17]

Such are the problems with attempts to pierce the corporate veil for the purpose of attaching responsibility to private individuals. We may find convincing the claim that as a CEO of Union Carbide, Warren Anderson never acts as an autonomous decision maker, no matter the great authority he undoubtedly wields. True, the lesson of the Nuremberg Trials is that guilt is individual; the notion of collective guilt has no place in American law. Yet, this is precisely the problem with attempts at the prosecution of individuals in many cases of corporate wrongdoing, for placing the blame in an exceedingly difficult undertaking, made more complicated by the corporation's very structure. For some corporations at least, no provision is made to accommodate issues of the public good. In such circumstances, an executive may find that resisting the ride of impending corporate decisions can take exceptional moral willpower. Moreover, we may have no way of knowing whether a given executive dissented from the board's joint decision. The matter of diffused responsibility is intimately connected with the corporation's internal structure of shared liability, but if everybody shares liability, then surely nobody does.

The judgments of the courts in these matters amply demonstrate their debility in handling prosecution of corporate wrongdoing. Once again, the courts are reluctant to utilize the full weight of the law against such corporations because too many innocent parties stand to suffer, whereas CEO's are largely protected from prosecution due to the corporation's traditional composition which diffuses personal responsibility. The result is that many corporations continue their abuses much in the manner as a repeat criminal or psychopathic individual would.

The problem is that such corporations may be criminally liable, but we exact mainly civil penalties. We've already considered why civil penalties are self-defeating — for one thing, the punishment exacted tends to ricochet, depriving workers of jobs, communities of their major industry, and consumers of needed products and optimal prices derived from the possible absence of competition should such fines effectively close a company down.

Yet, the history of the prosecution of corporate wrongdoing is the fullest exemplification of "thinking in a rut." If one fine doesn't work, and a company's transgression is repeated, then the court's policy is to levy another fine — usually not much greater than the one that preceded it. Companies write off these fines as external dis-economies, and learn that they are less costly than the technology needed to correct the abuses. As a result, the abuses continue. Commenting on the apparent lack of moral responsibility exercised by corporations, *The New Yorker* editorialized, "Corporations need to function the way they function — it is the only way they make sense. Yet there is no point in denying that they feel less responsibility to the people of, say, Bhopal than to the people who hold their stocks and bonds. This is neither good nor bad; it is merely a fact."[18]

We would do well to be skeptical of such laments of moral impotence. Corporations are, after all, made in the image and likeness of man; they are what we make them to be. They exist or perish at the sufferance of broader social interests. Corporations, like governments, are human institutions; that is sufficient cause to judge them on the basis of morality.

As a result of incidents like those at Bhopal, we loudly cry out for greater governmental regulation. The prosecutorial attempts against Lester Crown of General Dynamics also offer us some hope for changes in the conduct of corporate officers and powerbrokers. Whether such attempts will succeed — or whether even they should succeed — remain to be seen, but I will propose yet another way.

Let us return to the metaphor struck a few paragraphs above, comparing corporations to repeat criminals or psychopathic individuals. We find a useful ambiguity here. Corporations are not persons, but they sometimes behave *like* persons. In some respects, the recalcitrant corporation acts much like a repeat criminal in bearing some measure of responsibility for its conduct; in other respects, the corporation behaves like a psychopathic individual, breaking the law much as a person does who is out of control.

This ambiguity has confused the issue in the minds of many theorists, some of whom argue too tightly the "repeat criminal" analogy, while others argue too closely to the "psychopath" analogy. But the confusion is really very easy to resolve. The analogies have been pushed too far. Recalcitrant corporations can be viewed either way, depending on which point of view better serves the public interest. The courts cannot find human beings both criminally insane and morally responsible for their actions, but corporations are not human beings and sometimes good reasons will be found for treating them as "out of control," and sometimes as morally responsible.

In what ways are corporations like repeat criminal offenders? For one thing, certain intentional constructs can be discerned in corporate behavior. These intentions are collectively emergent from the corporation's charter, its executive leadership and statement of goals. These serve as the corporation's "rationale" for (sometimes) engaging in illegal conduct. To the extent that this rationale can be amended or changed, corporations can be said to be morally responsible for their actions.

In what ways are corporations like psychopathic individuals? This is a little more complicated. Psychopathic behavior in individuals is characterized as "spasmodic anti-social behavior," according to Brendan A. Maher in *Principles of Psychopathology: An Experimental Approach*. Many bases of comparison can be found between the psychopathic personality and the incorrigible corporation. Recall our discussion about the ineffectuality of fines levied against corporations (especially in the case of Hooker Chemical and Plastics Corporation,) and contrast this with the following comment from Maher: ". . . in spite of frequent punishments for impulsive antisocial activity, the psychopath appears not to learn anything from his own experience."[19]

Maher describes several traits as characteristic of the psychopathic individual:

> . . . we should notice that the positive attributes, such as antisocial behavior, emotional shallowness, and vanity, are accompanied by certain negative attributes. Notable among these are the absence of overt anxiety and the absence of guilt. Also, the psychopath's behavioral insensitivity to punishment requires explanation in any satisfactory account of the determinates of this pathological pattern.[20]

Recalling our cautions about metaphors, we must not be too strongly taken up by the analogies drawn here. For example, no relevant comparison comes to mind about the psychopath's trait of vanity and the makeup of the modern corporation. Yet, when Warren Anderson backs off from claims of moral responsibility by Union Carbide for the Bhopal accident, one is tempted to draw a comparison between this and the psychopath's absence of guilt. The environmental record of Hooker Chemical aptly exemplifies the psychopath's insensitivity to punishment. The analogy suggested here is straightforward enough: the incorrigible corporation is to the law-abiding corporation in the way that the criminal psychopath is to the moral person. If we sometimes find comparing the average corporation to a moral person a useful, if sometimes misleading, analogy, then the comparison between the recalcitrant corporation and the psychopathic individual may also serve us here. The question, "What is the *nature* of the corporation," is misdirected when discussing moral corporate conduct, a question about as out of date as the cosmologist's questions about the nature of the universe. We should be asking instead, "How should we *treat* corporations?" The answer here is obvious enough. We treat them as constructs set up to serve the public good. Now we can carry the insight one step further. When the corporation obstructs rather than advances the public good, when the corporation acts more like a criminal psychopath than as a model citizen, the offender ought to be confined in the interests of public safety. Unfortunately, a corporation is not sufficiently like a human being to allow for conventional methods of confinement; we are left to the devices of fines and regulations — the very devices we had assumed at the outset to have been ineffective when used against the recalcitrant corporation. Stronger measures are apparently called for.

In so suggesting, however, we return to the familiar problem of the effects any disruption of the corporation may have on its workers, its neighboring community, or the consumer deprived of its goods or services. However, now that we're clear about the role of the analogy in clarifying our thinking and in offering creative options, we see there is really no need to cling to our analogy too tightly. What we may propose for corporations which engage in repeated, calculated moral and legal wrongdoing is a sentence of "corporate corporal punishment." Therefore, we can propose something analogous to a "beheading."

The decision-making apparatus of most large corporations is a complicated and involved construction, including not only the President and the Chairman of the Board, but also the Board of Directors itself, the legions of Vice-Presidents and other important Corporate Executive Officers, and stockholders who carry large holdings in the corporation. At least on paper, this is correct (actual practice may vary.) Yet, we may well agree that each of them ought to have a voice in the conduct of the corporation. When they do not exercise that prerogative, and the corporation engages in wrongdoing, then they are remiss in their duties to the corporation and to the public at large. This proposal will insure that they do not commit such sins of omission in the future.

The proposal sketched here remains, above all, a proposal. I offer it in the spirit of further discussion. As such, I do not offer detailed guidelines for how such a corporate "beheading" should take place (though I will make some general suggestions.) I do not consider in any depth the sorts of legal obstacles that stand in the way. I do however assert that sufficient justification exists for implementing a proposal of this general sort.

How might this punishment be meted out? We may suggest a complete reorganization of the decision-making organization, including the Company President, the Chairman of the Board, the Board of Directors itself, and every executive officer at or above the level of Vice-President. We can further recommend the dissolution of shareholders' stock for all shareholders who possess 1% or more of the outstanding stock of the corporation. The figure as it is presented here is arbitrary, but the idea is to minimize the effects of this decision on the smallest shareholders, who presumably have little or no voice in the corporation's conduct (unlike the case of Lester Crown, who holds a sizable portion of General Dynamics stock.) The confiscated stocks will then be turned over to the company's employees in equal shares, provided (say) that the employee has been working for this company for six months or more.

Clearly, this proposal calls for drastic action. We can conceive of the idea as a last resort measure, to be taken when all other reasonable recourse has been exhausted. The point is, however, that the usual sorts of judicial sanctions, while they work well enough against most corporations, completely fail to modify the behavior of those corporations we compared to repeat criminal offenders or psychopathic individuals. The sanctions proposed here are directed at an aberrant minority of corporations. However, when appropriate, these penalties should not be invoked lightly. Therefore, several conditions must be prevalent for this recommendation to take effect. First, the transgressions a corporation commits must be sufficiently grievous, involving loss of life or extreme environmental damage. There must be some correlation to criminal justice's concept of a capital offense. Second, the implementation of this proposal should not apply to first-time offenders. Our main goal is behavior modi-

fication, and the conventional sanctions (fines and regulations) may be sufficient to accomplish that job with regard to most corporate legal transgressions.
However, we may think of "corporate corporal punishment" as another instrument the court can draw out of its judicial toolbox when the corporation has
repeatedly shown disdain for the law, and little likelihood exists for its
rehabilitation.

One advantage to this proposal is that it provides relief to the innocent.
Closing down a company altogether is an unsavory proposition, but the "beheading" called for here has a surgical benefit: removing the head, while leaving
the body unharmed. Workers have the opportunity, at least, to continue their
employment without relocation. As a further benefit, communities that rely on
the corporation's plants as their main industry will continue to hold on to their
main industry. And consumers will continue to have access to the corporation's
products and services, and to the pricing effects of its competitive impact such
as it might be.

A further advantage to this proposal is that it can be seen as a way to advance
what many regard as an economic ideal: corporate democracy. Corporate democracy or (as it is sometimes called) "economic democracy" is the organization of economic authority according to a Rousseauean interpretation of the
social contract when applied to business.[21] It is a hypothetical contract between
the company, workers and consumers. The Rousseauean interpretation demands an identification between the "rulers" and the "ruled" — in this instance, an identification of management with the workers.

Usually, in the West, economic democracy comes into play where no conflicts of private property rights stand in the way. For example, a company may
shut down a plant which serves as the major industry in a community, giving the
employees the dismal choice of relocation or unemployment. Economic democracy stands as a broadening of options, nullifying the apparent dilemma, and
offering a chance for a community and its workers to buy the company from its
parent and keep it in operation.

In much the same way, worker controlled factories offer a broadening of
options where a corporation's transgressions of the law are grievous and repetitive. Furthermore, a precedent may be in the making for this sort of activity in
the proposal made by New Orleans councilmen to "municipalize" their power
company. I offer this discussion as an extension of, and a justification of, the
New Orleans example. The New Orleans case also represents a possible response to the anticipated charge that the proposal is "socialistic" in its outlook.
Like the councilmen of New Orleans, many of whom are elected, conservative
Republicans, I share their answer that the proposal is not ideologically-tied; it is
merely a practical response to an aggravated problem.[22]

One might object, however, that I have strayed from the terms of the original
analogy. We compared the recalcitrant corporation to a psychopathic individual. But the courts do not execute psychopaths, they restrain them. Objectors
may point out that I am engaging in a species of fallacious special pleading by
appealing for unusual and inappropriate modes of punishment, or of begging
the question because I sometimes compare such corporations to repeat criminals and sometimes as criminal psychopaths. However, I do not think these are
serious objections.

My answer is that the objections fail to take cognizance of the role of the
analogy. We do not need a point-by-point correspondence between the of-

fending corporation and the psychopath or repeat offender. We need to know only that there is enough of a likeness between the two to warrant more drastic action to be taken than is conventionally applied: the offending corporation, like the criminal psychopath, represents a great danger to society; we have compassionate ways of restraining psychopaths, but no effective way of restraining the incorrigible corporation. The object in employing the analogy to criminal psychopaths is one of exploring creative options, not metaphysical analysis about the nature of the corporation. For the same reason, the objection of special pleading is also ill-conceived. The purpose of a thought-experiment is not critical discovery (and it is in this context that charges of special pleading carry the most weight,) but creative exploration of options. I do grant, however, that my position has metaphysical import. I am bringing a nominalist outlook to bear on the problem, employing Occam's razor in the effort to avoid the proliferation of unnecessary entities. Corporations really *aren't* persons; they are only somewhat *like* persons when corrective action is called for.

This difference in outlook makes all the difference in the world. For example, with regard to human beings, I have strong, personal moral reservations about the use of capital punishment. I question the truth of its adherent's strongest claim in the defense of its use — viz., its supposed deterrent powers.[23] Moreover, I object to capital punishment on the grounds of moral compassion, and because of the "de-civilizing" effects I believe wide-spread executions have on the moral fabric of society at large. This might well surprise the reader, since I openly advocate something similar for the corporation when it grievously breaks the law. However, the object of my proposal is not deterrence so much as it is protection from the menace of "psychopathic" corporations. My proposal may sound overly harsh, but the corporation, I repeat, is *not* a person; it is a human artifact.

There is a sense in which I want to pattern my sentiments after a remark made by John Kenneth Galbraith to the effect that, where financial dealings are concerned, "nothing is being lost but someone else's money."[24] In this context, however, the remark proves to be a bit cavalier. The financial insanity of incorrigible corporations can cause terrible tragedies, as in the cases of Bhopal and Love Canal. Moreover, given the implementation of the proposal, not only is money being lost, but in many cases the careers of executives. The consolation I offer is small, but perhaps adequate: this measure is directed at no individual in the corporation; it is directed against the chartered corporation itself — a corporation which sometimes enjoys rights and other protections, and must accordingly conduct itself in a socially responsible manner. The liability of individual executives in the corporation may be limited, but we discern enough responsibility on their parts to be liable to at least this extent.

No stigma need attach to any executive who is displaced under the terms of this proposal, but its implementation is only the other side of the coin from when an executive comes to benefit (whether through her efforts or not) from those conditions under which a corporation becomes prosperous. I expect, moreover, that most executives who are disenfranchised by the implementation of this proposal will find niches in other companies. In any case, the (usually temporary) setback in their careers is justly proportionate to the advantages they enjoyed by corporate veils of liability and equal to their responsibility for their sin of omission, their failure to speak for the record in protest.

Notes

1. *Dartmouth College v. Woodward*, 4 Wheat 518.636 (1819).

2. See, for example, Milton Friedman's discussion of 'The Social Responsibility of Business', in *The New York Times Magazine*, September 13, 1970 reprinted in Hoffman and Moore, *Business Ethics: Readings and Cases in Corporate Morality* (McGraw-Hill, New York) 1984, pp. 126–131.

3. In what may be the definitive history of the origins of business enterprise in England, Ephraim Lipson devotes a lengthy discussion to the struggle between the towns and the Church to gain separate legal jurisdiction. Lipson writes:
There appear to be no indications that English towns ever formed confederacies for their mutual support after the manner of continental towns, but there are signs of sporadic co-operation. We also get occasional glimpses of the process by which their efforts to achieve emancipation forced the townsmen to recognize the need for corporate action. The men of Bury St. Edmunds assessed themselves for a sum of money to maintain their contest with the abbey, and we may infer that in other towns a growing sense of corporate consciousness was fostered by the pressure of like circumstances. Ephraim Lipson, *The Economic History of England*, 'The Middle Ages', Vol. 1 (Barnes and Noble, New York) 12th Ed., 1962, p. 208.

4. 'Corporation, Business', *The Encyclopedia Britannica*, Vol. 5, pp. 182–189.

5. Thomas Donaldson, *Corporations and Morality* (Prentice-Hall, Englewood Cliffs, NJ) 1982, p. 3.

6. *First National Bank of Boston v. Bellotti*, 435 U.S. 765, April 26, 1978; reprinted in Hoffman and Moore, *op. cit.*, pp. 215–221.

7. Monroe Beardsley, *Thinking Straight* (Prentice-Hall, Englewood Cliffs, NJ) 4th Ed., 1975, p. 113.

8. *Ibid.*, p. 112.

9. *Ibid.*, p. 165.

10. Donaldson, *op. cit.*, p. 18. See also Justice Rehnquist's dissent in *First National Bank of Boston v. Bellotti*, where he also makes use of the metaphor of "invisible persons" in a "deductively binding" use of the metaphor. (Reprinted in Hoffman and Moore, *op. cit.*, pp. 220–221.)

11. Gary Whitney, 'Case Study — Hooker Chemical and Plastics', reprinted in Thomas Donaldson, *Cases Studies in Business Ethics* (Prentice-Hall, Englewood Cliffs, NJ) 1984, pp. 66–70. See also 'Hooker Chemical and Love Canal' in Tom L. Beauchamp, *Case Studies in Business, Society, and Ethics*, (Prentice-Hall, Englewood Cliffs, NJ) 1983, pp. 107–115.

12. Donaldson, *op. cit.*, *Corporations and Morality*, p. 11.

13. A timely example of the need for more stringent powers of enforcement against corporate wrongdoing may be seen in the aftermath of the Exxon Valdez accident of March, 1989. Regarding Exxon's irresponsibility in the matter, *The Los Angeles Times* editorialized: "The Exxon Valdez spill has demonstrated that Americans cannot rely on the good will of corporations to clean up their own messes adequately, although there are companies that value their public image so highly that they will do the right thing. The Alaskan tragedy makes the case for strong federal regulations and controls closely monitored and strongly enforced. There must be stiff penalties for failure to comply." 'The Risks of Underregulation', *The Los Angeles Times*, May 6, 1989.

14. *Business Week*, No. 2925, December 16, 1985, p. 28; See also: 'Lester Crown Blames the System: General Dynamics' Biggest Shareholder Steps Forward to Defend His Troubled Company and Its Departing Chief', *The New York Times*, June 16, 1985, Sec. 3.

15. Neil Glixon, 'Uncollared Crime: The Riddle of Guiltlessness', *Commonweal*, November 29, 1985, p. 662.

16. *Ibid.*

17. 'The Talk of the Town', *The New Yorker*, January 13, 1986, p. 18.

18. *Ibid.*, p. 18.

19. Brendan A. Maher, *Principles of Psychopathology: An Experimental Approach* (McGraw-Hill, New York) 1966, p. 213.

20. *Ibid.*, p. 213.

21. For a survey article on this subject, see Drew Christie, "Recent Calls for Economic Democracy', in *Ethics*, Vol. 95, October, 1984, pp. 112–128.

22. 'New Orleans Begins Plan Toward Utility Takeover', *The Wall Street Journal*, Western edition, January 30, 1985, p. 16.

23. For a representative discussion of the arguments for and against capital punishment, see Hugo A. Bedau, Ed., *The Death Penalty in America* (Oxford University Press, Oxford) 3rd ed., 1982.

24. John Kenneth Galbraith, *The Great Crash 1929* (Houghton-Mifflin, Boston) 1979, p. xiv.

◆ ◆ ◆

DISCUSSION QUESTIONS

1. Would a company punished according to French's "Hester Prynne Sanction" be treated justly and fairly? What ends does such punishment serve? Retribution? Deterrence?

2. Corlett takes the Hester Prynne Sanction to task on several fronts. One of his most important objections is that French's plan does not prevent innocent people from being hurt. Do you agree? Is this issue as serious as Corlett thinks?

3. Were the Stevens and Nestlé "vendettas" that Shannon describes morally appropriate as punishment? Did they achieve their ends?

4. Rafalko claims that "corporate beheading" protects the innocent and advances economic democracy. Does this make his proposal superior to those of French and Shipp?

CASE 7.1

◆ ◆ ◆

Beech-Nut's Imitation Apple Juice

In 1988, the Beech-Nut Nutrition Corporation and two of its top executives admitted that they had knowingly sold adulterated apple juice. In fact, the baby food, although described on the label as "100% fruit juice," contained little if any apple juice. The company agreed to pay a $2 million fine, but the ultimate cost to Beech-Nut was closer to $25 million when the settlement of a class action suit, legal fees, and lost sales are included. The two executives, Neils L. Hoyvald, the firm's former president and CEO, and John F. Lavery, former vice-president of manufacturing, were fined $100,000 each and sentenced to jail terms of a year and a day. (A major part of the conviction and Hoyvald's imprisonment were dismissed when an appeals court ruled that the trial had taken place in the wrong court.)

This example of corporate wrongdoing combines fraud with a coverup and was apparently driven by ongoing and intense financial pressure at Beech-Nut. In 1977, Beech-Nut changed suppliers of the concentrate used to produce its apple juice when it was offered the product at 20 percent below market rates by Interjuice Trading Corporation. This resulted in an annual savings of $250,000 — no small amount for a company that was financially strapped. Despite misgivings about the juice by Jerome LiCari, Beech-Nut's director of research and development, laboratory tests could not prove that the juice was counterfeit. By 1981, however, LiCari believed that there was enough circumstantial evidence to suggest that the concentrate was a blend of synthetic ingredients, and he claims that he notified senior management of his belief. By that time, however, Hoyvald had apparently promised Nestlé, the Swiss food concern that had bought Beech-Nut, that the company would turn around financially in 1982. Beech-Nut had been sold to Nestlé in 1979 and had lost $2.5 million in fiscal 1981. But Hoyvald pledged a profit of $700,000 for the following year, and the parent company apparently communicated to him that he must deliver. As Hoyvald put it, "The pressure was on." Changing suppliers and buying a more expensive concentrate would have made a profit impossible to achieve. Also, some Beech-Nut officials still pointed to the fact that there was no absolute proof that the apple juice was adulterated. (It is worth noting, however, that although Beech-Nut's policy was to stay with the concentrate as long as it could not be proven that it was counterfeit, other companies reversed the burden of proof and terminated a supplier if it could not prove that its product was genuine.) Some Beech-Nut officials also claimed that even if the juice were fake, it was not doing anyone any harm. The juice in the bottles might not be apple juice, but it was not a health hazard.

By mid-1982, however, a private detective hired by an industry association found proof that the concentrate was synthetic and presented it to Beech-Nut. The company did stop buying the concentrate at that time. But instead of publicly admitting the error, destroying or relabeling the inventory, and paying a fine, Hoyvald chose a strategy that would buy enough time to see the $3.5 million worth of juice sitting in warehouses. The company refused to cooperate with an investigation against the suppliers and waited a few months before recalling the product in the United States. The product then was offered at large discounts to offshore distributors. To keep one step ahead of state law enforcement officials, inventory was even moved from one state to another. Hoyvald apparently believed that Beech-Nut's very existence was at stake. When asked by one of the prosecutors why the juice had simply not been destroyed, he replied, "And I could have called up Switzerland and told them I had just closed the company down. Because that is what would have been the result of it." ◆

Discussion Questions

1. How seriously unethical is what Beech-Nut did? How seriously wrong is what Hoyvald and Lavery did?

2. How do you distinguish corporate from personal responsibility? Should the parent company, Nestlé, be held responsible for anything that happened?

3. Is the company's difficult financial condition an extenuating circumstance?

4. How relevant is the claim that the counterfeit juice did not hurt any babies who drank it?

5. If you were the judge in this case, what punishments would you assign the corporation and the individual executives?

6. What would the punishments look like if you used French's Hester Prynne Sanction, Shipp's modified vendetta, or Rafalko's beheading proposal?

Sources

Buder, Leonard, "2 Former Executives of Beech-Nut Guilty in Phony Juice Case," *New York Times*, February 18, 1988, A1, D3.

Traum, James, "Into the Mouths of Babes," *This World*, August 7, 1988, 14–15.

"What Led Beech-Nut Down the Road to Disgrace," *Business Week*, February 22, 1988, 124–128.

CASE 7.2

◆ ◆ ◆

Sentencing a Corporation to Prison

In 1988, Federal Judge Robert G. Doumar handed down an extremely unusual punishment for a corporation convicted of wrongdoing—he sentenced it to three years in prison. The Maryland-based Allegheny Bottling Company was found guilty of three years of price-fixing, and Judge Doumar wanted a penalty that would be sterner than the typical fine. "The corporation," explained the jurist, "cannot come in here, profit to the tune of $10 million and walk away with a $1 million fine." The punishment he chose, on top of such a fine, was clearly unexpected.

Judge Doumar later suspended the sentence and $50,000 of the fine, but he placed the company on probation. The judge explained that in the case of a corporation, imprisonment amounted to placing restrictions on the company's ability to operate. He ordered that four of the company's senior executives perform up to two years of full-time community service. And he threatened that if the company failed to do so, he would close down its operations.

Allegheny Bottling, a Pepsi bottling franchise, was accused of collaborating with the Mid-Atlantic Coca-Cola Bottling Company to set wholesale prices. Before Allegheny's sentencing, the price-fixing scheme had already led to convictions of Morton Lapides, former chairman of Allegheny, and James Harford, former president of Mid-Atlantic Coca-Cola. Both men were sentenced to three years in prison, with all but six months suspended. Harford was also sentenced to three years of community service. In his order that four of Allegheny's executives perform community service, Judge Doumar specified that their positions and salaries must be similar to those of the executives already sentenced.

Attorneys for the company objected, pointing out that there was no precedent for imprisoning a corporation. ◆

Discussion Questions

1. It is obviously difficult to punish a corporation, and one of the most frustrating aspects of trying to do is that a fine can ultimately be passed along to stockholders, employees, or consumers — that is, people who had no hand in the wrongdoing pay the penalty. Is the Allegheny case a model of how to address this particular problem?

2. Two specific top executives were sentenced to prison and community service, Allegheny was ordered to have four other senior managers perform community service, and the company was ordered to pay a fine. How does this serve justice, broadly understood? Is such a model appropriately retributive for the crime? Would it deter other corporations? Most important, does it make any sense to sentence a corporation to imprisonment?

Source

Hicks, Jonathan P., "Corporate Prison Term for Allegheny Bottling," *New York Times*, September 1, 1988, D2.

ADDITIONAL READINGS

Corlett, J. Angelo, "Corporate Responsibility and Punishment," *Public Affairs Quarterly*, 2, no. 1 (January 1988), 1–16.
——— , "The 'Modified Vendetta Sanction' as a Method of Corporate-Collective Punishment," *Journal of Business Ethics*, 8 (1989), 937–942.
May, Larry, *The Morality of Groups* (Notre Dame, In: University of Notre Dame Press, 1987).
——— , "Group Ontology and Legal Strategy: A Reply to Tam," *Business & Professional Ethics Journal*, 8, no. 1 (1988), 83–88.
Risser, David T., "Punishing Corporations: A Proposal," *Business & Professional Ethics Journal*, 8, no. 3 (1988), 83–91.
Tam, Victor C. K., "Review Essay: May on Corporate Responsibility and Punishment," *Business & Professional Ethics Journal*, 8, no. 1 (1988), 65–81.

CHAPTER 8

◆ ◆ ◆

Business and Honesty

If there is a stereotyped image of moral abuse in business, it is the seller of used cars who cons an innocent buyer with the idea that "this car was only used by a little old lady to drive to church on Sundays." At the same time, hard bargaining and adept deal making accomplished by bluffing or being less than fully candid with an adversary are acceptable and even admired in business. When does morally acceptable good negotiating ability cross the boundary and become unethical lying? Is deception ever or always allowed in business?

This section begins with a classic piece by Albert Carr, who argues that business is comparable to a game. Deception in business, he argues, is thus no less moral than bluffing in poker. Norman Bowie, by contrast, appeals to the ideas of Immanuel Kant and Sissela Bok in a challenge to Carr's view. And even though Thomas Carson, Richard Wokutch, and Kent Murrmann generally reject Carr's position, they nonetheless offer a conditional defense for using bluffing in business. Finally, Jennifer Jackson focuses on questions of honesty in marketing and also suggests conditions under which deception is morally permissible.

Albert Z. Carr

IS BUSINESS BLUFFING ETHICAL?

A respected businessman with whom I discussed the theme of this article remarked with some heat, "You mean to say you're going to encourage men to bluff? Why, bluffing is nothing more than a form of lying! You're advising them to lie!"

I agreed that the basis of private morality is a respect for truth and that the closer a businessman comes to the truth, the more he deserves respect. At the same time, I suggested that most bluffing in business might be regarded simply as game strategy — much like bluffing in poker, which does not reflect on the morality of the bluffer.

I quoted Henry Taylor, the British statesman who pointed out that "falsehood ceases to be falsehood when it is understood on all sides that the truth is not expected to be spoken" — an exact description of bluffing in poker, diplomacy, and business. I cited the analogy of the criminal court, where the criminal is not expected to tell the truth when he pleads "not guilty." Everyone from the judge down takes it for granted that the job of the defendant's attorney is to get his client off, not to reveal the truth; and this is considered ethical practice. I mentioned Representative Omar Burleson, the Democrat from Texas, who was quoted as saying, in regard to the ethics of Congress, "Ethics is a barrel of worms"[1] — a pungent summing up of the problem of deciding who is ethical in politics.

I reminded my friend that millions of businessmen feel constrained every day to say *yes* to their bosses when they secretly believe *no* and that this is generally accepted as permissible strategy when the alternative might be the loss of a job. The essential point, I said, is that the ethics of business are game ethics, different from the ethics of religion.

He remained unconvinced. Referring to the company of which he is president, he declared: "Maybe that's good enough for some businessmen, but I can tell you that we pride ourselves on our ethics. In thirty years not one customer has ever questioned my word or asked to check our figures. We're loyal to our customers and fair to our suppliers. I regard my handshake on a deal as a contract. I've never entered into price-fixing schemes with my competitors. I've never allowed my salesmen to spread injurious rumors about other companies. Our union contract is the best in our industry. And, if I do say so myself, our ethical standards are of the highest!"

He really was saying, without realizing it, that he was living up to the ethical standards of the business game — which are a far cry from those of private life. Like a gentlemanly poker player, he did not play in cahoots with others at the table, try to smear their reputations, or hold back chips he owed them.

But this same fine man, at that very time, was allowing one of his products to be advertised in a way that made it sound a great deal better than it actually was. Another item in his product line was notorious among dealers for its

From *Harvard Business Review*, 46 (1968), 143–153. Reprinted by permission of *Harvard Business Review*. "Is Business Bluffing Ethical?" by Albert Z. Carr, January/February, 1968. Copyright © 1968 by the President and Fellows of Harvard College; all rights reserved.

"built-in obsolescence." He was holding back from the market a much-improved product because he did not want it to interfere with sales of the inferior item it would have replaced. He had joined with certain of his competitors in hiring a lobbyist to push a state legislature, by methods that he preferred not to know too much about, into amending a bill then being enacted.

In his view these things had nothing to do with ethics; they were merely normal business practice. He himself undoubtedly avoided outright falsehoods — never lied in so many words. But the entire organization that he ruled was deeply involved in numerous strategies of deception.

PRESSURE TO DECEIVE

Most executives from time to time are almost compelled, in the interest of their companies or themselves, to practice some form of deception when negotiating with customers, dealers, labor unions, government officials, or even other departments of their companies. By conscious misstatements, concealment of pertinent facts, or exaggeration — in short, by bluffing — they seek to persuade others to agree with them. I think it is fair to say that if the individual executive refuses to bluff from time to time — if he feels obligated to tell the truth, the whole truth, and nothing but the truth — he is ignoring opportunities permitted under the rules and is at a heavy disadvantage in his business dealings.

But here and there a businessman is unable to reconcile himself to the bluff in which he plays a part. His conscience, perhaps spurred by religious idealism, troubles him. He feels guilty; he may develop an ulcer or a nervous tic. Before any executive can make profitable use of the strategy of the bluff, he needs to make sure that in bluffing he will not lose self-respect or become emotionally disturbed. If he is to reconcile personal integrity and high standards of honesty with the practical requirements of business, he must feel that his bluffs are ethically justified. The justification rests on the fact that business, as practiced by individuals as well as by corporations, has the impersonal character of a game — a game that demands both special strategy and an understanding of its special ethics.

The game is played at all levels of corporate life, from the highest to the lowest. At the very instant that a man decides to enter business, he may be forced into a game situation, as is shown by the recent experience of a Cornell honor graduate who applied for a job with a large company.

This applicant was given a psychological test which included the statement, "Of the following magazines, check any that you have read either regularly or from time to time, and double-check those which interest you most. *Reader's Digest, Time, Fortune, Saturday Evening Post, The New Republic, Life, Look, Ramparts, Newsweek, Business Week, U.S. News & World Report, The Nation, Playboy, Esquire, Harper's, Sports Illustrated.*"

His tastes in reading were broad, and at one time or another he had read almost all of these magazines. He was a subscriber to *The New Republic*, an enthusiast for *Ramparts*, and an avid student of the pictures in *Playboy*. He was not sure whether his interest in *Playboy* would be held against him, but he had a shrewd suspicion that if he confessed to an interest in *Ramparts* and *The New Republic*, he would be thought a liberal, a radical, or at least an intellectual, and his chances of getting the job, which he needed, would greatly diminish. He therefore checked five of the more conservative magazines. Apparently it was a sound decision, for he got the job.

He had made a game player's decision, consistent with business ethics.

A similar case is that of a magazine space salesman who, owing to a merger, suddenly found himself out of a job.

The man was 58, and, in spite of a good record, his chance of getting a job elsewhere in a business where youth is favored in hiring practice was not good. He was a vigorous, healthy man, and only a considerable amount of gray in his hair suggested his age. Before beginning his job search he touched up his hair with black dye to confine the gray to his temples. He knew that the truth about his age might well come out in time, but he calculated that he could deal with that situation when it arose. He and his wife decided that he could easily pass for 45, and he so stated his age on his résumé.

This was a lie; yet within the accepted rules of the business game, no moral culpability attaches to it.

THE POKER ANALOGY

We can learn a good deal about the nature of business by comparing it with poker. While both have a large element of chance, in the long run the winner is the man who plays with steady skill. In both games ultimate victory requires intimate knowledge of the rules, insight into the psychology of the other players, a bold front, a considerable amount of self-discipline, and the ability to respond swiftly and effectively to opportunities provided by chance.

No one expects poker to be played on the ethical principles preached in churches. In poker it is right and proper to bluff a friend out of the rewards of being dealt a good hand. A player feels no more than a slight twinge of sympathy, if that, when — with nothing better than a single ace in his hand — he strips a heavy loser, who holds a pair, of the rest of his chips. It was up to the other fellow to protect himself. In the words of an excellent poker player, former President Harry Truman, "If you can't stand the heat, stay out of the kitchen." If one shows mercy to a loser in poker, it is a personal gesture, divorced from the rules of the game.

Poker has its special ethics, and here I am not referring to rules against cheating. The man who keeps an ace up his sleeve or who marks the cards is more than unethical; he is a crook, and can be punished as such — kicked out of the game, or in the Old West, shot.

In contrast to the cheat, the unethical poker player is one who, while abiding by the letter of the rules, finds ways to put the other players at an unfair disadvantage. Perhaps he unnerves them with loud talk. Or he tries to get them drunk. Or he plays in cahoots with someone else at the table. Ethical poker players frown on such tactics.

Poker's own brand of ethics is different from the ethical ideals of civilized human relationships. The game calls for distrust of the other fellow. It ignores the claim of friendship. Cunning deception and concealment of one's strength and intentions, not kindness and openheartedness, are vital in poker. No one thinks any the worse of poker on that account. And no one should think any the worse of the game of business because its standards of right and wrong differ from the prevailing traditions of morality in our society.

DISCARD THE GOLDEN RULE

This view of business is especially worrisome to people without much business experience. A minister of my acquaintance once protested that business cannot possibly function in our society unless it is based on the Judeo-Christian system of ethics. He told me:

"I know some businessmen have supplied call girls to customers, but there are always a few rotten apples in every barrel. That doesn't mean the rest of the fruit isn't sound. Surely the vast majority of businessmen are ethical. I myself am acquainted with many who adhere to strict codes of ethics based fundamentally on religious teachings. They contribute to good causes. They participate in community activities. They cooperate with other companies to improve working conditions in their industries. Certainly they are not indifferent to ethics."

That most businessmen are not indifferent to ethics in their private lives, everyone will agree. My point is that in their office lives they cease to be private citizens; they become game players who must be guided by a somewhat different set of ethical standards.

The point was forcefully made to me by a Midwestern executive who has given a good deal of thought to the question:

"So long as a businessman complies with the laws of the land and avoids telling malicious lies, he's ethical. If the law as written gives a man a wide-open chance to make a killing, he'd be a fool not to take advantage of it. If he doesn't, somebody else will. There's no obligation on him to stop and consider who is going to get hurt. If the law says he can do it, that's all the justification he needs. There's nothing unethical about that. It's just plain business sense."

This executive (call him Robbins) took the stand that even industrial espionage, which is frowned on by some businessmen, ought not to be considered unethical. He recalled a recent meeting of the National Industrial Conference Board where an authority on marketing made a speech in which he deplored the employment of spies by business organizations. More and more companies, he pointed out, find it cheaper to penetrate the secrets of competitors with concealed cameras and microphones or by bribing employees than to set up costly research and design departments of their own. A whole branch of the electronics industry has grown up with this trend, he continues, providing equipment to make industrial espionage easier.

Disturbing? The marketing expert found it so. But when it came to a remedy, he could only appeal to "respect for the golden rule." Robbins thought this a confession of defeat, believing that the golden rule, for all its value as an ideal for society, is simply not feasible as a guide for business. A good part of the time the businessman is trying to do unto others as he hopes others will *not* do unto him.[2] Robbins continued:

"Espionage of one kind or another has become so common in business that it's like taking a drink during Prohibition — it's not considered sinful. And we don't even have Prohibition where espionage is concerned; the law is very tolerant in this area. There's no more shame for a business that uses secret agents than there is for a nation. Bear in mind that there already is at least one large corporation — you can buy its stock over the counter — that makes millions by providing counterespionage service to industrial firms. Espionage in business is not an ethical problem; it's an established technique of business competition."

"We Don't Make the Laws."

Wherever we turn in business, we can perceive the sharp distinction between its ethical standards and those of the churches. Newspapers abound with sensational stories growing out of this distinction:

- We read one day that Senator Philip A. Hart of Michigan has attacked food processors for deceptive packaging of numerous products.[3]
- The next day there is a Congressional to-do over Ralph Nader's book, *Unsafe At Any Speed*, which demonstrates that automobile companies for years have neglected the safety of car-owning families.[4]
- Then another Senator, Lee Metcalf of Montana, and journalist Vic Reinemer show in their book, *Overcharge*, the methods by which utility companies elude regulating government bodies to extract unduly large payments from users of electricity.[5]

These are merely dramatic instances of a prevailing condition; there is hardly a major industry at which a similar attack could not be aimed. Critics of business regard such behavior as unethical, but the companies concerned know that they are merely playing the business game.

Among the most respected of our business institutions are the insurance companies. A group of insurance executives meeting recently in New England was startled when their guest speaker, social critic Daniel Patrick Moynihan, roundly berated them for "unethical" practices. They had been guilty, Moynihan alleged, of using outdated actuarial tables to obtain unfairly high premiums. They habitually delayed the hearings of lawsuits against them in order to tire out the plaintiffs and win cheap settlements. In their employment policies they used ingenious devices to discriminate against certain minority groups.[6]

It was difficult for the audience to deny the validity of these charges. But these men were business game players. Their reaction to Moynihan's attack was much the same as that of the automobile manufacturers to Nader, of the utilities to Senator Metcalf, and of the food processors to Senator Hart. If the laws governing their businesses change, or if public opinion becomes clamorous, they will make the necessary adjustments. But morally they have, in their view, done nothing wrong. As long as they comply with the letter of the law, they are within their rights to operate their businesses as they see fit.

The small business is in the same position as the great corporation in this respect. For example:

In 1967 a key manufacturer was accused of providing master keys for automobiles to mail-order customers, although it was obvious that some of the purchasers might be automobile thieves. His defense was plain and straightforward. If there was nothing in the law to prevent him from selling his keys to anyone who ordered them, it was not up to him to inquire as to his customers' motives. Why was it any worse, he insisted, for him to sell car keys by mail, than for mail-order houses to sell guns that might be used for murder? Until the law was changed, the key manufacturer could regard himself as being just as ethical as any other businessman by the rules of the business game.[7]

Violations of the ethical ideals of society are common in business, but they are not necessarily violations of business principles. Each year the Federal Trade Commission orders hundreds of companies, many of them of the first magnitude, to "cease and desist" from practices which, judged by ordinary standards, are of questionable morality but which are stoutly defended by the companies concerned.

In one case, a firm manufacturing a well-known mouthwash was accused of using a cheap form of alcohol possibly deleterious to health. The company's chief executive, after testifying in Washington, made this comment privately:

"We broke no law. We're in a highly competitive industry. If we're going to stay in business, we have to look for profit wherever the law permits. We don't make the laws. We obey them. Then why do we have to put up with this 'holier than thou' talk about ethics? It's sheer hypocrisy. We're not in business to promote ethics: Look at the cigarette companies, for God's sake! If the ethics aren't embodied in the laws by the men who made them, you can't expect businessmen to fill the lack. Why, a sudden submission to Christian ethics by businessmen would bring about the greatest economic upheaval in history!"

It may be noted that the government failed to prove its case against him.

Cast Illusions Aside

Talk about ethics by businessmen is often a thin decorative coating over the hard realities of the game:

Once I listened to a speech by a young executive who pointed to a new industry code as proof that his company and its competitors were deeply aware of their responsibilities to society. It was a code of ethics, he said. The industry was going to police itself, to dissuade constituent companies from wrongdoing. His eyes shone with conviction and enthusiasm.

The same day there was a meeting in a hotel room where the industry's top executives met with the "czar" who was to administer the new code, a man of high repute. No one who was present could doubt their common attitude. In their eyes the code was designed primarily to forestall a move by the federal government to impose stern restrictions on the industry. They felt that the code would hamper them a good deal less than new federal laws would. It was, in other words, conceived as a protection for the industry, not for the public.

The young executive accepted the surface explanation of the code; these leaders, all experienced game players, did not deceive themselves for a moment about its purpose.

The illusion that business can afford to be guided by ethics as conceived in private life is often fostered by speeches and articles containing such phrases as, "It pays to be ethical," or, "Sound ethics is good business." Actually this is not an ethical position at all; it is a self-serving calculation in disguise. The speaker is really saying that in the long run a company can make more money if it does not antagonize competitors, suppliers, employees, and customers by squeezing them too hard. He is saying that oversharp policies reduce ultimate gains. That is true, but it has nothing to do with ethics. The underlying attitude is much like that in the familiar story of the shopkeeper who finds an extra twenty-dollar bill in the cash register, debates with himself the ethical problem — should he tell his partner? — and finally decides to share the money because the gesture will give him an edge over the s.o.b. the next time they quarrel.

I think it is fair to sum up the prevailing attitude of businessmen on ethics as follows:

We live in what is probably the most competitive of the world's civilized societies. Our customs encourage a high degree of aggression in the individual's striving for success. Business is our main area of competition, and it has been ritualized into a game of strategy. The basic rules of the game have been set by the government, which attempts to detect and punish business frauds. But as long as a company does not transgress the rules of the game set by law, it has the legal right to shape its strategy without reference to anything but its profits. If it takes a long-term view of its profits, it will preserve amicable relations, so far as possible, with those with whom it deals. A wise businessman will not seek advantage to the point where he generates dangerous hostility among employees, competitors, customers, government, or the public at large. But decisions in this area are, in the final test, decisions of strategy, not of ethics.

THE INDIVIDUAL AND THE GAME

An individual within a company often finds it difficult to adjust to the requirements of the business game. He tries to preserve his private ethical standards in situations that call for game strategy. When he is obliged to carry out company policies that challenge his conception of himself as an ethical man, he suffers.

It disturbs him when he is ordered, for instance, to deny a raise to a man who deserves it, to fire an employee of long standing, to prepare advertising that he believes to be misleading, to conceal facts that he feels customers are entitled to know, to cheapen the quality of materials used in the manufacture of an established product, to sell as new a product that he knows to be rebuilt, to exaggerate the curative powers of a medicinal preparation, or to coerce dealers.

There are some fortunate executives who, by the nature of their work and circumstances, never have to face problems of this kind. But in one form or another the ethical dilemma is felt sooner or later by most businessmen. Possibly the dilemma is most painful not when the company forces the action on the executive but when he originates it himself—that is, when he has taken or is contemplating a step which is in his own interest but which runs counter to his early moral conditioning. To illustrate:

- The manager of an export department, eager to show rising sales, is pressed by a big customer to provide invoices which, while containing no overt falsehood that would violate a U.S. law, are so worded that the customer may be able to evade certain taxes in his homeland.
- A company president finds that an aging executive, within a few years of retirement and his pension, is not as productive as formerly. Should he be kept on?
- The produce manager of a supermarket debates with himself whether to get rid of a lot of half-rotten tomatoes by including one, with its good side exposed, in every tomato six-pack.
- An accountant discovers that he has taken an improper deduction on his company's tax return and fears the consequences if he calls the matter to the president's attention, though he himself has done nothing illegal. Perhaps if he says nothing, no one will notice the error.
- A chief executive officer is asked by his directors to comment on a rumor that he owns stock in another company with which he has placed large

orders. He could deny it, for the stock is in the name of his son-in-law and he has earlier formally instructed his son-in-law to sell the holding.

Temptations of this kind constantly arise in business. If an executive allows himself to be torn between a decision based on business considerations and one based on his private ethical code, he exposes himself to a grave psychological strain.

This is not to say that sound business strategy necessarily runs counter to ethical ideals. They may frequently coincide; and when they do, everyone is gratified. But the major tests of every move in business, as in all games of strategy, are legality and profit. A man who intends to be a winner in the business game must have a game player's attitude.

The business strategist's decisions must be as impersonal as those of a surgeon performing an operation — concentrating on objective and technique, and subordinating personal feelings. If the chief executive admits that his son-in-law owns the stock, it is because he stands to lose more if the fact comes out later than if he states it boldly and at once. If the supermarket manager orders the rotten tomatoes to be discarded, he does so to avoid an increase in consumer complaints and a loss of goodwill. The company president decides not to fire the elderly executive in the belief that the negative reaction of other employees would in the long run cost the company more than it would lose in keeping him and paying his pension.

All sensible businessmen prefer to be truthful, but they seldom feel inclined to tell the *whole* truth. In the business game truth-telling usually has to be kept within narrow limits if trouble is to be avoided. The point was neatly made a long time ago (in 1888) by one of John D. Rockefeller's associates, Paul Babcock, to Standard Oil Company executives who were about to testify before a government investigating committee: "Parry every question with answers which, while perfectly truthful, are evasive of *bottom* facts."[8] This was, is, and probably always will be regarded as wise and permissible business strategy.

For Office Use Only

An executive's family life can easily be dislocated if he fails to make a sharp distinction between the ethical systems of the home and the office — or if his wife does not grasp that distinction. Many a businessman who has remarked to his wife, "I had to let Jones go today" or "I had to admit to the boss that Jim has been goofing off lately," has been met with an indignant protest. "How could you do a thing like that? You know Jones is over 50 and will have a lot of trouble getting another job." Or, "You did that to Jim? With his wife ill and all the worry she's been having with the kids?"

If the executive insists that he had no choice because the profits of the company and his own security were involved, he may see a certain cool and ominous reappraisal in his wife's eyes. Many wives are not prepared to accept the fact that business operates with a special code of ethics. An illuminating illustration of this comes from a Southern sales executive who related a conversation he had had with his wife at a time when a hotly contested political campaign was being waged in their state:

"I made the mistake of telling her that I had had lunch with Colby, who gives me about half my business. Colby mentioned that his company had a stake in the election. Then he said, "By the way, I'm treasurer of the citizens' committee for Lang. I'm collecting contributions. Can I count on you for a hundred dollars?'

"Well, there I was. I was opposed to Lang, but I knew Colby. If he withdrew his business, I could be in a bad spot. So I just smiled and wrote out a check then and there. He thanked me, and we started to talk about his next order. Maybe he thought I shared his political views. If so, I wasn't going to lose any sleep over it.

"I should have had sense enough not to tell Mary about it. She hit the ceiling. She said she was disappointed in me. She said I hadn't acted like a man, that I should have stood up to Colby.

"I said, 'Look, it was an either-or situation. I had to do it or risk losing the business.'

"She came back at me with, 'I don't believe it. You could have been honest with him. You could have said that you didn't feel you ought to contribute to a campaign for a man you weren't going to vote for. I'm sure he would have understood.'

"I said, 'Mary, you're a wonderful woman, but you're way off the track. Do you know what would have happened if I had said that? Colby would have smiled and said, "Oh, I didn't realize. Forget it." But in his eyes from that moment I would be an oddball, maybe a bit of a radical. He would have listened to me talk about his order and would have promised to give it consideration. After that I wouldn't hear from him for a week. Then I would telephone and learn from his secretary that he wasn't yet ready to place the order. And in about a month I would hear through the grapevine that he was giving his business to another company. A month after that I'd be out of a job.'

"She was silent for a while. Then she said, 'Tom, something is wrong with business when a man is forced to choose between his family's security and his moral obligation to himself. It's easy for me to say you should have stood up to him—but if you had, you might have felt you were betraying me and the kids. I'm sorry that you did it, Tom, but I can't blame you. Something is wrong with business!'"

This wife saw the problem in terms of moral obligation as conceived in private life; her husband saw it as a matter of game strategy. As a player in a weak position, he felt that he could not afford to indulge an ethical sentiment that might have cost him his seat at the table.

Playing to Win

Some men might challenge the Colbys of business—might accept serious setbacks to their business careers rather than risk a feeling of moral cowardice. They merit our respect—but as private individuals, not businessmen. When the skillful player of the business game is compelled to submit to unfair pressure, he does not castigate himself for moral weakness. Instead, he strives to put himself into a strong position where he can defend himself against such pressures in the future without loss.

If a man plans to take a seat in the business game, he owes it to himself to master the principles by which the game is played, including its special ethical outlook. He can then hardly fail to recognize that an occasional bluff may well be justified in terms of the game's ethics and warranted in terms of economic necessity. Once he clears his mind on this point, he is in a good position to match his strategy against that of the other players. He can then determine objectively whether a bluff in a given situation has a good chance of succeeding and can decide when and how to bluff, without a feeling of ethical transgression.

To be a winner, a man must play to win. This does not mean that he must be ruthless, cruel, harsh, or treacherous. On the contrary, the better his reputation for integrity, honesty, and decency, the better his chances of victory will be in the long run. But from time to time every businessman, like every poker player, is offered a choice between certain loss or bluffing within the legal rules of the game. If he is not resigned to losing, if he wants to rise in his company and industry, then in such a crisis he will bluff—and bluff hard.

Every now and then one meets a successful businessman who has conveniently forgotten the small or large deceptions that he practiced on his way to fortune. "God gave me my money," old John D. Rockefeller once piously told a Sunday school class. It would be a rare tycoon in our time who would risk the horse laugh with which such a remark would be greeted.

In the last third of the twentieth century even children are aware that if a man has become prosperous in business, he has sometimes departed from the strict truth in order to overcome obstacles or has practiced the more subtle deceptions of the half-truth or the misleading omission. Whatever the form of the bluff, it is an integral part of the game, and the executive who does not master its techniques is not likely to accumulate much money or power.

Notes

1. *The New York Times*, March 9, 1967.
2. See Bruce D. Henderson, "Brinkmanship in Business," HBR March-April 1967, p. 49.
3. *The New York Times*, November 21, 1966.
4. New York, Grossman Publishers, Inc., 1965.
5. New York, David McKay Company, Inc., 1967.
6. *The New York Times*, January 17, 1967.
7. Cited by Ralph Nader in "Business Crime" *The New Republic*, July 1, 1967, p. 7.
8. Babcock in a memorandum to Rockefeller (Rockefeller Archives).

Norman E. Bowie

THE ETHICS OF BLUFFING AND POKER

One of the classic expressions of [the] point of view [that business practice is analogous to poker, and hence a considerable amount of deception is not only common but could be universalized without undermining business practice] is Albert Z. Carr's "Is Business Bluffing Ethical?" In that article, Carr maintains that the proper analogy for understanding business ethics is that of poker:

> Poker's own brand of ethics is different from the ethical ideals of civilized human relationships. The game calls for distrust of the other fellow. It ignores the claim of friendship. Cunning deception and concealment of one's strength and intentions, not kindness and openheartedness, are vital in poker.[1]

As it is with poker, so it is with business:

> Most executives from time to time are almost compelled in the interests of their companies or themselves to practice some form of deception when negotiating with customers, dealers, labor unions, government officials, or even the departments of their companies. By conscious misstatements, concealment of pertinent facts, or exaggeration — in short, by bluffing — they seek to persuade others to agree with them. . . . A good part of the time the businessman is trying to do unto others as he hopes others will not do unto him. . . . A man who intends to be a winner in the business game must have a game player's attitude.[2]

Carr raises several important challenges to anyone discussing business ethics. Among the challenges that he raises are the following: (1) that the most appropriate analogy for understanding business is the game of poker, (2) that competition and negotiation require a form of deception that includes conscious misstatement and the concealment of pertinent facts, and (3) that a successful businessperson must "do unto others as he hopes others will not do unto him." . . .

Before responding to Carr's challenges, it seems important to indicate that Carr is not saying that business can ignore all moral rules. If it did, I think that Carr would agree with Kant that such a position would be self-defeating. However, Carr does think that business practice can and does require a great deal of deception: "conscious misstatements, concealment of pertinent facts, and exaggeration."

From Norman E. Bowie, "The Ethics of Bluffing and Poker" in *Business Ethics*, 2nd ed. (Englewood Cliffs, NJ: Prentice Hall, 1982), 54–64. Norman E. Bowie, *Business Ethics*, © 1982, pp. 54–64. Reprinted by permission of Prentice Hall, Englewood Cliffs, New Jersey.

[1] Albert Z. Carr, "Is Business Bluffing Ethical?" *Harvard Business Review*, (January–February 1968) 145.

[2] Ibid., p. 144.

Moreover, one does not need extensive experience in business to know that there are many types of deception, like bluffing, that are both widely practiced and widely accepted. A few examples suffice. It is common knowledge that auto dealers do not expect people to pay the sticker price for automobiles. A certain amount of bargaining is taken for granted. The same is true for real estate prices. The asking price for a house is seldom the selling price. At the initial bargaining session, labor leaders also overstate wage demands, and management also understates the wage increases it is willing to grant. In all these instances, the final price or wage contract is arrived at through a process that does resemble the poker game Carr uses as an analogy. The price or wage contract does depend in part on the strength of one's hand and on one's bluffing ability. In the late 1970's, one did need to pay the sticker price for small foreign cars with good gas mileage.

Surely the auto dealers and sellers of homes cannot be accused of immoral behavior when they post prices above those that they are willing to accept. Surely the labor leader is not behaving immorally when he overstates the wage increases that his union expects to receive.

But equally surely there are limits. Let us return to the real estate example. Suppose that I am willing to sell my home for $60,000 if that is the best price I can get. I ask $70,000. A potential buyer's initial offer is $60,000. I turn it down and tell him that $65,000 is my rock bottom price. He purchases the home for $65,000.[3]

Many people would characterize my behavior as shrewd bluffing rather than as an immoral lie. Most people would think more of me rather than less. However, suppose that I had manufactured the claim that someone else had promised me that they were in the process of writing up a contract for $65,000 for the house but that I would sell it to him since we were both members of Rotary International. In this case most people would agree that I had told an immoral lie. By the way, it would not improve the moral character of my action to have my brother pretend to make me an offer so that the prospective buyer would be pressured to actually buy. That would be a case of an immoral lie as well.

Sometimes how the vast majority of people feels about whether an action is a lie or merely bluffing cannot be determined. Consider the following examples from collective bargaining negotiations:

1. Management negotiators saying, "We can't afford this agreement," when it would not put the firm out of business but only reduce profits from somewhat above to somewhat below the industry average.
2. Union negotiators saying, "The union membership is adamant on this issue," when they know that, while one half of the membership is adamant, the other half couldn't care less.
3. Union negotiators saying, "If you include this provision, we'll get membership approval of the contract," when they know that they'll have an uphill battle for approval even with the provision.[4]

---

[3]These examples are adopted from Thomas L. Carson and Richard E. Wokutch, "Ethical Perspectives on Lying, Deception and Bluffing in Business," unpublished manuscript, pp. 1–2. (see below)

[4]Ibid., pp. 3–4.

Perhaps the debate on the line between harmless exaggeration and immoral deception is most intense in the discussion of advertising ethics. Horror stories concerning deceptive advertising abound. Language changes its meaning in many ads. "Noncancellable" and "guaranteed renewable" have technical meanings not at all what one would expect. Often age stipulations are thrown in. The physical world is subject to optical illusions that the advertiser can exploit as well. Marketing research has shown that, if housewives are given the choice between two boxes of cereal, one short and squat and the other tall and narrow, they will almost invariably choose the tall and narrow box, even if it contains less and costs more. Boxes and bottles are often much larger than needed for the quantity of material contained therein. Testimonials, until recently, were also under attack. And so it goes. To many, these practices indicate that advertising is an inherently deceptive industry.

Yet others would argue that much of what critics call "deceptive advertising" is nothing more than harmless bluffing. They argue that the purpose of advertising is to sell a product. To sell a product, you must put a product in its best light, you must emphasize its good points, you must exaggerate a bit. So long as this commercial context is understood, exaggeration, puffery, and hyperbole are not deceptive. The claim that one's product is the best or the use of other such superlatives should not cause anyone problems. Jules Henry speaks of the philosophy guiding the commercial context as the pecuniary philosophy. In the pecuniary philosophy, there is something known as pecuniary truth. A pecuniary pseudotruth is a false statement made as if it were true, but not intended to be believed. "No proof is offered for a pecuniary truth and no one looks for it." As Henry puts it,

> No sane American would think that literally everybody is "talking about the new Starfire," that Alpine cigarettes literally "put the men in menthol smoking," or that a woman wearing a Distinction foundation garment becomes so beautiful that her sisters literally want to kill her.[5]

Of course, some could criticize the whole commercial context and the so-called pecuniary philosophy that accompanies it. However, the critics should note that something like the pecuniary philosophy seems deeply embedded within human nature. Almost all of us try to sell ourselves. Whether searching for a job or searching for a mate, we engage in exaggeration, puffery, and hyperbole about ourselves. And we expect others to do the same. We also use the pecuniary language to talk about our children, our jobs, our neighborhoods, or our spouses. (Note that, for the last three items, hyperbole can be negative as well as positive.) Perhaps the world would be a better place if human beings could avoid hyperbole or puffery. Since such a change in human nature is unlikely, perhaps it would be more realistic to accept the pecuniary philosophy as operative in the commercial context — as well as elsewhere — and to discuss various rules or principles that might constrain pecuniary philosophy.

With these thoughts in mind, we need some criteria to distinguish the relatively harmless cases of puffery from the immoral lies and deceptions. A lie might be defined as a false statement uttered with the intention to mislead. The

---

[5]Jules Henry, "Advertising as a Philosophical System" in Thomas Beauchamp and Norman E. Bowie, eds., *Ethical Theory and Business* (Englewood Cliffs, N.J.: Prentice Hall, 1979), p. 470.

addition of the intentionality condition is extremely important. It allows many false statements not to be lies. Fortunately, mistaken utterances, although false, are not lies; otherwise, most of us would be frequent, if not habitual, liars. It also exempts poets. "He has the heart of a lion" is not a lie, although it is surely false. Sometimes advertisements are akin to poetry. "Esso puts a tiger in your tank" is false, but surely it is not a lie.

The intentionality condition is useful in areas beyond poetry. The Supreme Court decided in favor of a Federal Trade Commission (FTC) ruling that determined the Colgate-Palmolive's ad that Rapid Shave could soften even the toughness of sandpaper was deceptive. The television commercial depicted someone shaving sandpaper that had been generously lathered with Rapid Shave. Now the FTC admitted that Rapid Shave could soften sandpaper so that it could be shaved. However, the sandpaper needed to soak in Rapid Shave for approximately eighty minutes before it could be shaved. On the basis of this, the FTC declared the ad deceptive because the television viewer was deceived into believing that the actual experiment was being shown; the viewer was not informed about the eighty-minute wait.

Colgate-Palmolive disagreed that there was any deception. It compared its "experiment" with the use of mashed potatoes instead of ice cream in all television ice cream ads. Just as the television lights made the use of ice cream impossible, so the working time made an actual experiment impossible. The court turned down the analogy on the grounds that the mashed potatoes prop was not being used for additional proof of the quality of the product while the Rapid Shave commercial certainly was trying to provide additional proof. Perhaps the Rapid Shave decision could be generalized to make the following point: Within that pecuniary context, any deception or false statement that is not related to the cost, amount, or quality of the product is not an example of immoral deception in advertising. Such a principle would enable us to focus on the context in which advertising takes place.

Yet another criterion could be stated as follows: Any exaggeration that would not deceive the rational person is not inappropriate. No rational person will believe that the foam of Old Froshingslosh beer will really be on the bottom. (Whether such deception would be immoral within some other context is not a matter for discussion here.) Deception in advertising involves the use of false statements or inaccurate depictions of a product that are material to the consumer's decision to purchase and that are undertaken intentionally to mislead rational consumers. On that account, most advertising is not deceptive. However, equally on that account some advertising is deceptive and, more important, some advertising or marketing practices are deceptive. Packaging techniques are surely one example of a practice that deceives in terms of amount.

But what counts as a rational consumer? The federal agency that has confronted this question head on is the Federal Trade Commission. The commission has drawn a distinction between the rational consumer and the ignorant consumer. The ignorant consumer takes everything literally. He or she really does believe that, when Old Froshingslosh beer advertises that the foam will be on the bottom, it really will be on the bottom. The ignorant consumer does not show any common sense. It is generally agreed that, to require business practice to be so open and literal that even the ignorant consumer would not be deceived would stifle business and seriously affect productivity. On that point, the conventional wisdom seems correct. However, the definition of the "rational consumer" is fairly amorphous. Sometimes "rational consumer" is just a synonym for "average consumer." Advertisements, like television programs, would have to be aimed at those with the reading ability of a twelve-year-old. At other times "rational consumer" is given a more normative definition. It is equated with what a consumer should know. Perhaps the normative definition puts more responsibility on the consumer than does the definition that appeals to the average consumer.

Another way to handle this debate over where to draw the line between misstatement and fraud is to appeal to a criterion of public openness. A business practice is not deceptive when that business acknowledges the rules it is playing under. The ads for the auto dealers and for real estate make it perfectly clear that the "asking price" is not the "real price." An ad for a home that says "Asking $120,000" virtually announces that the homeowner is in a mood to deal. Auto ads for individual dealers stress the fact that they will match any other deal in town. They explicitly acknowledge the bargaining aspect of auto sales. Grocery store ads by and large contain none of this bargaining language. The price of oranges is not a function of an individual bargain worked out between the individual purchaser and the supermarket.

Deception enters when a businessperson announces that he or she is playing by one set of rules when in fact he or she is playing by another. Of course immorality also enters when one partner to a contract breaks his or her end. But, so long as the rules of the game are known, then most people will accept consequences of business practice that they might not accept in other circumstances. Consider the following case:

The Leaking Valve[6]

The Hawley Corporation, which ranks among the nation's one hundred largest manufacturing firms, had a persistent problem with a leaking valve assembly on the hydraulic presses it makes and distributes. Unable to remedy the defect on its own, Hawley engineers called in several vendors of this type of assembly and described the problem to them. The Hawley group explained that it hoped that the vendors would be willing to find a solution to the problem but that corporate policy did not permit paying for this sort of developmental work done outside the company.

Only one of the vendor firms, Allbright, Inc., decided to proceed on this basis with developing something that could answer Hawley's difficulty. Allbright reasoned that if it produced the remedy it would be in an excellent position to get the contract for supplying Hawley with the improved assembly.

The engineering department of the two firms worked together, and after a fairly lengthy effort a modification of the Hawley assembly was perfected that eliminated the leaking.

The Hawley purchasing department then sent our requests for bids on the

---

[6]This case and the subsequent case, "A Big Break for Fenwick Creations," was prepared by the Committee for Education in Business Ethics under a grant from the National Endowment for the Humanities.

new assembly to a number of vendors, Allbright included. Reston Corporation underbid Allbright and was awarded the order by Hawley.

Most of my students who analyze this case agree that Allbright had no right to the contract. Their argument is almost always the same: The rules were known and hence Allbright knew it was taking a risk when it agreed to assist Hawley.

One should compare this case with another:

A Big Break for Fenwick Creations

Fenwick Creations, a manufacturer of men's and women's sportswear, had come up with an exceptionally well-designed new line of clothes for tennis, jogging, and cycling. Initial response from buyers was so favorable that Fenwick's sales managers thought they had a good chance of finally attaining one of their goals: to get their merchandise into the locally prestigious Wilton-Cool and Company department store.

Wilton-Cool was known in the trade for acceptance of new lines. It was also known for making acceptance contingent upon special incentives from suppliers.

Fenwick's sales office offered to guarantee the resale of Wilton-Cool's total order, within a period of time agreeable to the department store. Fenwick offered further to take Wilton-Cool's statement about sales without a check of inventories by Fenwick.

Wilton-Cool accepted the proposition and ordered 500 articles of sportswear from Fenwick. After the previously arranged termination date, the department store claimed to have sold 325 of the items. In fact, 450 had been sold; but Fenwick abided by the guarantee. It was understood on both sides — though never stated — that what had occurred was standard practice and that prices charged by the supplier took these costs into account.

In this case, most of my students do not accept the morality of the practice. Even though the two businesses, Fenwick and Wilton-Cool, were aware of the rules, other relevant parties were not. The consumers were particularly adversely affected. Consumers believe that, in a competitive market economy, purchase decisions among businesses are made on the basis of quality and price. Those are the operative rules of the game. But clearly these rules are being violated in this case.

We now have a much better handle on what we mean by deceptive advertising. Deceptive advertising is advertising that is intentionally designed to mislead the rational consumer who knows the rules of the game about the cost, amount, or quality of a product.

But how does this discussion of advertising fit in with our larger analysis of the Kantian argument against lying. It does show that not all cases of "lying" will run afoul of the categorical imperative. Some types of "lies" can be universalized without being self-defeating. There are a few passages in Kant's writings where Kant seems to recognize the limitations of his views.

> Again, I may make a false statement (falsiloquium) when my purpose is to hide from another what is in my mind and when the latter can assume that such is my purpose, his own purpose being to make a wrong use of the truth. Thus, for instance, if my enemy takes me by the throat and asks where I keep my money, I need not tell him the truth, because he will abuse it; and my untruth is not a lie (mendacium) because the thief knows full well that I will not, if I can help it, tell him the truth and that he has no right to demand it of me.[7]

Nonetheless, there are clear instances of deceptive and fraudulent practices that do undermine the enterprise of business itself. The breaking of contracts and theft are paradigm cases. Such activities do run afoul of Kant's categorical imperative. It is clear that Kant would allow far less in the way of deceptive bluffing than would Carr. In Kantian language, Kant has a much higher number of business practices that he thinks would be self-defeating if universalized than does Carr. Let us now consider the dispute between Carr and Kant empirically. What business practices, if they became more common, would undermine business practice itself?

Let us take Carr's analogy seriously. Should the stockholders applaud a chief executive officer whose operating procedure is analogous to the operating procedure of a poker player? In Carr's view, "A good part of the time the businessman is trying to do unto others as he hopes other will not do unto him." But surely such a practice is very risky. The danger of discovery is great, and our experience of the past several years indicates that many corporations that have played the game of business like the game of poker have suffered badly. Moreover, if business practice consisted essentially of these conscious misstatements, exaggerations, and the concealment of pertinent facts, it seems clear that business practice would be inherently unstable. Contemporary business practice presupposes such stability, and business can only be stable if the chief executive officer has a set of moral standards higher than those that govern the game of poker.

This philosophical point, that deception must be very limited if society is to be stable, has been enriched by the appearance of Dr. Sissela Bok's book, *Lying: Moral Choice in Public and Private Life*, which reaffirms the centrality of the moral rule, "Do not lie." One of the points Dr. Bok most emphatically makes is that the existence of society itself depends upon the acceptance by the members of society of the rule "Do not lie."

> trust in some degree of veracity functions as a foundation of relations among human beings; when this trust shatters or wears away, institutions collapse. . . . A society, then, whose members were unable to distinguish truthful messages from deceptive ones, would collapse. But even before such a general collapse, individual choice and survival would be imperiled. The search for food and shelter could depend on no expectations from others. A warning that a well was poisoned or a plea for help in

---

[7]Immanuel Kant, *Lectures on Ethics*, trans. Louis Infield (New York: Harper & Row, Publishers, 1963), p. 227.

an accident would come to be ignored unless independent confirmation could be found.[8]

Dr. Bok's point can be restated so that it applies specifically to business.

Central to the philosophy of most businesspersons is the view that government should not intrude extensively into business. With respect to business, *laissez-faire* is the dominant view. However, even those with libertarian philosophies allow one important function to government. Government is to be the police officer that enforces the rules of business activity. Most important, government is to uphold the sanctity of contracts. This view is expressed clearly in the classical treatment of the merits of capitalism.

However, if business activity is to thrive, most people most of the time must uphold voluntarily the sanctity of contracts. No government can serve as an omnipresent police officer. Indeed, even within the competitive marketplace, the basic moral nature of persons must be assumed. Usually, people will keep to their contracts even when it does not work out to their advantage to do so. If this were not true, law enforcement would soon become impossibly burdensome. Indeed, we assume that even with limited cheating at least the police are honest. The uncovering of a dishonest cop is always a great shock. Commerce requires a basically honest society and honest police.

A cause of growing concern is the increased cheating on the part of an increasing number of citizens. Internal revenue spokespersons fear that, as American citizens face higher taxes through inflation and as they hear of cheating by others, they will tend to cheat on their own taxes. Internal revenue officials concede that enforcement agents could not deal with widespread cheating and that such a situation would undermine the income tax system. One need not wait for the collapse of the income tax to observe breakdowns in the market that result from breakdowns in the obligation to the sanctity of contracts.

Shoplifting has approached epidemic proportions. Since shoplifters are difficult to apprehend and even more difficult to convict, a partial "solution" is to figure into the retail price of a good a certain markup to cover the cost of shoplifting. The result is an increase on the price of goods. Of course as prices rise, one would expect shoplifting to increase. This is especially true when people realize that a portion of the price of their goods is set aside to cover shoplifting. Why shouldn't they shoplift, too, if they are already paying the cost of the shoplifters who shoplift with impunity?

If such a view becomes widespread, the market system will break down just the way a rationing scheme does when cheating is both widely known about and goes unpunished. Suppose that there is a ban on watering the lawn that is not enforced. Sam, who has followed the ban but who sees all his neighbors water the lawn, will be silly if he continues to refrain from watering his lawn. As a result, the rationing system breaks down.

All of this is fairly obvious. Bok's most significant point is that rather minor acts of deception like white lies, puffery, and exaggeration all contribute to a general instability. In other words, Carr underestimates the undesirable effects of such practices. If I were to summarize Bok's book in one sentence, I would

---

[8]Sissela Bok, *Lying: Moral Choice in Public and Private Life* (New York: Pantheon Books, 1978), pp. 19, 31.

say, "Even white lies, flattery, and deceptive practices that are *publicly known and accepted* undermine social institutions." Bok's critique of "white lies" and the use of placebos applies equally well to deception in business:

> Triviality surely does set limits to when moral inquiry is reasonable. But when we look more closely at practices such as placebo-giving, it becomes clear that all lies defended as "white" cannot be so easily dismissed. In the first place, the harmlessness of lies is notoriously disputable. What the liar perceives as harmless or even beneficial may not be so in the eyes of the deceived. Second, the failure to look at an entire practice rather than at their own isolated case often blinds liars to cumulative harm and expanding deceptive activities. Those who begin with white lies can come to resort to more frequent and more serious ones. Where some tell a few white lies, others may tell more. Because lines are so hard to draw, the indiscriminate use of such lies can lead to other deceptive practices. The aggregate harm from a large number of marginally harmful instances may, therefore, be highly undesirable in the end — for liars, those deceived, and honesty and trust more generally.[9]

In Bok's view even the bluffing that goes on in real estate and auto sales has its dangers. So does the hyperbole that accompanies advertising and the excessive demands that are characteristic of the early stages of collective bargaining negotiations. Those of us in academic life can see Bok's point when we consider what has happened as the result of grade inflation and the inflating of letters of recommendation. The professional and graduate schools are suspicious of high grades. Hardly anyone takes letters of recommendation seriously anymore.

In the area of business, a number of parents, like myself, have simply taught our children to regard all advertising as deceptive. Often, that type of teaching is not difficult. After eating three boxes of cereal so that one can send three box tops and 50 cents for a marvelous Star Wars toy, the toy almost never seems worth it. Children learn the lesson early. Jokes about used car salesmen are so ingrained in the public that honest used car ads just aren't taken seriously.

The growth of the large firm, the complexity of business decisions, the need for planning and stability, and the undesirable effects of puffery, exaggeration, and deception all count against Carr's view that the ethics of business should be the ethics of a poker game. Just how much puffery and exaggeration business practice can permit without serious undesirable consequences is a matter for further empirical investigation.

But how much deception, exaggeration, and puffery should business practice permit? . . . One condition that seemed to distinguish legitimate from illegitimate bluffing in our earlier examples was whether or not all parties knew that bluffing was taking place. The bluffing that goes on in used-car lots is legitimate because everyone knows that asking prices are just that. This openness condition, as I chose to call it, is often the basis for legislation as well. People should be free to speculate in stocks, but if an accountant, lawyer, or other person obtains inside information, that person is not free to buy or sell the stock of that company or the stock of any other company that would be significantly affected if the inside information were publicly known. In a context in which bluffing and exaggeration are permitted, open access to all relevant information is a moral necessity. Otherwise, the rules of the bluffing game are unfair. Poker is unfair when some of the players do not know the rules that are being used.

Thomas L. Carson, Richard E. Wokutch, and Kent F. Murrmann

BLUFFING IN LABOR NEGOTIATIONS: LEGAL AND ETHICAL ISSUES

More than a decade ago a *Harvard Business Review* article entitled "Is Business Bluffing Ethical?" (Carr, 1968) created a storm of controversy when the author defended bluffing and other questionable business practices on the grounds that they are just part of the game of business. The controversy over the ethics of bluffing and alleged deception in business negotiations erupted again recently with the publication of the Wall Street Journal article, "To Some at Harvard, Telling Lies Becomes a Matter of Course" (Bulkeley, 1979). This detailed a negotiations course taught at Harvard Business School in which students were allowed to bluff and deceive each other in various simulated negotiation situations. Student's grades were partially determined by the settlements they negotiated with each other, and hence some alleged that this course encouraged and taught students to bluff, lie to, and deceive negotiating partners. These controversies raised issues concerning the morality, necessity, and even the legality of bluffing in business negotiations which were never adequately resolved. It is the aim of this essay to shed some light on these issues.

In the first section of the paper we will describe briefly the nature of the collective bargaining process and then examine the role of bluffing in that process. The second section of the paper is a discussion of labor-law as it relates to bluffing. Then, in the third and fourth sections of the paper we will argue that bluffing and other deceptive practices in labor negotiations typically do constitute lying. Nevertheless, we will argue that bluffing is typically morally permissible but for different reasons than those put forth by Carr. In our conclusion we consider whether it is an indictment of our present negotiating practices and our economic system as a whole that, given the harsh realities of the marketplace, bluffing *is* usually morally acceptable.

THE NATURE OF COLLECTIVE BARGAINING

Collective bargaining is fundamentally a competitive process in which labor and management dispute and eventually decide the terms of employment. Through bargaining each party attempts to reach an agreement which each

From *Journal of Business Ethics*, 1 (1982), 13-22. Copyright © 1982 by D. Reidel Publishing Co., Dordrecht, Holland and Boston, U.S.A. Reprinted by permission of Kluwer Academic Publishers.

perceives to be at least minimally acceptable if not highly favorable in light of its vital interests. Typically there is a range of possible settlement points on wages (and other bargained issues) that each party would accept rather than fail to reach an agreement. This range exists with respect to wages, for instance, because the minimum wage that an employer could pay and still attract the needed employees is typically lower at any point in time than the maximum wage the employer could pay and still manage to operate a competitive business. Neither party knows the exact location of these extreme points. And, ordinarily there is no one economically optimal wage level within the range that can be established through reference to objective criteria that are acceptable to both parties.[1] Each party attempts to move the wage agreement toward its preferred end of the range. Also, each attempts to define a point on the range beyond which it would rather endure a work stoppage than accept a settlement. Thus, in practice, the top end of the range becomes the highest wage that management would pay rather than endure a work stoppage. The bottom end of the range becomes the minimum wage that labor would accept rather than endure a work stoppage. These extreme positions are the parties' respective "sticking points."

Factors Affecting Bargaining Success

Two factors are instrumental to the ability of either party to negotiate a favorable agreement, i.e., an agreement that both perceive to be more than minimally acceptable. The first factor is the ability to impose significant costs on the other party, or to credibly threaten the imposition of such costs, in order to pressure the other party to make concessions. Thus, in order to bargain successfully, labor must be able to instill in management the belief that labor would initiate a work stoppage, or other form of costly non-cooperation, in order to secure what it considers to be reasonable terms of employment. Likewise, in order for management to bargain successfully, it must convey to labor the perception that it would endure a work stoppage rather than accept what it believes to be unreasonable conditions.

The other key factor that affects one's bargaining success is the ability to accurately discern the other party's minimum acceptable conditions while vigilantly concealing one's own minimum terms. Such knowledge enables one to confidently drive the bargain to more favorable terms without risking an unwanted and costly work stoppage.

Bluffing and Bargaining Success

Bluffing typically plays a very important part concerning both of these factors. Bluffing is an act in which one attempts to misrepresent one's intentions or overstate the strength of one's position in the bargaining process. This is possible because neither party knows for sure the other party's true intentions or "sticking point." Bluffing often involves making deceptive statements. For instance, the union bargaining representative may boldly state, "There is no way that our people will accept such a small wage increase," when he/she knows full well that they would gladly accept management's offer rather than go out on strike. However, bluffing can be entirely nonverbal. Nodding confidently as one raises the bet while holding a poor hand in a game of poker is a paradigm case of bluffing. Getting up from the bargaining table in a huff and going out the door is another example of nonverbal bluffing. Through these and similar types of statements and behavior either party can convey to the other an exaggerated portrayal of its ability to impose or endure costs, and thereby can increase its actual ability to gain concessions in the bargaining process.

In addition, aggressive bluffing can be used to test the other party's resolve or otherwise prod the other party to concede certain points. This use of bluffing on different bargaining issues over a period of time, say spanning several bargaining sessions, can significantly increase one's understanding of the other party's true strength, and thus can enhance one's ability to accurately estimate the other party's sticking points on various issues.

There can be no doubt that bluffing is an important bargaining tool. It can be employed to create impressions of enhanced strength as well as to probe the other party to find out the level of its critical sticking points. Through these methods either party can attempt to gain a more favorable settlement than the other party would otherwise be willing to allow. And, labor and management alike are more apt to fully abide by those terms of employment that they know were established through a free and vigorous use of their best bargaining skills.

The Alleged Necessity of Bluffing

While bluffing can obviously be advantageous in labor negotiations, one might ask whether it is "economically necessary." This does not appear to be the case. Where one of the parties has an extremely strong negotiating position (e.g. an employer in a one company town with a high unemployment rate, a slavemaster, or a surgeon who is the only one capable of performing a new surgical procedure necessary to save one's life) wages and working conditions can simply be dictated by the stronger party.

What about the claim that bluffing is a necessary part of the negotiation of any *voluntary* labor agreement between parties of relatively equal power? This also seems false. Suppose that two very scrupulous parties are attempting to reach a wage settlement and neither wants to engage in bluffing. Assuming that they trust each other and honestly reveal their "sticking points," they could agree to some formula such as splitting the difference between the sticking points. This is of course unlikely to occur in real life, but only because few individuals are honest or trusting enough for our assumptions to hold.

THE LEGAL STATUS OF BLUFFING

The National Labor Relations Act, as amended (1970), provides the legal framework within which the collective bargaining process in the private sector of our economy is carried out. Sections 8(a)(5) and 8(b)(3) of the National Labor Relations Act provide that it shall be an unfair labor practice for a union or an employer in a properly constituted bargaining relationship to fail to bargain in good faith. The statute left it to the National Labor Relations Board and the courts to establish criteria for determining whether a party is bargaining in good faith. Over the years numerous such criteria have been established by the Board and the courts.

The Honest Claims Doctrine

Of particular interest with respect to the legal status of bluffing is the 'honest claims' doctrine, established by the U.S. Supreme Court in its Truitt Mfg. Co. decision (NLRB v. Truitt Mfg. Co., 1956). This states that "good faith necessarily requires that claims made by either party should be honest claims." The central issue in the Truitt Case was whether the employer would be required to substantiate its claim that it could not afford to pay a certain wage increase. In addition to enunciating its "honest claims" doctrine, the court declared that if an "inability to pay argument is important enough to present in the give and take of bargaining it is important enough to require some sort of proof of its accuracy" (NLRB v. Truitt Mfg. Co., 1956, p. 152). This "honest claims" policy has been consistently upheld and applied in numerous court decisions to this day. Thus, it is clear that the law requires honesty in collective bargaining. However, the "honest claims" requirement applies only to those types of claims that pertain directly to issues subject to bargaining, and the employer's ability to provide certain conditions of employment. Thus, the "honest claims" policy requires a union to refrain from presenting false information to management concerning the level of wages and fringe benefits provided by employers under other union contracts. Likewise, the employer must refrain from falsely claiming an inability to provide a certain benefit.

Bluffing and the Honest Claims Doctrine

How does the "honest claims" doctrine apply to the practice of bluffing? It is clear that bluffing that involves the presentation of false information about issues subject to bargaining (i.e., wages, hours, and condition of employment) is a violation. However bluffing about objective issues not subject to negotiation such as one's ability to withstand a strike (e.g. the size of the union strike fund, or the union membership's vote on the question of whether or not to go out on strike) is allowable. Also, bluffing that is limited to representations of one's bargaining intentions or one's willingness to impose or endure costs in order to win a more favorable contract does not constitute a violation. Of course, this type of bluffing is more effective and more prevalent because it cannot be as easily discredited through reference to objective information as can false statements about working conditions. In sum, though the Truitt decision requires honesty with regard to the making of claims concerning bargaining topics, it does not proscribe the more effective and important forms of bluffing commonly used in bargaining today.

BLUFFING AND THE CONCEPT OF LYING

Suppose (example 1) that I am a management negotiator trying to reach a strike settlement with union negotiators. I need to settle the strike soon and have been instructed to settle for as much as a 12% increase in wages and benefits if that is the best agreement I can obtain. I say that the company's final offer is a 10% increase. Am I lying? Consider also whether any of the following examples constitute lying:

2. Management negotiators misstating the profitability of a subsidiary to convince the union negotiating with it that the subsidiary would go out of business if management acceded to union wage demands.
3. Union officials misreporting the size of the union strike fund to portray a greater ability to strike than is actually the case.
4. Management negotiators saying, "We can't afford this agreement," when it would not put the firm out of business but only reduce profits from somewhat above to somewhat below the industry average.
5. Union negotiators saying, "The union membership is adamant on this issue," when they know that while one half of the membership is adamant, the other half couldn't care less.
6. Union negotiators saying, "If you include this provision, we'll get membership approval of the contract," when they know they'll have an uphill battle for approval even with the provision.

Defining Lying

What is lying? A lie must be a false statement,[2] but not all false statements are lies. If I am a salesman and say that my product is the best on the market and *sincerely believe this to be the case*, my statement is not a lie, even if it is untrue. A false statement is not a lie unless it is somehow deliberate or intentional. Suppose that we define a lie as an intentional false statement. According to this definition, I am telling a lie when I say, "This aftershave will make you feel like a million bucks." This definition implies that we lie when we exaggerate, e.g., a negotiator representing union workers making $10/hour but seeking a substantial raise says, "These are slave wages you're paying us." When I greatly exaggerate or say something in jest, I know that it is very improbable that the other person(s) will believe what I say. The reason that these examples do not appear to be lies is that they do not involve the intent to deceive. This suggests the following definition of lying:

1. A lie is a deliberate[3] false statement intended to deceive another person.

This definition is inadequate in cases in which a person is compelled to make false statements. For example, I may lie as a witness to a jury for fear of being killed by the accused. But it doesn't follow that I hope or intend to deceive them.[4] I may hope that my statements don't deceive anyone. We might say that what makes my statements lies is that I realize or foresee that they are likely to deceive others. This then suggests the following definition of lying:

2. A lie is a deliberate false statement which is thought to be likely to deceive others by the person who makes it.

This definition is also lacking because a person can lie even if he or she has almost no hope of being believed. A criminal protesting his or her innocence in court is lying no matter how unlikely it is that he/she thinks the argument will be convincing to the judge or jury. The following definition is more plausible than either (1) or (2):

3. A lie is a deliberate false statement which is either intended to deceive others or foreseen to be likely to deceive others.

Implications for Bluffing

It appears that this definition implies that the statements in our first three examples constitute lies. In examples (1) and (2) one is making deliberate false statements with the intent of deceiving others about matters relevant to the negotiations. In the first case I am making a deliberate false statement with the intent to deceive the other party into thinking that I am unwilling to offer more than 10%. One might object that this needn't be my intent in example (1). No one familiar with standard negotiating practices is likely to take at face value statements which a person makes about a "final offer." One might argue that in the two cases in question I intend and expect my statement that 10% is my best offer to be taken to mean my highest possible offer is something around 12%. If this is my intention and expectation, then my bluffing does not constitute a lie. To this we might add the observation that such intentions are quite uncommon in business negotiations. Even if I don't *expect* you to believe that 10% is my final position, I probably still *hope* or intend to deceive you into thinking that I am unwilling to offer as much as 12%. Examples (2) and (3) are clear instances of lying — they involve deliberate false statements intended to deceive others. It's not so clear, however, that examples (4), (5) and (6) constitute instances of lying. These cases do seem to involve the intent to deceive, but the statements involved are sufficiently ambiguous that it is not clear that they are untrue. We can still say that these are cases in which one affirms (or represents as true) statements which one knows to be dubious with the intent to deceive others. Morally speaking this may be just as bad or wrong as straightforward instances of lying.

An Alternative Definition of Lying

Our proposed definition of lying implies that bluffing in standard negotiation settings constitutes lying. There is at least one other approach to defining the concept of lying which does not have this consequence and it would be well for us to consider it here. In his *Lectures on Ethics*, Immanuel Kant (1775 – 1780) holds that a deliberate false statement does not constitute a lie unless the speaker has "expressly given" the other(s) to believe the he/she intends to speak the truth.[5] According to Kant's original view, when I make a false statement to a thief about the location of my valuables, I am not lying because "the thief knows full well that I will not, if I can help it, tell him the truth and that he has no right to demand it of me" (1775 – 1780, p. 227). According to this view, false statements uttered in the course of business negotiations do not constitute lies except in the very unusual circumstances that one promises to tell the truth during the negotiations. Kant's definition is open to serious objections. It seems to rule out many common cases of lying. For example, suppose that a child standing in line to see an X-rated movie claims to be 18 when he or she is only 15. This is a lie in spite of the fact that no explicit promise to tell the truth was made to the ticket seller. There does seem to be one relevant difference between the two cases in question. The ticket taker has a right to be told the truth and a right to the information in question; the thief has no right to the information on one's valuables. This suggests the following revision of Kant's definition:

4. A lie is a deliberate false statement which is (i) either intended to deceive others or foreseen to be likely to deceive others, and (ii) either the person who makes the statement has promised to be truthful or those to whom it is directed have a right to know the truth.

Many would take it to be a virtue of (4) that it implies that deliberate false statements made during the course of certain kinds of competitive activities do not constitute lies. Carr quoted the British statesman Henry Taylor who argued that "falsehood ceases to be falsehood when it is understood on all sides that the truth is not expected to be spoken" (1968, p. 143). Carr argued that in poker, diplomacy, and business, individuals (through mutually implied consent) forfeit their rights to be told the truth. It seems at least plausible to say this with respect to standard cases of negotiation. However, it is surely not the case in situations in which one of the parties is unfamiliar with standard negotiating procedures (e.g., children, immigrant laborers, naive individuals or the mentally impaired), and who enters into the discussion assuming that all of the parties will be perfectly candid.

If (4) is a correct definition of lying, then it does seem plausible to say that bluffing typically does not amount to lying. So, in order to defend our earlier claim, that bluffing usually involves lying we need to give reasons for thinking that (3) is preferable to (4). We are inclined to think that deliberate falsehoods uttered in the course of games and diplomacy as well as business do constitute lies, and are thus inclined to prefer (3) to (4). This is a case about which people have conflicting intuitions; it cannot be a decisive reason for preferring (3) to (4) or vice versa. A more decisive consideration in favor of (3) is the following case. Suppose that a management negotiator asks a union negotiator the size of the union strike fund. The union negotiator responds by saying it is three times its actual amount. Definition (4) implies that this statement is not a lie since the management negotiator didn't have a right to know the information in question and the union didn't explicitly promise to tell the truth about this. But surely this is a lie. The fact that management has no right to know the truth is just cause for withholding the information, but responding falsely is a lie nonetheless.

There is, to the best of our knowledge, no plausible definition of lying which allows us to say that typical instances of bluffing in labor and other sorts of business negotiations do not involve lying. We should stress that it is only bluffing which involves making false statements which constitutes lying. One is not lying if one bluffs another by making the true statement "We want a 30% pay increase." Similarly, it is not a lie if one bluffs without making any statements as in a game of poker or overpricing (on a price tag) a product where bargaining is expected (e.g., a used car lot or antique store).

The Concept of Deception

At this point it would be useful to consider the relationship between lying and the broader concept of deception. Deception may be defined as intentionally causing another person to have false beliefs. (It is not clear whether preventing someone from having true beliefs should count as deception.) As we have seen, lying always involves the intent to deceive others, or the expectation that they will be deceived as a result of what one says, or both. But one can lie without actually deceiving anyone. If you don't believe me when I lie and tell you that 10% is our final offer, then I haven't succeeded in deceiving you about anything. It is also possible to deceive another person without telling a lie. For example, I am not lying when I deceive a thief into thinking that I am at home by installing an automatic timer to have my lights turned on in the evening. Only deception which involves making false statements can be considered lying.

It seems that one can often avoid lying in the course of a business negotiation simply by phrasing one's statements very carefully. In negotiations, instead of lying and saying that 10% is the highest wage increase we will give, I could avoid lying by making the following true, but equally deceptive statement: "Our position is that 10% is our final offer" (without saying that this position is subject to change). It is questionable whether this is any less morally objectionable than lying. Most people prefer to deceive others by means of cleverly contrived true statements, rather than lies. Some who have strong scruples against lying see nothing wrong with such ruses. It is doubtful, however, whether lying is any worse than mere deception. Consider the following example. I want to deceive a potential thief into thinking that I will be at home in the late afternoon. I have the choice between (i) leaving my lights on, and (ii) leaving a note on my door which says "I will be home at 5 p.m." Surely this choice is morally indifferent. The fact that (ii) is an act of lying and (i) isn't, is not, itself, a reason for thinking that (i) is morally preferable to (ii).[6]

MORAL ISSUES IN LYING

Common sense holds that lying is a matter of moral significance and that lying is *prima facie* wrong, or wrong everything else being equal. This can also be put by saying that there is a presumption against lying, and that lying requires some special justification in order to be considered permissible. Common sense also holds that lying is not always wrong, it can sometimes be justified (Ross, 1960). Almost no one would agree with Kant's (1797) later view in "On the Supposed Right to Tell Lies from Benevolent Motives," that it is wrong to lie even if doing so is necessary to protect the lives of innocent people. According to this view it would be wrong to lie to a potential murderer concerning the whereabouts of an intended victim. Common sense also seems to hold that there is a presumption against simple deception.

Assuming the correctness of this view about the morality of lying and deception, and assuming that we are correct in saying that bluffing involves lying, it follows that bluffing and other deceptive business practices require some sort of special justification in order to be considered permissible.

We will now attempt to determine whether there is any special justification for the kind of lying and deception which typically occurs in labor and other sorts of business negotiations. Bluffing and other sorts of deceptive strategies are standard practice in these negotiations and they are generally thought to be acceptable. Does the fact that these things are standard practice or 'part of the game' show that they are justified? We think not. The mere fact that something is standard practice, legal, or generally accepted is not enough to justify it.

Standard practice and popular opinion can be in error. Such things as slavery were once standard practice, legal and generally accepted. But they are and *were* morally wrong. Bluffing constitutes an attempt to deceive others about the nature of one's intentions in a bargaining situation. The *prima facie* wrongness of bluffing is considerably *diminished* on account of the fact that the lying and deception involved typically concern matters about which the other parties have no particular right to know. The others have no particular right to know one's bargaining position—one's intentions. However, there is still some presumption against lying or deceiving other people, even when they have no right to the information in question. A stranger has no right to know how old I am. I have no obligation to provide him/her with this information. Other things being equal, however, it would still be wrong for me to lie to this stranger about my age.

In our view the main justification for bluffing consists in the fact that the moral presumption against lying to or deceiving someone holds only when the person or persons with whom you are dealing is/are not attempting to lie to or deceive you. Given this, there is no presumption against bluffing or deceiving someone who is attempting to bluff or deceive you on that occasion. The prevalence of bluffing in negotiations means that one is safe in presuming that one is justified in bluffing in the absence of any special reasons for thinking that one's negotiating partners are not bluffing (e.g., when one is dealing with an unusually naive or scrupulous person).

CONCLUSIONS

Granted that bluffing and deception can be permissible given the exigencies and harsh realities of economic bargaining in our society, isn't it an indictment of our entire economic system that such activities are necessary in so many typical circumstances? Even those who defend the practice of bluffing (Carr, 1968) concede that a great deal of lying and deception occurs in connection with the economic activities of our society. Much of this (particularly in the area of bargaining or negotiating) is openly condoned or encouraged by both business and labor. While lying and deception are not generally condoned in other contexts, they often occur as the result of pressures generated by the highly competitive nature of our society. For example, few would condone the behavior of a salesperson who deliberately misrepresents the cost and effectiveness of a product. However, a salesperson under pressure to sell an inferior product may feel that he/she must either deceive prospective customers or else find a new job.

Many people would argue that our economic system is flawed in that it allegedly encourages dishonesty and thus corrupts our moral character and makes us worse persons than we would have been otherwise. Such criticisms are frequently found in Marxist literature. This kind of criticism can be extended into other areas as well. The competitive arrangements of our economic system are not only blamed for encouraging dishonesty, but other kinds of allegedly unethical conduct as well. The so-called competitive business 'rat race' has been cited as a cause of personal treachery, backbiting, and sycophantic behavior. This, it seems to us is a very serious criticism which warrants careful consideration. We suggest the following three lines of response.

1. One could concede that the economic arrangements of our society are such as to elicit a great deal of unethical conduct, but argue that this is the case in any viable economic system — including various forms of socialism and communism. If this is so then the existence of immoral conduct which is associated with economic activities in our own society cannot be a reason to prefer some other sort of economic system. The record of the major socialist and communist countries would tend to support this view. There is deception in the bargaining involved in such things as the allocation of labor and raw materials for industry and setting production quotas for industry. There is also the same kind of gamesmanship involved in competing for desirable positions in society and (by all accounts) much greater opportunity and need for bribery. However, there have been viable feudalistic and caste societies which are much less competitive than our own which function with much less deception or occasions for deception. If one's place in society is determined by birth, then one will simply not have occasion to get ahead by deception.

2. While it must be conceded that there are other types of economic systems which involve less dishonesty than our own, these systems have other undesirable features which outweigh this virtue. In a feudal society or a centrally planned 'command' economy there might well be less occasion for bargaining about wages and prices and thus also less occasion for deceiving other people about such things. But such a society is surely less free than our own and also very likely to be less prosperous. There are strong reasons to desire that wages be determined by voluntary agreements, even if that allows for the possibility of dishonesty in negotiations.

3. It can be argued that the present objections to competitive economic systems such as our own rest on a mistaken view about the nature of moral goodness and the moral virtues. One's moral goodness and honesty are not a direct function of how frequently one tells lies. Thor Hyerdahl did not tell any lies during the many months in which he was alone on the Kon-Tikki. But we would not conclude from this that he was an exceptionally honest man during that period of time. Similarly, the fact that a businessperson who has a monopoly on a vital good or service does not misrepresent the price or quality of his/her goods or services does not necessarily mean that he/she is honest. There is simply no occasion or temptation to be dishonest. The extent to which a person possesses the different moral virtues is a function of how that person is *disposed* to act in various actual and possible situations. My courage or cowardice is a function of my ability to master fear in dangerous situations. Suppose that I am drafted into the Army and sent to serve in the front lines. If I desert my post at the first sign of the enemy we would not say that being drafted into the army has made me a more cowardly person. Rather, we could say that it has uncovered and actualized cowardly dispositions which I had all along. Similarly, competitive economic arrangements do not usually *cause* people to become dishonest or treacherous, etc. However these arrangements often actualize dispositions to act dishonestly or treacherously which people had all along. This is not to deny that the economic institutions of our society can in some cases alter a person's basic behavioral dispositions and thereby also his/her character for the worse. For example, the activities of a negotiator may cause him/her to be less truthful and trusting in his/her personal relationships. Our claim is only that most of the 'undesirable moral effects' attributed to our economic institutions involve actualizing pre-existing dispositions, rather than causing any fundamental changes in character.

Notes

1. It could however be argued on utilitarian grounds that, given a decreasing marginal utility for money, there is a presumption to settle as favorably as possible for the employees since they are *generally* poorer than the stockholders.

2. Arnold Isenberg however disputes this in "Conditions for Lying," in *Ethical Theory and Business*. Tom Beauchamp and Norman Bowie (eds.) (Prentice Hall, Englewood Cliffs, N.J., 1979), pp. 466–468. He holds that a true statement can be a lie provided that one does not believe it. He defines a lie as follows: "A lie is a statement made by one who does not believe it with the intention that someone else be led to believe it. This definition leaves open the possibility that a person should be lying even though he says what is true" (p. 466). We feel that this is most implausible. For if what one says is true, this is always sufficient to defeat the claim that it is a lie.

3. There is however some question here as to what it means to make a *deliberate* false statement. Must one believe that what one says is false or is it enough that one does not believe it? Roderick Chisholm and Thomas Feehan hold that the latter is all that is necessary in "The Intent to Deceive," *Journal of Philosophy* 74 (1977), 143–159. This makes the concept of lying broader than it would otherwise be.

4. Frederick Siegler considers this kind of example in "Lying," *American Philosophical Quarterly* 3 (1966), 128–136. But he argues that it does not count against the view that a necessary condition of a statement's being a lie is that it is intended to deceive someone. The example only shows that it is not necessary that the liar, him/herself, intend to deceive the others. But it does not count against the view that the lie must be intended by *someone* to deceive others. For, in our present example, *the criminal intends* that the witness' statements deceive others. However, a slight modification of the present example generates a counter-example to his claim that a lie must be intended by someone or other to deceive. Suppose that a witness makes a deliberate false statement, *x* for fear of being killed by the friends of the accused. He/she is lying even if the accused's friends believe that *x* is true, in which case neither they nor anyone else intend that the witness' statements deceive the jury.

5. Kant's analysis of lying offered here differs from the one presented in Kant's later and more well known work. "On the Supposed Right to Tell Lies from Benevolent Motives" (1797) in Barauch Brody (ed.), *Moral Rules and Particular Circumstances* (Prentice-Hall, 1970), pp. 31–36. There he says that any intentional false statement is a lie (p. 32) Kant also gives a different account of the morality of lying in these two works. His well-known absolute prohibition against lying is set forth only in the latter work.

6. We owe this example to Bernard Gert.

Bibliography

Bulkeley, W. M. 1979, "To Some at Harvard, Telling Lies Becomes a Matter of Course," *Wall Street Journal*, January 15, pp. 1, 37.

Carr, A. Z. 1968, "Is Business Bluffing Ethical?," *Harvard Business Review* 46, 143–153.

Chisholm, R. and T. Feehan: 1977, "The Intent to Deceive," *Journal of Philosophy* 74, 143–159.

Isenberg, A. 1965, "Conditions for Lying," in T. Beauchamp and N. Bowie (eds.), *Ethical Theory and Business* (Prentice-Hall, Englewood Cliffs, N.J., 1979), pp. 466–468.

Kant, I. 1775–1780, *Lectures on Ethics* (Louis Infield, Trans., Harper and Row, New York, 1963).

Kant, I. 1797, "On a Supposed Right to Tell Lies from Benevolent Motives," in B. Brody (ed.), *Moral Rules and Particular Circumstances* (Prentice-Hall, Englewood Cliffs, N.J., 1970), pp. 31–36.

National Labor Relations Act, as amended, 29 USC 151 *et seq.* (1970).

NLRB v. *Truitt Mfg. Co.* 351US149, 38LRRM2042 (1956).

Ross, D. 1930, *The Right and the Good* (Oxford University Press, Oxford).

Siegler, F. 1966, "Lying," *American Philosophical Quarterly* 3, 128–136.

Jennifer Jackson
HONESTY IN MARKETING

What standards of honesty are morally obligatory in marketing practices, specifically in trade and advertising? An undertaking to tell the truth, the whole truth and nothing but the truth may be altogether appropriate in the court-room. Would it not be absurd, though, to incorporate such an undertaking into a code of practice for trade and advertising: absurd, because wholly self-defeating? The market could barely function under so severe a constraint.

The necessity of having some teaching against fraudulent practices in society is obvious enough. It is easy to see that trust is a precondition of living in a community. Only imagine a society in which trust in the word of others were not possible. Any joint ventures in such a society would be highly problematic. Does not co-operation depend on at least a modicum of reliability? Without it each of us would have to become largely self-reliant and our having to be so would crowd out all activities except those devoted to obtaining and preserving the bare necessities of life. We need, then, a moral teaching that enables us to maintain the conditions of trust. What are the implications in regard to honesty? Should lying be deemed 'wrong' or 'inadvisable'? If 'wrong', absolutely or conditionally?

I will address these general questions here with an eye to the implications of my answers for marketing practices. I will suggest that what we need is a middle of the road teaching: that lying is wrong but conditionally, not absolutely; that, accordingly, *everyone* has a right not to be lied to — though a right which may in certain cases be overridden or waived. Deceptive practices which do not involve lying, I will suggest, are not as such to be deemed wrong — but they will be so in some cases — as if they involve a betrayal of trust or, if they are practised against people known to be especially vulnerable. Finally, I will warn against the tendency of codes to seek to impose too high standards. Critical in this respect, is the interpretation to be put on the notion of especially vulnerable persons entitled on that account to special protection. We should resist any suggestion that the reasonable man who does *not* need special protection has to be ever rational, has to be one who can be relied upon always to act sensibly.

DO PEOPLE HAVE A RIGHT NOT TO BE LIED TO?

It might be thought that no such right could be justified in terms of social necessity. While if lying became widespread and generally tolerated, that would be socially disastrous, the same cannot be supposed if people simply follow a counsel to 'lie as little as possible — only when you have to'.

But arguably such a counsel is too indefinite to prevent people from lying regularly. Is not a firm and specific teaching with reasonably clear-cut obedience rules what we need? — such as, that people have a right not to be lied to, that accordingly we are not even to think of lying as an option, i.e. it is not a

From *Journal of Applied Philosophy*, 7, no. 1 (1990), 51–60. Reprinted by permission.

possible means to consider in our pursuit of legitimate or even noble aims: it is 'unjust'.

But how strict a teaching do we need to have? Should we, like St Augustine & Kant, maintain that lying is always wrong, that the right not to be lied to is absolute rather than *prima facie*? While the question as to what is a sensible ruling on what to teach depends merely on matters of fact, the facts at issue are not very easy to prove.

Those who have taken to heart the teaching that lying is always wrong seem to have been driven to ludicrous expedients to conform to the teaching, e.g. the notorious resource of 'mental reservation' by which you could avoid telling a lie by silently qualifying what you said aloud. When the English Catholic priest, John Ward, was asked by his captors in 1606 whether he was a priest and whether he had ever been across the seas, he replied 'no' to both questions though in fact the correct answer was 'yes'. Upon evidence being produced that his answers were false he claimed that he had not lied since in denying that he was a priest he had mentally added 'of Apollo' and in saying that he had not been across the seas he had reserved 'Indian' before 'seas'.[1] St Francis, when asked whether a certain fugitive had passed that way, "put his hand in the sleeve of his cloak and replied that he had not passed that way—meaning through the sleeve".[2]

St Alfonso de Liguori suggests a form of equivocation of which either of the aforementioned could also have availed themselves to avoid lying. Wherever the truthful answer to a question is 'yes' you can still answer 'no' truthfully if you say: 'I say no'—this is always a truthful answer in as much as the speaker does in fact say 'no'. Peter Singer[3] notes that the resource of mental reservation is still defended in some quarters—in Charles McFadden's *Medical Ethics*, a text published in 1967. McFadden advises doctors and nurses to use the method of mental reservation when they consider it necessary to deceive patients. If, for instance, a feverish patient asks what his temperature is, and the doctor thinks it better that he not know, the doctor is advised to say, 'Your temperature is normal today', while making the mental reservation that it is normal for someone in the patient's precise physical condition.

But if we reject the teaching that lying is always wrong, does our teaching become inconsistent? So it might seem since we have said (1) that people should be taught that lying is unjust and therefore 'not an option', and now we are saying (2) that the right not to be lied to is only *prima facie*, that therefore in some circumstances, where the right is overridden, lying is not unjust. But isn't this to teach: (1) never lie and (2) sometimes lie?

It is not. In saying that lying is not an option we do not mean to suggest that it is never morally defensible to lie, only that since people have a *prima facie* right not to be lied to, it is only defensible to lie to them if, in the circumstances, the right does not apply as, e.g., if unless we lie we infringe another right. As we have already observed, where there is a conflict of *prima facie* rights one must take priority—e.g. someone's right to be rescued may override someone else's right not to be lied to (or not to have a confidence betrayed). In such cases it is not that we are committing a lesser injustice to avert a greater injustice. It is rather that the extent of one right is limited by that of another in which case the former simply does not apply.

Thus, while a firm would not be justified in lying to the public merely in order to increase its profits, it might be justified in lying to the public on some occasion in order to stay in business in the area — putting its employees' rights to their jobs over the public's right not to be lied to.

Nor would a trade or advertising practice offend against the middle of the road teaching I am advocating, that we have a conditional *prima facie* right not to be lied to, if those lied to had waived their right — as people do in games of bluff. Perhaps some of the gimmickry and patent nonsense in advertisements is recognised by the public to be merely playful and fanciful: is it not positively enjoyed? (Visiting a children's ward recently, I noticed that the young patients only seemed interested in watching the TV, played continuously in the ward, during the adverts.)

DELIBERATELY DECEPTIVE PRACTICES

While I have argued in support of a general right not to be lied to, I do not think that we should consider deliberately deceptive practices which do not involve lying to be wrong as such. This might sound strange to some: to those who assume that the only difference between deliberate deceptions which involve lying and those which do not, is that the former are verbal methods of deception, the latter, non-verbal. And what significance can there be morally between whether you deceive a person one way or the other? People can surely act lies as well as speak them. And may not the person deceived be equally harmed if he is taken in by a non-verbal trick or lie?

In regard to the first point, let us agree that lies can be acted as well as spoken. We may communicate a falsehood non-verbally, e.g. by a gesture, a nod of the head. But the acted deceit is not a lie unless it is a *communication*. Nor, indeed, is a false statement intended to deceive necessarily a lie, as it need not be a communication. Thus, if I, realising that you have your ear pressed against the keyhole of my door, say something false aloud in order to deceive you, I am not lying to you. I cannot be lying to you as I am not in communication with you. In Shakespeare's *Much Ado*, for example, Benedick and Beatrice are both successively and deliberately tricked by false statements they are intended to overhear: in neither case are they lied to. Likewise in *Twelfth Night* Malvolio is gulled by Maria's forged 'epistle of love' dropped for that purpose in his path: again, it is not a communication *to* him.

As to the second point, that non-verbal deception can be every bit as harmful as lying to the person deceived, that is true but irrelevant. The wrongness of lying does not depend on the person who is deceived being harmed thereby at all. Indeed, one reason for advocating a firm teaching against lying, just is that many individual lies we would otherwise be tempted to tell do *not* hurt the person deceived. The point in advocating the quite firm teaching against lying is that the practice does social harm, not that individual lies necessarily harm those who are lied to.

Deliberate deceptive practices need not involve lying, verbally or non-verbally. But are not the non-lying deliberately deceptive practices just as intolerable as the lying practices? Not necessarily, I will suggest.

Deliberate deception seems so entrenched in social life as we know it — that it is difficult to imagine what life would be like without it. Don't we all deliberately deceive each other constantly without a second thought (women wear make-up, quarrelsome couples feign harmony in public, we smile at each other's feeble jokes though inwardly we are not amused)? Now, to be sure, the fact that we think nothing of acting in a certain way is hardly proof of the innocence of the practice. Nor is complaisance about a practice that is long-standing necessarily justified. Just as the harm to our health of a long-standing common practice may escape our notice (e.g. the risks of sunbathing) so may the ill consequences of a long-established social practice go undetected.

But the practice of deliberate deception, lying apart, is something, I suggest, which we not only can, but ought to, tolerate. It is something, moreover, which we should not merely condone on account of the difficulties of stamping it out, but should positively uphold because it brings us benefits, it enriches our lives. We need to be able to practise deception in order to preserve our privacy and privacy is something which many of us, quite reasonably, cherish.

No doubt there are some who would dispute the desirability of protecting privacy, who regard secrecy as essentially discreditable; concealment as proof of guilt, or, at least, as proof of the inadequacies of human relationships in society as we know it, and of the compromises forced upon us in the present state of the world. Sisela Bok[4] invites us to imagine what it would be like to live (a) in a society in which no one could keep a secret from anyone else, in which our personal plans, actions, fears and hopes were all transparent or (b) in a society in which everyone could keep secrets impenetrable at will, in which no secret codes could be broken. Surely social institutions and individual relationships would in either society not only be amazingly different but radically impoverished.

WHOM ARE WE ENTITLED TO TRUST?

Yet though deliberate deception, lying apart, should not be deemed wrong as such, it may be wrong in certain cases — is so, for example, if it involves a betrayal of trust. Now there are many situations where we are misled, sometimes deliberately, sometimes inadvertently, by the behaviour of others though no betrayal of trust is involved. Perhaps, I have come to rely on the sound of my neighbour's car starting, to wake me up in the morning. But though I count on this, I have no right to expect it. Even if my neighbour happens to know that I rely on him in this way he is not obliged to give me notice of his departures from routine though it might be the friendly thing to do. There is a betrayal of trust only if (1) trust has been extended and (2) the person who trusts is *entitled* to do so.

Consider the following case. On a Sunday morning I anticipate that my sociable neighbour, if he sees me about, will drop in for a chat. I wish to be left undisturbed — but also, not to hurt his feelings. So, seeing that my neighbour is hovering about in his front garden, I put on hat and coat, take up my umbrella, walk out the front door, ostentatiously lock it and exchange a friendly greeting with my neighbour as I hurry down the path and out the gate. Thereafter I furtively creep along the hedge and round to the back of my house and quietly let myself back inside. The whole purpose of this exercise has been to deceive my neighbour into thinking that I am out. But I have not lied to him. Nor have I betrayed his trust.

My contention is that such antics do not require any excuse. I do not have to plead in self-defence, e.g. that I have work to do, papers to mark, letters to write. Moreover, since such trickery is innocent, it is no reflection on my character if I positively enjoy fooling my neighbour in this way — if it amuses me.

But while we do not have a general right (a right against everyone) not to be deliberately deceived by them, we do have a special right against some not to be deceived by them and this just because we are *entitled* to put our trust in them. Are not health professionals, e.g. obliged not only to advise us disinterestedly, i.e. to impart advice which they believe we would be prudent to follow, but also to give us advice which is honest and relevantly informative? The requirement (legal and moral) for doctors to obtain informed consent for invasive treatment suggests that in some circumstances they at least are so obliged.

But though health professionals would seem to have at least a *prima facie* duty not deliberately to deceive their patients we cannot generalise to all other professional relationships. The police hardly acknowledge any such duty in their dealings with suspects. Jerome H. Skolnick, commenting on contemporary police practice in the USA, remarks that "deception is considered by police and courts to be as natural to detecting as pouncing is to a cat".[5] And, after all, the relationship of constable to suspect is hardly analogous to that of doctor to patient or attorney to client. It is surely no dereliction of policemen's duty to give positively unhelpful advice to suspects. The police, it will be said, are providing a service to the law-abiding public not to 'the criminal classes'.

Thus it is standard practice for police when interrogating suspects, simulating a fatherly concern, to *pretend* to give helpful advice, saying e.g. 'you have a right to consult an attorney, but you had better talk to us straight away rather than delay matters unnecessarily'. Since police know very well that attorneys, if consulted, invariably caution their clients *not* to waive their right to 'maintain silence'[6] this police advice to suspects is (a) deliberately deceptive and (b) malevolent.

Should we regard the relationship of business man to customer or client (or of business man to business man) as analogous to that of police constable to suspect or to that of doctors to patient or as different again? Do we extend our trust to traders and advertisers beyond what the law binds them to? If we do trust them further, are we entitled so to do?

The relationship between constable and suspect is not characteristically on a voluntary footing: suspects do not usually choose to 'help' police with their enquiries, whereas patients usually choose to put themselves in their doctor's hands — but they do so on the understanding that the doctors will use the power surrendered to them disinterestedly and honestly.

The relationship between salesman and customer likewise is usually voluntary. But does the customer engage in trade only on the understanding that the salesman is acting disinterestedly and honestly?

Even within the context of trade and sales dealings we may not safely generalise concerning the underlying understanding on which negotiation is entered: this may vary from culture to culture and within cultures. In some sales contexts, e.g. the market bazaar, it is quite evident that the parties bargaining are fully aware that the strategy to be followed is one of bluff and counter-bluff, each side striving to achieve the better deal by disguising from one another what price they are willing to settle for. As in games of bluff participants challenge their opponents to try to deceive them.

In other sales contexts, though, bazaar-style evasiveness and bluff are out of place. A shop, jealous of its good name, may give customers to understand that it is committed to honest dealing; i.e. that it does not deliberately deceive its customers — even so, we do not expect, even in the most reputable of shops, the salesman to advise us that down the road the same make of camera he is recommending to us is being sold off at half price by a rival shop.

Is there any injustice in condoning a variety of standards regarding 'openness' in trade dealings within a society — provided all respect the bottom line legal constraints, e.g. on lying? Though the conventionally higher standards of openness in reputable firms are not legally enforced, there is obvious and effective remedy, through complaints procedures and adverse publicity, against individual salesmen who flout these standards. The variety of standards gives us a choice as consumers: some of us prefer to pay more and play safe or save time, others, to haggle in the market, to hunt for a bargain. Sometimes as ignorant consumers we seek and expect reliable advice from salesmen. Other times, preening ourselves on our expertise, we scheme to outsmart the salesman. We choose with whom to deal, knowing the standard of openness to be expected.

We are, however, entitled to expect those with whom we deal at least to obey the law and the law, in fact, does not prohibit lying merely. It prohibits advertising practices which are deceptive in effect, whether or not intentionally, if they mislead the reasonable man 'to a material degree', i.e. as regards the cost, quantity or quality of what is for sale.

Thus, for example, deceptive packaging or labelling is not allowed, not even if advertisers take the precaution of printing a disclaimer over it unless, according to Widgery LCJ (*Norman v. Bennett and Another*, 1974) the disclaimer is as "bold, precise and compelling as the trade description itself" and "as effectively brought to the notice of any person to whom the goods may be supplied".[7] Where an odometer was altered and a disclaimer stuck on it 'not guaranteed' (*Newman v. Hackney London Borough Council*, 1982) and where an odometer was transferred from one car to another and a disclaimer attached — "With deep regret due to Customers' Protection Act we can no longer verify that the mileage shown on this vehicle is correct" (*Corfield v. Starr*, 1981) neither disclaimer was deemed a defence.[8]

Similarly, the protection of the law may be extended to customers who are misled by outsize packaging. Suppose that we are buying a jar of moisturising cream at the chemists. The weight of contents is clearly and correctly stated on the jar. But does that information convey to the ordinary buyer any idea of the amount of cream in the jar? Do we not go rather by the size of the jar? Thus in *R v A.F. Pears Ltd*, 1982, Pears was found guilty of supplying goods to which a false trade description was applied although the jar of moisturising cream in question was correctly labelled concerning the weight of its contents. What was not apparent before purchase was that the jar had a double skin — had the inner container followed the contents of the outer, the capacity would have been substantially larger.[9]

While we are entitled to trust traders and advertisers to keep within the law, there is always going to be a grey area of indeterminacy about the standards which apply. Traders and advertisers are legally obliged not to mislead a customer as regards the suitability of goods for the customer's purpose (Trade Descriptions Act 1968, 2[d]). But how far (legally and morally) is the seller obliged to go to make sure of this? Suppose the customer is buying a child's toy, clearly labelled 'unsuitable for under fives'. Is the seller obliged to quiz the customer about the age of the person for whom he is buying the toy? Is he obliged at least to draw the customer's attention to the label? Or, may he assume the customer can (and does) read? What if the customer reads out, but casually dismisses, a caution — perhaps in front of, but not to, the salesman? Perhaps the customer consults his companion as to the suitability of the toy for a younger child — should the salesman butt in? Would it signify whether the grounds of unsuitability related merely to the complexity of the toy and not its safety?

Returning, now, to our question as to whether we are entitled to trust traders and advertisers beyond what the law binds them to, the answer would seem to be: it all depends on the circumstances. Promises may be morally, though not legally, binding, and a promise may be made implicitly if not explicitly. If a shop with an established name proclaims its commitment to customer service and advice, does it not therewith give its customers an undertaking they are entitled to trust — even if the very same phrases uttered by a street trader would not so entitle customers?

But while traders can assume obligation to customers not forced upon them by the law, offering, e.g., 'disinterested' advice, they are not morally obliged to make such undertaking and, if they do not, we have no right to expect more of them than precisely what the law requires. In so saying, am I condoning shady practices, i.e. practices which conform to the letter but not the spirit of the law?

SHADY PRACTICES

The resourceful trader or advertiser will perhaps keep one step ahead of the law finding ways to gull customers that are not as the law stands illegal. Is this type of enterprise 'unethical'? Is it unethical if a bakery boasts dietary advantages for its bread when the truth is merely that its slices are thinner?[10] Is it unethical to advertise six cans for a pound when singles sell for 16p?[11]

THE CASE AGAINST SHADY PRACTICES

In so far as people in trade and advertising lay claim to professional status, it may be argued that they must accept self-regulation, must evolve codes imposing stricter standards on themselves and their colleagues than the bottom line constraints staked out by law. Is not self-regulation a definitive criterion of professionalism? But, of course, this argument cuts no ice with those in trade and advertising who do not aspire to professional status, who brush aside such aspirations as wrong-headed, declaring, perhaps, that 'business is business'.

Here, then is another argument against engaging in shady practice.

Premises
1. People have a general right that just laws be upheld.
2. Upholding a law means not merely obeying it, but supporting it: it means acting in keeping with the spirit, not seeking ways round it.

Conclusion

In business we are obliged to repudiate shady practices.

THE CASE FOR 'SHADY PRACTICES'

Those who defend the permissibility of acting against the spirit of the law will naturally object to such conduct being labelled pejoratively as 'shady practice'. They will reject the foregoing argument on the ground that its first premiss is untenable. People do indeed have a right against certain appointed officials, e.g. health and safety inspectors, or the police, that just laws by *upheld* — but against everyone? In other words, they will argue that people do not have a general right that just law be upheld, only that it be obeyed. Why, after all, should advertisers tie their own hands with self-imposed constraints additional to those imposed by the law? It is the business of law, is it not, to fix whatever constraints are necessary to protect consumers? Additional constraints self-imposed by business must be superfluous.

We might defend the advertisers who argue thus by invoking the game analogy. Provided everyone understands the rules of the advertiser's game, viz. that we have no right to trust their claims except so far as the law decrees, is it not permissible for them to gull and cajole us if they can into preferring their product over rivals? Or is this game analogy inappropriate here in as much as we consumers are unwilling participants? But then not all games are voluntary — they are compulsory for schoolchildren. Perhaps anyway we relish the game and would not want to live in a society in which goods for sale were all in plain wraps with nothing but the bare facts concerning ingredients and costs proclaimed. Is shopping a game in which we delight to pit our wits against the sellers? The rules of the game safeguard our right to accurate information about quality, quantity and cost but otherwise, for the sake of the game, we are pleased to waive whatever right we might have against the advertisers' deceptive tricks: rights waived are not infringed.

SOCIALLY RESPONSIBLE TRADE AND ADVERTISING

Yet, surely, we all have an obligation to act responsibly. And is it not *irresponsible* to exploit other people's weaknesses? Is it not undeniable, moreover, that advertising characteristically does precisely that? Do not our weaknesses constitute the very foundation of an enterprise culture? If we were more rational, less self-indulgent, we would have little time for many consumer goods.

Only consider how, for example, advertisers would fare in Plato's *Republic*. The guardians being super-rational would themselves provide scant custom; advertisers would have to ply their trade almost exclusively among the lower orders. The guardians after all, eschew all worldly pleasures; eat and drink only to keep fit, copulate only to produce more guardians and in no case indulge in sensual pleasure for pleasure's sake (since that way, according to Plato, lies corrupting addiction).

But while advertisers depend on and benefit from our weaknesses, it does not follow that they are taking 'unjust' advantage of us as implied by the term 'exploit'. Though advertisers benefit from our weaknesses it does not follow that they seek to make or keep us weak. Judges and policemen earn their living off criminality: we need not assume that they seek to encourage it. (Of course, those who live off other people's misfortune, e.g. undertakers, pawnbrokers, may not be much liked by those who need their services — the prejudice is natural if unreasonable.)

The British Code of Advertising Practice defends the role of the Alcoholic Drinks Industry arguing that it does not seek to encourage people to acquire the habit or to abuse it, e.g. by increasing their consumption. Rather it addresses itself to moderate stable adult drinkers inviting them to try alternative brands 'instead of' rather than 'in addition to'. In keeping with this legitimate intent BCAP rules that, "Advertisers should not engage as models people under 25, or people who look as though they may be under 25, if these people are shown in any advertisement either drinking, or about to drink" (1988, 5.2) and "people featured in cigarette advertisements should both be and clearly be seen to be adults of 25 or over" (1988, 3.3).

Of course such precautions at best only limit the extent to which the non-targeted are captivated alongside the targeted. Thus the point in restricting the age of drinkers and smokers to adults is to avoid encouraging youths to emulate their peers. But do not youths aspire to appear older than they are? If drinking and smoking is represented as exclusively for grown-ups, youths will want to do it. Perhaps advertisements for these commodities should only portray guzzling toddlers and puffing octogenarians.

At any rate, we can accept that socially responsible trade and advertising: (1) does not seek to take advantage of the specially vulnerable; (2) seeks to protect the specially vulnerable. (2) indicates a positive obligation that codes of practice such as BCAP rightly acknowledge. (Thus BCAP requires special precautions to protect those who are generally vulnerable, e.g. children, and also to protect all of us who in certain situations become specially vulnerable, e.g. in regard to unmanageable aspects of our anatomies such as baldness and obesity.)

Strictures in codes of advertising or trading practices which go further than the law to protect the specially vulnerable are, then, morally defensible. But strictures aimed at protecting the reasonable man from his own imprudence are another matter. Should not the Drinks and Tobacco Industries be wary of broadening their obligation as suggested in BCAP (1985) to protect the 'immature' and the 'socially insecure', those with 'physical' or 'social' incapacity and those under stress? (243.1.4). Can their industries survive if they cater merely to those who are mature, fit, stress-free and successful?

The wording at this point of the latest edition of BCAP 1988 is marginally more circumspect, though not yet, I think, sufficiently so: "advertisers should not exploit the young, the immature, or those with mental or social incapacities" (C.XII 5.1). Of course advertisers should not 'exploit' anyone. We may readily consider, moreover, that the young and the mentally handicapped merit special protection. But should we not hesitate to extend that protection to the immature and those with social incapacities, unless those categories are more precisely defined?

At any rate, the reasonable man is quite capable of acting childishly and of manifesting social ineptitudes. But the reasonable man, I maintain, is within his right in acting imprudently — weakness is not as such vice. That granted, the reasonable, albeit foolish, consumer is fair game for traders and advertisers provided only they keep within the letter of the law.

We have here of course been discussing only whether such treatment from traders and advertisers is morally defensible. There may be prudential considerations which dictate otherwise.

CONCLUSION

Recently, I received a letter from a distinguished business man who observed: "It is frankly almost impossible to operate a business without telling lies, although I suppose you could say this of life in general". That is a sentiment, no doubt, with which many reputable businessmen would agree. But only, I suggest, because they fail to see any moral significance in the distinction between lying and other forms of deliberate deception — the latter are seen as merely alternative *methods* to the same end. But notice that it is perfectly possible to follow a quite firm teaching against lying both in business and elsewhere in life. The firm teaching need not be an absolute prohibition.

A quite firm teaching against deliberate deception (lying apart) would be quite another matter — or so it has been argued here. Thus a teaching that we have a general right not to be lied to but no general right not to be deliberately deceived makes sense. Is there any harm though in adopting a code such as BCAP which runs these together and prohibits both? There is. Demands which are unrealistically high do not get taken seriously; they get converted from 'requirements' to 'ideals'. If we merge the 'wrongness' of deliberate deception with the wrongness of lying, the net effect may be more dishonesty in practice, not less.

All the same I have conceded that there are circumstances where deception, even *unintended* deception, is morally indefensible: advertisements which mislead reasonable people to a material degree or, advertisements which prey upon the specially vulnerable who are predictably unreasonable. Thus I have argued here that where the specially vulnerable are concerned everyone, traders and advertisers included, has an obligation both not to take advantage of them and to seek ways to protect them. There is no corresponding general obligation, I have argued, not to take advantage of but to seek ways to protect, the reasonable, i.e. average, man from his own imprudence.

Notes

1. Johann P. Sommerville (1988) The 'new art of lying': equivocation, mental reservation, and casuistry, in: Edmund Leites (Ed.) *Conscience and Casuistry in Early Modern Europe* (Cambridge, Cambridge University Press, p. 160).

2. Ibid., p. 173.

3. Peter Singer (1981) *The Expanding Circle* (Oxford, Clarendon Press), p. 65.

4. Sisela Bok (1984) *Secrets* (Oxford, Oxford University Press), pp. 15ff.

5. Jerome H. Skolnick (1985) Deception by police, in: Frederick A. Elliston & Michael Feldberg (Eds) *Moral Issues in Police Work* (Totowa, NJ, Rowman & Allenheld), p. 75.

6. Ibid., p. 88.

7. C. J. Miller & B. W. Harvey (1985) *Consumer and Trading Law: cases and materials* (London, Butterworth), p. 493.

8. Ibid., p. 497.

9. Ibid., p. 497.

10. George C.S. Benson (1982) *Business Ethics in America* (Lexington, MA, D.C. Heath & Co.), p. 715.

11. Ivan L. Preston (1983) Reasonable consumer or ignorant consumer? How the FTC decides, in: Tom L. Beauchamp & Norman E. Bowie (Eds) *Ethical Theory and Business* (Englewood Cliffs, NJ, Prentice-Hall), p. 351.

DISCUSSION QUESTIONS

1. Carr argues that bluffing in business is not lying but simply "game strategy." Do you agree? Is this distinction morally significant?

2. Evaluate the following criticism of Carr: Carr's argument is based on a false analogy. Poker players freely choose to participate in every game they play. No one is forced to play. Weak or aspiring players may watch experts in order to learn the game. They may also practice their skills in games in which no money is at stake. And players may leave the game at any time with no harm to their overall welfare. As long as one lives in a capitalist economy, however, one is forced to be a player in business — if only as a consumer. There is nothing analogous to practicing the game with no money at risk. The only practical way to quit a game one dislikes is to move from one economy to another, that is, from one game to another. Carr's game analogy, then, is one of forced competition between players of unequal skill and experience, and this cannot be defended ethically.

3. Bowie concludes his criticism of Carr by arguing that bluffing in business is legitimate only when all parties know that bluffing is taking place. "Poker is unfair," notes Bowie, "when some of the players do not know the rules that are being used." As a consumer, do you feel you always know when bluffing will be used against you?

4. Carson, Wokutch, and Murrmann argue that bluffing is indeed lying. Nonetheless, they believe that deception in negotiation is morally justified if you have reason to believe that your negotiating partner is also bluffing. Is this argument any different from saying that if you know that a thief is planning to break into your house, then you do nothing wrong by stealing from him or her first?

5. Jackson begins her discussion of honesty in marketing by remarking that while telling "the truth, the whole truth and nothing but the truth" is appropriate in the courtroom, it would be an absurd standard for advertising. "The market," writes Jackson, "could barely function under so severe a constraint." Do you agree? Why should standards of truthfulness be lower in business than in law?

6. Jackson believes that some deceptive practices should be restricted, for example, those that exploit young people or those who are mentally handicapped. However, she opposes additional restrictions aimed at protecting people from their own foolishness. "The reasonable man," she writes, "is within his right in acting imprudently — weakness is not as such vice. That granted, the reasonable, albeit foolish, consumer is fair game for traders and advertisers provided only they keep within the letter of the law." Do you agree with Jackson that marketers do nothing unethical when they appeal to people's weaknesses?

CASE 8.1

◆ ◆ ◆

The Borland Scam

Borland International, Inc., is a computer software company that made $27 million in 1990 on sales of $226 million. Founded in 1983 by Philippe Kahn, the company has been so successful that in 1991 it acquired its arch rival, the Ashton-Tate Corporation. The merger made Borland the leading manufacturer of database software. It more than doubled the company's revenues and increased the number of employees to about 2,000.

Borland's past, however, is as inauspicious as the company's future is promising. As Kahn explained in the following excerpt from an interview with *Inc.* magazine, the company got its start by tricking an advertising salesman from *Byte* magazine.

Inc.: The story goes that Borland was launched by a single ad, without which we wouldn't be sitting here talking about the company. How much of that is apocryphal?

Kahn: It's true: one full-page ad in the November 1983 issue of *Byte* magazine got the company running. If it had failed, I would have had nowhere else to go.

Inc.: If you were so broke, how did you pay for the ad?

Kahn: Let's put it that we convinced the salesman to give us terms. We wanted to appear only in *Byte* — not any of the other microcomputer magazines — because *Byte* is for programmers, and that's who we wanted to reach. But we couldn't afford it. We figured the only way was somehow to convince them to extend us credit terms.

Inc.: And they did?

Kahn: Well, they didn't *offer*. What we did was, before the ad salesman came in — we existed in two small rooms, but I had hired extra people so we would look like a busy, venture-backed company — we prepared a chart with what we pretended was our media plan for the computer magazines. On the chart we had *Byte* crossed out. When the salesman arrived, we made sure the phones were ringing and the extras were scurrying around. Here was this chart he thought he wasn't supposed to see, so I pushed it out of the way. He said, "Hold on, can we get you in *Byte*?" I said, "We don't really want to be in your book, it's not the right audience for us." "You've got to try," he pleaded. I said, "Frankly, our media plan is done, and we can't afford it." So he offered good terms, if only we'd let him run it just once. We expected we'd sell maybe $20,000 worth of software and at least pay for the ad. We sold $150,000 worth. Looking back now, it's a funny story; then it was a big risk.

Kahn recalls this episode as a "funny story," but it might just as easily be characterized as an ethically questionable sting operation. The salesman from *Byte* was lied to and manipulated. If the ad flopped, *Byte* apparently would not have been paid. Still, there is no denying that Kahn's plan worked and that thousands of customers and employees are the beneficiaries of his cleverness. ◆

Discussion Questions

1. Was there anything morally wrong with Kahn's actions?

2. *Byte* could easily have checked out the company to determine if it was what it appeared to be, so the matter was not totally in Kahn's hands. Kahn would say that no one got hurt and that many people benefited. Do you agree?

3. Would you call Kahn's actions dishonest? Smart business? Both?

4. How do you think Carr would evaluate Kahn's operation? Would he see Kahn as playing by the rules of the game or as going too far?

Sources

"'Ashton-Tate Is Not an Active Force Anymore'," *Business Week*, July 22, 1991, 22–23.
"Managing by Necessity," *Inc.*, March 1989, 33, 36.

CASE 8.2

Truth and Business School

In January 1979, the *Wall Street Journal* reported about a course in negotiation at the Harvard Business School that aimed to teach students about "strategic misrepresentation." Prof. Howard Raiffa's Competitive Decision Making course paired students off in negotiation games and graded them according to how successful they were. As in real negotiations, concealing facts, bluffing, and lying could frequently let students cut better deals than they could with the truth alone. Raiffa defended the course by arguing that he was not teaching his students to lie. Rather, he claimed to be showing them that their adversary in a negotiation might lie to them. He also structured the semester so that in the later, more complex games, lying was not necessarily rewarded. ◆

Discussion Questions

1. Is there anything unethical about a course like this? Does it encourage unethical behavior as well as teach students to protect themselves against an opponent's dishonesty?

2. If Carr is right that no one expects total honesty in negotiation, could there be any objection whatsoever to what the course was doing — even if it did lead to more lying in the future?

Source

Bulkeley, William M., "To Some at Harvard, Telling Lies Becomes a Matter of Course," *Wall Street Journal*, January 15, 1979, 1, 22.

CASE 8.3

The Latest Books of "Late" Authors

The latest books by some best-selling authors are neither new nor written by the writer named on the cover. The publishing industry has apparently found ways to continue issuing "new" works under the names of writers who have been dead for several years. Critics of this practice contend that book jackets and promotional material are written to mislead readers who do not know the truth into believing that the author is still alive and writing.

In some cases, the publisher issues works that for one reason or another were not published during an author's lifetime. Yet the publisher does not inform the reader that the author is dead. The case of L. Ron Hubbard is a classic example of this practice. Someone who did not know that Hubbard died in 1986 might easily think that the author was still writing after reading the jacket of the latest L. Ron Hubbard book.

At least five recent novels of V. C. Andrews, however, were not written by Andrews at all. After the author died in 1986, her family selected a writer to continue working on stories that Andrews had begun and others that simply fit her style. Even though Pocket Books mentions Andrews's death and the family's decision inside the book, the cover still lists V. C. Andrews as the author.

The industry defends the practice by noting that it is nothing new. Publishers point to the Nancy Drew series that was published under a single name (Carolyn Keene) but was actually written by a variety of authors. They also claim that although they do not advertise an author's death, they do not really conceal it either. ◆

Discussion Questions

1. Is this practice an example of dishonesty and misrepresentation or clever marketing?

2. If readers are ignorant of an author's death, is it the publisher's responsibility to inform them of that fact? Isn't it relatively easy for a consumer to find out whether a writer is alive or not? What is the seller's responsibility? What is the buyer's responsibility?

3. If V. C. Andrews's family has approved of the practice and if the new writer is writing books in Andrews's style, is there anything wrong with putting "V. C. Andrews" on the cover of a new novel?

Source

McDowell, Edwin, "Sales Rise for Authors Who Perish and Publish," *New York Times*, March 4, 1991, D6.

ADDITIONAL READINGS

Bok, Sissela, *Lying: Moral Choice in Public and Private Life* (New York: Vintage Books, 1978).

Carson, Thomas, "On the Definition of Lying: A Reply to Jones and Revisions," *Journal of Business Ethics*, 7 (1988), 509–514.

Michelman, James H., "Deception in Commercial Negotiation," *Journal of Business Ethics*, 2 (1983), 255–262.

Sullivan, Roger J., "A Response to 'Is Business Bluffing Ethical?'," *Business & Professional Ethics Journal* 3, no. 2 (1983), 1–18.

Wokutch, Richard E., and Thomas L. Carson, "The Ethics and Profitability of Bluffing in Business," *Westminster Institute Review*, 1, no. 2 (May 1981, rev. 1986) in *Ethical Issues in Business: A Philosophical Approach*, edited by Thomas Donaldson and Patricia Werhane (Englewood Cliffs, NJ: Prentice Hall, 1988), 77–83.

———, "The Moral Status of Bluffing and Deception in Business," in *Profits and Professions*, edited by Wade L. Robison, Michael S. Pritchard, and Joseph Ellin (Clifton, NJ: Humana Press, 1983), 141–155.

◆ ◆ ◆

CHAPTER 9

Insider Trading

No issue better captures the controversy over the ethics of contemporary American business than insider trading. During the 1980s, Wall Street was rocked by the ever increasing number of individuals arrested for making illegal profits from acting on information unknown to the trading public. Two of the most influential men on Wall Street — Ivan Boesky and Michael Milken — wound up in jail because of insider trading. John Shad, the former head of the Securities and Exchange Commission, was so appalled over the dishonesty in the securities industry that he gave millions of dollars to establish an ethics program at the Harvard Business School.

Yet despite the dramatic headlines and the public outcry over insider trading, the practice is by no means condemned by all economists and philosophers. Some point to the fact that the stock markets of nations that allow insider trading are not harmed by it. Others contend that insider trading is actually beneficial and makes the market more efficient. Even ethicists who decry the practice do so for different reasons. Some claim fraud and unfairness, while others assert that the problem is one of a breach of trust. This chapter explores the range of opinions on the issue.

Bill Shaw defends insider trading, claiming that the practice will make for greater efficiency. A stock's price, he argues, will more accurately reflect its real value. William Irvine opposes insider trading, but he rejects the traditional claims that insider trading harms shareholders all the time and that the practice is always morally objectionable. Irvine, instead, argues that insider trading is unethical because shareholders are kept uninformed about matters that have a major impact on their interests. Patricia Werhane also rejects insider trading, but she bases her argument on both economic and moral grounds. Insider trading, she contends, makes the economy less competitive and, thereby, less efficient. She also believes that it is unfair. Jennifer Moore sides with Werhane's objections to insider trading, but she rejects arguments based on fairness, property rights, and harm to ordinary investors. She bases her argument on the claim that insider trading breaches a fiduciary duty.

Bill Shaw

SHOULD INSIDER TRADING BE OUTSIDE THE LAW?

Insider trading is good for the U.S. economy, for the corporation that is traded, and for the insiders (of course), and it does not necessarily amount to fraud on investors. Looking beyond the financial pages, and certainly beyond the 6:00 news, you can find a number of economic, legal, and moral arguments supporting this view.

Prof. Henry G. Manne, now dean of the George Mason University School of Law, crystallized the most radical position on this topic with his 1966 *Insider Trading and the Stock Market*. Essentially, Manne sought a return to simpler times — common law, pre-1934 Securities Exchange Act times. He saw knowledge as a valuable thing, whether it be knowledge that advances our cultural well-being or, more practically, knowledge that takes a business from marginal solvency to Fortune 500 status. This widely recognized insight led Manne and others to assign property rights to this information. The originator of the information (the individual or corporation that spent hard-earned bucks producing it) owns and controls this asset just as it does other proprietary goods — securities, real estate, patents, or copyrights. This assignment of ownership and exclusive use is essential to encouraging the production of additional information.

In a society that values freedom, especially economic freedom, self-interested owners of information ought to be permitted to use this asset to its highest and best use.

By employing information in the most efficient manner, as we do with all other privately owned goods, private wealth is maximized, and, in the spirit of Adam Smith, social wealth is thus maximized as well.

SOCIETAL EFFECTS

A reconsideration and revision of the insider trading prohibition would have a number of positive effects. It would also have a downside. The changes would make themselves felt on three levels: societal or systemic, corporate, and individual.

Without getting too technical, it should at least be noted that the securities industry operates on the proposition that information relating to the performance of a firm affects its stock price. The price increase/decrease will depend on how market experts perceive that information. If it appears that fourth quarter earnings will be much higher than expected, or that an innovative new product will soon be released, one would expect the stock price of that firm to increase when the information is made public; the opposite result would follow from the publication of an unfavorable court action or the loss of key personnel.

This evaluative process, led by market professionals, enhances the effi-

From *Business and Society Review*, 66 (1988), 34–37. Reprinted by permission of the publisher.

ciency of our national and regional exchanges by moving securities prices close to, if not perfectly in line with, a stock's real or intrinsic value. These adjustments take place quickly and in an unbiased (i.e., impersonal, objective) way. Thus, traders cannot expect to make a "quick kill" on the market unless they control nonpublic, inside information.

The paradigm just described is known as the "efficient capital market hypothesis." It is a given in the investment community, and it admits to the reality of insiders earning above-normal returns. Proponents of insider trading argue that the social value of such trades is immense. By pumping new information into the market, stock prices adjust quickly to real values. The insider's message — encoded in "who's buying, who's selling signals" rather than in volume trades per se — contributes more in the way of social benefits than it extracts in price.

DOGS AND GEMS

This same positive account may be rendered in another way. If insiders enter the market buying or selling, the traders with whom they deal will either profit more or lose less than they would have if the insider had abstained. By bidding up the price of a "gem" the insider is preventing the seller from experiencing the full, post-announcement gain, but the seller is making some gain, and in fact more than would have been made in the absence of such trading. By the same token, in depressing the price of a "dog," the insider is protecting the buyer from experiencing the full, postannouncement loss; the buyer's purchase is made at a price below that which would have been quoted in the absence of insider trades. Since the investors who are selling to or buying from the insider obviously do not know of the nonpublic, inside information, their perspective on the market remains the same.

Still, if it doesn't seem quite "fair" for insiders to utilize their positional advantage, trading on an informational disparity, consider the situation that exists today in the absence of such trading.

Even when insiders sit tight with the nonpublic information they possess, they at least know when not to sell and when not to buy. We tolerate that situation because it seems preferable to the alternative. If full and immediate disclosure of all nonpublic information were compelled by law, the economic freedom of the firm would be compromised and its economic interests would be diminished. For example, if an energy firm was compelled to announce its oil discoveries before it contracted for drilling rights, the loss of control over the information it developed would be extremely costly to the firm when it sought mineral leases. It appears then that our society is going to have to buy into some level of unfairness. The creation of a system of informational parity seems unlikely.

A NEW PARADIGM

Suppose now that the corporate proprietor of insider information, a computer chip firm, believed it to be in the company's best interest to license or permit insider trading. It could operate in the following way: The board of directors, or some appropriate committee thereof, could be charged with the responsibility of selecting employees who had notably contributed to the success of the firm. Permitting these selected employees to inside trade would be a way of rewarding their efforts over and above their base salary and fringe package. This licensing process permits the firm to cut its wage bill to a minimum while still attracting to its employ the brightest and most creative minds.

In effect, the firm is making entrepreneurs out of managers. Managers are notoriously risk-averse. They need to be nudged, encouraged, and booted into a more aggressive posture if the firm is to achieve and maintain a winning edge.

As an alternative to a board-designated list of insiders, the firm could simply adopt a hands-off policy, not involving itself in the selection process. This approach gives implicit approval to those who created the information to trade on it. It takes the lid off and allows employees to rewrite their compensation package whenever the opportunity arises to trade on nonpublic information.

THE DOWNSIDE

There is the possibility that the "candidates" for insider trading permits (or in firms with a hands-off policy, all employees) will create such turmoil as they jockey for position that the efficient operation of the firm will suffer. They will be so concerned with creating megatrade events that the long-term viability of the firm will be sacrificed to the short-term goal. The rate of development of promising projects and the timing of new releases could become secondary to efforts to line up financial backers and tippees in order to take advantage of the trading opportunities. At the very least, it must be said that the culture of such a firm would be significantly impacted by this strategy, and it is by no means certain that this work environment would attract and hold the most talented and productive work force.

With regard to the financing of this strategy, although the debits may not show up on the balance sheet, it is not without its price. Just as compensation packages, with their mix of salary, insurance, retirement, stock options, and other fringes, come out of someone's pocket, so, too, do inside trade profits. Investors will find themselves with less of a good stock or more of a bad one.

Once the lid is off, insiders will have the same opportunity to sell on nonpublic bad news, by emptying their portfolios or selling short, as they will to buy on undisclosed good news. There is a moral hazard lurking within this brew: the deliberate creation of bad news, or a perverse incentive to advance high-risk projects. If the insider locks into a no-lose or risk-neutral position, the genius of this strategy is undone.

COST OF COMPENSATION

There is a question mark as well with regard to the cost of insider compensation. In the normal compensation scheme, shareholders can choose among different benefits packages. But if the ban on insider trading is lifted, there is scarcely any means of accounting for the cost or controlling it.

Whereas in theory this strategy is an attractive way of inducing employee zeal, there is really no sound method of determining the marginal contribution that is purchased by each new dollar of inside trade profit. Is the amount of trade profits appropriate, or do employees become like proverbial "kids in the candy store"? Cost-benefit analysis, so dear to the calculations of the business community, flies out the window. The likelihood of tipping friends, relatives, and financial backers exacerbates the problem, bringing into the picture a whole contingent of free riders who have contributed nothing to the success of the firm.

Finally, in a system that rolls back the ban on insider trading, you can be assured that the message will not be lost on the financial community. Before a single sale is made, specialists and market makers will adjust their bid and ask prices, and traders their reservation prices. The initial adjustment is likely to be a negative one; it will have a discounting effect on the price of the security to account for the possibility of insider trading. Market experts have always taken positions against this possibility, but never to such a great extent.

A long-term price depression could spell hard times for the firm — an increase in the cost of capital and an increase in the number of takeover bids are just two possibilities.

NUDGING EFFECT

A price depression, however, is not an inevitable result. It really depends on how the market perceives the alleged productivity gains that are touted by insider trade proponents. If indeed the firm performs consistently above its historical levels, if there is some evidence that the strategy is working, one might safely guess that stock prices will be adjusted upward accordingly.

Clearly, neither the SEC nor the Justice Department is much impressed by efficiency arguments. If the "nudging" effect of insider trading is good, full disclosure would be that much better, the government contends. Further, the government insists, there are many different mixes of incentive packages, and, on balance, not all of them could be worse than letting an insider write his or her own. The bottom line is that the legislative and judicial branches in this country consider disclosure or abstinence from trading on the basis of nonpublic information to be fraudulent. No one in Washington is going to challenge this position in an election year or in any other.

FORM OVER SUBSTANCE

There is an opening, nevertheless, for the argument that insider trading is not fraudulent. Suppose that firm X, convinced of the economic soundness of insider trading, announced loudly and publicly that it intended to license such trading in its securities. It is difficult to see, under these circumstances, that such trading would be considered fraudulent.

Prior to the 1934 Act, common-law courts did not invoke insider trading unless there was some exceptional circumstance, such as express or implied misrepresentation of value or of the identity of the trader. Judges reasoned that fraud was an intentional tort that required, first of all, the breach of some duty to the plaintiff. In what has been described as a "triumph of form over substance," common-law judges found that the duty of corporate officers and employees was owed to the corporation, not to the stockholders; the fact that they traded on unequal information was simply the way of the world. Even today in the federal courts, trading on a disparity of information, even unfairness in the treatment of shareholders by fiduciaries, is not fraud and is not regarded as a violation of SEC rules.

If firm X announces its intentions and investors are forewarned of what lies ahead, how can it be said that they are defrauded? How can the firm or its insiders breach a duty toward shareholders if they have no such duty to breach? How can investors prove that they have suffered damages as a result of stock prices which are adjusted to account for inside information? In our scenario, shareholders have received all the normal attributes of stock ownership, minus only the assurance that the stock will not be traded on inside information. They got what they paid a discounted price for — no one deceived them, no one breached a duty toward them, and no one compelled them to make a purchase.

LOOKING ABROAD

In Japan, insider trading is an unspoken part of the business culture — there has been only one reported case under the limited insider trading prohibition currently in effect. Hong Kong has repealed the insider prohibitions it put into effect in 1974. France has a narrow prohibition against such trading, but it is hardly considered immoral, and the total number of suits and sanctions is negligible. West Germany relies on voluntary inside trading guidelines — the practice is proscribed but not illegal. These guidelines are enforced, or not, through employment contracts; it is a choice the firm makes itself. Great Britain, like common-law jurisdictions in the United States prior to 1934, applied no sanctions against insider trading until recently — in fact, too recently to analyze the level of enforcement.

These examples are relevant only for the purpose of documenting the official versus the real attitudes toward insider trading in other nations. Both sets of attitudes seem to be more tolerant. Insider trading probably would not be much different or more harmful in the United States. This is not to say that we should pattern our legal institutions after theirs, nor is it a suggestion that practices regarded as moral in other countries are the best that we are capable of achieving. It is important to note, however, that insider trading is not regarded as an abomination throughout the world, and since most countries do have legal and moral proscriptions against fraud, one must admit the possibility that our judgment is faulty.

The American people are indignant about insider trading because they view it as fraud and theft. While this is not necessarily the case, the efficiency argument is not likely to sway anybody's opinion. Moreover, there is surely no moral compulsion to insider trade; there is no cause for righteous indignation at the ban. Ivan Boesky is no modern-day hero — he just wanted to make a few million dollars. For now, live with the law. Don't break it. Get it changed.

William B. Irvine

INSIDER TRADING: AN ETHICAL APPRAISAL

To engage in insider trading is, roughly speaking, to buy or sell securities on the basis of privileged information. Suppose, for example, that the president of a company learns that another company wants to take his over. Suppose he secretly buys a large amount of his company's stock and makes a handsome profit when the public at large is finally informed of the takeover. This president has engaged in a classic bit of insider trading.

Insider trading does not necessarily involve a *purchase* of stock. Sometimes, a company employee will possess privileged information which, when made public, will hurt his company's stock. This person might respond by selling stock he owns, or even by selling short his company's stock;[1] and by doing so, he is engaging in insider trading. Furthermore, insider trading does not have to involve the purchase or sale of a company's *stock*. Indeed, much insider trading involves not stock, but rather stock options.[2] By buying options, a person can leverage his investment so that his profits will be far greater than if he had bought or sold stock.

Another important thing to realize about insider trading is that the person doing the trading doesn't have to be an employee of the company whose securities he trades. He can, to begin with, be an "agent" of the company. Suppose, for example, that the company hires a printer to print up pamphlets explaining an as-yet-unannounced takeover to the company's shareholders. In printing these pamphlets, the printer will have access to privileged information; and if he trades on the basis of this information, he will be engaged in insider trading even though he is an agent of the company rather than one of its employees.[3] Furthermore, a person who is neither an employee of a company nor its agent can also engage in insider trading. Suppose, for example, that the president of a company informs his sister of a coming takeover that has not yet been announced to the public, and suppose that she buys stock on the basis of this information. In doing so, she is engaged in insider trading.

The above examples demonstrate that the term 'insider trading' is, to some extent, a misnomer; for "insider trading" is not restricted to "insiders." Instead, it is possible for "outsiders" (e.g., print shop employees and relatives of insiders) to engage in "insider trading."

Another problem with the term 'insider trading', as used on Wall Street, is that it is ambiguous. Besides referring to "objectionable" trades made on the basis of privileged information, 'insider trading' can refer to perfectly legal trades made by a corporate insider. Suppose, for example, that the president of a corporation decides to buy the stock of his company and that he makes this decision not on the basis of any privileged information he possesses, but because he has confidence in the long-term prospects of his company. This sort of "insider trading" is not only legal — as long as he informs the Securities and

From *Business and Professional Ethics Journal*, 6, no. 4 (1986), 3–33. Reprinted by permission of the author.

Exchange Commission (SEC) of the trade—but desirable as well: The share-holders of the company should be glad that company employees and directors have a personal stake in the company, for it will give them an added incentive to make the company prosper.

Thus, the term 'insider trading' is objectionable for two reasons: It is mis-leading, since it is possible for outsiders to engage in "insider trading"; and it is ambiguous since it is used to refer both to trades made on the basis of privileged information and to trades made by insiders on the basis of non-privileged information. A more appropriate piece of terminology for "insider trading" would be 'trading on the basis of inside information'. Nevertheless, in the remainder of this paper I will follow standard practice and refer to cases in which people trade on the basis of inside information as cases of insider trading.

In what follows, I will distinguish between two different types of insider trading, primary and secondary. *Primary* insider trading involves people who have voluntarily assumed an obligation to look out for the interests of the shareholders. This will include not only the employees and directors of a corporation, but those—like the printer described above—who have con-tracted with the company. (Notice that in accepting the work, the printer has, in effect, assumed an obligation to protect the interests of the shareholders by keeping certain information confidential.) *Secondary* insider trading, on the other hand, involves people who have not voluntarily assumed an obligation to look out for the interests of the shareholders. Thus, the president's sister (described above) who engaged in insider trading was engaged in secondary insider trading.

The above characterization of insider trading is, to be sure, rather vague. What, we might wonder, do we mean when we say that information is "privi-leged"? Does insider trading involve *any* sort of trading on the basis of privi-leged information, or only some sorts? And does it make any difference, morally speaking, *how* the person trading on the basis of inside information obtained the information in question? In what follows, I will not attempt to answer these questions. This is because I will focus my attention not on insider trading in general, but on certain paradigmatic cases of insider trading. My goal is not so much to produce a full-scale analysis of the ethics of insider trading, but to attack certain popular views concerning the morality of insider trading.

1. THE LEGAL ASPECTS OF INSIDER TRADING

The laws concerning insider trading have evolved over many decades. In the 1920s, there were few sanctions against insider trading. Nearly all investors, both big and small, bought and sold stock with the assumption that insider trades were going on. The goal of many investors was not to stamp out insider trading, but rather to obtain inside information themselves so that they might profit from it.

The Great Crash of 1929 was followed by a period of reform. In the Securities Exchange Act of 1934, legislators made their first real attempt to curb insider trading. To be sure, legislators chose a blunt instrument for their battle against insider trading. Rather than make it illegal to engage in insider trading, they made it illegal for "insiders" to engage in short-term trades of stock. (Notice that insider trades will almost always be short-term trades.) If, for example, an insider bought and sold his company's stock within a six-month period, he was forced to give up any profit he might have realized; and to prevent insiders from hiding their short-term trades, legislators also forced "insiders" to reveal their stock holdings periodically.[5]

The Securities Exchange Act did not have much to say about "insider trades" as conducted by outsiders. The closest it came to prohibiting such trades was in section 10(b), in which it prohibited persons from employing "in connection with the purchase or sale of any security . . . any manipulative or deceptive device or contrivance. . . ."

This law left unresolved many issues concerning exactly what counts as insider trading.

In the late 1960s, for example, the SEC tried to argue that stock analyst Raymond Dirks had engaged in insider trading. As the result of careful investigation, Mr. Dirks uncovered a massive insurance company fraud and instigated trades on the basis of his discovery before making the discovery public. (He advised some institutional investors to sell their stock in the insurance company and thus avoid the plunge in stock prices that would result when news of the fraud leaked out.) The SEC argued that in advising these trades, Dirks was involved in insider trading. Indeed, in advising these trades, Dirks *was* involved in trading on the basis of what can reasonably be called privileged information. The Supreme Court, however, decided that because of the manner in which Dirks obtained the information, the case could not properly be called a case of insider trading.[6]

Another case that raises questions concerning what counts as insider trading is that of R. Foster Winans. In the early 1980s, Winans was a reporter for the *Wall Street Journal*. One of his jobs was to write the "Heard on the Street" column, in which the *Journal* either praises or criticizes companies. On various occasions, Winans allegedly leaked the contents of coming columns to investors in return for payments. These investors in turn made money by, for example, buying the stocks of companies that were about to be praised in the *Journal*.[7]

The interesting thing about this case is that the information that the investors traded on the basis of was "inside" information, but was not "privileged" in the normal sense of the word. It was not information that "belonged to" the company whose securities were traded; instead, it was simply information regarding a reporter's opinion of a certain stock. Winans's conviction for "insider trading" has been appealed to the Supreme Court, which, in its judgment, is expected to clarify insider trading laws.[8]

Let me pause here to make a confession concerning the Winans case. I was an unwitting beneficiary of Mr. Winans's scheme. In 1983, I owned shares in an obscure company called American Surgery Centers. This was one of the stocks recommended by Mr. Winans in his column: He allegedly recommended it so that his roommate, who owned shares in the company, could profit. In part because of Mr. Winans's recommendation, I saw my American Surgery Centers shares rise from under $2 per share to nearly $20 per share.[9] This gives lie to the common claim that insider trading always harms "innocent investors." I will have more to say about this claim below.

Despite laws prohibiting it, insider trading was widespread in the middle 1980s, when merger mania was at its peak. Even the casual follower of the stock market could not help noticing that stocks of companies had a tendency to rise or fall in the days before the companies in question made important announcements. Why such lawlessness? Because the worst that could happen to you if you were caught making an insider trade is that you would have to give back your profits. As Senator Alphonse D'Amato put it at the time, this "provides little in the way of deterrence since the violators' only risk is being returned to their original [financial] position."[10] What about the stigma that would result from being caught engaging in insider trading? With the stigma came benefits. In particular, a case can be made that in the early 1980s, getting caught engaging in insider trades was, more than anything, a form of free advertising: It showed other investors that you had contacts and therefore were desirable as an investment advisor or portfolio manager.

In 1984, a new law, the Insider Trading Sanctions Act (sponsored by Sen. D'Amato), was passed. This was an insider trading law with real teeth. It amended the Securities and Exchange Act of 1934 to

> permit the Securities and Exchange Commission, whenever it appears that any person has traded in securities while in possession of material nonpublic information, to seek an order in a district court action requiring the violator, or anyone who aided and abetted the violation, to pay a civil penalty of up to three times the profit gained or loss avoided as a result of the unlawful transaction.[11]

Notice the changes from the Securities Exchange Act: The emphasis was enlarged from insiders to "any person," and the penalties became very real.

With passage of this law, the SEC had a powerful new weapon with which to fight insider trading. It started looking for cases in which people had traded on the basis of "material nonpublic information" and soon discovered Dennis Levine, who, as a managing director of a major Wall Street firm, had allegedly made $12.6 million by illegally trading stocks and options on the basis of nonpublic information.[12] He later pleaded guilty and agreed to cooperate with the SEC's investigation of insider trading.[13]

It was largely as the result of Levine's cooperation that the SEC was able to build a case against arbitrager Ivan Boesky. On November 14, 1986, Boesky was "apprehended." He agreed to pay a $100 million penalty for trading on insider information, and to plead guilty to certain other criminal charges.[14] His arrest had a chilling effect on the stock market. On November 18, for example, stock prices fell dramatically, as stocks whose prices had risen as the result of takeover speculation (fueled, in part, by insider trading) plunged.[15]

There was an ironic twist to Boesky's arrest. Because he was cooperating with authorities, these same authorities — whose chief ambition was to fight insider trading — allowed Boesky to engage in insider trading before his "apprehension" was made public: They allowed him to sell off stock in a fund he managed, stock that would fall when news of his apprehension became public.[16]

The story probably won't end with Boesky, for in the six weeks before he was arrested, he was cooperating with authorities: He allowed them to tape his telephone conversations and wire him for sound.[17] As a result of his cooperation, there are likely to be new waves of arrests in the future.[18] Because of the Insider Trading Sanctions Act, large-scale insider trading of the sort seen in the middle 1980s is probably a thing of the past.

One thing that we probably will see in the future, though, is disputes concerning the exact meaning of the phrase "material nonpublic information." The courts will have to decide for themselves where and how to draw the line that separates legal trades from illegal insider trades.

So, insider trading is certainly wrong from a legal point of view. What about the ethics of insider trading, though? In what follows, I will ask two questions about insider trading: Is there anything wrong with it, ethically speaking; and if there is, what is the nature of the wrong?

This second question is a question that often arises in connection with issues in applied ethics. It is not unusual for people to have a strong feeling that some activity is morally objectionable without having a good notion of *why* it is morally objectionable. One example of this is Richard Wasserstrom's claim that extramarital sex is wrong because it involves the breaking of an important promise.[19] The victims of marital infidelity know instinctively that they have been wronged, but how likely are they to identify the wrong as a broken promise?

Let us now begin our investigation of the moral status of insider trading, beginning with an examination of primary insider trading.

2. PRIMARY INSIDER TRADING: THE SEARCH FOR "BODIES"

To keep our examination of the morality of primary insider trading in sharp focus, consider the following paradigmatic case of primary insider trading. Mr. Bossman is the chairman of the board of directors of Lilliputian Inc. On June 1, he and the other directors receive a buyout offer from Gargantuan Industries. Gargantuan offers to buy each outstanding share of Lilliputian for $50; this offer is quite attractive since Lilliputian shares have a current market value of only $25. The directors of Lilliputian tell Gargantuan that they will inform it of their decision on July 1, one month after the initial contact. They request that Gargantuan keep the offer secret until then, and Gargantuan is glad to do so since it wants more than anything to avoid rival takeover bids.

Suppose that on June 2, the day after getting the offer, Bossman calls his broker and tells him to purchase a large block of Lilliputian stock.[20] Suppose, too, that the timing of this purchase is no coincidence: It isn't as if he has been planning the purchase for months; rather, he is making the purchase simply so he can capitalize on the takeover offer.

Suppose, finally, that on July 1, Bossman and the other directors of Lilliputian announce to the world that they favor the takeover.

What has Lilliputian stock been doing during June? It was at $25 per share on June 1, when the takeover offer was made. On June 2 it rose to $28 per share largely because of Bossman's buying. (His sudden interest in Lilliputian stock meant increased demand for it; and as long as the supply remained constant, this meant a higher price for Lilliputian shares.) After this spurt, Lilliputian stock sank back to $25, where it remained until July 1, when the takeover announcement sent it soaring to $50 per share.

Now, according to the standard view concerning primary insider trading, Bossman, by engaging in insider trading, has done something morally objectionable. This is because (i) Bossman has a duty to look out for the interests of the shareholders and (ii) by engaging in insider trading, Bossman is harming the shareholders rather than looking out for their interests. In short, Bossman's insider trading is morally objectionable because in making such trades, he is not fulfilling his obligation to the shareholders. This, according to the standard view concerning insider trading, is the nature of the moral crime one commits by engaging in primary insider trading.

I agree that Bossman has an obligation to look out for the interests of the shareholders — more precisely, he has an obligation to take steps to maximize their return on their investment.[21] What I question, though, is the notion that by engaging in insider trading, Bossman has harmed the shareholders. Contrary to popular opinion, Bossman's insider trading does not do uniform harm to the shareholders. Rather, shareholders fall into three categories.

In the first category, which is by far the largest, shareholders are neither benefitted nor harmed by his insider trading. In this category, we find long-term owners of Lilliputian stock who did not have any intention of selling during June. These shareholders saw the price of the stock rise from $25 to $50, and are glad for its having done so.

In the second category, we find those who are benefitted by Bossman's insider trading. One of these shareholders is Ms. Selleck, who on June 2 put in an order to sell shares of Lilliputian "at the market" — i.e., immediately and for the best price her broker could obtain. (This is probably the most common kind of order an investor will place with his broker but, as we shall see, it is not the only kind of order.) We can even suppose — although this is not necessary for my argument — that when she sold her shares, some of them ended up in the hands of Bossman.

Suppose that Selleck ends up getting $28 per share for her stock. Many people will claim that Selleck is a victim of Bossman's insider trading, but I reject this claim. Instead, I think it is fairly clear that Selleck is a beneficiary of Bossman's insider trade; for notice that if it had not been for Bossman's sudden interest in Lilliputian shares, they would not have jumped to $28 on June 2, and Selleck would have got only $25 per share for her Lilliputian stock. Bossman's insider trading resulted in her getting $3 per share more than she otherwise would have got.

And Ms. Selleck is not the only beneficiary of Bossman's insider trading. Another beneficiary is Ms. Long. On June 2, she was on the verge of selling her Lilliputian shares: She had owned them for two years, and in that time they hadn't done a thing. The sudden jump Lilliputian shares took on that day, however, convinced her to hold on to her shares. (She suspected — rightly, as it turns out — that something was up.) Had it not been for Bossman's insider trading, she would have sold her shares for far less than the $50 that she ultimately obtained.

In the third category of Lilliputian shareholders, we find the "victims" of Bossman's insider trading. One person who was harmed by Bossman's insider trading was Mr. Hurt. On June 2, Hurt, like Selleck, placed an order to sell his Lilliputian stock; but whereas Selleck placed a "market order," Hurt placed a good-for-the-day "limit order": He instructed his broker not to sell immediately and for the best price the broker could obtain, but rather to sell if and only if the price of the stock rose to $28 a share.[22] Because of Bossman's insider trading, Hurt's limit order was triggered, and his stock was sold — maybe even to Bossman. Bossman's insider trading harmed Hurt, for if it hadn't been for Bossman's purchase, Hurt's order would have expired untransacted, and Hurt (we can presume) would still be holding his Lilliputian shares at the end of the month when they rose in value to $50.

Notice that the subtle difference between Selleck and Hurt — the first placed a market order and the second placed a limit order — resulted in Selleck's being a beneficiary of Bossman's insider trading and Hurt's being a victim: Bossman's trade left Selleck better off than she would otherwise have been and left Hurt worse off.

Hurt is not the only victim of Bossman's insider trading. Any Lilliputian shareholder who sold his shares because of the sudden jump in price these shares took on June 2 (a shareholder might have regarded the sudden jump as a God-given opportunity to get out of a stock that had gone nowhere for years) can also be counted as a victim.

So we find that some shareholders are helped by Bossman's insider trading, some are harmed, and some are neither helped nor harmed. What is the overall effect on the shareholders? It depends upon how we tell the story. One thing that is clear, though, is that we can tell the story so that Bossman's insider trading benefits more shareholders than it harms. Indeed, we can tell the story so that Bossman's insider trading benefits some shareholders while harming none at all. (Here is the story: Selleck is the only Lilliputian shareholder to sell her shares during the month. She is benefitted by Bossman's insider trading, and no one is harmed.)

The above discussion shows that the popular view concerning insider trading is mistaken. When we survey the scene after primary insider trading has taken place, we do not find victims everywhere. Instead, the search for victims is not an easy one, and sometimes produces no "bodies" whatsoever.

3. THE REAL CRIME IN CASES OF PRIMARY INSIDER TRADING

So much for the popular view that Bossman's insider trading is morally objectionable because in engaging in it, Bossman is harming the shareholders. I have shown above that it is altogether possible for Lilliputian shareholders to be better off if Bossman engages in insider trading than if he doesn't and consequently for his insider trading to benefit the shareholders.

Thus, it might appear that by engaging in insider trading, Bossman not only wasn't breaking his promise to look out for the interests of the shareholders, but was instead doing what was required to keep his promise. It might appear, in other words, that in the case described Bossman has a moral obligation to engage in insider trading!

This appearance, I would like to suggest, is misleading. I think that Bossman's insider trading is indeed morally objectionable. I also think, though, that we are missing his real moral crime if, like most people, we look no further than the insider trading itself. For it is my contention that Bossman's real crime — committed together with the other Lilliputian directors — was not his insider trading, but rather *his keeping from the shareholders information that they had a right to possess.*

Consider Bossman's options on June 1. He can either (1) reveal the takeover offer to Lilliputian shareholders or (2) keep it secret for a month,[23] and if he keeps it secret for a month, he can either (2a) engage in insider trading in the meantime or (2b) refrain from doing so. According to the popular view, Bossman is best serving the interests of Lilliputian shareholders if he makes choice (2b). I have shown that this view is mistaken since the shareholders might well benefit from his making choice (2a) instead. And I would now like to argue that the shareholders would be better off still if he made neither of these choices, but instead made choice (1).

To see why I say this, consider what happens during June if Bossman makes either choice (2a) or choice (2b). Many Lilliputian shareholders will sell their shares for between $25 and $28. They will sell them for a variety of reasons that are utterly unconnected with the coming takeover. Some will trade simply to raise cash so they can meet unforseen expenses. (Ms. Selleck, for example, sold her Lilliputian shares so she could pay her son's orthodontist bill.) Others will sell because whatever theory of investing they follow (mistakenly) yields a "sell signal" for Lilliputian stock. Depending on how "big" Lilliputian is, there could be hundreds or even thousands of Lilliputian investors who sell their shares during June. (Indeed, it is possible for millions of "shareholders" to be harmed in a single transaction—one made, for example, by a large pension fund.) *It is these shareholders*, I wish to maintain, *who are the real victims in the story told above*; for notice that because the Lilliputian directors kept them in the dark, they got only $25 to $28 per share for stock that was arguably worth $50 per share. In other words, *the real crime Bossman (and the other directors) committed was not insider trading, but rather the crime of withholding from the shareholders information that it was in their vital interest to possess.*

Any shareholder who sold his Lilliputian shares during June has, I think, a legitimate complaint against the Lilliputian directors. They could have informed him of the takeover; and if they had informed him, he would have got far more for his shares than he did. By keeping the takeover a secret, they have failed to look out for his interests.

The crime of insider trading, I think, pales in comparison to the crime of needlessly keeping shareholders in the dark about a takeover. The former crime, in most cases, will harm the shareholders far less than the latter crime. Indeed, notice that in many cases, the former crime will in fact *mitigate* some of the harm done to the shareholders by the latter crime: Insider trading can result in shareholders' getting more for each share they sell than they would have got if the directors engaged in no insider trading whatsoever. (Of course, the shareholders would get even more for their shares if the directors immediately announced the takeover offer to the world.)

This is not to say that Bossman's insider trading isn't morally objectionable. It *is* objectionable, since by engaging in insider trading, Bossman is taking steps to benefit personally from the wrong he is doing the shareholders by keeping them in the dark. It is bad enough to wrong someone; it is even worse to take steps to benefit while in the process of wronging them; and it is worst of all to wrong them just so you can benefit.

In order for the directors to be justified in keeping a takeover proposal secret, it must be the case that the interests of the shareholders as a group are best served by their doing so—it must be the case, that is, that the benefits the shareholders as a group will derive from being kept in the dark outweigh the harm done to those particular shareholders who sell their shares "prematurely." Generally, this will not be the case; and if it is not the case, then by failing to inform the shareholders of a takeover offer the directors are failing to keep their promise to look out for the interests of the shareholders and are consequently wronging the shareholders.

Another thing to notice about the crime of insider trading is that it is, for the most part, a crime that can be committed only when the larger crime of with-holding information from the shareholders has been committed. If the corporate directors do their duty to the shareholders and inform them immediately of corporate events that have a major impact on their well-being as shareholders, insider trading is virtually impossible: You can't insider trade on the basis of public information.

In summary, then, in their fascination with insider trading cases, the public and the SEC are guilty of overlooking a far greater crime perpetrated against the shareholders, the crime of keeping from them information that they have a right to possess.

4. SOME OBJECTIONS AGAINST THE FOREGOING ANALYSIS

Let me now consider some of the objections that might be raised against my analysis of "the crime of primary insider trading."

Some, to begin with, will argue that I am mistaken in thinking that if takeover offers were disclosed to shareholders, insider trading would be nearly impossible. Those raising this objection will point out that informing the shareholders would require a mass mailing, and that such a mailing would not only take time, but would require that many people — e.g., the employees of a print shop — be informed of the takeover. Thus, any attempt to inform the shareholders of the takeover offer would only increase the chance that insider trading will take place; and this means that the directors are best serving the interests of the shareholders when they keep takeover offers secret.

The problem with this first objection is that it mistakenly takes me to advocate the use of mass mailings to inform shareholders of takeover offers. I do not. Instead, I think the directors should inform the shareholders by simply informing the press that they have received and are considering a takeover offer. What if a shareholder doesn't get the news? No problem, since the announcement will cause the shares of the "target" company to rise immediately. Thus, even those shareholders who don't get the news will be prevented from selling their shares at a price that is substantially below their "real" value.

A second objection is that I am mistaken if I think that companies are best serving their shareholders by keeping them informed of everything that is going on in the company. Some secrecy is necessary if a company is to keep ahead of its competitors.

In reply to this, let me state that I am not advocating that a company tell its shareholders *everything* that is going on in the company. Some things, e.g., product formulations, *should* be kept secret. Similarly, in the case of companies that work on defense projects, the company may be justified in keeping secret from the shareholders much of what their company does. (It should, of course, inform the shareholders that secrets are being kept.) All I am advocating is that the company inform shareholders immediately of corporate events that have a major impact on their well-being as shareholders. Certainly, takeover proposals fall in this category; for notice that if the takeover succeeds, they will in many cases cease to be shareholders.

A third objection is that it is unrealistic for me to think that companies can conduct takeover negotiations in full public view. Such negotiations are difficult and would be nearly impossible if the shareholders were allowed to look over the shoulders of the negotiators.

My reply to this objection is that I am not advocating that companies conduct takeover negotiations in "full public view." The directors of a company are not obligated to disclose the details of a takeover offer to the shareholders; they are obligated only to say enough about the takeover offer to put the shareholders on their guard. They might, for example, announce simply that they have received a takeover offer at a substantially-above-market price. They don't need to disclose the name of the suitor or the exact terms of the takeover proposal; and they can conduct all negotiations behind closed doors.

There are two ways in which critics of my analysis might respond to this last reply.

In the first place, they might argue that current securities laws prohibit companies from making incomplete disclosures of the kind I have described. In reply to this, I can only point out (i) that companies *do* make such announcements and are not punished for doing so,[24] and (ii) that even if securities laws *did* prohibit incomplete disclosures, such laws are detrimental to the shareholders — the very people the laws are supposed to protect — and should be repealed.

In the second place, critics of my analysis might argue that there are cases in which a company trying to take over another company makes the whole takeover offer contingent on the "target" company's directors' keeping the offer secret. (The first company might do this to preclude rival takeover bids.) In such cases as this, they will argue, the directors will be best serving the interests of the shareholders if they keep the shareholders in the dark about the takeover offer. There may be cases in which this is true, but I think that in most takeover cases, the directors of the "target" company should refuse to take an "oath of silence": I think that to take such an oath would be to betray the trust the shareholders have placed in them.

Here is a rather different sort of objection that might be raised against my analysis of the ethical implications of primary insider trading. Some will argue that I am mistaken if I think that by immediately disclosing "major corporate events" to the shareholders, a company will benefit all of them and harm none of them. For suppose that on the day of the announcement, some shareholder had placed a limit order to sell his shares of stock at an above-market price. When the directors make their announcement, his limit order will be triggered, and he will be forced to give up his stock and give it up at a price much lower than it would get under the takeover offer.

I admit that some will be harmed by the takeover announcement. Nevertheless, I think that in most cases, the interests of the shareholders are better served by immediate disclosure than by keeping the takeover a secret. Notice that while immediate disclosure may harm a handful of shareholders, delayed disclosure can harm thousands: It can mean that they receive a price for their shares that is much lower than the takeover offer. (In general, the amount of harm done is proportional to the amount of time between when the takeover is proposed and when the proposal is disclosed to the public.) Notice, too, that by judicious use of trading halts — in which a company asks an exchange to halt trading in a stock until an announcement has been made — the number of victims of the takeover announcement can be kept to a minimum.[25]

In short, I am willing to sacrifice the well-being of some shareholders — e.g., those who put themselves at risk by placing limit orders — in order to benefit a far greater number of shareholders. The directors have an obligation not to maximize the well-being of each individual shareholder, but to maximize the well-being of the shareholders as a group.

Here is one last objection that might be raised against my analysis of the ethical implications of primary insider trading. Some will argue that if the directors of a "target" company take my advice and inform the shareholders that they have received a takeover offer, they might unintentionally mislead the shareholders. By announcing a takeover offer, they will create in many share-holders an expectation that the offer is going to be accepted. These share-holders will be both disappointed and financially harmed if the directors subse-quently decide against the takeover offer; for their rejection of the offer will probably cause the price of their company's stock to fall.

In response to this criticism, I have several things to say. In the first place, it seems to me that for the directors to say *nothing* about a takeover offer is to mislead the shareholders. (Many shareholders assume — often incorrectly — that their directors would inform them if a takeover were in the works.) Therefore, if it is wrong, as is suggested above, to mislead the shareholders, then it is wrong *not* to inform them of takeover proposals. In the second place, when I advocate that the directors announce takeover proposals, I am assuming that they will be careful how they word their announcements, and in particular, that they will not make them overly optimistic. If, for instance, they know from the start that they are unlikely to accept a takeover proposal, they should tell their shareholders as much. In the third place, those who owned shares of a company at the time a takeover proposal was announced will not, in most cases, be harmed if the takeover proposal is subsequently rejected. The rejection may cause the price of the stock to fall, but it is unlikely that it will fall below where it was before the announcement was made. Indeed, even though the takeover proposal in question is rejected, shareholders can benefit from its having been announced: For by announcing it, the directors might well stimulate rival takeover offers from other companies, offers that will be beneficial to the shareholders. In summary, the "dangers" of misleading the shareholders by announcing a takeover proposal seem not all that dangerous.

5. A CASE IN WHICH SECRECY IS DESIRABLE

Above I have advocated that it is wrong for the directors of a corporation to keep the shareholders "needlessly" in the dark and that this is the real crime in cases of primary insider trading. I would now like to consider a case in which it looks as if there is good reason for the directors to keep the shareholders in the dark about a corporate event that will have a major impact on their well-being as shareholders.

In the case I have in mind,[26] an oil company makes an incredible discovery of oil in a place almost no one thought oil could be. They determine that the oil formation in question contains massive amounts of oil, but they simultaneously realize that in order to benefit fully from their discovery, they will have to buy up oil leases all around the area. Furthermore, they realize that these leases will be much cheaper if they keep their discovery a secret. (This raises the issue of whether the company has a moral obligation to inform those it buys the leases from of its find. In what follows, though, I will sidestep this question and concern myself only with the obligation the company has to its shareholders.)

Now, in this case it is arguably in the interests of the shareholders *as a group* for the directors of the company to keep them in the dark about the oil discovery. It is true that informing them immediately of their find will prevent some shareholders from prematurely selling their shares. Nevertheless, by keeping the shareholders in the dark about the find, the directors can cause the ultimate jump in stock price to be far greater than it would otherwise be. (The longer the company keeps quiet about its discovery, the more leases it will be able to buy cheaply; the more leases it buys cheaply, the more it will profit from its discovery; and the more it profits from its discovery, the more investors will bid up the price of its stock.) In this case, the corporate directors have an obligation to keep the shareholders in the dark, since by doing so they are looking out for the interests of the shareholders as a group.

Notice that the above argument won't succeed if there is a way for the directors to have their cake and eat it too—namely, for them to inform the shareholders of the find and, at the same time, to buy the oil leases on the sly. There does not appear to be any way for them to do this, though. If the directors inform the shareholders of the oil find, the news will almost certainly get back to the people from whom the company wishes to buy leases.

What the directors could do in such cases, I think, is keep the shareholders in the dark, but simultaneously engage in a program to raise the price of the stock. The directors might, for example, announce a substantial dividend increase. Such an announcement will cause the price of the stock to rise and won't—if it is done properly—tip off the world to the company's oil find.

At this point, an intriguing possibility arises. Notice that insider trading, if it took place in such a case, would accomplish much the same as an announcement of a dividend increase: It would cause a rise in the price of the company's stock without thereby revealing the company's oil find to the world. Some might suggest that in such a case, the directors of the corporation have an obligation to engage in insider trading—that to do so is to maximize the well-being of the shareholders as a group. There may indeed be cases in which insider trading would benefit the shareholders as a group. Probably they will be rare, though.

6. A CASE OF SECONDARY INSIDER TRADING

Above we have examined primary insider trading. Now let us consider a case of secondary insider trading.

Consider again the story of Mr. Bossman's insider trade. I neglected to mention it above, but Bossman's broker was named Mr. Brooks. I also neglected to mention that after placing his order with Brooks, Bossman told him the reason for his transaction and invited him to place a similar order so that he—Brooks—could also benefit from the coming takeover. (In giving Brooks this tip, Bossman was repaying numerous "hot tips" Brooks had given him in the past.) Bossman's only warning to Brooks was that he send in his—Bossman's—order before sending in his own, so that Bossman would get the lowest possible price. Suppose, then, that after sending in Bossman's order, Brooks sent in his own order; and suppose he ended up purchasing a fair number of shares — purchasing them, let us assume, from Selleck. (Thus, part of the shares Selleck sold went to Bossman and part went to Brooks.)

The questions I will now address are these: Did Brooks, by buying the Lilliputian shares, do anything morally objectionable? And if he did, what was the nature of his moral wrongdoing?

The first thing to notice is that the case of Brooks, because it involves secondary insider trading, cannot be treated in the same way as we treated Bossman's primary insider trade. Bossman, by joining the board of directors, assumed an obligation to look out for the interests of the shareholders. That he had such an obligation was of key importance in our discussion of his insider trading. Brooks, however, is under no such obligation. (Notice that when Bossman hired Brooks, he did so in his capacity as a private investor, not in his capacity as a Lilliputian director. Thus, while Brooks is an agent of Bossman, he is not likewise an agent of Lilliputian.) This means that if Brooks did something wrong in engaging in insider trading, his crime was substantially different from that committed by Bossman.

It is also important to notice that I was careful to tell the above story so that Brooks didn't break any promises he might have made to Bossman. In particular, by buying Lilliputian shares, Brooks was not breaking the promise that he, as Bossman's broker, would look out for Bossman's interests. If Bossman hadn't encouraged Brooks to buy Lilliputian shares, though, Brooks might well have been wronging Bossman by buying them.

The popular view is that Brooks *did* do something morally objectionable in buying Lilliputian stock. Let me now describe some of the theories given concerning the nature of his wrongdoing.

One common view is that by engaging in secondary insider trading, Brooks is harming the shareholders of Lilliputian in general and is harming Selleck in particular. Our comments about the consequences of Bossman's insider trading, however, show this view to be mistaken. For in the same way that Bossman's insider trade can benefit Lilliputian shareholders, Brooks's insider trade can benefit them. In particular, it might well be that because of Brooks's insider trade, Selleck got a higher price for her shares than she would otherwise have got.

Another common view — let us call it the Unfair Advantage Theory — holds that Brooks has wronged Selleck by taking unfair advantage of her.[27] When he bought her Lilliputian shares, he knew something she didn't know, but would have benefitted from knowing; therefore, he took unfair advantage of her when he bought her shares without first informing her of what he knew.

The Unfair Advantage Theory strikes me as quite implausible. In general, I don't think parties to a transaction have any moral obligation to divulge what they know before it takes place. If the transaction takes place between "competent" people and if the selling party makes no claims about what he is selling but instead makes it clear that he is selling it "as is" (even though he may know of various "defects" in what he is selling), then I don't think any moral wrong has been done.[28]

Notice that if we took seriously the suggestion that by withholding information from another party to a transaction we are wronging them, we would have to draw the conclusion that the stock market as it now exists is a veritable den of iniquity; for in virtually every transaction that takes place, the parties to the transaction *do* withhold information. Indeed, given the manner in which stock exchanges currently operate, it is almost impossible for investors *not* to withhold information. This is because exchanges are so thoroughly anonymous: The sellers of a stock rarely, if ever, know who the buyers are.

I take the anonymity of exchanges, by the way, to be a plus rather than a minus. There are real benefits to be had from an anonymous system of trading, in which all trades are conducted on an "as is" basis. A stock exchange in which buyers and sellers tried to — or, worse still, were forced to — tell what they knew about their stocks before completing a transaction would be grotesquely inefficient. The costs of such a system of stock transactions would far outweigh any alleged moral benefits.[29]

In summary, the mere fact that Brooks knew something Selleck didn't and failed to inform her of what he knew does not mean that he has wronged her. The Unfair Advantage Theory does not get us very far.

Another attempt to explain the wrong Brooks has done in engaging in insider trading is the Theft Theory. According to this theory, in buying Lilliputian stock, Brooks is engaged in a kind of theft.

Of course, Brooks did not steal Selleck's shares: Rather, he bought them. What, then, did he steal? According to the Theft Theory, he stole the information on which he based his transaction. This, incidentally, appears to be the theory favored by the prosecuting attorney in the case against Ivan Boesky.[30]

It should be apparent that while the Theft Theory may apply to some cases of insider trading (and probably does apply to many of the cases that recently came to light on Wall Street), it does not apply to the case of Brooks. For in my story about Bossman and Brooks, it is clear that neither is guilty of theft of information. Bossman did not steal the information relating to the proposed takeover; he obtained it as part of his proper duties as corporate director. And Brooks did not steal the information from Bossman. Rather, Bossman made him a gift of the information. Theft has not taken place.

What has instead taken place is a misappropriation of property. By engaging in insider trading, Brooks is taking steps to benefit from the gift of something that was not Bossman's to give — viz., information of the takeover offer.

This brings us closer to the crime that I think Brooks has committed. To better understand the nature of this crime, let us consider an analogical case from outside the world of investing.

Suppose that while Al is on vacation, he asks his neighbor Bob to pick up his mail for him. Implicit in this request is the understanding that Bob will not tamper with or open Al's mail, will take care not to lose Al's mail, and will promptly turn over all of Al's mail when Al returns. Suppose that Bob agrees to pick up Al's mail and in so doing implicitly agrees to these conditions.

One of the things that arrives in the mail while Al is away is a box containing a new VCR. Bob realizes this and decides to open the box and use the VCR; and when Al gets back from his vacation, Bob turns all his mail over to him — except the VCR. Bob goes on using the VCR for a few weeks — without Al's knowledge — and then re-boxes it and places it on Al's doorstep, doing his best to make it look as if it were just delivered.

Bob's crime in this case is clear: He is not so much stealing Al's property as temporarily withholding from Al something that is rightfully his. (If Bob's intention were to deprive Al of his VCR permanently, then Bob *would* be stealing Al's property.) Bob's crime, then, is analogous to that of Bossman, if, at any rate, my analysis of primary insider trading is correct; for like Bob, Bossman has temporarily withheld from Lilliputian shareholders something that is right-fully theirs — namely, information concerning the takeover proposal.

Now suppose that while Al's VCR is still in Bob's possession, Bob invites his friend Charlie over to watch video-taped movies. When Charlie arrives, Bob explains exactly how he came to have the VCR. Suppose that Charlie, after hearing this explanation, responds by sitting down to enjoy a few movies.

I think it is clear that in the circumstances described, Charlie, like Bob, is wronging Al; for I think that Charlie has a moral obligation to inform Al of what Bob has done — in short, to take steps to see that Al regains what is rightfully his. Rather than watch movies, Charlie should report what he knows to Al.

Charlie's crime, I think, resembles stockbroker Brooks's crime in certain respects. Brooks has learned that Bossman (and the other directors) are with-holding from Lilliputian shareholders information that they have a moral (if not legal) right to possess. Realizing this, the proper thing for Brooks to do is not to buy some Lilliputian stock for himself, but rather to inform Lilliputian share-holders of the wrong that is being done them.

Despite this similarity, though, we should not make the mistake of thinking that Brooks's crime is identical to Charlie's. For notice that there are some important differences between the case of Brooks and that of Charlie. The most striking difference is this: While it is fairly easy for Charlie to tell Al what he knows, it will typically be extremely difficult for Brooks to tell the Lilliputian shareholders what he knows. There are thousands of these shareholders, and they are spread across the country. He might try calling the editor of the *Wall Street Journal* and asking him to write a story about the takeover. The editor is not likely to take this suggestion seriously, though. And for Brooks to try to inform the world by, say, buying ads in newspapers would be prohibitively expensive.

Another important difference is this: Lilliputian shareholders will be far more skeptical of Brooks's report than Al will be of Charlie's. For suppose that Brooks somehow succeeds in telling Lilliputian shareholders of the proposed takeover. Many of them simply won't believe him. They will instead take him to be engaged in some sort of maneuver to drive up artificially the price of Lilliputian shares — no doubt so he can sell his own shares at a higher price.

In summary, not only will Brooks have a hard time fulfilling his moral obligation to tell Lilliputian shareholders of the proposed takeover, but they are unlikely to believe him if he succeeds. It is for these reasons that I think Brooks may be excused if he takes no steps to tell Lilliputian shareholders what he knows.

Notice, though, that if Brooks were not some obscure stockbroker but were instead an investor with a national reputation (like Ivan Boesky), we can no longer forgive him for remaining silent about the proposed takeover. It will, after all, be far easier for a big-name investor to get the news out: The *Wall Street Journal*, for example, will take his claims quite seriously. And if he has a good reputation, Lilliputian shareholders will, for the most part, believe what he tells them. Thus, there are grounds for distinguishing between cases of secondary insider trading that involve "small fry" and those that involve "big fish."

At this point, many may admit that Brooks could be forgiven if he simply remained silent about the proposed takeover. They will go on, however, to remind us that he did not simply remain silent, but engaged in insider trading instead. To do this, they will insist, was wrong.

Let us, then, take a closer look at Brooks's situation. I would like to suggest that when Brooks reacted to his discovery of the takeover offer by engaging in insider trading, he was not necessarily doing something morally objectionable; I would also like to suggest that whether or not he was doing something morally objectionable depends primarily upon whether his insider trades harmed or helped Lilliputian shareholders.

It is easy to forget, but Brooks's insider trading could benefit Lilliputian shareholders. Suppose, for example, that when he places his order for Lilliputian shares, Brooks places a huge order. Indeed, the order is so huge, that it drives the price of Lilliputian stock immediately up to $50 per share. Notice that in this instance of insider trading, Brooks would benefit a vast number of Lilliputian shareholders (viz., those who would have otherwise sold shares for under $50 per share), while gaining very little himself (since he buys most of his Lilliputian stock at $50 per share, he won't benefit much from the ultimate takeover). In this case, the Lilliputian shareholders owe Brooks a debt of gratitude. Indeed, if there were any justice in the world, they would replace Bossman with Brooks as chairman of their board of directors.

Or consider a second scenario. Suppose that Brooks places an order somewhat smaller than the one just described. Suppose, though, that the order is still large enough to make the price of Lilliputian stock jump a few points. Suppose that this jump does not trigger any limit orders, but instead benefits those who, like Selleck, have placed "market orders" to sell Lilliputian shares. In such a case, Brooks's insider trading has again helped rather than harmed Lilliputian shareholders.

In the two cases described above, I don't think that Brooks is doing anything morally objectionable in purchasing Lilliputian shares on the basis of inside information. His actions in either case have not harmed Lilliputian shareholders, but rather have benefitted them. Thus, his actions are precisely those that a utilitarian would advise him to take—namely, those that maximize the general utility. It may be true that in doing so, he has increased his own utility, but the utilitarian will not object to this. It is, in other words, better for Brooks to benefit the Lilliputian shareholders by benefitting himself than for Brooks to sit back and do nothing.

Notice that if Brooks had another course of action open to him—if, in particular, he could somehow inform Lilliputian shareholders of the wrong being done them—then *this* is the course of action a utilitarian would advise him to take. In the cases just described, though, we are assuming that Brooks does not, as a practical matter, have another course of action open to him.

Some will object to this by protesting that when Brooks engages in insider trading, he is taking steps to benefit from the wrongdoing of others—namely, the wrong the Lilliputian directors do to the shareholders by keeping them in the dark about the takeover offer. They will go on to claim that it is morally objectionable to take steps to benefit from the wrongdoing of others, and will conclude that it is morally objectionable for Brooks to buy Lilliputian stock.

In reply to this, I can only point out, as I have elsewhere,[31] that it is *not necessarily* morally objectionable to take steps to benefit from the wrongdoing of others. Consider, for example, companies that make a profit by selling burglary insurance. These companies are taking steps to benefit from the wrongdoing of others — viz. burglars — but are not thereby doing anything morally objectionable.

It is, I admit, morally objectionable to take steps to benefit from the wrongdoing of others when by taking these steps you somehow facilitate the wrongdoing or augment the amount of harm done by the wrongdoing. I also admit that if Brooks's insider trading had harmed Lilliputian shareholders, his trades would have been morally objectionable. I would like to reiterate, though, that in the cases just described, his trades benefit Lilliputian shareholders rather than harm them.

It might now be objected that because of the anonymous nature of the stock exchange, Brooks can never be certain whether his trades will harm or help Lilliputian shareholders. He can't know beforehand, for example, whether or not there are "limit orders" that his purchase will trigger. (If his purchase triggers limit orders, it might cause some Lilliputian investors to sell who would not otherwise have sold; and this will harm them.) And since he can't be certain of whether his trades will help or harm Lilliputian shareholders, he should refrain from making such trades.

I, for one, am not impressed by this objection. Whenever one acts, one cannot be certain of the consequences of one's act. From this it does not follow that the right thing to do is to do nothing at all. Similarly, in the case of Brooks, from the mere fact that a trade *might* harm Lilliputian shareholders, it does not follow that he should not make the trade — particularly if there is good reason to think that the trade in question will *probably* help them.

In summary, "outsiders" who learn of takeover proposals have a moral obligation to inform the shareholders of the proposal — if, at any rate, it would be in the interests of the shareholders to possess this information. Often, however, it will as a practical matter be impossible for outsiders to inform shareholders of what they know. In these circumstances, an outsider who engages in secondary insider trading might or might not be doing something morally objectionable; it depends upon whether his trades harm the shareholders of the takeover target.

7. SOME CONCLUSIONS

In this paper, I have argued that the standard view concerning primary insider trading is mistaken. According to this view, a corporate insider who engages in insider trading necessarily wrongs the shareholders. This view is embodied in the insider trading laws, which, in cases of insider trading, call for the corporate insider to be punished and call for the shareholders to be compensated for their losses. I have argued, though, that primary insider trading does not necessarily harm the shareholders. What almost always *does* harm them is being kept in the dark about events that have a major impact on their well-being as shareholders. Thus, insider trading, while morally objectionable, is the lesser of two crimes that are typically involved in cases of insider trading. The "real" crime in cases of primary insider trading is the failure of the directors of the corporation to keep the shareholders informed.

In this paper, I have also argued against the common view concerning secondary insider trading. Contrary to popular belief, it is not always the case that a person engaged in secondary insider trading is doing something morally objectionable — and he might even be doing something morally laudable. And when a person engaged in secondary insider trading *is* doing something morally objectionable, his crime is importantly different from that of a person engaged in primary insider trading.

All this suggests that the laws against insider trading — both primary and secondary — fail to mirror the moral terrain. There are cases in which engaging in insider trading is illegal but not morally objectionable; and there are cases in which withholding news of takeover offers from shareholders is legal but not morally permissible.

If we must have laws to deal with cases of insider trading, these laws should focus their attention not on the insider trades themselves, but on the corporate secrecy that makes insider trading possible. If we had laws requiring immediate disclosure of takeover offers, insider trading on the basis of such offers would be nearly impossible, and laws against this sort of insider trading would become redundant. Notice, too, that laws requiring corporations to divulge certain information to the shareholders would be nothing new. Corporations are currently required, for example, to make periodic reports of corporate earnings to the shareholders. All we need to do is expand these reporting requirements.

It is, by the way, worth noting that there is a chance that the proposals I have made concerning the ethics of insider trading might someday become the law of the land. Quite recently, the Supreme Court agreed to hear a case in which the shareholders of Basic Inc. charge that their directors wronged them by withholding from them information concerning a takeover proposal. The shareholders' lawsuit charges that for more than a year Basic "repeatedly denied" that takeover discussions were being held, when in fact they were. The lawsuit also charges that because of these denials, shareholders "sold their shares at an artificially low price before the takeover."[32] Should the Supreme Court find that the occurrence of merger negotiations are a "material fact" that must be disclosed to shareholders,[33] they will in essence be agreeing with my claim that the shareholders have a right to be informed of takeover proposals.

Notes

1. To sell a stock short is to sell shares that you have not bought, but have merely borrowed. By selling short, you can make a profit if the price of the stock subsequently declines; for when you buy shares to repay your share debt, your cost will be less than the proceeds of your original sale.

2. By buying a stock option, one gains the right to buy or sell a certain number of shares of the stock in question for a certain price on or before a certain date.

3. Employees of printing firms have an unfortunate tendency to engage in insider trading. For descriptions of two cases in which print shop employees allegedly engaged in insider trading, see "Bowne Unit Ex-Aide Tied to Insider Trading . . .," *Wall Street Journal* (hereafter abbreviated *WSJ*), 20 July 1984, p. 33; and "SEC Charges 8 People of Insider Trades . . .," *WSJ*, 23 May 1985, p. 27.

4. For more information about this filing requirement, see Jack Clark Francis's *Investments: Analysis and Management*, 3rd ed. (New York: McGraw-Hill, 1980), p. 83.

5. These provisions can be found in Section 16 of the Securities Exchange Act of 1934. Those who appreciate the English language, however, will do better to consult, e.g., Francis's lucid explanation of Section 16. (Ibid.)

6. Paul Blustein, "Disputes Arise over Value of Laws on Insider Trading," *WSJ*, 17 November 1986, p. 14.

7. See "SEC's Inquiry Widens As It Questions Broker, Others in Journal Case," *WSJ*, 2 April 1984, pp. 1 and 18; and "Winans Gets 18-Month Term in Trading Case," *WSJ*, 7 August 1985, p. 2.

8. Stephen Wermiel, "Supreme Court Agrees to Hear Winans Case," *WSJ*, 16 December 1986, p. 4.

9. In case the reader takes this remark as evidence of my ability as an investor, let me end my confession with one last comment: I did not do the sensible thing and sell my American Surgery Centers shares at $20; instead, I sold them at various prices considerably below $20 and still hold a few at their current price of 25 cents per share.

10. Bruce Ingeroll, "Senate Approves Stiffer Penalties of Insider Trades," *WSJ*, 2 July 1984, p. 8.

11. *Digest of Public General Bills and Resolutions*, 1984 ed. (Washington, D.C.: The Library of Congress, 1984), pt. 1, p. 391.

12. Scott McMurray and Daniel Hertzberg, "Drexel Official Accused by SEC of Inside Trades," *WSJ*, 13 May 1986, p. 3.

13. James B. Stewart, "Levine Pleads Guilty, Agrees to Cooperate," *WSJ*, 6 June 1986, p. 3.

14. James B. Stewart and Daniel Hertzberg, "Fall of Ivan F. Boesky Leads to Broader Probe of Insider Information," *WSJ*, 17 November 1986, pp. 1 and 14.

15. Cynthia Crossen, "Industrials Sink 43.31 as Investors Fear Fallout from Boesky Probe," *WSJ*, 19 November 1986, p. 57.

16. George Anders, "Boesky Fund Sold Big Blocks of Securities," *WSJ*, 20 November 1986, p. 3.

17. Daniel Hertzberg and James B. Stewart, "SEC Is Probing Drexel on 'Junk Bonds,' . . .," *WSJ*, 18 November 1986, p. 3.

18. The events that have transpired since this paper was written (in early 1987) have shown this prediction to be correct.

19. "Is Adultery Immoral?" in *Today's Moral Problems* (New York: Macmillan Publishing, 1975), pp 240–252.

20. This would be a foolish thing for him to do, given the current restrictions against insider trading. It would make more sense for Bossman to pass on the information to some trustworthy person who would make the purchase for Bossman and turn over most of the profits to him. It would also make more sense for Bossman to purchase Lilliputian options rather than Lilliputian stock.

21. To be sure, a debate can arise on exactly how this should be accomplished. E.g., should he maximize long-term or short-term return on investment?

22. Investors often do this sort of thing to try to get additional profit from their sale. In exchange for this profit, though, they must be willing to undertake a risk — the risk that their order won't be transacted.

23. Actually, these aren't the only choices open to corporate directors: They can also choose to lie to their shareholders regarding the takeover proposal. Suppose, for example, that on June 2, a number of shareholders call Lilliputian to ask whether the company knows of any reason for the jump in the stock's price and in particular whether Lilliputian has received a takeover offer. Bossman could, under these circumstances, instruct his underlings to reply to these inquiries as follows: "Lilliputian has received no takeover offer and Lilliputian directors know of no reason for the recent jump in stock price." In making such an announcement, Lilliputian directors are lying to — or at least misleading — the shareholders. (For actual examples of this sort of thing, see "Texas Gulf Says 6 Months Needed to Weigh Ore Find . . . ," *WSJ*, 24 April 1964, p. 7; and Stephen Wermiel's "High Court to Rule When Merger Talks Are 'Material' to Shareholder Interests," *WSJ*, 24 February 1987, p. 2.)

24. When, for example, PC Acquisition Inc. offered to take over Purolator Courier Corp. in early 1987, Purolator announced that its directors were meeting to consider a takeover offer. It disclosed neither the identity of the company making the offer nor the terms of the offer. See Teri

Agins's "Purolator Board Backs Buyout for $268 Million," *WSJ*, 2 March 1987, p. 3; and Beatrice E. Garcia's "An Appraisal: . . . ," *WSJ*, 2 March 1987, p. 41.

25. During a trading halt, investors cannot buy or sell a stock. When trading reopens, it is often at a substantially different price than when the halt began. If the new price is above the price specified by a limit order to sell, the transaction will take place at the higher price — i.e., to the benefit of whoever placed the limit order.

26. The facts in my case approximate those in Texas Gulf Sulphur's discovery of a large mineral deposit in 1963. See Francis, *Investments: Analysis and Management*, pp. 83–84.

27. For one version of this theory, see "The Carberry Theory," *WSJ*, 29 December 1986, p. 18.

28. The case of Brooks, by the way, raises an interesting thought. Notice that Brooks is not "selling as is" something — viz. shares of stock — that he knows to be "defective"; rather, he is buying something from an owner who does not realize their true value. (Should we say that he is "buying them as is"?) Applied ethicists have had much more to say about cases in which a person withholds information about something he is selling than about cases in which a person withholds information about something he is buying. Further discussion of this would, however, carry us beyond the present topic.

29. One exception to this is the "new issues" market. When a company sells "new" shares of stock directly to investors, it is required to disclose a vast amount of information about the shares to would-be buyers. The costs of meeting this requirement are great, but not nearly as great as they would be if *every* seller of stock had to "inform" would-be buyers.

30. "The Carberry Theory," *WSJ*, 29 December 1986, p. 18.

31. "The Ethics of Investing," *Journal of Business Ethics* (April, 1987), pp. 233–242.

32. Stephen Wermiel, "High Court to Rule when Merger Talks are 'Material' to Shareholder Interests," *WSJ*, 24 February 1987, p. 2.

33. Since this paper was written, the Supreme Court has handed down its opinion in the Basic Inc. case. In this opinion the Supreme Court said that under some circumstances, companies do have a legal obligation to tell shareholders when they have received merger offers. More precisely, the court said that "the question of when merger talks are material must be decided on a case-by-case basis, taking into account the 'significance the reasonable investor would place on the withheld or misrepresented information,' the likelihood that the merger will take place and the importance of the merger to the companies." At the same time, though, the court said it did not see the need for "any change in companies' practice of silence or 'no comment' about the existence of merger talks." (Stephen Wermiel and Thomas E. Ricks, "Supreme Court Decision Eases Filing of Suits over False Merger-Talks Data," *WSJ*, 8 March 1988, pp. 3 and 18.

Patricia H. Werhane

THE ETHICS OF INSIDER TRADING

> Insider trading is the reverse of speculation. It is reward without risk, wealth generated — and injury done to others — by an unfair advantage in information . . . [T]he core principle is clear: no one should profit from exploitation of important information not available to the public.[1]

Insider trading in the stock market is characterized as the buying or selling of shares of stock on the basis of information known only to the trader or to a few persons. In discussions of insider trading it is commonly assumed that the privileged information, if known to others, would affect their actions in the market as well, although in theory this need not be the case. The present guidelines of the Securities and Exchange Commission prohibit most forms of insider trading. Yet a number of economists and philosophers of late defend this kind of activity both as a viable and useful practice in a free market and as a practice that is not immoral. In response to these defenses I want to question the value of insider trading both from a moral and an economic point of view. I shall argue that insider trading both in its present illegal form and as a legalized market mechanism violates the privacy of concerned parties, destroys competition, and undermines the efficient and proper functioning of a free market, thereby bringing into question its own raison d'etre. It does so and therefore is economically inefficient for the very reason that it is immoral.

That insider trading as an illegal activity interferes with the free market is pretty obvious. It is like a game where there are a number of players each of whom represents a constituency. In this sort of game there are two sets of rules — one ostensive set and another, implicit set, functioning for some of the players. In this analogy some of the implicit rules are outlawed, yet the big players manage to keep them operative and are actually often in control of the game. But not all the players know all the rules being played or at least they are ignorant of the most important ones, ones that determine the big wins and big losses. So not all the players realize what rules actually manipulate the outcome. Moreover, partly because some of the most important functioning rules are illegal, some players who do know the implicit rules and could participate do not. Thus not everyone in a position to do so plays the trading game the same way. The game, then, like the manipulated market that is the outcome, is unfair — unfair to some of the players and those they represent — unfair not only because some of the players are not privy to the most important rules, but also because these "special" rules are illegal so that they are adopted only by a few of even the privileged players.

But suppose that insider trading was decriminalized or not prohibited by SEC regulations. Then, one might argue, insider trading would not be unfair

From *Journal of Bussiness Ethics*, 8 (1989), 841–845. ©1989 Kluwer Academic Publishers. Reprinted by permission of Kluwer Academic Publishers.

because anyone could engage in it without impunity. Although one would be trading on privileged knowledge, others, too, could trade on *their* privileged information. The market would function more efficiently since the best-informed and those most able to gain information would be allowed to exercise their fiscal capabilities. The market itself would regulate the alleged excesses of insider trading. I use the term "alleged" excesses because according to this line of reasoning, if the market is functioning properly, whatever gains or losses are created as a result of open competition are a natural outcome of that competition. They are not excesses at all, and eventually the market will adjust the so-called unfair gains of speculators.

There are several other defenses of insider trading. First, insider information, e.g., information about a merger, acquisition, new stock issue, layoffs, etc., information known only to a few, *should* be and remain private. That information is the property of those engaged in the activity in question, and they should have the right to regulate its dissemination. Second and conversely, even under ideal circumstances it is impossible either to disseminate information to all interested parties equally and fairly, or alternately, to preserve absolute secrecy. For example, in issuing a new stock or deciding on a stock split, a number of parties in the transaction from brokers to printers learn about that information in advance just because of their participation in making this activity a reality. And there are always shareholders and other interested parties who claim they did not receive information of such an activity or did not receive information of such an activity or did not receive it at the same time as other shareholders even when the information was disseminated to everyone at the same time. Thus it is, at best, difficult to stop insider trading or to judge whether a certain kind of knowledge is "inside" or privileged. This is not a good reason to defend insider trading as economically or morally desirable, but it illustrates the difficulties of defining and controlling the phenomenon.

Third, those who become privy to inside information, even if they take advantage of that information before it becomes public, are trading on probabilities, not on certainties, since they are trading before the activity actually takes place. They are taking a gamble, and if they are wrong the market itself will "punish" them. It is even argued that brokers who do not use inside information for their clients' advantage are cheating their clients.

Finally, and more importantly, economists like Henry Manne argue that insider trading is beneficial to outsiders. Whether it is more beneficial than its absence is a question Manne admits he cannot answer. But Manne defends insider trading because, he argues, it reduces the factor of chance in trading both for insiders and outsiders. When shares are traded on information or probabilities rather than on rumor or whim, the market reflects more accurately the actual economic status of that company or set of companies. Because of insider trading, stock prices go up or down according to real, factual information. Outsiders benefit from this because stock prices more closely represent the worth of their company than shares not affected by insider trading. Insider trading, then, actually improves the fairness of the market, according to this argument, by reflecting in stock prices the fiscal realities of affected corporations thereby benefitting all traders of the stocks.[2]

These arguments for insider trading are persuasive. Because outsiders are allegedly not harmed from privileged information not available to them and may indeed benefit from insider trading, and because the market punishes rash speculators, insider trading cannot be criticized as exploitation. In fact, it makes the market more efficient. Strong as these arguments are, however, there is something amiss with these claims. The error, I think, rests at least in part with the faulty view of how free markets work, a view which stems from a misinterpretation that derives from a misreading of Adam Smith and specifically a misreading of Smith's notions of self-interest and the Invisible Hand.

The misinterpretation is this. It is sometimes assumed that an unregulated free market, driven by competition and self interest, will function autonomously. The idea is that the free market works something like the law of gravity — autonomously and anonymously in what I would call a no-blooded fashion. The interrelationships created by free market activities based on self-interested competition are similar to the gravitational relationships between the planets and the sun: impersonal, automatic interactions determined by a number of factors including the distance and competitive self-interest of each of the market components. The free market functions, then, despite the selfish peculiarities of the players just as the planets circle the sun despite their best intentions to do otherwise. Given that picture of the free market, so-called insider trading, driven by self-interest but restrained by competitive forces, that is, the invisible hand, is merely one gravitational mechanism — a complication but not an oddity or an aberration in the market.

This is a crude and exaggerated picture of the market, but I think it accounts for talk about the market *as if* it functioned in this independent yet forceful way, and it accounts for defenses of unrestrained self-interested actions in the market place. It allows one to defend insider trading because of the positive market fall-out from this activity, and because the market allegedly will control the excesses of self-interested economic activities.

The difficulty with this analysis is not so much with the view of insider trading as a legitimate activity but rather with the picture of economic actors in a free market. Adam Smith himself, despite his 17th century Newtonian background, did not have such a mechanical view of a laissez-faire economy. Again and again in the *Wealth of Nations* Smith extols the virtues of unrestrained competition as being to the advantage of the producer and the consumer.[3] A system of perfect liberty, he argues, creates a situation where "[t]he whole of the advantages and disadvantages of the different employments of labour and stock . . . be either perfectly equal or continually tending to equality."[4] Yet for Smith the greatest cause of inequalities of advantage is any restrictive policy or activity that deliberately gives privileges to certain kinds of businesses, trades, or professions.[5] The point is that Smith sees perfect liberty as the necessary condition for competition, but perfect competition occurs only if both parties in the exchange are on more or less equal grounds, whether it be competition for labor, jobs, consumers, or capital. This is not to imply that Smith favors equality of outcomes. Clearly he does not. But the market is most efficient and most fair when there is competition between equally matched parties.

Moreover, Smith's thesis was that the Invisible Hand works because, and only when, people operate with restrained self-interest, self-interest restrained by reason, moral sentiments, and sympathy, in Smith's case the reason, moral sentiments and sympathies of British gentlemen. To operate otherwise, that is, with unrestrained self-interest, where that self-interest causes harm to others would "violate the laws of justice"[6] or be a "violation of fair play,"[7] according to Smith. This interferes with free competition just as government regulation would because the character of competition, and thus the direction of the Invisible Hand, depends on the manner in which actors exploit or control their own self-interests. The Invisible Hand, then, that "masterminds" the free market is not like an autonomous gravitational force. It depends on the good will, decency, self-restraint, and fair play of those parties engaging in market activities.[8] When self-interests get out of hand, Smith contends, they must be regulated by laws of justice.[9]

Similarly, the current market, albeit not Smith's ideal of laissez-faire, is affected by how people operate in the market place. It does not operate autonomously. Unrestrained activities of insider traders affect competition differently than Smithian exchanges which are more or less equal exchanges between self-interested but restrained parties. The term "insider trading" implies that some traders know more than others, that information affects their decision-making and would similarly affect the trading behavior of others should they become privy to that information. Because of this, the resulting market is different than one unaffected by insider trading. This, in itself, is not a good reason to question insider trading. Henry Manne, for example, recognizes the role of insider trading in influencing the market and finds that, on balance, this is beneficial.

Insider trading, however, is not merely a complication in the free market mechanism. Insider trading, whether it is legal or illegal, affects negatively the ideal of laissez-faire of *any* market, because it thwarts the very basis of the market: competition, just as "insider" rules affect the fairness of the trader even if that activity is not illegal and even if one could, in theory, obtain inside information oneself. This is because the same information, or equal information, is not available to everyone. So competition, which depends on the availability of equal advantage by all parties is precluded. Insider trading allows the insider to indulge in greed (even though she may not) and that, by eschewing stock prices, works against the very kind of market in which insider trading might be allowed to function.

If it is true, as Manne argues, that insider trading produces a more efficient stock market because stock prices as a result of insider trading better reflect the underlying economic conditions of those companies involved in the trade, he would also have to argue that competition does not always produce the best results in the marketplace. Conversely, if competition creates the most efficient market, insider trading cannot, because competition is "regulated" by insiders. While it is not clear whether outsiders benefit more from insider trading than without that activity, equal access to information would allow (although not determine) every trader to compete from an equal advantage. Thus pure competition, a supposed goal of the free market and an aim of most persons who defend insider trading, is more nearly obtained without insider trading.

Insider training has other ethical problems. Insider trading does not protect the privacy of information it is supposed to protect. To illustrate, let us consider a case of a friendly merger between Company *X* and Company *Y*. Suppose this merger is in the planning stages and is not to be made public even to the shareholders for a number of months. There may be good or bad reasons for this secrecy, e.g., labor problems, price of shares of acquired company, management changes, unfriendly raiders, competition in certain markets, etc. By law, management and others privy to knowledge about the possible merger cannot trade shares of either company during the negotiating period. On the other hand, if that information is "leaked" to a trader (or if she finds out by some other means), then information that might affect the merger is now in the hands of persons not part of the negotiation. The alleged privacy of information, privacy supposedly protected by insider traders, is now in the hands of not disinterested parties. While they may keep this information a secret, they had no right to it in the first place. Moreover, their possession of the information has three possible negative effects.

First, they or their clients in fact may be interested parties to the merger, e.g., labor union leaders, stockholders in competing companies, etc., the very persons for whom the information makes a difference and therefore are the objects of Company X and Y's secrecy. Second, insider trading on privileged information gives unfair advantages to these traders. Even if outsiders benefit from insider trading, they are less likely to benefit as much nor as soon as insider traders for the very reason of their lack of proximity to the activity. Insider traders can use information to their advantage in the market, an advantage neither the management of X or Y nor other traders can enjoy. Even if the use of such information in the market makes the market more efficient, this is unfair competition since those without this information will not gain as much as those who have such knowledge. Even if insider trading does contribute to market stabilization based on information, nevertheless, one has also to justify the fact that insider traders profit more on their knowledge than outsiders, when their information becomes an actuality simply by being "first" in the trading of the stock. Do insider traders deserve this added profit because their trading creates a more propitious market share knowledge for outsiders? That is a difficult position to defend, because allowing insider trading also allows for the very Boeskyian greed that is damaging in any market.

Third, while trading X and Y on inside information may bring their share prices to the value most closely reflecting their real price-earnings ratio, this is not always the case. Such trading may reflect undue optimism or pessimism about the possible outcome of the merger, an event that has not yet occurred. So the prices of X and Y may be overvalued or undervalued on the basis of a probability, or, because insider traders seldom have all the facts, on guesswork. In these cases insider trading deliberately creates more risk in the market since the stock prices of X and Y are manipulated for not altogether solid reasons. So market efficiency, the end which allegedly justifies insider trading is not guaranteed.

What Henry Manne's defenses of insider trading do show is what Adam Smith well knew, that the market is neither independent nor self-regulatory. What traders do in the market and how they behave affects the direction and kind of restraint the market will exert on other traders. The character of the market is a product of those who operate within it, as Manne has demonstrated in his defense of insider trading. Restrained self-interest creates an approximation of a self-regulatory market, because it is that that allows self-interested individuals and companies to function as competitively as possible. In the long run the market will operate more efficiently too, because it precludes aberrations such as those exhibited by Ivan Boesky's and David Levine's behavior, behavior that created market conditions favorable to no one except themselves and their clients.

Notes

1. George Will, 'Keep Your Eye on Guiliani', *Newsweek*, March 2, 1987, p. 84.

2. See Henry Manne, *Insider Trading and the Stock Market* (The Free Press, New York, 1966), especially Chapters X and XI.

3. Adam Smith, *The Wealth of Nations*, ed. R. A. Campbell and A. S. Skinner (Oxford University Press, Oxford, 1976). l.x.c, II.v.8-12

4. *Wealth of Nations*, l.x.a.1.

5. *Wealth of Nations*, l.x.c.

6. *Wealth of Nations*, IV.ix.51.

7. Adam Smith, *The Theory of Moral Sentiments*, ed. D. D. Raphael and A. L. Macfic (Oxford University Press, Oxford, 1976), II.ii.2.1.

8. See Andrew Skinner, *A System of Social Science* (Clarendon Press, Oxford, 1979), especially pp. 237ff.

9. See, for example, *The Wealth of Nations*, II.ii.94, IV. v.16.

Jennifer Moore

WHAT IS REALLY UNETHICAL ABOUT INSIDER TRADING?

"Insider trading," as the term is usually used, means the buying or selling of securities on the basis of material, non-public information. It is popularly believed to be unethical, and many, though not all, forms of it are illegal. Insider trading makes for exciting headlines, and stories of the unscrupulousness and unbridled greed of the traders abound. As it is reported in the media — complete with details of clandestine meetings, numbered Swiss bank accounts and thousands of dollars of profits carried away in plastic bags — insider trading has all the trappings of a very shady business indeed.[1] For many, insider trading has become the primary symbol of a widespread ethical rot on Wall Street and in the business community as a whole.[2]

For a practice that has come to epitomize unethical business behavior, insider trading has received surprisingly little ethical analysis. The best ethical assessments of insider trading have come from legal scholars who argue against the practice. But their arguments rest on notions such as fairness or ownership of information that require much more examination than they are usually given.[3] Proponents of insider trading are quick to dismiss these arguments as superficial, but offer very little ethical insight of their own. Arguing almost solely on grounds of economic efficiency, they generally gloss over the ethical arguments or dismiss them entirely.[4] Ironically, their refusal to address the ethical arguments on their merits merely strengthens the impression that insider trading is unethical. Readers are left with the sense that while it might reduce efficiency, the prohibition against insider trading rests on firm *ethical* grounds. But can we assume this? Not, I think, without a good deal more examination.

From *Journal of Bussiness Ethics*, 9 (1990), 171-182. ©1990 Kluwer Academic Publishers, Reprinted by permission of Kluwer Academic Publishers.

This paper is divided into two parts. In the first part, I examine critically the principal ethical arguments against insider trading. The arguments fall into three main classes: arguments based on fairness, arguments based on property rights in information, and arguments based on harm to ordinary investors or the market as a whole. Each of these arguments, I contend, has some serious deficiencies. No one of them by itself provides a sufficient reason for outlawing insider trading. This does not mean, however, that there are no reasons for prohibiting the practice. Once we have cleared away the inadequate arguments, other, more cogent reasons for outlawing insider trading come to light. In the second part of the paper, I set out what I take to be the real reasons for laws against insider trading.

The term "insider trading" needs some preliminary clarification. Both the SEC and the courts have strongly resisted pressure to define the notion clearly. In 1961, the SEC stated that corporate insiders — such as officers or directors — in possession of material, non-public information were required to disclose that information or to refrain from trading.[5] But this "disclose or refrain" rule has since been extended to persons other than corporate insiders. People who get information from insiders ("tippees") and those who become "temporary insiders" in the course of some work they perform for the company, can acquire the duty of insiders in some cases.[6] Financial printers and newspaper columnists, not "insiders" in the technical sense, have also been found guilty of insider trading.[7] Increasingly, the term "insider" has come to refer to the kind of information a person possesses rather than to the status of the person who trades on that information. My use of the term will reflect this ambiguity. In this paper, an "insider trader" is someone who trades in material, non-public information — not necessarily a corporate insider.

I. ETHICAL ARGUMENTS AGAINST INSIDER TRADING

Fairness

Probably the most common reason given for thinking that insider trading is unethical is that it is "unfair." For proponents of the fairness argument, the key feature of insider trading is the disparity of information between the two parties to the transaction. Trading should take place on a "level playing field," they argue, and disparities in information tilt the field toward one player and away from the other. There are two versions of the fairness argument: the first argues that insider trading is unfair because the two parties do not have *equal* information; the second argues that insider trading is unfair because the two parties do not have equal *access* to information. Let us look at the two versions one at a time.

According to the equal information argument, insider trading is unfair because one party to the transaction lacks information the other party has, and is thus at a disadvantage. Although this is a very strict notion of fairness, it has its proponents[8] and hints of this view appear in some of the judicial opinions.[9] One proponent of the equal information argument is Saul Levmore, who claims that "fairness is achieved when insiders and outsiders are in equal positions. That is, a system is fair if we would not expect one group to envy the position of the other." As thus defined, Levmore claims, fairness "reflects the 'golden rule' of impersonal behavior — treating others as we would ourselves."[10] If Levmore is correct, then not just insider trading, but *all* transactions in which there is a disparity of information are unfair, and thus unethical. But this claim seems overly broad. An example will help to illustrate some of the problems with it.

Suppose I am touring Vermont and come across an antique blanket chest in the barn of a farmer, a chest I know will bring $2500 back in the city. I offer to buy it for $75, and the farmer agrees. If he had known how much I could get for it back home, he probably would have asked a higher price — but I failed to disclose this information. I have profited from an informational advantage. Have I been unethical? My suspicion is that most people would say I have not. While knowing how much I could sell the chest for in the city is in the interest of the farmer, I am not morally obligated to reveal it. I am not morally obligated to tell those who deal with me *everything* that it would be in their interest to know.

U.S. common law supports this intuition. Legally, people are obligated not to lie or to misrepresent a product they are selling or buying. But they are not required to reveal everything it is in the other party's interest to know.[11] One might argue that this is simply an area in which the law falls short of ethical standards. But there is substantial ethical support for the law on these matters as well. There does seem to be a real difference between lying or misrepresentation on the one hand, and simple failure to disclose information on the other, even though the line between the two is sometimes hard to draw.[12] Lying and misrepresentation are forms of deception, and deception is a subtle form of coercion. When I successfully deceive someone, I cause him to do something that does not represent his true will — something he did not intend to do and would not have done if he had known the truth. Simply not revealing information (usually) does not involve this kind of coercion.

In general, it is only when I owe a *duty* to the other party that I am legally required to reveal all information that is in his interest. In such a situation, the other party believes that I am looking out for his interests, and I deceive him if I do not do so. Failure to disclose is deceptive in this instance because of the relationship of trust and dependence between the parties. But this suggests that trading on inside information is wrong, *not* because it violates a general notion of fairness, but because a breach of fiduciary duty is involved. Cases of insider trading in which no fiduciary duty of this kind is breached would not be unethical.

Significantly, the Supreme Court has taken precisely this position: insider trading is wrong because, and when, it involves the violation of a fiduciary duty to the other parties to the transaction.[13] The Court has consistently refused to recognize the general duty to *all* investors that is argued for by proponents of the fairness argument. This is particularly clear in *Chiarella v. US*, a decision overturning the conviction of a financial printer for trading on inside information:

> At common law, misrepresentation made for the purpose of inducing reliance upon the false statement is fraudulent. But one who fails to disclose material information prior to the consummation of a transaction commits fraud *only when he is under a duty to do so*. And the duty to disclose arises when one party has information "that the other party is entitled to know because of a fiduciary or other similar relation of trust and confi-

dence between them." . . . The element required to make silence fraudulent — a duty to disclose — is absent in this case. . . .

We cannot affirm petitioner's conviction without recognizing a general duty between all participants in market transactions to forgo actions based on material, nonpublic information. Formulation of such a broad duty, which departs radically from the established doctrine that duty arises from a specific relationship between two parties . . . should not be undertaken absent some explicit evidence of congressional intent. . . .[14]

The court reiterated that "there is no *general* duty to disclose before trading on material nonpublic information" in *Dirks v. SEC.*[15] It is worth noting that if this reasoning is correct, the legal and ethical status of insider trading depends on the understanding between the fiduciary and the party he represents. Insider trading would not be a violation of fiduciary duty, and thus would not be unethical, unless (1) it were clearly contrary to the interests of the other party or (2) the other party had demanded or been led to expect disclosure. We shall return to this point below.

There is a second ethical reason for not requiring all people with informational advantages to disclose them to others: there may be relevant differences between the parties to the transaction that make the disparity of information "fair." Perhaps I invested considerable time, effort and money in learning about antiques. If this is true, I might deserve to reap the benefits of these efforts. We frequently think it is fair for people to benefit from informational advantages of their own making; this is an important justification for patent law and the protection of trade secrets. "Fairness" is often defined as "treating equals equally." But equals in what respect? Unless we know that the two parties to a transaction *are* equal in the relevant way, it is difficult to say that an informational advantage held by one of them is "unfair."

My point here is different from the frequently heard claim that people should be allowed to profit from informational advantages because this results in a more efficient use of information. This latter claim, while important, does not really address the fairness issue. What I am arguing is that the notion of fairness offered by proponents of the equal information argument is itself incomplete. We cannot make the notion of fairness work for us unless we supply guidelines explaining who are to count as "equals" in different contexts. If we try, we are likely to end up with results that seem intuitively *un*fair.

For these reasons, the "equal information" version of the fairness argument seems to me to fail. However, it could be argued that insider trading is unfair because the insider has information that is not *accessible* to the ordinary investor. For proponents of this second type of fairness argument, it is not the insider's information advantage that counts, but the fact that this advantage is "unerodable," one that cannot be overcome by the hard work and ingenuity of the ordinary investor. No matter how hard the latter works, he is unable to acquire non-public information, because this information is protected by law.[16]

This type of fairness argument seems more promising, since it allows people to profit from informational advantages of their own making, but not from advantages that are built into the system. Proponents of this "equal access" argument would probably find my deal with the Vermont farmer unobjectionable, because information about antiques is not in principle unavailable to the farmer. The problem with the argument is that the notion of "equal access" is not very clear. What does it mean for two people to have equal access to information?

Suppose my pipes are leaking and I call a plumber to fix them. He charges me for the job, and benefits by the informational advantage he has over me. Most of us would not find this transaction unethical. True, I don't have "equal access" to the information needed to fix my pipes in any real sense, but I could have had this information had I chosen to become a plumber. The disparity of information in this case is simply something that is built into the fact that people choose to specialize in different areas. But just as I could have chosen to become a plumber, I could have chosen to become a corporate insider with access to legally protected information. Access to information seems to be a relative, not an absolute, matter. As Judge Frank Easterbrook puts it:

> People do not have or lack "access" in some absolute sense. There are, instead, different costs of obtaining information. An outsider's costs are high; he might have to purchase the information from the firm. Managers have lower costs (the amount of salary foregone); brokers have relatively low costs (the value of the time they spent investigating). . . . The different costs of access are simply a function of the division of labor. A manager (or a physician) always knows more than a shareholder (or patient) in some respects, but unless there is something unethical about the division of labor, the difference is not unfair.[17]

One might argue that I have easier access to a plumber's information than I do to an insider trader's, since there are lots of plumbers from whom I can buy the information I seek.[18] The fact that insiders have a strong incentive to keep their information to themselves is a serious objection to insider trading. But if insider trading were made legal, insiders could profit not only from trading on their information, but also on selling it to willing buyers. Proponents of the practice argue that a brisk market in information would soon develop — indeed, it might be argued that such a market already exists, though in illegal and clandestine form.[19]

The objections offered above do not show conclusively that *no* fairness argument against insider trading can be constructed. But they do suggest that a good deal more spadework is necessary to construct one. Proponents of the fairness argument need to show how the informational advantages of insider traders over ordinary investors are different in kind from the informational advantages of plumbers over the rest of us — or, alternatively, why the informational advantages of plumbers are unfair. I have not yet seen such an argument, and I suspect that designing one may require a significant overhaul of our traditional ideas about fairness. As it stands, the effectiveness of the fairness argument seems restricted to situations in which the insider trader owes a duty to the person with whom he is trading — and as we will see below, even here it is not conclusive because much depends on how that duty is defined.

The most interesting thing about the fairness argument is not that it provides a compelling reason to outlaw insider trading, but that it leads to issues we cannot settle on the basis of an abstract concept of fairness alone. The claim that parties to a transaction should have equal information, or equal access to information, inevitably raises questions about how informational advantages are (or should be) acquired, and when people are entitled to use them for profit. Again, this understanding of the limits of the fairness argument is reflected in common law. If insider trading is wrong primarily because it is unfair, then it should be wrong no matter *who* engages in it. It should make no difference whether I am a corporate insider, a financial printer, or a little old lady who heard a takeover rumor on the Hudson River Line. But it does make a difference to the courts. I think this is because the crucial questions concerning insider trading are not about fairness, but about how inside information is acquired and what entitles people to make use of it. These are questions central to our second class of arguments against insider trading, those based on the notion of property rights in information.

Property Rights in Information

As economists and legal scholars have recognized, information is a valuable thing, and it is possible to view it as a type of property. We already treat certain types of information as property: trade secrets, inventions, and so on—and protect them by law. Proponents of the property rights argument claim that material, non-public information is also a kind of property, and that insider trading is wrong because it involves a violation of property rights.

If inside information is a kind of property, whose property is it? How does information come to belong to one person rather than another? This is a very complex question, because information differs in many ways from other, more tangible sorts of property. But one influential argument is that information belongs to the people who discover, originate or "create" it. As Bill Shaw put it in a recent article, "the originator of the information (the individual or the corporation that spent hard-earned bucks producing it) owns and controls this asset just as it does other proprietary goods."[20] Thus if a firm agrees to a deal, invents a new product, or discovers new natural resources, it has a property right in that information and is entitled to exclusive use of it for its own profit.

It is important to note that it is the firm itself (and/or its shareholders), and not the individual employees of the firm, who have property rights in the information. To be sure, it is always certain individuals in the firm who put together the deal, invent the product, or discover the resources. But they are able to do this only because they are backed by the power and authority of the firm. The employees of the firm—managers, officers, directors—are not entitled to the information any more than they are entitled to corporate trade secrets or patents on products that they develop for the firm.[21] It is the firm that makes it possible to create the information and that makes the information valuable once it has been created. As Victor Brudney puts it,

> The insiders have acquired the information at the expense of the enter-
> prise, and for the purpose of conducting the business for the collective
> good of all the stockholders, entirely apart from personal benefits from
> trading in its securities. There is no reason for them to be entitled to trade
> for their own benefit on the basis of such information. . . .[22]

If this analysis is correct, then it suggests that insider trading is wrong because it is a form of theft. It is not exactly like theft, because the person who uses inside information does not deprive the company of the use of the information. But he does deprive the company of the *sole* use of the information, which is itself an asset. The insider trader "misappropriates," as the laws puts it, information that belongs to the company and uses it in a way in which it was not intended—for personal profit. It is not surprising that this "misappropriation theory" has begun to take hold in the courts, and has become one of the predominant rationales in prosecuting insider trading cases. In *U.S. v. Newman*, a case involving investment bankers and securities traders, for example, the court stated:

> In *US v. Chiarella*, Chief Justice Burger . . . said that the defendant "misappropriated"—stole to put it bluntly—valuable nonpublic information entrusted to him in the utmost confidence." That characterization aptly describes the conduct of the connivers in the instant case. . . . By sullying the reputations of [their] employers as safe repositories of client confidences, appellee and his cohorts defrauded those employers as surely as if they took their money.[23]

The misappropriation theory also played a major role in the prosecution of R. Foster Winans, a *Wall Street Journal* reporter who traded on and leaked to others the contents of his "Heard in the Street" column.[24]

This theory is quite persuasive, as far as it goes. But it is not enough to show that insider trading is always unethical or that it should be illegal. If insider information is really the property of the firm that produces it, then using that property is wrong *only when the firm prohibits it*. If the firm does not prohibit insider trading, it seems perfectly acceptable.[25] Most companies do in fact forbid insider trading. But it is not clear whether they do so because they don't want their employees using corporate property for profit or simply because it is illegal. Proponents of insider trading point out that most corporations did not prohibit insider trading until recently, when it became a prime concern of enforcement agencies.[26]

If insider trading is primarily a problem of property rights in information, it might be argued, then it is immoral, and should be illegal, only when the company withholds permission to trade on inside information. Under the property rights theory, insider trading becomes a matter of *contract* between the company, its shareholders and its employees. If the employment contract forbids an employee from using the company's information, then it is unethical (and illegal) to do so.

A crucial factor here would be the shareholders' agreement to allow insider information. Shareholders may not wish to allow trading on inside information because they may wish the employees of the company to be devoted simply to advancing shareholder interests. We will return to this point below. But if shareholders did allow it, it would seem to be permissible. Still others argue that shareholders would not need to "agree" in any way other than to be told this information when they were buying the stock. If they did not want to hold stock in a company whose employees were permitted to trade in inside information, they would not buy that stock. Hence they could be said to have "agreed."

Manne and other proponents of insider trading have suggested a number of reasons why "shareholders would voluntarily enter into contractual arrangements with insiders giving them property rights in valuable information."[27] Their principal argument is that permitting insider trading would serve as an incentive to create more information—put together more deals, invent more new products, or make more discoveries. Such an incentive, they argue, would create more profit for shareholders in the long run. Assigning employees the right to trade on inside information could take the place of more traditional (and expensive) elements in the employee's compensation package. Rather than giving out end of the year bonuses, for example, firms could allow employees to put together their own bonuses by cashing in on inside information, thus saving the company money. In addition, proponents argue, insider trading would improve the efficiency of the market. We will return to these claims below.

If inside information really is a form of corporate property, firms may assign employees the right to trade on it if they choose to do so. The only reason for not permitting firms to allow employees to trade on their information would be that doing so causes harm to other investors or to society at large. Although our society values property rights very highly, they are not absolute. We do not hesitate to restrict property rights if their exercise causes significant harm to others. The permissibility of insider trading, then, ultimately seems to depend on whether the practice is harmful.

Harm

There are two principal harm-based arguments against insider trading. The first claims that the practice is harmful to ordinary investors who engage in trades with insiders; the second claims that insider trading erodes investors' confidence in the market, causing them to pull out of the market and harming the market as a whole. I will address the two arguments in turn.

Although proponents of insider trading often refer to it as a "victimless crime," implying that no one is harmed by it, it is not difficult to think of examples of transactions with insiders in which ordinary investors are made worse off. Suppose I have placed an order with my broker to sell my shares in Megalith Co., currently trading at $50 a share, at $60 or above. An insider knows that Behemoth Inc. is going to announce a tender offer for Megalith shares in two days, and has begun to buy large amounts of stock in anticipation of the gains. Because of his market activity, Megalith stock rises to $65 a share and my order is triggered. If he had refrained from trading, the price would have risen steeply two days later, and I would have been able to sell my shares for $80. Because the insider traded, I failed to realize the gains that I otherwise would have made.

But there are other examples of transactions in which ordinary investors *benefit* from insider trading. Suppose I tell my broker to sell my shares in Acme Corp., currently trading at $45, if the price drops to $40 or lower. An insider knows of an enormous class action suit to be brought against Acme in two days. He sells his shares, lowering the price to $38 and triggering my sale. When the suit is made public two days later, the share price plunges to $25. If the insider had abstained from trading, I would have lost far more than I did. Here, the insider has protected me from loss.

Not all investors buy or sell through such "trigger" orders. Many of them make their decisions by watching the movement of the stock. The rise in share price might have indicated to an owner of Megalith that a merger was imminent, and she might have held on to her shares for this reason. Similarly, the downward movement of Acme stock caused by the insider might have suggested to an owner that it was time to sell. Proponents of insider trading argue that large trades by insiders move the price of shares closer to their "real" value, that is, the value that reflects all the relevant information about the stock. This makes the market more efficient and provides a valuable service to all investors.[28]

The truth about an ordinary investor's gains and losses from trading with insiders seems to be not that insider trading is never harmful, but that it is not systematically or consistently harmful. Insider trading is not a "victimless crime," as its proponents claim, but it is often difficult to tell exactly who the victims are and to what extent they have been victimized. The stipulation of the law to "disclose *or* abstain" from trading makes determining victims even more complex. While some investors are harmed by the insider's trade, to others the insider's actions make no difference at all; what harms them is simply *not having complete information* about the stock in question. Forbidding insider trading will not prevent these harms. Investors who neither buy nor sell, or who buy or sell for reasons independent of share price, fall into this category.

Permitting insider trading would undoubtedly make the securities market *riskier* for ordinary investors. Even proponents of the practice seem to agree with this claim. But if insider trading were permitted openly, they argue, investors would compensate for the extra riskiness by demanding a discount in share price:

> In modern finance theory, shareholders are seen as investors seeking a return proportionate with that degree of systematic or market-related risk which they have chosen to incur. . . . [The individual investor] is "protected" by the price established by the market mechanism, not by his personal bargaining power or position. . . . To return to the gambling analogy, if I know you are using percentage dice, I won't play without an appropriate adjustment of the odds; the game is, after all, voluntary.[29]

If insider trading were permitted, in short, we could expect a general drop in share prices, but no net harm to investors would result. Moreover, improved efficiency would result in a bigger pie for everyone. These are empirical claims, and I am not equipped to determine if they are true. If they are, however, they would defuse one of the most important objections to insider trading, and provide a powerful argument for leaving the control of inside information up to individual corporations.

The second harm-based argument claims that permitting insider trading would cause ordinary investors to lose confidence in the market and cease to invest there, thus harming the market as a whole. As former SEC Chairman John Shad puts it, "if people get the impression that they're playing against a marked deck, they're simply not going to be willing to invest."[30] Since capital markets play a crucial role in allocating resources in our economy, this objection is a very serious one.

The weakness of the argument is that it turns almost exclusively on the *feelings* or *perceptions* of ordinary investors, and does not address the question of whether these perceptions are justified. If permitting insider trading really does harm ordinary investors, then this "loss of confidence" argument becomes a compelling reason for outlawing insider trading. But if, as many claim, the practice does not harm ordinary investors, then the sensible course of action is to educate the investors, not to outlaw insider trading. It is irrational to cater to the feelings of ordinary investors if those feelings are not justified. We ought not to outlaw perfectly permissible actions just because some people feel (unjustifiably) disadvantaged by them. More research is needed to determine the actual impact of insider trading on the ordinary investor.[31]

II. IS THERE ANYTHING WRONG WITH INSIDER TRADING?

My contention has been that the principal ethical arguments against insider trading do not, by themselves, suffice to show that the practice is unethical and should be illegal. The strongest arguments are those that turn on the notion of a fiduciary duty to act in the interest of shareholders, or on the idea of inside information as company "property." But in both arguments, the impermissibility of insider trading depends on a contractual understanding among the company, its shareholders and its employees. In both cases, a modification of this understanding could change the moral status of insider trading.

Does this mean that there is nothing wrong with insider trading? No. If insider trading is unethical, it is so *in the context* of the relationship among the firm, its shareholders and its employees. It is possible to change this context in a way that makes the practice permissible. But *should* the context be changed? I will argue that it should not. Because it threatens the fiduciary relationship that is central to business management, I believe, permitting insider trading is in the interest neither of the firm, its shareholders, nor society at large.

Fiduciary relationships are relationships of trust and dependence in which one party acts in the interest of another. They appear in many contexts, but are absolutely essential to conducting business in a complex society. Fiduciary relationships allow parties with different resources, skills and information to cooperate in productive activity. Shareholders who wish to invest in a business, for example, but who cannot or do not wish to run it themselves, hire others to manage it for them. Managers, directors, and to some extent, other employees, become fiduciaries for the firms they manage and for the shareholders of those firms.

The fiduciary relationship is one of moral and legal obligation. Fiduciaries, that is, are bound to act in the interests of those who depend on them even if these interests do not coincide with their own. Typically, however, fiduciary relationships are constructed as far as possible so that the interests of the fiduciaries and the parties for whom they act *do* coincide. Where the interests of the two parties compete or conflict, the fiduciary relationship is threatened. In corporations, the attempt to discourage divergences of interest is exemplified in rules against bribery, usurping corporate opportunities, and so forth. In the past few years, an entire discipline, "agency theory," has developed to deal with such questions. Agency theorists seek ways to align the interests of agents or fiduciaries with the interests of those on behalf of whom they act.

Significantly, proponents of insider trading do not dispute the importance of the fiduciary relationship. Rather, they argue that permitting insider trading would *increase* the likelihood that employees will act in the interest of shareholders and their firms.[32] We have already touched on the main argument for this claim. Manne and others contend that assigning employees the right to trade on inside information would provide a powerful incentive for creative and entrepreneurial activity. It would encourage new inventions, creative deals, and efficient new management practices, thus increasing the profits, strength, and overall competitiveness of the firm. Manne goes so far as to argue that permission to trade on insider information is the only appropriate way to compensate entrepreneurial activity, and warns: "[I]f no way to reward the entrepreneur within a corporation exists, he will tend to disappear from the corporate scene."[33] The entrepreneur makes an invaluable contribution to the firm and its shareholders, and his disappearance would no doubt cause serious harm.

If permitting insider trading is to work in the way proponents suggest, however, there must be a direct and consistent link between the profits reaped by insider traders and the performance that benefits the firm. It is not at all clear that this is the case — indeed, there is evidence that the opposite is true. There appear to be many ways to profit from inside information that do not benefit the firm at all. I mention four possibilities below. Two of these (2 and 3) are simply ways in which insider traders can profit without benefiting the firm, suggesting that permitting insider trading is a poor incentive for performance and fails firmly to link the interests of managers, directors and employees to those of the corporation as a whole. The others (1 and 4) are actually harmful to the corporation, setting up conflicts of interest and actively undermining the fiduciary relationship.[34]

1. Proponents of insider trading tend to speak as if all information were positive. "Information," in the proponents' lexicon, always concerns a creative new deal, a new, efficient way of conducting business, or a new product. If this were true, allowing trades on inside information might provide an incentive to work ever harder for the good of the company. But information can also concern *bad* news — a large lawsuit, an unsafe or poor quality product, or lower-than-expected performance. Such negative information can be just as valuable to the insider trader as positive information. If the freedom to trade on positive information encourages acts that are beneficial to the firm, then by the same reasoning the freedom to trade on negative information would encourage harmful acts. At the very least, permitting employees to profit from harms to the company decreases the incentive to avoid such harms. Permission to trade on negative inside information gives rise to inevitable conflicts of interest. Proponents of insider trading have not satisfactorily answered this objection.[35]

2. Proponents of insider trading also assume that the easiest way to profit on inside information is to "create" it. But it is not at all clear that this is true. Putting together a deal, inventing a new product, and other productive activities that add value to the firm usually require a significant investment of time and energy. For the well-placed employee, it would be far easier to start a rumor that the company has a new product or is about to announce a deal than to sit down and produce either one — and it would be just as profitable for the employee. If permitting insider trading provides an incentive for the productive "creation" of information, it seems to provide an even greater incentive for the non-productive "invention" of information, or stock manipulation. The invention of information is in the interest neither of the firm nor of society at large.

3. Even if negative or false information did not pose problems, the incentive argument for insider trading overlooks the difficulties posed by "free riders" — those who do not actually contribute to the creation of the information, but who are nevertheless aware of it and can profit by trading on it. It is a commonplace of economic theory that if persons can benefit from a good without paying for it, they will generally do so. If there is no way to exclude those who do not "pay" from enjoying a benefit, no one will have an incentive to pay for it, there

will be no incentive to produce it, and the good will not be supplied. In the case of insider trading, an employee's contribution to the creation of positive information constitutes the "payment." Unless those who do not contribute can be excluded from trading on it, there will be no incentive to produce the desired information; it will not get created at all.

4. Finally, allowing trading on inside information would tend to deflect employees' attention from the day-to-day business of running the company and focus it on major changes, positive or negative, that lead to large insider trading profits. This might not be true if one could profit by inside information about the day-to-day efficiency of the operation, a continuous tradition of product quality, or a consistently lean operating budget. But these things do not generate the kind of information on which insider traders can reap large profits. Insider profits come from dramatic changes, from "news" — not from steady, long-term performance. If the firm and its shareholders have a genuine interest in such performance, then permitting insider trading creates a conflict of interest for insiders. The ability to trade on inside information is also likely to influence the types of information officers announce to the public, and the timing of such announcements, making it less likely that the information and its timing is optimal for the firm. And the problems of false or negative information remain.[36]

If the arguments given above are correct, permitting insider trading does not increase the likelihood that insiders will act in the interest of the firm and its shareholders. In some cases, it actually causes conflicts of interest, undermining the fiduciary relationship essential to managing the corporation. This claim, in turn, gives corporations good reason to prohibit the practice. But insider trading remains primarily a private matter among corporations, shareholders, and employees. It is appropriate to ask why, given this fact about insider trading, the practice should be *illegal*. If it is primarily corporate and shareholder interests that are threatened by insider trading, why not let corporations themselves bear the burden of enforcement? Why involve the SEC? There are two possible reasons for continuing to support laws against insider trading. The first is that even if they wish to prohibit insider trading, individual corporations do not have the resources to do so effectively. The second is that society itself has a stake in the fiduciary relationship.

Proponents of insider trading frequently point out that until 1961, when the SEC began to prosecute insider traders, few firms took steps to prevent the practice.[37] They argue that this fact indicates that insider trading is not truly harmful to corporations; if it were, corporations would have prohibited it long ago. But there is another plausible reason for corporations' failure to outlaw insider trading: they did not have the resources to do so, and did not wish to waste resources in the attempt to achieve an impossible task.[38] There is strong evidence that the second explanation is the correct one. Preventing insider trading requires continuous and extensive monitoring of transactions and the ability to compel disclosure, and privately imposed penalties do not seem sufficient to discourage insider trading.[39] The SEC is not hampered by these limitations. Moreover, suggests Frank Easterbrook, if even a few companies allow insider trading, this could make it difficult for other companies to prohibit it. Firms that did not permit insider trading would find themselves at a competitive disadvantage, at the mercy of "free riders" who announce to the public that they prohibit insider trading but incur none of the enforcement costs.[40] Outlawing the practice might be worth doing simply because it enables corporations to do what is in all of their interests anyway — prohibit trading on inside information.

Finally, the claim that the fiduciary relationship is purely a "private" matter is misleading. The erosion of fiduciary duty caused by permitting insider trading has social costs as well as costs to the corporation and its shareholders. We have already noted a few of these. Frequent incidents of stock manipulation would cause a serious crisis in the market, reducing both its stability and efficiency. An increase in the circulation of false information would cause a general decline in the reliability of information and a corresponding decrease in investor trust. This would make the market less, not more efficient (as proponents of the practice claim). Deflecting interests away from the task of day-to-day management and toward the manipulation of information could also have serious negative social consequences. American business has already sustained much criticism for its failure to keep its mind on producing goods and services, and for its pursuit of "paper profits."

The notion of the fiduciary duty owed by managers and other employees to the firm and its shareholders has a long and venerable history in our society. Nearly all of our important activities require some sort of cooperation, trust, or reliance on others, and the ability of one person to act in the interest of another — as a fiduciary — is central to this cooperation. The role of managers as fiduciaries for firms and shareholders is grounded in the property rights of shareholders. They are the owners of the firm, and bear the residual risks, and hence have a right to have it managed in their interest. The fiduciary relationship also contributes to efficiency, since it encourages those who are willing to take risks to place their resources in the hands of those who have the expertise to maximize their usefulness. While this "shareholder theory" of the firm has often been challenged in recent years, this has been primarily by people who argue that the fiduciary concept should be widened to include other "stakeholders" in the firm.[41] I have heard no one argue that the notion of managers' fiduciary duties should be eliminated entirely, and that managers should begin working primarily for themselves.

III. CONCLUSION

I have argued that the real reason for prohibiting insider trading is that it erodes the fiduciary relationship that lies at the heart of our business organizations. The more frequently heard moral arguments based on fairness, property rights in information, and harm to ordinary investors, are not compelling. Of these, the fairness arguments seem to me the least persuasive. The claim that a trader must reveal everything that it is in the interest of another party to know, seems to hold up only when the other is someone to whom he owes a fiduciary duty. But this is not really a "fairness" argument at all. Similarly, the "misappropriation" theory is only persuasive if we can offer reasons for corporations not to assign the right to trade on inside information to their employees. I have found these in the fact that permitting insider trading threatens the fiduciary relationship. I do believe that lifting the ban against insider trading would cause harms to shareholders, corporations, and society at large. But again, these harms stem primarily from the cracks in the fiduciary relationship caused by permitting insider trading, rather than from actual trades with insiders. Violation of fiduciary duty, in short, is at the center of insider trading offenses, and it is with good reason that the Supreme Court has kept the fiduciary relationship at the forefront of its deliberations on insider trading.

Notes

1. See, for example, Douglas Frantz, *Levine & Co.* (Avon Books, NY, 1987).

2. This is certainly true of former SEC chair John Shad, one of the leaders of the crusade against insider trading, who recently donated millions of dollars to Harvard University to establish a program in business ethics. Also see Felix Rohatyn of the investment banking house Lazard Frères: " . . . [A] cancer has been spreading in our industry. . . . Too much money is coming together with too many young people who have little or no institutional memory, or sense of tradition, and who are under enormous economic pressure to perform in the glare of Hollywood-like publicity. The combination makes for speculative excesses at best, illegality at worst. Insider trading is only one result." *The New York Review of Books*, March 12, 1987.

3. An important exception is Lawson. 'The Ethics of Insider Trading', 11 *Harvard Journal of Law and Public Policy* 727 (1988).

4. Henry Manne, for example, whose book *Insider Trading and the Stock Market* stimulated the modern controversy over insider trading, has nothing but contempt for ethical arguments. See *Insider Trading and the Law Professors*, 23 Vanderbilt Law Review 549 (1969): "Morals, someone once said, are a private luxury. Carried into the area of serious debate on public policy, moral arguments are frequently either a sham or a refuge for the intellectually bankrupt." Or see Jonathan R. Macey, *Ethics, Economics and Insider Trading: Ayn Rand Meets the Theory of the Firm*, 11 Harvard Journal of Law and Public Policy 787 (1988): "[I]n my view the attempt to critique insider trading using ethical philosophy—divorced from economic analysis—is something of a non-starter, because ethical theory does not have much to add to the work that has already been done by economists."

5. *In re Cady, Roberts*, 40 SEC 907 (1961).

6. On tippees, see *Dirks v. SEC*, 463 US 646 (1983) at 659; on 'temporary insiders', see *Dirks v. SEC*, 103 S. Ct. 3255 (1983) at 3261 n. 14, and *SEC v. Musella* 578 F. Supp. 425.

7. See *Maternia v. SEC*, 725 F. 2d 197, involving a financial printer and the Winans case, involving the author of the *Wall Street Journal's* 'Heard on the Street' column, *Carpenter v. US*, 56 LW 4007; *U.S. v. Winans*, 612 F. Supp. 827. It should be noted that the Supreme Court has not wholeheartedly endorsed these further extensions of the rule against insider trading.

8. See Kaplan, '*Wolf v. Weinstein*: Another Chapter on Insider Trading', 1963 *Supreme Court Review* 273. For numerous other references, see Brudney, 'Insiders, Outsiders and Informational Advantages Under the Federal Securities Laws', 93 *Harvard Law Review* 339, n. 63.

9. See *Mitchell v. Texas Gulf Sulphur Co.*, 446 F. 2d 90 (1968) at 101; *SEC v. Great American Industries*, 407 F. 2d, 453 (1968) at 462; *Birdman v. Electro-Catheter Corp.*, 352 F. Supp. 1271 (1973) at 1274.

10. Saul Levmore, 'Securities and Secrets: Insider Trading and the Law of Contracts', 68 *Virginia Law Review* 117.

11. See Anthony Kronman, 'Mistake, Disclosure, Information, and the Law of Contracts', 7 *Journal of Legal Studies* 1 (1978). The Restatement (Second) of Torts § 551(2)e (Tent. Draft No. 11, 1965) gives an example which is a very similar example to the one above, involving a violin expert who buys a Stradivarius (worth $50,000) in a second-hand instrument shop for only $100.

12. It seems clear that sometimes failure to disclose can *be* a form of misrepresentation. Such could be the case, for example, when the seller makes a true statement about a product but fails to reveal a later change in circumstances which makes the earlier statement false. Or if a buyer indicates that he has a false impression of the product, and the seller fails to correct the impression. A plausible argument against insider trading would be that failure to reveal the information to the other party to the transaction allows a false impression of this kind to continue, and thus constitutes a form of deception. It is not clear to me, however, that insider trading is a situation of this kind.

13. An important question is whether trades involving the violation of *another kind* of fiduciary duty, constitute a violation of 10b-5. I address this second type of violation below.

14. *Chiarella v. US*, 445 U.S. 222, at 227–228; 232–233. Italics mine.

15. 445 US at 233. Italics mine.

16. The equal access argument is perhaps best stated by Victor Brudney in his influential article, 'Insiders, Outsiders and Informational Advantages Under the Federal Securities Laws', 93 *Harvard Law Review* 322.

17. Easterbrook, *Insider Trading, Secret Agents, Evidentiary Privileges, and the Production of Information*, 1981 Supreme Court Review 350.

18. Robert Frederick brought this point to my attention.

19. Manne, *Insider Trading and the Stock Market* (Free Press, New York, 1966), p. 75

20. Bill Shaw, 'Should Insider Trading Be Outside The Law', *Business and Society Review* 66, p. 34. See also Macey, 'From Fairness to Contract: The New Direction of the Rules Against Insider Trading', 13 *Hofstra Law Review* 9 (1984).

21. Easterbrook points out the striking similarity between insider trading cases and cases involving trade secrets, and cites *Perrin v. US*, 444 US 37 (1979), in which the court held that it was a federal crime to sell confidential corporate information.

22. Brudney, 'Insiders, Outsiders, and Informational Advantages', 344.

23. *U.S. v. Newman*, 664 F. 2d 17.

24. *U.S. v. Winans*, 612 F. Supp. 827. The Supreme Court upheld Winans' conviction, but was evenly split on the misappropriation theory. As a consequence, the Supreme Court has still not truly endorsed the theory, although several lower court decisions have been based on it. *Carpenter v. US*, 56 LW 4007.

25. Unless there is some other reason for forbidding it, such as that it harms others. See p. 176 first column below.

26. Easterbrook, 'Insider Trading As An Agency Problem', *Principles and Agents: The Structure of Business* (Harvard University Press, Cambridge, MA, 1985).

27. Carlton and Fischel, 'The Regulation of Insider Trading', 35 *Stanford Law Review* 857. See also Manne, *Insider Trading and the Stock Market*.

28. Manne, *Insider Trading and the Stock Market*; Carlton and Fischel, 'The Regulation of Insider Trading'.

29. Kenneth Scott, 'Insider Trading: Rule 10b-5, Disclosure and Corporate Privacy', 9 *Journal of Legal Studies* 808.

30. 'Disputes Arise Over Value of Laws on Insider Trading', *The Wall Street Journal*, November 17, 1986, p. 28.

31. One area that needs more attention is the impact of insider trading on the markets (and ordinary investors) of countries that permit the practice. Proponents of insider trading are fond of pointing out that insider trading has been legal in many overseas markets for years, without the dire effects predicted by opponents of the practice. Proponents reply that these markets are not as fair or efficient as U.S. markets, or that they do not play as important a role in the allocation of capital.

32. See Frank Easterbrook, 'Insider Trading as an Agency Problem'. I speak here as if the interests of the firm and its shareholders are identical, even though this is sometimes not the case.

33. Manne, *Insider Trading and the Stock Market*, p. 129.

34. For a more detailed discussion of the ineffectiveness of permitting insider trading as an incentive, see Roy Schotland, 'Unsafe at any Price: A Reply to Manne, *Insider Trading and the Stock Market*', 53 *Virginia Law Review* 1425.

35. Manne is aware of the "bad news" objection, but he glosses over it by claiming that bad news is not as likely as good news to provide large gains for insider traders. *Insider Trading and the Stock Market*, p. 102.

36. There are ways to avoid many of these objections. For example, Manne has suggested "isolating" non-contributors so that they cannot trade on the information produced by others. Companies could also forbid trading on "negative" information. The problem is that these piecemeal restrictions seem very costly — more costly than simply prohibiting insider trading as we do now. In addition, each restriction brings us farther and farther away from what proponents of the practice actually want: unrestricted insider trading.

37. Frank Easterbrook, 'Insider Trading as an Agency Problem.'

38. *Ibid.*

39. Penalties did not begin to become sufficient to discourage insider trading until the passage of the Insider Trading Sanctions Act in 1984. Some argue that they are still not sufficient, and that that is a good reason for abandoning the effort entirely.

40. Easterbrook, 'Insider Trading as an Agency Problem.'

41. See Freeman and Gilbert, *Corporate Strategy and the Search for Ethics* (Prentice-Hall, Englewood Cliffs, NJ, 1988).

DISCUSSION QUESTIONS

1. Shaw points out that some insider trading seems inevitable. "Even when insiders sit tight with the nonpublic information they possess," argues Shaw, "they at least know when not to sell and when not to buy." How do you evaluate this fact from an ethical perspective? Are the actions of buying on insider information and not buying on insider information morally equivalent?

2. Irvine argues that insider trading does not necessarily harm shareholders. What about the effect on other groups? Anheuser-Busch, for example, claimed that its acquisition of Campbell Taggart cost an extra $80 million because insider trading caused Campbell Taggart's stock to rise $5.00 per share. Was Anheuser-Busch harmed in a way that is ethically significant?

3. Werhane points out that one argument in favor of insider trading claims that insider information "*should* be and remain private" and "is the property of those engaged in the activity in question, and they should have the right to regulate its dissemination." One of Werhane's objections to insider trading, however, is based precisely on the idea of privacy of information. With which view of privacy do you agree?

4. Much of Moore's argument rests on the idea that insider trading violates a fiduciary duty. She considers the example of buying an antique chest worth $2,500 for $75 from an unknowing farmer, and she concludes that "while knowing how much I could sell the chest for in the city is in the interest of the farmer, I am not morally obligated to reveal it." Do you agree? Moore argues that "I am not morally obligated to tell those who deal with me *everything* that it would be in their interest to know." How do you determine when concealing information violates a duty toward someone else?

CASE 9.1

◆ ◆ ◆

The Small Investor

To most people, insider trading involves the kind of big-dollar conspiracies portrayed in the movie *Wall Street* and made legendary by former arbitrageur Ivan Boesky. Boesky's trading on inside information led to millions of dollars in profits for him and millions in losses to both corporations and individual investors. The FMC corporation claimed that Boesky's buying of FMC stock on inside information raised the costs of its recapitalization by an additional $225 million. And a group of Carnation shareholders argued that Boesky's $28.3 million profit from Nestlé's takeover of Carnation was made at their expense. They say that they sold their stock at "artificially depressed and stabilized prices" while Boesky, with knowledge of the upcoming takeover, kept his shares.

However, not all cases of insider trading involve big deals, huge profits, or even manipulation of the stock market itself. Thomas Hartnett, a former employee of General Electric, was accused by the SEC of making $8,472 in the sale of 10 call option contracts for RCA stock. (A call option gives the buyer the right to buy stock at a set price. Each of Hartnett's contracts entitled him to buy 100 shares of RCA stock.) On December 6, 1986, Hartnett learned from one of his employees at GE that the company intended to buy RCA. Hartnett asked the employee to make a copy of a binder that contained the details of GE's proposed offer; later that day, he ordered the call options from his broker at a cost of $1,805. The takeover was announced on December 11 and, predictably, the price of RCA stock increased. The following day, Hartnett sold the options for a little over $10,000. When accused by the SEC, Hartnett agreed to repay his profits and pay a penalty of the same amount. ◆

Discussion Questions

1. Is there anything unethical in Hartnett's actions? Was anyone hurt? If so, who? Was there a breach of "fiduciary responsibility," as Moore would claim?

2. Remember that Hartnett traded in options, not stock itself. Does this make any difference from an ethical standpoint?

3. In comparison to the huge amount of money some insiders made, we are dealing here with a relatively small amount. Another individual who traded on inside information about the same takeover made $2 million. Does that make what Hartnett did less serious from an ethical standpoint? Should they both receive the same punishment? If not, what would be the difference?

4. It could be argued that Hartnett was singled out to be an example for other small insiders. One SEC official stated that Hartnett's case "should disabuse people of the notion that they can trade in a relatively small quantity of stock or options and not be noticed." If this were part of the SEC's motivation in prosecuting Hartnett, how does it affect your assessment of the case or of the penalty?

5. Hartnett's employee was not charged with wrongdoing by the SEC, but did he do anything morally wrong by divulging the upcoming takeover and acceding to Hartnett's request for a copy of the details of GE's offer? Should he be punished as well?

Sources

"Carnation Investors Are Seeking Damages from Boesky Scandal," *Wall Street Journal*, February 24, 1987, 5.

Conlin, Kevin, "$2.1 Million Penalty in Insider Case," *New York Times*, August 8, 1986, D1, D4.

Kotlowitz, Alex, "FMC Charges Boesky's Trading Raised Costs of Recapitalization $225 Million," *Wall Street Journal*, December 19, 1986, 8.

Power, William, "Former GE Executive Accused by SEC of Insider Trading in RCA Takeover," *Wall Street Journal*, September 9, 1986, 7.

CASE 9.2

◆ ◆ ◆

Printers and Reporters

Two of the most controversial insider trading cases center around individuals who were neither arbitrageurs nor people directly associated with the companies whose stock they traded. Vincent Chiarella worked as a printer for a financial printing company and R. Foster Winans was a writer for the *Wall Street Journal*.

Chiarella worked for Pandick Press, a printing company specializing in highly sensitive documents connected with upcoming takeovers and mergers. Despite Pandick's precautions to keep even its printers unaware of companies' identities, Chiarella was able to guess takeover targets correctly five times. He backed up his hunches with investments in the target companies and made $30,000. The SEC forced Chiarella to return his profits to the people who sold him the stock. Because Chiarella had nonpublic market information, argued the SEC, he should be regarded as a corporate insider. He therefore should have disclosed what he knew to the shareholders whose stock he was buying, and failure to do so constituted fraud and deception. The SEC also claimed that Chiarella "misappropriated," that is, stole, information from his employer. Pandick had signs around the office saying that trading on information from documents being printed was both illegal and against company rules. Chiarella claimed, however, that he was simply making calculated guesses and could just as easily have been wrong as right. The Supreme Court ultimately overturned Chiarella's conviction and ruled that he was an outsider, not an insider, and had no special relationship of trust and confidence with those from whom he bought the shares. The Court also argued that it could not rule on whether a conviction under the "misappropriation" theory was legitimate because the prosecution had failed to present this theory during the trial.

R. Foster Winans wrote a column of stock tips entitled "Heard on the Street" for the *Wall Street Journal,* and he sold advance information about stories he planned to write to several investors. Winans made about $30,000; his associates, who traded on the information before Winans's columns were published, netted nearly $700,000. Winans was charged with breaking a fiduciary duty to his employer and, like Chiarella, with stealing inside information. His employer had policies prohibiting the divulging of information from stories before they were published and barring employees from trading in the stock of companies about which they were reporting. Winans's attorney, however, argued that what his client sold was not inside information about companies but gossip and rumors available to anyone on Wall Street. Winans's conviction on mail and wire fraud was upheld by the Supreme Court, but the Court's failure to clearly endorse misappropriation leaves that charge controversial. ◆

Discussion Questions

1. What do you think of Chiarella's actions? Should he be regarded as an insider or not?

2. Even if, as the Supreme Court argued, Chiarella had no special relationship with the shareholders of the companies in whose stocks he traded, what was his relationship with the companies who hired the printing company he worked for? Did he have a fiduciary duty that was violated by his "guessing"?

3. Was the information that Chiarella used rightfully the private property of Pandick and not his? Was his using it the same as stealing?

4. Did Chiarella really do anything morally wrong? Was anyone hurt by his actions?

5. Would your assessment of this case differ if Chiarella actually knew which companies were involved in the upcoming mergers? Does it matter that he claimed to be taking an educated guess that could have been wrong?

6. What about Winans's case? He too is not an insider the way that a CEO, director, or corporate employee is, but are his responsibilities the same as theirs?

7. What moral obligation does he owe to his employer?

8. Was anyone harmed in his case? Investors? Companies? Fellow employees? The *Wall Street Journal* claimed that it and its parent company, Dow Jones, were harmed. Do you agree? If a newspaper's reputation is harmed, does this lead to any tangible damage?

9. Winans concedes that what he did was the result of bad judgment, but do you think it was also morally wrong?

Sources

"Did the Winans Decision Go Too Far?," *Business Week*, July 8, 1985, 29–30.

"A Duty to Disclose?," *Newsweek*, September 10, 1984, 64.

Glaberson, William B, "The Winans Case: The Law Is on Trial, Too," *Business Week*, April 15, 1985, 142.

Greenhouse, Linda, "Supreme Court Rules for Printer," *New York Times*, March 19, 1980, D1, D18.

"The Journal Bares Its Soul," *Newsweek*, April 16, 1984, 74–75.

"Strict Views of the Law," *Newsweek*, March 31, 1980, 49.

"Supreme Court Ruling Clarified," *New York Times*, March 25, 1980, D2.

"Too Much Was Heard on the Street," *Newsweek*, April 9, 1984, 72.

"Trouble on the Street," *Newsweek*, February 4, 1985, 59.

Yang, Catherine, "Insider Trading: The High Court Hasn't Ended the Confusion," *Business Week*, November 30, 1987, 34.

ADDITIONAL READINGS

Lawson, Gary, "The Ethics of Insider Trading," *Harvard Journal of Law and Public Policy*, 11, no. 3, (1988), 727–783.

Manne, Henry, *Insider Trading and the Stock Market* (New York: The Free Press, 1966).

Parkman, Allen M, Barbara C. George, and Maria Boss, "Owners or Traders: Who Are the Real Victims of Insider Trading?," *Journal of Business Ethics*, 7 (1988), 965–971.

Seligman, Daniel, "An Economic Defense of Insider Trading," *Fortune*, July 13, 1981, 72–82.

Werhane, Patricia H, "The Indefensibility of Insider Trading," *Journal of Business Ethics*, 10 (1992), 729–731.

CHAPTER 10

◆ ◆ ◆

Employee Rights

M any discussions of business ethics employ the language of "rights"—the right to privacy, the right to work, and the like. Some individuals have gone so far as to propose a Bill of Rights for employees. Does it make sense to speak of a special set of employee rights? If so, what are they?

David Ewing proposes a specific bill of rights for employees, and he is followed by three thinkers who offer arguments on specific aspects of the employee rights debate. Patricia Werhane rejects the doctrine of "employment at will." Anita Superson suggests that workers have the right to know about on-the-job hazards. And Robert Dahl pushes the claim for employee rights even further by advocating economic democracy. Tibor Machan, however, flatly denies the existence of a special set of workers' rights.

David W. Ewing

A PROPOSED BILL OF RIGHTS

What should a bill of rights for employees look like?
First, it should be presented in the form of clear and practical injunctions, not in the language of desired behavior or ideals.

In 1789, when James Madison and other members of the first U.S. Congress settled down to write the Bill of Rights (the first ten amendments to the Constitution), Madison insisted on using the imperative "shall" instead of the flaccid "ought," which had been used in the declarations of rights by the states, from which the ideas for the federal Bill of Rights were taken. For instance, where Virginia's historic Declaration of Rights of 1776 stated that "excessive bail ought not to be required," and where the amendments proposed in 1788 by Virginia legislators were identically worded, the amendment proposed by Madison (and later accepted) read: "Excessive bail shall not be required. . . ."

The imperative has precisely the same advantage in a bill of rights for members of a corporation, government bureau, university administration, or other organization. An analogy is a traffic light. It does not contain various shades of red but just one shade which means clearly and unequivocally, "Stop." Nor does a stop sign say "Stop If Possible" or "Stop If You Can." It says simply "Stop."

Second, as a general rule, it is wise to phrase a bill of rights in terms of negative injunctions rather than positive ones. A bill of rights does not aim to tell officials what they can do so much as it aims to tell them what they cannot do. It is not like the delegation of powers found in constitutions. Here again it is instructive to recall the writing of the federal Bill of Rights in 1789. Madison insisted that the positive grants of government powers had been well provided for in the main body of the Constitution and did not need to be reiterated in the first ten amendments.

In addition, a "Thou shalt not" type of commandment generally can be more precise than a "Thou shalt" type of commandment; the latter must be worded and interpreted to cover many possibilities of affirmative action. Since it is more precise, a "Thou shalt not" injunction is more predictable — not quite as predictable as a traffic light, but more so than most positive injunctions can be.

Also, since it is more limited, a negative injunction is less of a threat to the future use of executive (and legislative) powers. For instance, the injunction "Congress shall make no law respecting an establishment of religion" (first item in the U.S. Bill of Rights) inhibits Congress less, simply because it is so precise, than a positive command such as "Congress shall respect various establishments of religion" (rejected by the Founding Fathers when proposed in the 1789 discussions), which is more protean and expansible.

Third, an organization's bill of rights should be succinct. It should read more like a recipe in a cookbook than the regulations of the Internal Revenue Service. It is better to start with a limited number of rights that apply to familiar situations and that may have to be extended and amended in a few years than try to write a definitive listing for all time. Rights take time to ingest.

Fourth, a bill of rights should be written for understanding by employees and lay people rather than by lawyers and personnel specialists. It should not read like a letter from a credit company or a Massachusetts auto insurance policy. If an organization desires to make everything clear for experts, it could add a supplement or longer explanation that elaborates in technical terms on the provisions and clarifies questions and angles that might occur to lawyers.

Fifth, a bill of rights should be enforceable. Existence as a creed or statement of ideals is not enough. While creeds indeed may influence behavior in the long run, in the short run they leave too much dependent on good will and hope.

The bill of rights that follows is one person's proposal, a "working paper" for discussion, not a platform worked out in committee. . . . The slight variations in style are purposeful — partly to reduce monotony and partly to suggest different ways of defining employee rights and management prerogatives.

1. *No organization or manager shall discharge, demote, or in other ways discriminate against any employee who criticizes, in speech or press, the ethics, legality, or social responsibility of management actions.*

Comment: This right is intended to extend the U.S. Supreme Court's approach in the *Pickering* case to all employees in business, government, education, and public service organizations.

What this right does not say is as important as what it does say. Protection does not extend to employees who make nuisances of themselves or who balk, argue, or contest managerial decisions on normal operating and planning matters, such as the choice of inventory accounting method, whether to diversify the product line or concentrate it, whether to rotate workers on a certain job or specialize them, and so forth. "Committing the truth," as Ernest Fitzgerald called it, is protected only for speaking out on issues where we consider an average citizen's judgment to be as valid as an expert's — truth in advertising, public safety standards, questions of fair disclosure, ethical practices, and so forth.

Nor does the protection extend to employees who malign the organization. We don't protect individuals who go around ruining other people's reputations, and neither should we protect those who vindictively impugn their employers.

Note, too, that this proposed right does not authorize an employee to disclose to outsiders information that is confidential.

This right puts publications of nonunionized employees on the same basis as union newspapers and journals, which are free to criticize an organization. Can a free press be justified for one group but not for the other? More to the point still, in a country that practices democratic rites, can the necessity of an "underground press" be justified in any socially important organization?

2. *No employee shall be penalized for engaging in outside activities of his or her choice after working hours, whether political, economic, civic, or cultural, nor for buying products and services of his or her choice for personal use, nor for expressing or encouraging views contrary to top management's on political, economic, and social issues.*

Comment: Many companies encourage employees to participate in outside activities, and some states have committed this right to legislation. Freedom of choice of products and services for personal use is also authorized in various state statutes as well as in arbitrators' decisions. The third part of the statement extends the protection of the First Amendment to the employee whose ideas about government, economic policy, religion, and society do not conform with the boss's. It would also protect the schoolteacher who allows the student newspaper to espouse a view on sex education that is rejected by the principal. . . . , the staff pyschologist who endorses a book on a subject considered taboo in the board room, and other independent spirits.

Note that this provision does not authorize an employee to come to work "beat" in the morning because he or she has been moonlighting. Participation in outside activities should enrich employees' lives, not debilitate them; if on-the-job performance suffers, the usual penalties may have to be paid.

3. *No organization or manager shall penalize an employee for refusing to carry out a directive that violates common norms of morality.*

Comment: The purpose of this right is to take the rule of the *Zinman* case a step farther and afford job security (not just unemployment compensation) to subordinates who cannot perform an action because they consider it unethical or illegal. It is important that the conscientious objector in such a case hold to a view that has some public acceptance. Fad moralities — messages from flying saucers, mores of occult religious sects, and so on — do not justify refusal to carry out an order. Nor in any case is the employee entitled to interfere with the boss's finding another person to do the job requested.

4. *No organization shall allow audio or visual recordings of an employee's conversations or actions to be made without his or her prior knowledge and consent. Nor may an organization require an employee or applicant to take personality tests, polygraph examinations, or other tests that constitute, in his opinion, an invasion of privacy.*

Comment: This right is based on policies that some leading organizations have already put into practice. If an employee doesn't want his working life monitored, that is his privilege so long as he demonstrates (or, if an applicant, is willing to demonstrate) competence to do a job well.

5. *No employee's desk, files, or locker may be examined in his or her absence by anyone but a senior manager who has sound reason to believe that the files contain information needed for a management decision that must be made in the employee's absence.*

Comment: The intent of this right is to grant people a privacy right as employees similar to that which they enjoy as political and social citizens under the "searches and seizures" guarantee of the Bill of Rights (Fourth Amendment to the Constitution). Many leading organizations in business and government have respected the principle of this rule for some time.

6. *No employer organization may collect and keep on file information about an employee that is not relevant and necessary for efficient management. Every employee shall have the right to inspect his or her personnel file and challenge the accuracy, relevance, or necessity of data in it, except for personal evaluations and comments by other employees which could not reasonably be obtained if confidentiality were not promised. Access to an employee's file by outside individuals and organizations shall be limited to inquiries about the essential facts of employment.*

Comment: This right is important if employees are to be masters of their employment track records instead of possible victims of them. It will help to eliminate surprises, secrets, and skeletons in the clerical closet.

7. *No manager may communicate to prospective employers of an employee who is about to be or has been discharged gratuitous opinions that might hamper the individual in obtaining a new position.*

Comment: The intent of this right is to stop blacklisting. The courts have already given some support for it.

8. *An employee who is discharged, demoted, or transferred to a less desirable job is entitled to a written statement from management of its reasons for the penalty.*

Comment: The aim of this provision is to encourage a manager to give the same reasons in a hearing, arbitration, or court trial that he or she gives the employee when the cutdown happens. The written statement need not be given unless requested; often it is so clear to all parties why an action is being taken that no document is necessary.

9. *Every employee who feels that he or she has been penalized for asserting any right described in this bill shall be entitled to a fair hearing before an impartial official, board, or arbitrator. The findings and conclusions of the hearing shall be delivered in writing to the employee and management.*

Comment: This very important right is the organizational equivalent of due process of law as we know it in political and community life. Without due process in a company or agency, the rights in this bill would all have to be enforced by outside courts and tribunals, which is expensive for society as well as time-consuming for the employees who are required to appear as complainants and witnesses. The nature of a "fair hearing" is purposely left undefined here so that different approaches can be tried, expanded, and adapted to changing needs and conditions.

Note that the findings of the investigating official or group are not binding on top management. This would put an unfair burden on an ombudsperson or "expedited arbitrator," if one of them is the investigator. Yet the employee is protected. If management rejects a finding of unfair treatment and then the employee goes to court, the investigator's statement will weigh against management in the trial. As a practical matter, therefore, employers will not want to buck the investigator-referee unless they fervently disagree with the findings.

In Sweden, perhaps the world's leading practitioner of due process in organizations, a law went into effect in January 1977 that goes a little farther than the right proposed here. The new Swedish law states that except in unusual circumstances a worker who disputes a dismissal notice can keep his or her job until the dispute has been decided by a court.

Every sizable organization, whether in business, government, health, or another field, should have a bill of rights for employees. Only small organizations need not have such a statement — personal contact and oral communications meet the need for them. However, companies and agencies need not have identical bills of rights. Industry custom, culture, past history with employee unions and associations, and other considerations can be taken into account in the wording and emphasis given to different provisions.

For instance, Booz, Allen and Hamilton, the well-known consulting company, revised a bill of rights for its employees in 1976 (the list included several of the rights suggested here). One statement obligated the company to "Respect the right of employees to conduct their private lives as they choose, while expecting its employees' public conduct to reflect favorably upon the reputation of the Firm." The latter part of this provision reflects the justifiable concern of a leading consulting firm with outward appearances. However,

other organizations — a mining company, let us say, or a testing laboratory —
might feel no need to qualify the right of privacy because few of their employees
see customers.

In what ways can due process be assured? There are certain procedures that
the organization itself can establish. In addition, society can undertake to assure
due process for employees.

Patricia H. Werhane

EMPLOYEE AND EMPLOYER RIGHTS IN AN INSTITUTIONAL CONTEXT

The common law principle of Employment at Will (EAW) states that in the
absence of a specific contract or law, an employer may hire, fire, demote,
or promote any employee (not covered by contract or law) when that employer
wishes. The theory is that employers have rights — rights to control what
happens in the workplace. These include decisions concerning all business
operations, extending of course to the hiring and placement of employees.
Although EAW is a common-law doctrine, until recently it virtually dictated
employment relationships.

What are the justifications for EAW? How would one defend this idea?
EAW is sometimes justified on the basis of property rights. It is contended that
the rights to freedom and to property ownership are valid rights and that they
include the right to use freely and to improve what one owns. According to this
view, an employer has the right to dispose of her business and those who work
for that business (and thus affect it) as she sees fit. Instituting employee rights
such as due process or the protection of whistle blowers, for example, would
restrict an employer's freedom to do what she wishes with her business, thus
violating property rights.

In the twentieth century, employer property rights have changed. Businesses
are mainly corporations owned by a large number of changing shareholders and
managed by employees who usually own little or no stock in the company. The
board of directors represents the owner – shareholder interests, but most business decisions are in the hands of managers. Despite this division of ownership
from management, however, proprietory ownership rights of employers have
translated themselves into management rights. Contemporary management
sees itself as having the rights to control business and therefore to control
employment. From a utilitarian perspective, control of a company by its managers is thought of as essential for maximum efficiency and productivity. To
disrupt this would defeat the primary purpose of free enterprise organizations.
Moreover, according to its proponents, EAW preserves the notion of "freedom of contract," the right of persons and organizations to enter freely into
binding voluntary agreements (e.g., employment agreements) of their choice.

From Patricia H. Werhane, "Employee and Employer Rights in an Institutional Context," in
Ethical Theory and Business, 3rd ed., edited by Tom Beauchamp and Norman E. Bowie (Englewood
Cliffs, NJ: Prentice Hall, 1988), 267–271. Reprinted by permission of the author.

That managers see themselves in the role of proprietors is, of course, too simple a description. In complex organizations there is a hierarchy of *at-will* relationships. Each manager is an at-will employee, but sees himself as proprietor of certain responsibilities to the organization and as being in control of certain other employees whom the manager can dismiss at will, albeit within certain guidelines of legal restraint. That manager, in turn, reports to someone else who is herself an at-will employee responsible to another segment of the organization. These at-will relationships are thought to preserve equal employee and employer freedoms because, just as a manager can demote or fire an at-will employee at any time, so too an employee, any employee, can quit whenever he or she pleases for any reason whatsoever. Notice a strange anomaly here. Employees have responsibilities to their managers and are not free to make their own choices in the workplace. At the same time, employees are conceived of as autonomous persons who are at liberty to quit at any time.

Notice, too, that there is sometimes a sort of Social Darwinist theory of management functioning in many of these relationships. Managers are so-titled because it is felt that they are the most capable. By reason of education and experience and from the perspective of their position, they allegedly know what is best for the organization or the part of the organization they manage. This gives them the right to manage other employees. The employees they manage (who themselves may be managers of yet other employees) have roles within the organization to carry out the directives of their managers, and so on.

The employee–manager hierarchy of at-will employment relationships is both more complex and more simple in union–management relationships. It is more complex because often the relationship is specified or restricted by a number of well-defined rules for seniority, layoffs, dismissals, and so on. It is more simple because by and large union employees are *employees*, not managers. Their role responsibilities defined by hierarchical relationships are clear-cut, and those wishing to change or move up to management usually must give up union membership.

This oversimplified, crude, overstated, overview of hierarchical employment relationships in business may not currently exist in the ways I have described in any business. Yet such relationships are at least *implicit* in many businesses and perpetuated in the law by a continued management or employer-biased interpretation of the principle of EAW.

Despite the fact that the principle of EAW is defended on a number of grounds — including that it allegedly protects equal employee and manager freedoms, that it promotes efficiency, and that it preserves the notion of freedom of contract — EAW violates all of these for the following reasons. EAW does not preserve equal freedoms because in most employment relationships employer–managers are in positions of greater power than employees. This in itself does not undermine EAW, but the potential abuse of this power is what is at issue. Employees and managers allegedly have equal rights — rights to be fired or to quit at any time for any reason. But an at-will employee is seldom in a position within the law to inflict harm on an employer. Legally sanctioned at-will treatment by employers of employees can, however, harm employees. This is because when an employee is fired arbitrarily without some sort of grievance procedure, a hearing or an appeal, he cannot demonstrate that he was fired without good reason. Employees who have been fired have much more difficulty getting new jobs than those who have not been fired, even when that treatment was unjustified. Because arbitrarily fired employees are treated like those who deserved to lose their jobs, EAW puts such employees at an unfair disadvantage compared with other workers. The principle of EAW, then, does not preserve equal freedoms because it is to the advantage of the employer or manager and to the unfair disadvantage of the fired employee.

Worse, at-will practices violate the very right upon which EAW is allegedly based. Part of the appeal of EAW is that it protects the freedom of contract — the right to make employment agreements of one's choice. Abolishing EAW is coercive, according to its proponents, because this forces employers involuntarily to change their employment practices. But at-will employment practices too are or can be coercive. This is because when an employee is fired without sufficient reasons employers or managers place this person involuntarily in a personally harmful position unjustified by her behavior, a position that an employee would never choose. Thus the voluntary employment agreement according to which such practices are allowed is violated.

It is argued that EAW maximizes efficiency. But what is to prevent a manager from hiring a mentally retarded son-in-law or firing a good employee on personal grounds, actions that themselves damage efficiency? On a more serious level, if managers have prerogatives, these are based on a claim to the right to freedom — the freedom to conduct business as one pleases. But if this is a valid claim, then one must grant equal freedoms to everyone, including employees. Otherwise managers are saying that *they* have greater rights than other persons. This latter claim brings into question a crucial basis of democratic capitalism, namely that every person has *equal* rights, the most important of which is the equal right to freedom. The notion of equal rights does not necessarily imply that employees and managers have equal or identical prerogatives in business decision making or in managing a company. But what is implied is that the exercise of freedom requires a respect for the equal exercise of freedom by others, although the *kind* of exercises in each case may be different. EAW practices, then, are inconsistent practices because they do not preserve equal freedoms, they do not protect freedom of contract for both parties, and they do not guarantee efficiencies in the workplace. A number of thinkers contend that the principle should be abolished or disregarded in the law.

Interestingly, however, one can *defend* at least some employee rights from a consistent interpretation of the principle of EAW. This is because to be consistent the demands of EAW, principally the demand of management for the freedom to control business, require an equal respect for employee freedoms. In other words, if EAW is to be justified on the basis of the right to freedom, it can only be justified for that reason if it respects everyone's freedoms equally. Otherwise, managers' alleged freedoms are merely unwarranted licenses to do anything they please, even abridging employee rights, and thus have no moral or constitutional basis. Such equal respect for employee rights cannot always be interpreted as equal participation in management decisions. Extending and respecting employee freedoms requires balancing equal but not necessarily identical liberties. The free exercise of management employment decisions, however, does seem to require that employees be given reasons, publicly stated and verifiable, for management decisions that affect employees, including hiring and firing. In this way voluntary choices in the job market are truly equal to management employment choices. Moreover, freedom of choice in management decision making requires allowing legitimate whistle blowing, conscientious objection, and even striking without employer retaliation when an employee is asked to perform illegal, immoral, and/or socially dangerous jobs, or when such practices occur in the workplace. I am suggesting that a proper interpretation of EAW is not inconsistent with granting some employee rights. It is the misinterpretation of EAW that has served as a basis for the exercise of management prerogatives at the expense of employee rights.

Employers and managers, of course, will not always be happy to grant these freedoms to employees, because such freedoms are often seen as giving employees too many rights. Other managers identify extending employee freedoms with participatory management programs that, they argue, would abridge management responsibilities. Neither of these consequences, however, necessarily follows from extending employee rights. On the other hand, continuing the present imbalance of freedoms in the workplace perpetuates injustices. Worse, from the perspective of management this is a highly risky policy in an age of employee enlightenment and a concern for employee rights. Many managers are sympathetic to arguments defending employee rights. However, they fear that instituting employee rights in the workplace entails government regulation of and intervention in the affairs of business, all of which is intrusive, expensive, and time-consuming. But there is no reason why businesses cannot voluntarily institute employment reforms, and in the climate of a surging interest in employee rights, such voluntary actions would help prevent government intervention and regulation.

Turning to a second moral justification for employee rights, balancing employee and employer freedoms in the workplace is also justified because of what I shall call the reciprocal nature of employment relationships. Employment relationships, which are by and large hierarchical role relationships, tend to be destructive of employee rights, yet this need not be so, and in fact quite the contrary is required. The reasons for this are the following. In the workplace both management and employees have role responsibilities that are a source of job accountability. A person holding a job is held accountable for a certain performance; it is sometimes not considered unjust to dismiss someone for failure to perform his or her job even if the employer pays poorly and sometimes even if the employer does not respect other employee rights. Employee job accountability in this context is usually described as first-party duties of the employee to a manager or to the organization for whom one works. However, this description is incomplete. There are, in addition, duties on the part of the manager or the institution to the employee who is held accountable. These obligations arise in part from the role responsibilities of the party to whom an employee is answerable and in part because of the nature of the relationship. These obligations, which are often neglected in an analysis of accountability, are reciprocal or correlative obligations implied by role responsibility to the employee in question. This notion of reciprocity, I shall argue, is crucial in employment relationships.

The notion of reciprocity in any social relationship is grounded on the basic fact that each party is a person or a group of persons. As the philosopher Carol Gould puts it,

> Reciprocity may be defined as a social relation among agents in which each recognizes the other as an agent, that is, as equally free, and each acts

with respect to the other on the basis of a shared understanding and a free agreement to the effect that the actions of each with respect to the other are equivalent.[1]

This does not mean that each party must treat the other in the same way in every respect, but rather that each treats the other with equal respect and as equal possessors of rights and benefits. Because they are social relationships between persons or between persons and institutions developed by persons, accountability relationships entail this notion of reciprocity.

Reciprocity in accountability relationships operates in part, as follows. If I am accountable for my actions to a certain group or institution because of my role in that group or institution, this accountability implicitly assumes a reciprocal accountability to me on the part of the institution to whom I am answerable. The obligations in each relationship are not necessarily contractual, but the strength of my role obligations depends at least in part on equally forceful, though obviously not identical, role obligations of the second party to me. And if no such reciprocal obligations exist, or if they are not respected, my accountability to that individual, group, or institution weakens.

What this brief analysis of role accountability suggests in the workplace is that when taking a job an employee has responsibilities connected with that job, responsibilities that are often only implicitly stated. At the same time, accountability does not consist merely of first-party duties of employees to employers or managers; it is also defined in reciprocal relationships with the party to whom one is accountable. The reason for this is that employee–employer relationships are both social and contractual arrangements. They are social because they are relationships entered into between persons or between persons and organizations created and run by persons. They are at least implicitly contractual ones voluntarily entered into and freely dissolvable by both parties. Therefore, if employees are accountable to managers or employers, managers or employers are also accountable for upholding their part of the agreement by being reciprocally accountable, albeit in different ways, to their employees.

The reciprocal nature of employee–employer relationships entails some important employee rights, in particular the rights to fair treatment and respect. What might constitute such fair treatment and respect? Obviously, fair pay or a living wage in exchange for work is an essential part of just treatment in the workplace. But if, in addition to working, employees are expected to respect and be fair to their employers, then employers have reciprocal obligations that go beyond merely offering fair pay. Employee respect demands from a manager a correlative respect for employee privacy, employee information, and for due process in the workplace, even for at-will employees.

Due process demands not that employees not be dismissed, but rather that any employer action meet impartial standards of reasonableness, the same sort of reasonableness expected of employees. Similarly, if an employee is to respect his or her employer and the decisions of that employer, the employer needs to honor the privacy of the employee as a human being, including protecting with confidentiality personnel information and respecting the privacy of employee activities outside the workplace. Respect for the employee also involves keeping the employee well-informed about his or her job, the quality of his or her work, and the stability of the company. This is a two-pronged responsibility. It entails not only the requirement that all employees are equally entitled to information, but the recognition that all employees actually in fact *have* such information. Employees have rights not merely to be informed but also to be communicated with in ways they understand.

The employee rights just enumerated — the rights to privacy, to employee information, and the right to due process — are moral rights that result from the nature of role accountability in the workplace. Like the right to freedom that is implied by a consistent interpretation of EAW, these rights are moral rather than legal rights, so employers need not respect them. But if the reciprocal requirements of employment accountability relationships are not met by employers or managers, those employers or managers undermine the basis for employee accountability in the workplace.

Note

1. Carol Gould, "Economic Justice, Self-Management and the Principle of Reciprocity," in *Economic Justice*, ed. Kenneth Kipnis and Diana T. Meyers (Totowa, N.J.: Rowman and Allanheld, 1985), pp. 213–214.

Anita M. Superson

THE EMPLOYER–EMPLOYEE RELATIONSHIP AND THE RIGHT TO KNOW

I

Dangers lurk in the workplace. It has been reported that more than 2,200,000 workers are disabled, and more than 14,000 are killed annually as a result of accidents on the job.[1] The causes include safety hazards such as fires, explosions, electrocution, dangerous machinery, as well as health hazards such as loud noise, harmful dusts, asbestos particles, toxic gases, carcinogens, and radiation.[2] The fact that these and other dangers exist is problem enough; but even more problematic is that an employee's awareness of such dangers, prior to being exposed to them, is often minimal, at best. If an employee is to have any say in what happens to his person, what needs to be established — at least more firmly than it is currently — is an employee's[3] right to know about the presence of health and safety hazards in the workplace.

In what follows, I shall first examine the current status of an employee's right to know. I shall argue that it is the very nature of the employer–employee relationship that gives rise to an employee's limited awareness of on-the-job hazards. Next, I shall offer what I think are the philosophical justifications for an employee's right to know. Finally, in light of these justifications, I shall argue

From *Business and Professional Ethics Journal*, 3, no. 1 (1983), 45–58. Reprinted by permission of the author.

that establishing an employee's right to know will, in fact, benefit both the employee and the employer, and be one step toward achieving a fiduciary relationship.

Throughout this essay, I compare the employer–employee relationship to that of the physician and patient. Although there are some disparities between the two, the comparison is helpful in that it points out that the moral basis for establishing a right to know for a patient is the same as for an employee, yet the two are not accorded the same recognition by the law. To show that the right to know for patients is not recognized as being the same for employees, yet that it is based on the same philosophical foundation for the same reasons, only strengthens the argument for establishing a right to know in the workplace.

II

In the medical setting a person's right to know about risks involved in different kinds of treatment has been recognized under the guise of informed consent. Recently, there have been many attempts in the law and in various health codes to ensure that patients have given informed consent to medical treatments or experimentation. In *Canterbury* v. *Spence*, 1972, Circuit Court Judge Spotswood W. Robinson III ruled that since "every human being of adult years and sound mind has a right to determine what shall be done with his own body," a physician has a "duty of reasonable disclosure of the choices with respect to proposed therapy and the dangers inherently and potentially involved."[4] Similarly, the American Hospital Association's *Patient's Bill of Rights* (1973) states that "The patient has the right to receive from his physician information necessary to give informed consent prior to the start of any procedure and/or treatment."[5] Again, the Nuremberg Code, which focuses on guidelines used in human experimentation carried out in Nazi Germany, specifies that the human subject "should have sufficient knowledge and comprehension of the elements of the subject matter involved as to enable him to make an understanding and enlightened decision."[6] These and other such examples show that through informed consent, a patient's or research subject's right to know about the risks and hazards involved in medical procedures is firmly entrenched. We shall see later that this right is protected by the law. Though the amount of information given to patients may vary among physicians, consent forms must be signed by the patient or by his next of kin. This is true for all patients undergoing most invasive forms of treatment (e.g., surgery).

But the headway that has been made in the medical setting is, unfortunately, unparalleled in the workplace. It was not until 1980 that the Occupational Safety and Health Administration (OSHA) of the United States Department of Labor established the legal right of an employee to "access to employer maintained exposure and medical records relevant to employees exposed to toxic substances and harmful physical agents."[7] In 1983, OSHA issued a final rule requiring

> chemical manufacturers and importers to assess the hazards of chemicals which they produce and import, and all employers having workplaces in the manufacturing division . . . to provide information to their employees concerning hazardous chemicals by means of hazard communica-

tion programs including labels, material safety data sheets, training, and access to written records. In addition, distributors of hazardous chemicals are required to ensure that containers they distribute are properly labeled, and that a material safety data sheet is provided to their customers. . . .[8]

On the same note, the National Institute for Occupational Safety and Health (NIOSH) reported that workers had the right to know whether or not they were exposed to hazardous chemical and physical agents regulated by the Federal Government.[9] Finally, the National Labor Relations Act (NLRA) recognizes a labor union's right to information that is relevant to a collective bargaining issue, including safety rules and practices.[10] Although these regulations are a step in the direction of securing a worker's right to know, they are insufficient.

First, though the OSHA rulings recently have been expanded from simply permitting access to an employer's exposure and medical records to requiring assessment of the hazards of chemicals and providing information about such chemicals to an employee by means of labels and material safety data sheets, they fail to extend protection through information to many workers. The 1983 regulation applies only to employees in the manufacturing division, yet does not apply to employees in other divisions such as mining, construction, trade, etc. The reasoning underlying OSHA's restriction to manufacturing is that it has determined that the employees in this division "are at the greatest risk of experiencing health effects from exposure to hazardous chemicals."[11] The agency thus hoped to regulate that sector in which it could be most effective for the greatest number of employees. So, although warning labels and safety data sheets, as well as the assessment of hazards which they necessitate, certainly are positive steps toward securing a worker's right to know, they apply to about only fifty percent of all workers.[12]

Second, the OSHA rulings apply only to employees which the agency defines as "a current employee, a former employee, or an employee being assigned or transferred to work where there will be exposure to toxic substances or harmful physical agents."[13] The rulings exclude provision of information regarding hazards to the *prospective* employee. This is problematic because the prospective employee is often faced with a similar choice, that is, the choice of whether or not to take on a job which entails working in hazardous conditions. Yet providing this information to prospective employees may raise problems in itself. Employers may find this too time-consuming a task to perform for *each* person contending for a position; or, they may feel an obligation to provide this information only to employees since it is this group of persons which has pledged some degree of loyalty to the company. These problems, though, should be worked around for the sake of the prospective employee who will avoid the trouble of committing himself to a job if he knows in advance that the hazardous working conditions outweigh the benefits of taking on the job.

Third, the OSHA rulings do not apply to all safety and health hazards. The 1980 ruling regulates "toxic substances and harmful physical agents," and the 1983 ruling regulates "hazardous chemicals." Clearly, these rulings do not account for a whole spectrum of on-the-job hazards, some of which were mentioned at the outset of this essay. A worker's right to know of these hazards has yet to be firmly established.

This is not to imply that an employer has no responsibility to keep his workplace safe. In fact, in 1970, the Occupational Safety and Health Act

(OSHAct) was passed, establishing safety and health standards for all workers other than those employed by federal, state, and local governments. The Act requires an employer to ensure that his workplace is "free from recognized hazards that are causing or likely to cause death or serious physical harm."[14] But this act, too, is insufficient. It has been reported[15] that the Act protects against only "recognized hazards," defined as those which "can be detected by the common human senses, unaided by testing devices, and which are generally known in the industry to be hazards." Indeed, this leaves many hazards unaccounted for. It is those hazards not prohibited by law about which the employee may not be informed.

The NIOSH report is inadequate in similar ways. The Institute recognizes a worker's right to know only whether or not they were *exposed* to hazardous chemical and physical agents regulated by the Federal Government. Its inadequacies are that it does not recognize a right to know of hazards prior to exposure to them, and that like the OSHA rulings, it applies only to chemical and physical agents, rather than all on-the-job hazards.

Finally, the National Labor Relations Act accords some protection to employees who belong to labor unions but is also limited. It established that labor unions had a right to "information that is in the hands of the employer and is relevant to bargainable issues."[16] An employee's right to know about hazardous working conditions is usually recognized as being "relevant to bargainable issues." But what sometimes occurs is a conflict between the employee's right to know and the company's right to keep trade secrets. A trade secret has been defined under the Restatement of Torts as "any formula, device, or information, used in a business which gives its holder a competitive advantage over those without the secret."[17] Now if a labor union requests information about job hazards, but this information will expose an employer's trade secrets, thereby jeopardizing his competitive advantage, the employer need not necessarily release this information. And in different cases, the law has favored both sides.

In *Borden Chemical*, an administrative law judge of the National Labor Relations Board determined that Borden had refused to bargain in good faith when it failed to release information to the labor union. It was then ordered to supply the information to the union. The reason behind the ruling was that Borden failed to show that disclosure of the information would damage its competitive position.[18] Essentially, Borden failed to show how its trade secrets would reach its competitors.[19] In *Colgate-Palmolive*, however, an administrative law judge ruled that the employer was obliged to reveal a list of chemicals in the workplace *except* those constituting trade secrets.[20] Colgate-Palmolive apparently showed how it would be disadvantaged were its trade secrets to be revealed. We can surmise from these two cases and from the OSHA and NIOSH rulings that an employee's right to know is not accorded full protection by the law, and, in fact, may be denied by the law.

III

Why is the right to know in the workplace not firmly grounded? It is the argument of this section that protection of such a right is limited because of the very nature of the employer–employee relationship.

This relationship can be best defined as a nonfiduciary one, meaning that there is little or no trust on behalf of each party in the actions of the other party. This lack of trust stems from the expectations each party has for forming a personal relationship. In most cases, the expectations dictate a non-personal interaction. The employer often does not have a psychological investment in his employees. The employee often feels the same; he views himself as a person for hire, whose function is to perform a certain job for the company or institution in exchange for wages and perhaps a few fringe benefits. If the employee does not like his job for whatever reason, he is free to leave. The employer is also free (for the most part) to fire any employee who is not performing his job in what the employer judges to be a favorable way. As a result, many employees remain with a certain company for only a short period of time, thus making it difficult to come to know their employer personally, if this be at all possible.

Both the employer and employee normally do not enter into their relation thinking that they can trust each other to look out for the other's best interests. Probably the only form of trust existent between the two parties is that the employer will pay the employee a wage that at least matches the work he puts out, and that the employee will perform the job he is asked to do in a way that is normally expected. These are the roles both the employer and employee expect each other to take on. It would be difficult to establish a fiduciary relationship under such expectations. What adds to the difficulty is that often the employer and employee do not even know each other at any kind of personal level. I ask rhetorically: How can a fiduciary relationship be established if no relationship has been established?

Another feature of the employer–employee relationship which adds to its nonfiduciary nature is the reasons both the employee and the employer have for entering into their relationship. The employee enters a relationship with his employer primarily for monetary reasons; he seeks employment in order to earn wages with which he can secure the goods he needs to live. The employer, on the other hand, enters a relationship primarily for the sake of profit-making. His position in respect to that of the employee is one of power. It derives its power from the fact that the employer offers the employee a benefit—wages —if he accepts and performs a job. The employer stands to benefit directly from his employee. He needs a certain job to be done; the company's profits depend upon whether the task is accomplished. And the financial success of the company is directly related to the employer.

Both the expectations of the employee and employer, as well as the reasons for each entering into the relationship, make it likely that an employer would use his employee merely as a means to his own end, to borrow a notion from Kant. That is, the employer, seeking to augment his profits (the end), may use the employee merely as a means to achieve that end. One way in which he could do this is to fail to inform an employee about hazardous work conditions. Failure to inform an employee about these hazards is to deny him information that may affect his decision to stay on the job. And by remaining on the job, the employee works in part for the employer's benefit, that is, to increase the company's profits. In this way, the employee is used as a means to the employer's end.

More specifically, if the expectations of both the employer and employee of each other are as I have described, it is easy for the former to use the latter as a means to an end because being so far removed on a personal level from the employee, he does not feel a sense of obligation towards the employee's welfare. All he has invested in the relationship is that the job gets done. And since the employee does not view the relationship as a fiduciary one, he has no basis for trusting the employer to ensure that the workplace is free from hazards, or at least to inform him of the hazards that do exist. Indeed it would be nice for the employer to do either; yet the employee probably does not expect it, and certainly cannot trust his employer to do so.

And, if the reasons the employer and employee have for entering their relationship are as I have described, this is another reason why an employer may use his employee merely as a means to his own end. If the employer is aware of the power he holds over his employee, that is, that he to a large extent controls the employee's means of livelihood, he may feel no obligation to inform the employee about on-the-job hazards. In fact, somewhat ironically, the employer may even go so far as to view the employee as using *him*, the *employer*, as a means to an end. This belief is based upon the fact that the employee may take on a job solely for the purpose of obtaining money, perhaps with minimum effort put forth, and that the employee is free to leave when he so desires. If the employer has this attitude toward his employee, it becomes easier for him not to inform the employee of hazards in the workplace.

The nature of the employer–employee relationship differs from that of the physician–patient in these two respects. Specifically, the expectations of the physician and patient are of a much more trusting nature. Oftentimes, the physician and patient have established a personal relationship; they, for example, know somewhat about each other's life-styles, values, etc. Patients generally expect and trust their physician to act in their best interests. They expect that physicians will inform them of the hazards and risks involved in various medical treatments, and that together they will arrive at a decision about what is the best course of action to take. And if the physician fails to inform his patient about these hazards and risks, the patient usually assumes that the information was withheld for his, the patient's, own benefit.

Furthermore, the reasons for the patient and physician entering a relationship are different from that of the employer and employee. Patients seek the advice of a physician because, simply put, they want to be treated for an illness. They expect that the physician will do this, and will give the patient information on forms of treatment. This is what the patient pays for, and thus expects to receive. The physician, in turn, should feel that he has an obligation to provide this information to the patient, unless he can justify withholding it.

The physician's reasons for entering the relationship are different from the employer's. Rather than being solely, or at least primarily, profit-motivated, physicians often view their role as one of benefitting the sick. Certainly there are many physicians who enter the profession for monetary reasons: I do not wish to deny this. Yet, as any physician would admit, there are easier ways to make money. Still, the physician, like the employer, is in a power position. But the source of the physician's power is different. He does not stand to benefit from performing a certain therapy on any *particular* patient (unless, of course, the patient is indeed unique), for it is likely that another patient will choose to undergo that treatment. And, more importantly, physicians will always have patients seeking their services because persons will always get sick. Unless a physician is so inadequate, he can rest assured that he will be in business for a long time. This gives him less reason to deny patients information they need concerning the hazards of treatment. Thus, a physician's power position is not as threatened by loss of profit as is an employer's. He therefore has less reason than an employer to use a person merely as a means to his own end.

Moreover, an employer's reasons for withholding information are often different from those of the physician. While the physician may feel he is acting in the patient's best interests (whether or not he is certainly is open to debate) when he withholds information concerning the risks of treatment, this is not often the case with the employer. The employer withholds information about on-the-job hazards not because he wishes to protect the employee, or to act in the employee's best interests, but because he wants to protect his *own* interests. He wants the company to profit, and this may be possible only if certain hazardous assignments are made. The employer may feel that he is justified in withholding information about risks from the employee. After all, the employee does not have to stay on *this* job; he is free to leave. The employer's reasons for withholding information are thus, unlike those of most physicians, self-interested.

It is these features of the employer–employee relationship, namely, the expectations of both parties, their reasons for entering into the relationship, and the employer's reasons for withholding information, which all contribute to the nonfiduciary nature of this relationship. These features may, of course, all be a result of the capitalist system. If this be so, some persons may argue that the very nature of the employer–employee relationship can be changed only by changing the socio-economic system. I believe this is false, and in Section V I will argue that establishing an employee's right to know will, in fact, make headway in changing the relationship into one that is fiduciary in nature.

IV

We have seen that the nature of the employer–employee relationship is such that it is difficult to establish an employee's right to know. Employers, on the one hand, find little or no reason to give their employees information about hazards in the workplace. In turn, employees find little or no reason to expect to receive this information. The differences in the nature of the relationship are, in all probability, responsible for the dissimilarities in the establishment of the right to know. But should this difference exist? Is there a difference in the choices faced by a person as patient versus a person as employee that will justify the difference in the recognition of the right to know?

I suggest that there is not. Although many disparities exist between the relationships, an important similarity grounds the right to know. It is this: in both cases, the person wants to know the dangers involved for the *same* reasons. He wants to know the risks that may be incurred to his body so that he can decide whether or not to expose himself to those risks. The information is needed for him to make a reasonable choice.

In both situations, the moral basis of the right to know lies in the principle of autonomy. Much talk has been generated about this principle since Mill and Kant recognized its importance. Although the literature offers a variety of definitions, this principle is usually defined in such a way as to include the notion of making one's own decisions affecting one's own life without coercion from others. In order for one to make a responsible decision, he must be

informed about the choices with which he is faced. Just as a patient must be
informed about the risks involved in a certain treatment in order for him to
decide if he wants that treatment, an employee, too, must be informed about the
hazards involved in working under certain conditions if he is to make a responsible, autonomous choice about whether or not to subject his person to such
risks. In either case, if such information is not disclosed, the person's autonomy
has been placed in jeopardy.

The choice faced by both the patient and the employee is one of whether or
not to subject one's person to risk of harm. It may be objected that the harms
which may be incurred in the workplace are less serious than those which may
be incurred in the medical setting. But this is simply not true. The harms
incurred in the workplace may be just as serious, and may not be as immediate as
those incurred in the medical setting. For example, side-effects from an operation or from taking certain drugs are often known by the patient and/or his
physician soon after they are incurred. Harms resulting from on-the-job hazards, however, often take considerable time to manifest themselves, and often
require long-term exposure to take effect. For example, chronic berylliosis,
constituted by coughing, dyspnea, and anorexia, may appear years after exposure to beryllium.[21] And cancer may take years to manifest itself after exposure
to coal tar, paraffin, asbestos, vinyl chloride, and benzene. Other toxic materials
do not produce side-effects in the exposed person, but instead in his or her
children. These are either mutagenic in nature, in which case they change the
genetic makeup of the offspring, or teratogenic, in which case they are capable
of causing birth defects in the offspring.[22] This is not to imply that all harms
incurred in the medical setting are immediate, and those incurred on the job are
made manifest years after exposure; instead, the point is that many do follow
this pattern.

Because the harms incurred in the workplace often are made manifest years
later, it is more difficult for an employer to face liability charges. In the medical
realm, patients can be awarded damages either in battery or in negligence.
Traditionally, patients can sue physicians for damages in battery if they are
touched, treated, or researched upon without consent.[23] In a British Columbia
case, it was reported[24] that a patient who suffered loss of smell and partial loss of
taste after surgery was awarded damages in battery because she was unaware of
these risks at the time of her consent. In America, failure to disclose risks to
patients "is considered a breach of the physician's general duty of care to give
reasonable information and advice to his patient."[25] To be awarded damages in
battery, the patient need only establish that "what was done differed substantially from that to which he assented."[26]

Patients can sue also for damages in negligence. In Canada, it is reported that
the physician should inform the patient of the nature and seriousness of treatment lest he be held negligent. The duty in negligence "is based on the nature of
the physician – patient relationship as a trust, thus imposing a basic requirement
of honesty upon the physician."[27] In order for a physician to be found negligent,
the patient must show that there was a breach of the duty of disclosure and that
he, the patient, would not have consented had the required disclosure been
given, and that he suffered a loss as a result.[28]

Although a patient can sue for damages in either battery or negligence, an
employee has no such privilege. Establishment of workmen's compensation has

prevented the right to sue in tort.[29] Prior to the establishment of workmen's compensation, employees could settle under tort law and receive payments for both loss of income as well as for "pain and suffering." Workmen's compensation statutes, however, include payment for loss of income, but only limited payment for "pain and suffering."[30] One source reports that *no* payment for pain and suffering is included.[31] Thus, employers do not have to pay for the full consequences of their negligence. Employees themselves must shoulder most of the burden of costs for employer negligence. This seems especially unjust when we are reminded of the fact that an employee's right to know is not firmly established.

One basis, then, for establishing a right to know in the workplace is that it ensures that an employee is given information necessary for him to be able to make a choice which may significantly affect his life. Informing an employee of workplace hazards puts him in the position of deciding whether or not he wants to be exposed to hazards, and thereby is one step in the direction of promoting his autonomy. Establishment of a right to know is especially important for the worker since he does not have much recourse against his employer if damages ensue.

Another basis for establishing this right lies in the notion of fairness of contract. When a person is hired for a job, there is an implicit contract made between the employer and employee, the terms of which spell out that person X will do job A and will be paid by person Y. This contract requires, like any fair contract, that both parties know what they are contracting to. It is insufficient that an employee know he is consenting to do a certain job in a certain way at a certain pace, and so on. If hazards which may produce harm to his person are involved, he should be made aware of them before he enters the contract. If he is not made aware of the hazards, and enters the contract with the employer, he is not giving fully informed consent to the relevant terms of the contract. The contract is thus unfair.

A third basis for establishing an employee's right to know is partly economic, partly moral. It lies in Milton Friedman's notion of business' social responsibility, namely, "to use its resources and engage in activities designed to increase its profits so long as it stays within the rules of the game, which is to say, engages in open and free competition, without deception or fraud."[32] The moral justification for the right to know, using Friedman's terms of business' social responsibility, lies in his normative judgment that business should not engage in deceptive practices. Though Friedman does not spell out what this entails, surely withholding information from the prospective employee — information which is likely to influence his decision — is a deceptive practice, prohibited even on Friedman's libertarian analysis of business in the free market system.

An economic justification for the right to know also can be found in Friedman and other free market advocates. It is this: in order to ensure that the free market really *is* free, persons should be able to enter the occupation of their choosing (at least insofar as they meet the qualifications). This choice must be informed. If information about job hazards is withheld, the choice will not be fully informed. And if the choice is not fully informed, it is not truly free. Thus, ignoring the right to know, besides violating moral principles such as autonomy and fairness of contract, violates one of the fundamental economic bases of the free market system.

V

If an employee's right to know becomes firmly established, certain implications are likely to follow. On the negative side, the employer will be faced with the difficult task of determining how much and what kind of information ought to be given to the employee. The employer will have to devote time and effort to find out just what hazards exist, and to convey the results of his findings to the employee. And if the risks involved in taking on a certain job are very high, or very serious, the employer may have difficulty in hiring someone for the job. Also, the company's trade secrets undoubtedly will sometimes be revealed.

While I do not wish to diminish the inconvenience these implications bring to the employer, none is too important to override the employee's right to know. Indeed, there certainly are ways to lessen the inconvenience while still bringing about the desired effects.

More importantly though, it is reasonable to assume that both parties are likely to benefit by establishing an employee's right to know.

It benefits the employee in several ways. First, since the employer will have to ascertain what are hazards in the workplace, he may eliminate at least some of them for the sake of attracting employees. Thus, the environment may be safer for the employee. Second, if the employee is presented with the relevant information about on-the-job hazards, it places into the hands of the *employee* the informed decision of whether or not to accept a position. The employee can then make his *own* choice of whether or not to expose himself to those hazards. Moreover, informing the employee of hazards in the workplace ensures him that the contract made with his employer is fair and not based upon deception. In these ways, it establishes trust in the employer.

The employer, too, benefits. Once he has given such information to his employee, if the employee willingly accepts the job knowing that to which he has consented, and is in some way harmed, the employer would decrease his liability in many cases. After all, it was the employee's decision to expose himself to the hazards. He knew what to expect, and is responsible for his decision. The employer, in many cases, will avoid paying compensation.

Most important is that the right to know may go so far as to establish a fiduciary relationship between employer and employee, much the same as that existent between many patients and their physicians. Part of what is involved in such a relationship is that both parties trust each other to look after each other's best interests. The employer can accomplish this by improving his work environment, by informing his employee of existent hazards, and the like.

The employee, also, can look out for his employer's best interests by unifying his goals with the goals of his employer. If the employee is made aware of risks involved in taking on a certain job, and yet he consents to taking on that job (assuming, of course, that he understands the risks and is not coerced into the job perhaps by another person or because he is unable to find an alternative), he has invested a part of himself into that relationship. He admits his willingness to work for an employer to achieve his employer's goals. The goals of the employer are then shared with the employee. And since the employee knows he is not being deceived about the conditions under which he works, he may have more incentive to do his job well. This, too, is likely to benefit the employer.

It is interesting to note, in conclusion, that the very nature of the employer–employee relationship which makes it difficult to secure an employee's right to know can, in fact, be changed into one of a fiduciary nature through the establishment of a right to know. We have seen that though the philosophical basis for securing a right to know in the workplace is the same as in the medical setting and that the harms which may possibly be incurred are similar, this right is more firmly grounded in the medical setting than in the workplace. What needs to be firmly established for the benefit of both the employer and employee in order to make headway in achieving a fiduciary relationship is an employee's right to know.

Notes

*I am greatly indebted to George Brenkert for his initial suggestion to write this paper, for his very helpful comments on earlier versions, as well as for his encouragement to send it out.

1. Manuel G. Velasquez, *Business Ethics: Concepts and Cases* (Englewood Cliffs, NJ: Prentice-Hall, Inc., 1982), p. 311.

2. See Nicholas A. Ashford, *Crisis in the Workplace: Occupational Disease and Injury* (Cambridge, MA: The MIT Press, 1976), pp. 68–83, for a thorough and interesting description of these hazards.

3. Although I shall use the term 'employee' throughout this essay, my arguments shall apply also to the prospective employee since he is faced with a similar choice, that is, whether or not to accept a job in a hazardous work environment.

4. *Canterbury* v. *Spence*, US Court of Appeals, District of Columbia Circuit, May 19, 1972, 464 Federal Reporter, 2nd Series, 772.

5. "A Patient's Bill of Rights," American Hospital Association, reprinted in Mappes & Zembaty (eds.), *Biomedical Ethics* (New York: McGraw-Hill, Inc., 1981), pp. 87–89.

6. "Declaration of Helsinki," World Medical Association, reprinted in Mappes & Zembaty, *ibid.*, pp. 145–147.

7. *Federal Register*, Vol. 45, no. 102, Friday, May 23, 1980, Rules and Regulations, Dept. of Labor, Occupational Safety and Health Administration, 23CFR Part 1910, 35212.

8. *Federal Register*, Vol. 48 no. 228, Friday, November 25, 1983, Rules and Regulations, Dept. of Labor, Occupational Safety and Health Administration, 29CFR Part 1910, 53280.

9. Ruth R. Faden and Tom L. Beauchamp, "The Right to Risk Information and the Right to Refuse Health Hazards in the Workplace," in *Ethical Theory of Business* (2nd Ed.), Tom L. Beauchamp and Norman E. Bowie (eds.), (Englewood Cliffs, NJ: Prentice-Hall, Inc., 1983), pp. 196–206.

10. Tim D. Wermager, "Union's Right to Information vs. Confidentiality of Employer Trade Secrets: Accommodating the Interests Through Procedural Burdens and Restricted Disclosure," 66 *Iowa Law Review*, 1333–1351, July, 1981.

11. *Federal Register*, Vol. 48 no 228, Friday, November 25, 1983, Rules and Regulations, Dept. of Labor, Occupational Safety and Health Administration, 29CFR Part 1910 53284.

12. *Ibid.*, Table I, p. 53285.

13. *Ibid.*, Vol. 45, p. 35215.

14. The Occupational Safety and Health Act of 1970 (Public Law 91-596), Section 5(a)(I), reprinted in Ashford, pp. 545–575.

15. Robert Stewart Smith, *The Occupational Safety and Health Act: Its Goals and Its Achievements* (Washington, D.C.: American Enterprise Institute for Public Policy Research, 1976), p. 9.

16. Wermager, *op. cit.*, p. 1333.

17. David Carey Fraser, "Trade Secrets and the NLRA: Employee's Right to Health and Safety Information," 14 *University of San Francisco Law Review*, 495–524, Spring, 1980.

18. Wermager, *op. cit.*, pp. 1335–1336.

19. Wermager, *op. cit.*, p. 1343.

20. Wermager, *op. cit.*, p. 1345.

21. Ashford, *op. cit.*, p. 76.

22. Ashford, *op. cit.*, p. 78.

23. Karen Lebacqz and Robert J. Levine, "Informed Consent in Human Research: Ethical and Legal Aspects," in *Encyclopedia of Bioethics*, Vol. 2, Warren T. Reich, ed.-in-chief, (New York: The Free Press, 1978), pp. 754–762.

24. Gilbert Sharpe, LLM, "Recent Canadian Court Decisions on Consent," *Bioethics Quarterly*, Vol. 2 No. I (Spring, 1980), 56–63.

25. Sharpe, *ibid.*, p. 58.

26. Sharpe, *ibid.*, p. 61.

27. Janice R. Dillon, "Informed Consent and the Disclosure of Risks of Treatment: The Supreme Court of Canada Decides," *Bioethics Quarterly*, Vol. 3 No. 3&4, (Fall/Winter, 1981), 156–162.

28. Dillon, *ibid.*, p. 160.

29. Ashford, *op. cit.*, p. 350.

30. Ashford, *op. cit.*, p. 392.

31. "Occupational Health Risks and the Worker's Right to Know." 90 *Yale Law Journal*, 1792–1810, July, 1981.

32. Milton Friedman, *Capitalism and Freedom* (Chicago: The University of Chicago Press, 1962), p. 133.

Robert A. Dahl

DEMOCRACY IN THE WORKPLACE: IS IT A RIGHT OR A PRIVILEGE?

Although political theorists who favor worker participation have often emphasized its potentialities for democratic character and its beneficial effects on democracy in the government of the state, a stronger justification, with a more Kantian flavor, seems to me to rest on a different argument: *if* democracy is justified in governing the state, it must *also* be justified in governing economic enterprises; and to say that it is *not* justified in governing economic enterprises is to imply that it is not justified in governing the state.

I can readily imagine several objections to this argument:

1. A system of self-governing enterprises would violate a superior right to property.
2. The assumptions that justify the democratic process do not apply to an economic enterprise. In particular—
   a. Decisions in economic enterprises are not *binding* in the same sense as decisions made and enforced by the government of a state.
   b. Generally speaking, employees are not as well qualified as others to run a company. Thus the argument for the democratic process fails. On the contrary, a government by the best qualified, that is, a system of guardianship or meritocracy, is justified by the marked differences in competence.

Rule by corporate managers, it might be argued, is such a system.

From *Dissent*, 31 (Winter 1984), 54–60. Reprinted by permission.

3. Michels's iron law of oligarchy operates so strongly in economic enterprises that democracy would prove to be a sham. Thus the effort to inaugurate the democratic process within firms is essentially a waste of time.

PROPERTY RIGHTS

As to property rights, transferring control over the decisions of a firm to its employees, it might be objected, would violate the right of owners to use their property as they choose. If, however, a right to property is understood in its fundamental moral sense as a right to acquire the personal resources necessary to political liberty and a decent existence, then self-governing enterprises would surely not, on balance, diminish the capacity of citizens to exercise that right: in all likelihood they would strengthen it. Even if property rights are construed in a narrower, more legalistic sense, the way a self-governed enterprise is owned *need not necessarily violate such a right*. As we shall see later on, it could entail a shift of ownership from stockholders to employees.

ARE DECISIONS BINDING

However, can the assumptions that justify the democratic process reasonably be applied to economic enterprises? For one thing, do economic enterprises make decisions that are binding on workers in the same way a state government makes decisions that citizens are compelled to obey? After all, laws made by the government of a state can be enforced by physical coercion, if need be. Even in a democratic state, a minority opposed to a law is nevertheless compelled to obey it. But a firm, it might be said, is nothing more than a sort of market within which people engage in voluntary individual exchanges: workers voluntarily exchange their labor in return for wages paid by the employer.

Decisions made by the government of a firm and by the government of the state, however, are in some crucial respects more similar than the classical liberal interpretation allows for. Like the government of the state, the government of a firm makes decisions that apply uniformly to all workers or a category of workers: decisions governing the place of work, time of work, product of work, minimally acceptable rate of work, equipment to be used at work, number of workers, number (and identity) of workers laid off in slack times, and whether there is to be any work at all — or if, instead, the plant is to be shut down. These decisions are enforced by sanctions, including the ultimate sanction of firing.

Have I now understated the difference? Unlike citizens of a state, you might object, workers are not compelled to obey managerial decisions. Their decision to do so is voluntary. Since a worker may choose to obey the management or not, he is free to leave the firm if he prefers not to obey; and since he cannot be punished by management for leaving, his decision to obey is perfectly free of all compulsion. But an objection along these lines exaggerates the differences between a worker's subjection to decisions made by the government of a firm and a citizen's subjection to decisions made by the government of the state.

Take a local government. A citizen who does not like a local ordinance is also "free" to move to another community. Indeed, if a citizen does not want to obey his country's laws, he is "free" — at least in all democratic states — to leave his country. Now if a citizen were perfectly free to leave, then citizenship would be wholly voluntary; for if a citizen found "voice" unsatisfactory, he could freely opt for "exit." But is not "exit" (or exile) often so costly, in every sense, that membership is for all practical purposes compulsory — whether it requires one to leave a country, a municipality, or a firm? But if so, then the government of a firm looks rather more like the government of a state than we are habitually inclined to believe because exit is too costly, membership in a firm is not significantly more voluntary or less compulsory than citizenship in a municipality or perhaps even in a country. In fact, citizenship in a democratic state is in one respect more voluntary than employment in a firm.

Within a democratic country, citizens may ordinarily leave one municipality and automatically retain or quickly acquire full rights of citizenship in another. Unlike a citizen of a democratic state, one who leaves a firm has no right to employment in another. Yet the decisions of firms, like the decisions of a state, can be enforced by the severe sanction of firing. Like a state, then, a firm can also be viewed as a political system in which relations of power exist between government and governed. If so, is it not appropriate to insist that the relationship between governors and governed should satisfy the criteria of the democratic process — as we properly insist in the domain of the state?

Let the firm be considered a political system, you might now agree. Within this political system, however, cannot the rights of workers be adequately protected by labor unions? But this objection not only fails to meet the problem of nonunion workers (who in the United States comprise about 80 percent of the work force); it also implicitly recognizes that in order to protect some fundamental right or interest, workers are entitled — have a right — to at least *some* democratic controls. What, then, is the nature and scope of this right or interest? To say that its scope is limited by an equally or more fundamental right to property runs afoul of our earlier analysis.

On what grounds, then, must the employees' *right* to democratic controls be restricted to the conventional (but by no means well-defined) limits of trade unions? Is this not precisely the question at issue: do workers have a fundamental right to self-government in their economic enterprises? If they have such a right, is it not obvious that, however essential conventional trade unions may be in reducing the impact of authoritarian rule in the government of a firm, an ordinary firm, even with a trade union, still falls very far short of satisfying the criteria of the democratic process?

DOES THE PRINCIPLE OF EQUALITY HOLD?

The government of large American corporations could be seen as a form of guardianship. Although managers are nominally selected by a board of directors, which in turn is nominally chosen by and legally accountable to stockholders, in reality new managers are typically co-opted by the existing management that also, in practice, chooses and controls its own board of directors. Guardianship has also been the ideal of many socialists, particularly the Fabians. In this view the managers of state-owned enterprises were to be chosen by state officials, to whom the top managers were to be ultimately responsible. In most countries, in fact, nationalized industries are governed by some such scheme. One could easily dream up still other meritocratic alternatives.

Thus in theory and practice both corporate capitalism and bureaucratic socialism have rejected democracy for economic enterprises; explicitly or by implication they uphold guardianship. Because of the overwhelming weight of existing institutions and ideologies probably most people, including many thoughtful ones, will find it hard to believe that employees are qualified to govern the enterprises in which they work. However, in considering whether a principle of democratic equality holds for business firms, it is important to keep two points in mind.

First, while we may reasonably compare the ideal or theoretically possible performance of one system with the ideal or theoretical performance of another, we cannot reasonably compare the actual performance of one with the ideal performance of another. Although a good deal of the discussion of self-governing enterprises that follows is necessarily conjectural, my aim is to compare how self-governing enterprises would probably perform in the real world with the actual performance of their main real-world alternative, the modern privately owned corporation.

Second, a principle of democratic equality does not require that citizens be equally competent in every respect. It is sufficient that they are qualified enough to decide which matters do or do not require binding decisions — for instance, which matters require general rules: of those that do, if citizens are competent to judge which they are sufficiently qualified to decide collectively through the democratic process; and if on matters they do not feel competent to decide for themselves they are qualified to set the terms on which they will delegate these decisions to others.

Except in exceedingly small firms, employees would surely choose to delegate some decisions to managers. In larger firms, they would no doubt elect a governing board or council, which in the typical case would probably be delegated the authority to select and remove the top executives. Except in very large enterprises, the employees might constitute an assembly for "legislative" purposes — to make decisions on such matters as the workers chose to decide, to delegate matters they prefer not to decide directly, and to review decisions on matters they had previously delegated as well as the conduct of the board and the managers in other ways. In giant firms, where an assembly would suffer all the infirmities of direct democracy on an excessively large scale, a representative government would have to be created.

Given the passivity of stockholders in a typical firm, their utter dependency on information supplied by management, and the extraordinary difficulties of contesting a managerial decision, it seems to me hardly open to doubt that employees are on the whole as well qualified to run their firms as are stockholders, and probably on average a good deal more. But, of course, that is not really the issue, given the separation of ownership from control to which Berle and Means called attention in 1932 in *The Modern Corporation and Private Property*. In a much more systematic study published in 1981, Edward Herman found that 64 percent of the 200 largest nonfinancial American corporations are controlled by inside management and another 17 percent by inside management with an outside board, or altogether 81 percent of the total, with 84 percent of the assets and 82 percent of the sales. Although it is reasonable to assume that the percentage of management-controlled firms would decline among smaller firms, the question remains whether workers are as qualified to govern economic enterprises as managers who gain their position by co-optation, producing a sort of co-optative guardianship. The question raises many familiar issues of democracy versus guardianship as alternative political regimes, notably the issues of competence; in making a judgment about the competence of workers, as about citizens in the state; in distinguishing knowledge about the *ends* the collective enterprise should seek from technical knowledge about the best *means* for achieving those ends. The argument might be made that as to ends, self-governing enterprises would produce lower rates of savings, investment, growth, and employment than the "society" might rationally (or at least reasonably) prefer; while as to means they would be unable to supply qualified management and would be less efficient than stockholder-owned firms like American corporations.

ENDS: SAVINGS, INVESTMENT, GROWTH, AND EMPLOYMENT

How would a system of self-governing enterprises affect savings, investment, employment, and growth? For example, would workers vote to allocate so much of enterprise earnings to wages that they would sacrifice investment in new machinery and future efficiencies? Would firms run democratically by their employees be more short-sighted than firms run hierarchically by managers? American corporate managers are frequently criticized nowadays for an excessive emphasis on short-run as against long-run returns. Would self-governing enterprises accentuate the sacrifice of deferred to immediate benefits, to the disadvantage and contrary to the collective preferences of their society? If so, would not the particular interests of workers in an enterprise conflict with the general interest?

Purely theoretical analysis by economists, whether critics or advocates of worker-managed firms, is ultimately inconclusive. Advocates of self-management agree that in contrast to conventional firms in which managers seek to maximize total profit for shareholders, the worker-members of self-governing firms would seek to maximize the per capita income of the members. In view of this, some critics have pointed out that members would have no incentive to expand savings, production, employment, or investment unless the effect were to increase their own per capita earnings; and they would have a definite incentive not to do so if they expected that by doing it they would reduce their own earnings. It follows that in some situations in which a conventional firm would expand in order to increase returns to shareholders, worker-managed firms would not.

Advocates of self-governing firms reply that in an economy of self-governing firms, the problem of employment is theoretically distinguishable from the problem of investment and growth. In the theoretical scenario just sketched out, expanding employment is a problem only at the level of the individual firm. At the level of the economy, however, it would be dealt with by insuring ease of entry for new firms. If unemployment existed and enterprises failed to respond to rising demand for their product by expanding employment, new firms would do so; hence both investment and employment would increase. As to investment, except in the circumstances just described, members of a self-managed enterprise would have strong incentives to invest, and thus to save, whenever doing so would increase the surplus available for distribution to themselves.

In the real world, however, these comparisons between theoretical models do not take us very far. As Peter Jay has remarked, it is hardly relevant to compare

> . . . the rational investment behavior of workers' cooperatives with the rational behavior of idealized capital enterprises working according to textbook optimization. If we actually lived in the latter world, we would hardly be considering the problem discussed in this paper at all.[1]

Turning then to the domain of practical judgment, it seems likely that in the real world, self-governing enterprises might stimulate as much saving, investment, and growth as American corporate enterprises have done, and perhaps more, because workers typically stand to incur severe losses from the decline of a firm. If we permit ourselves to violate the unenforceable injunction of some welfare economists against interpersonal comparisons, we can hardly deny that the losses incurred by workers from the decline of a firm are normally even greater than those investors suffer; for it is ordinarily much easier and less costly in human terms for a well-heeled investor to switch in and out of the securities market than for a worker to switch in and out of the job market. A moderately foresightful worker would therefore be as greatly concerned with long-run efficiencies as a rational investor or a rational manager, and perhaps more so.

This conjecture is supported by at least some experience showing that, given the opportunity, workers will make significant short-run sacrifices in wages and benefits in order to keep their firm from collapsing. They did so, for example, at both the Chrysler Corporation and the Rath Packing Company. When they own the company themselves, their incentive to sacrifice in order to save it is all the stronger. As a worker in one of the plywood co-ops put it, "If things get bad we'll all take a pay cut. You don't want to milk the cow, because if you milk the cow, there's nothing left. And *we* lose the company."

Perhaps an even more relevant example is the Mondragon complex of more than 80 worker cooperatives in Spain. During a period in which the Spanish economy was expanding generally, the sales of the Mondragon cooperatives grew at an impressive rate, averaging 8.5 percent annually from 1970 to 1979. Their market share increased from less than 1 percent in 1960 to over 10 percent in 1976. The percentage of gross value added in investment by the cooperatives between 1971 and 1979 averaged 36 percent, nearly four times the average rate of industry in the heavily industrialized Basque province in which Mondragon is located.[2] Moreover, when a recession in the Spanish economy led to declining profits in 1981, "investment [was] squeezed, but the workers [were] prepared to make sacrifices to keep their jobs, digging into their own pockets to keep the balance sheets in shape." Members chose to contribute

---

[1]Peter Jay, "The Workers' Cooperative Economy," in *The Political Economy of Co-operation and Participation*, A. Clayre, ed (Oxford: Oxford University Press, 1980), p. 20.

[2]Henk Thomas and Chris Logan, *Mondragon* (London: George Allen & Unwin, 1982, pp. 100–105.

more capital rather than cut their wages. Thus the members of one co-op voted to increase their capital contributions by amounts varying from $570 to $1,700, depending on a member's wage level.[3]

Nor have the self-managed enterprises of Yugoslavia, on the whole, followed the theoretical model described above. Though the causes are complex, with some exceptions they have not sacrificed investment to current income but, on the contrary, have maintained very high levels of investment.

A final observation on the problem of saving, investment, employment, and growth. The introduction of self-governing enterprises *could* be accompanied by the creation of new investment funds operating under democratic control. This was one of the aims of a proposal introduced in Parliament by the Danish Social Democrats in 1973. The proceeds of a payroll tax covering most Danish firms (about 25,000) would be divided, in effect, in two parts. One part — the smaller — would go to a national "Investment and Dividend Fund" that would be used both to beef up Danish investment and to provide a social dividend to Danish workers. Virtually every worker would receive certificates from the fund in an amount that would vary according to the number of years worked, but not according to the employee's wage or salary. The certificates would be nonnegotiable, but an employee would have the right to withdraw the value of his certificates after seven years or at the age of 67; upon death their value would be paid to the employee's estate. The other and larger part of the proceeds from the payroll tax would remain in the firm as share capital owned collectively by the employees, who would vote as enterprise-citizens, that is, one person, one vote. The employees' share of capital, however, and thus of voting rights, would not be permitted to increase beyond 50 percent — presumably a move to reassure private investors. Like the Meidner Plan in Sweden, the Danish proposal is intended to achieve several purposes: greater equalization of wealth, more democratic control of the economy, and, definitely not least in importance, a steady supply of funds for investment.

Thus it is not inconceivable that American workers might enter into a social contract that would require them to provide funds for investment, drawn from payrolls, in return for greater control over the government of economic enterprises. If self-governing enterprises proved to be better matched to the incentives of workers than hierarchically run firms, and thus more efficient, this country might have a recipe for economic growth that would outperform even the Japanese — and leave recent American performances far behind.

MEANS: MANAGERIAL SKILLS AND EFFICIENCY

A disastrous assumption of revolutionaries, exhibited with stunning naiveté in Lenin's *State and Revolution*, is that managerial skills are of trivial importance, or will arise spontaneously, or will be more than made up for by revolutionary enthusiasm. The historical record relieves one of all need to demonstrate the foolishness of such an assumption. The question is not, however, whether self-governing enterprises would need managerial abilities but whether workers and their representatives would select and oversee managers less competently than is now the case in American corporations, which are largely

[3]The *Economist*, October 31, 1981, p. 84.

controlled by managers whose decisions are rarely open to serious challenge, except when disaster strikes, and not always even then. If the self-governing enterprises were to become widespread, it would be wise to provide much wider opportunities than now exist in any country for employees to learn some of the tools and skills of modern management. One reason for the success of the Mondragon cooperatives is the prominent place they have assigned to education, including technical education at advanced professional levels. As a result, they have created their own managers. In the United States, at least, a significant proportion of both blue- and white-collar workers, often the more ambitious and aggressive among them, aspire to supervisory and managerial positions but lack the essential skills. Efficiency and economic growth flow from investments in human capital every bit as much as from financial capital, and probably more so. A system of self-governing enterprises would be likely to heighten — not diminish — efforts to improve a country's human capital.

If in the meantime skilled managers are in short supply, self-governing enterprises will have to compete for their services, as does Puget Sound Plywood, a worker-owned cooperative. The president and members of the board of trustees are elected by and from the members, who all receive the same pay. However, the president and the board in turn select a general manager from outside the membership at a salary sufficient to attract managers who thus earn considerably more than the members themselves.

Unless self-governing enterprises were less competent in recruiting skilled managers, they should be no less efficient in a narrow sense than American corporations at present. And unless they were more likely to evade the external controls of competition and regulation, they should not be less efficient in a broader sense. I have suggested why it is reasonable to expect neither of these to occur.

Yet if self-governing enterprises can be as efficient as orthodox firms, why have they so often failed? As everyone knows who is familiar with American and British labor history, the late 19th century saw waves of short-lived producer cooperatives both in Britain and in the United States. Their quick demise convinced trade union leaders that in a capitalist economy unionism and collective bargaining held out a much more realistic promise of gains for workers than producer cooperatives. In both countries, and in continental Europe as well, labor and socialist movements largely abandoned producer cooperatives as a major short-run objective. Most academic observers, including labor economists and social historians, concluded that the idea of labor-managed firms was a rejected and forlorn utopia irrelevant to a modern economy.

In recent years, however, a number of factors have brought about a reassessment of the relevance of the older experience. These include the highly unsatisfactory performance of both corporate capitalism and bureaucratic socialism, which has stimulated a search for an alternative to both, the introduction and survival — despite severe difficulties — of self-management in Yugoslavia; some stunning successes, such as the U.S. plywood cooperatives and the Mondragon group; formal economic analysis showing how a labor-managed market economy would theoretically satisfy efficiency criteria; growing awareness of the need to reduce the hierarchical structure of the workplace and increase participation by workers in order to increase productivity; and the seeming success of many new arrangements for worker participation, control, or ownership in Europe and the United States.

It has become clear that in the past labor-managed firms were often doomed from the start by weaknesses that are not inherent but remediable, such as shortages of credit, capital, and managerial skills. Moreover, in the past producer cooperatives have usually been organized in the worst possible circumstances, when employees desperately attempted to rescue a collapsing company by taking it over — often during a recession. It is hardly surprising that workers may fail to save a firm after management already has failed. What is surprising is that workers' cooperatives have sometimes succeeded where private management had failed. It was from the failure of privately owned companies that the plywood co-ops started.

I mentioned the Mondragon producer co-operatives as an example of success. They include the largest manufacturer of machine tools in the country, as well as one of the largest refrigerator manufacturers. During a period of a falling economy and rising unemployment in Spain from 1977 to 1981, employment in the Mondragon co-ops increased from 15,700 to about 18,500. Unless they are denied access to credit — the Mondragon complex has its own bank — self-governing enterprises have a greater resiliency than American corporations. For in times of stringency, when an orthodox private firm would lay off workers or shut down, in a self-governing enterprise the members can decide to reduce their wages, curtail their share of the surplus, if any, or following a prosperous period even contribute additional capital funds, as at Mondragon. As these and other cases show, self-governing enterprises are likely to tap the creativity, energies, and loyalties of workers to an extent that stockholder owned corporations probably never can, even with profit-sharing schemes.

Although rigorous comparisons of the relative efficiencies of labor-managed and conventional corporations are difficult and still fairly uncommon, the best analysis of a broad range of experiences in a number of different countries appears to support these conclusions: *participation by workers in decision-making rarely leads to a decline of productivity*; far more often it either has no effect or results in *an increase in productivity*.[4]

HOW MUCH INTERNAL DEMOCRACY?

Often the effects of more democratic structures have been greatly exaggerated by both advocates and opponents. Yet just as the democratization of the authoritarian structures of centralized monarchies and modern dictatorships has transformed relations of authority and power in the government of states, so there is every reason to believe that the democratization of the government of modern corporations would profoundly alter relations of authority and power in economic enterprises. Relationships of governors to governed of a sort that Americans have insisted on for 200 years in the public governments of the state would be extended to the hitherto private governments in the economy. If too often exaggerated, it is nonetheless a grievous mistake to underestimate the importance of democratic institutions in the domain of the state. It is also a mistake to underestimate the importance in the daily lives of ordinary people of authoritarian institutions in the sphere of work. To be sure, democratic structures do not

---

[4]The most rigorous analysis to date is in the studies contained in *Participatory and Self-Managed Firms*, Derek C. Jones and Jan Svejnar, eds. (Lexington, Mass.: Lexington Books, 1982).

escape Robert Michels's "iron law of oligarchy." But Michels's "law" is neither iron nor a law. At most it is a universal tendency in human organizations; and it is often offset, if never wholly nullified, by a universal tendency toward personal and group autonomy and the displacement of strictly hierarchical controls by at least some degree of mutual control. It is not unreasonable to expect that democratic structures in governing the workplace would satisfy the criteria of the democratic process neither markedly worse nor markedly better than democratic structures in the government of the state.

Tibor R. Machan

HUMAN RIGHTS, WORKERS' RIGHTS, AND THE "RIGHT" TO OCCUPATIONAL SAFETY

INTRODUCTION

I take the position of the nonbeliever.[1] I do not believe in special workers' rights. I do believe that workers possess rights as human beings, as do publishers, philosophers, disc jockeys, students, and priests. Once fully interpreted, these rights may impose special standards at the workplace, as they may in hospitals, on athletics fields, or in the marketplace.

HUMAN RIGHTS

Our general rights, those we are morally justified to secure by organized force (e.g., government), are those initially identified by John Locke: life, liberty, and property. That is, we need ask no one's permission to live, to take actions, and to acquire, hold, or use peacefully the productive or creative results of our actions. We may, morally, resist (without undue force) efforts to violate or infringe upon our rights. Our rights are (1) absolute, (2) unalienable, and (3) universal: (1) in social relations no excuse legitimizes their violation; (2) no one can lose these rights, though their exercise may be restricted (e.g., to jail) by what one chooses to do; and (3) everyone has these rights, whether acknowledged or respected by others or governments or under different descriptions (within less developed conceptual schemes).[2]

I defend this general rights theory elsewhere.[3] Essentially, since adults are rational beings with the moral responsibility to excel as such, a good or suitable community requires these rights as standards. Since this commits one to a virtuously self-governed life, others should respect this as equal members of the

From Tibor R. Machan, "Human Rights, Workers' Rights, and the 'Right' to Occupational Safety," in *Moral Rights in the Workplace*, edited by Gertrude Ezorsky (Albany: State University of New York Press, 1987), 45–50. Reprinted by permission of the State University of New York Press. © 1987 State University of New York Press.

community. Willful invasion of these rights — the destruction of (negative) liberty — must be prohibited in human community life.

So-called positive freedom — that is, the enablement to do well in life — presupposes the prior importance of negative freedom. As, what we might call, self-starters, human beings will generally be best off if they are left uninterfered with to take the initiative in their lives.

WORKERS' RIGHTS

What about special workers' rights? There are none. As individuals who intend to hire out their skills for what they will fetch in the marketplace, however, workers have the right to offer these in return for what others, (e.g., employers) will offer in acceptable compensation. This implies free trade in the labor market.

Any interference with such trade workers (alone or in voluntary coopera-tion) might want to engage in, with consent by fellow traders, would violate both the workers' and their traders' human rights. Freedom of association would thereby be abridged. (This includes freedom to organize into trade associations, unions, cartels, and so forth.)

Workers' rights advocates view this differently. They hold that the employee – employer relationship involves special duties owed by employers to employees, creating (corollary) rights that governments, given their purpose, should protect. Aside from negative rights, workers are owed respect of their positive rights to be treated with care and consideration.

This, however, is a bad idea. Not to be treated with care and consideration can be open to moral criticism. And lack of safety and health provisions may mean the neglect of crucial values to employees. In many circumstances em-ployers should, morally, provide them.

This is categorically different from the idea of enforcible positive rights. (Later I will touch on unfulfilled reasonable expectations of safety and health provisions on the job!) Adults aren't due such service from free agents whose conduct should be guided by their own judgments and not some alien authority. This kind of moral servitude (abolished after slavery and serfdom) of some by others has been discredited.

Respect for human rights is necessary in a moral society — one needn't thank a person for not murdering, assaulting, or robbing one — whereas being pro-vided with benefits, however crucial to one's well being, is more an act of generosity than a right.

Of course moral responsibilities toward others, even strangers, can arise. When those with plenty know of those with little, help would ordinarily be morally commendable. This can also extend to the employment relationship. Interestingly, however, government "regulation may impede risk-reducing change, freezing us into a hazardous present when a safer future beckons."[4]

My view credits all but the severely incapacitated with the fortitude to be productive and wise when ordering their affairs, workers included. The form of liberation that is then vital to workers is precisely the bourgeois kind: being set free from subjugation to others, including governments. Antibourgeois "liberation" is insultingly paternalistic.[5]

ALLEGING SPECIAL WORKERS' RIGHTS

Is this all gross distortion? Professor Braybrooke tells us, "Most people in our society . . . must look for employment and most (taking them one by one) have no alternative to accepting the working conditions offered by a small set of employers — perhaps one employer in the vicinity."[6] Workers need jobs and cannot afford to quibble. Employers can wait for the most accommodating job prospects.

This in part gives rise to special workers' rights doctrines, to be implemented by government occupational safety, health and labor-relations regulators, which then "makes it easier for competing firms to heed an important moral obligation and to be, if they wish, humane."[7]

Suppose a disadvantaged worker, seeking a job in a coal mine, asks about safety provision in the mine. Her doing so presupposes that (1) she has other alternatives, and (2) it's morally and legally optional to care about safety at the mine, not due to workers by right. Prior to government's energetic prolabor interventions, safety, health, and related provisions for workers had been lacking. Only legally mandated workers' rights freed workers from their oppressive lot. Thus, workers must by law be provided with safety, health care, job security, retirement, and other vital benefits.

Workers' rights advocates deny that employers have the basic (natural or human) private property rights to give them full authority to set terms of employment. They are seen as nonexclusive stewards of the workplace property, property obtained by way of historical accident, morally indifferent historical necessity, default, or theft. There is no genuine free labor market. There are no jobs to offer since they are not anyone's to give. The picture we should have of the situation is that society should be regarded as a kind of large team or family; the rights of its respective parts (individuals) flow not from their free and independent moral nature, but from the relationship of the needs and usefulness of individuals as regards the purposes of the collective.

By this account, everyone lacks the full authority to enter into exclusive or unilaterally determined and mutual agreements on his or her terms. Such terms — of production, employment, promotion, termination, and so on — would be established, in line with moral propriety, only by the agency (society, God, the party, the democratic assembly) that possesses the full moral authority to set them.

Let us see why the view just stated is ultimately unconvincing. To begin with, the language of rights does not belong within the above framework. That language acknowledges the reality of morally free and independent human beings and includes among them workers, as well as all other adults. Individual human rights assume that within the limits of nature, human beings are all efficacious to varying degrees, frequently depending upon their own choices. Once this individualist viewpoint is rejected, the very foundation for rights language disappears (notwithstanding some contrary contentions).[8]

Some admit that employers are full owners of their property, yet hold that workers, because they are disadvantaged, are owed special duties of care and considerateness, duties which in turn create rights the government should protect. But even if this were right, it is not possible from this position to establish enforcible *public* policy. From the mere existence of *moral* duties employers may have to employees, no enforcible public policy can follow;

moral responsibilities require freely chosen fulfillment, not enforced compliance.

Many workers' rights advocates claim that a free labor market will lead to such atrocities as child labor, hazardous and health-impairing working conditions, and so forth. Of course, even if this were true, there is reason to think that OSHA-type regulatory remedies are illusionary. As Peter Huber argues, "regulation of health and safety is not only a major obstacle to technological transformation and innovation but also often aggravates the hazards it is supposed to avoid."[9]

However, it is not certain that a free labor market would lead to child labor and rampant neglect of safety and health at the workplace. Children are, after all, dependents and therefore have rights owed them by their parents. To subject children to hazardous, exploitative work, to deprive them of normal education and health care, could be construed as a violation of their individual rights as young, dependent human beings. Similarly, knowingly or negligently subjecting workers to hazards at the workplace (of which they were not made aware and could not anticipate from reasonable familiarity with the job) constitutes a form of actionable fraud. It comes under the prohibition of the violation of the right to liberty, at times even the right to life. Such conduct is actionable in a court of law and workers, individually or organized into unions, would be morally justified, indeed advised, to challenge it.

A consistent and strict interpretation of the moral (not economic) individualist framework of rights yields results that some advocates of workers' rights are aiming for. The moral force of most attacks on the free labor market framework tends to arise from the fact that some so-called free labor market instances are probably violations of the detailed implications of that approach itself. Why would one be morally concerned with working conditions that are fully agreed to by workers? Such a concern reflects either the belief that there hadn't been any free agreement in the first place, and thus workers are being defrauded, or it reflects a paternalism that, when construed as paternalism proper instead of compassion, no longer carries moral force.

Whatever its motives, paternalism is also insulting and demeaning in its effect. Once it is clear that workers can generate their own (individual and/or collective) response to employers' bargaining power — via labor organizations, insurance, craft associations, and so on — the favorable air of the paternalistic stance diminishes considerably. Instead, workers are seen to be regarded as helpless, inefficacious, inept persons.

THE "RIGHT" TO OCCUPATIONAL SAFETY

Consider an employer who owns and operates a coal mine. (We could have chosen any firm, privately or "publicly" owned, managed by hired executives with the full consent of the owners, including interested stockholders who have entrusted, by their purchase of stocks, others with the goal of obtaining economic benefits for them.) The firm posts a call for jobs. The mine is in competition with some of the major coal mines in the country and the world. But it is much less prosperous than its competitors. The employer is at present not equipped to run a highly-polished, well-outfitted (e.g., very safe) operation. That may lie in the future, provided the cost of production will not be so high as to make this impossible.

Some of the risks will be higher for workers in this mine than in others. Some of the mineshafts will have badly illuminated stairways, some of the noise will be higher than the levels deemed acceptable by experts, and some of the ventilation equipment will be primitive. The wages, too, will be relatively low in hopes of making the mine eventually more prosperous.

When prospective employees appear and are made aware of the type of job being offered, and its hazards they are at liberty to (a) accept or reject, (b) organize into a group and insist on various terms not in the offing, (c) bargain alone or together with others and set terms that include improvements, or (d) pool workers' resources, borrow, and purchase the firm.

To deny that workers could achieve such things is not yet to deny that they are (negatively) free to do so. But to hold that this would be extraordinary for workers (and thus irrelevant in this sort of case) is to (1) assume a historical situation not in force and certainly not necessary, (2) deny workers the capacity for finding a solution to their problems, or (3) deny that workers are capable of initiative.

Now suppose that employers are compelled by law to spend the firm's funds to meet safety requirements deemed desirable by the government regulators. This increased cost of production reduces available funds for additional wages for present and further employees, not to mention available funds for future prospect sites. This is what has happened: The employee – employer relationship has been unjustly intruded upon, to the detriment not only of the mine owners, but also of those who might be employed and of future consumers of energy. The myth of workers' rights is mostly to blame.

CONCLUSION

I have argued that the doctrine of special workers' rights is unsupported and workers, accordingly, possess those rights that all other humans possess, the right to life, liberty, and property. Workers are not a special species of persons to be treated in a paternalistic fashion and, given just treatment in the community, they can achieve their goals as efficiently as any other group of human beings.[10]

Notes

1. I wish to thank the Earhart, Jon M. Olin, and Reason Foundations for making it possible, in part, for me to work on this project. I also wish to thank Bill Puka and Gertrude Ezorsky for their very valuable criticism of an earlier draft of this essay, despite their very likely disapproval of my views.

2. This observation rests, in part, on epistemological insights available, for example, in Hanna F. Pitkin, *Wittgenstin and Justice* (Berkeley, Calif.: University of California Press, 1972).

3. Tibor R. Machan, "A Reconsideration of Natural Rights Theory," *American Philosophical Quarterly* 19 (January 1980): 61 – 72.

4. Peter Huber, "Exorcists vs. Gatekeepers in Risk Regulation," *Regulation* (November/December 1983), 23.

5. But see Steven Kelman, "Regulation and Paternalism," *Rights and Regulation*, ed. T. R. Machan and M. B. Johnson (Cambridge, Mass.: Ballinger Publ. Co., 1983), 217 – 248.

6. David Braybrooke, *Ethics in the World of Business* (Totowa, N.J.: Rowman & Allanheld, 1983), 223.

7. Ibid., 224.

8. For an attempt to forge a collectivist theory of rights, see Tom Campbell, *The Left and Rights* (London and Boston: Routledge & Kegan Paul, 1983).

9. Huber, "Exorcists vs. Gatekeepers," 23.

10. Ibid. Huber observes that "Every insurance company knows that life is growing safer, but the public is firmly convinced that living is becoming ever more hazardous" (p. 23). In general, capitalism's benefits to workers have simply not been acknowledged, especially by moral and political philosophers! It is hardly possible to avoid the simple fact that the workers of the world believe differently, judging by what system they prefer to emigrate to whenever possible.

◆ ◆ ◆

DISCUSSION QUESTIONS

1. Does Ewing list anything that you think should not be thought of as an employee's right? Do you agree with Ewing's suggestion that these rights should be protected by a Constitutional amendment?

2. Werhane rejects the idea that employers should be able to fire employees "at will." Do you agree with her position? Is this an unwarranted intrusion on the rights of a corporation?

3. Superson suggests that the employer–employee relationship should be fiduciary in character, akin to that between a physician and his or her patients. Do you agree? Would this sort of relationship still allow employers to do business profitably? Would it put business under any unreasonable restrictions?

4. Dahl essentially argues that if democracy is the preferable form of government, it should also be applied in the workplace. Do you agree? If so, how should this be implemented?

5. Machan suggests that the notion of workers' rights to a safe environment has hurt owners, employees, and consumers. Using the example of a mine, Machan points out that comprehensive safety requirements raise the cost of production, which "reduces available funds for additional wages for present and future employees, not to mention available funds for future prospect sites." Assume that Machan's analysis is correct. Does it overthrow the idea of workers' rights to a safe environment?

CASE 10.1

◆ ◆ ◆

The Rights of Current Employees Versus the Rights of Their Unconceived Children

In 1982, Johnson Controls, Inc., instituted a policy designed to protect the health of unborn children. The Wisconsin manufacturer of automobile batteries banned potentially fertile women from working where they might be exposed to hazardous levels of lead, a substance that can cause fetal brain damage. A woman could risk such exposure only if she presented a written statement from her physician confirming that she was unable to bear children. A group of female employees challenged the policy; and, although a federal appeals court ruled in favor of the company in 1989, two years later the Supreme Court judged the policy to be discriminatory.

Critics of the policy contend that the company's motivation was less to protect the unborn than to avoid liability lawsuits that could result if a child with birth defects were born to an employee who had been exposed to high levels of lead. Other objections focus on the harm done to women prohibited from such jobs. Judge Frank H. Easterbrook, who dissented from the appeals court's majority decision, criticized the company's treatment of women as stereotypical. He argued that the extension of such policies to other companies meant that "20 million industrial jobs could be closed to women" and that "the law would allow employers to consign more women to 'women's work' while reserving better-paying but more-hazardous jobs for men." Joan E. Bertin of the American Civil Liberties Union echoed this sentiment when she contended that policies like these "will institutionalize the second-class employment status of all fertile women."

It is the concern with discrimination that surfaced in the Supreme Court's ruling that the company's policy constituted sex discrimination and thereby violated the Civil Rights Act of 1964. The Court pointed out that even though lead also affects the male reproductive system, Johnson Controls' restrictions applied only to women.

The situation at Johnson Controls was not unusual. Concern with dangers to the reproductive systems of women has led many companies to restrict women's options, while attention has not been given to the hazards that men face. A 1988 study of nearly two hundred large chemical and electronics companies in Massachusetts found that while nearly 20 percent restricted women's options because of reproductive risk, only one company restricted the job options of men whose partners were trying to become pregnant. Many companies apparently were either unaware of or just ignored the risk to their male employees. As one of the authors of the study reported, "For example, very low doses of glycol ethers have been found to cause toxic effects on sperm, and yet, of the 54 companies we surveyed that had glycol ethers in use, none excluded men from working with them." ◆

Discussion Questions

1. Do such policies violate the rights of women? Does a fetus that is not simply unborn, but unconceived have rights? If so, how do you resolve the conflict between the rights of the woman and the rights of the fetus?

2. What about the case of a woman who does not want children? Could the company defend its policy by arguing that she may change her mind some day and that the company is simply protecting the rights of the potential fetus?

3. Would it make any difference if the company's motivation were strictly to protect itself from expensive law suits?

4. Do you agree with the Supreme Court that the different ways that hazards to female and male reproductive systems are treated amount to discrimination? If so, does this mean that the policy of exclusion should apply to both sexes or to neither of them?

Sources

Lewin, Tamar, "Companies Ignore Men's Health Risk," *New York Times*, December 15, 1988, A24.

Patner, Andrew, "Court Upholds 'Fetal-Protection Policy' Barring Most Women from Certain Jobs," *Wall Street Journal*, October 3, 1989, B7.

Schmidt, William E., "Risk to Fetus Ruled as Barring Women from Jobs," *New York Times*, October 3, 1989, I16.

CASE 10.2

◆ ◆ ◆

Firings, Libel, and Due Process

An increasing number of people are turning to the courts with complaints that their former companies violated their rights by giving negative feedback about them to prospective employers. Claims of libel and defamation against former employers are now commonplace. Moreover, such suits do not even require direct communication between an old and new employer. If someone who was fired from one job is forced to reveal the reason for termination as part of applying for another, this "compelled self-publication" might also be considered defamation.

For example, after a Texas insurance broker had trouble getting a new job after being fired from one company, he learned that the reason was that his former boss made negative remarks about him to prospective employers, saying he was ruthless, disliked by his co-workers, a failure as a businessman, a sociopath, and a zero who lacked scruples. The former broker sued and was awarded more than $2 million by a jury.

Such cases are leading some corporations to resist firing inadequate employees who perform poorly. Other companies may delay termination until they have gone through the costly process of building a documented case that can stand up in court. Still other businesses have decided to do no more than verify a former employee's rank and dates of employment when prospective employers call. But this, of course, creates a new set of problems. Without information about someone's performance elsewhere, companies may quickly discover that they now have an incompetent or dishonest employee on their hands.

A small number of companies, however, have instituted internal peer-review boards to which employees may appeal if they disagree with managers' decisions about promotions, disciplinary actions, and even firings. This might alleviate some of the problems just described.

Such appeals committees are used by corporations such as Federal Express, Adolph Coors, Polaroid, and Citicorp. A typical committee consists of three employees and two managers. The process is informal, giving all parties and relevant witnesses a turn to speak privately to the committee. The outcome is binding on both sides. According to David Ewing, an expert on employee rights, the original decision being contested is overruled from 20 to 40 percent of the time.

In essence, these panels institutionalize employees' rights to due process. They provide a forum for the scrutiny of a supervisor's decision and they allow an employee's peers to have a major hand in the decision. It is interesting that employees are harsher on their peers than are their supervisors. "Workers," claims Ewing, "are terribly impatient with peers because they often are the ones who have to pick up the pieces." Many supervisors, not surprisingly, object to such a review process as undermining their authority and infringing on their rights. ◆

Discussion Questions

1. The courts are saying that employees who have been fired have legal rights that are violated by negative characterizations of their prior employment, but are there similar moral rights? To what moral rights are former employees entitled? Is it a violation of an individual's moral rights for one employer to tell another that that person was not a good worker? This would surely be wrong if the information were false, but what if it were true?

2. If you fired someone and received a call from a company to which your former employee had applied for a job, what would you say? How much protection is the applicant entitled to? How much consideration is the prospective employer entitled to?

3. Can peer-review boards effectively protect employee rights? Should they be mandatory at all corporations?

4. If you had just fired someone, would you object to defending your decision to a peer-review board? Would this violate your rights as a manager? Would it matter if you owned the company?

Sources

Ewing, David, "Corporate Due Process Lowers Legal Costs," *Wall Street Journal*, October 23, 1989, A14.

Reibstein, Larry, "More Firms Use Peer Review Panel to Resolve Employees' Grievances," *Wall Street Journal*, November 25, 1986, 32.

Stricharchuk, Gregory, "Fired Employees Turn the Reason for Dismissal into a Legal Weapon," *Wall Street Journal*, October 2, 1986, 33.

ADDITIONAL READINGS

Dalton, Dan R., and Idelene F. Kesner, "Commentary on At Will Employment: A Devil's Advocate," *Business & Professional Ethics Journal*, 5, no. 1 (1985), 73–74.

Donaldson, Thomas, "Employee Rights," in *Corporations and Morality* (Englewood Cliffs, NJ: Prentice Hall, 1982), 130–146.

Ewing, David, *Freedom Inside the Organization: Bringing Civil Liberties to the Workplace* (New York: E. P. Dutton, 1977).

Hiley, David R., "Employee Rights and the Doctrine of At Will Employment," *Business & Professional Ethics Journal*, 4, no. 1 (1984), 1–10.

Ladenson, Robert F., "Freedom of Expression in the Corporate Workplace," in *Profits and Professions*, edited by Wade L. Robison, Michael S. Pritchard, and Joseph Ellin (Clifton, NJ: Humana Press, 1983), 275–286.

Lynd, Staughton, "Company Constitutionalism," *Yale Law Journal*, 84, no. 4 (March 1978). Reprinted in *Individual Rights in the Corporation: A Reader on Employee Rights*, edited by Alan F. Westin and Stephen Salisbury (New York: Pantheon, 1980), 70–75.

Maitland, Ian, "Rights in the Workplace: A Nozickian Argument," *Journal of Business Ethics*, 8 (1989), 951–954.

Werhane, Patricia, "Accountability and Employee Rights," *The International Journal of Applied Philosophy*, 1 (Spring 1983), 15–26.

———, *Persons, Rights and Corporations* (Englewood Cliffs, NJ: Prentice Hall, 1985).

Westin, Alan F., and Stephen Salisbury, eds., *Individual Rights in the Corporation* (New York: Pantheon Books, 1980).

Woodhouse, Mark B., "Implementing Employee Rights: A Critique," in *Business Ethics*, edited by Milton Snoeyanbos, Robert Almeder, James Humber (New York: Prometheus Books, 1983), 328–333.

CHAPTER 11

◆ ◆ ◆

Employee Privacy

How much is an employer entitled to know about his or her employees? Must an employer always have the employee's consent to get sensitive information? At what point is an employee's privacy invaded? May an employer regulate what an employee does in his or her private life? These questions point to one of the most controversial issues in business ethics—privacy. At first glance, employers seem entitled to any information that bears directly on the company's interest. Yet employees are also entitled to a private life beyond the reach of their employer's control. How do we resolve the conflict?

This section begins with George Brenkert's classic discussion of the conditions that constitute a violation of the right to privacy. Brenkert focuses mainly on lie detectors, now largely outlawed, but his claim that information that does not relate to an employee's job performance is rightfully private applies to the varied methods a company could use to gather information. Joseph Des Jardins reflects on the brief legal history of privacy, and he endorses Brenkert's reading of the right. Considering the problems associated with gathering, using, and protecting information, Des Jardins emphasizes the importance of employee consent. Another endorsement of rights to privacy is offered by Richard Lippke, but he approaches the issue through the imbalance of power between employer and employees. This chapter closes with a discussion of privacy as it relates to an issue that many college students will face in trying to get their first jobs — drug testing. Despite the pervasive use of drug tests by corporations, Joseph Des Jardins and Ronald Duska argue that drug testing is rarely justified.

George G. Brenkert

PRIVACY, POLYGRAPHS, AND WORK

The rights of prospective employees have been the subject of considerable dispute, both past and present. In recent years, this dispute has focused on the use of polygraphs to verify the claims which prospective employees make on employment application forms. With employee theft supposedly amounting to approximately ten billion dollars a year, with numerous businesses suffering sizeable losses and even being forced into bankruptcy by employee theft, significant and increasing numbers of employers have turned to the use of polygraphs.[1] Their right to protect their property is in danger, they insist, and the use of the polygraph to detect and weed out the untrustworthy prospective employee is a painless, quick, economical, and legitimate way to defend this right. Critics, however, have questioned both the reliability and validity of polygraphs, as well as objected to the use of polygraphs as demeaning, affronts to human dignity, violations of self-incrimination prohibitions, expressions of employers' mistrust, and violations of privacy.[2] Though there has been a great deal of discussion of the reliability and validity of polygraphs, there has been precious little discussion of the central moral issues at stake. Usually terms such as "dignity," "privacy," and "property rights" are simply bandied about with the hope that some favorable response will be evoked. The present paper seeks to redress this situation by discussing one important aspect of the above dispute — the supposed violation of personal privacy. Indeed, the violation of "a right to privacy" often appears to be the central moral objection to the use of polygraphs. However, the nature and basis of this claim have not yet been clearly established.[3] If they could be, there would be a serious reason to oppose the use of polygraphs on prospective employees.

I.

There are three questions which must be faced in the determination of this issue. First, is the nature of the information which polygraphing seeks to verify, information which can be said to violate, or involve the violation of, a person's privacy? Second, does the use of the polygraph itself as the means to corroborate the responses of the job applicant violate the applicant's privacy? Third, even if — for either of the two preceding reasons — the polygraph does violate a person's privacy, might this violation still be justified by the appeal to more weighty reasons, e.g., the defense of property rights?

It might be maintained that only the last two questions are meaningful since "there is no such thing as violating a man's right to privacy by simply knowing something about him";[4] rather, a violation of one's right to privacy may occur because "we have a right that certain steps shall not be taken to find out facts, and because we have a right that certain uses shall not be made of facts."[5] Thus, it is said that to torture, to extort information by threat, to spy, etc. are all

From *Business and Professional Ethics Journal*, 1, no. 1 (1981), 19–35. Reprinted by permission of the author.

illegitimate ways to obtain information. If one obtains information in these ways one violates various rights of a person — and thereby also one's right to privacy.

If this view is correct, then an employer who knows, or comes to know, certain facts about a prospective employee would not as such violate the prospective employee's right to privacy. Only the use of certain means (e.g., spying or perhaps the polygraph) or the use of these facts in certain ways would violate this privacy. Thus, there could be no violation of rights of privacy by knowing certain information (the first question), only in the manner of obtaining it and the use of it (the second and third questions).

This view is, I believe, implausible when the (private) information concerned is intentionally sought, as it is in the case of polygraphs. In this case, it would seem, there are certain things which people (in their various roles as employers, government officials, physicians, etc.) and institutions (governments and businesses, etc.) ought not to know about individuals, however they might come to know these facts. Indeed, since they ought not to know such facts, those individuals who are the ultimate object of this knowledge may legitimately object to a violation of their rights and demand that steps should be taken to make sure that others do not come to know this information. For example, it would be wrong, however they went about it, for government officials to make it their business to know the details of the sexual practices of each particular citizen. It would be wrong, it has been claimed, for a physician to know by what means a patient intends to pay for the health care administered.[6] Finally, the following case suggests that there is information which an employer ought not to know about an employee. A warehouse manager had an employee who had confessed to a theft on the job take a polygraph test in order to determine whether others had helped him steal some of the missing goods. The employee answered "no" to each person he was asked about — and the polygraph bore him out, except in the case of one person. Each time he was asked about this person the employee would deny that he had helped him, but each time the polygraph reported a reaction indicative of lying. At last they asked him why each time they raised this person's name there was such a great physiological response. After some hesitation, the thief "took a deep breath and explained that one day a few weeks before, he had walked into the company bathroom and found the fellow in a stall masturbating." The employer's reaction suggests that such information he considered to be information he ought not to know — however he found it out:

> "I fired the thief, but I never said a word to the other guy. He was a good worker, and that's what counts. But I'll have to tell you this: Every time I saw him for months after that, I'd think about what the thief had told me, and I'd say to myself, 'God, I don't have any right to know that.' "[7]

It is not implausible then that there are various kinds of information which people and institutions ought not to know about individuals.[8] Surely to torture a person to get information or to extort information by threat is to violate a person's right not to be threatened or tortured as well as his right to privacy. But one may do the latter without resorting to such exotic means. One might simply ask the person about the matter which is rightfully private. Some people are weak, gullible, easily persuaded, desirous of pleasing, overly trusting, etc., etc.

They might not even know that they need not disclose certain information to this person or that institution. Thus, to hold that our right to privacy of information is violated only when other rights are violated (e.g., rights not to be threatened, or tortured) is to hold an overly positive and optimistic view of the actual condition of people.

Is it possible then to characterize the nature of privacy such that one might know what kinds of information are rightfully private? If an employer had or sought access to that information he would be said to violate the person's right to privacy. Quite often one suspects that people take the view that information about a person is private in the above sense, if that person does not want it known by others.[9] Thus, the determination of which information is protected by a right to privacy is subjectively, individually, based — it is whatever an individual does not want to be known.

There are, however, good reasons to reject this view. Though we may intelligibly talk about the privacy a person seeks and equate this with a state of affairs he wants or seeks in which he does not share himself and/or information about himself with others, we are not thereby talking about that person's right to privacy. A person might not want passers-by to know that he is bald; he may not want his doctor to know exactly which aches and pains he has; he may not want his neighbors to know about the toxic chemicals he is burying on his land. It does not follow, however, that passers-by, one's doctor, and neighbors violate a person's right to privacy in acquiring such information. It is indeed true that control of information about oneself is important in the formation of the kinds of relationships one wants to have with other people.[10] But it does not follow from this that, just because one wants — or does not want — to have a certain relationship with another person or institution, a certain piece of information which one does not want revealed to that person or institution is therefore private — that others in acquiring it would violate one's right to privacy. In this sense, privacy is not like property which is itself merely a cluster of rights. We may, on the contrary, speak intelligibly of the privacy a person seeks apart from any right to privacy to which a person may be entitled.

On the other hand, one may want some things to be public, to be exposed to the view of all, but this may also be unjustified. The person who exposes his sexual organs at mid-day on a busy downtown street or makes a practice of revealing his most intimate thoughts and feelings to unconcerned strangers may be condemned not simply for the offense he causes others but also for his refusal to treat such matters as private rather than public. Perhaps the latter sounds strange. But one should recall that it was not simply the violation of the rights of others which shocked and disturbed non-members of the late 60's and early 70's youth revolt, but the apparent lack of any sense by those who partook of that revolt that, with regard to themselves, they ought to treat certain matters as private rather than public.[11] When they were not condemned for not treating certain (personal) matters as private, excuses and explanations were found for their behavior. They were said to be ethically immature or morally blind.[12] My purpose, however, is not to discuss this or any other particular instance in which privacy has been rejected, but to indicate that both an obligation to privacy and a right to privacy constitute the social institution surrounding privacy.

Accordingly, privacy must be seen as part of a complex social practice within which we must distinguish (a) privacy itself, (b) privacy as a value, (c) the right to privacy, and (d) the obligation to privacy which this social institution imposes upon individuals. Consequently, we cannot simply identify "A does not want X to be known" with "Knowledge of X violates A's right to privacy," although the former may be identical with "X is private to A." Similarly, "A wants (or does not care if) X (is) to be made public" is not to be equated with "Knowledge or exposure of X does not violate A's (obligation to) privacy." "X is private to A," "Knowledge or exposure of X violates A's right to privacy," and "Knowledge or exposure of X ought to be kept private by A" are not, therefore, the same, even though on occasion and by extension we may so treat them. To distinguish these notions I will speak of X being "simply private," X being "rightfully private," and X being "obligatorily private."

Upon what basis then, if it is not simply a personal determination, do we maintain that certain information is rightfully private, that the knowledge of it by others constitutes a violation of one's right to privacy? There are two points to make here. First, there is no piece of information about a person which is by itself rightfully private. Information about one's financial concerns may be rightfully private vis-a-vis a stranger or a neighbor, but not vis-a-vis one's banker. The nature of one's sex life may be rightfully private with regard to most people, including future employers, but not to one's psychiatrist, sex therapist, or mate. Accordingly, the right to privacy involves a three place relation. To say that something is rightfully private is to say that A may withhold from or not share something, X, with Z. Thus to know whether some information, X, about a person or institution, A, is, or ought to be, treated as rightfully private, we must ask about the relationship in which A stands to Z, another person or institution. Because the threefold nature of this relation is not recognized, the view which we have argued is implausible, viz., that "none of us has a right over any fact to the effect that that fact shall not be known by others,"[13] is confused with the view which is plausible, viz., that there is no piece of information about people or institutions which is in itself private. It does not follow from this latter truth that the knowing of a piece of information by some particular person or institution may not be a violation of one's right to privacy — it may or may not be depending upon who or what knows it.

Second, then, to speak of the right to privacy is to speak of the right which individuals, groups, or institutions have that access to and information about themselves is limited in certain ways by the relationships in which they exist to others. In general, the information and access to which a person or institution is entitled with regard to another person and/or institution is that information and access which will enable the former to fulfill, perform, or execute the role the person or institution plays in the particular relationship. All other access and information about the latter is beyond the pale. Thus one cannot be a friend of another unless one knows more about another and has a special access to that person. Similarly, one cannot be a person's lawyer, physician, or barber unless one is entitled to other kinds of knowledge and access. It follows that to speak of one's right to privacy is not simply to speak of one's ability to control information and access to him, since one may be unable to control such access or information acquisition and still be said to have a right to such. Similarly, to speak of one's privacy is not to speak of a claim one makes, since one may not claim or demand that others limit their access to oneself and still have a right that they do so.[14] Such a situation might occur when one is dominated or oppressed by others such that one does not insist on — or claim — the rights one is entitled to. On the other hand, one might also, in certain situations, decide not to invoke one's right to privacy and thus allow others access to oneself which the present relationship might not otherwise permit. It is in this sense that individuals can determine for themselves which others and when others have access to them and to information about them.

II.

In order to determine what information might be legitimately private to an individual who seeks employment we must consider the nature of the employer/(prospective) employee relationship. The nature of this relationship depends upon the customs, conventions and rules of the society. These, of course, are in flux at any time — and particularly so in the present case. They may also need revision. Further, the nature of this relationship will depend upon its particular instances — e.g., that of the employer of five workers or of five thousand workers, the kind of work involved, etc. In essence, however, we have a complex relationship in which an employer theoretically contracts with a person(s) to perform certain services from which the employer expects to derive a certain gain for himself. In the course of the employee's performance of these services, the employer entrusts him with certain goods, money, etc.; in return for such services he delivers to the employee a certain remuneration and (perhaps) benefits. The goals of the employer and the employee are not at all, on this account, necessarily the same. The employee expects his remuneration (and benefits) even if the services, though adequately performed, do not result in the end the employer expected. Analogously, the employer expects to derive a certain gain for the services the employee has performed even if the employee is not (fully) satisfied with his work or remuneration. On the other hand, if the employer is significantly unable to achieve the ends sought through the contract with the employee, the latter may not receive his full remuneration (should the employer go bankrupt) and may even lose his job. There is, in short, a complicated mixture of trust and antagonism, connectedness and disparity of ends in the relation between employer and employee.

Given this (brief) characterization of the relationship between employer and employee, the information to which the employer qua employer is entitled about the (prospective) employee is that information which regards his possible acceptable performance of the services for which he might be hired. Without such information the employer could not fulfill the role which present society sanctions. There are two aspects of the information to which the employer is entitled given the employer/employee relationship. On the one hand, this information will relate to and vary in accordance with the services for which the person is to be hired. But in any case, it will be limited by those services and what they require. In short, one aspect of the information to which the employer is entitled is "job relevant" information. Admittedly the criterion of job relevancy is rather vague. Certainly there are few aspects of a person which might not affect his job performance — aspects including his sex life, etc. How then does the "job relevancy" criterion limit the questions asked or the information sought? It does so by limiting the information sought to that which is directly connected with the job description. If a typist is sought, it is job relevant to know whether or not a person can type — typing tests are legitimate.

If a store manager is sought, it is relevant to know about his abilities to manage employees, stock, etc. That is, the description of the job is what determines the relevancy of the information to be sought. It is what gives the employer a right to know certain things about the person seeking employment. Accordingly, if a piece of information is not "job relevant" then the employer is not entitled qua employer to know it. Consequently, since sexual practices, political beliefs, associational activities, etc. are not part of the description of most jobs, that is, since they do not directly affect one's job performance, they are not legitimate information for an employer to know in the determination of the hiring of a job applicant.[15]

However, there is a second aspect to this matter. A person must be able not simply to perform a certain activity, or provide a service, but he must also be able to do it in an acceptable manner — i.e., in a manner which is approximately as efficient as others, in an honest manner, and in a manner compatible with others who seek to provide the services for which they were hired. Thus, not simply one's abilities to do a certain job are relevant, but also aspects of one's social and moral character are pertinent. A number of qualifications are needed for the purport of this claim to be clear. First, that a person must be able to work in an acceptable manner is not intended to legitimize the consideration of the prejudices of other employees. It is not legitimate to give weight in moral deliberations to the immoral and/or morally irrelevant beliefs which people hold concerning the characteristics of others. That one's present employees can work at a certain (perhaps exceptional) rate is a legitimate consideration in hiring other workers. That one's present employees have prejudices against certain religions, sexes, races, political views, etc. is not a morally legitimate consideration. Second, it is not, or should not be, the motives, beliefs, or attitudes underlying the job relevant character traits, e.g., honest, efficient, which are pertinent, but rather the fact that a person does or does not perform according to these desirable character traits. This is not to say, it should be noted, that a person's beliefs and attitudes about the job itself, e.g., how it is best to be done, what one knows or believes about the job, etc., are irrelevant. Rather it is those beliefs, attitudes and motives underlying one's desired character traits which are not relevant. The contract of the employer with the employee is for the latter to perform acceptably certain services — it is not for the employee to have certain underlying beliefs, motives, or attitudes. If I want to buy something from someone, this commercial relation does not entitle me to probe the attitudes, motives, and beliefs of the person beyond his own statements, record of past actions, and the observations of others. Even the used car salesman would correctly object that his right to privacy was being violated if he was required to submit to Rorschach tests, an attitude survey test, truth serums, and/or the polygraph in order to determine his real beliefs about selling cars. Accordingly, why the person acts the way in which he acts ought not to be the concern of the employer. Whether a person is a good working colleague simply because he is congenial, because his ego needs the approval of others, or because he has an oppressive superego is, in this instance, morally irrelevant. What is relevant is whether this person has, by his past actions, given some indication that he may work in a manner compatible with others.

Consequently, a great deal of the information which has been sought in preemployment screening through the use of polygraph tests has violated the privacy of individuals. Instances in which the sex lives, for example, of applicants have been probed are not difficult to find. However, privacy violations have occurred not simply in such generally atypical instances but also in standard situations. To illustrate the range of questions asked prospective employees and the violations of privacy which have occurred we need merely consider a list of some questions which one of the more prominent polygraph firms includes in its current tests:

> Have you ever taken any of the following without the advice of a doctor? If Yes, please check: Barbiturates, Speed, LSD, Tranquilizers, Amphetamines, Marijuana, Others.
>
> In the past five years about how many times, if any, have you bet on horse races at the race track?
>
> Do you think that policemen are honest?
>
> Did you ever think about committing a robbery?
>
> Have you been refused credit or a loan in the past five years?
>
> Have you ever consulted a doctor about a mental condition?
>
> Do you think that it is okay to get around the law if you don't actually break it?
>
> Do you enjoy stories of successful crimes and swindles?[16]

Such questions, it follows from the above argument, are for any standard employment violations of one's right to privacy. An employer might ask if a person regularly takes certain narcotic drugs, if he is considering him for a job which requires handling narcotics. An employer might ask if a person has been convicted of a larceny, etc. But whether the person enjoys stories about successful larcenists, whether a person has ever taken any prescription drugs without the advice of a doctor, or whether a person bets on the horses should be considered violations of one's rightful privacy.

The upshot of the argument in the first two sections is, then, that some information can be considered rightfully private to an individual. Such information is rightfully private or not depending on the relationship in which a person stands to another person or institution. In the case of the employer/employee relationship, I have argued that that information is rightfully private which does not relate to the acceptable performance of the activities as characterized in the job description. This excludes a good many questions which are presently asked in polygraph tests, but does not, by any means, exclude all such questions. There still remain many questions which an employer might conceivably wish to have verified by the use of the polygraph. Accordingly, I turn in the next section to the question whether the verification of the answers to legitimate questions by the use of the polygraph may be considered a violation of a person's right to privacy. If it is, then the violation obviously does not stem from the questions themselves but from the procedure, the polygraph test, whereby the answers to those questions are verified.

III.

A first reason to believe that use of the polygraph occasions a violation of one's right to privacy is that, even though the questions to be answered are job relevant, some of them will occasion positive, lying reactions which are not necessarily related to any past misdeeds. Rather, the lying reaction indicated by the polygraph may be triggered because of unconscious conflicts, fears and hostilities a person has. It may be occasioned by conscious anxieties over other past activities and observations. Thus, the lying reaction indicated by the polygraph need not positively identify actual lying or the commission of illegal activities. The point, however, is not to question the validity of the polygraph. Rather, the point is that the validity of the polygraph can only be maintained by seeking to clarify whether or not such reactions really indicate lying and the commission of past misdeeds. But this can be done only by the polygraphist further probing into the person's background and inner thoughts. However, inasmuch as the questions can no longer be restrained in this situation by job relevancy considerations, but must explore other areas to which an employer is not necessarily entitled knowledge, to do this will violate a person's right to privacy.

It has been suggested by some polygraphists that if a person has "Something Else" on his mind other than the direct answer to the questions asked, a "something else" which might lead the polygraph to indicate a deceptive answer, the person might, if he so feels inclined,

> tell the examiner about this "outside troubling matter" . . . but as a special precaution obtain the examiner's promise that the disclosure of this information is secret and . . . request that the matter be held in strict confidence. The examiner will comply with your wishes. The examiner does not wish to enter into your personal problems since they tend to complicate the polygraph examination.[17]

What this suggests, however, is that a person go ahead, under the threat of the polygraph indicating that one is lying, and tell the polygraphist matters that are rightfully private. This is supposedly acceptable since one "requests" that it be held in strict confidence. But it surely does not follow that a violation of one's right to privacy does not occur simply because the recipient promises not to pass the information on. If, under some threat, I tell another person something which he has no right to know about me, but I then get his promise that he will treat the information confidentially and that it will not be misused in any way, my right to privacy has still been violated.[18] Accordingly, whether the polygraphist attempts to prevent job applicants from producing misleading deceptive reactions by allowing them to reveal what else is on their minds or probes deceptive reactions once they have occurred to ascertain whether they might not be produced by job irrelevant considerations, he violates the right to privacy of the job applicant.

A second reason why the polygraph must be said to violate a job applicant's right to privacy relates to the monitoring of a person's physiological responses to the questions posed to him. By measuring these responses, the polygraph can supposedly reveal one's mental processes. Now even though the questions posed are legitimate questions, surely a violation of one's right to privacy occurs. Just because I have something which you are entitled to see or know, it does not follow that you can use any means to fulfill that entitlement and not violate my privacy. Consider the instance of two good friends, one of whom has had some dental work done which puts him in a situation such that he can tune in the thoughts and feelings of his friend. Certain facts about, and emotional responses of, his friend — aspects which his friend (we will assume) would usually want to share with him — simply now stream into his head. Even though the friendship relation generally entitles its members to know personal information about the other person, the friend with the dental work is not entitled to such information in this direct and immediate way. This manner of gaining this information simply eliminates any private reserves of the person; it wholly opens his consciousness to the consciousness of another. Surely this would be a violation of his friend's right to privacy, and his friend would rightfully ask that such dental work be modified. Even friends do not have a right to learn in this manner of each other's inner thoughts and feelings.

Such fancy dental work may, correctly, be said to be rather different from polygraphs. Still the point is that though one is entitled to some information about another, one is not entitled to use any means to get it. But why should the monitoring by an employer or his agent of one's physiological responses to legitimate questions be an invasion of privacy — especially if one has agreed to take the test? There are several reasons.

First, the claim that one freely agrees or consents to take the test is surely, in many cases, disingenuous.[19] Certainly a job applicant who takes the polygraph test is not physically forced or coerced into taking the exam. However, it is quite apparent that if he did not take the test and cooperate during the test, his application for employment would either not be considered at all or would be considered to have a significant negative aspect to it. This is surely but a more subtle form of coercion. And if this be the case, then one cannot say that the person has willingly allowed his reactions to the questions to be monitored. He has consented to do so, but he has consented under coercion. Had he a truly free choice, he would not have done so.

Now the whole point of the polygraph test is, of course, not simply to monitor physiological reactions but to use these responses as clues, indications, or revelations of one's mental processes and acts. The polygraph seeks to make manifest to others one's thoughts and ideas. However, unless we freely consent, we are entitled to the privacy of our thoughts, that is, we have a prima facie right not to have our thoughts exposed by others, even when the information sought is legitimate. Consider such analogous cases as a husband reading his wife's diary, a person going through a friend's desk drawers, a stranger reading personal papers on one's desk, an F.B.I. agent going through one's files. In each of these cases, a person attempts to determine the nature of someone else's thoughts by the use of clues and indications which those thoughts left behind. And, in each of these cases, though we may suppose that the person seeks to confirm answers to legitimate questions, we may also say that, if the affected person's uncoerced consent is not forthcoming, his or her right to privacy is violated. Morally, however, there is no difference between ascertaining the nature of one's thoughts by the use of a polygraph, or reading notes left in a drawer, going through one's diary, etc. Hence, unless there are overriding considerations to consent to such revelations of one's thoughts, the use of the polygraph is a violation of one's right to privacy.[20]

Second, it should be noted that even if a person voluntarily agreed to the polygraph test, it need not follow that there is not a violation of his privacy. It was argued in Section I that there are certain aspects of oneself which are obligatorily private, that is, which one ought to keep private. Accordingly, it may be wrong for one voluntarily to reveal various aspects of oneself to others, even though in so doing one would be responding to legitimate demands. For example, consider a person being interviewed by a health officer who is legitimately seeking information from the person about venereal diseases. Suppose that the person does not simply admit to having such a disease but also — instead of providing a corrobative statement from a physician — reveals the diseased organs. Further, suppose that the health officer is not shocked or offended in any way. The person has been asked legitimate questions, he has acted voluntarily, but still he has violated his own privacy. This is not the kind of access to oneself one ought to afford a bureaucrat. Now it may well be that, analogously, one ought not to allow employers access to one's physiological reactions to legitimate questions, for the reason that such access also violates one's obligatory privacy. To act in this way sets a bad precedent, it signifies that those with power and authority may disregard the privacy of an individual in order to achieve aims of their own. Thus, even if a job applicant readily agreed to reveal certain aspects of himself in a polygraph test, it would not follow without more argument that he was not violating his own privacy.

Finally, if we value privacy not simply as a barrier to the intrusion of others but also as the way by which we define ourselves as separate, autonomous persons, individuals with an integrity which lies at least in part in the ability to make decisions, to give or withhold information and access, then the polygraph strikes at this fundamental value.[21] The polygraph operates by turning part of us over which we have little or no control against the rest of us. If a person were an accomplished yogi, the polygraph would supposedly be useless — since that person's physiological reactions would be fully under his control. The polygraph works because most of us do not have that control. Thus, the polygraph is used to probe people's reactions which they would otherwise protect, not expose to others. It uses part of us to reveal the rest of us. It takes the "shadows" consciousness throws off within us and reproduces them for other people. As such, the use of the polygraph undercuts the decision-making aspect of a person. It circumvents the person. The person says such and such, but his uncontrolled reactions may say something different. He does not know — even when honest — what his reactions might say. Thus it undercuts and demeans that way by which we define ourselves as autonomous persons — in short, it violates our privacy. Suppose one said something to another — but his Siamese and undetached twin, who was given to absolute truth and who correctly knew every thought, past action, and feeling of the person said: "No, he does not really believe that." I think the person would rightfully complain that his twin had better remain silent. Just so, I have a right to complain when my own feelings are turned on me. This subtle form of self-incrimination is a form of invading one's privacy. An employer is entitled to know certain facts about one's background, but this relationship does not entitle him — or his agents — to probe one's emotional responses, feelings, and thoughts.

Thus, it follows that even if the only questions asked in a polygraph test are legitimate ones, the use of the polygraph for the screening of job applicants still violates one's privacy. In this case, the violation of privacy stems from the procedure itself, and not the questions. Accordingly, one can see the lameness of the defense of polygraphing which maintains that if a person has nothing to hide, he should not object to the polygraph tests. Such a defense is mistaken at least on two counts. First, just because someone believes something to be private does not mean that he believes that what is private is wrong, something to be ashamed about or to be hidden. Second, the polygraph test has been shown to violate a person's privacy, whether one person has really something to hide or not--whether he is dishonest or not. Consequently, if the question is simply whether polygraphing of prospective employees violates their privacy the answer must be affirmative.

IV.

There remains one possible defense of the use of polygraphs for screening prospective employees. This is to admit that such tests violate the applicant's privacy but to maintain that other considerations outweigh this fact. Specifically, in light of the great amount of merchandise and money stolen, the right of the employers to defend their property outweighs the privacy of the applicant. This defense is specious, I believe, and the following arguments seek to show why.

First, surely it would be better if people who steal or are dishonest were not placed in positions of trust. And if the polygraphs were used in only these cases, one might well maintain that the use of the polygraph, though it violates one's privacy, is legitimate and justified. However, the polygraph cannot be so used, obviously, only in these cases — it must be used more broadly on both honest and dishonest applicants. Further, if a polygraph has a 90% validity then out of 1,000 interviewees, a full 100 will be misidentified.[22] Now if 10% of the interviewees are thieves, then 10 out of the 100 will steal, but 90 would not; in addition 90 out of the 900 would be thieves, and supposedly correctly identified. This means that 90 thieves would be correctly identified, 10 thieves would be missed, and 90 honest people would be said not to have cleared the test. Thus, for every thief "caught," one honest person would also be "caught" — the former would be correctly identified as one who would steal, while the latter could not be cleared of the suspicion that he too would steal. The point, then, is that this means of defending property rights is one that excludes not simply thieves but honest people as well — and potentially in equal numbers. Such a procedure certainly appears to constitute not simply a violation of privacy rights, but also, and more gravely, an injustice to those honest people stigmatized as not beyond suspicion and hobbled in their competition with others to get employment. If then using polygraph tests to defend property rights is not simply like preventing a thief from breaking into the safe, but more like keeping a thief from the safe plus binding the leg of an innocent bystander in his competition with others to gain employment, then one may legitimately doubt that this procedure to protect property rights is indeed defensible.[23]

Second, it has been claimed that just as the use of blood tests on suspected drunken drivers and the use of baggage searches at the airport are legitimate, so too is the polygraphing of prospective employees. Both of the former kinds of searches may also be said to violate a person's privacy; still they are taken to be justified whether the appeal is to the general good they produce or to the protection of the rights of other drivers or passengers and airline employees. However, neither the blood test nor the baggage search is really analogous to the use of the polygraph on job applicants. Blood tests are only administered to those drivers who have given police officers reason to believe that they (the drivers) are driving while under the influence of alcohol. The polygraph, however, is not applied only to those suspected of past thefts; it is applied to others as well. Further, the connection between driving while drunk and car accidents is quite direct; it immediately endangers both the safety and lives of others. The connection between polygraph tests of a diverse group of applicants (some honest and some dishonest) and future theft is not nearly so direct nor do the thefts endanger the lives of others. Baggage searches are a different matter. They are similar to polygraphing in that they are required of everyone. They are dissimilar in that they are made because of fears concerning the safety of other people. Further, surely there is a dissimilarity between officials searching one's baggage for lethal objects which one is presently trying to sneak on board, and employers searching one's mind for the true nature of one's past behavior which may or may not lead to future criminal intentions. Finally, there are signs at airports warning people, before they are searched, against carrying weapons on airplanes; such weapons could at that time be declared and sent, without prejudice, with the regular baggage. There is no similar aspect to polygraph tests. Thus, the analogies suggested do not hold. Indeed, they suggest that we allow for a violation of privacy only in very different circumstances than those surrounding the polygraphing of job applicants.

Third, the corporate defense of polygraphs seems one-sided in the sense that employers would not really desire the universalization of their demands. Suppose that the businesses in a certain industry are trying to get a new government contract. The government, however, has had difficulties with other corporations breaking the rules of other contracts. As a result it has lost large sums of money. In order to prevent this in the present case it says that it is going to set up devices to monitor the reactions of board members and top managers when a questionnaire is sent to them which they must answer. Any business, of course, need not agree to this procedure but if it does then it will be noted in their file regarding this and future government contracts. The questionnaire will include questions about the corporations' past fulfillment of contracts, competency to fulfill the present contract, loopholes used in past contracts, collusion with other companies, etc. The reactions of the managers and board members, as they respond to these questions, will be monitored and a decision on the worthiness of that corporation to receive the contract will be made in part on this basis.

There can be little doubt, I think, that the management and directors of the affected corporations would object to the proposal even though the right of the government to defend itself from the violation of its contracts and serious financial losses is at stake. It would be said to be an unjustified violation of the privacy of the decision-making process in a business; an illegitimate encroachment of the government on free enterprise. But surely if this is the legitimate response for the corporate job applicant, the same kind of response would be legitimate in the case of the individual job applicant.

Finally, it is simply false that there are not other measures which could be taken which could not help resolve the problem of theft. The fact that eighty percent of industry does not use the polygraph is itself suggestive that business does not find itself absolutely forced into the use of polygraphs. It might be objected that that does not indicate that certain industries might need polygraphs more than others — e.g., banks and drug companies more than auto plants and shipyards. But even granting this point there are other measures which businesses can use to avoid the problem of theft. Stricter inventory controls, different kinds of cash registers, educational programs, hot lines, incentives, etc. could all be used. The question is whether the employer, management, can be imaginative and innovative enough to move in these directions.

In conclusion, it has been argued that the use of the polygraph to screen job applicants does indeed violate a prospective employee's privacy. First, it is plausible that the privacy of (prospective) employees may be violated by the employer acquiring certain kinds of information about them. Second, using a polygraph an employer may violate an employee's privacy even when the employer seeks the answers to legitimate questions. Third, other moral considerations employers have raised do not appear to outweigh the employee's right to privacy. Accordingly, on balance, a violation of the privacy of a job applicant occurs in the use of the polygraph. This constitutes a serious reason to oppose the use of the polygraph for such purposes.[24]

Notes

1. Cf. Harlow Unger, "Lie Detectors: Business Needs Them to Avoid Costly Employee Rip-offs," *Canadian Business*, Vol. 51 (April, 1978), p. 30. Other estimates may be found in "Outlaw Lie-Detector Tests?", *U.S. News & World Report*, Vol. 84, No. 4, (January 1978), p. 45, and Victor Lipman, "New Hiring Tool: Truth Tests," *Parade* (October 7, 1979), p. 19.

2. Both the AFL-CIO and the ACLU have raised these objections to the use of the polygraph for screening job applicants; cf. *AFL-CIO Executive Council Statements and Reports: 1956–1975* (Westport, Conn.: Greenwood Press, 1977), p. 1422. See also ACLU Policy #248.

3. See, for example, Alan F. Westin, *Privacy and freedom* (New York: Atheneum, 1967), p. 238.

4. Judith Jarvis Thomson, "The Right to Privacy," *Philosophy and Public Affairs*, Vol. IV (Summer, 1975), p. 307.

5. *Ibid.*

6. Cf. "A Model Patient's Bill of Rights," from George J. Annas, *The Rights of Hospital Patients* (New York: Avon Books, 1975), p. 233.

7. Frye Gaillard, "Polygraphs and Privacy," *The Progressive*, Vol. 38 (September, 1974), p. 46.

8. Cf. James Rachels' comment on the importance of the privacy of medical records in "Why Privacy Is Important," *Philosophy and Public Affairs*, Vol IV (Summer, 1975), p. 324.

9. Alan Westin's definition of privacy suggests this view; cf. Alan F. Westin, *Privacy and Freedom*, p. 7. Also, Rachels' account of privacy suggests this view at times; cf. "Why Privacy Is Important," *Philosophy and Public Affairs*, pp. 326, 329.

10. Rachels emphasizes this point in his article; cf. "Why Privacy is Important."

11. John W. Chapman discusses the "deadly danger" which "the moral psychology of the young" poses for privacy in his essay "Personality and Privacy." I take it that one of the major theses of his article is that, morally considered, the young ought to treat certain aspects of themselves and their relations to others as private. CF. John W. Chapman, "Personality and Privacy," in *Privacy*, eds. J. Roland Pennock and John W. Chapman (New York: Atherton Press, 1971).

12. *Ibid.*, pp. 239, 240.

13. Judith Jarvis Thomson, "The Right to Privacy," p. 307.

14. Alan Westin characterizes privacy in terms of the "claim" which people make; cf. *Privacy and Freedom*, p. 7.

15. This would have to be qualified for security jobs and the like.

16. John E. Reid and Associates, *Reid Report* (Chicago: By the author, 1978), passim.

17. John E. Reid and Associates, *The Polygraph Examination* (Chicago: By the author, n.d.), p. 7.

18. It should be further pointed out that the polygraphist/job-applicant relation is not legally or

morally a privileged relation. What one tells one's physician one can expect to be treated confidentially. There is no similar expectation that one may entertain in the present case. At most one may hope that as another human being he will keep his promise. On the other hand, the polygraphist is an agent of the employer and responsible to him. There is and can be then no guarantee that the promise of the polygraphist will be kept.

19. The reasons why people do not submit to the polygraph are many and various. Some might have something to hide; others may be scared of the questions, supposing that some of them will not be legitimate; some may feel that they are being treated like criminals; others may fear the jaundiced response of the employer to the applicant's honest answers to legitimate questions; finally some may even object to the polygraph on moral grounds, e.g., it violates one's right to privacy.

20. See Section IV below.

21. Cf. Jeffrey H. Reiman, "Privacy, Intimacy, and Personhood," *Philosophy and Public Affairs*, Vol. VI (Fall, 1976).

22. Estimates of the validity of the polygraph range widely. Professor David Lykken has been reported as maintaining that the most prevalent polygraph test is correct only two-thirds of the time (cf. Bennett H. Beach, "Blood, Sweat and Fears," *Time*, September 8, 1980, p. 44). A similar figure of seventy percent is reported by Richard A. Sternbach et. al., "Don't Trust the Lie Detector," *Harvard Business Review*,, Vol. XL (Nov.–Dec., 1962), p. 130. Operators of polygraphs, however, report figures as high as 95% accuracy; cf. Sternbach, p. 129.

23. This argument is suggested by a similar argument in David T. Lykken, "Guilty-Knowledge Test: The Right Way to Use a Lie Detector," *Psychology Today*, (March, 1975), p. 60.

24. I wish to thank the following for their helpful comments on earlier versions of the present paper: Tom Donaldson, Norman Gillespie, Ken Goodpaster, Betsy Postow, William Tolhurst, and the editors of this journal.

Joseph R. Des Jardins
PRIVACY IN EMPLOYMENT

It would be convenient if we could begin a paper on privacy rights in employment by citing a commonly accepted definition of privacy and proceeding to develop the paper by applying that definition to employment situations. Unfortunately, there is little consensus regarding the definition, nature, and justification of privacy rights in general. Statutory protection of privacy is a relatively recent development in American legal history. The U.S. Constitution, for example, makes no explicit reference to a general right of privacy. It is not found among the numerous political rights mentioned in the Bill of Rights. The legal discussion of privacy typically is traced to the 1890 *Harvard Law Review* article by Samuel Warren and Louis Brandeis and the 1965 Supreme Court decision in *Griswold* V. *Connecticut*. Indeed, it was not until this 1965 decision that the Supreme Court recognized any Constitutional basis for privacy. Further, the very meaning of privacy is so confused that in 1977 the congressionally established Privacy Protection Study Commission reported that after two years of study its members could reach no consensus on a definition of privacy.

Fortunately, we do not need to settle upon one precise definition of the

From Joseph R. Des Jardins, "Privacy in Employment," in *Moral Rights in the Workplace*, edited by Gertrude Ezorsky (Albany: State University of New York Press, 1987) 127–139. Reprinted by permission of the State University of New York Press. © 1987 State University of New York Press.

general civil right of privacy before considering the range of privacy rights in employment. In fact, one good way to sharpen a definition is to fix its context and reflect upon the use of the word within that particular situation. With this in mind, this paper considers the extent and justification of an employee's claim to privacy in the workplace.

There tend to be three general meanings to "privacy" used in the legal and philosophical literature on this topic: (1) the proprietary relationship that a person has to his/her own name or likeness; (2) the right to be "let alone" within one's own zone of solitude; and (3) the right to control information about oneself. There may be other ways to understand privacy, but these seem to cover the most obvious cases.

The origin of the first meaning of privacy is in tort law and often is traced to a New York statute passed after a well-publicized case involving the unauthorized use of a woman's likeness in a commercial endorsement. This use of a person's likeness or name without consent was said to involve an invasion of personal privacy.

I will not be concerned with this sense of privacy here. It is unlikely that employees need to be much concerned with privacy in this sense. Further, it seems clear that what really is at issue in this definition would be more a matter of ownership or property rights and not specifically a matter of privacy. The confusion with privacy arises because of the special nature of what is claimed as property (i.e., one's own name or likeness). But the unauthorized use of a person's name or likeness is neither a necessary nor sufficient condition for a violation of privacy. For example, monitoring an employee's phone conversation would violate her privacy although no unauthorized use of her name or likeness was involved. On the other hand, we would not say that an employee's privacy was violated when, for example, her identification photograph was used in a personnel file or when her name was used in conversations among other employees without consent. Employment is an essentially social activity and as such it requires the relatively unrestricted use of a person's name among co-workers. Granting employees a right to privacy in this first sense would make most work activities terribly difficult if not altogether impossible.

A more common understanding of privacy centers around the notion of being "let alone." Beginning with the Warren and Brandeis article in 1890 and the 1965 decision in *Griswold* v. *Connecticut*, this sense of privacy has dominated the legal discussions. Privacy as a right "to be let alone" is also the understanding typically found in ordinary linguistic usage. Since this is such a common understanding of privacy and since I will suggest that it is inadequate for employment contexts, it will be useful to consider this view in some detail.

In their article, Warren and Brandeis were concerned that certain technological advances and business practices, notably the practice among some newspapers of printing stories and photographs of private parties, were causing an increasing threat to the solitude of individual citizens. They defended the right of privacy as "the next step which must be taken for the protection of the person, and for securing to the individual . . . the right 'to be let alone.' "[1]

It was not until 1965, however, that the Supreme Court recognized Constitutional protection of this right to privacy. In *Griswold* v. *Connecticut*, the Court ruled that the Constitution guaranteed citizens a "zone of privacy" around their person that could not be violated by government. The Court found privacy within the "penumbra" of rights established by the First, Third, Fourth, and

Fifth Amendments. By doing so, the Court found privacy implicit in the liberty-based rights established by the Bill of Rights.

Much of the discussion concerning the right of privacy in employment begins with this definition of privacy. The aim of some employee-rights advocates is to preserve the integrity of this zone within the workplace. According to this view, a citizen's right "to be let alone" should not be lost when he or she enters into an employment agreement. Some defenders of employee rights use this definition in developing extensive lists of privacy rights in the workplace. These lists include not only such issues as privacy of personnel records and freedom from polygraph and psychological testing, but also surveillance at work, restrictions upon afterhours activities, peace and quiet at work, employee lounges, privacy of personal property at work, and employee grooming, dress, and manners.[2]

Unfortunately there are problems with this definition of privacy. Phrases like *right to be let alone* and *zone of privacy* are quite vague, and their application tends to be much broader than is appropriate. It is difficult to see how a legitimate claim to be let alone can be consistently maintained at the same time in which one wishes to participate in an essentially social and cooperative activity like work. The difficulty with this second definition is that it confuses privacy with the more general right of liberty. Liberty, understood as the freedom from interference, can be used to generate a variety of specific rights. Free speech, freedom of religious worship, freedom of press, and private property have all been thought of as liberty-based rights. It seems that both Warren and Brandeis and the Griswold decision assume that privacy is simply another liberty-based right. It is understandable that they do so. In the *Griswold* case, the court stated that the Connecticut law might require police searches of the bedrooms of married couples. Certainly this would be an unjustified interference with personal liberty. Being free from interference is virtually synonymous with Warren and Brandeis' definition of privacy as the right to be "let alone." Certainly privacy can be closely related to liberty. Indeed, in many cases a right to privacy can be justified by appeal to liberty. Nevertheless, the justification of a right claim is independent of the definition of that right. It seems a confusion between justification and definition may underlie much of the problem with this second definition of privacy.

Violating someone's liberty is neither necessary nor sufficient for violating privacy. We can imagine a situation in which a "peeping tom" monitors someone's activities from a distance. While this would violate privacy it would not be an interference with their liberty, in any straightforward sense. Further, some coercive activities could well violate liberty without affecting the privacy of the person coerced. For example, subliminal advertising would, if effective, violate liberty without necessarily violating privacy. These examples show not only that privacy cannot be identified with liberty, but also that not all privacy claims can be justified by appeal to liberty.[3]

This brings us to the third understanding of privacy, privacy as involving information about oneself and the right to privacy as the right to control that information. To understand this view, let us return to the concerns of Warren and Brandeis. It seems that Mrs. Warren was troubled by the publicity that inevitably followed her social gatherings and parties. No doubt Mrs. Warren wanted to be "let alone," and Warren and Brandeis certainly were correct in identifying her concern as involving privacy. But surely Mrs. Warren's objections were to the publication of personal information and not simply with the violation of her liberty. No one was, after all, directly interfering with her parties. Her privacy was violated not by an interference with her actions, but when she lost control over information that was essentially private. More precisely, her privacy was violated when people who had no legitimate claim to this information (i.e., newspaper reporters and their readers) came to know the details of her parties. Her privacy was not violated when invited guests, for example, came to know about the party.

Despite the centrality of the Court's concern with the "fundamental liberties of citizens," it is also true that this informational sense of privacy played a crucial role in the *Griswold* case. Justice Douglas' majority opinion abhorred the violation of marital intimacy that would occur if government agents came to know the details of the sexual lives of married citizens.

These examples suggest that the right to privacy does not involve, as some have argued, merely the control that a person has over information about herself.[4] Rather, the relationship that exists between the persons involved also plays a crucial role. Because they were invited guests, some people could claim that they were entitled to know certain things about Mrs. Warren's party. Since no such relationship existed between Mrs. Warren and the general public, the public was not entitled to that information. In the *Griswold* case, the relationship that exists between a citizen and a liberal-democratic state makes it illegitimate for that state to come to possess intimate information about its citizens' married lives.

In an insightful article, George Brenkert recently has developed this view.[5] Brenkert claims that the right to privacy involved a three place relation between person, A, some information, X, and another person, Z. The right of privacy is violated only when Z comes to possess information X, *and* no relationship exists between A and Z that would justify Z's coming to know X. Following Brenkert, I shall say that the right to privacy is the "right of individuals, groups, or institutions that [have] access to and information about themselves is limited in certain ways by the relationships in which they exist to others."[6]

Note that this definition will help resolve some of the difficulties associated with the liberty-based understanding of privacy. If privacy receives its value simply by being derived from the more general right of liberty, then it would seem that privacy could be seriously restricted in the workplace. After all, one of the things one gives up when entering an employment agreement is the freedom to do as one chooses. The cooperative nature of work will require, at least, some restrictions on employee liberties. If privacy were justified solely by its derivation from liberty, privacy in employment would be similarly limited. But a good case can be made for protecting employee privacy even though the employee has voluntarily accepted a general restriction upon her liberty. Brenkert's definition allows the employee to retain various privacy rights while relinquishing the general claim to liberty. It does this by recognizing that specific relationships between people can justify limiting access to information in certain ways. Consequently, even if an appeal to liberty cannot justify an employee's privacy claims, the nature of the employment relationship itself can.

Accordingly, the nature and extent of privacy rights in the workplace can be determined by identifying the relationship that exists between employer and employee. On one traditional view, the relationship that exists is that of an agent-principal. The employee is the agent of the employer and as such must comply with any legal request of the employer. On this view the only right that an employee can claim is the right to quit her job. At the same time, the employee has the obligations of obedience, loyalty, and confidentiality.[7] However, there are good reasons to reject this view. This model of the employer-employee relationship developed out of a common law tradition that viewed labor merely as one type of capital and the employee as merely one type of property. But surely this outdated model cannot be justified from a moral point of view since it does not treat both parties as autonomous moral agents. Consequently, the agent-principal model has come under increasing attack and is being replaced by a contractual model of the employer-employee relationship.[8]

The existence of a contractual relationship between employer and employee, whether the contract is implicit or explicit, will entail certain ground rules. These ground rules, in turn, can be used to generate the privacy rights that should exist within the workplace. Among these ground rules are, first, that contracts presuppose a legal framework to guarantee their enforcement. An unenforceable contract is an empty contract. Contracts also must be noncoercive, voluntary agreements between rational and free agents. Contracts involving children or mentally handicapped adults, or those involving a threat of force are invalid. Finally, contracts must be free from fraud and deception. This initial sketch can help us to begin to identify the nature of privacy rights in employment.

First, since the contract presupposes the existence of a legal framework, it must conform to the requirements of that legal system. In particular, obedience to tax, social security, equal opportunity, and health and safety laws would require an employer to collect and store certain information about all employees. Providing, of course, that this information is used only in the proper legal manner, an employer coming to know an employee's age, number of dependents, sex race, social security number, and so on would not violate the employee's privacy.

There is much other information that an employer can come to know about employees without violating employee privacy. Certainly information needed to insure that the contract is voluntary and free from fraud or deception can be required. Accordingly, prior to the employment agreement, an employer can require, under the threat of not hiring the potential employee, information about job qualifications, work experience, educational background, and other information relevant to the hiring decision. However, this relevancy test should be taken seriously. There is no reason to require information concerning marital status, arrest records (as opposed to conviction records), credit or other financial data, military records (unless required by law), or such things as religious convictions and sexual or political preferences. This information is irrelevant for deciding whether or not the employee is capable of fulfilling her part of the employment contract. Further, as Brenkert argues, the use of polygraph tests prior to employment is also suspect since it seeks information in ways that bypass the employee's consent.[9]

Only after the employment agreement has been reached does other information about employees become relevant. Health and insurance plans, for example, may require information about the employee. However, since the contract is already in force, since, in other words, the relationship is grounded upon mutual consent, such information can only be requested with the consent of the employee. Thus, if an employee can choose not to participate in health or insurance packages, the medical examination required for such participation cannot be required (although, of course, there may be other reasons to require a medical examination). After the employment agreement has been reached, and the employer is satisfied with the employee's qualifications for the job, there is a prima facie prohibition against collecting or verifying evaluative information without the employee's consent. This would rule out such things as electronic or other covert surveillance, polygraph or psychological tests, background checks by third parties, and unconsented searches of an employee's desk, files, or locker.

Finally, since the contract does require the voluntary agreement of both parties, the use of third parties to gather or verify information about employees should be limited only to those cases in which the employee has given her uncoerced consent and in which the information sought is relevant to the employment relationship. Thus, checks with an employee's school to verify educational background can be justified, while credit agencies, private investigators, and police agencies are highly suspect as sources of information.

Two further issues need to be considered before this preliminary examination of privacy in employment will be complete. First, we need to consider how employers can use information about employees that has been legitimately collected, and second, we need to discuss employee access to and control over that information once the employer has come to know it.

Given the important function consent plays in the employment contract, we can say that, in general, employers should use personal information about employees only in those instances for which consent was granted. For example, social security numbers given to comply with legal requirements should not be used as employee identification numbers. Medical information released for insurance purposes should not be used during an evaluation for promotion. Information relevant for evaluations should not become the object of office gossip.

More importantly, the information an employer collects about an employee is not a commodity that can be exchanged, sold, or released in the marketplace. Accordingly, the release of information to a landlord, credit grantor, or any other third party without the employee's consent is a violation of that employee's privacy. Release of information to law enforcement agencies without either the employee's consent or a warrant also violates employee privacy. Releasing information about an employee to a credit agency, either in response to a credit check or in exchange for information about other present or potential employees, is another clear violation of employee privacy. In short, there is a prima facie prohibition against the release of any information about an employee to a third party without the employee's explicit consent.

Finally, the number of people within a company who have access to employee files should be strictly limited. Immediate supervisors ought not to have access to an employee's medical file, for example. Consent granted by employees should restrict not only the use to which personal information is put, but also the parties to whom that information is available. If an employee has not consented to release information to a particular person, release of that information again represents a prima facia violation of that employee's privacy.

The last issue to consider involves an employee's access to, and control over, information already released to an employer. In general, the rule here should be that employees ought to have access to all personal information within an employer's possession. A separate but equally important rule is that employees ought to be informed about the exact extent of the information an employer has. Access rights to personal information will prove empty unless employees know what files exist. Of course, third parties who come to possess information about an employee while providing services to the employer have similar obligations to make available the information they possess.

A morally legitimate contract must involve parties who are free and equal. An agreement between radically unequal parties easily can become coercive. To insure that this not occur in the employment agreement, it is important that neither party occupy a significantly superior position. When one party possesses a great deal more information about the other party, the relationship can become unequal and the agreement unfair. This needs special protection in employment relationships where employers typically have significant resources available for collecting and storing information about employees. Without knowledge of and access to their own personnel files, employees will be at an unfair "competitive disadvantage." As a result, this will undermine the legitimacy of the employment contract.

Of course, there can be exceptions to this rule. In some cases a third party (e.g., a physician or evaluating supervisor) may receive a pledge of confidentiality as a condition for providing information about an employee. In some cases, this pledge of confidentiality might restrict an employee's access. We should consider exactly why and when such restrictions are justified.

It may be the case that some information necessary to fulfill the employment contract can only be acquired with a promise of confidentiality to a third party. Its necessity to the contract would justify an employer coming to know this information, but does the promise of confidentiality justify restricting an employee's access? Consider two examples: In order to provide medical insurance, a medical examination might be required. The physician may request that the medical records be kept confidential. (Perhaps she thinks it unwise for the employee to have access without her being present to explain and interpret the report.) Or a supervisor is requested to evaluate an employee. The supervisor expects the evaluation to be kept confidential. Should the employee have access to such records? It seems to me that if the information is essential to the employment contract (as a medical exam might be necessary for insurance or an evaluation necessary for promotion), then access can be limited. However, if it is essential, then employee consent would be an appropriate precondition. Similar to standard practice with student recommendations, employees should be asked to sign a waiver of access rights. Employees who desire the medical insurance or promotion, for example, would waive their access rights. Those who choose not to waive their rights must acknowledge that they are jeapordizing these other goods. In general, there ought to be a presumption of access, but with employee consent confidential information can be excluded.

Before moving on, two caveats are in order. First, we should distinguish between evaluations made for promotion purposes from those made to determine satisfactory performance levels. Since the employee likely will desire the benefits of promotion, consent to limit access will be to everyone's advantage. However, we can imagine some workers who would rather not be evaluated on job performance at all. Unsatisfactory workers could hinder legitimate evaluations somewhat by refusing to waive their access rights. To overcome this potential problem, a time limit could be established, perhaps six months or a year, in which all evaluations could be kept confidential. After that time, we could assume that the employer is satisfied with job performance and make future evaluations open to employee inspection. (This latter issue may be more a concern of an employee's right to due process than a privacy concern.)

Second, some evaluations involve comparisons of employees. Since access here may involve violating another employee's privacy, some limitation may be in order. However, it would seem that if all parties consented, the same conditions should apply to these files that apply to single employee evaluation files.

Nevertheless, an employee's right to see, copy, challenge, respond to, and know about personal information held by an employer is very strong. Since numerous decisions involving an employee's life prospects are made on the basis of this information, simple justice requires that the information be accurate, complete, and relevant. To guarantee this, employees must have access to this information; they must be able to correct it when it is mistaken, and they must be allowed to challenge it when it is in question. To do otherwise would make the employment relationship radically unequal and unfair, and thereby make the contract fundamentally coercive.

More needs to be done to specify the exact extent of privacy rights in employment. Different employment situations will no doubt require different privacy rights. IBM employees, for example, likely will have different specific privacy rights than employees of the CIA. Government employees might have more extensive rights than employees in the private sector. This paper has attempted to sketch a framework into which the details of particular employment situations can be fit.

Notes

1. Louis D. Brandeis and Samuel Warren, "The Right to Privacy," *Harvard Law Review* 4 (1890): 193.

2. See, for example, the chapter on "Privacy in Employment" in Robert Ellis Smith, *Privacy* (New York: Anchor, Doubleday 1979).

3. For more developed analyses of the relationship between privacy and liberty, see Hyman Gross, "Privacy and Autonomy," *Privacy: Nomos XIII*, ed. J.R. Pennock and J.W. Chapman (New York: Lieber Atherton, 1971) and H.J. McCloskey, "Privacy and the Right to Privacy," *Philosophy*, vol. 55, no. 211 (1980).

4. For example, see Alan Westin, *Privacy and Freedom* (New York: Atheneum Publishers, 1976), 7.

5. George Brenkert, "Privacy, Polygraphs, and Work," *Business and Professional Ethics Journal*, vol. 1, no. 1 (1982), 19–35.

6. Ibid., 23.

7. For a good discussion of this model, see Phillip Blumberg, "Corporate Responsibility and the Employee's Duty of Loyalty and Obedience: A Preliminary Inquiry," *Oklahoma Law Review*, vol. 24, no. 3 (August 1971).

8. Besides the Blumberg article, also see David Ewing, "Your Right to Fire," *Harvard Business Review*, vol. 61, no. 2 (March-April 1983), 32–42 and Norm Bowie, "The Moral Contract Between Employer and Employee," *The Work Ethic in Business*, ed. W.M. Hoffman and T.J. Wyly (Cambridge, Mass.: Oelgeschlager, Gunn, and Hair, 1981), 195–202.

9. Brenkert, "Privacy, Polygraphs, and Work."

Richard L. Lippke
WORK, PRIVACY, AND AUTONOMY

Employees today face what many believe are unjustified assaults on their privacy. At present, the most well-known and controversial such assault is the urine test. Estimates are that about 30% of the Fortune 500 companies in the United States require a urine test as part of the employment application process. Proponents of such testing warn of the dangers of rampant drug use and abuse in our society. They insist on the need to safeguard co-worker and consumer health and safety, and the need to maintain productivity. Opponents of testing conjure up images of Orwell's *1984*—of large and powerful institutions run amok, forcing innocent people to urinate while under the intense (and let us hope not prurient) supervision of official inspectors. Opponents lambast testing as an invasion of privacy and as a form of self-incrimination. Their most effective tactic has been to raise the specter of inaccurate tests; of persons unfairly scored with the scarlet letter of drug use.

Unfortunately, in the public debate over these issues there is little in the way of patient and careful analysis. . . . I will maintain that the philosophical defenses of employee privacy that have been offered are either incomplete or misguided. At times, they say too little about the value of privacy. Or, they offer suspect models of the employer/employee relationship. Or, they fail to convincingly show how we should deal with the conflict between privacy and other, competing values.

I will begin my analysis by arguing that privacy is valuable because of its relation to autonomy. For the purposes of this discussion, I will define autonomy as the capacity of persons to make rationally reflective choices about their ends and activities. All areas of persons' lives are assumed to be fit subjects for the exercise of their autonomy. Unless the relation between privacy and autonomy is kept clearly in view, we will not be able to establish the need for restrictions on the information employers may gather or on the means they may use. More importantly, I will argue that we must examine the privacy issue in the context of an understanding of how the contemporary organization of work in the United States affects the autonomy of workers. Simply put, workers in the U.S. face myriad assaults to their autonomy. I will show how failure to recognize this and to incorporate it into philosophical analyses of employee privacy inevitably weakens the case that can be made on behalf of employees. I will argue that when the reality of work is ignored, workers are more likely to be blamed for behavior that arguably stems (at least in part) from the system of private property rights in productive resources that deprives them of control over their working lives.

Though I will focus exclusively on the value of autonomy, I will not try to argue that it is the only value we should pay attention to in assessing the current organization of work in the U.S. I would contend that autonomy is an essential value, but I concede that other values are important as well. Others who have offered critiques of the current organization of work have tried to show that it undermines values like self-respect and welfare.[1] . . .

From *Public Affairs Quarterly*, 3 (April 1989), 41–55. Reprinted by permission.

There are difficulties in defining what privacy is. However, I do not think we need to be detained by them.[2] Generally, there is a consensus that it involves two things: (1) control over some information about ourselves; and (2) some control over who can experience or observe us.[3] In the abstract, it is hard to further specify how much control privacy involves and over what types of information it ranges. This is because whether any given piece of information about me is private in relation to someone else depends on the type of relationship I have to that individual. What is private in relation to my spouse is very different from what is private in relation to an employer or working associate.

Joseph Kupfer has recently offered a compelling analysis of the value of privacy.[4] Two of the ways in which privacy is valuable are especially relevant to the employer/employee relationship, so I will concentrate on them. First, Kupfer argues that privacy plays an essential role in individuals coming to have an "autonomous self-concept," that is, a concept of themselves as in control of their own lives:

> An autonomous self-concept requires identifying with a particular body whose thoughts, purposes, and actions are subject to one's control . . . autonomy requires awareness of control over one's relation to others, including their access to us . . . privacy contributes to the formation and persistence of autonomous individuals by providing them with control over whether or not their physical and psychological existence becomes part of another's experience.[5]

Kupfer does not argue that privacy is intrinsically good. He argues that it is causally related to the formation and maintenance of an autonomous self-concept. An autonomous self-concept is, in turn, a necessary condition of the basic good of autonomy. In other words, unless individuals conceive of themselves as able to determine their own courses of action, their own life-plans, they cannot be autonomous. If individuals are to develop and maintain an autonomous self-concept, others must grant them control over information about themselves and control over who can experience them and when. Kupfer offers some empirical evidence to substantiate the claim that lack of privacy defeats the formation and maintenance of an autonomous self-concept.[6]

As Kupfer notes, the most autonomous person is one who evaluates his deepest convictions, or the most fundamental aspects of his life-plan. Privacy is essential to individuals having the concept that they can do this. It allows them to engage in this self-scrutiny without intrusion and distraction. When the most intimate aspects of their lives are up for scrutiny, individuals are vulnerable to ridicule or manipulation by others. It is vitally important for them to be able to remove themselves from observation and criticism by those they feel they cannot trust.

A second way in which privacy is valuable is that individuals subjected to invasions of their privacy seem less likely to conceive of themselves as *worthy* of autonomy:

> Privacy is a trusting way others treat us, resulting in a conception of ourselves as worth being trusted. In contrast, monitoring behavior or collecting data on us, projects a disvaluing of the self in question.[7]

Close, intrusive supervision and constant correction (or the threat of it) are inimical to individuals developing and maintaining a sense of themselves as worthy of autonomy. In contrast, social practices that respect privacy give the individual a chance to make mistakes or do wrong, and thus convey the message that the individual is worthy of acting autonomously. .The sense that they are worthy of acting autonomously may, as Kupfer notes, increase the confidence of individuals in themselves, and so they may exercise their autonomy to an even greater extent. . . .

With this brief characterization of some of the ways in which privacy is valuable in hand, I turn first to consider the issues raised by the *content* of information that businesses might acquire about employees or prospective employees. Both George Brenkert and Joseph Des Jardins offer arguments designed to restrict the types of information employers may justifiably gather about employees to information that is "job relevant." Both also construe the employer/employee relationship in contractual terms, relying, apparently, on the fact that the courts are increasingly viewing the relationship in that fashion.

Des Jardins argues that the contractual model is a marked improvement over the old principal/agent model, where the moral and legal rights seemed to be largely on the side of the employer and the moral and legal duties on the side of the employee. The contractual model presumes the existence of a legal framework to enforce the contract. More importantly, "contracts also must be non-coercive, voluntary agreements between rational and free agents."[8] And, they must be free from fraud and deception.

Des Jardins explores the implications of this model for the issue of privacy in the employment context. He argues that the employer is entitled to make sure that the contract is free from fraud and deception. The employer can legitimately acquire information about the prospective employee's job qualifications, work experience, educational background, and "other information relevant to the hiring decision."[9] Information is "relevant" if it has to do with determining whether or not the employee is capable of fulfilling her part of the contract. In a similar vein, Brenkert argues that the "job relevance" requirement limits the information sought "to that which is directly connected with the job description."[10] Brenkert admits that aspects of a person's social and moral character (for example, honesty, ability and willingness to cooperate with others) are job relevant. What both Brenkert and Des Jardins want to rule out as job relevant is information about such things as a prospective employee's political or religious beliefs and practices, her sexual preferences, marital status, credit or other financial data, and the like. One of Brenkert's complaints about the use of polygraph tests is that they often involve asking employees for information that *is not* job relevant.

I am sympathetic with the idea of such content restrictions, but I believe the arguments of Des Jardins and Brenkert are seriously flawed. In the first place, we should be wary of the contractual model of the employer/employee relationship. . . .

The danger in using this model is that it may lead us to ignore a crucial imbalance of power that exists in the marketplace. Individual employees rarely have bargaining power equal to that of their prospective employers. First, there are typically more potential employees available to firms than there are job openings available. Many jobs require little training or pre-existing expertise, and so workers can often be easily replaced. The threat that "there is always someone to take your place" is not an idle one for most workers. Unemployment in the economy generally and the problems workers face in moving to areas where there are jobs contribute to this buyers' market that is to the advantage of firms. Second, firms seem able to absorb underemployment more easily than workers can absorb unemployment. While firms need employees, they rarely need them as desperately as workers need jobs. As a result of these two factors, individual workers are rarely in a position to bargain on anything like equal terms with their perspective employers.[11]

This imbalance of power renders most workers practically unable to resist the demands for information that precede and accompany employment offers, and makes all the more urgent the content restrictions Des Jardins and Brenkert advocate. After all, what is the point of urging such restrictions if the wage-labor agreement is one between relative equals? Why not just leave the sorts of information to be exchanged up to the negotiations between employer and employee?

. . . My point is that the contractual model is very misleading if used as a way to conceive of the reality of work in the U.S. It suggests a type of equality that does not exist, and if its descriptive and normative functions are run together, it distorts our perception of where the balance of power lies in the relationship between workers and employers.

Leaving aside the problems with the contractual model, it does not seem that Des Jardins and Brenkert help us to understand the moral basis for the content restrictions they advocate. The appeal to the notion of "job relevance" raises more questions than it answers. Lots of information both would prevent employers from obtaining is, arguably, job relevant. For instance, if all of my employees are politically and religiously conservative, knowing where prospective employees stand on these matters may very well be job relevant if my employees have to work closely together. After all, an atheist with socialist leanings may not get along at all with my employees and thereby disrupt productivity. Neither may a union supporter, a homosexual, or someone who is financially reckless or sexually promiscuous. I am not suggesting that we should cater to the prejudices of existing employees in making hiring decisions. What I am suggesting is that Brenkert's and Des Jardins' arguments invoke a concept that is far from unproblematic.[12]

Even if the notion of "job relevance" was unproblematic, the argument would be incomplete. What we want is an argument that connects job relevance up with some moral value or values. In other words, why (morally speaking) limit employer access to only job relevant information? What is at stake in doing so?

If we turn back to the analysis of the value of privacy, the answer emerges. Suppose that employers are allowed to gather all of the sorts of information that the notion of "job relevance" is meant to exclude, and to use that information in making employment-related decisions. The result might be that business hiring and promotion decisions will wind up shaping peoples' lives in rather dramatic ways. Consider the likely chilling effects on employees. They may be reluctant to try out any new ideas or activities that may, at some future date, come back to haunt them. As we saw, privacy vitally contributes to our concept of ourselves as in control of our own lives. Part of this is that it protects our sense of self-determination by enabling us to engage in a "no holds barred" examination of all aspects of our lives. It allows us to experiment with different courses of our lives, if only in thought. These different courses may not be popular, especially to employees who are very conscious of the bottom line.

There is also the very real danger that all sorts of mistaken inferences about employee behavior will be made from access to such information. For instance, suppose that a polygraph test uncovers the fact that a person sometimes fantasizes about theft. It seems clear that a person who fantasizes about theft may be a long way from behaving as a thief. We do not understand the connections between the "inner workings" of people's minds and their behavior anywhere near well enough to allow employers to make such predictions in an accurate fashion.[13]

In short, the content restrictions Des Jardins and Brenkert favor are morally justified as ways of limiting the perceived power that businesses have over the lives of their employees. We should discourage invasions of privacy that will likely result in individuals narrowing the exploration and examination of their lives, or that will decrease their sense that they control and are responsible for their lives. In a work environment without such restrictions, and where employers are already in a position to impose their wills on employees in other ways, it seems unlikely that employees will have as rich and lively a sense of their own autonomy. In turn, they will be less prone to exercise their autonomy.

It seems clear that many of the most controversial *means* of acquiring information about employees may provide employers with information that is, on any reasonable interpretation of the notion, job relevant. Surveillance to prevent theft or to maintain productivity provides such information. Urine tests will provide such information, though they will also provide information about off-the-job drug or alcohol use that is, less obviously, job relevant. Searches of employee desks or lockers, and even polygraph tests (where the questions are suitably restricted) will provide such information. Physical exams and skills tests will do so, though few have seen these as controversial.

Numerous writers have argued against the use of at least some of these means. One popular objection to some of these means is that they are so inaccurate. Polygraph tests, in particular, seem gravely defective in this way, and to a lesser extent, so do urine tests. The concern about accuracy is a concern about fairness, about the possibility of unfairly accusing individuals of actions they are innocent of. I think that the inaccuracy issue is a very serious one, but I do not believe we should base our case against such tests on it alone, or even primarily. The reason for this is simple: suppose through various technological developments such tests are made *very* accurate. Are we then to conclude that there is nothing objectionable about them? I think not. I will try to show that there are other objectionable features to such tests.

A second objection might be that such means of acquiring information are somehow too intrusive. It is important to ask what this means. Is it that such methods come too close to us, crossing some physical or psychological boundary that is morally significant? Administering the polygraph test does require that various devices be attached to our bodies, so maybe it is the actual physical contact that matters. It is hard to imagine anything more intrusive in this regard than a physical exam. Urine tests are not intrusive in this way, however, and neither are surveillance or forays through employee desks and lockers. Thus, physical contact does not seem to be a necessary condition of intrusiveness. It might be a sufficient condition, but we need to know precisely what is so objectionable about such contact. It does not seem objectionable in the same way that battery is, where the concern is with shielding individuals from physical harm. . . .

What all of these methods of acquiring information seem to have in common is that they are ways of checking on the things employees say about themselves or the ways employees present themselves. In this regard, I do not see how a urine test or surveillance is all that much different than the required disclosure of information about work experience or educational background. Perhaps some methods are more intrusive, as a matter of degree, than others. Employees are increasingly finding that not even their own bodies are safe havens, let alone their desks and lockers. At every turn, they are hounded by employee efforts to catch them speaking or acting in ways contrary to what are deemed the employer's interests.

The proliferation of these methods of acquiring contradicting information seems likely to have two sorts of effects on workers. First, all such methods implicitly remind the worker where the balance of power lies in the working world. Again, most workers are not in a position to refuse to cooperate with the use of such methods and workers are highly vulnerable to any negative employer reactions to the information so gleaned.[14] The more a worker is checked on, tested, spied upon, and so on, the less likely she is to feel that she controls her own life in the working world. The aggregate and cumulative effects of many (by themselves seemingly innocent) attempts to check on workers might be an increased sense on the part of workers that the workplace is an oppressive environment. It is distressing that so many employees apparently submit to polygraph or urine tests without any reluctance. Can this be because they have already internalized the message that in the workplace their lives are not their own?

Second, random or across-the-board drug testing, or surveillance without "reasonable cause" implicitly tells employees that they are not trustworthy. It is important to keep in mind that in spite of statistics on the use of drugs by workers (estimates as high as one in six use drugs either on or off the job), the vast majority of workers are probably "clean" and honest. However, instead of there being a presumption that employees will act responsibly, the presumption behind the use of these methods of gathering information is that they cannot be trusted to act responsibly. Individuals who find themselves with a presumption of doubt against them may simply react with resentment. That is bad enough and a potential cost to employers. What is worse is the tendency such methods might have to undermine the employees' sense of trustworthiness, and therefore their sense that they are worthy of acting autonomously. Again, one valuable thing about privacy is that it affirms an individual's sense that she is worthy of autonomy. The more she lacks that sense, the more she is prone to tolerate invasions of her privacy, with the resulting debilitating effects on her autonomy.

In the abstract, concerns about the effects of such methods on employee autonomy might appear legitimate, but not of a sufficiently compelling nature to convince us that their use is wholly objectionable. If they are employed in a work environment that is otherwise supportive of employee autonomy, they might be only minor threats. Therefore, in order to strengthen the case against the use of such methods, it will help here to focus attention on how the organization of work in the U.S. *already* undermines the autonomy of most workers to an extraordinary extent.

As numerous critics of the organization of work in the U.S. have pointed out, the majority of workers are routinely subjected to a hierarchical, authoritarian management structure that deprives them of any significant input into the economic decisions directly affecting their working lives. Most have very little input into decisions about the organization of work at even the shop-floor level, let alone at levels above it. As Adina Schwartz argues, most workers are subjected to a division of labor where they are confined to increasingly narrowly-defined tasks determined and supervised by others:

> These routine jobs provide people with almost no opportunities for formulating aims, for deciding on means for achieving their ends, or for adjusting their goals and methods in light of experience.[15]

Work technology is decided by others, as are productivity quotas, criteria for evaluation, discipline procedures, and plant closings or employee lay-offs. Even the attitudes with which work is to be done are prescribed and pressures are put on workers to "be a loyal member of the team" or to "please the customer at all costs." . . .

Thus, each concession made to management's desire to gather information using the methods we have been discussing adds to an already impressive arsenal of weapons at its disposal for the assault on employee autonomy. The question is *not* whether we should endorse the use of methods that undermine employee autonomy in a setting where that autonomy is otherwise affirmed and nurtured. The question is whether we should endorse the use of methods that might further erode employee autonomy. For instance, random or across-the-board urine tests do not send a messsage to workers that they are untrustworthy in a context where their trustworthiness is normally affirmed. Instead, it sends a message that is likely repeated to workers in a thousand different ways throughout their working lives. A verdict wholly in favor of employees on all of the privacy issues we have been considering will, by itself, come nowhere near establishing working conditions supportive of employee autonomy.

Another way to put the preceding point about the organization of work in the U.S. is to say that property rights, with their supporting political-social institutions and practices, give some individuals a considerable amount of *power* over the lives of others. It is with this in mind that we should consider attempts to override the privacy of employees by appeals to the property rights of the owners and stockholders.

Proponents of gathering information about employees may admit that privacy is a value and that it is threatened by the means employers want to use to gather information. But, they will argue, the property rights of the owners and stockholders are valuable as well. They will rightly demand to be shown that the privacy rights of workers ought to prevail over these property rights. . . .

What this plausible-sounding argument ignores is how property rights in productive resources differ from privacy rights. The right to privacy is such that respecting it provides individuals with an increased sense of control (a necessary condition of autonomy) over their own lives. Respecting it does *not* provide individuals with increased control over the lives of others. Property rights as they exist in the U.S. are, as we have seen, not like this. They do give some power over the lives of others. And, importantly, a verdict in favor of the owners and stockholders will mean a further extension of that already considerable control.

Hence, the issue is not the rather abstract one of whether privacy rights are more or less important than property rights in relation to the autonomy of the

bearers of those rights. Rather, since property rights as currently institutionalized give some power over the lives of others, the issue is whether to preserve or
increase that power, *or* curtail it. Indeed, once the connection between property
rights and power is revealed in this way, those rights become fit subjects for
critical scrutiny. If we are concerned about the autonomy of workers, we can
hardly ignore the existence of working conditions that systematically and pervasively undermine it.

A second reason for not allowing the issues to be framed simply in terms of
conflicting rights is that this is likely to exonerate the existing organization of
work from any blame for generating the employee behavior that is viewed as
irresponsible. This irresponsible behavior is taken as a *given*, and various
methods for collecting information about employees are proposed. The need to
gather such information is implicitly attributed solely to defects in the character
of employees. Those who seek to defend workers against invasions of their
privacy are likely to be portrayed as condoning dishonesty, drug use, and the
like. This portrayal is, of course, unfair, but it gains credence from the implicit
assumption that such behaviors simply exist and must be countered. Thus, the
debate about conflicting rights begins, and employers are all too easily depicted
as the innocent victims of their unscrupulous, irresponsible, and ungrateful
employees.

Many critics of the organization of work in the U.S. will argue that it is the
character of that work itself which is a very significant factor in producing such
"problem" behaviors. The research that exists in this area strongly suggests that
this is a possibility we should not ignore.[16] It is surprising that in the popular and
philosophical discussions of these issues, the following sorts of questions are so
rarely asked: Why is it that employees show up drunk or drugged for work?
Why is it that they shirk work and responsibility? Why is it that they lie about
their credentials or exaggerate them? Why is it that they engage in theft or
sabotage? When the question asked is whether the employee privacy that is
violated in order to counter such behaviors outweighs or is outweighed by the
right to property, the preceding sorts of questions are suppressed. Behaviors
which may be symptomatic of a morally sick organization of work are viewed as
the underlying cause of the conflict. Then, in a twist of bitter irony, the
property rights in which that organization of work is anchored are brought in to
beat back the challenge posed by the employees' privacy rights.

Appeals to co-worker health and safety, or to the health and safety of consumers and members of the general public, are also used to justify invasions of
worker privacy. No one wants their airline pilot to be high on cocaine or their
nuclear power plant operator to be blitzed on Jim Beam. Moreover, protecting
people's health and safety does *not* ipso facto give them power over the lives of
others. Health and safety are obviously essential conditions for the preservation
and exercise of autonomy, perhaps more essential than privacy. So, it would
seem that health and safety considerations ought to prevail over privacy considerations.

In response to this, I begin by noting that we should not isolate the issue of
whether or not we can invade the privacy of workers to protect health and
safety from the larger issue of the role of the current organization of work in
generating dangerous behavior. The issue is not simply whether health and
safety outweighs privacy, but also whether fundamental changes in the organization of work would lessen or eliminate the behavior that makes overriding

privacy seem so reasonable. It is hard to say whether and to what extent the means many would now use to gather information about employees would be used in a more democratically and humanely organized economy. Such an economy would eliminate or at least lessen the specter of unemployment, and so the felt need to lie about or exaggerate credentials in order to obtain work might be eliminated. Such an economy would give workers more real control over their working lives, and would eliminate the division between those who make decisions at work and those who simply implement the decisions of others. Such an economy would give workers more control over the products of their labor, and give them the power to discipline other workers. How such changes would affect employee morale, productivity, and the sense of responsibility for work performed are things we can only speculate about.

It seems likely that such changes will *not* eliminate all dangerous or destructive behavior on the part of workers. I do not wish to rule out, once and for all, the use of means of acquiring information that encroach on privacy. What I do want to suggest, in closing, is that in a more democratically and humanely organized economy, decisions about what measures to use and when to use them would not be made unilaterally by some people and then simply imposed on others. If we are going to respect the autonomy of persons, then we must give them input into decisions like this that vitally affect their lives.

Notes

1. See, for instance, David Schweickart, *Capitalism or Worker Control? An Ethical and Economic Appraisal* (New York: Praeger Publishers, 1980); Gerald Doppelt, "Conflicting Social Paradigms of Human Freedom and the Problem of Justification," *Inquiry*, vol. 27 (1984), pp. 51–86.

2. For a useful discussion of the difficulties in defining privacy, see H. J. McCloskey, "Privacy and the Right to Privacy," *Philosophy*, vol. 55 (1980), pp. 17–38.

3. For instance, see Joseph Kupfer, "Privacy, Autonomy, and Self-Concept," *American Philosophical Quarterly*, vol. 24 (1987), pp. 81–89. Also, Richard Wasserstrom, "Privacy," in *Today's Moral Problems*, Richard Wasserstrom (ed.) (New York: Macmillan Publishing Co., 1979), pp. 392–408.

4. Kupfer, "Privacy, Autonomy, and Self-Concept," pp. 81–89. For a similar analysis, see Jeffrey H. Reiman, "Privacy, Intimacy, and Personhood," *Philosophy and Public Affairs*, vol. 6 (1976), pp. 26–44.

5. Kupfer, "Privacy, Autonomy, and Self-Concept," p. 82.

6. *Ibid.*, pp. 81–82.

7. *Ibid.*, p. 85.

8. Joseph R. Des Jardins, "Privacy in Employment," in *Moral Rights in the Workplace*, Gertrude Ezorsky (ed.) (Albany, NY: State University of New York Press, 1987), pp. 127–139, 131.

9. *Ibid.*, p. 132.

10. George G. Brenkert, "Privacy, Polygraphs, and Work," in *Contemporary Issues in Business Ethics*, Joseph R. Des Jardins and John J. McCall (eds.) (Belmont, CA: Wadsworth, 1985), pp. 227–237, 231.

11. For those who might say that labor unions provide workers with such equality, I point out that, at present, less than 15% of U.S. workers are represented by labor unions.

12. Brenkert, "Privacy, Polygraphs, and Work," p. 231. Brenkert admits that the criterion of job relevance is "rather vague," yet proceeds to use it.

13. One of the most frightening prospects employees face is the availability of so-called "genetic marker" tests. These tests will allow employers to tell which individuals have genetic *tendencies* for such things as alcoholism, heart attacks, and cancer. Suppose businesses decide to

gather and use such information in making employment-related decisions. Though there are things individuals can do to counteract their tendencies, they might find themselves labeled due to their genetic tendencies, and so denied jobs or promotions. This threatens their abilities to determine how their lives will go *in spite of* their genetic tendencies.

14. In light of this vulnerability, I think we can better understand the vocal opposition to polygraphs and drug tests based on their inaccuracy. Most workers who are victims of inaccurate tests cannot simply fall back on adequate unemployment compensation or secure comparable employment.

15. Adina Schwartz, "Meaningful Work," *Ethics*, vol. 92 (1982), pp. 634–646, 634. Cf. also Edward Sankowski, "Freedom, Work, and the Scope of Democracy," *Ethics*, vol. 91 (1981), pp. 228–242.

16. See, for instance, *Work in America: Report of a Special Task Force to the Secretary of Health, Education, and Welfare* (Cambridge, MA: MIT Press, 1973); Harry Braverman, *Labor and Monopoly Capital: The Degradation of Work in the Twentieth Century* (New York: Monthly Review Press, 1974).

Joseph R. Des Jardins and Ronald Duska
DRUG TESTING IN EMPLOYMENT

According to one survey, nearly one-half of all Fortune 500 companies were planning to administer drug tests to employees and prospective employees by the end of 1987.[1] Counter to what seems to be the current trend in favor of drug testing, we will argue that it is rarely legitimate to override an employee's or applicant's right to privacy by using such tests or procedures.[2]

OPENING STIPULATIONS

We take privacy to be an "employee right" by which we mean a presumptive moral entitlement to receive certain goods or be protected from certain harms in the workplace.[3] Such a right creates a *prima facie* obligation on the part of the employer to provide the relevant goods or, as in this case, refrain from the relevant harmful treatment. These rights prevent employees from being placed in the fundamentally coercive position where they must choose between their job and other basic human goods.

Further, we view the employer–employee relationship as essentially contractual. The employer–employee relationship is an economic one and, unlike relationships such as those between a government and its citizens or a parent and a child, exists primarily as a means for satisfying the economic interests of the contracting parties. The obligations that each party incurs are only those that it voluntarily takes on. Given such a contractual relationship, certain areas of the employee's life remain their own private concern and no employer has a

From *Business and Professional Ethics Journal*, 6, no. 3 (1986), 3–21. Reprinted by permission of authors.

right to invade them. On these presumptions we maintain that certain information about an employee is rightfully private, i.e. the employee has a right to privacy.

THE RIGHT TO PRIVACY

According to George Brenkert, a right to privacy involves a three-place relation between a person A, some information X, and another person B. The right to privacy is violated only when B deliberately comes to possess information X about A, and no relationship between A and B exists which would justify B's coming to know X about A.[4] Thus, for example, the relationship one has with a mortgage company would justify that company's coming to know about one's salary, but the relationship one has with a neighbor does not justify the neighbor's coming to know that information. Hence, an employee's right to privacy is violated whenever personal information is requested, collected and/or used by an employer in a way or for any purpose that is *irrelevant to* or *in violation of* the contractual relationship that exists between *employer and employee*.

Since drug testing is a means for obtaining information, the information sought must be relevant to the contract in order for the drug testing not to violate privacy. Hence, we must first decide if knowledge of drug use obtained by drug testing is job relevant. In cases where the knowledge of drug use is *not* relevant, there appears to be no justification for subjecting employees to drug tests. In cases where information of drug use is job relevant, we need to consider if, when, and under what conditions using a means such as drug testing to obtain that knowledge is justified.

IS KNOWLEDGE OF DRUG USE JOB RELEVANT INFORMATION?

There seem to be two arguments used to establish that knowledge of drug use is job relevant information. The first argument claims that drug use adversely affects job performance thereby leading to lower productivity, higher costs, and consequently lower profits. Drug testing is seen as a way of avoiding these adverse effects. According to some estimates twenty-five billion ($25,000,000,000) dollars are lost each year in the United States because of drug use.[5] This occurs because of loss in productivity, increase in costs due to theft, increased rates in health and liability insurance, and such. Since employers are contracting with an employee for the performance of specific tasks, employers seem to have a legitimate claim upon whatever personal information is relevant to an employee's ability to do the job.

The second argument claims that drug use has been and can be responsible for considerable harm to the employee him/herself, fellow employees, the employer, and/or third parties, including consumers. In this case drug testing is defended because it is seen as a way of preventing possible harm. Further, since employers can be held liable for harms done both to third parties, e.g. customers, and to the employee or his/her fellow employees, knowledge of employee drug use will allow employers to gain information that can protect themselves from risks such as liability. But how good are these arguments? We turn to examine the arguments more closely.

THE FIRST ARGUMENT: JOB PERFORMANCE AND KNOWLEDGE OF DRUG USE

The first argument holds that drug use leads to lower productivity and consequently implies that a knowledge of drug use obtained through drug-testing will allow an employer to increase productivity. It is generally assumed that people using certain drugs have their performances affected by such use. Since enhancing productivity is something any employer desires, any use of drugs that reduces productivity affects the employer in an undesirable way, and that use is, then, job relevant. If such production losses can be eliminated by knowledge of the drug use, then knowledge of that drug use is job-relevant information. On the surface this argument seems reasonable. Obviously some drug use in lowering the level of performance can decrease productivity. Since the employer is entitled to a certain level of performance and drug use adversely affects performance, knowledge of that use seems job relevant.

But this formulation of the argument leaves an important question unanswered. To what level of performance are employers entitled? Optimal performance, or some lower level? If some lower level, what? Employers have a valid claim upon some *certain level* of performance, such that a failure to perform up to this level would give the employer a justification for disciplining, firing or at least finding fault with the employee. But that does not necessarily mean that the employer has a right to a maximum or optimal level of performance, a level above and beyond a certain level of acceptability. It might be nice if the employee gives an employer a maximum effort or optimal performance, but that is above and beyond the call of the employee's duty and the employer can hardly claim a right at all times to the highest level of performance of which an employee is capable.

That there are limits on required levels of performance and productivity becomes clear if we recognize that job performance is person related. It is person related because one person's best efforts at a particular task might produce results well below the norm, while another person's minimal efforts might produce results abnormally high when compared to the norm. For example a professional baseball player's performance on a ball field will be much higher than the average person's since the average person is unskilled at baseball. We have all encountered people who work hard with little or no results, as well as people who work little with phenomenal results. Drug use by very talented people might diminish their performance or productivity, but that performance would still be better than the performance of the average person or someone totally lacking in the skills required. That being said, the important question now is whether the employer is entitled to an employee's maximum effort and best results, or merely to an effort sufficient to perform the task expected.

If the relevant consideration is whether the employee is producing as expected (according to the normal demands of the position and contract) not whether he/she is producing as much as possible, then knowledge of drug use is irrelevant or unnecessary. Let's see why.

If the person is producing what is expected, knowledge of drug use on the grounds of production is irrelevant since, *ex hypothesi* the production is satisfactory. If, on the other hand, the performance suffers, then, to the extent that it slips below the level justifiably expected, the employer has *prima facie* grounds for warning, disciplining or releasing the employee. But the justification for this is the person's unsatisfactory performance, not the person's use of drugs. Accordingly, drug use information is either unnecessary or irrelevant and consequently there are not sufficient grounds to override the right of privacy. Thus, unless we can argue that an employer is entitled to optimal performance, the argument fails.

This counter-argument should make it clear that the information which is job relevant, and consequently which is not rightfully private, is information about an employee's level of performance and not information about the underlying causes of that level. The fallacy of the argument which promotes drug testing in the name of increased productivity is the assumption that each employee is obliged to perform at an optimal, or at least quite high, level. But this is required under few, if any, contracts. What is required contractually is meeting the normally expected levels of production or performing the tasks in the job description adequately (not optimally). If one can do that under the influence of drugs, then on the grounds of job performance at least, drug use is rightfully private. If one cannot perform the task adequately, then the employee is not fulfilling the contract, and knowledge of the cause of the failure to perform is irrelevant on the contractual model.

Of course, if the employer suspects drug use or abuse as the cause of the unsatisfactory performance, then she might choose to help the person with counseling or rehabilitation. However, this does not seem to be something morally required of the employer. Rather, in the case of unsatisfactory performance, the employer has a *prima facie* justification for dismissing or disciplining the employee.

Before turning to the second argument which attempts to justify drug testing, we should mention a factor about drug use that is usually ignored in talk of productivity. The entire productivity argument is irrelevant for those cases in which employees use performance enhancing drugs. Amphetamines and steroids, for example, can actually enhance some performances. This points to the need for care when tying drug testing to job performance. In the case of some drugs used by athletes, for example, drug testing is done because the drug-influenced performance is too good and therefore unfair, not because it leads to inadequate job performance. In such a case, where the testing is done to ensure fair competition, the testing may be justified. But drug testing in sports is an entirely different matter than drug testing in business.

To summarize our argument so far. Drug use may affect performances, but as long as the performance is at an acceptable level, the knowledge of drug use is irrelevant. If the performance is unacceptable, then that is sufficient cause for action to be taken. In this case an employee's failure to fulfill his/her end of a contract makes knowledge of the drug use unnecessary.

THE SECOND ARGUMENT: HARM AND THE
KNOWLEDGE OF DRUG USE TO PREVENT HARM

Even though the performance argument is inadequate, there is an argument that seems somewhat stronger. This is an argument based on the potential for drug use to cause harm. Using a type of Millian argument, one could argue that drug testing might be justified if such testing led to knowledge that would enable an employer to prevent harm. Drug use certainly can lead to harming others. Consequently, if knowledge of such drug use can prevent harm, then, knowing whether or not one's employee uses drugs might be a legitimate concern of an employer in certain circumstances. This second argument claims that knowledge of the employee's drug use is job relevant because employees who are under the influence of drugs can pose a threat to the health and safety of themselves and others, and an employer who knows of that drug use and the harm it can cause has a responsibility to prevent it. Employers have both a general duty to prevent harm and the specific responsibility for harms done by their employees. Such responsibilities are sufficient reason for an employer to claim that information about an employee's drug use is relevant if that knowledge can prevent harm by giving the employer grounds for dismissing the employee or not allowing him/her to perform potentially harmful tasks. Employers might even claim a right to reduce unreasonable risks, in this case the risks involving legal and economic liability for harms caused by employees under the influence of drugs, as further justification for knowing about employee drug use.

This second argument differs from the first in which only a lowered job performance was relevant information. In this case, even to allow the performance is problematic, for the performance itself, more than being inadequate, can hurt people. We cannot be as sanguine about the prevention of harm as we can about inadequate production. Where drug use can cause serious harms, knowledge of that use becomes relevant if the knowledge of such use can lead to the prevention of harm and drug testing becomes justified as a means for obtaining that knowledge.

As we noted, we will begin initially by accepting this argument on roughly Millian grounds where restrictions on liberty are allowed in order to prevent harm to others. (The fact that one is harming oneself, if that does not harm others is not sufficient grounds for interference in another's behavior according to Mill.) In such a case an employer's obligation to prevent harm may over-ride the obligation to respect an employee's privacy.

But let us examine this more closely. Upon examination, certain problems arise, so that even if there is a possibility of justifying drug testing to prevent harm, some caveats have to be observed and some limits set out.

JOBS WITH POTENTIAL TO CAUSE HARM

To say that employers can use drug testing where that can prevent harm is not to say that every employer has the right to know about the drug use of every employee. Not every job poses a serious enough threat to justify an employer coming to know this information.

In deciding which jobs pose serious enough threats certain guidelines should be followed. First the potential for harm should be *clear* and *present*. Perhaps all jobs in some extended way pose potential threats to human well-being. We suppose an accountant's error could pose a threat of harm to someone somewhere. But some jobs like those of airline pilots, school bus drivers, public transit drivers and surgeons, are jobs in which unsatisfactory performance poses a clear and present danger to others. It would be much harder to make an argument that job performances by auditors, secretaries, executive vice-presidents for public relations, college teachers, professional athletes, and the like, could cause harm if those performances were carried on under the influence of drugs. They would cause harm only in exceptional cases.[6]

NOT EVERY PERSON IS TO BE TESTED

But, even if we can make a case that a particular job involves a clear and present danger for causing harm if performed under the influence of drugs, it is not appropriate to treat everyone holding such a job the same. Not every job holder is equally threatening. There is less reason to investigate an airline pilot for drug use if that pilot has a twenty-year record of exceptional service than there is to investigate a pilot whose behavior has become erratic and unreliable recently, or than one who reports to work smelling of alcohol and slurring his words. Presuming that every airline pilot is equally threatening is to deny individuals the respect that they deserve as autonomous, rational agents. It is to ignore previous history and significant differences. It is also probably inefficient and leads to the lowering of morale. It is the likelihood of causing harm, and not the fact of being an airline pilot *per se*, that is relevant in deciding which employees in critical jobs to test.

So, even if knowledge of drug use is justifiable to prevent harm, we must be careful to limit this justification to a range of jobs and people where the potential for harm is clear and present. The jobs must be jobs that clearly can cause harm, and the specific employee should not be someone who is reliable with a history of such reliability. Finally, the drugs being tested should be those drugs, the use of which in those jobs is really potentially harmful.

LIMITATIONS ON DRUG TESTING POLICIES

Even when we identify those jobs and individuals where knowledge of drug use would be job relevant information, we still need to examine whether some procedural limitations should not be placed upon the employer's testing for drugs. We have said that in cases where a real threat of harm exists and where evidence exists suggesting that a particular employee poses such a threat, an employer could be justified in knowing about drug use in order to prevent the potential harm. But we need to recognize that as long as the employer has the discretion for deciding when the potential for harm is clear and present, and for deciding which employees pose the threat of harm, the possibility of abuse is great. Thus, some policy limiting the employer's power is called for.

Just as criminal law places numerous restrictions protecting individual dignity and liberty on the state's pursuit of its goals, so we should expect that some restrictions be placed on an employer in order to protect innocent employees from harm (including loss of job and damage to one's personal and professional reputation). Thus, some system of checks upon an employer's discretion in these matters seems advisable. Workers covered by collective bargaining agreements or individual contracts might be protected by clauses in those agreements that specify which jobs pose a real threat of harm (e.g. pilots but not cabin attendants) and what constitutes a just cause for investigating drug use. Local, state, and federal legislatures might do the same for workers not covered by employment contracts. What needs to be set up is a just employment relationship — one in which an employee's expectations and responsibilities are specified in advance and in which an employer's discretionary authority to discipline or dismiss an employee is limited.

Beyond that, any policy should accord with the nature of the employment relationship. Since that relationship is a contractual one, it should meet the condition of a morally valid contract, which is informed consent. Thus, in general, we would argue that only methods that have received the informed consent of employees can be used in acquiring information about drug use.[7]

A drug-testing policy that requires all employees to submit to a drug test or to jeopardize their job would seem coercive and therefore unacceptable. Being placed in such a fundamentally coercive position of having to choose between one's job and one's privacy does not provide the conditions for a truly free consent. Policies that are unilaterally established by employers would likewise be unacceptable. Working with employees to develop company policy seems the only way to insure that the policy will be fair to both parties. Prior notice of testing would also be required in order to give employees the option of freely refraining from drug use. It is morally preferable to prevent drug use than to punish users after the fact, since this approach treats employees as capable of making rational and informed decisions.

Further procedural limitations seem advisable as well. Employees should be notified of the results of the test, they should be entitled to appeal the results (perhaps through further tests by an independent laboratory) and the information obtained through tests ought to be kept confidential. In summary, limitations upon employer discretion for administering drug tests can be derived from the nature of the employment contract and from the recognition that drug testing is justified by the desire to prevent harm, not the desire to punish wrong doing.

EFFECTIVENESS OF DRUG TESTING

Having declared that the employer might have a right to test for drug use in order to prevent harm, we still need to examine the second argument a little more closely. One must keep in mind that the justification of drug testing is the justification of a means to an end, the end of preventing harm, and that the means are a means which intrude into one's privacy. In this case, before one allows drug testing as a means, one should be clear that there are not more effective means available.

If the employer has a legitimate right, perhaps duty, to ascertain knowledge of drug use to prevent harm, it is important to examine exactly how effectively, and in what situations, the *knowledge* of the drug use will prevent the harm. So far we have just assumed that the *knowledge* will prevent the harm. But how?

Let us take an example to pinpoint the difficulty. Suppose a transit driver, shortly before work, took some cocaine which, in giving him a feeling of invulnerability, leads him to take undue risks in his driving. How exactly is drug testing going to contribute to the knowledge which will prevent the potential accident?

It is important to keep in mind that (1) if the knowledge doesn't help prevent the harm, the testing is not justified on prevention grounds; (2) if the testing doesn't provide the relevant knowledge it is not justified either; and finally, (3) even if it was justified, it would be undesirable if a more effective means for preventing harm were discovered.

Upon examination, the links between drug testing, knowledge of drug use, and prevention of harm are not as clear as they are presumed to be. As we investigate, it begins to seem that the knowledge of the drug use even though relevant in some instances is not the most effective means to prevent harm.

Let us turn to this last consideration first. Is drug testing the most effective means for preventing harm caused by drug use?

Consider. If someone exhibits obviously drugged or drunken behavior, then this behavior itself is grounds for preventing the person from continuing in the job. Administering urine or blood tests, sending the specimens out for testing and waiting for a response, will not prevent harm in this instance. Such drug testing because of the time lapse involved, is equally superfluous in those cases where an employee is in fact under the influence of drugs, but exhibits no or only subtly impaired behaviour.

Thus, even if one grants that drug testing somehow prevents harm an argument can be made that there might be much more effective methods of preventing potential harm such as administering dexterity tests of the type employed by police in possible drunk-driving cases, or requiring suspect pilots to pass flight simulator tests.[8] Eye – hand coordination, balance, reflexes, and reasoning ability can all be tested with less intrusive, more easily administered, reliable technologies which give instant results. Certainly if an employer has just cause for believing that a specific employee presently poses a real threat of causing harm, such methods are just more effective in all ways than are urinalysis and blood testing.

Even were it possible to refine drug tests so that accurate results were immediately available, that knowledge would only be job relevant if the drug use was clearly the cause of impaired job performance that could harm people. Hence, testing behavior still seems more direct and effective in preventing harm than testing for the presence of drugs *per se*.

In some cases, drug use might be connected with potential harms not by being causally connected to motor-function impairment, but by causing personality disorders (e.g. paranoia, delusions, etc.) that affect judgmental ability. Even though in such cases a *prima facie* justification for urinalysis or blood testing might exist, the same problems of effectiveness persist. How is the knowledge of the drug use attained by urinalysis and/or blood testing supposed to prevent the harm? Only if there is a causal link between the use and the potentially harmful behavior, would such knowledge be relevant. Even if we get the results of the test immediately, there is the necessity to have an established causal link between specific drug use and anticipated harmful personality disorders in specific people.

But it cannot be the task of an employer to determine that a specific drug is causally related to harm-causing personality disorders. Not every controlled substance is equally likely to cause personality changes in every person in every case. The establishment of the causal link between the use of certain drugs and harm-causing personality disorders is not the province of the employer, but the province of experts studying the effects of drugs. The burden of proof is on the employer to establish that the substance being investigated has been independently connected with the relevant psychological impairment and then, predict on that basis that the specific employee's psychological judgment has been or will soon be impaired in such a way as to cause harm.

But even when this link is established, it would seem that less intrusive means could be used to detect the potential problems, rather than relying upon the assumption of a causal link. Psychological tests of judgment, perception and memory, for example, would be a less intrusive and more direct means for acquiring the relevant information which is, after all, the likelihood of causing harm and not the presence of drugs *per se*. In short, drug testing even in these cases doesn't seem to be very effective in preventing harm on the spot.

Still, this does not mean it is not effective at all. Where it is most effective in preventing harm is in its getting people to stop using drugs or in identifying serious drug addiction. Or to put it another way, urinalysis and blood tests for drug use are most effective in preventing potential harm when they serve as a deterrent to drug use *before* it occurs, since it is very difficult to prevent harm by diagnosing drug use *after* it has occurred but before the potentially harmful behavior takes place.

Drug testing can be an effective deterrent when there is regular or random testing of all employees. This will prevent harm by inhibiting (because of the fear of detection) drug use by those who are occasional users and those who do not wish to be detected.

It will probably not inhibit or stop the use by the chronic addicted user, but it will allow an employer to discover the chronic user or addict, assuming that the tests are accurately administered and reliably evaluated. If the chronic user's addiction would probably lead to harmful behavior of others, the harm is prevented by taking that user off the job. Thus regular or random testing will prevent harms done by deterring the occasional user and by detecting the chronic user.

There are six possibilities for such testing:

1. regularly scheduled testing of all employees;
2. regularly scheduled testing of randomly selected employees;
3. randomly scheduled testing of all employees;
4. randomly scheduled testing of randomly selected employees;
5. regularly scheduled testing of employees selected for probable cause; or finally,
6. randomly scheduled testing of employees selected for probable cause.

Only the last two seem morally acceptable as well as effective.

Obviously, randomly scheduled testing will be more effective than regularly scheduled testing in detecting the occasional user, because the occasional users can control their use to pass the tests, unless of course tests were given so often (a practice economically unfeasible) that they needed to stop altogether. Regular scheduling probably will detect the habitual or addicted user. Randomly selecting people to test is probably cheaper, as is random scheduling, but it is not nearly as effective as testing all. Besides, the random might miss some of the addicted altogether, and will not deter the risk takers as much as the risk aversive persons. It is, ironically, the former who are probably potentially more harmful.

But these are merely considerations of efficiency. We have said that testing without probable cause is unacceptable. Any type of regular testing of all employees is unacceptable. We have argued that testing employees without first establishing probable cause is an unjustifiable violation of employee privacy. Given this, and given the expense of general and regular testing of all employees (especially if this is done by responsible laboratories), it is more likely that random testing will be employed as the means of deterrence. But surely testing of randomly selected innocent employees is as intrusive to those tested as is regular testing. The argument that there will be fewer tests is correct on quantitative grounds, but qualitatively the intrusion and unacceptability are the same. The claim that employers should be allowed to sacrifice the well-being of (some few) innocent employees to deter (some equally few) potentially harmful employees seems, on the face of it, unfair. Just as we do not allow the state randomly to tap the telephones of just any citizen in order to prevent crime, so we ought not allow employers to drug test all employees randomly to prevent harm. To do so is again to treat innocent employees solely as a means to the end of preventing potential harm.

This leaves only the use of regular or random drug testing as a deterrent in those cases where probable cause exists for believing that a particular employee poses a threat of harm. It would seem that in this case, the drug testing is acceptable. In such cases only the question of effectiveness remains: Are the standard techniques of urinalysis and blood-testing more effective means for preventing harms than alternatives such as dexterity tests? It seems they are effective in different ways. The dexterity tests show immediately if someone is incapable of performing a task, or will perform one in such a way as to cause harm to others. The urinalysis and blood-testing will prevent harm indirectly by getting the occasional user to curtail their use, and by detecting the habitual or addictive user, which will allow the employer to either give treatment to the addictive personality or remove them from the job. Thus we can conclude that drug testing is effective in a limited way, but aside from inhibiting occasional users because of fear of detection, and discovering habitual users, it seems problematic that it does much to prevent harm that couldn't be achieved by other means.

Consider one final issue in the case of the occasional user. They are the drug users who do weigh the risks and benefits and who are physically and psychologically free to decide. The question in their case is not simply "will the likelihood of getting caught by urinalysis or blood-testing deter this individual from using drugs?" Given the benefits of psychological tests and dexterity tests described above, the question is "will the rational user be more deterred by urinalysis or blood-testing than by random psychological or dexterity tests?" And, if this is so, is this increase in the effectiveness of a deterrent sufficient to offset the increased expense and time required by drug tests?[9] We see no reason to believe that behavioral or judgment tests are not, or cannot be made to be, as effective in determining what an employer needs to know (i.e., that a particular employee may presently be a potential cause of harm). If the behavioral, dexterity and judgment tests can be as effective in determining a potential for harm, we see no reason to believe that they cannot be as effective a deterrent as drug tests. Finally, even if a case can be made for an increase in deterrent effect of drug testing, we are skeptical that this increased effectiveness will outweigh the increased inefficiencies.

In summary, we have seen that deterrence is effective at times and under certain conditions allows the sacrificing of the privacy rights of innocent employees to the future and speculative good of preventing harms to others.

However, there are many ways to deter drug use when that deterrence is legitimate and desirable to prevent harm. But random testing, which seems the only practicable means which has an impact in preventing harm is the one which most offends workers rights to privacy and which is most intrusive of the rights of the innocent. Even when effective, drug testing as a deterrent must be checked by the rights of employees.

THE ILLEGALITY CONTENTION

At this point critics might note that the behavior which testing would try to deter is, after all, illegal. Surely this excuses any responsible employer from being overly protective of an employee's rights. The fact that an employee is doing something illegal should give the employer a right to that information about his private life. Thus, it is not simply that drug use might pose a threat of harm to others, but that it is an *illegal* activity that threatens others. But again, we would argue that illegal activity itself is irrelevant to job performance. At best *conviction* records might be relevant, but, of course, since drug tests are administered by private employers we are not only ignoring the question of conviction, we are also ignoring the fact that the employee has not even been arrested for the alleged illegal activity.

Further, even if the due process protections and the establishment of guilt are acknowledged, it still does not follow that employers have a claim to know about all illegal activity on the part of their employees.

Consider the following example: Suppose you were hiring an auditor whose job required certifying the integrity of your firm's tax and financial records. Certainly, the personal integrity of this employee is vital to the adequate job performance. Would we allow the employer to conduct, with or without the employee's consent, an audit of the employee's own personal tax return? Certainly if we discover that this person has cheated on his/her own tax return we will have evidence of illegal activity that is relevant to this person's ability to do the job. Given one's own legal liability for filing falsified statements, the employee's illegal activity also poses a threat to others. But surely, allowing private individuals to audit an employee's tax returns is too intrusive a means for discovering information about that employee's integrity. The government certainly would never allow this violation of an employee's privacy. It ought not to allow drug testing on the same grounds. Why tax returns should be protected in ways that urine, for example, is not, raises interesting questions of fairness. Unfortunately, this question would take us beyond the scope of this paper.

VOLUNTARINESS

A final problem that we also leave undeveloped concerns the voluntariness of employee consent. For most employees, being given the choice between submitting to a drug test and risking one's job by refusing an employer's request is not much of a decision at all. We believe that such decisions are less than voluntary and thereby would hold that employers cannot escape our criticisms simply by including within the employment contract a drug-testing clause.[10] Furthermore, there is reason to believe that those most in need of job security will be those most likely to be subjected to drug testing. Highly skilled, professional employees with high job mobility and security will be in a stronger position to resist such intrusions than will less skilled, easily replaced workers. This is why we should not anticipate surgeons and airline pilots being tested, and should not be surprised when public transit and factory workers are. A serious question of fairness arises here as well.

Drug use and drug testing seem to be our most recent social "crises." Politicians, the media, and employers expend a great deal of time and effort addressing this crisis. Yet, unquestionably, more lives, health, and money are lost each year to alcohol abuse than to marijuana, cocaine and other controlled substances. We are well-advised to be careful in considering issues that arise due to such selective social concern. We will let other social commentators speculate on the reasons why drug use has received scrutiny while other white-collar crimes and alcohol abuse are ignored. Our only concern at this point is that such selective prosecution suggests an arbitrariness that should alert us to questions of fairness and justice.

In summary, then, we have seen that drug use is not always job relevant, and if drug use is not job relevant, information about it is certainly not job relevant. In the case of performance it may be a cause of some decreased performance, but it is the performance itself that is relevant to an employee's position, not what prohibits or enables him to do the job. In the case of potential harm being done by an employee under the influence of drugs, the drug use seems job relevant, and in this case drug testing to prevent harm might be legitimate. But how this is practicable is another question. It would seem that standard motor dexterity or mental dexterity tests, immediately prior to job performance, are more efficacious ways of preventing harm, unless one concludes that drug use invariably and necessarily leads to harm. One must trust the individuals in any system in order for that system to work. One cannot police everything. It might work to randomly test people, to find drug users, and to weed out the few to forestall possible future harm, but are the harms prevented sufficient to override the rights of privacy of the people who are innocent and to overcome the possible abuses we have mentioned? It seems not.

Clearly, a better method is to develop safety checks immediately prior to the performance of a job. Have a surgeon or a pilot or a bus driver pass a few reasoning and motor-skill tests before work. The cause of the lack of a skill, which lack might lead to harm, is really a secondary issue.

DRUG TESTING FOR PROSPECTIVE EMPLOYEES

Let's turn finally to drug testing during a pre-employment interview. Assuming the job description and responsibilities have been made clear, we can say that an employer is entitled to expect from a prospective employee whatever performance is agreed to in the employment contract. Of course, this will always involve risks, since the employer must make a judgment about future performances. To lower this risk, employers have a legitimate claim to some information about the employee. Previous work experience, training, education, and the like are obvious candidates since they indicate the person's ability to do the job. Except in rare circumstances drug use itself is irrelevant for determining an employee's ability to perform. (Besides, most people who are interviewing know enough to get their systems clean if the prospective employer is going to test them.)

We suggest that an employer can claim to have an interest in knowing (a) whether or not the prospective employee *can* do the job and (b) whether there is reason to believe that once hired the employee *will* do the job. The first can be determined in fairly straightforward ways: past work experience, training, education, etc. Presumably past drug use is thought more relevant to the second question. But there are straightforward and less intrusive means than drug testing for resolving this issue. Asking the employee "Is there anything that might prevent you from doing this job?" comes first to mind. Hiring the employee on a probationary period is another way. But to inquire about drug use here is to claim a right to know too much. It is to claim a right to know not only information about what an employee *can* do, but also a right to inquire into whatever background information *might* be (but not necessarily *is*) causally related to what an employee *will* do. But the range of factors that could be relevant here, from medical history to psychological dispositions to family plans, is surely too open-ended for an employer to claim as a *right* to know.

It might be responded that what an employer is entitled to expect is not a certain level of output, but a certain level of effort. The claim here would be that while drug use is only contingently related to what an employee *can* do, it is directly related to an employee's *motivation* to do the job. Drug use then is *de facto* relevant to the personal information that an employer is *entitled* to know.

But this involves an assumption mentioned above. The discussion so far has assumed that drugs will adversely affect job performance. However, some drugs are performance *enhancing* whether they are concerned with actual *output* or *effort*. The widespread use of steroids, pain-killers, and dexadrine among professional athletes are perhaps only the most publicized instances of performance enhancing drugs. (A teacher's use of caffeine before an early-morning class is perhaps a more common example.) More to the point, knowledge of drug use tells little about motivation. There are too many other variables to be considered. Some users are motivated and some are not. Thus the motivational argument is faulty.

We can conclude, then, that whether the relevant consideration for prospective employees is output or effort, knowledge of drug use will be largely irrelevant for predicting. Employers ought to be positivistic in their approach. They should restrict their information gathering to measurable behavior and valid predictions, (What has the prospect done? What can the prospect do? What has the prospect promised to do?) and not speculate about the underlying *causes* of this behavior. With a probationary work period always an option, there are sufficient non-intrusive means for limiting risks available to employers without having to rely on investigations into drug use.

In summary, we believe that drug use is information that is rightfully private and that only in exceptional cases can an employer claim a right to know about such use. Typically, these are cases in which knowledge of drug use could be used to prevent harm. However, even in those cases we believe that there are less intrusive and more effective means available than drug testing for gaining the information that would be necessary to prevent the harm. Thus, we conclude that drug testing of employees is rarely justified, and mostly inefficacious.

Notes

*Versions of this paper were read to the Department of Philosophy at Southern Connecticut State University and to the Society of Business Ethics. The authors would like to thank those people, as well as Robert Baum and Norman Bowie, the editors of *Business and Professional Ethics Journal* for their many helpful comments. Professor Duska wishes to thank the Pew Memorial Trust for a grant providing released time to work on this paper.

1. *The New Republic*, March 31, 1986.

2. This trend primarily involves screening employees for such drugs as marijuana, cocaine, amphetamines, barbituates, and opiates (e.g., heroin, methadone and morphine). While alcohol is also a drug that can be abused in the workplace, it seldom is among the drugs mentioned in conjunction with employee testing. We believe that testing which proves justified for controlled substances will, *a fortiori*, be justified for alcohol as well.

3. "A Defense of Employee Rights," Joseph Des Jardins and John McCall, *Journal of Business Ethics* 4, (1985). We should emphasize that our concern is with the *moral* rights of privacy for employees and not with any specific or prospective *legal* rights. Readers interested in pursuing the legal aspects of employee drug testing should consult: "Workplace Privacy Issues and Employee Screening Policies" by Richard Lehe and David Middlebrooks in *Employee Relations Law Journal* (Vol. 11, no. 3) pp. 407–421; and "Screening Workers for Drugs: A Legal and Ethical Framework" by Mark Rothstein, in *Employee Relations Law Journal* (vol. 11, no. 3) pp. 422–436.

4. "Privacy, Polygraphs, and Work," George Brenkert, *Business and Professional Ethics Journal* vol. 1, no. 1 (Fall 1981). For a more general discussion of privacy in the workplace see "Privacy in Employment" by Joseph Des Jardins, in *Moral Rights in the Workplace* edited by Gertrude Ezorsky, (SUNY Press, 1987). A good resource for philosophical work on privacy can be found in "Recent Work on the Concept of Privacy" by W.A. Parent, in *American Philosophical Quarterly* (Vol. 20, Oct. 1983) pp. 341–356.

5. *U.S. News and World Report* Aug. 1983; *Newsweek* May 1983.

6. Obviously we are speaking here of harms that go beyond the simple economic harm which results from unsatisfactory job performance. These economic harms were discussed in the first argument above. Further, we ignore such "harms" as providing bad role-models for adolescents, harms often used to justify drug tests for professional athletes. We think it unreasonable to hold an individual responsible for the image he/she provides to others.

7. The philosophical literature on informed consent is often concerned with "informed consent" in a medical context. For an interesting discussion of informed consent in the workplace, see Mary Gibson, *Worker's Rights* (Rowman and Allanheld, 1983) especially pp. 13–14 and 74–75.

8. For a reiteration of this point and a concise argument against drug testing see Lewis L. Maltby, "Why Drug Testing is a Bad Idea," *Inc.* June 1987, pp. 152–153. "But the fundamental flaw with drug testing is that it tests for the wrong thing. A realistic program to detect workers whose condition puts the company or other people at risk would test for the condition that actually creates the danger. The reason drunk or stoned airline pilots and truck drivers are dangerous is their reflexes, coordination, and timing are deficient. This impairment could come from many situations — drugs, alcohol, emotional problems — the list is almost endless. A serious program would recognize that the real problem is workers' impairment, and test for that. Pilots can be tested in flight simulators. People in other jobs can be tested by a trained technician in about 20 minutes — at the job site." p. 152.

9. This argument is structurally similar to the argument against the effectiveness of capital punishment as a deterrent offered by Justice Brennan in the Supreme Court's decision in *Furman v. Georgia*.

10. It might be argued that since we base our critique upon the contractual relationship between employers and employees, our entire position can be underminded by a clever employer who places within the contract a privacy waiver for drug tests. A full answer to this would require an account of the free and rational subject that the contract model presupposes. While acknowledging that we need such an account to prevent just any contract from being morally legitimate, we will have to leave this debate to another time. Interested readers might find "The Moral Contract between Employers and Employees" by Norman Bowie, in *The Work Ethic in Business*, edited by Hoffman and Wyly (Oelgeschlager and Gunn, 1981) pp. 195–202, helpful here.

DISCUSSION QUESTIONS

1. In the course of his discussion, Brenkert claims that even if job applicants consented to a polygraph test (or any similarly revealing test), they may still be violating their own privacy. Explain why Brenkert makes this claim. Are there rights, such as privacy, that we cannot give up?

2. Consider how Des Jardins's discussion of privacy applies to people with AIDS. Is it a violation of privacy for a company to test prospective employees to determine if they are HIV positive? What are morally acceptable grounds for companies to require such a test? How much are companies entitled to know about a prospective employee's health?

3. Lippke approaches privacy differently from Brenkert and Des Jardins. Contending that the power imbalance between employer and employee already erodes the latter's autonomy, Lippke sees invasions of privacy as additional, unwarranted threats to autonomy. Is it possible to respect employee autonomy while at the same time letting corporations gather the information about their workers that they believe they need?

4. Des Jardins and Duska argue that drug testing is rarely justified; yet such tests are now commonplace in American corporations. Who is right on this issue?

CASE 11.1

Love and Business

Most of the public controversy about invasions of employees' privacy has centered on a company's attempt to find out if its workers are doing something illegal, such as using drugs. More pressing, however, is the practice by many companies of regulating its employees' lives in an area that is not simply legal, but also normal, healthy, and the source of great joy — personal relationships. Numerous corporations limit the kinds of relationships its employees may enter. In some cases, they are barred from dating co-workers; in other cases, competitors.

A major U.S. food corporation, for example, does not let its employees date one another. Nonetheless, two executives met and fell in love. Despite the fact that the man and woman worked in different parts of the company and had no formal business relationship with each other, their actions now jeopardized both of their jobs. For a year they lived together secretly. Before they publicly announced their plans to marry, however, the man left the company.

In 1982, the Coca-Cola Company fired Amanda Blake, a manager of data processing at the Coca-Cola bottler in Northampton, Massachusetts, when she refused to break her engagement with an accountant at a rival Pepsi bottler. An attorney representing the company said that she might have accidentally leaked confidential information to her husband. In a similar case in 1979, Virginia Rulon-Miller lost her job as a marketing manager at IBM because she continued to date a former IBM account manager who now worked for a competitor. Former IBM Chairman Thomas J. Watson, Jr., however, at one time had said that "we have concern with an employee's off-the-job behavior only when it reduces his ability to perform regular job assignments." Rulon-Miller sued and received a judgment of $300,000.

Critics of these restrictions claim that they are unwarranted intrusions into employees' private lives. Moreover, they argue that finding a suitable companion is not only critical to one's well-being but also can be so difficult that such restrictions are an unreasonable price to pay for a job. Proponents, however, argue that the matter is not so simple. Personal relationships between co-workers can lead to favoritism and even to an unfair competitive advantage over other workers. One member of the relationship may be in a position to pass along useful information that his or her partner's peers lack. And even if there are no problems when the relationship is going well, there may be significant problems if it sours. Particularly if the former lovers work together, their professional relationship may be affected. There may be tension, hostility, and difficulty communicating with each other in a way that affects their own performance and that of their colleagues. Relationships with competitors are seen as even more dangerous because of the risk of the spread of confidential information that could cost a company sales and, ultimately, jobs. ◆

Discussion Questions

1. Is there anything wrong with a company's regulating its employees' personal relationships? If you think so, you would probably argue that this part of an employee's life is not any of the company's business. But how do you respond to the claim that because this relationship might affect the company, it becomes the company's business?

2. If you support such policies, how do you respond to the claim that it is generally considered unethical for companies to use gender and race as criteria for promotions even if such policies result in lost sales in particular areas?

3. Should such restrictions apply to friendships as well as romantic relationships? Don't the same dangers of favoritism and breach of security apply?

Sources

"Privacy," *Business Week*, March 28, 1988, 61–68.
"What's in a Job?," *Wall Street Journal*, October 23, 1985, 35.

CASE 11.2

◆ ◆ ◆

High-Tech Invasions of Privacy

New technologies usually give business increased efficiency, new abilities, and higher profits. But they sometimes also create new ethical issues, as is the case with technologies that allow for the secret surveillance of employees.

Computers allow employers to track the speed and efficiency of workers in a variety of positions: data-entry clerks, telephone operators, supermarket checkout clerks, airline reservation agents, and customer-service representatives for transportation companies. Directory-assistance operators, for example, are allowed 25 seconds to handle a request, with computers logging their performance. Computers also can track an employee's entire day by recording sign-on and sign-off times at his or her terminal. At one airline, reservation agents' computers record whether they exceed their allowed 30 minutes for lunch, two 15-minute breaks, and 10 minutes for visits to the restroom. Experts estimate that as many as 20 million workers are regularly monitored at their computers.

Other kinds of surveillance that employees object to include being secretly monitored on the telephone by supervisors and being observed by hidden cameras. General Electric has used pinhole lenses mounted in walls and ceilings to scrutinize the actions of employees it suspects of wrongdoing. An employee union filed suit in 1991 against the Amoco Corporation after learning that the company had installed a hidden camera in the women's shower room. The camera had been used to catch a man who had been sneaking into the room, and the company said that people were photographed only above the shoulders. Nonetheless, the employees claimed that their privacy had been violated.

Corporate concern with employee misdeeds has even led to claims that the privacy of innocent third parties has been violated. In 1991, Procter & Gamble wanted to discover which one of its employees was passing company secrets to a reporter. The company contacted local law enforcement officials who had Cincinnati Bell search the records of all 655,000 customers in two particular area codes.

Companies who use electronic monitoring claim that such practices are necessary in order to measure employee productivity, to ensure courtesy for customers, and to prevent theft. Opponents of monitoring claim it is an invasion of privacy. But they also contend that it rewards quantity rather than quality and that it can have an adverse effect on employees. A 1990 study of more than 700 telephone workers claimed that among monitored employees, 81 percent had symptoms or complaints of depression and 54 percent had stiff or sore wrists. The percentages for employees who were not monitored were 69 percent and 24 percent, respectively, suggesting that monitoring itself was a source of stress. Critics also argue that eavesdropping on personal phone calls can reveal information about an employee that the worker is entitled to keep private. For example, Barbara Otto, a director of a working women's advocacy group, notes that employers may "discover that employees are spending weekends with a person of the same sex or talking about forming a union." ◆

Discussion Questions

1. Is there anything unethical about electronic monitoring? Does the extent to which it is used, as described in this case study, constitute an unwarranted invasion of privacy?

2. Critics of such surveillance contend that the contemporary workplace has become an "electronic sweatshop." Do you agree? Opponents of listening in on telephone calls claim that eavesdropping would be unobjectionable only if the employee were notified by some signal, for example, a tone, before the surveillance began. Companies object, however, saying that the whole point of the practice is to monitor an employee's performance when he or she does not know a supervisor is listening. Companies would never catch a thief, they contend, if they had to publicly announce whenever they were observing workers. What would you propose as a way of protecting the legitimate, if conflicting, interests of all the parties involved?

Sources

"Is Your Boss Spying on You?," *Business Week*, January 15, 1990, 74–75.

Kilborn, Peter T., "Workers using Computers Find a Supervisor Inside," *New York Times*, December 23, 1990, 1, 17.

"Nowhere to Hide," *Time*, November 11, 1991, 34–40.

"Surveillance in the Shower," *New York Times*, December 10, 1991, A22.

ADDITIONAL READINGS

Garrett, Thomas M., and Richard J. Klonoski, "Private Lives and Company Lives," in *Business Ethics*, 2nd ed. (Englewood Cliffs, NJ: Prentice Hall, 1986), 46–53.

Thompson, Judith Jarvis, "The Right to Privacy," *Philosophy and Public Affairs*, 4 (Summer 1975), 295–322.

Westin, Alan, *Privacy and Freedom* (New York: Atheneum Publishers, 1976).

CHAPTER 12

◆ ◆ ◆

Whistleblowing

What should an employee do if he or she uncovers evidence of wrongdoing by the corporation or by another employee? Is it morally permissible to "blow the whistle"? Is it obligatory? Does it matter if not blowing the whistle will lead to physical harm or if it will only contribute to the company's (or customers') losing money?

Despite the fact that whistleblowing takes place fairly infrequently and that whistleblowers are generally punished rather than rewarded for their courage and integrity, this issue has persisted as an important topic in business ethics. This chapter presents a range of different positions. Richard De George specifies three conditions that must be met for whistleblowing to be morally permissible and another two that make it morally required. Gene James criticizes De George's position as too limited, and he also justifies anonymous whistleblowing. David Goldberg also criticizes De George and argues that whistleblowing is more obligatory than merely permissible. Ronald Duska focuses on the concept that makes most people uneasy about whistleblowing — loyalty — and argues that an employee does not have even a prima facie obligation of loyalty to his or her company. Natalie Dandekar, however, asserts that whistleblowing is not intrinsically virtuous and that not all whistleblowing should be fully legitimated.

Richard T. De George
WHISTLE BLOWING

As a general rule, people have a moral obligation to prevent serious harm to others if they are able to do so and can do so with little cost to themselves. As the cost increases, the obligation decreases. If one can save another's life only at the expense of one's own life, one is not morally obliged to do so, and giving up one's life for another is usually considered an act of heroic virtue. What is one's obligation as an employee to prevent one's company from harming others? The question is a complicated one and leads us to a consideration of what has become known as *whistle blowing.*

KINDS OF WHISTLE BLOWING

Whistle blowing is a term used for a wide range of activities that are dissimilar from a moral point of view. Sometimes the term refers to disclosures made by employees to executives in a firm, perhaps concerning improper conduct of fellow employees or superiors who are cheating on expense accounts, or are engaging in petty or grand theft. Students are sometimes said to "blow the whistle" on fellow students whom they see cheating on exams. In these cases, whistle blowing amounts to reporting improper activities to an appropriate person. This can be called *internal whistle blowing,* for the disclosure or allegation of inappropriate conduct is made to someone within the organization or system. Generally, one believes an investigation will follow and a sanction will be imposed. In the classroom situation, if the students are on the honor system, they have agreed to report cheating and are morally obliged to do so. If they are not on the honor system, such reporting may be morally permissible, but is not usually required. A similar analysis applies on the job as well.

Internal whistle blowing is frequently not an act of either corporate disloyalty or disobedience. In fact, it is more often than not a form of corporate loyalty. But it does involve disloyalty or disobedience to one's immediate superior or to one's fellow workers. If done from moral motives, the intent of such whistle blowing is to stop dishonesty or some immoral practice or act, to protect the interests and reputation of the company, or to increase the company's profits. For these reasons, it is in the company's interest to encourage such whistle blowing, so long as it does not turn the firm into a sort of police-state, where everyone watches and reports on everyone else.

Someone who reports sexual harassment is also sometimes said to blow the whistle on the offender; this is often because simply speaking to the person has no effect. In this case, the charge is about an offense not against the organization or system, but against oneself; the whistle blowing might be called personal, as opposed to impersonal whistle blowing, in which the potential or actual injury is to others or to the organization rather than to oneself. *Personal*

From Richard T. De George, "Whistle Blowing," in *Business Ethics*, 3rd ed. (New York: Macmillan, 1990), 200–216. Reprinted by permission of the publisher.

whistle blowing is, in general, morally permitted but not morally required, unless other aspects of the case show that there is immediate danger to others.

Because workers have a right not to be sexually harassed, they should have a means by which to report such harassment if simply speaking to the harasser proves ineffective. Similarly, workers who have other rights violated should also have channels through which to get their legitimate complaints heard and acted on. Acts of personal whistle blowing are usually within the organization. But if serious enough, the whistle blower who gets no satisfaction internally might have to report to someone outside. Only a shortsighted firm would force external whistle blowing; a well-managed firm would be so structured as to take care of such cases internally. This is in the best interests not only of the firm but also of the workers and their morale.

Whistle blowing sometimes refers to government employees who divulge to a governmental regulatory or investigative bureau unethical practices in their division or office. It sometimes refers to reporting such things as cost overruns to congressional committees or to the media. (The former is still considered external whistle blowing, because one goes outside the division or office to alert someone in another part of the government system.) Sometimes whistle blowing refers to leaks by government employees to the media. We can call all these kinds of disclosure *governmental whistle blowing.*

This sort of whistle blowing is different from private-sector whistle blowing, which is by employees on their employers. The obligations one has to one's government are considerably different from obligations to a nongovernmental employer. The reason is that government employees are related to their government both as citizens and as employees and the harm done by governmental employees may have effects not only on the particular division in which they are employed but also on the government and country as a whole. The law recognizes this difference, and Congress has passed special legislation governing and protecting certain kinds of governmental whistle blowers.[1] The laws do not protect those who break the law by revealing classified information, but they protect from dismissal those who reveal waste, overspending, or illegal or corrupt activity within the government bureaucracy. The legislation has been enforced only sporadically, and those who have blown the whistle have usually not fared well in terms of promotion or career advancement, even if they have kept their jobs. No administration has yet signaled that such people, if they have the best interests of the country at heart, are to be rewarded and made examples to be emulated.

We shall restrict our discussion to a specific sort of whistle blowing — namely, *nongovernmental, impersonal, external whistle blowing.* We shall be concerned with (1) employees of profit-making firms, who, for moral reasons, in the hope and expectation that a product will be made safe, or a practice changed, (2) make public information about a product or practice of the firm that due to faulty design, the use of inferior materials, or the failure to follow safety or other regular procedures or state of the art standards (3) threatens to produce serious harm to the public in general or to individual users of a product. We shall restrict our analysis to this type of whistle blowing because, in the first place, the conditions that justify whistle blowing vary according to

[1] U.S. Merit Systems Protection Board, *Whistle Blowing and the Federal Employee*, Washington, D.C.: U.S. Government Printing Office, 1981.

the type of case at issue. Second, financial harm can be considerably different from bodily harm. An immoral practice that increases the cost of a product by a slight margin may do serious harm to no individual, even if the total amount when summed adds up to a large amount, or profit. (Such cases can be handled differently from cases that threaten bodily harm.) Third, both internal and personal whistle blowing cause problems for a firm, which are for the most part restricted to those within the firm. External, impersonal whistle blowing is of concern to the general public, because it is the general public rather than the firm that is threatened with harm.

As a paradigm, we shall take a set of fairly clear-cut cases — namely, those in which serious bodily harm, including possible death, threatens either the users of a product or innocent bystanders because of a firm's practice, the design of its product, or the action of some person or persons within the firm. (Many of the famous whistle-blowing cases are instances of such situations.) We shall assume clear cases where serious, preventable harm will result unless a company makes changes in its product or practice.

Cases that are less clear are probably more numerous, and pose problems that are difficult to solve — for example, how serious is *serious*, and how does one tell whether a given situation is serious? We choose not to resolve such issues, but rather to construct a model embodying a number of distinctions that will enable us to clarify the moral status of whistle blowing, which may, in turn, provide a basis for working out guidelines for more complex cases.

Finally, the only motivation for whistle blowing we shall consider here is moral motivation. Those who blow the whistle for revenge, and so on, are not our concern in this discussion.

Corporations are complex entities. Sometimes those at the top do not want to know in detail the difficulties encountered by those below them. They wish lower management to handle these difficulties as best they can. On the other hand, those in lower management frequently present only good news to those above them, even if those at the top do want to be told about difficulties. Sometimes, lower management hopes that things will be straightened out without letting their superiors know that anything has gone wrong. For instance, sometimes a production schedule is drawn up that many employees along the line know cannot be achieved. The manager at each level has cut off a few days of the production time actually needed, to make his projection look good to those above. Because this happens at each level, the final projection is weeks, if not months, off the mark. When difficulties develop in actual production, each level is further squeezed and is tempted to cut corners in order not to fall too far behind the overall schedule. The cuts may consist of not correcting defects in a design, or of allowing a defective part to go through, even though a department head and the workers in that department know that this will cause trouble for the consumer. Sometimes a defective part will be annoying; sometimes it will be dangerous. If dangerous, external whistle blowing may be morally mandatory.

Producing goods that are known to be defective, or that will break down after a short period of time, is sometimes justified by producers, who point out that the product is warrantied and that it will be repaired for consumers free of charge. They claim it is better to have the product available for the Christmas market, for the new-model season for cars, or for some other target date, even if it must later be recalled and fixed, rather than have the product delayed beyond the target date.

When the product is so defective as to be dangerous, the situation from a moral point of view is much more serious than when only convenience is at stake. If the danger is such that people are likely to die from the defect, then clearly it should be repaired before being sold. There have been instances, however, when a company, knowing that its product was dangerous, did a cost-benefit analysis. The managers of the company determined how many people were likely to be killed, and what the cost to the company would be if a certain percentage of the deceased persons' families successfully sued the company. They then compared this figure with the cost of repairing the defect, or of repairing it immediately rather than at a later date, through a recall. They also estimated the cost to the company if they were not only sued but also fined. If the loss from immediate repair substantially exceeded the probable cost of suits and fines, they continued production.

Such a cost-benefit analysis might seem, at first glance, to resemble a utilitarian calculation. However, a utilitarian calculation would not fail to consider the effect on all parties. The cost-benefit analysis is made exclusively from the standpoint of the company. How much, we have to ask, is a human life worth? If a defective part will probably cause fifty or sixty deaths, can we simply calculate the probability of a certain number of people suing, and then weigh that cost against the cost of replacing the part? An adequate moral utilitarian calculation would include the deaths and the injuries, plus the inconvenience for all the purchasers, and weigh these factors against the dollars saved. The equation is not difficult to solve. We know that we all have a moral obligation not to harm others, when we can prevent it. In such cases, the equation of deaths to dollars is an equation which, from a moral point of view, will always balance out in favor of lives saved. This realization often provides the moral motivation for whistle blowers.

A variety of corporate activities have led people to disclose publicly the internal actions of their companies. In some cases, companies were dumping toxic wastes into a water supply, knowing that it would harm the people who lived near the supply. In other cases, papers were signed by employees certifying that a dangerous defect had been repaired, when in fact no repairs had been made. In the Bay Area Rapid Transit case three engineers saw a dangerous defect in the system. When their warnings were systematically ignored, and they were told to keep quiet, they felt it was their moral duty to make the danger known to the public.[2]

The whistle blower usually fares very poorly at the hands of his company, as we mentioned before. Most are fired. In some instances, they have been blackballed in the whole industry. If they are not fired, they are frequently shunted aside at promotion time, and treated as pariahs. Those who consider making a firm's wrongdoings public must therefore be aware that they may be fired, ostracized, and condemned by others. They may ruin their chances of future promotion and security, and they also may make themselves a target for revenge. Only rarely have companies praised and promoted such people. This is not surprising, because the whistle blower forces the company to do what it did not want to do, even if, morally, it was the right action. This is scandalous. And it is ironic that those guilty of endangering the lives of others — even of

[2]Robert M. Anderson, Robert Perrucci, Dan E. Schendel, and Leon E. Trachtman, *Divided Loyalties: Whistle-Blowing at BART*, West Lafayette, Ind.: Purdue University, 1980.

indirectly killing them — frequently get promoted by their companies for increasing profits.

Because the consequences for the whistle blower are often so disastrous, such action is not to be undertaken lightly. Moreover, whistle blowing may, in some cases, be morally justifiable without being morally mandatory. The position we shall develop is a moderate one, and falls between two extreme positions: that defended by those who claim that whistle blowing is always morally justifiable, and that defended by those who say it is never morally justifiable.

WHISTLE BLOWING AS MORALLY PROHIBITED

Whistle blowing can be defined in such a way that it is always morally permissible, or in such a way that it is always morally obligatory. Initially, however, we can plausibly consider as morally neutral the act of an employee making public a firm's internal operations, practices, or policies that affect the safety of a product. In some cases whistle blowing may be morally prohibited, in some cases it may be morally permissible, and in some it may be morally mandatory.

Each of the two extreme positions on whistle blowing, although mistaken, is instructive. The view that whistle blowing is always morally prohibited is the more widely held view. It is held not only by most managers but also by most employees. There is a strong tradition within American mores against "ratting," or telling on others. We find this to be true of children, in and out of school, and in folk wisdom: "Don't wash your dirty linen in public." There is ample evidence that when someone does blow the whistle on his or her company — even for moral reasons, and with positive results for the public — he or she is generally ostracized, not only by the management of the firm but also by fellow employees. The whistle blower is perceived as a traitor, as someone who has damaged the firm — the working family — to which he or she belongs. In so doing, he or she has hurt and offended most of those within the firm.

Rarely are whistle blowers honored as heroes by their fellow workers. A possible explanation might be that, by this action, the whistle blower has implied that fellow workers who did not blow the whistle are guilty of immorality, complicity in the wrongdoings of the company, or cowardice. The whistle blower did what the others were obliged to do but failed to do. His or her presence is therefore a constant reminder of their moral failure. Such a scenario may describe some situations, but whatever the scenario, the evidence is overwhelming that the whistle blower is not considered a hero by fellow workers.

How can we justify this feeling of most workers and managers that an employee ought not blow the whistle on the firm for which he or she works? Are they not operating under a double standard if they themselves wish to be preserved from injury caused by other firms, even if the means of achieving that protection is the result of someone in another firm blowing the whistle?

The most plausible, and most commonly stated, rationale for not blowing the whistle is given in terms of loyalty. When people join a company, it is claimed, they become part of an organization composed of fellow employees. They are not simply automatons filling positions. They are people with feelings, who are engaged in a joint enterprise. In accepting employment, employees at every level owe something to the employing firm as well as to those with whom they work. Employees owe not only a certain amount of work but also a certain positive attitude toward that work and to their fellow workers. Without such a positive attitude (which we can characterize roughly as loyalty), a worker is either indifferent or disaffected. An indifferent or disaffected worker is clearly not a team player, and typically contributes only enough work to keep from being fired. Given the chance, such a worker would gladly leave the firm for a job with another company. Such employees lack loyalty to their employer.

Now, if the indifferent or disaffected worker were to blow the whistle on his or her employer, one might doubt that he or she did so from noble or moral motives. One might be mistaken in assuming ignoble motives, but the natural tendency would be to see the whistle blowing as stemming from the worker's indifference or disaffection. Therefore, it is unlikely that those workers who feel a sense of obligation or loyalty to the firm will look kindly on the whistle blower or the whistle blowing.

This leaves us to consider the loyal worker. What is the basis of this loyalty, and to what extent is it owed the company or employer? In one view, loyalty is based appropriately on gratitude. The firm or employer, after all, gives the worker a job, which is no small consideration in a society in which 4 percent unemployment is considered normal, and in which unemployment for some groups in the society has recently reached 18 percent. To be disloyal to one's employer is to bite the hand that feeds one—hardly an admirable or praise-worthy action. But even if the worker feels no gratitude, both the worker and the employer profit from their mutual contract, because if workers are to be more than cogs in an impersonal machine, they come to see the company as their company. Workers, in any event, have a stake in the firm for which they work. The stake is appropriately translated into positive concern for the firm, if not full identification with it—a concern that is in part what people mean by *loyalty.*

But even if we concede that an employee appropriately feels loyalty to a firm or to those within it, we cannot agree that such loyalty involves or demands that a worker engage in immoral activities for the firm. Nor need we admit that loyalty is always the overriding consideration in an employee's actions. The flaw in the argument of those who claim that whistle blowing is always immoral is that they make loyalty to a firm the worker's highest obligation, and consider it to be always overriding.

On the other hand, those who argue that whistle blowing is always at least morally permissible typically approach such acts from the point of view of the right of free speech. Workers do not give up the right of free speech—a civil right—by taking employment. They usually make no pledge of loyalty; and any claim that employers make regarding an employee's obligation to be loyal to their firm is wishful thinking, or self-serving ideological hogwash that they try to foist on naive employees. There is no obligation of employee loyalty, either as a result of a contract or as an implied condition of employment. But there is the right of free speech.

The right of free speech, of course, is a limited right. One is not free to yell "fire" in a crowded theater when there is no fire. One is legally prohibited from making libelous statements. But one is not prevented from making true statements, whether they be about one's employer or about others. American citizens freely criticize their government and their elected leaders. It would be strange if they did not have a similar right to criticize their employers. More-over, the argument continues, if the actions of their employers, or of some members of the firm, are morally suspect, or if actions of the firm may in some way damage consumers, workers, or innocent bystanders, or if these actions threaten the interests of shareholders or of other interested parties, then workers clearly have the right to speak out in whatever way, and in whatever forum, they desire. By doing so they violate no commitment to loyalty because there is no such commitment; they are simply exercising their right to free speech. It may be imprudent at times to speak out, and they may suffer from the often unjust reactions of others, but whistle blowing, or speaking out about a company's practices, is not immoral; it is always a morally defensible act.

This extreme position has much to recommend it. But it is extreme because it makes the right of free speech always overriding, and it fails to consider the harm done to one's firm or fellow workers by the usual kind of whistle blowing. In denying any obligation of loyalty, it implicitly denies any consideration of the harm that one's actions may do to those with whom one is associated, and fails to consider whether there are morally preferable alternatives — or perhaps even morally required alternatives.

Each of the two positions we have described as extreme suffers from the same defect. Each makes absolute one aspect of a complex situation and fails to consider the conflict of obligations, rights, and responsibilities that usually arise in the conditions that lead to whistle blowing. If neither loyalty nor the right to free speech is always overriding, and if neither always determines the morality of a case, it is sometimes possible for loyalty to be overriding, sometimes for the right of free speech to be overriding — and it is possible, therefore, that at times neither be overriding, and that both may give way to some other consideration. This suggests that sometimes whistle blowing may be immoral — as when loyalty is overriding — and that sometimes it is morally justified — as when the right to free speech is overriding.

On whom rests the onus of justification? Should we assume that whistle blowing is generally morally justifiable, and require that anyone who claims that a given act of whistle blowing is immoral make out that case? Or should we assume that whistle blowing is generally immoral, and require moral justifica-tion for those acts that are morally permissible or obligatory? Tradition has placed the onus on those who justify whistle blowing, the common assumption being that it is morally prohibited. We have already noted the general attitude of most workers to whistle blowing, and their negative reaction to the whistle blower. Moreover, unless we are to indict most workers as moral cowards, the relatively rare incidence of whistle blowing indicates that most workers do not feel it is their moral obligation to blow the whistle. Although these considera-tions do not by themselves show that workers feel it is immoral to blow the whistle, they at least tend to put the onus on those who would claim it is morally obligatory. Finally, the literature on whistle blowing has developed in such a way that those who justify it have assumed the need to do so.

That whistle blowing needs justification makes sense, moreover, if it is seen as an instance of disobedience to the corporation or organization. Frequently, whistle blowers are in fact told by their superiors to mind their own business. To blow the whistle is to go beyond what they are paid to do, and is to fly in the face of orders given by a legitimate superior within the firm or organization. Disobedience typically requires justification if it is to be considered moral —

whether it is a case of civil disobedience, disobedience to the corporation, or a child's disobedience to his or her parents. Under the appropriate conditions, obedience is the expected and required moral way to act. Disobedience may be morally justified, but if it is, the onus is on the disobedient person or his spokesman to make out the case.

To admit that whistle blowing is often an instance of disobedience to the corporation, and that at least sometimes one (i.e., the corporation) is owed obedience leads us to the conclusion that at least sometimes whistle blowing is morally wrong. That it is sometimes morally wrong seems the general consensus in American society, and there is no reason to challenge the consensus. But sometimes whistle blowing is morally permissible, and sometimes is even morally obligatory; therefore it is appropriate to accept the onus of spelling out and justifying the conditions that render it such.

WHISTLE BLOWING AS MORALLY PERMITTED

The kind of whistle blowing we are considering involves an employee somehow going public, revealing information or concerns about his or her firm in the hope that the firm will change its product, action, or policy, whatever it is that the whistle blower feels will harm, or has harmed others, and needs to be rectified. We can assume that when one blows the whistle, it is not with the consent of the firm, but against its wishes. It is thus a form of disloyalty and of disobedience to the corporation. Whistle blowing of this type, we can further assume, does injury to a firm. It results in either adverse publicity or in an investigation of some sort, or both. If we adopt the principle that one ought not to do harm without sufficient reason, then, if the act of whistle blowing is to be morally permissible, some good must be achieved to outweigh the harm that will be done.

There are five conditions that, if satisfied, change the moral status of whistle blowing. If the first three are satisfied, the act of whistle blowing will be morally justifiable and permissible. If the additional two are satisfied, the act of whistle blowing will be morally obligatory.

Whistle blowing is morally permissible if

1. The firm, through its product or policy, will do serious and considerable harm to the public, whether in the person of the user of its product, an innocent bystander, or the general public.

Because whistle blowing causes harm to the firm, this harm must be offset by at least an equal amount of good, if the act is to be permissible. We have specified that the potential or actual harm to others must be serious and considerable. That requirement may be considered by some to be both too strong and too vague. Why specify "serious and considerable" instead of saying, "involve more harm than the harm that the whistle blowing will produce for the firm?" Moreover, how serious is "serious?" And how considerable is "considerable?"

There are several reasons for stating that the potential harm must be serious and considerable. First, if the harm is not serious and considerable, if it will do only slight harm to the public, or to the user of a product, the justification for whistle blowing will be at least problematic. We will not have a clear case. To assess the harm done to the firm is difficult; but though the harm may be rather vague, it is also rather sure. If the harm threatened by a product is slight or not certain, it might not be greater than the harm done to the firm. After all, a great many products involve some risk. Even with a well-constructed hammer, one can smash one's finger. There is some risk in operating any automobile, because no automobile is completely safe. There is always a trade-off between safety and cost. It is not immoral not to make the safest automobile possible, for instance, and a great many factors enter into deciding just how safe a car should be. An employee might see that a car can be made slightly safer by modifying a part, and might suggest that modification; but not making the modification is not usually grounds for blowing the whistle. If serious harm is not threatened, then the slight harm that is done, say by the use of a product, can be corrected after the product is marketed (e.g., as a result of customer complaint). Our society has a great many ways of handling minor defects, and these are at least arguably better than resorting to whistle blowing.

To this consideration should be added a second. Whistle blowing is frequently, and appropriately, considered an unusual occurence — a heroic act. If the practice of blowing the whistle for relatively minor harm were to become a common occurence, its effectiveness would be diminished. When serious harm is threatened, whistle blowers are listened to by the news media, for instance, because it is news. But relatively minor harm to the public is not news. If many minor charges or concerns were voiced to the media, the public would soon not react as it is now expected to react to such disclosures. This would also be the case if complaints about all sorts of perceived or anticipated minor harm were reported to government agencies, although most people would expect that government agencies would act first on the serious cases, and only later on claims of relatively minor harm.

There is a third consideration. Every time an employee has a concern about possible harm to the public from a product or practice we cannot assume that he or she makes a correct assessment, nor can we assume that every claim of harm is morally motivated. To sift out the claims and concerns of the disaffected worker from the genuine claims and concerns of the morally motivated employee is a practical problem. It may be claimed that this problem has nothing to do with the moral permissibility of the act of whistle blowing; but whistle blowing is a practical matter. If viewed as a technique for changing policy or actions, it will be justified only if effective. It can be trivialized. If it is, then one might plausibly claim that little harm is done to the firm, and hence the act is permitted. But if trivialized, it loses its point. If whistle blowing is to be considered a serious act with serious consequences, it should be reversed for disclosing potentially serious harm, and will be morally justifiable in those cases.

Serious is admittedly a vague term. Is an increase in probable automobile deaths from 2 in 100,000 to 15 in 100,000 over a one-year period serious? Although there may be legitimate debate on this issue, it is clear that matters that threaten death are prima facie serious. If the threatened harm is that a product may cost a few pennies more than otherwise, or if the threatened harm is that a part or product may cause minor inconvenience, that harm — even if multiplied by thousand or millions of instances — does not match the seriousness of death to the user or the innocent bystander.

The harm threatened by unsafe tires — for example, sold as premium quality but blowing out at 60 or 70 mph — is serious, for such tires can easily lead to death. The dumping of metal drums of toxic waste into a river, where the drums will rust, leak, and cause cancer or other serious ills to those who drink the river water or otherwise use it, threatens serious harm. The use of substandard concrete in a building, such that the building is likely to collapse and kill people, poses a serious threat to people. Failure to X-ray pipe fittings, as required in building a nuclear plant, is a failure that might lead to nuclear leaks; this may involve serious harm, for it endangers the health and lives of many.

The notion of *serious* harm might be expanded to include serious financial harm, and kinds of harm other than death and serious threats to health and body. But as we noted earlier, we shall restrict ourselves here to products and practices that produce or threaten serious harm or danger to life and health. The difference between producing harm and threatening serious danger is not significant for the kinds of cases we are considering.

2. Once employees identify a serious threat to the user of a product or to the general public, they should report it to their immediate superior and make their moral concern known. Unless they do so, the act of whistle blowing is not clearly justifiable.

Why not? Why is not the weighing of harm sufficient? The answer has already been given in part. Whistle blowing is a practice that, to be effective, cannot be routinely used. There are other reasons as well. First, reporting one's concerns is the most direct, and usually the quickest, way of producing the change the whistle blower desires. The normal assumption is that most firms do not want to cause death or injury, and do not willingly and knowingly set out to harm the users of their products in this way. If there are life-threatening defects, the normal assumption is, and should be, that the firm will be interested in correcting them, if not for moral reasons, at least for prudential reasons — viz., to avoid suits, bad publicity, and adverse consumer reaction. The argument from loyalty also supports the requirement that the firm be given the chance to rectify its action, procedure, or policy before it is charged in public. Additionally, because whistle blowing does harm to the firm, harm in general is minimized if the firm is informed of the problem and allowed to correct it. Less harm is done to the firm in this way, and if the harm to the public or the users is also averted, this procedure produces the least harm, on the whole.

The condition that one report one's concern to one's immediate superior presupposes a hierarchical structure. Although firms are usually so structured, they need not be. In a company of equals, one would report one's concerns internally, as appropriate.

Several objections may be raised to this condition. Suppose one knows that one's immediate superior already knows of the defect and the danger. In this case reporting it there would be redundant, and condition 2 would be satisfied. But one should not presume without good reason that one's superior does know. What may be clear to one individual may not be clear to another. Moreover, the assessment of risk is often a complicated matter. To a person on one level what appears as unacceptable risk may appear as legitimate to a person on a higher level, who may see a larger picture, and know of offsetting compensations, and the like.

However, would not reporting one's concern effectively preclude the possibility of anonymous whistle blowing, and so put one in jeopardy? This might of course be the case, and this is one of the considerations one should weigh before blowing the whistle. We will discuss this matter later on. If the reporting is done tactfully, moreover, the voicing of one's concerns might, if the problem is apparent to others, indicate a desire to operate within the firm, and so make one less likely to be the one assumed to have blown the whistle anonymously.

By reporting one's concern to one's immediate superior or other appropriate person, one preserves and observes the regular practices of firms, which on the whole promote their order and efficiency; this fulfills one's obligation of minimizing harm, and it precludes precipitous whistle blowing.

> 3. If one's immediate superior does nothing effective about the concern or complaint, the employee should exhaust the internal procedures and possibilities within the firm. This usually will involve taking the matter up the managerial ladder, and, if necessary — and possible — to the board of directors.

To exhaust the internal procedures and possibilities is the key requirement here. In a hierarchically structured firm, this means going up the chain of command. But one may do so either with or without the permission of those at each level of the hierarchy. What constitutes exhausting the internal procedures? This is often a matter of judgment. But because going public with one's concern is more serious for both oneself and for the firm, going up the chain of command is the preferable route to take in most circumstances. This third condition is of course satisfied if, for some reason, it is truly impossible to go beyond any particular level.

Several objections may once again be raised. There may not be time enough to follow the bureaucratic procedures of a given firm; the threatened harm may have been done before the procedures are exhausted. If, moreover, one goes up the chain to the top and nothing is done by anyone, then a great deal of time will have been wasted. Once again, prudence and judgment should be used. The internal possibilities may sometimes be exhausted quickly, by a few phone calls or visits. But one should not simply assume that no one at any level within the firm will do anything. If there are truly no possibilities of internal remedy, then the third condition is satisfied.

As we mentioned, the point of the three conditions is essentially that whistle blowing is morally permissible if the harm threatened is serious, and if internal remedies have been attempted in good faith but without a satisfactory result. In these circumstances, one is morally justified in attempting to avert what one sees as serious harm, by means that may be effective, including blowing the whistle.

We can pass over as not immediately germane the questions of whether in nonserious matters one has an obligation to report one's moral concerns to one's superiors, and whether one fulfills one's obligation once one has reported them to the appropriate party.

WHISTLE BLOWING AS MORALLY REQUIRED

To say that whistle blowing is morally permitted does not impose any obligation on an employee. Unless two other conditions are met, the employee does not have a moral obligation to blow the whistle. To blow the whistle when one is not morally required to do so, and if done from moral motives (i.e., concern for one's fellow man) and at risk to oneself, is to commit a supererogatory act. It is an act that deserves moral praise. But failure to so act deserves no moral blame. In such a case, the whistle blower might be considered a moral hero. Sometimes he or she is so considered, and sometimes not. If one's claim or concern turns out to be ill-founded, one's subjective moral state may be as praiseworthy as if the claim were well-founded, but one will rarely receive much praise for one's action.

For there to be an obligation to blow the whistle, two conditions must be met, in addition to the foregoing three.

4. The whistle blower must have, or have accessible, documented evidence that would convince a reasonable, impartial observer that one's view of the situation is correct, and that the company's product or practice poses a serious and likely danger to the public or to the user of the product.

One does not have an obligation to put oneself at serious risk without some compensating advantage to be gained. Unless one has documented evidence that would convince a reasonable, impartial observer, one's charges or claims, if made public, would be based essentially on one's word. Such grounds may be sufficient for a subjective feeling of certitude about one's charges, but they are not usually sufficient for others to act on one's claims. For instance, a newspaper is unlikely to print a story based simply on someone's undocumented assertion.

Several difficulties emerge. Should it not be the responsibility of the media or the appropriate regulatory agency or government bureau to carry out an investigation based on someone's complaint? It is reasonable for them to do so, providing they have some evidence in support of the complaint or claim. The damage has not yet been done, and the harm will not, in all likelihood, be done to the complaining party. If the action is criminal, then an investigation by a law-enforcing agency is appropriate. But the charges made by whistle blowers are often not criminal charges. And we do not expect newspapers or government agencies to carry out investigations whenever anyone claims that possible harm will be done by a product or practice. Unless harm is imminent, and very serious (e.g., a bomb threat), it is appropriate to act on evidence that substantiates a claim. The usual procedure, once an investigation is started or a complaint followed up, is to contact the party charged.

One does not have a moral obligation to blow the whistle simply because of one's hunch, guess, or personal assessment of possible danger, if supporting evidence and documentation are not available. One may, of course, have the obligation to attempt to get evidence if the harm is serious. But if it is unavailable — or unavailable without using illegal or immoral means — then one does not have the obligation to blow the whistle.

5. The employee must have good reasons to believe that by going public the necessary changes will be brought about. The chance of being successful must be worth the risk one takes and the danger to which one is exposed.

Even with some documentation and evidence, a potential whistle blower may not be taken seriously, or may not be able to get the media or government agency to take any action. How far should one go, and how much must one try? The more serious the situation, the greater the effort required. But unless one has a reasonable expectation of success, one is not obliged to put oneself at great risk. Before going public, the potential whistle blower should know who (e.g., government agency, newspaper, columnist, TV reporter) will make use of the evidence, and how it will be handled. The whistle blower should have good reason to expect that the action taken will result in the kind of change or result that he or she believes is morally appropriate.

The foregoing fourth and fifth conditions may seem too permissive to some and too stringent to others. The conditions are too permissive for those who wish everyone to be ready and willing to blow the whistle whenever there is a chance that the public will be harmed. After all, harm to the public is more serious than harm to the whistle blower, and, in the long run, if everyone saw whistle blowing as obligatory, without satisfying the last two conditions, we would all be better off. If the fourth and fifth conditions must be satisfied, then people will only rarely have the moral obligation to blow the whistle.

If, however, whistle blowing were mandatory whenever the first three conditions were satisfied, and if one had the moral obligation to blow the whistle whenever one had a moral doubt or fear about safety, or whenever one disagreed with one's superiors or colleagues, one would be obliged to go public whenever one did not get one's way on such issues within a firm. But these conditions are much too strong, for the reasons already given. Other conditions, weaker than those proposed might be suggested. But any condition that makes whistle blowing mandatory in large numbers of cases may possibly reduce the effectiveness of whistle blowing. If this were the result, and the practice were to become widespread, then it is doubtful that we would all be better off.

Finally, the claim that many people very often have the obligation to blow the whistle goes against the common view of the whistle blower as a moral hero, and against the commonly held feeling that whistle blowing is only rarely morally mandatory. This feeling may be misplaced. But a very strong argument is necessary to show that although the general public is morally mistaken in its view, the moral theoretician is correct in his or her assertion.

A consequence of accepting the fourth and fifth conditions stated is that the stringency of the moral obligation of whistle blowing corresponds with the common feeling of most people on this issue. Those in higher positions and those in professional positions in a firm are more likely to have the obligation to change a firm's policy or product — even by whistle blowing, if necessary — than are lower-placed employees. Engineers, for instance, are more likely to have access to data and designs than are assembly-line workers. Managers generally have a broader picture and more access to evidence than do nonmanagerial employees. Management has the moral responsibility both to see that the expressed moral concerns of those below them have been adequately considered and that the firm does not knowingly inflict harm on others.

The fourth and fifth conditions will appear too stringent to those who believe that whistle blowing is always a supererogatory act, that it is always moral heroism, and that it is never morally obligatory. They might argue that, although we are not permitted to do what is immoral, we have no general moral obligation to prevent all others from acting immorally. This is what the whistle blower attempts to do. The counter to that, however, is to point out that whistle blowing is an act in which one attempts to prevent harm to a third party. It is not implausible to claim both that we are morally obliged to prevent harm to others at relatively little expense to ourselves, and that we are morally obliged to prevent great harm to a great many others, even at considerable expense to ourselves.

The five conditions outlined can be used by an individual to help decide whether he or she is morally permitted or required to blow the whistle. Third parties can also use these conditions when attempting to evaluate acts of whistle blowing by others, even though third parties may have difficulty determining whether the whistle blowing is morally motivated. It might be possible successfully to blow the whistle anonymously. But anonymous tips or stories seldom get much attention. One can confide in a government agent, or in a reporter, on condition that one's name not be disclosed. But this approach, too, is frequently ineffective in achieving the results required. To be effective, one must usually be willing to be identified, to testify publicly, to produce verifiable evidence, and to put oneself at risk. As with civil disobedience, what captures the conscience of others is the willingness of the whistle blower to suffer harm for the benefit of others, and for what he or she thinks is right.

PRECLUDING THE NEED FOR WHISTLE BLOWING

The need for moral heroes shows a defective society and defective corporations. It is more important to change the legal and corporate structures that make whistle blowing necessary than to convince people to be moral heroes.

Because it is easier to change the law than to change the practice of all corporations, it should be illegal for any employer to fire an employee, or to take any punitive measures, at the time or later, against an employee who satisfies the first three aforementioned conditions and blows the whistle on the company. Because satisfying those conditions makes the action morally justifiable, the law should protect employees when acting in accordance with what their conscience demands. If the whistle is falsely blown, the company will have suffered no great harm. If it is appropriately blown, the company should suffer the consequences of its actions being made public. But to protect a whistle blower by passing such a law is no easy matter. Employers can make life difficult for whistle blowers without firing them. There are many ways of passing over an employee. One can be relegated to the back room of the firm, or be given unpleasant jobs. Employers can find reasons not to promote one or to give one raises. Not all of this can be prevented by law, but some of the more blatant practices can be prohibited.

Second, the law can mandate that the individuals responsible for the decision to proceed with a faulty product or to engage in a harmful practice be penalized. The law has been reluctant to interfere with the operations of companies. As a result, those in the firm who have been guilty of immoral and illegal practices have gone untouched even though the corporation was fined for its activity.

A third possibility is that every company of a certain size be required by law to have an inspector general or an internal operational auditor, whose job it is to uncover immoral and illegal practices. This person's job would be to listen to the moral concerns of employees, at every level, about the firm's practices. He or she should be independent of management, and report to the audit committee of the board, which, ideally, should be a committee made up entirely of outside board members. The inspector or auditor should be charged with making public those complaints that should be made public if not changed from within. Failure on the inspector's part to take proper action with respect to a worker's complaint, such that the worker is forced to go public, should be prima facie evidence of an attempt to cover up a dangerous practice or product, and the inspector should be subject to criminal charges.

In addition, a company that wishes to be moral — that does not wish to engage in harmful practices or to produce harmful products — can take other steps to preclude the necessity of whistle blowing. . . It can establish channels whereby those employees who have moral concerns can get a fair hearing without danger to their position or standing in the company. Expressing such concerns, moreover, should be considered a demonstration of company loyalty and should be rewarded appropriately. The company might establish the position of ombudsman, to hear such complaints or moral concerns, or an independent committee of the board might be established to hear such complaints and concerns. Someone might even be paid by the company to present the position of the would-be whistle blower, who would argue for what the company should do from a moral point of view, rather than what those interested in meeting a schedule or making a profit would like to do. Such a person's success within the company could depend on his success in precluding whistle blowing, as well as the conditions that lead to it.

Unions and professional organizations should become concerned with the problem of whistle blowing. They should support their members who feel obligated to blow the whistle on a company; they should defend and support members in their endeavors, and prevent them from being fired or abused on the job. They can also establish channels of their own, to which members can report concerns, and then follow up such concerns and force appropriate action.

Although we have concentrated on a specific type of nongovernmental, impersonal, external whistle blowing that threatens serious physical harm to the public, the analysis provides a model for dealing with other kinds of whistle blowing as well.

In all cases, because whistle blowing involves disloyalty or disobedience at some level, we start by requiring that it be justified, rather than assuming it needs no justification. If the action needs no justification, it is probably not an instance of whistle blowing. To distinguish the various kinds of whistle blowing, listing conditions that make it morally permissible and those that make it morally required is useful as a guide. In personal whistle blowing, there are many instances in which it is permitted but not obligatory. Many people may prefer to change employers rather than blow the whistle, and this may be perfectly justifiable. In all cases, one must weigh the harm done to individuals against the good to be achieved and the rights to be protected.

Whistle blowing is a relatively recent phenomenon in the workplace. It is one more indication of the falsity of the Myth of Amoral Business. Whistle blowing should also alert corporations to what can and should be done if they wish to be both moral and excellent. When corporate structures preclude the need for whistle blowing, they protect both workers' rights and the public's good.

Gene G. James
WHISTLE-BLOWING: ITS MORAL JUSTIFICATION*

INTRODUCTION

Whistle-blowing may be defined as the attempt of an employee or former employee of an organization to disclose what he or she believes to be wrongdoing in or by the organization. Like blowing a whistle to call attention to a thief, whistle-blowing is an effort to make others aware of practices one considers illegal or immoral. If the wrongdoing is reported to someone higher in the organization, the whistle-blowing may be said to be *internal*. If the wrongdoing is reported to outside individuals or groups, such as reporters, public interest groups, or regulatory agencies, the whistle-blowing is *external*. If the harm being reported is primarily harm to the whistle-blower alone, such as sexual harassment, the whistle-blowing may be said to be *personal*. If it is primarily harm to other people that is being reported, the whistle-blowing is *impersonal*. Most whistle-blowing is done by people currently employed by the organization on which they are blowing the whistle. However, people who have left an organization may also blow the whistle. The former may be referred to as *current* whistle-blowing, the latter as *alumni* whistle-blowing. If the whistle-blower discloses his or her identity, the whistle-blowing may be said to be *open*; if the whistle-blower's identity is not disclosed, the whistle-blowing is *anonymous*.

Whistle-blowers differ from muckrakers because the latter do not have any ties to the organizations whose wrongdoing they seek to disclose. Whistle-blowers also differ from informers and stool pigeons because the latter usually have self-interested reasons for their disclosures, such as obtaining prosecutorial immunity. The term *whistle-blower*, on the other hand, is usually used to refer to people who disclose wrongdoing for moral reasons. However, unless whistle-blowing is arbitrarily defined as disclosure of wrongdoing for moral reasons, the distinction cannot be a sharp one. Thus, although most whistle-blowers act for moral reasons, one cannot take for granted that their motives are praiseworthy.

The organization involved may be either private or public. It may also be either an organization for profit such as a commercial corporation or a nonprofit organization such as a philanthropic foundation. The public organizations that are the most frequent targets of whistle-blowing are, of course, government agencies, from the county or city level to the federal. Whistle-blowing at the federal level may concern either activities that involve national security or

*This article is a substantial revision and expansion of an earlier article "In Defense of Whistle-Blowing" initially published in the first edition of *Business Ethics: Readings and Cases in Corporate Morality*, eds., Michael Hoffman and Jennifer Moore, and reprinted in a number of places. A much shorter edited version of the current article will appear in the second edition of the above work.

From Gene G. James, "Whistle-Blowing: Its Moral Justification," in *Essentials of Business Ethics*, edited by Peter Madsen and Jay Shafritz (New York: Penguin Books, 1990), 160–190. Reprinted by permission of the author.

more ordinary activities such as waste, fraud, or permitting activities that are harmful to the public. Whistle-blowing that concerns national security usually involves agencies such as the National Security Council and the CIA, but it may also involve private commercial firms such as defense contractors. This type of whistle-blowing raises a number of issues not raised by more ordinary whistle-blowing, in particular the issue of balancing the public's right to know against the need for secrecy. One major problem here is that appeal to secrecy and classification of information have frequently been used to hide illegal and immoral activities. Although some of the comments in this article apply to whistle-blowing involving national security, because it raises issues that are more complicated than whistle-blowing involving most commercial firms, or government agencies dealing with domestic matters, the present discussion is limited to whistle-blowing of the latter type.

Whistle-blowers almost always experience retaliation. If they work for private firms and are not protected by unions or professional organizations, they are likely to be fired. They are also likely to receive damaging letters of recommendation, and may even be blacklisted so that they cannot find work in their profession. If they are not fired, they are still likely to be transferred, given less interesting work, denied salary increases and promotions, or demoted. Their professional competence is usually attacked. They are said to be unqualified to judge, misinformed, etc. Since their actions may threaten both the organization and their fellow employees, attacks on their personal lives are also frequent. They are called traitors, rat finks, disgruntled, known trouble-makers, people who make an issue out of nothing, self-serving, and publicity seekers. Their life-styles, sex lives, and mental stability may be questioned. Physical assaults, abuse of their families, and even murder are not unknown as retaliation to whistle-blowing.

WHISTLE-BLOWING AND THE LAW[1]

The law does not at present offer whistle-blowers very much protection. Agency law, the area of common law which governs relations between employees and employers, imposes a duty on employees to keep confidential any information learned through their employment that might be detrimental to their employers. However, this duty does not hold if the employee has knowledge that the employer either has committed or is about to commit a felony. In this case the employee has a positive obligation to report the offence. Failure to do so is known as misprision and makes one subject to criminal penalties.

One problem with agency law is that it is based on the assumption that unless there are statutes or agreements to the contrary, contracts between employees and employers can be terminated at will by either party. It therefore grants employers the right to discharge employees at any time for any reason or even for no reason at all. The result is that most employees who blow the whistle, even those who report felonies, are fired or suffer other retaliation. One employee of thirty years was even fired the day before his pension became effective for testifying under oath against his employer, without the courts doing anything to aid him.

This situation has begun to change somewhat in recent years. In *Pickering v. Board of Education* in 1968, the Supreme Court ruled that government employees have the right to speak out on policy issues affecting their agencies provided doing so does not seriously disrupt the agency. A number of similar decisions have followed and the right of government employees to speak out on policy issues now seems firmly established. But employees in private industry cannot criticize company policies without risking being fired. In one case involving both a union and a company doing a substantial portion of its business with the federal government, federal courts did award back pay to an employee fired for criticizing the union and the company, but did not reinstate or award him punitive damages.

A few state courts have begun to modify the right of employers to dismiss employees at will. Courts in Oregon and Pennsylvania have awarded damages to employees fired for serving on juries. A New Hampshire court granted damages to a woman fired for refusing to date her foreman. A West Virginia court reinstated a bank employee who reported illegal interest rates. The Illinois Supreme Court upheld the right of an employee to sue when fired for reporting and testifying about criminal activities of a fellow employee. However, a majority of states still uphold the right of employers to fire employees at will unless there are statutes or agreements to the contrary. To my knowledge only one state, Michigan, has passed a law prohibiting employers from retaliating against employees who report violations of local, state, or federal laws.

A number of federal statutes contain provisions intended to protect whistle-blowers. The National Labor Relations Act, Fair Labor Standards Act, Title VII of the 1964 Civil Rights Act, Age Discrimination Act, and the Occupational Safety and Health Act all have sections prohibiting employers from taking retaliatory actions against employees who report or testify about violations of the acts. Although these laws seem to encourage and protect whistle-blowers, to be effective they must be enforced. A 1976 study[2] of the Occupational Safety and Health Act showed that only about 20 percent of the 2,300 complaints filed in fiscal years 1975 and 1976 were judged valid by OSHA investigators. About half of these were settled out of court. Of the sixty cases taken to court at the time of the study in November 1976, one had been won, eight lost, and the others were still pending. A more recent study[3] showed that of the 3,100 violations reported in 1979, only 270 were settled out of court and only sixteen litigated.

Since the National Labor Relations Act guarantees the right of workers to organize and bargain collectively, and most collective-bargaining agreements contain a clause requiring employers to have just cause for discharging employees, these agreements would seem to offer some protection for whistle-blowers. In fact, however, arbitrators have tended to agree with employers that whistle-blowing is an act of disloyalty which disrupts business and injures the employer's reputation. Their attitude seems to be summed up in a 1972 case in which the arbitrator stated that one should not "bite the hand that feeds you and insist on staying for future banquets."[4] One reason for this attitude, pointed out by David Ewing, is that unions are frequently as corrupt as the organizations on which the whistle is being blown. Such unions, he says, "are not likely to feed a hawk that comes to prey in their own barnyard."[5] The record of professional societies is not any better. They have generally failed to come to the aid or defense of members who have attempted to live up to their codes of professional ethics by blowing the whistle on corrupt practices.

THE MORAL JUSTIFICATION OF WHISTLE-BLOWING

Under what conditions, if any, is whistle-blowing morally justified? Some people have argued that whistle-blowing is never justified because employees have absolute obligations of confidentiality and loyalty to the organization for which they work. People who argue this way see no difference between employees who reveal trade secrets by selling information to competitors, and whistle-blowers who disclose activities harmful to others.[6] This position is similar to another held by some business people and economists that the sole obligation of corporate executives is to make a profit for stockholders. If this were true, corporate executives would have no obligations to the public. However, no matter what one's special obligations, one is never exempt from the general obligations we have to our fellow human beings. One of the most fundamental of these obligations is to not cause avoidable harm to others. Corporate executives are no more exempt from this obligation than other people. Corporations in democratic societies are chartered with the expectation that they will function in ways that are compatible with the public interest. If they cease to behave this way, they violate the understanding on which they are based and may legitimately be penalized or even have their charters revoked. Corporations in democratic societies are also chartered with the expectation that they will not only obey the laws governing their activities, but will not do anything that undermines basic democratic processes, such as bribing public officials. In addition to having the obligation to make money for stockholders, corporate executives have the obligation to see that these expectations are complied with. They also have obligations to the company's employees, e.g., to maintain a safe working place. It is the failure of corporate executives to fulfill obligations of the types mentioned that creates the need for whistle-blowing.

Just as the special obligations of corporate executives to stockholders cannot override their more fundamental obligations to others, the special obligations of employees to employers cannot override their more fundamental obligations. In particular, obligations of confidentiality and loyalty cannot take precedence over the fundamental duty to act in ways that prevent unnecessary harm to others. Agreements to keep something secret have no moral standing unless that which is to be kept secret is itself morally justifiable. For example, no one can have an obligation to keep secret a conspiracy to murder someone, because murder is an immoral act. It is for this reason also that employees have a legal obligation to report an employer who has committed or is about to commit a felony. Although there are obvious differences between the situations of employees who work for government agencies and those who work for private firms, if we leave aside the special case in which national security is involved, then the same principles apply to both. The Code of Ethics of Government Service to which all government employees are expected to conform requires that employees put loyalty to moral principles and the national interest above loyalty to political parties or the agency for which they work. Nor can one justify participation in an illegal or immoral activity by arguing that one was merely following orders. Democratic governments repudiated this type of defense at Nuremberg.

It has also been argued that whistle-blowing is always justified because it is an exercise of the right to free speech. However, the right to free speech is not absolute. An example often used to illustrate this is that one does not have the right to shout "Fire" in a crowded theater because that is likely to cause a panic in which people may be injured. Analogously, one may have a right to speak out on a particular subject, in the sense that there are no contractual agreements which prohibit one from doing so, but it nevertheless may be the case that it would harm innocent people, such as one's fellow workers and stockholders who are not responsible for the wrongdoing being disclosed. The mere fact that one has the right to speak out does not mean that one ought to do so in every case. But this kind of consideration cannot create an absolute prohibition against whistle-blowing because one must weigh the harm to fellow workers and stockholders caused by the disclosure against the harm to others caused by allowing the organizational wrong to continue. Furthermore, the moral principle that one must consider all people's interests equally prohibits giving priority to one's own group. There is, in fact, justification for not giving as much weight to the interests of the stockholders as to those of the public, because stockholders investing in corporate firms do so with the knowledge that they undergo financial risk if management acts in imprudent, illegal, or immoral ways. Similarly, if the employees of a company know that it is engaged in illegal or immoral activities and do not take action, including whistle-blowing, to terminate the activities, then they too must bear some of the guilt for the actions. To the extent that these conditions hold, they nullify the principle that one ought to refrain from whistle-blowing because speaking out would cause harm to the organization. Unless it can be shown that the harm to fellow workers and stockholders would be *significantly greater* than the harm caused by the organizational wrongdoing, the obligation to avoid unnecessary harm to the public must take precedence. Moreover, as argued above, this is true even when there are specific agreements which prohibit one from speaking out, because such agreements are morally void if the organization is engaged in illegal or immoral activities. In that case one's obligation to the public overrides one's obligation to maintain secrecy.

If the foregoing arguments are sound, then neither the position that whistle-blowing is never justified because it involves violations of loyalty and confidentiality, nor the position that whistle-blowing is always right because it is an exercise of the right to free speech, is a morally justifiable position. The right to free speech confers a presumption in favor of whistle-blowing, making it a morally permissible action, unless: (a) one is bound by specific agreements to maintain secrecy, and (b) the harm resulting from the wrongdoing isn't great. If these two conditions hold, then one's right to free speech is overridden by the special agreement into which one has entered. Furthermore, even if the harm resulting from the wrongdoing is great, there may be situations in which one ought not blow the whistle because the harm from blowing the whistle would be even greater. However, these are special situations. In general, the fundamental obligation to prevent avoidable harm to others overrides special obligations of confidentiality and loyalty, creating an obligation to blow the whistle on illegal or immoral activities.

CRITERIA FOR JUSTIFIABLE WHISTLE-BLOWING

The argument in the foregoing section is an attempt to show that unless special circumstances hold, one has an obligation to blow the whistle on illegal or immoral actions — an obligation that is grounded on the fundamental human duty to avoid preventable harm to others. In this section I shall attempt to spell out in greater detail the conditions under which blowing the whistle is morally obligatory. Since Richard De George has previously attempted to do this, I shall proceed by examining the criteria he has suggested.[7]

De George believes there are three conditions that must hold for whistle-blowing to be morally permissible, and two additional conditions that must hold for it to be morally obligatory. The three conditions that must hold for it to be morally permissible are:

1. The firm, through its product or policy, will do serious and considerable harm to the public, whether in the person of the user of its product, an innocent bystander, or the general public.
2. Once an employee identifies a serious threat to the user of a product or to the general public, he or she should report it to his or her immediate superior and make his or her moral concern known. Unless he or she does so, the act of whistle-blowing is not clearly justifiable.
3. If one's immediate superior does nothing effective about the concern or complaint, the employee should exhaust the internal procedures and possibilities within the firm. This usually will involve taking the matter up the managerial ladder, and, if necessary — and possible — to the board of directors.

The two additional conditions which De George thinks must hold for whistle-blowing to be morally obligatory are:

4. The whistle-blower must have, or have accessible, documented evidence that would convince a reasonable, impartial observer that one's view of the situation is correct, and that the company's product or practice poses a serious and likely danger to the public or to the user of the product.
5. The employee must have good reason to believe that by going public the necessary changes will be brought about. The chance of being successful must be worth the risk one takes and the danger to which one is exposed.[8]

One problem with these criteria is that they are intended to apply only to situations involving commercial firms. However, as pointed out above, if national security is not involved, then there are many similarities between the issues facing whistle-blowers in corporate settings and those facing them in governmental settings. Consequently, I shall treat the proposed criteria as if they were intended to cover all acts of whistle-blowing not involving national security. Some of the comments that follow may also be applicable to whistle-blowing involving national security, but it is not my intention to address this topic here.

De George intends for the proposed criteria to apply to situations in which a firm's policies or products cause physical harm to people. Indeed, the first criterion he proposes is intended to restrict the idea of harm even more narrowly to threats of serious bodily harm or death. He offers the following reasons in support of restricting the concept of harm in this way: (1) Non-physical harm, such as financial harm to one's interests as a result of fraud, seems to be quite different from physical harm. (2) To suffer non-physical harm is not as serious an injury as suffering physical harm. For example, "An immoral practice that increases the cost of a product by a slight margin may do serious harm to no individual, even if the total amount when summed adds up to a large amount."[9] (3) "If the harm threatened by a product is slight or not certain, it might not be greater than the harm done to the firm [by the whistle-blowing]."[10] (4) Even if the policy or product does cause minor harm to the public, there may be routine procedures by which the harm can be eliminated. "The slight harm that is done, say, by the use of a product, can be corrected after the product is marketed (e.g., as a result of customer complaint)."[11]

De George apparently believes that situations which involve threats of serious bodily harm or death are so different from those involving other types of harm that the kind of considerations which justify whistle-blowing in the former situations could not possibly justify it in the latter. Thus, he says, referring to the former type of whistle-blowing: "We shall restrict our analysis to this type of whistle-blowing because, in the first place, the conditions that justify whistle-blowing vary according to the type of case at issue."[12] A few sentences later he adds: "As a paradigm, we shall take a set of fairly clear-cut cases, namely, those in which serious bodily harm — including possible death — threatens either the users of a product or innocent bystanders."[13]

One problem in restricting discussion to clear-cut cases of this type, regarding which one can get almost universal agreement that whistle-blowing is justifiable, is that it leaves us with no guidance when we are confronted with more usual situations involving other types of harm. Although De George states that his "analysis provides a model for dealing with other kinds of whistle-blowing as well,"[14] his criteria in fact provide no help in deciding whether one should blow the whistle in situations involving such wrongs as sexual harassment, violations of privacy, industrial espionage, insider trading, and a variety of other harmful actions. A second problem is that even if we were to restrict our attention to the type of situations De George suggests, his criteria are formulated in such a way that they cover only possible harm to users of a firm's products and the general public. He totally ignores, for example, possible harm to workers because of unsafe work practices.

No doubt, one of the reasons De George restricts his treatment the way he does is to avoid having to define harm. This is indeed a problem. For if we fail to put any limitations on the idea of harm, it seems to shade into the merely offensive or distasteful and thus offer little help in resolving moral problems. But, on the other hand, if we restrict harm to physical injury, as De George does, it then applies to such a limited range of cases that it is of minimal help in most of the moral situations which confront us. The only defensible way of dealing with this problem, in my opinion, is to first recognize that the notion of harm, like most moral concepts, is not amenable to precise definition. No matter how carefully we define it, borderline cases are likely to arise. However, this is precisely what we should expect. As Aristotle pointed out, it is the mark of an educated person not to look for more precision than a subject matter allows. The most difficult moral problems are frequently those in which we are confronted with shades of gray rather than black-and-white situations. This is not to say that we should not strive for as much precision as possible without arbitrarily limiting the situations taken into consideration. This can be done in the case of harm by correlating it with violations of fundamental human rights such as the rights to due process, privacy, and property, in addition to the right to freedom from physical harm. Thus, not only situations which involve threats of physical harm, but also those involving actions such as sexual harassment which violates the right to privacy and causes psychological harm, compiling unnecessary records on people, and financial harm due to fraudulent actions, are situations which may justify whistle-blowing. Correlating harm with the violation of fundamental human rights does not, of course, relieve us of the necessity to deal with borderline cases, since there is no way to avoid these in making moral decisions. But it does provide a guideline for helping decide when whistle-blowing is justified. Fortunately, the law recognizes that people may be harmed in a number of ways and makes most infractions of fundamental human rights illegal. The fact that a company or agency is engaged in illegal actions is, therefore, always a prima facie reason for blowing the whistle, whether or not the action causes physical injury.

A still greater problem with De George's analysis is that even in cases where there is a threat of serious physical harm or death, he believes that this only makes whistle-blowing morally permissible, rather than creating a strong prima facie obligation in favor of whistle-blowing. His primary reasons for believing this seem to be those stated in criterion 5. Unless one has reason to believe that the whistle-blowing will eliminate the harm, and the cost to oneself is not too great, he does not believe whistle-blowing is morally obligatory. He maintains that this is true even when the person involved is a professional whose code of ethics requires her or him to put the public good ahead of private good. He argued in an earlier article, for example:

> The myth that ethics has no place in engineering has . . . at least in some corners of the engineering profession . . . been put to rest. Another myth, however, is emerging to take its place — the myth of the engineer as moral hero. . . . The zeal . . . however, has gone too far, piling moral responsibility upon moral responsibility on the shoulders of the engineer. This emphasis . . . is misplaced. Though engineers are members of a profession that holds public safety paramount, we cannot reasonably expect engineers to be willing to sacrifice their jobs each day for principle and to have a whistle ever at their sides.[15]

He contends that engineers have only the obligation "to do their jobs the best they can."[16] This includes reporting their concerns about the safety of products to management, but does *not* include "the obligation to insist that their perceptions or . . . standards be accepted. They are not paid to do that, they are not expected to do that, and they have no moral or ethical obligation to do that."[17] He also states that even though engineers are better qualified than other people to determine cost versus safety features of products, decisions about acceptable risk should be left to management. Under ideal conditions he thinks the public itself should make this kind of decision. "A panel of informed people, not necessarily engineers, should decide . . . acceptable risk and minimum standards."[18] This information should then be provided to consumers so they can decide whether they wish to buy the product.

To take a specific case, De George maintains that even though some Ford engineers had grave misgivings about the safety of Pinto gas tanks, and several people had been killed when tanks exploded after rear-end crashes, the engineers did not have an obligation to make their misgivings public. De George's remarks are puzzling because the Pinto case would seem to be exactly the kind of clear-cut situation which he says provides the paradigm for justified whistle-blowing. Indeed, if the Ford engineers did not have an obligation to blow the whistle, it is difficult to see what cases could satisfy his criteria. They knew that if Pintos were struck from the rear by vehicles traveling thirty miles per hour or more, their gas tanks were likely to explode, seriously injuring or killing people. They also knew that if they did not speak out, Ford would continue to market the Pinto. Finally, they were members of a profession whose code of ethics requires them to put public safety above all other obligations.

De George's remarks suggest that the only obligation the Ford engineers had was to do what management expected of them by complying with their job descriptions, and that so long as they did that no one should find fault with them or hold them accountable for what the company did. It is true that when people act within the framework of an organization, it is often difficult to assess individual responsibility. One reason for this is that organizational decisions are frequently the product of groups or committees rather than of individuals. Another is that because committee members often serve temporary terms, none of the people who helped make a particular decision may be members when it is implemented. Implementation is also likely to be the responsibility of others. Finally, even when decisions are made by individuals, they may have little control over the outcome. The result is frequently that no one feels responsible for the consequences of an organizational decision. Top management does not because it only formulates policy rather than implementing it. Those at the bottom and middle of the chain of authority do not because they merely implement it. If challenged to assume moral responsibility for their actions, those at the top respond that they never intended those consequences, while those at the bottom reply they were simply carrying out orders. But as De George points out, absence of the feeling of obligation does not mean absence of obligation. The fact that one is acting as a member of an organization does not relieve one of moral obligations. The exact opposite is true. Because most of the actions we undertake in organizational settings have more far-reaching consequences than those we undertake in our personal lives, our moral obligation to make sure that we do not harm others is *increased* when we act as a member of an organization. The amount of moral responsibility one has for any particular organizational action depends on the extent to which: (a) the consequences of the action are foreseeable, and (b) one's own action or failure to act is a cause of those consequences. It is important to include failure to act here, because frequently it is easier to determine what will happen if we do not act than if we do, and because we are morally responsible for not preventing harm as well as for causing it.

De George thinks that the Ford engineers would have had an obligation to blow the whistle only if they believed doing so would have been likely to prevent the harm involved. But we have an obligation to warn others of danger even if we believe they will ignore our warnings. This is especially true if the danger will come about partly because we did not speak out. De George admits that the public has a right to know about dangerous products. If that is true, then those who have knowledge about such products have an obligation to inform the public. This is not usurping the public's right to decide acceptable risk; it is simply supplying people with the information necessary to exercise that right.

De George's comments also seem to imply that in general it is not justifiable to ask people to blow the whistle if it would threaten their jobs. It is true that we would not necessarily be justified in demanding this if it would place them or their families' lives in danger. But this is not true if only their jobs are at stake. It is especially not true if the people involved are executives and professionals who are accorded respect and high salaries not only because of their specialized knowledge and skills, but also because of the special responsibilities we entrust to them. Frequently, as in the case of engineers, they also subscribe to codes of ethics which require them to put the public good ahead of their own or the organization's good. Given all this, it is difficult to understand why De George does not think the Ford engineers had an obligation to blow the whistle in the Pinto case.

Although De George rejects the view that loyalty to an organization creates an absolute prohibition against whistle-blowing, he believes that it is one of three factors which collectively create a presumption that it is not justified, so that the burden of justification always falls on the whistle-blower. The reasons he gives for loyalty creating a presumption against whistle-blowing are: (1) "There is a strong tradition within American mores against 'ratting,' or telling on others. We find this to be true of children . . . and . . . folk wisdom."[19] (2) The view of the vast majority of workers is, therefore, that the whistle-blower is a kind of traitor. (3) Workers owe a debt of gratitude to their company or organization for their job, "no small consideration in a society in which 4 percent unemployment is considered normal."[20] The second factor which he believes creates a presumption that whistle-blowing is not justified is that it may be seen as an act of disobedience. "Disobedience typically requires justification if it is to be considered moral—whether . . . civil disobedience, disobedience to the corporation, or a child's disobedience to its parents. Under the appropriate conditions, obedience is the expected and required moral way to act."[21] The third factor is that whistle-blowing is likely to harm the organization's reputation, subjecting it to bad publicity and possible investigation.

The fact that whistle-blowing harms the organization is one of the reasons De George believes that for it to be justified it must disclose threats of serious bodily harm or death. It was argued above that this is far too narrow a criterion. The belief that whistle-blowing is an act of disloyalty and disobedience, on the other hand, seems to underlie his second and third criteria that for whistle-blowing to be justified, the whistle-blower must have first reported the wrongdoing to his or her immediate superior and, if nothing was done, taken the complaint as far up the managerial ladder as possible.

Some of the problems with adopting these suggestions as general criteria for justified whistle-blowing are: (1) It may be one's immediate supervisor who is responsible for the wrongdoing. (2) Organizations differ considerably in both their procedures for reporting, and how they respond to, wrongdoing. (3) Not all wrongdoing is of the same type. If the wrongdoing is of a type that threatens people's health or safety, exhausting channels of protest within the organization may result in unjustified delay in correcting the problem. (4) Exhausting internal channels of protest may give people time to destroy evidence needed to substantiate one's allegations. (5) Finally, it may expose the employee to possible retaliation, against which she or he might have some protection if the wrongdoing were reported to an external agency.

His fourth criterion, that the whistle-blower have documented evidence which would convince an impartial observer, is intended to reduce incidences of whistle-blowing by curbing those who would blow the whistle on a mere suspicion of wrongdoing. It is true that one should not make claims against an organization based on mere guesses or hunches, because if they turn out to be false one will have illegitimately harmed the organization and innocent people affiliated with it. But De George also wishes to curb whistle-blowing because he thinks that if it were widespread, that would reduce its effectiveness. He argues that "any condition that makes whistle-blowing mandatory in large numbers of cases may possibly reduce [its] . . . effectiveness. . . . If this were the result, and the practice were to become widespread, then it is doubtful that we would all be better off."[22] Another argument against the claim that "many people very often have the obligation to blow the whistle," in his opinion, is that it "goes against the common view of the whistle-blower as a moral hero, and against the commonly held feeling that whistle-blowing is only rarely morally mandatory."[23] De George's fourth and fifth criteria are, therefore, deliberately formulated in such a way that if they are satisfied, "people will only rarely have the moral obligation to blow the whistle."[24]

De George's fear, that unless strict criteria of justification are applied to whistle-blowing it might become widespread, is unjustified. If it is true, as he himself claims, that there is a strong tradition in America against "ratting," that most workers consider themselves to have an obligation of loyalty to their organization, and that whistle-blowers are commonly looked upon as traitors, then it is unlikely that whistle-blowing will ever be a widespread practice. (The last statement that whistle-blowers are usually seen as traitors, incidentally, contradicts the one quoted in the preceding paragraph that they are commonly thought of as moral heroes.) However, there is a more basic reason that whistle-blowing will never become widespread. Workers usually have a feeling of loyalty to their organization according to De George. What is the basis of this feeling? De George gives the following answer to this question:

> In one view, loyalty is based appropriately on gratitude. . . . But even if the worker feels no gratitude, both the worker and the employer profit from their mutual contract. . . . The worker . . . has a stake in the firm for which he or she works. The stake is appropriately translated into positive concern for the firm, if not full identification with it — a concern that is in part what people mean by *loyalty*.[25]

In other words what people call loyalty to the organization is frequently merely self-interest, the very same factor that accounts for organization wrongdoing. Furthermore, contrary to De George, if the organization is engaged in wrongdoing, it is *not* morally appropriate for self-interest to be translated into loyalty to the organization. Indeed, even if it is genuine loyalty based on gratitude that makes a worker feel an obligation to the organization, as argued above, this cannot override one's obligation to blow the whistle on activities harmful to the public.

De George argues both: (1) whistle-blowing is not likely to be effective unless it is done by a previous loyal employee who blows the whistle publicly for moral reasons, and (2) if whistle-blowing is not likely to be effective, then it is not morally justified. He states, e.g., that for whistle-blowing to be effective the whistle-blower "must usually be willing to be identified, to testify publicly, to produce verifiable evidence, and to put oneself at risk."[26] He attempts to support this claim by drawing a parallel between the whistle-blower and the civil disobedient. "As with civil disobedience, what captures the conscience of others is the willingness of the whistle-blower to suffer harm for the benefit of others, and for what he or she thinks is right."[27] And he maintains that if a whistle-blower is "disaffected" from the organization for which she or he works, then the whistle-blowing is not likely to be taken seriously. Thus he thinks that it is necessary to determine the whistle-blower's motives before one can determine whether whistle-blowing is justified. He concedes that this may be difficult, but argues that it is a practical rather than a theoretical problem. "To sift out the claims and concerns of the disaffected worker from the genuine claims and concerns of the morally motivated employee is a practical problem. It may be claimed that this problem has nothing to do with the moral permissibility of the act of whistle-blowing; but whistle-blowing is a practical matter. If viewed as a technique for changing policy or actions, it will be justified only if effective."[28]

One problem with these claims is that they contradict his stipulation in criterion 5 that one does not have an obligation to blow the whistle if the personal cost is great. However, they also raise several other questions. Is it true that anonymous whistle-blowing is likely to be ineffective? If whistle-blowing is likely to be ineffective, is it morally unjustified? Is it necessary for the whistle-blower to testify openly for whistle-blowing to be justified? Or is anonymous whistle-blowing sometimes justified? Is it necessary that in addition to testifying openly, the whistle-blower must show a "willingness to suffer" in order for whistle-blowing to be either effective or morally justified? Does one need to determine the whistle-blower's motives in order to decide whether whistle-blowing is justified?

In my opinion, whenever anonymous whistle-blowing is ineffective, it is more likely to be due to lack of documentation than to its anonymity. It should not be forgotten, e.g., that one of the most effective and dramatic whistle-blowing incidents in recent years, Deep Throat's disclosure of Richard Nixon's betrayal of the American people, was an instance of anonymous whistle-blowing. Moreover, anonymity is a matter of degree. For whistle-blowing to be anonymous, the whistle-blower's identity does not have to be unknown to everyone, only to those on whom the whistle is blown and the general public. A few key investigators may know her or his identity.

The statement that for whistle-blowing to be morally justified, it must be probable that it will end the wrongdoing has already been responded to above, where it was argued that we have an obligation to warn others about possible harm even if we think they will ignore our warnings. One reason people may disregard warnings of danger is that whistle-blowers are sometimes unable to adequately document threats of harm. De George believes that if one is unable to document wrongdoing without recourse to illegal or immoral means, this relives one of the obligation to blow the whistle. He argues:

> One does not have an obligation to blow the whistle simply because of one's hunch, guess, or personal assessment of possible danger, if supporting evidence and documentation are not available. One may, of course, have the obligation to attempt to get evidence if the harm is serious. But if it is unavailable — or unavailable without using illegal or immoral means — then one does not have the obligation to blow the whistle.[29]

I have already indicated above that I do not think one has an obligation to blow the whistle on possible wrongdoing on the basis of a mere guess or hunch because this might harm innocent people. But if one has good reason to believe that wrongdoing is occurring, even though one cannot document it without oneself engaging in illegal or immoral actions, this does not relieve one of the obligation to blow the whistle. Indeed, if this were true, one would almost never have an obligation to blow the whistle, because employees are rarely in a position to satisfy De George's fourth criterion that the whistle-blower "must have, or have accessible, documented evidence that would convince a reasonable, impartial observer that one's view of the situation is correct." Indeed, it is precisely because employees are rarely ever in a position to supply this type of documentation without themselves resorting to illegal or immoral actions that they have an obligation to inform others who have the authority to investigate the possible wrongdoing. The attempt to secure such evidence on one's own may even thwart the gathering of evidence by the proper authorities. Thus, instead of De George's criterion being a necessary condition for justifiable whistle-blowing, the attempt to satisfy it would prevent its occurence. One has an obligation to gather as much evidence as one can so that authorities will have probable cause for investigation. But, if one is convinced that wrongdoing is occurring, one has an obligation to report it even if one is unable to adequately document it. One will have then done one's duty even if the authorities ignore the report.

The claim that it is usually necessary for the whistle-blower to speak out openly for whistle-blowing to be morally justified implies that anonymous whistle-blowing is rarely, if ever, justified. Is this true? It has been argued that anonymous whistle-blowing is never justified because it violates the right of people to face their accusers. But, as Frederick Elliston has pointed out, although people should be protected from false accusations it is not necessary for the identity of whistle-blowers to be known to accomplish this. "It is only necessary that accusations be properly investigated, proven true or false, and the results widely disseminated."[30]

Some people believe that because the whistle-blower's motive is not known in anonymous whistle-blowing, this suggests that the motive is not praiseworthy and in turn raises questions about the moral justification of anonymous whistle-blowing. De George apparently believes this, because in addition to stating that only public whistle-blowing by previously loyal employees who display their sincerity by their willingness to suffer is likely to be effective and morally justified, he mentions at several places that he is restricting his attention to whistle-blowing for moral reasons. He says, e.g., that "the only motivation for whistle-blowing we shall consider . . . is moral motivation."[31] However, in my opinion, concern with the whistle-blower's motive is irrelevant to the moral justification of whistle-blowing. It is a red herring which takes attention away from the genuine moral issue involved: whether the whistle-blower's claim that the organization is doing something harmful to others is true. If the claim is true, then the whistle-blowing is justified regardless of the motive. If the whistle-blower's motives are not moral, that makes the act less praiseworthy, but this is a totally different issue. As De George states, whistle-blowing is a "practical matter." But precisely because this is true, the justification of whistle-blowing turns on the truth or falsity of the disclosure, not on the motives of the whistle-blower. Anonymous whistle-blowing is justified because it can both protect the whistle-blower from unjust attacks and prevent those who are accused of wrongdoing to shift the issue away from their wrongdoing by engaging in an irrelevant ad hominem attack on the whistle-blower. Preoccupation with the whistle-blower's motives facilitates this type of irrelevant diversion. It is only if the accusations prove false or inaccurate that the motives of the whistle-blower have any moral relevance. For it is only then, and not before, that the whistle-blower rather than the organization should be put on trial.

The view that whistle-blowing is prima facie wrong because it goes against the tradition that "ratting" is wrong is indefensible because it falsely assumes both that we have a general obligation to not inform others about wrongdoing and that this outweighs our fundamental obligation to prevent harm to others. The belief that whistle-blowers should suffer in order to show their moral sincerity, on the other hand, is not only false and irrelevant to the issue of the moral justification of whistle-blowing, but is perverse. There are *no* morally justifiable reasons a person who discloses wrongdoing should be put at risk or made to suffer. The contradictory view stated by De George that "one does not have an obligation to put oneself at serious risk without some compensating advantage to be gained,"[32] is also false. Sometimes doing one's duty requires one to undertake certain risks. However, both individuals and society in general should attempt to reduce these risks to the minimum.

Notes

1. For discussion of the legal aspects of whistle-blowing see Lawrence E. Blades, "Employment at Will vs. Individual Freedom: On Limiting the Abusive Exercise of Employer Power," *Columbia Law Review*, vol. 67 (1967); Philip Blumberg, "Corporate Responsibility and the Employee's Duty of Loyalty and Obedience: A Preliminary Inquiry," *Oklahoma Law Review*, vol. 24 (1967); Clyde W. Summers, "Individual Protection Against Unjust Dismissal: Time for a Statute," *Virginia Law Review*, vol. 62 (1976); Arthur S. Miller, "Whistle Blowing and the Law," in Ralph Nader, Peter J. Petkas, and Kate Blackwell, *Whistle Blowing*, New York: Grossman Publishers, 1972; Alan F. Westin, *Whistle Blowing!*, New York: McGraw-Hill, 1981. See also vol. 16, no. 2, Winter 1983, *University of Michigan Journal of Law Reform*, special issue, "Individual Rights in the Workplace: The Employment-At-Will Issue."

2. For a discussion of this study which was conducted by Morton Corn, see Frank von Hipple, "Professional Freedom and Responsibility: The Role of the Professional Society," *Newsletter on Science, Technology and Human Values*, vol. 22, January 1978.

3. See Westin, op. cit.

4. See Martin H. Marlin, "Protecting the Whistleblower From Retaliatory Discharge," in the special issue of the *University of Michigan Journal of Law Reform*, op. cit.

5. David W. Ewing, *Freedom Inside the Organization*, New York: E. P. Dutton, 1977, pp. 165–166.

6. For a more detailed discussion of this argument, see Gene G. James, "Whistle Blowing: Its Nature and Justification," *Philosophy in Context*, vol. 10 (1980).

7. See Richard T. De George, 2nd ed., *Business Ethics*, New York: Macmillan, 1986. Earlier versions of De George's criteria can be found in the first edition (1982), and in "Ethical Responsibilities of Engineers in Large Organizations," *Business and Professional Ethics Journal*, vol. 1, no. 1, Fall 1981.

8. De George, *Business Ethics*, 2nd ed., pp. 230–234.

9. *Ibid.*, p. 223.

10. *Ibid.*, p. 230.

11. *Ibid.*

12. *Ibid.*, p. 223.

13. *Ibid.*

14. *Ibid.*, p. 237.

15. De George, "Ethical Responsibilities of Engineers in Large Organizations," p. 1.

16. *Ibid.*, p. 5.

17. *Ibid.*

18. *Ibid.*, p. 7.

19. De George, *Business Ethics*, 2nd ed., p. 226.

20. *Ibid.*, p. 227.

21. *Ibid.*, p. 229.

22. *Ibid.*, p. 235.

23. *Ibid.*

24. *Ibid.*

25. *Ibid.*, p. 227.

26. *Ibid.*, p. 236.

27. *Ibid.*

28. *Ibid.*, p. 231.

29. *Ibid.*, p. 234.

30. Frederick A. Elliston, "Anonymous Whistleblowing," *Business and Professional Ethics Journal*, vol l. no. 2, Winter 1982.

31. De George, *Business Ethics*, 2nd ed., p. 223.

32. *Ibid.*, p. 234.

David Theo Goldberg

TUNING IN TO WHISTLE BLOWING

In thinking about whistle blowing it is not uncommon to distinguish between those conditions under which it is considered morally permissible, that is, where persons will have a right of sorts to call attention to some corporate or government wrongdoing, and those conditions under which it is morally obligatory or required. Richard De George perhaps captures the general sense of the distinction in laying out the conditions for permissibility and obligation. Accordingly, employees should be considered to have a right to blow the whistle when:

a. the corporation, government agency, or its representatives (are about to) undertake a practice or develop a product which does or will cause serious and considerable harm to individuals or society at large;

b. the suspicion or charge of (potential) wrongdoing has been brought to the attention of immediate superiors;

c. no appropriate action has been taken to remedy the wrong-doing even when one has proceeded up the chain of command (De George, 1982: 161; and De George, 1981: 6).

From *Business and Professional Ethics Journal*, 7, no. 2 (1987), 85–94. Reprinted by permission of the author.

We should note a few things about this characterization of permissibility. First, as Gene James points out in criticism of De George, (a) may be too stringently stated to capture cases where permissibility will seem reasonable to most. Sometimes it may be thought reasonable to have the whistle blown not where there is actual wrongdoing but a strong likelihood of it. Second, to report a reasonable suspicion of (potentially) serious harm, to bring it to the notice of one's superiors, is not in itself to blow the whistle. It is perhaps simply plain good professional sense. Moreover, (b) and (c) may be too strongly stated as requirements, for the wrongdoing may be the responsibility of one's superiors. It cannot be a condition of the moral permissibility of whistle blowing that one be urged to confront alone those who have power over one, where it is their very actions that may be at issue (James, 1984: 249–259).

Whistle blowing becomes increasingly obligatory, more pressingly a moral duty on De George's view, the more serious and considerable the (potential) harm at issue and the greater the degree to which intra-corporate or intra-agency resolution has been exhausted. In particular, De George adds two further conditions which must be met for whistle blowing to be obligatory:

d. there must be documentation of the (potentially) harmful practice or defect; and
e. there is good reason to believe that public disclosure will effect the necessary action to avoid the present or prevent similar future wrongdoing.

It is common knowledge that whistle blowers frequently experience retaliation and suffering for their civic-mindedness: loss of employment and reputation, unemployability, loss of home, and divorce, all of which not infrequently leads to attempted suicide. Thus De George concludes that though blowing the whistle may often be morally permissible it is much less pressingly obligatory (De George, 1981, 1, 7, 11).

Whether De George has correctly identified the specific conditions for the difference between permissibility and obligation, between right and duty to blow the whistle, the distinction will no doubt seem intuitively appealing to most.[1] Nevertheless, I want to suggest that the very distinction is questionable. To begin with De George's conditions, why should merely having documented evidence and good sense of effectiveness be the cutting point of the distinction? Surely we would want to require documentable and not just documented evidence (d) as a condition of *permissibility*, at least a reasonable degree of documentable evidence, for otherwise we stand in danger of licensing idle accusation. And proceeding without some reasonable chance of success would be irrational, so (e) would seem a rational constraint upon permissibility as well.

However, I do not mean by this to plead for strengthening the case for permissibility; after all, this is De George's strategy. I want rather to collapse the distinction in favor of obligation.[2] After all, reason dictates that if employees are to have a right to whistle blowing, then they must be protected from reprisals in exercising the right. (Under some interpretations being so protected lies at the heart of what it means to have a right.) The recent strengthening of protective legislation for whistle blowers would seem to acknowledge this.[3] But this undermines De George's primary reason for stressing permissibility over obligation. So if conditions (a) through (e) are met there is a duty; and if (d) and (e) are unavailable so too is the right.

Consider the case of the space shuttle *Challenger* which exploded shortly after take-off on January 28, 1986 killing all seven astronauts aboard. The Rogers Commission concluded that the explosion was due to failure in a seal between solid rocket booster joints. Roger Boisjoly was a senior engineer expert in rocket seals at Morton Thiokol, Inc., the corporation that built the shuttle. In the year prior to the explosion Boisjoly and other engineers had expressed increasing concern both to Morton Thiokol management and to NASA officials about seal erosion especially at low temperatures. In August 1985 these concerns resulted in the formation of a Seal Erosion Task Team at the corporation to test for causes of erosion. Yet the corporation failed to make available resources necessary to carry out the Task Team's charge. For example, crucial tests were delayed for three-and-a-half months and finally rescheduled for just thirteen days prior to the *Challenger* lift-off. At a critical pre-launch teleconference on January 27, 1986 between NASA officials, senior management at Morton Thiokol, and concerned engineers (prompted by the forecast that the launch temperature was to be unseasonably low), Boisjoly and his fellow engineers strongly recommended against launching at that time. At the insistence of a senior NASA official, this recommendation was unanimously overruled by the four senior Morton Thiokol managers present. As a result, *the initial engineering recommendations were revised by a corporate vice-president to support the managers' decision to launch*. After the conference Boisjoly returned to his office to write: "I sincerely hope that this launch does not result in a catastrophe. I personally do not agree with some of the statements made in [the vice-president's] written summary stating that [the *Challenger*] is okay to fly." The following morning he watched as his worst fears were realized. A month later, testifying in closed session before two members of the Rogers Commission with the corporate vice-president who had revised the engineers' recommendation, Boisjoly and another engineer provided crucial supporting documentation to contradict the vice-president's interpretation of data and events. As a result Boisjoly was increasingly alienated at Morton Thiokol, and by mid-year resulting ill health led him to request an extended sick leave.[4]

On De George's view it would appear that Roger Boisjoly was permitted but not obliged to blow the whistle both immediately prior to and in the investigation after launch. He had grave misgivings about human and product safety, and knowledge of at least questionable practice on the part of Morton Thiokol management and NASA administration. Moreover, he had unsuccessfully pursued the issue with his superiors. Thus conditions (a) through (c) were met. Yet so were (d) and (e), for Boisjoly had documented evidence in hand, and was aware of further documentable evidence. De George's overriding reason why Boisjoly was permitted but not required to blow the whistle is the severe personal difficulty he was bound to confront in his relations with his employer.

On my view, by contrast, either Boisjoly had an obligation to blow the whistle or he was not permitted to. It seems clear to me, as it did to Boisjoly at the time, that in spite of the likely personal consequences he was required to reveal to the Rogers Commission the details of the pre-launch teleconference and alteration by Thiokol officials of the data supporting their recommendation to launch. For De George the prevailing principle in the distinction between right and duty is the sufferance likely to the individual whistle blower. But unless we are reduced to egoism as the grounds of ethical justification,[5] the effects of the act must be assessed not just for the individual actor but impartially for all those who might be affected. In general, the consequences of whistle blowing must include the benefits to the public at large, the trust it would engender in public and corporate administration, and the dampening effect it would have on corporate negligence at public expense. Without Boisjoly's evidence NASA still might not be subjected to the stringent oversight conditions it now operates under.

It is a more difficult question whether Boisjoly was obliged to undertake further action immediately prior to launch. Clearly, the most striking difference in De George's conditions between the pre- and post-launch moments concerns the certainty of disastrous consequences. And while this has bearing on the question, Boisjoly's pre-launch misgivings were sufficiently grave to militate against the distinction between right and obligation in this case. Indeed, one might plausibly argue that the obligation is more pressing where there is strong possibility of *preventing* impending harm. However, the difficulty in identifying the appropriate authority to whom to reveal his misgivings may give pause to insisting upon an obligation facing Boisjoly here. Obviously there seemed to be little sympathy for Boisjoly's position at NASA or Thiokol. For the obligation to hold, the appropriate person to approach would have to occupy a position of the highest authority from which a decision not to launch could be effected immediately. The immediacy of the moment rules out members of Congress or government agencies. This likely leaves only someone with Presidential access. Thus, whether Boisjoly had an obligation to blow the whistle on January 27, 1986 turns on whether he could reasonably be held to have access to persons at this level. This speaks to condition (e), and so if it turns out that because of inaccessibility Boisjoly failed to have an obligation here he would fail both on my and on De George's account. Yet De George would still grant Boisjoly a *right* to blow the whistle for conditions (a) through (d) remain intact; and extending permissibility given the likelihood of failure to effect anything strikes me not only as odd but as undermining the very point of the project.

Perhaps it will help to look at the issue thus. Accepting conditions (a) through (c) as providing necessary grounds for a duty to blow the whistle encourages the social expectation that serious (potential) harms to individual or social wellbeing will be reported, and the reporters protected. This is surely far preferable to leaving the report to individual caprice. In other words, by considering whistle blowing a duty rather than mostly a right we place emphasis upon its requirement. This would imply that an agent who fails to meet the conditions of obligation — that is, where there is reasonably documentable evidence of harmful wrongdoing, a reasonable chance of success, and where the possibilities of retaliation are minimized — may in a sense be considered complicit with the wrong. Such a person may be guilty, at least, of an act of omission if not commission. Here, Aristotle's distinction between acting by reason of and acting from ignorance may be revealing (Aristotle, III.1: 1110b15 ff). A person acting by reason of ignorance cannot be expected to have known better and is not responsible for a wrong following from the act. By contrast, acting from ignorance implies that the agent ought reasonably to have known better and is responsible for any ensuing wrong. For example, if the CEO of Morton Thiokol had received senior management's recommendation to launch without any indication of altered data or engineers' misgivings and had signed off on it, he may be said to have acted by reason of ignorance. If however he signed in spite of warnings that he failed to pursue he may be said to be acting from — virtually hiding behind — his ignorance. Accordingly, corporate or government agents who act by reason of ignorance may be excused provided they correct their ways when their wrongs are brought to their notice; indeed, the appropriate attitude of such people may be grateful apology. One acting *from* ignorance should be held responsible; the attitude likely here when confronted no doubt will be evasive. Similarly, a bystander who genuinely and understandably overlooks and so fails to report the wrongdoing is excusable; the revealing attitude here is likely to be genuine incredulity. By contrast, one who fails to blow the whistle because of turning a blind eye is wanting at the very least in moral character; again, the revealing disposition here is likely to be evasion.

It is not necessary that this plea for a strengthened moral commitment to the obligation of whistle blowing result in an increasingly accusatory or vindictive society. Nor need professionals become moral martyrs (cf. De George, 1981: 1). For in strengthening the plea on behalf of whistle blowing I have also strengthened the conditions for its requirement. Whistle blowing covers cases only of serious not trivial harm. The appropriate motive is to right a relatively serious social wrong. Thus retributive recourse against the wrongdoers, though perhaps not completely misplaced, should be considered a probable implication not a necessary condition of righting the wrong. The principle at issue here is not unlike that at the basis of strict liability. A corporation may be obliged to rectify a harm even though it is not blameable for bringing the harm about: the concern is to undo the harm. This too should be the primary concern in blowing the whistle, though of course where there is individual responsibility that will have to be answered for. On the other hand, we want to avoid cases like the famous Goodrich and BART ones where the principal wrongdoers remain untarnished while the whistle blowers suffer the consequences of their moral mindedness. Again, changing social attitudes, more supportive professional codes and societies, and toughened legislation should help in straightening out our commitments here. The *Challenger* case was instrumental in effecting legislation in support of whistle blowers, and NASA has since introduced a formal policy to protect those with information that might prevent harms (Boisjoly and Curtis, 1990: 403).[6]

Theoretical support for my argument may be derived from any of the major traditions in moral theorizing. I have suggested above that the general utility of an act of whistle blowing under the conditions specified will tend to outweigh those generated by a policy of permissibility. The social benefits will almost invariably override the individual disbenefits accruing to whistle blowers and to those responsible for the (potential) harm, even once we have discounted for the slight increase in social disutility administering policies of this kind may generate. As indicated, these benefits will include the diminishing of harms to the innocent including loss of life, increased trust in public and corporate administration, the encouragement to pursue the public good over narrow self-interest, and so on. Indeed, increased social utility is generally so probable as to support an unexceptional rule utilitarian principle, that is, a general moral rule requiring whistle blowing without exception, subject to the conditions stipulated, even in a particular case where individual disbenefits are likely to outweigh the social benefits. We would likely get a similar principle from contractarian considerations: Rationally self-interested bargainers subject to some equal constraints on the information from which they bargain will likely agree on a rule requiring whistle blowing under the kinds of conditions specified. For it is rational to want to be apprised of potential harms to oneself and to social welfare in general.

This principle could be derived also from more straightforwardly deontological considerations: it treats rational agents with the respect due them by requiring that they be furnished with the information necessary to make autonomous decisions concerning matters affecting their well-being. Moreover, it would be at least consistent with, if not positively required by, the principle of honesty considered so central to deontological concerns. Finally, though my argument issues strong support for an obligation to blow the whistle where conditions are seen to require it, there is no reason why the underlying justification cannot be right-based. So, for example, the duty may be derivative from something like the basic "*rights* of persons progressively to choose how they shall live" (Mackie, 1980).

Thus, that blowing the whistle under something like the range of conditions specified but not otherwise is derivative from very different moral theories suggests convergence upon its obligatoriness, and not as De George would have it upon permissibility. If we really are to whistle the dutiful tune, we need some general agreement as to what constitutes the range of serious harms, and what a reasonable system of social support.

Notes

*The author would like to express appreciation to the referees and editor of this journal for their helpful comments and suggestions on an earlier draft of this paper.

1. Though James criticizes the scope of De George's conditions, he accepts the distinction.

2. There is a sense in which my strategy here can be likened to James Rachels' in resolving the moral dilemma between active and passive euthanasia in favor of the former (Rachels, 1975). Of course, the common objections to Rachels' argument are inapplicable here for they turn on the reluctance to grant killing moral sanction (Steinbock, 1980).

3. Further support may be gathered from the fact that professional codes tend to include a canon, principle, or rule requiring members of the professional society to warn the public of serious (potential) harm of professional activities.

4. I have taken the details of the case from Russell Boisjoly and Curtis (1990).

5. For present purposes, ethical egoism may be taken as the view that everyone ought to act only out of self-interest. The claimed justification is that this would maximize the good.

6. Commission chairman Rogers warned Morton Thiokol management that ". . . if it appears that you're punishing the two people . . . who are right about the decision and objected to the launch which ultimately resulted in criticism of Thiokol and then they're demoted or feel that they are retaliated against, then that is a very serious matter. It would seem to me . . . they should be promoted, not demoted or pushed aside." Quoted in Boisjoly and Curtis (1990: 402).

References

Aristotle. *Nicomachean Ethics.*

Boisjoly, Russell and Ellen Foster Curtis, "A Case Study in Management Practice, Corporate Loyalty, and Business Ethics," in *Business Ethics: Readings and Cases in Corporate Morality*, 2nd ed., pp. 397–404. Edited by W. M. Hoffman and J. M. Moore. New York: McGraw-Hill, 1990.

De George, Richard, "Ethical Responsibilities of Engineers in Large Organizations," *Business and Professional Ethics Journal* 1, 1 (Fall): 1–14, 1981.

De George, Richard. *Business Ethics.* New York: Macmillan, 1982.

James, Gene. "In Defense of Whistle Blowing," in *Business Ethics: Readings and Cases in Corporate Morality*, pp. 249–260. Edited by W. M. Hoffman and J. M. Moore. New York: McGraw-Hill, 1984.

Mackie, John. "Can There Be a Right-Based Moral Theory?" in *Midwest Studies in Philosophy, III*, pp. 350–360. Edited by P. French, T. Uehling, and H. Wettstein. Minneapolis: University of Minnesota Press, 1980.

Rachels, James. "Active and Passive Euthanasia," *The New England Journal of Medicine*, 292, 1975.

Steinbock, B., ed. *Killing and Letting Die*. Englewood Cliffs: Prentice-Hall, 1980.

Ronald Duska

WHISTLEBLOWING AND EMPLOYEE LOYALTY

There are proponents on both sides of the issue — those who praise whistleblowers as civic heroes and those who condemn them as "finks." Maxwell Glen and Cody Shearer, who wrote about the whistleblowers at Three Mile Island say, "Without the *courageous* breed of assorted company insiders known as whistleblowers — workers who often risk their livelihoods to disclose information about construction and design flaws — the Nuclear Regulatory Commission itself would be nearly as idle as Three Mile Island. . . . That whistleblowers deserve both gratitude and protection is beyond disagreement."[1]

Still, while Glen and Shearer praise whistleblowers, others vociferously condemn them. For example, in a now infamous quote, James Roche, the former president of General Motors said:

> Some critics are now busy eroding another support of free enterprise — the loyalty of a management team, with its unifying values and cooperative work. Some of the enemies of business now encourage an employee to be *disloyal* to the enterprise. They want to create suspicion and disharmony, and pry into the proprietary interests of the business. However this is labelled — industrial espionage, whistle blowing, or professional responsibility — it is another tactic for spreading disunity and creating conflict.[2]

From Roche's point of view, not only is whistleblowing not "courageous" and not deserving of "gratitude and protection" as Glen and Shearer would have it, it is corrosive and impermissible.

Discussions of whistleblowing generally revolve around three topics: (1) attempts to define whistleblowing more precisely, (2) debates about whether and when whistleblowing is permissible, and (3) debates about whether and when one has an obligation to blow the whistle.

In this paper I want to focus on the second problem, because I find it

From Ronald Duska, "Whistleblowing and Employee Loyalty," in *Contemporary Issues in Business Ethics*, 2nd ed., edited by Joseph R. Des Jardins and John J. McCall (Belmont, CA: Wadsworth Publishing Company, 1990), 142–146. Reprinted by permission of the author.

somewhat disconcerting that there is a problem at all. When I first looked into the ethics of whistleblowing it seemed to me that whistleblowing was a good thing, and yet I found in the literature claim after claim that it was in need of defense, that there was something wrong with it, namely that it was an act of disloyalty.

If whistleblowing is a disloyal act, it deserves disapproval, and ultimately any action of whistleblowing needs justification. This disturbs me. It is as if the act of a good Samaritan is being condemned as an act of interference, as if the prevention of a suicide needs to be justified.

In his book *Business Ethics*, Norman Bowie claims that "whistleblowing . . . violate(s) a *prima facie* duty of loyalty to one's employer." According to Bowie, there is a duty of loyalty that prohibits one from reporting his employer or company. Bowie, of course, recognizes that this is only a *prima facie* duty, that is, one that can be overriden by a higher duty to the public good. Nevertheless, the axiom that whistleblowing is disloyal is Bowie's starting point.[3]

Bowie is not alone. Sissela Bok sees "whistleblowing" as an instance of disloyalty:

> The whistleblower hopes to stop the game; but since he is neither referee nor coach, and since he blows the whistle on his own team, his act is seen as a *violation of loyalty*. In holding his position, he has assumed certain obligations to his colleagues and clients. He may even have subscribed to a loyalty oath or a promise of confidentiality. . . . Loyalty to colleagues and to clients comes to be pitted against loyalty to the public interest, to those who may be injured unless the revelation is made.[1]

Bowie and Bok end up defending whistleblowing in certain contexts, so I don't necessarily disagree with their conclusions. However, I fail to see how one has an obligation of loyalty to one's company, so I disagree with their perception of the problem and their starting point. I want to argue that one does not have an obligation of loyalty to a company, even a *prima facie* one, because companies are not the kind of things that are properly objects of loyalty. To make them objects of loyalty gives them a moral status they do not deserve and in raising their status, one lowers the status of the individuals who work for the companies. Thus, the difference in perception is important because those who think employers have an obligation of loyalty to a company fail to take into account a relevant moral difference between persons and corporations.

But why aren't companies the kind of things that can be objects of loyalty? To answer that we have to ask what are proper objects of loyalty. John Ladd states the problem this way. "Granted that loyalty is the wholehearted devotion to an object of some kind, what kind of thing is the object? Is it an abstract entity, such as an idea or a collective being? Or is it a person or group of persons?"[5] Philosophers fall into three camps on the question. On one side are the idealists who hold that loyalty is devotion to something more than persons, to some cause or abstract entity. On the other side are what Ladd calls "social atomists," and these include empiricists and utilitarians, who think that at most one can only be loyal to individuals and that loyalty can ultimately be explained away as some other obligation that holds between two people. Finally, there is a moderate position that holds that although idealists go too far in postulating some super-personal entity as an object of loyalty, loyalty is still an important and real relation that holds between people, one that cannot be dismissed by reducing it to some other relation.

There does seem to be a view of loyalty that is not extreme. According to Ladd, "loyalty" is taken to refer to a relationship between persons — for instance, between a lord and his vassal, between a parent and his children, or between friends. Thus the object of loyalty is ordinarily taken to be a person or a group of persons."[6]

But this raises a problem that Ladd glosses over. There is a difference between a person or a group of persons, and aside from instances of loyalty that relate two people such as lord/vassal, parent/child, or friend/friend, there are instances of loyalty relating a person to a group, such as a person to his family, a person to his team, and a person to his country. Families, countries, and teams are presumably groups of persons. They are certainly ordinarily construed as objects of loyalty.

But to what am I loyal in such a group? In being loyal to the group am I being loyal to the whole group or to its members? It is easy to see the object of loyalty in the case of an individual person. It is simply the individual. But to whom am I loyal in a group? To whom am I loyal in a family? Am I loyal to each and every individual or to something larger, and if to something larger, what is it? We are tempted to think of a group as an entity of its own, an individual in its own right, having an identity of its own.

To avoid the problem of individuals existing for the sake of the group, the atomists insist that a group is nothing more than the individuals who comprise it, nothing other than a mental fiction by which we refer to a group of individuals. It is certainly not a reality or entity over and above the sum of its parts, and consequently is not a proper object of loyalty. Under such a position, of course, no loyalty would be owed to a company because a company is a mere mental fiction, since it is a group. One would have obligations to the individual members of the company, but one could never be justified in overriding those obligations for the sake of the "group" taken collectively. A company has no moral status except in terms of the individual members who comprise it. It is not a proper object of loyalty. But the atomists go too far. Some groups, such as a family, do have a reality of their own, whereas groups of people walking down the street do not. From Ladd's point of view the social atomist is wrong because he fails to recognize the kinds of groups that are held together by "the ties that bind." The atomist tries to reduce these groups to simple sets of individuals bound together by some externally imposed criteria. This seems wrong.

There do seem to be groups in which the relationships and interactions create a new force or entity. A group takes on an identity and a reality of its own that is determined by its purpose, and this purpose defines the various relationships and roles set up within the group. There is a division of labor into roles necessary for the fulfillment of the purposes of the group. The membership, then, is not of individuals who are the same but of individuals who have specific relationships to one another determined by the aim of the group. Thus we get specific relationships like parent/child, coach/player, and so on, that don't occur in other groups. It seems then that an atomist account of loyalty that restricts loyalty merely to individuals and does not include loyalty to groups might be inadequate.

But once I have admitted that we can have loyalty to a group, do I not open myself up to criticism from the proponent of loyalty to the company? Might not the proponent of loyalty to business say: "Very well. I agree with you. The atomists are short-sighted. Groups have some sort of reality and they can be proper objects of loyalty. But companies are groups. Therefore companies are proper objects of loyalty."

The point seems well taken, except for the fact that the kinds of relationships that loyalty requires are just the kind that one does not find in business. As Ladd says, "The ties that bind the persons together provide the basis of loyalty." But all sorts of ties bind people together. I am a member of a group of fans if I go to a ball game. I am a member of a group if I merely walk down the street. What binds people together in a business is not sufficient to require loyalty.

A business or corporation does two things in the free enterprise system: It produces a good or service and it makes a profit. The making of a profit, however, is the primary function of a business as a business, for if the production of the good or service is not profitable, the business would be out of business. Thus nonprofitable goods or services are a means to an end. People bound together in a business are bound together not for mutual fulfillment and support, but to divide labor to make a profit. Thus, while we can jokingly refer to a family as a place where "they have to take you in no matter what," we cannot refer to a company in that way. If a worker does not produce in a company or if cheaper laborers are available, the company — in order to fulfill its purpose — should get rid of the worker. A company feels no obligation of loyalty. The saying "You can't buy loyalty" is true. Loyalty depends on ties that demand self-sacrifice with no expectation of reward. Business functions on the basis of enlightened self-interest. I am devoted to a company not because it is like a parent to me; it is not. Attempts of some companies to create "one big happy family" ought to be looked on with suspicion. I am not devoted to it at all, nor should I be. I work for it because it pays me. I am not in a family to get paid, I am in a company to get paid.

The cold hard truth is that the goal of profit is what gives birth to a company and forms that particular group. Money is what ties the group together. But in such a commercialized venture, with such a goal, there is no loyalty, or at least none need be expected. An employer will release an employee and an employee will walk away from an employer when it is profitable for either one to do so.

Not only is loyalty to a corporation not required, it more than likely is misguided. There is nothing as pathetic as the story of the loyal employee who, having given above and beyond the call of duty, is let go in the restructuring of the company. He feels betrayed because he mistakenly viewed the company as an object of his loyalty. Getting rid of such foolish romanticism and coming to grips with this hard but accurate assessment should ultimately benefit everyone.

To think we owe a company or corporation loyalty requires us to think of that company as a person or as a group with a goal of human fulfillment. If we think of it in this way we can be loyal. But this is the wrong way to think. A company is not a person. A company is an instrument, and an instrument with a specific purpose, the making of profit. To treat an instrument as an end in itself, like a person, may not be as bad as treating an end as an instrument, but it does give the instrument a moral status it does not deserve; and by elevating the instrument we lower the end. All things, instruments and ends, become alike.

Remember that Roche refers to the "management team" and Bok sees the name "whistleblowing" coming from the instance of a referee blowing a whistle in the presence of a foul. What is perceived as bad about whistleblowing in business from this perspective is that one blows the whistle on one's own team, thereby violating team loyalty. If the company can get its employees to view it as a team they belong to, it is easier to demand loyalty. Then the rules governing teamwork and team loyalty will apply. One reason the appeal to a team and team loyalty works so well in business is that businesses are in competition with one another. Effective motivation turns business practices into a game and instills teamwork.

But businesses differ from teams in very important respects, which makes the analogy between business and a team dangerous. Loyalty to a team is loyalty within the context of sport or a competition. Teamwork and team loyalty require that in the circumscribed activity of the game I cooperate with my fellow players, so that pulling all together, we may win. The object of (most) sports is victory. But winning in sports is a social convention, divorced from the usual goings on of society. Such a winning is most times a harmless, morally neutral diversion.

But the fact that this victory in sports, within the rules enforced by a referee (whistleblower), is a socially developed convention taking place within a larger social context makes it quite different from competition in business, which, rather than being defined by a context, permeates the whole of society in its influence. Competition leads not only to victory but to losers. One can lose at sport with precious few consequences. The consequences of losing at business are much larger. Further, the losers in business can be those who are not in the game voluntarily (we are all forced to participate) but who are still affected by business decisions. People cannot choose to participate in business. It permeates everyone's lives.

The team model, then, fits very well with the model of the free market system, because there competition is said to be the name of the game. Rival companies compete and their object is to win. To call a foul on one's own teammate is to jeopardize one's chances of winning and is viewed as disloyalty.

But isn't it time to stop viewing corporate machinations as games? These games are not controlled and are not ended after a specific time. The activities of business affect the lives of everyone, not just the game players. The analogy of the corporation to a team and the consequent appeal to team loyalty, although understandable, is seriously misleading, at least in the moral sphere where competition is not the prevailing virtue.

If my analysis is correct, the issue of the permissibility of whistleblowing is not a real issue since there is no obligation of loyalty to a company. Whistleblowing is not only permissible but expected when a company is harming society. The issue is not one of disloyalty to the company, but of whether the whistleblower has an obligation to society if blowing the whistle will bring him retaliation.

Notes

1. Maxwell Glen and Cody Shearer, "Going After the Whistle-blowers," *Philadelphia Inquirer*, Tuesday, August 2, 1983, Op-ed page, p. 11A.

2. James M. Roche, "The Competitive System, to Work, to Preserve, and to Protect," *Vital Speeches of the Day* (May 1971): 445.

3. Norman Bowie, *Business Ethics* (Englewood Cliffs, N.J.: Prentice-Hall, 1982), pp. 140–143.

4. Sissela Bok, "Whistleblowing and Professional Responsibilities," *New York University Education Quarterly* 2 (1980): 3, and here p. 294.

5. John Ladd, "Loyalty," *The Encyclopedia of Philosophy* 5:97.

6. *Ibid.*

Natalie Dandekar

CAN WHISTLEBLOWING BE FULLY LEGITIMATED? A THEORETICAL DISCUSSION

Whistleblowing as a phenomenon seems puzzling. The whistleblower presumably acts to bring a wrongful practice to public attention so that those with power are enabled to correct the situation. Bok observes, "Given the indispensable services performed by so many whistleblowers, strong public support is often merited."[1] Yet Myron and Penina Glazer[2] report that in over two thirds of the sixty-four cases they documented whistleblowers suffered severe negative consequences.[3] When a social practice issues in consequences which marginalize or endanger the agent, when the agent may become a pariah for "committing the truth" it is impossible to claim that practice is regarded as fully legitimate. I am interested in exploring the paradox. Why, in the case of whistleblowing, does committing truth result in punitive sanctions? How might we, as a society, increase the probability that this virtue is rewarded rather than punished? Why have we been so slow to do just that?

To answer these questions, I consider all four topics Duska[4] considers central to a theoretical discussion of whistleblowing, (1) definition;[5] (2) whether and when whistleblowing is permissible; or (3) obligatory; and (4) appropriate mechanisms for institutionalizing whistleblowing. In Section 1, I discuss two important recent definitions of whistleblowing, concluding that whistleblowing is a specific type of action: going public with privileged information about a legitimate organization in order to prevent non-trivial public harm. In Section 2, I explore the moral ambiguity inherent in whistleblowing and the complications this affords to Goldberg's persuasive case for seeing a case of potential whistleblowing as either inappropriate or obligatory.[6] In Section 3, citing studies which show that whistleblowers often suffer outrageous costs, I explore legitimation factors which might safeguard the morally responsible whistleblower.

I. WHISTLEBLOWING DEFINED

Two recent books about whistleblowing differ in their definition of the term. For the Glazers, whistleblowing is defined by Norman Bowie's six ideal requirements:

From *Business and Professional Ethics Journal*, 10, no. 1 (1990), 89–108. Reprinted by permission of the author.

B1. the act stems from appropriate moral motives of preventing unnecessary harm to others;

B2. the whistleblower uses all available internal procedures for rectifying the problematic behavior before public disclosure (except when special circumstances preclude this);

B3. the whistleblower has evidence that would persuade a reasonable person;

B4. the whistleblower perceives serious danger that can result from the violation;

B5. the whistleblower acts in accordance with his or her responsibilities for avoiding/exposing moral violations; and

B6. the whistleblower's action has some reasonable chance of success.[7]

In contrast, Deborah Johnson, writing as a consultant for an NSF project on whistleblowing research[8] concluded that a fully defined case of whistleblowing occurs when

J1. an individual performs an action or series of actions intended to make information public;

J2. the information is made a matter of public record;

J3. the information is about possible or actual nontrivial wrongdoing in an organization; and

J4. the individual who performs the action is a member or former member of the organization.[9]

As Heacock and McGee point out, managers define whistleblowing to include going outside the normal chain of command even if not actually going public with damaging information. Thus, whistleblowing can include internal reporting of wrongdoing in or by the organization.[10] Like Davis,[11] I am willing to see going outside the normal chain of command as a form of going public.[12]

The definitions offered by Johnson and Bowie differ with respect to whether a whistleblower's motivation should be included (B1), whether whistleblowing will succeed (B6), and whether the whistleblower is a member or former member of the organization (J4). Johnson's focus on action, exclusive of any reference to the whistleblower's motivation seems preferable since, as Johnson observes,

> reasons for acting, the degree of certainty that the whistleblower has about the wrongdoing and whether or not the whistleblower has tried to remedy the wrongdoing by internal mechanisms . . . will bear on our understanding of when whistleblowing is permissible and when it is morally obligatory, but these factors should not be confused with definitional features.[13]

An additional reason for adopting Johnson's perspective arises when one considers a case of mixed motives. The *Wall Street Journal*[14] describes a former GE employee who spoke about time card fraud in a GE sponsored assertiveness training session. For six years afterward, Mr. Gravitt

> confronted executives with evidence . . . (until he) was fired (or laid off) . . . (He also) testified before the House subcommittee about mischarging as a way of life at GE.

Now he hopes to win a bountiful settlement, so "people will know they can do something to correct what isn't right."

Mr. Gravitt meets Johnson's definitional criteria though not those of Bowie. Since, it seems wrong to dismiss his case simply because he might realize monetary gain, it seems appropriate to dismiss motivation as a definitional issue. The action — going public with possible or actual nontrivial wrongdoing — seems the more appropriate focus for definition.

There are however two points on which I think Johnson's definition could be improved. First, Johnson's stipulation that "whistleblowing always takes place in the context of an organization"[15] should be amended to include the point that the wrongdoers be persons of presumed respectability and the organization a legitimate one. This seems a little noted aspect of whistleblowing, but as with Gravitt's case where the reporter notes GE "prides itself on a favorable public image," presumptive organizational respectability consistently characterizes whistleblowers' self-reports. When they suspect wrongful practices, they feel surprise. Knowing the organization values its good reputation, the whistleblower sees the wrongful practice as a sign of deterioration but remediable.[16] Amazed that higher management avoids imposing remedies to restore reputable practice, the whistleblower is moved to protest.

Second, where Johnson stipulates the actor is a member or former member of the organization, I think the criterion should be broadened. The whistleblower must have privileged access and be trusted to maintain the confidentiality of this information. But not every privileged insider must be a member or former member of the organization. A rough survey of the ways whistleblowers have obtained incriminating information shows privileged access can result from six distinct relationships.[17]

Most often the whistleblower is a member/former member trusted with privileged information. Yet within the category of trusted employee, distinctions can be usefully drawn isolating four subcategories.

First, the whistleblower may have earned access to incriminating information through quite legal acts of loyalty. For example, when he brought charges against Senator Thomas Dodd, James Boyd was Dodd's chief aide and had worked devotedly on Senator Dodd's behalf for eleven years.

A second pattern involves a worker who colludes with the criminal practice. Thus, Dr. Arthur Console, medical director of Squibb, pressured by profit oriented superiors, pushed others to certify drugs they had not fully tested. After changing careers, he conscientiously reported the ongoing practice at Squibb.[18]

Third, a worker afraid to face reprisals may share data with a less obviously assailable colleague. A staff psychologist at the Veterans Administration Hospital in Leavenworth, Kansas learned that a staff physician was conducting a drug-testing project using patients who could suffer harm from the drug's side effects. Believing the opinion of a trained physician would carry more weight with hospital administrators, he asked Dr. Mary McAnaw, then chief of surgery at the hospital to accompany him when he discussed his concerns. In this way she learned of the hospital administration's complicity and eventually blew the whistle.[19]

Fourth, company arrogance may lead to information about wrongful practices being available to all employees, though the company hides these practices from the public. Karen Silkwood seems to have worked for such an arrogantly abusive corporation.

However my rough survey also reveals two patterns by which a whistle-blower may learn of an incriminating practice without being a member of an organization. Fifth, someone who is not a member of the organization, may be given access to their records. Thus, Dr. Carl Johnson, a public health physician established the probability of wrongful practices at the Rocky flats nuclear weapons plants.[20] The company never gave him direct access to specifically incriminating information[21] but accepted that he had a right to acquire health-related data about their employees. In another such instance, Thomas Applegate, a private detective "hired by Cincinnati Gas and Electric to investigate timecard fraud among workers at the construction site of the Zimmer nuclear power plant in Ohio . . . inadvertently uncovered much more serious construction problems."[22] After utility officials ignored his warnings, he alerted the NRC. When no official body would pay attention, he sought help from GAP, a public interest watchdog group,[23] which forced additional investigations uncovering such gross violations the plant was cancelled.[24]

Sixth, the whistleblower may be a relative of the victim of wrongful practices, even if neither are members of the supposedly respectable organization. For example, in cases of nursing home abuse, drugged/senile patients are in no position to bring charges of wrongdoing. But some relatives have done so on their behalf. Mental patients too require someone else act e.g. to prevent fiscally wasteful practices, since testimony of the mentally deranged is unlikely to be believed trustworthy. Thus, a concerned relative may become a whistleblower on a wrongful organizational practice even when generally grateful for the care provided by the organization to the needy relative.

Gaining access to information, the whistleblower must be an insider in some sense, but it seems too restrictive to require the whistleblower be a member/former member of the organization accused of wrongdoing. Of the six distinct patterns of acquiring privileged information, two — the clue follower, who is not made directly privy to information about a wrongful practice but is given an opportunity to obtain clues, and the caring relative who, like the clue follower, discerns the outlines of a wrongful practice by observation — find themselves in possession of information because both have been trusted with privileged access though they are not members of the organization. Yet even these, when they go public, in some sense betray the trust which led to confidentiality.

II. THE MORAL AMBIGUITY OF WHISTLEBLOWING

The whistleblower's act is intrinsically liable to moral ambiguity because whistleblowing (a) involves betrayal of confidentiality and (b) the organization is presumptively legitimate. Because the organization accused is legitimate and so presumably staffed by persons of at least ordinary moral probity, whistleblowing shares the moral ambiguity of insubordinate accusations which reject the judgement of a majority of normally competent individuals who find a dubious practice at least minimally acceptable.

In a case of price-fixing those charged include some "described as having high moral character. . . ."[25] A sympathetic analysis of their motivation showed these morally respectable perpetrators generally practiced some form of self-deception, excusing their wrongdoing as only trivially wrong, or offset by some non-trivial good. Knowing pricefixing to be illegal, some claimed that it helps stabilize the market, or serves the corporate good, ends which outweigh illegality. Others claimed the law was wrong, and pricefixing should not be illegal.[26]

When respectable persons go along, their behavior suggests that the apparently wrongful practice is not thoroughly vicious. This undercuts the impetus to whistleblowing, and may also explain some of the anger that those who go along feel toward the whistleblower who won't.

The premise that private vices produce public goods, as in Adam Smith's theoretical conclusion that individual greed works through an Invisible Hand to produce the common welfare, may also promote hanging back in this respect. When respectable persons, obviously competent to engage in moral reasoning, have chosen to go along, an onlooker may wonder if this wrong nonetheless serves the common welfare in the long run, with whistleblowing morally compromised by that possibility.

Core elements of whistleblowing foster a condition of moral ambiguity. The whistleblower perceives the wrongful practice as a source of non-trivial public harm and the effort to bring the practice to public attention as serving the public interest. But from the perspective of ordinary citizens, the organization accused is respectable, so there is some doubt about the degree to which the wrongful practice will harm the public. Moreover, the person bringing the charge is betraying a trust on behalf of protecting the public interest. Paradoxically the one who betrays a trust claims to be more trustworthy than those who remain loyal to an apparently respectable corporation.

Apart from these sources of moral ambiguity, whistleblowing is liable to two other kinds of moral defect. The first stems from the motivation and character of the whistleblower.

> (T)he disappointed, the incompetent, the malicious and the paranoid all too often leap to accusations in public . . . (while) ideological persecution throughout the world traditionally relies on insiders willing to inform on their colleagues or even on their family members.[27]

HUAC operated in an environment characterized by two factors: the communist party was illegal and ordinary citizens feared that communism might lead to society-wide harm. Thus those who chose to inform on communists acted in accordance with the definition of whistleblowing suggested above: bringing unlawful practices presumed harmful to the general public to the attention of those in a position to protect the public against the continuance of the practice. Even under Bowie's idealistic description of whistleblowing, the issue persists. For during that period of public hysteria, some testimony was motivated by a concern for preventing the spread of communism. However, the illegality reported and the harm feared seem less dangerous to the public than the practice of reporting and the climate thus engendered. Witchhunts illustrate the necessity to limit the powers of a wrongly aroused public opinion.

As Johnson noticed, once whistleblowing is defined, it remains worthwhile to discover under what circumstances it is permissible and when it is morally obligatory.[28] It may also be worth exploring the conditions under which whistleblowing is simply not the morally correct response to a situation. De George[29] suggests whistleblowing is *permissible* when

    a. a practice or product does or will cause serious harm to individuals or society at large;

b. the charge of wrongdoing has been brought to the attention of immediate superiors; and
c. no appropriate action has been taken to remedy the wrongdoing.

If, in addition

d. there is documentation of the potentially harmful practice or defect; and
e. there is good reason to believe public disclosure will avoid the present or prevent similar future wrongdoing,

then according to De George whistleblowing becomes increasingly *obligatory*. But, since it is common knowledge that whistleblowers frequently suffer extreme retaliation, De George concludes that whistleblowing is to be understood as morally permissible, rather than obligatory.[30] Against this, Goldberg convincingly argues that if employees are to have a right, then they must be protected from reprisals in exercising the right. If conditions (a) through (e) are met and (d) and (e) are unavailable so too is the right.[31] It follows that some whistleblowing is obligatory. So, it is more than ever important to distinguish situations in which it does not pander to the wrongful arousal of public opinion or witchhunting. De George's conditions, unfortunately compatible with anticommunist witchhunts, need supplementation. Legitimate whistleblowing must be limited to cases where the wrongfulness ascribed is not the product of emotional distortion, rationalization, or prejudice.[32]

Whistleblowing is a morally ambiguous activity on a complex concatenation of grounds: it necessarily involves a betrayal of trust on behalf of a public interest which itself is on some occasions morally ambiguous; it indicts otherwise morally competent individuals and organizations concerned with being perceived as legitimate; sometimes it arouses public opinion, a frequently contaminated process. Understandably, whistleblowers are not always perceived as moral heros.

Nonetheless when an outsider—an investigative reporter, or a political opponent, or a lawyer on behalf of a defendent—proves a corporation or government bureaucracy is wasting public funds, or endangering the lives of those who rely upon their integrity, the exposer reaps social rewards. Reporters enhance a valued reputation for sleuthing. Political opponents generally realize gains from making a case against corruption. Lawyers earn money and respect for success in prosecuting wrongdoing.

However, privileged insiders do best to serve as valuable but anonymous informants for outsiders. For if identified, they suffer outrageous costs. Once the charge becomes a threat to some superior, whistleblowers risk retaliation. Westin[33] suggests every whistleblower suffers loss of reputation. Supervisors redescribe them as disgruntled troublemakers, people who make an issue out of nothing, self-serving publicity seekers or troubled persons who distort and misinterpret situations due to their own psychological imbalance and irrationality.[34]

Yet character assassination barely begins to describe the consequences of submitting well-founded important alerts, serving to prevent harm in obvious ways. Some who work in private industry are fired, even black-listed so they cannot continue in their profession. Of sixty four, the Glazers found forty one lost their jobs; twenty eight suffered long periods of idleness, and eighteen of these changed careers entirely. A ". . . career switch usually meant . . . a reduction in their standard of living . . . or a painful realization that closure was still beyond their farthest reach."[35] Others suffered transfer with prejudice, or demotion. Staff were transferred away. Letters of recommendation subtly or overtly mentioned the trouble caused by this employee's actions. When possible, the letter attacked professional competence and impugned professional judgement.

Even when evidence entirely supports the rightness of whistleblowing and the public benefit accruing therefrom, whistleblowers may find themselves unemployable in their chosen fields. Dr. Carl Johnson, after alerting the public to negligent practices at Rocky Flats nuclear weapons plants, had been "horribly mistreated and discredited" for many years, only finding rehabilitation after death.[36]

As mentioned earlier, other employees often feel that with respect to loyalty, they are morally superior. They are loyal. The whistleblower is disloyal. For this, other employees may shun, vilify, or physically attack whistleblowers.[37] Death threats may be aimed at the whistleblower and her family.[38]

Analysis shows whistleblowing is morally ambiguous. It is a betrayal of trust, and an accusation against a respectable person, corporate or natural. But when legitimate, it is also morally obligatory. So, the original puzzle remains: too often praiseworthy whistleblowing, deserving societal reward, results in severe social penalties for the whistleblower. As one writer put it, "It's a hell of a commentary on our contemporary society when you must . . . become an insolvent pariah . . . to live up to your own ethical standards by 'committing the truth' and exercising your First Amendment rights."[39]

Where whistleblowing is a legitimate, responsible, morally obligatory action, this must be remedied. But how?

III. SAFEGUARDING LEGITIMATE WHISTLEBLOWING

In the early 1970s one who brought a charge of sexual harassment suffered character assassination and reprisals from more "loyal" employees, just as other whistleblowers of that period did. But, by the middle of the 1980s one who brings a charge of sexual harassment is less likely to be perceived as a disloyal employee.[40] Her supervisor may even confront a harasser on her behalf.[41] Courts often support the legitimate complainant with continued job security and awards.

The difference in outcome can be related to several specific and to some extent imitable factors. First, the power imbalance between the one bringing the charge, and the respectable institution, is mitigated:

a. because of consciousness raising techniques, those bringing charges of sexual harassment have a well-defined constituency willing to offer support;
b. sexual harassment offers a specific legal ground; and
c. organizations like the Women's Rights Litigation Clinic at Rutgers University Law School offer litigants well trained legal help, at a more affordable cost than is otherwise generally available.

Thus, the disparity of resources between the corporation and the claimant is made less overwhelming. Second, susceptible bureaucracies have established internal procedures for sensitizing employees to the issues that give rise to these complaints.[42] Two factors may be noted:

a. education about sexual harassment is mandated as part of the legal settlement for a proven sexual harassment case; and
b. sexual harassment is a "new" form of wrong.

By contrast, with respect to the power imbalance, only one organization correlates efforts on behalf of most whistleblowers

"organized . . . by a group of young attorneys to defend and investigate problems of national security resisters, such as Daniel Ellsberg. By the mid-1970s, their mission had expanded to . . . issues concerning waste and mismanagement . . . in large organizations (and) . . . gave whistleblowers an institutional home."[43]

Perhaps, in imitation of sexual harassment litigation, the Government Accountability Project (GAP) would do well to train lawyers in a variety of locations, and for a variety of specific purposes. The approach taken by GAP's Kohn in focussing on environmental whistleblowers suggests specificity is possible.[44]

A second potentially imitable factor pertaining to the protecting whistleblowers relates to the law itself. While an employee who discovers criminal behavior is enjoined to blow the whistle or become personally liable to criminal penalties, only five states prohibit private employers from retaliating.[45] All but nine states have a public policy exception that limits an employer's right to fire at will.[46] Nevertheless, state by state exceptions limit the effectiveness of this tort. For example, Maryland law does not require any investigation into underlying charges of wrongdoing. California law protects whistleblowers who testify before special legislative committees[47] but those who give depositions may not be covered.[48]

Public sector employees under the Civil Service Reform Act of 1978 fall under language which seems to protect them for disclosures within a wide latitude. In addition to crimes, "an employee may now complain of mismanagement, gross waste of funds, abuse of authority or substantial and specific danger to public health and safety."[49] But those charged with protecting confidentiality of public sector employees apparently put whistleblowers at risk of reprisal, and "courts have struck an uneasy balance between the employee's First Amendment right to freedom of speech and the efficient operation of government agencies. Thus public employee's First Amendment rights . . . vary from court to court."[50] Unions and professional societies generally fail to defend members who live up to professional codes of ethics by blowing the whistle.[51] Arbitrators, too, tend to see whistleblowing as an act of disloyalty which disrupts business and injures the employer's reputation.[52]

Unpredictability of legal protection may reflect the vagueness of the law enjoining that "possible acts of dishonest, improper actions or behavior, . . . should be reported."[53] MacKinnon found that when company policies were unspecific, cases alleging sexual harassment tended to be dismissed as personal rather than job related difficulties. This suggests that vague law might promote dismissive court responses. Thus, more specificity both of lawyers and laws might eventuate in a more protective environment for legitimate whistleblowing.

Another category of imitative practice might focus on educational sensitizing sessions, to establish some practices as no longer subject to social toleration. Educational procedures which create sensitivity about sexual harassment have been among the most productive means of fostering community tolerance. It therefore seems appropriate to suggest that the institution of procedures sensitizing and empowering employees to prevent other kinds of wrongful practices should be included among punishments meted out for corporate wrongdoing. It is important that others within the company be persuaded that loyalty to the company does not entail support of wrongful behavior.[54]

Another possibly imitable factor may be called "moral newness." As Calhoun[55] points out feminist moral critique begins in an abnormal moral context where moral ignorance is the norm and only a limited group are morally aware. Under these circumstances one need neither be morally defective nor morally corrupt to be at risk of wrongdoing. As public consensus emerges on the wrongness of the newly sensitive area, wrongdoers become the subject of reproach. Yet there is an excusatory element, an acknowledgement that at the level of social practice, the wrongdoer is part of an oppressive system. The complications of accomodating to a new consciousness allows for educational lapses. Normally ethical individuals might be ignorant; they occupy an abnormal moral context in process of being normalized. To realize a new level of moral behavior in the workplace, when presumably this level reflects new sensitivities makes it easier for individuals to accept responsibility for change.

In 1974 when Catherine MacKinnon undertook to establish that sexual harassment fit the legal contours of discrimination she created a kind of moral newness as the draft copy of her book circulated. Courts came to agree with her analysis, so that by 1979, her published book cites favorable precedents establishing sexual harassment as a legal claim.[56] The very term, sexual harassment, is a neologism which "facilitate(s) . . . seeing moral issues where we had not previously and drawing connections between these and already acknowledged moral issues.[57]

Newness seems paradoxically to smooth the path for those bringing the charge. Where the accusation focusses upon a newly normalized moral context, the wrongdoer is accused more of ignorance than of vice, willful complicity, or self-deception. The wrongdoing is real, yet the wrongdoer is not ipso facto morally flawed. Rather, moral newness raises "the possibility of morally unflawed individuals committing serious wrongdoing."[58]

In pursuit of moral newness, perhaps the foolish sounding term whistleblowing should be replaced with a neologism of more apparent dignity. The Glazers suggest "ethical resistance." Other routes to moral newness, such as institutional ombuds or compliance officers, offer hope.[59] But they also pose risks since moral newness is endangered by familiarity/friendship within an organization. Bok warns that "many a patient representative in hospitals (experiences) . . . growing loyalty to co-workers and to the institution."[60] So the method for remedying defects within the corporate structure turns into a management tool, leaving the dissenter "little choice between submission and open revolt." Another risk involves what James Thomson calls domestication[61] co-opting the dissenter as the insider who might eventually persuade. Then the doubter's conscience is assuaged. But his position is made predictable. Hirschman concludes this predictability means a fatal loss of power with the dissenter left hoping even the tiniest influence is worth exerting.

Sensitivity to the need for remedy against deterioration can be blunted by the familiar and domesticated. As sexual harassment becomes a normal moral concept and newness thins, potential wrongdoers may practice techniques of self-deception. A colleague mentioned hearing an instance of sexual harassment that began with the offender saying "you will probably call this sexual harassment, but . . ." This demonstrates how fragile it is and yet how important it is to retain the lens of moral newness.

Re-inventing newness might serve as a means in restoring quality in legitimate organizations. One step to legitimating whistleblowing may be recognition that legitimate organizations suffer remediable deteriorations in quality. Perhaps eventually we could realize the ideal in which loyalty to an organization means loyalty to ethical standards characteristic of the organization at its finest. But until then whistleblowing deserves far greater legitimation than it evokes.

CONCLUSION

To answer the questions asked at the beginning of this paper, not all whistleblowing should be fully legitimated. The moral ambiguities of whistleblowing preclude any assumption that all whistleblowing is intrinsically virtuous. However, some whistleblowing is morally justified and of indispensible service to society. Such whistleblowers should find legitimacy in new forms of social practice. At least they should be saved from suffering punitive sanctions. I argue two sorts of changes might promote such legitimation. The first requires redressing the power imbalance by means of specificity in laws and educational methods. The second, closely allied with the first, requires recognition that organizations suffer quality deterioration. Moral newness can serve to disintegrate misplaced familiarity and help repair quality deterioration within an organization by means of rhetorical neologisms, educational and legal consensus building techniques.

Notes

*I should like to thank the anonymous readers and the editor for their helpful suggestions through several revisions.

1. Sissela Bok, "Whistleblowing and Professional Responsibility," *New York University Education Quarterly*, Vol. 11, #4 Summer 1980, p. 2.

2. Myron Peretz Glazer and Penina Migdal Glazer, *The Whistleblowers, Exposing Corruption in Government and Industry* (New York: Basic Books, 1989).

3. Glazer and Glazer, p. 206

4. Ronald Duska, "Whistleblowing and Employee Loyalty," in J. R. Des Jardins and J. J. McCall, *Contemporary Issues in Business Ethics* (Belmont, CA: Wadsworth, 1985), pp. 295–300.

5. A good summary of the recent literature of definition is provided by Marian V. Heacock and Gail W. McGee, "Whistleblowing: An Ethical Issue in Organizational and Human Behavior," *Business & Professional Ethics Journal*, Vol. 6, No. 4, pp. 35–45.

6. David Theo Goldberg, "Tuning in To Whistleblowing," *Business & Professional Ethics Journal*, Vol. 7, No. 2, pp. 85–94.

7. Norman Bowie, *Business Ethics* (Englewood Cliffs, N. J.: Prentice-Hall, 1982), p. 143, cited in Glazer and Glazer, p. 4.

8. Frederick Elliston, John Keenan, Paula Lockhart and Jane van Schaick, *Whistleblowing*

Research: Methodological and Moral Issues (New York: Praeger, 1984), work conducted under a grant from NSF jointly sponsored by the National Endowment for the Humanities.

9. Elliston, *et al.*, p. 15. (In the text, the authors attribute the definition to Dr. Johnson who worked as a consultant on the project. p. 23.)

10. However, with reference to the legitimation of the practice, Heacock and McGee suggest that the external whistleblower may suffer most. "External whistleblowing, in the absence of specific mechanisms to facilitate it, may be construed as a violation of the privilege of employment with a firm." (p. 37.) Alternatively, Lee suggests that with respect to job loss in the private sector, the whistleblower is more fortunate than many in that all but nine states allow plaintiffs to use the law of personal injury in case of unjust discharge by private sector employers if and only if the employer discharges an employee without just cause and the employee can articulate a claim involving the public good. For discussion of these and related points, see Barbara A. Lee, "Something Akin to a Property Right: Protections for Employee Job Security" in *Business & Professional Ethics Journal*, Vol. 8, No. 3, pp. 63–82.

11. Davis appropriately notices that "taking the information out of channels to try to stop the organization from doing something he believes is morally wrong" is sufficient to cause organizational members to regard the informer as a whistleblower. cf. Michael Davis, "Avoiding the Tragedy of Whistleblowing," *Business & Professional Ethics Journal*, Vol. 8, No. 3, pp. 3–20.

12. I think that Davis' observation can be accomodated to the claim that the whistleblower goes public by noticing the onionlike structure of the public-private distinction: what is private belongs on the inside of each enveloping segment, all the surrounding outer layers are perceived as public from that perspective.

13. Elliston, *et al.*, p. 17.

14. Gregory Stricharchuk, "Bounty Hunter, Ex-Foreman May Win Millions for His Tale about Cheating at GE," *Wall Street Journal*, June 23, 1988, pp. 1 and 12.

15. Elliston, *et al.*, p. 13.

16. cf. Albert O. Hirschman's discussion of remediable flaws in deteriorating institutions growing out of an effort to connect economic and political theorizing. Albert O. Hirschman, *Exit, Voice and Loyalty, Responses to Decline in Firms, Organizations and States* (Cambridge, MA: Harvard University Press, 1970).

17. Ralph Nader, Peter J. Petkas and Kate Blackwell, eds., *Whistle Blowing* (New York: Bantam, 1972); Charles Peters and Taylor Branch, *Blowing the Whistle* (New York: Praeger, 1972); Alan Westin, ed., *Whistle Blowing! Loyalty and Dissent in the Corporation* (New York: McGraw-Hill, 1981); Greg Mitchell, *Truth . . . and Consequences* (New York: Dembner Books, 1981).

18. Glazer and Glazer, pp. 97ff.

19. Glazer and Glazer, pp. 84–85. This point may hold against one of Davis' suggestions about the way in which a conscientious employee may avoid the tragedy of whistleblowing by using some alternative informant to pass information. cf. Davis, p. 14.

20. Pamela Reynolds, "Respect in Death, For Nuclear Safety He Took a Stand" *Boston Globe*, Jan. 11, 1989, p. 1.

21. Reynolds, p. 47.

22. Glazer and Glazer, pp. 30–31.

23. This is described more fully below.

24. Glazer and Glazer, p. 31.

25. Mike W. Martin, *Self-Deception and Morality* (Lawrence, Kansas: University Press of Kansas, 1986) p. 7.

26. Martin, p. 17.

27. Bok, p. 3.

28. In Elliston, *et al.*, p. 17.

29. Richard De George, *Business Ethics* (New York: Macmillan, 1982).

30. Richard De George, "Ethical Responsibilities of Engineers in Large Organizations," *Business & Professional Ethics Journal*, Vol. 1, No. 1, pp. 1–14, and *Business Ethics* (New York: Macmillan, 1982), p. 161.

31. Goldberg, *Ibid.*

32. Ronald Dworkin, "Should Homosexuality and Pornography be Crimes?" *The Yale Law*

Journal, Vol. 75, p. 986, reprinted in A. K. Bierman and James A. Gould, eds., *Philosophy for a New Generation* (New York: Macmillan, 1981), pp. 279–292.

33. Alan F. Westin, *Ibid*.

34. Westin, pp. 22 ff, 34–35, 50 and 102; Elliston, *et al.*, pp. 99 ff.

35. Glazer and Glazer, p. 210.

36. Reynolds, p. 47.

37. cf. Hirschman, Westin and Salisbury. Also, Albert Robbins, "Dissent in the Corporate World: When Does an Employee Have the Right to Speak out?" *Civil Liberties Review 5*, (Sept/Oct 1978), pp. 6–10, 15–17; Phillip I. Blumberg, "Corporate Responsibility and the Employee's Duty of Loyalty and Obedience: A Preliminary Inquiry," *Oklahoma Law Rev.* 24, (Aug. 1971), pp. 297–318.

38. Glazer and Glazer, p. 160.

39. Cited in Glazer and Glazer, p. 207.

40. Natalie Dandekar, "Contrasting Consequences: Bringing Charges of Sexual Harassment Compared with Other Cases of Whistleblowing," *Journal of Business Ethics*, Vol. 9, No. 2 (1990), pp. 151–158.

41. Danielle Coviello, "Interviews with students who have reported sexual harassment from employers," unpublished paper, Bentley College, Women and Society course, Ph. 291 Sec. 002, May 1989.

42. Dandekar, p. 156.

43. Glazer and Glazer, p. 61.

44. Steven Kohn, *Protecting Environmental and Nuclear Whistleblowers: A Litigation Manual*, Nuclear Information and Resource Service, GAP, 1985.

45. David Lindorff, "How to Blow the Whistle — Safely," *Working Mother*, June, 1987, p. 25; John Conway, "Protecting the Private Sector At Will Employee Who 'Blows the Whistle': A Cause of Action Based Upon Determinants of Public Policy," *Wisconsin Law Review* 77 (1977), pp. 777–812; Alfred Feliu, "Discharge of Professional Employees: Protecting Against Dismissal for Acts Within a Professional Code of Ethics" *Columbia Human Rights Law Review* 11, (1980), pp. 149–187.

46. Stephen M. Kohn and Michael D. Kohn, "An Overview of Federal and State Whistleblower Protections," *Antioch Law Journal* (Summer, 1986), pp. 102–111.

47. Elliston, *et al.*, p. 106.

48. Rosemary Chalk, "Making the World Safe for Whistle-blowers" *Technology Review*, Jan. 1988, pp. 48–58.

49. Elliston, *et al.*, p. 109.

50. Elliston, p. 112.

51. Glazer and Glazer, pp. 97 ff.

52. Martin H. Marlin, "Current Status of Legal Protection for Whistleblowers," paper delivered at the Second Annual Conference on Ethics in Engineering, Illinois Institute of Technology, 1982, cited in Gene James, "In Defense of Whistle Blowing" in W. Michael Hoffman and Jennifer Mills Moore, eds., *Business Ethics, Readings and Cases in Corporate Morality* (New York: McGraw-Hill, 1984), pp. 249–252.

53. Bank of America policy as cited for *Miller v. Bank of America*, cited in Mackinnon, p. 62.

54. Michael Davis, whose interest coincides with mine in trying to support organizational change which would obviate the tragedies of whistleblowing suggests in addition that employees should receive training in how to present bad news effectively. I think there is merit in this suggestion, and I would like to see him explore the means by which this might actually be accomplished. (Davis, p. 15.) Perhaps Hirschman's conception of remediable defects in an organization also deserves more attention than those who discuss whistleblowing have yet given it. (Hirschman, pp. 33, 45–53, 59 and 77–106.)

55. Cheshire Calhoun, "Responsibility and Reproach," *Ethics*, 99 (January 1989), p. 396.

56. Catherine A. MacKinnon, *Sexual Harassment of Working Women* (New Haven: Yale University Press, 1979), p. xi.

57. Calhoun, p. 397.

58. Calhoun, p. 389.

59. cf. also, Monte Throdahl, "Anyone Can Whistle," describing the internal institutionalization of whistleblowing activities at Monsanto through the Environmental Policy Staff, in A. Pablo Iannone, ed. *Contemporary Moral Controversies in Business* (Oxford University Press, New York, 1989), pp. 219–220.

60. Bok, p. 8.

61. James C. Thomson, Jr. "How Could Vietnam Happen? An Autopsy," *Atlantic Monthly* (April, 1968), pp. 45–57 cited in Hirschman, p. 115.

DISCUSSION QUESTIONS

1. As De George points out, a whistleblower is commonly described as a "rat," "snitch," or "fink." Not surprisingly, then, the fellow workers of a whistleblower generally do not support their colleague. How would you react to a whistleblower at your company? How would you react to someone in your class who blew the whistle on a group of students who were cheating? Would the student whistleblower be doing something morally right or morally wrong?

2. James points out that under De George's criteria, engineers at Ford would not have been required to blow the whistle on the Pinto. James claims that this is a major weakness in De George's position. Do you agree?

3. James defends anonymous whistleblowing. How do you evaluate such an action from an ethical perspective?

4. Goldberg asserts that in his view, Roger Boisjoly either had an obligation to blow the whistle or was not permitted to. Do you agree?

5. Duska argues that whistleblowing needs no formal defense because an employee has no obligation of loyalty to a corporation. "Companies," claims Duska, "are not the kinds of things that are properly objects of loyalty." Do you agree? By contending that loyalty to corporations is misplaced, Duska implies that loyalty properly directed is a good thing. Is loyalty really a moral virtue? If not, how could it become one?

6. In the course of her discussion, Dandekar observes that whistleblowing is a betrayal of trust. If we accept this description, how does the act of blowing the whistle fare from a deontological perspective?

CASE 12.1

The Pattern of Retaliation

As you have seen in this chapter, there is considerable debate about the conditions under which an employee may or must blow the whistle on corporate wrongdoing. However these issues are settled, there is no question that whistleblowers regularly face retaliation for their actions. For example, a study of 55 whistleblowers in government and industry by Myron and Penina Glazer claims that these individuals can be subject to a range of penalties. Whistleblowers are no longer shown sensitive documents or involved in policy decisions. They are also arbitrarily transferred, demoted, and even dismissed. Because they are usually blacklisted in their original industries, whistleblowers almost always end up in a completely different, and lower paying, profession.

The Glazers claim that the retaliation stems from the fact that whistle-blowers "break the unwritten law of social relationships . . . they break a norm — the norm of loyalty." As Don Rosendale, himself a victim of such retaliation, explains: "Corporations, most of them anyway, are male-bonding fraternities made up of team players, men who blend in, men who don't rock the boat. I had been the antithesis of those things. The term 'whistleblower' has no gender, but to snitch is not considered manly; 'one of the boys' is never a tattletale." ◆

Discussion Questions

1. The retaliation that whistleblowers experience is so universal that it forces the question: Is it wrong to publicize wrongdoing? Do whistleblowers in fact deserve to be punished for what they do? Is a whistleblower a "snitch" and a "tattletale"? Is whistleblowing ethically different from "truth telling"? Is whistleblowing any different from testifying as a witness in a court case against someone already charged with a crime?

2. Is a whistleblower disloyal in a way that merits punishment? Should employees be loyal to a corporation or to a boss? *Exactly* what does loyalty mean in this context?

3. What about a whistleblower's loyalty or responsibilities to people he or she may be supporting financially? How should their interests be considered?

4. Whistleblowers usually have trouble finding new jobs because they have reputations as troublemakers. Is this a justifiable label?

5. Would you hire a whistleblower? Why or why not?

Sources

Glazer, Myron Peretz, and Penina Migdal Glazer, "The Whistle-Blower's Plight," *New York Times*, August 13, 1986, 123.

Hamilton, Joan, "Blowing the Whistle Without Paying the Piper," *Business Week*, June 3, 1991, 138–139.

Rosendale, Don, "A Whistleblower," *New York Times Magazine*, June 7, 1987, 59.

CASE 12.2

♦ ♦ ♦

More Questions and Alternative Scenarios for the Challenger Disaster

The explosion of the space shuttle Challenger in January 1986 is without question the worst disaster in this nation's space program. The seven astronauts aboard died, and the shuttle was grounded until it could fly safely. The explosion resulted from the failure of O-rings to seal in the booster rocket joints, apparently because of unusually low temperatures that day in Florida. The catastrophe is also remembered as a classic example of alleged retribution against whistleblowers by their employer—Morton Thiokol, Inc., maker of the shuttle's booster rockets. Some Thiokol employees were critical of the company and of NASA in their testimony before the presidential commission investigating the accident, and they believed that they were punished as a result. Most notable among these individuals was Roger Boisjoly, an engineer who for several months had voiced concerns about the O-rings and whose warnings against launching Challenger were ignored.

For a year before the Challenger explosion, Boisjoly conducted research into concerns that low temperatures could compromise critical joints and seals in the shuttle's booster rockets. He advised his superiors about his concerns, but they did not view the matter with the same degree of urgency. On the evening before the Challenger liftoff, Boisjoly and other engineers opposed the launch because of the low temperature. After NASA officials objected, Thiokol senior managers overruled the engineers and authorized the flight. After the disaster, Boisjoly was initially placed on the investigating team. But after testifying before the Rogers Commission about the disagreement over launching the shuttle, his position was changed and he was isolated from NASA and the effort to redesign the seal. After the commission chairman criticized the company for what appeared to be punishment of Boisjoly and Allan McDonald, another engineer whose testimony was critical of Thiokol and NASA, both men were given their jobs back. A couple of months later, however, Boisjoly left Thiokol on extended sick leave. ♦

Discussion Questions

1. It is generally conceded that the Thiokol engineers did what they could to prevent the Challenger launch. But did they? In view of what was at stake, did they have a moral responsibility to do more? What more could they have done?

2. Consider the following scenario: After the engineers are overruled, Boisjoly calls a major television news reporter and goes public with his concerns. The story is aired, the flight is stopped, and Boisjoly is eventually eased out of the company. How do you assess the moral character of Boisjoly's actions? Are there conditions under which a whistleblower has a moral obligation to publicize a matter outside company channels? Even if his or her job will be at risk?

3. Imagine that when the reporter checks with an engineer at NASA, she is told that Boisjoly is absolutely wrong and that the risk is minimal. Not having enough time to check out the facts, the reporter chooses to kill the story and tells Boisjoly of her decision. Boisjoly then calls another reporter and anonymously claims that a terrorist group has planted a bomb on the shuttle. As a rocket engineer, Boisjoly is able to convince the reporter that the threat is genuine. The story runs, the flight is postponed, and the shuttle launches safely on a warmer day. The original reporter never reveals that Boisjoly called her, and Boisjoly keeps his job. Assess the moral character of Boisjoly's actions. Are there conditions under which a whistleblower has a moral obligation to resort to deception or law breaking?

4. Imagine that Boisjoly's original story is reported, the flight is delayed, and Boisjoly is gradually eased out of the company. The news story causes a precipitous drop in Thiokol's stock price. The price remains depressed for a year while the O-ring problem is solved. The next launch is successful, but a massive unrelated computer malfunction causes the shuttle to burn up during reentry. NASA decides to cancel such space flights for good, costing Thiokol millions of dollars and hundreds of jobs. Assess the moral character of Boisjoly's actions.

Sources

Boisjoly, Russell P., Ellen Foster Curtis, and Eugene Melican, "Roger Boisjoly and the Challenger Disaster: The Ethical Dimensions," *Journal of Business Ethics*, 8 (1989), 217–230.

Rossiter, Al, Jr., "Company Sidelines Exec Who Objected to Challenger Launch," *Sunday Star-Ledger*, May 11, 1986, I, 10.

ADDITIONAL READINGS

Bok, Sissela, "Whistleblowing and Professional Responsibility," *New York Education Quarterly*, 4 (1980), 2–7.

———, *Secrets* (New York: Vintage, 1983).

Davis, Michael, "Avoiding the Tragedy of Whistleblowing," *Business & Professional Ethics Journal*, 8, no. 4, (1988), 3–19.

De George, Richard T., "Ethical Responsibilities of Engineers in Large Organizations: The Pinto Case," *Business & Professional Ethics Journal*, 1, no. 1 (1981) 1–14.

Elliston, Frederick A., "Civil Disobedience and Whistleblowing: A Comparative Appraisal of Two Forms of Dissent," *Journal of Business Ethics*, 1 (1982), 23–28.

———, "Anonymity and Whistleblowing," *Journal of Business Ethics*, 1 (1982), 167–177.

———, *Business & Professional Ethics Journal*, 1, no. 2 (1981) 59–70.

CHAPTER 13

◆ ◆ ◆

Advertising

One of the supposed great virtues of free market capitalism is that every decision made by buyers, sellers, and producers is done so freely. Capitalism is theoretically a system without control and manipulation. In this spirit, advertising informs consumers about available goods and services, thus helping them decide how best to meet their needs. Advertising, however, is regularly criticized as aiming not just to inform, but to produce. That is, companies allegedly use advertising to create the needs in the consumer that their products will then meet. Is this true? Even if it is, is there anything wrong with it?

We begin with Robert Arrington's defense of advertising in which he rejects the idea that advertising controls consumer behavior. Richard Lippke's view of advertising is not so flattering, however, inasmuch as he concludes that persuasive mass advertising undermines autonomy. John Waide objects to "associative advertising" (ads that link their products to values such as friendship, acceptance by others, excitement, and power) because of the harm it does to consumers. Finally, Lynda Sharp Paine focuses on the special issues raised by advertising directed at children.

Robert L. Arrington

ADVERTISING AND BEHAVIOR CONTROL

Consider the following advertisements:

1. "A woman in *Distinction Foundations* is so beautiful that all other women want to kill her."
2. Pongo Peach color for Revlon comes "from east of the sun . . . west of the moon where each tomorrow dawns." It is "succulent on your lips" and "sizzling on your finger tips (and on your toes goodness knows)." Let it be your "adventure in paradise."
3. "Musk by English Leather—The Civilized Way to Roar."
4. "Increase the value of your holdings. Old Charter Bourbon Whiskey —The Final Step Up."
5. Last Call Smirnoff Style: "They'd never really miss us, and it's kind of late already, and it's quite a long way, and I could build a fire, and you're looking very beautiful, and we could have another martini, and it's awfully nice just being home . . . you think?"
6. A Christmas Prayer. "Let us pray that the blessing of peace be ours — the peace to build and grow, to live in harmony and sympathy with others, and to plan for the future with confidence." New York Life Insurance Company.

These are instances of what is called puffery — the practice by a seller of making exaggerated, highly fanciful or suggestive claims about a product or service. Puffery, within ill-defined limits, is legal. It is considered a legitimate, necessary, and very successful tool of the advertising industry. Puffery is not just bragging; it is bragging carefully designed to achieve a very definite effect. Using the techniques of so-called motivational research, advertising firms first identify our often hidden needs (for security, conformity, oral stimulation) and our desires (for power, sexual dominance and dalliance, adventure) and then they design ads which respond to these needs and desires. By associating a product, for which we may have little or no direct need or desire, with symbols reflecting the fulfillment of these other, often subterranean interests, the advertisement can quickly generate large numbers of consumers eager to purchase the product advertised. What woman in the sexual race of life could resist a foundation which would turn other women envious to the point of homicide? Who can turn down an adventure in paradise, east of the sun where tomorrow dawns? Who doesn't want to be civilized and thoroughly libidinous at the same time? Be at the pinnacle of success — drink Old Charter. Or stay at home and dally a bit — with Smirnoff. And let us pray for a secure and predictable future, provided for by New York Life. God willing. It doesn't take very much motivational research to see the point of these sales pitches. Others are perhaps a little less obvious. The need to feel secure in one's home at night can be used to sell window air conditioners, which drown out small noises and

From *Journal of Business Ethics* 1, no. 1 (February 1982), 3–12. Copyright © 1982 by D. Reidel Publishing Co., Dordrecht, Holland and Boston, U.S.A. Reprinted by permission of Kluwer Academic Publishers.

provide a friendly, dependable companion. The fact that baking a cake is symbolic of giving birth to a baby used to prompt advertisements for cake mixes which glamorized the "creative" housewife. And other strategies, for example involving cigar symbolism, are a bit too crude to mention, but are nevertheless very effective.

Don't such uses of puffery amount to manipulation, exploitation, or down-right control? In his very popular book *The Hidden Persuaders*, Vance Packard points out that a number of people in the advertising world have frankly admitted as much:

> As early as 1941 Dr. Dichter (an influential advertising consultant) was exhorting ad agencies to recognize themselves for what they actually were — "one of the most advanced laboratories in psychology." He said the successful ad agency "manipulates human motivations and desires and develops a need for goods with which the public has at one time been unfamiliar — perhaps even undesirous of purchasing." The following year *Advertising Agency* carried an ad man's statement that psychology not only holds promise for understanding people but "ultimately for controlling their behavior."[1]

Such statements lead Packard to remark: "With all this interest in manipulating the customer's subconscious, the old slogan 'let the buyer beware' began taking on a new and more profound meaning."[2]

B. F. Skinner, the high priest of behaviorism, has expressed a similar assess-ment of advertising and related marketing techniques. Why, he asks, do we buy a certain kind of car?

> Perhaps our favorite TV program is sponsored by the manufacturer of that car. Perhaps we have seen pictures of many beautiful or prestigeful persons driving it — in pleasant or glamorous places. Perhaps the car has been designed with respect to our motivational patterns: the device on the hood is a phallic symbol; or the horsepower has been stepped up to please our competitive spirit in enabling us to pass other cars swiftly (or, as the advertisements say, "safely"). The concept of freedom that has emerged as part of the cultural practice of our group makes little or no provision for recognizing or dealing with these kinds of control.[3]

In purchasing a car we may think we are free. Skinner is claiming, when in fact our act is completely controlled by factors in our environment and in our history of reinforcement. Advertising is one such factor.

A look at some other advertising techniques may reinforce the suspicion that Madison Avenue controls us like so many puppets. T.V. watchers surely have noticed that some of the more repugnant ads are shown over and over again, *ad nauseum*. My favorite, or most hated, is the one about A-1 Steak Sauce which goes something like this: Now, ladies and gentlemen, what is hamburger? It has succeeded in destroying my taste for hamburger, but it has surely drilled the name of A-1 Sauce into my head. And that is the point of it. Its very repetitious-ness has generated what ad theorists call *information*. In this case it is indirect information, information derived not from the content of what is said but from the fact that it is said so often and so vividly that it sticks in one's mind — i.e., the information yield has increased. And not only do I always remember A-1

Sauce when I go to the grocers, I tend to assume that any product advertised so often has to be good—and so I usually buy a bottle of the stuff.

Still another technique: On a recent show of the television program "Hard Choices" it was demonstrated how subliminal suggestion can be used to control customers. In a New Orleans department store, messages to the effect that shoplifting is wrong, illegal, and subject to punishment were blended into the Muzak background music and masked so as not to be consciously audible. The store reported a dramatic drop in shoplifting. The program host conjectured whether a logical extension of this technique would be to broadcast subliminal advertising messages to the effect that the store's $15.99 sweater special is the "bargain of a lifetime." Actually, this application of subliminal suggestion to advertising has already taken place. Years ago in New Jersey a cinema was reported to have flashed subthreshold ice cream ads onto the screen during regular showings of the film—and, yes, the concession stand did a landslide business.[4]

Puffery, indirect information transfer, subliminal advertising—are these techniques of manipulation and control whose success shows that many of us have forfeited our autonomy and become a community, or herd, of packaged souls?[5] The business world and the advertising industry certainly reject this interpretation of their efforts. *Business Week*, for example, dismissed the charge that the science of behavior, as utilized by advertising, is engaged in human engineering and manipulation. It editorialized to the effect that "it is hard to find anything very sinister about a science whose principle conclusion is that you get along with people by giving them what they want."[6] The theme is familiar: businesses just give the consumer what he/she wants; if they didn't they wouldn't stay in business very long. Proof that the consumer wants the products advertised is given by the fact that he buys them, and indeed often returns to buy them again and again.

The techniques of advertising we are discussing have had their more intellectual defenders as well. For example, Theodore Levitt, Professor of Business Administration at the Harvard Business School, has defended the practice of puffery and the use of techniques depending on motivational research.[7] What would be the consequences, he asks us, of deleting all exaggerated claims and fanciful associations from advertisements? We would be left with literal descriptions of the empirical characteristics of products and their functions. Cosmetics would be presented as facial and bodily lotions—and powders which produce certain odor and color changes; they would no longer offer hope or adventure. In addition to the fact that these products would not then sell as well, they would not, according to Levitt, please us as much either. For it is hope and adventure we want when we buy them. We want automobiles not just for transportation, but the feelings of power and status they give us. Quoting T. S. Eliot to the effect that "Human kind cannot bear very much reality," Levitt argues that advertising is an effort to "transcend nature in the raw," to "augment what nature has so crudely fashioned." He maintains that "everybody everywhere wants to modify, transform, embellish, enrich and reconstruct the world around him." Commerce takes the same liberty with reality as the artist and the priest—in all three instances the purpose is "to influence the audience by creating illusions, symbols, and implications that promise more than pure functionality." For example, "to amplify the temple in men's eyes, (men of cloth) have, very realistically, systematically sanctioned the embellishment of the houses of the gods with the same kind of luxurious design and expensive decoration that Detroit puts into a Cadillac." A poem, a temple, a Cadillac — they all elevate our spirits, offering imaginative promises and symbolic interpretations of our mundane activities. Seen in this light, Levitt claims, "Embellishment and distortion are among advertising's legitimate and socially desirable purposes." To reject these techniques of advertising would be "to deny man's honest needs and values."

Phillip Nelson, a Professor of Economics at SUNY-Binghamton, has developed an interesting defense of indirect information advertising.[8] He argues that even when the message (the direct information) is not credible, the fact that the brand is advertised, and advertised frequently, is valuable indirect information for the consumer. The reason for this is that the brands advertised most are more likely to be better buys — losers won't be advertised a lot, for it simply wouldn't pay to do so. Thus even if the advertising claims made for a widely advertised product are empty, the consumer reaps the benefit of the indirect information which shows the product to be a good buy. Nelson goes so far as to say that advertising, seen as information and especially as indirect information, does not require an intelligent human response. If the indirect information has been received and has had its impact, the consumer will purchase the better buy even if his explicit reason for doing so is silly, e.g., he naively believes an endorsement of the product by a celebrity. Even though his behavior is overtly irrational, by acting on the indirect information he is nevertheless doing what he ought to do, i.e., getting his money's worth. "'Irrationality' is rational," Nelson writes, "if it is cost-free."

I don't know of any attempt to defend the use of subliminal suggestion in advertising, but I can imagine one form such an attempt might take. Advertising information, even if perceived below the level of conscious awareness, must appeal to some desire on the part of the audience if it is to trigger a purchasing response. Just as the admonition not to shoplift speaks directly to the superego, the sexual virtues of TR-7's, Pongo Peach, and Betty Crocker cake mix present themselves directly to the id, bypassing the pesky reality principle of the ego. With a little help from our advertising friends, we may remove a few of the discontents of civilization and perhaps even enter into the paradise of polymorphous perversity.[9]

The defense of advertising which suggests that advertising simply is information which allows us to purchase what we want, has in turn been challenged. Does business, largely through its advertising efforts, really make available to the consumer what he/she desires and demands? John Kenneth Galbraith has denied that the matter is as straightforward as this.[10] In his opinion the desires to which business is supposed to respond, far from being original to the consumer, are often themselves created by business. The producers make both the product and the desire for it, and the "central function" of advertising is "to create desires"? Galbraith coins the term "The Dependence Effect" to designate the way wants depend on the same process by which they are satisfied.

David Braybrooke has argued in similar and related ways.[11] Even though the consumer is, in a sense, the final authority concerning what he wants, he may come to see, according to Braybrooke, that he was mistaken in wanting what he did. The statement "I want *x*," he tells us, is not incorrigible but is "ripe for revision." If the consumer had more objective information than he is provided by product puffing, if his values had not been mixed up by motivational research strategies (e.g., the confusion of sexual and automotive values), and if he had an expanded set of choices instead of the limited set offered by profit-hungry corporations, then he might want something quite different from what he presently wants. This shows, Braybrooke thinks, the extent to which the consumer's wants are a function of advertising and not necessarily representative of his real or true wants.

The central issue which emerges between the above critics and defenders of advertising is this: do the advertising techniques we have discussed involve a violation of human autonomy and a manipulation and control of consumer behavior, *or* do they simply provide an efficient and cost-effective means of giving the consumer information on the basis of which he or she makes a free choice. Is advertising information, or creation of desire?

To answer this question we need a better conceptual grasp of what is involved in the notion of autonomy. This is a complex, multifaceted concept, and we need to approach it through the more determinate notions of (a) autonomous desire, (b) rational desire and choice, (c) free choice, and (d) control or manipulation. In what follows I shall offer some tentative and very incomplete analyses of these concepts and apply the results to the case of advertising.

(A) AUTONOMOUS DESIRE

Imagine that I am watching T.V. and see an ad for Grecian Formula 16. The thought occurs to me that if I purchase some and apply it to my beard, I will soon look younger — in fact I might even be myself again. Suddenly I want to be myself! I want to be young again! So I rush out and buy a bottle. This is our question: was the desire to be younger manufactured by the commercial, or was it "original to me" and truly mine? Was it autonomous or not?

F. A. von Hayek has argued plausibly that we should not equate nonautonomous desires, desires which are not original to me or truly mine, with those which are culturally induced.[12] If we did equate the two, he points out, then the desires for music, art, and knowledge could not properly be attributed to a person as original to him, for these are surely induced culturally. The only desires a person would really have as his own in this case would be the purely physical ones for food, shelter, sex, etc. But if we reject the equation of the nonautonomous and the culturally induced, as von Hayek would have us do, then the mere fact that my desire to be young again is caused by the T.V. commercial — surely an instrument of popular culture transmission — does not in and of itself show that this is not my own, autonomous desire. Moreover, even if I never before felt the need to look young, it doesn't follow that this new desire is any less mine. I haven't always liked 1969 Aloxe Corton Burgundy or the music of Satie, but when the desires for these things first hit me, they were truly mine.

This shows that there is something wrong in setting up the issue over advertising and behavior control as a question whether our desires are truly ours *or* are created in us by advertisements. Induced and autonomous desires do not separate into two mutually exclusive classes. To obtain a better understanding of autonomous and nonautonomous desires, let us consider some cases of a desire which a person does not *acknowledge* to be his own even though he *feels* it. The kleptomaniac has a desire to steal which in many instances he repudiates, seeking by treatment to rid himself of it. And if I were suddenly overtaken by a desire to attend an REO concert, I would immediately disown this desire, claiming possession or momentary madness. These are examples of desires which one might have but with which one would not identify. They are experienced as foreign to one's character or personality. Often a person will have what Harry Frankfurt calls a second-order desire, that is to say, a desire *not* to have another desire.[13] In such cases, the first-order desire is thought of as being nonautonomous, imposed on one. When on the contrary a person has a second-order desire to maintain and fulfill a first-order desire, then the first-order desire is truly his own, autonomous, original to him. So there is in fact a distinction between desires which are the agent's own and those which are not, but this is not the same as the distinction between desires which are innate to the agent and those which are externally induced.

If we apply the autonomous/nonautonomous distinction derived from Frankfurt to the desires brought about by advertising, does this show that advertising is responsible for creating desires which are not truly the agent's own? Not necessarily, and indeed not often. There may be some desires I feel which I have picked up from advertising and which I disown — for instance, my desire for A-1 Steak Sauce. If I act on these desires it can be said that I have been led by advertising to act in a way foreign to my nature. In these cases my autonomy has been violated. But most of the desires induced by advertising I fully accept, and hence most of these desires are autonomous. The most vivid demonstration of this is that I often return to purchase the same product over and over again, without regret or remorse. And when I don't, it is more likely that the desire has just faded than that I have repudiated it. Hence, while advertising may violate my autonomy by leading me to act on desires which are not truly mine, this seems to be the exceptional case.

Note that this conclusion applies equally well to the case of subliminal advertising. This may generate subconscious desires which lead to purchases, and the act of purchasing these goods may be inconsistent with other conscious desires I have, in which case I might repudiate my behavior and by implication the subconscious cause of it. But my subconscious desires may not be inconsistent in this way with my conscious ones; my id may be cooperative and benign rather than hostile and malign.[14] Here again, then, advertising may or may not produce desires which are "not truly mine."

What we are to say in response to Braybrooke's argument that insofar as we might choose differently if advertisers gave us better information and more options, it follows that the desires we have are to be attributed more to advertising than to our own real inclinations? This claim seems empty. It amounts to saying that if the world we lived in, and we ourselves, were different, then we would want different things. This is surely true, but it is equally true of our desire for shelter as of our desire for Grecian Formula 16. If we lived in a tropical paradise we would not need or desire shelter. If we were immortal, we would not desire youth. What is true of all desires can hardly be used as a basis for criticizing some desires by claiming that they are nonautonomous.

(B) RATIONAL DESIRE AND CHOICE

Braybrooke might be interpreted as claiming that the desires induced by advertising are often irrational ones in the sense that they are not expressed by an agent who is in full possession of the facts about the products advertised or about the alternative products which might be offered him. Following this line of thought, a possible criticism of advertising is that it leads us to act on irrational desires or to make irrational choices. It might be said that our autonomy has been violated by the fact that we are prevented from following our rational wills or that we have been denied the "positive freedom" to develop our true, rational selves. It might be claimed that the desires induced in us by advertising are false desires in that they do not reflect our essential, i.e., rational, essence.

The problem faced by this line of criticism is that of determining what is to count as rational desire or rational choice. If we require that the desire or choice be the product of an awareness of *all* the facts about the product, then surely every one of us is always moved by irrational desires and makes nothing but irrational choices. How could we know all the facts about a product? If it be required only that we possess all of the *available* knowledge about the product advertised, then we still have to face the problem that not all available knowledge is *relevant* to a rational choice. If I am purchasing a car, certain engineering features will be, and others won't be, relevant, *given what I want in a car*. My prior desires determine the relevance of information. Normally a rational desire or choice is thought to be one based upon relevant information, and information is relevant if it shows how other, prior desires may be satisfied. It can plausibly be claimed that it is such prior desires that advertising agencies acknowledge, and that the agencies often provide the type of information that is relevant in light of these desires. To the extent that this is true, advertising does not inhibit our rational wills or our autonomy as rational creatures.

It may be urged that much of the puffery engaged in by advertising does not provide relevant information at all but rather makes claims which are not factually true. If someone buys Pongo Peach in anticipation of an adventure in paradise, or Old Charter in expectation of increasing the value of his holdings, then he/she is expecting purely imaginary benefits. In no literal sense will the one product provide adventure and the other increased capital. A purchasing decision based on anticipation of imaginary benefits is not, it might be said, a rational decision, and a desire for imaginary benefits is not a rational desire.

In rejoinder it needs to be pointed out that we often wish to purchase subjective effects which in being subjective are nevertheless real enough. The feeling of adventure or of enhanced social prestige and value are examples of subjective effects promised by advertising. Surely many (most?) advertisements directly promise subjective effects which their patrons actually desire (and obtain when they purchase the product), and thus the ads provide relevant information for rational choice. Moreover, advertisements often provide accurate indirect information on the basis of which a person who wants a certain subjective effect rationally chooses a product. The mechanism involved here is as follows.

To the extent that a consumer takes an advertised product to offer a subjective effect and the product does not, it is unlikely that it will be purchased again. If this happens in a number of cases, the product will be taken off the market. So here the market regulates itself, providing the mechanism whereby misleading advertisements are withdrawn and misled customers are no longer misled. At the same time, a successful bit of puffery, being one which leads to large and repeated sales, produces satisfied customers and more advertising of the product. The indirect information provided by such large-scale advertising efforts provides a measure of verification to the consumer who is looking for certain kinds of subjective effect. For example, if I want to feel well dressed and in fashion, and I consider buying an Izod Alligator shirt which is advertised in all of the magazines and newspapers, then the fact that other people buy it and that this leads to repeated advertisements shows me that the desired subjective effect is real enough and that I indeed will be well dressed and in fashion if I purchase the shirt. The indirect information may lead to a rational decision to purchase a product because the information testifies to the subjective effect that the product brings about.[15]

Some philosophers will be unhappy with the conclusion of this section, largely because they have a concept of true, rational, or ideal desire which is not the same as the one used here. A Marxist, for instance, may urge that any desire felt by alienated man in a capitalistic society is foreign to his true nature. Or an existentialist may claim that the desires of inauthentic men are themselves inauthentic. Such concepts are based upon general theories of human nature which are unsubstantiated and perhaps incapable of substantiation. Moreover, each of these theories is committed to a concept of an ideal desire which is normatively debatable and which is distinct from the ordinary concept of a rational desire as one based upon relevant information. But it is in the terms of the ordinary concept that we express our concern that advertising may limit our autonomy in the sense of leading us to act on irrational desires, and if we operate with this concept we are driven again to the conclusion that advertising may lead, but probably most often does not lead, to an infringement of autonomy.

(C) FREE CHOICE

It might be said that some desires are so strong or so covert that a person cannot resist them, and that when he acts on such desires he is not acting freely or voluntarily but is rather the victim of irresistible impulse or an unconscious drive. Perhaps those who condemn advertising feel that it produces this kind of desire in us and consequently reduces our autonomy.

This raises a very difficult issue. How do we distinguish between an impulse we *do* not resist and one we *could* not resist, between freely giving in to a desire and succumbing to one? I have argued elsewhere that the way to get at this issue is in terms of the notion of acting for a reason.[16] A person acts or chooses freely if he does so for a reason, that is, if he can adduce considerations which justify in his mind the act in question. Many of our actions are in fact free because this condition frequently holds. Often, however, a person will act from habit, or whim, or impulse, and on these occasions he does not have a reason in mind. Nevertheless he often acts voluntarily in these instances, i.e., he could have acted otherwise. And this is because if there *had been* a reason for acting otherwise of which he was aware, he would in fact have done so. Thus acting from habit or impulse is not necessarily to act in an involuntary manner. If, however, a person is aware of a good reason to do x and still follows his impulse to do y, then he can be said to be impelled by irresistible impulse and hence to act involuntarily. Many kleptomaniacs can be said to act involuntarily, for in spite of their knowledge that they likely will be caught and their awareness that the goods they steal have little utilitarian value to them, they nevertheless steal.

Here their "out of character" desires have the upper hand, and we have a case of compulsive behavior.

Applying these notions of voluntary and compulsive behavior to the case of behavior prompted by advertising, can we say that consumers influenced by advertising act compulsively? The unexciting answer is: sometimes they do, sometimes not. I may have an overwhelming, T.V. induced urge to own a Mazda Rx-7 and all the while realize that I can't afford one without severely reducing my family's caloric intake to a dangerous level. If, aware of this good reason not to purchase the car, I nevertheless do so, this shows that I have been the victim of T.V. compulsion. But if I have the urge, as I assure you I do, and don't act on it, or if in some other possible world I could afford an Rx-7, then I have not been the subject of undue influence by Mazda advertising. Some Mazda Rx-7 purchasers act compulsively; others do not. The Mazda advertising effort *in general* cannot be condemned, then, for impairing its customers' autonomy in the sense of limiting free or voluntary choice. Of course the question remains what should be done about the fact that advertising may and does *occasionally* limit free choice. We shall return to this question later.

In the case of subliminal advertising we may find an individual whose subconscious desires are activated by advertising into doing something his calculating, reasoning ego does not approve. This would be a case of compulsion. But most of us have a benevolent subconsciousness which does not overwhelm our ego and its reasons for action. And therefore most of us can respond to subliminal advertising without thereby risking our autonomy. To be sure, if some advertising firm developed a subliminal technique which drove all of us to purchase Lear jets, thereby reducing our caloric intake to the zero point, then we would have a case of advertising which could properly be censured for infringing our right to autonomy. We should acknowledge that this is possible, but at the same time we should recognize that it is not an inherent result of subliminal advertising.

(D) CONTROL OR MANIPULATION

Briefly let us consider the matter of control and manipulation. Under what conditions do these activities occur? In a recent paper on "Forms and Limits of Control" I suggested the following criteria.[17]

A person C controls the behavior of another person P *if*

1. *C* intends *P* to act in a certain way *A*;
2. *C*'s intention is causally effective in bringing about *A*; and
3. *C* intends to ensure that all of the necessary conditions of *A* are satisfied.

These criteria may be elaborated as follows. To control another person it is not enough that one's actions produce certain behavior on the part of that person; additionally one must intend that this happen. Hence control is the intentional production of behavior. Moreover, it is not enough just to have the intention; the intention must give rise to the conditions which bring about the intended effect. Finally, the controller must intend to establish by his actions any otherwise unsatisfied necessary conditions for the production of the intended effect. The controller is not just influencing the outcome, not just having input; he is as it were guaranteeing that the sufficient conditions for the intended effect are satisfied.

Let us apply these criteria of control to the case of advertising and see what happens. Conditions (1) and (3) are crucial. Does the Mazda manufacturing company or its advertising agency intend that I buy an Rx-7? Do they intend that a certain number of people buy the car? *Prima facie* it seems more appropriate to say that they *hope* a certain number of people will buy it, and hoping and intending are not the same. But the difficult term here is "intend." Some philosophers have argued that to intend A it is necessary only to desire that A happen and to believe that it will. If this is correct, and if marketing analysis gives the Mazda agency a reasonable belief that a certain segment of the population will buy its product, then, assuming on its part the desire that this happen, we have the conditions necessary for saying that the agency intends that a certain segment purchase the car. If I am a member of this segment of the population, would it then follow that the agency intends that I purchase an Rx-7? Or is control referentially opaque? Obviously we have some questions here which need further exploration.

Let us turn to the third condition of control, the requirement that the controller intend to activate or bring about any otherwise unsatisfied necessary conditions for the production of the intended effect. It is in terms of this condition that we are able to distinguish brainwashing from liberal education. The brainwasher arranges all of the necessary conditions for belief. On the other hand, teachers (at least those of liberal persuasion) seek only to influence their students — to provide them with information and enlightenment which they may absorb *if they wish*. We do not normally think of teachers as controlling their students, for the students' performances depend as well on their own interests and inclinations.

Now the advertiser — does he control, or merely influence, his audience? Does he intend to ensure that all of the necessary conditions for purchasing behavior are met, or does he offer information and symbols which are intended to have an effect only *if* the potential purchaser has certain desires? Undeniably advertising induces some desires, and it does this intentionally, but more often than not it intends to induce a desire for a particular object, *given* that the purchaser already has other desires. Given a desire for youth, or power, or adventure, or ravishing beauty, we are led to desire Grecian Formula 16, Mazda Rx-7's, Pongo Peach, and Distinctive Foundations. In this light, the advertiser is influencing us by appealing to independent desires we already have. He is not creating those basic desires. Hence it seems appropriate to deny that he intends to produce all of the necessary conditions for our purchases, and appropriate to deny that he controls us.[18]

Let me summarize my argument. The critics of advertising see it as having a pernicious effect on the autonomy of consumers, as controlling their lives and manufacturing their very souls. The defense claims that advertising only offers information and in effect allows industry to provide consumers with what they want. After developing some of the philosophical dimensions of this dispute, I have come down tentatively in favor of the advertisers. Advertising may, but certainly does not always or even frequently, control behavior, produce compulsive behavior, or create wants which are not rational or are not truly those of the consumer. Admittedly it may in individual cases do all of these things, but it is innocent of the charge of intrinsically or necessarily doing them or even, I think, of often doing so. This limited potentiality, to be sure, leads to the question whether advertising should be abolished or severely curtailed or regulated because of its potential to harm a few poor souls in the above ways. This is a very difficult question, and I do not pretend to have the answer. I only hope that the above discussion, in showing some of the kinds of harm that can be done by advertising and by indicating the likely limits of this harm, will put us in a better position to grapple with the question.

Notes

1. Vance Packard, *The Hidden Persuaders* (Pocket Books, New York, 1958), 20–21.
2. Ibid., 21.
3. B. F. Skinner, "Some Issues Concerning the Control of Human Behavior: A Symposium," in Karlins and Andrews (eds.), *Man Controlled* (The Free Press, New York, 1972).
4. For provocative discussions of subliminal advertising, see W. B. Key, *Subliminal Seduction* (The New American Library, New York, 1973), and W. B. Key, *Media Sexploitation* (Prentice-Hall, Inc., Englewood Cliffs, N.J., 1976).
5. I would like to emphasize that in what follows I am discussing these techniques of advertising from the standpoint of the issue of control and not from that of deception. For a good and recent discussion of the many dimensions of possible deception in advertising, see Alex C. Michalos, "Advertising: Its Logic, Ethics, and Economics" in J. A. Blair and R. H. Johnson (eds.), *Informal Logic: The First International Symposium* (Edgepress, Pt. Reyes, Calif., 1980).
6. Quoted by Packard, op. cit., 220.
7. Theodore Levitt, "The Morality (?) of Advertising," *Harvard Business Review* 48 (1970), 84–92.
8. Phillip Nelson, "Advertising and Ethics," in Richard T. De George and Joseph A. Pichler (eds.), *Ethics, Free Enterprise, and Public Policy* (Oxford Universtiy Press, New York, 1978), 187–198.
9. For a discussion of polymorphous perversity, see Norman O. Brown, *Life Against Death* (Random House, New York, 1969), chapter III.
10. John Kenneth Galbraith. *The Affluent Society*; reprinted in Tom L. Beauchamp and Norman E. Bowie (eds.), *Ethical Theory and Business* (Prentice-Hall, Englewood Cliffs, 1979), 496–501.
11. David Braybrooke, "Skepticism of Wants, and Certain Subversive Effects of Corporations on American Values," in Sidney Hook (ed.), *Human Values and Economic Policy* (New York University Press, New York, 1967); reprinted in Beauchamp and Bowie (eds.), op. cit., 502–508.
12. F. A. von Hayek, "The *Non Sequitur* of the 'Dependence Effect,'" *Southern Economic Journal* (1961); reprinted in Beauchamp and Bowie (eds.), op. cit., 508–512.
13. Harry Frankfurt, "Freedom of the Will and the Concept of a Person." *Journal of Philosophy* LXVIII (1971), 5–20.
14. For a discussion of the difference between a malign and a benign subconscious mind, see P. H. Nowell-Smith, "Psycho-analysis and Moral Language," *The Rationalist Annual* (1954); reprinted in P. Edwards and A. Pap (eds.), *A Modern Introduction to Philosophy*, Revised Edition (The Free Press, New York, 1965), 86–93.
15. Michalos argues that in emphasizing a brand name—such as Bayer Aspirin—advertisers are illogically attempting to distinguish the indistinguishable by casting a trivial feature of a product as a significant one which separates it from other brands of the same product. The brand name is said to be trivial or unimportant "from the point of view of the effectiveness of the product or that for the sake of which the product is purchased" (op. cit., 107). This claim ignores the role of indirect information in advertising. For example, consumers want an aspirin *they can trust* (trustworthiness being part of "that for the sake of which the product is purchased"), and the indirect information conveyed by the widespread advertising effort for Bayer aspirin shows that this product is judged trustworthy by many other purchasers. Hence the emphasis on the name is not at all irrelevant but rather is a significant feature of the product from the consumer's standpoint, and attending to the name is not at all an illogical or irrational response on the part of the consumer.

16. Robert L. Arrington, "Practical Reason, Responsibility and the Psychopath," *Journal for the Theory of Social Behavior* 9 (1979), 71–89.

17. Robert L. Arrington, "Forms and Limits of Control," delivered at the annual meeting of the Southern Society for Philosophy and Psychology, Birmingham, Alabama, 1980.

18. Michalos distinguishes between appealing to people's tastes and molding those tastes (op. cit., 104), and he seems to agree with my claim that it is morally permissible for advertisers to persuade us to consume some article *if* it suits our tastes (105). However, he also implies that advertisers mold tastes as well as appeal to them. It is unclear what evidence is given for this claim, and it is unclear what is meant by *tastes*. If the latter are thought of as basic desires and wants, then I would agree that advertisers are controlling their customers to the extent that they intentionally mold tastes. But if by molding tastes is meant generating a desire for the particular object they promote, advertisers in doing so may well be appealing to more basic desires, in which case they should not be thought of as controlling the consumer.

Richard L. Lippke

ADVERTISING AND THE SOCIAL CONDITIONS OF AUTONOMY

In *The New Industrial State*, John Kenneth Galbraith charged that advertising creates desires rather than responds to them.[1] His thesis raised in stark terms the issue of who is controlling whom in the marketplace. Yet, Galbraith did not provide a rigorous analysis of autonomy, and his remarks about the effects of advertising on individuals were often more suggestive than carefully worked out.

The claim that advertising is inimical to the autonomy of individuals has been taken up and discussed by philosophers, economists, and social theorists. Typically, these discussions provide first, an analysis of autonomy, and second, some empirical conjecture about whether or not advertising can be said to subvert it. The focus of most of these discussions has been on whether or not advertising can be justly accused of manipulating individuals into wanting and therefore purchasing specific products or services. Less attention has been paid to what I believe is another major theme in Galbraith's writings — that mass-advertising induces in individuals beliefs, wants, and attitudes conducive to the economic and political interests of corporations in advanced capitalist societies like the United States. Galbraith's concern seems to be not only that advertising is hostile to individual autonomy, but that it is an aspect of the ability of corporations to dominate the lives of other members of society.

What the effects of mass-advertising are on individuals is, it must be admitted, ultimately an empirical question. In spite of this, I will try to show how we might reasonably conclude that advertising undermines autonomy, especially under the social conditions that exist in advanced capitalist countries like the United States.[2] Recent discussions of advertising have not only failed to consider one crucial way in which advertising might subvert autonomy; they have also ignored important aspects of the broader social context of advertising. Specifically, they have paid scant attention to the ways in which other social

From *Business and Professional Ethics Journal*, 8, no. 4 (1988), 35–58. Reprinted by permission of the author.

conditions also undermine autonomy. My analysis will emphasize the complex interplay between and amongst the various social conditions that affect the autonomy of individuals.

In addition to providing an analysis of autonomy, I will show how autonomy requires social conditions for its development and continued viability. I will show how the content and methods of *persuasive* mass-advertising are likely to suppress the development of the abilities, attitudes and knowledge constitutive of dispositional autonomy. Yet, my view is that its full impact on autonomy should be considered in light of the ways in which political and economic institutions distribute the other social conditions of autonomy.

My primary focus will be on persuasive as opposed to informational advertising. Though the distinction is not a sharp one, I take the latter to involve information about the features, price, and availability of a product or service. Persuasive advertising, in contrast, often contains very little direct informational content about a product or service. Whereas the former presupposes some interest on the part of individuals in the product or service, the latter seeks to cultivate an interest. This typically involves tying the product or service to the satisfaction of individuals' other, sometimes subconscious desires. It seems fair to say that current informational advertising is woefully deficient. The information that is presented is often incomplete or misleading, or both. As a result, even informational ads are deceptive or manipulative at times.[3] To that extent, they undercut the abilities of persons to make informed choices and may be destructive to the intellectual honesty that is one of the constituents of dispositional autonomy. Also, in the context of massive persuasive advertising, informational advertising is likely to reinforce the content of its persuasive counterpart. Nonetheless, the two can be roughly distinguished and my remarks will be predominantly directed against persuasive advertising.

Implicit in my analysis will be the claim that one criterion for judging social orders is the extent to which they provide all of their members with the social conditions of autonomy. I will not attempt to argue for this claim here, though it is by no means an uncontroversial one. I note only that my claim is a relatively modest one — that this is *one* criterion for judging social orders. Critics of my approach may point out that many individuals seem to lack a strong desire for the sort of autonomous life I elucidate. We should not, however, be misled by this appearance. Many persons will assent to the principle that, *ceteris paribus*, the choices of individuals ought to be respected. Yet, as Lawrence Haworth shows, it makes little sense to urge such respect where peoples' choices do not reflect an autonomous way of living.[4] This suggests there may be sound reasons to hold that autonomy is a central value. Its value may be obscured for many people by, among other things, persuasive mass-advertising.

One reason that we value autonomy is relevant to Galbraith's thesis that advertising is an aspect of the dominance of large corporations over the lives of individuals in advanced capitalist societies. Persons who are nonautonomous seem much more likely to be dominated by others. Such domination need not be consciously intended or effected by the more powerful.[5] They may simply act in ways that they perceive to be in their own interests. Nonautonomous individuals may respond by passively assimilating the interests of the more powerful. I suspect that something like this is true when it comes to corporations, advertising, and its effects on individuals. Though I cannot hope to fully support Galbraith's thesis here, I will touch on it in numerous places throughout my discussion.[6]

I.

Recent discussions of advertising and autonomy are inadequate because they fail to isolate the crucial way in which the content of advertising might be subversive to autonomy. Roger Crisp, a critic of advertising, develops and tries to support the claim that ads are manipulative in an objectionable fashion. He argues that advertising "links, by suggestion, the product with my unconscious desires for [for instance] power and sex."[7] Crisp claims that persuasive advertising leaves persons unaware of their real reasons for purchasing a product, and so precludes their making rational purchasing decisions. Crisp then argues that "many of us have a strong second-order desire not to be manipulated by others without our knowledge, and for no good reason."[8] If persons become aware of how persuasive advertising affects them, by locking onto their unconscious desires, they will likely repudiate the desires induced by advertising. Such repudiated desires will not be regarded by individuals as theirs. Hence, Crisp believes he has shown how advertising is subversive to autonomy.

Crisp's approach seems to attribute both too much and too little power to advertising. Too much, because there is reason to doubt that most adults are manipulated by particular ads in the way Crisp describes. Perhaps children are so manipulated at times, and this is cause for concern. Most adults, though, seem quite able to resist what I will call the "explicit content" of ads. The explicit content of ads is the message to "buy X," along with information about where it may be purchased, its features, and how much it costs. Most individuals learn at an early age that many ads are out to persuade them, even manipulate them. They become wary of ads and this explains why they often resist their explicit consent quite easily. Even if persons do have the second-order desire Crisp attributes to them, it is not the explicit content of ads that manipulates them *without their knowledge*. The challenge is to develop an account of how advertising can have power over individuals who very often realize ads are designed to manipulate them.

This brings us to the way in which Crisp's account attributes too little power to advertising. In addition to encouraging persons to buy Brand X, many ads have what I will term an "implicit content" that consists of messages about, broadly speaking, the consumer lifestyle. This lifestyle consists of a set of beliefs, attitudes, norms, expectations, and aspirations that I will, in due course, attempt to summarize. While individuals may be aware that they are being sold particular products, the crucial issue is the extent to which they are aware of being "sold" this implicit content. As Samuel Gorovitz remarks, "it is an error to focus too narrowly on the cognitive content of advertising by looking at the truth of its claims and the validity of its inferences."[9] Instead, we should consider how the images and emotional content of ads affect our beliefs, aspirations, expectations, and attitudes. Crisp does not really consider where some of the unconscious desires ads supposedly lock onto might originate.

In an important defense of advertising, Robert Arrington argues that it rarely, if ever, subverts the autonomy of individuals. He maintains that a desire is autonomous so long as it is endorsed by an individual on reflection. In other words, the (first-order) desire is autonomous if the person has a second-order desire to have and satisfy it.[10] Advertising, he contends, rarely leads persons to have first-order desires for products that they subsequently repudiate. Perhaps, as we saw earlier, this is because many individuals resist the explicit content of even the most manipulative ads.

Arrington also argues that ads do not violate autonomy by inducing persons to make irrational choices based on faulty or inadequate information. The only information needed for a rational choice, on his view, is information relevant to the satisfaction of individuals' particular desires. He claims that ads often provide the information relevant to the satisfaction of such desires.

Even if we accept his arguments as stated, Arrington's defense of advertising is seriously incomplete. He ignores the very real possibility that it violates autonomy *not* by manipulating persons' desires and choices with respect to particular products, but by suppressing their capacities to make rational choices about the implicit content of ads. If advertising induces uncritical acceptance of the consumer lifestyle as a whole, then Arrington's vindication of it with respect to the formation of particular desires or the making of particular choices *within* that lifestyle is hardly comforting. Arrington consistently ignores the possibility that the beliefs, attitudes, and desires particular ads cater to may themselves be influenced by ads in ways that ought to trouble anyone who values human autonomy.

II.

As a first step in building my case, I offer an account of autonomy that draws on recent work on the concept. Robert Young notes that a person has "dispositional autonomy" to the extent that the person's life is "ordered according to a plan or conception which fully expresses [that person's] own will."[11] In a similar vein, Gerald Dworkin suggests that autonomy is a "global" concept: "It is a feature that evaluates a whole way of living one's life and can only be assessed over extended periods of a person's life. . . ."[12] Autonomy is a matter of degree, an achievement that depends in part on the capacities and virtues of individuals, and in part, as we shall see, on the existence of certain social conditions.[13]

Dworkin's analysis employs the well-known distinction between first and second-order desires and abilities. He summarizes his account as follows:

> Putting the various pieces together, autonomy is conceived of as a second-order capacity of persons to reflect critically upon their first-order preferences, desires, wishes, and so forth and the capacity to accept or attempt to change these in light of higher-order preferences and values.[14]

Similarly, Lawrence Haworth interprets autonomy in terms of the notion of "critical competence."[15] Autonomous persons are competent in the sense of being active and generally successful in giving effect to their intentions. They are critical in that they deliberate not only about means to their ends, but about the ends themselves, including those of central significance in their lives. While not engaged in continuous ratiocination, they are nonetheless disposed to critically examine their beliefs, desires, attitudes, and motivations. They subject claims they are confronted with and norms others urge on them to rational scrutiny.

Importantly for our purposes, autonomous individuals should be understood as ones who scrutinize the political, social, and economic institutions under which they live. These institutions, and the patterns of habit and expectation they establish, shape the possibilities individuals can envision and determine the areas in which they can exercise their autonomy. Autonomous individuals want to shape their own lives. Hence, of necessity they will be interested in the social forces and institutions that significantly affect their lives, especially since these forces and institutions are often humanly alterable.

Autonomy is not a capacity that develops in isolation from the social conditions that surround individuals. It requires individuals to have certain abilities, motivations, and knowledge (or at least awareness) of alternative belief-systems and lifestyles. It also requires venues in which they can reasonably expect to display these abilities and act on these motivations. Obviously, individuals must not be subjected to things like coercion, deception, brainwashing, and harassment. Being shielded from these is a necessary social condition of the development and exercise of autonomy. Yet, there are other social conditions that while perhaps not, strictly speaking, necessary ones, are such that they foster and support autonomy in vital ways. Societies differ in the extent to which they provide these conditions for all individuals, and thus in the extent to which they enable autonomy.

III.

What is the importance of noting the numerous social conditions of autonomy in the context of an analysis of persuasive mass-advertising? Very simply that advertising, as a possible threat to autonomy, does not exist in a social vacuum. We cannot assume that individuals encounter mass-advertising with already finely-honed skills of critical competence. The extent to which they do so is a function of the distribution of other social conditions of autonomy. The absence of social conditions of autonomy in one area will often reinforce or exacerbate the effects of their absence in other areas. Thus, in any attempt to gauge how much of a threat to autonomy persuasive mass-advertising represents, we must consider these and other background social conditions of autonomy.

In advanced capitalist countries like the United States, many individuals spend significant portions of their working lives in conditions destructive to autonomy. As Adina Schwartz and others have argued, hierarchical, authoritarian management structures, typical in such industrialized countries, thwart the autonomy of workers in obvious ways.[16] Very few have meaningful input into the decisions affecting their working lives. The tasks they perform are determined by management, as are the methods used in carrying them out. Work technology is decided by management, as are productivity quotas, discipline procedures, and criteria for evaluation. Workers are not allowed or expected to exercise even the *minimal* autonomy of determining the ends they will pursue or the means used to pursue them. This is one way in which the institutions of advanced capitalism enable corporations to impose their interests on individuals.

Often connected with the character of work is unequal access to quality education. While certain ways of organizing work may simply deny individuals avenues along which to exercise their autonomy, lack of education or poor quality education undermines it in more basic ways.[17] Reduced educational and cultural experiences often result in restricted intellectual abilities and dispositions. The kinds of rational skills needed for autonomy and the motivation to employ them seem to be the products of a liberal education in the classic sense. Individuals who lack ready access to such education are likely to have an impoverished awareness of different ways of conceiving of their lives and their social relations. This makes them ideal candidates for the tutelage in the consumer lifestyle effected by mass-advertising.

Much of that which is sponsored by advertising on TV, radio, and in magazines is hardly such as to encourage the development of autonomy.[18] Program content on commercial networks is often mindless, melodramatic, simplistic in its approach to the problems of human life — or worse, violent, sexist, or subtly racist. Even commercial network news programs seem to emphasize entertainment. Dramatic visual images, "sound bites," and fifteen second summaries of events are the rule. Commercial sponsorship of the media opens the way for the exercise of subtle control over program content. But the more likely effect of that sponsorship is an emphasis on gaining and holding an audience. That which cannot do so does not get sponsored. Yet, I think we should be wary of those who claim that what the public does not choose to consume in the way of mass media reflects its autonomous choices. Other factors, such as lack of education, mindless work, and the impact of advertising may figure in such choices. In any case, what ads are wrapped around must be factored into any analysis of their likely effects.

We should also pay attention to the ways in which institutions distribute political power, and therefore the abilities of individuals to act on and realize their interests. In this regard, the existence of formally democratic political structures is often misleading. Notoriously, access to political power depends on wealth or economic power in various ways. Here again, the political and economic institutions of advanced capitalism facilitate the dominance of corporations and their constituents.

IV.

I come, at last, to the central argument of my paper. My strategy in what follows will be to amass considerations that make a plausible case for the claim that persuasive mass-advertising is detrimental to autonomy. If there is a case to be made, it is not one that can be made by showing how advertising falls into categories that are traditionally viewed as hostile to autonomy — coercion, deception, manipulation, and brainwashing. While advertising is sometimes deceptive and often manipulative, and in some ways akin to brainwashing, its overall character is not easily assimilable to any of these. I am inclined to think that the way to conceptualize its character is in terms of the notion of *suppression*. Advertising suppresses autonomy by discouraging the emergence of its constitutive skills, knowledge, attitudes, and motivations.

One general feature of mass-advertising is simply its pervasiveness. Individuals are inundated with ads, no matter where they go or what activities they engage in. David Braybrooke refers to the "aggregative and cumulative effects" of ads.[19] The quantity of ads and their near inescapability are such that even the most diligent will be hard-pressed to avoid absorbing some of their implicit content. Many television shows and magazines feature or cater to the consumer lifestyle and this reinforces the implicit content.

The pervasiveness of ads is often coupled with an absence of views that challenge or reject their implicit content. In assessing the likely impact of mass-advertising, we must pay attention to societal measures to counter its effects. For instance, in the United States, there are few if any public service announcements urging individuals to be wary of ads, exposing the tactics of manipulation and seduction ads employ. Also, it is unlikely that such announcements would ever be repeated often enough, or have anything like the appeal of ads which promise persons sex, power, prestige, etc., if only they will buy the associated products. It seems clear that our society's educational and religious institutions, which might serve to counter ads, are ill-equipped to raise and deal with complex issues such as the nature of the good life. These are issues which ads greatly oversimplify and offer a virtual unanimity of opinion about. In many cases, attempts to educate children (and adults) about ads are sporadic and unsophisticated. To the extent that this is so, it is unlikely that such education will be forceful enough to effectively counter the advertising barrage.

Stanley Benn writes that one of the unique features of rational suasion is that it invites response and criticism.[20] It presupposes the possibility of a dialogue between or amongst the parties involved. Yet, we might wonder how far most individuals are from having a meaningful dialogue in their lives with advertising. What competing conceptions of the good life has advertising vanquished in an open, rational dialogue? If individuals lack appealing and coherent alternatives to what ads tell them about how to live, they cannot make critical, rational choices about such matters.

It is bad enough that advertising has the character of a loud, persistent bully. What is worse is that it often is not directed only at adults who might be capable of responding critically. The concern about the effects of advertising on the vulnerable, especially children, is not simply that many ads are so manipulative that they trick the vulnerable into wanting things they do not need or which are not good for them. It is also that the implicit content of ads gets absorbed by children, and habits are set up that *carry forward* into their adult lives. The ways in which they habitually perceive their lives and the social world, the alternatives they see as open to them, and the standards they use to judge themselves and others, are all shaped by advertising, perhaps without their ever being aware of it.[21]

I now turn to an analysis of the implicit content of persuasive mass-advertising. This content is a function of both the methods of conveying messages in ads and the messages conveyed. What follows are some of the key facets of this implicit content. I do not claim that my analysis is exhaustive, only that it is thorough enough to support my contention that the character of advertising is such as to suppress autonomy.

I begin with the facet of the content and methods of ads that Jules Henry refers to as the encouragement of "woolly mindedness."[22] Ads subtly encourage the propensity to accept emotional appeals, oversimplification, superficiality, and shoddy standards of proof for claims. Evidence and arguments of the most ridiculous sorts are offered in support of advertising claims. Information about products is presented selectively (i.e. bad or questionable features are ignored), the virtues of products are exaggerated, and deception and misinformation are commonplace. The meanings of words are routinely twisted so that they are either deceptive or wholly lost (e.g. consider the use of words like 'sale' or 'new and improved'). Also, ads encourage the belief that important information about our lives must be entertainingly purveyed and such that it can be passively absorbed.

All of these are what we might term "meta-messages." They are messages about how to deal with messages, or more precisely, about how to approach claims made by others. They are messages that tell individuals, among other things, that they cannot believe or trust what others say, that anything (or nothing!) can be proved, that evidence contrary to one's claims may be ignored, and that words can mean whatever anyone wants them to mean. They tell persons that success in communication is a matter of persuading others *no matter how it is done*. Such attitudes about thought and communication starkly oppose the habits and attitudes constituitive of critical competence: clarity, rigor, precision, patience, honesty, effort, etc. Henry remarks that advertising would never succeed in a world filled with logicians.[23] Though we may not want such a world, we should be aware of how advertising promotes sophistry and attitudes supportive of it.

Complementing the meta-messages is the pervasive emphasis on ease and gratification. As Henry points out, austerity and self-restraint are anathema to advertisers.[24] Mass production requires the existence of ready and willing consumers. Lifestyles contrary to consumption are either absent from ads (and from TV shows) or are ridiculed in them. Predominant messages in ads are "take it easy," "relax and enjoy yourself," and most especially "buy it now!" In moderation, there may be nothing objectionable about such messages. However, where not balanced by other messages, and so not made liable to critical examination, they encourage attitudes subversive to autonomy. In order to formulate, assess, and carry out life-plans of their own choosing, individuals must possess self-control and seriousness of purpose. They must also have the capacity to resist temptations or momentary distractions.

More insidious, though, is a further implied message — that persons ought to let advertisers show them how to live the good life. What could be more inviting than a life that demands so little beyond ease and gratification (especially to children, who are less attuned to the values of self-control and delayed gratification)? Freedom is divorced from self-direction and equated with passivity and consumption. Control over one's life becomes simply the ability to satisfy one's consumer desires. Alternative conceptions of freedom are drowned out. Opposing lifestyles are saddled with a burden of justification. Those who resist the easy gratifications of the consumer marketplace are likely to be perceived as square, eccentric, boring, or life-denying. The scorn of others thus becomes a barrier to the critical examination of life.

While one of the main messages of advertising is to accept a lifestyle of ease and gratification, individuals who buy into that lifestyle cannot be allowed to relax if that means not buying products. Fear and insecurity are the motifs of advertising. There are always new products and services to be sold and individuals must be convinced that they will not experience true or complete gratification until they buy this or that product. As John Waide remarks, advertising cultivates and thrives on "sneer group pressure"[25] Other persons are portrayed as constantly ready to judge negatively those who have not tried the newest product that promises to make their lives more appealing in some fashion. Advertising is fundamentally divisive in this regard. It encourages the view that social relationships are competitive, that persons are out to "top" one another rather than help and support one another. The internalization of this competitive model is likely to deprive individuals of the care and counsel of others, two things that vitally contribute to the sustained critical examination of their lives. Individuals need others to provide them feedback about their conduct and projects, as well as to present them with alternative beliefs, outlooks, and commitments.[26]

Numerous writers have commented on the confusion about values ads promote. Many ads tell individuals that if they will only buy X, they will acquire friendship, self-esteem, sex appeal, power, etc. Collectively, these ads tell individuals that they will be able to satisfy some of their most important desires (ones Waide refers to as being for "non-market goods"[27]) through the purchase and use of consumer products. Where they have bought these products and still not found the relevant satisfactions, advertising has a ready answer: buy more or better products!

It is doubtful that there are areas of peoples' lives where clear thinking is of more importance. It is equally doubtful that consumer products can make a significant contribution to the satisfaction of the desires for such non-market goods. More to the point, at best ads can only *distract* individuals from clear thinking about such things as why they lack self-esteem, or why they feel powerless, or why their friendships or marriages are unsatisfactory. At worst, they can fill individuals' minds with pseudo-truths or pseudo-values bearing on issues of central significance in their lives. Numerous examples come to mind: how women are encouraged by ads to conceive of their self-worth in terms of unrealistic standards of physical beauty; how having fun is portrayed in ads for beer, wine, and alcohol; ideas about nutrition courtesy of the junk food industry; how racial disharmony, homosexuality, and poverty are missing from the social world of ads; and so on.

Finally, in light of my earlier claim that autonomous individuals will be disposed to critically scrutinize the institutions they live under, it is important to point out how the portrayal of consumption as the good life serves a political function. This portrayal provides individuals with standards and expectations against which to judge not only their own lives, but the institutions that shape and mold their lives. Consumption is presented as the reward for "making it," and as a way of ameliorating, if not curing, boredom, powerlessness, lack of self-esteem, etc. Political and economic institutions then come to be measured by the extent to which they provide individuals access to consumer goods. Of course, there is no guarantee that, judged against this criterion, a society's political and economic institutions will fare well. In this way, even mass-advertising may provide individuals with a basis for criticizing their institutions.

However, the basis is a very limited one. Individuals may only be concerned with whether they might get more or less consumer goods if institutions were organized differently (or run by members of a different political party). Other, competing criteria against which to judge institutions are likely to have a hard time getting a hearing in societies dominated by mass-advertising. In this way, advertising serves as a force that *legitimizes* the political and economic status quo. It deadens individuals to a more extensive critical scrutiny of the institutions they live under. The ways in which their political and economic institutions distribute the social conditions of autonomy, and therefore allow the economic interests of corporations to dominate their lives, are rarely considered or seriously discussed.

One of the supposed virtues of advanced capitalist societies where mass-advertising is ubiquitous is that they afford individuals a wide range of choices. Within the ambit of the consumer lifestyle, that may be so. But, what about some of the more basic choices individuals have about how to live their lives or about how to organize their political and economic affairs? Are these choices many individuals in such societies realize they have, let alone can conceive of an array of alternatives about? My contention is that many in such societies are in no position to make critically competent choices about these more basic issues and that advertising significantly contributes to their inability to do so.

V.

It is not enough for defenders of advertising to respond to the preceding analysis by pointing out that *some* individuals seem to resist absorbing much of its implicit content. No doubt this is true. It is also true that many interactions of a more mundane sort between and amongst individuals fall short of being fully autonomous ones. The use of emotional appeals is widespread, as are other forms of manipulation. There are many insecure or servile individuals who are influenced by others in ways that likely fail the tests of critical competence. Few would suggest that societies be judged harshly for allowing such interactions to go on. Yet, it might be argued, why should we think societies ought to treat persuasive mass-advertising any differently? Why not, instead, think it reasonable to let individuals watch out for themselves in the face of mass-advertising? After all, some seem to.

This is a formidable objection, but it fails to take account of the differences between individuals' encounters with advertising and their encounters with other individuals. The latter typically have three features that the former lack. First, encounters with other individuals are often either voluntarily sought out or at least voluntarily maintained. Yet, advertising is not easily avoided. It begins to work its influence on individuals when they are young and it never lets up. It is omni-present. Second, even where individual encounters with other individuals are not fully voluntary (e.g. familial or work relationships), they typically serve some important value or function in individuals' lives. This is less obviously true with respect to persuasive mass-advertising. Third, encounters with other individuals, if found unsatisfactory, can be altered by the participants. Individuals can ask, or insist, that others not deceive or manipulate them. Sometimes this works. With advertising, individuals can, at best, try to shut it out or be wary of it. It is not an agent whose "conduct" can be altered by direct appeals.

Also, the fact that some individuals manage to resist the effects of persuasive mass-advertising might be explained by their having greater access to the other social conditions of autonomy (e.g. education). Surely that does not show that a society need do nothing about an institution in its midst that arguably plays a very significant role in suppressing the autonomy of what is perhaps a very large majority of its members. As Tom Beauchamp notes, a source of influence need not be completely controlling in order to be an object of concern.[28]

Defenders of advertising might at this point argue that the actions of corporations are protected by the moral right of free speech. Joseph Des Jardins and John McCall maintain, however, that we should distinguish commercial speech from moral, religious, and political speech. They argue that some types of speech are more valuable to human life than others. Moral, religious, and political speech "contribute to the pursuit of meaning and value in human existence," while commercial speech "in offering an item for sale appears a rather mundane concern."[29] The latter only encourages persons to deliberate about various and competing consumer choices.

Des Jardins and McCall are mostly concerned about providing a rationale for governmental efforts to regulate deceptive commercial speech. Their argument relies on a conception of human autonomy similar to my own. Still, it seems to me that there exists a simpler and more straightforward justification for attempts to regulate deceptive commercial speech, one that appeals to the notion of the sorts of voluntary informed exchanges which are supposed to be the backbone of free enterprise economic systems. Deceptive commercial speech vitiates the *informedness* of such exchanges and it is often possible to prove ads deceptive.

Additionally, Des Jardins and McCall fail to distinguish between the explicit and implicit content of persuasive mass-advertising. The latter, as we have seen, *is* rich in moral and political content. Thus, by their argument, if we should reject restrictions on political, religious, and moral speech, we should equally reject the curtailment of persuasive mass-advertising.[30] Nevertheless, I think that most of the traditional arguments for free speech will not serve defenders of persuasive advertising. Frederick Schauer develops and assesses several of these arguments.[31] I will concentrate on three central ones.

First, there is what Schauer calls the "argument from truth." This argument alleges that there is a causal link between freedom of speech and the discovery of truth. Schauer suggests we modify this argument to emphasize the elimination of error so as to avoid the complications that attend the notion of "objective truth."[32] The modified argument suggests that allowing the expression of contrary views is the only rational way of recognizing human fallibility, thus making possible the rejection or modification of erroneous views. It holds that we can increase the level of rational confidence in our views by comparing them to other views and seeing whether ours survive all currently available attacks. The suppression of speech, as John Stuart Mill noted, is inconsistent with a recognition of human fallibility.

A second argument is what Schauer refers to as the "argument from democracy." It is an argument that presupposes the acceptance of democratic principles for the organization of the state. It then consists of two parts:

1. in order for the people as sovereign electorate to vote intelligently, all relevant information must be available to them; and
2. as political leaders are to serve their citizens' wishes, the latter must be able to communicate their wishes on all matters to the government.

In short, since democracy implies that government is the servant of the people, the people must retain the right to reject and criticize their government. Yet, this requires no prior restrictions by the government on information available to the citizens.

A third argument has been developed by Thomas Scanlon, and is referred to by Schauer as the "argument from autonomy."[33] This argument claims that the province of thought and decision-making is morally beyond the reach of the state's powers. The state is alleged to have no ultimate authority to decide matters of religious, moral, political, or scientific doctrine. Autonomous persons cannot accept, without independent consideration, the judgment of others as to what they should believe or do, especially on these matters. Thus, it is held that individuals must be free from governmental intrusion into the process of choice.

It is important to note, in general, that all three of these arguments presuppose that it is government suppression of speech that threatens individual thought-processes and choices. Historically, this may have been true, but the development of persuasive mass-advertising poses a different sort of threat. Schauer repeatedly claims that the province of individual thought and decision-making is inherently (as a causal matter) beyond the control of the state. He claims that the area of individual conscience is "under the exclusive control of the individual" because of the "internal" nature of thought.[34] While this may only underestimate the power of the state to influence thoughts and feelings, it surely ignores the possibility that persuasive mass-advertising significantly influences these in the ways detailed earlier.

With regard to the argument from truth, it is not fair to portray advertising as simply offering "truths" for consideration that compete against other beliefs in the marketplace of ideas. Whatever "truths" it offers (and I suspect they are small ones) threaten to drown out all other claims, or to render them tedious or irrelevant by comparison. Worse, as we have seen, its implicit content encourages beliefs and attitudes about thought and decision-making that are hostile to those necessary to sort through claims and weed out the false or misleading ones.

Similar remarks hold for the argument from democracy. Especially relevant here is the political content of persuasive mass-advertising, with its emphasis on consumption-as-the-good-life as the standard against which to measure political and economic systems. More insidious than its insistence on this essentially status quo – preserving standard is its implicit denial of the value of political debate and activity. Consumption is where individuals are told they will find satisfaction, and a host of pseudo-issues about such a life are offered as the central focus for individuals' care and concern.

Finally, if advertising is inimical to autonomy in the ways I have claimed throughout this paper, it is obvious that the argument from autonomy cannot be invoked on its behalf. Those who defend persuasive mass-advertising on the basis of its contribution to individual choice would seem to have an extremely limited notion of the range of choices that individuals have about their lives.

Virginia Held makes the important point that in societies like the United States, it is no longer adequate to construe the right to free expression simply as a right not to be interfered with:

> But in a contemporary context this leaves those with economic resources free to express themselves through the media: they can buy time on TV or own a station, they can buy up or start a newspaper, and so on. At the same time, those without economic resources can barely be heard.[35]

Held's concern is with a society's taking steps to *enable* its members to freely express themselves. Though she does not directly address the issue of persuasive mass-advertising, it is likely that she would view the nearly unchecked power of corporations to express their interests through the media with alarm.

VI.

What to do about persuasive mass-advertising is, I think, a daunting problem. Throughout my analysis, I have insisted that we consider the effects of advertising in conjunction with the effects of other social conditions that might impact on autonomy. The question we must ask ourselves, then, is what changes in our political and economic institutions are necessary in order to provide all persons with the social conditions of autonomy. Since advanced capitalist countries like the United States are now plagued in various ways by the dominance of corporate interests, we might hope that enhancing the social conditions of autonomy for all persons will result in the cultivation, expression, and realization of more varied (and autonomous) interests.

While some will think that the only way to accomplish this result is to abandon capitalism altogether, I want to consider changes that are somewhat more modest. First, in order to modify the organization of work so as to provide a venue for the realization of worker autonomy, we might adopt the sorts of worker participation mechanisms institutionalized in countries like West Germany and Sweden.[36] These mechanisms guarantee workers participation in the economic decisions that vitally affect their lives. Second, we would need to guarantee to all individuals the level and quality of education necessary for them to develop the skills, dispositions, and knowledge constituitive of dispositional autonomy. Third, we would need to take steps to lessen if not eliminate the influence of wealth and economic power over the decisions of democratically elected political officials. This might include such things as the development of a public financing scheme for all political campaigns and the institutionalization of mechanisms to guarantee the independence of government officials from those they regulate or purchase products and services from. Fourth, steps must be taken to divorce the media from their almost exclusive reliance on commercial financial support and to provide individuals with increased access to the means of expression. Virginia Held offers a number of valuable proposals about how to effect these ends.[37] These include having more public financing of the media and having commercial sponsors buy nonspecific time on the airwaves. Both measures would reduce the pressure to produce programming that is successful according to narrow commercial criteria. The hope is that this will lead to greater experimentation in the media, and thus to the creation of a more diverse cultural life.

Obviously, the preceding changes would need to be considered at greater length. But, let me instead turn to advertising and its role in the suppression of autonomy. As an aspect of the dominance of corporate interests in advanced capitalist societies, it is important to neither over-estimate nor under-estimate its significance. On the one hand, without complementary changes of the sort just discussed, attempts to regulate or restrict advertising seem likely to have only minimal impact on the development and maintenance of autonomy. At most, such regulation or restriction would eliminate one barrier to autonomy. On the other hand, it may be argued that the saluatory effects of such complementary changes will be undermined if no steps are taken to regulate or restrict persuasive mass-advertising. Workers might remain imbued with the mentality promulgated in ads and so unwittingly express views conducive to corporate interests. Attempts to cultivate a more educated populace would still be opposed by the barrage of ads with its implicit content.

Unfortunately, it is hard to come up with a feasible approach to the regulation or restriction of advertising. Since the thrust of my argument has been against persuasive advertising, it might be suggested that we attempt to legislate a distinction between it and informational advertising. The idea would then be to restrict if not eliminate the former while permitting the latter. Perhaps simply providing information about the price, character, and availability of products and services poses little threat to autonomy and may even facilitate it.

One serious problem with this approach will be that of defining "persuasive." For instance, if individuals are shown using and enjoying a product, will that have to be considered an attempt at persuasion? Or, if a product is displayed in a pictorially pleasing manner, will that be considered persuasive? Also, assuming this difficulty can be overcome in a reasonable manner, won't the amount of regulation required necessitate the creation of a massive bureaucracy? It should be noted that corporations confronted with restrictions on persuasive advertising are likely to respond creatively in attempts to circumvent the rules.

An alternative approach would be to try to restrict the overall quantity of advertising without regard to a distinction between informational and persuasive types. It might be feasible to restrict the number of ads on TV to a certain number per hour, but can we do something similar with magazines, radio, and newspapers? Even if we had the will to do so, at least two serious problems remain:

1. a mere reduction in the quantity of ads (persuasive and otherwise) may not greatly lessen their impact in terms of selling the consumer lifestyle — especially in the absence of steps to counter this implicit content;
2. the difficulties in formulating and enforcing such restrictions would be formidable.

On the latter point, think about the enormous number of venues for advertising (currently existing as well as those that might soon be available) that we would have to regulate.

It is not easy to avoid drawing a pessimistic conclusion from the preceding remarks. Perhaps those more inventive than I can come up with proposals to restrict persuasive advertising that evade these problems and others like them. What cannot be evaded is the political reality that any proposed restrictions will be steadfastly, and I suspect effectively, resisted by corporations and advertisers. On this score, the only hope may lie with the sorts of institutional changes sketched earlier. It is possible that a better educated populace with more democratic control over its corporations can take the necessary steps to curtail the suppression of autonomy effected by current mass-advertising.

Notes

1. John Kenneth Galbraith, *The New Industrial State* (Boston, MA: Houghton Mifflin, 1967), especially pp. 198–218. See also the selection by Galbraith, "Persuasion — and Power," in Joseph R. Des Jardins and John J. McCall (eds.), *Contemporary Issues in Business Ethics* (Belmont, CA: Wadsworth, 1985): 142–147.

2. I will limit my claims to countries with schemes of political and economic organization like

those in the United States. Obviously, my claims would have to be weakened or modified if they were to be made applicable to countries with significantly different institutions.

3. On the ways in which many ads deceive by presenting information in misleading ways, see, for instance, Tom L. Beauchamp, "Manipulative Advertising," *Business and Professional Ethics Journal* 3 (Spring/Summer 1984): 1–22.

4. Lawrence Haworth, *Autonomy: An Essay in Philosophical Psychology and Ethics* (New Haven, CT: Yale University Press, 1986), especially chapter 8.

5. Tom Beauchamp distinguishes between the responses of individuals to advertising and the intentions of those who create the advertising. My remarks in what follows concern the responses of individuals. I do not wish to suggest that corporations consciously intend all of the effects I delineate. See Beauchamp, "Manipulative Advertising," p. 7.

6. Virginia Held has also touched on the theme of the dominance of corporate interests. See her *Rights and Goods: Justifying Social Action* (New York: The Free Press, 1984), especially chapter 12.

7. Roger Crisp, "Persuasive Advertising, Autonomy, and the Creation of Desire," *Journal of Business Ethics* 6 (1987): 413–418, p. 414.

8. Ibid., p. 414.

9. Samuel Gorovitz, "Advertising Professional Success Rates," *Business and Professional Ethics Journal* 3 (Spring/Summer 1984): 31–45, p. 41.

10. Robert Arrington, "Advertising and Behavior Control," reprinted in Des Jardins and McCall *Contemporary Issues in Business Ethics*, pp. 167–175.

11. Robert Young, *Personal Autonomy: Beyond Negative and Positive Liberty* (New York: St. Martin's Press, 1986), p. 8.

12. Gerald Dworkin, *The Theory and Practice of Autonomy* (Cambridge: Cambridge University Press, 1988), pp. 15–16.

13. Young distinguishes between internal constraints on autonomy (e.g. lack of self-control) and external constraints (e.g. lack of liberty). See his *Personal Autonomy*, p. 35.

14. Dworkin, *The Theory and Practice of Autonomy*, p. 20.

15. Haworth, *Autonomy*, pp. 42–43.

16. Adina Schwartz, "Meaningful Work," *Ethics* 92 (July 1982): 632–646. See also Edward Sankowski, "Freedom, Work, and the Scope of Democracy," *Ethics* 91 (January 1981): 228–242; and Carole Pateman, *Participation and Democratic Theory* (Cambridge: Cambridge University Press, 1970).

17. Of course, the lack of avenues for the exercise of autonomy will often result in atrophy of the abilities and motivations that are its constituents.

18. For more on advertising and program content, see Virginia Held, "Advertising and Program Content," *Business and Professional Ethics Journal* 3 (Spring/Summer 1984): 61–76. See also the accompanying commentaries by Clifford Christians and Norman Bowie.

19. David Braybrooke, *Ethics and the World of Business* (Totowa, NJ: Rowman and Allanheld, 1983), pp. 327–328.

20. Stanley I. Benn, "Freedom and Persuasion," *Australasian Journal of Philosophy* 45 (December 1967): 259–275.

21. Cf. Lynda Sharp Paine, "Children As Consumers," *Business and Professional Ethics Journal* 3 (Spring/Summer 1984): 119–145. Paine argues persuasively that children ought not be viewed as capable of making responsible consumer choices. She does not emphasize the effects of advertising on the habits of thought and perception of children.

22. Jules Henry, *Culture Against Man* (New York: Random House, 1963), p. 49.

23. Ibid., p. 48.

24. Ibid., p. 75.

25. John Waide, "The Making of Self and World in Advertising," *Journal of Business Ethics* 6 (1987): 73–79.

26. Also, if most persons can be induced to fear the judgment of others and adopt the consumer lifestyle, the result will be a remarkably homogenous collection of otherwise isolated individuals. Advertising superficially promotes individuality by telling persons they can only truly find themselves with this or that product. Of course, it tells every individual the same thing. Ethnic or individual diversity is worn away.

27. Waide, "The Making of Self and World in Advertising," p. 73.

28. Beauchamp, "Manipulative Advertising," p. 3.

29. Joseph R. Des Jardins and John J. McCall, "Advertising and Free Speech," in Des Jardins and McCall, *Contemporary Issues in Business Ethics*, p. 105.

30. Also, Burton Leiser argues that the United States Supreme Court has seen fit to extend constitutional protection to commercial speech. See his "Professional Advertising: Price Fixing and Professional Dignity versus the Public's Right to a Free Market," *Business and Professional Ethics Journal* 3 (Spring/Summer 1984): 93–107.

31. Frederick Schauer, *Free Speech: A Philosophical Inquiry* (Cambridge: Cambridge University Press, 1982). Schauer notes problems with each of these arguments that I will ignore here.

32. Ibid., pp. 24–25.

33. Thomas Scanlon, "A Theory of Freedom of Expression," *Philosophy and Public Affairs* 6 (Winter 1972): 204–226.

34. Schauer, *Freedom of Speech*, p. 68. See also p. 53.

35. Virginia Held, "Advertising and Program Content," *Business and Professional Ethics* Journal 3 (Spring/Summer 1984): 61–76, p. 73.

36. On this, see G. David Garson, *Worker Self-Management in Industry: The West European Experience* (New York: Praeger Publishers, 1977).

37. See her "Advertising and Program Content," pp. 66–74. Also, see *Rights and Goods*, Chapter 12.

John Waide

THE MAKING OF SELF AND WORLD IN ADVERTISING

In this paper I will criticize a common practice I call associative advertising. The fault in associative advertising is not that it is deceptive or that it violates the autonomy of its audience — on this point I find Arrington's arguments persuasive.[1] Instead, I will argue against associative advertising by examining the virtues and vices at stake. In so doing, I will offer an alternative to Arrington's exclusive concern with autonomy and behavior control.

Associative advertising is a technique that involves all of the following:

1. The advertiser wants people[2] to buy (or buy more of) a product. This objective is largely independent of any sincere desire to improve or enrich the lives of the people in the target market.

2. In order to increase sales, the advertiser identifies some (usually) deep-seated non-market good for which the people in the target market feel a strong desire. By 'non-market good' I mean something which cannot, strictly speaking, be bought or sold in a marketplace. Typical non-market goods are friendship, acceptance and esteem of others. In a more extended sense we may regard excitement (usually sexual) and power as non-market goods since advertising in the U.S.A. usually uses versions of these that cannot be bought and sold. For example, "sex appeal" as the theme of an advertising campaign is not the

From *Journal of Business Ethics*, 6 (1987), 73–79. ©1987 by D. Reidel Publishing Co. Reprinted by permission of Kluwer Academic Publishers.

market-good of prostitution, but the non-market good of sexual attractiveness and acceptability.

3. In most cases, the marketed product bears only the most tenuous (if any) relation to the non-market good with which it is associated in the advertising campaign. For example, soft drinks cannot give one friends, sex, or excitement.

4. Through advertising, the marketed product is associated with the non-market desire it cannot possibly satisfy. If possible, the desire for the non-market good is intensified by calling into question one's acceptability. For example, mouthwash, toothpaste, deodorant, and feminine hygiene ads are concocted to make us worry that we stink.

5. Most of us have enough insight to see both (a) that no particular toothpaste can make us sexy and (b) that wanting to be considered sexy is at least part of our motive for buying that toothpaste. Since we can (though, admittedly, we often do not bother to) see clearly what the appeal of the ad is, we are usually not lacking in relevant information or deceived in any usual sense.

6. In some cases, the product actually gives at least partial satisfaction to the non-market desire—but only because of advertising.[3] For example, mouthwash has little prolonged effect on stinking breath, but it helps to reduce the intense anxieties reinforced by mouthwash commercials on television because we at least feel that we are doing the proper thing. In the most effective cases of associative advertising, people begin to talk like ad copy. We begin to sneer at those who own the wrong things. We all become enforcers for the advertisers. In general, if the advertising images are effective enough and reach enough people, even preposterous marketing claims can become at least partially self-fulfilling.

Most of us are easily able to recognize associative advertising as morally problematic when the consequences are clear, extreme, and our own desires and purchasing habits are not at stake. For example, the marketing methods Nestlé used in Africa involved associative advertising. Briefly, Nestlé identified a large market for its infant formula—without concern for the well-being of the prospective consumers. In order to induce poor women to buy formula rather than breastfeed, Nestlé selected non-market goods on which to base its campaigns—love for one's child and a desire to be acceptable by being modern. These appeals were effective (much as they are in advertising for children's clothing, toys, and computers in the U.S.A.). Through billboards and radio advertising, Nestlé identified parental love with formula feeding and suggested that formula is the modern way to feed a baby. Reports indicate that in some cases mothers of dead babies placed cans of formula on their graves to show that the parents cared enough to do the very best they could for their children, even though we know the formula may have been a contributing cause of death.[4]

One might be tempted to believe that associative advertising is an objectionable technique only when used on the very poorest, most powerless and ignorant people and that it is the poverty, powerlessness, and ignorance which are at fault. An extreme example like the Nestlé case, one might protest, surely doesn't tell us much about more ordinary associative advertising in the industrialized western nations. The issues will become clearer if we look at the conceptions of virtue and vice at stake.

Dewey says "the thing actually at stake in any serious deliberation is not a difference of quantity [as utilitarianism would have us believe], but what kind of person one is to become, what sort of self is in the making, what kind of a world is making."[5] Similarly, I would like to ask who we become as we use or are used by associative advertising. This will not be a decisive argument. I have not found clear, compelling, objective principles — only considerations I find persuasive and which I expect many others to find similarly persuasive. I will briefly examine how associative advertising affects (a) the people who plan and execute marketing strategies and (b) the people who are exposed to the campaign.

(a) Many advertisers[6] come to think clearly and skillfully about how to sell a marketable item by associating it with a non-market good which people in the target market desire. An important ingredient in this process is lack of concern for the well-being of the people who will be influenced by the campaign. Lloyd Slater, a consultant who discussed the infant formula controversy with people in both the research and development and marketing divisions of Nestlé, says that the R&D people had made sure that the formula was nutritionally sound but were troubled or even disgusted by what the marketing department was doing. In contrast, Slater reports that the marketing people simply did not care and that "those guys aren't even human" in their reactions.[7] This evidence is only anecdotal and it concerns an admittedly extreme case. Still, I believe that the effects of associative advertising[8] would most likely be the same but less pronounced in more ordinary cases. Furthermore, it is quite common for advertisers in the U.S.A. to concentrate their attention on selling something that is harmful to many people, e.g., candy that rots our teeth, and cigarettes. In general, influencing people without concern for their well-being is likely to reduce one's sensitivity to the moral motive of concern for the well-being of others. Compassion, concern, and sympathy for others, it seems to me, are clearly central to moral virtue.[9] Associative advertising must surely undermine this sensitivity in much of the advertising industry. It is, therefore, *prima facie* morally objectionable.

(b) Targets of associative advertising (which include people in the advertising industry) are also made worse by exposure to effective advertising of this kind. The harm done is of two kinds:

(1) We often find that we are buying more but enjoying it less. It isn't only that products fail to live up to specific claims about service-life or effectiveness. More often, the motives ('reasons' would perhaps not be the right word here) for our purchases consistently lead to disappointment. We buy all the right stuff and yet have no more friends, lovers, excitement or respect than before. Instead, we have full closets and empty pocket books. Associative advertising, though not the sole cause, contributes to these results.

(2) Associative advertising may be less effective as an advertising technique to sell particular products than it is as an ideology[10] in our culture. Within the advertising which washes over us daily we can see a number of common themes, but the most important may be "You are what you own."[11] The quibbles over which beer, soft drink, or auto to buy are less important than the over-all message. Each product contributes its few minutes each day, but we are bombarded for hours with the message that friends, lovers, acceptance, excitement,

and power are to be gained by purchases in the market, not by developing personal relationships, virtues, and skills. Our energy is channeled into careers so that we will have enough money to *be* someone by buying the right stuff in a market. The not very surprising result is that we neglect non-market methods of satisfying our non-market desires. Those non-market methods call for wisdom, compassion, skill, and a variety of virtues which cannot be bought. It seems, therefore, that insofar as associative advertising encourages us to neglect the non-market cultivation of our virtues and to substitute market goods instead, we become worse and, quite likely, less happy persons.

To sum up the argument so far, associative advertising tends to desensitize its practitioners to the compassion, concern, and sympathy for others that are central to moral virtue and it encourages its audience to neglect the cultivation of non-market virtues. There are at least five important objections that might be offered against my thesis that associative advertising is morally objectionable.

First, one could argue that since each of us is (or can easily be if we want to be) aware of what is going on in associative advertising, we must want to participate and find it unobjectionable. Accordingly, the argument goes, associative advertising is not a violation of individual autonomy. In order to reply to this objection I must separate issues.

(a) Autonomy is not the main, and certainly not the only, issue here. It may be that I can, through diligent self-examination neutralize much of the power of associative advertising. Since I can resist, one might argue that I am responsible for the results — *caveat emptor* with a new twist.[12] If one's methodology in ethics is concerned about people and not merely their autonomy, then the fact that most people are theoretically capable of resistance will be less important than the fact that most are presently unable to resist.

(b) What is more, the ideology of acquisitiveness which is cultivated by associative advertising probably undermines the intellectual and emotional virtues of reflectiveness and self-awareness which would better enable us to neutralize the harmful effects of associative advertising. I do not know of specific evidence to cite in support of this claim, but it seems to me to be confirmed in the ordinary experience of those who, despite associative advertising, manage to reflect on what they are exposed to.

(c) Finally, sneer group pressure often makes other people into enforcers so that there are penalties for not going along with the popular currents induced by advertising. We are often compelled even by our associates to be enthusiastic participants in the consumer culture. Arrington omits consideration of sneer group pressure as a form of compulsion which can be (though it is not always) induced by associative advertising.

So far my answer to the first objection is incomplete. I still owe some account of why more people do not complain about associative advertising. This will become clearer as I consider a second objection.

Second, one could insist that even if the non-market desires are not satisfied completely, they must be satisfied for the most part or we would stop falling for associative advertising. This objection seems to me to make three main errors:

(a) Although we have a kind of immediate access to our own motives and are generally able to see what motives an advertising campaign uses, most of us lack even the simple framework provided by my analysis of associative advertising. Even one who sees that a particular ad campaign is aimed at a particular non-market desire may not see how all the ads put together constitute a cultural bombardment with an ideology of acquisitiveness — you are what you own. Without some framework such as this, one has nothing to blame. It is not easy to gain self-reflective insight, much less cultural insight.

(b) Our attempts to gain insight are opposed by associative advertising which always has an answer for our dissatisfactions — buy more or newer or different things. If I find myself feeling let down after a purchase, many voices will tell me that the solution is to buy other things too (or that I have just bought the wrong thing). With all of this advertising proposing one kind of answer for our dissatisfactions, it is scarcely surprising that we do not usually become aware of alternatives.

(c) Finally, constant exposure to associative advertising changes[13] us so that we come to feel acceptable as persons when and only when we own the acceptable, fashionable things. By this point, our characters and conceptions of virtue already largely reflect the result of advertising and we are unlikely to complain or rebel.

Third, and perhaps most pungent of the objections, one might claim that by associating mundane marketable items with deeply rooted non-market desires, our everyday lives are invested with new and greater meaning. Charles Revson of Revlon once said that "In the factory we make cosmetics: in the store we sell hope."[14] Theodore Levitt, in his passionate defense of associative advertising, contends that[15]

> Everyone in the world is trying in his [or her] special personal fashion to solve a primal problem of life — the problem of rising above his [or her] own negligibility, of escaping from nature's confining, hostile, and unpredictable reality, of finding significance, security, and comfort in the things he [or she] must do to survive.

Levitt adds: "Without distortion, embellishment, and elaboration, life would be drab, dull, anguished, and at its existential worst."[16] This objection is based on two assumptions so shocking that his conclusion almost seems sensible.

(a) Without associative advertising would our lives lack significance? Would we be miserable in our drab, dull, anguished lives? Of course not. People have always had ideals, fantasies, heroes, and dreams. We have always told stories that captured our aspirations and fears. The very suggestion that we require advertising to bring a magical aura to our shabby, humdrum lives is not only insulting but false.

(b) Associative advertising is crafted not in order to enrich our daily lives but in order to enrich the clients and does not have the interests of its audience at heart. Still, this issue of intent, though troubling, is only part of the problem. Neither is the main problem that associative advertising images somehow distort reality. Any work of art also is, in an important sense, a dissembling or distortion. The central question instead is whether the specific appeals and images, techniques and products, enhance people's lives.[17]

A theory of what enhances a life must be at least implicit in any discussion of the morality of associative advertising. Levitt appears to assume that in a satisfying life one has many satisfied desires — *which* desires is not important.[18] To propose and defend an alternative to his view is beyond the scope of this paper. My claim is more modest — that it is not enough to ask whether desires are satisfied. We should also ask what kinds of lives are sustained, made possible, or fostered by having the newly synthesized desires. What kind of self and world are in the making, Dewey would have us ask. This self and world are always in the making. I am not arguing that there is some natural, good self which advertising changes and contaminates. It may be that not only advertising, but also art, religion, and education in general, always synthesize new desires.[19] In each case, we should look at the lives. How to judge the value of these lives and the various conceptions of virtue they will embody is another question. It will be enough for now to see that it is an important question.

Now it may be possible to see why I began by saying that I would suggest an alternative to the usual focus on autonomy and behavior control.[20] Arrington's defense of advertising (including, as near as I can tell, what I call associative advertising) seems to assume that we have no standard to which we can appeal to judge whether a desire enhances a life and, consequently, that our only legitimate concerns are whether an advertisement violates the autonomy of its audience by deceiving them or controlling their behavior. I want to suggest that there is another legitimate concern — whether the advertising will tend to influence us to become worse persons.[21]

Fourth, even one who is sympathetic with much of the above might object that associative advertising is necessary to an industrial society such as ours. Economists since Galbraith[22] have argued about whether, without modern advertising of the sort I have described, there would be enough demand to sustain our present levels of production. I have no answer to this question. It seems unlikely that associative advertising will end suddenly, so I am confident that we will have the time and the imagination to adapt our economy to do without it.

Fifth, and last, one might ask what I am proposing. Here I am afraid I must draw up short of my mark. I have no practical political proposal. It seems obvious to me that no broad legislative prohibition would improve matters. Still, it may be possible to make small improvements like some that we have already seen. In the international arena, Nestlé was censured and boycotted, the World Health Organization drafted infant formula marketing guidelines, and finally Nestlé agreed to change its practices. In the U.S.A., legislation prohibits cigarette advertising on television.[23] These are tiny steps, but an important journey may begin with them.

Even my personal solution is rather modest. *First*, if one accepts my thesis that associative advertising is harmful to its audience, then one ought to avoid doing it to others, especially if doing so would require that one dull one's compassion, concern, and sympathy for others. Such initiatives are not entirely without precedent. Soon after the surgeon general's report on cigarettes and cancer in 1964, David Ogilvy and William Bernbach announced that their agencies would no longer accept cigarette accounts and *New Yorker* magazine banned cigarette ads.[24] *Second*, if I am even partly right about the effect of associative advertising on our desires, then one ought to expose oneself as little as possible. The most practical and effective way to do this is probably to banish commercial television and radio from one's life. This measure, though rewarding,[25] is only moderately effective. Beyond these, I do not yet have any answers.

In conclusion, I have argued against the advertising practice I call associative advertising. My main criticism is two-fold: (a) Advertisers must surely desensitize themselves to the compassion, concern, and sympathy for others that are central emotions in a virtuous person, and (b) associative advertising influences its audience to neglect the non-market cultivation of our virtues and to substitute market goods instead, with the result that we become worse and, quite likely, less happy persons.

Notes

*An earlier draft of this paper was presented to the Tennessee Philosophical Association, 10 November 1984. I am indebted to that group for many helpful comments.

1. Robert L. Arrington, 'Advertising and Behavior Control', *Journal of Business Ethics* 1, pp. 3–12.

2. I prefer not to use the term 'consumers' since it identifies us with our role in a market, already conceding part of what I want to deny.

3. Arrington, p. 8.

4. James B. McGinnis. *Bread and Justice* (New York: Paulist Press, 1979) p. 224. McGinnis cites as his source INFACT Newsletter, September 1977, p. 3. Formula is often harmful because poor families do not have the sanitary facilities to prepare the formula using clean water and utensils, do not have the money to be able to keep up formula feeding without diluting the formula to the point of starving the child, and formula does not contain the antibodies which a nursing mother can pass to her child to help immunize the child against common local bacteria. Good accounts of this problem are widely available.

5. John Dewey, *Human Nature and Conduct* (New York: Random House, 1930), p. 202.

6. This can be a diverse group including (depending upon the product) marketing specialists, sales representatives, or people in advertising agencies. Not everyone in one of these positions, however, is necessarily guilty of engaging in associative advertising.

7. This story was told by Lloyd E. Slater at a National Science Foundation Chatauqua entitled 'Meeting World Food Needs' in 1980–1981. It should not be taken as a condemnation of marketing professionals in other firms.

8. One could argue that the deficiency in compassion, concern, and sympathy on the part of advertisers might be a result of self-selection rather than of associative advertising. Perhaps people in whom these moral sentiments are strong do not commonly go into positions using associative advertising. I doubt, however, that such self-selection can account for all the disregard of the audience's best interests.

9. See Lawrence A. Blum, *Friendship, Altruism and Morality* (Boston: Routledge and Kegan Paul, 1980) for a defense of moral emotions against Kantian claims that emotions are unsuitable as a basis for moral judgement and that only a purely rational good will offers an adequte foundation for morality.

10. I use 'ideology' here in a descriptive rather than a pejorative sense. To be more specific, associative advertising commonly advocates only a part of a more comprehensive ideology. See Raymond Geuss, *The Idea of a Critical Theory* (Cambridge University Press, 1981). pp. 5–6.

11. For an interesting discussion, see John Lachs, 'To Have and To Be', *Personalist* 45 (Winter, 1964), pp. 5–14; reprinted in John Lachs and Charles Scott, *The Human Search* (New York: Oxford University Press, 1981), pp. 247–255.

12. This is, in fact, the thrust of Arrington's arguments in 'Advertising and Behavior Control'.

13. I do not mean to suggest that only associative advertising can have such ill effects. Neither am I assuming the existence of some natural, pristine self which is perverted by advertising.

14. Quoted without source in Theodore Levit, 'The Morality (?) of Advertising', *Harvard Business Review*, July-August 1970; reprinted in Vincent Barry, *Moral Issues in Business*, (Belmont, CA: Wadsworth Publishing Company, 1979), p. 256.

15. Levitt (in Barry), p. 252.

16. Levitt (in Barry), p. 256.

17. 'Satisfying a desire would be valuable then if it sustained or made possible a valuable kind of life. To say this is to reject the argument that in creating the wants he [or she] can satisfy, the advertiser (or the manipulator of mass emotion in politics or religion) is necessarily acting in the best interests of his [or her] public." Stanley Benn, 'Freedom and Persuasion', *Australasian Journal*

of Philosophy 45 (1969); reprinted in Beauchamp and Bowie, *Ethical Theory and Business*, second edition (Englewood Cliffs, NJ: Prentice-Hall, 1983), p. 374.

18. Levitt's view is not new. "Continual success in obtaining those things which a man from time to time desires — that is to say, continual prospering — is what men call felicity." Hobbes, *Leviathan* (Indianapolis: Bobbs-Merrill, 1958), p. 61.

19. This, in fact, is the principal criticism von Hayek offered of Galbraith's argument against the "dependence effect". F. A. von Hayek, *'The Non Sequitur* of the "Dependence Effect"', *Southern Economic Journal*, April 1961; reprinted in Tom L. Beauchamp and Norman E. Bowie, *Ethical Theory and Business*, second edition (Englewood Cliffs, New Jersey: Prentice-Hall, 1983), pp. 363–366.

20. Taylor R. Durham, 'Information, Persuasion, and Control in Moral Appraisal of Advertising', *The Journal of Business Ethics* 3, 179. Durham also argues that an exclusive concern with issues of deception and control leads us into errors.

21. One might object that this requires a normative theory of human nature, but it seems to me that we can go fairly far by reflecting on our experience. If my approach is to be vindicated, however, I must eventually provide an account of how, in general, we are to make judgements about what is and is not good (or life-enhancing) for a human being. Clearly, there is a large theoretical gulf between me and Arrington, but I hope that my analysis of associative advertising shows that my approach is plausible enough to deserve further investigation.

22. The central text for this problem is *The Affluent Society* (Houghton Mifflin, 1958). The crucial passages are reprinted in many anthologies, e.g., John Kenneth Galbraith. 'The Dependence Effect', in W. Michael Hoffman and Jennifer Mills Moore, *Business Ethics: Readings and Cases in Corporate Morality* (New York: McGraw-Hill, 1984), pp. 328–333.

23. "In March 1970 Congress removed cigarette ads from TV and radio as of the following January. (The cigarette companies transferred their billings to print and outdoor advertising. Cigarette sales reached new records.)" Stephen Fox, *The Mirror Makers: A History of American Advertising and its Creators* (New York: William Morrow and Co., 1984), p. 305.

24. Stephen Fox, pp. 303–304.

25. See, for example, Jerry Mander, *Four Arguments for the Elimination of Television* (New York: Morrow Quill Paperbacks, 1977).

Lynn Sharp Paine

CHILDREN AS CONSUMERS: AN ETHICAL EVALUATION OF CHILDREN'S TELEVISION ADVERTISING

Television sponsors and broadcasters began to identify children as a special target audience for commercial messages in the mid-1960s.[1] Within only a few years, children's television advertising emerged as a controversial issue. Concerned parents began to speak out and to urge the networks to adopt codes of ethics governing children's advertising. By 1970, the issue had attracted the attention of the Federal Trade Commission (FTC) and the Federal Communications Commission (FCC). The FCC received some 80,000 letters in support of a proposed rule "looking toward the elimination of sponsorship and commercial content in children's programming."[2] Public attention to the contro-

From *Business and Professional Ethics Journal*, 3, nos. 3 & 4 (1983), 119–146. Reprinted by permission of the author.

versy over children's television advertising peaked between 1978 and 1980, when the FTC, under its authority to regulate unfair and deceptive advertising, held public hearings on its proposal to ban televised advertising directed to or seen by large numbers of young children. More recently parents have complained to the FCC about so-called program-length commercials, children's programs designed around licensed characters.[3]

As this brief chronology indicates, children's television advertising has had a history of arousing people's ethical sensibilities. In this paper I want to propose some explanations for why this is so and to argue that there are good ethical reasons that advertisers should refrain from directing commercials to young children. However, because so much of the public debate over children's advertising has focused on the FTC's actions rather than explicitly on the ethical aspects of children's advertising, a few preliminary remarks are called for.

First, it is important to bear in mind that the ethical propriety of directing television advertising to young children is distinct from its legality. Even if advertisers have a constitutional right to advertise lawful products to young children in a nondeceptive way, it is not necessarily the right thing to do.[4] Our system of government guarantees us rights that it may be unethical to exercise on certain occasions. Terminology may make it easy to lose sight of the distinction between "having a right" and the "right thing to do," but the distinction is critical to constitutional goverance.[5] In this paper I will take no position on the scope of advertisers' First Amendment rights to freedom of speech. I am primarily interested in the moral status of advertising to young children.

A second preliminary point worth noting is that evaluating the ethical status of a practice, such as advertising to young children, is a different exercise from evaluating the propriety of governmental regulation of that practice. Even if a practice is unethical, there may be legal, social, economic, political, or administrative reasons that the government cannot or should not forbid or even regulate the practice. The public policy issues faced by the FTC or any other branch of government involved in regulating children's advertising are distinct from the ethical issues facing advertisers. The fact that it may be impossible or unwise for the government to restrict children's advertising does not shield advertisers from ethical responsibility for the practice.

Finally, I want to point out that public opinion regarding children's advertising is a measure neither of its ethical value nor of the propriety of the FTC's actions. Two critics of the FTC declared that it had attempted to impose its conception of what is good on an unwilling American public.[6] There is reason to doubt the writers' assumption about the opinions of the American public regarding children's advertising,[7] but the more critical point is the implication of their argument: that the FTC's actions would have been appropriate had there been a social consensus opposing child-oriented advertising. Majority opinion, however, is neither the final arbiter of justified public policy, nor the standard for assaying the ethical value of a practice like children's advertising. As pointed out earlier, constitutional limits may override majority opinion in the public policy arena. And although publicly expressed opinion may signal ethical concerns (as I suggested in mentioning the letters opposing commercial sponsorship of children's television received by the FCC), social consensus is not the test of ethical quality. We cannot simply say that children's advertising is ethically all right because many people do not object to it or because people's objections to it are relatively weak. An ethical evaluation requires that we probe our ethical principles and test their relation to children's advertising. Publicly expressed opposition may signal that such probing is necessary, but it does not establish an ethical judgment one way or the other.

Public focus on the FTC has had the unfortunate effect of diverting attention from the ethical propriety of children's television advertising and emphasizing the legal and political dimensions of the FTC's actions. It has also had the unfortunate effect of putting advertisers and manufacturers of children's products in an adversarial mode vis-a-vis their critics. In this mode reasoned discussion of children's abilities and perceptions and children's proper role, if any, in the marketplace can proceed only with great difficulty. For purposes of this discussion, I will set aside the legal and public policy questions involved in government restrictions on children's advertising. Instead, as promised, I will explore the ethical issues raised by the practice of directing television advertising to young children. In the process of this investigation, I will necessarily turn my attention to the role of consumers in a free market economy, to the capacities of children as they relate to consumer activities, and to the relationships between adults and children within the family.

By *young children* I mean children who lack the conceptual abilities required for making consumer decisions, certainly children under eight. Many researchers have investigated the age at which children can comprehend the persuasive intent of advertising.[8] Depending on the questions employed to test comprehension of persuasive intent, the critical age has been set as low as kindergarten age or as high as nine or ten.[9] Even if this research were conclusive, however, it would not identify the age at which children become capable of making consumer decisions. Comprehending persuasive intent is intellectually less complex than consumer decisionmaking. Even if children appreciate the selling intent behind advertising, they may lack other conceptual abilities necessary for responsible consumer decisions. Child psychologists could perhaps identify the age at which these additional abilities develop. For purposes of this discussion, however, the precise age is not crucial. When I use the term *child* or *children* I am referring to "young children" — those who lack the requisite abilities.

Children's advertising is advertising targeted or directed to young children. Through children's advertising, advertisers attempt to persuade young children to want and, consequently, to request the advertised product.[10] Although current voluntary guidelines for children's advertising prohibit advertisers from explicitly instructing children to request that their parents buy the advertised product, child-oriented advertising is designed to induce favorable attitudes that result in such requests.[11] Frequently child-oriented ads utilize themes and techniques that appeal particularly to children: animation, clowns, magic, fantasy effects, superheroes, and special musical themes.[12] They may also involve simply the presentation of products, such as cereals, sweets, and toys, that appeal to young children with announcements directed to them.[13] The critical point in understanding child-directed advertising, however, is not simply the product, the particular themes and techniques employed, or the composition of the audience viewing the ad, but whether the advertiser intends to sell to or through children. Advertisers routinely segment their markets and target their advertising.[14] The question at issue is whether children are appropriate targets.

Advertising directed to young children is a subcategory of advertising seen by them, since children who watch television obviously see a great deal of advertising that is not directed toward them — ads for adult consumer products, investment services, insurance, and so on. Occasionally children's products are advertised by means of commercials directed to adults. The toy manufacturer Fisher-Price, for example, at one time advertised its children's toys and games primarily by means of ads directed to mothers.[15] Some ads are designed to appeal to the whole family. Insofar as these ads address young children they fall within the scope of my attention.

My interest in television advertising directed to young children, as distinct from magazine or radio advertising directed to them, is dictated by the nature of the medium. Television ads portray vivid and lively images that engage young children as the printed words and pictures of magazines, or even the spoken words of radio, could never do. Because of their immediacy television ads can attract the attention of young children who have not yet learned to read. Research has shown that young children develop affection for and even personal relationships with heavily promoted product characters appearing on television.[16] At the same time, because of their immaturity, these children are unable to assess the status of these characters as fictional or real, let alone assess whatever minimal product information they may disclose.[17] Technical limitations make magazine advertising and radio advertising inherently less likely to attract young children's attention. Consequently, they are less susceptible to ethical criticisms of the sort generated by television advertising.

CHILDREN AS CONSUMERS

The introduction of the practice of targeting children for televised commercial messages challenged existing mores. At the obvious level, the practice was novel. But at a deeper level, it called into question traditional assumptions about children and their proper role in the marketplace. The argument advanced on behalf of advertising to children by the Association of National Advertisers (ANA), the American Association of Advertising Agencies (AAAA), and the American Advertising Federation (AAF) reflects the rejection of some of these traditional assumptions:

> Perhaps the single most important benefit of advertising to children is that it provides information to the child himself, information which advertisers try to gear to the child's interests and on an appropriate level of understanding. This allows the child to learn what products are available, to know their differences, and to begin to make decisions about them based on his own personal wants and preferences. . . . Product diversity responds to these product preferences and ensures that it is the consumer himself who dictates the ultimate success or failure of a given product offering.[18]

The most significant aspect of this argument supporting children's advertising is its vision of children as autonomous consumers. Children are represented as a class of consumers possessing the relevant decisionmaking capacities and differing from adult consumers primarily in their product preferences. Children are interested in toys and candy, while adults are interested in laundry detergent and investment services. That children may require messages tailored to their level of understanding is acknowledged, but children's conceptual abilities are not regarded as having any other special significance. Advocates of children's advertising argue that it gives children "the same access to the marketplace which adults have, but keyed to their specific areas of interest."[19]

When children are viewed in this way — as miniature adults with a distinctive set of product preferences — the problematic nature of advertising to them is not apparent. Indeed, it appears almost unfair not to provide children with televised information about products available to satisfy their special interests. Why should they be treated differently from any other class of consumers?

There are, however, significant differences between adults and young children that make it inappropriate to regard children as autonomous consumers. These differences, which go far beyond different product preferences, affect children's capacities to function as responsible consumers and suggest several arguments for regarding advertising to them as unethical. For purposes of this discussion, the most critical differences reflect children's understanding of self, time, and money.

Child-development literature generally acknowledges that the emergence of a sense of one's self as an independent human being is a central experience of childhood and adolescence.[20] This vague notion, "having a sense of one's self as an independent human being," encompasses a broad range of capacities — from recognition of one's physical self as distinct from one's mother to acceptance of responsibility for one's actions and choices. Normally children acquire these capacities gradually in the course of maturation. While this mastery manifests itself as self-confidence and self-control in an ever-widening range of activities and relationships, it depends more fundamentally upon the emergence of an ability to see oneself as oneself. The reflexive nature of consciousness — the peculiar ability to monitor, study, assess, and reflect upon oneself and even upon one's reflections — underlies the ability to make rational choices. It permits people to reflect upon their desires, to evaluate them, and to have desires about what they shall desire. It permits them to see themselves as one among others and as engaging in relationships with others. Young children lack — or have only in nascent form — this ability to take a higher-order perspective on themselves and to see themselves as having desires or preferences they may wish to cultivate, suppress, or modify. They also lack the self-control that would make it possible to act on these higher-order desires if they had them.

Closely related to the sense of self, if not implicit in self-reflection is the sense of time. Children's understanding of time — both as it relates to their own existence and to the events around them — is another area where their perspectives are special. Preschoolers are intrigued with "time" questions: "When is an hour up?" "Will you be alive when I grow up?" "When did the world begin and when will it end?" "Will I be alive for the time after I die?" Young children's efforts to understand time are accompanied by a limited ability to project themselves into the future and to imagine themselves having different preferences in the future. It is generally true that children have extremely short time horizons. But children are also struggling with time in a more fundamental sense: they are testing conceptions of time as well as learning to gauge its passage in conventional markers.[21] Young children's developing sense of time goes hand in hand with their developing sense of self. Their capacity for self-reflection, for evaluating their desires, and for making rational choices is intimately related to their understanding of their own continuity in time.

Young children are in many ways philosophers: they are exploring and questioning the very fundamentals of existence.[22] Since they have not accepted many of the conventions and assumptions that guide ordinary commercial life, they frequently pose rather profound questions and make insightful observations. But although young children are very good at speculation, they are remarkably unskilled in the sorts of calculations required for making consumer judgments. In my experience, many young children are stymied by the fundamentals of arithmetic and do not understand ordinal relations among even relatively small amounts — let alone the more esoteric notions of selling in exchange for money. Research seems to support the observation that selling is a difficult concept for children. One study found that only 48 percent of six-and-a-half- to seven-and-a-half-year-olds could develop an understanding of the exocentric (as distinct from egocentric) verb *to sell*.[23] A five-year-old may know from experience in making requests that a $5.00 trinket is too expensive, but when she concludes that $5.00 is also too much to pay for a piano, it is obvious that she knows neither the exchange value of $5.00, the worth of a piano, nor the meaning of *too expensive*.[24]

What is the significance of the differences between adults and young children I have chosen to highlight — their differing conceptions of self, time, and money? In the argument for advertising quoted earlier, it was stated that advertising to children enables them "to learn what products are available, to know their differences, and to begin to make decisions about them based on [their] own personal wants and preferences." Ignore, for the moment, the fact that existing children's advertising, which concentrates so heavily on sugared foods and toys, does little either to let children know the range of products available or differences among them and assume that children's advertising could be more informative.[25] Apart from this fact the critical difficulty with the argument is that because of children's, shall we say, "naive" or "unconventional" conceptions of self, time, and money, they know very little about their own personal wants and preferences — how they are related or how quickly they will change — or about how their economic resources might be mobilized to satisfy those wants. They experience wants and preferences but do not seem to engage in critical reflection, which would lead them to assess, modify, or perhaps even curtail their felt desires for the sake of other more important or enduring desires they may have or may expect to have in the future. Young children also lack the conceptual wherewithal to engage in research or deliberative processes that would assist them in knowing which of the available consumer goods would most thoroughly satisfy their preferences, given their economic resources. The fact that children want so many of the products they see advertised is another indication that they do not evaluate advertised products on the basis of their preferences and economic resources.[26]

There is thus a serious question whether advertising really has or can have much at all to do with children's beginning "to make decisions about [products] based on [their] own personal wants and preferences" until they develop the conceptual maturity to understand their own wants and preferences and to assess the value of products available to satisfy them.[27]

If children's conceptions of self, time, and money are not suited to making consumer decisions, one must have reservations about ignoring this fact and treating them as if they were capable of making reasonable consumer judgments anyway.

There is another reason to question the validity of treating children as a parallel with other consumers. The argument for advertising to children envisions them as similar to other classes of consumers with distinctive product interests, but it appeals ultimately to the principle of consumer sovereignty.[28] Advocates of children's advertising argue that by informing children through advertising, they can "ensure that it is the consumer himself [the child] who dictates the ultimate success or failure of a given product offering." Under the principle of consumer sovereignty, the consumer is king. The preferences he expresses through his purchasing behavior determine what products succeed in the market and set the standard for what products are offered. But who is the "consumer" when children's products are at issue? Children may eat the candy or play with the toys purchased by their parents, but does this entitle them to be regarded as the "consumers" of these products? Should children who are unable to assess a product's effectiveness in satisfying their consumer preferences be the arbiters of a product's success simply because they are the final users?

Whenever the funds for a purchase do not come from the pocket of the user, the identity of the "true consumer" — if we are bent on identifying one and only one consumer — is unclear. But there is no reason to insist that there is only one consumer in such instances. Indeed, when parents buy children's products for their offspring it is much more accurate to regard both parent and child as the relevant consumers. As argued earlier, children alone lack the capacity for responsible autonomous consumer decisions. Moreover, both parent and child have interests in the purchase. Not only does the parent supply the funds and make the decision to buy while the child uses the product, but the parent derives satisfaction from the child's enjoyment of the product. As a consequence of the common and interlocking interests of parents and children, a toy that is the right price, that the child wants, and that the parent wants for the child provides much more consumer satisfaction than a toy that the child wants but that the parent does not want for the child. Whether we view the child alone as the relevant consumer, or include the parent as well, can make a significant difference in which products we regard as successful and which as unsuccessful. It will also make a difference in our assessment of the contribution children's advertising makes to consumer satisfaction.

The argument for children's advertising treats the child as the only consumer who should determine the ultimate success or failure of a product. This view implies for parents a rather minimal role in their children's consumer activities: it implies that parents should simply effectuate their children's consumer desires.[29] Anyone who agrees that children's conceptions of self, time, and money do not equip them to make responsible consumer decisions and who respects the interlocking interests of parents and their children will find the notion of children as sovereign consumers — and the parental role it implies — problematic. But how far should a parent go in influencing and directing a child's consumer activities? Most parents want to promote and support their children's developing independence, but surely renouncing all responsibility for their children's decisions is not the most effective way to do this. Should a parent restrict herself to attempting to determine what the child's desires would be if they were consistent and informed by price and value information? Or is it legitimate to go further and to permit the child only those consumer goods that reflect the parent's desires for the child? I raise these questions not to explore them but to contrast these visions of the parental role with the vision implied by the notion of the child as the sovereign consumer.

CONSUMER SOVEREIGNTY AND ADVERTISING TO CHILDREN

The seeds of an ethical argument against children's advertising may be apparent. To claim that a practice is unethical is to claim that it violates some ethical or moral principle that is or ought to be accepted. (I am, by the way, using the terms *ethical* and *moral* interchangeably.) There are several principles upon which ethical challenges to children's advertising have been based. The principles requiring veracity, fairness, and respect as well as the principle against causing harm were all appealed to in the FTC proceedings I mentioned. A somewhat different case against children's advertising can be grounded on a principle widely recognized in the business world — the principle of consumer sovereignty, the very principle that advocates of children's advertising invoked in the argument discussed above.

The principle of consumer sovereignty has a venerable heritage. Adam Smith's famous hypothesis of the invisible hand implicitly invokes the principle that consumer desires should be the touchstone for designing an economic system. The free market's efficiency in satisfying consumer desires has traditionally been a source of its moral justification. Many believe that, as compared with other systems, a free market leads to the greatest satisfaction of consumer preferences at the least cost and thus results in the most efficient allocation of economic resources. In addition to its role in justifying the free market economy as a whole, consumer sovereignty is often appealed to in specific cases. As illustrated above, business interests sometimes justify their practices by invoking consumer satisfaction or consumer demand.

Satisfying the principle of consumer sovereignty is not an all-or-nothing proposition. Some products and practices promote consumer satisfaction more than others, but there is no ultimate or perfect practice. Since consumers' preferences are so varied, following the principle of consumer sovereignty is a matter of choosing practices that do more than the available alternatives to promote consumer satisfaction.

As the medium through which producers communicate with consumers, advertising serves an essential function in promoting consumer satisfaction. A competitive free market can achieve the impressive benefits claimed for consumers only if consumers themselves are knowledgeable about products and their prices. Advertising is an obvious way to provide this information. By informing consumers of the availability, quality, and prices of products, advertising facilitates consumer satisfaction. It can also enhance consumer satisfaction by sharpening consumers' understanding of what their preferences actually are. To the extent that advertising serves these functions, it promotes the speed and accuracy with which the market responds to consumers' actual preferences and thus enhances consumer satisfaction.

It is unquestionable that advertising has the potential to promote consumer satisfaction. But it is also clear that false, misleading, or even merely uninformative advertising detracts from it. I have suggested that child-oriented advertising, too, diminishes consumer satisfaction. In order to develop an argument to support that suggestion, it is necessary first to outline briefly how children's advertising works.

HOW CHILDREN'S ADVERTISING WORKS

According to a recent textbook on marketing, the purpose of advertising is to "communicate information, imagery, and purchasing incentives" to prospective buyers.[30] As a description of the purpose of children's advertising, this statement is not quite accurate. Typically, the prospective buyers of products advertised to children are adults, who may never see the ads, and not the children to whom the information and imagery are communicated. In contrast with advertising addressed to adults who will themselves decide whether to purchase the advertised product, child-oriented advertising provides purchasing incentives to individuals who can influence, but who cannot make, the ultimate purchase decision. The desire for the product and the decision to buy lie with different individuals.

Although advertising through children poses the special problem of linking the child's desire for the product with the parent's purchase decision, it is apparently an effective way to sell certain products. From the frequency with which ads for sugared foods and toys, for example, are targeted to children, we can conclude that some companies believe they sell more toys and sweets by advertising to children than by advertising to adults. This must mean that many children ask their parents to buy toys and sweets they see advertised on television and that a significant number of parents accede to these requests. Although toys, sweets, and fast-food restaurants are the staples of children's advertising, they are not the only products promoted through children. Other snack foods and items like records are also targeted to children.[31] It has even been suggested that child-oriented advertising may be more effective than adult advertising for some adult products.[32]

The sales success attributed to children's advertising is thus apparently based on children requesting advertised products they would not otherwise request and on parents purchasing items they would not otherwise purchase — either because they would not have known about the advertised product or because they would not have purchased it had it not been requested by the child. Research seems to support the conclusion that there is a positive relationship between children's television viewing and purchase requests. Both experiments and surveys show that exposure to advertising increases the number of requests children make: heavier viewers make more requests.[33]

From the advertiser's perspective, there are three critical points in the process by which children's television advertising works: (1) the point at which the child develops a desire for the advertised product; (2) the point at which the child requests the product; and (3) the point at which the parent purchases the product. The first steps, getting the child to want the product and to request it, are facilitated by children's natural suggestibility. As noted earlier, children want a large proportion of the items advertised to them. They also tend to make more purchase requests as they watch more television. Their natural suggestibility and enthusiasm for the products advertised to them can be attributed largely to their lack of familiarity with concepts of cost or worth, to their lack of knowledge or understanding of the economic resources available to them, and to their youthful concepts of self, time, and money that I elaborated earlier. They neither understand their own preferences nor recognize a distinction between what they want and what they are willing to pay for.

Compared with product desires advertising stimulates among mature viewers, children's consumer desires are quite unsophisticated. Mature viewers generally regard advertising critically, noting missing information and possible exaggerations.[34] Their interest in a product, even if initially aroused by an advertisement, is nevertheless tempered by an understanding, not necessarily explicit or even conscious, that the product will cost money and by some evaluation of its merits in relation to its cost and in relation to other possible expenditures. Children's consumer desires lack this background complexity. They are not informed by considerations of value or worth, nor by an understanding of a product's relationship to longer-term and future desires. Even though children's product desires are in this sense "raw" and certainly do not reflect genuine consumer judgment, they are full-fledged desires that frequently lead children to ask their parents to buy the product.

The final step in the children's advertising process — the parents' decision to buy — is actually the most critical one. No matter how effectively an ad arouses children's interest in a product, the ad is not effective from a business standpoint unless parents are motivated and financially equipped to make the purchase. Judging from the widespread use of children's advertising, however, many parents do decide to satisfy their children's purchase requests. The rationale behind children's advertising is that parents who would not otherwise buy a product will do so if their children request it.

Parents' responsiveness to their children's purchase requests is attributable, I believe, to parents' natural inclination to satisfy their children's desires. Parents want to please their children in ways that elicit immediate and obvious happiness and, consequently, do not like to frustrate their children's desires. The disposition to honor children's present desires reflects the affection parents feel for their children and the positive value placed on shared emotional experiences. Parents' inclinations to see their children's immediate desires satisfied and to share the resulting, if temporary, delight operate quite independently of parental desires to see their children's interests maximally satisfied over the longer term. Sometimes parental desires for children's immediate pleasure and for their long-term well-being conflict. It is frequently necessary to refuse children's requests for the sake of their own longer-term or future desires, and it would be irrational, if not irresponsible, not to do so.[35]

It is up to parents to provide the consumer judgments their children are incapable of making. Every purchase decision parents face requires assessment from several points of view: from the perspective of the family budget, other comparable products, and the interests and needs of various family members. But when a child initiates a consumer decision by making a request, a new factor is introduced. In addition to all the considerations that would be relevant had the potential purchase come directly to the parent's attention, the parent must also take into account the child's express desire for the item and the parent's own predisposition to satisfy that desire. The child's potential unhappiness over the denial of the request is not the critical factor, although, by the same token, the strength of the child's desire for the product should not be totally ignored.

This review of the process through which children's advertising works indicates that advertising directed to children affects the consumer decisions faced by parents in two main ways. It increases the number of requests to which they must respond, and it alters the factors relevant to their purchase decisions. The effectiveness of advertising via children is attributable to the ease with which indiscriminate children lacking concepts to evaluate economic worth are persuaded to want what they see and parents' natural inclination to satisfy their children's desires. These factors in combination account for the fact that products that would not attract the attention of or withstand the scrutiny of many potential adult purchasers can nevertheless be sold to them through their children. A parent may buy what he regards as a worthless or overpriced item when requested by his child, provided that it is not too costly in absolute terms and its purchase would not seriously interfere with other parental desires, whereas the same parent may not buy the product on the basis of its merits assessed independently of the child's wishes.[36] The child's request itself introduces a new factor into the parent's decision.

To facilitate discussion, I want to classify the reasons a parent might have for purchasing an item into two categories. "Child-satisfaction" reasons are those which stem from the parent's desire to satisfy the child's request. "Product-related" reasons are those which would govern the parent's purchase decision in the absence of the child's request. Product-related reasons are not necessarily unrelated to the child. This category might include the product's value for developing the child's interests and capacities or the parent's belief that the child would like the product, as well as more general financial considerations.

Employing this vocabulary, we can now say that increased sales resulting from children's advertising can be attributed in part to parents' child-satisfaction motivation. Even when parents have no product-related motivation to purchase a product, their child-satisfaction desires may be strong enough to supply the motivation to buy. Children's advertising may also promote sales by channeling to parents information that would not otherwise reach them. Parents may buy items they hear of through their children for product-related reasons and not only for child-satisfaction reasons.

Given the variety of consumer preferences, we can assume that both explanations of the success of children's advertising are operative. Certainly there may be some occasions on which parents are glad to learn of products their children point out and willingly buy them for product-related reasons. However, it would be unwarranted to assume that most, or even a large proportion, of the increased sales resulting from children's advertising can be explained by children's drawing attention to products their parents want to buy for product-related reasons. Parents' natural inclinations to look out for their children's welfare and to satisfy their children's desires guarantee that they will be generally attentive and receptive to consumer goods available to express those dispositions. It is much more likely that the greater share of increased sales resulting from children's advertising is attributable to the child-satisfaction motivations supplied by children's requests.

THE EFFECTS OF CHILDREN'S ADVERTISING ON CONSUMER SATISFACTION

This analysis of the process through which children's advertising works provides the backdrop for the critical question: Does child-focused advertising promote consumer satisfaction? Or is there some alternative that would make a greater contribution to consumer satisfaction?

Before looking at the effect of children's advertising on aggregate consumer satisfaction, I want to look at the consumers most directly affected — the child viewers and their parents. I have argued that children's television advertising introduces two new elements into a parent's purchase decision: it introduces the child's desire for the advertised item and it activates the parent's desire to satisfy the child. These two elements are added to the product-related considerations that would otherwise determine the parent's decision. Analysis of the effectiveness of children's television advertising suggests that the products advertised to children are those which would not sell as well if advertised directly to their parents. They are likely to be products many parents would not buy solely for product-related reasons, presumably because product considerations alone are not sufficiently compelling. This group — the parents who would not buy if not asked by their children — are the critical market for children's advertisers. If the products are ones which parents would buy without the motivations provided by their children's requests, advertising to children rather than directly to parents would have no incremental effect on sales.

Parents in the critical group face a difficult decision when advertising arouses their children's interests in consumer products. They must choose between acting on their product-related judgment and satisfying their children's requests for the products. As diagram I shows, if they do not or cannot buy for product-related reasons, they will frustrate their children's express wishes and their own wishes to please their children. On the other hand, yielding to their children's desires puts them in the position of acting against their own better judgment.

DIAGRAM I.   Child-Oriented Advertising

	Parent's Product-Related Desires	Parent's Child-Satisfaction Desires	Desire for Product
The parent chooses not to buy for product-related reasons.	S	U	U
The parent buys the product to satisfy the child but would not buy the same product on product-related grounds.	U	S	S

S = Satisfied; U = Unsatisfied.

From the point of view of consumer satisfaction the parent's product-related judgment ought to prevail.[37] In contrast to the child's raw desire for the product, the parent's product-related desire is presumably based on a genuine consumer judgment informed by considerations of economic value and by appreciation of the child's longer-term and future interests. The parent's product-related judgment more closely approximates an evaluation of the product's contribution to consumer satisfaction than does the child's desire for the product. Because of the limitations described earlier, the child's desire cannot be assumed to represent a judgment of the product's worth to him.

From the perspective of the intensity of their children's desires, however, parents may be inclined to grant their children's requests. Parents who exercise their best consumer judgment and deny their children's requests may find that as a result their children experience unhappiness, anger, or disappointment.[38] Parents thus face a difficult choice: even if acting on their product-related judgment will maximize consumer satisfaction over the longer term, consumer desires will be thwarted whether they accede to or deny their children's requests.

As noted earlier, advertisers presumably direct commercials to children because they believe it is the most effective way to sell their products. I suggested that the resultant increase in sales can be accounted for at least in part by children's receptivity to persuasion and by the desire of parents to accommodate their children. If it is correct to assume that the products advertised are those which many adults would not buy solely for product-related reasons and that television advertising increases the number of purchase requests to which parents must respond, then for some parents child-oriented advertising has the effect of increasing the number of occasions on which they rationally and ethically ought to deny their children's requests.

From the standpoint of consumer satisfaction, child-oriented advertising has some serious drawbacks. For a significant number of children and their parents it introduces sources of frustration that would not exist if children's products were advertised to adults or not advertised on television at all. The dissatisfactions that these children and parents experience when parents deny their children's product requests and the dissatisfactions that follow when parents grant product requests against their better judgment would be lessened if child-oriented advertising were eliminated. Without child-focused advertising, parents would less frequently face the necessity to choose between their children's consumer requests and their own consumer judgments. While it is certainly true that children may develop desires for products they see advertised in ads not directed to them, the likelihood that those desires will be stimulated is greatly enhanced when the ads are child-focused.[39]

Adam Smith's hypothesis of the invisible hand suggests that profitability or sales is an indicator of a company's success in satisfying consumers. Regardless of whether this is true as a general matter,[40] it appears that increased sales and increased consumer satisfaction do not correspond when those sales are achieved through child-oriented advertising. Additional sales resulting from child-focused advertising are accompanied by increased consumer satisfaction when parents' consumer judgments correspond with their children's requests. But when, as is frequently the case, increased sales do not reflect such correspondence, the net effect on consumer satisfaction is negative. Taking into account the additional disappointment children experience when their requests are denied leads to the conclusion that, on balance, child-oriented advertising detracts from rather than adds to consumer satisfaction.

Some supporters of children's television advertising argue that parental opposition is based on parents' weakness or their reluctance to stand up to their children by refusing consumer requests. They argue that children will be better off if parents refuse their children's requests and somewhat disingenuously advise parents to do so.[41] While urging parents to deny their children's requests is sound advice in a world where children's advertising exists, it is not an effective response to the argument that children's advertising should not encourage the requests in the first place. As I have tried to show, child viewers and their parents would be better off still if there were no child-focused advertising. Moreover, the proffered advice to parents puts advertisers in the rather peculiar and morally questionable position of deliberately stimulating in children desires that they acknowledge ought to be denied. If advertisers sincerely believed that the parents' decisions on the merits of children's products ought to prevail, would they not then advertise directly to the parents?

I have suggested that the principle of consumer sovereignty should lead advertisers to prefer adult-oriented advertising over children's advertising. But it may be objected that children may want and request products they see advertised even though the ads are not targeted to them. Does my argument suggest that advertisers ought for this reason to stop advertising altogether?

Advertising, as I indicated earlier, plays a very important role in our economic system. Advertising assists consumers in shaping their preferences and in acting on them. Its function is accomplished most satisfactorily when it is addressed to mature consumers. Even with the negative aspects of adult-focused advertising resulting when children are influenced by it, consumers — children and adults alike — are better off with it than without it. Of course, some forms of advertising are more desirable, effective, or tasteful than others. The consumer benefits that result from advertising to children could be produced with diminished attendant costs to consumer satisfaction through adult-oriented advertising. The argument developed here does not lead to the abolition of advertising altogether. It leads to concentrating on developing the kinds of advertising that make the greatest contributions to consumer satisfaction.

The effects of children's advertising on consumer satisfaction actually extend far beyond the child viewers of commercials and their parents. We have seen that when advertising to children works to the advantage of advertisers it does so in part because some parents act contrary to their product-related judgments and satisfy their children's purchase requests. These purchases contribute to the advertiser's sales goals but do not represent increased consumer satisfaction. Since the market responds to consumer behavior and not to actual consumer satisfaction, such purchases contribute ultimately to the misallocation of resources. Resources that would otherwise be utilized to produce goods of greater value to consumers will be channeled into the production of less desirable goods, diminishing the welfare of many consumers as well as of companies that would flourish within a more efficient market.

CONSUMER RESPONSIBILITY AND ADVERTISING TO CHILDREN

In order for the market to fulfill its potential as an efficient allocator of resources, producers, advertisers, and consumers all must do their part. I have argued that in their role as purveyors of information and shapers of consumer preferences, advertisers ought to try to enhance consumer satisfaction. There are numerous ways they can do this: by avoiding advertising to children; by providing truthful product information; by not encouraging unrealistic product expectations. They can also enhance consumer satisfaction by encouraging responsible consumer behavior through the focus and content of their ads.

As my argument against children's advertising suggests, consumers, too, bear responsibility for the market's effectiveness in providing them what they want. At the very least, consumers should spend their money in ways that accurately reflect their preferences. This consumer responsibility is actually rather difficult to fulfill and more complex than it first appears. It requires understanding what one's desires actually are — sorting out priorities, identifying conflicting desires, understanding and anticipating how one's desires will change over time, and allocating one's economic resources to reflect these desires. In addition to a high level of self-awareness and self-control, responsible consumer behavior also requires knowledge of the range of available products and of the components of quality in the product desired — or at least recognition of the risk involved in failing to acquire this information. To the extent that consumers fail to align their expenditures with their preferences, the market becomes increasingly inefficient. It will generate goods and services to satisfy the preferences consumers express through their pocketbook rather than their actual preferences.

When consumers are confused about their preferences, the market's response will be confused. An example drawn from the service sector will illustrate the point. Consumers of child-care services repeatedly deplore the shortage of high-quality care-givers — both institutional and individual — while at the same time offering low wages to individual care-givers and refusing to pay institutional fees adequate to attract superior teachers. People's actual preferences and priorities are unclear. Do they give highest priority to what they say they prefer — quality child care — or to the preferences they express through their market behavior — cheap child care?

This view of consumer responsibility imposes special obligations on parents whose children are too young to exercise responsible consumer judgment. These parents should take special care to evaluate their children's consumer requests and to provide their children with a model of responsible consumer conduct. As their children mature, parents should teach their children the elements of responsible consumer behavior.

Without denying the responsibilities of consumers for their own behavior and for the effects of their behavior on the market, one can also acknowledge the responsibilities of advertisers to encourage responsible consumerism or, at the very least, not to discourage it. Television ads targeted to children diminish consumer satisfaction, as I argued earlier. They also discourage responsible consumer behavior through their implication that children, who lack the essential capacities necessary for responsible consumer decisions, are nevertheless capable of making such decisions. In addition, child-directed advertising discourages responsible consumer decisions among parents by making those decisions harder.

CHILDREN'S ADVERTISING AND BASIC ETHICAL PRINCIPLES

My evaluation of children's advertising has proceeded from the principle of consumer sovereignty, a principle of rather narrow application. Unlike more general ethical principles, like the principle of veracity, the principle of consumer sovereignty applies in the specialized area of business. Addressing the issue of children's advertising from the perspective of special business norms rather than more general ethical principles avoids the problem of deciding whether the specialized or more general principles should have priority in the moral reasoning of business people.[42] Nevertheless, children's advertising could also be evaluated from the standpoint of the more general ethical principles requiring veracity and fairness and prohibiting harmful conduct.

Veracity

The principle of veracity, understood as devotion to truth, is much broader than
a principle prohibiting deception. Deception, the primary basis of the FTC's
complaint against children's advertising, is only one way of infringing the
principle of veracity. Both critics and defenders of children's advertising agree
that advertisers should not intentionally deceive children and that they should
engage in research to determine whether children are misled by their ads. The
central issue regarding veracity and children's advertising, however, does not
relate to deception so much as to the strength of advertisers' devotion to truth.
Advertisers generally do not make false statements intended to mislead children. Nevertheless, the particular nature of children's conceptual worlds makes
it exceedingly likely that child-oriented advertising will generate false beliefs or
highly improbable product expectations.

Research shows that young children have difficulty differentiating fantasy
and reality[43] and frequently place indiscriminate trust in commercial characters
who present products to them.[44] They also develop false beliefs about the
selling characters in ads[45] and in some cases have unreasonably optimistic
beliefs about the satisfactions advertised products will bring them.[46]

This research indicates that concern about the misleading nature of children's advertising is legitimate. Any parent knows — even one who has not
examined the research — that young children are easily persuaded of the existence of fantasy characters. They develop (what seem to their parents) irrational
fears and hopes from stories they hear and experiences they misinterpret. The
stories and fantasies children see enacted in television commercials receive the
same generous and idiosyncratic treatment as other information. Children's
interpretations of advertising claims are as resistant to parental correction as
their other fantasies are. One can only speculate on the nature and validity of the
beliefs children adopt as a result of watching, for example, a cartoon depicting a
pirate captain's magical discovery of breakfast cereal. Certainly, many ads are
designed to create expectations that fun, friendship, and popularity will accompany possession of the advertised product. The likelihood that such expectations will be fulfilled is something young children cannot assess.

To the extent that children develop false beliefs and unreasonable expectations as a result of viewing commercials, moral reservations about children's
advertising are justified. To the extent advertisers know that children develop
false beliefs and unreasonable expectations, advertisers' devotion to truth and to
responsible consumerism are suspect.

Fairness and Respect for Children

The fact that children's advertising benefits advertisers while at the same time
nourishing false beliefs, unreasonable expectations, and irresponsible consumer desires among children calls into play principles of fairness and respect.
Critics have said that child-oriented advertising takes advantage of children's
limited capacities and their suggestibility for the benefit of the advertisers. As
expressed by Michael Pertschuk, former chairman of the FTC, advertisers
"seize on the child's trust and exploit it as weakness for their gain."[47] To
employ as the unwitting means to the parent's pocketbook children who do not
understand commercial exchange, who are unable to evaluate their own con-

sumer preferences, and who consequently cannot make consumer decisions based on those preferences does indeed reflect a lack of respect for children. Such a practice fails to respect children's limitations as consumers, and instead capitalizes on them. In the language of Kant, advertisers are not treating children as "ends in themselves": they are treating children solely as instruments for their own gain.

In response to the charge of unfairness, supporters of children's advertising sometimes point out that the children are protected because their parents exercise control over the purse strings.[48] This response demonstrates failure to appreciate the basis of the unfairness charge. It is not potential economic harm that concerns critics: it is the attitude toward children reflected in the use of children's advertising that is central. As explained earlier, the attitude is inappropriate or unfitting.

Another frequent response to the charge of unfairness is that children actually do understand advertising.[49] A great deal of research has focused on whether children distinguish programs from commercials, whether they remember product identities, whether they distinguish program characters from commercial characters, and whether they recognize the persuasive intent of commercials.[50] But even showing that children "understand" advertising in all these ways would not demonstrate that children have the consumer capacities that would make it fair to advertise to them. The critical questions are not whether children can distinguish commercial characters from program characters,[51] or even whether they recognize persuasive intent, but whether they have the concepts of self, time, and money that would make it possible for them to make considered consumer decisions about the products they see advertised. Indeed, if children recognize that commercials are trying to sell things but lack the concepts to assess and deliberate about the products advertised, the charge that advertisers are "using" children or attempting to use them to sell their wares is strengthened. Intuitively, it seems that if children were sophisticated enough to realize that the goods advertised on television are for sale, they would be more likely than their younger counterparts to request the products.[52]

Harm to Children

Another principle to which appeal has been made by critics of television advertising is the principle against causing harm. The harmful effects of children's advertising are thought to include the parent-child conflicts generated by parental refusals to buy requested products, the unhappiness and anger suffered by children whose parents deny their product requests, the unhappiness children suffer when advertising-induced expectations of product performance are disappointed, and unhappiness experienced by children exposed to commercials portraying life-styles more affluent than their own.[53]

Replies to the charge that children's advertising is harmful to children have pinpointed weaknesses in the claim. One supporter of children's advertising says that the "harm" to children whose parents refuse their requests has not been adequately documented.[54] Another, claiming that some experts believe conflicts over purchases are instructive in educating children to make choices, denies that parent-child conflict is harmful.[55] As these replies suggest, demonstrating that children's advertising is harmful to children, as distinct from being misleading or unfair to them, involves much more than showing that it has the effects enumerated. Agreement about the application of the principle against causing harm depends on conceptual as well as factual agreement. A conception of harm must first be elaborated, and it must be shown to include these or other effects of advertising. It is not obvious, for example, that unhappiness resulting from exposure to more different life-styles is in the long run harmful.

Research indicates that children's advertising does contribute to the outcomes noted.[56] Certainly, child-oriented television advertising is not the sole cause of these effects, but it does appear to increase their frequency and even perhaps their intensity.[57] I believe that a conception of harm including some of these effects could be developed, but I will not attempt to do so here. I mention this argument rather to illustrate another general ethical principle on which an argument against children's advertising might be based.

A NOTE ON MORAL THEORY

My analysis of the ethical status of child-oriented advertising has proceeded from what Professor R. M. Hare has called "first-level" moral principles, generally accepted ethical principles that guide us in our daily lives as workers, family members, and members of the human community.[58] Without attempting to justify the principles of consumer sovereignty, honesty, respect, and nonmaleficence, I have tried to show how they bear on children's advertising. In order to justify the principles I have relied on, it would be necessary to engage in the sort of moral reasoning Professor Hare has called "second-level" or "critical" moral reasoning. I have here omitted this critical reasoning to avoid straying too far from the central theme of children's advertising.

CONCLUSION

How might advertisers implement their responsibilities to promote consumer satisfaction and consumer responsibility and satisfy the principles of veracity, fairness, and nonmaleficence? There are degrees of compliance with these principles: some marketing strategies will do more than others to enhance consumer satisfaction, for example. One way compliance can be improved is by eliminating child-oriented television advertising for children's products and substituting advertising geared to mature consumers. Rather than employing the techniques found in advertising messages targeted to children under eleven,[59] advertisers could include product information that would interest adult viewers and devise ways to let child viewers know that consumer decisions require responsible decisionmaking skills. If much of the information presented is incomprehensible to the five-year-olds in the audience, so much the better.[60] When they reach the age at which they begin to understand consumer decisionmaking, they will perhaps have greater respect for the actual complexity of their responsibilities as consumers.

The problems of child-oriented advertising can best be dealt with if advertisers themselves recognize the inappropriateness of targeting children for commercial messages. I have tried to show why, within the context of a free market economy, the responsibilities of advertisers to promote consumer satisfaction and not to discourage responsible consumer decisions should lead advertisers away from child-oriented advertising. The problem of what types of ads are appropriate given these constraints provides a challenging design problem for the many creative people in the advertising industry. With appropriate inspiration and incentives, I do not doubt that they can meet the challenge.

Whether appropriate inspiration and incentives will be forthcoming is more doubtful. Children's advertising seems well entrenched and is backed by powerful economic forces,[61] and it is clear that some advertisers do not recognize, or are unwilling to acknowledge, the ethical problems of child-focused advertising.[62] The trend toward programming designed around selling characters is especially discouraging.

Even advertisers who recognize that eliminating child-oriented advertising will promote consumer satisfaction and consumer responsibility may be reluctant to reorient their advertising campaigns because of the costs and risks of doing so. Theoretically, only advertisers whose products would not withstand the scrutiny of adult consumers should lose sales from such a reorientation. It is clear that in the short run a general retreat from children's advertising would result in some lost revenues for makers, advertisers, and retail sellers of products that do not sell as well when advertised to adults. It is also possible that television networks, stations, and entrenched producers of children's shows would lose revenues and that children's programming might be jeopardized by the lack of advertisers' interest in commercial time during children's programs.

On the other hand, a shift away from children's advertising to adult advertising could result in even more pressure on existing adult commercial time slots, driving up their prices to a level adequate to subsidize children's programming without loss to the networks. And there are alternative means of financing children's television that could be explored.[63] The extent to which lost revenues and diminished profits would result from recognizing the ethical ideals I have described is largely a question of the ability of all the beneficiaries of children's television advertising to respond creatively. The longer-term effect of relinquishing child-focused advertising would be to move manufacturers, advertisers, and retailers in the direction of products that would not depend for their success on the suggestibility and immaturity of children. In the longer run, the result would be greater market efficiency.

Notes

*An earlier version of this paper was delivered at a workshop on advertising ethics at the University of Florida in April 1984. I want to thank Robert Baum for organizing the workshop and to express my appreciation to all the workshop participants who commented on my paper, but especially to Katherine Clancy, Susan Elliott, Kathleen Henderson, Betsy Hilbert, Craig Shulstad, and Rita Weisskoff. I also want to acknowledge the helpful criticisms of Eric Douglas, Paul Farris, and Anita Niemi.

1. Richard P. Adler, "Children's Television Advertising: History of the Issue," in *Children and the Faces of Television*, ed. Edward L. Palmer and Aimee Dorr (New York: Academic Press, 1980), p. 241; hereafter cited as Palmer and Dorr.

2. Adler, p. 243.

3. Daniel Seligman, "The Commercial Crisis," *Fortune* 108 (November 14, 1983):39.

4. For discussion of the constitutionality of banning children's advertising, see C. Edwin

Baker, "Commercial Speech: A Problem in the Theory of Freedom," *Iowa Law Review* 62 (October 1976):I; Martin H. Redish, "The First Amendment in the Marketplace: Commercial Speech and the Values of Free Expression," *George Washington Law Review* 39 (1970–1971):429; Gerald J. Thain, "The 'Seven Dirty Words' Decision: A Potential Scrubbrush for Commercials on Children's Television?" *Kentucky Law Journal* 67 (1978–1979):947.

5. This point has been made by others. See, e.g., Ronald Dworkin, "Taking Rights Seriously," in *Taking Rights Seriously* (Cambridge, MA: Harvard University Press, 1977), pp. 188ff.

6. Susan Bartlett Foote and Robert H. Mnookin, "The 'Kid Vid' Crusade," *Public Interest* 61 (Fall 1980):91.

7. One survey of adults found the following attitudes to children's commercials: strongly negative (23%); negative (50%); neutral (23%); positive (4%). These negative attitudes are most pronounced among parents of kindergarten-age children. The survey is cited in Thomas S. Robertson, "Television Advertising and Parent–Child Relations," in *The Effects of Television Advertising on Children*, ed. Richard P. Adler, Gerald S. Lesser, Laurene Krasny Meringoff, et al. (Lexington, MA: Lexington Books, 1980), p. 197; hereafter cited as Adler et al.

8. E.g., M. Carole Macklin, "Do Children Understand TV Ads?" *Journal of Advertising Research* 23 (February-March 1983):63–70; Thomas Robertson and John Rossiter, "Children and Commercial Persuasion: An Attribution Theory Analysis," *Journal of Consumer Research* 1 (June 1974):13–20. See also summaries of research in David Pillemer and Scott Ward, "Investigating the Effects of Television Advertising on Children: An Evaluation of the Empirical Studies," Draft read to American Psychological Assn., Div. 23, San Francisco, California, August 1977; John R. Rossiter, "The Effects of Volume and Repetition of Television Commercials," in Adler et al., pp. 160–162; Ellen Wartella, "Individual Differences in Children's Responses to Television Advertising," in Palmer and Dorr, pp. 312–314.

9. Wartella, p. 313.

10. Compare the definition of "child-oriented television advertising" adopted by the FTC in its Final Staff Report and Recommendation: "advertising which is in or adjacent to programs either directed to children or programs where children constitute a substantial portion of the audience." See "FTC Final Staff Report and Recommendation," *In the Matter of Children's Advertising*, 43 *Federal Register* 17967, March 31, 1981, p. 2.

11. *Self-Regulatory Guidelines for Children's Advertising*, by Children's Advertising Review Unit, Council of Better Business Bureaus, Inc., 3d ed. (New York, 1983), p. 6.

12. F. Earle Barcus, "The Nature of Television Advertising to Children," in Palmer and Dorr, pp. 276–277.

13. Barcus, p. 275.

14. Research has been developed to support advertisers targeting child audiences. See, e.g., Gene Reilly Group, Inc., *The Child* (Darien, CT: The Child, Inc., 1973), cited in Robert B. Choate, "The Politics of Change," in Palmer and Dorr, p. 329.

15. Thomas Donaldson and Patricia H. Werhane, *Ethical Issues in Business* (Englewood Cliffs, NJ: Prentice-Hall, Inc., 1979), p. 294. In a telephone interview a representative of Fisher-Price's advertising agency told me that Fisher-Price continues to focus its advertising on parents because most Fisher-Price toys appeal to the very young.

16. See "FTC Final Staff Report and Recommendation," pp. 21–22, n. 51, for a description of studies by Atkin and White. Atkin found that 90% of the three-year-olds studied and 73% of the seven-year-olds thought that selling characters like them. White found that 82% of a group of four- to seven-year-olds thought that the selling figures ate the products they advertised and wanted the children to do likewise.

17. Studies indicate that there is very limited use of product information in children's television advertising. Predominant are "appeals to psychological states, associations with established values, and unsupported assertions about the qualities of the products"; Barcus, p. 279.

18. Submission before the FTC, 1978, quoted in Emilie Griffin, "The Future Is Inevitable: But Can It Be Shaped in the Interest of Children?" in Palmer and Dorr, p. 347.

19. Griffin, p. 344.

20. E.g., Frances L. Ilg, Louise Bates Ames, and Sidney M. Baker, *Child Behavior*, rev. ed. (New York: Harper & Row, 1981).

21. On the child's conception of time, see Jean Piaget, *The Child's Conception of Time* (New York: Basic Books, 1970).

22. Some intriguing illustrations of children's philosophical questions and observations are recounted in Gareth B. Matthews, *Philosophy and the Young Child* (Cambridge, MA: Harvard University Press, 1980).

23. "FTC Final Staff Report and Recommendation," pp. 27–28, citing the work of Geis.

24. My five-year-old son reasoned thus to explain why a five-dollar piano would be too expensive.

25. Toys, cereals, and candies are the products most heavily promoted to children; Barcus, pp. 275–276.

26. The FTC concluded on the basis of relevant literature that children tend to want whatever products are advertised on television; "FTC Final Staff Report and Recommendation," p. 8. For data on the extent to which children want what they see advertised on television, see Charles K. Atkin, "Effects of Television Advertising on Children," in Palmer and Dorr, pp. 289–290.

27. The results of one study of children's understanding of television advertising messages suggested that although "parents cannot 'force' early sophistication in children's reactions to television advertising, their attention and instruction can enhance the process." Focusing on children's capacities to understand advertising rather than on their capacities to make decisions, the article supports the general proposition that the child's conceptual world differs in many ways from that of the adult. The critical question is, of course: even if we can promote earlier understanding of advertising and consumer decisions, should we do so? See John R. Rossiter and Thomas S. Robertson, "Canonical Analysis of Developmental, Social, and Experimental Factors in Children's Comprehension of Television Advertising," *Journal of Genetic Psychology* 129 (1976):326.

28. For discussion of consumer sovereignty, see Norman Bowie, *Business Ethics* (Englewood Cliffs, NJ: Prentice-Hall, Inc., 1982), pp. 80–88.

29. Gene Reilly Group, Inc., advising advertisers who target children, says that "the mother can simply be a 'purchasing agent' for the child"; quoted in Choate, p. 329.

30. Paul W. Farris and John A. Quelch, *Advertising and Promotion Management* (Radnor, PA: Chilton Book Co., 1983), p. 2.

31. Barcus, pp. 275–276.

32. William Melody, *Children's Television* (New Haven: Yale University Press, 1973), pp. 79–80.

33. Atkin, pp. 290–291; Thomas S. Robertson, "Television Advertising and Parent-Child Relations" in Adler et al., pp. 204–207.

34. "FTC Final Staff Report and Recommendation," pp. 22–23, cites work of Roberts to support the notion that adults "counter-argue" when faced with commercial messages.

35. Herbert Spencer cautioned against "the selfishness of affection which sacrifices the higher interests of a child to gain immediate pleasurable emotion"; *The Principles of Ethics*, vol. 2, sec. 434 (1897; rpt. Indianapolis, IN: Liberty Classics, 1978), p. 361.

36. One study found that a parent will pay 20% more for an advertised product with child appeal—even when a less expensive, nonadvertised product is no different; Melody, p. 80.

37. Atkin, p. 301. Toys and candies are denied more often than cereals. It is estimated that parents reject one-third to one-half of children's requests for products.

38. About one-third to one-half of the children involved in various research projects became unhappy, angry, or expressed disappointment after denials of food and toy requests. The rate was considerably higher among heavy television viewers; Atkin, pp. 299–301.

39. This is certainly the belief underlying advertisers' use of child-oriented advertising. See Melvin Helitzer and Carl Heyel, *The Youth Market: Its Dimensions, Influence and Opportunities for You* (New York: Media Books, 1970), cited in Melody, pp. 79–80.

40. For criticism of the view that profit maximization guarantees maximal satisfaction of consumer wants, see Alan H. Goldman, *The Moral Foundations of Professional Ethics* (Totowa, NJ: Rowman and Littlefield, 1980), pp. 247–257.

41. *Comments of M & M/Mars, Children's Television Advertising Trade Regulation Rule-Making Proceeding*, Federal Trade Commission (November 1978), pp. 4–5 and 67.

42. For general discussion of this issue see Goldman, chap. 5.

43. See T. G. Bever, M. L. Smith, B. Bengen, and T. G. Johnson, "Young Viewers' Troubling Response to TV Ads," *Harvard Business Review*, November-December 1975, pp. 109–120.

44. "FTC Final Staff Report and Recommendation," pp. 21–22, n. 51, describes the work of Atkin supporting the conclusion that children trust selling characters. Atkin found in a group of three- to seven-year-olds that 70% of the three-year-olds and 60% of the seven-year-olds trusted the characters about as much as they trusted their mothers.

45. "FTC Final Staff Report and Recommendation," at pp. 21–22, n. 51, describes the work of White, who found that many children in a group of four- to seven-year-olds she studied believe that the selling figures eat the advertised products and want the children to do likewise and that the selling figures want the children to eat things that are good for them.

46. Atkin, p. 300.

47. Quoted in Foote and Mnookin, p. 92.

48. June Esserman of Child Research Services, Inc., quoted in *Comments of M & M/Mars*, p. 4.

49. *Comments of M & M/Mars*, p. 5. See also Macklin, n. 8, *supra*.

50. See n. 8, *supra*.

51. For a similar view of the relevance of children's ability to distinguish commercial characters from program characters, see Scott Ward, "Compromise in Commercials for Children," *Harvard Business Review*, November-December 1978, p. 133.

52. Recent research indicates that as children become more aware of advertising's persuasive intent, the frequency of their requests does not decline. This finding is contrary to earlier research purportedly showing that awareness of persuasive intent leads to a decline in number of requests; Rossiter, pp. 163–165.

53. Atkin, pp. 298–301.

54. Foote and Mnookin, p. 95.

55. *Comments of M & M/Mars*, p. 64. Cf. n. 27, *supra*.

56. Atkin, pp. 298–301. See also Scott Ward and Daniel B. Wackman, "Children's Purchase Influence Attempts and Parental Yielding," *Journal of Marketing Research*, August 1972, p. 318.

57. For example, one study found that heavy viewers of Saturday morning television got into more arguments with their parents over toy and cereal denials than did light viewers; Atkin, pp. 298–301. See also Ward and Wackman, p. 318.

58. R. M. Hare, *Moral Thinking* (Oxford: Clarendon Press, 1981).

59. The majority of advertising directed to children is targeted to children two-to-eleven or six-to-eleven years of age; "FTC Final Staff Report and Recommendation," p. 46.

60. For the view that children's special capacities and limitations should be respected but that children should not be "contained" in a special children's world isolated from that of adults, see Valerie Polakow Suransky, *The Erosion of Childhood* (Chicago: University of Chicago Press, 1982).

61. It was estimated that the coalition established to fight the FTC proceedings in 1978 put together a "war chest" of $15–30 million. According to news reports the coalition included several huge law firms, the national advertising association, broadcasters and their associations, the U.S. Chamber of Commerce, the Grocery Manufacturers of America, the sugar association, the chocolate and candy manufacturers, cereal companies and their associations, and more; Choate, p. 334. It is interesting to note that supporters of children's advertising tend not to be people who spend a great deal of time with children.

62. "In the area of children's products, the U.S. is an advertiser's paradise compared with many countries"; Christopher Campbell, International Marketing Director at the Parker Brothers subsidiary of General Mills, quoted in Ronald Alsop, "Countries' Different Ad Rules Are Problem for Global Firms," *Wall Street Journal*, September 27, 1984, p. 33. According to Alsop, "The other countries' aim is to protect kids from exploitation."

63. It is interesting to note that in 1949 42% of the children's programs broadcast were presented without advertiser sponsorship; Melody, p. 36.

DISCUSSION QUESTIONS

1. Arrington defends advertising by denying that it controls consumer behavior. Reflecting on your personal experience, decide whether Arrington's denial is accurate.

2. In the course of his discussion, Lippke refers to John Kenneth Galbraith's contention that advertising creates desires rather than responds to them. Do you find that advertising ever does this to you? If so, are these desires strong enough to lead you to buy something you otherwise would not have?

3. Part of Lippke's assault on advertising is that it encourages bad thinking. He writes, for example, "Ads subtly encourage the propensity to accept emotional appeals, oversimplification, superficiality, and shoddy standards of proof for claims." Do you agree with this accusation? Even if it is true, does it lead to any great harm to an individual or to society? Does this make advertising ethically suspect?

4. Waide offers an unusual and particularly interesting criticism of advertising by claiming that associative advertising makes us more selfish and materialistic and less sensitive to others. Has advertising had that effect on you or others you know?

5. Paine argues that advertisers should refrain from directing commercials to young children. Do you agree? What is your opinion of cartoon programs whose featured characters are used to promote products? Do you think that this practice takes unfair advantage of children?

CASE 13.1

Airfares

The airline industry is perennially under fire for its advertisements. Consumer groups regularly charge that airfare ads are misleading and deceptive — and more like a huckster's "come-on" than an ethical advertisement. The average flier, critics contend, pays considerably more than the advertised fare.

One common complaint is that the advertised fare is only half the real cost; that is, it is only the one-way cost of a round-trip ticket. The large print in the center of the ad may list the fare between New York and San Francisco at $139. However, this fare is available only with the purchase of a round-trip ticket for $378. The actual one-way fare is a substantially higher $643. Industry critics argue that it is wrong for the airlines to advertise the low figure as a one-way fare when it is not actually available as such. They claim that this same practice would be illegal if, for example, a clothing store advertised shoes at $30 but would sell them only in $60 pairs.

A related complaint contends that the advertised fares invariably require certain conditions to be met: for instance, the fare is nonrefundable, the trip must include a Saturday night's stay, reservations must be made at least 14 days before departure, and the ticket must be purchased within 24 hours of making the reservation. Many, if not most, travelers cannot meet these conditions, and critics charge again that the advertisements describe products that are, for all practical purposes, unavailable to the average customer.

Industry defenders object to the criticism that the ads are misleading and point out that the ads do inform consumers about relevant restrictions. Some airlines do prominently display appropriate disclaimers. For example, in the middle of a Delta airlines ad is a large and readable "Fares are each way, based on round trip." But in most print ads, that information can be found only in the small print at the bottom of the page. And on television ads the conditions appear in an unreadable paragraph that appears in the commercial's final seconds.

The greatest controversy, however, revolves around an airline practice called *yield management*. This is a computer-based technique aimed at producing the greatest profit per flight by changing the mix of discount and full-fare seats as the day of departure draws closer. The airlines probably allot from 5 to 20 percent of their seats for the lowest advertised fares; then they work with the remaining seats until the flight takes off. The lowest fare available will thus depend on how the airline's computers and yield management specialists analyze the demand for a particular flight. If early demand is high, more seats will be held at the higher fares. If demand slackens, however, the airline will increase the number of seats at lower fares. The technology is so sophisticated that each flight is analyzed at least every 24 hours and as often as each hour to determine if the flight has the best combination of low- and high-price seats.

The consequence of yield management for consumers is that the lowest available fare on a particular flight may vary by hundreds of dollars from one day to the next. A traveler may buy a ticket for a flight on Monday at a higher fare, and the airline may decide on Wednesday that the flight will not fill unless it increases the number of lower fares. Thus, the earlier traveler will pay more than customers buying closer to departure. The airlines, of course, hope that the opposite will happen — that as departure approaches, more customers will be willing to pay the higher fare because they need that particular flight.

Critics of the practice claim that yield management is nothing more than a classic "bait and switch" practice. Again, they contrast the airlines' actions with those of other industries. In most retail stores, if an advertised item is sold out, customers are offered a raincheck or a similar or even superior product at the sale price. As Stephen Gardner, assistant attorney general for Texas, describes the situation, "Nobody except the airlines in this country right now can advertise something that they don't have at a price they wouldn't sell it to you for if they did have it." The only warning consumers have of this practice is a general disclaimer: "Fares may not be available on all flights and are subject to change." The airlines generally will not discuss yield management, but the practice can mean the difference between an airline's making and losing money at the end of a year. ◆

Discussion Questions

1. Are the criticisms against the airlines' advertising practices justified? Is it misrepresentation to advertise a one-way price if it is available only with a round-trip purchase?

2. If a fare requires a round-trip purchase or other conditions to be met, how prominently should those restrictions be stated in an advertisement?

3. Is there anything unethical about yield management? Is there anything wrong with selling two customers the same service for different prices?

4. As you have read, critics of the airlines argue that if other industries acted as the airlines do, they would be charged with breaking the law. Is this a fair comparison or is this argument based on a false analogy? An empty seat on an airline loses all value as soon as the plane takes off; that does not happen to a pair of shoes. Even if the shoes are no longer in fashion, they still have some value because the merchant can sell them at a steep discount. Can such differences justify variations in what would be considered ethical business practices between businesses that sell "hard goods" and those that sell a product whose value can change dramatically in a short time — for example, airlines, car rental companies, and sellers of food or other perishable goods?

5. Isn't yield management simply one of the clearest examples of prices varying by forces of supply and demand? If so, and if every traveler freely agrees to fly at the given price when he or she buys the ticket, is there any way to object to yield management?

Sources

Cowan, Alison Leigh, "Mirage of Discount Air Fares Is Frustrating to Many Fliers," *New York Times*, April 22, 1991, A1, D4.
Meier, Barry, "U.S. and States Trade Shots in Battle over Air-Fare Ads," *New York Times*, October 7, 1989, I, 48.

CASE 13.2

Sexual Persuasion

Few practices are so commonplace in contemporary advertising as using sex to sell a product. Even if the product has nothing to do with sex, advertisers will hint that purchasing it — the right car, perfume, alcohol, piece of clothing — will significantly improve our love lives. In fact, using sex to pitch everything from jeans to cologne is so common that most of us probably never question whether anything inappropriate is being done. Yet from an ethical perspective, this practice raises several questions: Does such advertising misrepresent the nature of the product? Does it thus make a false claim? Is the use of sex an ethically questionable attempt to manipulate buyers through appeals to the unconscious part of their personality?

Some ads use sex in an obvious and heavy-handed way. Beautiful women simply decorate an advertisement. Commodities such as automobiles, electronic equipment, and power tools are displayed by women whose beauty has nothing whatsoever to do with the product. The strategy is used to get the attention of a male audience — an attractive, provocatively dressed woman increases the odds that the ad will be read or watched. Of course, opponents of this practice argue that such ads use women strictly as sexual objects. And it might also be claimed that sexual response is an intensely personal part of our lives and should be respected as such, not used as the hook for catching the attention of an audience.

Other ads also use sex that is irrelevant to the product, but in this case they do so for shock value. Among the most famous examples are the nudes in ads for Calvin Klein products. First came the artistic Obsession ads in the 1980s. But then in 1991 came an advertising supplement for Calvin Klein jeans, a collection of 116 photographs that contained numerous provocative shots featuring nudity and lovemaking. Among the most striking was a shot that subsequently ran as an ad by itself — a man standing in the shower and barely covering his genitals with a pair of Calvin Klein jeans. Again, it can be asked whether this is an ethically appropriate use of human sexuality.

Other advertisements use sex in a way that at least relates to the product being sold. The cover illustrations on book jackets — whether they are Gothic romances, mysteries, or even science fiction novels — often portray a sexual event or character from the story. Similarly, provocative scenes that appear in the previews of motion pictures and on the packages of videocassettes do come from the films being promoted. Nonetheless, the book jackets and film clips usually suggest that the plot of the novel or film revolves around sex more than it actually does. This raises the question of whether the product is being misrepresented.

The issue of misrepresentation also arises with ads that include the product as an integral part of a pleasurable, romantic, or sexual event. Many beer ads, for example, are built around attractive young men and women flirting and enjoying themselves at beach parties or bars. Numerous print ads for cigarettes and hard alcohol do the same. Fragrance companies do this more blatantly than anyone else. The unmistakable implication is that smoking brand X, drinking cognac Y, or wearing perfume Z leads to the pleasure portrayed. Perhaps the message is that simply using the product will likely include us in activities that may lead to sex. Or are we to think that the product will even somehow make us more attractive sexually? It is highly unlikely, however, that either alcohol or cigarettes have sexual benefits. Although alcohol may initially lower inhibitions, drinking, at least among men, generally impairs, not enhances, sexual performance. Similarly, smoking can decrease the oral pleasure connected with sex because it dulls the sense of taste, and, as nonsmokers will attest, it makes kissing less pleasurable. And although people do wear perfume and cologne in romantic settings and in order to be more attractive, someone else will not decide to have sex with them just because of the scent they are wearing that night. When looked at in this light, then, we can ask whether these advertisements mislead the audience. Do they imply that products have properties that they actually lack? Do they at least exaggerate?

Advertisers would no doubt defend themselves by saying not only that these ads suggest no sexual benefits from using the product, but also that average consumers understand the ads for what they are — attempts to portray products favorably and to generate positive feelings toward them. Thus, advertisers hope that consumers will feel positive about beer *X* from seeing it being enjoyed by young, healthy, sexy people in swimsuits.

From an ethical standpoint, however, this is not an effective defense. It may answer the charge of misrepresentation, but it actually reinforces an accusation of manipulation. Sexually provocative ads aim to build an automatic, unthinking connection between the product and pleasure. The ads are designed not simply to portray a sexual situation, but to arouse the audience sexually, at least to a mild degree. Sex in these advertisements is thus used in an attempt to build a classic psychological association between the product and pleasurable feelings. The psychological association, of course, is not the Pavlovian "bell/saliva" relationship but one of "product *X*/sexual pleasure." When the consumer is shopping, the hope is that the sight of the product will act as a trigger; the erotic pleasure will be reexperienced; and the consumer, desiring more of the same, will buy the product.

It is the "automatic, unthinking" part of all of this that poses ethical problems. A sexual response to a sexy or provocative advertisement is generally beyond our conscious control, and this raises the issue of manipulation. Some critics of advertising even contend that some ads portray sexual symbols and images "subliminally," that is, in a way that registers only in the unconscious. And if this is true, the charge of manipulation would seem to be even stronger.

Surely no one suggests that sexy advertisements make consumers unthinking robots who cannot resist buying an expensive cologne. But if these ads simply weaken a customer's resistance because of the association between the product and sexual pleasure, the question of manipulation still remains. ◆

Discussion Questions

1. Is there anything ethically objectionable about using sex in advertisements?

2. Is it fair to interpret sexy advertisements as implying that the products in question will make us sexier and improve our love lives? Do the commercials claim something else? Or do they claim nothing?

3. Is it misrepresentation to suggest that alcohol or cigarettes will make us more appealing sexually?

4. What is your opinion of advertisements that seek to build a psychological association between a product and sexual pleasure? Is it wrong for an ad to appeal directly to a part of our being that we do not have complete and conscious control over? From an ethical standpoint, are either of these practices manipulative?

◆ ◆ ◆

ADDITIONAL READINGS

Beauchamp, Tom L, "Manipulative Advertising," *Business & Professional Ethics Journal*, 3, nos. 3 & 4 (1983) 1–22.

Crisp, Roger, "Persuasive Advertising, Autonomy, and the Creation of Desire," *Journal of Business Ethics*, 6 (1987), 413–418.

Galbraith, John Kenneth, "The Dependence Effect," in *The Affluent Society*, 4th ed. (New York: New American Library, 1984), 121–128.

Goldman, Alan, "Ethical Issues in Advertising," in *Just Business*, edited by Tom Regan (New York: Random House, 1983), 235–270.

Held, Virginia, "Advertising and Program Content," *Business & Professional Ethics Journal*, 3, nos. 3 & 4 (1983) 61–76.

Leiser, Burton, "The Ethics of Advertising," in *Ethics, Free Enterprise, and Public Policy*, edited by Richard T. De George and Joseph A. Picheler, (New York: Oxford University Press, 1978), 173–186.

Levitt, Theodore, "The Morality (?) of Advertising," *Harvard Business Review*, 48 (July/August 1970), 84–92.

Machan, Tibor R, "Advertising: The Whole or Only Some of the Truth?," *Public Affairs Quarterly*, 1, no. 4 (October 1987), 59–71.

Santilli, Paul C., "The Informative and Persuasive Functions of Advertising," *Journal of Business Ethics*, 2 (1983), 27–33.

von Hayek, F. A., "The *Non Sequitur* of the 'Dependence Effect'," *Southern Economic Journal*, 2 (April 1961); 346–348.

CHAPTER 14

◆ ◆ ◆

Affirmative Action and Discrimination

One of our most troubling moral lapses is the ease with which we discriminate against one another on such grounds as race, gender, ethnicity, and the like. It should both trouble and humble all of us that although the United States prides itself at being more than two centuries old, racial and sexual discrimination was made illegal little more than two decades ago. The power and long-term effects of discrimination, however, could not be eradicated by simply banning the practice. American corporations thus instituted *affirmative action* programs that aimed to address past wrongs by taking race and gender into account in a positive way. Yet such programs spawned a host of ethical questions. If making decisions on the basis of race and sex was wrong in the "bad old days," why is it right now? Isn't this practice equally indefensible and discriminatory? What about the innocent people who are hurt in the process? And how long does remedial action have to go on? Isn't a quarter century enough to set things right, and isn't it time to allow everyone to compete equally?

Issues related to discrimination and affirmative action have occupied philosophers throughout the last twenty years. Thomas Nagel begins this chapter with a defense of preferential hiring. Nagel believes that it advances the public good, even though it is intrinsically undesirable. Leo Groarke supports affirmative action on yet other grounds — as a form of restitution. Evelyn Pluhar defends the practice against the charge that it unfairly sacrifices the interest of those who are denied jobs because of it. And Laura Purdy explicitly defends hiring apparently less qualified women. Sidney Hook, however, completely rejects any form of racial preference as reverse discrimination.

Thomas Nagel

A DEFENSE OF AFFIRMATIVE ACTION

The term "affirmative action" has changed in meaning since it was first introduced. Originally it referred only to special efforts to ensure equal opportunity for members of groups that had been subject to discrimination. These efforts included public advertisement of positions to be filled, active recruitment of qualified applicants from the formerly excluded groups, and special training programs to help them meet the standards for admission or appointment. There was also close attention to procedures of appointment, and sometimes to the results, with a view to detecting continued discrimination, conscious or unconscious.

More recently the term has come to refer also to some degree of definite preference for members of these groups in determining access to positions from which they were formerly excluded. Such preference might be allowed to influence decisions only between candidates who are otherwise equally qualified, but usually it involves the selection of women or minority members over other candidates who are better qualified for the position.

Let me call the first sort of policy "weak affirmative action" and the second "strong affirmative action." It is important to distinguish them, because the distinction is sometimes blurred in practice. It is strong affirmative action — the policy of preference — that arouses controversy. Most people would agree that weak or precautionary affirmative action is a good thing, and worth its cost in time and energy. But this does not imply that strong affirmative action is also justified.

I shall claim that in the present state of things it is justified, most clearly with respect to blacks. But I also believe that a defender of the practice must acknowledge that there are serious arguments against it, and that it is defensible only because the arguments for it have great weight. Moral opinion in this country is sharply divided over the issue because significant values are involved on both sides. My own view is that while strong affirmative action is intrinsically undesirable, it is a legitimate and perhaps indispensable method of pursuing a goal so important to the national welfare that it can be justified as a temporary, though not short-term, policy for both public and private institutions. In this respect it is like other policies that impose burdens on some for the public good.

THREE OBJECTIONS

I shall begin with the argument against. There are three objections to strong affirmative action: that it is inefficient; that it is unfair; and that it damages self-esteem.

The degree of inefficiency depends on how strong a role racial or sexual preference plays in the process of selection. Among candidates meeting the

From Thomas Nagel, "A Defense of Affirmative Action." Testimony before the Subcommittee on the Constitution of the Senate Judiciary Committee, June 18, 1981. Reprinted by permission of the author.

basic qualifications for a position, those better qualified will on the average perform better, whether they are doctors, policemen, teachers, or electricians. There may be some cases, as in preferential college admissions, where the immediate usefulness of making educational resources available to an individual is thought to be greater because of the use to which the education will be put or because of the internal effects on the institution itself. But by and large, policies of strong affirmative action must reckon with the costs of some lowering in performance level: the stronger the preference, the larger the cost to be justified. Since both the costs and the value of the results will vary from case to case, this suggests that no one policy of affirmative action is likely to be correct in all cases, and that the cost in performance level should be taken into account in the design of a legitimate policy.

The charge of unfairness arouses the deepest disagreements. To be passed over because of membership in a group one was born into, where this has nothing to do with one's individual qualifications for a position, can arouse strong feelings of resentment. It is a departure from the ideal — one of the values finally recognized in our society — that people should be judged so far as possible on the basis of individual characteristics rather than involuntary group membership.

This does not mean that strong affirmative action is morally repugnant in the manner of racial or sexual discrimination. It is nothing like those practices, for though like them it employs race and sex as criteria of selection, it does so for entirely different reasons. Racial and sexual discrimination are based on contempt or even loathing for the excluded group, a feeling that certain contacts with them are degrading to members of the dominant group, that they are fit only for subordinate positions or menial work. Strong affirmative action involves none of this: it is simply a means of increasing the social and economic strength of formerly victimized groups, and does not stigmatize others.

There is an element of individual unfairness here, but it is more like the unfairness of conscription in wartime, or of property condemnation under the right of eminent domain. Those who benefit or lose out because of their race or sex cannot be said to deserve their good or bad fortune.

It might be said on the other side that the beneficiaries of affirmative action deserve it as compensation for past discrimination, and that compensation is rightly exacted from the group that has benefited from discrimination in the past. But this is a bad argument, because as the practice usually works, no effort is made to give preference to those who have suffered most from discrimination, or to prefer them especially to those who have benefited most from it, or been guilty of it. Only candidates who in other qualifications fall on one or the other side of the margin of decision will directly benefit or lose from the policy, and these are not necessarily, or even probably, the ones who especially deserve it. Women or blacks who don't have the qualifications even to be considered are likely to have been handicapped more by the effects of discrimination than those who receive preference. And the marginal white male candidate, who is turned down can evoke our sympathy if he asks, "Why me?" (A policy of explicitly *compensatory* preference, which took into account each individual's background of poverty and discrimination, would escape some of these objections, and it has its defenders, but it is not the policy I want to defend. Whatever its merits, it will not serve the same purpose as direct affirmative action.)

The third objection concerns self-esteem, and is particularly serious. While strong affirmative action is in effect, and generally known to be so, no one in an affirmative action category who gets a desirable job or is admitted to a selective university can be sure that he or she has not benefited from the policy. Even those who would have made it anyway fall under suspicion, from themselves and from others: it comes to be widely felt that success does not mean the same thing for women and minorities. This painful damage to esteem cannot be avoided. It should make any defender of strong affirmative action want the practice to end as soon as it has achieved its basic purpose.

JUSTIFYING AFFIRMATIVE ACTION

I have examined these three objections and tried to assess their weight, in order to decide how strong a countervailing reason is needed to justify such a policy. In my view, taken together they imply that strong affirmative action involving significant preference should be undertaken only if it will substantially further a social goal of the first importance. While this condition is not met by all programs of affirmative action now in effect, it is met by those which address the most deep-seated, stubborn, and radically unhealthy divisions in the society, divisions whose removal is a condition of basic justice and social cohesion.

The situation of black people in our country is unique in this respect. For almost a century after the abolition of slavery we had a rigid racial caste system of the ugliest kind, and it only began to break up twenty-five years ago. In the South it was enforced by law, and in the North, in a somewhat less severe form, by social convention. Whites were thought to be defiled by social or residential proximity to blacks, intermarriage was taboo, blacks were denied the same level of public goods — education and legal protection — as whites, were restricted to the most menial occupations, and were barred from any positions of authority over whites. The visceral feelings of black inferiority and untouchability that this system expressed were deeply ingrained in the members of both races, and they continue, not surprisingly, to have their effect. Blacks still form, to a considerable extent, a hereditary social and economic community characterized by widespread poverty, unemployment, and social alienation.

When this society finally got around to moving against the caste system, it might have done no more than to enforce straight equality of opportunity, perhaps with the help of weak affirmative action, and then wait a few hundred years while things gradually got better. Fortunately it decided instead to accelerate the process by both public and private institutional action, because there was wide recognition of the intractable character of the problem posed by this insular minority and its place in the nation's history and collective consciousness. This has not been going on very long, but the results are already impressive, especially in speeding the advancement of blacks into the middle class. Affirmative action has not done much to improve the position of poor and unskilled blacks. That is the most serious part of the problem, and it requires a more direct economic attack. But increased access to higher education and upper-level jobs is an essential part of what must be achieved to break the structure of drastic separation that was left largely undisturbed by the legal abolition of the caste system.

Changes of this kind require a generation or two. My guess is that strong affirmative action for blacks will continue to be justified into the early decades of the next century, but that by then it will have accomplished what it can and will no longer be worth the costs. One point deserves special emphasis. The goal to be pursued is the reduction of a great social injustice, not proportional representation of the races in all institutions and professions. Proportional racial representation is of no value in itself. It is not a legitimate social goal, and it should certainly not be the aim of strong affirmative action, whose drawbacks make it worth adopting only against a serious and intractable social evil.

This implies that the justification for strong affirmative action is much weaker in the case of other racial and ethnic groups, and in the case of women. At least, the practice will be justified in a narrower range of circumstances and for a shorter span of time than it is for blacks. No other group has been treated quite like this, and no other group is in a comparable status. Hispanic-Americans occupy an intermediate position, but it seems to me frankly absurd to include persons of oriental descent as beneficiaries of affirmative action, strong or weak. They are not a severely deprived and excluded minority, and their eligibility serves only to swell the numbers that can be included on affirmative action reports. It also suggests that there is a drift in the policy toward adopting the goal of racial proportional representation for its own sake. This is a foolish mistake, and should be resisted. The only legitimate goal of the policy is to reduce egregious racial stratification.

With respect to women, I believe that except over the short term, and in professions or institutions from which their absence is particularly marked, strong affirmative action is not warranted and weak affirmative action is enough. This is based simply on the expectation that the social and economic situation of women will improve quite rapidly under conditions of full equality of opportunity. Recent progress provides some evidence for this. Women do not form a separate hereditary community, characteristically poor and uneducated, and their position is not likely to be self-perpetuating in the same way as that of an outcast race. The process requires less artificial acceleration, and any need for strong affirmative action for women can be expected to end sooner than it ends for blacks.

I said at the outset that there was a tendency to blur the distinction between weak and strong affirmative action. This occurs especially in the use of numerical quotas, a topic on which I want to comment briefly.

A quota may be a method of either weak or strong affirmative action, depending on the circumstances. It amounts to weak affirmative action — a safeguard against discrimination — if, and only if, there is independent evidence that average qualifications for the positions being filled are no lower in the group to which a minimum quota is being assigned than in the applicant group as a whole. This can be presumed true of unskilled jobs that most people can do, but it becomes less likely, and harder to establish, the greater the skill and education required for the position. At these levels, a quota proportional to population, or even to representation of the group in the applicant pool, is almost certain to amount to strong affirmative action. Moreover it is strong affirmative action of a particularly crude and indiscriminate kind, because it permits no variation in the degree of preference on the basis of costs in efficiency, depending on the qualification gap. For this reason I should defend quotas only where they serve the purpose of weak affirmative action. On the whole, strong affirmative action is better implemented by including group preference as one factor in appointment or admission decisions, and letting the results depend on its interaction with other factors.

I have tried to show that the arguments against strong affirmative action are clearly outweighed at present by the need for exceptional measures to remove the stubborn residues of racial caste. But advocates of the policy should acknowledge the reasons against it, which will ensure its termination when it is no longer necessary. Affirmative action is not an end in itself, but a means of dealing with a social situation that should be intolerable to us all.

Leo Groarke

AFFIRMATIVE ACTION AS A FORM OF RESTITUTION

1. INTRODUCTION

Though it has not been clearly recognized by philosophers and other commentators, the common sense defense of affirmative action or "employment equity"[1] appeals to principles of restitution. It is because some groups have suffered, and other groups have benefited, from discrimination that it seems that we should compensate the former by awarding them preferential treatment paid for by the latter (in the sense that they must lose their right to equal treatment). Philosophers have nonetheless defended affirmative action in ways that reject this appeal to restitution. In contrast, I defend it, arguing (1) that alternative attempts to defend affirmative action fail; and (2) that ordinary affirmative action programs are not in keeping with the principles of restitution. Present programs should not, I argue, be rejected out of hand, though we are obliged to supplement and amend them in keeping with the proposals I suggest.

2. AFFIRMATIVE ACTION: A CRITIQUE

In some ways, the appeal to restitution which is the implicit basis of affirmative action is persuasive and compelling. In North America, women, natives, blacks and other groups have suffered, and white males have benefited, from discrimination in the past, and it seems reasonable to alleviate this injustice by asking the latter to compensate the former. The appeal to restitution this implies (and the notion that affirmative action can be defended by obvious and intuitive principles of justice) is, however, problematic as soon as one considers the internal make up of the groups affected by affirmative action programs. As many commentators have pointed out, the costs of such programs are borne by young white males (candidates for jobs and programs awarded to other groups), though it is *older* white males who have been the main perpetrators and benefi-

From *Journal of Business Ethics*, 9 (1990), 207–213. © 1990 Kluwer Academic Publishers. Reprinted by permission of Kluwer Academic Publishers.

ciaries of discrimination (cf. Carr, 1982). It follows that standard affirmative action violates the principles of restitution, for they suggest that those who have gained unjust advantage (in this case, older white males) should compensate those who have been disadvantaged.

Though it has received less attention, an analogous problem arises when one considers the victims of discrimination, for they are, first and foremost, *older* individuals who belong to discriminated groups (e.g., older women who pursued jobs and careers when discrimination was accepted). The problem is that restitution requires that they be compensated for their losses, though they receive no compensation from standard affirmative action programs. Instead, the benefits provided are made available to other, younger members of the groups that they belong to (cf. Wolf-Devine, 1988).

Looked at from the point of view of restitution, it seems to follow that ordinary affirmative action neither compensates nor taxes the appropriate individuals (the main victims, and the main beneficiaries of discrimination). If analogous principles were used in dealing with individuals, they would not force John to return to Jacinth property he has wrongly acquired, but force Jack (i.e. someone else entirely) to provide benefits to Jill. Such sanctions would obviously be a travesty of justice and it needs to be explained why ordinary affirmative action should not be viewed in the same light.

Rather than meet this challenge, commentators who defend affirmative action usually ignore the problems it implies, employing categories that gloss over the distinction between older and younger members of the groups that they discuss. Judith Jarvis Thomson's oft quoted defense of preferential hiring is, for example, founded on the following analogy between affirmative action and the way a dining club might decide to allocate tables when there are not enough to go around.

> . . . suppose that we have of late had reason to be especially grateful to one of the members, whom I'll call Smith: Smith has done a series of very great favors for the club. It seems to me we might, out of gratitude to Smith, adopt the following policy: for the next six months, if two members arrive at the same time, and there is only one available table, then Smith gets in first, if he's one of the two; whereas if he's not, then the headwaiter shall toss a coin. . . .
>
> It seems to me that there would be no impropriety in our taking these actions—by which I mean to include that there would be no injustice in our taking them. Suppose another member, Jones, votes No. Suppose he says "Look, I admit we all benefited from what Smith did for us. But still, I'm a member and a member in as good standing as Smith is. So I have a right to an equal chance (and equal share), and I demand what I have a right to." I think we may rightly feel that Jones merely shows insensitivity: he does not adequately appreciate what Smith did for us. Jones, like all of us, has a right to an equal chance at such benefits as the club has available for distribution to the members; but there is no injustice in a majority's refusing to grant the members this equal chance, in the name of a debt of gratitude to Smith. (Thomson, 1981, 297–298)

According to Thomson, justice, or at least common decency, similarly shows that society has a debt to blacks, women and others, and that it is reasonable to use preferential hiring as one way of repaying it.

The problem with Thomson's claim is her assumption that different members of society are equally responsible for the debt it owes to groups which have suffered from discrimination, and that members of these groups are equally entitled to be compensated. A better analogy would compare the situation that precipitates affirmative action to a dining club in which the oldest members of the club have treated its employees unfairly. In such circumstances, it hardly need be said that it would be wrong to rectify this injustice by forcing new members of the club who have not mistreated the employees (and who can ill afford to pay) to provide the necessary compensation. Such a proposal would be all the more objectionable if it forced them to make restitution, not to the employees who have been mistreated, but to new employees. If the new employees have suffered some discrimination, they deserve to be compensated to this extent (and the new members deserve to pay), but justice and common decency require that the major beneficiaries should be the old employees. In an analogous way, restitution demands that the major costs of restitution be paid for by the club's older members.

Thomson's arguments make affirmative action plausible only by glossing the distinctions which seem to demonstrate its injustice (the distinctions between older and younger members of the groups in question). The same mistake characterizes many other thinkers (see, e.g., Martin, 1976; Dworkin, 1981: esp. pp. 326–327; and Boxill, 1984) who justify affirmative action by arguing that social goals must take precedence over the rights of young white males, ignoring the principle that society's debts should be paid by those who have incurred them. It is not that young white males have an explicit right to the jobs they lose because of affirmative action (the straw man position Boxill attributes to those who criticize it), but that they have a right not to have to pay for other people's debts. Analogously, older women, blacks and others have a right to enjoy the compensation that is paid to debts owed primarily to them. Granting that there are social goals that must be met (this is not in question), justice still requires that this be done in a way that respects the demands of restitution (as we shall see, this is not difficult to accomplish).

In answer to such arguments, one might try to justify affirmative action by appealing to present, rather than past, discrimination. So construed, it need not be seen as an attempt to pay debts owed by (and to) older members of the groups it deals with, and is not so obviously unjust. It is in keeping with this that commentators like Thomson and Boxill have argued that discrimination persists in North American society, and that younger members of the relevant groups can, therefore, be reasonably compensated or asked to pay its cost. Thomson, for example, writes that "Large-scale, blatant, overt wrongs have presumably disappeared; but it is only within the last twenty-five years (perhaps the last ten years in the case of women), that it has become at all widely agreed in this country that blacks and women must be recognized as having, not merely this or that particular right normally recognized as belonging to white males, but all of the rights and respect which go with full membership in the community." (Thomson, 1981: 299). The problem is that these very comments, especially as they were made in 1973, themselves suggest that the major victims and beneficiaries of discrimination are older individuals, and that they should, therefore, be the focus of attempts to make up for past discrimination. Thus morality, justice and restitution all demand that attempts to make up for past discrimination should be aimed, first and foremost, at its *major* victims, and that compensation should be provided by its *major* beneficiaries.

This being said, the emphasis on past discrimination this implies is all the more important given that claims about present discrimination are frequently exaggerated, founded as they are, on a misperception of inequities that persist. Laura Purdy (Purdy, 1987) has, for example, argued for affirmative action for women in university hiring by appealing to empirical studies which demonstrate discrimination in the 1960s and the early 1970s, failing to take seriously the possibility that they are out of date.[2] As she suggests, there continue to be relatively few women in academe, though it is a mistake to conclude that this is the result of present discrimination (in particular, discriminatory hiring practices). On the contrary, statistics show that women graduates have received more than their fair share of new positions, and that the continued lack of women faculty has been primarily the result of constraints on university funding which have meant that there have been almost no available positions (see Groarke, 1983). The problem is that more than one's fair share of a handful of positions cannot bring about a significant change in the overall ratio of male and female faculty and it is this (not present discrimination) which perpetuates the inequities that have existed in the past.[3] Discriminated groups are in this sense the victims of past (not present) discrimination and an economy which has not provided them with opportunities that can sufficiently alter its effects. It is in view of this that Lisa Newton (Newton, 1987) suggests that those groups which have suffered from discrimination will make real inroads into professional positions when, and only when, the economy significantly expands. She therefore rejects affirmative action policies, suggesting that such inroads, and the opportunities they require, are even more unlikely when the economy "is burdened by the enormous weight of the nonproductive administrative procedure [and the "procedural monsters"] required to implement them." (206–207)

3. AFFIRMATIVE ACTION AS RESTITUTION

Given the various objections to affirmative action, many commentators have concluded that it should be rejected out of hand (see, for example, Newton, 1987). Such a move ignores rather than rectifies the enormous discrimination that has existed in the past, however, and it follows that justice demands some restitution, though it must be restitution that is not susceptible to the criticisms we have already noted. Despite an almost universal failure to consider how this might be achieved, it can be easily accomplished by designing affirmative action programs that make more of an attempt to abide by the principles of restitution. In particular, this requires more of an attempt to (1) compensate those individuals who are the main victims of discrimination, and (2) ensure that such compensation is provided by those who have been its main beneficiaries. The first objective requires programs that provide benefits to older women, blacks, etc. The second requires an arrangement that ensures that they are funded by older white males.

One way to satisfy these requirements is by instituting ordinary affirmative action in circumstances where it has the requisite effects. The experience needed for senior (as opposed to entry level) positions in universities, business, or government means, for example, that it is older individuals who apply for such positions, and that affirmative action in this context benefits and burdens the appropriate groups (on the one hand, older blacks, women, natives, etc.; on the other, older white males, who are disadvantaged when other individuals are favoured). This being said, the possibilities for restitution such opportunities provide are extremely limited, both because there are few positions of this nature, and because those who have suffered from discrimination usually lack the qualifications they demand. Given that it is particularly important that qualified individuals occupy influential roles, it is, moreover, difficult to argue for strong affirmative action policies along these lines, though it can be said that preference should be given, all things being equal, to individuals from groups that have suffered from discrimination.[4] More comprehensive kinds of affirmative action are, however, needed if it is to compensate, in any serious way, for past discrimination.

The best way to overcome the shortcomings of such programs from the point of view of restitution is by compensating the victims of past discrimination in ways that go beyond job allocation. Given the enormous economic losses they have suffered,[5] this can be accomplished by instituting programs that provide financial benefits. Among other things, such programs should include pension reform, tax breaks and other economic benefits that are targeted at older members of those groups which have suffered from discrimination. Pension reform is, in particular, needed to alleviate the plight of many older women, blacks and others whose work has not been recognized by regular pension plans, and who have been denied careers that can provide them with adequate support in later life (women over sixty-five are said to occupy the lowest economic rung in North America). More generally, the details of such programs need to be determined by looking at the needs of these specific individuals. The principle that the costs of affirmative action should be borne by those who have most benefited from discrimination, can be satisfied by taxing older white males to pay for the programs this implies. As we have already noted, they have benefited from discrimination (by not having to compete with women, blacks and others for careers, and by enjoying laws and social programs that favour their interests), and it is in view of this that this burden is appropriate.

A third way to redress the debts owed to the victims of discrimination is by instituting affirmative action programs as we now know them. To see how they can be understood as restitution to the victims of past discrimination, we need note that the losses they have suffered are not restricted to the economic losses that attend the loss of well paid professional positions. On the contrary, they have also suffered because their exclusion from universities, governments, businesses, hospitals and other major institutions has meant that their interests have not been adequately represented in social goals and policies. It is in view of this that such losses can be alleviated by ordinary affirmative action that entails a more equitable distribution of positions to the groups that they belong to. The hiring of younger women can, for example, help rectify women's lack of social power, and thus protect women's interests. In some cases, such women may not have the same concerns as older women, but their interests are likely to be closer than those of men and there is no other way to ensure that women have a more significant share of the positions (and the influence) held by particular professions.

It may, however, seem that it is difficult to make ordinary affirmative action programs compatible with the principle that they be paid for by those who have benefited from discrimination, but this can be accomplished by tying them to retirement policies. Especially in circumstances where opportunities are scarce, such policies play an important role in dealing with discrimination, for a decision to allow individuals to keep their positions past normal retirement age prolongs the effects of past discrimination, perpetuating the inequities it produced (the lack of women faculty in universities, for example).[6] Such problems are exacerbated by the high salaries of individuals with a great deal of seniority, for it follows that the attempt to finance this decision greatly limits the ability of an institution to pursue other goals. Given such considerations, one way to make more opportunities available for groups which have suffered from discrimination is by restricting the ability of older white males to work past normal retirement age, thereby freeing the resources and positions that are needed for effective affirmative action programs. Adopting such a policy is one way to ensure that the costs of such programs are borne primarily by older white males who are denied the opportunity to continue in their positions.[7] Such policies are, it should be noted, possible even if one rejects mandatory retirement (the practice of requiring retirement of all individuals who reach normal retirement age), for one may make exceptions in the case of exceptional individuals (allowing them to continue past normal retirement), thus allowing exceptions to the rule. Though there are other alternatives, one way to institute such a policy is by requiring all individuals who reach the normal age of retirement to compete for their positions in an open competition (exceptionally qualified individuals will win such competitions, other individuals will not). In the present context, the important point is that the principles of restitution show that older individuals should pay the costs of affirmative action and such moves will, like the other policies we have already noted, help ensure this is the case.

4. AN OBJECTION: REVERSE DISCRIMINATION

One way to assess the proposed affirmative action programs is in terms of their relationship to the standard criticism of affirmative action, reverse discrimination. It should in this regard be noted that, in addition to making affirmative action consistent with the principles of restitution, these proposals minimize the charges of reverse discrimination that can be raised against it. The standard claim is that affirmative action discriminates against young white males, but this is not a serious issue in the present case, for the proposed programs are designed so that their disadvantages are not borne by young white males. One might answer that they merely shift the burden to older white males, but this is justified by the principles of restitution. Indeed, the debt they owe to the victims of discrimination has been (especially in discussions of retirement policy — see, e.g. Brett, 1987) too long ignored and the proposed programs are important because they can rectify this oversight.

One might answer that the proposed affirmative action still implies unjust discrimination in individual cases where restitution cannot justify the penalties imposed on particular older white males. An older white male growing up in extreme poverty in an area where whites suffer discrimination may, for example, have been more disadvantaged than a successful upper class black who was insulated from discrimination, and one might therefore ask why he (the white) should be taxed to make, for example, financial benefits available to the latter (cf. Sher, 1987 and Simon, 1982). There is, it must be said, something to such concerns and it is in view of them that it makes sense to try to minimize such possibilities. In instituting economic benefits for older individuals (in terms of pension reform, e.g.), it thus makes sense to restrict them to those in need, especially as such obligations (in contrast to obligations to those better off) must rank high on our list of priorities and cannot be easily overridden by competing obligations to other groups in society (the need to support education, pollution control, and so on). Such a move will to some extent eliminate the specific case that we have noted (disqualifying the wealthy black from consideration), though it must simply be accepted that it is impossible to design social programs that ensure that no individual receives unwarranted benefits or taxes. On the contrary, some exceptions cannot be avoided when one works on such a grand scale and the limited reverse discrimination this implies must simply be accepted as the cost of rectifying past injustice (social programs must rely on generalizations which inevitably have exceptions). This does not show that the proposed affirmative action policies should be rejected, however, for such exceptions *are* exceptions and, therefore, the lesser evil when compared with the injustice of making no attempt to rectify past discrimination. Given the pervasiveness of the latter and a reasonable attempt to minimize reverse discrimination, any serious commitment to the eradication of discrimination must give priority to affirmative action and the discrimination it addresses, not to the much less serious reverse discrimination it may sometimes cause.

5. CONCLUSION

Given the kinds of affirmative action that are usually defended, some of the proposed alternatives may seem radical. This is because they are unfamiliar, however, and not because they are problematic from a moral point of view. On the contrary, they are a straightforward application of the principles of restitution and not open to the standard criticisms of affirmative action policies. It is not these proposals, but the failure of commentators to consider them which is difficult to understand.[8] The closest one appears to come in Thomson's remark that ". . . it isn't only the young male applicant for a university job who has benefited from the exclusion of blacks and women: the older white male, now comfortably tenured, also benefited. . . . Well, presumably, we can't demand that he give up his job, or share it. But it seems to me in place to expect the occupants of comfortable professional chairs to contribute in some way, to make some form of return to the young white male who bears the cost, and is turned away. . . . I find the outcry now heard against preferential hiring in the universities objectionable: it would also be objectionable that those of us who are now securely situated should placidly defend it, with no more than a sigh of regret for the young white male who pays for it." (Thomson, 1981, 301 – 302). There is something to these sentiments, though it should by now be clear that they greatly underestimate the obligations of older faculty who have benefited from discrimination (it isn't that they have *also* benefited, it is that they have been the *major* beneficiaries), completely ignore the debt owed to older members of discriminated groups, and fail to propose any concrete means of ensuring that older white males meet the obligations that they countenance. Contra Thomson, it is not difficult to design programs that achieve these ends.

Notes

1. This new name highlights the fact that affirmative action allocates a more equitable number of jobs to women, natives, blacks and other groups, but it is unfortunately ambiguous (perhaps purposely so). Whatever label one applies, it must be accepted that affirmative action promotes inequity in the sense that it grants preference to individuals of a particular sex, race, etc. Rather than hide this fact, a defense of affirmative action must show that such inequity is the lesser of two evils, and justified as a way of dealing with the greater evils perpetrated by discrimination now or in the past. The term "affirmative action" might (like "employment equity") also be said to be a loaded term, but it can at least be said that it does not so blatantly assume that the standard objection to such policies (viz., the claim that they promote inequity) is mistaken.

2. The books she cites were published in 1965 and 1976, but they depend on earlier studies. According to her own account, things have improved.

3. It must be said that Purdy tends to be very careless in considering alternative explanations of the problems she discusses. At one point, for example, she attributes a 1973–1975 rise in the acceptance of papers by women at the Archeological Institute of America annual conference to the introduction of blind referring (and the elimination of sexual bias), not considering other obvious possibilities (more submissions from women, random fluctuations, or improvements in the quality of women's papers as more women gain professional qualifications), and failing to even discuss the question of whether its attitudes in 1975 are representative of general trends in academe in 1987 (see her note 11).

4. This is, in effect, applying the kind of affirmative action Thomson proposes to these specific cases. Such programs are particularly important, for the individuals they benefit can act as important role models that help undermine the stereotypes that promote discrimination.

5. In the case of women, for example, the financial rewards from occupying one third, one half, or an even greater portion of the positions held by older male doctors, lawyers, judges, professors, etc. is difficult to exaggerate.

6. Especially as male faculty seem very reluctant to retire when they are given the opportunity to continue. The only survey I know of was conducted at the University of Manitoba when it adopted an open policy in response to the Manitoba Supreme Court's ruling against mandatory retirement. Of eighteen individuals scheduled to retire, fourteen indicated that they planned to continue teaching, two of them on a part time basis. As the university concludes, such prospects leave the university with "a pretty bleak picture in the area of staff renewal" (Weston, 1983).

7. Younger white males will still be disadvantaged by ordinary affirmative action, though this disadvantage will be much less onerous given the extra positions such policies would make available.

8. One can only point to the relative ability (and inability) of different social classes to protect their interests. Women and other groups have, for example, gained enough of a hearing to demand the redress of inequities, while older white males have retained the power to see that such debts are not paid by them (in contrast, young white males occupy an almost powerless position in the present social ladder). I hasten to add that I am not suggesting that different groups have *intentionally* pursued their own interests and disregarded those of other groups. On the contrary, the moral is how difficult it is to see past one's own interests.

Bibliography

Boxill, Bernard R.: 1984, 'The Morality of Preferential Hiring', in James P. Sterba, ed. *Morality In Practice* (Wadsworth, Belmont), pp. 208–216.

Brett, Nathan: 1987, 'Equality Rights in Retirement', in Deborah Poff and Wilfrid Waluchow, eds. *Business Ethics In Canada* (Prentice-Hall, Scarborough), pp. 218–233.

Carr, C. R.: 1982, 'Unfair Sacrifice — Reply to Pluhar's 'Preferential Hiring and Unjust Sacrifice'', *Philosophical Forum* 14, No. 1, 94–97.

Dworkin, Ronald: 1981, 'The Rights of Allan Bakke', in John Arthur, ed. *Morality and Moral Controversies* (Prentice-Hall, Englewood Cliffs), pp. 318–322.

Groarke, Leo: 1983, 'Beyond Affirmative Action', *Atlantis: A Women's Studies Journal* 9, No. 1, 13–24.

Martin, Michael: 1976, 'Pedagogical Arguments for Preferential Hiring and Tenuring of Women Teachers in University', in Gould and Wartofsky, eds. *Women and Philosophy* (G.P. Putnam, New York).

Newton, Lisa H.: 1987, 'Bakke and Davis: Justice, American Style', in Mappes and Zembaty, eds. *Morality and Social Policy*; 3rd edn. (McGraw-Hill, Toronto), pp. 205–206.

Purdy, Laura M: 1987, 'In Defense of Hiring Apparently Less Qualified Women', in Mappes and Zembaty, eds. *Morality and Social Policy*; 3rd edn. (McGraw-Hill, Toronto), pp. 227–232.

Sher, George: 1987, 'Justifying Reverse Discrimination in Employment', in Mappes and Zembaty, eds. *Morality and Social Policy*; 3rd edn. (McGraw-Hill, Toronto), pp. 219–226.

Simon, Robert: 1982, 'Preferential Hiring: A Reply to Judith Jarvis Thomson', in Mappes and Zembaty, eds. *Morality and Social Policy*; 2nd edn. (McGraw-Hill, Toronto), pp. 178–182.

Thomson, Judith Jarvis: 1981, 'Preferential Hiring', in Arthur, ed. *Morality and Moral Controversies* (Prentice-Hall, Englewood Cliffs), pp. 287–301.

Weston, Julia: 1983, 'When Retirement is No Longer Mandatory', *University Affairs*, January.

Wolf-Devine, Celia: 1988, 'An Inequality in Affirmative Action', *Journal of Applied Philosophy* 5, 107–108.

Evelyn B. Pluhar

PREFERENTIAL HIRING AND UNJUST SACRIFICE

Many philosophers have denied that preferential hiring is an acceptable means of rectifying the injustice committed against those disadvantaged by discrimination.[1] Two of the most important objections to preferential hiring which have recently been discussed are the allegations (1) that it confers benefits on those who do not deserve them and (2) that it unfairly sacrifices the interests of those who are denied jobs on its basis.[2] The first of these allegations has been attacked successfully by philosophical defenders of preferential hiring, most notably by Bernard Boxill,[3] and will not, therefore, be discussed here. The second allegation, however, while it has been attacked vigorously,[4] remains very troublesome. It will be argued here that the case which has been made against it is seriously incomplete. In this paper I hope to complete that case, thereby showing that preferential hiring cannot be rejected on that ground. I shall confine my attention to the implications of preferential hiring for whites and blacks, leaving open to what extent the conclusions drawn will apply to other relevant groups.

It is clear that the debate on preferential hiring takes place within a social context. As Alison Jagger points out, "the whole debate on preferential hiring makes sense only within a certain set of assumptions."[5] Most importantly, we assume that jobs should be competed for, that competence should be a major

From *The Philosophical Forum*, 12, no. 3 (Spring 1981), 214–224. Reprinted by permission of the publisher.

factor in the awarding of jobs, and that equality of opportunity for job competition is desirable. It is not my task here to either dispute or defend these assumptions:[6] I merely wish to acknowledge them. With these assumptions in mind, I hope to further the debate by using the same analytic tools that have been employed effectively by the disputants thus far, *viz.*, analogies designed to isolate the relevant features of this complex ethical issue so as to clarify the issue as a whole. I shall argue that key analogies developed by those on opposite sides of the debate are defective in crucial respects and then proceed to sketch analogies which I believe do clarify and help resolve the issue.

It is a fact that blacks have been denied equality of opportunity with whites. That denial has produced disadvantages for blacks and corresponding advantages for whites in today's competitive economic market. Preferential hiring is one of several measures intended to rectify this situation. That the situation needs rectification seems clear. The existing imbalance of opportunities which results from discrimination has not been caused by blacks, and it will continue to exist in the future, resulting in yet more undeserved misery for blacks and profit for whites, unless correction takes place. I am of course not asserting that all whites have equal opportunities. I do assert, however, that on the average blacks have lesser opportunities than whites. Thus, although one may wish to abolish all inequality of opportunity, this cannot be an objection against concentrating on one common type of such inequality. I shall argue that even individual whites who are innocent of discrimination owe blacks the rectification which preferential hiring makes possible.

It might be argued that blacks are owed *more* than rectification, i.e., correction, of their present disadvantages in opportunity, that the suffering each living black has undergone *in the past* due to discrimination should be compensated, and perhaps even that some legitimate interpretation of inheritance would justify extra compensation for the suffering of now dead ancestors of living blacks. Such arguments, if successful, would justify the imposition of much heavier burdens on whites than preferential hiring exacts. I shall not attempt such arguments here because I do not think they are necessary to justify preferential hiring. I therefore prefer to follow Irving Thalberg's approach to the issue:[7] he regards restoration of equal opportunity rather than exaction of damages as the goal of preferential hiring.[8] Past discrimination will therefore be regarded here as causally rather than morally relevant to present disadvantage. For that reason I shall also not consider the case of the black competitor who has qualifications superior to those of his white competitors. Perhaps he should receive compensation for past disadvantage, but preferential hiring is obviously not a relevant means of gaining such compensation for him. I shall for the same reason use the term "rectification" (of present imbalance) rather than "compensation" (for present *or past* imbalance).

Those who believe that preferential hiring unjustly sacrifices the interests of the individual denied a job on its basis think that such an individual is done a double injustice. (1) The typical young white denied a job in this way is not responsible for the harm done his[9] black competitor, yet he is asked to pay for it; (2) it is held that other whites who already have jobs or who do not have black competitors make no comparable payment. I will discuss both these allegations of injustice, with emphasis on the latter. Although much progress has been made in dispatching the former, the latter has sometimes been conceded[10] rather than attacked, and when attacked not successfully handled. Does the individual excluded from a job by preferential hiring suffer from either of the two injustices above?

Let us consider the first allegation of injustice. The typical young white, [11] while his ancestors were perhaps guilty of discrimination against blacks, may well be innocent of such discrimination himself. I will here consider the case of those whites who are innocent.[12] Such a person has, however, benefited from the inequality of opportunity which favors members of his race. Any white in a society in which there is considerably discrimination against blacks thus comes to enjoy thereby corresponding educational, social, and economic advantages. The young white did not, however, ask for these advantages and I will suppose that he could not have turned them down. Suppose he is not competing with a black who is equally, or almost as, qualified for the position, and that he is denied the position on the basis of preferential hiring. Is he not being punished unjustly? Robert Hoffman thinks it obvious that such treatment is immoral: "it is morally absurd to penalize him for an evil that he could not have prevented."[13] It would be just to impose losses on an individual *responsible* for the disadvantaged state of another, "But," argues Barry Gross, "here the person 'punished,'" the person from whom the compensation is exacted, is often not the criminal."[14]

Now, it would indeed be unjust to "punish" an innocent person, but it is not the case that preferential hiring constitutes "punishment" for a white denied a job on its basis. Bernard Boxill supplies the beginnings of a proper response with a simple analogy.[15] If Tom steals Dick's bicycle and gives it to an unsuspecting Phil, and Phil then discovers the truth, he is clearly obligated to return it to Dick. Even if Dick has passed on, Phil should return the bicycle to Dick's bicycle-impoverished heirs. Surely the return is not a "punishment" of or a penalty on Phil. Indeed, one hasn't the slightest temptation to think that poor Phil is being unjustly deprived of his innocently acquired bicycle.

As Boxill himself realizes, however, the analogy is defective. Unfair advantages innocently acquired cannot simply be returned to their rightful owners. He cites a counter-analogy by Fullenwider, who is arguing against preferential hiring.[16] Suppose Dick has ordered a construction company to pave his driveway, but someone has directed the workmen to Phil's home instead, in his absence, and *his* driveway is subsequently paved. Phil, let us suppose, had no intention of paving his driveway now or in the near future. Boxill agrees with Fullenwider that it would be unjust to require Phil to pay Dick the cost of the paving job.[17] Phil cannot hand over his driveway as he could hand over a bicycle, and to demand money would be to force him to buy an unwanted, albeit handsome, driveway. However, Boxill rightly does not agree with Fullenwider's conclusion that preferential hiring would likewise exact an unfair burden on an innocent party.

As Boxill notes, the driveway analogy is in fact *also* defective. The young white, unlike Phil in the story, has not only accepted his unfairly gained advantages, but he has in addition *built on them*. While he cannot simply return his initial advantage, as Phil cannot jerk his driveway out and plaster it on Dick's property, he can and should pay *something* for the benefits that have thus been made possible. As Boxill points out, if the driveway owner began making profits on his illicitly acquired pavement (say, by renting it as parking space), we would look differently at the matter.[18]

Since both the bicycle and driveway analogies are defective, I would like to propose a third analogy which incorporates relevant features of both. Suppose Tom has stolen valuable land from Dick, then given it to an unsuspecting Phil. Phil invests a good deal of money and effort into the land and, years later, has made it into a prosperous farm. Phil then discovers the theft perpetrated by a now-dead Tom. What are his obligations to a now-impoverished Dick? He is not obligated to return the land in its present state: to ask this would be to ask him to return much more than he initially received. Nor can he physically separate the land from the improvements he has made and return it to Dick, as he could a bicycle. He does, however, owe Dick *something*, unlike in the driveway analogy (though like the somewhat outlandish modification of it suggested by Boxill, where a profit is made), because he has benefited from the initial injustice. He has had an opportunity denied to Dick, and it is this imbalance of opportunity existing now which must be rectified.

With this analogy in mind, let us return to the preferential hiring case. How much does the young white owe the young black with whom he is competing? He does not owe the equivalent of all the advantages he *now has* over his black counterpart, for these are in part due to his own efforts. His counterpart might well have exerted the same efforts had he been provided with the same opportunities, but this is not the point. Preferential hiring is intended to restore *equal opportunity* between white and black competitor, not to reverse the positions of the advantaged and disadvantaged. If, as we are supposing, the former is innocent, such a reversal would indeed be unjustly punitive. By the same token, it would be wrong for Phil, the present landowner, simply to trade positions with the cheated Dick. Thus, although the young white can neither simply transfer his social, educational, and economic advantages nor pay their equivalent in money to his disadvantaged black counterpart without being unjustly penalized, he *can* and it seems *should* give up the competitive edge which he has unfairly though innocently received over his black competitor. Boxill sums up the conclusion of this argument eloquently:

> . . . by refusing to allow him [the white] to get the job because of an unfair [initial] advantage, preferential hiring makes the competition fairer.[19]

Therefore, the first allegation of injustice (i.e., that preferential hiring would penalize an innocent individual to benefit a wronged one) has not been borne out.

Let us now turn to the second allegation of injustice. It is all very well, so the objection goes, to say that the young white who has had greater opportunity to become what he is should forfeit his competitive edge to the black who has been denied equal opportunity, but the trouble is that such rectification is not done across the board. *Other* young whites who have no black competitors suffer no such loss. Nor, and this is even more troubling, are the vastly greater number of already employed individuals made to suffer such a loss. These already employed individuals have had the opportunity to benefit even more from their unfair advantages, yet they are not threatened by "preferential firing." Preferential hiring, it is held, is unjust above all because it demands an unequal distribution of burdens.

This second allegation of injustice is more troublesome than the first. One of the most eloquent defenders of preferential hiring, Boxill, stops short of answering it. James Nickel, another defender, frankly concedes the charge:

Rather than trying to deny this, it is probably more plausible to argue that the fact that there is some unfairness in the distribution of this burden does not settle the question of whether using preferential policies is acceptable or wise.[20]

This concession, moreover, is hardly mitigated by Nickel's pointing out other instances of unequal burdens exacted by society: either the inequality of burdens is just as questionable morally, or the burdens are only *apparently* unequal.[21] Before we settle for regarding preferential hiring as, at best, a necessary evil, however, let us see if we cannot dispose of the second allegation of injustice.

I propose to throw light on the allegation by extending the land analogy developed earlier. Suppose Tom has cheated a number of individuals of their land, then given parcels of it to unsuspecting farmers. The land is very rich and the new owners very industrious, and in a few years each is a prosperous farm and home owner. Meanwhile the rightful owners are languishing in poverty. Suppose the thefts are then discovered and an authority appointed to see that justice is done. I have already argued what the obligation of any one of the cheated group would be, and I shall not repeat that discussion here. But what if only *one* present landowner, Phil, is asked for payment? Suppose it is simply more *expedient* to single out Phil than to let the burden rest equally on all. Perhaps, e.g., Phil but not the others is applying for a loan to improve the property, or his being penalized will cause less economic dislocation than would result if all were asked to pay. He is simply unlucky in being in the wrong place at the wrong time. It seems clear that such treatment is outrageously unjust. Is such treatment parallel to the treatment involved in the case of preferential hiring, as its opponents allege (and as Nickel, a proponent, concedes)? The young white, it is held, simply has the misfortune of competing with a black equally or somewhat less qualified for the position than he, and thus loses his chance at that position. Young whites similar to him in other relevant respects but *without* such competition are not held back and, it is held, those whites who, benefiting from unfair competition in the past, are now secure in their jobs, are left undisturbed. If the latter were summarily turned out of their jobs ("preferentially fired"), there would be economic chaos and presumably political hell to pay. But such is not the case if only *some* young whites are burdened.

I shall argue that the picture painted above is not at all a fair representation of the burdens imposed by preferential hiring. First, however, I will discuss an unsuccessful attack that has been made on the second allegation of injustice. George Sher argues that it is fair for those young whites who have black competitors to lose prospective positions while the other whites suffer no such handicap on the ground that the former

> will benefit more than the others from its [discrimination's] effects on their competitors. They will benefit more because unless they are restrained, they, but not the others, will use their competitive edge to claim jobs which their competitors would otherwise have gotten. Thus it is only because they stand *to gain* the most from the *original* discrimination, that the by-passed individuals stand *to lose* the most from *reverse* discrimination. This is surely a valid reply to the charge that reverse discrimination does not distribute the burden of compensation equally.[22]

I fail to see how this serves as an answer to the charge, however. To return to the land analogy: Phil has the most to gain if *his* land is not expropriated and given to one of the men initially cheated. His neighbor Harry has nothing to gain or lose from Phil's situation. Is *this* a reason for expropriating Phil's land? In fairness to Sher, however, I must point out that in a footnote he tries to supply a more relevant relationship between the black competitor of the young white and the other whites who are not in that competitive situation, particularly those who have jobs:

> While many such individuals have undoubtedly benefited from the effects of discrimination upon *their original* competitors, few if any are likely to have benefited from a reduction in the abilities of the *currently best qualified* competitor. As long as none of them have so benefited, the best qualified applicant in question will stand to gain the most from that *particular* effect of past discrimination, and so reverse discrimination against him will remain fair.[23]

The situation is hardly so tidy, however. Advantages and disadvantages are not individuated in this fashion. Rectification is owed to all those who are unjustly disadvantaged from all those who have benefited from correspondingly unfair advantages. The young white may agree that he has more to gain if he succeeds than another white who has *already* succeeded by using his unfair advantages and still wonder why *he* should be singled out. Sher has no answer for that young white.

I suggest that preferential hiring would indeed be unjust if it required that only a few individuals bear the burden of compensation, but deny that it makes such a requirement. Those who make the second allegation of injustice against preferential hiring have ignored the fact that it is but *one* available means of rectification. The picture of preferential hiring as capricious and insensitive, sketched by its opponents (and some of its proponents), is a picture taken out of context. There would be little point in establishing a policy of preferential hiring for those who are being held back by the effects of discrimination if other measures were not simultaneously being taken to overcome these competitive disadvantages. Preferential hiring is intended to function hand in hand with other programs designed to alleviate financial disadvantage and sharply upgrade educational opportunity. To those who object that these other measures are sufficient, I reply that they are *not*: not for rectification. Those blacks competing with whites now have been robbed of their competitive edge by initial (including continuing) discrimination. To deny them jobs in favor of whites who are equally or somewhat better qualified is to put at best small quality differences before justice. It would also be unjust to *limit* rectification to preferential hiring. Inequality of opportunity should be rectified *wherever* it occurs. *Therefore, it is the distribution of the burden of an entire package of rectifying measures which matters.*

The correct answer to the second allegation of injustice is that payment need not *and cannot* be made in the same coin. An individual lucky enough to have a job already, gained in part on the strength of undeserved advantages,[24] owes part of his income to those who are unjustly disadvantaged, income to be used in financing programs to offset their lack of equal opportunity. He does not owe the job itself, assuming he is not responsible for the injustice, for the reasons already discussed: "preferential firing" is unjust because it would impose losses which exceed the value of the undeserved benefits. Progressive taxation would equalize burdens for those with incomes. Since blacks with incomes would also contribute to these programs, they should receive other kinds of rectification; e.g., preferential treatment in promotions and salaries. An individual who is *applying* for a job and has a black competitor equally or almost as qualified as he is pays in another coin: he is asked to forfeit his competitive edge (or to forfeit the flip of a coin in the case of equal qualifications) and to look elsewhere. The kind of rectification which ought to be required of individuals differs according to their circumstances. There is no reason why burdens should be unequal.

Consider the land analogy once more. Suppose the land that was stolen was parceled out free to "deserving" individuals; i.e., those with enough skill and capital to become prosperous farmers, and that these individuals (who are innocent of wrong-doing) prosper while the former owners do poorly. The theft is discovered and a central authority appointed to dispense justice. Now suppose that one parcel of good land remains to be given away, and that there are two applicants. One is a son of one of the other farmers; the other is one of those cheated of the land. The former is quite experienced and can easily raise capital to improve the land; the latter is not quite as experienced and has very little capital, for understandable reasons. It seems clear that (1) the land should be given to the latter individual and (2) the other prospering farmers should provide him with capital, as well as contributing funds to help the other deprived rightful owners in every way possible. The authority's action of distributing the rectifying burdens in all sorts of coin has, in such a case, resulted in justice. This situation is, it seems to me, relevantly similar to the situation in which preferential hiring should occur.

I would like to suggest, however, that there can be special circumstances which should influence our views on what kinds of costs are to be exacted from the various members of an unfairly advantaged group. In particular, we should ask ourselves whether in some circumstances the burden imposed on an individual by preferential hiring is too heavy. In many academic fields, for example, the job market is quite poor at present, especially for young aspirants. There are so few openings in some fields that it is almost impossible to get a position. Many a young white, encouraged rather than warned by his advisors, has invested a tremendous amount of energy and emotion in an academic career only to discover when he begins job seeking (or is forced to look for yet another temporary position) that he has little chance of success. Suppose such a person does land a campus interview, does very well, but is rejected in favor of a black competitor who is equally or almost as qualified as he is. This could severely threaten his career, for although there are not many black candidates as yet for many academic fields, there also are precious few openings. Is this not asking too much? Or suppose there is a general economic depression which makes new jobs extremely scarce. Should the young white, already severely limited in his opportunities, be given the additional handicap which preferential hiring imposes, when older whites with jobs bear a much lighter burden?

The burden on young whites in such circumstances is indeed disproportionately severe and should be lightened, but *not* by abandoning preferential hiring. The burden of a bad job market falls most heavily on the disadvantaged. Obviously, whatever opportunities remain for positions are *more* open to those who can compete for them, and the ability to compete depends on the advantages one has or has not received. Moreover, the burden on the young white in such circumstances in not *quite* as heavy as it might seem. He does not have a right to a *career*: he has the right to *compete* for any opening in his chosen field, and he retains that right. Nor can he charge that the competition he lost due to preferential hiring was *unfair*, if the argument against the first allegation of injustice is correct.[25] Nevertheless, he has been put in a more difficult position than his older white counterpart, and his burden ought to be lightened. Others who have benefited from injustice to blacks, however innocently, who are fortunate enough to have relatively secure positions, should in such special circumstances help their young would-be colleagues and co-workers.[26] Payment in some coin to the young whites to alleviate their too-heavy burdens, especially measures aimed at improving their competitive standing (e.g., research fellowships for academics, job-retraining and job-retooling programs), should be provided. This can be done most effectively through professional organizations. Such actions ought to be considered very seriously at present.

Consider a modification of the land analogy. Suppose the farming market were extremely tight, but that the central authority otherwise faced the same decision between the two applicants as sketched before. I believe we would, in his place, still decide to give the land to the person who is disadvantaged. It would however, be appropriate in this situation for the already established farmers to give aid to the young loser of the competition (as well as aid to the winner and to others in his group.) Thus burdens would remain equal.

In conclusion: I have argued that preferential hiring does not unjustly sacrifice the interests of those excluded from jobs on its basis. It is one legitimate means of rectifying the inequality of opportunity which discrimination causes. It must not be forgotten that it is but *one* such means, that it should be treated as one part of a package of policies having the same goal. It is no simple matter to determine what the most efficacious and just policies should be and to fashion them into a coherent overall policy, but intelligent persons of good will should be able to succeed in this task. Justice requires that it be done.

Notes

*This paper has profited from discussion with my husband and colleague, Werner S. Pluhar. I am also indebted to the editor of [*The Philosophical Forum*] for helpful criticisms.

1. For convenience's sake, the term "discrimination" will in this paper be short for "discrimination on the basis of irrelevant characteristics."

2. *Cf.*, e.g., A. H. Goldman, "Reparations to Individuals or Groups?", *Reverse Discrimination*, ed. Barry Gross (New York: Prometheus Books, 1977), p. 322; Barry Gross, "Is Turn About Fair Play?", *ibid.*, pp. 386–387; Robert Hoffman, "Justice, Merit, and the Good," *ibid.*, p. 368; and Robert Simon, "Preferential Hiring: A Reply to Judith Jarvis Thompson," *Equality and Preferential Treatment*, eds. M. Cohen, T. Nagel, T. Scanlan (Princeton: Princeton University Press, 1977), pp. 40–48.

3. Bernard Boxill, "The Morality of Preferential Hiring," *Philosophy and Public Affairs*, 7, No. 3 (Spring 1978). Cf. also Alison Jagger, "Relaxing the Limits on Preferential Treatment," *Social Theory and Practice*, 4, No. 2 (Spring 1977).

4. Boxill, *op cit.*; George Sher, "Justifying Reverse Discrimination in Employment," *Equality and Preferential Treatment*, pp. 54–55.

5. Jagger, p. 234.

6. They have in fact been defended persuasively by reference to Rawls's principle of maximizing the lot of those most disadvantaged in a society. See, e.g., Alan H. Goldman, "Reverse

Discrimination and the Future: A Reply to Irving Thalberg," *The Philosophical Forum*, 6, Nos. 2 – 3 (1974), 325.

7. Irving Thalberg, "Reverse Discrimination and the Future," *Sex Equality*, ed. Jane English (Engelwood Cliffs: Prentice-Hall, 1977), pp. 161 – 169.

8. I do not deny that preferential hiring might *also* be justified as a means of exacting damages for past injustices, as Goldman argues in "Reverse Discrimination and the Future: A Reply to Irving Thalberg," *op. cit*. But, as Goldman himself points out, "there are two distinct grounds of justification for reverse discrimination," (p. 321), one of them being the Thalberg type of approach.

9. Following basic English, the masculine pronoun will here be used in its generic sense.

10. James Nickel, "Preferential Policies in Hiring and Admissions: A Jurisprudential Approach," *Reverse Discrimination*, pp. 338 – 339.

11. By "young" I am referring simply to the age group *most likely* to be of relevance here.

12. I do not imply that all or most whites are innocent, but some clearly are, and it is they who are claimed to be most wronged by preferential hiring.

13. Hoffman, p. 368.

14. Gross, p. 386.

15. Boxill, p. 265.

16. Fullenwider, "Preferential Hiring and Compensation," *Social Theory and Practice*, 3 (1975), 316 – 317.

17. Boxill, p. 265.

18. *Ibid.*, pp. 266 – 267.

19. *Ibid.*, p. 266.

20. Nickel, pp. 338 – 339.

21. E.g., the preference of veterans to nonveterans in the job market cited by Nickel on p. 339.

22. Sher, pp. 54 – 55.

23. *Ibid.*, p. 54, note 7.

24. This point also applies to those who gain jobs in the absence of black competition.

25. Cf. my p. 218. See also Boxill, p. 266.

26. Judith Jarvis Thompson also suggests that tenured white professors provide some form of compensation to young whites who are denied jobs on the basis of preferential hiring in her "Preferential Hiring," *Equality and Preferential Treatment*, p. 39. She does not, however, there consider the question of what is owed by tenured professors to blacks. The question of what constitutes a fair burden cannot be settled without taking this into account.

Laura M. Purdy

IN DEFENSE OF HIRING APPARENTLY LESS QUALIFIED WOMEN

A Man's mind — what there is of it — has always the advantage of being masculine — as the smallest birchtree is of higher kind than the most soaring palm — and even his ignorance is of a sounder quality.

George Elliot,
Middlemarch, Ch. 2

There are relatively few women in academe, and it is reasonable to believe that discrimination — conscious and unconscious, subtle and overt, individual and institutional — is responsible for this state of affairs.[1] Affirmative action programs have been promoted to try to neutralize this discrimination. One form requires academic departments to search actively for female candidates; if a woman with qualifications at least as good as those of the leading male contender is found, she is to be hired.

Does this policy create new and serious injustice, as some contend?[2] If a woman and a man were equally qualified, and one could be sure that prejudice against women played no part in the decision to hire, such a policy would certainly be an imposition on the department's freedom to hire the most compatible-seeming colleague. (This is not to say that such an imposition could never be justified: we might, for example, believe that the importance of creating role models for female students justifies some loss of freedom on the part of departments.) However, it is widely conceded that there is prejudice against women among academics, with the result that women are not getting the appointments they deserve. My intent here is to consider how this happens. I will argue that women are often not perceived to be as highly qualified as they really are. Thus when the qualifications of candidates are compared, a woman may not be thought equally (or more highly) qualified, even when she is. Affirmative action programs which require hiring of equally qualified women will therefore be ineffective: the hiring of women perceived to be less qualified is needed if discrimination against women is to cease.

Some people think that the latter course is both unnecessary and unfair. Alan Goldman, for instance, maintains that it is unnecessary because the procedural requirements of good affirmative action programs are sufficient to guarantee equal opportunity. He also believes it to be unfair because it deprives the most successful new Ph.D.'s of their just reward — a good job.[3] I will argue that neither of these claims is true and that there is a good case for hiring women perceived to be less well qualified than their male competitors.

The general difficulty of forming accurate assessments of candidates' merit

From *Journal of Social Philosophy*, 15, no. 2 (Summer 1984), 26–33. Used by permission of the editor.

is well-known, and it is probable that the better candidate has sometimes been taken for the worse. It is reasonable to believe, however, that the subjective elements in evaluations lead to systematic lowering of women's perceived qualifications. I have two arguments for this claim. The first is that past prejudice biases the evidence and the second is that present prejudice biases perception of the evidence. Let us examine each in turn.

Why then may women be better qualified than their records suggest? One principal reason is that many men simply do not take women seriously:

> You might think that the evaluation of a specific performance would be an objective process, judged on characteristics of performance itself rather than on assumptions about the personality or ability of the performer. Yet performance is rarely a totally objective process. Two people may view the same event and interpret it differently. In the same way, it is possible for someone to view two people acting in exactly the same way and yet come to different conclusions about that behavior.[4]

Studies by Rosenthal and Jacobson provide experimental support for this claim. They found that students reported one group of rats to run mazes faster than another identical group, when they had previously been told that the first group was brighter. Ann Sutherland Harris quite plausibly concludes that such studies have important implications for women:

> If male scholars believe that women are intellectually inferior to men — less likely to have original contributions to make, less likely to be logical, and so on — will they not also find the evidence to support their beliefs in the women students in their classes, evidence of a far more sophisticated nature than the speed at which one rat finds its way through a maze? Their motives will be subconscious. Indeed, they will firmly believe that their judgment is rational and objective.[5]

What grounds are there for maintaining that this does not occur whenever women are evaluated? Other studies suggest additional hurdles for women that bias the evidence upon which they are judged. For instance, male students (though not female ones) rate identical course syllabi higher when the professor is said to be a man.[6]

Sociologist Jessie Bernard suggests that bias occurs whether women present accepted ideas or novel ones. In one study, a man and woman taught classes using the same material. The man engaged the students' interest: he was thought both more biased and more authoritative than the equally competent woman. According to Bernard, she was taken less seriously because she did not "look the part."[7] To support her position that novel ideas are less well received from women than men, Bernard mentions the case of Agnes Pockels, whose discoveries in physics were ignored for years. She cites this as an example of the general inability to see women in "the idea-man or instrumental role. We are simply not used to looking for innovation and originality from women"[8] The consequences of failing to take new ideas seriously may be even more detrimental to women than the failure to be taken seriously as a teacher. Bernard argues: "The importance of priority . . . highlights the importance of followers, or, in the case of science, of the public qualified to judge innovations. If an innovation is not recognized — even if recognition takes the form of rejection and a fight — it is dead."[9]

Additional persuasive evidence that women's ideas are not taken seriously by men comes from a study by Daryl and Sandra Bem, replicating a previous study by Philip Goldberg with women. A number of scholarly articles were submitted to a group of undergraduate men, who were to judge how good they were. Each paper was read by each man, but the paper read by half the students was attributed to a man, that read by the other half, to a woman. The results were striking: the "man's" article was rated higher than the "woman's" in most cases.[10] Does this prejudice continue to operate at more advanced levels?

One significant study showed more papers by women were chosen for presentation at the annual meeting of a national professional organization when they were submitted anonymously.[11] This suggests that whether a woman's work is published or not will also depend more on the reviewers' conception of women than upon the merits of the piece — at least until blind reviewing becomes the rule. Furthermore, there is evidence that even when a woman is recognized as having done a good job at some task, her performance is more likely than a man's to be attributed to factors other than ability. Hence others are less likely to expect future repeated success on her part.[12] And, unsuccessful performance by a male is more likely than that of a female to be attributed to bad luck.[13] Studies have also shown that male applicants for scholarship funds were judged more intelligent and likeable than their female counterparts,[14] and that males were favored over females for study abroad programs.[15] In addition, until very recently, recommendations written for women were more likely to mention personal appearance in an undermining way (as well as marital status) than those written for men.[16] These facts have obvious repercussions for candidates' overall records. Hence if the hypotheses considered so far here are true, then women are systematically undervalued with respect to some of the most widely-used indicators of quality.

Much of this bias could be neutralized if women were able to attract the best faculty as mentors. Bernard stresses the importance of mentors:

> The association of the graduate student with his mentor may make all the difference between success or lack of it in his subsequent career. If a top man takes him under his wing, doors will open for him and he will be in the club. If no one takes him on, he may never arrive professionally. He will not be recommended for the best jobs; he will not be in.[17]

The existence of a first-rate mentor is doubly important for women, if the results of a study by Gail Pheterson, Sara Kiesler, and Philip Goldberg are valid.[18] It suggests that women's performances will be taken seriously if an authority publicly recognizes their worth. This is because it is sometimes difficult to judge quality and in an ambiguous case, sexual stereotypes tend to step in to "help" the viewer decide. But there is no need for this when an individual acknowledged to be an expert has affirmed the value of the work.

Kay Deaux reports that this tendency is particularly evident when the judge has little training in the area to be evaluated. This is presumably not the case when faculties judge candidates within their own discipline. But it is plausible to believe that the uncertain nature of standards and the ambiguous performances in academe — especially in the conflict-ridden humanities — creates some of the same pressures. Bernard provides more support for this hypothesis when, in another context, she comments: "Because there are so few objective criteria for judging the worth of a person and because so much competition is

judgmental in nature, academic people depend on recognition from one another to a greater extent than do those in professions where autonomous
competition is the rule."[19]

Thus graduate school mentors could help talented women achieve the professional recognition they deserve. Unfortunately women are less likely to
enjoy the advantages of a good mentor. The best graduate schools have few
women on their faculties and not every such woman will be interested in or
capable of helping others advance. The men in such schools, with their poor
record of hiring women, appear to be among the most prejudiced against them
and hence cannot be counted on for help here.[20] The failure to take women
seriously in graduate schools downgrades their apparent quality. This diminishes their chance of obtaining a prestigious post where they will have the
opportunity to do significant research; in the current market, it also diminishes the probability that they will find any job in their field.

As if this were not enough, they run the risk of having their already undervalued qualifications devalued again when they are candidates for a position.
This conclusion is supported by a study which showed that the same dossier
was often ranked higher by academic departments when it was attributed to a
man than when it was attributed to a woman.[21] Research on interviews also
suggests that both men and women are systematically biased against women.[22]

I have been arguing that women are likely to be more highly qualified than
they seem. This fact alone would support a policy of hiring women perceived
to be less qualified. However, I think there is another sound argument for such
a policy. Women may sometimes be less qualified than their male competitors
because as students they faced stumbling-blocks the men did not. Hence some
women probably deserve their weak recommendations and dearth of publications because their work is less fully developed and their claims less well
supported than a man's might be. This can occur because women's social role
often precludes opportunities for informal constructive criticism; it may also
be the result of the lack of a mentor to push her to her limits. Finally, a woman is
likely to have had to work in a debilitating environment of lowered
expectations.[23]

Goldman argues that it would be wrong to hire such a woman if there were a
more qualified candidate: ". . . the white male who has successfully met the
requirements necessary to attaining maximal competence attains some right to
that position. It seems unjust for society to set standards of achievement and
then to thwart the expectations of those who have met those standards."[24]

But surely hiring is ultimately intended to produce the best scholar and
teacher, not to reward the most successful graduate student. Consequently, if
there are grounds for believing that women turn into the former, despite not
having been the latter according to the traditional criteria, it is reasonable to
hold that they should sometimes be hired anyway. And there are such grounds.

The obstacles encountered by women in academe are well-documented and
there is no need to elaborate at length upon them here. What matters is the
nature of the person they create. Until very recently, at every stage of schooling, fewer girls than boys continued.[25] There is considerable evidence that
women graduate students have higher academic qualifications than their male
counterparts.[26] This appears to be because only the very highly qualified get
into graduate school.[27] Harris argues that it ". . . is worth remembering that
women candidates for graduate school are the survivors of a long sifting

process — only the very best of the good students' go on to graduate school."[28] A report issued by women at the University of Chicago supports this claim — the grade averages of women students entering graduate school were significantly higher than those of men.[29]

Once there, women have somewhat higher attrition rates than men. But Harris thinks that this is "largely explained by the lack of encouragement and the actual discouragement experienced by women graduate students for their career plans. . . . It is not surprising that some women decide that they are not cut out to be scholars and teachers."[30] She argues that if women were not highly committed, the attrition rate would be much higher; ". . . only the hardiest survive."[31]

In light of all these facts, a temporary policy of hiring women perceived to be less well qualified would be reasonable, to see if the hypothesis that they will bloom is borne out. Such a policy is less risky than it might seem since junior faculty members are on probation and can be fired if they do not start to fulfill their promise.

In conclusion, there are good grounds for at least a trial of the policy I am proposing with regard to hiring in academe, since existing affirmative action programs have not been and cannot be effective.[32] I have tried to show why women may often seem less qualified than they really are, and why they may be more promising than they seem. Unless faculty members take these factors into account, no improvement in the position of women can be expected, for women are likely to seem less worthy of being hired than their male competitors when they are judged in the usual manner. Requiring departments to hire women perceived to be less well qualified may well turn out to be the most efficacious way to force departments to recognize and remedy the situation. It might also have a more generally beneficial side-effect of promoting faculty-members' awareness of their own biases as they struggle to distinguish between truly mediocre women and those merely perceived to be so!

Notes

1. The general trend continues to be that the more prestigious the post or institution, the fewer women there are to be found. See, for instance, "Status of Female Faculty Members, 1979–80," *The Chronicle of Higher Education*, 29 September 1980.

2. See Alan Goldman, "Affirmative Action," *Philosophy and Public Affairs*, Vol. 5, n. 2 (Winter 1976), 178.

3. Ibid.

4. Kay Deaux, *The Behavior of Women and Men* (Monterey, Ca.: Brooks/Cole Publishing Co., 1976), p. 24.

5. Ann Sutherland Harris reports this study in "The Second Sex in Academe" in *And Jill Came Tumbling After: Sexism in American Education*, ed. Judith Stacey et al. (New York: 1974), p. 299.

6. Jessie Bernard, *Academic Women* (New York: Meridian Press, 1965), pp. 255–257. "The 'teachers' were selected by the department as being of about equal competence in communications skills. They were given two written lectures to deliver to sections of Sociology 1 . . . . both young people were given the lectures in advance, and they agreed on how to interpret all major points in their presentations, which were to be identical. One spoke to each section and a week later each spoke to the other section" (p. 256).

7. Ibid.

8. Ibid.

9. Ibid.

10. Reported by Deaux, p. 25.

11. This study appeared in "On Campus with Women," March 1977, Association of American Colleges, and was reported in *Ms.*, Vol. 7, n. 5 (November 1978), 87. *Ms.* writes: "In 1973, at the last annual conference held before the policy was initiated, 6.3 percent of the papers selected were from women scholars. In 1975, 17 percent of the papers selected were from women scholars." The organization in question is the Archaeological Institute of America.

12. Veronica F. Nieva and Barbara Gutek, "Sex Effects on Evaluation.," *Academy of Management Review*, Vol. 5, n. 2 (1980), p. 267.

13. Ibid., p. 270.

14. Ibid., p. 268.

15. Ibid.

16. Jennie Farley, "Academic Recommendations: Males and Females as Judges and Judged," *AAUP Bulletin*, Vol. 64, n. 2 (May 1978), p. 84.

17. Bernard, p. 140.

18. Reported by Deaux, p. 25.

19. Bernard, p. 193.

20. See Harris, above.

21. L. S. Fidell, "Empirical Verification of Sex Discrimination in Hiring Practices in Psychology," *American Psychologist*, Vol. 60 (1970), 1049–98.

22. Robert L. Dipboye, Richard D. Arvey, and David E. Terpstra, "Sex and Physical Attractiveness of Raters and Applicants as Determinants of Resume Evaluations," *Journal of Applied Psychology*, Vol. 62, n. 3 (June 1977), p. 288. This study was limited to undergraduate students, however, so it should not be assumed that it can be generalized to the educated population we are concerned with here.

23. Nieva and Gutek, p. 271.

24. Goldman, p. 191.

25. See Harris and Barnard in Stacey et al., pp. 302–305.

26. Harris, pp. 304–305.

27. Ibid.

28. Ibid.

29. Ibid.

30. Ibid.

31. Ibid.

32. Ibid., pp. 297–298. My own experience at the prestigious Ivy League institution where I took my Ph.D. was far from encouraging. When I arrived, there were no women faculty members. The class before mine, numbering about 10, contained no women, and I was the only woman in my class of about 10. Twice in my first year I was present in groups addressed by professors as "Gentlemen." One of these occasions was especially fraught with emotion. I and four men gathered at a professor's office to return one of the crucial 4-hour field exams required of first-year students. The professor beamed at us and said, "Well, we'll see how you did, gentlemen!"

See *Sex Discrimination in Higher Education*, ed. Jennie Farley, (Ithaca: ILR Publications, 1981).

Sidney Hook

RATIONALIZATIONS FOR REVERSE DISCRIMINATION

The progress of civilization is marked, among other things, by the abolition of the blood feud. This is the practice of continued hostility over generations often marked by murder based on the views of collective, inherited guilt for a crime committed in the past. Although the blood feud often involves murder, those who engage in it deny that their killing is murder if murder is defined as the killing of the innocent. But since it is not difficult to establish the innocence of most victims of blood feuds, when that is established, other rationalizations are sought for the practice. Sometimes religious justifications are introduced. There is the biblical pronouncement "I shall visit the sins of the fathers upon the heads of the children unto the third and fourth generation." Yet no one can morally justify such a view of collective guilt over time. The law in all enlightened jurisdictions recognizes that guilt is individual.

There is, to be sure, a distinction between collective guilt and collective responsibility; one can accept the validity of the latter concept in some situations without accepting the former. In the West, however, the responsibility for the commission of immoral or illegal acts is generally recognized as individual, not collective. Since invidious discrimination against persons on the basis of race, color, sex or national origin is rightfully regarded as immoral today, no one can reasonably object to the punishment of individual persons guilty of such discrimination. The punishment may take many forms in order to redress the sufferings of those victimized. But it is clear that current applications of affirmative action, by going beyond the outlawing of present day discrimination and requiring preferential hiring practices on the basis of race and sex, constitute a form of punishment based on the concept of collective rather than individual guilt and responsibility. This is evidenced by the manifest injustices committed against white males who by no stretch of the imagination can be regarded as responsible for present or past practices of invidious discrimination. I myself am acquainted with half a dozen young white males who, after long years of intense preparation, have been prevented from achieving an academic career in the humanities, and are compelled to look elsewhere for work by the refusal of administrative officers in the institutions where they applied even to grant them interviews. This was an injustice not only to these highly qualified candidates but to all students — black and white — in the institutions which accepted less academically qualified applicants in place of those summarily rejected for reasons of race or sex.

There are some situations in which the claims of justice may be overridden on behalf of other values — e.g., safety and social stability. And there are some advocates of affirmative action based on reverse discrimination who do in fact acknowledge its injustice with respect to young white males and to student bodies but insist that these are the necessary and unavoidable costs of beneficent social policy. Such judgments are based on empirical estimates of consequences.

From *New Perspectives*, 17 (Winter 1985), 9–11. Reprinted by permission.

I doubt, however, whether anyone can establish that the results of quota systems, lax or discriminatory open admissions policies or reverse discrimination in hiring practices have contributed to the quality and discipline of the educational experience or that strict application of the merit principle would pose a threat to basic peace and social order. On the contrary, were the Supreme Court to reverse itself and mandate that the claims of the seniority system were subordinate to those of the affirmative action quota programs, the result would be chaos and conflict in many institutions and industries. Indeed, on the basis of *their* empirical experience, a majority of whites and blacks in some opinion surveys have time and again declared themselves opposed to reverse discrimination and quotas.

Militant advocates of discriminatory affirmative action programs insist that despite the objections raised, these programs are based on justice. They assert that even if minorities and women are given equal opportunities in the present, even if they are not subjected to any invidious discrimination, they still suffer collectively under the weight of past discrimination. They claim that despite enlightened treatment of minorities and women in the recent past, despite all encouragement and remedial programs, these victimized groups suffer from the cumulative effects of the previous discrimination against their forbearers, and that among these effects from the distant past are loss of confidence, self-contempt and lower expectations resulting from the absence of role models in many areas of life.

It is further argued that even if some women and members of minority groups have not themselves suffered directly from the environment in which they grew up, they have suffered debilitating consequences *indirectly* from the discrimination against their brothers and sisters of earlier times and that present day society should therefore make amends to them even if by so doing it does less than justice to some white males. The latter, it is asserted, even if not guilty themselves of having wronged minorities and women, have profited from the wrongs imposed and the opportunities denied to minorities and women by the past policies of the community.

This line of argument seems to me to be very far fetched and invalid. For one thing, the present descendants of *any* group that suffered severe discrimination in the past, could, by the same mode of argument, make similar claims for preferential treatment and hiring. Faced by such claims in any particular situation, we would have to determine the relative degree, intensity and duration of the injustices of the past with respect to each candidate. Anyone who knows the history of the United States knows of the persecutions to which the Jews, the Irish, the Mormons, the Chinese and Japanese were subjected, to mention only major groups. Yet none of these groups has asked for preferential treatment. All they have ever demanded is that one equitable standard by applied to all. Of course, our knowledge of American history also tells us that none of the aforementioned groups, even when periodically subjected to mayhem, suffered the evils and consequences of slavery. But surely there are *some* individuals from discriminated groups not recognized today as protected minorities for purposes of preferential treatment who have suffered as much as or more than *some* present day individual blacks who may be competing for the same position. It would be absurd to attempt to undertake an inquiry in each individual case to make comparative evaluations.

Secondly, if it is the community which is responsible for the injustice of the past to minorities and women, why should the burden of compensating such injustices now fall upon young white males alone? To allege that the white male who may himself be from a poor and underprivileged family has necessarily profited from the deprivations and psychic damage of present day descendents of the enslaved is a claim that borders on fantasy. Wisdom suggests that instead of correcting the injustices of yesterday by creating the new injustices of today, it is better to recognize a statute of limitations on present day accountability for man's inhumanity to man in the distant past.

In many areas, society has already long acknowledged the need for a statute of limitations on the obligations incurred by injustices of the past when the effect of attempting to counteract or undo long past wrongs is to create new and possibly greater wrongs. There is no doubt that property was unjustifiably seized or fraudulently acquired by early American settlers from the native population. But even if it were possible to establish the truth about these spoliations centuries ago, to contest or deny legitimate title to the current possessions of those who purchased them in good faith would generate social chaos. Similar considerations apply to the current recognition of squatters rights. Even in the area of criminal law, except for treason and capital crimes, statutes of limitation of varying durations are the rule. In various state jurisdictions, contractual obligations lapse after a certain period of time.

There is one particular response that is often made to the proposal that we recognize a statute of limitations on accountability for injustices of the distant past and conscientiously and honestly abide in the present and future by the merit principle. This response invokes a deceptive analogy: "If you handicap a runner at the outset of the race," say the advocates of preferential hiring, "by burdening him with heavy chains, you cannot make it a fair race by removing the chains from his limbs when the race has been half run. He will still suffer unfairly from the effects of that handicap."

Of course, this is perfectly true for the individual runner in this particular race and possibly in subsequent races in which he engages. He is certainly entitled to special consideration and treatment to overcome his handicap. This is nothing but a simple application of the principle of justice on which there is universal agreement, viz., that any person who has been unfairly discriminated against in the past is entitled to compensatory treatment. But surely this does not entitle the descendants of the originally handicapped person who are running against others in subsequent races to a privilege of handicap over them. Who knows but that the ancestors of the others in the race were also handicapped unjustly in past races.

There is also something very nebulous about postulating the harm done to individuals by social practices that undermine their self-confidence. The same conditions that depress and discourage one person may inspire another to revolt against these conditions, or to rise to a challenge. Further, when we have to make a choice between specific candidates, how do we balance the possible lack of confidence of a minority because of past discrimination against members of his group and the danger of a crisis of self-confidence that often arises when one profits from discrimination and subsequently encounters the judgment of one's professional peers that the post or award was not earned by merit but by special favor?

To give weight to possible injustices from the past, and their alleged continuing debilitating effect on individuals in the present, without tracing the spe-

cific proximate causes of discriminatory actions, encourages fantastic specula-
tions of a conflicting kind. Because some blacks have said that they prefer their
present status in the United States to that of the present African descendants of
blacks whose ancestors were not sold by their chiefs of kidnapped by Arab
raiders into slavery, should the relatively superior status of American blacks, as
compared to what would have been their lot if their ancestors had remained in
Africa, be entered into the equation when calculating what society owes them?
This would be absurd. Here we are dealing with hypothetical possibilities that
defy not only quantification but significant comparison.

Another questionable assumption by those who speculate about the might-
have-beens of the past is that we can retroactively determine what would have
been the vocational interests of members of discriminated-against minorities if
they had not experienced any prejudice against them. We therefore can reasonably assess — so it is argued — the advantages thereby gained by contemporary
white males in particular fields from the cumulative frustrations of the lives of
the minorities in the past and make it clear what the former owe the latter. This
presupposes, among other things, that in the absence of persecution and discrimination, all groups will manifest interest in various vocational fields
roughly in the same proportions. It overlooks the variety of cultural, religious
and historical factors that may operate in determining the vocational orienta-
tions of different groups. (It is, moreover, an elementary fallacy to infer merely
from the statistical inequalities of representation, without evidence of individual discrimination, an overall practice of past or present discrimination. No
informed person or one with a sense of humor would infer from the fact that 92
percent of the captains of tug boats in New York harbor and adjoining waters
are Swedish, and from the fact that no a single Jew is among them, that the
industry is anti-Semitic or, for that matter, anti-black.)

One must acknowledge that the experiences of the blacks who endured
slavery and the Jim Crow laws of the post-Reconstruction era were worse than
the humiliations and handicaps of any other minority group in this country
except the American Indians. But one cannot convert this acknowledgement
into a sufficient criterion for public policy in making positions available to the
descendants of blacks regardless of their qualifications. After all, there are black
immigrants to the United States who were never slaves or were slaves for a
short time before being liberated. And how shall we assess the effects of
oppression on persons of mixed blood? Implicit in the very essence of a social
policy of preferential treatment based on race is the assumption that members of
victimized minorities in the past were a compact, passive mass, incapable of
differentiated responses and lacking all initiative and responsibility for making
choices, however limited, that would in some way have altered their lot.
Stripped of its moralistic rhetoric, the reverse discrimination approach represents a condescending and disparaging attitude towards an entire race, an attitude which many blacks quite properly resent.

We should also question the assumption that minorities were seriously
handicapped because they were deprived of role models, especially in the
educational system at the level of college and university life. The fact that there
were once no role models for aspiring black athletes in some professional
sports, particularly major league baseball, a field from which American blacks
were unfairly and shamefully excluded, did not prevent blacks from acquiring

the skills of star players and—once Jackie Robinson broke the color bar—from achieving outstanding careers in all major sports. The best players were recruited for baseball, football and basketball teams, regardless of the percentage of black and white players represented on the team in relation to the distribution of blacks and whites in the general population. In this field we do not hear of setting up numerical goals and definite time periods within which these goals are to be achieved.

There is no reason to doubt the potential ability of blacks, other minorities and women when given the opportunities in an atmosphere free of invidious discrimination to reach achievement comparable to those of the general population. It requires, of course, the sacrifice or postponement of immediate gratifications in order to achieve success. Preferential treatment, quota systems, reverse discrimination of any variety, are likely in actual effect to harm the prospects of achievement for blacks by wrongly suggesting to them that there is a shortcut to success.

The black experience in professional sports may in fact be taken as a paradigm case of how to combat invidious discrimination without a demand for reverse discrimination. If the bars of racial discrimination are removed in *all* fields and remedial programs are introduced to supplement the educational activities of those interested in learning, who is to predict what the outcome will be? One thing, however, is certain. Just as skill and success in athletics are not simply gifts bestowed at birth but are the result of harnessing native talents to a hard and sustained discipline, so too will meaningful achievement in any field of endeavor depend upon that same sort of effort and commitment.

DISCUSSION QUESTIONS

1. Nagel argued in 1981 that strong affirmative action (hiring lesser qualified candidates because of their race or sex) was justified because it advanced a critical social goal. He anticipated that strong affirmative action for blacks would be necessary until the early decades of the next century and for a shorter time for women and other minorities. Do you agree with his general argument? Do you agree with his timetable?

2. Nagel admits that strong affirmative action is intrinsically undesirable. How would a deontological thinker evaluate weak and strong affirmative action?

3. Groarke makes the critical point that ordinary affirmative action programs neither compensate the main victims nor tax the main beneficiaries of discrimination. How serious a problem is this from an ethical perspective? How should this matter be addressed?

4. If you failed to get a job because of a company's preferential hiring program, would you find Pluhar's arguments persuasive that you had no moral grounds to claim that you were treated unjustly?

5. Do you agree with Purdy's claim that women often seem less qualified than they actually are?

6. Hook opposes affirmative action programs because they are based on the notion of "collective guilt." Do you agree with Hook that this idea is morally questionable?

7. Hook questions the assumption that women and minorities were harmed by the absence of role models in the professions. He claims that the absence of role models in professional sports did not prevent black athletes from excelling. Does this overthrow the role model argument?

CASE 14.1

Did It Work?

Opponents of affirmative action claim that the more than two decades of such programs have achieved their goal — greater representation of racial minorities and women in the work force. Moreover, they claim that continuation of affirmative action will amount to nothing more than reverse discrimination against white men. But did affirmative action succeed in ending racial discrimination and ensuring that blacks would be judged in business strictly on merit?

The gains over the last twenty-five years are impressive. The percentage of blacks in the work force has risen by 50 percent. In 1966, only 1 percent of all managers in the United States were black; in 1989, that figure was 5 percent. In the 1960s, fewer than 15 percent of black families had middle-class incomes, but by 1988, a third of all black families had incomes between $25,000 and $50,000.

However, not all the statistics are this positive. Blacks make up nearly 13 percent of the work force in the private sector, but they hold only 5 percent of the professional positions. Nearly 60 percent of whites work as managers, professionals, or administrators, while fewer than 25 percent of blacks do so. More than 50 percent of blacks work as service personnel or laborers, as compared to 38 percent of whites. Moreover, many jobs that allowed blacks to move into the middle class — public sector professional positions, high-paying factory jobs, positions in corporate community relations and affirmative action offices — are being eliminated in the shift to a lower-paying service economy and an overall financial belt-tightening by business and government. This makes future prospects uncertain at best.

Incomes of blacks also continue to lag behind those of whites. In 1970, the median income of a black family was 61 percent that of a white family; in 1988, the difference had increased by another 4 percent. In 1988, 32 percent of blacks were living in poverty (income of less than $12,092 for a family of four), as compared to only 10 percent of whites. A 1984 Census Bureau study found that the median net worth of a black family was only 9 percent of the median net worth of a white family. The same pattern held among middle-class blacks and whites, with the median net worth of blacks being 54 percent that of whites with the same income. It is disturbing that not even greater access to higher education allowed blacks to keep pace with whites. In 1979, white male college graduates between the ages of 25 and 34 earned 12 percent more than similarly schooled black men; in 1989, the difference had more than doubled to 26 percent. Also, in 1979, the median earnings of whites between 25 and 64 were 18 percent higher than those of blacks; in 1989, the gap was 32 percent. ◆

Discussion Questions

1. In light of the statistics presented in the case study, has affirmative action worked?

2. To what do you attribute the fact that most blacks are worse off economically in relation to whites? Is this in some way still the consequence of past discrimination? Is it the result of present bias?

3. The policies of the Reagan and Bush administrations were generally unsympathetic to affirmative action. Does the increasing disparity between the economic fortunes of whites and blacks suggest that these policies were ethically questionable, making matters worse rather than better?

4. What should happen now? Should affirmative action programs be eliminated? Should we continue what we have been doing over the last quarter century? Should we initiate programs that are more aggressive than those in the past?

Sources

"The Black Middle Class," *Business Week*, March 14, 1988, 62–70.
"Male College Grads: The Racial Pay Gap Is Widening," *Business Week*, March 18, 1991, 20.
"Race in the Workplace: Is Affirmative Action Working?," *Business Week*, July 8, 1991, 50–62.

CASE 14.2

◆ ◆ ◆

Life-Style Discrimination?

"Discrimination" has traditionally been thought of as related mainly to race or gender. Some people, however, claim that businesses have begun discriminating against them on new grounds—how they live. For example, one of the fastest growing costs in business is employee health care. Many companies address this problem by allowing only people with healthy life-styles to work for them. If you smoke or drink—on or off the job—you would not be hired at many firms. Companies defend the practice as an effective way to contain costs. Critics label it *life-style discrimination*."

The issue is how many of an employee's activities in life are legitimately an employer's concern. Many employees argue that all that counts is whether they can perform the job. Unhealthy life-styles may be responsible for as much as 25 percent of a corporation's health care costs, however; and many companies argue that this fact makes an employee's habits their business.

Not surprisingly, many companies do not want to hire smokers because of the link between smoking and illness. Smokers among state employees in

Kansas spent nearly 70 percent more time in the hospital than nonsmokers in 1990. Employees at Control Data Corporation who smoke a pack or more of cigarettes a day had health care expenses nearly 120 percent higher than those of nonsmokers. Consequently, many companies flatly refuse to hire smokers. Others have instituted policies requiring that every smoker eventually quit smoking. At such companies, smoking — even in the privacy of one's home — could jeopardize one's job.

Smoking, however, is not the only habit that employers are worrying about. Mountain climbing, motorcycling, skydiving, and flying a private airplane are grounds for not being hired by at least one Georgia company. At one time, the Atlanta city government refused to hire people with a high cholesterol reading. And other factors have been found to correlate with higher health care costs. One study by the Control Data Corporation found that health care costs for obese employees were 11 percent higher than those for employees who were not overweight. The same study also showed that people with high blood pressure spent 25 percent more days in the hospital than their healthier coworkers, and employees who did not regularly use seat belts and were in car accidents spent 54 percent more time in the hospital than did those who used them.

Although some companies exclude risky employees altogether, other firms handle the situation differently. Some insist that employees share the burden of the consequences of their habits. For example, companies may make employees who smoke or are overweight contribute more than $100 to their annual health care premium. Other businesses take a more positive approach, rewarding employees for losing weight or exercising regularly.

Although companies cite financial benefits from monitoring employee life-styles, many employees understandably oppose the practice. They charge that hiring decisions or the assessing of health care costs based on private, nonbusiness practices is discriminatory. More than twenty states agree with this point of view and have laws that prohibit employer discrimination for off-the-job smoking or, in some cases, for any legal off-the-job activity. ◆

Discussion Questions

1. Critics of the practices described in this case study call them life-style discrimination. Not every case of treating people differently, however, is discrimination. Do you think these practices are discriminatory?

2. Discrimination is frequently thought to require not only that victims be treated differently, but also that they be stigmatized as inferior because of some trait that is out of their control, such as their race or sex. If a company said that it simply saw nonsmokers as less expensive employees, not as naturally superior human beings, would that constitute an adequate defense against the charge of discrimination?

3. Are all of the habits, activities, or characteristics described in the case study within an employee's control? Does that make any difference in how you assess these practices from an ethical perspective?

4. Are any of the following legitimate grounds on which to base employment decisions: smoking, drinking, blood pressure levels, weight, involvement in an exercise program?

5. If one group of employees can be predicted to have higher health care costs than other employees, is it fair to make everyone share these costs

equally? Yet, if the point of insurance is precisely to spread the cost of hardships over many individuals, is it fair to treat different members of the pool differently?

6. One study showed that people who are married or who otherwise have strong social ties are healthier than unmarried or socially isolated people. Indeed, the difference in the mortality of the two groups is roughly the same as the effect of smoking. Would this make one's marital status, or at least the character of one's social life, a legitimate matter of corporate inquiry?

Sources

"If You Light Up On Sunday, Don't Come In On Monday," *Business Week*, August 26, 1991, 68–72.

James, Frank E., "Study Lays Groundwork for Tying Health Costs to Workers' Behavior," *Wall Street Journal*, April 14, 1987, 35.

"Living Alone Can Be Hazardous to Your Health," *Business Week*, March 5, 1990, 20.

"None of an Employer's Business," *New York Times*, July 7, 1991, E10.

"No Smoking Or No Work," *New York Times*, February 28, 1988, 47.

ADDITIONAL READINGS

Blackstone, William, and Robert Heslep, *Social Justice and Preferential Treatment* (Athens: University of Georgia Press, 1977).

Cohen, Marshall, Thomas Nagel, and Thomas Scanlon, eds., *Equality and Preferential Treatment* (Princeton, NJ: Princeton University Press, 1977).

Goldman, Alan, *Justice and Reverse Discrimination* (Princeton, NJ: Princeton University Press, 1979).

Gross, Barry R., *Reverse Discrimination* (Buffalo, NY: Prometheus Books, 1977).

Hettinger, Edwin C., "What Is Wrong with Reverse Discrimination?," *Business & Professional Ethics Journal*, 6, no. 3 (1986) 39–55.

Lindgren, J. Ralph, "The Irrelevance of Philosophical Treatments of Affirmative Action," *Social Theory and Practice*, 7, no. 1 (Spring 1981), 1–19.

Newton, Lisa, "Reverse Discrimination as Unjustified," *Ethics* 83, no. 4 (July 1973), 308–312.

Sher, George, "Justifying Reverse Discrimination in Employment," *Philosophy & Public Affairs*, 4 (Winter 1975), 159–170.

———, "Reverse Discrimination, the Future, and the Past," *Ethics*, 90 (October 1979), 81–87.

Thompson, Judith Jarvis, "Preferential Hiring," *Philosophy & Public Affairs*, 2 (1973), 364–384.

van den Haag, Ernest, "Reverse Discrimination: A Brief Against It," *National Review*, 29, no. 16 (April 1977), 492–495.

Wasserstrom, Richard, "A Defense of Programs of Preferential Treatment," *National Forum: The Phi Kappa Phi Journal*, 58, no. 1 (Winter 1978), 15–18.

CHAPTER 15

◆ ◆ ◆

Sexual Harassment and Comparable Worth

The issues concerning affirmative action discussed in the preceding chapter stem from the blatant discrimination that was common against women and racial minorities — discrimination that civil rights legislation was designed to stop. Women charge, however, that they continue to be victimized in less overt ways. They report being harassed sexually and working at jobs that are undervalued. Despite legal remedies aimed at guaranteeing equality and respect for human dignity, women claim that sexual harassment and pay inequity persist. They call for harassment simply to stop, and they argue that salaries should be based on the *comparable worth* of jobs.

Susan Dodds, Lucy Frost, Robert Pargetter, and Elizabeth Prior begin this chapter with an explication of the notion of sexual harassment. Larry May and John Hughes explain its coercive nature. Then we consider comparable worth. June O'Neill's article argues against the concept, while two other pieces support it. Laurie Shrage provides an extensive defense against liberal, not conservative, critics, while Judith Olans Brown, Phyllis Tropper Bauman, and Elaine Millar Melnick offer only limited support.

Susan M. Dodds, Lucy Frost, Robert Pargetter, and Elizabeth W. Prior

SEXUAL HARASSMENT

Mary has a problem. Her boss, Bill, gives her a bad time. He is constantly making sexual innuendoes and seems always to be blocking her way and brushing against her. He leers at her, and on occasions has made it explicitly clear that it would be in her own best interests to go to bed with him. She is the one woman in the office now singled out for this sort of treatment, although she hears that virtually all other attractive women who have in the past worked for Bill have had similar experiences. On no occasion has Mary encouraged Bill. His attentions have all been unwanted. She has found them threatening, unpleasant and objectionable. When on some occasions she has made these reactions too explicit, she has been subjected to unambiguously detrimental treatment. Bill has no genuinely personal feelings for Mary, is neither truly affectionate nor loving: his motivation is purely sexual.

Surely this is a paradigmatic case of sexual harassment. Bill discriminates against Mary, and it seems that he would also discriminate against any other attractive woman who worked for him. He misuses his power as an employer when he threatens Mary with sex she does not want. His actions are clearly against her interests. He victimizes her at present and will probably force her to leave the office, whatever the consequences to her future employment.

Not all cases of sexual harassment are so clear. Indeed, each salient characteristic of the paradigmatic case may be missing and yet sexual harassment still occurs. Even if all the features are missing, it could still be a case of sexual harassment.

We aim to explicate the notion of sexual harassment. We note that our aim is not to provide an analysis of the ordinary language concept of sexual harassment. Rather we aim to provide a theoretical rationale for a more behavioral stipulative definition of sexual harassment. For it is an account of this kind which proves to be clearly superior for policy purposes. It provides the basis for a clear, just and enforceable policy, suitable for the workplace and for society at large. Of course ordinary language intuitions provide important touchstones. What else could we use to broadly determine the relevant kind of behavior? But this does not mean that all ordinary language considerations are to be treated as sacrosanct. Sexual harassment is a concept with roots in ordinary language, but we seek to develop the concept as one suitable for more theoretical purposes, particularly those associated with the purposes of adequate policy development.

In brief we aim to provide an account which satisfies three desiderata. The account should:

a. show the connection between harassment in general and sexual harassment
b. distinguish between sexual harassment and legitimate sexual interaction
c. be useful for policy purposes.

From *Social Theory and Practice*, 14 (Summer 1988), 111–130. Reprinted by permission.

1. SEXUAL HARASSMENT AND SEXUAL DISCRIMINATION

It seems plausible that minimally harassment involves discrimination, and more particularly, sexual harassment involves sexism. Sexual discrimination was clearly part of the harassment in the case of Mary and Bill.

The pull towards viewing sexual harassment as tied to sexual discrimination is strengthened by consideration of the status of most harassers and most harassees. In general, harassers are men in a position of power over female harassees. The roles of these men and women are reinforced by historical and cultural features of systematic sexual discrimination against women. Generally, men have control of greater wealth and power in our society, while women are economically dependent on men. Men are viewed as having the (positive) quality of aggression in sexual and social relations, while women are viewed as (appropriately) passive. These entrenched attitudes reflect an even deeper view of women as fundamentally unequal, that is in some sense, less fully persons than men. Sexual harassment, then, seems to be just one more ugly manifestation of the sexism and sexual inequality which is rampant in public life.

MacKinnon sees this connection as sufficient to justify treating cases of sexual harassment as cases of sexual discrimination.[1] Sexual discrimination, for MacKinnon, can be understood through two approaches. The first is the "difference approach," under which a "differentiation is based on sex when it can be shown that a person of the opposite sex in the same position is not treated the same." The other is the "inequality approach," which "requires no comparability of situation, only that a rule or practice disproportionately burden one sex because of sex."[2] Thus, even when no comparison can be made between the situation of male and female employees (for example, if the typing pool is composed entirely of women, then the treatment a woman in the pool receives cannot be compared with the treatment of a man in the same situation), if a rule or practice disproportionately burdens women, because they are women, that rule or practice is sexually discriminatory. For MacKinnon all cases of sexual harassment will be cases of sexual discrimination on one or other of these approaches.

Closer consideration reveals, however, that while discrimination may be present in cases of harassment, it need not be. More specifically, while sexual discrimination may be (and often is) present in cases of sexual harassment, it is not a necessary feature of sexual harassment.

The fact that in most cases women are (statistically, though not necessarily) the objects of sexual harassment, is an important feature of the issue of sexual harassment, and it means that in many cases where women are harassed, the harassment will involve sexual discrimination. However, sexual harassment need not entail sexual discrimination.

Consider the case of Mary A and Bill A, a case very similar to that of Mary and Bill. The only relevant difference is that Bill A is bisexual and is sexually attracted to virtually everyone regardless of sex, appearance, age or attitude. Perhaps all that matters is that he feels that he has power over them (which is the case no matter who occupies the position now occupied by Mary A). Mary A or anyone who filled her place would be subjected to sexual harassment.

The point of this variant case is that there appears to be no discrimination, even though there clearly is harassment. Even if it is argued that there is discrimination against the class of those over whom Bill A has power, we can still describe a case where no one is safe. Bill A could sexually harass anyone. This particular case clearly defeats both of MacKinnon's conceptual approaches to sexual discrimination; it is neither the case that Bill A treats a man in Mary A's position differently from the way in which he treats Mary A, nor is it the case that (in Bill A's office) the burden of Bill A's advances is placed disproportionately on one sex, because of that person's sex (for the purpose of sex, perhaps, but not on account of chromosomes).[3]

A different point, but one worth making here, is that there is a difference between sexual harassment and sexist harassment. A female academic whose male colleagues continually ridicule her ideas and opinions may be the object of sexist harassment, and this sexist harassment will necessarily involve sexual discrimination. But she is not, on this basis, the object of sexual harassment.

2. NEGATIVE CONSEQUENCES AND INTERESTS

Perhaps sexual harassment always involves action by the harasser which is against the interests of the harassee, or has overall negative consequences for the harassee.

However, consider Mary B who is sexually harassed by Bill B. Mary B gives in, but as luck would have it, things turn out extremely well; Mary B is promoted by Bill B to another department. The long term consequences are excellent, so clearly it has been in Mary B's best interests to be the object of Bill B's attentions. One could also imagine a case where Mary B rejects Bill B, with the (perhaps unintentional) affect that the overall consequences for Mary B are very good.

Crosthwaite and Swanton argue for modification of this view. They urge that, in addition to being an action of a sexual nature, an act of sexual harassment is an action where there is no adequate consideration of the interests of the harassee. They in fact suggest that this is both a necessary and sufficient condition for sexual harassment.[4]

We think it is not sufficient. Consenting to sex with an AIDS carrier is not in an antibody-negative individual's best interests. If the carrier has not informed the other party, the antibody-positive individual has not given adequate consideration to those interests. But this case need not be one of sexual harassment.

Nor is this condition necessary for sexual harassment. Of course Bill B may believe that it is in Mary B's interests to come across. (A sexual harasser can be deceitful or just intensely egotistical.) Bill B may believe that it would conform with Mary B's conception of her interests. And, as we noted earlier, it may even be objectively in her own best interests. Yet still we think this would not prevent the action of Bill B against Mary B — which is in other ways similar to Bill's actions against Mary — being a case of sexual harassment.

In general, harassment need not be against the interests of the harassee. You can be harassed to stop smoking, and harassed to give up drugs. In these cases the consequences may well be good, and the interests of the harassee adequately considered and served, yet it is still harassment. This general feature seems equally applicable to sexual harassment.

3. MISUSE OF POWER

Bill has power over Mary and it is the misuse of this power which plays an important role in making his treatment of Mary particularly immoral. For, on almost any normative theory, to misuse power is immoral. But is this misuse of power what makes this action one of sexual harassment?

If it is, then it must not be restricted to the formal power of the kind which Bill has over Mary — the power to dismiss her, demote her, withhold benefits from her, and so on. We also usually think of this sort of formal power in cases of police harassment. But consider the harassment of women at an abortion clinic by Right-To-Lifers. They cannot prevent the women having abortions and indeed lack any formal power over them. Nonetheless, they do possess important powers — to dissuade the faint-hearted (or even the over-sensitive), and to increase the unpleasantness of the experience of women attending the clinic.

Now consider the case of Mary C. Bill C and Mary C are coworkers in the office, and Bill C lacks formal power over Mary C. He sexually harasses her — with sexual innuendoes, touches, leers, jokes, suggestions, and unwanted invitations. To many women Bill C's action would be unpleasant. But Mary C is a veteran — this has happened to her so many times before that she no longer responds. It is not that she desires or wants the treatment, but it no longer produces the unpleasant mental attitudes it used to produce — it just rolls off her. She gives the negative responses automatically, and goes on as though nothing had happened.

It would still seem to us that Mary C has been sexually harassed. But what power has Bill C misused against Mary C? He has not used even some informal power which has caused her some significantly unpleasant experience.

Crosthwaite and Swanton also argue against the necessary connection between misuse of power and sexual harassment. They note that one case where there is a lack of power and yet harassment takes place (like the Mary C and Bill C case), is the case where there is a use of pornographic pictures and sexist language by work colleagues. They also note that there are cases in which a sexually-motivated misuse of power leads to events advantaging the woman in the long run. Misuse of power cannot in itself therefore constitute sexual harassment.[5]

4. ATTITUDES, INTENTIONS AND EXPERIENCES

In our discussions so far, it seems that we have not taken into account, to any significant extent, how Mary and Bill feel about things. It may be argued that what defines or characterizes sexual harassment is the mental state of the harasser, or harassee, or both.

Bill wanted to have sex with Mary. He perceived her as a sex object. He failed to have regard for her as a person. He failed to have regard for how she might feel about things. And his actions gave him egotistical pleasure. These attitudes, intentions and experiences may help constitute Bill's action as a case of sexual harassment.

Mary also had very specific kinds of mental states. She found Bill's actions unpleasant, and unwanted. She wished Bill would not act in that way towards her, and she disliked him for it. She was angry that someone would treat her in that way, and she resented being forced to cope with the situation. So again we have attributed attitudes and mental experiences to Mary in describing this case as one of sexual harassment.

We do not want to have to label as sexual harassment all sexual actions or approaches between people in formally structured relationships. Cases of sexual harassment and non-harassing sexual interaction may appear very similar (at least over short time intervals). It seems that in the two kinds of cases only the mental features differ. That is, we refer to attitudes, intentions or experiences in explaining the difference between the two cases. But attention to this feature of sexual harassment is not enough in itself to identify sexual harassment.

We will now consider one of the more salient features of the mental attitudes of Bill and Mary, and show that sexual harassment is not dependent on these or similar features. Then we shall describe a case where the mental experiences are very different, but where sexual harassment does, in fact, still occur.

Consider the claim that Bill uses (or tries to use) Mary as a sex object. The notion of sex object is somewhat vague and ill-defined, but we accept that it is to view her as merely an entity for sexual activity or satisfaction, with no interest in her attributes as a person and without any intention of developing any personal relationship with her.

This will not do as a sufficient condition for sexual harassment. We normally do not think of a client sexually harassing a prostitute. And surely there can be a relationship between two people where each sees the other merely as a sex object without there being harassment. Nor is viewing her merely as a sex object a necessary condition.[6] For surely Bill could love Mary deeply, and yet by pursuing her against her wishes, still harass her.

Now consider the claim that what is essential is that Mary not want the attentions of Bill. This is not a sufficient condition — often the most acceptable of sexual approaches is not wanted. Also a woman may not want certain attentions, and even feel sexually harassed, in situations which we would not want to accept as ones of sexual harassment.

Imagine that Mary D is an abnormally sensitive person. She feels harassed when Bill D comments that the color she is wearing suits her very well, or even that it is a cold day. Bill D is not in the habit of making such comments, nor is he in the habit of harassing anyone. He is just making conversation and noting something (seemingly innocuous) that has caught his attention. Mary D feels harassed even though she is not being harassed.

Perhaps this condition is a necessary one. But this too seems implausible. Remember Mary C, the veteran. She is now so immune to Bill C that she has no reaction at all to his approaches. He does not cause unpleasantness for her; she does not care what he does. Yet nonetheless Bill C is harassing Mary C.

Mary E and Bill E interact in a way which shows that sexual harassment is not simply a matter of actual attitudes, intentions or experiences. Bill E is infatuated with Mary E and wants to have sex with her. In addition to this, he genuinely loves her and generally takes an interest in her as a person. But he is hopeless on technique. He simply copies the brash actions of those around him and emulates to perfection the actions of the sexual harasser. Most women who were the object of his infatuation (for instance, someone like our original Mary) would feel harassed and have all the usual emotions and opinions concerning the harasser. But Mary E is different. Outwardly, to all who observe the public interactions between them, she seems the typical harassee—doing her best to politely put off Bill E, seeming not to want his attentions, looking as though she is far from enjoying it. That is how Bill E sees it too, but he thinks that that is the way women are.

Inwardly Mary E's mental state is quite different. Mary E is indifferent about Bill E personally, and is a veteran like Mary C in that she is not distressed by his actions. But she decides to take advantage of the situation and make use of Bill E's attentions. By manipulating the harassing pressures and invitations, she believes she can obtain certain benefits that she wants and can gain certain advantages over others. The attention from Bill E is thus not unwanted, nor is the experience for her unpleasant. In this case neither the harasser nor the harassee have mental states in any way typical of harassers and harassees, yet it is a case of sexual harassment.

Such a case, as hypothetical and unlikely as it is, demonstrates that the actual mental states of the people involved cannot be what is definitive of sexual harassment. They are not even necessary for sexual harassment.

5. A BEHAVIORAL ACCOUNT OF SEXUAL HARASSMENT

The case of Mary E and Bill E persuades us that we require a behavioral account of sexual harassment. For a harasser to sexually harass a harassee is for the harasser to behave in a certain way towards the harassee. The causes of that behavior are not important, and what that behavior in turn causes is not important. The behavior itself constitutes the harassment.

But how then are we to specify the behavior that is to count as sexual harassment? We shall borrow a technique from the functionalist theory of the mind.

Functionalists usually identify mental states in terms of the functional roles they play. However some functionalist theories allow a variation on this. If we talk instead of the kind of mental state which *typically* fills a functional role or the functional role *typically* associated with a mental state, we maintain the functionalist flavor, but allow unusual combinations of kinds of inner states and kinds of functional roles to be accommodated. We shall follow a similar technique when describing the kinds of behavior associated with sexual harassment.

Consider the behavior which is typically associated with a mental state representing an attitude which seeks sexual ends without any concern for the person from whom those ends are sought, and which typically produces an unwanted and unpleasant response in the person who is the object of the behavior. Such behavior we suggest is what constitutes sexual harassment. Instances of the behavior are instances of sexual harassment even if the mental states of the harasser or harassee (or both) are different from those typically associated with such behavior. The behavior constitutes a necessary and sufficient condition for sexual harassment.

According to this view, the earlier suggestion that attitudes, intentions and experience are essential to an adequate characterization of sexual harassment is correct. It is correct to the extent that we need to look at the mental states typical of the harasser, rather than those present in each actual harasser, and at those typical of the harassee, rather than those present in each actual harassee.

The empirical claim is that connecting these typical mental states is a kind of behavior—behavior not incredibly different from instance to instance, but with a certain sameness to it. Thus it is a behavior of a definite characteristic *type*. This type of behavior is sexual harassment.

This proffered account may at first appear surprising. But let us look at some of its features to alleviate the surprise, and at the same time increase the plausibility of the account.

Most importantly, the account satisfies our three desiderata: to show the connection between harassment in general and sexual harassment, to distinguish between sexual harassment and legitimate sexual interaction, and to assist in guiding policy on sexual harassment.

The relationship between harassment and sexual harassment is to be accounted for in terms of a behavioral simplicity. This at first may seem to be a sweeping suggestion, since *prima facie*, there need to be no descriptive similarity between sexual harassment, harassment by police, harassment of homosexuals, harassment of Jews, and so on. But the behavioral elements on which each kind of harassment supervenes will have enough in common to explain our linking them all as harassment, while at the same time being sufficiently different to allow for their differentiation into various kinds of harassment. The most plausible similarity, as we shall argue later, will be in the presence of certain behavioral dispositions, though the bases for these dispositions may differ.

Our approach allows for an adequate distinction between sexual harassment and legitimate sexual approaches and interactions. The approach requires that this be a behavioral difference. There is something intrinsically different about the two kinds of activity. Given that the typical causal origin of each of the kinds of behavior is different and so too is the typical reaction it in turn produces, it is to be expected that there would be a difference in the behavior itself. It is important to note that the constitutive behavior will be within a particular context, in particular circumstances. (The importance of this is well illustrated in cases such as a student and her lecturer at a university.[7]) Further it will include both overt and covert behavior (subtle differences count). In many cases it will also be behavior over a time interval, not just behavior at a time.

From the policy guiding perspective the account is very attractive. It is far easier to stipulate a workable, practical, defensible, and legally viable policy on harassment if it is totally definable in behavioral terms. Definition in terms of mental experiences, intentions and attitudes spells nothing but trouble for a viable social policy on sexual harassment.

The analysis we have offered entails that if there were no such characteristic kind of behavior there would be no sexual harassment. This seems to be right. In this case no legislation to ground a social policy would be possible. We would instead condemn individual actions on other moral grounds—causing pain and distress, acting against someone's best interests, misusing power, and so on.

In addition to satisfying these three desiderata, our account has numerous other positive features. First our account is culturally relative. It is highly likely that the kind of behavior constitutive of sexual harassment will vary from culture to culture, society to society. That is, it will be a culture-relative kind of behavior that determines sexual harassment. In any culture our reference to the typical mental states of the harasser and harassee will identify a kind of behavior that is constitutive of sexual harassment in that culture. This kind of behavior matches well with the empirical observations. There is so much variation in human behavior across cultures that behavior which may be sexual harassment in one need not be in another. The same is true of other kinds of human behavior. In the middle east, belching indicates appreciation of a meal. In western society, it is considered bad manners. The practice of haggling over the price of a purchase is acceptable (indeed expected) in some societies, and unacceptable in others. But in almost any culture, some kind of behavior may reasonably be judged to be sexual harassment.

Second, while we have cast our examples in terms of a male harasser and female harassee, there is nothing in the account which necessitates any gender restriction on sexual harassment. All that is required is that the behavior is sexual in nature and has other behavioral features which make it an instance of sexual harassment. The participants could be of either sex in either role, or of the same sex.

We acknowledge that we use the notion of an action being sexual in nature without attempting any explication of that notion. Such an explication is a separate task, but we believe that for our purposes there is no problem in taking it as primitive.

Third, the account allows for the possibility of sexual harassment without the presence of the mental states typical of the harasser or the harassee. There is an important connection between these typical mental states and sexual harassment, but it does not restrict instances of sexual harassment to instances where we have these typical mental states.

Further as the account focuses on behavior, rather than mental states, it explains why we feel so skeptical about someone who behaves as Bill behaves, yet pleads innocence and claims he had no bad intentions. The intentions are not essential for the harassment, and such a person has an obligation to monitor the responses of the other person so that he has an accurate picture of what is going on. Moreover, he has an obligation to be aware of the character of his own behavior. He also has an obligation to give due consideration to the strength and the weight of the beliefs upon which he is operating before he makes a decision to act in a manner that may have unpleasant consequences for others. Strength of belief concerns the degree of confidence it is rational to have in the belief, given the evidence available. Weight of belief concerns the quality of the evidential basis of the belief, and the reasonableness of acting on the evidence available.[8] If a person is acting in a way which has a risk of bad consequences for others, that person has an obligation to be aware of the risks and to refrain from acting unless he has gained evidence of sufficient strength and weight to be confident that the bad consequences will not arise. In the case of someone who wishes to engage in legitimate sexual interaction and to avoid sexual harassment, he must display a disposition to be alive to the risks and to seek appropriate evidence from the other person's behavior, as to whether that person welcomes his attentions. He must also display a disposition to refrain from acting if such evidence is lacking.

In the case of Mary E and Bill E, Bill E relies on the harassing behavior of other men as a guide to his actions regarding Mary E. Mary E has displayed standard forms of avoidance behavior (although she has ulterior motives). Bill E does not pay sufficient heed to the strength and weight of the beliefs which guide his actions, and it is just fortunate that Mary E is not harmed by what he does. Given Bill E's total disregard of Mary E's interests and reactions, it seems that his behavior could have caused, just as easily, significant distress to any other Mary who might have filled that role. A policy intended to identify sexual harassment should not rely on such luck, although the actual mental states (where they are as atypical as Mary E's) may mitigate blameworthiness. Bill E's harassing behavior should be checked and evaluated, regardless of any of Mary's actual mental states.[9]

Consider an example taken from an actual case[10] which highlights this obligation. Suppose Tom is married to Jane. He invites Dick (an old friend who has never met Jane) home to have sex with Jane. He tells Dick that Jane will protest, but that this is just part of the game (a game she very much enjoys). Dick forces Jane, who all the time protests violently, to have sex with him. Jane later claims to have been raped. Dick has acted culpably because he has acted without giving due consideration to the weight of the belief which guided his action, that is, to how rational it was to act on the belief given such a minimal evidential base. The only evidence he had that Jane did consent was Tom's say-so, and the consequences of acting on the belief were very serious. All of Jane's actions indicated that she did not consent.

In the case of Bill E and Mary E, Bill has an obligation to consider the strength and weight of the beliefs which guide his action before he acts. He is not justified in claiming that he is innocent, when he has been provided with signals that indicate that Mary does not welcome his attentions.

We acknowledge that it will be difficult in many situations to obtain sufficient evidence that a proposed act will not be one of sexual harassment. This will be true especially in cases where the potential harassee may believe that any outward indication of her displeasure would have bad consequences for her. The awareness of this difficulty is probably what has led others to promote the policy of a total ban on sexual relationships at the office or work place. While we acknowledge the problem, we feel that such a policy is both unrealistic and overrestrictive.

Fourth, the account allows an interesting stance on the connection between sexual harassment and morality. For consequentialist theories of morality, it is possible (though unlikely) that an act of sexual harassment may be, objectively, morally right. This would be the case if the long term good consequences outweighed the bad effects (including those on the harassee at the time of the harassment). For other moral theories it is not clear that this is a possibility, except where there are sufficiently strong overriding considerations present, such as to make the sexual harassment morally permissible. From the agent's point of view, it would seem that the probable consequences of sexual harassment (given the typical attitude of the typical harasser and the typical effects on the typical harassee) will be bad. Hence it is very likely, on any moral theory, that the agent evaluation for a harasser will be negative. The possible exceptions are where the harasser's actual mental state is not typical of a harasser, or the harassee's is not typical of a harassee.

Further, on this account many of the salient features of the case of Mary and Bill — such as misuse of power, discrimination, unfair distribution of favors, and so on — are not essential features of sexual harassment. They are usually immoral in their own right, and their immorality is not explained by their being part of the harassment. But the behavior characteristic of sexual harassment will be constituted by features which we commonly find in particular instances of sexual harassment. For sexual harassment must supervene on the behavioral features which constitute its instances, but there is a range of such behavior, no one element of which need be present on any particular occasion. Similarly the morality of an instance of sexual harassment (at least for the consequentialist) will supervene on the morality of those same features of behavior.

6. OBJECTIONS TO THE BEHAVIORAL ACCOUNT

It may be objected that we have made no significant progress. We acknowledged at the beginning of the paper that many different kinds of behavior were instances of sexual harassment, even though there seemed to be no specific kind of behavior commonly present in all these instances.

Our reply is to concede the point that there is no first order property commonly possessed by all the behaviors. However, other important similarities do exist.

The property of being an instance of sexual harassment is a second order property of a particular complex piece of behavior. It is a property of the relevant specific behavioral features, and these features may be from a list of disjunctive alternatives (which may be altered as norms of behavior change). Also, the behavior of a typical harassee will possess the property of being an instance of avoidance behavior. Avoidance behavior is a disposition. Hence, even if two lots of behavior are descriptively similar they may differ in their dispositional properties. Finally the behavior of the typical harasser will possess the property of being sexually motivated, which again is dispositional in nature.

A second objection goes as follows: couldn't we have the very same piece of behavior and yet have no sexual harassment? To take the kind of example well tried as an objection to behaviorism, what would we say about the case of two actors, acting out a sexual harassment sequence?

There are a variety of replies we may make here. We could "bite the bullet" and admit the case to be one of sexual harassment. On the model proposed, we may do this while still maintaining that the behavior in this case is not morally wrong. Or, instead, we could insist that certain kinds of behavior only become harassment when they are carried on over a sufficiently lengthy time interval, the circumstances surrounding the behavior also being relevant. The case of the actors would not count as an instance of harassment because the behavior has not been recurrent over a sufficiently long period of time, especially as the behavior before and after the acting period are significantly different. Also the circumstances surrounding an acting exercise would be typically different from those of an instance of sexual harassment.

Still another response to the acting example is to argue that if the actual mental states of "harasser" and "harassee" are sufficiently different from those of the prototypical harasser and harassee, there can be no sexual harassment as there will be behavioral differences. This is not a logical necessity, but a physical one given the causal relations which hold between the mental states and the behavior. We should also keep in mind that many of the features of sexual harassment are dispositional. Thus, even if such features of sexual harassment are not manifested in particular circumstances, they would in other circumstances, and it is in these other circumstances that the observable behavior would be significantly different if it is the manifestation of harassment from that which would be associated with non-harassment.[11]

A third objection to our behavioral account focuses on our use of the mental state *typical* of harassers and harassees. We have noted that it is possible that some instances of harassment will involve a harasser or harassee with mental states significantly different from those of the typical harasser or harassee. So it is possible that the harassee is not even offended or made to feel uncomfortable, and it is possible that the harasser did not have intentions involving misuse of power against, and disregard for the interests of, the harassee. It is even possible that one or both of the harasser and harassee could know about the atypical mental states of the other. Why, at least in this last case, insist that the behavior is sufficient for sexual harassment?

From our concern to provide an account of sexual harassment adequate for policy purposes, we would be inclined to resist this kind of objection, given the clear advantage in policy matters of a behavioral account. But there is more to say in reply to this objection. Policy is directed at the action of agents, and in all cases except where at least one of the agents involved has justified beliefs about the atypical actual mental states of the agents involved, it is clearly appropriate to stipulate behavior associated with the states of mind typical of harassers and harassees as sexual harassment. For agents ought to be guided by what it is reasonable to predict, and rational prediction as to the mental states of those involved in some kind of behavior will be determined by the mental states typically associated with that behavior. So only in cases where we have reliable and justified knowledge of atypical mental states does the objection have any substance at all.

But even in these cases it seems the behavior should not be regarded as innocuous. Instances of behavior all form parts of behavioral patterns. People are disposed to behave similarly in similar circumstances. Hence we ought not to overlook instances of behavior which would typically be instances of sexual harassment. Agents ought not be involved in such patterns of behavior. It is for similar reasons that while we allow for cultural relativity in the behavior constitutive of sexual harassment, this relativity should not be taken to legitimate patterns of behavior which do constitute sexual harassment but which are taken as the standard mode of behavior by a culture.[12]

There are three final notes about our account of sexual harassment. Provided that the kind of behavior so specified is characteristically different from behavior having other typical causes and effects, the desired distinction between sexual harassment and other kinds of sexual activity is assured.

The required connection between sexual harassment and other forms of harassment seems assured by a kind of behavioral similarity. Other forms of harassment are not sexual and vary in many ways from the pattern of behavior characteristic of sexual harassment. But there will be corresponding accounts for each kind of harassment in terms of typical causes and typical effects. The connection between all the different kinds of harassment may well be revealed by looking at these typical causes and typical effects. But despite the noted differences, the contention is that there will be an empirically verifiable behavioral similarity, and this will justify the claim that they are all forms of harassment. It may be that the relevant features of the behavior characteristic of the various forms of harassment are dispositional.

We have made two claims about the behavior constitutive of sexual harassment, and we should now see how they relate. The behavior is identified in terms of its typical causes and typical effects, that is, in terms of the typical mental states of harassers and harassees. But harassment is recognized by reference to features of the behavior itself, and any legislation to ground social policy will also refer to such features. The philosophical claim is that there will be a range of such behavior features some combination of which will be present in each case of sexual harassment. The empirical job is to tell us more about the nature of such behavior and help determine the practical social policy and legislation.[13]

Notes

1. Catherine MacKinnon, *Sexual Harassment of Working Women* (London: Yale University Press, 1979), Ch. 6.

2. MacKinnon, p. 225.

3. Given that sexual harassment is possible between men, by a woman harassing a man, among co-workers, and so on, MacKinnon's view of sexual harassment as nothing but one form of sexual discrimination is even less persuasive. It is also interesting that the problems which MacKinnon recognizes in trying to characterize the "offence" of sexual harassment (p. 162 ff.), indicate a need for a behavioral analysis of sexual harassment, like the one we offer.

4. Jan Crosthwaite and Christine Swanton, "On the Nature of Sexual Harassment," *Women and Philosophy: Australasian Journal of Philosophy*, supplement to 64 (1986): 91–106; pp. 100–101.

5. Crosthwaite and Swanton, p. 99.

6. If it is, it needs to be connected to a general view that women are sex objects, for pornographic pin-ups and sexist jokes and language may harass a woman without anyone viewing *that* woman as a sex object. [See Nathalie Hadjifotiou, *Women and Harassment at Work* (London: Pluto Press, 1983), p. 14.] Note that we have urged that sexual harassment should be a special case of harassment. But what is the general form of the sex object account? It seems implausible that for each form of harassment there is something corresponding to the notion of sex object.

7. See, for example, Billie Wright Dzeich and Linda Weiner, *The Lecherous Professor: Sexual Harassment on Campus* (Boston: Beacon Press, 1984).

8. For a discussion of this concept of weight see Barbara Davidson and Robert Pargetter, "Weight" *Philosophical Studies* 49 (1986): 219–230.

9. Some might say that this behavioristic account of sexual harassment is similar to having strict liability for murder, that is to say, that mental states do need to be taken into account when judging and penalizing someone's actions. What we are arguing for is a way of *identifying* sexual harassment, not how (or even if) it should be *penalized*. The appropriate response to a case of sexual harassment may very well take mental states into account, along with the harm caused, or likely to be caused, and so forth. One advantage of our account is that it demands that potential harassers become aware of their behavior and to be alert to the responses of those around them. The response of Bill E (that he thought women liked to be treated that way) ought not be considered adequate especially in public life where a person's livelihood could hang in the balance.

10. This example is based on the British case, D.P.P. v. Morgan (1975), 2 All E.R. 347 (House of Lords): Morgan (1975), 1 All E.R. 8 (Court of Appeal); see also Frank Jackson, "A Probabilistic Approach to Moral Responsibility," in Ruth Barcan Marcus, *et al.* (eds.), *Logic, Methodology and Philosophy of Science VII* (North Holland, 1986), pp. 351–366.

11. For a useful account of dispositional properties, their manifestations, and their categorical bases, see Elizabeth Prior, Robert Pargetter and Frank Jackson, "Three Theses about Dispositions," *American Philosophical Quarterly* 19 (1982): 251–258.

The case of pressing solicitation by a prostitute towards a reluctant john can be viewed in the same manner as that of the actors. It is quite likely that there would be sufficient difference in the mental states of the pressing prostitute and the typical harasser to yield behavioral differences (for instance the prostitute is more interested in making money than having sex so her behavior will reflect this insofar as, say, she would not keep on pressing if the john proved to have no money). The pressing behavior of the prostitute may be seen as a nuisance by the reluctant john, but it is not sexual harassment.

12. What will be culturally relative are types of behavior incidental to their being viewed as constituting sexual harassment in a particular culture. Acceptable standards concerning modes of address, physical proximity, touching, and so forth will vary among cultures, so the behavior patterns which will constitute sexual harassment will also vary. Of course we must be careful not to confuse socially accepted behavior with behavior which is not sexually harassing, especially in cultures where men have much greater power to determine what is to count as socially acceptable behavior. However, so long as there are typical mental states of harassers and harassees, the behavior which constitutes sexual harassment will be identifiable in each culture.

13. We acknowledge useful comments from Robert Young and various readers for this journal.

Larry May and John C. Hughes
IS SEXUAL HARASSMENT COERCIVE?

A number of recent lawsuits filed under Title VII of the 1964 Civil Rights Act have brought the problem of sexual harassment into the footlights of contemporary political and moral discussion.[1] Is sexual harassment a purely private matter between two individuals, or is it a social problem? If sexual harassment is to be treated as something more than a purely personal dispute, how do we distinguish the social problem from benevolent forms of social interaction between members of a work hierarchy? We will argue here that sexual harassment of women workers is a public issue because it is inherently coercive, regardless of whether it takes the form of a threat for noncompliance, or of a reward for compliance. We will further argue that the harm of harassment is felt beyond the individuals immediately involved because it contributes to a pervasive pattern of discrimination and exploitation based on sex.

The term *sexual harassment* refers to the intimidation of persons in subordinate positions by those holding power and authority over them in order to exact sexual favors that would ordinarily not have been granted. Sexual harassment of male subordinates by female superiors is conceivable, and probably occurs, albeit infrequently. Positions of authority are more likely to be occupied by males, while women are predominantly relegated to positions of subservience and dependency. Furthermore, strong cultural patterns induce female sexual passivity and acquiescence to male initiative.[2] These factors combine to produce a dominant pattern of male harassment of females. However, it might bear reflecting that the poisoning of the work environment that may result from sexual intimidation may affect members of both sexes, so that sexual harassment should be viewed as more than merely a women's issue.

Truly systematic empirical studies of the incidence of sexual harassment are yet to be done. Most of the studies by social scientists to date suffer from severe methodological flaws. Nevertheless, they reveal a pattern of sexual harassment of working women that is too strong to ignore. Perhaps the most telling study is that conducted by Peggy Crull.[3] Working with a self-selected sample, Crull

From Larry May and John C. Hughes, "Is Sexual Harassment Coercive?," in *Moral Rights in the Workplace*, edited by Gertrude Ezorsky (Albany, NY: SUNY Press, 1987), 115–122. Reprinted by permission of the State University of New York Press. © 1987 State University of New York.

sought to discern the nature, extent, and effects of sexual harassment on women, as well as the predominant relationship between harasser and victim. Her data show the victims of harassment to be likely to occupy low-status and low-paying positions of economic vulnerability. Fifty-three percent of the victims on her survey were clerical workers (including secretaries, typists, and general office help), with another 15 percent occupying service positions (waitresses, hospital aids, and the like). The most frequent pattern involved verbal harassment, but over half of Crull's respondents also reported incidents of physical harassment that persisted over time despite their protestations, with 39 percent reporting fondling. Twelve percent claimed to have been physically restrained during incidents of sexual harassment.

What is perhaps most significant in Crull's finding is that 79 percent of the men involved held power to fire or promote the victim, while only 16 percent threatened an explicit employment sanction. Seventy-nine percent of the victims complained about the incident to the harasser or to someone in authority (often though not always the same person), but in only 9 percent of the cases did the behavior stop. Forty-nine percent of the women who complained felt their claims were not taken seriously, while 26 percent experienced retaliation for their complaints. Crull also discovered that whether the victim complained or not, her experience of harassment placed her job in jeopardy. A full 24 percent of Crull's respondents were soon fired, while another 42 percent were pressured into resigning by the intolerable working conditions that resulted from the behavior of their supervisors. If this figure is not striking enough, 83 percent claimed the harassment interfered in some way with their job performance. Indeed, 96 percent reported symptoms of emotional stress, with 63 percent reporting symptoms of physical stress. Twelve percent sought some form of therapeutic help in dealing with these symptoms. Faced with such results, it seems fair to say that sexual harassment is a problem that must be taken seriously.

I.

Like most interpersonal transactions, sexual advances may take many forms. There is of course the sincere proposal, motivated by genuine feelilng for another, made in a context of mutual respect for the other's autonomy and dignity. Such offers are possible between members of a work hierarchy, but are of no concern here. Rather, we are interested in advances that take the following forms: (1) Sexual threat: "If you don't provide a sexual benefit, I will punish you by withholding a promotion or a raise that would otherwise be due, or ultimately fire you." (2) Sexual offer: "If you provide a sexual benefit, I will reward you with a promotion or a raise that would otherwise not be due." There are also sexual harassment situations that are merely annoying, but without demonstrable sanction or reward. It is worth noting at the outset that all three forms of sexual harassment have been proscribed under recently promulgated Equal Employment Opportunity Commission guidelines implementing Title VII.[4]

Sexual harassment in the form of threats is coercive behavior that forces the employee to accept a course of conduct she wouldn't otherwise accept. What is wrong with this? Why can't she simply resist the threats and remain as before? Viewed in the abstract, one can seemingly resist threats, for unlike physical restraint, threatening does not completely deny individual choice over her alternatives. A person who is physically restrained is literally no longer in control of her own life. The victim is no longer reaching decisions of her own and autonomously carrying them out. Threats do not have this dramatic effect on a person's autonomy. Rather, the effect of the threat is that the recipient of a threat is much less inclined to act as she would have absent the threat — generally out of fear. Fear is the calculation of expected harm and the decision to avoid it. Reasonably prudent individuals will not, without a sufficiently expected possibility of gain, risk harm. The first thing wrong with sexual threats then is that, for the reasonable person, it now takes a very good reason to resist the threat, whereas no such strength of reasoning was required before to resist a sexual advance.

Sexual threats are coercive because they worsen the objective situation the employee finds herself in. To examine this claim, consider her situation before and after the threat has been made (preproposition stage and postproposition stage).[5] In the proposition stage, a secretary, for example, is judged by standards of efficiency to determine whether she should be allowed to retain her job. She would naturally view her employer as having power over her, but only in the rather limited domain concerning the job-related functions she performs. Her personal life would be her own. She could choose her own social relationships, without fear that these decisions might adversely affect her job. In the postproposition stage, she can no longer remain employed under the same conditions while not choosing to have relations with her employer. Further, the efficient performance of job-related functions is no longer sufficient for the retention of her job. She can no longer look to her supervisor as one who exercises power merely over the performance of her office duties. He now wields power over a part of her personal life. This may help to explain Crull's finding that many women leave their jobs after such a proposition has been tendered. They cannot simply go on as before, for their new situation is correctly perceived as worse than the old situation.

It is the worsening of the woman's situation after the threat has been made that contributes to the likelihood of her acquiescence to the threat. The perception of job insecurity created by the threat can only be alleviated by her acceptance of the sexual proposition. But what of the woman who prefers to have a sexual relationship with her employer than not to do so? Has this woman also been made objectively worse off than she was before the threat occurred? We contend that she has, for before the threat was made she could pursue her preference without feeling forced to do so. If the liaison developed and then turned sour, she could quit the relationship and not so clearly risk a worsening of her employment situation. Now, however, her continued job success might be held ransom to the continued sexual demands of her employer. This also may adversely affect other women in the business organization. What the employer has done is to establish a precedent for employment decisions based upon the stereotype that values women for their sexuality rather than for their job skills. This has a discriminatory impact on women individually and as a group. Focusing on this effect will shed some light on the harm of both sexual threats and sexual offers.

II.

Consider the following case.[6] Barnes was hired as an administrative assistant by the director of a federal agency. In a preemployment interview, the director, a male, promised to promote Barnes, a female, within ninety days. Shortly after beginning her job, (1) the director repeatedly asked her for a date after work hours, even though she consistently refused; (2) made repeated remarks to her that were sexual in nature; and (3) repeatedly told her that if she did not cooperate with him by engaging in sexual relations, her employment status would be affected. After consistently rebuffing him, she finally told him she wished for their relationship to remain a strictly professional one. Thereafter the director, sometimes in concert with others, began a campaign to belittle and demean her within the office. Subsequently she was stripped of most of her job duties, culminating in the eventual abolition of her job. Barnes filed suit, claiming that these actions would not have occurred but for the fact that she was a woman.

Under Title VII, it is now widely accepted that the kind of sexual threat illustrated by this case is an instance of sex discrimination in employment.[7] Such threats treat women differently than men in employment contexts even though gender is not a relevantly applicable category for making employment-related decisions. The underlying principle here is that like persons should be treated alike. Unless there are relevant differences among persons, it is harmful to disadvantage one particular class of persons. In the normal course of events, male employees are not threatened sexually by employers or supervisors. The threats disadvantage a woman in that an additional requirement is placed in her path for successful job retention, one not placed in the path of male employees. When persons who are otherwise similarly situated are distinguished on the basis of their sex, and rewards or burdens are apportioned according to these gender-based classifications, illegal sex discrimination has occurred. Applying this theory of discrimination to Barnes' complaint, the federal appellate court ruled:

> So it was, by her version, that retention of her job was conditioned upon submission to sexual relations — an exaction which the supervisor would not have made of any male. It is much too late in the day to contend that Title VII does not outlaw terms of employment for women which differ appreciably from those set for men and which are not genuinely and reasonably related to the performance on the job. . . . Put another way, she became the target of her superior's sexual desires because she was a woman and was asked to bow to demands as the price for holding her job.[8]

There is a second way in which this behavior might be viewed as discriminatory. Sexual threats also contribute to a pervasive pattern of disadvantaged treatment of women as a group. Under this approach, the harm is not viewed as resulting from the arbitrary and unfair use of gender as a criterion for employment decisions. Rather, emphasis is on the effect the classification has of continuing the subordination of women as a group. The harm results regardless of whether the specific incident could be given an employment rationale or not. Sexual harassment perpetuates sex discrimination, and illustrates the harm that occurs for members of a group that have historically been disadvantaged. This theory was applied to sexual harassment in another federal lawsuit, *Tomkins* v. *Public Service Gas and Electric Co.*[9] The plaintiff's lawyers argued that employer tolerance of sexual harassment and its pattern of reprisals had a disparate impact upon women as an already disadvantaged group and was inherently degrading to all women.

Sexual threats are harmful to the individual woman because she is coerced and treated unfairly by her employer, disadvantaging her for no good reason. Beyond this, such practices further contribute to a pervasive pattern of disadvantaged status for her and all women in society. The sexual stereotyping makes it less likely, and sometimes impossible, that women will be treated on the basis of job efficiency, intelligence, or administrative skill. These women must now compete on a very different level, and in the case where sexual threats are common or at least accepted, this level is clearly inferior to that occupied by men. The few male employees who are harassed in the workplace suffer the first harm but not the second. We shall next show that there are also two harms of sexual offers in employment, only one of which can also be said to befall men.

III.

The harm of sexual offers is much more difficult to identify and analyze. Indeed, some may even see sexual offers as contributing to a differentiation based on sex that advantages rather than disadvantages women, individually and as a group. After all, males cannot normally gain promotions by engaging in sexual relations with their employers. We shall argue, on the contrary, that a sexual offer disadvantages the woman employee by changing the work environment so that she is viewed by others, and may come to view herself, less in terms of her work productivity and more in terms of her sexual allure. This change, like the threat, makes it unlikely that she can return to the preproposition stage even though she might prefer to do so. Furthermore, to offset her diminished status and to protect against later retaliation, a prudent woman would feel that she must accept the offer. Here, sexual offers resemble the coercive threat. The specific harm to women becomes clearer when one looks at the group impact of sexual offers in employment. Women are already more economically vulnerable and socially passive than men. When sexual offers are tendered, exploitation of a woman employee is accomplished by taking advantage of a preexisting vulnerability males generally do not share.

Seduction accomplished through sexual offers and coercive threats blend together most clearly in the mixed case of the sexual offer of a promotion with the lurking threat of retaliation if the offer is turned down. Both combine together to compel the woman to engage in sexual relations with her employer. Gifts are so rare in economic matters that it is best to be suspicious of all offers and to look for their hidden costs. As Crull's study showed, only 16 percent of those harassed were explicitly threatened. Yet 24 percent were fired, and another 42 percent reported that they were forced to resign. This evidence leads us to surmise that sexual offers often contain veiled threats and are for that reason coercive.

Why are the clearly mixed cases, where there is both an offer and a (sometimes only implied) threat, coercive rather than noncoercive? To return to our initial discussion, why is it that one is made worse off by the existence of these proposals? In one sense they enable women to do things they couldn't otherwise do, namely, get a promotion that they did not deserve, thus seeming to be noncoercive. On the other hand, if the woman prefers not having sexual relations with her employer (while retaining her job) to having sexual relations with him (with ensuing promotion), then it is predominantly a threat and more clearly coercive. The best reason for not preferring the postproposition stage is that she is then made worse off if she rejects the proposition, and if she accepts, she nonetheless risks future harm or retaliation. This latter condition is also true for more straightforward offers, as we shall now show.

A number of contemporary philosophers have argued that offers place people in truly advantageous positions, for they can always be turned down with the ensuring return to the preoffer stage.[10] In the case of sexual offers, however, the mere proposal of a promotion in exchange for sexual relations changes the work environment. Once sexual relations are seriously proposed as a sufficient condition for employment success, the woman realizes that this male employer sees her (and will probably continue to see her) as a sex object as well as an employee. A prudent woman will henceforth worry that she is not being regarded as an employee who simply happens to be a woman, but rather as a woman made more vulnerable by the fact that she happens to be an employee. If she accepts the offer, she lends credence to the stereotype, and because of this, it is more likely that she may experience future offers or even threats. She would thus worry about her ability to achieve on the basis of her work-related merits. If she rejects the offer, she would still worry about her employer's attitude toward her status as a worker. Furthermore, because of the volatility of sexual feelings, these offers cannot be turned down without the risk of offending or alienating one's employer, something any employee would wish to avoid. She may reasonably conclude from these two considerations that neither postoffer alternative is desirable. This is one of the hidden costs of sexual offers in the workplace.

It may be claimed that such environmental changes are no different for men who can also be the objects of sexual offers in the workplace. One needs to show that the changed environment is worse for those who are women. Sexual employment offers take advantage of unequal power relations that exist between employer and employee so as to force a particular outcome further benefitting those who are already in advantageous positions. But beyond this, sexual offers are doubly exploitative for female employees, because women already enter the employment arena from a position of vulnerability. As we have indicated, this is true because of the history of their economic powerlessness and because of their culturally ingrained passivity and acquiescence in the face of male initiatives. Women enter the employment arena much more ripe for coercion than their male colleagues. Thus, women are more likely to be harmed by these offers.

This may partially explain Crull's finding that women frequently experience extreme stress and sometimes even require professional therapy when harassed in this way. Men are not similarly harmed by sexual offers because they do not have the same history of sexual exploitation. Men are likely to regard such seductive offers either humorously or as insults to be aggressively combatted, while women have been socialized to be passive rather than combative in such situations. The woman to whom the offer is made becomes less sure of her real abilities by virtue of the proposal itself. This self-denigrating response to an unwelcomed proposal is a vestige of women's history of subordination. Even without the veiled threat, sexual offers can cause women to act in ways they would not choose to act otherwise. To this extent, these sexual offers are coercive.

Most offers are not coercive because one would prefer to have the offer made. This is because one of the postoffer alternatives (rejecting the offer) is equivalent to the preoffer alternative (having no offer at all). Sexual offers made by male employers to female employees are different, however, because they more closely resemble threats than ordinary offers.[11] As we have shown, the preoffer alternative — being employed, unpromoted, yet able to obtain promotion according to one's merits — is different from, and preferable to, either of the postoffer alternatives — accepting the promotion, and having sexual relations with her employer, with all of its negative consequences, or rejecting the offer of promotion, but with the risk that the promotion may now prove unobtainable on the basis of merit. By blocking a return to the more preferable preoffer alternative, the male employer has acted similarly to the employer who uses sexual threats. The woman is forced to choose between two undesirable alternatives because she cannot have what she would have chosen before the proposal was made. Stressing these hidden costs, which are much greater for women than for men, exposes the coercive element inherent in sexual offers as well as in sexual threats. We are thus led to conclude that both of these employment practices are harmful to women and recently were properly proscribed by the U.S. Equal Employment Opportunity Commission.

Notes

1. For a careful analysis of these cases we recommend Catherine MacKinnon's book, *Sexual Harassment of Working Women* (New Haven, Conn.: Yale University Press, 1979).

2. For the historical evidence, see William Chaffe, *Women and Equality* (New York: Oxford University Press, 1977). For the sociological evidence, see J. R. Feagin and C. B. Feagin, *Discrimination American Style* (Englewood Cliffs, N.J.: Prentice-Hall, 1978).

3. Peggy Crull, "The Impact of Sexual Harassment on the Job: a Profile of the Experiences of 92 Women," *Sexuality in Organizations*, ed. D. A. Neugarten and J. M. Shafritz (Oak Park, Ill.: Moore Publishing Co., 1980), 67–72.

4. 45 Fed. Reg. 74, 677 (1980); 29 C.F.R. 1604.11 (a).

5. We proceed from the general analysis developed by Robert Nozick, "Coercion," *Philosophy, Science and Method*, ed. Morgenbesser, Suppes, and White (New York: St. Martin's Press, 1969). A very large literature has grown out of this analysis. We recommend the essays by Bernard Gert, Michael Bayles, and especially Virginia Held, collected in *NOMOS XIV: Coercion* (New York: Lieber Atherton, 1973).

6. Summary of the facts for *Barnes* v. *Costel*, 561 F.2d 984 (D.C. Cir. 1977).

7. For more elaboration, see Section II of our essay, "Sexual Harassment," *Social Theory and Practice* (1980), 256–268.

8. 561 F.2d 989, 990, 992 n. 68 (D.C. Cir. 1977).

9. 568 F.2d 1044 (3rd Cir. 1977).

10. See Michael Bayles, "Coercive Offers and Public Benefits," *The Personalist*, vol. 55 (1974); Donald Vandeveer, "Coercion, Seduction and Rights," *The Personalist*, vol. 58 (1977); and Nozick, "Coercion," among others.

11. Some other employment offers have been seen as coercive also. See David Zimmerman, "Coercive Wage Offers," *Philosophy and Public Affairs*, vol. 10 (1981).

June O'Neill

AN ARGUMENT AGAINST COMPARABLE WORTH

The traditional goal of feminists has been equal opportunity for women — the opportunity for women to gain access to the schools, training, and jobs they choose to enter, on the same basis as men. This goal, however, basically accepts the rules of the game as they operate in a market economy. In fact the thrust has been to improve the way the market functions by removing discriminatory barriers that restrict the free supply of workers to jobs. By contrast, the more recent policy of "comparable worth" would dispense with the rules of the game. In place of the goal of equality of opportunity it would substitute a demand for equality of results, and it would do this essentially through regulation and legislation. It proposes, therefore, a radical departure from the economic system we now have, and so should be scrutinized with the greatest care.

The topics I will cover in this paper and the main points I will make are as follows:

1. The concept of comparable worth rests on a misunderstanding of the role of wages and prices in the economy.

2. The premises on which a comparable worth policy is based reflect a misconception about the reasons why women and men are in different occupations and have different earnings. Both the occupational differences and the pay gap to a large extent are the result of differences in the roles of women and men in the family and the effects these role differences have on the accumulation of skills and other job choices that affect pay. Discrimination by employers may account for some of the occupational differences, but it does not, as comparable worth advocates claim, lower wages directly in women's occupations.

3. Comparable worth, if implemented, would lead to capricious wage differentials, resulting in unintended shortages and surpluses of workers in different occupations with accompanying unemployment. Moreover, it would encourage women to remain in traditional occupations.

4. Policies are available that can be better targeted than comparable worth on any existing discriminatory or other barriers. These policies include the equal employment and pay legislation now on the books.

THE CONCEPT OF COMPARABLE WORTH

By comparable worth I mean the view that employers should base compensation on the inherent value of a job rather than on strictly market considerations. It is not a new idea — since the time of St. Thomas Aquinas, the concept of the "just price," or payment for value, has had considerable appeal. Practical considerations, however, have won out over metaphysics. In a free market, wages and

From June O'Neill, "An Argument Against Comparable Worth," *Comparable Worth: An Issue for the 80's*, vol. 1 (Washington, D.C.: U.S. Commission on Civil Rights, 1984). Reprinted by permission.

prices are not taken as judgments of the inherent value of the worker or the good itself, but reflect a balancing of what people are willing to pay for the services of these goods with how much it costs to supply them. Market prices are the efficient signals that balance supply and demand. Thus, in product markets we do not require that a pound of soybeans be more expensive than a pound of Belgian chocolates because it is more nutritious, or that the price of water be higher than that of diamonds because it is so much more important to our survival. If asked what the proper scale of prices should be for these products, most people — at least those who have taken Economics I — would give the sensible answer that there is no proper scale — it all depends on the tastes and needs of millions of consumers and the various conditions that determine the costs of production and the supplies of these products.

What is true of the product market is equally true of the labor market. There is simply no independent scientific way to determine what pay should be in a particular occupation without recourse to the market. Job skills have "costs of production" such as formal schooling and on-the-job training. Different jobs also have different amenities that may be more or less costly for the employer to provide — for example, parttime work, safe work, flexible hours, or a pleasant ambience. And individuals vary in their talents and tastes for acquiring skills and performing different tasks. The skills required change over time as the demand for products changes and as different techniques of production are introduced. And these changes may vary by geographic region. In a market system, these changing conditions are reflected in changing wage rates, which in turn provide workers with the incentive to acquire new skills or to migrate to different regions.

The wage pattern that is the net outcome of these forces need not conform to anyone's independent judgment based on preconceived notions of comparability or of relative desirability. The clergy, for example, earn about 30 percent less than brickmasons.[1] Yet the clergy are largely college graduates; the brickmasons are not. Both occupations are more than 95 percent male — so one cannot point to sex discrimination. Possibly the reason for the wage disparity lies in unusual union power of construction workers and is an example of market imperfections. But other explanations are possible too. The real compensation to the clergy, for example, may include housing and spiritual satisfaction as fringe benefits. On the other hand, the high risk of unemployment and exposure to hazards of brickmasons may be reflected in additional monetary payments. If enough people require premiums to become brickmasons and are willing to settle for nonmonetary rewards to work as clergy, and if the buyers of homes are willing to pay the higher costs of brickmasons, while churchgoers are satisfied with the number and quality of clergy who apply, the market solution may well be satisfactory.[2]

One can also think of examples of jobs that initially may seem quite comparable but that would not command the same wage, even in nondiscriminatory and competitive markets. The following example is based on a case that has been used before, but it illustrates the point so well it bears repeating.[3] Consider two jobs — one a Spanish-English translator and the other a French-English translator. Most job evaluators would probably conclude that these jobs are highly comparable and should be paid the same. After all, the skills required, the mental demands, the working conditions, and responsibility would seem to be nearly identical. But "nearly" is not equal, and the difference in language may in fact give rise to a legitimate pay differential. The demand for the two languages may differ — for example, if trade with Spanish-speaking countries is greater. But the supply of Spanish-English translators may also be greater. And this would vary by geographic area. It would be difficult to predict which job will require the higher wage and by how much in order to balance supply and demand.

What the market does is to process the scarcity of talents, the talents of heterogeneous individuals and the demands of business and consumers in arriving at a wage. The net outcome would only coincidentally be the same as a comparable worth determination. There are simply too many factors interacting in highly complex ways for a study to find the market clearing wage.

WHY ABANDON THE MARKET?

The argument for abandoning market determination of wages and substituting "comparable worth," where wage decisions would be based on an independent assessment of the "value" of occupations, is based on the following premises: (1) the pay gap between women and men is due to discrimination and has failed to narrow over time; (2) this discrimination takes the form of occupational segregation, where women are relegated to low-paying jobs; and (3) pay in these female-dominated occupations is low simply because women hold them.

The Pay Gap

In 1983 the pay gap, viewed as the ratio of women's to men's hourly pay, was about 72 percent overall (Table 1).[4] Among younger groups the ratio is higher (and the pay gap smaller) — a ratio of 89 percent for 20–24-year-olds and 80 percent for the age 25–34 years old. Among groups age 35 and over the ratio is about 65 percent.

What accounts for the pay gap? Clearly, not all differentials reflect discrimination. Several minorities (Japanese and Jewish Americans, for example) have higher than average wages, and I do not believe anyone would ascribe these differentials to favoritism towards these groups and discrimination against others.

A growing body of research has attempted to account for the pay gap, and the researchers have come to different conclusions. These studies, however, use different data sources, refer to different populations and control for many, but not always the same set of variables. Even the gross wage gap — the hourly earnings differential before adjusting for diverse characteristics — varies from study to study, ranging from 45 to 7 percent depending on the type of population considered. Studies based on national samples covering the full age range tend to show a gross wage gap of 35 to 40 percent. Studies based on more homogeneous groups, such as holders of advanced degrees or those in specific professions, have found considerably smaller gross wage gaps.

After adjusting for various characteristics, the wage gap narrows. Generally, the most important variables contributing to the adjustment are those that measure the total number of years of work experience, the years of tenure on current job, and the pattern or continuity of previous work experience.

Traditional home responsibilities of married women have been an obstacle to their full commitment to a career. Although women are now combining work and marriage to a much greater extent than in the past, older women in the labor force today have typically spent many years out of the labor force raising their families. Data from the National Longitudinal Survey (NLS) indicate that in 1977 employed white women in their forties had worked only 61 percent of the years after leaving school, and employed black women had worked 68 percent of the years.[5] By contrast, men are usually in the labor force or the military on a continuing basis after leaving school.

In a recent study I examined the contribution of lifetime work experience and other variables using the NLS data for men and women aged 25 to 34. White women's hourly wage rate was found to be 66 percent of white men's — a wage gap of 34 percent. This wage gap narrowed to 12 percent after accounting for the effects of male-female differences in work experience, job tenure, and schooling, as well as differences in plant size and certain job characteristics, such as the years of training required to learn a skill, whether the occupation was hazardous, and whether the occupation had a high concentration of women.

The gross wage gap between black men and black women was 18 percent. The gross wage gap was smaller for blacks than for whites because job-related characteristics of black women and black men are closer than those of white women and white men. Black women have somewhat fewer years of work experience in their teens and early twenties than white women, which may be related to earlier childbearing. They are more likely to work continuously and full time later on, however, and thus accumulate more total work experience and longer tenure on their current jobs than white women. The adjustment for differences in the measured characteristics cited above narrowed the wage gap of black men and women to 9 percent.

Are the remaining unaccounted-for differences a measure of discrimination in the labor market?

If all the productivity differences between women and men are not accurately identified and measured, labor market discrimination would be overestimated by the unexplained residual. Many variables were omitted from this analysis and from other studies because relevant data are not available. These include details on the quality and vocational orientation of education; on the extent of other work-related investments, such as job search; and on less tangible factors, such as motivation and effort. Differences in these factors could arise from the priority placed on earning an income versus fulfilling home responsibilities. If women, by tradition, assume the primary responsibility for homemaking and raising children, they may be reluctant to take jobs that demand an intense work commitment.

On the other hand, the unexplained residual may underestimate discrimination if some of the included variables, such as years of training to learn a job, or the sex typicality of occupations, partially reflect labor market discrimination. Some employers may deny women entry into lengthy training programs or be reluctant to hire them in traditionally male jobs. It is difficult with available data to distinguish this situation from one where women choose not to engage in training because of uncertainty about their long-run career plans or choose female occupations because they are more compatible with competing responsibilities at home.

TABLE 1   *Female-Male Ratios of Median Usual Weekly Earnings of Full-Time Wage and Salary Workers, by Age, 1971-1983*

I. Unadjusted Ratios

Age	May 1971	May 1973	May 1974	May 1975	May 1976	May 1977	May 1978	2nd Quarter 1979	Annual Average 1979	1982	1983
16-19	.89	.82	.82	.86	.86	.88	.86	.85	.87	.88	.94
20-24	.78	.77	.76	.76	.80	.78	.75	.75	.76	.83	.84
25-34	.65	.64	.65	.66	.67	.65	.66	.67	.66	.72	.73
35-44	.59	.54	.55	.57	.55	.56	.53	.58	.58	.60	.60
45-54	.57	.57	.57	.59	.57	.56	.54	.57	.56	.59	.58
55-64	.62	.63	.60	.63	.61	.59	.60	.60	.58	.60	.62
Total, 16 years and over	.62	.62	.61	.62	.61	.61	.61	.62	.62	.65	.66

II. Adjusted for Male-Female Differences in Full-time Hours[1]

Age	May 1971	May 1973	May 1974	May 1975	May 1976	May 1977	May 1978	2nd Quarter 1979	Annual Average 1979	1982	1983
16-19	.94	.86	.87	.90	.90	.92	.91	.90	.92	.91	.96
20-24	.85	.83	.82	.82	.86	.84	.80	.81	.82	.88	.89
25-34	.73	.72	.72	.73	.74	.72	.73	.74	.73	.79	.80
35-44	.66	.61	.61	.63	.61	.62	.59	.64	.64	.66	.66
45-54	.62	.62	.62	.63	.62	.61	.59	.63	.61	.64	.63
55-64	.67	.69	.65	.67	.67	.65	.65	.66	.64	.65	.67
Total, 16 years and over	.68	.68	.67	.68	.68	.67	.67	.68	.68	.71	.72

[1] Female-male earnings ratios were adjusted for differences in hours worked by multiplying by age-specific male-female ratios of average hours worked per week (for nonagricultural workers on full-time schedules).

Source: [Data from] Earnings by age and sex are from unpublished tabulations from the Current Population Survey provided by the Bureau of Labor Statistics, U.S. Department of Labor. Hours data are from U.S. Bureau of Labor Statistics, Employment and Earnings series, January issues, annual averages.

Occupational Segregation

Although occupational segregation clearly exists, it is in large part the result of many of the same factors that determine earnings: years of schooling, on-the-job training, and other human capital investments, as well as tastes for particular job characteristics. In a recently completed study, I found that women's early expectations about their future life's work — that is, whether they planned to be a homemaker or planned to work outside the home — are strongly related to the occupations they ultimately pursue.[6] Many women who initially planned to be homemakers, in fact, become labor force participants, but they were much more likely to pursue stereotyped female occupations than women who had formed their plans to work at younger ages. Early orientation influences early training and schooling decisions, and as a result women may be locked into or out of certain careers. Some women, however, by choice, maintain an ongoing dual career — combining work in the home with an outside job — and this leads to an accommodation in terms of the number of hours that women work and other conditions that influence occupational choice.

Women and men were also found to differ sharply in the environmental characteristics of their occupations. Women were less likely to be in jobs with a high incidence of outdoor work, noisy or hazardous work, or jobs requiring heavy lifting. These differences may reflect employer prejudice or the hostile attitudes of male coworkers, but they may also reflect cultural and physical differences.

In sum, a substantial amount of the differences in wages and in occupations by sex has been statistically linked to investments in work skills acquired in school or on the job. Varied interpretations of these results are possible, however. Thus, the precise amount that can be labeled as the result of choices made by women and their families rather than the result of discrimination by employers is not known.

The Trend in the Pay Gap

A major source of frustration to feminists and a puzzle to researchers has been the failure of the gap to narrow over the post-World War II period, despite large increases in women's labor force participation. In fact, the gap in 1982 is somewhat larger than it was in 1955.

The wage gap would not, however, narrow significantly over time unless the productivity or skill of women in the labor force increased relative to men's, or discrimination in the workplace diminished. Because the gross wage gap widened somewhat after 1955, either discrimination increased or women's skills decreased relative to men's. Findings from a recent study suggest that changes in skill, as measured by the changes in the education and work experience of men and women in the labor force, strongly contributed to an increase in the wage gap.[7]

In 1952 women in the labor force had completed 1.6 more years of schooling than men. This difference narrowed sharply so that by 1979 it had disappeared. One reason for this is that the educational level of men advanced more rapidly than that of women during the 1950s. Aided by the GI bill educational benefits, more men attended college. Another reason is that the labor force participation of less educated women increased more rapidly than the participation of highly educated women. Thus, the female labor force became increasingly less selective over time in terms of schooling attainment.

The rise in the number of women in the labor force may also have had an effect on the lifetime work experience of the average working women. A large number of less experienced women entering the labor force may have diluted the experience level of the working women. Although the total number of years of work experience of women is not available for periods of time before the late 1960s, data on job tenure — years with current employer — show that in 1951 men's job tenure exceeded women's job tenure by 1.7 years. This difference widened to 2.7 years in 1962 and then slowly declined, reaching 1.9 years in 1978 and 1.5 years in 1981.

The decline in working women's educational level relative to men's alone would have caused the pay gap to widen by 7 percentage points. The initial widening in the job tenure differential contributed another 2 percentage points to the gap. Together the change in education and job tenure would have increased the wage gap by more than it actually increased. Possibly then, discrimination declined during this period even though the wage gap widened. Since the mid-1960s, educational and work experience differences have moved in different directions. Male educational attainment rose slightly more than that of working women, which alone would have widened the pay gap slightly. Difference in work experience declined overall. Recently (between 1979 and 1983), a narrowing has occurred in the wage gap, from 68 percent to 72 percent overall.

Evidence from the NLS and other sources suggests that the pay gap is likely to narrow perceptibly in the next decade. Not only are young women working more continuously, but they are also getting higher pay for each year of work experience than they were in the late 1960s. This could reflect a reduction in sex discrimination by employers or a greater willingness of women to invest in market skills, or both. Women's career expectations also seem to be rising. In response to an NLS question asked in 1973, 57 percent of women between 25 and 29 indicated their intention to hold jobs rather than be homemakers when they reach age 35. Among women reaching ages 25 to 29 in 1978, 77 percent expressed their intention to work.

Young women have also greatly increased their educational level relative to men. Female college enrollment increased significantly during the 1970s, while male enrollment fell between 1975 and 1980. Moreover, women have made impressive gains in professional degrees during the 1970s. Work roles and work expectations of women and men may well be merging. As these younger women become a larger component of the female labor force, it is anticipated that the overall wage gap will be reduced.

Are Women's Occupations Underpaid?

A major contention of comparable worth supporters is that pay in women's occupations is lower because employers systematically downgrade them. The argument differs from the idea that pay in women's occupations is depressed because of an oversupply to these occupations. An oversupply could arise either because large numbers of women entering the labor force choose these occupations (which is compatible with no discrimination) or because women are barred from some causing an oversupply in others (a discriminatory situation). Although comparable worth advocates have taken the view that overcrowding is caused by restrictive measures, they have lately come to believe that this explanation is not the whole cause of "low payment" in women's jobs.[8] The argument is made that employers can pay less to women's jobs regardless of supply considerations, simply reflecting prejudice against such jobs because they are held by women.

The ability of firms to wield such power is highly questionable. If a firm underpaid workers in women's occupations, in the sense that their wages were held below their real contributions to the firm's receipts, other firms would have a strong incentive to hire workers in these occupations away, bidding up the wages in these occupations. Thus, competition would appear to be a force curtailing employer power. This process could only be thwarted by collusion, an unrealistic prospect considering the hundreds of thousands of firms.

Killingsworth (1984) has suggested that the market for nurses may be an example of collusion by a centralized hospital industry that has conspired to hold wages down. Without more careful analysis of the hospital industry, it is difficult to verify whether this is a valid hypothesis. Basic facts about wages and supply in nursing, however, suggest that collusion either does not exist or is ineffective. Despite a perennial "shortage" of nurses that seems to have existed as far back as one can go, the number of nurses has increased dramatically, both absolutely and as a percentage of the population. In 1960 there were 282 registered nurses per 100,000 population. In 1980 there were 506 nurses per 100,000. This rate of increase is even more rapid than the increase in doctors over the past decade, and the supply of doctors has been rapidly increasing. Why did the increase occur? Were women forced into nursing because they were barred from other occupations? That does not seem to be the case in recent times. What has happened is that nursing, along with other medical professions, has experienced a large increase in demand since the middle 1960s when medicare and medicaid were introduced, and private health insurance increased. As a result, the pay of nurses increased more rapidly than in other fields. Between 1960 and 1978 the salary of registered nurses increased by 250 percent, while the pay of all men rose by 206 percent and the pay of all women rose by 193 percent. During the 1970s the rate of pay increase for nurses slowed, which is not surprising considering the increase in supply. And entry of women into nursing school has recently slowed, suggesting a self-correcting mechanism is at work.

Another way to attempt to evaluate the contention that lower pay in female-dominated occupations reflects discrimination is through statistical analysis of the determinants of earnings in occupations. In a recent study, I asked the question — after accounting for measurable differences in skill, do these predominantly female occupations still pay less? In an analysis of data on more than 300 occupations, I found that after adjusting for schooling, training, part-time work, and environmental conditions (but not actual years of work experience or job tenure, which were not available), the female proportion in an occupation was associated with lower pay in that occupation for both women and for men. But the effect was not large. For each 10 percentage point increase in the percent female in an occupation, the wage in the occupation went down by 1.5 percent. Again, however, one is left with a question mark. Are there other characteristics of occupations that women, on the average, may value more highly than men because of home responsibilities or differences in tastes and for which women, more so than men, are willing to accept a lower wage in exchange? Characteristics that come to mind might be a long summer vacation, such as teaching provides, or a steady 9 to 5 job close to home that certain office or shop jobs may provide. The true effect of sex on occupational differences or wage rates is, therefore, another unresolved issue. There are many good reasons why women would be in lower paying occupations than men, even in the absence of sex discrimination on the part of employers. That does not rule out the existence of discrimination, but it weakens the case for seeking an alternative to the market determination of occupational wage rates.

COMPARABLE WORTH IN PRACTICE— THE WASHINGTON STATE EXAMPLE

What would happen if wages were set in accordance with comparable worth standards and independently of market forces? Any large-scale implementation of comparable worth would necessarily be based on job evaluations that assign points for various factors believed to be common to disparate jobs. For example, in the State of Washington, where a comparable worth study was commissioned, a job evaluation firm assisted a committee of 13 politically chosen individuals in rating the jobs used as benchmarks in setting pay in State employment. The committee's task was to assign points on the basis of knowledge and skills, mental demands, accountability, and working conditions. In the 1976 evaluation a registered nurse at level IV was assigned 573 points, the highest number of points of any job—280 points for knowledge and skills, 122 for mental demands, 160 for accountability, and 11 for working conditions. A computer systems analyst at the IV level received a total of only 426 points—212 points for knowledge and skills, 92 points for mental demands, 122 points for accountability, and no points for working conditions. In the market, however, computer systems analysts are among the highest paid workers. National data for 1981 show that they earn 56 percent more than registered nurses. The Washington job evaluation similarly differs radically from the market in its assessment of the value of occupations throughout the job schedule. A clerical supervisor is rated equal to a chemist in knowledge and skills and mental demands, but higher than the chemist in accountability, thereby receiving more total points. Yet the market rewards chemists 41 percent higher pay. The evaluation assigns an electrician the same points for knowledge and skills and mental demands as a level I secretary and 5 points less for accountability. Auto mechanics are assigned lower points than the lowest level homemaker or practical nurse for accountability as well as for working conditions. Truckdrivers are ranked at the bottom, assigned lower points on knowledge and skills, mental demands, and accountability than the lowest ranked telephone operator or retail clerk. The market, however, pays truckdrivers 30 percent more than telephone operators, and the differential is wider for retail clerks.

Should the market pay according to the comparable worth scale? Or is the comparable worth scale faulty? In Washington State, AFSCME, the American Federation of State, County, and Municipal Employees, brought suit against the State on the grounds that failure to pay women according to the comparable worth scale constituted discrimination. Judge Jack E. Tanner agreed and ruled in favor of the union. The decision was based largely on the fact that the State had conducted the study. Whether or not the study was a reasonable standard for nondiscriminatory wage patterns was never an issue. The State, in fact, was disallowed from presenting a witness who would have critically evaluated the study.

What would happen if comparable worth were to be adopted as a pay-setting mechanism? Take the example of registered nurses and computer systems analysts. Nurses are 95 percent female. If a private firm employing both occupations were required to adopt the rankings from the Washington State comparable worth study, it would likely have to make a significant pay adjustment. It could either lower the salary of systems analysts below that of nurses or raise the pay of nurses above systems analysts. If it lowered the pay of systems analysts, it would likely find it impossible to retain or recruit them. The more popular remedy would be to raise the pay of nurses. If the firm did so, it would also be compelled to raise its prices. Most likely, demand for the firm's product would fall, and the firm would of necessity be required to cut back production. It would seek ways of lowering costs—for example, by reducing the number of registered nurses it employed, trying to substitute less skilled practical nurses and orderlies where possible. Some women would benefit — those who keep their jobs at the higher pay. But other women would lose — those nurses who become unemployed, as well as other workers who are affected by the cutback.

Of course, if the employer is a State government, the scenario may be somewhat different. The public sector does not face the rigors of competition to the same extent as a private firm. I suspect this is one reason why public sector employees seem to be in the forefront of the comparable worth movement. The public sector could not force workers to work for them if the remedy was to lower the wage in high-paying male jobs. But that is not usually what employee groups request. It can, however, pay the bill for the higher pay required to upgrade wages in female-dominated occupations by raising taxes. But in the long run, the State may have financing problems, since taxpayers may not be willing to foot the bill, and the result would be similar to that in the private firm — unemployment of government workers, particularly women in predominantly female occupations, as government services are curtailed.

CONCLUDING REMARKS

Advocates of comparable worth see it as a way of raising women's economic status and, quite expectedly, tend to minimize costs. A typical comment is as follows (Center for Philosophy and Public Policy):

> Certainly, the costs incurred would vary widely depending on the scope of the approach chosen. But the economic costs of remedying overt discrimination should not prove staggering. Employers and business interests have a long history of protesting that fair treatment of workers will result in massive economic disruption. Similar claims were made preceding the abolishment of child labor and the establishment of the minimum wage, and none of the dire predictions came to pass.

Evidently the author is unaware of the numerous economic studies showing the disemployment effects of the minimum wage. However, what this statement fails to see is that comparable worth is in a bigger league than the child labor law or the minimum wage laws that have actually been implemented. It is far more radical. Instituting comparable worth by means of studies such as the one conducted in Washington State could be more like instituting a $15 an hour minimum wage or passing sweeping legislation like Prohibition. Moreover, the costs in terms of economic distortion would be much more profound than the dollars required to pay the bills. Curiously, this is recognized by one comparable worth proponent,[9] who then suggests "that we give very serious consideration to the idea that firms that do raise pay for 'disadvantaged occupations' get special tax incentives for capital equipment that will raise the productivity of these workers. We can't expect firms to swallow these losses; that's crazy." Barrett is willing to go to these lengths because she thinks it might be a way to raise the incomes of poor women heading families on welfare. Long-term welfare recipients, however, are not the women holding the jobs covered by comparable worth schemes. The work participation of women in this situation is very low. Moreover, the lesson of studies of minimum wage effects has been that those who are most vulnerable to disemployment as a result of wage hikes that exceed national market rates are the disadvantaged—those with little education, poor training, and little work experience. Comparable worth would hurt, not help, these women. Subsidies to try to prevent these effects from occurring would be impractical to implement and prohibitively costly.

With all the difficulties that would ensue from implementing comparable worth, it is striking that it would not achieve many of the original goals of the women's movement such as the representation of women as electricians, physicists, managers, or plumbers. In fact, it would likely retard the substantial progress that has been made in the past decade. Younger women have dramatically shifted their school training and occupational choices. They have been undertaking additional training and schooling because the higher pay they can obtain from the investment makes it worthwhile. Raising the pay of clerical jobs, teaching, and nursing above the market rates would make it less rewarding to prepare for other occupations and simply lead to an oversupply to women's fields, making it still harder to find a stable solution to the problem of occupational segregation.

Another byproduct of comparable worth is that it diverts attention away from the real problems of discrimination that may arise. Such problems need not be confined to women in traditional jobs. Pay differences between men and women performing the same job in the same firm at the same level of seniority may no longer be an important source of discrimination. The form discrimination more likely takes is through behavior that denies women entry into on-the-job training or promotions on the same basis as men. The obvious solution is the direct one—namely, allowing or encouraging women whose rights are being denied to bring suit. Existing laws were intended to cover this very type of problem.

The pay-setting procedure in all levels of government employment is another area where remedies other than comparable worth would be more direct and effective. Governments usually do not have the flexibility to meet market demands. The need to adhere to rigid rules under considerable political pressure may result in paying wages that are too high in some occupations and too low in others. (By "too high" I mean that an ample supply of workers could be obtained at a lower wage). This could occur if the private plants covered in a pay survey for a particular occupation are themselves paying above market—for example, as the result of a powerful union. Such a situation could lead to unnecessary pay differentials between certain occupations that are male dominated (which are more likely to be represented by such strong unions) and other male, mixed, and female occupations whose private sector wages are more competitive. Comparable worth is not the solution, however, since it does not address the problem. Paysetting procedures can be improved by changing the nature of the pay surveys and by introducing market criteria—for example, by considering the length of the queue to enter different government jobs and the length of time vacancies stay open. Such changes may help women and also improve the efficiency of government.

Dramatic changes have occurred in women's college enrollment, in labor force participation, and in entrance into formerly male occupations, particularly in the professions. These changes are taking place because of fundamental changes in women's role in the economy and in the family—changes that themselves reflect a response to rising wage rates as well as changing social attitudes. Pay set according to comparable worth would distort wage signals, inducing inappropriate supply response and unemployment. If women have been discouraged by society or barred by employers from entering certain occupations, the appropriate response is to remove the barriers, not try to repeal supply and demand. Comparable worth is no shortcut to equality.

Notes

1. These statistics are based on the median hourly earnings of workers in these occupations in 1981. Rytina, 1982.

2. If brickmasons' wages are artificially high because of union power, the market would be unstable. More workers would desire to be brickmasons than would be hired at the artificially high wage. Would comparable worth policy help the situation? Not likely. A comparable worth solution would likely require higher pay for clergy than for brickmasons because of the heavy weight placed on readily measured items like education. A wage for clergy that is too high would also be unstable. Only the removal of the union power or restrictions on unions would satisfactorily resolve the issue.

3. This example was originated by Sharon Smith and described in Killingsworth (1984), who notes it is cited in Gold (1983).

4. The commonly cited pay gap — where women are said to earn 59 cents out of every dollar earned by men — is based on a comparison of the annual earnings of women and men who work year round and are primarily full time. In 1982 this ratio was 62 percent. This figure is lower than the figure of 72 percent cited above because the annual earnings measure is not adjusted for differences in hours worked during the year, and men are more likely than women to work overtime or on second jobs.

5. O'Neill, 1984.

6. O'Neill, 1983.

7. O'Neill, 1984.

8. Hartmann, 1984.

9. Barrett, 1983.

References

Barrett, Nancy, 1984. "Poverty, Welfare and Comparable Worth," in Phyllis Schlafly, ed., *Equal Pay for Unequal Work, A Conference on Comparable Work.*

Hartmann, Heidi I. 1984. "The Case for Comparable Worth," in Phyllis Schlafly, ed. *Equal Pay for Unequal Work, A Conference on Comparable Work.*

Killingsworth, Mark, 1984. *Statement on Comparable Worth.* Testimony before the Joint Economic Committee, U.S. Congress, Apr. 10, 1984.

O'Neill, June, 1983. "The Determinants and Wage Effects of Occupational Segregation." Working Paper, The Urban Institute.

O'Neill, June, 1984. "Earnings Differentials: Empirical Evidence and Causes," in G. Schmid, ed., *Discrimination and Equalization in the Labor Market: Employment Policies for Women in Selected Countries.*

O'Neill, June, 1984. "The Trend in the Male–Female Wage Gap in the United States." *Journal of Labor Economics,* October.

Rytina, Nancy F. 1982. "Earnings of Men and Women: A Look at Specific Occupations." *Monthly Labor Review,* April 1982.

Laurie Shrage

SOME IMPLICATIONS OF COMPARABLE WORTH

On one side we hear that woman's position can never be improved until
women themselves are better; and on the other, that women can never
become better until their position is improved — until the laws are made
more just, and a wider field opened to feminine activity. But we constantly hear the same difficulty stated about the human race in general.
There is a perpetual action and reaction between individuals and institutions; we must try and mend both by little and little — the only way in
which human things can be mended.

George Eliot[1]

1. INTRODUCTION

The passage of the Equal Pay Act in 1963 established the principle of "equal pay
for equal work" in the American legal system. Workers who perform identical
work must be paid equivalent wages, regardless of a worker's sex or race.
However, due to historic occupational segregation, the vast majority of men
and women do not perform work that is essentially similar in content. Moreover, occupational categories in which the incumbents are predominantly
women (nurse, clerical worker, nursery school teacher, and the like) provide,
on average, lower wages than those awarded to jobs predominantly performed
by men.

The persistent gap in wages between male and female dominated professions
involving similar training, experience, and working conditions, indicates *prima
facie* that wage differentials are affected by gender discrimination. For the past
decade, feminist civil rights organizations have affirmed the existence of
gender-based wage discrimination, and the need to compensate women more
equitably for their work. The remedy they commonly advocate appeals to the
principle of comparable worth: jobs which are dissimilar in content, but comparable in terms of their value to an employer, should be rewarded equally. While
the idea of "equal pay for jobs of comparable worth" is widely accepted among
feminists, it is established neither in the law nor in the academy.

Despite its narrow base of support, the comparable worth movement has
made considerable progress. Several labor unions have successfully negotiated
wage adjustments based on comparable worth studies, and many states have
passed or rewritten legislation which will facilitate the litigation of comparable
worth complaints.[2] In response to these gains, conservative political economists have criticized the doctrine of comparable worth for promoting regulations that threaten to disrupt our free market economy.[3] Business and management experts too have begun to question the validity of job evaluation
techniques that have served management in the past, but which now form the
basis of comparable worth demands.

From *Social Theory and Practice*, 13, no. 1 (Spring 1987), 77–102. Reprinted by permission.

Recently, comparable worth has attracted criticism not only from conservatives but from progressives as well. Critics on the left argue that comparable worth primarily serves the class interests of middle-class white women, and fails to address the needs of minorities, the poor, and working class people.[4] Because the principle of comparable worth ties compensation to job merit — rather than, for example, to employee need — its enforcement, these critics allege, will primarily benefit those in our society whose work carries high social status (in other words, white-collar, managerial and professional workers over blue-collar, skilled or unskilled manual laborers).

Although proponents of comparable worth have frequently addressed the concerns of conservative critics, they have not similarly confronted the issues raised by social progressives.[5] Since comparable worth is motivated by a concern for equality, its proponents should be especially sensitive to the charge that their goals reflect some degree of middle-class elitism. This paper will examine the theoretical assumptions behind the demand for comparable worth, in order to see if it can be maintained in light of the criticisms raised by progressive theorists.

2. THE THEORY OF COMPARABLE WORTH AND ITS JUSTIFICATION

The demand for comparable worth contains five distinct components:

1. Work which is dissimilar in content, but which requires similar levels of training, experience, and responsibility, and is performed under similar conditions, is of comparable value to employers. Workers whose work is of comparable value should receive equal compensation from employers, regardless of race or sex.

2. The occurrence of systemic economic discrimination against women and minorities in our society can be inferred from a pervasive pattern of salary differentials — a pattern in which wages paid for work performed predominantly by women and minorities average approximately 60–75 percent of wages paid to white men for work of comparable value.

3. The job evaluation system developed by business and management experts, and which have a long history of use by employers, are helpful for comparing jobs in terms of their value to an employer.

4. However, job evaluation techniques that are currently in use must be reexamined to eliminate sex and ethnic bias both in their form (for example, how job factors are weighted, which factors are chosen, how jobs are described, and so forth) and in their application (for example, whether women and minorities participate in administering them).[6]

5. Public and private employers must conduct their own bias-free job evaluation studies to determine the extent to which wage differentials in their institutions have been affected by race or gender, and must then make appropriate adjustments to their wage structure if inequities are found to exist.[7] If employers do not voluntarily undertake these actions, then such studies and adjustments should be brought about by union negotiations, or by state or federal law.

Parts (1), (4) and (5) summarize the prescriptive components of the demand for comparable worth: that adjustments to wages should be made in accordance with the principle of equal pay for work of comparable value, using the findings of gender and ethnic neutral job evaluation techniques. Parts (2) and (3) summarize the empirical presuppositions of comparable worth theory: that statistical data on existing wage differentials, together with the findings of unbiased job evaluation studies, strongly imply the existence of systemic race and sex discrimination in our society in the setting of compensation levels. Components (2) and (3) provide some justification for (1), (4) and (5) in that if discrimination against women and minorities in the form of wage suppression exists, and if we believe the wage structure should be equitable, it follows that some steps to remedy this situation should be taken. However, what does not follow from these claims is that the remedy morally and practically required is the one proposed in (1), (4) and (5). Hence, to justify the prescriptive components of the theory, additional considerations and principles which indicate their unique remedial potential must be brought forth. In this section I will explore and develop some of these considerations.

Economists report that "women who work full time all year earn about 60 percent of what full-time men earn."[8] Despite the entrance of women in past years into jobs traditionally held by men, and despite a dramatic increase in the number of women in the work force, the gap in earnings between women and men has remained constant, or has even slightly increased, since 1955. Conversely, workers in male-dominated occupations earn 30–50% more than those in integrated or female-dominated occupations, and "the more an occupation is dominated by women, the less it pays."[9]

Some of the differences in earnings between men and women can be explained by the amount of labor supplied, in other words, the number of hours worked. This is one example of a so-called "human capital" or "productivity-related job content" variable that economists and sociologists attempt to isolate and hold constant, in order to explain some portion of the wage gap. By identifying relevant variables, social scientists attempt to determine whether factors which are independent of employer bias (such as an employee's years of training, previous experience, or the level of responsibility a job demands) can account for salary differentials between male- and female-dominated occupations. While some portion of the earnings gap can be predicted by observing variation in "human capital" characteristics other than gender or race, even conservative critics find that these correlations leave a significant portion of the gap in wages (perhaps 60 percent) unexplained.[10]

Some social scientists maintain that the unpredicted portion of the wage gap merely reflects the degree of difficulty involved in measuring certain "human capital" variables. By contrast, other scholars claim that the "unexplained" portion of the wage gap is predictable when wage differentials are correlated with human capital features, such as race and sex. However, such correlations imply the occurrence of sex and race discrimination in the evolution of the wage structure; thus, they raise controversial issues. Nevertheless, according to civil rights attorney Winn Newman, the occurrence of discrimination can be inferred from "a consistent pattern of underpayment of women's jobs . . . in virtually every work place, public and private, in this country."[11] To further support the claim that current wage differentials are caused, in part, by sex and race discrimination, he argues:

> If Jack and Jill . . . went up the hill, and Jack reached the top before Jill, you don't necessarily have a violation of the law. You can't necessarily infer discrimination. But on the other hand, if all the Jacks and all the Jims

and all the Joes reach the top of the hill before all the Jills and all the Janets and all the Joannes, then commonsense suggests . . . that the explanation as to why all of the women lagged behind all of the men is sex discrimination.[12]

Of course, without the initial assumption of gender equality with respect to climbing ability, commonsense might suggest that the explanation lies in Jill's inherent inferiority. Comparable worth assumes at a minimum that Jill and Jack are equally equipped to climb. Consequently, a convincing interpretation of the statistical data on earnings will very likely make reference to sex and race discrimination. Yet, this passage points to some confusion in our thinking about discrimination, and to why some social scientists ignore its explanatory power.

The theories of liberal economists generally make little use of the notion of discrimination because discrimination — as liberals conceive of it — is difficult to observe and measure. For them "discrimination in hiring and promotion" refers to the extent to which individual employers make decisions based upon their own biases or prejudices against particular segments of the population. To determine the extent of this phenomenon, one must measure the number of intentionally discriminatory acts of individuals. Thus, even where all Jills earn less than all Jacks, let alone in a single instance, commonsense will not dictate that discriminatory acts by employers have necessarily occurred. It is at least theoretically possible that all Jills have engaged in intentional action which is causally responsible for this state of affairs. Indeed, some would argue that given that all Jills have been socialized in a similar fashion, it is more plausible to assume that they have acted in a common fashion than to assume that their employers have.[13] To assume common intentional action on the part of employers is to postulate a conspiracy, which is not only unlikely, but the product of paranoid thinking.

Some explanations of social phenomena employ a conception of discrimination that differs from the liberal model. By "discrimination in hiring and promotion," some theorists are referring to implicit principles of social organization which have adverse consequences for certain social groups, but which are generally not recognized by individuals because they are subsumed or entailed by the accepted, unquestioned values of their society. On this model, sex discrimination is implicit in a society which is organized so that all Jills are paid less than all Jacks for comparable work. Employers may promote and perpetuate discrimination of this sort even if their individual actions happen to be relatively free of personal bias or the intention to discriminate. Indeed, they perpetuate economic discrimination against women and minorities when their actions are merely consistent with dominant cultural beliefs and stereotypes. In short, one need not be aware of the principles which organize our social institutions in order to behave "normally," just as one need not be aware of the syntactical rules of one's native language in order to speak grammatically. Nevertheless, as social theorists, we can recognize the existence of rules which structure our social interaction, and which reproduce a social hierarchy that places women and minorities in the weakest economic positions. Because this type of discrimination focuses on structural features of cultural systems or institutions, it is variously referred to as "structural," "systemic" or "institutional discrimination."[14]

Given the statistical data on earnings, few would dispute that discrimination against women and minorities, as our second model defines it, exists in our society. What remains at issue, however, is how to reorganize our society in order to achieve a more equitable wage structure. In other words, even if components (2) and (3) are valid, do they justify the prescriptive claims in (1), (4) and (5)?

Comparable worth proponents are skeptical of the proposition that free market competition will in its course bring about an equitable wage structure. For instance, according to some liberal economists, discriminatory practices based on race and sex should prove unprofitable to an employer. However, even if this is true — even if reserving well paid work for white males is economically harmful — the disappearance of this custom once it has been established may disrupt the lives of those who have, or simply feel they have, benefited from it. According to economists Ray Marshall and Beth Paulin, "to suggest that the elimination of discrimination in internal labor markets is optimal for the profit-maximizing firm is to misunderstand the importance of order (and security) in the efficient operation of the production process in these markets."[15] Clearly, the economic utility of a practice cannot be assessed without regard to its historical context, which means that in some settings a segregated, hierarchical work force may boost an employer's profits.

Some liberal economists argue that if employers pay low wages to women and minorities for certain types of work, the labor supply for these jobs will decrease, forcing a rise in wage levels. However, this cycle will be interrupted, allowing wages to remain low, when the reserve of unemployed and unskilled workers — homemakers, immigrants, and so on — is larger than the number of jobs. Where shortages do occur, employers have other options besides raising wages. They can demand more overtime from fewer employees, hire temporary workers, cut back in service or production, or look for cheaper labor markets. Such actions by employers, have been common for example, in response to recurring shortages of nurses.[16]

Proponents of comparable worth also doubt that the current level of regulation on the market is high enough to bring about an equitable wage structure. In other words, they believe the achievement of equal pay for substantively equal work, together with the Title VII prohibitions against sex and race discrimination in hiring, are not sufficient to correct historical wage suppression. Women and minorities who work in occupations which have been traditionally dominated by their sex or race will continue to feel the effect of past discrimination on their wages: their wages are and will remain lower than they would be if these jobs were, or had been, performed predominantly by white men.[17] The great majority of women and minority men work in segregated occupations.[18] Moreover, efforts to integrate the work force have primarily benefited younger, college-educated persons,[19] leaving most of the work force untouched. Therefore, policies which raise the wages of traditionally undervalued occupations are necessary, both to compensate equitably those unaffected by new opportunities for mobility into jobs traditionally held by white males, and to attract white males into occupations from which they have been historically absent.

Since progressive political theorists doubt the therapeutic effects of the forces of supply and demand, they should be sympathetic to the demand for regulations that are designed to correct existing inequities. Moreover, since discrimination against certain economic classes in society and the underpayment of labor similarly reflect implicit structures of discrimination, theorists on the left should have little difficulty recognizing systemic economic discrimination based on race and sex. Despite these areas of compatibility between radical political philosophy and comparable worth theory, some radical theorists argue that comparable worth wrongly implies that once the market is corrected for sex and race discrimination and other imperfections through regulation, the wage structure in our society will be fair. Comparable worth theorists assume, according to these critics, that all white males in our society (including working class men), are equitably compensated for their work, and once women and minorities receive equal rates of compensation for comparable work, their wages too will be equitable. In other words, the doctrine uncritically assumes that wide differentials in pay are fair as long as they are correlated with features other than race or gender. For this reason they charge the doctrine of comparable worth with legitimating an elitist system of compensation, and with overlooking the injustices of our society's class system.[20]

In the following sections, I will try to respond to the serious issues raised by leftist critics of comparable worth. In doing so, I will avoid debating the more general principles of distributive justice on which their criticisms are based. Instead, I am more concerned with showing which principles of fair distribution actually underlie the demand for comparable worth, rather than arguing for the ultimate acceptability of any specific principle. In particular, I will argue that proponents of comparable worth need not, as radicals have claimed, embrace liberal, meritocratic principles of justice. I will argue this by showing, first, that comparable worth proponents are not committed to the view that the wages white men generally receive for their labor are fair. At most, they assume that the rate of compensation white males receive is, on average, less exploitative than the rate received by women and minority workers. Second, I will show that in making judgments regarding the relative worth of different job categories, comparable worth proponents are not endorsing meritocratic compensation, but are merely urging consistent application of accepted standards of reward. These defenses will be developed in the next two sections.

3. EQUALITY AND WORTH

The theory of comparable worth is based on the fundamental assumption that the wages workers receive should not reflect their race or sex. Such attributes are irrelevant to the value of the work performed, and thus, to equitable rates of compensation.[21] In other words, the theory presupposes a fundamental equality of ability, talent and intelligence between persons of different gender and color. One consequence of the assumption of equality is the desire to have compensation levels set with consistency and impartiality. This means that whatever standards are employed to establish pay rates, they should be applied without regard to an employee's gender or race.

The theory's use of the concept of "worth" may be misleading. The crucial assumption underlying the theory's claims about worth is *not* that wages should be proportionate to worth, but that the labor of women and minorities is of equal worth to the labor of white men. If salary levels among white males were roughly equivalent — in other words, if large disparities in pay did not exist — then comparable worth would entail comparable salary levels and differentials for women and minorities. Moreover, it is consistent with the doctrine of comparable worth to acknowledge that some white male workers are compensated unfairly under the present system. At most, comparable worth assumes, as I have already stated, that the wages white male workers receive are, on average, less exploitative than the wages received by women and minorities.

I am not claiming that comparable worth is inconsistent with liberal, meritocratic principles. Instead, I am arguing these principles are neither entailed, nor presupposed, by the doctrine of comparable worth. Indeed, the idea of comparable worth is even consistent with tying wage levels to workers' needs, as long as the needs of women and minorities are not underrated in this process. If such principles of compensation were the norm, the supporters of comparable worth might modify their demand to one for equal pay for workers with comparable needs. The demand to pay women and minorities what their jobs are worth is made simply to ensure that women and minorities are not treated differently than white males in relation to the distribution of income.

Although the doctrine of comparable worth is not inconsistent with liberal theory, liberals are likely to find less justification for it. The reason for this is that liberals have difficulty recognizing systemic discrimination, a point I raised earlier. Since the model of discrimination they invoke involves decisions individuals make on the basis of personal biases, discrimination will be difficult to identify and measure. Yet, it is unnecessary to establish the existence of discrimination in this sense for feminist purposes. Feminists are not interested in finding individuals to hold responsible for sex discrimination, but in changing social institutions and principles which adversely affect women.

4. DOES COMPARABLE WORTH REFLECT CLASS BIAS?

Comparable worth advocates often emphasize statistics which show that women with college degrees, on average, earn less than men without high school diplomas; for example, childcare workers are often paid less than janitors, and librarians are often paid less than truck drivers. These comparisons suggest that proponents place a high value on credentials gained through formal education. According to Brigitte Berger:

> In arguing for awarding higher value to educational credentials in a bias-free job evaluation model yet to be constructed, comparable worth activists fall prey to a credentialing bias that has little to do with the value of work. If this comparable worth vision should take hold and become the accepted definition of the value of work in America, a blatant antiworking class and antiblue-collar work bias will be introduced under the disguise of justice and equality. . . . [C]omparable worth, if enacted, would benefit in the main the type of white-collar credentialed jobs in which women predominate. . . . It is one of the more aggressively elitist visions of modern life that has surfaced in recent decades.[22]

Comparable worth proponents are not arguing for awarding higher value to credentials gained through formal education. They are merely in favor of rewarding these credentials impartially, without regard to the sex or race of the person who has earned them. If women with formal credentials are earning less than men without them, and men without formal credentials are earning significantly less than men with them, then women are being compensated at a lower rate than men for work dependent upon such achievements. Comparable worth proponents are in favor of women receiving an equal rate of return on their achievements, and do not necessarily favor a higher rate of compensation for formal credentials relative to other qualifications, *per se*. Thus, the criticism that the comparable worth movement is guilty of a credentialing bias shows a fundamental misunderstanding of its aims.

In current job evaluation studies that comparable worth proponents endorse, formal training represents only one of a composite of job worth factors. Other factors include effort, level of responsibility, and work conditions. For example, in the controversial Washington state job evaluation study used by the AFSCME in its discrimination suit against the state, "a clerical supervisor is rated equal to a chemist in knowledge and skills and mental demands, but higher than the chemist in accountability, thereby receiving more total points."[23] A clerical supervisor is likely to have less formal education than a chemist. In the past, comparable worth proponents have criticized existing job evaluation methods for overlooking skills and work demands often found in connection with jobs traditionally held by women and minorities (including many blue-collar jobs), rather than for awarding too little value to formal credentials. To redress inequities that result from the underevaluation of such skills, Ronnie Steinberg notes that "comparable worth studies . . . examine potential wage discrimination in jobs such as garment worker, launderer, food service worker, institutional caretaker, retail sales worker, and entry-level clerk typist."[24] A further fact which attests to the sensitivity of comparable worth proponents to blue-collar interests is that labor unions representing blue-collar workers have overwhelmingly supported the demand for comparable worth through contract negotiations, lawsuits and lobbying for favorable legislation.[25]

Comparable worth supporters focus on factors such as education to illustrate dramatically that women receive a lower rate of return on comparable credentials. Donald Treiman, Heidi Hartmann, and Patricia Roos estimate that "about 40 percent of the earnings gap between male- and female-dominated occupations can be attributed to differences in job characteristics and 60 percent to differences in the rate of return of these characteristics."[26] For instance, providing supervision is a job content characteristic that is generally highly compensated. Yet, supervisors in female-dominated occupations may not be compensated equivalently for the task of supervision compared to supervisors in male-dominated categories.[27] Because of this situation, comparable worth supporters are demanding equal rates of return for comparable skills and qualifications, regardless of the sex or race of the employees.

Unfortunately, in stressing comparisons between formally educated female workers and formally uneducated male workers, comparable worth proponents may have made themselves vulnerable to the misunderstanding that their demands are anti–blue-collar. Such comparisons are useful, however, to counter the objection that women, on average, are paid less than men only because the average women's level of education or job training is lower than the average man's. It is indeed the case that the average woman's "human capital investment" is lower. But this discrepancy does not account for the entire wage gap. If it did, then we would expect to see women compensated at a level equal to their comparably educated male cohorts. But this does not generally happen. In short, the human capital theory simply cannot "explain such facts as why a woman with a college degree made on average only as much as a man with an eighth grade education," which is the point of these comparisons.[28]

In addition, comparisons between men and women with comparable credentials are made to counter the objection that certain skills are scarce, and therefore can command higher wages. Winn Newman argues that if there were a shortage of workers in every male-dominated professional category, you could possibly justify providing all these workers with wages higher than, for example, the wages of a librarian; but there is no such shortage of workers. Nevertheless, librarians with master's degrees are typically paid less than workers in male-dominated jobs requiring a bachelor's.[29] In sum, analogies between women workers who are college educated and men who are not are drawn, not to affirm the superiority of mental work over manual, but to illustrate decisively how our society systematically undervalues the training and skills women possess.

The presumption that comparable worth is a middle-class reform has also led to the charge that it is anti-minority. Blue-collar jobs are disproportionately filled by minority men and women, and hence, if comparable worth contained an anti–working-class bias, it would adversely affect minority workers. Yet, as I have argued, comparable worth is neither anti–blue-collar nor pro–white-collar. Moreover, comparable worth pertains as much to wage discrimination based on race as it does to discrimination based on gender. According to Ronnie Steinberg, the director of a New York State comparable pay study, "the processes perpetuating undervaluation are the same, whether the source of differential treatment is race or sex or ethnicity."[30] Steinberg's study examines jobs held disproportionately by minority males — such as youth division aide, window washer, and elevator operator — for possible wage discrimination. Furthermore, Joy Ann Grune reports that minority women "experience slightly greater degrees of occupational segregation than do white women."[31] If this is true, then the interests of minority women will be well served by comparable worth, since it aims to reward more equitably those whose wages have suffered because of occupational segregation.

Leftist intellectuals are in an awkward position when they tell women and minorities who have struggled to obtain their credentials that their expectation of comparable compensation and social privileges is anti–working class. Denigrating the worth of these credentials when women and minorities achieve them reflects not a pro–working class position, but one that is anti-women and anti-minority. While comparable worth advocates do not claim that formal credentials outweigh all other factors, they do assume that these credentials have positive value, in other words, that they reflect worthwhile achievements. To argue against comparable worth on these grounds is like arguing against busing because the practice assumes that black children ought to have an equal opportunity to attain a formal education. Since this assumption grants positive value to having such an education, it is also open to the charge of elitism. Because the aim of these movements is the elimination of discrimination based on sex or race in the distribution of social goods, to criticize these movements by denigrating the achievements they aim to reward fairly, or facilitate access to, is to reject reform out of an unrealistic desire for revolution. The result, of course, is not revolution, but continuation of the *status quo*.

5. THE POTENTIAL IMPACT OF COMPARABLE WORTH

Marshall and Paulin claim that "in 1950, 70 percent of American households were headed by men whose income was the sole source of family income: in 1984, less than 15 percent of families fit this 'traditional' model, even though many of our employment policies assume it still to be pervasive."[32] A woman's paycheck is not merely a secondary, but often primary source of income for herself and her family. Yet, in our society, over one-third of American families headed by women have incomes below the poverty level and the great majority of persons living in poverty are women and children.[33]

Drew Christie has claimed that a major drawback of comparable worth is that it is likely to have little impact on the problem commonly referred to as "the feminization of poverty."[34] He argues that comparable worth is likely to benefit few women because the greatest push for comparable worth is coming from labor unions, and the majority of female workers are not union members (this includes women who work for small companies, who work part-time, or who work in occupations that are unorganized). However, these claims do not provide an argument against comparable worth, but rather reveal the need for women workers to affiliate in greater numbers with labor organizations. If the gains from comparable worth disputes are to be achieved by and distributed to members of labor organizations, then a subsidiary goal of comparable worth strategists should be to organize in occupations that are dominated by women. Furthermore, Christie's argument ignores the extent to which union settlements set precedents that benefit non-union workers as well, leading one to expect that non-union women will benefit from the efforts of their organized cohorts.

Comparable worth could have more extensive impact on our society than its opponents will allow. According to Roslyn Feldberg:

> While conservatives have fought hard against comparable worth, radicals have been reluctant to fight for it. In part I think that reluctance stems from seeing the narrow presentations in comparable worth litigation as the natural limits of the concept. . . . By taking seriously the value of women's work and their right to equitable wages, comparable worth not only can increase women's earnings but can also set the stage for ending their economic dependency. . . . Its theoretical and political impact will reach far beyond the liberal framework in which it was conceived and force a rethinking of assumptions underlying gender hierarchy and the dominance of the market.[35]

We have seen that comparable worth challenges both gender and racial bias in wage differentials, and the ability of market mechanisms to correct this bias. Nevertheless, Feldberg is correct to point out that the principle of comparable worth has been narrowly applied. For example, due to the kinds of complaints that have been litigated, comparable worth supporters have generally confined themselves to urging equal pay for comparable jobs within the conventional wage-labor market. However, there is no need to limit the demand for equal pay to this range of work. The doctrine of comparable worth has implications for work falling outside the system of monetary exchange (work which is therefore often invisible as "work"), such as the job of homemaking. If we assume that the relative value of a job can be assessed — its value relative to other types of jobs—then we can estimate the relative value of housework, in monetary terms, by comparing it to jobs performed for wages outside the home. Comparisons of this sort can be used to support the demand for pay for housework equal to that of comparably valued work, and thus to support the general demand for "wages for housework."

The confinement of women to unpaid labor in the home contributes substantially to women's economic and social subordination. In return for her full-time housework, the "housewife" receives neither social status nor economic independence. To achieve greater economic independence for women, feminist reformers argue for the unrestricted right of women to enter the paid labor force. In addition, some feminists assert the need for "wages for housework," that is, for granting a woman a legally protected right to some portion of her spouse's (or the biological father's) income, or for awarding a mother a state-subsidized income. These latter reformers argue that the work women perform in the home contributes to, among other things, the reproduction and maintenance of society's labor force. It is, therefore, socially necessary and valuable work, for which women should be compensated in monetary terms. Moreover, in order for a woman to both raise a family and perform work that grants her an income, the work of raising a family must become recognized as socially valuable work: it must become paid work.[36] In other words, the unrestricted right to enter the paid labor force is not sufficient to guarantee women both economic independence and the freedom to be mothers and wives.

The theory of comparable worth lends additional support to the case for wages for housework. For example, the following chart shows that many common tasks of a homemaker are comparable to work performed in other occupations.[37] In the leftmost column of the chart, the work of a homemaker is compared to that of a nursemaid, a dietitian, a maintenance "man," chauffeur, and so forth. Although the rate per hour in the middle section of the chart reflects the "going rate" and not necessarily an equitable rate of compensation for these jobs, the composite comparison offers us a rough way to reach an estimate of the social and monetary value of an average homemaker's work. (This chart is based on 1972 statistics, and thus the rates should be adjusted upward to account for inflation.) If we assume that the underpayment of labor in all cases constitutes economic exploitation, then the failure to provide homemakers with monetary compensation (or its equivalent in terms of property, support or pension rights) is exploitative.

Job	Hours per week	Rate per hour	Value per week
Nursemaid	44.5	$2.00	$89.00
Dietitian	1.2	4.50	5.40
Food buyer	3.3	3.50	11.55
Cook	13.1	3.25	42.58
Dishwasher	6.2	2.00	12.40
Housekeeper	17.5	3.25	56.88
Laundress	5.9	2.50	14.75
Seamstress	1.3	3.25	4.22

(continued)

Job	Hours per week	Rate per hour	Value per week
Practical nurse	0.6	3.75	2.25
Maintenance man	1.7	3.00	5.10
Gardener	2.3	3.00	6.90
Chauffeur	2.0	3.25	6.50

TOTAL $257.53 or $13,391.56 a year (1972)

Ronnie Steinberg argues:

> Until women pointed out the possibility of making such comparisons across sex-segregated occupational groups, no one thought to make them. Comparing women's jobs to men's jobs was a culturally irrelevant activity with obvious financial benefits to employers who could pay incumbents of these jobs less for doing equivalent work.[38]

By encouraging comparisons which force a reevaluation of traditionally devalued categories of work, the theory of comparable worth will make its greatest impact. If work performed inside the home were treated as comparable to work performed outside, then states which do not recognize a homemaker's right to some portion of her spouse's financial assets might be forced to change their laws.

6. CONCLUSION

This paper tries to demonstrate how the concept of systemic discrimination can be used to acquire a better understanding of the statistical data on wage differentials and, consequently, of the way in which inequitable distributions of income are to be redressed. By introducing this concept, we can give greater credibility to claims of discrimination—claims for which there is little evidence in terms of the liberal model. I have argued that claims of discrimination can be sustained, not by observing individual acts or intentions, but by observing a pattern of wage disparities that signifies the existence of rules which implicitly organize our social institutions and which adversely affect specific portions of our population. In saying these rules are implicit, I mean that they are not usually recognized explicitly by members of our society. Nevertheless we can, and indeed must, recognize them in constructing our social policies. The prescriptions of comparable worth theory constitute social policy proposals which recognize and aim to redress implicit structures of discrimination. In sum, the concept of systemic discrimination provides a powerful theoretical tool for challenging our economic system and for motivating institutional, judicial or legislative reform.

Alison Jaggar argues that one major problem with the theory of comparable worth

> is that it provides little indication how the worth of a job should be measured. Should it be measured by the length of training or degree of

skill required for its performance, by the amount of stress or danger it involves or by the social indispensability of its product? Questions can be raised about the interpretation and appropriateness of all these criteria.[39]

It is certainly true that job evaluation is no straightforward matter and that much thought needs to be given to the criteria used. Nevertheless job evaluation systems are employed quite extensively and have been for some time. The need for job evaluation was not first raised by the demands of the comparable worth movement, but rather by the need to compensate workers in a society that did not, and still does not, believe in setting one wage for all. So long as we continue to be such a society, we should not allow gender or race to be a factor in the job evaluation methods employers use. It is true that devising fair job evaluation methods will raise numerous theoretical problems pertaining to the justification of value claims; perhaps it is in this area of the debate that philosophers can make their most useful contribution.[40]

Notes

1. *The Writings of George Eliot: Essays and Uncollected Papers* (Boston: Houghton Mifflin Company, 1908), pp. 332–333.

2. The most significant case so far is *AFSCME* (American Federation of State, County and Municipal Employees) v. *State of Washington*. On the basis of comparable worth studies, the state was held to be guilty of intentional and pervasive discrimination (1983). The state appealed the ruling, and, on September 4, 1985, won its appeal. However, the state legislature authorized the state to negotiate an out-of-court settlement with the union, and a pact was soon signed and ratified. The pact provides for salary increases of 2.5 to 10 percent per year (through 1992) for select underpaid job classes. See *The New York Times*, March 20, 1986, Section C, p. 7. See also Mary Heen, "A Review of Federal Court Decisions under Title VII of the Civil Rights Act of 1964," in *Comparable Worth and Wage Discrimination*, Helen Remick, ed. (Philadelphia: Temple University Press, 1984), pp. 197–219. For a review of Federal and State legislation on comparable worth, see Virginia Dean, Patti Roberts, and Carroll Boone, "Comparable Worth under Various Federal and State Laws," *Comparable Worth and Wage Discrimination*, pp. 238–266.

3. For an apocalypse-threatening diatribe in this vein, see Jeremy Rabkin, "Comparable Worth as Civil Rights Policy: Potentials for Disaster," in *Comparable Worth: Issue for the 80's* (Washington, D.C.: U.S. Commission on Civil Rights, 1984), Vol. 1, pp. 187–195.

4. Drew Christie, "Comparable Worth and Distributive Justice," a paper presented on April 25, 1985 in Chicago to a meeting of the Radical Philosophy Association held in conjunction with the American Philosophical Association Western Division meetings.

5. For an excellent rebuttal of the claim that current wage differentials reflect the free play of neutral forces existing in a free market, see Donald Treiman and Heidi Hartmann, eds., *Women, Work, and Wages: Equal Pay for Jobs of Equal Value* (Washington, D.C.: National Academy Press, 1981).

6. For a summary of how sex bias can enter job evaluation systems, see Helen Remick, "Major Issues in *a priori* Applications," in *Comparable Worth and Wage Discrimination*, pp. 106–108.

7. Remick, p. 99.

8. Paula England, "Explanations of Job Segregation and the Sex Gap in Pay," in *Comparable Worth: Issue for the 80's*, Vol. 1, p. 54. In 1981, the median weekly earnings of full-time black male workers was 76 percent of white male workers' earnings. In the same year black women who worked full-time earned 77 percent of what black men earned. These figures are based on a table of data on gender differences in income and earnings compiled in Solomon Polachek, "Women in the Economy: Perspectives on Gender Inequality," in *Comparable Worth: Issue for the 80's*, Vol. 1, p. 36.

9. Andrea Beller, "Occupational Segregation and the Earnings Gap," in *Comparable Worth: Issue for the 80's*, Vol. 1, p. 23. According to Paula England, "each one percent female in an occupation was found to have a net depressing effect on annual earnings of $30 for males and $17

for females. This means that the difference between the median annual earnings of full-time workers in two occupations of equivalent value in their combinations of skill demands, but differing in that one is 90 percent female and one is 90 percent male, is $1,360 for women and $2,400 for men." Paula England, "Explanation of Job Segregation and the Sex Gap in Pay," pp. 61–62.

10. England, "Explanation of Job Segregation and the Sex Gap in Pay," p. 60.

11. Winn Newman, Statement to the U.S. Commission on Civil Rights at their Consultation on Comparable Worth, June 7, 1984, in *Comparable Worth: Issue for the 80's*, Vol. 2, p. 87.

12. Newman, p. 87.

13. See June O'Neill, "An Argument Against Comparable Worth," in *Comparable Worth: Issue for the 80's*, Vol. 1, p. 183; and Polachek, "Women in the Economy: Perspectives on Gender Inequality," pp. 34–53.

14. The data on occupational segregation, like the data on wage differentials, attest to the existence of systemic race and sex discrimination in employment, and can be redressed by affirmative action in hiring and promotion, as well as by comparable worth.

15. Ray Marshall and Beth Paulin, "The Employment and Earnings of Women: The Comparable Worth Debate," in *Comparable Worth: Issue for the 80's*, Vol. 1, p. 202.

16. See Joy Ann Grune, "Pay Equity Is a Necessary Remedy for Wage Discrimination," in *Comparable Worth: Issue for the 80's*, Vol. 1, p. 169.

17. See Ronnie Steinberg, "Identifying Wage Discrimination and Implementing Pay Equity Adjustments," in *Comparable Worth: Issue for the 80's*, Vol. 1, p. 99. Steinberg states that "systematic undervaluation means that the wages paid to women and men engaged in historically female or minority work are artificially depressed relative to what those wages would be if these jobs had been and were being performed by white males."

18. According to Ray Marshall and Beth Paulin, in 1979 "80 percent of women were in occupations where women constituted 70 percent or more of total employment." Marshall and Paulin, "The Employment and Earnings of Women: The Comparable Worth Debate," p. 199. Paula England states that "by 1970, about 70 percent of either men or women would have had to change occupational categories to achieve the same sex mix within each occupation that exists within the labor force." Paula England, "Socioeconomic Explanations of Job Segregation," in Remick, ed., *Comparable Worth and Wage Discrimination*, p. 29. I have not seen corresponding statistics for minority men in the literature on comparable worth.

19. England, "Explanations of Job Segregation and the Sex Gap in Pay," p. 55. Also see Beller, "Occupational Segregation and the Earnings Gap," p. 32.

20. Christie, "Comparable Worth and Distributive Justice."

21. While our legal system recognizes that, in some cases, a person's gender or religion is inherent to the work performed (a *bona fide* occupational qualification") — for example, being Jewish is inherent to being a cantor; being female is inherent to modeling women's clothes, acting a woman's part in a play, being a wetnurse or a private attendant, and so on — these characteristics should not be relevant to determining the salary levels for such work.

22. Brigitte Berger, "Comparable Worth at Odds with American Realities," in *Comparable Worth: Issue for the 80's*, Vol. 1, p. 71.

23. O'Neill, "An Argument Against Comparable Worth," p. 184. Social scientists appeal to the concepts of "human capital characteristic" and "job worth factor" to correlate both per capita income and salary differentials with productivity — and thereby to establish the comparative value of particular employees or jobs. Thus, in the context of paid work, "worth" becomes operationally defined as "productivity." However, it is not only questionable whether some of the factors standardly used measure productivity, but also whether the worth of an employee to an employer is completely a matter of productivity. (I am grateful to P. Dalton for this point.)

24. Ronnie Steinberg, Statement to the U.S. Commission on Civil Rights at their Consultation on Comparable Worth, June 7, 1984, in *Comparable Worth: Issue for the 80's*, Vol. 2, p. 56.

25. For an overview of the involvement of organized labor in the comparable worth movement, see Lisa Portman, Joy Ann Grune, and Eve Johnson, "The Role of Labor," in *Comparable Worth and Wage Discrimination*, pp. 219–237.

26. Donald Treiman, Heidi Hartmann, and Patricia Roos, "Assessing Pay Discrimination Using National Data," in *Comparable Worth and Wage Discrimination*, p. 147.

27. Steinberg, "Identifying Wage Discrimination and Implementing Pay Equity Adjustments," p. 103–104.

28. Marshall and Paulin, "The Employment and Earnings of Women: The Comparable Worth Debate" p. 202. Nor can human capital theory explain why unskilled, male-dominated entry level jobs pay more than unskilled, female-dominated entry level jobs. Presumably the human capital investment in male and female unskilled labor is the same. Moreover, since the supply of unskilled workers of both sexes is higher than the number of jobs, the scarcity hypothesis does not explain this differential either.

29. Newman, *Comparable Worth: Issue for the 80's*, p. 99.

30. Steinberg, *Comparable Worth: Issue for the 80's*, p. 56.

31. Joy Ann Grune, Statement to the U.S. Commission on Civil Rights at their Consultation on Comparable Worth, June 7, 1984, in *Comparable Worth: Issue for the 80's*, Vol. 2, p. 109.

32. Marshall and Paulin, "The Employment and Earnings of Women: The Comparable Worth Debate," p. 197.

33. Helen Remick, *Comparable Worth and Wage Discrimination*, p. ix.

34. Christie, "Comparable Worth and Distributive Justice."

35. Roslyn Feldberg, "Comparable Worth: Toward Theory and Practice in the United States," in *Signs* 10 (1984): 328.

36. According to Gisela Bock and Barbara Duden, our contemporary notion of "housework," and the association of this type of work with women, arose in the 17th and 18th centuries with the transition from a pre-capitalist, pre-industrial economy to an industrial capitalist one. They argue that in the transition to modern production, the need for the efficient (and cheap) reproduction and maintenance of the worker forced the basic family unit structure to homogenize across class and ethnic groups. The family structure which evolved to suit the needs of capitalist production was one that linked the relatively modern chores of homemaking and childrearing to the wife's economic role. See Gisela Bock and Barbara Duden, "Labor of Love — Love as Labor: On the Genesis of Housework in Capitalism," in *From Feminism to Liberation*, Edith Hoshino Altbach, ed. (Cambridge, Mass.: Schenkman Publishing Company, Inc., 1980), pp. 153–192.

37. This chart is taken from Ann Crittenden Scott, "The Value of Housework," in *Feminist Frameworks*, A. Jaggar and P. Rothenberg, eds. (New York: McGraw Hill, 1984), p. 315.

38. Steinberg, "Identifying Wage Discrimination and Implementing Pay Equity Adjustments," p. 104. It could be argued that the unwaged labor of the wife has benefits for employers too, who can hire workers who will work for less because their costs for house care and childcare are low — the cost of maintaining a wife who receives only her subsistence in return for 12 hours plus of daily toil. However, this suggests that the recent entry of large numbers of women into waged, traditionally male dominated jobs marks both a decrease in the exploitation of women and a restructuring of sex roles, rather than reflecting a need at this stage in capitalist production to enlarge the work force or the aspirations of middle-class families for a certain standard of living.

39. Alison Jaggar, *Feminist Politics and Human Nature* (New Jersey: Rowman and Allanheld, 1983), p. 204.

40. I am grateful to Sandra Bartky, Elizabeth Segal, Daniel Segal, and the *STP* editors for their helpful comments and suggestions on earlier drafts of this paper. I am also grateful to the Radical Philosophy Association for their session on comparable worth where these ideas were first presented. Finally, I am indebted to Norman Segal, of Mudge, Rose, Guthrie, Alexander, and Ferdon, for his assistance in examining the judicial history of comparable worth.

Judith Olans Brown, Phyllis Tropper Baumann, and Elaine Millar Melnick

EQUAL PAY FOR JOBS OF COMPARABLE WORTH: AN ANALYSIS OF THE RHETORIC

A. DEFINITIONS: THE HEART OF THE DEBATE

"Comparable worth" means that workers, regardless of their sex, should earn equal pay for work of comparable value to their common employer. Imprecise use of the phrase hinders meaningful discussion. Comparable worth is equated indiscriminately with comparable work, work of equal worth, work of equal value, or pay equity; however, these terms are not synonymous. Comparable worth theory addresses wage inequities that are associated with job segregation. The basic premise of comparable worth theory is that women should be able to substantiate a claim for equal wages by showing that their jobs and those of male workers are of equal value to their common employer. The doctrine allows comparison of jobs which are different but which require comparable skills, effort and responsibility.[1] In other words, this doctrine permits comparison of jobs which do not come within the ambit of the Equal Pay Act requirement of equal pay for jobs which are "substantially equal."

Opponents of comparable worth, however, focus on jobs that are not demonstrably equivalent and where a comparable worth claim is thus not present. Their rhetoric too often sacrifices accuracy to ideology.[2] In a popular but mistaken example, comparable worth opponents ask why such unrelated workers as nurses (not generally unionized) and truck drivers (highly unionized) should receive the same wages.[3] Opponents also ask why nurses and teamsters, who do not even work for the same employer, should receive the same pay. The response must emphasize that comparable worth cases always involve the same employer. The cases also always involve occupations which, according to a rational standard, are of comparable value to that employer.

The nurse/truck driver example implies that comparable worth requires equal pay for randomly selected job categories simply because the jobs being compared are ordinarily performed by members of one sex. What is really at issue, however, is equal pay for demonstrably equivalent jobs, as measured by either job content or a standard of experience, skill, or responsibility. An appropriate index against which to measure nurses' salaries might be the salaries of hospital sanitarians. Similarly, the appropriate comparable job for a truck driver is one which, although perhaps different in job content, is rated as equivalent in a job evaluation study, or which is capable of being so rated.[4]

Comparable worth doctrine differs from the Equal Pay Act formula in that it permits comparison of jobs which are not substantially similar in content. The Equal Pay Act of 1963 requires equal pay for work of equal skill, effort and

From *Harvard Civil Rights–Civil Liberties Law Review*, 21 (Winter 1986), 127–170. Permission granted by the Harvard Civil Rights–Civil Liberties Law Review. Copyright © 1986 by the President and Fellows of Harvard College.

responsibility performed under similar working conditions. But the statute requires pay equality only for jobs which are *substantially equal*. If the jobs are relatively equivalent yet not sufficiently similar to meet that standard, no Equal Pay Act violation exists.

[In 1981 the Supreme Court] eliminated the requirement that Title VII plaintiffs prove the substantial equality of the jobs being compared.[5] . . . All Title VII plaintiffs alleging gender-based discrimination are comparing jobs which may have dissimilar functions but are of comparable value to the common employer.

The question for Title VII plaintiffs invoking comparable worth theory then becomes how to demonstrate that their jobs and those of male workers are of equal value to their common employer. [After the Court's 1981 decision] plaintiffs need not demonstrate job equivalency. Nor does a successful comparable worth claim require proof of undervaluation due to historical discrimination.[6] Instead, comparable worth requires proof that the employer's male and female workers perform work of comparable value and that the female workers are paid less. Such a demonstration necessarily depends upon the evaluation of jobs which are different in content.

B. JOB EVALUATION: THE RED HERRING OF THE COMPARABLE WORTH DEBATE

Job evaluation techniques provide a method for comparing jobs which are dissimilar in content. Job evaluation is a formal procedure which classifies a set of jobs on the basis of their relative value to the employer. Although the courts are uncomfortable with the concept of comparable worth, the technique of job evaluation has been familiar to American industry for decades.[7] Contrary to the claims of comparable worth critics, job evaluation does not require governmental participation. Evaluation merely eliminates resort to guesswork or unsubstantiated assertions of comparability. It provides a way of identifying situations in which wages remain artificially low because of sex, but where men and women are not performing identical or nearly identical operations.

Formal job evaluation originated in the late nineteenth century as part of a generalized expansion of organizational techniques and a restructuring of workplace control systems. Indeed, job evaluation was such a familiar method for comparing jobs that it provided the theoretical underpinning for the Equal Pay Act of 1963.[8] The various evaluation techniques all use similar methods to inject objectivity and equality into pay structures. The first stage requires a formal description of the duties, requirements and working conditions of each job within the unit being evaluated. Next, jobs are evaluated in terms of "worth" to the organization. The outcome of these two processes is a ranking of all jobs in the evaluation unit. The third stage involves setting wage rates for each job in accordance with the evaluation — the higher the ranking, the higher the wages. The job itself, not the worker performing it, is the subject of evaluation.

Any attempt to raise wages on the basis of comparable worth turns on effective use of wage rate, job classification, promotion policy and contractual data. Job evaluations assemble the relevant information in a form useful to employers, employees, and courts. Firmly grounded in existing industrial relations practice, job evaluation itself is hardly controversial. What is new is the use of this practice to address sex discrimination in wages.

Women in diverse occupations have begun to use job evaluation to demonstrate the discriminatory nature of their employers' male/female pay discrepancies.[9] The public rhetoric that characterizes job evaluation as an impossible task of comparing "apples and oranges" merely ignores the factual basis of the technique. The employer has already fashioned a wholly rational hierarchy of "apples and oranges" on the basis of relative worth to the employer. Unfortunately, the mistaken but popular notion of job evaluation has nonetheless prejudiced the courts against evaluation techniques that are essential to plaintiffs' cases.

C. ARGUMENTS AGAINST COMPARABLE WORTH: THE CRUX OF THE RHETORIC

Intense hostility has surrounded the idea of comparable worth. In order to understand this hostility, it is necessary to examine the arguments used by opponents of comparable worth. These arguments involve three related contentions: the male/female earnings gap results, at least in large part, from factors unrelated to discrimination by particular employers; comparable worth analysis is logistically impossible since there is no objective basis for establishing comparisons between different jobs; and, third, pay equity based on comparable worth would cripple the so-called free market.

1. The Non-Discriminatory Nature of the Wage Gap

The argument that the wage gap between men and women results from non-discriminatory factors is clearly expressed in a report by the U.S. Civil Rights Commission. In its findings, the Civil Rights Commission states that:

> The wage gap between female and male earnings in America results, at least in significant part from a variety of things having nothing to do with discrimination by employers, including job expectations resulting from socialization beginning in the home; educational choices of women who anticipate performing child-bearing and child-rearing functions in the family and who wish to prepare for participation in the labor force in a manner which accommodates the performance of those functions, like the desire of women to work in the kinds of jobs which accommodate their family roles and the intermittency of women's labor force participation.

Essentially, one can reduce the Commission's argument to three basic propositions: women choose low-paying jobs because of their sociological predisposition; women make educational choices which lead to low-paying jobs; and the interrupted participation of women in the labor force leads to lower pay.

The first contention is misguided; comparable worth does not raise job *access* issues. Instead, it addresses situations where women who are already employed are paid less for jobs demonstrably similar to those of male co-workers. In comparable worth cases, women are not socialized to hold "easier" jobs: they are paid less for work of equivalent value. While the effect of socialization on job expectations is relevant to a woman's choice to become a nurse rather than a doctor, it does not address why female nurses are paid less than male orderlies or sanitarians at the same hospital. Comparable worth theory addresses inequities subsequent to access. The Commission simply misses the point in arguing that disadvantage results from the victim's choice, based on her own lower expectations.

The second and third contentions reflect the analytical framework used by human capital theorists to account for employment discrimination.[10] The touchstone of human capital theory as an explanation of wage differentials is productivity. Wages are viewed as a return on investments in human capital. The argument proceeds from the premise that individuals make investments in their productive capacity through education and training. These investments have costs, but they also produce returns in the form of higher wages. The male/female wage differential, therefore, merely reflects the different investments that men and women make.

Mincer and Polachek provide the classic formulation of the theory that women's lower wages merely reflect lower investments in human capital.[11] Productivity of men and women arguably differs . . . [due to] differences in education, training, or length of experience. [However] comparable worth theory does not rely on generalized statistical assertions; it requires a demonstration that in a particular case no other factor appears capable of explaining a proven disparity.

2. Comparing "Apples and Oranges"

The second major argument espoused by opponents of comparable worth is that no objective technique exists for comparing jobs that are not identical in content. The Civil Rights Commission contends that in comparable worth litigation job evaluations are inherently subjective and cannot establish jobs' intrinsic worth. Instead, the Commission claims that such studies function only "to establish rational pay-setting policies within an organization, satisfactory to the organization's employees and management."

This objection, though partially valid, goes too far. Although job evaluation is not absolutely objective, it is a well-established technique in American industry for determining relative wage levels. Representatives of business interests successfully sought to incorporate the concepts of job evaluation into the definition of equality in the Equal Pay Act of 1963. They argued that such a course was necessary because the use of job evaluation techniques was so widespread in industry. For example, E. G. Hester, the director of industrial relations research for Corning Glass, told the Senate Committee on Labor and Public Welfare of his company's concern over the proposed equality criteria. According to Mr. Hester, the proposed criteria would require equal pay "for equal work on jobs the performance of which requires equal skills." He asserted that his approach:

> . . . could give a great deal of difficulty to that large part of American industry and business which has relied upon systematic methods of job evaluation for establishment of equitable rate relationships. Such job evaluation plans depend for their reliability upon other factors than skill alone.

Mr. Hester's statement to the Committee included evidence of the extent to which job evaluation was used. He argued that:

With this general acceptance of job evaluation throughout industry on the part of both management and labor, we feel it most desirable that legislation related to the equal-pay principle incorporate in its language, recognition of job evaluation (or job classification) principles that have been developed, accepted, and are in general use.

In arguing for the incorporation of job evaluation principles, Mr. Hester conceded that job evaluation was "not a precise science governed by natural laws" but still lauded it as "a systematic approach to establish relative job order. . . ." He pointed out that industries using job evaluation principles had customarily constructed the hierarchy on the basis of "effort, skill, responsibility, and working conditions." The Equal Pay Act incorporates these same four factors.

Even a cursory examination of industrial relations practices demonstrates that business and industry have long used specific techniques to determine the relative wage rates of jobs which are dissimilar in content. While evaluation techniques are not absolutely objective, they are a logical starting point in any meaningful wage determination process. Comparable worth cases do not require an abstract showing of intrinsic value. Instead, plaintiffs' cases turn on proof that the employer's job worth determinations are gender-based. Since comparable worth cases always address alleged discrimination of a particular employer, they compare "pay-setting policies within an organization." The Commission itself admits that this use of job evaluation is "rational."

3. Laissez-Faire Economics and Antidiscrimination Law

The third argument commonly raised against comparable worth is that it requires an unwarranted intrusion into the market. Again, the Civil Rights Commission report provides an example. The Commission notes that: "The setting of wages is not and cannot be divorced from the forces of labor supply and demand. These factors heavily influence the setting of pay in many jobs and play an important role in setting wages for virtually all other jobs." The Commission then argues that there is nothing in the language or legislative history of Title VII to indicate that Congress intended to prevent employers from relying on the operation of the market in setting wages.

Courts have also made this assertion. However, any statute governing the employment relationship must by its very nature interfere with an employer's absolute freedom to determine wages by reference to the market. The enactment of Title VII indicates congressional intent to intervene in the market to further significant policy interests.

Those who argue that comparable worth is an unwarranted interference insist that supply and demand curves create the wage disparity at issue. Thus, comparable worth theory is not a legitimate response to discrimination but rather a specious definition of discrimination. If there is no impermissible discrimination, they argue, there is no social justification for judicial interference with market forces. A recent article called equal pay for work of comparable worth "a fallacious notion that apples are equal to oranges and that prices for both should be the same, even if that means overriding the law of supply and demand."[12] Market forces are the only relevant measure of value.

The argument's proponents would cloak impermissible sex-based discrimination in the putative legality of "market operation." Yet the argument sidesteps the contention of comparable worth proponents that, despite a pay differential, the jobs are equivalent according to a rational standard. Extolling the overriding authority of supply and demand is to ignore the possibility that the "law" conflicts with Title VII, which like other regulatory legislation necessarily interferes with a laissez-faire economy. The market-based argument against comparable worth is nonetheless instructive since it links criticisms of the allegedly spurious nature of comparable worth with antipathy to the remedy — interference with the market — that comparable worth purportedly implies. It is this connection which is critical to an understanding of judicial opinions in the comparable worth area, since judges often defer to the operation of the market.

Notes

1. See, e.g. Newman and Wilson, "Comparable Worth: A Job Inequity By Any Other Name," in *Manual On Pay Equity: Raising Wages for Women's Work* 54 (J. Grune ed. undated) (on file with Harv. C.R.-C.L. L. Rev.).

2. President Reagan even dismissed comparable worth as a "cockamamie idea." Connant & Paine, "A Loss for Comparable Worth," *Newsweek*, Sept. 16, 1985, 36.

3. See, e.g. Krucoff, "Money: The Question of Men, Women, and 'Comparable Worth,'" *Wash. Post*, Nov. 13, 1979, B5, col. 1.

4. The point is not to assert that equal pay *must* be based on similarity of job content, although it may be so based. Jobs which are quite different in content may properly be the basis for an equal pay claim if it can be demonstrated that they are of equal worth. A case brought under the British Equal Pay Act of 1970 provides an illustration. In *Hayward v. Cammell Laird Shipbuilders Ltd.* IRLR 463 (1984), ICR 71 (1985), a female cook employed in the works cafeteria at the employer's shipyard sought equal pay with men employed as painters, thermal insulation engineers and joiners. An independent expert appointed by the industrial tribunal hearing the claim assessed the various jobs under five factors: physical demands, environmental demands, planning and decisionmaking, skill and knowledge required, and responsibility involved. On the basis of this evaluation he found the jobs to be of equal value.

5. "Respondent's claims of discriminatory undercompensation are not barred by § 703(h) of Title VII merely because respondents do not perform work equal to that of male jail guards." *Gunther*, 452 U.S. at 181.

6. For a discussion of the historic undervaluation of women's jobs, see Blumrosen, "Wage Discrimination, Job Segregation, and Title VII of the Civil Rights Act of 1964," 12 *U. Mich. J.L. Ref.* 397 (1979).

7. See, e.g. *Laffey v. Northwest Airlines*, 567 F.2d 429 (D.C. Cir. 1976), vacating and remanding in part, aff'g in pertinent part, 366 F. Supp. 763 (D.D.C. 1973), cert. denied. 434 U.S. 1080 (1978) (Court of Appeals agreeing with District Court judge who found, after testimony from expert witnesses on job evaluation presented by both plaintiff and defendant, that "pursers" and "stewardesses" performed substantially equal work even though jobs had different titles, descriptions and responsibilities).

8. The "effort, skill, responsibility and working conditions" criteria which the Equal Pay Act uses to determine whether jobs are equal were derived from then-current job evaluation systems.

9. See American Federation of State, County, and Municipal Employees, AFL-CIO (AFSCME), *Guide to Comparable Worth, in Pay Equity: A Union Issue for the 1980's* 11–12 (1980). Unions representing women workers have begun to use evaluation techniques to demonstrate the extent to which women's work is undervalued and underpaid. AFSCME bargained for job evaluation studies in San Jose, California, Lane County, Oregon, and statewide in Minnesota, Wisconsin, and Michigan. *Manual on Pay Equity: Raising Wages for Women's Work* 152–153 (J. Grune ed. undated) (on file with Harv. C.R.-C.L. L. Rev.). The trend has been especially pronounced in the public sector where 100 municipalities are now re-evaluating their job classification systems. See Noble, "Comparable Worth: How It's Figured," *New York Times*, Feb. 27, 1985, p. C7, col. 1

10. See Amsden, "Introduction," in *The Economics of Women and Work* 13–18 (A. Amsden ed. 1980).

11. See Mincer & Polachek, "Family Investments in Human Capital: Earnings of Women," 82 *J. Pol. Econ.* 76 (1974) (supp.).

12. Smith, "The EEOC's Bold Foray into Job Evaluation," *Fortune,* Sept. 11, 1978, 58. The author goes on to talk of the "enormous inflationary effect" of comparable worth, which "at the extreme [would] raise the aggregate pay of the county's 27.3 million full-time working women high enough . . . [to] add a staggering $150 billion a year to civilian payrolls." *Id.* at 59. The statement is typical of the hyperbole on which comparable worth arguments often are based. The author fails to acknowledge that no comparable worth advocate has suggested that all American working women will benefit from the implementation of the doctrine — only those doing work of demonstrably comparable value to that of a male worker of the same employer.

◆ ◆ ◆

DISCUSSION QUESTIONS

1. How seriously wrong is sexual harassment? Where do you draw the line between innocent flirting and sexual harassment?

2. Dodds, Frost, Pargetter, and Prior characterize sexual harassment as "threatening [a woman] with sex she does not want." Does this description seem accurate to you? Does it affect your appraisal of the ethical nature of sexual harassment? If so, how?

3. Do you agree with May and Hughes that in addition to being coercive, sexual harassment also contributes to "a pervasive pattern of disadvantaged treatment of women as a group"?

4. O'Neill points out that the idea that jobs have intrinsic value has been rejected by modern economics in favor of the extrinsic measures of the market. What would you say to the claim that the notion of a *just wage* is morally superior to that of market value and that modern, market economics has a critical moral flaw?

5. Brown, Baumann, and Melnick argue that comparable worth makes sense only when different jobs for the same employer are compared. For example, they dismiss as "mistaken" the comparison frequently made between nurses and truck drivers. Do you agree with this limitation? Is it morally indefensible to inquire about the equity of salaries for jobs for different employers or jobs in different industries?

6. Shrage bases her defense of comparable worth on the idea that discrimination is "systemic" in nature. If she is right, does this mean that the limited defense of comparable worth by Brown, Baumann, and Melnick is flawed?

7. Do you agree with advocates of comparable worth that the pay differentials in question resulted from prior discrimination?

CASE 15.1

◆ ◆ ◆

Ontario's Ground-Breaking Comparable Worth Program

Beginning January 1, 1990, all employers — public and private — in the Canadian province of Ontario were legally required to begin implementing the policy of comparable worth in their compensation programs. The law requires that if 60 percent of the people performing a particular job at a business are women, employers with more than 10 workers must evaluate the position in terms of skill, effort, responsibility, and working conditions. Payroll expenditures were expected to increase by up to 5 percent throughout the province in order to reach pay equity. Companies with 10 to 49 employees did not have to comply until January 1993.

In one method of evaluating jobs, positions are assigned points for each of the categories listed in the accompanying table. The highest possible score is 2,350; jobs with totals within three points of one another are considered equal. If the salaries for such jobs are different, the assumption is that the lower-paying job has been undervalued and must be raised within five years until equity is reached. The following comparison at a Toronto automobile company found that a receptionist and a warehouseman had comparable jobs even though the former was making $6.81 per hour to the latter's $9.36.

	Receptionist	*Warehouseman*
Education	106 points	80 points
Experience	79	86
Complexity	81	76
Supervision of others	0	0
Independence of action	55	55
Consequence of errors	46	51
Confidentiality	14	0
Contacts	48	33
Physical skill and effort	44	76
Working conditions	19	38
TOTAL	492	495

Comparisons at one of the province's regional boards of education also revealed the predicted pattern — jobs generally held by women (clerks, secretaries, switchboard receptionists, health assistants, and child care workers) paid less than comparable jobs held by men (caretakers, grasscutters, maintenance workers, maintenance foremen, and audiovisual technicians). Salary differences ranged from 6 to 25 percent.

The Canadian program is considerably more aggressive than anything found in the United States. A number of American cities and states require that salaries in public agencies conform to the principle of comparable worth, but the requirement does not apply to private businesses. Many corporations are implementing programs on their own, although they are more likely to term them *internal equity*, not comparable worth. Pay adjustments have been made at one bank between commercial bankers (mainly women) and the more highly paid investment bankers (mainly men). Similar corrections were made at a newspaper between the largely female staff of sales representatives who sell ads over the telephone and their more highly paid male counterparts who call on clients. In a program at BankAmerica, the definition of physical labor was expanded to include factors that affected employees in female-dominated jobs — eye strain from working at computer terminals and muscle strain from standing all day at a teller's window. ◆

Discussion Questions

1. Do you agree with the Ontario law?
2. Do you find the comparison between the receptionist and the warehouseman reasonable? Do you find the attempts of the U.S. corporations reasonable?
3. How would you evaluate the Ontario program from an ethical point of view?
4. Does the program exact any costs that are morally unacceptable?
5. Would you support a federally mandated, all-inclusive, Ontario-like program for the United States?

Sources

"Comparable Worth: It's Already Happening," *Business Week*, April 18, 1986, 52, 56.
Freudenheim, Milt, "A New Ontario Law Matches Women's Wages With Men's," *New York Times*, July 27, 1989, A1, A18.

CASE 15.2

◆ ◆ ◆

New Forms of Harassment

For many years in business, the only behavior considered to be sexual harassment was a manager's making sexual intercourse a condition of a woman's getting a job or being promoted. Although such quid pro quo arrangements still count as harassment, many more activities are now recognized as falling into the same category. Unwelcome sexual advances, requests for sexual favors, and offensive verbal or physical contact are also proscribed. Indeed, for conduct to fit the Equal Employment Opportunity Commission's definition of sexual harassment, it must simply have the effect of "unreasonably interfering with an individual's work performance or creating an intimidating, hostile or offensive working environment."

The most celebrated case of a supervisor's allegedly creating a "hostile or offensive working environment," of course, is that of the U.S. Supreme Court's Clarence Thomas. During Thomas's 1991 confirmation hearings, law professor Anita Hill claimed that she had been the victim of sexual harassment by Thomas when she worked for him ten years earlier at the EEOC. Hill said that Thomas made repeated sexual overtures, described pornographic films he watched, and made obscene comments.

Hill's experiences are not uncommon. Studies reveal that anywhere from 40 to 70 percent of female workers have experienced some form of harassment, usually consisting of sexually suggestive looks or gestures, sexual teasing, jokes, remarks or questions, or physical contact. A survey by the National Law Journal found such practices prevalent even among attorneys — 60 percent of the 900 women in the top 250 law firms surveyed had experienced harassment.

One of the most interesting developments in the way sexual harassment has been handled from a legal standpoint, however, is the use of a new standard for determining whether an environment is offensive — that of the "reasonable woman." When courts face questionable situations, the law has traditionally appealed to the notion of how the "reasonable man" would view things. Judges handling offensive environment cases, however, have begun to apply the perspective of a reasonable woman. Judges Robert R. Beezer and Lex Kozinski of the Ninth Circuit of the U.S. Court of Appeals, for example, wrote that, "Conduct that many men consider unobjectionable may offend many women. . . . Because women are disproportionately victims of rape and sexual assault, women have a stronger incentive to be concerned with sexual behavior. Men, who are rarely victims of sexual assault, may view sexual conduct in a vacuum." Accordingly, nude pictures at the workplace, unwelcome love letters, and massages may provoke dramatically different responses in men and women. The courts are thus recognizing that sexual harassment is primarily about power, not sex, and that subtle or visual features of an environment can, to the average woman, be as menacing and fear-inducing as an explicit threat or demand for sexual favors.

One of the most controversial cases, however, claims that even a company's advertisements can be a factor in sexual harassment. In 1991, several female employees of a Minnesota plant of Stroh's Brewery charged that the company's latest campaign of television commercials created a climate in the brewery that tolerated sexual harassment. Stroh's, makers of Stroh's and Old Milwaukee beer, had for years advertised Old Milwaukee through commercials featuring men in outdoor settings sitting around and drinking beer at the end of the day, saying, "It dooesn't get any better than this." In the new ads, after this line is uttered, the "Swedish bikini team" suddenly arrives at the men's campsite to entertain them. The female employees claim that by treating women as sex objects in the commercials, Stroh's encourages the same attitude in its plants. They say that the brewery at which they work has suggestive graffiti and nude calendars and that women have been subjected to sexual abuse of a direct, physical sort. Lori Peterson, the women's attorney, argues that the commercials' offensiveness is clear when an analogy is made to racial stereotypes. "Imagine," she remarks, "our collective horror at seeing black men drop out of the sky to serve white men beer, tap-dance and shine shoes for them. Why is this scenario seen as horrible but similar caricatures of women (with oversized chests and undersized minds) still accepted?" ◆

Discussion Questions

1. In precisely what ways is sexual harassment morally objectionable? Does it matter whether a quid pro quo is intended or whether a hostile environment is the issue?

2. Do you agree with the law that nude calendars can constitute sexual harassment?

3. It is estimated that only 3 percent of women who experience sexual harassment take any formal action. One study of 832 working women found that of the nearly 50 percent who said they had been harassed, none had filed a legal complaint and only 22 percent told anyone what happened. Women are reluctant to speak out because of embarrassment and because, even if they win, they fear reprisals and harm to their careers and reputations. Do these facts make you think that sexual harassment is more or less serious from an ethical standpoint?

4. How defensible is the "reasonable woman" standard from an ethical point of view? Should gender be an irrelevant factor in moral deliberations?

5. Many men argue that sexual or flirtatious remarks, looks, and gestures are just their way of being friendly or humorous. Does this affect your evaluation of such actions from an ethical standpoint? What would make a joke or a look morally offensive?

6. What is your reaction to the "Swedish bikini team" commercials? Does advertising of that sort contribute to sexual harassment, either directly or indirectly? Is it morally objectionable on any other grounds?

Sources

"Bikini Ad Prompts a Sexual Harassment Suit," *New York Times*, November 9, 1991, 11.

DeWitt, Karen, "The Evolving Concept of Sexual Harassment," *New York Times*, October 13, 1991, 28.

"Ending Sexual Harassment: Business Is Getting the Message," *Business Week*, March 18, 1991, 90–100.

Garland, Susan, and Troy Segal, "Thomas Vs. Hill: The Lessons for Corporate America," *Business Week*, October 21, 1991, 32.

"Harassment Rules Often Not Pushed, *New York Times*, October 20, 1991, 1, 22.

Kolbert, Elizabeth, "Sexual Harassment at Work Is Pervasive, Survey Suggests," *New York Times*, October 11, 1991, A1, A17.

"Nude Pictures Are Ruled Sexual Harassment," *New York Times*, January 23, 1991, A14.

Rosenthal, Andrew, "A Terrible Wrong Has Been Done, But to Whom?," *New York Times*, October 13, 1991, IV, 1, 5.

"Sexual Harassment: It's About Power, Not Sex," *New York Times*, October 22, 1991, C1, C12.

◆ ◆ ◆

ADDITIONAL READINGS

Comparable Worth: Issue for the 80's. Washington, DC: U.S. Commission on Civil Rights, 1984.

Gold, Michael Evan, *A Dialogue on Comparable Worth.* Ithaca, NY: Cornell University Press, 1983.

Remick, Helen, *Comparable Worth and Wage Discrimination.* Philadelphia: Temple University Press, 1984.

CHAPTER 16

◆ ◆ ◆

Mergers and Acquisitions

As you have seen, most problems in business ethics come from the way that corporations deal with their employees, customers, or society in general. However, the explosion of mergers and acquisitions in the 1980s has produced a new set of ethical issues related to how businesses deal with one another. Should corporations themselves be seen as just another commodity that can be bought and sold? What ethical problems arise from hostile takeovers — attempts to buy a company whose board and management do not want to sell? Is more good than harm produced by such unwilling acquisitions?

We begin with Michael Jensen's claim that despite the public criticisms of takeovers, these deals serve important economic functions and particularly benefit stockholders. Patricia Werhane explores two issues ignored by Jensen — the rights of employees and the responsibilities of stockholders. Lisa Newton then offers two essays in which she details still other reasons against takeovers, ranging from "pain to individuals, loss of freedom or dignity for individuals, injustice, damage to the common good, violation of accepted moral principles, and betrayal of humanity's highest ideals" to the fact that "the corporate raiders have yet to make their first widget, grow their first carrot, or deliver their first lunch."

Michael C. Jensen

TAKEOVERS: FOLKLORE AND SCIENCE

From 1981 to 1983, the number of large U.S. corporate acquisitions grew at a rate roughly double that of the 1970s and even exceeded the one realized during the famous merger wave of the 1960s. The drama of 2,100 annual takeovers valued at more than $1 million — much of it played out in heated, public battles — has generated an enormous amount of criticism, not only from politicians and the media but also from high-level corporate executives.

Commenting in the *Wall Street Journal* on the Bendix and Martin Marietta takeover battle, for example, Lee Iacocca, chairman of Chrysler, argued:

"It's not a merger. It's a three-ring circus. If they're really concerned about America, they'd stop it right now. It's no good for the economy. It wrecks it. If I were in the banking system I'd say no more [money] for conglomerates for one year."

A former director at Bendix added:

"I think . . . it's the kind of thing corporate America ought not to do, because the poor stockholder is the one whose interest is being ignored in favor of the egos of directors and executives. And who the hell is running the show — the business of making brakes and aerospace equipment — while all of this is going on?"

In a 1984 *New York Times* piece on the "surge of corporate mergers," Felix Rohatyn noted:

"All this frenzy may be good for investment bankers now, but it's not good for the country or investment bankers in the long run. We seem to be living in a 1920s, jazz age atmosphere."

Just as the public outcry over excesses on Wall Street in the early 1930s led to the Glass-Steagall Act regulating banking, so the latest criticisms of mergers have brought enormous political pressure to bear on Congress to restrict takeovers. The July 1983 report of the SEC Advisory Committee on Tender Offers contained 50 recommendations for new regulations. Democratic Representative Peter Rodino has cosponsored a bill that would require advance notice of proposed acquisitions resulting in assets of $5 billion and 25,000 employees and a judgment by the Antitrust Division of the Justice Department or the FTC whether such acquisitions "serve the public interest."

The popular view underlying these proposals is wrong, however, because it ignores the fundamental economic function that takeover activities serve. In the corporate takeover market, management teams compete for the right to control — that is, to manage — corporate resources. Viewed in this way, the market for control is an important part of the managerial labor market, which is very different from, and has higher stakes than, the normal labor market. After all, potential chief executive officers do not simply leave their applications with personnel officers. Their on-the-job performance is subject not only to the

From *Harvard Business Review*, (November/December 1984), 109–121. Reprinted by permission of the *Harvard Business Review*. "Takeovers: Folklore and Science" by Michael Jensen, November/December 1984. Copyright ©1984 by the President and Fellows of Harvard College; all rights reserved.

normal internal control mechanisms of their organizations but also to the scrutiny of the external market for control.

Imagine that you are the president of a large billion-dollar corporation. Suddenly, another management team threatens your job and prestige by trying to buy your company's stock. The whole world watches your performance. Putting yourself in this situation leads to a better understanding of the reasons behind the rhetoric, maneuverings, and even lobbying in the political and regulatory sectors by managers for protection from unfriendly offers.

The Bendix attempt to take control of Martin Marietta in 1982 gained considerable attention because of Marietta's unusual countertakeover offer for Bendix, called the "Pac-Man defense," whose principle is: "My company will eat yours before yours eats mine."[1] Some describe this kind of contest as disgraceful. I find it fascinating because it makes clear that the crucial issue is not whether the two companies will merge but which managers will be in control.

At the end of the contest, Bendix held 67% of Martin Marietta while Martin Marietta held 50% of Bendix. United Technologies then entered as Martin Marietta's friend and offered to buy Bendix. But it was Allied, coming in late, that finally won the battle with its purchase of all of Bendix's stock, 39% of Martin Marietta's, and a promise not to buy more. When the dust had cleared, shareholders of Bendix and Martin had both won; their respective shares gained roughly 38% in value (after adjusting for marketwide stock price change). Allied's shareholders, on the other hand, lost approximately 8.6%.[1]

Given the success and history of the modern corporation, it is surprising how little the media, the legal and political communities, and even business executives understand the reasons behind the complexities and subtleties of takeover battles. Prior to the last decade, the academic community made little progress in redressing this lack of understanding. But research efforts in business schools across the country have recently begun to overcome it.

In this article I summarize the most important scientific evidence refuting the myths that swirl around the controversy. The research shows that:

- Takeovers of companies by outsiders do not harm shareholders of the target company; in fact, they gain substantial wealth.
- Corporate takeovers do not waste resources; they use assets productively.
- Takeovers do not siphon commercial credit from its uses in funding new plant and equipment.
- Takeovers do not create gains for shareholders through creation of monopoly power.
- Prohibition of plant closings, layoffs, and dismissals following takeovers would reduce market efficiency and lower aggregate living standards.
- Although managers are self-interested, the environment in which they operate gives them relatively little leeway to feather their nests at shareholders' expense. Corporate control-related actions of managers do not generally harm shareholders, but actions that eliminate actual or potential takeover bids are most suspect as exceptions to this rule.
- Golden parachutes for top-level executives are, in principle, in the interest of shareholders. Although the practice can be abused, the evidence indicates that shareholders gain when golden parachutes are adopted.
- In general, the activities of takeover specialists benefit shareholders.

Before exploring the evidence, I consider why shareholders are the most important constituency of the modern corporation and why their interests must be held paramount when discussing the current wave of acquisitions and mergers.

THE NATURE OF THE CORPORATION

Stockholders are commonly portrayed as one group in a set of equal constituencies, or "stakeholders," of the company. In fact, stockholders are not equal with these other groups because they are the ultimate holders of the rights to organization control and therefore must be the focal point for any discussion concerning it.

The public corporation is the nexus for a complex set of voluntary contracts among customers, workers, managers, and the suppliers of materials, capital, and risk bearing. The rights of the interacting parties are determined by law, the corporation's charter, and the implicit and explicit contracts with each individual.

Corporations, like all organizations, vest control rights in the constituency bearing the residual risk.[3] (Residual risk is the risk associated with the difference between the random cash inflows and outflows of the organization.) In partnerships and privately held companies, for example, these residual claims and the organizational control rights are restricted to major decision agents (directors and managers); in mutuals and consumer cooperatives, to customers; and in supplier cooperatives, to suppliers.

Corporations are unique organizations because they make no restrictions on who can own their residual claims and this makes it possible for customers, managers, labor, and suppliers to avoid bearing any of the corporate residual risk. Because stockholders guarantee the contracts of all constituents, they bear the corporation's residual risk. The absence of restrictions on who can own corporate residual claims allows specialization in risk bearing by those investors who are most adept at the function. As a result, the corporation realizes great efficiencies in risk bearing that reduce costs substantially and allow it to meet market demand more efficiently than other organizations.

Although the identities of the bearers of residual risk may differ, all business organizations vest organizational control rights in them. For control to rest in any other group would be equivalent to allowing that group to "play poker" with someone else's money and would create inefficiencies that lead to the possibility of failure. Stockholders as the bearers of residual risk hold the right to control of the corporation, although they delegate much of this control to a board of directors who normally hire, fire, and set the compensation of at least the CEO.

Proof of the efficiency of the corporate organizational form shows dramatically in market performance. In principle, any marketer can supply goods and services. In reality, all organizational forms compete for consumers, managers, labor, and supplies of capital and other goods. Those that supply the goods demanded by customers at the lowest price win out. The dominance of the corporate form of organization in large-scale nonfinancial activities indicates that it is winning much of this competition.

ACQUISITION FOLKLORE

Takeovers can be carried out through mergers, tender offers, and proxy fights, or sometimes through elements of all three. A tender offer made directly to the stockholders to buy some or all of their shares for a specified price during a specified time period does not require the approval of the target company's management or board of directors. A merger, however, is negotiated with the company's management and, when approved by its board of directors, is submitted to the shareholders for approval. In a proxy contest the votes of the stockholders are solicited, generally for the election of a new slate of directors.

Takeovers frequently begin with what is called a "friendly" merger offer from the bidder to the target management and board. If management turns down the offer, the bidder can, and often does, take the offer directly to the shareholders in the form of a tender offer. At this point, target company managers usually oppose the offer by issuing press releases condemning it as outside the shareholders' best interest, by initiating court action, by requesting antitrust action against the bidder, by starting a countertakover move for the bidder, and by other actions designed to make the target company a less desirable acquisition.

Target company management often casts about for a "white knight" — a friendly merger partner who will protect the "maiden" from the advances of the feared raider and, more important, who will pay a higher price. When the company doesn't find a white knight, and an unfriendly bidder takes it over, its leaders will likely look for new jobs. The takeover process penalizes incompetent or self-serving managers whose actions have lowered the market price of their corporation's stock. Although the process operates with a lag, the forces are strong and persistent. Of course — as a result of economies of scale or other efficiencies — some efficient managers lose their jobs after a takeover through no fault of their own.

This kind of romantic language has been used to offer comic relief, but it contributes to the atmosphere of folklore that surrounds a process fundamental to the corporate world. The resulting myths and misunderstandings distort the public's perception and render a meaningful dialogue impossible.

Folklore: Takeovers harm the shareholders of target companies.

Fact: The pejorative term *raider* used to label the bidding company in an unfriendly takeover suggests that the bidder will buy control of a company, pillage it, and leave the stockholders with only a crumbling shell.

More than a dozen studies have painstakingly gathered evidence on the stock price effect of successful takeovers (see *Exhibit I* for a summary of the results).[4]

Exhibit I   *Abnormal Stock Price Increases from Successful Takeovers**

	Target Companies	Bidding Companies
Tender offers	30%	4%
Mergers	20%	0%
Proxy contests	8%	N.A.†

* Adjusted to eliminate the effects of marketwide price changes.
† Not applicable.

According to these studies, companies involved in takeovers experience abnormal increases in their stock prices for approximately one month surrounding the initial announcement of the takeover. (Abnormal stock price changes are stock price changes customarily adjusted by regression analysis to eliminate the effects of marketwide forces on all corporations.)[5] The exhibit shows that target company shareholders gain 30% from tender offers and 20% from mergers.

Because tender offers are often extended for less than 100% of the outstanding shares and because not all takeover announcements result in acquisitions, stock prices do not increase at the announcement of the offer by the full amount of the premium offered. Consequently, average target stockholder returns in takeovers are actually higher than the estimates in *Exhibit I* because the abnormal stock price changes it summarizes generally exclude the purchase premiums shareholders receive when they surrender their shares.

The shareholders of bidding companies, on the other hand, earn only about 4% from tender offers and nothing from mergers. If the much feared raiding has taken place, it seems to be of a peculiar, Robin Hood variety.

When an insurgent group, led by a dissatisfied manager or a large stockholder, attempts to gain controlling seats on the board of directors of a company (thereby taking over the company through an internal proxy fight), shareholders also gain. As *Exhibit I* shows, the stock prices of these companies gain 8% on average.

Because target companies are usually a lot smaller than the bidders, you cannot calculate total returns to both parties from the data in *Exhibit I*. An analysis of more than 180 tender-offer acquisitions, however, indicates statistically significant gains to target and acquiring company shareholders equal to an average 8.4% of the total market value of the equity of both companies.[6]

In sum, contrary to the argument that merger activity wastes resources without benefiting stockholders, stockholders earn substantial gains in successful takeovers. In the Texaco takeover of Getty, for example, Getty Oil shareholders realized abnormal stock price gains of $4.7 billion, or 78.6% of the total equity value, and Texaco shareholders, abnormal returns of $1.3 billion or 14.5%. Gains for both totaled $6 billion, 40% of the sum of their equity values. Gulf stockholders earned abnormal returns of $6.2 billion (79.9%) from the Socal takeover, and Socal stockholders earned $2.8 billion (22.6%). The total gains of $9 billion in this merger represent a 44.6% increase in the total equity values of both companies.

In light of these shareholder benefits, the cries to eliminate or restrain unfriendly takeovers seem peculiar (and in some cases self-serving). In a January 5, 1983 *Wall Street Journal* article, Peter Drucker called for such controls: "The question is no longer whether unfriendly takeovers will be curbed but only when and how." He went on to say:

"The recent shoot-out between Bendix and Martin Marietta has deeply disturbed even the staunchest laissez-faire advocates in the business community. And fear of the raider and his unfriendly takeover bid is increasingly distorting business judgment and decisions. In company after company the first question is no longer: Is this decision best for the business? But, will it encourage or discourage the raider?"

Such arguments may comfort concerned managers and board members who want protection from the discipline of competition in the market for managers.

But they are based on false premises. The best way to discourage the competing manager (that's what *raider* means) is to run a company to maximize its value. "Will this decision help us obtain maximum market value?" is the only logically sensible interpretation of "What is best for the business?"

Folklore: Takeover expenditures are wasted.

Fact: Purchase prices in corporate takeovers represent the transfer of wealth from the stockholders of bidding companies to those of target organizations, not the consumption of wealth. In a takeover, the resources represented in the cash received by the target shareholders can still be used to build new plant and equipment or for R&D.

The only resources consumed are those used to arrange the transaction, such as the time and fees of managers, lawyers, economists, and financial consultants. These expenses are often large in dollar terms; the financial fees of the U.S. Steel/Marathon Oil merger were more than $27 million, and those received by four investment banking firms in the Getty takeover hit a record by exceeding $47 million. But they are a tiny fraction of the dollar value of the acquisition; total financial and legal fees usually amount to only about .7%. More significantly, they help shareholders achieve their much larger gains of 4% to 30%.

In fact, the stock price change is the best measure of the takeover's future impact on the organization. The vast scientific evidence on the theory of efficient markets indicates that, in the absence of inside information, a security's market price represents the best available estimate of its true value.[7] The evidence shows that market prices incorporate all current public information about future cash flows and the value of individual assets in an unbiased way. Stock prices change, of course, in response to new information about individual assets. Because market prices are efficient, however, the new information is equally likely to cause them to decrease or increase, after allowing for normal returns. Positive stock price changes, then, indicate a *rise* in the total profitability of the merged companies. Furthermore, because evidence indicates it does not come from the acquisition of market power, this increased profitability must come from the company's improved productivity.

Folklore: The huge bank credit lines used to carry out large takeovers siphon credit from the financial system and crowd out "legitimate" borrowing for productive investments.

Fact: First, the increases in shareholder wealth I've discussed indicate that takeover activities are productive investments; credit lines are not wasted. Second, companies that make acquisitions with stock or other securities, or with cash on hand or capital acquired from the sale of assets, do not use bank credit.

More important, even when companies accomplish takeovers with bank loans, they do not waste credit because most, if not all, of it is still available for real investment such as new plant and equipment. Let me illustrate the point by using a simple example.

When an acquiring company borrows from a bank for an acquisition, it receives the funds in the form of a credit to its bank account. When target company stockholders deposit receipts from the takeover in their accounts, the bank's total deposits remain unchanged because the acquirer's deposits are reduced by the same amount.

Now, however, the portfolios of the target company shareholders are unbalanced. In response, they can make new investments either directly or by purchasing newly issued shares, and if they do so the credit goes directly into productive real investments. If they take the opposite course of action and reduce their bank debt, the bank will have the same amount of loans and deposits as before the acquisition; total outstanding credit is unchanged and there is no waste.

Alternatively, target company shareholders can purchase securities from other investors, but the sellers then are in the same position as the target company shareholders after the acquisition.

If the recipients of the funds from the takeover don't make new investments or pay down debt, they must increase either their cash holdings or their consumption. If their wealth hasn't changed, they have no reason to change either their cash balances or their consumption, and, therefore, the proceeds will go to make new investments and/or reduce debt. If investor wealth increases, investors will increase their consumption and their cash balances. The value of the consumption and cash balance increases will only be a small fraction of the wealth increase (the capital gains, not the proceeds) from the takeover; the remainder will go for new investments and/or debt reduction. The increase in cash balances and consumption will be the same as that coming from increases in wealth generated by any other cause. Thus, takeovers waste no more credit than any other productive investment.

Folklore: By merging competitors, takeovers create a monopoly that will raise product prices, produce less, and thereby harm consumers.

Fact: The evidence from four studies of the issue indicates that takeover gains come not from the merger's creation of monopoly market power but from its productive economies and synergy.

If the gains did come from the creation of companies with monopolistic powers, industry competitors would benefit, in turn, from the higher prices and would enjoy significant increases in profits and stock prices. Furthermore, the stock prices of rivals would fall if the FTC or the Antitrust Division of the Justice Department cancelled or challenged the merger.

The evidence indicates, however, that competitors gain when two other companies in the same industry merge. But these gains are not related to the creation of monopolistic power or industry concentration. Moreover, the stock prices of competitors do not fall on announcement of antitrust prosecution or cancellation of the acquisition. This evidence supports the hypothesis that takeover gains stem from real economies in production and distribution realized through the takeover and that it signals the availability of similar gains for rival companies.[8]

In fact, the evidence raises serious doubts about the wisdom of FTC or Justice Department policies concerning mergers. The cancellation of an acquisition erases virtually all the stock price increases occurring on its announcement—with no apparent offsetting benefits to anyone.[9]

Folklore: Consolidating facilities after a takeover leads to plant closings, layoffs, and employee dismissals—all at great social cost.

Fact: No evidence with which I am familiar indicates that takeovers produce more plant closings, layoffs, and dismissals than would otherwise have occurred.

This charge raises a serious question, however, about the proper criteria for evaluation of the social desirability of takeovers. The standard efficiency yard-stick measures increases in the aggregate real standard of living. By these criteria the wealth gains from takeovers (and their associated effects) are good as long as they do not come from the creation of monopolistic market power. Therefore, even if takeovers lead to plant closings, layoffs, and dismissals, their prohibition or limitation would generate real social costs and reduce aggregate human welfare because of the loss of potential operating economies.

Some observers may not agree that the standard efficiency criterion is the best measure of social desirability. But the adoption of any other criterion threatens to paralyze innovation. For example, innovations that increase stan-dards of living in the long run initially produce changes that reduce the welfare of some individuals, at least in the short run. The development of efficient truck and air transport harmed the railroads and their workers; the rise of television hurt the radio industry. New and more efficient production, distribution, or organizational technology often imposes similar short term costs.

The adoption of new technologies following takeovers enhances the overall real standard of living but reduces the wealth of those individuals with large investments in older technologies. Not surprisingly, such individuals and com-panies, their unions, communities, and political representatives will lobby to limit or prohibit takeovers that might result in new technologies. When suc-cessful, such politics reduce the nation's standard of living and its standing in international competition.

Folklore: Managers act in their own interests and are in reality unans-werable to shareholders.

Fact: Because executive compensation is related to company size, critics charge that a top officer's desire for wealth and an empire drives merger activity while the stockholders pay the bill. But as *Exhibit I* shows, there is no systematic evidence that bidding company managers are harming shareholders to build empires. Instead, the evidence is consistent with the synergy theory of take-overs. This theory argues that the stock price increases for target companies come from the increase in value obtained by consolidating or altering control of the assets of the companies involved, perhaps because of cost savings from economies of scale or from a highly complementary combination of employees and assets in production and distribution.

The evidence shows that target companies get a large share of the gains; indeed, the gains in mergers go to the target companies while virtually none accrue to bidding companies on the average. Bidding wars such as the DuPont-Seagram-Mobil competition for control of Conoco push up the gain for target companies.

The zero returns to bidders in mergers noted in *Exhibit I* are puzzling. For several reasons, however, this particular estimate has more uncertainty built into it and is probably biased downward. My own assessment is that the returns to bidding companies in mergers are closer to the 4% shown for bidders in tender offers. An examination of the total dollar gains to both bidding and target company shareholders shows that both get about the same amount of dollars but not of percentage gains. The disparity results because bidding companies are generally larger than target companies and the same dollar gains translate into different percentage gains. Because the stock prices of larger companies vary more widely relative to gains in an acquisition than do the stock prices of target companies, their returns cannot be estimated as precisely.

Furthermore, bidders often engage in a prolonged acquisition program. The benefits for target companies from a particular merger occur around the time of the takeover announcement and therefore can be more easily estimated than the bidders' benefits, which may be spread out over several acquisitions.

Often the stock price of a company that seeks several acquisitions reflects the projected benefits of future deals at an early date.[10] When a particular acquisition is announced, the bidder's stock price will change only to the extent that there is a difference between the actual and the previously expected profitability of the merger and on average this will be zero in an efficient market. And because mergers involve negotiations that do not occur in tender offers, more information about the intentions of bidders will leak than will information about the identity of the target; the effect on the bidder's price will therefore be spread out over time.

The record of several large takeovers shows mixed evidence on the returns to acquiring shareholders. In the $13.2 billion takeover of Gulf, Socal shareholders earned $2.77 billion (22.6%) after adjustment for the effects of market-wide price changes (from January 23, 1984 to May 3, 1984). Similarly, in the $10.1 billion takeover of Getty Oil, Texaco shareholders earned $1.3 billion (14.5%, from December 13, 1983 to February 7, 1984). In contrast, Allied shareholders lost $100 million (−8.6%) in the acquisition of Bendix; DuPont lost $800 million (−10.0%) in the takeover of Conoco, while Conoco shareholders realized a gain of 71%, or about $3.2 billion.[11]

On the other hand, Occidental Petroleum shareholders did not lose in Occidental's takeover of Cities Service, whose shareholders gained about $350 million (12.5%).[12] Mesa Petroleum initiated the Cities Service war with a bid of $45 per share. Cities Service countered with a bid for Mesa Petroleum. Gulf Oil then announced completion of negotiations to merge with Cities Service for $63 per share; Cities Service stock immediately gained over 43%, or $1.25 billion. In contrast, the Gulf stock price fell over 14%, or slightly over $900 million. The $350 million difference between the gain to Cities Service shareholders and the loss to Gulf shareholders measures the market's estimate of the net increase in value from the merger.

Citing antitrust difficulties with the FTC, Gulf cancelled its acquisition of Cities Service seven weeks later. Cities Service countered with a breach of contract suit against Gulf for $3 billion. All the earlier gains in the price of Cities Service stock were eliminated, but only one-third of the Gulf loss was recovered — perhaps because the market forecast that legal action might hold Gulf liable for part of the premium offered to Cities Service shareholders or that Gulf would make more overpriced takeover attempts. Within four weeks of the Gulf cancellation, Cities Service merged with Occidental for a $350 million premium — an amount identical to the estimated value of the net merger gains from the aborted combination of Cities Service and Gulf.

A good way for a company to become a takeover target is to make a series of acquisitions that reduce value but allow the value to be recovered through divestiture. A bidder that realizes it can make money by selling off the pieces at a profit will likely seize the initiative. Victor Posner's attack on Marley Company in 1981 is an extreme example. Marley, which manufactured water-cooling towers and heat exchangers, took control of Wylain, a manufacturer of air conditioning, heating, and pumping systems, for an 87% premium over Wylain's previous market value. Marley's stock price fell 21%. Posner bought 11.2% of Marley during the first six months of 1980. Unable to find a white knight, Marley sold its assets, dissolved, and distributed the proceeds in June 1981. Posner received $21.9 million for his investment of $12.5 million in Marley.[13]

MANAGER-SHAREHOLDER CONFLICTS

The interests of managers and shareholders conflict on many, but certainly not all, issues. The divergence intensifies if the company becomes the target of an unfriendly takeover. *Exhibit I* indicates that target shareholders benefit when the bidders offer substantial premiums over current market value. During a takeover top managers of target companies can lose both their jobs and the value of their talents, knowledge, and income that are particular to the organization. Threatened with these losses, such officers may try to reduce the probability of a successful unfriendly takeover and benefit themselves at the expense of shareholders.

Management Struggles

The attempt by Carter Hawley Hale to acquire Marshall Field is an interesting example of a management struggle to retain control. Marshall Field, a high-quality department and specialty store chain, enjoyed less growth than other retailers but consistently rejected merger bids. In early 1978, Carter Hawley Hale, another retailer, offered $42 per share for Marshall Field stock, which was selling for less than $20. Resisting, Marshall Field filed a lawsuit that argued the acquisition would violate securities and antitrust laws. It informed shareholders that the asking price was inadequate and made several defensive acquisitions that aggravated potential antitrust problems and made it less attractive to Carter Hawley. Marshall Field's board authorized top officials to take "such action as they deemed necessary" to defeat the offer. After Carter Hawley withdrew the offer, Marshall Field's stock fell back to $20 per share.

In April 1984, another retailer, The Limited, tried to take over Carter Hawley Hale, whose stock then experienced abnormal gains of 49% in the ensuing conflict. Carter Hawley filed suit against The Limited, claiming securities law violations and antitrust problems, and gave up 33% of its voting rights through the sale of $300 million of convertible preferred stock to General Cinema Corporation. Carter Hawley then gave General Cinema a six-month option to buy the Waldenbook chain, one of its most profitable subsidiaries, and repurchased 51% of its own shares. As a result The Limited withdrew its offer in May and Carter Hawley stockholders lost $363 million—the entire 49% abnormal stock price gain.

Both of these cases show what happens to stock prices when acquisition bids fail. *Exhibit II* summarizes the general evidence obtained from ten studies on stock price behavior during unsuccessful takeover attempts. The average abnormal stock price changes surrounding unsuccessful takeover bids are uniformly small and negative, ranging from −1% to −5%. The exception is the 8% positive return to shareholders of companies subjected to unsuccessful proxy contests. It is interesting that a proxy contest causes an abnormal stock price gain even when the challengers fail, perhaps because the contest threat motivates incumbent managers to change their strategies.

Exhibit II   *Abnormal Stock Price Changes from Unsuccessful Bids* *

	Target Companies	Bidding Companies
Tender offers	−3%	−1%
Mergers	−3%	−5%
Proxy contests	8%	N.A.†

* Adjusted to eliminate the effects of marketwide price changes.
† Not applicable.

The uncertainty of the estimates, however, means that only the −5% return for unsuccessful bidders is statistically significantly different from zero. The other negative returns can arise by chance if the true returns from such unsuccessful offers are actually zero. In conclusion, the Marshall Field experience that target company shareholders essentially lose all the offered premiums when an acquisition bid fails, fits the general evidence.

Exhibit II, however, simplifies the story. Sometimes stockholders benefit greatly from opposition to takeover bids.

Uncoordinated, independent decisions by individual shareholders regarding the acceptance or rejection of a tender offer can cause most of the takeover gains to go to bidding company stockholders.[14] If target managers act as the agents for all target shareholders in negotiating with the bidder for a higher price, however, this "free rider" problem can be alleviated.

Empirical evidence also indicates that some managerial opposition benefits target shareholders. For example, on the failure of a tender offer, target stock prices do not on average immediately lose the 30% average increase in price they earned when the offer was made. In fact, they generally stay up, apparently in anticipation of future bids. And target companies that receive at least one more bid in the two years following the failure of a tender offer on average realize another 20% increase in price. Those targets that do not receive another bid, however, lose the entire initial price increase.[15] Apparently, a little opposition in a merger battle is good, but too much can be disastrous if it prohibits takeover of the company.

The Corporate Charter

Corporate charters specify governance rules and establish conditions for mergers, such as the percentage of stockholders who must approve a takeover. Since constraints on permissible charter rules differ from state to state, changing the state of incorporation will affect the contractual arrangement among shareholders and the probability that a company will be a takeover target. It is alleged that some states desiring to increase their corporate character revenues make their statutes appealing to corporate management. Allegedly, in doing so they provide management with great freedom from stockholder control and therefore provide little shareholder protection. Delaware, for example, has few constraints in its rules on corporate charters and hence provides much contractual freedom for shareholders. William L. Cary, former chairman of the Securities and Exchange Commission, has criticized Delaware and argued that the state is leading a "movement towards the least common denominator" and "winning a race for the bottom."[16]

But a study of 140 companies switching their state of incorporation reveals no evidence of stock price declines at the time of the change, even though most switched to Delaware.[17] In fact, small abnormal price increases are usually associated with the switch. This evidence is inconsistent with the notion that such charter changes lead to managerial exploitation of shareholders.

Without switching their state of incorporation, companies can amend corporate charters to toughen the conditions for the approval by shareholders of mergers. Such antitakeover amendments may require a "super majority" for approval or for the staggered election of board members and can thus lower the probability that the company will be taken over and thereby reduce shareholder wealth. On the other hand, the amendments can also benefit shareholders by increasing the plurality required for takeover approval and thus enable management to better represent their common interests in the merger negotiations.

Two studies of adoption of antitakeover amendments in samples of 100 and 388 companies reveal no negative impact on shareholder wealth.[18] One exception may arise if the super-majority provisions grant effective power to block mergers to a manager-stockholder. The market value of R.P. Scherer, for example, fell 33.8% when shareholders adopted an 80% super-majority merger approval provision. Because the wife of Scherer's CEO owned 21.1% of the stock, she then had the power to block a proposed takeover by FMC. In fact, FMC withdrew its offer after Scherer stockholders approved the 80% majority provision and the price of Scherer stock plummeted.

Repurchase Standstill Agreements

Currently available evidence suggests that management's opposition to takeovers reduces shareholder wealth only when it eliminates potential takeover bids. In a privately negotiated or targeted repurchase, for example, a company buys a block of its common stock from a holder at a premium over market price—often to induce the holder, usually an active or a potential bidder, to cease takeover activity. Such repurchases, pejoratively labeled "greenmail" in the press, generate statistically significant abnormal stock price declines for shareholders of the repurchasing company and significantly positive returns for the sellers.[19] These stock price declines contrast sharply with the statistically significant abnormal stock price increases associated with *nontargeted* stock repurchases found in six studies.[20]

The managers of target companies also may obtain standstill agreements, in which one company agrees to limit its holdings in another. Announcements of such agreements are associated with statistically significant abnormal stock price declines for target companies. Because these agreements almost always lead to the termination of an acquisition attempt, the negative returns seem to represent the merger gains lost by shareholders.

Again, however, the issue is not clearcut because closer examination of the evidence indicates that these takeover forays by competing managers benefit target shareholders. Within ten days of an acquisition of 5% or more of a company's shares, the SEC requires the filing of information giving the identity of the purchaser, purpose of acquisition, and size of the holding. The significantly positive increase in stock price that occurs with the initial purchase announcement indicates that potential dissident activity is expected to benefit shareholders even given the chance that the venture will end in a targeted repurchase. Moreover, this is confirmed by the fact that on average during the period from the SEC filing through the targeted repurchase of the shares, target company shareholders earn statistically significant positive abnormal returns.[21]

Thus, when you look at the whole process, repurchase agreements are clearly not "raiding" or "looting" but are profitable for the target shareholders —although not as profitable as a takeover. The stock price decline at repurchase seems due to the repurchase premium that is effectively paid by the nonselling shareholders of the target firm and to the unraveling of takeover expectations with consequent loss of the anticipated takeover premium.

Because, on average, target shareholders lose the anticipated takeover premiums shown in *Exhibit I* when a merger or takeover fails for any reason, we cannot easily tell whether they were hurt by a repurchase. If the takeover would have failed anyway and if the target company's stock price would have fallen even more without the repurchase, then the repurchase benefited target company shareholders. Such additional price declines might be caused, for example, by the costs of dealing with a disgruntled minority shareholder.

Although the issue requires further study, current evidence implies that prohibition of targeted large-block repurchases advocated by some may hurt target shareholders. Moreover, since shareholders can amend corporate charters to restrict targeted repurchases, there is little justification for regulatory interference by the state in the private contractual arrangements among shareholders. Such repurchase restrictions might well restrict the vast majority of stock repurchases that clearly benefit shareholders. In addition, by reducing the profitability of failed takeovers, such restrictions would strengthen the position of entrenched managers by reducing the frequency of takeover bids. Doing so would deprive shareholders of some of the stock price premiums associated with successful mergers.

Going Private

The phrase *going private* means that publicly owned stock is replaced with full equity ownership by an incumbent management group and that the stock is delisted. On occasion, when going private is a leveraged buy out, management shares the equity with private investors. Some believe that incumbent managers as buyers are exploiting outside shareholders as sellers in these minority freeze outs.

Advocating restrictions on going-private transactions, in 1974 Securities and Exchange Commissioner A.A. Sommer, Jr. argued:

"What is happening is, in my estimation, serious, unfair, and sometimes disgraceful, a perversion of the whole process of public financing, and a course that inevitably is going to make the individual shareholder even more hostile to American corporate mores and the securities markets than he already is."[22]

Study of stockholder returns in 72 goingprivate transactions, however, reveals that the average transaction offers a premium 56% over market price and that abnormal stock price increases on announcement of the offer average 30%. The gains apparently arise from savings of registration and other public ownership expenses, improved incentives for decision makers under private ownership, and increased interest and depreciation tax shields. Outside shareholders are not harmed in going-private transactions.[23]

Golden Parachutes

Some companies provide compensation in employment contracts for top-level managers in the event that a takeover occurs — that is, golden parachutes. Allied agreed, for example, to make up the difference for five years between Bendix CEO William Agee's salary in subsequent employment and his former annual $825,000 salary in the event of a change in control at Bendix. Much confusion exists about the propriety and desirability of golden parachutes, even among senior executives.

But the detractors fail to understand that the parachutes protect stockholders as well as managers. Think about the problem in the following way: top-level managers and the board of directors act as stockholders' agents in deals involving hundreds of millions of dollars. If the alternative providing the highest value to stockholders is sale to another company and the retirement of the current management team, stockholders do not want the managers to block a bid in fear of losing their own jobs. Stockholders may be asking managers to sacrifice position and wealth to negotiate the best deal for them.

Golden parachutes are clearly desirable when they protect stockholders' interests. Like anything else, however, they may be abused. For example, a stockholder doesn't want to pay managers so much for selling the company that they hurry to sell at a low price to the first bidder. But that is a problem with the details of the parachute's contractual provisions and not with the existence of the parachute itself. An analysis of 90 companies shows that adoption of golden parachutes on average has no negative effect on stock prices and provides some evidence of positive effects.[24]

The thing that puzzles me about most golden parachute contracts is that they pay off only when the manager leaves his job and thus create an unnecessary conflict of interest between shareholders and executives. Current shareholders and the acquiring company will want to retain the services of a manager who has valuable knowledge and skills. But the officer can collect the golden parachute premium only by leaving; the contract rewards him or her for taking an action that may well hurt the business. As the bidder assimilates the knowledge that turnover among valuable top-level managers after the acquisition is highly likely, it will reduce its takeover bid. A company can eliminate this problem by making the award conditional on transfer of control and not on the manager's exit from the company.

Selling the 'Crown Jewels'

Another often criticized defensive tactic is the sale of a major division by a company faced with a takeover threat. Some observers claim that such sales prove that managers will do anything to preserve their tenure, even to the extent of crippling or eliminating major parts of the business that appear attractive to outside bidders. Such actions have been labeled a "scorched earth policy."

Studies of the effects of corporate spinoffs, however, indicate they generate significantly positive abnormal returns.[25] Moreover, when target managers find a white knight to pay more for the entire company than the initial, hostile bidder, shareholders clearly benefit.

In the same way, when an acquirer is interested mainly in a division rather than the whole company, shareholders benefit when target management auctions off the unit at a higher price. Brunswick's sale of its Sherwood Medical Industries division to American Home Products shows how the sale of a crown jewel can benefit shareholders. Whittaker Corporation made a hostile takeover bid for Brunswick in early 1982. In defense, Brunswick sold a key division, Sherwood Medical, to American Home Products through a negotiated tender offer for 64% of Brunswick's shares. American Home Products then exchanged these shares with Brunswick for Sherwood's stock. Because its main interest lay in acquiring Sherwood, Whittaker withdrew its offer.[26]

The value of the Whittaker offer to Brunswick shareholders ranged from $605 million to $618 million, depending on the value assigned to the convertible debentures that were part of the offer. The total value to Brunswick shareholders of the management strategy, selling off the Sherwood division, was $620 million. Moreover, because of the structure of the transaction, the cash proceeds went directly to the Brunswick shareholders through the negotiated tender offer. The $620 million value represents a gain of $205 million (49%) on the total equity value of Brunswick prior to the initial Whittaker offer. The Brunswick shareholders were $2 million to $15 million better off with the management strategy, hardly evidence of a scorched-earth policy.

Takeover Artists

Recently, criticism has been directed at corporate takeover specialists who are said to take advantage of a company's vulnerability in the market and thus ultimately harm shareholders. While acting in their own interests, however, these specialists also act as agents for shareholders of companies with entrenched managers. Returning to the Marshall Field story, for example, Carl Icahn launched a systematic campaign to acquire the chain after it had avoided takeover. When it looked as if he would achieve the goal, Marshall Field initiated a corporate auction and merged with BATUS (British American Tobacco Company, U.S.) for $30 per share in 1982. After adjustment for inflation, that price was slightly less than the $20 price of Field's stock in 1977, when it defeated Carter Hawley's $42 offer.

Takeover specialists like Icahn risk their own fortunes to dislodge current managers and reap part of the value increases available from redeploying the assets or improving the management. Evidence from a study of 100 such instances indicates that when such specialists announce the purchase of 5% or more of a company's shares, the stockholders of that company on average earn significantly positive abnormal returns of about 6%.[27]

THE EFFECTIVENESS OF THE MARKET

The corporation has contributed much to the enhancement of society's living standards. Yet the details of how and why this complex institution functions and survives are poorly understood, due in part to the complexity of the issues involved and in part to the political controversy that historically surrounds it. Much of this controversy reflects the actions of individuals and groups that wish to use the corporation's assets for their own purposes, without purchasing them.

One source of the controversy comes from the separation between managers and shareholders—a separation necessary to realize the large efficiencies in risk bearing that are the corporation's comparative advantage. The process by which internal control mechanisms work so that professional managers act in the shareholders' interest is subtle and difficult to observe. When internal control mechanisms are working well, the board of directors will replace top-level managers whose talents are no longer the best ones available for the job.[28]

When these mechanisms break down, however, stockholders receive some protection from the takeover market, where alternative management teams compete for the rights to manage the corporation's assets. This competition can take the form of mergers, tender offers, or proxy fights. Other organizational forms such as nonprofits, partnerships, or mutual insurance companies and savings banks do not benefit from the same kind of external market.

The takeover market also provides a unique, powerful, and impersonal mechanism to accomplish the major restructuring and redeployment of assets continually required by changes in technology and consumer preferences. Recent changes occurring in the oil industry provide a good example.

Scientific evidence indicates that activities in the market for corporate control almost uniformly increase efficiency and shareholders' wealth. Yet there is an almost continuous flow of unfavorable publicity and calls for regulation and restriction of unfriendly takeovers. Many of these appeals arise from managers who want protection from competition for their jobs and others who desire more controls on corporations. The result, in the long run, may be a further weakening of the corporation as an organizational form and a reduction in human welfare.

Notes

Author's note: I am indebted to Armen Alchian, Karl Brunner, Harry DeAngelo, Leo Herzel, Charles Plosset, Richard Rosett, Richard Ruback, Clifford Smith, Jr., Robert Sproull, Alan Underberg and Ned Wass for comments and assistance.

1. For further analysis, see Leo Herzel and John R. Schmidt, "SEC is Probing 'Double Pac-Man' Takeover Defense," *Legal Times*, April 18, 1983, p. 27.

2. For further insight, see Claude W. McAnally, III, "The Bendix-Martin Marietta Takeover and Stockholder Returns," unpublished masters thesis, Massachusetts Institute of Technology, 1983.

3. The only exception is the nonprofit organization, against which there are no residual claims. For a discussion of the critical role of donations in the survival of nonprofits, the nature of the corporation, and competition and survival among organizational forms, see Eugene F. Fama and Michael C. Jensen, "Separation of Ownership and Control," *Journal of Law and Economics*, June 1983, p. 301, and also "Agency Problems and Residual Claims," *Journal of Law and Economics*, June 1983, p. 327.

4. For a summary, see Michael C. Jensen and Richard S. Ruback, "The Market for Corporate Control: The Scientific Evidence," *Journal of Financial Economics*, April 1983, p. 5. The original studies are: Peter Dodd and Richard S. Ruback, "Tender Offers and Stockholder Returns: An Empirical Analysis," *Journal of Financial Economics*, December 1977, p. 351; D. Kummer and R. Hoffmeister, "Valuation Consequences of Cash Tender Offers," *Journal of Finance*, May 1978, p. 505; Michael Bradley, "Interfirm Tender Offers and the Market for Corporate Control," *Journal of Business*, October 1980, p. 345; Peter Dodd, "Merger Proposals, Management Discretion and Stockholder Wealth," *Journal of Financial Economics*, June 1980, p. 1; Michael Bradley, Anand Desai, and E. Han Kim, "The Rationale Behind Interfirm Tender Offers: Information or Synergy?" *Journal of Financial Economics*, April 1983, p. 183; Richard S. Ruback, "Assessing Competi-

tion in the Market for Corporate Acquisitions," *Journal of Financial Economics*, April 1983, p. 141; Paul Asquith, "Merger Bids, Uncertainty, and Stockholder Returns," *Journal of Financial Economics*, April 1983, p. 51; Peggy Wier, "The Costs of Antimerger Lawsuits: Evidence from the Stock Market," *Journal of Financial Economics*, April 1983, p. 207; Peter Dodd and Jerold B. Warner, "On Corporate Governance: A Study of Proxy Contests," *Journal of Financial Economics*, April 1983, p. 401; Paul H. Malatesta, "The Wealth Effect of Merger Activity and the Objective Functions of Merging Firms," *Journal of Financial Economics*, April 1983, p. 155; Paul Asquith, Robert E. Bruner, and David W. Mullins, Jr. "The Gains to Bidding Firms from Merger," *Journal of Financial Economics*, April 1983, p. 121; Katherine Schipper and Rex Thompson, "Evidence on the Capitalized Value of Merger Activity for Acquiring Firms," *Journal of Financial Economics*, April 1983, p. 85; Katherine Schipper and Rex Thompson, "The Impact of Merger-Related Regulations on the Shareholders of Acquiring Firms," *Journal of Accounting Research*, Spring 1983, p. 184; Michael Bradley, Anand Desai, and E. Han Kim, "Determinants of the Wealth Effects of Corporate Acquisitions Via Tender Offer: Theory and Evidence," University of Michigan Working Paper (Ann Arbor: December 1983); Frank H. Easterbrook and Gregg A. Jarrell, "Do Targets Gain from Defeating Tender Offers?" unpublished manuscript, University of Chicago, 1983; Gregg A. Jarrell, "The Wealth Effects of Litigation by Targets: Do Interests Diverge in a Merge?" unpublished manuscript, University of Chicago, 1983.

5. Financial economists have used abnormal price changes or abnormal returns to study the effects of various events on security prices since Eugene F. Fama, Lawrence Fisher, Michael C. Jensen, and Richard Roll used them to measure the impact of stock splits in "The Adjustment of Stock Prices to New Information," *International Economic Review*, February 1969, p. 1. Stephen J. Brown and Jerold B. Warner provide a detailed discussion in "Measuring Security Price Performance," *Journal of Financial Economics*, September 1980, p. 205, and in "Using Daily Stock Returns in Event Studies," *Journal of Financial Economics*, forthcoming.

6. Bradley, Desai, and Kim, "Determinants of the Wealth Effects of Corporate Acquisitions Via Tender Offer."

7. For an introduction to the literature and empirical evidence on the theory of efficient markets, see Edwin J. Elton and Martin J. Gruber, *Modern Portfolio Theory and Investment Analysis* (New York: Wiley, 1984), New York: Wiley, 1984), Chapter 15, p. 375, and the 167 studies referenced in the bibliography. For some anomalous evidence on market efficiency, see the symposia in the *Journal of Financial Economics*, June/September 1978, p. 95.

8. B. Espen Eckbo, "Horizontal Mergers, Collusion, and Stockholder Wealth," *Journal of Financial Economics*, April 1983, p. 241; Robert Stillman, "Examining Antitrust Policy Towards Horizontal Mergers," *Journal of Financial Economics*, April 1983, p. 225; B. Espen Eckbo and Peggy Wier, "Antimerger Policy and Stockholder Returns: A Reexamination of the Market Power Hypothesis," University of Rochester Managerial Economics Research Center Working Paper No. MERC 84-09, (Rochester, N.Y.: March 1984); and B. Espen Eckbo, University of Rochester Managerial Economics Research Center Working Paper No. MERC 84-08, "Horizontal Mergers, Industry Structure, and the Market Concentration Doctrine," (Rochester, N.Y.: March 1984).

9. Wier, "The Costs of Antimerger Lawsuits: Evidence from the Stock Market."

10. Schipper and Thompson, "Evidence on the Capitalized Value of Merger Activity for Acquiring Firms."

11. For a further look, see Richard S. Ruback, "The Conoco Takeover and Stockholder Returns," *Sloan Management Review*, Winter 1982, p. 13.

12. This discussion is based on Richard S. Ruback, "The Cities Service Takeover: A Case Study," *Journal of Finance*, May 1983, p. 319.

13. For a detailed analysis, see David W. Mullins, Jr. *Managerial Discretion and Corporate Financial Management*, Chapter 7, unpublished manuscript, Harvard Business School, 1984.

14. See S. Grossman and O. Hart, "Takeover Bids, the Free-Rider Problem, and the Theory of the Corporation," *Bell Journal of Economics*, Spring 1980, p. 42; and Michael Bradley, "Interfirm Tender Offers and the Market for Corporate Control," *Journal of Business*, October 1980, p. 345.

15. See Bradley, Desai, and Kim, "The Rationale Behind Interfirm Tender Offers."

16. William L. Cary, "Federalism and Corporate Law: Reflections upon Delaware," *Yale Law Journal*, March 1974, p. 663.

17. Peter Dodd and Richard Leftwich, "The Market for Corporate Charters: 'Unhealthy Competition' Versus Federal Regulation," *Journal of Business*, July 1980, p. 259.

18. Harry DeAngelo and Edward M. Rice, "Antitakeover Charter Amendments and Stockholder Wealth," *Journal of Financial Economics*, April 1983, p. 329; and Scott C. Linn and John J. McConnell, "An Empirical Investigation of the Impact of 'Antitakeover' Amendments on Common Stock Prices," *Journal of Financial Economics*, April 1983, p. 361.

19. Larry Y. Dann and Harry DeAngelo, "Standstill Agreements, Privately Negotiated Stock Repurchases, and the Market for Corporate Control," *Journal of Financial Economics*, April 1983, p. 275; and Michael Bradley and L. MacDonald Wakeman, "The Wealth Effects of Targeted Share Repurchases," *Journal of Financial Economics*, April 1983, p. 301.

20. Bradley and Wakeman, "The Wealth Effects of Targeted Share Repurchases"; Larry Dann, "The Effect of Common Stock Repurchase on Stockholder Returns," unpublished dissertation, University of California, Los Angeles, 1980; Larry Dann, "Common Stock Repurchases: An Analysis of Returns to Bondholders and Stockholders," *Journal of Financial Economics*, June 1981, p. 113; Ronald Masulia, "Stock Repurchase by Tender Offer: An Analysis of the Causes of Common Stock Price Changes," *Journal of Finance*, May 1980, p. 305; Ahron Rosenfeld, University of Rochester, Managerial Economics Research Center Monograph and Theses No. MERC MT-82-01, 1982, "Repurchase Offers: Information Adjusted Premiums and Shareholders' Response"; Theo Vermaelen, "Common Stock Repurchases and Market Signalling," *Journal of Financial Economics*, June 1981, p. 139.

21. Richard S. Ruback and Wayne H. Mikkelson, "Corporate Investments in Common Stock," Sloan School of Management Working Paper #1559-84, (Cambridge: M.I.T., 1984); and Clifford G. Holderness and Dennis Sheehan, University of Rochester Managerial Economics Research Center Working Paper No. MERC 84-06, "Evidence on Six Controversial Investors" (Rochester: N.Y.: August 1984).

22. A.A. Sommer, Jr., " 'Going Private': A Lesson in Corporate Responsibility," Law Advisory Council Lecture, Notre Dame Law School, reprinted in *Federal Securities Law Reports*, Commerce Clearing House, Inc., 1974, p. 84.

23. Harry DeAngelo, Linda DeAngelo, and Edward M. Rice, "Going Private: Minority Freezeouts and Stockholder Wealth," *Journal of Law and Economics*, October 1984; and Harry DeAngelo, Linda DeAngelo, and Edward M. Rice, "Going Private: The Effects of a Change in Corporate Ownership Structure," *Midland Corporate Finance Journal*, Summer 1984.

24. Richard A. Lambert and David F. Larcker, "Golden Parachutes, Executive Decision-Making and Shareholder Wealth," *Journal of Accounting and Economics*, forthcoming.

25. See Katherine Schipper and Abbie Smith, "Effects of Recontracting on Shareholder Wealth: The Case of Voluntary Spin-offs," *Journal of Financial Economics*, December 1983, p. 437; Gailen Hite and James Owers, "Security Price Reactions Around Corporate Spin-off Announcements," *Journal of Financial Economics*, December 1983, p. 409; J. Miles and J. Rosenfeld, "The Effect of Voluntary Spin-off Announcements on Shareholder Wealth," *Journal of Finance*, December 1983, p. 1597; Gailen Hite and James E. Owers, "The Restructuring of Corporate America: An Overview," *Midland Corporate Finance Journal*, Summer 1984; Scott C. Linn and Michael Rozeff, "The Effects of Voluntary Spin-offs on Stock Prices: The Anergy Hypothesis," *Advances in Financial Planning and Forecasting*, Fall 1984; Scott C. Linn and Michael Rozeff, "The Corporate Sell-off," *Midland Corporate Finance Journal*, Summer 1984; Scott C. Linn and Michael Rozeff, "The Effects of Voluntary Sell-offs on Stock Prices," unpublished manuscript, University of Iowa, 1984; and Abbie Smith and Katherine Schipper, "Corporate Spin-offs," *Midland Corporate Finance Journal*, Summer 1984.

26. For a further analysis, see Leo Herzel and John R. Schmidt, "Shareholders Can Benefit from Sale of 'Crown Jewels,' " *Legal Times*, October 24, 1983, p. 33.

27. For analysis of the effects of purchases by six so-called raiders, Bluhdorn, Icahn, Jacobs, Lindner, Murdock, and Posner, see Holderness and Sheehan, "The Evidence on Six Controversial Investors."

28. For evidence on the relation between poor performance and executive turnover, see Anne Coughlan and Ronald Schmidt, "Executive Compensation, Management Turnover and Firm Performance: An Empirical Investigation," *Journal of Accounting and Economics*, forthcoming.

Patricia H. Werhane

TWO ETHICAL ISSUES IN
MERGERS AND ACQUISITIONS

With the recent rash of mergers and friendly and unfriendly takeovers, questions have been raised concerning the ethical propriety of these actions. Some of these have to do with the tactics companies engage in when trying to acquire a company or when trying to avoid being acquired. These include the so-called "poison-pill" tactics, greenmailing, and the institution of golden parachutes by the corporations that are threatened with acquisition, problems in good faith bargaining (as illustrated in the Texaco-Pennzoil case), the granting of lock-up options, and the usual anti-trust problems. Other issues include the rights of bondholders on both sides of a merger or acquisition, rights that are often considered secondary in light of shareholder interests, and the question of the rights of individual stockholders who are usually neglected in face of institutional shareholder power.[1]

However, two important issues have not surfaced as questionable practices deriving from mergers and takeovers, one having to do with the rights of employees in mergers and the second concerning the responsibilities of shareholders during these activities. Employees in the acquiring and in the acquired company are expected to carry out their job responsibilities both during the process of the merger or takeover and after its completion. They are supposed to carry on as if nothing had happened, despite rumors, threats of their jobs, or upheavals on all levels of management. Although employees are drastically affected by a merger or an acquisition because in almost every case a number of jobs are shifted or even eliminated after a merger, in fact except for top management, employees at all levels are usually the last to find out about a merger transaction. Yet few commentators have thought this was an issue, and almost nothing has been said about the *rights* of employees during and after a merger or acquisition. It is as if the question of how employees are affected in these sorts of transactions was unimportant or incidental to the fiduciary benefits or losses of the negotiation. Second, although a merger is said to be for the fiduciary benefit of shareholders of both parties, and indeed, this is allegedly the primary justification for a merger or an acquisition, insufficient attention has been paid to the *responsibilities* of shareholders in these activities. If shareholders are the fiduciary beneficiaries of mergers and takeovers then it would appear that they have some responsibilities or obligations attached to these benefits, but little is said about such responsibilities. In this paper I shall analyze these two issues. Although these appear to be two disparate ethical questions, at the end of the paper I shall suggest how they are related.

I.

Let us turn first to the question of employee rights in a merger or acquisition. In any merger or takeover, whether or not in the end it is financially successful,

From *Journal of Business Ethics*, 7 (1988), 41–45. ©1988 by D. Reidel Publishing Co. Reprinted by permission of Kluwer Academic Publishers.

there is a great deal of employee uneasiness or stress. This occurs primarily in the corporation to be acquired, but employees in the acquiring company, too, may have these worries to a lesser extent. These stresses occur because of the secrecy, ambiguity, and uncertainty surrounding the merger. No employee is sure of his or her job, of his or her status in the newly-formed company created out of the merger or acquisition, or even of the status of the division or department in which he or she is employed. Little information is disseminated to any employee. In most mergers only the top management is privy to the negotiations, and what is occuring is kept secret to prevent stock fluctuations, competing offers, and other market changes. Such secrecy seems necessary so that the merger can take place with the smallest amount of fiscal damage, but the result is the dissemination of ungrounded rumors which creates fear and thus unrest or even psychological trauma for almost every employee. In many merger situations preoccupation with the process of the takeover or the acquisition by top management is such that sometimes employee interests are neglected or even forgotten. Economic interests supersede any other concerns.

It is not that top management seeks to abrogate employee rights or injure employees. In fact it is often the converse when the merger or acquisition is seen as beneficial to the acquiring or acquired company. Indeed some mergers often preserve jobs when the acquiring or acquired company is in financial or marketing difficulty. Moreover, it is often argued, and not without justification, that mergers and acquisitions protect jobs in the long run by increasing efficiently through a larger organization which can provide more capital for growth, or by expanding a market share through a merger of two similar competing enterprises. At the same time, mergers and acquisitions provide an opportunity to streamline certain divisions and to "weed out" aging, unproductive or superfluous employees. Thus increased productivity, efficiency, and profitability created by the merger or acquisition allow for expansion and provide more employment and more stable employment in the long run.

Now these arguments are all viable economic arguments based on the more general contention that a good merger serves economic interests more fully than not merging and that, from a moral point of view, in the long run the greatest economic happiness for more persons is served by this sort of transaction. What, then is at issue? The question is, do economic interests, important economic interests which affect employees as well as top management, take precedent over basic employee rights, at least under certain economic conditions?

First, what sorts of rights are entitled in these circumstances, and why is it I have called them *basic* employee rights? Employees (or at least most employees) are adults. It has been argued at length elsewhere,[2] that because employees are rational adults, they have certain rights in the workplace, those rights accorded all rational adults equally by our Constitution and Bill of Rights simply because they are persons. Included in these are the obvious ones, especially the right to freedom or the right not to be coerced which includes the right not to be forced into some situation not of one's own choice.[3] Freedom, however, is not merely a negative right to be left alone, because freedom includes the right to exercise choice. Part of the exercise of freedom is illustrated in an employee's right to choose a job and to quit at any time. But another less emphasized part of the exercise of freedom is the control over one's future. For if I cannot control what happens to me at least within the limits of the kinds of choices and actions I am capable of, I am thereby coerced, because I find myself in situations not warranted by my own behavior. So employees have a second right — the right to information which affects their job, their company, and their career. Withholding that kind of information when it is available takes away self-control of one's job and future and therefore is paramount to restricting an employee's freedom of choice. Third, because the right to freedom entails its *exercise*, employees, having chosen to work and where they will work, should be allowed to participate in decisions which affect their employment.[4]

Notice that none of these rights is an absolute or unlimited right. Rather, each right is an equal right in balance with equal rights of others. That is, I have a right to control my future so long as exercising that right does not interfere with the equal rights of another person to do likewise. So an employee's right to information is both a limited and an equal right. Every employee has an equal right to employment information when that information affects her job and future, but not a right to all company information when that does not entail letting out a trade secret (e.g., the recipe for Coca Cola). It is also often contended that employees do not have rights to information when such publicity might affect adversely the market or a proposed merger or acquisition. What this view shows is that shareholder rights supersede employee rights. But if rights are equal rights, one must carefully weigh the sometimes conflicting claims of employees to information and protection of shareholder rights to their fiduciary interests. Note that this claim is different from the right of a company to protect a trade secret. In the latter case the protection of a trade secret does not interfere with employee *rights*. Not revealing the trade secret does not hurt employees because it is not their secret, and protecting the secret usually protects the jobs and interests of employees as well. But in the former case (protecting merger secrets) not informing employees *can* affect their freedom of choice; so it is important to employee rights. While some secrecy is justified, an employee should have a right to at least as much knowledge about such activities as, any other "outsiders" who often know far in advance of such affairs, since it is to the express disadvantage of an employee not to have this information. Notice, too, that in these instances shareholders, too, often do not have such information and this is unfair to them as well for the same reasons.

Similarly, the right to participate in management decisions is an equal employee right, not an unlimited one. The problem is that top management often does not include middle management or other employees in its decision-making particularly when that concerns a merger or acquisition. Yet unless one can argue conclusively that top management always represents shareholder interests, shareholders who are seldom informed or consulted about these decisions, just as employees are not consulted, then there is no justification for excluding employees from participation in these decisions just as there is no excuse for excluding shareholders until the moment before the actual merger.

Failing to honor these rights in the workplace creates two fatal problems. First, when a corporation does not respect the rights of its employees, it is threatening its own claims to those rights. It is saying that it has rights or more extensive rights than people or some people. But this implies that so-called rights are neither equal nor universal, and this implication undermines the justification for a corporate defense of *its* rights. Second, in not upholding employee rights the corporation is in contradiction with itself. It has hired responsible adults whom it holds liable to act as morally decent persons and to perform satisfactorily in whatever jobs those persons are assigned. If employees are accountable for their performance in the workplace, if they are expected to be loyal and have other responsibilities to their employer, that employer has reciprocal responsibilities to that employee, responsibilities which are correlative to what is expected on the employer's part including respect for the employee as a person. This has to be a "good faith" employer responsibility, because although an employer can hold an employee responsible for his job performance, it is more difficult in fact for employees to hold an employer equally liable except by striking. But by not respecting the employee as a rational adult, that is, in not respecting her *equal rights*, the corporation is asking more of that employee in terms of job responsibility than it should expect, and the employee – employer accountability relationship thereby weakens or breaks down.

In the case of mergers and acquisitions the basic employee rights that are not always respected include the right to information, the right to participate in the management decision to accept or fight the merger, and job protection for long-time loyal "at will" employees. Management argues that even if such rights are accorded in the workplace under "normal" circumstances, such rights may need to be bracketed in merger situations, because economic interests outweigh respect for these rights in these economic instances.

But do economic interests supersede rights of employees in these sorts of cases? If one were starving, basic needs might supersede rights to information or participation. But the case is much less clear for mergers. Basic needs are not at stake here. In general if economic interests override rights, then one could imagine extreme situations where one could justify slave labor for example if greater economic interests are served. It is this sort of argument that white South Africans use to justify apartheid — the contention that under apartheid black South Africans are economically better off than any other blacks in Africa. Second, only 50% of all mergers are economically successful.[5] So even to make an argument that economic interests of employees will be better protected in the long run with a merger or any other major corporate reorganization which requires setting aside employee rights is not a very strong argument. Third, even when the merger is fiscally successful, there is much data to suggest that employee stress engendered by such activities translates into lowered productivity, preoccupation with self-preservation, loss of trust in top management and thereby in middle management who by implication must share blame, parochialism rather than teamwork, unwarranted power struggles, loss of efficiency and momentum, and even resignations of good people who, fearing their future unemployment, go elsewhere to better and apparently more secure jobs.[6] In nonutilitarian terms, the lack of respect for employee *rights* translates into an equal loss of commitment, loyalty, responsibility, and trust.

A defender of top management's prerogative to concentrate on fiscal interests in a merger or acquisition might counter argue as follows. A merger or acquisition is carried out only when it is in the best interests of the shareholders. Shareholders have rights, one of which is to do what they please with their shares, in this case shares of a company, so long as they do not harm others. Therefore a focus on economic interests in a merger situation merely respects these rights. However, this point is based on the premise that such shareholders' rights are equal to or more important than political rights. And that contention is unjustified for the same reason that defending the priority of economic interests is unjustified. For if shareholder rights outweigh the right to freedom which includes the right to information, a variety of abhorrent scenarios could be justified too.

Does this mean that mergers are morally wrong and should be abolished? No, that is not the argument. Mergers and acquisitions are neither right or wrong. It is the fiduciary preoccupation of a merger which negatively affects employees and employee rights that is at issue. The latter are at least as important as the former; yet they are seldom taken into account. And by not taking employee considerations into account both the acquired company and the acquiring one threaten the viability of their own rights as well as the success of the merger.

II.

Examining briefly the question of shareholder responsibility, particularly as it relates to a merger activity, in any merger, fiduciary responsibilities to shareholders are taken very seriously, for it is the shareholder who stands to benefit or lose in any stock exchange or acquisition. Shareholder pressure can force an unfriendly takeover, for example, if shareholders are thereby to gain a good price for their holdings. Shareholders, then, have rights to maximize the earnings or the price of their shares simply because they own them. Yet along with rights one also has responsibilities. For example, if one owns property on which chemical dumping is taking place, dumping for which the owner is paid, that property owner has responsibilities to contain the contamination of the chemical so that it does not damage other properties in the neighborhood. Similarly, shareholders have responsibilities connected with their right to maximize their gain as shareholders. At a minimum, they have a responsibility to be sure that management is looking after their interests. Now most of the time an individual shareholder has trouble exercising her responsibilities since she has few voting shares. But institutional shareholders such as universities and pension funds can wield a great deal of influence in corporate decision-making simply because of the number of shares they own. This has been seen to a small extent by those institutional shareholders who have withdrawn their interests in companies who do not adopt the Sullivan Principles in their South African subsidiaries. Such withdrawals have made a difference. Yet while institutions claim they are concerned, we do not always see institutional shareholders pressuring corporations who use "poison pills" or establish large "golden parachutes," questionable practices by any account, and certainly not in shareholders' best interests. What I am suggesting is that along with fiduciary rights shareholders, particularly institutional shareholders, have responsibilities, responsibilities they need to exercise particularly when mergers and acquisitions are taking place. Otherwise they cannot complain when a merger does not take place because of a poison pill tactic, when a merger is not a success, or when millions of dollars of profit are syphoned into golden parachutes.

III.

Finally, what do employee rights have to do with shareholder responsibilities? There is the obvious sense that rational persons cannot be held responsible without according to them the rights which should be accorded to them just because they are persons. So if employees have responsibilities, they need to be accorded the correlative rights implied in these responsibilities. Conversely, one cannot expect to have rights of any sort without assuming the entailing responsibility. So if shareholders have fiduciary rights, by implication they also have responsibilities connected with those rights.

Secondly, using rights talk again, in addition to the relation between rights and responsibilities, rights have two other characteristics: they are universal, that is, if X is a human right, X applies to everyone, and they are equal, that is, X applies to everyone equally. Shareholders who argue that they have fiduciary rights, also contend that they have the right to exercise that fiduciary claim freely and, along with that, that they have a right to enough information about the corporation to exercise that claim intelligently. This is fair enough, but if rights are universal and equal claims, and if employees are rational adults, they too have a right freely to decide on their job options and a claim to enough information to exercise that option intelligently. Those rights are often not respected by top management in merger activities. Shareholders ordinarily recognize their own rights, but they seldom consider them as equal rights of employees. If shareholders have responsibilities, perhaps one of them should be to see whether the rights they expect are being respected in the workplace of which they have a share. Most shareholders, even large institutional shareholders, of course, will argue that this is too much to expect of them. Yet not exercising their prerogatives as shareholders when such exercise might reduce both fiduciary losses and employee stress and unrest is irresponsible, because preventable harm is allowed to occur, harm which is in the shareholders' power to lessen.

Finally, shareholders might take an interest in employees for more practical reasons. If morale is bad and trust is undermined, the resulting loss of productivity and efficiency and even the loss of good managers is not in the self-interest of the shareholder. So shareholder responsibility is not only a moral obligation, it may be a smart business investment as well.

Notes

1. See David Pauly, 'Merger Ethics Anyone?' *Newsweek*, December 9, 1985, pp. 45–47 for a litany of these issues.

2. See Patricia H. Werhane, *Persons, Rights, and Corporations* (Englewood Cliffs: Prentice-Hall, Inc., 1985), especially Part II. See also, Adina Schwartz, 'Meaningful Work', *Ethics* 92 (1982), pp. 634–646.

3. See Eric Mack, 'Natural and Contractual Rights', Ethics 84 (1977), pp. 153–159.

4. Schwartz, *op. cit.*

5. See Price Pritchett, *After the Merger: Managing the Shockwaves* (Homewood, Illinois: Dow-Jones-Irwin, 1985), p. 32.

6. Pritchett, *op. cit.*

Lisa H. Newton

CHARTING SHARK-INFESTED WATERS: ETHICAL DIMENSIONS OF THE HOSTILE TAKEOVER

In the new, amorphous, and somewhat contradictory field of "business ethics," the "hostile takeover" plays a unique role: of all of the dilemma situations we introduce as fuel for our classes, this one must be (as I write this) the newest, the most amorphous, and the most contradictory. It is (as we shall understand it) a set of practices arising wholly within the practice of business in the context of free-market capitalism, not appearing in response to some larger societal initiative. It arrived on the scene with no ethical labels attached or flags flying, and our first task will be to extract and lay out the ethical issues involved. And yet in the very short time since it arrived on the scene, it seems to have given rise to more moral outrage than anything since topless bathing suits. It seems only a short while ago, in the first wave of takeovers, that we had nothing but admiration for the "financial geniuses" who could make tens of millions in a matter of days. But now all we hear, *Time*[1] and *Times*[2] again, is that the "takeover madness," merger mania, takeover boom, is hazardous to our health and perilous for the country.

When moral outrage floods the popular press, the ethicist with pretensions to social relevance is obligated at least to investigate and find out where all the noise is coming from. And when the noise-occasioning phenomenon turns out to be as new and as puzzling as the field of business ethics itself, it begins to seem likely that efforts to understand its logic and clarify its ethical dimensions will pay off in some increase in general enlightenment for the whole field, even if concrete suggestions for remedying this particular evil are not forthcoming. Indeed, given the present volume of the noise, and the normal speed of academic publication, it seems very improbable that suggestions here advanced will find their way into public view before the whole "corporate takeover" flurry has run its course and receded into the curious pages of business history. Analytic effort had therefore best be directed at the most general aspects of the problem.

Along that line, a preliminary delineation of the subject matter is in order. Specifically, this paper will not discuss (1) the state of the law, (2) the friendly merger, or (3) the fine points of the economics. (1) The law at this point is a daily soap opera broadcast direct from the Delaware courts, where a bombshell a day seems to be an essential ingredient in the plotline. It is of the essence of novelty in any practice, that the law on it must be unsettled, for we make law on a case by case basis, wherever possible saving legislation until the end of the changes. Uncertainty is inevitable, as is injury to those who, in the course of their business, zigged, when, the court later decides, they should have zagged. As Bayless Manning points out, "it is an unfortunate aspect of the common law process that, since it decides today on the events of yesterday, any novel swerve in doctrine is likely to sideswipe some poor devil . . ." in that case, the board

From *Journal of Business Ethics*, 7 (1988), 81–87. ©1988 by D. Reidel Publishing Co. Reprinted by permission of Kluwer Academic Publishers.

of directors of Trans Union Corporation, for selling the company by a process the judge thought to be insufficiently businesslike, so they were eventually liable for $23.5 million.[3] "Poison pills" are illegal[4] or legal,[5] depending on what newspaper you pick up, similarly "greenmail," "lockups" and other "shark repellents." There is no future in speculating on the next tack of an apparently baffled court in an uncharted sea of novelty. (2) "Friendly" mergers have been part of the scene forever, and we have at least figured out how to forestall the worst (monopolistic) abuses, and to absorb any undesirable side effects into the larger fabric of the economy. The hostile takeover is new, at least at its current size and frequency, and involves new kinds of funding, corporate maneuvering, legal and human consequences. (3) And the fine points of the economic consequences we will leave to the experts: the economics employed in this paper goes no further than Adam Smith and common sense.

A. LOGIC

On these strictures, then, we proceed with the logic of the takeover boom, which turns out to be simplicity itself. We shall make three assumptions:

Assumption 1:

Greed. Each person involved in any financial transaction wishes to become, and stay, as rich as possible. We shall call this proposition "G" in what follows.

Assumption 2:

Fiduciary obligation. A person who is hired by a group of people to advance their interests (manage their money or other assets) has an absolute obligation to do everything to ensure that they become, and stay, as rich as possible. We shall call this proposition "F."

Assumption 3:

Necessity of investment. An enterprise that is expected to maximize wealth, at least over the long run, requires the investment of resources at the outset of the enterprise for the tools, buildings, lands, livestock, or other durable assets which will be employed to produce that profit. We shall call this proposition "N."

Each of these assumptions could be qualified and elaborated upon, but not in any way that changes its usefulness for us. Thus G obviously does not entail that people *always* act selfishly, but warns you, while you are in the market, that you had best assume they will. F does not permit money managers to break the law, but does require a certain blindness to large-scale economic or ethical consequences of F-dictated behavior; the client/employer/stockholder is the sole object of F-responsibility. N is not true for *all* enterprises; I can hang out my shingle as a philosophical consultant tomorrow with no investment needed at all. (Dentists are not so lucky.) We assume further that those durable assets could be turned into money again (the fundamental reversibility of all market transactions), let us assume the same amount of money it took to buy them (corrected for inflation). Enterprises for which N is not true are henceforth outside the scope of this paper.

Those assumptions made, nothing slows the hostile takeover machine on the road to total liquidation, total debt, total bankruptcy, of all business. Assume only that a raider materializes, bent on making money (and by G, one surely will). Let us assume further, that he finds a company that is worth more dead than alive — i.e., the total value of whose assets, if sold, is higher than the total value of its outstanding stock. By N, this will be true of a significant number of companies, especially those holding quantities of inflation-prone assets (timberlands, oil reserves, etc.). For the value of all the stock in a going company, after all, equals only the present value of anticipated future dividends to the shareholders, and the market value of one share of an untroubled company is probably the best measure of the fractional worth of that company's future operations. (When the company comes under attack, all hell breaks loose, as we shall see, and no figures are reliable gauges of value.) That calculation takes account of the fact that an enormous amount of money is sunk in assets which not only cannot be liquidated, if the company is to keep going, but have, at some expense, to be maintained and occasionally replaced. Then all the raider need do is obtain control of the company to ensure himself an enormous profit on the transaction. Note that the amount, by which the value of the assets if sold exceeds the present expectation of profit from continued operation (total stock value), tends to be increased if the company has any fields lying fallow, forests, oil fields, or Research and Development operations geared to develop new technology to compete with the Japanese (although intelligent market analysts feed the R&D operations into their anticipation of future earnings, and value the stock accordingly). *Anything* held for the future increases the profit to be made from buying up a majority of the outstanding stock (thus gaining control) and immediately selling off all the assets.

Yes, but is it in the stockholders' interest to sell the stock to the raider? The stockholders bought the stock, after all, to make money (G) from the dividends it yields, not primarily for the chance to sell it again at a profit (although that's the way the sophisticated institutional investors might work). The company as it stands may be a very reasonable mix of current profitability and preparation for the long-term, and may show every sign of being a very good bet for long-term earnings. Why should a stockholder trade in a good bet for the long term for the quick cash that would be realized if he tendered his stock to a greedy raider anxious to carve up the company for dinner? It would be in his interest to hang on to the stock, right?

Wrong, for two reasons, one stemming from the realities of the takeover process, the other from the nature of the contemporary stockholder. The hostile takeover process is not instantaneous. The raider makes an offer for the stock, noticeably above current market price; everybody sits tight except the target company's board of directors, who scurry around spreading shark repellent; before that activity gets too far advanced, the raider comes back with a higher offer; by this time the target may have found a "white knight" company to join the bidding, and the price goes still higher. Eventually the price offered per share may, indeed, be higher than the amount (per share) to be realized by selling off the assets: but then, that price is only being offered for a controlling interest (51%) of the shares. Tender the shares now, and the purchase price is very generous, too generous; wait, and you may find the company sold from under you, and your stock exchanged for high-risk notes. In either case, the long-term bet is off, no longer one of your options. So you might as well sell now and get the high price (for at least part of your shares).

Of course, if you are in fact a typical individual stockholder, you still theoretically have a choice: it is always possible to hold on to your shares and hope the raider will fail and the company can go forward as before. By G, very few individual shareholders will avail themselves of that option. By F, none of the great fund managers who mange anywhere up to 70% of the outstanding stock of American companies have that option at all. Fund managers spend full time watching the stock market. They know that whatever the relation between book value and the stock price prior to the takeover attempt (and the latter may well have *exceeded* the former), (1) the inflated stock price at takeover time is surely higher than any simple sale and cash distribution would yield, (2) they can put that cash immediately back into the market — with a little luck they can even pick the next takeover target — at a far higher profit than the orderly yield on investment. In short, they are *not* typically individual stockholders, or anything like. Hence the tendency, on the part of target companies, to treat these short-term investors differently from those in for the long term. (This tendency is heartily deplored by T. Boone Pickens, short-termer *par excellence*, who feels discriminated against when this sort of thing happens.)[6] But by F, the fund managers have no choice. That is what they must do; that is not their own money to make moral choices with.

So as soon as a raider appears, there is very good reason to tender your shares to him — quickly, while the offer lasts. This disposition is completed by the entrance of the other actors in these swift dramas: the lawyers and investment bankers to cement the deal; the arbitrageurs (ultra short-termers) to gobble up the stock while still low, who will make money only if the takeover goes through to completion: the issuers of the bonds that will be paid off by the sale of the target company's assets (the "junk bonds," as they are called, because of their high risk), ensuring that the company must be "busted up" and sold off as soon as the acquisition is complete. Once the process has begun, no one has any interest in stopping it except the management of the target company, who may lose their jobs in the takeover. But they cannot oppose it: there is no doubt that the sudden inflation of stock value is of great benefit to those of the target's shareholders who are in a position to move quickly in the market, i.e., the institutional fund managers; since the majority of publicly held stock is held by the funds, that means a majority of the shareholders will profit from the takeover (even though the late minority may be badly hurt); the managers of a company have a fiduciary responsibility to benefit their shareholders (and that means a majority of the shareholders); therefore, by F, it would follow logically that managers and boards of directors of target companies may not do what they ordinarily *do* do, which is fight. By G, they may certainly promote their own interests by ensuring that if they are in fact tossed out their boardroom windows, they will float gently to the ground with the aid of (reasonably) large golden parachutes, but it would seem that they may do nothing to save the company.

Then why *do* they fight? Because they love the company? Because it is a damnable shame to see a good organization, product of human skill and effort, functioning profitably now and prepared to function profitably into the foreseeable future, destroyed merely for the present cash? Is a company more than a cash machine for (the majority of) its shareholders? Not by this theory it isn't, and no right of defense pertains to it. We may wish to examine alternative theories before we finish, if only to account for the furious defense efforts on the part of the threatened targets. For now, they remain mysterious.

By the Adam Smith assumptions made at the outset, no alternative to sheer corporate entropy appears. As John Maynard Keynes pointed out a half century ago, as more money comes into the investment market the natural result is that "enterprise becomes the bubble on a whirlpool of speculation."[7] You do not, after all, have to be a financial genius to play the takeover game. *Any* number can play. By *N*, many companies can be liquidated for more than the price of their outstanding stock; by *G*, someone's bound to realize that and start a take-over attempt; by *F*, the target managers may not oppose it and, as soon as the arbitrageurs start to run up the price of the stock, the managers of the funds must tender their shares. So there is no stopping the process of liquidation until the last asset has been sold, the last Research and Development facility dismantled, the last equity turned into debt. And that last means that any of the normal reversals in the business world — recession, mismanagement or sheer bad luck — will plunge the highly leveraged remainder companies straight into bankruptcy. Can we afford this?

B. ETHICS

The logic of the takeover boom may be pure simplicity; the ethics is a little more difficult. There are a series of signs by which we may recognize situations that demand moral scrutiny: pain to individuals, loss of freedom or dignity for individuals, injustice, damage to the common good, violation of accepted moral principles, and betrayal of humanity's highest ideals, for instance. When hostile takeovers result in (to take those signs in order) abrupt termination of employment and pensions, jobless futures, vast wealth for fast-moving shareholders and expropriation for others, significant sectors of the economy teetering on the edge of bankruptcy, abrupt termination of all (non-monetary) debts and understandings in the local community, and the publicly trumpeted triumph of pure greed over faithfulness, for instance, scrutiny may begin forthwith. Our problem is that none of the specific results of the takeover boom are specifically evil, or at least evil enough to fight. Felix Rohatyn, surely an undisputed expert on takeovers, having invented them, now says that "today things are getting badly out of hand."[8] Whose hand? And why is that bad? It isn't against the law, nor noticeably immoral; something just feels wrong. Nor have we remedies, at law or at morals, for things getting out of hand. Others of the trade are likely to express themselves in much the same language: Henry Kaufman of Salomon Brothers finds the situation "generally disturbing," and "unwholesome."[9] Since when is *that* against the law? Like Hamlet, we find ourselves trying to take up arms against a sea of troubles, and arms are notoriously ineffective against seas. When we begin (as Rohatyn does) to spell out the badnesses we condemn, each one chameleonlike assumes the color of the surrounding business world, and our attack loses the name of action.

Thus the joblessness, the dissolution of headquarters and wholesale termination of personnel after takeovers, done to raise cash quickly to service the enormous debt incurred in the process, is no different (at least to the unemployed) from other joblessness, brought on by plant closings for economic reasons, obsolescence of skills due to technological change, competition or other market changes. Here is pain indeed, loss of dignity and freedom, abrogation of individual futures and family security, but it's all part of the free market game.[10] We will try to help the individuals (that's what the parachutes are for, not to mention unemployment compensation), but attempts to provide guarantees of job security end up guaranteeing only the progressive obsolescence of all American industry. If we accept the free market system at all, we cannot select nondiscriminatory disemployment as the prohibitable evil. Onwards, then; what about the injustice of two-tier pricing — full value for 51% of the stock, significantly less for those who move more slowly and get squeezed out at the back end? But why is it unjust to buy only what you want to buy? Suppose as a purchaser of oranges I make a (fully public) announcement that I will pay a dollar an orange for oranges delivered to my doorstep before Friday a week, but only a quarter an orange thereafter — what's wrong with that? (or with the stipulation that I'll only pay full price for 200 oranges so if you deliver more I'll have to prorate your batch?) So described, it certainly sounds innocent enough. Is it worth it to pass a law against it? "What other business practices would be adversely affected by any law that would curb two-tier pricing?

The injury to the economy occasioned by the vast debt ($1.4 trillion corporate debt load, according to the same article) carries somewhat more credibility as an evil. We have depended, perhaps more than we know, on the prudence of corporate directors to keep American companies in condition to weather hard times — cycles, recessions, new competitive pressures, etc. We expect them to keep a thin layer of fat on their companies, so that in lean days the belt can be tightened without cutting the company in half. One thing we expect them to do, for instance, is keep the company's debt under control, so that they can borrow more money if they need it (to invest in new equipment in order to stay competitive if the technology changes, e.g.), and so that service on the debt will not be so large as to bankrupt the company in a sudden downturn. It is this debt that is "getting out of hand" in the takeover mania; companies are reaching the point where they may find it difficult to survive at all, let alone develop and install the new tools and techniques they will need to catch up with the Japanese. This aspect of takeover activity should surely be curbed in the national interest.

But how can we outlaw debt? "Neither a borrower nor a lender be," Polonius advised, and had we taken his advice our economy would still be in the caves, and so might we be. The only limit on debt is the risk perceived by the lender to himself, and lenders here, the most experienced in the country, sure that the assets of the company will be sufficient to pay off the debt, do not seem to be worried. We may have this odd feeling in the pit of the stomach that these happy lenders are under the charm of the new no-fault money back guaranteed society, and are certain that while individual bankruptcies may be a risk, massive defaults will be picked up by the Government and no one will really suffer in the end — in short, the perception of the lender may be fatally flawed.[11] But our system is hardly geared to tell the largest banks when they lend unwisely, even when they seem to be turning into casinos, or to take arms against seas of troubles in the pit of the stomach. We are going to have to change our minds about the desirability of certain market freedoms before we can limit the kinds of bets banks can make on the future as they see it.

Damage to the local community falls into the same category as damage to employees; any economically dictated plant closing does the same damage, and legislation to curb these closings, popular as it may be in the legislatures of the affected states, does nothing except hinder inevitable movements of capital and labor into better employment elsewhere, and create a drag on the economy as a whole. And as for the final candidate for evil — the triumph of (the sin of) avarice over the long-term altruistic fidelity to company, customer and community that we associate with the stodgy firms of our recent past — what is that but the amoral root of the whole capitalist ethic, which claims that greed is no sin,[12] but is the engine that drives all mankind to achieve public good through private acquisitiveness? Could it be that the whole capitalist orientation is wrong?

Where *is* the sin, then, the offense or harm that cries out for public remedy? Even today our lawmakers are in session, pondering remedies for the unacceptable depredations of the raiders. What shall we ask them to do?

As rapidly as the press disapproval has expanded, proposed remedies have spread out in their wake. As is normal in such cases, the remedies are aimed only at the problem at hand, and fail noticeably to square with the presuppositions set forth at the beginning (the Market in its Natural State). We will take on (very briefly) a typical set of recommendations, to give a feel for the level of the debate and a view of the shortcomings of the answer. As before, we shall not primarily be interested in these remedies *per se*, but in observing what happens when we attempt to discern moral corrections for evil in a field that disdains the former and rejects the latter.

C. ACTION?

The remedies we shall look at are chosen as typifying current thinking on the subject. They showed up in a *New York Times* article by economist Leonard Silk, who conjures up the usual evils of takeovers (debt, primarily) abjuring all insight into why they are bad, then launches into suggestions for reform. First he wants tax reform noting (correctly) that by "encouraging debt and discouraging equity, the tax laws have helped fuel takeovers."[13] His fourth suggestion is "impose greater restraint on financial institutions," the ones that fund the takeovers by issuing the "junk bonds"; his fifth is like unto it, "avoid excessive money and credit creation"; and his seventh. "Let the Securities and Exchange Commission write better rules for mergers and acquisitions." In short, make more rules. Regulate more. This is no more than a candid recognition that there is no "free market" in this nation, not where this sort of activity is concerned.[14] Twiddle the economic motivators that lie entirely in government hands — the tax provisions, the rules for the banks, the SEC provisions — and you alter, sometimes violently, the activities of those free marketeers who find their livelihood in the markets of Wall Street. Recommendations two, three and six are directed not at government but at the actors in the takeover drama, and echo even more strangely in the Adam Smith structure we presumed at the start. Second recommendation, "*Change the attitude* of institutional investors, to reward management for long-term performance"; third, "*Alter accounting conventions* so as not to discriminate in favor of acquisitions over research and development and capital expenditures"; and sixth, "*Prevent abusive takeovers* in which companies with a history of good and responsible management are taken over for the sake of 'busting them up' and extracting immediate financial gain."[15] (emphasis added) Deep down we *know* we should reward management for long-term performance, invest in Research and Development, invest in new equipment, and protect companies with a history of good and responsible management. But how can we? By *G*, the investors want financial gain, by *F*, the fund managers who handle most of the stock must get it for them, by N, the easiest way to do that is to fuel those junk bond bust-up takeovers, sell the stock at the highest point, and plunge the cash into new investment, and by F again, no one in the target has any right to stop them. What are these "recommendations" but wishful thinking, harking back to an earlier age of business management when ignorance — and a heavy-handed regulatory climate — prevented these magnificent opportunities for money-making from seeing the light? Yet these suggestions are, at this writing, the state of the art in thinking about hostile takeovers.

How shall we stop them, then? There is always the second route suggested above — to appeal to all actors not to do what they are doing, or think what they are thinking, lest they bankrupt the lot of us. In some part, those actors are probably unwilling to listen to us; in large part, they are legally unable to — that is not their own money, and if they see a sure route to a quick profit, they are obligated to take it. Should they want moral sanction to back them up further, there is a school of "shark defender" academics, led by Michael Jensen of Harvard, cheering them on with increasingly ingenious rationalizations for acquisition.[16] So the route of voluntary change is not very hopeful. Once that route fails, there is the first route: legislate them out of existence. Pass laws that make hostile takeovers impossible to initiate (you must post all cash up front), or carry through (you must gain consent of the Board of Directors of the target) or fund (no junk bonds) or make legal in time for profit (SEC antitrust hangups). In short, forget the "free market" rhetoric and recognize the takeover phenomenon for what it is: an intricate *pas-de-deux* with an administration that loves the rich with a devotion perhaps unequalled in the history of administrations, and that is willing to write the provisions, tax and otherwise, that will ensure their unlimited prosperity.

But that means that we must recognize that our market economy is the creation of our government, and that we must take responsibility for its wanderings as if they were, which they really are, choices of ours. In the mechanistic climate of his times, Adam Smith gave us an Eternal Machine to admire, working only on everlasting and automatically operative laws. Now we can see it as the creature it always was — born of its own historical time, appropriately buried when the world changed around it and rendered it nonfunctional, but curiously Undead in the literature of the very acquisitive, reviving and spawning new myths to paralyze social action at crucial junctures of economic change. We may be grateful, in the end, to the hostile takeover frenzy, for the threatened bankruptcy or destruction of most of our productive enterprise has unmasked the apparition for us all to see, even those of us once thought wealthy and respectable. Is it finally time to drive a stake through its heart?

Notes

1. Most coherently, in a one-page interview with Felix Rohatyn, p. 51 in the December 23, 1985 issue, in the course of a multipage cover story on "Merger Tango."

2. At greatest length (to date of this writing) in the Business section of *The New York Times* Sunday, December 29, 1985: "The Peril Behind the Takeover Boom," byline Leonard Silk. This is the article whose "possible remedies" will be examined later.

3. *Smith v. Van Gorkom*, 488 A.2d 858 (Del. 1985). Bayless Manning, "Reflections and

Practical Tips on Life in the Boardroom After *Van Gorkom*," *The Business Lawyer* 41 1–14 (November 1985).

4. *Norlin Corp. v. Rooney, Pace Inc.*, 744 F2d 255 (1984) *McAndrews V. Revlon*, Del. Ch. October 1985.

5. *Moran V. Household International Inc.*, 490 A.2d 1059 (Del. Ch. 1985).

6. T. Boone Pickens, Jr., "Professions of a Short-Termer," *Harvard Business Review*, May–June 1986. p. 77.

7. J. M. Keynes, *The General Theory of Employment, Interest and Money* (New York: Harcourt Brace, 1936). Chapter 12 cited in Warren A. Law, "A Corporation Is More Than Its Stock," *Harvard Business Review*, May–June 1986, p. 81.

8. *Time*, supra. Such vague quotes may appear unfair to the speaker. But it is possible to be clear, and precise, even to *Time*; the vagueness lies in the subject, not in Rohatyn, *Time*, or me.

9. Cited in Leonard Silk, "Peril Behind Takeover . . ." *supra.*

10. See Steven Prokesch, "People Trauma in Mergers," *The New York Times*, November 19, 1985.

11. As Law (*supra*) points out, the investors' perceptions of what is good for the company may be skewed by the fact that they obtain immediately all the upside returns of leverage, but the downside risk is diffused among creditors and may be obviated by government action (p. 82). The perception of the employees, of course, is skewed just the other way.

12. Surely you saw William Safire's column, "Ode to Greed," in *The New York Times*, January 5, 1986.

13. Silk, *op. cit.*

14. Maybe you didn't see Newton Minow's and David Sawyier's column, "The Free Market Blather Behind Takeovers," *The New York Times*, December 10, 1985.

15. Silk, *op. cit.*

16. For a sampling of Jensen's work, start with "Takeovers: Folklore and Science," *Harvard Business Review*, November-December 1984: 109–121. Go on to read Jensen and Ruback, "The Market for Corporate Control: The Scientific Evidence," *Journal of Financial Economics*, April 1983. If you *really* want to know how his mind works, look up "How to Detect a Prime Takeover Target," *The New York Times*, March 9, 1986, especially the part about how increased leverage "gives managers a crisis (the threat of bankruptcy) to help overcome resistance to retrenchment, which the payout of free cash flow often requires. The crisis makes cutbacks, reassignments and layoffs more acceptable to employees."

Lisa H. Newton

THE HOSTILE TAKEOVER: AN OPPOSITION VIEW

1. RIGHTS AND CONSEQUENCES

Given the nature and prestige of the players, we might be tempted to think that the *hostile takeover* is just one more game businessmen play. But the business literature on the subject sounds atypically harsh notes, describing this activity in the unbusinesslike language of threat and attacks, followed by occasionally desperate and increasingly sophisticated defenses — the junk-bond bust-up takeover versus the Pac-Man, Poison Pill, Crown Jewel Option defenses ranged against the two-tier tender offer and finally the launching of the golden parachutes.

In this colorful literature, the most noticeable feature of a corporate takeover is its terrible human cost. *Fortune* magazine entitled a 1984 article, "Help! My Company Has Just Been Taken Over," and began the article with the story of the suicide of a corporate executive precipitated by his termination following a takeover. "There are more mergers than ever these days," the author warns, "and their human toll is higher than ever too."[1] A more recent *New York Times* article, entitled " 'People Trauma' in Mergers" documents the anxiety and feelings of betrayal experienced by employees — increasingly, down to the hourly level — when the prospect of takeover looms into view. Trust is broken, loyalty ebbs, and, if none of the above is of any interest to managers, productivity plummets.[2] The fact that these alarms come from publications inside the business world is significant; outsiders might be expected to see human effects more clearly than the economic realities that underlie the takeover activity, yet here are the insiders suddenly concluding that the realities of profit may actually be less important than the injuries to the people caught up in it against their will. The hostile corporate takeover is simply *not* business as usual. It is assault with a deadly weapon; and the question seems to be, how can it be right?

Let us backtrack for the moment. A practice requires moral scrutiny if it regularly derogates from human dignity, causes human pain, or with no apparent reason treats one class of human beings less well than another. Any practice that regularly throws people out of work does at least the first two of those (work being possibly the largest factor in self-worth and the major instrument to creature satisfactions), and unless we find the raider's urgent need for self-aggrandizement as a worthy reason for dismembering working units, it probably does the third also. To be sure, all manner of evil things can happen to people in non-takeover situations; part of the fun of being alive is the risk, and part of being in business is knowing that your livelihood may depend on the next quarter's earnings. But as a general moral principle, if I, by my voluntary act and for my own profit, increase the riskiness of your life, no matter how high the base risk and no matter how small the increment by which I raise it for you, then

From Lisa H. Newton, "The Hostile Takeover: An Opposition View," in *Ethical Theory and Business*, 3rd ed., edited by Tom L. Beauchamp and Norman Bowie (Englewood Cliffs, NJ: Prentice Hall, 1988), 301–310. Reprinted by permission of the author.

I owe you an explanation. The hostile takeover regularly disemploys at least some people who would not have been unemployed absent the takeover; that makes it, by the above, a proper candidate for moral scrutiny, without presumption one way or another on the results of the scrutiny.

A further problem, if it is a problem, is that a takeover deliberately destroys something — a company, corporation, an instance of human association. In the other cases, it can be said that the association itself "decided" to do something to make itself better, or more efficient. But when it is taken over, it does nothing — it is killed, and the atmosphere of the threat of death hangs over the entire proceeding, from the raider's first phone call to the final resolution (usually the acquisition of the company by some party other than the raider). Does it make any difference, that a company is destroyed? Is that an evil over and above all the other disruptions that takeovers occasion? Or is it, strictly speaking, meaningless, beyond the sufferings of the individuals?

We have, in short, two very separate and distinct questions. First, does the hostile corporate takeover serve some ordinary and necessary role in the economy? Whatever the present injuries, is the practice justified in the long run as improving the economic condition of the greatest number? That very pragmatic question is accompanied by a second, metaphysical one: Is the corporation the type of thing whose demise could or should be regretted? Could it have some right to live, to persevere in existence — a right appropriately exercised in management's series of "defenses"? Ordinarily we assume that only individual human beings have dignity, worth, or rights (beyond the uninteresting legal "rights" bestowed on the corporation to permit it to conduct business). But that assumption fits poorly with the fact that people will willingly die for their associations when they will not willingly sacrifice their lives for personal interests; that fact needs further examination before we dismiss the association as a merely instrumental good. We will pursue, then, two separate and logically independent lines of inquiry: First, on straightforward utilitarian reasoning, does the business practice that we know as the *hostile takeover* serve the public interest by performing some useful role in the economy, or are there good utilitarian reasons for limiting or prohibiting it? Second, does the corporation have some right to exist that is violated by any business practice that ends its existence without the consent of its present governors? Along the line of the firs inquiry, we will argue, first, that the hostile takeover is damaging to the economy (and the people in it) in the short and middle run and, second, that this practice is a deadly symptom of a long-term process in our relation to material goods, a loss of "ownership," which ought to be noted and, as far as possible, reversed. On the line of the second inquiry, we will argue that "the association," usually the political association, has been invested with dignity since Aristotle's day, and that its right to self-defense is firmly grounded in individual rights of undisputed worth. Therefore the corporation, acting through its present management, has the right and (sometimes) the duty to defend itself when its existence is threatened, apart from any arguments about immediate effects on the wealth of individuals.

II. RESPONSIBLE OWNERSHIP PROFITS

Takeovers are generally defended on the utilitarian grounds that they are in the public interest. The "takeover" is simply capital flowing from one sector of the economy to a more profitable one, in this instance, to buy up the stock of a company the value of whose assets is significantly greater than the value of its outstanding stock. Where stock is undervalued, an inefficiency exists in the economy; whether through management ineptness or other market conditions, the return on the shareholder's investment is not as high as it could be. It would be maximized by selling off the assets and distributing the proceeds among the owners; but then, by the above, it is management's duty to do that. The takeover merely does the job that the managers were supposed to do, and the prospect of a takeover, should the stock become undervalued, is an excellent incentive to management to keep the shareholders' interest in mind.

Moreover, defenses against takeovers often involve managers in apparent conflicts of interest. They are protecting their jobs rather than meeting their fiduciary obligations to stockholders. Theory in this instance concurs with current case law; there should be no regulation of takeovers beyond (not very rigorous) anti-trust scrutiny, and defensive moves on the part of management are morally and probably legally illegitimate. To be sure, people get hurt in takeovers, but the shareholders profit, and control of the corporation belongs by statute to them. Against these considerations, what arguments can be raised that unregulated takeover activity is harmful, wrong, contrary to the public interest, and ought to be stopped by new legislation?

The best approach to a response may be to peel an onion: All of the evils seem to be related, differing primarily in the level of analysis suited to elicit them. Beginning with the surface, then, we may note the simple disruption caused by hostile takeover activity: The raider's announcement that a certain percentage of shares of a company have been purchased, more to follow, immediately puts the company in play in a deadly game from which it will not emerge intact. Productive activity, at least at the upper levels of the target (where salaries are highest), stops. Blitzkrieg raider tactics are met with poison pills, sales of crown jewels and other defenses — often of questionable legality. Orderly planning disappears. Employees, terrified for their jobs, spend their days in speculation and the search for another job.[3] Other bidders emerge from the Midwest, from abroad, from next door. Nobody sleeps. All the players hire lawyers, financiers, banks, and start paying them incredible amounts of money. (In the takeover of Revlon by Pantry Pride in the fall of 1985, the investment bankers' share alone came to over $100 million, legal fees to over $10 million, and the negotiated "golden parachutes" to $40 million. Added up, the costs of the takeover — not one penny of which went to shareholders — came to close to 9 percent of the $1.83 billion deal.)[4] However the game ends, people are exhausted, betrayed, out of work, and demoralized. The huge debt incurred by the acquiring company, secured by the assets of the target (by the infamous *junk bonds*), requires the immediate dismemberment of the company for financial survival (more on this later), and financial health, under those circumstances, is out of the question. And all this to what end?

"Hostile takeovers create no new wealth," Andrew Sigler pointed out to the House Committee on Energy and Commerce, "They merely shift ownership, and replace equity with large amounts of debt." He continues:

> More and more companies are being pushed — either in self-defense against the raiders or by the raiders once they achieve control — into unhealthy recapitalizations that run contrary to the concepts of sound management I have learned over thirty years. This type of leveraging

exposes companies to inordinate risks in the event of recession, unantici-
pated reverses, or significant increases in interest rates. . . . Generation
after generation of American managers have believed that there *must* be a
solid equity basis for an enterprise to be successful in the long term. This
long-term equity base absorbs — in exchange for the expectation of
higher returns — the perils of depression, product failure, strikes, and all
the other dangers that characterize business in a free economy. That
healthy conservatism is now being replaced by a new game in which the
object is to see how far that equity base can be squeezed down by layers of
debt. And too much of this debt is carrying interest rates far in excess of
those a prudent manager can possibly be comfortable with.[5]

At a second level, then, the takeover has two deleterious effects on the
management of corporations: First, when the takeover materializes, equity is
inevitably transformed into debt, leaving the company terribly vulnerable to
foreseeable reverses, second anticipating takeover attempts, management may
well be tempted to aim for short-term profits and engage in aggressive accounting practices to show higher current earnings. These practices may weaken the
company and deceive long-term investors, but they will be reflected in a higher
stock price and thus one more resistant to attack.[6] As Peter Drucker put it,
"Fear of the raider and his unfriendly takeover bid is increasingly distorting
business judgment and decisions. In company after company the first question
is no longer: Is this decision best for the business? But, will it encourage or
discourage the raider?"[7] Fear of the raider may encourage the managers of a
company to put up their own money as well as to incur debts well beyond
prudence, to take the company privately in a "leveraged buyout." All the same
risks, including bankruptcy in the event of any reversal, attend the buyout as
attend the takeover.[8] Nor is it clear that the damaging effects of these maneuvers
are limited to the domestic scene: As Harold Williams (chairman of the Securities and Exchange commission during the Carter administration) points out,

> The pursuit of constantly higher earnings can compel managers to avoid
> needed writedowns, capital programs, research projects, and other bets
> on the long term. The competitiveness of U.S. corporations has already
> been impaired by the failure to make long-term commitments. To com-
> pound the problem because of fears of takeovers is a gift to foreign
> competitors that we cannot afford.[9]

The alarms, confusions, and pains first noted as the result of hostile takeover
activity, are then compounded by what seems to be very imprudent business
practice. But imprudent for whom? Do the target shareholders, at least, get
some profit from the takeover — and if they do, does that not justify it? Michael
Jensen, one of a new breed of scholar known as the "shark defenders," argues
that they do and that does. He dismisses worries about shareholders' welfare as
"folklore," and insists that "science" shows otherwise.[10] His evidence for this
claim is interesting:

> More than a dozen studies have painstakingly gathered evidence on the
> stock price effect of successful takeovers. . . . According to these stud-
> ies, companies involved in takeovers experience abnormal increases in
> their stock prices for approximately one month surrounding the initial

announcement of the takeover. . . . The evidence shows that target company shareholders gain 30% from tender offers and 20% from mergers.[11]

But isn't the raider's effect pure artifice? Let his initiative be withdrawn — because of government opposition, or because he has agreed to purchase no more stock for whatever reason — and the same studies show that the stock immediately reverts to its previous value.[12] So it was not, really, that the company's stock was too low. It was rather that the flurry of activity, leading to speculation that the stock might be purchased at an enormous premium, fueled the price rise all by itself. Or could it be that certain professional investors find out about the raid before the public does, buy the target's stock at the lowest point, sending it up before the announcement, wait for the announcement, ride the stock to the top, then sell off before the defense moves, government action, or "targeted repurchase" (see the section on "greenmail," below) stop the takeover bid and send the stock back down to its true market value? As Jensen's figures confirm,[13] that value is often a bit *lower* than the starting value of the stock; after all those payouts we are dealing with a much poorer company. Nothing but evil, for all concerned except professional fund managers and investment bankers, seems to come of this takeover activity.

Hence, at the first level there is disruption and tens of millions of dollars' worth of unproductive expense; at the second level there is very dubious business practice. At a third, there is the betrayal of the stakeholders. Current laws, as discussed earlier, force the directors of the target company to consider only shareholder rights and interests, to the probable disadvantage of the other stakeholders: employees, retirees, creditors, host communities, customers, and suppliers. But each of these has helped to build the company to its present state, relying on the company's character and credit-worthiness; the employees and retirees, especially, have worked in expectation of future benefits that may depend in part on the good faith of management, good faith that can hardly be presumed in a raider.[14] The mid-career, upper middle-level managers are especially vulnerable to redundancy and the least likely to be able to transfer their acquired skills and knowledge elsewhere.

Some elimination of positions resulting from duplication is inevitable in any merger, of course, hostile or otherwise, and when carried out under normal conditions succeeds at least in making the company more efficient, even if the cost to the individual is very high. But only some of the people-cutting in these extravagant takeovers stems from real redundancy. Companies are paying such high takeover prices that they have to engage in deep cost-cutting immediately, even to the elimination of personnel crucial to continued operations. The "efficiency" achieved may not serve the company well in the long run, but the raider's calculations rarely run very long. As a consequence, middle-management employees (who are, on the whole, not stupid, and read the same business publications as we do) seem to have taken all this into account and reoriented their work lives accordingly:

> Management turnover at all levels is on the rise and employee loyalty is at a low, according to consultants, executive recruiters and the companies themselves. And there is growing evidence, they say, that merger mania is an important reason for both problems, spreading fear about layoffs and

dissatisfaction with other changes in the corporate environment. These problems, in turn, promise to make it harder for companies to realize the anticipated efficiencies that many of them pointed to in justifying their acquisitions. . . . Critics of the takeover binge maintain that the short shrift given to 'people issues' . . . [is] one reason why perhaps half to two-thirds of mergers and acquisitions ultimately fail.[15]

Do we owe anything to people who have worked for a company and who may actually love the company and may be devastated by its dismemberment or transformation? At present, our law does not recognize, or even have any language to describe, the rights possessed by those who have contributed to the growth of an association, have participated in it and loved it, and now see it threatened. The fact that such rights are by no means absolute does not mean they are not there. Classical political theory has the vocabulary to discuss them, under the rubric of the "just war"; discussion of the implications of that doctrine for the hostile takeover issue will occupy the final section of this paper. Rights or no rights, and prudential considerations (as discussed earlier) aside, the condition of the stakeholders ought not, in charity, to be ignored; yet our institutions make no provision for them. Here we have, in the center of the most civilized sector of the civilized world, an open wound, a gap of institutional protection most needed by those who have worked hardest, which we struggle to paper over with the "unemployment benefits" fashioned for different people in different circumstances. Law and business practice seem to require a callousness toward human need and human desert that is incompatible with our notions of justice.

Inevitable disruption, mandated imprudence, and legally required injustice are the first three levels of palpable wrong in the hostile takeover phenomenon. It may be that the fourth layer, the last under consideration in this section, has more worrisome implications than all of the above. The thesis is simple: At primary risk in all of this is our concept of ownership. For all of human history, we have been able to trust property owners (individuals or groups) to take care of their property, because it was in their interest to do so, and outside of military and government property, that was how the property of the world was cared for. With the corporate takeover, that may no longer be the case for the kind of property that looms too large in Western economics, the publicly held corporation. And this development is very alarming.

To begin with the concepts: Ordinarily we use the concepts of *ownership* and *property* interchangeably; even etymologically, they are indistinguishable. But the concept does have two distinct aspects: the primary aspect of a legally protected complex of rights and duties obtaining between the owner and other *persons* and the less prominent aspect of a diffuse set of nonlegal duties, or imperatives, incumbent upon the owner to take care of the *owned thing*, itself. This duty of care has a history of its own; the duty to the thing, analogous to the duty of *stewardship* when the property of others is in question, attaches naturally to the legal owner.

Ownership has the longest history of any concept still extant in the West, certainly longer than its ultimate derivative, *personhood*. Aristotle assumed that the union of man and property, along with the union of man and woman, lay at the foundation of the household and hence of all society. Ownership is presupposed, and discussed, throughout the earliest books of the Bible. The list of *what* was owned was very short: animals, people (slaves), land, tools, buildings, and personal effects. Except for the last item, all were essential to survival, and all required care. The duty arises from that fact.

Whether ownership is single or shared, the duty corresponds to personal interest. If I own a sheep, it is very much in my interest, and incumbent upon me, to take care of the beast and see that it thrives. If you and I together own a sheep, the same interest applies to both of us, the same imperative follows, and we shall divide up the responsibilities of caring for it. If you and I and 998 others own it, enormous practical difficulties attend that care. But however small my interest in that sheep, it is still in my interest that the animal should thrive. Similarly, partial ownership in a whole herd of sheep, or a farm, or a factory, or a business that owns several factories, does not necessitate a change in the notion of *ownership*.

Liquidation consumes something that is owned, or turns it into money that can be spent on consumption. The easiest way to liquidate a sheep is to eat it. The way to liquidate most owned things is to sell them. Then you no longer own the thing, and your responsibilities terminate; but so, of course, does all future good you might have gotten of the thing. Part of the cultural evolution of ownership has been the elaboration of a tension between retention and liquidation, saving and spending, with the moral weight of the most successful cultures on the side of thrift and preservation. The business system probably depends as much on Ben Franklin's "A penny saved is a penny earned" as it does on Adam Smith's invisible hand." The foreseen result of the *hand*, we may remember, was to increase the wealth, the assets, of a nation. For the herdsman it is self-evident that if you slaughter or sell all your sheep, you will starve in the next year; for Smith, it was equally self-evident that it is in a businessman's interest, whatever business he may be in, to save his money and invest it in clearing more land, breeding more beasts, or building more plants, to make more money in the future. Hence the cleared land, the herds, and the factories — the assets of the nation — increase without limit, and all persons, no matter how they participate in the economy, in fact share in this increased wealth. Presupposed is the willingness of all players in the free enterprise game to acquire things that need care if they are to yield profit, hence to render that care, and to accept that responsibility, over the long run. Should that willingness disappear, and the population suddenly show a preference for liquidation, all bets are off for the wealth of the nation.

And the problem is, of course, that the developments of ownership made possible in the last century create excess tendencies toward liquidation. If several thousand of us jointly own several thousand shares of stock, we may in theory bear the traditional responsibilities of owners for those companies, but we shall surely not *feel* them. And if we purchased those shares not for the sake of investing in the companies, but for the sake of having money available to us at some future time (say, in a pension fund), we will have acquired them for a purpose that is directly contrary to our concerns as owners. We will be involved in a conflict of interest and obligation with ourselves: On the one hand, we should be protecting and nurturing the company(s) we (partially) own, plowing profit back into improvements in plant on occasion, even if that means no profit this year; on the other, if it seems we could get more money if the company were liquidated and the proceeds shared around, we should work toward that end. Suppose that we several thousand owners hire a fund manager to make sure our pension fund provides us with as much pension as possible. That manager, hired with those instructions, is not an owner, and has *no* responsibility toward the companies. On the contrary, his entire obligation is to us and the increase of our money. Where liquidation serves that purpose, it is his job to bring it about. Ownership, for such a manager, is no more than present legal title to property, a way station between sums of money, and its whole moral framework has become totally irrelevant. To complete the picture, let only the tax structure subsidize that liquidation in cases of takeover:

> Accounting procedures and tax laws . . . shift much of the cost of acquisitions to taxpayers through the deductibility of interest payments and the revaluation of assets in ways that reduce taxes . . . I suspect that many of the acquisitions that proved profitable for acquirers did so largely because of tax benefits and the proceeds from busting up the target company. If liquidation is subsidized by the tax system, are we getting more liquidations than good business would dictate?[16]

The answer is probably yes.

Institutional investors — those gargantuan funds — now own up to 70 percent of the stock of the publicly owned corporations. It must be unprecedented in human history that majority ownership of such entities lies with "owners" whose interests may be best served by the destruction of the object owned. In the case of companies that own large holdings of natural resources, forests, or oil reserves, it is usually the case that the assets sold separately will yield more than the companies' stock. (As Minow and Sawyier grimly put it, under current practices such companies "are worth more dead than alive.")[17] Any company, in fact, that regularly works for the long term (funding research and development, for example), can be profitably liquidated: Whatever those raiders may be, they do not need to be geniuses to figure out which companies to attack. The only limits on the process of liquidation of the country's assets by the managers hired by those investors, or by the raiders that cater to their own interests, might be the success of new and inventive defenses.

The evils of the takeover market, then, go to the philosophical base of our market system, striking at the root of moral habits evolved over 2500 years. The corporate raiders have yet to make their first widget, grow their first carrot, or deliver their first lunch. *All* they do is turn money into money, cantilevering the profit off the shell of responsible ownership. No doubt capital is more productively lodged in some places than others, but it follows from no known economic theory that it is more beneficial to the world when lodged in T. Boone Picken's bank account than when lodged wherever it was before he got it. Possibly it will end up facilitating some industrial projects — he has no intention of keeping it in a mattress, after all — but only in those that promise quick profits. We need not look to him to revitalize our smokestack industries and make them competitive on the world markets. The whole productive capacity of the American economy seems at the mercy of moneymen on the rampage, with all productive companies under threat of being taken over, taken apart, and eradicated. Surely this condition cannot be healthy or good.

In sum: This section has tried to provide a series of pragmatic arguments that the present rash of corporate takeover activity is harmful to the stakeholders, to the economy, and to the general public, from all of which it would follow that regulation is justified. In the next section we attempt to provide a defense for the proposition that a corporation has a real right to exist, hence to resist takeover.

III. THE ASSOCIATION AS WORTH KEEPING

Individuals may be hurt by the corporate takeover. The corporation, on the other hand, is usually killed. Does this fact add anything to the list of injuries, or is it simply a shorthand way of saying that the individuals are no longer part of it? Does the corporation have a right to life — a right to persevere in existence, as itself, under its own laws and practices, at least to the extent that would give it a presumptive right to mount a defense against hostile takeover?

The disutility of unregulated takeover activity, implying the desirability of some regulation in the public interest, was the theme of the last section. In this section we ask a different question: Can the corporation be seen as an entity analogous to an individual human being, with rights, including the right to defend itself (through the actions of its officers) regardless of the utilities involved in each case? The law is unsympathetic to defensive moves in takeover situations, suggesting that the right in question here is not derivable from any acknowledged legal rights or present powers of the corporation. It must be found, if it is to be found anywhere, as a logical derivation from other recognized rights of the corporation or, more likely, of the individuals who make it up.

We may begin the inquiry by noting that over the last decade, philosophical students of the corporation have been moving cautiously in the direction of grounding their moral discourse, in the assumption that the corporation is a moral individual like other moral individuals.

It is possible, however, that a corporation may be capable of assuming moral responsibility and still not have rights, but it is not likely. Our attribution of rights rests heavily on the attribution of moral agency, which alone confers worth or dignity on the human, and moral agency is the condition for attribution of moral responsibility. In the literature, the development continues, and recent work (e.g., Patricia Werhane's *Persons, Rights, and Corporations*) accepts that corporations have, indeed, moral rights, even if only "secondarily."[18]

There is, however, one body of literature precisely on the point of our question, albeit not one that deals with "the corporation" as this paper understands the corporation. Since Saint Augustine, the right of a nation to defend itself against foreign aggression has been recognized. While the political association, as Aristotle and Augustine understood it, may seem an odd model for Phillips Petroleum and Continental Group, it is possible that the literature articulating any collectivity's right of defense may help us formulate one for the modern corporation.

The queerness of attributing a "right" to a collectivity rather than to an individual was not generally noticed in discussions of the Just War, most likely because its recognition predates the theory of individual rights by several centuries; nations had rights long before we did. But if we are to make sense of this right in a modern political context, it must be restated in terms compatible with individual rights theory. Michael Walzer undertakes this task in *Just and*

Unjust Wars. For Walzer, the right of the political association to exist comes from the general right of *social contract* — the right of people to join together in any voluntary association, preeminently the state, the association charged with the whole governance of a people. (This is the right primarily challenged in *aggression*, which threatens to abrogate it permanently.) Like Burke before him. Walzer does not understand the agreement that binds the state as a set of real "contracts."

> What actually happens is harder to describe. Over a long period of time, shared experiences and cooperative activity of many different kinds shape a common life. . . . The moral standing of any particular state depends on the reality of the common life it protects and the extent to which the sacrifices required by that protection are willingly accepted and thought worthwhile.[19]

Again,

> The right of a nation or people not to be invaded derives from the common life its members have made . . . and not from the legal title they hold or don't hold.[20]

So the fact of the common life, which has been made by the participants in it, is the immediate source of the right to defend it, presumably necessarily mediated by the desire of participants to defend it. Walzer is likely correct that the right of the state to defend itself stems from the right of a people to create a common life, to adorn and embellish it, to examine and reform it, and by spending themselves on it, to make it valuable — a variety of the rather prosaic right of association. And the reason why people exercise that right in the formation of permanent associations, which build up a history for themselves, is that associations extend individual life in dimensions that the individual otherwise cannot control — in time, in space, in power. To the limited and partial individual, participation in an association provides immortality, global reach, and collective power. The individual needs the association for these benefits, and in this way the right of association is grounded in human nature. When my association is attacked, my basic security in these insecurity-ridden areas is very much endangered, and that is why I so justifiably resent any attacks on it.

Has this argument any validity for the corporation? Here the relatively recent moves to articulate the internal order of a corporation precisely as a historical culture, with a set of values and commitments all its own, may have some relevance. It would be tempting to argue that a corporation that has, as have the best companies of the recent literature, earnestly pursued excellence in all respects, taken care of its employees, stayed close to its customers, produced the highest quality product, and really cared about its communities, has somehow earned the right to exist, while the others have not.[21] Temptation must be resisted: the difficulties of discerning the "excellent" companies from the others are insurmountable. But maybe we don't have to make that judgment: If a corporation, even in theory, can be the kind of collectivity that the state is, and can serve the purposes in human life that a state can serve, then good or bad, it shares in the state's presumptive right to defend itself.

To summarize this section: The association provides those individuals who voluntarily and fully participate in it with goods they can not get elsewhere —

social recognition, material reward, and above all the extension of the limited self in space, time, and power. These are the reasons why the right of association exists and is exercised, and why the result of that exercise has, derived from that right, the right to stay in being and to expect its officers to mount a defense for it should that turn out to be necessary. But that is all we need to establish the right to defend itself against hostile takeover attempts.

That conclusion does not entail, of course, that present officers may do anything they like in the course of a defense; as Walzer points out, there are standards of justice in war as well as standards to determine if a war as a whole is just. (At present, for instance, the payment of greenmail to a raider — a premium price to obtain his stock and only his stock, to persuade him to go away and leave the company alone — raises questions of acceptable practice in the event of a takeover, more than the poison pills, ESOPs, and Crown Jewel Options designed to make a company significantly poorer in the event of takeover.)

CONCLUSION

We have argued that as a matter of right, and as a matter of utility, the takeover game should be ended. Capital is not unlimited; in a country rapidly losing out to foreign competition in part because of outdated plant, and declining in its quality of urban life in part because of obsolete and crumbling infrastructure, there are plenty of worthwhile uses for capital. Law that turns the attentions of the restless rich away from cannibalizing productive corporations, toward investing in the undercapitalized areas of the economy, would be a great public service.[22]

Notes

1. Myron Magnet, "Help! My Company Has Just Been Taken Over," *Fortune*, July 9, 1984, pp. 44–51. See also Joel Lang, "Aftermath of a Merger," *Northeast Magazine*, April 21, 1985, pp. 10–17.

2. Steven Prokesch, " 'People Trauma' in Mergers," *New York Times*, November 19, 1985.

3. *Ibid.*

4. *Wall Street Journal*, November 8, 1985.

5. Testimony of Andrew C. Sigler, Chairman and Chief Executive Officer of Champion International Corporation, representing the Business Roundtable, before hearings of the Subcommittee on Telecommunications, Consumer Protection and Finance of the House Committee on Energy and Commerce, Thursday, May 23, 1985.

6. Some of these considerations I owe to conversations and correspondence with S. Bruce Smart, Jr.

7. Drucker, *Wall Street Journal*, January 5, 1983.

8. Leslie Wayne, "Buyouts Altering Face of Corporate America," *New York Times*, November 23, 1985.

9. Harold M. Williams, "It's Time for a Takeover Moratorium," *Fortune*, July 22, 1985. pp. 133–136.

10. Michael Jensen, "Takeovers: Folklore and Science," *Harvard Business Review* 62 (November–December 1984): 109–121.

11. P. 112. The footnote on the studies cites. For a summary of these studies, Michael C. Jensen and Richard S. Ruback, "The Market for Corporate Control: The Scientific Evidence,"

Journal of Financial Economics (April 1983). The studies are cited individually in the same footnote; *ibid.*, p. 120.

12. *Ibid.*, p. 116.

13. *Ibid.*

14. Another point owed to conversations and correspondence with S. Bruce Smart, Jr.

15. Prokesch, " 'People Trauma' in Mergers."

16. Williams, "It's Time for a Takeover Moratorium," pp. 133–136.

17. Newton Minow and David Sawyier, "The Free Market Blather Behind Takeovers" Op-ed, *The New York Times*, December 10, 1985.

18. Patricia H. Werhane, *Persons, Rights, and Corporations* (Englewood Cliffs, N.J.: Prentice-Hall, 1985), p. 61.

19. Michael Walzer, *Just and Unjust Wars* (New York: Basic Books, 1977) p. 54.

20. *Ibid.*, p. 55.

21. Criteria freely adapted from Thomas J. Peters and Robert H. Waterman, Jr., *In Search of Excellence* (New York: Harper and Row, 1982).

22. In developing the ideas for this paper. I have profited enormously from conversations with Lucy Katz, Philip O'Connell, Stuart Richardson, Mark Shanley, Andrew Sigler, S. Bruce Smart, Jr., and C. Roger Williams.

DISCUSSION QUESTIONS

1. Much of Jensen's position depends on his belief in the primacy of stock-holders. Does he provide a convincing argument for this position?

2. Most takeovers are financed by large amounts of borrowed money. What is the impact of this fact on Jensen's argument?

3. Do you agree with Werhane's general contention that shareholders have responsibilities as well as rights? Do you agree that one of those responsibilities is to be concerned about the rights of employees? Would it ever be the share-holders' responsibility to turn down a merger or acquisition that would be profitable for them?

4. In light of Newton's analysis of the logic and ethics of hostile takeovers, do legislatures have a moral duty to make them illegal?

5. Newton remarks that "the evils of the takeover market, then, go to the philosophical base of our market system." Does this imply a critical moral flaw in contemporary capitalism?

6. Jensen and Newton take diametrically opposed positions on takeovers. From an ethical perspective, which do you think is the better position?

CASE 16.1

ESOPs

The central event that takes place in a merger or acquisition is, of course, a change in ownership. Traditionally, a company is now owned by new outside owners — another company or a group of investors. With the onset of leveraged buyouts (LBOs), companies began to be bought by insiders — typically, a small group of senior managers. The newest twist in insider ownership, however, is for a company to hand over ownership to its employees through an employee stock-ownership plan (ESOP). However, such plans carry new ethical dilemmas.

Hundreds of American corporations have instituted ESOPs in the last few years, thus making their employees the single largest owner of the company's stock. Avis, Procter & Gamble, Anheuser-Busch, and Polaroid are a few of the best known. Tax laws grant corporations numerous financial benefits from such plans, and in at least one case — Polaroid — instituting an ESOP protected the company from a hostile takeover. ESOPs give employees as direct a stake as possible in the corporation's fate, and, as a result, morale and productivity have soared in the most successful cases.

Traditionalists are concerned about the fact that ESOPs change the balance of power at a corporation. Managers and board members have typically held a monopoly on power at a company. At some ESOP corporations, however, an employee representative has been appointed to the board of directors. And technically, ESOPs that hold a majority of a company's stock could replace directors or managers or even sell the company. ESOPs could thus lay the groundwork for a kind of "economic democracy."

One concern regarding ESOPs is whether they put an employee's future financial security too much at risk. One of their main appeals is that they allow corporations to use the transfer of stock to employees to reduce or even end traditional pension benefits. An employee's pension is thus directly tied to how well the company's stock performs between hiring and retiring. Consider an employee who started at a company at $40,000 and retired after 30 years of service. If the company's stock did poorly and appreciated at a rate of only 4 percent per year, the employee's pension would be only about $26,000 annually. But if the stock grew at 12 percent a year (only slightly more than the 10 percent typical for stocks), the pension would be a considerably fatter $89,000.

Another basic question related to ESOPs is what a company then owes its employee-owners. Specifically, does it owe them jobs? This question came up at the Weirton Steel Corporation, a company bought by its unionized employees through an ESOP in 1984. Trumpeted as an early success story for ESOPs, Weirton faced hard times and decided to eliminate 1,000 of its 8,200 jobs. Most of these cuts have been handled through attrition and early retirement, but there have been layoffs among union members. Moreover, at the same time, a small number of new employees started working at the company, hired by a contractor who was updating some of the steel company's equipment. Weirton owner-employees predictably objected, asking, "How can we be laid off if we own the company? And if there are jobs to be had, why should they go to outsiders?" Complicating matters is the fact that 30 percent of the company's stock is owned by public shareholders, some of whom are objecting that company policies are favoring the employees. ◆

Discussion Questions

1. How much power should employees be entitled to in an ESOP?
2. Is there anything questionable from an ethical standpoint about the connection between pensions and stock price?
3. Should an ESOP guarantee employment for all employees?
4. How do you fairly and equitably handle the competing interests of employee-owners and investor-owners?

Sources

"ESOPs: Are They Good For You?," *Business Week*, May 15, 1989, 116–123.
"How Can We Be Laid Off If We Own the Company?," *Business Week*, September 9, 1991, 66.

CASE 16.2

Should Investors Have to Give Some Money Back?

If a leveraged buyout (LBO) fails — particularly an LBO undertaken as a defense against a hostile takeover — should people who profited from the deal have to return money to the company? Investors, of course, say "no." But retired employees of Kaiser Steel Corporation think otherwise.

In 1984, Kaiser was the target of corporate raider Irwin L. Jacobs, and the company defended itself by going private. This move cost Kaiser more than $200 million to buy back its stock, with Jacobs alone receiving more than $60 million, including $14 million in greenmail. But Kaiser was unable to operate profitably under its new level of debt, and so in 1987 it filed for bankruptcy, discontinued retirees' medical insurance, and reduced pensions. As a result, Kaiser is suing Jacobs and a variety of investment firms on behalf of Kaiser's retirees and creditors, hoping to get back some of the money it paid out in 1984. The company claims that Jacobs knew that Kaiser's liabilities, especially the retirees' medical benefits, put it in a precarious financial position even in 1984. Yet he continued in his bid and helped push the corporation over the edge. Jacobs, of course, denies this and contends that the company was financially healthy at the time.

The legal concept at issue is "fraudulent conveyance" — the practice of transferring assets out of an insolvent company or transferring so many assets out of a company that it lacks enough money to operate. The idea is to protect people to whom a company already owes money. The law is thus intended to prevent somebody from absconding with company assets and leaving creditors and pensioners to hold the bag. Kaiser's retirees argue that Jacobs and the investment houses did just that and that the company's subsequent financial woes resulted from their unscrupulous profiteering. Kaiser also sued its former management and board in connection with the LBO and has received a settlement of $17 million.

The Kaiser case is not unique. Similar arguments have been advanced in the case of several other companies whose failed LBOs landed them in bankruptcy court. Creditors for these companies are suing former shareholders, lenders, and accountants, asking for the return of profits and fees generated by the original deals years earlier. ◆

Discussion Questions

1. The central question here is whether there are conditions under which people who made money on a deal are obligated to return it years later. What conditions would have to be met for it to be morally obligatory for profits and fees to be returned? Are these conditions met in the Kaiser case?

2. Assess the moral status of fraudulent conveyance as it relates to LBOs. How much would people have to know about a company's financial position for us to say that they were not morally entitled to their profits? Would ordinary stockholders agreeing to sell their stock to the company know enough about the situation to be morally culpable?

3. Kaiser claims that the exchange of stock for cash in its LBO was not a normal stock transaction but what it calls a "mandatory redemption." If the trade was indeed "mandatory," does this mean that stockholders should not be considered morally responsible for harm that subsequently befell the company?

4. Who is morally responsible for the retirees' plight? Jacobs and investment advisors? Former management? The retirees themselves? Current management? Or is this just one of those things that happens in business and no one is really responsible?

Source

"Are Investors Liable For LBOs Gone Bust?," *Business Week*, August 5, 1991, 74–76.

ADDITIONAL READINGS

Bruner, Robert F., and Lynn Sharp Paine, "Management Buyouts and Managerial Ethics," *California Management Review*, Winter 1988, 89–106.

Cooke, Robert A., and Earl C. Young, "Mergers from an Ethical Perspective," *Business & Professional Ethics Journal*, 5, nos. 3 & 4 (1985), 111–128.

Manning, Rita C., "Dismemberment, Divorce and Hostile Takeovers: A Comment on Corporate Moral Personhood," *Journal of Business Ethics*, 7 (1988), 639–643.

Serpa, Roy, "The Often Overlooked Ethical Aspect of Mergers," *Journal of Business Ethics*, 7 (1988), 359–362.

CHAPTER 17

◆ ◆ ◆

Doing Business in a Global Economy

Business in America has changed dramatically in the last forty years. Basic manufacturing has declined as the service industry has grown. The use of computers, robots, and other advances in high technology has grown exponentially. And work force demographics are such that business will soon cease to be dominated by white males. One of the most important changes, however, is that business is now done on an international, not a national, playing field. This change has brought with it new ethical issues.

Richard De George begins our discussion of international business with an overview of the ethical dilemmas faced by multinational corporations. Norman Bowie takes up the perennial debate over cultural relativism. And Thomas Donaldson offers two essays that explore two particularly pressing issues in international business: first, questions that arise when a multinational company adopts a corporate practice which is morally and/or legally prohibited in its home country, but allowed in a host country, and second, the problem of determining whether it is morally acceptable to subject foreign citizens to technological risks higher than those faced by either home country citizens or more favored foreign citizens.

Richard T. De George

ETHICAL DILEMMAS FOR MULTINATIONAL ENTERPRISE: A PHILOSOPHICAL OVERVIEW

First World multinational corporations (MNCs) are both the hope of the Third World and the scourge of the Third World. The working out of this paradox poses moral dilemmas for many MNCs. I shall focus on some of the moral dilemmas that many American MNCs face.

Third World countries frequently seek to attract American multinationals for the jobs they provide and for the technological transfers they promise. Yet when American MNCs locate in Third World countries, many Americans condemn them for exploiting the resources and workers of the Third World. While MNCs are a means for improving the standard of living of the underdeveloped countries, MNCs are blamed for the poverty and starvation such countries suffer. Although MNCs provide jobs in the Third World, many criticize them for transferring these jobs from the United States. American MNCs usually pay at least as high wages as local industries, yet critics blame them for paying the workers in underdeveloped countries less than they pay American workers for comparable work. When American MNCs pay higher than local wages, local companies criticize them for skimming off all the best workers and for creating an internal brain-drain. Multinationals are presently the most effective vehicle available for the development of the Third World. At the same time, critics complain that the MNCs are destroying the local cultures and substituting for them the tinsel of American life and the worst aspects of its culture. American MNCs seek to protect the interests of their shareholders by locating in an environment in which their enterprise will be safe from destruction by revolutions and confiscation by socialist regimes. When they do so, critics complain that the MNCs thrive in countries with strong, often right-wing, governments.[1]

The dilemmas the American MNCs face arise from conflicting demands made from opposing, often ideologically based, points of view. Not all of the demands that lead to these dilemmas are equally justifiable, nor are they all morally mandatory. We can separate the MNCs that behave immorally and reprehensibly from those that do not by clarifying the true moral responsibility of MNCs in the Third World. To help do so, I shall state and briefly defend five theses.

THESIS I: MANY OF THE MORAL DILEMMAS MNCs FACE ARE FALSE DILEMMAS WHICH ARISE FROM EQUATING UNITED STATES STANDARDS WITH MORALLY NECESSARY STANDARDS.

Many American critics argue that American multinationals should live up to and implement the same standards abroad that they do in the United States and

From Richard T. De George, "Ethical Dilemmas for Multinational Enterprise: A Philosophical Overview," in *Ethics and the Multinational Enterprise*, edited by W. Michael Hoffman, Ann E. Lange, and David A. Fedo (Washington, DC: University Press of America, 1986), 39–46. Reprinted by permission.

that United States mandated norms should be followed.[2] This broad claim confuses morally necessary ways of conducting a firm with United States government regulations. The FDA sets high standards that may be admirable. But they are not necessarily morally required. OSHA specifies a large number of rules which in general have as their aim the protection of the worker. However, these should not be equated with morally mandatory rules. United States wages are the highest in the world. These also should not be thought to be the morally necessary norms for the whole world or for United States firms abroad. Morally mandatory standards that no corporation — United States or other — should violate, and moral minima below which no firm can morally go, should not be confused either with standards appropriate to the United States or with standards set by the United States government. Some of the dilemmas of United States multinationals come from critics making such false equations.

This is true with respect to drugs and FDA standards, with respect to hazardous occupations and OSHA standards, with respect to pay, with respect to internalizing the costs of externalities, and with respect to foreign corrupt practices. By using United States standards as moral standards, critics pose false dilemmas for American MNCs. These false dilemmas in turn obfuscate the real moral responsibilities of MNCs.

THESIS II: DESPITE DIFFERENCES AMONG NATIONS IN CULTURE AND VALUES, WHICH SHOULD BE RESPECTED, THERE ARE MORAL NORMS THAT CAN BE APPLIED TO MULTINATIONALS.

I shall suggest seven moral guidelines that apply in general to any multinational operating in Third World countries and that can be used in morally evaluating the actions of MNCs. MNCs that respect these moral norms would escape the legitimate criticisms contained in the dilemmas they are said to face.

1. *MNCs should do no intentional direct harm.* This injunction is clearly not peculiar to multinational corporations. Yet it is a basic norm that can be usefully applied in evaluating the conduct of MNCs. Any company that does produce intentional direct harm clearly violates a basic moral norm.

2. *MNCs should produce more good than bad for the host country.* This is an implementation of a general utilitarian principle. But this norm restricts the extent of that principle by the corollary that, in general, more good will be done by helping those in most need, rather than by helping those in less need at the expense of those in greater need. Thus the utilitarian analysis in this case does not consider that more harm than good might justifiably be done to the host country if the harm is offset by greater benefits to others in developed countries. MNCs will do more good only if they help the host country more than they harm it.

3. *MNCs should contribute by their activities to the host country's development.* If the presence of an MNC does not help the host country's development, the MNC can be correctly charged with exploitation, or using the host country for its own purposes at the expense of the host country.

4. *MNCs should respect the human rights of its employees.* MNCs should do so whether or not local companies respect those rights. This injunction will

preclude gross exploitation of workers, set minimum standards for pay, and prescribe minimum standards for health and safety measures.

5. *MNCs should pay their fair share of taxes.* Transfer pricing has as its aim taking advantage of different tax laws in different countries. To the extent that it involves deception, it is itself immoral. To the extent that it is engaged in to avoid legitimate taxes, it exploits the host country, and the MNC does not bear its fair share of the burden of operating in that country.

6. *To the extent that local culture does not violate moral norms, MNCs should respect the local culture and work with it, not against it.* MNCs cannot help but produce some changes in the cultures in which they operate. Yet, rather than simply transferring American ways into other lands, they can consider changes in operating procedures, plant planning, and the like, which take into account local needs and customs.

7. *MNCs should cooperate with the local government in the development and enforcement of just background institutions.* Instead of fighting a tax system that aims at appropriate redistribution of incomes, instead of preventing the organization of labor, and instead of resisting attempts at improving the health and safety standards of the host country, MNCs should be supportive of such measures.

THESIS III: WHOLESALE ATTACKS ON MULTINATIONALS ARE MOST OFTEN OVERGENERALIZATIONS. VALID MORAL EVALUATIONS CAN BE BEST MADE BY USING THE ABOVE MORAL CRITERIA FOR CONTEXT-AND-CORPORATION-SPECIFIC STUDIES AND ANALYSIS.

Broadside claims, such that all multinationals exploit underdeveloped countries or destroy their culture, are too vague to determine their accuracy. United States multinationals have in the past engaged — and some continue to engage — in immoral practices. A case by case study is the fairest way to make moral assessments. Yet we can distinguish five types of business operations that raise very different sorts of moral issues: (1) banks and financial institutions; (2) agricultural enterprises; (3) drug companies and hazardous industries; (4) extractive industries; and (5) other manufacturing and service industries.

If we were to apply our seven general criteria in each type of case, we would see some of the differences among them. Financial institutions do not generally employ many people. Their function is to provide loans for various types of development. In the case of South Africa they do not do much — if anything — to undermine apartheid, and by lending to the government they usually strengthen the government's policy of apartheid. In this case, an argument can be made that they do more harm than good — an argument that several banks have seen to be valid, causing them to discontinue their South African operations even before it became financially dangerous to continue lending money to that government. Financial institutions can help and have helped development tremendously. Yet the servicing of debts that many Third World countries face condemns them to impoverishment for the foreseeable future. The role of financial institutions in this situation is crucial and raises special and difficult moral problems, if not dilemmas.

Agricultural enterprises face other demands. If agricultural multinationals buy the best lands and use them for export crops while insufficient arable land is left for the local population to grow enough to feed itself, then MNCs do more harm than good to the host country — a violation of one of the norms I suggested above.

Drug companies and dangerous industries pose different and special problems. I have suggested that FDA standards are not morally mandatory standards. This should not be taken to mean that drug companies are bound only by local laws, for the local laws may require less than morality requires in the way of supplying adequate information and of not producing intentional, direct harm.[3] The same type of observation applies to hazardous industries. While an asbestos company will probably not be morally required to take all the measures mandated by OSHA regulations, it cannot morally leave its workers completely unprotected.[4]

Extractive industries, such as mining, which remove minerals from a country, are correctly open to the charge of exploitation unless they can show that they do more good than harm to the host country and that they do not benefit only either themselves or a repressive elite in the host country.

Other manufacturing industries vary greatly, but as a group they have come in for sustained charges of exploitation of workers and the undermining of the host country's culture. The above guidelines can serve as a means of sifting the valid from the invalid charges.

THESIS IV: ON THE INTERNATIONAL LEVEL AND ON THE NATIONAL LEVEL IN MANY THIRD WORLD COUNTRIES THE LACK OF ADEQUATE JUST BACKGROUND INSTITUTIONS MAKES THE USE OF CLEAR MORAL NORMS ALL THE MORE NECESSARY.

American multinational corporations operating in Germany and Japan, and German and Japanese multinational corporations operating in the United States, pose no special moral problems. Nor do the operations of Brazilian multinational corporations in the United States or Germany. Yet First World multinationals operating in Third World countries have come in for serious and sustained moral criticism. Why?

A major reason is that in the Third World the First World's MNCs operate without the types of constraints and in societies that do not have the same kinds of redistributive mechanisms as in the developed countries. There is no special difficulty in United States multinationals operating in other First World countries because in general these countries *do* have appropriate background institutions.[5]

More and more Third World countries are developing controls on multinationals that insure the companies do more good for the country than harm.[6] Authoritarian regimes that care more for their own wealth than for the good of their people pose difficult moral conditions under which to operate. In such instances, the guidelines above may prove helpful.

Just as in the nations of the developed, industrial world the labor movement serves as a counter to the dominance of big business, consumerism serves as a watchdog on practices harmful to the consumer, and big government serves as a restraint on each of the vested interest groups, so international structures are necessary to provide the proper background constraints on international corporations.

The existence of MNCs is a step forward in the unification of mankind and in the formation of a global community. They provide the economic base and substructure on which true international cooperation can be built. Because of their special position and the special opportunities they enjoy, they have a special responsibility to promote the cooperation that only they are able to accomplish in the present world.

Just background institutions would preclude any company's gaining a competitive advantage by engaging in immoral practices. This suggests that MNCs have more to gain than to lose by helping formulate voluntary, UN (such as the code governing infant formulae),[7] and similar codes governing the conduct of all multinationals. A case can also be made that they have the moral obligation to do so.

THESIS V: THE MORAL BURDEN OF MNCs DO NOT EXONERATE LOCAL GOVERNMENTS FROM RESPONSIBILITY FOR WHAT HAPPENS IN AND TO THEIR COUNTRY. SINCE RESPONSIBILITY IS LINKED TO OWNERSHIP, GOVERNMENTS THAT INSIST ON PART OR MAJORITY OWNERSHIP INCUR PART OR MAJORITY RESPONSIBILITY.

The attempts by many underdeveloped countries to limit multinationals have shown that at least some governments have come to see that they can use multinationals to their own advantage. This may be done by restricting entry to those companies that produce only for local consumption, or that bring desired technology transfers with them. Some countries demand majority control and restrict the export of money from the country. Nonetheless, many MNCs have found it profitable to engage in production under the terms specified by the host country.

What host countries cannot expect is that they can demand control without accepting correlative responsibility. In general, majority control implies majority responsibility. An American MNC, such as Union Carbide, which had majority ownership of its Indian Bhopal plant, should have had primary control of the plant. Union Carbide, Inc. can be held liable for the damage the Bhopal plant caused because Union Carbide, Inc. did have majority ownership.[8] If Union Carbide did not have effective control, it is not relieved of its responsibility. If it could not exercise the control that its responsibility demanded, it should have withdrawn or sold off part of its holdings in that plant. If India had had majority ownership, then it would have had primary responsibility for the safe operation of the plant.

This is compatible with maintaining that if a company builds a hazardous plant, it has an obligation to make sure that the plant is safe and that those who run it are properly trained to run it safely. MNCs cannot simply transfer dangerous technologies without consideration of the people who will run them, the local culture, and similar factors. Unless MNCs can be reasonably sure that the plants they build will be run safely, they cannot morally build them. To do so would be to will intentional, direct harm.

The theses and guidelines that I have proposed are not a panacea. But they suggest how moral norms can be brought to bear on the dilemmas American multinationals face and they suggest ways out of apparent or false dilemmas. If MNCs observed those norms, they could properly avoid the moral sting of their critics' charges, even if their critics continued to level charges against them.

Notes

1. The literature attacking American MNCs is extensive. Many of the charges mentioned in this paper are found in Richard J. Barnet and Ronald E. Muller, *Global Reach: The Power of the Multinational Corporations*, New York: Simon & Schuster, 1974, and in Pierre Jalee, *The Pillage of the Third World*, translated from the French by Mary Klopper, New York and London: Modern Reader Paperbacks, 1968.

2. The position I advocate does not entail moral relativism, as my third thesis shows. The point is that although moral norms apply uniformly across cultures, U.S. standards are not the same as moral standards, should themselves be morally evaluated, and are relative to American conditions, standard of living, interests, and history.

3. For a fuller discussion of multinational drug companies see Richard T. De George, *Business Ethics*, 2nd ed., New York: Macmillan, 1986, pp. 363–367.

4. For a more detailed analysis of the morality of exporting hazardous industries, see my *Business Ethics*, 367–372.

5. This position is consistent with that developed by John Rawls in his *A Theory of Justice*, Cambridge, Mass.: Harvard University Press, 1971, even though Rawls does not extend his analysis to the international realm. The thesis does not deny that United States, German, or Japanese policies on trade restrictions, tariff levels, and the like can be morally evaluated.

6. See, for example, Theodore H. Moran, "Multinational Corporations: A Survey of Ten Years' Evidence," Georgetown School of Foreign Service, 1984.

7. For a general discussion of UN codes, see Wolfgang Fikentscher, "United Nations Codes of Conduct: New Paths in International Law," *The American Journal of Comparative Law*, 30 (1980), pp. 577–604.

8. The official Indian Government report on the Bhopal tragedy has not yet appeared. The Union Carbide report was partially reprinted in the *New York Times*, March 21, 1985, p. 48. The major *New York Times* reports appeared on December 9, 1984, January 28, 30, and 31, and February 3, 1985.

Norman E. Bowie
BUSINESS ETHICS AND CULTURAL RELATIVISM

Business people doing business abroad know full well that ethical practices, including ethical practices in business, differ among cultures. You can't rely on what is ethical in the U.S. when you do business abroad. How should American companies practice business in other countries? A popular way of raising this issue is to ask whether U.S. multinationals should follow the advice "When in Rome, do as the Romans do."

In discussing this issue, a distinction must be made between home and host countries. The home country is where the corporation has its charter of incorporation. Usually the multinational has major facilities in the home country and has had a long history of business practice there. The host country is any other country where the multinational does business. If European and Japanese companies build manufacturing plants in the U.S., the United States is the host country. The fact that we are a host country comes as something of a shock to most Americans. We are used to being the home country. Foreign firms face their own version of the U.S. multinational question: When in America, should you do as the Americans do?

Some companies have answered the question in the negative. Japanese companies have been reluctant to adopt American unions or American management techniques; they have brought their own ways of managing with them. Is that appropriate? If it is, should American multinationals export their management philosophy when they build plants in Japan? When two cultures have different moral traditions and a corporation does business in both, how should the company behave? There are at least four possibilities. The first is that the company follow the moral practices of its own country. Most Americans would find this option unacceptable and would not, for example, want foreign companies to treat American women the way women allegedly are treated in certain other countries.

Another alternative is for the company to follow the moral practices of the host country. Most Americans would find that option unacceptable as well. If that option were required, American corporations would have to treat women in foreign countries where they do business as women are treated in those countries. In many cases Americans would object, just as they would object if American corporate officials treated black South Africans the way South Africa does.

The principle "When in Rome do as the Romans do" might seem like a reasonable and tolerant position to adopt, and many officers and managers of multinationals often speak as if this is the position they have adopted. Who are we, they argue, to impose our moral standards on the rest of the world? For

From Norman E. Bowie, "Business Ethics and Cultural Relativism," in *Essentials of Business Ethics*, edited by Peter Madsen and Jay M. Shafritz (New York: Penguin Books, 1990), 366–382. Portions of this paper are based on an earlier article, "The Moral Obligations of Multinational Corporations in *Problems of International Justice*, Steven Luper-Foy, Ed., Westview Press, 1988. Used with permission of the author.

example, the Foreign Corrupt Practices Act, which prohibits the payment of unrecorded bribes to foreign governments or officials, has come under intense attack. After all, if the payment of bribes is morally acceptable in country x, why should we impose our moral views about bribery on that country? Besides, if American multinationals don't bribe, German and Japanese multinationals will — or so the argument goes. Former President Jimmy Carter's attempt to include a country's record on violating or not violating fundamental human rights when making foreign policy decisions came under the same kind of criticism.

Philosophers have given a name to the when-in-Rome-do-as-the-Romans-do position. Cultural relativism is the doctrine that what is right or wrong, good or bad, depends on one's culture. If the Irish consider abortion to be morally wrong, abortion *is* morally wrong in Ireland. If the Swedes do not consider abortion to be morally wrong, then abortion is *not* morally wrong in Sweden. There is no universal principle to which the Swedes and the Irish can appeal that determines whether abortion really is wrong or not.

This relativistic way of thinking has always been prominent in the thinking of many social scientists. After all, the discoveries by anthropologists, sociologists, and psychologists documented the diversity of moral beliefs and punctured some of the pseudo-justifications that had been given for the superiority of white Western male ways of thinking. Philosophers, by and large, welcomed the corrections to prejudicial moral thinking but nonetheless found the doctrine of cultural relativism to be seriously flawed. That people and cultures disagree as to what is right or wrong, good or bad, and behave accordingly can be accepted as a fact. But what implications does this fact have for ethical decision making? Some have argued that the diversity of "moral" behavior shows that the theory of moral relativism is true. How do relativists establish their position? Many relativists have pointed to the fact that different individuals and cultures hold different views about what constitutes moral behavior as evidence for the truth of their position. Philosophers are virtually unanimous in the opinion that this is an invalid argument.

First, many philosophers claim that the "facts" aren't really what they seem. Several writers refer to the fact that in some cultures, after a certain age parents are put to death. In our culture such behavior would be murder. We take care of our parents. Does this difference in behavior prove that the two cultures disagree about matters of ethics? No, it does not. Suppose the other culture believes that people exist in the afterlife in the same condition that they leave their present life. It would be very cruel to have one's parents exist eternally in an unhealthy state. By killing them when they are relatively active and vigorous, you insure their happiness for all eternity. The underlying ethical principle of this culture is that children have duties to their parents, including the duty to be concerned with their parents' happiness as they approach old age. This ethical principle is identical with our own. What looked like a difference in ethics between our culture and another turned out, upon close examination, to be a difference based on factual evidence alone.

Here is another example that shows how the "facts" really aren't what they seem. Cultures differ in physical setting, in economic development, in the state of their science and technology, in their literacy rate, and in many other ways. Even if there were universal moral principles, they would have to be applied in these different cultural contexts. Given the different situations in which cultures exist, it would come as no surprise to find universal principles applied in different ways. Hence the differences in so-called ethical behavior among cultures would be superficial differences only. The cultures would agree on fundamental universal moral principles. One commonly held general principle appeals to the public good; it says that social institutions and individual behavior should be ordered so that they lead to the greatest good for the greatest number. Many different forms of social organization and individual behavior are consistent with this principle. The point of these two arguments is that superficial differences among cultures on so-called ethical behavior may not reflect genuine disagreement about ethics. Unless the relativist can establish basic differences about matters of ethics, the case for relativism cannot be made.

This discussion is important because it shows that ethical judgments are bound up in some complicated way with the facts. The existence of simple, safe birth-control methods has implications for sexual morality. The existence of sophisticated mechanical techniques for prolonging human life has implications for medical ethics. Since our ethical judgments depend in part upon what the facts are, the first step in resolving disputes about ethics should be to determine whether or not the disputants are disagreeing over the facts. If the disagreement is factual, it will need to be resolved before tackling any ethical disagreement. If the factual disagreement is resolved, the ethical disagreement often dissolves.

Some philosophers have made the strong claim that ultimately all the disagreement between cultures is either about the facts or about nothing more than the attempt to apply universal moral principles to specific situations. These philosophers claim that the apparent diversity in behavior among cultures is only apparent, and that ultimately cultures do agree on certain fundamental ethical standards. A discussion of this claim would take us beyond philosophy to anthropology, history, theology, and a host of other disciplines. The analysis thus far, though, should have established the early contention that you can't claim that cultural relativism is true just because cultures have different moral standards.

Another common strategy for criticizing relativism is to show that the consequences of taking the perspective of ethical relativism lead to some rather bizarre results. One of the bizarre results is that if relativism is true, then agreement on morals is, in principle, impossible. Of course, in this context *agreement* means agreement on the basis of reasons. There can be agreement by force. That's equivalent to "Worship my God or I'll cut off your head." Why there can be no rational agreement is obvious when an examination is made of the definition of relativism. Cultural relativism is the view that what is right or wrong is determined by culture. So if one culture says that abortion is right and another says it is wrong, that has to be the end of the matter. Abortion *is* morally permissible in some cultures and morally wrong in others.

But suppose a person from one culture moves to another and tries to persuade the other culture to change its view. Suppose someone moves from a culture where slavery is immoral to one where slavery is morally permitted. Normally, if a person were to try to convince the culture where slavery was permitted that slavery was morally wrong, we would refer to such a person as a moral reformer. But if cultural relativism were true, there would be no place for the concept of a moral reformer. Slavery is right in those cultures that say it is right and wrong in those cultures that say it is wrong. If the reformer fails to persuade a slaveholding country to change its mind, the reformer's antislavery position was never right. If the reformer is successful in persuading a country to change its mind, the reformer's antislavery views would be wrong — until the country did, in fact, change its view. Then the reformer's antislavery view was right. Now that's a bizarre result.

Underlying these two objections is the broader objection that relativism is inconsistent with our use of moral language. When Russia and the United States argue about the moral rights of human beings, they seem to be genuinely disagreeing about a matter of ethics. How unfortunate it would be if that dispute had to be resolved by nonrational means, since rational agreement is in principle impossible. People do marshal arguments in behalf of ethical views. If relativism is true, such arguments are doomed to failure or are a mere subterfuge to creating agreement. Similarly, we do have a place in our language for the concept of a moral reformer. Is this use of language really deviant, as it would have to be if relativism were true?

By virtue of the arguments developed so far, we see that you can't move from the facts of diversity in so-called ethical behavior and disagreement in ethics to moral relativism. The facts really don't establish ethical relativism, and the facts about our use of moral language are inconsistent with a relativist theory.

Although these arguments are powerful ones, they do not deliver a knockout blow to cultural relativism. A cultural relativist might admit that cultural relativism doesn't follow from the fact of cultural diversity. However, in the absence of universal moral principles, cultural relativists could argue that cultural relativism is the only theory available to help make sense of moral phenomena. Some cultural practices might be shown to be based on common moral principles, but the relativists doubt that all can.

Similarly, the cultural relativist might argue that our language does reflect a commitment to universal moral principles but that since we are mistaken about the existence of such principles, our language should be reformed. We should talk differently. At one time people used to talk and act as if the world were flat. Now they don't. Surely we can change our ethical language in the same way. Future historians could note that people used to talk as if there were universal moral principles, but of course we don't talk that way anymore. The cultural relativist insists that the only knockout blow against cultural relativism is to establish the truth or correctness of at least one universal moral principle that applies to all cultures.

Such confidence by the cultural relativist might not be warranted. Consider this argument against cultural relativism.[1] A spectrum of moral positions is laid out in Figure 1.

Figure 1

Individual Relativism	Cultural Relativism	Universalism

Individual relativism is the view that what is right or wrong, good or bad, depends on the feelings or attitudes of the individual. If an individual believes abortion is wrong, then abortion is wrong for that individual. If another individual believes abortion is not wrong, then abortion is not wrong for *that* individual. There is no valid cultural norm that will tell us which individual is objectively right.

The strategy is to show that any argument the cultural relativist uses against universalism can also be used by the individual relativist against cultural relativism. Similarly, any argument the cultural relativist uses against the individual relativist can be used by the universalist against the cultural relativist. The cultural relativist is constantly fighting a war on two fronts.

For example, against an individual relativist, a cultural relativist would often argue that if individual relativism were the prevailing view, a stable society would be impossible. Arguments from Thomas Hobbes or decision theory would prove the point. If individual relativism were the prevailing norm, life would be "nasty, brutish, and short" in the words of Hobbes' *Leviathan* (1650).

But in the world of 1989, any arguments that appeal to social stability will have to be applied universally. In the atomic age and in an age where terrorism is in some societies an acceptable form of political activity, the stability problems that afflict individual relativism equally afflict cultural relativism. If the necessity for social stability is a good argument for a cultural relativist to use against an individual relativist, it is an equally good argument for a universalist to use against a cultural relativist.

Multinational CEOs are likely to accept the argument thus far, however, because multinationals need a stable international environment if they are to make a profit in the long run. As any adviser for any multinational will tell you, one of the chief factors affecting an investment decision in a foreign country is the political stability of both that individual country and of the region surrounding it. An unstable country or region is highly inimical to the conduct of international business.

On the other hand, if the cultural relativist argues that there is no objective basis for asserting a universal moral principle, an individual relativist could make the same charge against the cultural relativist. What justification can a culture give for saying that the moral principles of some people are right but that the moral values of others, e.g., the reformer or prophet, are wrong? My hypothesis is that the types of argument available for the cultural relativist against the individual relativist are also available to the universalist against the cultural relativist. The real battle in ethics is not between the cultural relativist and the universalist but between the individual relativist and the universalist.

Even if this argument succeeds, the international business person has not been helped very much. She still doesn't know what her company should do when behaving abroad, and executives with other companies don't know what to do when they practice business in the United States. Despite appearances to the contrary, a great deal of morality has already been internationalized, either explicitly, by treaty or by belonging to the U.N.; or implicitly, through language and conduct.

For example, American business leaders engaged in business abroad often complain that the Foreign Corrupt Practices Act puts American business at a competitive disadvantage in doing business abroad. They argue that bribery is standard business practice abroad and that our laws against bribery put American firms at a disadvantage. You get the impression from reading the press that the U.S. is fairly unique in making bribery illegal and that bribery is a common practice in many parts of the world.

Such an impression is seriously mistaken, however. As Michael Bogdan, Professor of International Law at the University of Lund, Sweden, has pointed out, bribery — at least of public officials — is prohibited by the laws of practically every nation.[2] Member countries of the OECD have adopted guidelines, albeit voluntary ones, against bribery. Both the International Chamber of Commerce and the Permanent Council of the Organization of American States have called on states to pass antibribery legislation outlawing the bribery of officials in host countries. Sweden has enacted such a law. Finally the General Assembly of the United Nations adopted Resolution 3514, condemning bribery among other practices. Research has also shown that U.S. multinationals were involved in Middle East scandals nearly twice as often as multinational corporations of other nationalities.[3] Moreover, for those scandals involving non-U.S. multinationals, the host countries in the Mideast generally originated the investigation. The notion that bribery is generally permitted and practiced abroad does not stand up to empirical scrutiny.

Whereas the explicit acceptance of a universal morality has often been commented upon, the implicit acceptance of universal standards has not. Note the following: The words *democracy* and *democratic* have become honorific terms. Nearly all national states claim they are democracies — people's democracies, worker democracies, but democracies nonetheless. The August 4, 1986 issue of *Newsweek* carried a story about repression and the denial of civil rights in Chile. The president of Chile responded to his critics by calling his dictatorship "a democratic government with authority." I have yet to come across a state that brags that it is not a democracy and has no intention of being one. (Some nations do indicate they don't want to be a democracy like the U.S.)

A notion of shared values can be of assistance here as well. There is a whole range of behavior — e.g., torture, murder of the innocent, racism — that nearly all agree is wrong. A government accused of torture does not respond by saying that a condemnation of torture is just a matter of subjective morality. It doesn't respond by saying, "We think torture is right but you don't." Rather, the standard response is to deny that any torture took place. If the evidence of torture is too strong, a finger will be pointed either at the victim or at the morally outraged country: "They do it too." In this case the guilt is spread to all. Even the Nazis denied that genocide took place. What is important to note is that *no* state replies that there is nothing wrong with genocide or torture.

This conceptual argument is buttressed by another. Suppose an anthropologist discovers a large populated South Pacific island. How many tribes are on the island? Part of the answer to that question will be determined by seeing if such things as killing and murder are permitted, and if so, against whom? If they are not permitted, that counts as evidence that there is only one tribe. If people on the northern half of the island permit stealing directed against southerners but do not permit northerners to steal from one another, that provides evidence that there are at least two tribes. What often distinguishes one society from another is the fact that society *A* does not permit murder, lying, and stealing against members of *A* — society *A* couldn't permit that and still be a society, but society *A* does permit that kind of behavior against society *B*. What this strategy shows is that one of the criteria for having a society is that there be a shared morality among the individuals that comprise it.

What follows from this is that there are certain basic rules that must be followed in each society; e.g., don't lie, don't commit murder. There is a moral minimum in the sense that if these specific moral rules aren't generally followed, then there won't be a society at all. These moral rules are universal, but they are not practiced universally. That is, members of society *A* agree that they should not lie to each other, but they think it is permissible to lie to the members of other societies. Such moral rules are not relative; they simply are not practiced universally.

However, multinational corporations are obligated to follow these moral rules. Since the multinational is practicing business in the society, and since these moral norms are necessary for the existence of the society, the multinational has an obligation to support those norms. Otherwise multinationals would be in the position of benefiting from doing business with the society while at the same time engaging in activity that would undermine the society. Such conduct would be unjust.

Since the norms constituting a moral minimum are likely to be few in number, it can be said that the argument thus far has achieved something — i.e., multinationals are obligated to follow the moral norms required for there to be a society at all — but it hasn't achieved very much, and most issues surrounding multinationals do not involve alleged violations of these norms. Perhaps a stronger argument can be found by making explicit the morality of the marketplace. That there is an implicit morality in the market is a point that is often ignored by most economists and many business people.

Although economists and business people assume that individuals are basically self-interested, they must also assume that people involved in business transactions will honor their contracts. In most economic exchanges the transfer of product for money is not simultaneous. You deliver and I pay, or vice versa. As the economist Kenneth Boulding put it:

> . . . without an integrative framework, exchange itself cannot develop, because exchange, even in its most primitive forms, involves trust and credibility.[4]

Boulding's point can be illustrated by considering whether a business person should keep her contract when it is to her advantage not to. The contract device is extremely useful in business. The hiring of employees, the use of credit, the ordering and supplying of goods, and the notion of warranty, to name but a few, all make use of the contract device. Indeed, the contract is such an important part of business operation that it is often overlooked. This is a serious blunder. I maintain that if contract breaking were universalized, then business practice would be impossible. If a participant in business were to universally advocate violating contracts, such advocacy would be self-defeating, just as the universal advocacy of lying and cheating are self-defeating in a given society.

In fact, one can push this analysis to the generalization that business practice requires the adoption of a minimum standard of justice. In the U.S., a business person who engages in the practice of giving bribes or kickbacks is behaving unjustly. Why? Because the person is receiving the benefits of the rules against such activities without supporting the rules personally. This is an example of freeloading. A freeloader is one who accepts the benefits without paying any of the costs. A similar argument could be used against activities such as theft, fraud, and the use of kickbacks. All these activities take a free ride at the expense of honesty. If all people were dishonest, no one could gain an advantage from theft and fraud.

This argument does not show that if bribery really is an accepted moral practice in country X, that moral practice is wrong. What it does show is that practices in country X that permit freeloading are wrong, and if bribery can be construed as freeloading, then it is wrong.

To establish this point, consider what would happen if everyone bribed. A bribe undermines the competitive process so that a purchaser pays more than the competitive price; it is designed to enable a firm to get a contract without making the lowest bid possible. But the successful briber freeloads off those who offered competitive bids. Consider an example: Suppose in a two-firm universe that the two firms are sufficiently alike to be able to build an airport in a foreign country for $50 million. Neither could afford to build for less than that. Suppose firm A bids $50 million and firm B bribes official X to give it the contract for $60 million, in return for a $5-million bribe. The foreign country would pay $10 million more than it needed to pay. In practice, the briber has to free-ride off those who make competitive bids. Otherwise, if everyone bribed, they would bid the cost of the project up to where the country cannot afford it. If the contract is lost by all parties, nobody wins the contract and the bribery has become self-defeating.

The implications of this analysis for multinationals are broad and important. If activities that are permitted in other countries violate the morality of the marketplace, e.g., undermine contracts or involve free-loading on the rules of the market, they are nonetheless morally prohibited to multinationals that operate there. Such multinationals are obligated to follow the moral norms of the market. Contrary behavior is inconsistent and ultimately self-defeating.

Our analysis here has rather startling implications. If the moral norms of a host country are in violation of the moral norms of the marketplace, then the multinational is obligated to follow the norms of the marketplace. Systematic violation of marketplace norms would be self-defeating. Moreover, whenever a multinational establishes businesses in a number of different countries, the multinational provides something approaching a universal morality — the morality of the marketplace itself. If Romans are to do business with the Japanese, then whether in Rome or Tokyo, there is a morality to which members of the business community in both Rome and Tokyo must subscribe — even if the Japanese and Romans differ on other issues of morality. As we have seen from our analysis of lying, contract breaking, theft, fraud, kickbacks, and bribery, these activities, prohibited by norms of the market, are quite extensive.

However, many would point out that the norms of the market are not extensive enough. They have nothing to say about how companies should behave in countries where human rights are violated, e.g., should companies behave in South Africa as the law requires them to? Violating the rights of a minority class allegedly is not a violation of market morality. Does that mean that when in South Africa a company should do as the South African government does?

It seems that the answer to this last question should be no, but some arguments for a negative answer are needed. First, an argument can be made that the morality of the market does require that the rights of economic agents in the country be recognized and respected. Business activity on the market model assumes that contracts are made voluntarily. An involuntary contract is usually not considered to be a valid contract. Market morality explicitly requires that market transactions be voluntary and hence implicitly recognizes the right to liberty of participants in business. What justifies the voluntariness requirement? The right to liberty.

But what about the right to liberty in the political realm? What arguments can be given for civil and political liberty? A common argument is to appeal to a general right to liberty. Think of the argument in the Declaration of Independence. If economic, political, and civil liberties are *all* justified by the human right to liberty, then a recognition of the right to liberty brings with it a recognition of the other rights that are justified by it as well. You have to take the whole package. Thus it would be wrong for business to behave in South Africa as the South African government does.

Does that mean that American companies shouldn't do business in South Africa? That depends on whether or not international business can serve as a catalyst for democratic reform and the promotion of human rights. If business actively promotes democracy and human rights, despite laws against such activity on the part of business, then a moral argument can be made to justify business activity there. The multinational is serving the moral end of making the government less repressive. By the way, this is precisely the argument that many have used to justify business practice in South Africa. Indeed the South African situation can serve as an interesting case study. The point of the Sullivan principles, a set of ten criteria for ethical corporate behavior offered by Rev. Leon Sullivan, is to provide moral guidelines so that a company may be morally justified in having plants in South Africa without becoming part of the system of exploitation. The Sullivan principles also prevent profit-seeking corporations from morally justifying immoral behavior. No company can passively do as the South Africans do and then claim that their presence will bring about a more democratic, less racist regime. After all, if it is plausible to argue that capitalism can help create a democracy, it seems equally plausible to argue that a totalitarian regime may corrupt capitalism. The Sullivan principles help keep multinationals with South African facilities morally honest.

Moreover, the morality of the Sullivan principles depends on an empirical claim that profit-seeking corporations behaving in accordance with marketplace morality and acknowledging universally recognized human rights will in fact help transform totalitarian or repressive regimes into more democratic, more human regimes. If that transformation does not take place within a reasonable amount of time, the moral justification for having facilities in that country disappears. Leon Sullivan recognized that point when he set May 31, 1987, as the deadline for reform of the South African government. When the deadline passed, he insisted that American companies suspend operations in South Africa.

At this point some special remarks must be made about our relationship with the Soviet Union, since some hold that because there is little evidence that doing business with the Soviets will end their oppressive regime, the U.S. should not do business with them. An obvious response to that charge is to point out how much less oppressive the Soviet Union is under Gorbachev and *glasnost*. But suppose Gorbachev disappears from the scene?

Another argument remains. The ability to destroy one another perversely binds us in a special relationship. Even if increased business transactions between the two countries do not transform the Soviet system of government, moral justification for doing business with the Soviets remains. If such business transactions lessen the chance of war between us and the Soviets, then such business activity is justified on those grounds alone. Hence, there need be no inconsistency in saying that a multinational has an obligation not to do business in South Africa but does not have a similar obligation with respect to the Soviet Union. What is needed is a similar code or set of codes for doing business in the Soviet Union or in any other nondemocratic country. The existence of such a code would go far toward promoting the required consistency.

This brings up the human-rights issue again. Part of what it means to be a democracy is that respect be shown for fundamental human rights. The only justification for a multinational doing business with a regime that violates human rights is the claim that in so doing, the country's human rights record will improve. Again, business activity under that justification will have to be judged on results.

Hence, only in special circumstances is it right to do in Rome as the Romans do. Similarly it is only right in certain circumstances for the Japanese to do in New York as the Japanese do in Tokyo. What settles this question are moral principles that either have been accepted by all parties — as in U.N. treaties and other multinational agreements — or the principles of morality required by the practice of business itself. Since the practice of business requires an underlying business ethic, the international practice of business brings with it an international ethic that must be practiced everywhere. And the ethic is a demanding one!

Notes

1. This is an adaptation of an argument against prudentialism by Derek Parfit, *Reasons and Persons* (New York: Oxford University Press, 1986), pp. 126–127.

2. Michael Bogdan, "International Trade and the New Swedish Provisions on Corruption," *American Journal of Comparative Law*, Vol. 29, no. 4 (Fall 1979), p. 665.

3. Kate Gillespie, "Middle East Response to the U. S. Foreign Corrupt Practices Act," *California Management Review*, Vol. XXIX, no. 4 (Summer 1987), pp. 21–22.

4. Kenneth Boulding, "The Basis of Value Judgments in Economics," in *Human Values and Economic Policy*, ed., Sidney Hook (New York: New York University Press, 1967), p. 68.

Thomas Donaldson

MULTINATIONAL DECISION-MAKING: RECONCILING INTERNATIONAL NORMS

Jurisprudence theorists are often puzzled when, having thoroughly analyzed an issue within the boundaries of a legal system, they must confront it again outside those boundaries. For international issues, trusted axioms often fail as the secure grounds of legal tradition and national consensus erode. Much the same happens when one moves from viewing a problem of corporate ethics against a backdrop of national moral consensus to the morally inconsistent backdrop of international opinion. Is the worker who appeals to extra-national opinion while complaining about a corporate practice accepted within his or her country, the same as an ordinary whistleblower? Is a factory worker in Mexico justified in complaining about being paid three dollars an hour for the same work a U.S. factory worker, employed by the same company, is paid eight dollars?[1] Is he justified when in Mexico the practice of paying workers three dollars an hour — and even much less — is widely accepted? Is an asbestos worker in India justified in drawing world attention to the lower standards of

From *Journal of Business Ethics* 4 (1985), 357–366. © 1985 by Thomas Donaldson. Reprinted by permission of Kluwer Academic Publishers.

in-plant asbestos pollution maintained by an English multinational relative to standards in England, when the standards in question fall within Indian government guidelines and, indeed, are stricter than the standards maintained by other Indian asbestos manufacturers?

What distinguishes these issues from standard ones about corporate practices is that they involve reference to a conflict of norms, either moral or legal, between home and host country. This paper examines the subclass of conflicts in which host country norms appear substandard from the perspective of home country, and evaluates the claim often made by multinational executives that the prevalence of seemingly lower standards in a host country warrants the adoption by multinationals of the lower standards. It is concerned with cases of the following form: A multinational company (C) adopts a corporate practice (P) which is morally and/or legally permitted in C's host country (B), but not in C's home country (A). The paper argues that the presence of lower standards in B justifies C's adopting the lower standards only in certain, well-defined contexts. It proposes a conceptual test, or ethical algorithm, for multinationals to use in distinguishing justified from unjustified applications of standards. This algorithm ensures that multinational practice will remain faithful at least to the enlightened standards of home country morality.

If C is a non-national, that is to say a multinational, corporation, then one may wonder why home country opinion should be a factor in C's decision-making. One reason is that although global companies are multinational in doing business in more than one country, they are uninational in composition and character. They are chartered in a single country, typically have over ninety-five percent of their stock owned by citizens of their home country, and have managements dominated by citizens of their home country. Thus, in an important sense the term 'multinational' is a misnomer. For our purposes it is crucial to acknowledge that the moral foundation of a multinational, i.e., the underlying assumptions of its managers infusing corporate policies with a basic sense of right and wrong, is inextricably linked to the laws and mores of the home country.

Modern textbooks dealing with international business consider cultural relativity to be a powerful factor in executive decision-making. Indeed they often use it to justify practices abroad which, although enhancing corporate profits, would be questionable in the multinational's home country. One prominent text, for example, remarks that "In situations where patterns of dominance-subordination are socially determined, and not a function of demonstrated ability, management should be cautioned about promoting those of inferior social status to positions in which they are expected to supervise those of higher social status".[2] Later, referring to multiracial societies such as South Africa, the same text offers managers some practical advice: ". . . the problem of the multiracial society manifests itself particularly in reference to promotion and pay. And equal pay for equal work policy may not be acceptable to the politically dominant but racial minority group . . ."[3]

Consider two actual instances of the problem at issue:

Charles Pettis. In 1966 Charles Pettis, employee of Brown and Root Overseas, Inc., an American multinational, became resident engineer for one of his company's projects in Peru: a 146 miles, $46 million project to build a highway across the Andes. Pettis soon discovered that Peruvian safety standards were far below those in the United States. The highway design called for cutting channels through mountains in areas where rock formations were unstable. Unless special precautions were taken, slides could occur. Pettis blew the whistle, complaining first to Peruvian government officials and later to U.S. officials. No special precautions were taken, with the result that thirty-one men were killed by slides during the construction of the road. Pettis was fired for his trouble by Brown and Root and had difficulty finding a job with another company.[4]

American bank in Italy. A new American bank in Italy was advised by its Italian attorneys to file a tax return that misstated income and expenses and consequently grossly underestimated actual taxes due. The bank learned, however, that most other Italian companies regarded the practice as standard operating procedure and merely the first move in a complex negotiating process with the Italian Internal Revenue Service. The bank initially refused to file a fallacious return on moral grounds and submitted an 'American style' return instead. But because the resulting tax bill was many times higher than what comparable Italian companies were asked to pay, the bank changed policy in later years to agree with 'Italian style'.[5]

A. THE MORAL POINT OF VIEW

One may well decide that home country standards were mandatory in one of the above cases, but not in the other. One may decide that despite conforming to Peruvian standards, Peruvian safety precautions were unacceptable, while at the same time acknowledging that however inequitable and inefficient Italian tax mores may be, a decision to file 'Italian style' is permissible.

Despite claims to the contrary, one must reject the simple dictum that whenever P violates a moral standard of country A, it is impermissible for C. Arnold Berleant has argued that the principle of equal treatment endorsed by most U.S. citizens requires that U.S. corporations pay workers in less developed countries exactly the same wages paid to U.S. workers in comparable jobs (after appropriate adjustments are made for cost of living levels in the relevant areas).[6] But most observers, including those from the less developed countries, believe this stretches the doctrine of equality too far in a way detrimental to host countries. By arbitrarily establishing U.S. wage levels as the benchmark for fairness one eliminates the role of the international market in establishing salary levels, and this in turn eliminates the incentive U.S. corporations have to hire foreign workers. If U.S. companies felt morally bound to pay Korean workers exactly the wages U.S. workers receive for comparable work, they would not locate in Korea. Perhaps U.S. firms should exceed market rate for foreign labor as a matter of moral principle, but to pay strictly equal rates would freeze less developed countries out of the international labor market.[7] Lacking, then, a simple formula of the sort, 'P is wrong when P violates A's norms', one seems driven to undertake a more complex analysis of the types and degrees of responsibilities multinationals possess.

The first task is to distinguish between responsibilities that hold as minimum conditions, and ones that exceed the minimum. We are reminded of the distinction, eloquently articulated by Kant, between perfect and imperfect duties.

Perfect duties are owed to a specific class of persons under specified conditions, such as the duty to honor promises. They differ from imperfect duties, such as the duty of charity, which although mandatory, allow considerable discretion as to when, how, and to whom they are fulfilled. The perfect-imperfect distinction, however, is not appropriate for corporations since it is doubtful whether economic entities such as corporations must assume the same imperfect burdens, e.g., of charity, as individual persons.

For purposes of discussing multinationals, then, it is best to recast the distinction into one between 'minimal' and 'enlightened' duties, where a minimal duty is one the persistent failure of which to observe would deprive the corporation of its moral right to exist, i.e., a strictly mandatory duty, and an enlightened duty is one whose fulfillment would be praiseworthy but not mandatory in any sense. In the present context, it is the determination of minimal duties that has priority since in attempting to answer whether P is permissible for C in B, the notion of permissibility must eventually be cashed in terms of minimal standards. Thus, P is not impermissible for C simply because C fails to achieve an ideal vision of corporate conduct; and C's failure to contribute generously to the United Nations is a permissible, if regrettable, act.

Because minimal duties are our target, it is appropriate next to invoke the language of rights, for rights are entitlements that impose minimum demands on the behavior of others.

B. THE APPEAL TO RIGHTS

Theorists commonly analyze the obligations of developed to less developed countries in terms of rights. James Sterba argues that "distant peoples" (e.g., persons in Third World countries) enjoy welfare rights that members of the developed countries are obliged to respect.[8] Welfare rights are defined as rights to whatever is necessary to satisfy "basic needs", and "basic needs", in turn, as needs "which must be satisfied in order not to seriously endanger a person's health and sanity".[9] It follows that multinationals are obliged to avoid workplace hazards that seriously endanger workers' health.

A similar notion is advanced by Henry Shue in his book, *Basic Rights*. The substance of a basic right for Shue is "something the deprivation of which is one standard threat to rights generally."[10] He considers it a "minimal demand" that "no individuals or institutions, including corporations, may ignore the universal duty to avoid depriving persons of their basic rights."[11] Since one's physical security, including safety from exposure to harmful chemicals or pollution, is a condition for one's enjoyment of rights generally, it follows that the right to physical security is a basic right that imposes specific obligations on corporations.

Equally important for our purposes is Shue's application elsewhere of the "no harm" principle to the actions of U.S. multinationals abroad.[12] Associated with Mill and traditional liberalism, the "no harm" principle reflects a rights based approach emphasizing the individuals's right to liberty, allowing maximal liberty to each so long as each inflicts no avoidable harm on others. Shue criticizes as a violation of the no-harm principle a plan by a Colorado based company to export millions of tons of hazardous chemical waste from the U.S. for processing and disposal in the West African nation of Sierra Leone.[13] Using the same principle, he is able to criticize any U.S. asbestos manufacturing corporation which, in order to escape expensive regulations at home, moves its plant to a foreign country with lower standards.[14]

Thus the Shue-Sterba rights based approach recommends itself as a candidate for evaluating multinational conduct. It is irrelevant whether the standards of B comply or fail to comply with home country standards; what is relevant is whether they meet a universal, objective minimum. In the present context, the principal advantage of a rights based approach is to establish a firm limit to appeals made in the name of host country laws and morals — at least when the issue is a clear threat to workers' safety. Clear threats such as in-plant asbestos pollution exceeding levels recommended by independent scientific bodies, are incompatible with employee's rights, especially their right not to be harmed. It is no excuse to cite lenient host country regulations or ill-informed host country public opinion.

But even as a rights oriented approach clarifies a moral bottom line for extreme threats to workers' safety, it leaves obscure not only the issue of less extreme threats, but of harms other than physical injury. The language of rights and harm is sufficiently vague so as to leave shrouded in uncertainty a formidable list of issues crucial to multinationals.

When refined by the traditions of a national legal system, the language of rights achieves great precision. But left to wander among the concepts of general moral theory, the language proves less exact. Granted, the celebrated dangers of asbestos call for recognizing the right to workers' safety no matter how broadly the language of rights is framed. But what are we to say of a less toxic pollutant? Is the level of sulfer-dioxide air pollution we should demand in a struggling nation, say, one with only a few fertilizer plants working overtime to help feed its malnourished population, the same we should demand in Portland, Oregon? Or taking a more obvious case, should the maximal level of thermal pollution generated by a poor nation's electric power plants be the same as West Germany's? Since thermal pollution raises the temperature of a given body of water, it lowers the capacity of the water to hold oxygen and in turn the number of 'higher' fish species, e.g., Salmon and Trout. But whereas the trade-off between more Trout and higher output is rationally made by the West German in favor of the Trout, the situation is reversed for the citizen of Chad, Africa. This should not surprise us. It has long been recognized that many rights, e.g., the right to medical care, are dependent for their specification on the level of economic development of the country in question.[15]

Nor is it clear how a general appeal to rights will resolve issues that turn on the interpretation of broad social practices. For example, in the Italian tax case mentioned earlier, the propriety of submitting an 'Italian' vs. 'American' style tax return hinges more on the appraisal of the value of honesty in a complex economic and social system, than on an appeal to inalienable rights.

C. AN ETHICAL ALGORITHM

What is needed, then, is a test for evaluating P more comprehensive than a simple appeal to rights. In the end nothing short of a general moral theory working in tandem with an analysis of the foundations of corporate existence is needed. That is, ultimately there is no escape for the multinational executive from merging the ordinary canons of economic decision-making, of profit maximization and market share, with the principles of basic moral theory.[16] But this formidable task, essential as it is, does not preclude the possibility of discovering lower-order moral concepts to clarify the moral intuitions already in use by multinational decision-makers. Apart from the need for general theories of multinational conduct there is need for pragmatic aids to multinational decision-making that bring into relief the ethical implications of views already held. This suggests, then, the possibility of generating an interpretive mechanism, or algorithm, that managers of multinationals could use in determining the implications of their own moral views about cases of the form, "Is P permissible for C when P is acceptable in B but not in A?"

The first step in generating such an ethical algorithm is to isolate distinct senses in which B's norms may conflict with the norms of A. Now, if P is morally and/or legally permitted in B, but not in A then either:

1. The moral reasons underlying B's view that P is permissible refer to B's relative level of economic development; or
2. The moral reasons underlying B's view that P is permissible are independent of B's relative level of economic development.

Let us call the conflict of norms described in (1) a 'type #1' conflict. In such a conflict, an African country that permits slightly higher levels of thermal pollution from electric power generating plants, or a lower minimum wage, than those prescribed in European countries would do so not because higher standards would be undesirable *per se*, but because its level of economic development requires an ordering of priorities. In the future when it succeeds in matching European economic achievements, it may well implement the higher standards.

Let us call the conflict of norms described in (2) a 'type #2' conflict. In such cases levels of economic development play no role. For example, low level institutional nepotism, common in many underdeveloped countries, is justified not on economic grounds, but on the basis of clan and family loyalty. Presumably the same loyalties should be operative even after the country has risen to economic success — as the nepotism prevalent is Saudia Arabia would indicate. The Italian tax case also reflects an Italian cultural style with a penchant for personal negotiation and an unwillingness to formalize transactions, more than a strategy based on level of economical development.

When the conflicts of norms occurs for reasons other than relative economic development (type #2), then the possibility is increased that there exists what Richard Brandt has called an "ultimate ethical disagreement". An ultimate disagreement occurs when two cultures are able to consider the same set of facts surrounding a moral issue while disagreeing on the moral issue itself. An ultimate disagreement is less likely in a type #1 case since after suitable reflection about priorities imposed by differing economic circumstance, the members of A may come to agree that *given* that facts of B's level of economic development, P is permissible. On the other hand, a type #2 dispute about what Westerners call "nepotism" will continue even after economic variables are discounted.[17]

The status of the conflict of norms between A and B, i.e., whether it is of type #1 or #2, does not fix the truth value of B's claim that P is permissible. P may or may not be permissible whether the conflict is of type #1 or #2. This, however, is not to say that the truth value of *B*'s claim is independent of the conflict's type status, for a different test will be required to determine whether *P* is permissible when the conflict is of type #1 than type #2. In a type #1 dispute, the following formula is appropriate:

> *P* is permissible if and only if the members of *A* would, under conditions of economic development relevantly similar to those of *B*, regard *P* as permissible.

Under this test, excessive levels of asbestos pollution would almost certainly not be tolerated by the members of *A* under relevantly similar economic conditions, whereas higher levels of thermal pollution would be. The test, happily, explains and confirms our initial moral intuitions.

Yet, when as in type #2 conflicts the dispute between *A* and *B* depends upon a fundamental difference of perspective, the step to equalize hypothetically the levels of economic development is useless. A different test is needed. In type #2 conflicts the opposing evils of ethnocentricism and ethical relativism must be avoided. A multinational must forego the temptation to remake all societies in the image of its home society, while at the same time rejecting a relativism that conveniently forgets ethics when the payoff is sufficient. Thus, the task is to tolerate cultural diversity while drawing the line at moral recklessness.

Since in type #2 cases *P* is in conflict with an embedded norm of *A*, one should first ask whether *P* is necessary to do business in *B*, for if not, the solution clearly is to adopt some other practice that is permissible from the standpoint of *A*. If petty bribery of public officials is unnecessary for the business of the Cummins Engine Company in India, then the company is obliged to abandon such bribery. If, on the other hand, *P* proves necessary for business, one must next ask whether *P* constitutes a direct violation of a basic human right. Here the notion of a right, specifying a minimum below which corporate conduct should not fall, has special application. If Polaroid, an American company, confronts South African laws that mandate systematic discrimination against non-whites, then Polaroid must refuse to comply with the laws. Thus, in type #2 cases, *P* would be permissible if and only if the answer to both of the following questions is 'no'.

a. It is possible to conduct business successfully in *B* without undertaking *P*?
b. Is *P* a clear violation of a basic human right?

What sorts of practice might pass both conditions (a) and (b)? Consider the practice of low-level bribery of public officials in some underdeveloped nations. In some South American countries, for example, it is impossible for any company, foreign or national, to move goods through customs without paying low-level officials a few dollars. Indeed, the salaries of such officials are sufficiently low that one suspects they are set with the prevalence of the practice in mind. The payments are relatively small, uniformly assessed, and accepted as standard practice by the surrounding culture. Here, the practice of petty bribery would pass the type #2 test and, barring other moral factors, would be permissible.

A further condition, however, should be placed on multinationals undertaking P in type #2 contexts. The companies should be willing to speak out against, and be willing to work for change of P. Even if petty bribery or low-level nepotism passes the preceding tests, it may conflict with an embedded norm of country A, and as a representative of A's culture, the company is obliged to take a stand. This would be true even for issues related exclusively to financial practice, such as the Italian tax case. If the practice of underestimating taxes due is (1) accepted in B, (2) necessary for successful business, and (3) does not violate any basic human rights, then it satisfies the necessary conditions of permissibility. Yet insofar as it violates a norm accepted by A, C should make its disapproval of the practice known.

To sum up, then, two complementary tests have been proposed for determining the ultimate permissibility of P. If P occurs in a type #1 context, then P is not permissible if:

The members of A would not, under conditions of economic development relevantly similar to those of B, regard P as permissible.

If P occurs in a type #2 context, then P is not permissible if either:

1. It is possible to conduct business successfully in B without undertaking P or
2. P is a direct violation of a basic human right.

Notice that the type #1 criterion is not reducible to the type #2 criterion. In order for the two criteria to have equivalent outcomes, four propositions would need to be true: (1) If P passes #1, it passes #2; (2) if P fails #1, it fails #2; (3) if P passes #2, it passes #1; and (4) if P fails #2, it fails #1. But none of these propositions is true. The possibility matrix below lists in rows A and B the only combinations of outcomes that are possible on the assumption that the two criteria are equivalent. But they are not equivalent because the combinations of outcomes in C and D are also possible. To illustrate, P may pass #2 and fail #1; for example, the practice of petty bribery may be necessary for business, may not violate basic human rights, but may nonetheless be unacceptable in A under hypothetically lowered levels of economic development; similarly, the practice of allowing a significant amount of water pollution may be necessary for business, may not violate basic rights, yet may be hypothetically unacceptable in A. Or, P may fail #2 and pass #1; for example, the practice of serving alcohol at executive dinners in a strongly Moslem country may not be necessary for business in B (and thus impermissible by criteria #2) while being thoroughly acceptable to the members of A under hypothetically lowered economic conditions. It follows, then, that the two tests are not mutually reducible. This underscores the importance of the preliminary step of classifying a given case under either type #1 or type #2. The prior act of classification explains, moreover, why not all cases in row C or in row D will have the same moral outcome. Consider, for example, the two Fail–Pass cases from row C mentioned above, i.e., the cases of water pollution and petty bribery. If classified as a type #1 case, the water pollution would *not* be permissible, while petty bribery, if classified as a type #2 case, *would* be.

	Criterion #1	Criterion #2
A	Fail	Fail
		equivalent outcomes
B	Pass	Pass

	Criterion #1	Criterion #2
C	Fail	Pass
		non-equivalent outcomes
D	Pass	Fail

D. SOME PRACTICAL CONSIDERATIONS AND OBJECTIONS

The algorithm does not obviate the need for multinational managers to appeal to moral concepts both more general and specific than the algorithm itself. It is not intended as a substitute for a general theory of morality or even an interpretation of the basic responsibilities of multinationals. Its power lies in its ability to tease out implications of the moral presuppositions of a manager's acceptance of 'home' morality and in this sense to serve as a clarificatory device for multinational decision-making. But insofar as the context of a given conflict of norms categorizes it as a type #1 rather than type #2 conflict, the algorithm makes no appeal to a universal concept of morality (as the appeal to basic human rights does in type #2 cases) save for the purported universality of the ethics endorsed by culture A. This means that the force of the algorithm is relativized slightly in the direction of a single society. When A's morality is wrong or confused, the algorithm can reflect this ethnocentricity, leading either to a mild paternalism or to the imposition of parochial standards. For example, A's oversensitivity to aesthetic features of the environment may lead it to reject a given level of thermal pollution even under hypothetically lowered economic circumstances, thus yielding a paternalistic refusal to allow such levels in B, despite B's acceptance of the higher levels and B's belief that tolerating such levels is necessary for stimulating economic development. Or, A's mistaken belief that the practice of hiring twelve year olds for full-time, permanent work, although happily unnecessary at its relatively high level of economic development, would be acceptable and economically necessary at a level of economic development relevantly similar to B's, might lead it both to tolerate and undertake the practice in B.

Nor is the algorithm a substitute for more specific guides to conduct such as the numerous codes of ethics now appearing on the international scene. A need exists for topic-specific and industry-specific codes that embody detailed safeguards against self-serving interpretations. Consider the Sullivan Standards, designed by the black American minister, Leon Sullivan, drafted for the purpose of ensuring non-racist practices by U.S. multinationals operating in South Africa. As a result of a lengthy lobbying campaign by U.S. activists, the Sullivan principles are now endorsed and followed by almost one third of all American multinationals with South African subsidiaries. Among other things, companies complying with the Sullivan principles must:

> Remove all race designation signs.
>
> Support the elimination of discrimination against the rights of Blacks to form or belong to government registered unions.
>
> Determine whether upgrading of personnel and/or jobs in the lower echelons is needed (and take appropriate steps).[18]

A variety of similar codes are either operative or in the process of development, e.g., the European Economic Community's Vredeling Proposal on labor-management consultations; the United Nation's Code of Conduct for Transnational Corporations and its International Standards of Accounting and Reporting; the World Health Organizations's Code on Pharmaceuticals and Tobacco; the World Intellectual Property Organization's Revision of the Paris Convention for the Protection of Industrial Patents and Trademarks; the International Chamber of Commerce's Rules of Conduct to Combat Extortion and Bribery; and the World Health Organization's Infant Formula code against advertising of breast-milk substitutes.[19]

Despite these limitations, the algorithm has important application in countering the well documented tendency of multinationals to mask immoral practices in the rhetoric of 'tolerance' and 'cultural relativity'. Utilizing it, no multinational manager can naively suggest that asbestos standards in Chile are permissible because they are accepted there. Nor can he infer that the standards are acceptable on the grounds that the Chilean economy is, relative to his home country, underdeveloped. A surprising amount of moral blindness occurs not because people's fundamental moral views are confused, but because their cognitive application of those views to novel situations is misguided.

What guarantees that either multinationals or prospective whistleblowers possess the knowledge or objectivity to apply the algorithm fairly? As Richard Barnet quips, "On the 56th floor of a Manhattan skyscraper, the level of self-protective ignorance about what the company may be doing in Colombia or Mexico is high".[20] Can Exxon or Johns Manville be trusted to have a sufficiently sophisticated sense of 'human rights', or to weigh dispassionately the hypothetical attitudes of their fellow countrymen under conditions of 'relevantly similar economic development'? My answer to this is 'probably not', at least given the present character of the decision-making procedures in most global corporations. I would add, however, that this problem is a contingent and practical one. It is no more a theoretical flaw of the proposed algorithm that it may be conveniently misunderstood by a given multinational, than it is of Rawl's theory that it may be conveniently misunderstood by a trickle-down capitalist.

What would need to change in order for multinationals to make use of the algorithm? At a minimum they would need to enhance the sophistication of their decision-making mechanisms. They would need to alter established patterns of information flow and collection in order to accommodate moral information. The already complex parameters of corporate decision-making would become more so. They would need to introduce alongside analyses of the bottom line analyses of historical tendencies, nutrition, rights, and demography. And they would need to introduce a new class of employee to provide expertise in these areas. However unlikely such changes are, I believe they are within the realm of possibility. Multinationals, the organizations capable of colonizing our international future, are also capable of looking beyond their national borders and applying — at a minimum — the same moral principles they accept at home.

Notes

*This is a revision of a paper entitled 'International Whistleblowing', to be published in *Conflicting Loyalties in the Workplace*, ed. by Frederick Elliston (Notre Dame, Indiana: University of Notre Dame Press).

1. An example of disparity in wages between Mexican and U.S. workers is documented in the case-study, 'Twin-Plants and Corporate Responsibilities', by John H. Haddox, in *Profits and Responsibility*, ed. Patricia Werhane and Kendall D'Andrade (New York: Random House, 1985).

2. Richard D. Robinson, *International Business Management: A Guide to Decision Making*, Second Edition (Hinsdale, Ill.: The Dryden Press, 1978), p. 241.

3. Robinson, p. 241.

4. Charles Peters and Taylor Branch, *Blowing the Whistle: Dissent in the Public Interest* (New York: Praeger Publishers, 1972), pp. 182–185.

5. Arthur Kelly, 'Italian Bank Mores', in *Case-Studies in Business Ethics*, ed. T. Donaldson (Englewood Cliffs: Prentice-Hall, Inc., 1984).

6. Arnold Berleant, 'Multinationals and the Problem of Ethical Consistency', *Journal of Business Ethics* 3 (August 1982), 185–195.

7. One can construct an argument attempting to show that insulating the economies of the less developed countries would be advantageous to the less developed countries in the long run. But whether correct or not, such an argument is independent of the present issue, for it is independent of the claim that if P violates the norms of A, then P is impermissible.

8. James Sterba, 'The Welfare Rights of Distant Peoples and Future Generations: Moral Side Constraints on Social Policy', in *Social Theory and Practice* 7 (Spring, 1981) p. 110.

9. Sterba, p. 111.

10. Henry Shue, *Basic Rights, Subsistence, Affluence, and U.S. Foreign Policy* (Princeton, N.J.: Princeton University Press, 1981) p. 34.

11. Shue, *Basic Rights*, p. 170.

12. Henry Shue, 'Exporting Hazards', *Ethics* 91 (July 1981): 579–606.

13. Shue, 'Hazards', pp. 579–580.

14. Considering a possible escape from the principle, Shue considers whether inflicting harm is acceptable in the event overall benefits outweigh the costs. Hence, increased safety risks under reduced asbestos standards might be acceptable insofar as the economic benefits to the country outweighed the costs. The problem, as Shue correctly notes, is that this approach fails to distinguish between the no-harm principle and a naive greatest happiness principle. Even classical defenders of the no-harm principle were unwilling to accept a simple-minded utilitarianism that sacrificed individual justice on the altar of maximal happiness. Even classical utilitarians did not construe their greatest happiness principle to be a 'hunting license'. (Shue, 'Hazards', pp. 592–593.)

Still another escape might be by way of appealing to the rigors of international economic competition. That is, is it not unreasonable to expect firms to place themselves at a competitive disadvantage by installing expensive safety equipment in a market where other firms are brutally cost conscious? Such policies, argue critics, could trigger economic suicide. The obligation not to harm, in turn, properly belongs to the government of the host country. Here, too, Shue's rejoinder is on-target. He notes first that the existence of an obligation by one party does not cancel its burden on another party; hence, even if the host country's government does have an obligation to protect their citizens from dangerous workplace conditions, its duty does not cancel that of the corporation. (Shue, 'Hazards', p. 600.) Second, governments of poor countries are themselves forced to compete for scarce foreign capital by weakening their laws and regulations, with the result that any 'competitive disadvantage' excuse offered on behalf of the corporation would also apply to the government. (Shue, 'Hazards', p. 601.)

15. Sterba himself reflects this consensus when he remarks that for rights ". . . an acceptable minimum should vary over time and between societies at least to some degree". (Sterba, 'Distant Peoples', p. 112.)

16. For the purpose of analyzing the moral foundations of corporate behavior, I prefer a social contract theory, one that interprets a hypothetical contract between society and productive organizations, and which I have argued for in my book, *Corporations and Morality*. Thomas Donaldson, *Corporations and Morality* (Englewood Cliffs: Prentice-Hall, 1982); See especially Chapter 3. There I argue that Corporations are artifacts; that they are in part the products of our moral and legal imagination. As such, they are to be molded in the image of our collective rights and societal ambitions. Corporations, as all productive organizations, require from society both recognition as single agents, and the authority to own or use land and natural resources, and to hire employees. In return for this, society may expect that productive organizations will, all other things being equal, enhance the general interests of consumers and employees. Society may reasonably expect that in doing so corporations honor existing rights and limit their activities to accord with the bounds of justice. This is as true for multinationals as it is for national corporations.

17. Richard Brandt, 'Cultural Relativism', in *Ethical Issues in Business*, Second Edition, ed. T. Donaldson and P. Werhane (Englewood Cliffs. N.J.: Prentice-Hall, Inc., 1983.)

18. See 'Dresser Industries and South Africa', by Patricia Mintz and Kirk O. Hanson, in *Case Studies in Business Ethics*, ed. Thomas Donaldson (Prentice-Hall, 1984).

19. For a concise and comprehensive account of the various codes of conduct for international business now under consideration, see 'Codes of Conduct: Worry over New Restraints on Multinationals', *Chemical Week* (July 15, 1981), 48–52.

20. Richard J. Barnet and Ronald Muller, *Global Reach: The Power of Multinational Corporations* (New York: Simon and Schuster, 1974), p. 185.

Thomas Donaldson

THE ETHICS OF RISK
IN THE GLOBAL ECONOMY

In India, The Philippines, Nigeria, and elsewhere, technology is spread thin on ancient cultures. In 1984, in Bhopal, India, the devastating potential of technology's hazards in a non-technological culture was brought home with awesome pain—over 2,000 dead and 200,000 injured. My aim here is to inquire about the justice of practices, like those in Bhopal, that subject foreign citizens to technological risks higher than those faced by either home country citizens or more favored foreign citizens. The object of exploration, hence, is the justice of the distribution of technological risks in and among nation states. What moral obligations underlie, what extra-national responsibilities should inform, the behavior of global actors such as Union Carbide and the United

From *Business and Professional Ethics Journal*, 5, nos. 3 & 4 (1985), 31–49. Reprinted by permission of the author.

States? The question not only intrigues us, it demands answers on behalf of those who have been harmed or who are presently at risk. Yet it appears disturbingly clear that the question as framed eludes answers because we possess no viable interpretive scheme for applying traditional moral precepts to the moral twilight created by the juxtaposition of differing legal and cultural traditions.

The key issue to address is obligation. In particular, what are the obligations of macro-agents or macro-organizations to third or fourth parties who are denied membership in those macro-organizations? The terms "macro-agents" or "macro-organizations" will be used interchangeably. They refer to key organizational actors in the international economy, and especially nation states and multi-national corporations. By "third party victims" I mean persons who are put at risk by a given macro-organization who are not themselves members of that organization, for example, innocent bystanders or citizens of another country; by "fourth party victims" I mean fetuses and future generations. In general, third and fourth party victims do not make policy decisions that affect the level or distribution of risk, and when harmed are entirely innocent. Both categories are to be contrasted to first-party victims such as corporate managers or government leaders, and second-party victims such as rank and file employees or national citizens.[1] These latter categories of persons, when harmed, may or may not be innocent.

The point about non-membership is important. We expect corporations to honor certain responsibilities toward their employees (no matter how frequently some may violate them), and when they fail to do so, we are able to appeal to accepted moral principles in criticizing their behavior. Similarly, we expect nation states to exercise special care over their citizens, and doing so is regarded as a *sine qua non* of a national legal system. Hence when states fail in this regard, we know what to say. But we do not know, or know as well, what to say about the responsibilities of the United States government to the citizens of Bangladesh, or of Dow Chemical to the man or woman in the street in Cubatao, Brazil.

Let us begin by sketching key elements of the disaster in Bhopal, India. Bhopal is by no means unique in the history of chemical catastrophes,[2] but it is striking for the enormity of its scale and, more importantly, the lesson it teaches.[3]

Although the entire story remains to be told, blame for the disaster is likely to be spread through a complex constellation of persons and acts. Cost cutting measures in the year prior severely weakened safety control. The refrigeration unit designed to cool the methyl isocyanate had been broken for some time, and more than a score of crucial safety devices specified in the safety handbook prepared by Union Carbide in the United States were conspicuously absent. The training, habits, and attitudes of Indian employees were lax and naive. Safety procedures specified in the book were routinely circumvented by technicians who, lacking adequate training, went on with their work blissfully ignorant of the dangers lurking behind their daily routines. In responding to the disaster, employees showed bad judgement and bad training: upon learning of the initial leak, the officer in charge opted to think about it over tea. Outside the plant, government regulatory authorities and city officials were entirely at a loss either to inspect and regulate the plant on an ongoing basis, or to respond appropriately to a disaster once it occurred.

Finally, Union Carbide itself, despite holding a majority of its subsidiary's stock and accepting responsibility for all major economic and safety decisions, failed to maintain an adequate system of safety accountability, and consequently, to exercise appropriate control over its subsidiary.

Yet Bhopal was not only a story about tragedy and human frailty, it is also a story about injustice. For the people who died and suffered were not citizens of the nation whose corporation held responsibility. To make matters worse, the people who suffered the most were slum dwellers, the poorest of the Indian poor, who had pitched their tents literally next to the walls of the Carbide plant.

Cultural variables muddy moral analysis. Whereas in the context of our own culture we can estimate with some assurance the value of goods sacrificed or put at risk by undertaking a given act or policy, in a foreign one our intuitions are opaque. Our extra-cultural vision may be sufficiently clear to allow us to understand a tradeoff between risk and productivity, between the dollar value of an increased gross national product on the one hand, and the higher dollar cost of the medical care necessary to accommodate higher levels of risk; but our vision is blurred by more ethnocentric tradeoffs. In many less developed countries a higher gross national product is only one of a handful of crucial goals informed by cultural tradition and experience.

This consideration highlights the second and more disruptive of two cultural variables that can sidetrack international risk analysis. The first is the level of gross marginal improvement in health or economic well-being, as statistically measurable by universally accepted norms of health and economic welfare. Let us call this marginal improvement in health or economic well being, as statistically measurable by universally accepted norms of health and economic welfare. Let us call this marginal value that of "statistical welfare." Since, as suggested above, the analyst is free to factor cultural values into the determination of extra-national responsibilities, he is free to integrate the concept of "statistical welfare" into overall risk analysis, and estimate tradeoffs from the standpoint of the foreign country. Furthermore, since the concept is by definition compatible with the objective, quantitative methods of analysis, the task is manageable. Armed with an appropriate statistical method, he may well conclude that the marginal welfare resulting from the use of a hazardous drug or piece of technology is positive in the United States, while negative in another country, or vice versa. The notion of marginal statistical welfare thus aids in sidestepping one version of cultural myopia and in weighting the effect local conditions can have on the character of tradeoffs between risks and benefits.

The second variable is that of marginal cultural welfare. In contrast to marginal statistical welfare, it cannot be interpreted through standard norms of health or economic well-being. A citizen of Zimbabwe, Africa, may be willing to trade off a few marginal dollars in per capita gross national product for the unquantifiable improvement in her nation's economic independence from earlier colonial powers. For the same improvement, she may even be willing to trade off a fraction of a percentage point in the nation's infant mortality rate. Similarly, a citizen of Pakistan may be more eager to preserve her country's Moslem heritage, a heritage with strict sexual differentiation in the division of labor, than to increase the country's economic welfare through integrating women into the work place.

My point is simply that in instances where the tradeoffs involve marginal cultural welfare it is doubtful how accurately a cultural stranger can estimate the value that a citizen of another culture places on key goods involved in social tradeoffs. Hence, short of abdicating risk analysis entirely to the other culture (a move I will show later to be unwise), no decisive or even objective decision-making mechanism appears to exist for assessing risk tradeoffs.

Still further, cultural variables can aggravate weaknesses of traditional methods of risk analysis. This is especially true of most methods' tendency to focus on dollars and bodies at the expense of social and cultural criteria, a tendency which, while faulted in domestic contexts, becomes pernicious when the difference between two countries' social and cultural habits are marked.

Consider the twin issues of distributing risk and pricing risk. It is well known that the techniques of cost-benefit analysis are often mute regarding issues of distributive justice. That is, they tend to bypass questions of the fairness of a practice from the perspective of its relative impact on social subclasses, such as the poor, the infirm, or the members of a minority ethnic group. Such silence is less neglectful in the context of a national legal system whose rules have as a central function the protection of individual rights.[4] But in the context of international transactions, where the legal strictures affecting a macro agent's domestic activities do not (and in an important sense *can* not) regulate its activities in a separate legal jurisdiction, the silence is morally corrupting. Clearly pesticide risks to field workers must be weighed against the crying need of a poor country for greater food production; but when that development is carried entirely on the backs of the poor, when the life expectancy of the field worker is cut by a decade or more while the life expectancy of the urban elite *increases* by a decade, then distributive moral factors should trump consequential cost benefit considerations offered in the name of overall welfare.

The common and sometimes criticized distinction in risk analysis between voluntary assumptions of risks is of little help. If we are uneasy over the assumption that the decision of a lower class worker in the U.S. to take a high risk job is "voluntary," despite that worker's limited technological sophistication and pressing financial needs, then surely we must reject the label of "voluntary," despite that worker's limited technological sophistication and pressing financial needs, then surely we must reject the label of "voluntary" when applied to the starving, shoeless laborer in Bangladesh, who agrees to work in a pesticide infected field.

Finally, the tendency in cost-benefit analysis to tie costs to the market prices can distort risk tradeoffs in less developed countries. The dominant assumption of most risk analysis — and of cost-benefit analysis in particular — that risks must be balanced against costs, means that in the instance of life-threatening risks human life must be assigned a price. Despite the apparent barbarity of the very concept, defenders point out that most of us are willing to assume non-zero risks to our life for the sake of reducing cost and frequently do so when we, say, buy a smaller car or accept a higher paying, but riskier job.[5] But while assigning a price to human life may have beneficial consequences against the backdrop of a single, developed country, i.e., it may help policy makers better allocate scarce safety-promoting resources, in the Third World it can unfairly relativize human worth. Since the market price of a life is tied to the capacity of a person to generate income, and since in most parts of the Third World the absence of a capital infrastructure limits the average individual's productive capacity, it follows that in the Third World a human life will be given a lower price.

If cultural variables confound risk analysis, then how can such analysis address international problems? One tempting solution must be abandoned, namely, reliance on international market pressures for acceptable risk distribution. What the market does unsuccessfully in a national context, it fails utterly to do in an international context. As Charles Perrow has pointed out, even in the developed countries "there is no impersonal fair market that rewards those that risk their lives with higher wages."[6] The "jumpers" or "glow boys" in the nuclear industry, temporary workers "who dash into a radioactive area to make repairs, will be hired for two or three weeks' work, at only six dollars an hour . . . Textile workers are not compensated for brown lung disease, nor are chemical plant workers compensated for cancer showing up ten or twenty years after exposure."[7]

The average level of unemployment in the Third World today exceeds forty percent, a figure that has frustrated the application of neo-classical economic principles to the international economy on a score of issues. With full employment, market forces will *ceteris paribus* encourage workers to make tradeoffs between job opportunities using safety as a variable. But with massive unemployment, market forces in Third World countries drive the unemployed to the jobs they are lucky enough to land, regardless of safety.

Does some criterion exist, itself not bound by culture or nation, that can give objectivity to intercultural assessments of risk distribution? At first glance nothing seems appropriate. The recent and monumental analysis of distributive justice undertaken by John Rawls[8] explicitly exempts international considerations from the reach of his two famous principles, i.e., that everyone is entitled to maximal liberty, and that inequalities in the distribution of primary goods are unjust unless everyone, including the average person in the worst affected group, stands to benefit. Rawls' reasons for nationalizing distributive justice are tied to his belief that distributive claims can be evaluated meaningfully only against a background scheme of cooperation that yields goods subject to distribution. Since nation states are customarily the agents which provide the mechanisms necessary for facilitating cooperative arrangements and for pooling and distributing the fruits of such arrangements, and since such mechanisms are conspicuously not provided on the international scale, it seems both idealistic and implausible to speak seriously of distributive justice on an international scale.

Yet, even if Rawls is correct in limiting the application of the two principles, it is noteworthy that many problems of risk assessment in a global context do not depend on *inter*-national distributive comparisons (distributions *among* nations) but on *intra*-national comparisons (distributions *within* a nation). Hence Rawls' principles have important application, even when *inter*-national distributive comparisons are excluded. For example, in assessing the fairness of exposing a disproportionate number of poor Indians to the risks of chemical accidents, Union Carbide need not enter into the moral calculus of distributing risk between Indians and U.S. citizens; it need only calculate the fairness of risk distribution among Indians. Insofar as it is unfair to distribute risks disproportionately among U.S. citizens without corresponding benefits for those at greatest risk (and sometimes not even fair when there are corresponding benefits), it is also unfair for an official of Union Carbide, or of the U.S. Government, to undertake activities in India that unfairly distribute risks among Indian citizens.[9] Hence Rawls' second principle need only be modified for application to problems of risk distribution within Third World countries. At a minimum the principle must be adjusted to include freedom from risk as one member of the bundle of primary goods normally covered by the second principle. It may also be argued that modification is needed to Rawls' condition of moderate scarcity, insofar as some Third World countries may manifest poverty sufficiently harsh that "fruitful ventures must inevitably break down".[10] Whether the application of the second principle in risk contexts must be limited to societies fulfilling the moderate scarcity proviso, or whether it need not be so limited — at least *vis a vis* the risk issue — is a question I wish to sidestep at this point. My suspicion is either the application need not be limited in the standard Rawlsian way for risk contexts, or that if it must be limited, the effects are negligible since no matter how poor by European or U.S. standards, most Third World countries are not at the point where "fruitful ventures must inevitably breakdown."

Turning next to *inter*-national issues, it is worth noting the possibility that for all his moral acumen Rawls is wrong about the scope of his own theory. As Brian Barry often notes, no scheme of cooperation need exist in order to demonstrate the unjustness of allowing toxic air pollution, generated in one country for the benefit of that country, to waft over into the unpolluted atmosphere of a second country.[11] And in Charles Beitz's influential book *Political Theory and International Relations*, Beitz points out that Rawls' argument for the inapplicability of his scheme seems not only to presuppose the *present* absence of such features as community and enforcement, but their *future* impossibility as well. What makes assertions of distributive justice and injustice meaningful, according to Beitz, are the shared features of agents to whom such assertions apply, such as rationality and purposiveness. To put it another way, what makes it wrong for me to refuse to spend $10 in order to save the life of a starving Ethiopian is our shared humanity, a humanity that may someday prompt international enforcement mechanisms.[12]

A distributive criterion for risks, then, may be appropriate for evaluating the actions of macro agents in international affairs, although the nature of that criterion remains unspecified. Giving precision to it is no easy matter, since Rawls' second principle of justice, even if applicable, must be weakened in the international context. It must be weakened because it is generally assumed that one has greater duties to one's fellow citizens than to strangers. For example, people may have a duty to help the homeless in America, but the duty no doubt stops short of providing them with special attention and love, as one is bound to do in the case of one's own children. And similarly, one may have a duty to aid the starving poor in Africa, but it does not extend to providing them social security benefits in old age, as it may be the case of one's fellow citizens. For this and other reasons, I shall not attempt here the complex task of shaping Rawls' principle to fit problems of international risk distribution (despite my belief that such a project is promising). Instead, I will show that, while not reducible to a single principle, a set of moral parameters exists that governs issues from the perspective of international distributive fairness. I plan to show how these parameters are confirmed in the context of an analysis of two pivotal moral considerations: namely, universalization under conditions of relevant similarity, and the distinction between, value-intrinsic and value-extrinsic associations.

It will help to provide concrete contexts for the problem. Consider two incidents, the first involving selling banned goods abroad.

Case #1 Morally speaking, selling banned goods abroad seems a clear example of double standards.[13] Nonetheless, developing countries sometimes argue that a given banned product is essential to meeting their standards.[14]

The U.S. Congress in 1979 passed legislation amending the Export Administration Act which gave the President broad powers to control exports.[15] But just thirty-six days after the signing of the order, on February 17, 1981, newly elected President Reagan revoked the order.[16] In a further move, President Reagan called for a repeal on the export restrictions affecting unapproved drugs and pharmaceutical products. (Banned pharmaceuticals, in contrast to other banned goods, have been subject to export restrictions for over forty years.) In defense of the Reagan initiative, drug manufacturers in the United States argued by appealing to differing cultural variables. For example, a spokesman for the American Ciba-Geigy Pharmaceuticals justified relaxing restrictions on the sale of its Entero-Vioform, a drug he agrees has been associated with blindness and paralysis, on the basis of culture-specific, cost-benefit analysis. "The government of India," he pointed out, "has requested Ciba-Geigy to continue producing the drug because it treats a dysentery problem that can be life-threatening."[17]

Before continuing, let us consider a second instance of international risk distribution, this time involving the world's worst pollution.

Case #2 A small triangle of land near Sao Paulo, Brazil, known as Cubatao, has more reported cases of cancer, stillbirths, and deformed babies than anywhere else in Brazil.[18] Factories, and especially petrochemical plants, dominate the landscape, where about 100,000 live and work. Cubatao has air considered unfit on a record number of days and has the highest level of pollutants in the rainfall recorded anywhere. In 1983, one hundred slum dwellers living alongside a gasoline duct were killed when the duct caught fire. The town was constructed during the heyday of the so-called "Brazilian miracle," a time when right-wing military rulers maintained pro-business labor laws, stable political conditions, and some of the highest profit margins in the world, conditions that allowed enormous influx of foreign investment. Even today, with the Brazilian miracle in disrepute, substantial foreign investment remains: Cubatao's 111 plants are owned by twenty-three foreign and Brazilian companies.

According to Marlise Simons of the *New York Times*, "Squatters have built rows of shacks above a vast underground grid of ducts and pipes that carry flammable, corrosive and explosive materials. Trucks lumber alongside loaded with poison, which has spilled in past accidents . . .' But we need the work,' one man said. 'We have nowhere else to go.'"[19]

The neglected responsibilities of importing countries to police more effectively incoming goods and of less developed countries in particular, such as Brazil, to improve pollution controls, are no doubt awesome. But while not forgetting these responsibilities I want for the moment to expand on the responsibilities of the exporting nations, and in particular of the developed nations. Now to hold the view that the former responsibilities preclude the latter amounts to adopting what I call the "sociocentric" view. This view holds that all nations, including Third World ones, have moral duties to tighten the inflow of dangerous goods and to insure an acceptable level of industrial risks. Government and corporate officials have fiduciary duties to their fellow citizens either through the fact of mutual citizenship, or, as in the case of the government official, because of a public trust. So far so good. But according to the sociocentric view, responsibilities for the citizens of other countries are exclusively of the officials and citizens of *those* countries.

The sociocentric view shares a packet of muddled assumptions with a sister theory, the doctrine of political realism, which is popular among international theorists perhaps because it accepts the convenient definition of statecraft as nothing more than maximizing the interests of one's nation. But these views utilize a vague premise to draw a false conclusion. The premise is that we have stronger duties to friends than to strangers; the conclusion is that our *moral* responsibilities to citizens in other countries — responsibilities other than, of course, those defined by explicit covenants — are either negligible or nonexistent. The premise is vague because it says nothing about the relative weight of duties to friends and strangers, nor about possible distinctions among kinds of friends, i.e., family members, next-door neighbors, or fellow citizens, and kinds of strangers, i.e., non-family members, passing acquaintances, citizens of foreign countries, and so on. While it may be true that a father is morally permitted to spend a dollar to repair his own child's bike instead of sending it to a starving child abroad, or a congresswoman to spend millions on national park improvement instead of sending it to Afghan rebels, this in itself cannot be extended to an unlimited endorsement of *national* favoritism.

Let us back up. Good reasons do exist for limited favoritism. The first is that social arrangements which define memberships in associations as well as the specific fiduciary duties of members, often turn out to be *efficient* means of maximizing shared values. For example, the institution of the family is a remarkably efficient way of raising the young. It is simply more efficient for a single person, or a small group of persons (as in a Kibbutz) to specialize in caring for a particular child or group of children, than it is for people in general to diffuse love and attention broadly. Nation states, too, are efficient means of organizing judicial arbitration, military defense, and resource control.

The efficiency gained from organizing society in a manner where emotional and geographical realities are recognized through associations and where "each takes care of his own," recommends the creation and development of *permanent* associations, i.e., ones whose habits and rules cannot be changed at whim. Hence when a family or nation finds itself in the happy position of possessing a relative abundance of goods or a comparative international advantage, it is not necessarily true that the surplus should be shared equally with other nations or families. To do so would necessitate the undoing of the very institutions and habits that benefit all persons in the long run.

A second reason sometimes offered for favoritism fails to justify state favoritism. The reason concerns what I have elsewhere called "value-intrinsic" associations, i.e., ones whose ends are by definition logically unobtainable without the existence of the associations themselves.[20] Such associations would no doubt include the family (in some version or other, although not necessarily in its present form) since part of the value of parenting — at least from the standpoint of the parent — appears to require the existence of the family for its realization. Hence, *ceteris paribus*, a certain amount of favoritism finds justification in associations, e.g., of family and friendship, where the favoritism seems essential for securing the value intrinsic to the association.

But the associations of family and friendship are to be contrasted with nation states, whose ends of providing judicial arbitration, military defense, and resource control could conceivably be met by other social arrangements (though perhaps not met as well). Hence, while it may be said that efficiency speaks not only on behalf of the existence of the nation state, but on behalf of a certain amount of state favoritism, additional state favoritism will be precluded insofar as the state is a value-extrinsic, not a value-intrinsic association.[21] Nation states or multinational corporations are unable to make appeals in the name of intrinsic value, for although patriotism and national pride may embody slight vestiges of our natural status as political animals, they are valued primarily for their instrumental value, that is, for their ability to secure collective goals such as self-defense, personal security, efficient legislation, and the protection of natural rights.

We may conclude that the amount of permissible favoritism by nation states or multinational corporations towards their own members in questions of international risk distribution is only the amount that can be justified in the name of efficiency. To put the matter in rule-consequential terms, a corporation or nation state is justified in adopting policies exhibiting favoritism to the extent that the favoritism itself is a non-eliminable aspect of policies which, if adopted by other relevantly similar states, would increase efficiency and thus maximize overall welfare.

The point is that precious little risk favoritism can be justified in this manner. I would stretch moral credibility, for example, to suppose that the toleration of frighteningly high levels of toxic pollution in Cubatao, Brazil, or of the export to Third World countries of most banned products — acts which tend to distribute risk to the favor of multinational corporations and First World citizens — could be justified in the name of rule-consequential sanctioned efficiency. It seems highly unlikely that these are non-eliminable aspects of policies that will maximize global welfare; rather the policies seem quite eliminable and of the sort which, if eliminated, would result in greater overall happiness. Hence, it is safe to conclude that the penchant for national egoism and for the favoring of fellow citizens over foreigners, or for favoring fellow employees and stockholders in the instance of the corporation, provides no justification for gross inequities in risk distribution.

But appeals to efficiency or to the duty to favor friends over strangers are not the only way to attempt to justify international risk inequities. A different, and in many respects more successful way, is through appeal to a nation's special needs, e.g., for economic development or the elimination of a particular problem. Lower safety, pollution, and import standards are explicitly maintained by some countries in order to achieve special ends. In Brazil, for example, lax standards of pollution enforcement are justified in the name of Brazil's desperate need for greater productivity, and the claim has a persuasive edge in a country where malnutrition is sufficiently widespread that by some estimates one in every five Brazilian children will suffer permanent brain damage.[22] In India, as mentioned earlier, special dysentery problems have prompted the government to encourage the import of drugs which, without such problems, would be considered unacceptably risky.[23] It seems morally arrogant to suppose that acts that encourage or tolerate lower standards abroad undertaken by the macro-agents of developed societies are impermissible simply for that reason. On the other hand, the convenient relativism of some corporate and government officials which excuses anything in the name of socio-centrism seems equally suspect.

Elsewhere I have argued for the need to distinguish cases of conflicting norms where the norms accepted by citizens of a host country appear inferior to those of the home country.[24] There I argued that a key distinction should be drawn between those instances in which from the standpoint of the foreign country (a) the reason for tolerating the "lower" norms refers to the country's relative level of economic development, and (b) the reason for tolerating them is related to inherent cultural beliefs, e.g., in religion or tradition. When an instance falls under the former (a) classification, a different moral analysis is required than when it falls under the latter. Here it makes sense to do what for cultural reasons cannot be done in the later instance (where inherent cultural beliefs intrude), namely, put ourselves in the shoes of the foreigner. To be more specific, it makes sense to consider ourselves and our own culture at a level of economic development relevantly similar to that of the other country. And, if, having done this, we find that *under such hypothetically altered social circumstances* we ourselves would accept the lower standards, then it is permissible to adopt the standards that appear inferior.

What lies behind the thought experiment is an age-old philosophical insight, namely, that when considering the universality of moral principles like must be compared to like, and cases must be evaluated in terms of morally relevant similarities. Hence, when considering the acceptability of practices abroad, the moralist must not err by applying wholesale, principles relevant to her own nation, but instead must ask herself what those principles would imply under the relevantly altered circumstances of the foreign nation.

Now as a practical matter of moral psychology, some acts of rational empathy are easier than others. This is reflected in the distinction between lower standards justified in terms of relative economic development and those that are not. It is relatively easy for us to empathize with the need for economic development in a poor nation, since economic well-being is an almost universally shared value, than to empathize with the need for a purer form of Muslim government, or for a more African, less European, social system. Indeed, the general principle governing the psychological possibility of rational empathy seems to be one restricting empathy to situations wherein the fundamental values motivating the decision-making of our object of empathy, are values that we share.

Let us be more specific. We can "test" the practices of shipping banned products abroad, and operating multinational branch facilities in Cubatao, by a thought experiment wherein we ask whether our own moral intuitions would find such practices acceptable were we in a state of social development relevantly similar to the countries in question. This test works in such cases because the values that presumably prompt the lower standards in foreign countries are ones we share, i.e., economic and medical well-being. For example, it makes sense to ask whether we in the United States would find levels of pollution equal to those in Cubatao justified here for the sake of economic progress, were we at Brazil's present level of economic development. If we answer yes, then we may conclude that it is permissible for U.S. multinationals to adopt the lower standards existing in Cubatao. If not, then the practice is not permissible. (I suspect, by the way, that we would *not* find Cubatao's pollution permissible.)

The same test is appropriate in the case of banned products. Were we at a hypothetically lowered state of economic development similar to Ghana or Colombia, would we allow Tris-Treated Sleepwear (sleepwear treated with a fire retardant known to be highly carcinogenic and hence banned from the United States market) to be bought and sold? Probably not. Yet, lest one think that the test always returns negative results, consider the case of India's special request for the drug, Entero-Vioform. Dysentery, a widespread and virulent health problem, is often associated with undeveloped societies because of their lack of modern systems of food handling and sanitation. It may well be that as we imagine ourselves in a relevantly similar social situation, the tradeoffs between the risks to minority sufferers and the widespread dysentery that would occur without the drug, would favor Entero-Vioform, despite its properly being banned in developed countries.

In instances where we fail to share the moral values that prompt lower safety standards, the test of rational empathy is inappropriate for reasons already stated. Here the final appeal can only be to a floor of universal rights, with the presumption in favor of permitting the lower standards unless doing so violates a basic right or conflicts with standards of *intra*-national risk distribution mentioned earlier.[25] Unable to make appeal to the values that must ultimately underlie social-welfare tradeoffs, we must presume the validity of the foreign culture's stance except in the instance where a universal human right is at stake, or where we doubt the actual acceptance of the lower norms by rank and file citizens. Appealing to rights here has special validity because rights are, by definition, moral concepts that specify moral minimums and prescribe, as it were, the lowest common denominator of permissibility.[26]

The preceding analysis has shown, then, that there are firm limits to the extent to which macro-actors can impose risks on third and fourth parties in foreign countries, even when such risks fall within existing moral and legal guiding principles already operative in the foreign country. Hence, risk sociocentrism must be abandoned. Although reached by a different route, it is noteworthy how similar in tone this conclusion is to Rawls' second principle of justice, wherein, it is necessary to demonstrate universal benefit to justify a systematic inequality.

The only remaining appeal possible for risk sociocentrism is to moral and social autonomy. The argument runs something like this: in individual affairs the value of freedom often overrides even that of moral propriety. Even if we suppose it morally wrong for a person to risk his health by drinking excessively at home, we do not want the law to restrict his activity. Hence, if the Third World countries wish to expose themselves to unreasonable risks it is not our business.

This argument will not wash. In its present form it falls prey to the obvious objection that coercion of others is not directly at issue here (as it is in the instance of law proscribing home drinking). Were multinational corporations and First World nations to restrict voluntarily their risk-imposing activities, they would be exercising *self-control*, not coercion; and while certainly affecting the actions of others, their decision not to refuse to distribute risk in certain ways would merely limit the range of options available to others (e.g., they would no longer be able to purchase certain banned goods). The actions would be what Mill thought of as "primarily self-regarding," not "primarily other regarding."[27]

Even if reformulated to refer to actions that may *discourage* (rather than coercively restrict) unreasonable risks, however, the argument fails. This is not only because in morality, as in law abiding or abetting an irresponsible action is itself colored by the shadow of the action's irresponsibility. It is also because in the instance of most Third World countries the agents who assume risks are surrogate ones, which is to say that they act on behalf of third parties to whom they are presumably responsible. Surrogate agency would be less damning were it true that both democracy and informed public opinion lay behind such agency. But in most Third World countries this is seldom the case. Most are far from democratic in the sense of democracy to which we are accustomed, and even when democratic, possess a level of technological sophistication sufficiently low to rule out the possibility of rational risk assessment. In Bhopal, India (which happens to be a good sized city), only one in a thousand households owns a telephone. It is arrogant self-delusion for us to imagine that such people make rational decisions about exposing themselves to the risks of methyl isocyanate.

The idea of a culture "choosing" to undertake risks when that culture lacks a sufficient political and technological infra-structure lies at the root of much unwitting technological imperialism. Again, consider Bhopal. Even the Indian employees of Union Carbide were unaware of methyl isocyanate's toxicity; most thought it was chiefly a skin-eye irritant, and almost none thought it could kill outright.

Outside the plant, the Indian regulatory apparatus was woefully unequal to its task. A few weeks before the disaster, the Union Carbide Plant had been granted an "environmental clearance certificate."[28] Enforcement was left not to the national government, but to the separate states. In Madhya Pradesh, the state in which Bhopal lies, fifteen factory inspectors were given the task of regulating 8,000 plants, while the inspectors themselves, sometimes lacking even typewriters and telephones, were forced to use public trains and buses to get from factory to factory. The inspectors responsible for the Bhopal area held degrees only in mechanical engineering, and knew little about chemical risks.[29] It should be added that India is considerably *more* advanced technologically, with a better technological infrastructure, than most of its Third World counterparts.

Bhopal offers many lessons about what Third World countries must do to reduce irrational technological risks, among which are the need for suitable zoning ordinances, better inspection and regulation of hazardous factories, and the acceptance of only those technologies that the local technological infrastructure is capable of handling. Similarly, there is little doubt that these same countries have unfulfilled responsibilities in other areas, including policies affecting the importation of banned products. Nicholas Ashford, for example, has offered a tidy list of recommendations: that such countries coordinate industrial development policy with environmental policy (frequently the Ministry of Industry does not talk to the Ministry of the Environment); that they develop a data base for the assessment of effects on productivity and safety of imported products; and, finally, that they maintain a centralized purchasing control mechanism for choosing products or technology that will enter the country.[30]

But realism demands that we recognize the unlikelihood of such reforms in the near future. We cannot justify our own irresponsibility by thrusting the moral burden on the shoulders of societies still adolescent in the age of technology.

To conclude, let me summarize the moral limitations shown to affect the distribution of risk in the global economy. Both market-dominated risk distribution and cultural relativism were rejected as solutions. We found each to be excessively permissive. Next, the issues of *intra*-national and *inter*-national risk distribution were separated. For *intra*-national issues, no convincing reason exists for deviating from traditional canons of distributive justice, for example, a modified version of Rawls' second principle. *Inter*-national issues, on the other hand, are more recalcitrant. Sociocentrism, however tempting, is wrongheaded. Claims for state favoritism, while sometimes defensible, were shown to be limited to those justifiable in the name of institutional efficiency. A thought-experiment relying on the principle of adjusting empathy to conditions of relevant similarity may be used to assess risk tradeoffs justified by appeal to marginal welfare, but the experiment succeeds only in instances where the values motivating decisions are shared by the macro-agent and the foreign culture. Otherwise, the empathy necessary for the thought experiment is lacking, and risk decisions must be cashed in terms of basic rights. Finally, existing facts about surrogate agency and technological infra-structure in Third World countries refute attempts to reintroduce sociocentrism into the ethics of risk assessment through appeal to national autonomy and freedom.

Notes

1. I have adopted this set of distinctions between first, second, third, and fourth party victims, from a somewhat different set appearing in Charles Perrow's book, *Normal Accidents*, (New York: Basic Books, 1984), p. 67.

2. In 1972 anywhere from 400 to 5,000 Iraqis were killed as a result of eating unlabeled, mercury-treated grain from the United States. In 1979 workers and livestock were poisoned in Egypt by the pesticide leptophos; and, more recently, hundreds died and were injured in Mexico City as a result of a liquified natural gas explosion. Nicholas A. Ashford, "Control the Transfer of Technology," in the *New York Times*, Sunday, December 9, 1984, p. 2.

3. The information used to construct the following description comes largely from an extended series of four articles appearing in the *New York Times* on December 9, 1984, shortly after the disaster, were written by Stuart Diamond. Mr. Diamond's account comes largely from interviews with workers, including Mr. Suman Dey, who was the senior officer on duty.

4. The view that the fundamental function of a legal system is the protection of rights is articulated systematically by Ronald Dworkin in *Taking Rights Seriously* (Cambridge, Mass.: Harvard University Press, 1978).

5. For an insightful account of the moral assumptions involved in risk analysis see Kristin S. Shrader-Frechette, *Risk Analysis and Scientific Method: Methodological and Ethical Problems with Evaluating Societal Hazards* (Hingham, MA: D. Reidel Publishing Co., 1985).

6. Perrow, *Normal Accidents*, p. 68.

7. Perrow, *Normal Accidents*, p. 68.

8. John Rawls, *A Theory of Justice* (Cambridge, Mass.: Harvard University Press, 1971).

9. Here I don't mean to assert the unquestionable applicability of Rawls' principle to *intra*-national risk assessment since to do so would necessarily involve a comparative assessment of Rawls' distributive approach in contrast to his competitors'. I want to claim only that *if* one accepts Rawls' principle as applying to analysis of one's own society, then one should also accept it in application to other societies. My own sympathies are Rawlsian, but I shall not presume their accuracy here.

10. Rawls' specific characterization of the "moderate scarcity" proviso (which he borrows from Hume) is that "natural and other resources are not so abundant that schemes of cooperation become superflous, nor are conditions so harsh that fruitful ventures must inevitably break down." See John Rawls' *A Theory of Justice* (Cambridge, Mass.: Belknap Press of Harvard University Press, 1971), pp. 127–128).

11. Brian Barry, "The Case for a New International Economic Order," *Ethics, Economics, and Law: Nomos Vol. XXIV*, ed. J. Roland Pennock and John W. Chapman (New York: New York University Press, 1982).

12. Beitz also notes that a common error prompting the denial of international distributive justice is the assumption that international mechanisms of community and enforcement must exactly resemble existing ones at the national level. Other arrangements, while different from those associated with nation states, would be capable of giving substance to distributive claims. Charles Beitz, *Political Theory and International Relations* (Princeton, N.J.: University Press, 1979), parts II and III, and "Cosmopolitan Ideals and National Sentiment," *The Journal of Philosophy*, Vol. LXXX, No. 10, October 1983, pp. 591–560.

13. A 1979 United Nations resolution stressed the need to "exchange information on hazardous chemicals and unsafe pharmaceutical products that have been banned in their territories and to discourage, in consultation with importing countries, the exportation of such products. Quoted in "Products Unsafe at Home Are Still Unloaded Abroad," in *New York Times*, Sunday, August 22, 1982, p. 22.

14. The problem, by the way, is not limited to the United States, since Europe exports even more hazardous products to developing countries than does the U.S.. See "Control the Transfer of Technology," by Nicholas Ashford in the *New York Times*, Sunday, December 9, 1984, p. 2F.

15. With this as a basis, President Carter issued on January 15, 1981, an executive order that asked for a comprehensive approach to hazardous exports. The complex notification schemes for alerting foreign countries about hazards were to be coordinated and streamlined. An annual list of all products banned in the U.S. was to be compiled and made available, and government officials were empowered to seek international agreements on hazardous exports. Finally, the order required the creation of export controls on those "extremely hazardous substances" that constituted a "substantial threat to human health or safety or the environment." See "Control the Transfer of Technology," p. 2F.

16. Industry opposition, described as "massive" by Edward B. Cohen, Executive director of the Carter Administration's Task Force on Hazardous Exports Policy, probably was what killed the Carter plan. See "Products Unsafe at Home," p. 22.

17. Quoted in "Products Unsafe at Home," p. 22.

18. Most of the information about Cubatao described here is from Marlise Simons, "Some Smell a Disaster in Brazil Industry Zone," *New York Times*, May 18, 1985, p. 4.

19. Simons, "Some Smell a Disaster," p. 4.

20. In February, 1985, I presented a paper, as yet unpublished, to the Great Expectations Philosophy Forum at Great Expectations Bookstore, Evanston, Illinois. This paper will eventually constitute Chapter 4 of a book I am finishing, entitled *Ethics in the International Order*.

21. "Duties to Strangers," especially pp. 20–26.

22. See "Controlling Interest," a film produced and distributed by California Newsreel. (California, 1977).

23. "Products Unsafe at Home," p. 4.

24. See "Multinational Decision-Making: Recycling International Norms," *Journal of Business Ethics*, (Summer, 1985).

25. In this paper I am able only to sketch what is worked out more fully in "Multinational Decision-Making: Reconciling International Norms" (cited above) regarding the thought-experiment of rational empathy and the use of basic rights in contexts where host country norms appear

substandard from the perspective of the host country. Anyone interested in the fuller account should refer to that paper.

26. In attempting to isolate the list of rights with true claim to cultural universality, we might, for example, consult international documents such as the U.N. Declaration.

27. See John Stuart Mill, *On Liberty.*

28. Surprisingly, the Union Carbide plant in Bhopal was considered almost a model for other plants. In contrast to a steel plant in the same state that had 25 fatalities in the past year, Union Carbide had in recent years only a single fatal accident.

29. Robbert Reinhold, "Disaster in Bhopal: Where Does Blame Lie?" *New York Times,* January 31, 1985, p. 1.

30. Ashford, "Control the Transfer of Technology," p. 2F.

◆ ◆ ◆

DISCUSSION QUESTIONS

1. De George observes that critics of multinational corporations claim that MNCs "are destroying local cultures and substituting for them the tinsel of American life and the worst aspects of its culture." Even if this negative characterization is true, why would it be of moral significance?

2. De George points out the flaw in applying U.S. standards to other countries. How would De George evaluate the following situation: A multinational corporation manufactures identical products in the United States and Mexico. The Mexican workers are paid well by Mexican standards, but they still receive much less than their American counterparts. Both American and Mexican products are sold for the same price in the United States. The Mexican operation thus generates substantially greater profits. Are the Mexican workers being treated badly? Does the corporation have a moral responsibility somehow to share its higher profits with Mexico or may the company simply appropriate all of its profits to itself?

3. Many people deal with the fact that cultures often differ in their moral norms by saying "when in Rome, do as the Romans do." Bowie, however, concludes his analysis of cultural relativism by claiming, "only in special circumstances is it right to do in Rome as the Romans do." What are those special circumstances? Do you agree with Bowie?

4. What do your ordinary ethical intuitions tell you is the proper way to handle the situation Donaldson discusses (a multinational company [C] adopts a corporate practice [P] that is morally and/or legally permitted in C's host country [B], but not in C's home country [A])?

5. Evaluate how satisfactory Donaldson's "ethical algorithm" is.

6. Do you agree with Donaldson's rejection of market-dominated risk distribution and cultural relativism? Do you agree with his use of Rawls' theory?

CASE 17.1

◆ ◆ ◆

The Ethics of Prison Labor

Is there anything unethical about using prisoners for profit? A six-month investigation by *Business Week* argued that Chinese prisons and labor camps are manufacturing a wide range of exports. It is illegal to import products made by prisoners into the United States, but many countries allow the practice because prison goods are inexpensive. Chinese officials deny using prison labor for exports. The *Business Week* study, however, claims that the true origin of such Chinese exports is concealed and that these products do find their way into American markets.

Critics of the practice denounce it as forced labor. They also claim that because China imprisons political dissidents, it makes matters worse by profiting from such a violation of its citizens' human rights. They argue that China should be punished for the practice — perhaps with higher tariffs that would raise the price of their goods and make their exports less attractive.

It is estimated that China's prison system contains 10 million inmates. Prisoners work up to 15 hours a day for little, if any, remuneration. American prisoners produce license plates or other goods sold by state governments, but Chinese prisoners manufacture everything from textiles to shoes to parts for electronics goods. One prison factory made $28 million in foreign-exchange earnings over a five-year period, making it a top textile company in its province. Each year China probably exports hundreds of millions of dollars worth of products produced from prison labor. China's annual trade surplus with the United States is currently $10 billion, a figure surpassed only by Japan and Taiwan. ◆

Discussion Questions

1. Is China doing anything unethical by using prison labor in this way? Is this really any different from practices in American prisons? Is there anything wrong with a country's benefiting from prison labor?

2. As a way of competing against cheap foreign labor, should the United States aggressively develop prison factories? What if it paid prisoners for their work, but at far below market rates?

3. From an ethical viewpoint, would it matter to you whether the Chinese prisoners doing the labor are rapists, murderers, or political dissidents? Dissent is regarded as a serious crime in China. Do other countries have a right to object to what China would regard as an internal matter?

4. Would there be anything unethical about officials in a foreign country saying that they objected so strongly to the way homeless people are treated in America that they were barring U.S. imports until the homeless were treated in a more humane manner?

5. Is the U.S. law barring imports produced by foreign prisoners ethically

justifiable? Whom does the law help? Whom does it hurt? Would a U.S. corporation be doing anything unethical if it successfully concealed from legal authorities the fact that it imported inexpensive Chinese prison goods and passed along the savings directly to the consumer in the form of low prices?

Source

"China's Ugly Export Secret: Prison Labor," *Business Week*, April 22, 1991, 42–46.

CASE 17.2

◆ ◆ ◆

The Mequiladoras

In 1965, The United States and Mexico reached an agreement that allowed U.S. companies to establish operations in Mexico free from nearly all tariffs and trade restrictions. Known as the *mequiladoras,* nearly 2,000 of these plants now exist just south of the border between the two countries where workers perform the final, labor intensive assembly of products from parts shipped primarily from the United States. Foreign-based multinational corporations employ roughly 500,000 workers. These companies, mostly headquartered in the United States, range from such giants as General Motors, General Electric, Zenith, and RCA to Cohart Products, Inc., a small, family-owned, pipe-fixture company from California.

Businesses are pulled to this region by cheap labor. The mequiladora industry is based on low Mexican wages, which range from about $25 to $50 a week for a 49-hour workweek. Compared to the nearly $15 per hour U.S. workers make in wages and benefits, the lower salaries of the Mexican workers are extremely attractive for many businesses. In addition, high Mexican unemployment leads to low absenteeism and high productivity from those workers who are employed.

Critics of the mequiladoras say that they are nothing more than modern day sweatshops. They say that the wages, even if high by Mexican standards, are still exploitative. Critics also allege a variety of questionable labor practices, such as ensuring a docile labor force by hiring obedient, teenage girls and then pressuring them to leave when they reach their late twenties. Living conditions for plant workers are difficult. Shortages of housing and water are severe. Shantytowns and unhealthy living conditions are not uncommon. Annual turnover at some factories is as high as 100 percent.

In addition to cheap labor, another appeal of doing business in Mexico is the absence of environmental regulations with the strict enforcement that companies face in the United States. As a result, substantial environmental damage has been done, including ongoing water and air pollution. Pollutants range from raw sewage to highly toxic industrial wastes, and their harm is not limited to Mexico. For example, a public health emergency was declared for months in an Arizona town because a river originating in Mexico was so polluted that it was apparently responsible for soaring rates of hepatitis in local residents. The water of some Texas wells has also been contaminated.

Not surprisingly, U.S. workers are strenuously opposed to the movement of jobs south of the border. For example, a Missouri company closed its Kansas City plant, putting out of work nearly 200 people who had been making $9.00 per hour. The work was then moved to Mexico, where the company offered $1.00 per hour. U.S. workers also claim that companies can keep wages lower by threatening to move U.S. operations to Mexico. Public officials cite the cost of unemployment that follows a U.S. corporation's move to Mexico.

Defenders of the mequiladoras argue that the lower Mexican wages can actually save American jobs by helping a company become more stable financially. They also point out that the only way American corporations can compete internationally is to take advantage of lower wages offshore. The average hourly cost of wages and benefits in 1989 in Singapore was $2.25; in South Korea, $2.94; and in Taiwan, $3.71. Jobs moved from the United States to Mexico, they argue, are at least staying in North America. ◆

Discussion Questions

1. Is there anything morally questionable about corporations' use of the mequiladora industry?

2. Are the local workers being exploited?

3. Should there be any restrictions on a corporation's ability to take advantage of low labor costs or less restrictive environmental rules in different places in the world?

Sources

"Charlie Crowder Sees Utopia, And It's A Border Town," *Business Week*, July 31, 1989, 35–36.

"Mexico: A New Economic Era," *Business Week*, November 12, 1990, 102–113.

Russell, James W., "U.S. Sweatshops Across the Rio Grande," *Business and Society Review* no. 50 (Summer 1987), 17–20.

Suro, Roberto, "Border Boom's Dirty Residue Imperils U.S.–Mexico Trade," *New York Times*, March 31, 1991, 1, 16.

ADDITIONAL READINGS

Barnet, Richard J., and Ronald E. Muller, *Global Reach: The Power of the Multinational Corporation* (New York: Simon & Schuster, 1974).

Donaldson, Thomas, *The Ethics of International Business* (Oxford: Oxford University Press, 1989).

Hoffman, W. Michael, Ann E. Lange, and David A. Fedo, eds., *Ethics and the Multinational Enterprise* (New York: University Press of America, 1986).

Tavis, Lee, ed., *Multinational Managers and Poverty in the Third World* (Notre Dame, IN: Notre Dame University Press, 1982).

◆ ◆ ◆

CHAPTER 18

Business and the Environment

Modern Western societies have developed a series of questionable and self-defeating beliefs about our natural environment: The earth holds unlimited resources for human consumption; humans may use (or abuse) the planet's plants, animals, and minerals as they want; and the earth can handle a virtually infinite amount of pollution. The last two centuries of conducting business according to these attitudes, however, have led to a hole in the earth's ozone layer, the threat of global warming, and carcinogens in the air and water. One of the most pressing challenges for the future is for corporations to be environmentally responsible as well as profitable.

This chapter begins with W. Michael Hoffman's argument for approaching ethical dilemmas with a biocentric, rather than a homeocentric point of view. David Hanson considers the specific problem of promoting economic development while restraining development. Then Peter Singer and Eric Katz address the issue of human use of other animals. Singer defends the rights of these animals, while Katz rejects them.

W. Michael Hoffman

BUSINESS AND ENVIRONMENTAL ETHICS

The business ethics movement, from my perspective, is still on the march. And the environmental movement, after being somewhat silent for the past twenty years, has once again captured our attention — promising to be a major social force in the 1990s. Much will be written in the next few years trying to tie together these two movements. This is one such effort.

Concern over the environment is not new. Warnings came out of the 1960s in the form of burning rivers, dying lakes, and oil-fouled oceans. Radioactivity was found in our food, DDT in mother's milk, lead and mercury in our water. Every breath of air in the North American hemisphere was reported as contaminated. Some said these were truly warnings from Planet Earth of eco-catastrophe, unless we could find limits to our growth and changes in our lifestyle.

Over the past few years Planet Earth began to speak to us even more loudly than before, and we began to listen more than before. The message was ominous, somewhat akin to God warning Noah. It spoke through droughts, heat waves, and forest fires, raising fears of global warming due to the buildup of carbon dioxide and other gases in the atmosphere. It warned us by raw sewage and medical wastes washing up on our beaches, and by devastating oil spills—one despoiling Prince William Sound and its wildlife to such an extent that it made us weep. It spoke to us through increased skin cancers and discoveries of holes in the ozone layer caused by our use of chlorofluorocarbons. It drove its message home through the rapid and dangerous cutting and burning of our primitive forests at the rate of one football field a second, leaving us even more vulnerable to greenhouse gases like carbon dioxide and eliminating scores of irreplaceable species daily. It rained down on us in the form of acid, defoliating our forests and poisoning our lakes and streams. Its warnings were found on barges roaming the seas for places to dump tons of toxic incinerator ash. And its message exploded in our faces at Chernobyl and Bhopal, reminding us of past warnings at Three Mill Island and Love Canal.

Senator Albert Gore said in 1988: "The fact that we face an ecological crisis without any precedent in historic times is no longer a matter of any dispute worthy of recognition."[1] The question, he continued, is not whether there is a problem, but how we will address it. This will be the focal point for a public policy debate which requires the full participation of two of its major players — business and government. The debate must clarify such fundamental questions as: (1) What obligation does business have to help with our environmental crisis? (2) What is the proper relationship between business and government, especially when faced with a social problem of the magnitude of the environment crisis? And (3) what rationale should be used for making and justifying decisions to protect the environment? Corporations, and society in general for that matter, have yet to answer these questions satisfactorily. In the first section of this paper I will briefly address the first two questions. In the final two sections I will say a few things about the third question.

From *Business Ethics Quarterly*, 1, no. 2 (April 1991), 169–184. Reprinted by permission.

I.

In a 1989 keynote address before the "Business, Ethics and the Environment" conference at the Center for Business Ethics, Norman Bowie offered some answers to the first two questions.

> Business does not have an obligation to protect the environment over and above what is required by law; however, it does have a moral obligation to avoid intervening in the political arena in order to defeat or weaken environmental legislation.[2]

I disagree with Bowie on both counts.

Bowie's first point is very Friedmanesque.[3] The social responsibility of business is to produce goods and services and to make profit for its shareholders, while playing within the rules of the market game. These rules, including those to protect the environment, are set by the government and the courts. To do more than is required by these rules is, according to this position, unfair to business. In order to perform its proper function, every business must respond to the market and operate in the same arena as its competitors. As Bowie puts this:

> An injunction to assist in solving societal problems [including depletion of natural resources and pollution] makes impossible demands on a corporation because, at the practical level, it ignores the impact that such activities have on profit.[4]

If, as Bowie claims, consumers are not willing to respond to the cost and use of environmentally friendly products and actions, then it is not the responsibility of business to respond or correct such market failure.

Bowie's second point is a radical departure from this classical position in contending that business should not lobby against the government's process to set environmental regulations. To quote Bowie:

> Far too many corporations try to have their cake and eat it too. They argue that it is the job of government to correct for market failure and then they use their influence and money to defeat or water down regulations designed to conserve and protect the environment.[5]

Bowie only recommends this abstinence of corporate lobbying in the case of environmental regulations. He is particularly concerned that politicians, ever mindful of their reelection status, are already reluctant to pass environmental legislation which has huge immediate costs and in most cases very long-term benefits. This makes the obligations of business to refrain from opposing such legislation a justified special case.

I can understand why Bowie argues these points. He seems to be responding to two extreme approaches, both of which are inappropriate. Let me illustrate these extremes by the following two stories.

At the Center's First National Conference on Business Ethics, Harvard Business School Professor George Cabot Lodge told of a friend who owned a paper company on the banks of a New England stream. On the first Earth Day in 1970, his friend was converted to the cause of environmental protection. He became determined to stop his company's pollution of the stream, and marched off to put his new-found religion into action. Later, Lodge learned his friend went broke, so he went to investigate. Radiating a kind of ethical purity, the friend told Lodge that he spent millions to stop the pollution and thus could no longer compete with other firms that did not follow his example. So the company went under, 500 people lost their jobs, and the stream remained polluted.

When Lodge asked why his friend hadn't sought help from the state or federal government for stricter standards for everyone, the man replied that was not the American way, that government should not interfere with business activity, and that private enterprise could do the job alone. In fact, he felt it was the social responsibility of business to solve environmental problems, so he was proud that he had set an example for others to follow.

The second story portrays another extreme. A few years ago "Sixty Minutes" interviewed a manager of a chemical company that was discharging effluent into a river in upstate New York. At the time, the dumping was legal, though a bill to prevent it was pending in Congress. The manager remarked that he hoped the bill would pass, and that he certainly would support it as a responsible citizen. However, he also said he approved of his company's efforts to defeat the bill and of the firm's policy of dumping wastes in the meantime. After all, isn't the proper role of business to make as much profit as possible within the bounds of law? Making the laws — setting the rules of the game — is the role of government, not business. While wearing his business hat the manager had a job to do, even if it meant doing something that he strongly opposed as a private citizen.

Both stories reveal incorrect answers to the questions posed earlier, the proof of which is found in the fact that neither the New England stream nor the New York river was made any cleaner. Bowie's points are intended to block these two extremes. But to avoid these extremes, as Bowie does, misses the real managerial and ethical failure of the stories. Although the paper company owner and the chemical company manager had radically different views of the ethical responsibilities of business, both saw business and government performing separate roles, and neither felt that business ought to cooperate with government to solve environmental problems.[6]

If the business ethics movement has led us anywhere in the past fifteen years, it is to the position that business has an ethical responsibility to become a more active partner in dealing with social concerns. Business must creatively find ways to become a part of solutions, rather than being a part of problems. Corporations can and must develop a conscience, as Ken Goodpaster and others have argued — and this includes an environmental conscience.[7] Corporations should not isolate themselves from participation in solving our environmental problems, leaving it up to others to find the answers and to tell them what not to do.

Corporations have special knowledge, expertise, and resources which are invaluable in dealing with the environmental crisis. Society needs the ethical vision and cooperation of all its players to solve its most urgent problems, especially one that involves the very survival of the planet itself. Business must work with government to find appropriate solutions. It should lobby for good environmental legislation and lobby against bad legislation, rather than isolating itself from the legislative process as Bowie suggests. It should not be ethically quixotic and try to go it alone, as our paper company owner tried to do, nor should it be ethically inauthentic and fight against what it believes to be environmentally sound policy, as our chemical company manager tried to do. Instead business must develop and demonstrate moral leadership.

There are examples of corporations demonstrating such leadership, even when this has been a risk to their self-interest. In the area of environmental moral leadership one might cite DuPont's discontinuing its Freon products, a $750-million-a-year-business, because of their possible negative effects on the ozone layer, and Proctor and Gamble's manufacture of concentrated fabric softener and detergents which require less packaging. But some might argue, as Bowie does, that the real burden for environmental change lies with consumers, not with corporations. If we as consumers are willing to accept the harm done to the environment by favoring environmentally unfriendly products, corporations have no moral obligation to change so long as they obey environmental law. This is even more the case, so the argument goes, if corporations must take risks or sacrifice profits to do so.

This argument fails to recognize that we quite often act differently when we think of ourselves as *consumers* than when we think of ourselves as *citizens*. Mark Sagoff, concerned about our over-reliance on economic solutions, clearly characterizes this dual nature of our decision making.[8] As consumers, we act more often than not for ourselves; as citizens, we take on a broader vision and do what is in the best interests of the community. I often shop for things I don't vote for. I might support recycling referendums, but buy products in nonreturnable bottles. I am not proud of this, but I suspect this is more true of most of us than not. To stake our environmental future on our consumer willingness to pay is surely shortsighted, perhaps even disastrous.

I am not saying that we should not work to be ethically committed citizen consumers, and investors for that matter. I agree with Bowie that "consumers bear a far greater responsibility for preserving and protecting the environment than they have actually exercised,"[9] but activities which affect the environment should not be left up to what we, acting as consumers, are willing to tolerate or accept. To do this would be to use a market-based method of reasoning to decide on an issue which should be determined instead on the basis of our ethical responsibilities as a member of a social community.

Furthermore, consumers don't make the products, provide the services, or enact the legislation which can be either environmentally friendly or unfriendly. Grass roots boycotts and lobbying efforts are important, but we also need leadership and mutual cooperation from business and government in setting forth ethical environmental policy. Even Bowie admits that perhaps business has a responsibility to educate the public and promote environmentally responsible behavior. But I am suggesting that corporate moral leadership goes far beyond public educational campaigns. It requires moral vision, commitment, and courage, and involves risk and sacrifice. I think business is capable of such a challenge. Some are even engaging in such a challenge. Certainly the business ethics movement should do nothing short of encouraging such leadership. I feel morality demands such leadership.

II.

If business has an ethical responsibility to the environment which goes beyond obeying environmental law, what criterion should be used to guide and justify such action? Many corporations are making environmentally friendly decisions where they see there are profits to be made by doing so. They are wrapping themselves in green where they see a green bottom line as a consequence. This rationale is also being used as a strategy by environmentalists to encourage more businesses to become environmentally conscientious. In December 1989 the highly respected Worldwatch Institute published an article by one of its senior researchers entitled "Doing Well by Doing Good" which gives numerous examples of corporations improving their pocketbooks by improving the environment. It concludes by saying that "fortunately, businesses that work to preserve the environment can also make a buck."[10]

In a recent Public Broadcast Corporation documentary entitled "Profit the Earth," several efforts are depicted of what is called the "new environmentalism" which induces corporations to do things for the environment by appealing to their self-interest. The Environmental Defense Fund is shown encouraging agribusiness in Southern California to irrigate more efficiently and profit by selling the water saved to the city of Los Angeles. This in turn will help save Mono Lake. EDF is also shown lobbying for emissions trading that would allow utility companies which are under their emission allotments to sell their "pollution rights" to those companies which are over their allotments. This is for the purpose of reducing acid rain. Thus the frequent strategy of the new environmentalists is to get business to help solve environmental problems by finding profitable or virtually costless ways for them to participate. They feel that compromise, not confrontation, is the only way to save the earth. By using the tools of the free enterprise system, they are in search of win-win solutions, believing that such solutions are necessary to take us beyond what we have so far been able to achieve.

I am not opposed to these efforts; in most cases I think they should be encouraged. There is certainly nothing wrong with making money while protecting the environment, just as there is nothing wrong with feeling good about doing one's duty. But if business is adopting or being encouraged to adopt the view that good environmentalism is good business, then I think this poses a danger for the environmental ethics movement — a danger which has an analogy in the business ethics movement.

As we all know, the position that good ethics is good business is being used more and more by corporate executives to justify the building of ethics into their companies and by business ethics consultants to gain new clients. For example, the Business Roundtable's *Corporate Ethics* report states:

> The corporate community should continue to refine and renew efforts to improve performance and manage change effectively through programs in corporate ethics . . . corporate ethics is a strategic key to survival and profitability in this era of fierce competitiveness in a global economy.[11]

And, for instance, the book *The Power of Ethical Management* by Kenneth Blanchard and Norman Vincent Peale states in big red letters on the cover jacket that "Integrity Pays! You Don't Have to Cheat to Win." The blurb on the inside cover promises that the book "gives hard-hitting, practical, *ethical* strategies that build profits, productivity, and long-term success."[12] Whoever would have guessed that business ethics could deliver all that! In such ways business ethics gets marketed as the newest cure for what ails corporate America.

Is the rationale that good ethics is good business a proper one for business ethics? I think not. One thing that the study of ethics has taught us over the past 2500 years is that being ethical may on occasion require that we place the interests of others ahead of or at least on par with our own interests. And this implies that the ethical thing to do, the morally right thing to do, may not be in our own self-interest. What happens when the right thing is not the best thing for the business?

Although in most cases good ethics may be good business, it should not be advanced as the only or even the main reason for doing business ethically. When the crunch comes, when ethics conflicts with the firm's interests, any ethics program that has not already faced up to this possibility is doomed to fail because it will undercut the rationale of the program itself. We should promote business ethics, not because good ethics is good business, but because we are morally required to adopt the moral point of view in all our dealings — and business is no exception. In business, as in all other human endeavors, we must be prepared to pay the costs of ethical behavior.

There is a similar danger in the environmental movement with corporations choosing or being wooed to be environmentally friendly on the grounds that it will be in their self-interest. There is the risk of participating in the movement for the wrong reasons. But what does it matter if business cooperates for reasons other than the right reasons, as long as it cooperates? It matters if business believes or is led to believe that it only has a duty to be environmentally conscientious in those cases where such actions either require no sacrifice or actually make a profit. And I am afraid this is exactly what is happening. I suppose it wouldn't matter if the environmental cooperation of business was only needed in those cases where it was also in business' self-interest. But this is surely not the case, unless one begins to really reach and talk about that amorphous concept "long-term" self-interest. Moreover, long-term interests, I suspect, are not what corporations or the new environmentalists have in mind in using self-interest as a reason for environmental action.

I am not saying we should abandon attempts to entice corporations into being ethical, both environmentally and in other ways, by pointing out and providing opportunities where good ethics is good business. And there are many places where such attempts fit well in both the business and environmental ethics movements. But we must be careful not to cast this as the proper guideline for business' ethical responsibility. Because when it is discovered that many ethical actions are not necessarily good for business, at least in the short-run, then the rationale based on self-interest will come up morally short, and both ethical movements will be seen as deceptive and shallow.

III.

What is the proper rationale for responsible business action toward the environment? A minimalist principle is to refrain from causing or prevent the causing of unwarranted harm, because failure to do so would violate certain moral rights not to be harmed. There is, of course, much debate over what harms are indeed unwarranted due to conflict of rights and questions about whether some harms are offset by certain benefits. Norm Bowie, for example, uses the harm principle, but contends that business does not violate it as long as it obeys environmental law. Robert Frederick, on the other hand, convincingly argues that the harm principle morally requires business to find ways to prevent certain harm it causes even if such harm violates no environmental law.[13]

However, Frederick's analysis of the harm principle is largely cast in terms of harm caused to human beings and the violation of rights of human beings. Even when he hints at the possible moral obligation to protect the environment when no one is caused unwarranted harm, he does so by suggesting that we look to what we, as human beings, value.[14] This is very much in keeping with a humanistic position of environmental ethics which claims that only human beings have rights or moral standing because only human beings have intrinsic value. We may have duties with regard to nonhuman things (penguins, trees, islands, etc.) but only if such duties are derivative from duties we have toward human beings. Nonhuman things are valuable only if valued by human beings.

Such a position is in contrast to a naturalistic view of environmental ethics which holds that natural things other than human beings are intrinsically valuable and have, therefore, moral standing. Some naturalistic environmentalists only include other sentient animals in the framework of being deserving of moral consideration; others include all things which are alive or which are an integral part of an ecosystem. This latter view is sometimes called a biocentric environmental ethic as opposed to the homocentric view which sees all moral claims in terms of human beings and their interests. Some characterize these two views as deep *versus* shallow ecology.

The literature on these two positions is vast and the debate is ongoing. The conflict between them goes to the heart of environmental ethics and is crucial to our making of environmental policy and to our perception of moral duties to the environment, including business'. I strongly favor the biocentric view. And although this is not the place to try to adequately argue for it, let me unfurl its banner for just a moment.

A version of R. Routley's "last man" example[15] might go something like this: Suppose you were the last surviving human being and were soon to die from nuclear poisoning, as all other human and sentient animals have died before you. Suppose also that it is within your power to destroy all remaining life, or to make it simpler, the last tree which could continue to flourish and propagate if left alone. Furthermore you will not suffer if you do not destroy it. Would you do anything wrong by cutting it down? The deeper ecological view would say yes because you would be destroying something that has value in and of itself, thus making the world a poorer place.

It might be argued that the only reason we may find the tree valuable is because human beings generally find trees of value either practically or aesthetically, rather than the atoms or molecules they might turn into if changed from their present form. The issue is whether the tree has value only in its relation to human beings or whether it has a value deserving of moral consideration inherent in itself in its present form. The biocentric position holds that when we find something wrong with destroying the tree, as we should, we do so because we are responding to an intrinsic value in the natural object, not to a value we give to it. This is a view which argues against a humanistic environmental ethic and which urges us to channel our moral obligations accordingly.

Why should one believe that nonhuman living things or natural objects forming integral parts of ecosystems have intrinsic value? One can respond to this question by pointing out the serious weaknesses and problems of human chauvinism.[16] More complete responses lay out a framework of concepts and beliefs which provides a coherent picture of the biocentric view with human beings as a part of a more holistic value system. But the final answer to the question hinges on what criterion one decides to use for determining moral worth — rationality, sentience, or a deeper biocentric one. Why should we adopt the principle of attributing intrinsic value to all living beings, or even to all natural objects, rather than just to human beings? I suspect Arne Naess gives as good an answer as can be given.

> Faced with the ever returning question of 'Why?,' we have to stop somewhere. Here is a place where we well might stop. We shall admit that the value in itself is something shown in intuition. We attribute intrinsic value to ourselves and our nearest, and the validity of further identification can be contested, and *is* contested by many. The negation may, however, also be attacked through a series of 'whys?' Ultimately, we are in the same human predicament of having to start somewhere, at least for the moment. We must stop somewhere and treat where we then stand as a foundation.[17]

In the final analysis, environmental biocentrism is adopted or not depending on whether it is seen to provide a deeper, richer, and more ethically compelling view of the nature of things.

If this deeper ecological position is correct, then it ought to be reflected in the environmental movement. Unfortunately, for the most part, I do not think this is being done, and there is a price to be paid for not doing so. Moreover, I fear that even those who are of the biocentric persuasion are using homocentric language and strategies to bring business and other major players into the movement because they do not think they will be successful otherwise. They are afraid, and undoubtedly for good reason, that the large part of society, including business, will not be moved by arguments regarding the intrinsic value and rights of natural things. It is difficult enough to get business to recognize and act on their responsibilities to human beings and things of human interest. Hence many environmentalists follow the counsel of Spinoza:

> . . . it is necessary that while we are endeavoring to attain our pur-pose . . . we are compelled . . . to speak in a manner intelligible to the multitude . . . For we can gain from the multitude no small advantages. . . .[18]

I understand the temptation of environmentalists employing a homocentric strategy, just as I understand business ethicists using the rationale that good ethics is good business. Both want their important work to succeed. But just as with the good ethics is good business tack, there are dangers in being a closet ecocentrist. The ethicists in both cases fail to reveal the deeper moral base of their positions because it's a harder sell. Business ethics gets marketed in terms of self-interest, environmental ethics in terms of human interest.

A major concern in using the homocentric view to formulate policy and law is that nonhuman nature will not receive the moral consideration it deserves. It might be argued, however, that by appealing to the interests and rights of human beings, in most cases nature as a whole will be protected. That is, if we are concerned about a wilderness area, we can argue that its survival is important to future generations who will otherwise be deprived of contact with its unique wildlife. We can also argue that it is important to the aesthetic pleasure of certain individuals or that, if it is destroyed, other recreational areas will become overcrowded. In this way we stand a chance to save the wilderness area without having to refer to our moral obligations to respect the intrinsic value of the spotted owl or of the old-growth forest. This is simply being strategically savvy. To trot out our deeper ecological moral convictions runs the risk of our efforts being ignored, even ridiculed, by business leaders and policy makers. It also runs head-on against a barrage of counter arguments that human interests take precedence over nonhuman interests. In any event it will not be in the best interest of the wilderness area we are trying to protect. Furthermore, all of the above homocentric arguments happen to be true — people will suffer if the wilderness area is destroyed.

In most cases, what is in the best interests of human beings may also be in the best interests of the rest of nature. After all, we are in our present environmental crisis in large part because we have not been ecologically intelligent about what is in our own interest — just as business has encountered much trouble because it has failed to see its interest in being ethically sensitive. But if the environmental movement relies only on arguments based on human interests, then it perpetuates the danger of making environmental policy and law on the basis of our strong inclination to fulfill our immediate self-interests, on the basis of our consumer viewpoints, on the basis of our willingness to pay. There will always be a tendency to allow our short-term interests to eclipse our long-term interests and the long-term interest of humanity itself. Without some grounding in a deeper environmental ethic with obligations to nonhuman natural things, then the temptation to view our own interests in disastrously short-term ways is that much more encouraged. The biocentric view helps to block this temptation.

Furthermore, there are many cases where what is in human interest is not in the interest of other natural things. Examples range from killing leopards for stylish coats to destroying a forest to build a golf course. I am not convinced that homocentric arguments, even those based on long-term human interests, have much force in protecting the interests of such natural things. Attempts to make these interests coincide might be made, but the point is that from a homocentric point of view the leopard and the forest have no morally relevant interests to consider. It is simply fortuitous if nonhuman natural interests coincide with human interests, and are thereby valued and protected. Let us take an example from the work of Christopher Stone. Suppose a stream has been polluted by a business. From a homocentric point of view, which serves as the basis for our legal system, we can only correct the problem through finding some harm done to human beings who use the stream. Reparation for such harm might involve cessation of the pollution and restoration of the stream, but it is also possible that the business might settle with the people by paying them for their damages and continue to pollute the stream. Homocentrism provides no way for the stream to be made whole again unless it is in the interests of human beings to do so. In short it is possible for human beings to sell out the stream.[19]

I am not saying that human interests cannot take precedence over nonhuman interests when there are conflicts. For this we need to come up with criteria for deciding on interspecific conflicts of interests, just as we do for intraspecific conflicts of interest among human beings.[20] But this is a different problem from holding that nonhuman natural things have no interests or value deserving of moral consideration. There are times when causing harm to natural things is morally unjustifiable when there are no significant human interests involved and even when there are human interests involved. But only a deeper ecological ethic than homocentrism will allow us to defend this.

Finally, perhaps the greatest danger that biocentric environmentalists run in using homocentric strategies to further the movement is the loss of the very insight that grounded their ethical concern in the first place. This is nicely put by Lawrence Tribe:

> What the environmentalist may not perceive is that, by couching his claim in terms of human self-interest—by articulating environmental goals wholly in terms of human needs and preferences — he may be helping to legitimate a system of discourse which so structures human thought and feeling as to erode, over the long run, the very sense of obligation which provided the initial impetus for his own protective efforts.[21]

Business ethicists run a similar risk in couching their claims in terms of business self-interest.

The environmental movement must find ways to incorporate and protect the intrinsic value of animal and plant life and even other natural objects that are integral parts of ecosystems. This must be done without constantly reducing such values to human interests. This will, of course, be difficult, because our conceptual ideology and ethical persuasion is so dominantly homocentric; however, if we are committed to a deeper biocentric ethic, then it is vital that we try to find appropriate ways to promote it. Environmental impact statements should make explicit reference to nonhuman natural values. Legal rights for nonhuman natural things, along the lines of Christopher Stone's proposal, should be sought.[22] And naturalistic ethical guidelines, such as those suggested by Holmes Rolston, should be set forth for business to follow when its activities impact upon ecosystems.[23]

At the heart of the business ethics movement is its reaction to the mistaken belief that business only has responsibilities to a narrow set of its stakeholders, namely its stockholders. Crucial to the environmental ethics movement is its reaction to the mistaken belief that only human beings and human interests are deserving of our moral consideration. I suspect that the beginnings of both movements can be traced to these respective moral insights. Certainly the significance of both movements lies in their search for a broader and deeper moral perspective. If business and environmental ethicists begin to rely solely on promotional strategies of self-interest, such as good ethics is good business, and of human interest, such as homocentrism, then they face the danger of cutting off the very roots of their ethical efforts.

Notes

This paper was originally presented as the Presidential Address to the *Society for Business Ethics*, August 10, 1990, San Francisco, CA.

1. Albert Gore, "What is Wrong With Us?" *Time* (January 2, 1989), 66.
2. Norman Bowie, "Morality, Money, and Motor Cars," *Business, Ethics, and the Environ-

ment: The Public Policy Debate, edited by W. Michael Hoffman, Robert Frederick, and Edward S. Petry, Jr. (New York: Quorum Books, 1990), p. 89.

3. See Milton Friedman, "The Social Responsibility of Business Is to Increase Its Profits," *The New York Times Magazine* (September 13, 1970).

4. Bowie, p. 91.

5. Bowie, p. 94.

6. Robert Frederick, Assistant Director of the Center for Business Ethics, and I have developed and written these points together. Frederick has also provided me with invaluable assistance on other points in this paper.

7. Kenneth E. Goodpaster, "Can a Corporation have an Environmental Conscience," *The Corporation, Ethics, and the Environment*, edited by W. Michael Hoffman, Robert Frederick, and Edward S. Petry, Jr. (New York: Quorom Books, 1990).

8. Mark Sagoff, "At the Shrine of Our Lady of Fatima, or Why Political Questons Are Not All Economic," found in *Busines Ethics: Readings and Cases in Corporate Morality*, 2nd edition, edited by W. Michael Hoffman and Jennifer Mills Moore (New York: McGraw-Hill, 1990), pp. 494-503.

9. Bowie, p. 94.

10. Cynthia Pollock Shea, "Doing Well By Doing Good," *World-Watch* (November/December, 1989), p. 30.

11. *Corporate Ethics: A Prime Business Asset*, a report by The Business Roundtable, February, 1988, p. 4.

12. Kenneth Blanchard, and Norman Vincent Peale, *The Power of Ethical Management* (New York: William Morrow and Company, Inc., 1988).

13. Robert Frederick, "Individual Rights and Environmental Protection," presented at the Annual Society for Business Ethics Conference in San Francisco, August 10 and 11, 1990.

14. Frederick.

15. Richard Routley, and Val Routley, "Human Chauvinism and Environmental Ethics," *Environmental Philosophy*, Monograph Series, No. 2, edited by Don Mannison, Michael McRobbie, and Richard Routley (Australian National University, 1980), pp. 121ff.

16. See Paul W. Taylor, "The Ethics of Respect for Nature," found in *People, Penguins, and Plastic Trees*, edited by Donald VanDeVeer and Christine Pierce (Belmont, California: Wadsworth, 1986), pp. 178-183. Also see R. and V. Routley, "Against the Inevitability of Human Chauvinism," found in *Ethics and the Problems of the 21st Century*, edited by K. E. Goodpaster and K. M. Sayre (Notre Dame: University of Notre Dame Press, 1979), pp. 36-59.

17. Arne Naess, "Identification as a Source of Deep Ecological Attitudes," *Deep Ecology*, edited by Michael Tobias (San Marcos, California: Avant Books, 1988), p. 266.

18. Benedict de Spinoza, "On the Improvement of the Understanding," found in *Philosophy of Benedict de Spinoza*, translated by R. H. M. Elwes (New York: Tudor Publishing Co., 1936), p. 5.

19. Christopher D. Stone, "Should Trees Have Standing?—Toward legal Rights for Natural Objects," found in *People, Penguins, and Plastic Trees*, pp. 86-87.

20. See Donald VanDeVeer, "Interspecific Justice," *People, Penguins, and Plastic Trees*, pp. 51-66.

21. Lawrence H. Tribe, "Ways Not to Think about Plastic Trees: New Foundations for Environmental Law," found in *People, Penguins, and Plastic Trees*, p. 257.

22. Stone, pp. 83-96.

23. Holmes Rolston, III, *Environmental Ethics* (Philadelphia: Temple University Press, 1988), pp. 301-313.

David P. Hanson

THE ETHICS OF DEVELOPMENT
AND
THE DILEMMAS OF
GLOBAL ENVIRONMENTALISM

Environmentalism is a pledge to preserve the possibilities of our world for future generations. It is based on an acceptance of interdependence and the need for self-restraint in the interests of those yet to come. The environmental ethic forces us to confront the economists' truth: resources are limited, and not all interests can be satisfied. Whose interests shall we defend? What resources are we willing to sacrifice?

Environmental problems are increasingly matters of international concern. They are the result in large part of well-established patterns of economic development. In considering what to do, we should evaluate environmental issues in the broadest possible context by looking at the impact of historical patterns of global economic and social change to determine if the present rate of economic development can be sustained.

A strong argument can be made that the poorer countries have a moral right to economic development. The technological and economic developments of the last century have led to a moral revolution in Western societies. From the perspective of those who are accustomed to developed standards of living, the lives of most people in traditional societies are nasty, brutish, and short. Economic and technological development has produced enormous advances in basic human values: nutrition, sanitation, health, longevity, education, and overall security.

Economic development has also brought a moral resolution in social relations. In traditional agricultural societies, the control of land has been a major basis for social power. The pace of technological change has generally been very slow. In the short term, potential production has been constant. As a result, peasant and master have generally fought over a fixed quantity, where the gains of one come at the expense of the other. In this struggle, landlords had the superior position as long as there were too many peasants and a scarcity of arable land. As a result, class relations in traditional societies have often been characterized by violence and exploitation by the few, who are very rich, against the many, who are very poor.

Resources in the developed societies are produced by larger groups of people acting in cooperation. Competition in the market economies occurs as much among these competing corporate bureaucracies as between individual pro-

From David P. Hanson, "The Ethics of Development and the Dilemmas of Global Environmentalism," in *Business, Ethics and the Environment: The Public Policy Debate*, edited by W. Michael Hoffman, Robert Frederick, and Edward S. Petry, Jr. (New York: Quorum Books, 1990), 185–194. Reprinted by permission of Greenwood Publishing Group, Inc., Westport, CT, from *Business, Ethics and the Environment: The Public Policy Debate*, edited by W. Michael Hoffman, Robert Frederick, and Edward S. Petry, Jr. Copyright © 1990 by the Center for Business Ethics at Bentley College.

ducers. The competitive position of companies in the market economies is increasingly determined by the judgment and skill employees bring to the production process. Even in the traditional manufacturing industries, quality and design have become as important as the more traditional criteria of cost and volume.

The increasing dependence of managerial elites on the commitment and skill of subordinates has led to increased demands for highly qualified personnel. Over the last fifty years, these processes have led to the development of a large middle class made up of managers, professionals, technicians, and skilled workers. With this has also come the development of a social ethic based on the acceptance of interdependency, consensus, professionalism, and the need for self-restraint.[1]

The reality of rapid and sustained economic growth in the Western societies has also transformed social conflicts. With economic growth, all can benefit in the long run. Social conflict becomes a barrier to the welfare of all rather than a tool for the prosperity of a few. The results of this transformation can be seen in the institutionalization of the welfare state and a general acceptance of environmental ideals.

The existing patterns of economic and technological development are historically unique. With few exceptions, the conditions of life for most people, in, for example, Mesopotamia in 2000 B.C. were not significantly different from the living standards of the average French citizen in the year 1500 A.D.

The pace of economic and technological development has accelerated dramatically in the last fifty years. Per capita energy consumption, a reasonable measure of technological and economic development, has risen thirty-fold in North America between 1870 and the present.[2]

If population growth can be curtailed, the availability of raw materials need not pose an obstacle to continued economic development. If we take care of the land, fertility can be sustained indefinitely. Few materials are ever lost from human use; they are only transformed and transported into different forms. The transformation of ore into iron, for example, does not make the metal any less available.

The major barriers to continued development are environmental. The traces of carbon dioxide (CO_2) and related gases in the atmosphere block the radiation of energy from the earth into space. Any significant increases in the atmospheric concentration of these gases will result in rising temperatures on earth.[3]

Unfortunately, the major energy source for economic development has been based on the conversion of mineral carbon into gaseous CO_2. Every year, we are dumping between 6 billion and 10 billion tons of CO_2 into the air. The amount of CO_2 in the atmosphere is increasing by almost 1 percent per year. If this rate of CO_2 dumping continues, we can expect an increase of 6 to 9 degrees Fahrenheit in the mean temperature of the earth over the next fifty years.[4]

The consequences for the human community are generally unfavorable. Climate zones should shift toward the poles. Both precipitation and the length of the growing season at high latitudes should increase. The increases should be most pronounced at higher latitudes. Arable lands located around 30 degrees north–south latitude are likely to become increasingly arid. A most serious consequence is likely to be the melting of the polar icecaps and the rising level of the ocean. A 3-foot rise in the water level would make many cities uninhabitable and, in many parts of the world, could significantly reduce the amount of arable land.[5]

The processes of climactic change will lead to environmental stress quite apart from the increase in final equilibrium temperatures. There will inevitably be a lag between the death of existing plant, animal, and human communities and the reestablishment of new species and technologies for life.

Unless we are willing to discount the welfare of future generations against our own, there is a compelling case for reducing the emission of carbon-based gases down to the level at which these gases are being removed from the atmosphere. Dumping at any higher level than zero net emission will slow the pace of change but may not change the result.[6]

Energy utilization in the developed economies can be reduced by at least half through conservation without significantly altering standards of living. Roughly equal amounts of energy are used for manufacturing, transportation, and heating and cooling. Major cuts in the amount of energy required for transportation and heating and cooling can be achieved through increased utilization of existing technology and through changes in the criteria and processes of public planning.[7]

There are limits to what can be achieved toward energy conservation in manufacturing. The amount of energy required to produce the steel, aluminum, and cement for building new houses, roads, and cars is fixed by the laws of chemistry and physics. There do not seem to be any viable low-energy substitutes for these materials in the construction of the public and private goods we associate with economic development.

To an extent, we can shift over to less polluting energy sources. Solar power might be able to supply up to one-quarter of all electric energy needs.[8] Biomass could also provide a closed-cycle, carbon-based fuel source. Geothermal, wind, and ocean thermal energy conversion processes may replace carbon fuels.

A changeover from carbon-based fuels is not likely to be easy or cheap. Many of these technologies are best suited for the production of electricity, which has the problem of high capital costs and low conversion efficiencies. The initially promising option of nuclear power has already been derailed by a record of high costs, high risks, and high opposition. Solar power will not be feasible in many parts of the world or for many industrial applications. Raising crops, such as sugar cane, for conversion to fuels will take abundant supplies of land, capital, and labor.

A failure to restrict carbon utilization while promoting worldwide economic development will severely complicate the problems of the greenhouse effect. Raising worldwide per capita consumption of carbon-based energy to just one-fourth of current U.S. levels would increase aggregate CO_2 production by almost 90 percent. Even if the developed countries then reduced their per capita carbon consumption to the "one-quarter U.S." level, the aggregate result would still be a 26 percent increase in global CO_2 emissions.[9]

Maintaining a balance between economic development and energy conservation will be far more difficult for the poorer countries. Among the developed countries of the Organization for Economic Cooperation and Development, there is no relation between per capita income and per capita energy consumption. The correlation between per capita income and energy consumption for all nations though is 0.88.[10]

In effect, the demand for material- and energy-intensive goods in the developed countries is becoming satiated. Much of the growth in the developed economies is in the design, manufacture, and distribution of intellect-intensive goods, such as computers and aircraft.[11] The relation between energy consumption and economic development is much stronger for poorer nations. The demand for energy-intensive basic construction materials and manufactured goods, such as houses, roads, telephone systems, airports, and cars, has not yet been met.

In the developed world, a transition to a low-pollution economy for a given level of economic development could be implemented relatively easily. The resources of capital and technology are readily available. Rising costs of energy production could be offset through the adoption of conservation technologies in housing and transportation. The problems posed by changing energy sources will be far more severe in the developing countries. The poorer countries have tended to specialize in the production of basic minerals and agricultural goods, surprisingly energy-intensive processes. World markets in most of these goods are highly price competitive. Poorer countries that unilaterally restrict their rate of carbon utilization are likely to face increasingly severe competitive disadvantages.

Population size is another long-term limit to environmental protection and economic development. For a given level of technology and per capita income, the level of CO_2 production will be directly related to population size. Thus, we may be able to maintain a smaller population at a higher standard of living, subject to the constraints of carbon utilization.

Population growth tends to be quite high in the poorer countries and almost zero in the developed countries. In the poorest countries, the rate of increase may be as high as 3.5 to 4 percent per year, and the population will double every seventeen to twenty-two years. Thus, the social dislocations caused by population growth are far greater in the poorer countries, which have the fewest resources, and far less in countries with abundant resources. The imposition of pollution restraints on developing countries, leading to an increased demand for scarce intellectual and capital resources, is likely to accentuate these difficulties.

Rapid population growth in the poorer countries compounds the social problems of economic development. The work force is usually divided between a large traditional agricultural sector and a small, relatively modernized urban sector. Population growth in the traditional sector generally outpaces economic growth in the modern sector. At the same time, the modernization of agriculture often leads to the displacement of inefficient, labor-intensive share-cropping systems for more productive plantations using seasonal wage labor. The results of these two trends are seen in rising unemployment levels, the explosive growth of the urban population, and widening gaps between rich and poor.[12]

Population growth in poorer countries often leads to greater pressures on land utilization. In parts of Africa and Latin America, overpopulation and population growth have led to overcultivation, erosion, and an actual drop in per capita agricultural production. In Latin America, Africa, and Southeast Asia, this has led to a search for new agricultural land through the widespread destruction of the rain forests. Between 15 and 30 percent of total CO_2 production is caused by this deforestation.[13]

The moral importance of encouraging development in the Third World must therefore be balanced against the practical imperative of limiting atmospheric pollution. Progress on either goal will require effective action on population growth. Can any of these goals be achieved?[14]

An honest answer is not a comforting one. The problems of population control, economic growth, and atmospheric pollution require effective responses that must be based on what will be possible, which is not necessarily what will be fair or equitable.

The priorities for action can be evaluated according to the consequences of failure. A failure to stabilize atmospheric CO_2 levels will lead to a progressive deterioration in the conditions of life for all—rich and poor alike. Partial solutions that only slow the rate of CO_2 buildup will merely postpone the greenhouse effects; they will not avoid them.

This is not true for the problem of population growth. To an extent, the problems of rapid population growth can potentially be offset by rapid economic and technological development. While a failure to control population growth is likely to result in a progressive immiseration of life, the effects will generally be confined to the poorer countries, where the population growth is outstripping resource development.

From a global perspective, the problems of economic development are less pressing. Like the issue of population growth, the consequences of a failure to develop are largely local. If we can solve the population problem, then a failure to promote economic development results in the persistence of the status quo rather than in a progressive reduction of human welfare. Furthermore, economic development is not an all-or-nothing proposition; any increase in income will potentially increase social welfare.

There are also differences in the capacities of government for effective action on these three issues. Our capacity for effective action on the tasks of economic development, population control, and pollution abatement is significantly limited by our reliance on the independent nation-state as the fundamental political unit. The division of the world into many small administrative units has created an incentive for governments to emphasize local over global issues. In both the developed and underdeveloped world, governments generally respond to local interests over international concerns. We cannot expect governments to act where the local costs significantly outweigh local benefits.

The division of the world into rich and poor states also poses problems. The invention of guns, large sailing ships, the factory system, and the corporation gave the European powers a vast military and economic advantage over the traditional societies. The result was the global expansion of Europe through colonialism and empire. The benefits to the home countries came in the forms of cheap resources and guaranteed markets. Colonialism broke down because the costs of occupation outstripped the benefits of market domination. It became easier to turn local administration over to local elites while maintaining ties of trade and investment.

The moral results of decolonization have been mixed. Independence is consistent with the strong ethical claim of all people for autonomy and self-determination. Forceful intervention by a stronger country into the affairs of a weaker one, even if the motives were to be good and results beneficial, is morally unacceptable. However, the colonial powers often turned authority over to local elites, who were likely to safeguard the interests of the colonial government in trade and investment ties. The end of colonialism has too often resulted in the emergence of ineffective or corrupt institutions of governance. Political control over trade ties with the outside world has often become a new source of power rivaling the traditional control over land. The results have often added a barrier to development: a tendency for Third World governments to emphasize short-term political and class interests over long-term popular development interests.

The end of colonialism has also put a new perspective on the roles of the Western powers. It is now the responsibility of the newly independent governments, not the colonial powers, to promote the interests of the developing societies. It is true, though, that lip service has been paid to international development efforts. Poor people can neither produce nor buy very much. Poor countries tend to be unstable and politically troubled. However, the desire of foreign governments to maintain existing military alliances, trade ties, and investment security guarantees encourages an accommodation with elites who may have little concrete interest in development.

The social and political interests of the upper classes in many developing countries also constitute major barriers to economic growth. Raising the income of the poor usually implies a radical shift in the positions and interests of the rich. If so, then development assistance programs will not be effective unless they are accompanied by substantial political changes in both the developing and the developed countries.[15]

What is to be done? How do we achieve the antithetical goals of restraining atmospheric pollution and promoting economic development? How can we encourage progress on population control, which may be a precondition for progress on either goal?

It is unrealistic to expect strong action by the poorer countries on problems of global pollution. On one hand, their contribution to both the magnitude of the problem and the effectiveness of the response are likely to be low. On the other hand, the costs to the poorer countries of limiting carbon-gas emissions, relative to available resources, are likely to be high. Countries that do not impose these costs on their local economies potentially enjoy cost advantages in international markets.

It is unlikely that the developed countries will be able to promote economic development effectively in the Third World. To the extent that the social structure and government policies of the developing countries constitute major impediments to development, the role of the developed countries is limited to encouragement and support. To the extent that these changes would upset existing political and economic ties, the developed countries are unlikely to support development efforts.

It is even more difficult for foreign governments to promote population control in the developing world. Economic development has a major effect on reducing family size. Where they are effective, family planning programs also reduce population growth. The effectiveness of these programs, however, depends heavily on an involved commitment by government and other social institutions. Neither economic development nor the necessary commitment to population control can be mandated from the outside.

It will be up to the developed countries to take effective leadership on the issue of carbon buildup in the atmosphere while essentially leaving the problems of population control and economic development to the poorer states.

The effectiveness of the response from the developed countries on the issue of pollution control will depend on their capacity for concerted action. Only by applying uniform rules for all developed countries can we avoid the conflict between economic advantage and environmental progress. Therefore, the desirability of program alternatives must be matched against the reasonable availability of international institutions through which they will be administered.

Fortunately, a major consolidation of political units at the supranational level has taken place among the developed nations over the last fifty years. World governance in the post-World War II period has been characterized by the development of specialized institutions such as the General Agreement on Tariffs and Trade, and International Monetary Fund (IMF), and the International Maritime Organization (IMO), which have been surprisingly effective. It is possible that institutions will develop to regulate global environmental conditions similar to the effective role played by the IMO in regulating oceanic pollution.

This does not answer the question of how the developed countries can encourage the less developed nations to follow suit. One possible tool is through influence over international energy markets and prices. Historically the consumption rate of carbon-based fuel in the developing world has declined when energy prices on international markets increased. The generally cooperative relation between the developed countries and the Organization of Petroleum Exporting Countries provides an example of how these market prices could be managed.

Unfortunately our ability to block the utilization of domestic coal or oil resources in countries such as China or to prevent deforestation in countries such as Brazil is limited given our lack of political control and their need for additional land and cheap energy. Other tools may be needed to encourage developing countries to pursue a domestic policy of environmental restraint.

The incentive might be based on a conditional acceptance of programs for capital subsidy and commodity price stabilization that many developing countries have been advocating in the United Nations and elsewhere. The penalty for noncompliance could come through conditional restrictions imposed by the developed countries on international credits and market access. The model for these programs could be taken from the role played by the IMF in encouraging domestic fiscal restraint.

Another key might be through technology transfer. Western countries could encourage the utilization of energy-efficient production techniques by reducing restrictions on the diffusion of the relevant technologies and by subsidizing the capital costs of energy-efficient equipment. A similar program of technology transfer has already been incorporated into the Law of the Sea treaty.

Another strategy might be to encourage developing countries to break away from the production of basic agricultural and industrial materials. Countries such as Mexico and Hong Kong have based development programs in large part on low-energy, labor-intensive manufacturing and assembly operations. Tourism and banking services are becoming increasingly important in many developing countries. Industries such as programming and software development are both highly labor intensive and potentially portable across national boundaries.

These programs are likely to be, at best, only partially effective. The experience of the IMF has shown that short-term considerations of domestic politics often override long-term incentives for reform from international agencies. Countries such as the People's Republic of China and the Soviet Union that have traditionally pursued policies of autarky are less likely to be swayed by incentives and penalties imposed by international institutions.

Even if the developing countries concentrated on low-pollution industries and adopted the best available technologies, development is likely to increase pollution levels. Development implies the acquisition of manufactured goods and a dramatic expansion of civil construction. The production of these goods is still energy intensive. In short, there are no easy solutions.

Notes

1. Rheinhard Bendix, *Work and Authority in Industry* (New York: Wiley, 1956); Amatai Etzioni, *The Comparative Analysis of Complex Organizations* (New York: Free Press, 1961).

2. Chauncey Starr, "Energy and Power," *Scientific American* (September 1971): 37 – 50.

3. C. Genthon et al., "Vostok Ice Core: Climate Response to CO_2 and Orbital Forcing Changes Over the Last Climactic Cycle," *Nature*, October 1, 1987, pp. 414 – 418. Other gases besides CO_2, such as methane and Freon, contribute significantly to the greenhouse effect. The concentrations of these gases have also been rising steadily in recent years, largely as a result of human activity. The distinctions among the sources and effects of these gases are not particularly relevant for this argument and will be ignored in the balance of this chapter. V. Ramanathan et al., "Trace Gas Trends and Their Potential Role in Climate Change," *Journal of Geophysical Research*, June 20, 1985, pp. 5547 – 5556.

4. Stephen H. Schneider, "The Changing Climate," *Scientific American* (September 1989): 70 – 79.

5. Michael Malik, "Fear of Flooding: Global Warming Could Threaten Low Lying Asia-Pacific Countries," *Far Eastern Economic Review*, December 22, 1988, pp. 20 – 21.

6. It is not clear how much CO_2, if any, we can safely release into the atmosphere. There are 740 million tons of CO_2 in the atmosphere. Each year natural processes release and absorb roughly 400 million tons of CO_2. The contribution from human activity is therefore a very small percentage of the total interchange. Schneider, "Changing Climate," p. 73.

Other factors complicate predictions about climate changes. The earth has been unusually warm for the last few thousand years. It is possible that any temperature rise induced by human activities will be offset by a naturally occurring shift toward a colder climate. Finally, mathematical models are still too imprecise to allow for confident predictions about the long-term results of atmospheric changes. Particularly troublesome are the effects of cloud cover and estimates on the rate at which CO_2 will be taken up by the oceans. The analysis in this chapter reflects the predominant view. See James E. Hansen, director, Goddard Institute for Space Studies, "The Greenhouse Effect: Impacts on Global Temperatures and Regional Heat Waves," testimony before U.S. Senate, Committee on Energy and Natural Resources, June 23, 1988.

7. Earl Cook, "The Flow of Energy in an Industrial Society," *Scientific American* (September 1971): 135 – 144; Arthur Rosenfeld and David Hafemeister, "Energy Efficient Buildings," *Scientific American* (April 1988): 78 – 85.

8. Yoshihiro Hamakawa, "Photovoltaic Power," *Scientific American* (April 1987): 92.

9. Calculations based on data in John H. Gibbons, Peter D. Blair, and Holly L. Gwin, "Strategies for Energy Use," *Scientific American* (September 1989): 136 – 143.

10. Between 1980 and 1986, the U.S. gross national product grew by 16 percent. During this period, steel consumption dropped by 7 percent, and energy consumption declined by 3 percent. Data from *Statistical Abstract of the United States, 1988* (Washington, D.C.: U.S. Government Printing Office, 1989), pp. 422, 681, 741.

11. Calculations based on data from ibid., pp. 805, 816.

12. James Clad and Margot Cohen, "Genesis of Dispair," *Far Eastern Economic Review*, October 20, 1988, pp. 24 – 30; "Development and Income Inequality Revisited," *Applied Economics* (April 1988): 509 – 531.

13. Schneider, "Changing Climate," p. 73; Lester A. Brown, Christopher Flavin, and Sandra Postel, "A World at Risk," in Lester A. Brown et al., *State of the World: 1989* (New York: Norton, 1989), pp. 1 – 20.

14. Several representatives from developing countries argued vigorously at a 1971 international conference in Founex, Switzerland, that the pollution and exhaustion of resources caused by economic activity in the developed countries are major barriers to the growth of the undeveloped economies. See "The Founex Report on Development and the Environment," *International Conciliation*, no. 586 (January 1972): 7 – 36; Miguel A. Ozorio de Almieda "The Confrontation between Problems of Development and the Environment," *International Conciliation*, no. 586 (January 1972): 37 – 56.

15. For a discussion of this point from the Alliance for Progress, see Walter LaFeber, "The Alliance in Retrospect," in Andrew MacGuire and Janet Welsh, eds., *Bordering on Trouble: Resources and Politics in Latin America* (Bethesda: Adler and Adler, 1986), pp. 337–388.

Peter Singer

THE PLACE OF NONHUMANS IN ENVIRONMENTAL ISSUES

When we humans change the environment in which we live, we often harm ourselves. If we discharge cadmium into a bay and eat shellfish from that bay, we become ill and may die. When our industries and automobiles pour noxious fumes into the atmosphere, we find a displeasing smell in the air, the long-term results of which may be every bit as deadly as cadmium poisoning. The harm that humans do the environment, however, does not rebound solely, or even chiefly, on humans. It is nonhumans who bear the most direct burden of human interference with nature.

By "nonhumans" I mean to refer to all living things other than human beings, though for reasons to be given later, it is with nonhuman animals, rather than plants, that I am chiefly concerned. It is also important, in the context of environmental issues, to note that living things may be regarded either collectively or as individuals. In debates about the environment the most important way of regarding living things collectively has been to regard them as species. Thus, when environmentalists worry about the future of the blue whale, they usually are thinking of the blue whale as a species, rather than of individual blue whales. But this is not, of course, the only way in which one can think of blue whales, or other animals, and one of the topics I shall discuss is whether we should be concerned about what we are doing to the environment primarily insofar as it threatens entire species of nonhumans, or primarily insofar as it affects individual nonhuman animals.

The general question, then, is how the effects of our actions on the environment of nonhuman beings should figure in our deliberations about what we ought to do. There is an unlimited variety of contexts in which this issue could arise. To take just one: Suppose that it is considered necessary to build a new power station, and there are two sites, A and B, under consideration. In most respects the sites are equally suitable, but building the power station on site A would be more expensive because the greater depth of shifting soil at that site will require deeper foundations; on the other hand to build on site B will destroy a favored breeding ground for thousands of wildfowl. Should the presence of the wildfowl enter into the decision as to where to build? And if so, in what manner should it enter, and how heavily should it weigh?

In a case like this the effects of our actions on nonhuman animals could be taken into account in two quite different ways: directly, giving the lives and welfare of nonhuman animals an intrinsic significance which must count in any moral calculation; or indirectly, so that the effects of our actions on nonhumans are morally significant only if they have consequences for humans. . . .

The view that the effects of our actions on other animals has no direct moral significance is not as likely to be openly advocated today as it was in the past; yet it is likely to be accepted implicitly and acted upon. When planners perform cost-benefit studies on new projects, the costs and benefits are costs and benefits for human beings only. This does not mean that the impact of the power station or highway on wildlife is ignored altogether, but it is included only indirectly. That a new reservoir would drown a valley teeming with wildlife is taken into account only under some such heading as the value of the facilities for recreation that the valley affords. In calculating this value, the cost-benefit study will be neutral between forms of recreation like hunting and shooting and those like bird watching and bush walking — in fact hunting and shooting are likely to contribute more to the benefit side of the calculations because larger sums of money are spent on them, and they therefore benefit manufacturers and retailers of firearms as well as the hunters and shooters themselves. The suffering experienced by the animals whose habitat is flooded is not reckoned into the costs of the operation; nor is the recreational value obtained by the hunters and shooters offset by the cost to the animals that their recreation involves.

Despite its venerable origin, the view that the effects of our actions on nonhuman animals have no intrinsic moral significance can be shown to be arbitrary and morally indefensible. If a being suffers, the fact that it is not a member of our own species cannot be a moral reason for failing to take its suffering into account. This becomes obvious if we consider the analogous attempt by white slaveowners to deny consideration to the interests of blacks. These white racists limited their moral concern to their own race, so the suffering of a black did not have the same moral significance as the suffering of a white. We now recognize that in doing so they were making an arbitrary distinction, and that the existence of suffering, rather than the race of the sufferer, is what is really morally significant. The point remains true if "species" is substituted for "race." The logic of racism and the logic of the position we have been discussing, which I have elsewhere referred to as "speciesism," are indistinguishable; and if we reject the former then consistency demands that we reject the latter too.[1]

It should be clearly understood that the rejection of speciesism does not imply that the different species are in fact equal in respect of such characteristics as intelligence, physical strength, ability to communicate, capacity to suffer, ability to damage the environment, or anything else. After all, the moral principle of human equality cannot be taken as implying that all humans are equal in these respects either — if it did, we would have to give up the idea of human equality. That one being is more intelligent than another does not entitle him to enslave, exploit, or disregard the interests of the less intelligent being. The moral basis of equality among humans is not equality in fact, but the principle of equal consideration of interests, and it is this principle that, in consistency, must be extended to any nonhumans who have interests.

There may be some doubt about whether any nonhuman beings have interests. This doubt may arise because of uncertainty about what it is to have an interest, or because of uncertainty about the nature of some nonhuman beings. So far as the concept of "interest" is the cause of doubt, I take the view that only a being with subjective experiences, such as the experience of pleasure or the experience of pain, can have interests in the full sense of the term; and that any being with such experiences does have at least one interest, namely, the interest in experiencing pleasure and avoiding pain. Thus consciousness, or the capacity for subjective experience, is both a necessary and a sufficient condition for having an interest. While there may be a loose sense of the term in which we can say that it is in the interests of a tree to be watered, this attenuated sense of the term is not the sense covered by the principle of equal consideration of interests. All we mean when we say that it is in the interests of a tree to be watered is that the tree needs water if it is to continue to live and grow normally; if we regard this as evidence that the tree has interests, we might almost as well say that it is in the interests of a car to be lubricated regularly because the car needs lubrication if it is to run properly. In neither case can we really mean (unless we impute consciousness to trees or cars) that the tree or car has any preference about the matter.

The remaining doubt about whether nonhuman beings have interests is, then, a doubt about whether nonhuman beings have subjective experiences like the experience of pain. I have argued elsewhere that the commonsense view that birds and mammals feel pain is well founded,[2] but more serious doubts arise as we move down the evolutionary scale. Vertebrate animals have nervous systems broadly similar to our own and behave in ways that resemble our own pain behavior when subjected to stimuli that we would find painful; so the inference that vertebrates are capable of feeling pain is a reasonable one, though not as strong as it is if limited to mammals and birds. When we go beyond vertebrates to insects, crustaceans, mollusks and so on, the existence of subjective states becomes more dubious, and with very simple organisms it is difficult to believe that they could be conscious. As for plants, though there have been sensational claims that plants are not only conscious, but even psychic, there is no hard evidence that supports even the most modest claim.[3]

The boundary of beings who may be taken as having interests is therefore not an abrupt boundary, but a broad range in which the assumption that the being has interests shifts from being so strong as to be virtually certain to being so weak as to be highly improbable. The principle of equal consideration of interests must be applied with this in mind, so that where there is a clash between a virtually certain interest and highly doubtful one, it is the virtually certain interest that ought to prevail.

In this manner our moral concern ought to extend to all beings who have interests. . . .

Giving equal consideration to the interests of two different beings does not mean treating them alike or holding their lives to be of equal value. We may recognize that the interests of one being are greater than those of another, and equal consideration will then lead us to sacrifice the being with lesser interests, if one or the other must be sacrificed. For instance, if for some reason a choice has to be made between saving the life of a normal human being and that of a dog, we might well decide to save the human because he, with his greater awareness of what is going to happen, will suffer more before he dies; we may also take into account the likelihood that it is the family and friends of the human who will suffer more; and finally, it would be the human who had the greater potential for future happiness. This decision would be in accordance with the principle of equal consideration of interests, for the interests of the dog get the same consideration as those of the human, and the loss to the dog is not discounted because the dog is not a member of our species. The outcome is as it is because the balance of interests favors the human. In a different situation — say, if the human were grossly mentally defective and without family or anyone else who would grieve for it — the balance of interests might favor the nonhuman.[4]

The more positive side of the principle of equal consideration is this: where interests are equal, they must be given equal weight. So where human and nonhuman animals share an interest — as in the case of the interest in avoiding physical pain — we must give as much weight to violations of the interest of the nonhumans as we do to similar violations of the human's interest. This does not mean, of course, that it is as bad to hit a horse with a stick as it is to hit a human being, for the same blow would cause less pain to the animal with the tougher skin. The principle holds between similar amounts of felt pain, and what this is will vary from case to case.

It may be objected that we cannot tell exactly how much pain another animal is suffering, and that therefore the principle is impossible to apply. While I do not deny the difficulty and even, so far as precise measurement is concerned, the impossibility of comparing the subjective experiences of members of different species, I do not think that the problem is different in kind from the problem of comparing the subjective experiences of two members of our own species. Yet this is something we do all the time, for instance when we judge that a wealthy person will suffer less by being taxed at a higher rate than a poor person will gain from the welfare benefits paid for by the tax; or when we decide to take our two children to the beach instead of to a fair, because although the older one would prefer the fair, the younger one has stronger preference the other way. These comparisons may be very rough, but since there is nothing better, we must use them; it would be irrational to refuse to do so simply because they are rough. Moreover, rough as they are, there are many situations in which we can be reasonably sure which way the balance of interests lies. While a difference of species may make comparisons rougher still, the basic problem is the same, and the comparisons are still often good enough to use, in the absence of anything more precise. . . .

The difficulty of making the required comparison will mean that the application of this conclusion is controversial in many cases, but there will be some situations in which it is clear enough. Take, for instance, the wholesale poisoning of animals that is euphemistically known as "pest control." The authorities who conduct these campaigns give no consideration to the suffering they inflict on the "pests," and invariably use the method of slaughter they believe to be cheapest and most effective. The result is that hundreds of millions of rabbits have died agonizing deaths from the artificially introduced disease, myxomatosis, or from poisons like "ten-eighty"; coyotes and other wild dogs have died painfully from cyanide poisoning; and all manner of wild animals have endured days of thirst, hunger, and fear with a mangled limb caught in a leg-hold trap.[5] Granting, for the sake of argument, the necessity for pest control — though this has rightly been questioned — the fact remains that no serious attempts have been made to introduce alternative means of control and thereby reduce the incalculable amount of suffering caused by present methods. It would not, presumably, be beyond modern science to produce a substance which, when eaten by rabbits or coyotes, produced sterility instead of a drawn-out death. Such methods might be more expensive, but can anyone doubt that if a similar amount of human suffering were at stake, the expense would be borne?

Another clear instance in which the principle of equal consideration of interests would indicate methods different from those presently used is in the timber industry. There are two basic methods of obtaining timber from forests. One is to cut only selected mature or dead trees, leaving the forest substantially intact. The other, known as clear-cutting, involves chopping down everything that grows in a given area, and then reseeding. Obviously when a large area is clear-cut, wild animals find their whole living area destroyed in a few days, whereas selected felling makes a relatively minor disturbance. But clear-cutting is cheaper, and timber companies therefore use this method and will continue to do so unless forced to do otherwise.[6] . . .

It is not merely the act of killing that indicates what we are ready to do to other species in order to gratify our tastes. The suffering we inflict on the animals while they are alive is perhaps an even clearer indication of our speciesism than the fact that we are prepared to kill them.[7] In order to have meat on the table at a price that people can afford, our society tolerates methods of meat production that confine sentient animals in cramped, unsuitable conditions for the entire durations of their lives. Animals are treated like machines that convert fodder into flesh, and any innovation that results in a higher "conversion ratio" is liable to be adopted. As one authority on the subject has said, "cruelty is acknowledged only when profitability ceases."[8] So hens are crowded four or five to a cage with a floor area of twenty inches by eighteen inches, or around the size of a single page of the *New York Times*. The cages have wire floors, since this reduces cleaning costs, though wire is unsuitable for the hens feet; the floors slope, since this makes the eggs roll down for easy collection, although this makes it difficult for the hens to rest comfortably. In these conditions all the birds' natural instincts are thwarted: They cannot stretch their wings fully, walk freely, dust-bathe, scratch the ground, or build a nest. Although they have never known other conditions, observers have noticed that the birds vainly try to perform these actions. Frustrated at their inability to do so, they often develop what farmers call "vices," and peck each other to death. To prevent this, the beaks of young birds are often cut off.

This kind of treatment is not limited to poultry. Pigs are now also being reared in cages inside sheds. These animals are comparable to dogs in intelligence, and need a varied, stimulating environment if they are not to suffer from stress and boredom. Anyone who kept a dog in the way in which pigs are frequently kept would be liable to prosecution, in England at least, but because our interest in exploiting pigs is greater than our interest in exploiting dogs, we object to cruelty to dogs while consuming the produce of cruelty to pigs. Of the other animals, the condition of veal calves is perhaps worst of all, since these animals are so closely confined that they cannot even turn around or get up and lie down freely. In this way they do not develop unpalatable muscle. They are also made anaemic and kept short of roughage, to keep their flesh pale, since white veal fetches a higher price; as a result they develop a craving for iron and roughage, and have been observed to gnaw wood off the sides of their stalls, and lick greedily at any rusty hinge that is within reach.

Since, as I have said, none of these practices cater to anything more than our pleasures of taste, our practice of rearing and killing other animals in order to eat them is a clear instance of the sacrifice of the most important interests of other beings in order to satisfy trivial interests of our own. To avoid speciesism we must stop this practice, and each of us has a moral obligation to cease supporting the practice. Our custom is all the support that the meat industry needs. The decision to cease giving it that support may be difficult, but it is no more difficult than it would have been for a white Southerner to go against the traditions of his society and free his slaves; if we do not change our dietary habits, how can we censure those slaveholders who would not change their own way of living?

Notes

1. For a fuller statement of this argument, see my *Animal Liberation* (New York: A New York Review Book, 1975), especially ch. 1.

2. *Ibid.*

3. See, for instance, the comments by Arthur Galston in *National History*, 83, no. 3 (March 1974): 18, on the "evidence" cited in such books as *The Secret Life of Plants.*

4. Singer, *Animal Liberation*, pp. 20–23.

5. See J. Olsen, *Slaughter the Animals, Poison the Earth* (New York: Simon and Schuster, 1971), especially pp. 153–164.

6. See R. and V. Routley, *The Fight for the Forests* (Canberra: Australian National University Press, 1974); for a thoroughly documented indictment of clear-cutting in America, see *Time*, May 17, 1976.

7. Although one might think that killing a being is obviously the ultimate wrong one can do to it, I think that the infliction of suffering is a clearer indication of speciesism because it might be argued that at least part of what is wrong with killing a human is that most humans are conscious of their existence over time, and have desires and purposes that extend into the future — see, for instance, M. Tooley, "Abortion and Infanticide," *Philosophy and Public Affairs*, vol. 2, no. 1 (1972). Of course, if one took this view one would have to hold — as Tooley does — that killing a human infant or mental defective is not in itself wrong, and is less serious than killing certain higher mammals that probably do have a sense of their own existence over time.

8. Ruth Harrison, *Animal Machines* (Stuart, London, 1964). This book provides an eye-opening account of intensive farming methods for those unfamiliar with the subject.

Eric Katz

DEFENDING THE USE OF ANIMALS BY BUSINESS: ANIMAL LIBERATION AND ENVIRONMENTAL ETHICS

In recent years much attention has been focused on the proper treatment of animals by business. Among those who care about animals, two concerns seem paramount: that animals are being used for the wrong purposes and that animals are being mistreated or abused, whether or not the purposes are justifiable. Thus, arguments are made against the use of animals for fur, food, or experimentation in the cosmetic industry; additionally, arguments are made against the treatment of animals in laboratories, on factory farms, and in zoological parks. In part, the role of business in the misuse and mistreatment of animals has received attention as a spillover from the organized protests against the use of animals in scientific and medical research.[1] Also in part, business has been scrutinized because of environmental concerns; the annual Canadian baby seal hunt and, more recently, the Exxon oil spill in Alaska draw attention to the killing and abuse of wild animals. But more directly, business has come under increasing attack from those who advocate the general principle that animals deserve moral consideration, that animals have both legal and moral rights, that animals should be "liberated" from the oppression and domination of humanity.

The animal liberation movement descends from the animal welfare or humane movement of the late nineteenth and early twentieth centuries, but its purposes and tactics clearly differ. The goals of animal liberation go far beyond urging the benevolent care of pets and animals used for labor. Animal liberation seeks to end all unnecessary cruelty and suffering that humans perpetrate on animal life, especially the use of animals in scientific experimentation, in industrial product testing, and in food production. Animal liberation thus advocates vegetarianism and alternative methods of research and experimentation. Most animal liberationists use traditional tactics for effecting social change; lobbying, boycotts, and philosophical and political arguments. But some elements of the movement have resorted to acts of violence, coercion, and terrorism. In 1989 demonstrators at Saks Fifth Avenue in New York protested the sale of furs and harassed wearers of fur coats who passed by the store. One splinter group, the Animal Liberation Front, is considered a terrorist organization by the FBI. Recently national attention was focused on this group because of the alleged bombing attempt of a surgical supply company that practiced vivisection in the sales demonstrations of its surgical tools.[2]

And so business is faced with the task of defending its treatment of animals from the moral arguments and political tactics of the animal liberation movement. In this chapter I present a method — or at least, several arguments — that business can employ to blunt these attacks. I suggest that the adoption by business of a more conscious environmentalism can serve as a defense against the animal liberation movement. This strategy may seem paradoxical: how can business defend its use of animals by advocating the protection of the environment? But the paradox disappears once we see that animal liberation and environmentalism are incompatible practical moral doctrines.

Arguments in favor of the direct moral consideration of animals follow two major lines of thought.[3] First, it is argued that no morally relevant criterion can be applied to all human beings to differentiate them from nonhuman animals. Traditional criteria such as rationality, autonomy, or linguistic capability are not possessed by all humans. Other criteria, such as the possession of an immortal soul, are problematic at best. Thus, the animal liberationist argues that a moral preference for humans over animals, insofar as it is based on mere species membership, is an irrational prejudice analogous to racial or sexual bias. Animal liberationists often label such arguments "speciesist."[4] Like racism or sexism, speciesism is a groundless bias in favor of one's own kind.

This first argument is essentially negative. It demonstrates the absence of a significant difference between humans and other animals in the establishment of moral consideration. The second argument for the moral consideration of animals is positive. It claims that moral standing is derived from the ability to feel pleasure and pain or, as it is commonly termed in the literature, sentience. As Peter Singer writes, "If a being suffers there can be no moral justification for refusing to take that suffering into consideration. . . . If a being is not capable of suffering, or of experiencing enjoyment or happiness, there is nothing to be taken into account."[5] Any moral agent must consider the pain and pleasure that result from his or her actions. This is the minimum requirement of morality. Since most animals experience pain and pleasure, a moral agent must take these experiences into account. Animals must be given moral standing, moral consideration. The capacity to suffer, to undergo experiences of pain and pleasure, is the primary moral similarity between human and nonhuman animals. Sentience, then, is the nonarbitrary, nonspeciesist basis of moral value.

These two lines of argument are generally combined to form the strongest case for the moral consideration of animals. Yet the two arguments are actually quite different; they derive from totally different philosophical roots. The second argument, with its focus on pain and pleasure, is an outgrowth of classical Benthamite utilitarianism. It is a consequentialist doctrine, in which pain and pleasure are the only two determinants of moral value.[6] The first argument, with its focus on rights, uses a deontological model of thought. Within this model, the central problem in normative ethics becomes the search for a moral criterion that is not directly connected to the results of an action. The possession of rights is not determined by the consequences of action but by the inherent qualities of the possessor. The differing supports for the moral consideration of animals suggest the possibility of differing critical attacks. Each line of thought can be subjected to a unique criticism that weakens the case for animal liberation and points in the direction of a more comprehensive doctrine of environmentalism.

The utilitarian criterion of sentience is problematic for at least two reasons. First, how far down the scale of animal life can one safely assume the experience of pain and pleasure? Is the kind of experience required for animal suffering (and hence for the moral consideration of animals) limited to the so-called higher animals — mammals, birds, and so on? One author suggests that insects have the requisite nervous system for the possible experience of pain.[7] Insects then would be serious candidates for moral consideration. Does this possibility suggest that the utilitarian basis of an animal liberation ethic can be pushed too far, offering a reductio ad absurdum of the position? Or does it place limits on the operational application of the concept of sentience, rendering only higher animals morally considerable? Both alternatives are problematic. The first case includes too many animals under the purview of moral consideration. The second presents a new, more subtle form of speciesism: only animals that resemble humans, who experience pain and pleasure in ways recognizable to us, gain entry into the moral kingdom.[8]

To a certain extent, this criticism is a theoretical quibble. Except for insects killed by pesticides, almost all animals used in business meet the minimum standards of sentient experience. Animals that are used in scientific research, that are hunted, or that are raised for food clearly do feel pain. Nevertheless, this mere theoretical criticism tends to demonstrate that the arguments in favor of the moral consideration of animals are not consistent. There are implications, weak points, and even holes in the arguments that are not addressed by advocates of animal liberation.

The second problem with the criterion of sentience is the contextual significance of pain. The utilitarian advocate of animal consideration contends that pain is an intrinsic evil, but the argument focuses on an abstract concept of pain separated from natural reality. In its concrete natural existence pain has an instrumental function in organisms: a warning of internal stress or external danger. Understood in context, pain is not an evil at all; it is an essential part of a successful organic life. An organism that does not feel pain cannot survive. It cannot reproduce itself, condemning its species to extinction. Once one adopts a more contextual environmental perspective, one can understand the role of pain in organic life. In the natural world pain serves a crucial positive function. But the hallmark of utilitarian animal liberation — the absolute, abstract denial of pain — ignores this context. It proscribes the infliction of any and all pain. Such a denial is both practically impossible and conceptually meaningless.[9]

The deontological concern for animal rights fares no better as a moral argument. The advocates of animal moral consideration claim that the denial of animal rights without a specific moral criterion shows a preference for human beings that is analogous to racism or sexism. The absence of a nonarbitrary moral criterion that distinguishes all humans from all nonhuman animals leaves no justifiable defense of preferential treatment for human beings. This animal rights argument rests on the claim that "marginal" cases of humanity — the severely retarded, the insane, comatose humans, newborns with severe birth defects, fetuses — are treated as normal or typical humans from the moral point of view. The crucial point is that even though marginal humans do not meet standards of moral consideration such as rationality or linguistic capability, they are given a full moral standing that is denied to animals — even when the animals are not inferior to the marginal humans. The moral consideration of marginal humans thus shows the speciesist bias in our treatment of animals.

This argument is empirically false. No observer of the contemporary world, or the history of humanity, could possibly believe that marginal humans are given full moral consideration. The cases obviously differ, but all in all, these humans are clearly deemed to have less moral value because of their reduced capacities. It is true, as animal rightists claim, that we do not eat retarded humans or babies. But we do perform scientific and medical experiments on marginal humans, and we generally find it easier to sacrifice their lives. The factual moral truth, however depressing as it might be, is that the hierarchy of moral value exemplified in the human treatment of animals is echoed and repeated in the human treatment of other humans. The animal rightist claim about human speciesism is hollow, for it assumes the equal treatment of all humans, a treatment that is superior to all animals.[10] There is not an arbitrary speciesist preference for humans. There is the imperfect application of ambiguous criteria such as rationality, autonomy, and linguistic capability. These criteria are used, not altogether consistently, to determine the moral considerability of various classes of humans and nonhumans alike. A recognition of this picture of moral thinking softens the sharpest attack of the animal rights advocates.

Defenders of the use of animals by business and industry thus can raise several problems for questioning the moral consideration of animals. These criticisms are supplemented by the adoption of an "environmental ethic," that is, a direct concern for the moral consideration of nature and natural processes.

The term *environmental ethic* has been used extensively since the mid-1970s to denote a more benign relationship between humanity and the natural world. Within academic philosophy the term has developed in several overlapping, but often contradictory, directions.[11] This is not the proper place for a review of these various formulations. Instead I will merely suggest that the most useful environmental ethic for business to adopt as a countermeasure to animal liberation is ecological holism. This ethic uses the normal functioning of natural ecological systems as the baseline for human decisions that affect the environment. The primary and direct ethical focus is on the continuation of environments, natural ecological systems, not the lives or experiences of individual natural entities. As Aldo Leopold wrote over forty years ago, "A thing is right when it tends to preserve the integrity, stability, and beauty of the biotic community. It is wrong when it tends otherwise."[12] Consequently the way animals live in and through natural ecological systems would be the model for their treatment by humans. Business, or any other human institution, would look to the operations of natural ecological systems as a guide to the proper behavior regarding animals and other natural beings.[13]

As a countermeasure to animal liberation, ecological holism reinforces the proper role of pain in organic life. Since pain is as necessary as pleasure in a successful organic life, it cannot, and should not, be considered a moral evil. Pain, and even death, are crucial aspects in the operation of natural systems. Pain is a warning to individual natural organisms. It is an instrumental good for the preservation of individual life. The death of individuals in nature is a means for reusing and redirecting the energy in the system. In being eaten by a predator, an organism "donates" its energy to another individual in the system. Its corpse decays into basic organic elements, donating its energy to the rest of the system. From an ecological point of view, it is thus a mistake to consider pain and death as merely intrinsic evils that must be eliminated.

Indeed, advocates of animal liberation have trouble with the basic natural process of predation. A utilitarian concerned with the lessening of pain in the world would be forced to prevent predation in the wild. The advocate of animal rights would also, it seems, consider the rights of the prey to be violated in the act of predation.[14] But the prevention of predation seems an absurd position to advocate; if the moral consideration of animals implies the implementation of such a moral policy, then animals cannot be morally considerable.

An environmental perspective acknowledges predation as a basic fact of natural existence. Killing other animals for food serves the interests of the individual carnivore by sustaining its life. Predation serves the interests of the carnivore species by preserving its function or niche in the ecological system. In addition, the killing of prey, often the weakest members of the herd, helps preserve and strengthen the species that is preyed upon. In sum, there is no ecological reason to attempt an elimination of pain, killing, and death in the animal kingdom.

Here the advocate of animal moral considerability can offer a serious objection: the use and mistreatment of animals by humans is not normally an act of predation in the wild. Indeed, the few humans who need to hunt for a food supply may be permitted to do so.[15] However, most of the harm inflicted on animals by humanity takes place through factory farming, scientific experimentation, and industrial testing. So, the objection goes, the beneficial instrumental value of pain in the wild is an irrelevant consideration. The pain of animals in slaughterhouses or research laboratories serves no useful natural function.

The answer to this objection lies in a consciously radical environmentalism. From the perspective of ecological holism, the pain of animals in factory farms, slaughterhouses, and research laboratories is not natural pain. The animals suffering the pain are domesticated animals. They are themselves irrelevant to a comprehensive environmental ethic.

This radical environmentalism is based on the fact that most domesticated species of animals are essentially human artifacts. For thousands of years they have been bred for the development of traits important for human life and human use. Recent advances in the technology of agriculture and recombinant DNA research only make this fact clearer. Consider the injection of antibiotics into beef cattle or the genetically altered Harvard mice that are susceptible to forms of cancer.[16] Thus, the animals used by business and industry are human creations designed to fulfill a specific human need. They are artifacts, living artifacts to be sure, but they are no more natural than the wooden table I am using to write this chapter. To consider them the moral equals of wild animals — who, analogously to autonomous humans, pursue their own goals in a natural system — is a serious category mistake.[17]

Nevertheless, there are proper and improper ways to treat human artifacts. Humans may be required to grant direct moral consideration to some artifacts. Works of art seem to be a paradigm example.[18] So the defender of the business use of animals may be led to a kind of moral pluralism in which various kinds of natural and artificial entities, human and nonhuman organisms, natural individuals and collectives, are each determined to have differing amounts of moral value. Adopting a serious environmental ethic may involve remapping the entire landscape of our moral obligations, so that we take into account wild and domestic animals, marginal humans, plants, ecosystems, nonliving natural entities, species, and even future generations. This remapping is clearly a formidable task, but I believe that it will yield more moral truth than the overly easy utilitarian and rights-based arguments proposed by the advocates of animal liberation.[19]

One possible direction for the development of moral pluralism is an emphasis on the context of moral decision making. I criticized the utilitarian consideration of animal pain as being too abstract. The value or disvalue of pain can be understood only in the exact context of an organism's life. This contextual approach to ethical decision making should be generalized to include all practical moral thought. An emphasis on context is inseparable from moral pluralism. This ethical viewpoint implies that there is no one objective overall moral standard. Various criteria — such as sentience, rationality, life, beauty, integrity — are applicable in varying situations. In one situation it may be morally obligatory to treat a dog better than a human; at a different time or situation the human would come first. The point is that no moral decision can be made abstracted from the context of real life. The concrete situation determines the proper moral outcome.

I conclude by returning to the defense of business in its use of animals for food, fur, and research. The argument presented here suggests that business can blunt the criticisms of the animal liberation movement if it adopts an ethic of ecological holism and moral pluralism. Business must stress that the primary value to be promoted in the human interaction with the animal kingdom is the natural fit with ecological processes.[20] Pain and death are not absolute or intrinsic evils. They serve important instrumental functions in the preservation of individuals, species, and systems. They need not be avoided at all costs. As long as animals are used in ways that respect their natural integrity or their natural functions in ecological systems, then they are being treated with the proper moral consideration. Human beings, as natural omnivores, are not acting directly against moral value when they raise and kill animals for food.[21] The human use of domestic animals falls outside the realm of environmental ethics; domestic animals are nothing more than living human artifacts. This conclusion does not deny that there are proper and improper ways of treating animals bred for human purposes; however, these moral constraints are not the absolutes proposed by animal liberationists. Consequently business should argue for a contextual approach to the human treatment of animals. Harms and benefits, value and disvalue, can be determined only in concrete situations. Before making a moral decision, the complex relationship between human and animal, society and nature, individual and species, must be understood.

I have consciously avoided presenting specific proposals. I recommend a general approach to applied ethics that eschews the determination of specific ethical commands abstracted from actual situations. Nevertheless, this defense of the use of animals by business and industry does not imply approbation of current practices. Many of the specific techniques of factory farming, to cite one example, cause pain and suffering that is unnecessary from even a perspective of ecological holism. Although I have argued that pain is not an absolute evil and that it is a mistake to consider it as an evil abstracted from a concrete situation, I am not suggesting that it is never an evil in specific contexts. It can be unnecessary. Humans can reform their practices so that they gain the benefits of using animals without mistreating them. Business and industry ought to modify existing technologies in the raising, harvesting, and slaughtering of animals, even as they defend themselves against the critical attacks of animal liberation.

A final impetus for reform would be the sincere adoption of environmentalist attitudes. An ethic of ecological holism would require major revisions in human activities regarding wildlife and the natural environment. Industry would be compelled to develop alternative technologies with low impact on natural evolutionary processes, such as solar power and organic pesticides. These reforms would affect the animal kingdom in positive ways, for reducing air and water pollution benefits all organic life. However, the reforms required by an attitude of environmentalism are miniscule compared to the reforms demanded by the animal liberation movement. That prudential reason alone should be enough to convince business to adopt an environmental ethic.

Notes

*I thank Michal McMahon for helpful comments on an earlier version of this chapter.

1. One medical researcher gave up fourteen years of research because of protests against animal use. See Sarah Lyall, "Pressed on Animal Rights, Researcher Gives Up Grant," *New York Times*, November 22, 1988, sec. 2, p. 1.

2. The antifur demonstration was reported in Carole Agus, "The Fur and the Fury," *Newsday*, February 21, 1989, pt. 2, pp. 16–18. For more on fur protests see James Hirsch, "Animal-Rights Groups Step Up Attacks on Furriers," *New York Times*, November 27, 1988, sec. 1, p. 50. In the last year, the *New York Times* has printed several articles on the "animal rights" movement — a sure sign of public acceptance of the merits of the debate. See Kirk Johnson, "Arrest Points Up Split in Animal-Rights Movement," *New York Times*, November 13, 1988, sec. 2, p. 40; Robert A. Hamilton, "Advocates of Animal Rights See Influence Grow in State," *New York Times*, November 27, 1988, sec. 23, p. 1; Katherine Bishop, "From Shop to Lab to Farm, Animal Rights Battle Is Felt," *New York Times*, January 14, 1989, sec. 1, p. 1; Barnaby J. Feder, "Research Labs Look Away from Laboratory Animals," *New York Times*, January 29, 1989, sec. 4, p. 24. The Trutt bombing case was originally reported by Robert D. McFadden, "A Bombing Is Thwarted in Norwalk," *New York Times*, November 12, 1988, sec. 1, p. 29, and McFadden, "Norwalk Bomb Inquiry: Did Suspect Have Help?" *New York Times*, November 14, 1989, sec. 2, p. 3.

3. These two lines are represented by Tom Regan, *The Case for Animal Rights* (Berkeley: University of California Press, 1983), and Peter Singer, *Animal Liberation: A New Ethics for Our Treatment of Animals* (New York: Avon Books, 1977).

4. Singer attributes the term *speciesism* to Richard Ryder, author of *Victims of Science* (London: Davis-Poynter, 1975); see *Animal Liberation*, pp. 7, 25.

5. Singer, *Animal Liberation*, p. 8.

6. Hedonistic utilitarianism, the moral doctrine that judges human action by the resulting pleasure and pain, derives from Jeremy Bentham: "Nature has placed mankind under the governance of two sovereign masters, *pain* and *pleasure*." *An Introduction to the Principles of Morals and Legislation* (1789; rpt. *The Utilitarians*, Garden City, N.Y.: Anchor, 1973), p. 17. Bentham extends the moral significance of pain and pleasure to the animal kingdom; in an oft-quoted passage, he writes: "The French have already discovered that the blackness of the skin is no reason why a human being should be abandoned without redress to the caprice of a tormentor. It may come one day to be recognized, that the number of the legs, the villosity of the skin, or the termination of the *os sacrum*, are reasons equally insufficient for abandoning a sensitive being to the same fate. What else is it that should trace the insuperable line? Is it the faculty of reason, or, perhaps, the faculty of discourse? But a full-grown horse or dog is beyond comparison a more rational, as well as a more conversable animal, than an infant of a day, or a week, or even a month, old. But suppose the case were otherwise, what would it avail? The question is not, Can they *reason*? nor, Can they *talk*? but, Can they *Suffer*?" *Utilitarians*, p. 381.

7. Jeffrey A. Lockwood, "Not to Harm a Fly: Our Ethical Obligations to Insects," *Between the Species* 4 (3) (1988): 204–211.

8. See John Rodman, "The Liberation of Nature?" *Inquiry* 20 (1977): 83–131, esp. 90–91.

9. One of the most important criticisms of the animal liberationist use of pain can be found in J. Baird Callicott, "Animal Liberation: A Triangular Affair," *Environmental Ethics* 2 (1980): 311–338, esp. 332–333. Another movement in ethics that emphasizes context is feminist ethics,

although many feminists advocate vegetarianism and other nonharmful treatment of animals. I argue that a proper attention to context permits the use and eating of animals. For feminist ethics in general see Carol Gilligan, *In a Different Voice: Psychological Theory and Women's Development* (Cambridge: Harvard University Press, 1982). For a feminist perspective on environmental issues, see Jim Cheney, "Ecofeminism and Deep Ecology," *Environmental Ethics* 9 (1987): 115–145; for a feminist perspective on animals, see Cora Diamond, "Eating Meat and Eating People," *Philosophy* 53 (1978): 464–479.

10. Many animals are treated better than humans. I provide my pet dog, for example, with a better life than millions of humans in the world. His nutritional and medical needs are met to a higher level (I am guessing) than any individual in the entire homeless population of New York City or in the famine regions of the Third World. Since we do not normally condemn this "preferential" treatment of pet animals, we can see that we are not speciesists.

11. The large literature on environmental ethics cannot be cited here. Some of the best book-length treatments of the subject are Mark Sagoff, *The Economy of the Earth* (Cambridge: Cambridge University Press, 1988), Holmes Rolston III, *Environmental Ethics: Duties to and Values in the Natural World* (Philadelphia: Temple University Press, 1988), and Paul Taylor, *Respect for Nature: A Theory of Environmental Ethics* (Princeton: Princeton University Press, 1986). Two excellent anthologies are Donald Scherer and Thomas Attig, eds., *Ethics and the Environment* (Englewood Cliffs, N.J.: Prentice-Hall, 1983), and Donald VanDeVeer and Christine Pierce, eds., *People, Penguins and Plastic Trees: Basic Issues in Environmental Ethics* (Belmont, Calif.: Wadsworth, 1986). Current debates in the field appear in the journal *Environmental Ethics*, edited by Eugene Hargrove, Department of Philosophy, University of Georgia, Athens. I have published an annotated bibliography of recent titles in the field: "Environmental Ethics: A Select Annotated Bibliography, 1983–1987," *Research in Philosophy and Technology* 9 (1989): 251–285.

12. Aldo Leopold, *A Sand County Almanac* (1949; rpt., New York: Ballantine, 1970), p. 262.

13. Rolston, *Environmental Ethics*, pp. 45–125.

14. For more on predation, see Steve F. Sapontzis, "Predation," *Ethics and Animals* 5 (2) (June 1984): 27–38, and J. Baird Callicott's review of Tom Regan's *The Case for Animal Rights* in *Environmental Ethics* 7 (1985): 365–372.

15. So argues Peter Wenz, despite his concern for the moral consideration of animals. See his *Environmental Justice* (Albany: SUNY Press, 1988), pp. 324–331.

16. The creation and patenting of the so-called Harvard mice is reported in "U.S. Plans to Issue First Patent on Animal Today," *New York Times*, April 12, 1988, sec. 1, p. 21, and Keith Schneider, "Harvard Gets a Mouse Patent, a World First," *New York Times*, April 13, 1988, sec. 1, p. 1.

17. See Callicott, "Animal Liberation," pp. 329–336, and Rodman, "Liberation of Nature?" pp. 93–118, for more on domestication and its significance for animal and environmental ethics.

18. For discussion, see Alan Tormey, "Aesthetic Rights," *Journal of Aesthetics and Art Criticism* 32 (1973): 163–170, and a reply by David Goldblatt, "Do Works of Art Have Rights?" *Journal of Aesthetics and Art Criticism* 35 (1976): 69–77.

19. The idea of a morally pluralistic system of ethical value is being discussed seriously in the literature. See Christopher Stone, *Earth and Other Ethics: The Case for Moral Pluralism* (New York: Harper & Row, 1987); Wenz, *Environmental Justice*, esp. pp. 310–343; Callicott, "Animal Liberation and Environmental Ethics: Back Together Again," *Between the Species* 4 (3) (1988): 163–169; and my two articles, "Organism, Community and 'The Substitution Problem,'" *Environmental Ethics* 7 (1985): 241–256, and "Buffalo-killing and the Valuation of Species," in *Values and Moral Standing*, ed. L. W. Sumner (Bowling Green: Bowling Green State University Press, 1986), pp. 114–123.

20. See Rolston, *Environmental Ethics*.

21. But they may be acting indirectly against their interests and the overall health of the biosphere. Meat production is one of the most inefficient means of converting biomass to protein. There would be more food for the human population of the earth if we ceased meat production and shifted to a basic vegetarian diet.

DISCUSSION QUESTIONS

1. Hoffman argues for using a biocentric as opposed to a homeocentric view in approaching ethical dilemmas. Is a biocentric view morally superior to a homeocentric view? Is it practical to apply?

2. Hanson asks, "How do we achieve the antithetical goals of restraining atmospheric pollution and promoting economic development? What would you propose? Is it morally acceptable for the developed nations to ask third world countries to fight global pollution by limiting economic development and thus to settle for a less comfortable style of life than people in developed countries enjoy?

3. Do nonhuman animals have rights or interests? If so, how should they be respected in our business dealings?

4. Evaluate Singer's attack on the meat industry.

5. Does Katz refute Singer and the "animal rights" arguments he summarizes?

6. Although Katz generally defends the use of animals by business, he does not approve of every practice. How do you think he would evaluate the way veal is produced?

CASE 18.1

Nuclear Power

In the 1950s, nuclear power was trumpeted as an energy source that would be so revolutionary it would produce electricity "too cheap to meter." Enthusiasm waned in the United States in the 1970s as concern grew about the disposal of nuclear wastes. The accident at Three Mile Island in 1979 and then the tragedy at Chernobyl in 1986 further accelerated public disenchantment with nuclear as a power source. Utility companies suffered major losses as they faced years of lawsuits trying to block proposed reactors. The operation of completed plants was delayed or halted altogether, costing utilities billions of dollars. Only 21 percent of the electricity generated in the United States comes from nuclear power plants.

Nonetheless, nuclear power is still thought of by some people as a safe and necessary source of electricity. France generates 75 percent of its electricity from nuclear power, Belgium 60 percent, and Germany 33 percent. Proponents argue that unlike power facilities that burn oil or coal, nuclear plants produce nothing that contributes to acid rain or the greenhouse effect. They also point to future American demands for electricity. The Department of Energy projects that by the year 2010, the United States will have to produce more than a third more electricity than it does now. By 2030, it will need nearly twice the current capacity. Supporters of nuclear power argue that nuclear reactors are the only practical source to meet such a demand. A report by the National Academy of Sciences notes, "Alternative energy technologies [e.g., solar and wind] are unable currently or in the near future to replace fossil fuels as the major electricity source for this country. If fossil fuels had to be replaced now as the primary source of electricity, nuclear power appears to be the most technically feasible alternative."

The problem with nuclear power that has yet to be solved, however, is the disposal of its highly toxic, long-lasting radioactive wastes. No chemical process can make a radioactive substance safe — only the passage of time can. Strontium-90 and cesium-137 have half-lives of thirty years and are unusually difficult to store. (A *half-life* is the time it takes a radioactive substance to become one-half as radioactive as it once was.) Carbon-14 has a half-life of 5,900 years; technetium-99, 21,300 years; plutonium, 24,000 years; and iodine-129, 16 million years. Nuclear power plants themselves have life spans of no more than forty years, after which, because of their radioactivity, they are usually sealed up. Nuclear scientists claim to have discovered a "transmutation" process that can decrease the time nuclear wastes are toxic. Nonetheless, instead of thousands or millions of years, a substance would still need hundreds of years of storage before its radioactivity reached a safe level. Moreover, transmutation produces plutonium, a substance used in nuclear weapons, and some people fear that this would increase the risk of terrorists's obtaining the materials needed to make such weapons.

The primary risk of nuclear waste to humans, of course, is that radioactive substances damage human tissue and can produce life-threatening diseases and genetic mutations. Any leakage of nuclear wastes into the food chain or the water supply will likely find its way into the human diet. Although some experts argue that it would be safe to store radioactive waste at a proposed permanent dump site deep in the earth in the supposedly impermeable geologic formations below Nevada's Yucca Mountain, others claim that there is no way to guarantee that any geological site will go unchanged for tens of thousands of years. ◆

Discussion Questions

1. Do the benefits of nuclear power outweigh its risks?

2. From an ethical standpoint, how do you take account of the risks radioactive wastes pose to future generations? Do future generations have rights?

3. Nuclear energy produces waste that remains toxic longer than the amount of time our species has lived on the planet. Some would say that the fact that we actually use nuclear power — leaving our descendants to worry about how to dispose of our toxic wastes — shows that homo sapiens is essentially irrational, self-destructive, selfish, and unethical. What is your reaction to this?

4. What would your reaction be to the idea that in order to avoid the risks of nuclear waste, Americans have a moral responsibility to curb their demand for electricity and to live more simply?

Sources

Browne, Malcolm W., "Modern Alchemists Transmute Nuclear Waste," *New York Times*, October 29, 1991, C1, 11.
Greenwald, John, "Time to Choose," *Time*, April 29, 1991, 54–61.
Parisi, Anthony J., "Nuclear Power: The Bottom Line Gets Fuzzier," *New York Times*, April 8, 1979, III, 1, 4.
"Running Out of Space for Nuclear Waste," *New York Times*, October 22, 1989, E7.

CASE 18.2

The Ethics of Dolphin/Human Interaction

In tales that reach back to ancient Crete, dolphins are said to be special creatures. We are told that they regularly aid lost ships, save drowning sailors, and form fast friendships with humans. Dolphins were even thought to be gods by some ancient peoples. This fascination with dolphins continues in the present. Even though we no longer consider dolphins to be divine, we have learned that they are surprisingly complex socially, emotionally, and intellectually. Accordingly, we now face a series of questions about the moral justifiability of our behavior toward them.

Research over the last two decades reveals that dolphins are more like humans than was once thought. Dolphins are air-breathing mammals, not fish, and they evidence many of the same higher characteristics as humans. The size and complexity of the dolphin brain compares favorably to that of the human brain. Dolphins can solve difficult, novel problems; they are aware of time; and they can handle abstract and relational concepts. They have a sophisticated level of language comprehension, including the ability to understand syntax, something heretofore thought to be an exclusively human ability. More than one study suggests that dolphins engage in self-reflection. Dolphins appear to experience a range of emotions and to have distinct personalities, and their actions seem to result from deliberation and choice.

At the same time, the fact that dolphins live in the ocean and have an evolutionary history much different from humans leads to important differences between the two species. Dolphins possess a sonar sense that we humans lack, a sense that is superior to anything our technology has been able to devise. They use whistles to communicate with one another at a speed and at frequencies often beyond the ability of human hearing to perceive. Their system of communication may be more nonverbal than ours is, but they live a much more intensely social life than we do.

Both the similarities and the differences between dolphins and humans raise important philosophical questions. For example, we humans have traditionally reserved for ourselves the category of "person," with its special rights and privileges. Yet the advanced characteristics of dolphins suggest that they are probably "nonhuman persons." Does this mean, then, that they have moral standing and "rights"?

The question of whether dolphins have moral standing is an interesting philosophical issue in its own right. The specifics about dolphin/human inter-action, however, make it much more than that because it raises the question of the ethical justifiability of our behavior toward the dolphins. Clashes between human and dolphin interests take place daily in the fishing and entertainment industries, and dolphins generally do poorly in the exchange. For example, approximately four hundred dolphins are held in captivity in the United States alone for purposes of research and entertainment at facilities such as Sea World and Marine World. In addition, despite recent progress regarding how tuna is caught in the eastern tropical Pacific, and despite decisions by companies such as Star-Kist to no longer sell tuna caught on dolphins, as many as three hundred dolphins still die each day in the nets of tuna boats. (In the eastern tropical Pacific, dolphins and tuna frequently school together. Tuna boats will often set their nets around a school of dolphin hoping to find tuna beneath them. Dolphins are regularly killed or injured in this process. Approximately 7 mil-lion dolphins have died because of this practice.)

The Marine Mammal Protection Act of 1972 allows 20,500 dolphins to die annually from American tuna fishing despite the fact that the original version of the bill aimed to bring the deaths to zero. The law also allows the United States to refuse to import fish from foreign boats causing too many dolphin deaths, and a federal court ordered such an embargo on Mexican tuna in 1990. Mexico objected to the U.S. action and appealed to an international trade body, arguing that the embargo was an unfair trade practice. A panel of the Geneva-based General Agreement on Tariffs and Trade (GATT) sided with Mexico, saying that a GATT member nation has no right to limit trade that harms the environment beyond its borders. For the time being, however, Mexico has agreed to table its case rather than take it to GATT's General Council. ◆

Discussion Questions

1. Do dolphins have rights? If so, which ones? Life? Liberty? Self-determination?

2. How do we evaluate situations in which there is a conflict between human interests and dolphin interests? In trying to resolve such a clash, how do we properly take account of the differences between dolphins and humans and avoid anthropocentrism, that is, irrational prejudice in favor of our own species?

3. Does our need for food and our desire for maximum profit justify the technology we currently employ in tuna fishing? Does human curiosity about dolphins defend keeping them captive for research and education? Does human pleasure at watching dolphins perform (and the ability to make a profit at this) make it ethically justifiable to keep dolphins captive?

4. Do you agree with Mexico and the GATT panel?

5. The National Marine Fisheries Service (NMFS) is the federal agency that regulates how dolphins should be treated. NMFS is a branch of the Department of Commerce, not the Department of the Interior. This implies that dolphins are an economic resource. From an ethical viewpoint, is this defensible?

Sources

Aridjis, Homero, "Defending Dolphins," *New York Times*, October 7, 1991 A17.

White, Thomas I., "Is a Dolphin a Person?," *Discovering Philosophy* (Englewood Cliffs, NJ: Prentice Hall, 1991), 72–96.

———, "Ethics at Sea: The Dolphin/Tuna Controversy," in *Business, Ethics and the Environment: The Public Policy Debate*, edited by W. Michael Hoffman, Robert Frederick, and Edward S. Petry, Jr. (New York: Quorum Books, 1990), 233–245.

◆ ◆ ◆

ADDITIONAL READINGS

Hoffman, W. Michael, Robert Frederick, and Edward S. Petry, Jr., eds., *Business, Ethics and the Environment* (New York: Quorum Books, 1990).

———, *The Corporation, Ethics and the Environment* (New York: Quorum Books, 1990).

Newton, Lisa H., "The Chainsaws of Greed: The Case of Pacific Lumber," *Business & Professional Ethics Journal*, 8, no. 3 (1988), 29–61.

Regan, Tom, ed., *Earthbound: New Introductory Essays in Environmental Ethics* (New York: Random House, 1984).

Singh Jang B., and V. C. Lakhan, "Business Ethics and the International Trade in Hazardous Wastes," *Journal of Business Ethics*, 8 (November 1989), 889–899.

Stone, Christopher, *Should Trees Have Standing?* (Los Altos, CA: William Kaufman, Inc., 1972).